Signs of Life in the U.S.A.

Fourth Edition

Signs of Life in the U.S.A.

Readings on Popular Culture for Writers

Sonia Maasik
University of California, Los Angeles

Jack Solomon
California State University, Northridge

BEDFORD/ST. MARTIN'S   Boston ◆ New York

This one's for Pooh.

For Bedford/St. Martin's

Developmental Editor: John E. Sullivan III
Production Editor: Deborah Baker
Senior Production Supervisor: Joe Ford
Marketing Manager: Brian Wheel
Editorial Assistants: Carrie Thompson, Christine Turnier–Vallecillo
Production Assistant: Tina Lai
Copyeditor: Lisa Wehrle
Text Design: Gretchen Toles for Anna George Design
Cover Design: Mark McKie
Cover Art: Photographs © 2002 Getty Images
Composition: Pine Tree Composition, Inc.
Printing and Binding: R.R. Donnelley & Sons Company

President: Joan E. Feinberg
Editorial Director: Denise B. Wydra
Editor in Chief: Karen S. Henry
Director of Marketing: Karen Melton
Director of Editing, Design, and Production: Marcia Cohen
Managing Editor: Elizabeth M. Schaaf

Library of Congress Control Number: 2002112258

Manufactured in the United States of America.

7 6 5 4 3 2
f e d c b a

For information, write: Bedford/St. Martin's, 75 Arlington Street, Boston, MA 02116
(617-399-4000)

ISBN: 0–312–39784–4

Acknowledgments

Melissa Algranati, "Being an Other," from *Becoming American, Becoming Ethnic: College Students Explore Their Roots,* edited by Thomas Dublin. Copyright © 1996 by Melissa Algranati. Reprinted by permission of the author.

Acknowledgments and copyrights are continued at the back of the book on pages 809–15, which constitute an extension of the copyright page. It is a violation of the law to reproduce these selections by any means whatsoever without the written permission of the copyright holder.

Preface for Instructors

We were well along in our work on the fourth edition of *Signs of Life in the U.S.A.* when we awoke on that terrible morning in September to the news that America was under attack. Even as we watched the live coverage of the fall of the World Trade Center towers, the fire at the Pentagon, and the mysterious disappearance of United Flight 93, we knew that we were witnessing a historic intervention. "Nothing will ever be the same" became a refrain that grew in volume throughout that awful day and continued in the weeks that followed. And the impact of the events of 9/11 (a date that has entered the American vocabulary as permanently as the words "Pearl Harbor") was powerful in the realm of American popular culture, where our national devotion to entertainment and celebrity worship suddenly looked not simply trivial but unworthy of a nation at war.

Indeed, one of the first consequences of the attacks was a string of cancellations of high-profile popular cultural events: The Latin Grammys vanished; the Emmy Awards ceremony was canceled, postponed, canceled, and postponed; and the NFL nixed its weekend schedule, a move that did not happen when John F. Kennedy was assassinated. The brightest luminaries among the pantheon of entertainment celebrities appeared quite frankly embarrassed and bewildered, not knowing how to respond appropriately to the dramatic change in the national mood. And a number of movies featuring terrorist themes were pulled from pending release.

So what, we wondered, could be the place of a book devoted to the study of popular culture in such a changed world? Was it still appropriate to teach students critical thinking and writing skills through popular cultural analysis? Had life simply become too serious for such study?

v

As the days went by, it became increasingly clear not only that it *was* appropriate to continue with our work but that the national response to the September 11 attacks only underscored the very premise upon which every edition of *Signs of Life in the U.S.A.* has been founded. That premise has been both that the traditional distinction between "high" (or culturally approved) and "low" (mass or popular) culture has come to be irrelevant in a world where string quartets are essential components of heavy metal recordings and operatic tenors perform stadium gigs, and where the terms "American culture" and "popular culture" are becoming virtually synonymous. America's passionate turn to popular culture in the immediate aftermath of the attacks dramatically illustrated this point. From the star-studded Concert for New York to a World Series and Super Bowl that were celebrated as national memorials and morale builders, it became clear that popular culture had not become too trivial for serious attention; in fact, it had become more important than ever before. Indeed, our own students complained that it was a mistake to cancel the Emmy Awards (when that was what looked to be the plan) and a mistake to tone down their glitter when they were rescheduled, while many parents found that their children were best able to cope with the attacks by understanding them through the lens of *Harry Potter.* In short, Americans turned to popular culture for comfort and support in the aftermath of September 11, finding there a common ground upon which they could rally and recover.

As the months passed, it also became clear that while travel would be a mess for years to come and that the economic impact of the attacks would scar many lives, popular culture would return pretty much to normal. Movies like *Collateral Damage,* once held back, were successfully released. Hollywood glitter and self-promotion returned. And very few, if anyone, complained. It wasn't simply a matter that too much money was involved to let popular culture languish (though, of course, that contributed to the rapid return to business as usual in the entertainment industry): Americans simply didn't want to see it languish. And so, with such powerful evidence of the essential place that popular culture holds in American culture as a whole, its study appears to be more important than ever before.

Then and Now

Things have not always appeared this way, of course. When the first edition of *Signs of Life in the U.S.A.* appeared, the study of popular culture was still embroiled in the "culture wars" of the early 1990s, a struggle for academic legitimacy in which the adherents of cultural studies ultimately prevailed. Since then, accordingly, more and more scholars and teachers have come to recognize the importance of understanding what Michel de Certeau has called "the practice of everyday life" and the value of using popular culture as a thematic ground for educating students in critical thinking and writing. Once excluded from academic study on the basis of a naturalized distinction between "high" and "low" culture that contemporary cultural analysis has shown to be historically contingent, popular culture has come to be an accepted part of the curriculum, widely studied in freshman composition classrooms, as well as in upper-division undergraduate courses and graduate seminars.

But recognition of the important place that popular culture has assumed in our society has not been restricted to the academy. Increasingly, Americans are realizing that American culture and popular culture are virtually one and the same, and that whether we are looking at our political system, our economy, or simply our national consciousness, the power of popular culture to shape our lives is strikingly apparent. Sometimes this realization has been fraught with controversy, as when after a spate of schoolyard shootings in the late 1990s a host of politicians and pundits pointed their fingers at violent entertainment as the culprit behind the violence. At other times, the growing influence of popular culture has been received more enthusiastically, as in the widespread belief in the Internet as a medium of economic and educational reform and revival. But whether the recognition is tinged with controversy or splashed with enthusiasm, at no time in our history have Americans been more aware of the place of popular culture in their lives.

For this reason, we believe that learning to think and write critically about popular culture is even more important today than it was when we published the first edition of this book. As the boundary between "culture" and popular culture blurs and even disappears, it is all the more essential that our students understand how popular culture works and how it generates meaning. This is why we continue to make semiotics the guiding methodology behind *Signs of Life in the U.S.A.* For semiotics leads us, and our students, to take an analytic stance towards popular culture, one that avoids the common pitfalls of uncritical celebration or simple scapegoating.

The reception of the first three editions of this text has demonstrated that the semiotic approach to popular culture has indeed found a place in America's composition classrooms. Composition instructors have seen that students feel a certain sense of ownership toward the products of popular culture — and that using popular culture as a focus can help students overcome the sometimes alienating effects of traditional academic subject matter. At the same time, the semiotic method has helped instructors lead their students to analyze critically the popular cultural phenomena that they enjoy writing about and so learn the critical thinking and writing skills that their composition classes are designed to impart.

The Book's Organization

Reflecting the broad academic interest in cultural studies, we've assumed an inclusive definition of popular culture. This definition can be seen in the book's organization. Its two sections — Cultural Productions and Cultural Constructions — highlight the essential cultural connection between the things we do and the things we believe. The four chapters in the first section focus on the marketing and consumption of the products of mass production, from sport utility vehicles to TV shows, music, and movies. The five chapters in the second part of the book may seem a bit more sobering, but they are inextricably linked to the text's first half. In addressing spatial semiotics, gender issues, race relations, the culture of sports, and American icons, these chapters show how ideologies work to construct us as consumers and producers.

The Critical Method: Semiotics

Signs of Life departs from some textbook conventions in that it makes explicit an interpretive approach — semiotics — that can guide students' analyses of popular culture. We've made this approach explicit because it has struck us that while students enjoy assignments that ask them to look at popular cultural phenomena, they often have trouble distinguishing between an argued interpretive analysis and the simple expression of an opinion. Some textbooks, for example, suggest assignments that involve analyzing a TV program or film, but they don't always tell a student how to do that. The semiotic method provides that guidance.

At the same time, semiotics reveals that there's no such thing as a pure, ideologically neutral analysis. Anthologies typically present analysis as a "pure" category: They present readings that students are asked to analyze, but articulate no conceptual framework and neither explore nor define theoretical assumptions and ideological positions. Being self-conscious about one's point of view, however, is an essential part of academic writing, and we can think of no better place for students to learn that lesson than in a writing class.

We've found through experience that a semiotic approach is especially well suited to this purpose. As a conceptual framework, semiotics teaches students to formulate cogent, well-supported interpretations. It emphasizes the examination of assumptions and the way language shapes our apprehension of the world. And, because it focuses on *how* beliefs are formulated within a social and political context (rather than just judging or evaluating those beliefs), it's ideal for discussing sensitive or politically charged issues. As an approach used in literature, media studies, anthropology, art and design coursework, sociology, law, and market research (to name only some of its more prominent field applications), semiotics has a cross-disciplinary appeal that makes it ideal for a writing class of students from a variety of majors and disciplines. We recognize that semiotics has a reputation for being highly technical or theoretical; rest assured that *Signs of Life* does not require students or instructors to have a technical knowledge of semiotics. We've provided clear and accessible introductions that explain what students need to know.

We also recognize that adopting a theoretical approach may be new to some instructors, so we've designed the book to allow instructors to be as semiotic with their students as they wish. The book does not obligate instructors or students to spend a lot of time with semiotics — although we do hope you'll find the approach intriguing and provocative.

The Editorial Apparatus

With its emphasis on popular culture, *Signs of Life* should generate lively class discussion and inspire many kinds of writing and thinking activities. The general introduction provides an overall framework for the book, acquainting students with the semiotic method they can use to interpret the topics raised in each chapter. It is followed by a section on Writing about Popular Culture that not only provides a brief introduction to writing about popular culture but additionally features three sample student essays that demonstrate different approaches to writing critical essays on pop culture topics. The chapters start with a frontispiece, a provocative visual image related to the chapter's topic, and an introduction that suggests ways to "read" the topic, presents model interpretations, and links the issues raised by the reading selections. Every chapter introduction contains three types of boxed questions designed to stimulate student thinking on the topic. The Exploring the Signs questions invite students to reflect on an issue in a journal entry or other prewriting activity, whereas the Discussing the Signs questions trigger class activities such as debates, discussions, or small group work. Reading the Net questions invite students to explore the chapter's topic on the Internet, both for research purposes and for texts to analyze.

The readings themselves are followed by two sorts of assignments. The Reading the Text questions help students comprehend the selections, asking them to identify important concepts and arguments, explain key terms, and relate main ideas to each other and to the evidence presented. The Reading the Signs questions are writing and activity prompts designed to produce clear analytic thinking and strong persuasive writing; they often make connections among reading selections from different chapters. Most assignments call for analytic essays, while some invite journal responses, in-class debates, group work, or other creative activities. Complementing the readings in each chapter are images that serve as visual texts that can be discussed. We've also included a Glossary of semiotic terms, which can serve as a ready reference of key terms and concepts used in the chapter introductions. Finally, the instructor's manual (*Editors' Notes to Accompany Signs of Life in the U.S.A.*) provides suggestions for organizing your syllabus, encouraging student responses to the readings, and using popular culture and semiotics in the writing class.

What's New in the Fourth Edition

Few subjects move so quickly as does the pace of popular culture, and the fourth edition of *Signs of Life* reflects this essential mutability through its substantial revision of the third edition. First, we have updated our readings, adding selections that focus on issues and trends important in the new millennium. We have also updated the exemplary topics in our introductions used to model the critical assignments that follow and have readjusted the focus of some chapters to reflect changing conditions. A new chapter on sports ("It's Not Just a Game") has been added to reflect what we call the growth of the "sports-and-entertainment postindustrial complex" — that amalgamation of athletics with the culture industry that has transformed the nature of modern sport. A new design updates the look of the book, and new photographs with questions in each chapter help students learn to think critically about visual popular culture.

From the beginning, *Signs of Life* was predicated on the premise that in a postindustrial, McCluhanesque world, the image has been coming to supplant the printed word in American, and global, culture. That is one of the reasons we chose semiotics, which provides a rational basis for the critical analysis of images, as the guiding methodology for every edition of our book. Each edition of *Signs of Life* has accordingly included images for critical analysis and in this, the fourth edition of the book, we have increased the number of images while modifying the shape of the book to make their presentation more effective. Each chapter now includes an image with discussion and writing questions. The images supplement the readings, offering a visual perspective designed to *enhance* the critical understanding modeled by the texts, not to replace them; we believe that while the semiotic interpretation of images can help students in the honing of their writing skills, it should not be a substitute for learning critical thinking through the analysis of written texts.

Even as we revise this text to reflect current trends, popular culture continues to evolve. The inevitable gap between the pace of editing and publishing, on the one hand, and the flow of popular culture, on the other, need not affect its use in the classroom, however. The readings in the text, and the semiotic method we propose, are designed to show students how to analyze and write critical essays about any topic they choose. They can, as one of our student writers does, choose a topic that appeared before they were born, or they can turn to the latest box office or prime-time hit to appear after the publication of this edition of *Signs of Life*. To put it another way, the practice of everyday life may itself be filled with evanescent fads and trends, but it is not itself a fad. As the vital texture of our lived experience, popular culture provides a stable background against which students of every generation can test their critical skills.

Acknowledgments

The vastness of the terrain of popular culture has enabled many users of the third edition of this text to make valuable suggestions for the fourth edition. We have incorporated many such suggestions and thank all for their comments on our text: Joy Barta, University of California, Riverside; Lisa Berman, Miami-Dade Community College; Anthony C. Bleach, Lehigh University; Jami Carlaccio, University of Wisconsin, Milwaukee; Robin Carstensen, Texas A&M

University; Barbara Chiarello, University of Texas–Arlington; Gina Claywell, Murray State University; David J. Daniels, Indiana University; Dale Dittmer, Bowling Green State University; Sharara Drew, Tufts University; Garett Euridge, Denison University; Jennifer Fickling, Cabrillo College; Linda Girard, Parkland College; Angela Gulick, Parkland College; Lori Harrison-Kahan, Boston College; Rebecca Hooker, University of New Mexico; Kevin Howarth, Kent State University; Dawnelle A. Jager, Syracuse University; Benedict Jones, University of California, Riverside; Glynis Kinna, University of Illinois at Chicago; April L. Mason, Kent State University; Meghan Mercier, Syracuse University; Jennifer Musial, Bowling Green State University; Brigid-Elizabeth N. Reardon, Indiana University; T. V. Reed, Washington State University; Alexis Rizzuto, Syracuse University; Cristina Lucia Stasia, Syracuse University; Cheryl Strayed, Syracuse University; Emily Walker, Indiana University; and Randall Lee Wolff, Murray State University. We would also like to thank those reviewers who examined *Signs of Life* in depth: Patricia Fillipi, University of Minnesota; Claudia Milstead, University of Tennessee; Inez Schaechterle, Bowling Green State University; Annette Wannamaker, Eastern Michigan University; and David M. Wright, Mt. Hood Community College. If we have not included something you'd like to work on, you may still direct your students to it, using this text as a guide, not as a set of absolute prescriptions. The practice of everyday life includes the conduct of a classroom, and we want all users of the fourth edition of *Signs of Life in the U.S.A.* to feel free to pursue that practice in whatever way best suits their interests and aims.

We'd like especially to thank our friends Andrew and Anna, who helped us with one of our favorite photographic images in this text, and our friend Jim Moyle, who once again generously provided us Internet access when we were away from home. Steve Steinberg, too, proved generous in offering suggested readings. And once again, we wish to thank heartily the people at Bedford/St. Martin's who have enabled us to make this fourth edition a reality, particularly Chuck Christensen and Joan Feinberg, who have now been at the helm through six of our textbook projects. Very special thanks are due our editor, John Sullivan, who continues to embody, as we said in the last edition, the best combination of diplomacy, creativity, critical insight, and good cheer that characterizes such editorial legends as Maxwell Perkins. Deborah Baker ably guided our manuscript through the rigors of production, while Carrie Thompson handled the innumerable questions and details that arise during textbook development. Alice Lundoff expertly researched and obtained permission for art, and Chris Stripinis cleared text permissions. In addition, Elizabeth Schaaf, Lisa Wehrle, and Coleen O'Hanley contributed their intelligence and superb competence to the production of this book.

Contents

Chapter 3.
Video Dreams: *Television, Music, and Cultural Forms*   *223*

POPULAR SIGNS

*Or, Everything You Always
Knew about American Culture
(But Nobody Asked)*

It was a year in which the most famous soprano in America was named Tony. A year in which "reality" was a television programming sensation, and *Collateral Damage* a new Schwarzenegger flick just due for release. It was a time when alien invaders were held at bay by prime-time heroes with names like Buffy and Scully and Mulder, and New York City was a giant television setting famous for its "Friends" and its really good "Sex." Then, without warning, "September 11," or simply "9/11," became a part of American history, and nothing, almost everyone said, would ever be the same.

As the nation mourned the destruction of the World Trade Center and the deaths of over three thousand innocent people, it looked like this might be true. With the shock waves from the terrorist attacks washing over the entire country, the reverberations were felt everywhere, not least in the vast realm of America's popular culture, where suddenly our fascination with entertainment and the men and women who entertain us appeared to be both frivolous and irrelevant. In short order, the Emmy award ceremony — that glittering testimonial to American celebrity worship — was postponed, and the Latin Grammys canceled. *Collateral Damage,* an about-to-be-released thriller featuring international terrorism, itself became collateral damage and, along with Tim Allen's *Big Trouble,* stayed in the can. Even the NFL, which had played on in spite of the assassination of President John F. Kennedy, scrapped its weekend football schedule.

The Day the Music Didn't Die

But even as America geared up for an unconventional and uncertain war on terror, and firefighters and police began to emerge as a new class of American hero, there were signs of remarkable resilience in America's popular culture. With the fires still smoldering in the ruins of the World Trade Center, Sir Paul McCartney led an all-star cast of pop legends at Madison Square Garden to raise money for victims of the attacks. The NFL pushed back the Super Bowl one week and returned to the gridiron, while the World Series went on as scheduled. *The Mole* went under, a casualty of a sudden disenchantment with reality programming, but *Survivor Africa* soldiered on. Meanwhile, two fantasy heroes named Harry and Frodo challenged box office history, and, after a discreet four-month gap, *Collateral Damage* was released after all. And finally, with U2 presiding over a star-spangled halftime testimonial to the victims of 9/11, Super Bowl XXXVI marked a crucial milepost in America's recovery.

That America returned so quickly to its popular culture, indeed relied upon it to help cope with the disaster, is itself a sign of just how important that culture is to us and how enduring. Far from being a mere frivolity that we could easily do without, our popular culture, in effect, *is* our culture, constituting the essential fiber of our everyday lives. From the way we entertain ourselves to the goods and services we consume, we are enveloped in a popular cultural environment that we can no longer do without. To see this, just try to imagine a world without television, or movies, or sports, or music, or shopping malls, or advertising, or DVD, MTV, or MP3.

Pop Culture Is Us

Given the importance of popular culture to our lives and the life of our country, it may seem surprising that until recently its study was largely excluded from university curricula. Equated with "low" or "mass" culture, popular culture was subordinated to the "high" culture that academia was charged with preserving and propagating. Not until the advent of cultural studies, which was first pioneered in English universities and which came to America in the late 1980s, did the study of popular culture become a common, and accepted, topic for university study. But as the barrier between high and low culture, privileged and popular, continues to erode in a world where the Three Tenors perform Pink Floyd-like stadium gigs and Mel Gibson plays Hamlet, where *Romeo and Juliet* is a rap opera and string quartets have been part of the rock scene ever since the Beatles' "Yesterday," the study of pop culture is emerging as a mainstay of contemporary education.

This has been especially true in American composition classrooms, which have been taking the lead in incorporating popular culture into academic study, both because of the inherent interest value of the subject and because

Traditional examples of "high" and "low" culture: the symphony and the circus.

of its profound familiarity to most students. Your own expertise in popular culture means not only that you may know more about a given topic than your instructor but that you may use that knowledge as a basis for learning the critical thinking and writing skills that your composition class is charged to teach you. This book is designed to show you how to do that — how to write about American popular culture as you would write about any other academic subject.

We have prepared *Signs of Life in the U.S.A.,* in other words, because we believe that you are already a sophisticated student of American culture. Think of all you already know. Just list all the performers you can name. Or television series. Or movies. Do you always pick the green M&Ms — especially when in mixed company — or know the difference between Tupac and Wu Long? Face it, you're an expert. So isn't that a good place to start learning how to write college essays, with what you know already? We all write best when we can write from our strengths, and this book is intended to let you tap into your own storehouse of information and experience as you learn to write college essays.

Signs of Life in the U.S.A., then, is designed to let you exploit your knowledge of popular culture so that you may grow into a better writer about any subject. You can interpret the popularity of programs like *The West Wing,* for example, in the same manner as you would interpret, say, a short story, because *The West Wing,* too, constitutes a kind of *sign.* A sign is something, *anything,* that carries a meaning. A stop sign, for instance, means exactly what it says: "Stop when you approach this intersection," while carrying the implied message "or risk getting a ticket." Words, too, are signs: You read them to figure out what they mean. You were trained to read such signs, but that training began so long ago that you may well take your ability to read for granted. But all your life you have been encountering, and interpreting, other sorts of signs that you were never formally taught to read. You know what they mean anyway. Take the way you wear your hair. When you get your hair cut, you are not simply removing hair: You are making a statement, sending a message about yourself. It's the same for both men and women. For men, think of the different messages you'd send if you got a buzzcut to match a goatee, or grew your hair out long, or shaved your head. What does a woman communicate when she chooses beaded braids rather than the sleek Gwyneth Paltrow look? Why was your hair short last year and long this year (or long last year and short this year)? Aren't you saying something with the scissors? In this way, you make your hairstyle into a sign that sends a message about your identity. You are surrounded by such signs. Just look at your classmates.

The world of signs could be called a kind of text, the text of America's popular culture. We want you to think of *Signs of Life in the U.S.A.* as a window onto that text. What you read in this book's essays and introductions should lead you to study and analyze the world around you. Let the readings guide you to your own interpretations, your own readings, of the text of America.

We have chosen nine "windows" in this edition of *Signs of Life in the U.S.A.*, each of which looks out onto a separate, but often interrelated, segment of the American scene. We have put some of the scenery directly into this book, as when we include actual ads in our chapter on advertising or cartoons that you can interpret directly. Where it is impossible to put something directly into a textbook, like a TV show or a movie, we have included essays that help you think about specific programs and films, and assignments that invite you to go out and interpret a TV show or movie of your own choosing. Each chapter also includes an introduction written to alert you to the kinds of signs you will find there, along with advice on how to go about interpreting them.

We have designed *Signs of Life in the U.S.A.* to reflect the many ways in which culture shapes our sense of reality and of ourselves, from the things that we buy to the ways that culture, through such media as television and the movies, constructs our ethnic and gender identities. This text thus introduces you to both the entertainment and the ideological sides of popular culture — and shows how the two sides are mutually interdependent. Indeed, one of the major lessons you can learn from this book is how to find the ideological underpinnings of some of the most apparently innocent entertainments and consumer goods.

Signs of Life in the U.S.A. accordingly begins with a chapter on "Consuming Passions," because America is a consumer culture, and so the environment within which the galaxy of popular signs functions is, more often than not, a consumerist one. This is true not only for obvious consumer products like blue jeans and sport utility vehicles (SUVs) but for such traditionally non-consumer items as political candidates and college campuses as well, both of which are often marketed like any other consumer product. It is difficult to find anything in contemporary America that is not affected in one way or another by our consumerist ethos or by consumerism's leading promoter, the advertiser. Thus, the second chapter, "Brought to You B(u)y," explores the world of advertising, for advertising provides the grease, so to speak, that lubricates the engine of America's consumer culture. Because television (including MTV) and film are the sources of many of our most significant cultural products, we include a chapter on each. Chapters on sports, gender, race, popular icons, and public space round out our survey of everyday life.

Throughout, the book invites you to go out and select your own "texts" for analysis (an advertisement, a film, a fashion fad, a political opinion, a building, and so on). Here's where your own experience is particularly valuable, because it has made you familiar with many different kinds of popular signs and their backgrounds, with the particular popular cultural *system* or environment to which they belong.

The nine "windows" you will find in *Signs of Life in the U.S.A.* are all intended to reveal the common intersections of entertainment and ideology that can be found in contemporary American life. Often what seems to be simply entertainment, like a TV show, is actually quite political, while what seems purely political, like a gender conflict, can be cast as entertainment as well — as in movies like *Thelma and Louise*. The point is to see that little in American life is "merely" entertainment; indeed, just about everything we do has a meaning, often a profound one.

The Semiotic Method

To find this meaning, to interpret and write effectively about the signs of popular culture, you need a method, and it is part of the purpose of this book to introduce such a method to you. Without a methodology for interpreting signs, writing about them could become little more than descriptive reviews or opinion pieces. There is nothing wrong with writing descriptions and opinions, but one of your tasks in your writing class is to learn how to write academic essays, that is, analytical essays that present theses or arguments that are well supported by evidence. The method we draw on in this book — a method that is known as *semiotics* — is especially well suited for analyzing popular culture. Whether or not you're familiar with this word, you are already practicing sophisticated semiotic analyses every day of your life. Reading this page is an act of semiotic decoding (words and even letters are signs that must be interpreted), but so is figuring out just what your classmate *means* by wearing a particular shirt or dress. For a semiotician (one who practices semiotic analysis), a shirt, a haircut, a television image, anything at all, can be taken as a sign, as a message to be decoded and analyzed to discover its meaning. Every cultural activity for the semiotician leaves a trace of meaning, a kind of blip on the semiotic Richter scale, that remains for us to read, just as a geologist reads the earth for signs of earthquakes, volcanoes, and other geological phenomena.

Many who hear the word *semiotics* for the first time assume that it is the name of a new, and forbidding, subject. But in truth, the study of signs is neither very new nor forbidding. Its modern form took shape in the late nineteenth and early twentieth centuries through the writings and lectures of two men. Charles Sanders Peirce (1839–1914) was an American philosopher and physicist who first coined the word *semiotics,* while Ferdinand de Saussure (1857–1913) was a Swiss linguist whose lectures became the foundation for what *he* called *semiology.* Without knowing of each other's work, Peirce and Saussure established the fundamental principles that modern semioticians or semiologists — the terms are essentially interchangeable — have developed into the contemporary study of semiotics.

The application of semiotics to the interpretation of popular culture was pioneered in the 1950s by the French semiologist Roland Barthes (1915–1980) in a book entitled *Mythologies* (1957). The basic principles of semiotics had already been explored by linguists and anthropologists, but Barthes took the matter to the heart of his own contemporary France, analyzing the cultural significance of everything from professional wrestling to striptease, from toys to plastics.

It was Barthes, too, who established the political dimensions of semiotic analysis. Often, the subject of a semiotic analysis — a movie, say, or a TV program — doesn't look political at all; it simply looks like entertainment. In our society (especially in the aftermath of the Watergate and Monicagate scandals), *politics* has become something of a dirty word, and to *politicize* something seems somehow to contaminate it. So you shouldn't feel alarmed if at first it feels a little odd to search for a political meaning in an apparently neutral topic. You may even think that to do so is to read too much into that topic. But Barthes's point — and the point of semiotics in general — is that all social behavior is political in the sense that it reflects some personal or group interest. Such interests are encoded in what are called *ideologies,* or worldviews that express the values and opinions of those who hold them. Politics, then, is just another name for the clash of ideologies that takes place in any complex society in which the interests of all those who belong to it constantly compete with one another.

Take, for example, the way people have responded to the movie *Forrest Gump.* Those viewers who like the film tend to share its conservative political values: its celebration of individual responsibility and capitalist enterprise. The same viewers, on the other hand, are less likely to enjoy Oliver Stone's *Nixon,* a film that gives a less-than-flattering portrait of one of American conservatism's leading standard-bearers of the last century. In each case, the viewers' responses are shaped in part by their ideological and political interests, not simply by their tastes in movie styles.

While not all movies are as manifestly political as these two are, careful analysis usually can uncover some set of political values at the heart of a film, although those values may be subtly concealed behind an apparently apolitical facade. Indeed, the political values that guide our social behavior are often concealed behind images that don't look political at all. Consider, for example, the depiction of the "typical" American family in the classic TV sitcoms of the fifties and sixties, particularly all those images of happy, docile housewives. To most contemporary viewers, those images looked "normal" or natural at the time that they were first broadcast — the way families and women were supposed to be. The shows didn't seem at all ideological. To the contrary, they seemed a retreat from political rancor to domestic harmony. But to a feminist semiotician, the old sitcoms were in fact highly political, because the happy housewives they presented were really images designed to *convince* women that their place is in the home, not in the workplace competing with men. Such images — or signs — did not reflect reality; they reflected, rather, the interests of a patriarchal, male-centered society. If you think not, then ask yourself why there were shows called *Father Knows Best, Bachelor Father,* and *My Three Sons,* but no *My Three Daughters*? And why did few of the women in the shows have jobs or ever seem to leave the house? Of course, there was always *I Love Lucy,* but wasn't Lucy the screwball character that her husband Ricky had to rescue from one crisis after another?

Such are the kinds of questions that semiotics invites us to ask. They may be put more generally. When analyzing any popular cultural phenomenon, always ask yourself questions like these: Why does this thing look the way it does? Why are they saying this? Why am I doing this? What are they really saying? What am I really doing? In short, take nothing for granted when analyzing any image or activity.

Take, for instance, the reason you may have joined a health club (or decided not to). Did you happen to respond to a photo ad that showed you a gorgeous girl or guy (with a nice-looking guy or girl in the background)? On the surface of the ad, you simply see an image showing — or *denoting* — a patron of the club. You may think: "I want to look like that." But there's probably another dimension to the ad's appeal. The ad may *show* you someone with a nice body, but what it is suggesting — or *connoting* — is that this club is a good place to pick up a hot date. That's why that other figure appears in the background. That's supposed to be *you.* The one in the foreground is the sort of person you're being promised you'll find at the club. The ad doesn't say this, of course, but that's what it wants you to think because that's a more effective way of getting you to join. Suggestion, or connotation, is a much more powerful stimulant than denotation, but it is often deliberately masked in the signs you are presented with every day. Semiotics, one might say, reveals all the denotative smoke screens around you.

Health club membership drives, you may think, aren't especially political (though actually they are when you think of the kinds of bodies that they are telling you are desirable to have), but the powerful effect of a concealed suggestion is used all the time in actual political campaigns. The now infamous Willie Horton episode during the 1988 presidential campaign provides a classic instance. What happened was this: Some Republican supporters of George Bush's candidacy ran a series of TV ads featuring the photographic image of one Willie Horton, a convicted rapist from Massachusetts who murdered someone while on parole. On the surface, the ads simply showed, or denoted, this fact. But what they connoted was racial hatred and fear (Willie Horton is black), and they were very effective in prompting white voters to mistrust Massachusetts governor Michael Dukakis and to vote instead for George Bush.

Signs, in short, often conceal some interest or other, whether political, or commercial, or whatever. And the proliferation of signs and images in an era of electronic technology has simply made it all the more important that we learn to decode the interests behind them.

Semiotics, accordingly, is not just about signs and symbols: It is equally about ideology and power. This makes semiotics sound rather serious, and often the seriousness of a semiotic analysis is quite real. But reading the text of modern life can also be fun, for it is a text that is at once popular and accessible, a "book" that is intimately in touch with the pulse of American life. As such, it is constantly changing. The same sign can change meaning if something else comes along to change the environment in which it originally appeared. Take the return of the VW Beetle.

Interpreting Popular Signs

In 1998, after a hiatus of some twenty-five years, the Volkswagen New Beetle returned to the American automotive marketplace. But the return of the Beetle was not only a consumer event; it was also a sign, an indicator of a broader trend within American popular culture. The question is, of what?

One of the key elements in a semiotic analysis is to situate your topic within its historical context, and this is especially important in analyzing the cultural significance of the VW Beetle because of the dramatic changes that have occurred within its history. Originally conceived as a kind of propagandistic challenge to America's ability to provide automotive transport to the common person, the Volkswagen, or "people's wagon," was Adolf Hitler's answer to the Model T. It was expressly designed to connote the superiority of the Third Reich and to be a symbol of Germany's triumphant entry to the center of world power and prosperity.

The defeat of Nazi Germany put a swift end to that significance, and when the VW Beetle first appeared in American showrooms in the 1950s, its meaning changed accordingly. During an era of postwar prosperity when U.S. automobiles, the biggest and gaudiest on earth, were signifiers of American affluence, the humble Beetle was a car for the prudent and the penny-pinching. One of the first subcompact "economy cars," the VW Beetle, with its under-one-thousand-dollar price tag, served as a kind of reverse status symbol, identifying its owner as someone who didn't have a lot of money to spend. Realizing this, the advertisers for the VW decided to make a virtue of necessity and so used humor to market their product as a homely but sensible alternative in a marketplace of tail-finned extravagance and status sedans.

This humor, and the low cost of the Beetle, contributed to the next stage of the VW's semiotic history, which intersected with the rise of the 1960s youth culture. For then the Beetle, along with its wildly popular Microbus cousin, became the car of the counterculture, a cheap set of wheels for free-wheeling hippies who disdained the muscle cars, luxury chariots, and ordinary autos of the rest of America. Indeed, original Beetles and Microbuses — preferably plastered with Grateful Dead stickers — retain something of that significance to this day, mixing memory and nostalgia for many an aging baby boomer.

The Beetle disappeared from the American road in the 1970s as the hippie scene turned yuppie and a host of more fuel-efficient Japanese subcompacts (in those days they were known simply as "Toyotas" and "Datsuns") provided a more functional alternative in the wake of an exponential increase in gas prices. Volkswagen scrapped the Beetle and turned to the Rabbit, which never developed a cultural significance at all.

But, as they say, that was then, and this is now. The question for our semiotic analysis is what does the Beetle signify today? It certainly isn't a sign

of Nazi prosperity, nor is it simply a perky economy car (it's a bit too expensive for that). It's no signifier of the counterculture either. But it is a sign, a signifier of current popular cultural preoccupations. To see what it is a signifier of, we need to look at the current *system* in which the Beetle functions as a sign.

To establish the system in which a sign functions and gets its meaning, we need to look at some things with which the sign can be *associated,* or related, for from a semiotic perspective, the meaning of a sign largely lies in its relations to other signs, both in its similarities and in its differences to them. In other words, when looking at a popular cultural sign, you want to ask "what is this thing like?" as well as "how is it different from some of the things that it resembles?" By asking such questions, you establish a set of associations and differences. You can then approach the semiotic significance of your topic.

Let's return to the Beetle to see how this works. So ask yourself, with what things can the return of the Beetle be associated? It would be useful to begin with those products that are closest to it: other automobiles. But this association, while essential to our analysis, only takes us so far, because every year witnesses the introduction of new automobile lines as manufacturers seek to stimulate consumption through the introduction of new models and styles. The Beetle's return, in other words, is part of the *system* of automobile production and consumption, but without any way of distinguishing the Beetle from other cars within the system, its meaning would be limited to "new car offering in a marketplace that continually offers new models in order to stimulate consumption." This *is* a part of the Beetle's meaning, but there is a lot more to it than that.

Here is where we can consider the role of *difference* in a semiotic analysis. Among the new model car offerings of 1999 were a host of SUVs, sedans, pickups, sports cars, subcompacts — in short, the whole array of automotive lines. What made the Beetle different was, in large part, the fact that it was a revival (with some modifications) of a popular, and culturally acclaimed, auto from the golden age of American motoring: the 1950s and 1960s. What ended this era was the Arab oil embargo of 1973, which sent gas prices on an irreversible sky rocket and prompted carmakers to search for more functional and fuel-efficient automotive designs (Chrysler's bland K Car might represent the epitome of this chapter in automotive history). The Beetle, which was not as fuel efficient as the new subcompacts from Japan and Detroit, was a casualty of the gasoline spike, and it can be argued that the flair of automotive design was as well.

The return of the Beetle, then, marked a return to an earlier era of car design. So, what significance can we find in this? To answer this question, we can look back to the primary system in which the Beetle figures — the system of new car offerings at the end of the millennium — and look for some more associations or similarities. What we find are a number of other automobiles that represent the revival of earlier, largely abandoned styles from the golden age of American motoring. These include the return of the sporty two-seater, inaugurated by the Mazda Miata and most recently reproduced by the return of the two-seated Thunderbird, as well as the revival of the Mini. There are also Chrysler's PT Cruiser, which, while being a new design, was intended to suggest the styling of a 1950s hot-rod jalopy, and Chevrolet's SSR, another new model with a 1940s profile.

So, there has been a pattern of what might be called nostalgic revivals in the automotive marketplace. This pattern already provides a clue as to the cultural significance of the return of the Beetle, but before describing that meaning it would be useful to broaden our perspective a bit to see whether the pattern we have found within the system of car production can be found within the broader system of American consumer behavior. And, sure enough, it can.

Indeed, the last five or ten years have seen quite a number of revivals from the 1950s and 1960s. In 2001, for example, S&H Greenstamps, an icon of fifties and sixties consumer culture that disappeared years ago along with such relatives as Blue Chip Stamps and Plaid Stamps, staged a digitalized comeback as Greenpoints. In the realm of entertainment, movies such as *Ocean's 11* and *The Rat Pack,* along with the emergence of a lounge music scene, represented a revival of the Sinatra/Martin/Davis/Lewis/Bishop era.

We could continue searching for related revivals, but the outline of a significant pattern is already emerging. Clearly, the turn of the century witnessed a number of popular cultural revivals. Such revivals arguably signify a certain nostalgia for a bygone era, a desire to return to the products and images of the past. This raises another question in our analysis so far: Why should Americans desire to return to the past?

Here you need to look at a much broader context in your semiotic analysis: the overall mood and state of American consciousness. By the end of the millennium, that mood was at once jaunty — in the wake of the huge stock market run-up of the 1990s — and uncertain, as Americans worried about what Y2K would bring. At times of uncertainty, we tend to cling to those things that we know, the old verities as it were. In a consumer culture, those things include tried-and-true consumer goods like, well, VW Beetles or Ford Thunderbirds. The return of such vehicles reflects a calculated gamble on the part of their manufacturers that Americans would embrace them as signifiers of a more certain and comforting past. But they are also signifiers of that end-of-the-nineties jauntiness, for these, like the PT Cruiser, are also fun cars, deliberately and strikingly cute and whimsical rather than being simply functional. As such they are representative signs of their times indeed.

But wouldn't you interpret the owner of a PT Cruiser differently from the owner of a VW Beetle? Or what about a Thunderbird buyer? Or a Mini purchaser? All these cars can be associated together and all bear a similar meaning in one context, but there are also their differences to consider. These differences help to establish an even more precise significance for the Beetle, and so, to conclude our analysis, we must turn to them.

What differences can you note between the image of a Beetle owner and, say, a PT Cruiser driver? Though there may be a number of differences to note, gender difference is especially striking here, for the Beetle, with its bright green and yellow color options, as well as its low-octane cuteness, has especially become the choice of women consumers. With its relatively low, but not bargain basement, price tag, the Beetle has become a favorite choice for better-off young people, especially women in their early careers. While not being nearly as connotative as the Beetle of the 1960s, then, the current model has already assumed a certain significance, sending an identifiable image. Since Americans have always used their automobiles to make statements about themselves and construct a personal image, we can interpret just what sort of person is likely to drive what sort of car. Indeed we do this all the time, as do market researchers, who, as you will see further in our chapter on advertising, commonly construct consumer profiles on the basis of the products that they buy. And after all, don't you interpret others on the basis of the cars they drive? Isn't your own car a lifestyle signifier?

The Classroom Connection

The interpretive analysis we have sketched out here is intended to illustrate the kind of thought process that goes into a semiotic analysis. The historical surveying and contextualization, the comparative associations and analytic distinctions, and the drawing of interpretive conclusions are what come first in the writing process. Once you have done that, you will have your thesis, or argument, which will then form the structural backbone of your written analysis. Your paper will present that thesis and defend it with the evidence that your semiotic thinking produced. This process is, in essence, no different from the more conventional interpretive analyses you will be asked to perform in your college writing career. It is in the nature of all interpretations to make connections and mark differences to go beyond the surface of a text or issue toward a meaning. The skills you already have as an interpreter of the popular signs around you — of images, objects, and forms of behavior — are the same skills that you develop as a writer of critical essays that present an argued point of view and the evidence to defend it.

Because most of us tend to identify closely with our favorite popular cultural phenomena and have strong opinions about them, it can be more difficult to adopt the same sort of analytic perspective toward popular culture that we do toward, say, texts assigned in a literature class. Still, that is what you should do in a semiotic interpretation: You need to set your opinions aside in order to pursue an interpretive argument with evidence to support it. Note how in our interpretation of the VW Beetle we didn't say whether we like the car: Our concern was what it might mean within a larger cultural context. It is not difficult to express an opinion, but that isn't the goal of analytic writing. Analytic writing requires the martialing of supporting evidence, just like a lawyer needs evidence to argue a case. So by learning to write analyses of our culture, by searching for supporting evidence to underpin your interpretive take on modern life, you are also learning to write critical arguments.

"But how," you (and perhaps your instructor) may ask, "can I know that a semiotic interpretation is right?" Good question — it is commonly asked by those who fear that a semiotic analysis might read too much into a subject. But then, it can be asked of the writer of any interpretive essay, and the answer in each case is the same. No one can ever absolutely *prove* the truth of any argument in the human sciences; what you do is *persuade* your audience through the use of pertinent evidence. In writing analyses about popular culture, that evidence comes from your knowledge of the system to which the object you are interpreting belongs. The more you know about the system, the more convincing your interpretations will be. And that is true whether you are writing about popular culture or about more traditional academic subjects.

But often our interpretations of popular culture involve issues that are larger than those involved in music or entertainment. How, for instance, are we to analyze fully the widespread belief — as reflected in the classic TV sitcoms mentioned earlier — that it is more natural for women to stay at home and take care of the kids than it is for men to do so? Why, in other words, is the concept of housewife so easy to accept, while the idea of a househusband may seem ridiculous? How, in short, can we interpret some of our most basic values semiotically? To see how, we need to look at those value systems that semioticians call *cultural mythologies.*

Of Myths and Men

As we have seen, in a semiotic analysis we do not search for the meanings of things in the things themselves. Rather, we find meaning in the way we can relate things together, either through association or differentiation. We've done this with the Beetle's place in popular culture, but what about with beliefs? This book asks you to explore the implications of social issues like gender norms that involve a great many personal beliefs and values that we do not always recognize *as* beliefs and values. Rather, we think of them as truths (as in, "Of course it's odd for a man to stay home and take care of the house!"). But from a semiotic perspective, our values too belong to systems from which they take their meaning. Semioticians call these systems of belief *cultural mythologies.*

A cultural mythology, or *myth* for short, is not some fanciful story from the past; indeed, if this word seems confusing because of its traditional association with such stories, you may prefer to use the phrase *value system.* Consider the value system that governs our traditional thinking about gender roles. Have you ever noticed how our society presumes that it is primarily the role of women — adult daughters — to take care of aging and infirm parents? If you want to look at the matter from a physiological perspective, it might seem that men would be better suited to the task: In a state of nature, men are physically stronger and so would seem to be the natural protectors of the aged. And yet, though our cultural mythology holds that men should protect the nuclear family, it tends to assign to women the care of extended families. It is culture that decides here, not nature.

But while cultural myths guide our behavior, they are subject to change. You may have already experienced a transitional phase in the myths surrounding courtship behavior. In the past, the gender myths that formed the rules of the American dating game held that it is the role of the male to initiate proceedings (he calls) and for the female to react (she waits by the phone). Similarly, the rules once held that it is invariably the responsibility of the male to plan the evening and pay the tab. These rules are changing, aren't they? Can you describe the rules that now govern courtship behavior?

A cultural mythology or value system, then, is a kind of lens that governs the way we view our world. Think of it this way: Say you were born with rose-tinted lenses permanently attached over your eyes, but you didn't know they were there. Because the world would look rose-colored to you, you would presume that it *is* rose-colored. You wouldn't wonder whether the world might look otherwise through different lenses. But in the world there are other kinds of lenses, and reality does look different to those who wear them. Those lenses are cultural mythologies, and no culture can claim to have the one set of lenses that sees things as they really are.

The profound effect our cultural mythologies have on the way we view reality, on our most basic values, is especially apparent today when the myths of European culture are being challenged by the worldviews of the many other cultures that have taken root in American soil. European American culture, for example, upholds a profoundly individualistic social mythology that values individual rights before those of the group, but traditional Chinese culture believes in the primacy of the family and the community over the individual. Maxine Hong Kingston's short story "No Name Woman" poignantly demonstrates how such opposing ideologies can collide with painful results in its tale of a Chinese woman who is more or less sacrificed to preserve the interests of her village. The story, from *The Woman Warrior* (1976), tells of a young woman who gives birth to a baby too many months after her husband's departure to America with most of her village's other young men for it to be her husband's child. The men had left to earn the money in America that keeps the impoverished villagers from starving. They may be away for years and so need to be assured that their wives will remain faithful to them in their absence lest they refuse to go at all. The unfortunate heroine of the tale — who, to sharpen the agony, had probably been the victim of rape rather than the instigator of adultery — is horribly punished by the entire village as an example to any other wives who might disturb the system. The heroine ends a tragic suicide.

That Kingston wrote "No Name Woman" as a self-conscious Asian American, one whose identity fuses both Chinese and Euro-American values, reveals the fault lines between conflicting mythologies. As an Asian, Kingston understands the communal values behind the horrific sacrifice of her story's heroine, and her story makes sure that her Euro-American readers understand this too. But, as an American and as a feminist, she is outraged by the violation of an individual woman's rights on behalf of the group (or mob, which is how the village behaves in the story). Kingston's own sense of personal conflict in this clash of mythologies—Asian, American, and feminist—offers a striking example of the inevitable conflicts that America itself will face as it changes from a monocultural to a multicultural society.

To put this another way, from the semiotic perspective, *how* you interpret something is very much a product of *who* you are, for culture is just another name for the frames that shape our values and perceptions. Traditionally, American education has presumed a monocultural perspective, a melting-pot view that no matter what one's cultural background, truth is culture-blind. Langston Hughes took on this assumption many years ago in his classic poem "Theme for English B," where he writes, "I guess I'm what/I feel and see and hear," and wonders whether "my page will be colored" when he writes. "Being me, it will not be white," the poet suggests, but while he struggles to find what he holds in common with his white instructor, he can't suppress the differences. In essence, that is the challenge of multicultural education: to identify the different cultural codes that inform the mythic frameworks of the many cultures that share America while searching for what holds the whole thing together.

That meaning is not culture-blind, that it is conditioned by systems of ideology and belief that are codified differently by different cultures, is a foundational semiotic judgment. Human beings, in other words, construct their own social realities, and so who gets to do the constructing becomes very important. Every contest over a cultural code is, accordingly, a contest for power, but the contest is usually masked because the winner generally defines its mythology as the truth, as what is most natural or reasonable. Losers in the contest become objects of scorn and are quickly marginalized, declared unnatural, or deviant, or even insane. The stakes are high as myth battles myth, with truth itself as the highest prize.

This does not mean that you must abandon your own beliefs when conducting a semiotic analysis, only that you cannot take them for granted and must be prepared to argue for them. We want to assure you that semiotics will not tell you what to think and believe. It *does* assume that what you believe reflects some cultural system or other and that no cultural system can claim absolute validity or superiority. The readings and chapter introductions in this book contain their own values and ideologies, and if you wish to challenge those values you can begin by exposing the myths that they may take for granted.

To put this another way, everything in this book reflects a political point of view, and if you hold a different one it is not enough to simply presuppose the innate superiority of your own point of view—to claim that one writer is being political while you are simply telling the truth. This may sound heretical precisely because human beings operate within value systems whose political invisibility is guaranteed by the system. No mythology, that is to say, begins by saying, "this is just a political construct or interpretation." Every myth begins, "this is the truth." It is very difficult to imagine from within the myth any alternatives. Indeed, as you read this book, you may find it upsetting to see that some traditional beliefs — such as the "proper" roles of men and women in society — are socially constructed and not absolute. But the outlines of the myth, the bounding (and binding) frame, best appear when challenged by another myth, and this challenge is probably nowhere more insistent than in America, where so many of us are really "hyphenated" Americans, citizens combining in our own persons two (or more) cultural traditions.

Getting Started

Mythology, like culture, is not static, however, and so the semiotician must always keep his or her eye on the clock, so to speak. History, time itself, is a constant factor in a constantly changing world. Since the previous editions of this book, American popular culture has moved on. In this edition, we have tried to reflect those changes, but inevitably, further changes will occur in the time it takes for this book to appear on your class syllabus. That such changes occur is part of the excitement of the semiotic enterprise: There is always something new to consider and interpret. What does not change is the nature of semiotic interpretation: Whatever you choose to analyze in the realm of American popular culture, the semiotic approach will help you understand it.

It's your turn now. Start asking questions, pushing, probing. That's what critical writing is all about, but this time *you're* part of the question. Arriving at answers, conclusions, is the fun part here, but answers aren't the basis of analytic thinking: Questions are. You always begin with a question, a query, a hypothesis, something to explore. If you already knew the answer, there would be no point in conducting the analysis. We leave you to it to explore the almost infinite variety of questions that the readings in this book raise. Many come equipped with their own "answers," but you may (indeed will and should) find such answers raise further questions. To help you ask those questions, keep in mind the two elemental principles of semiotics that we have explored so far:

1. The meaning of a sign can be found not in itself but in its *relationships* (both differences and similarities) with other signs within a *system*. To interpret an individual sign, then, you must determine the general system in which it belongs.
2. What we call social "reality" is a human construct, the product of a cultural *mythology* or *value system* that intervenes between our minds and the world we experience. Such cultural myths reflect the values and ideological interests of its builders, not the laws of nature or logic.

Perhaps our first principle could be more succinctly phrased, "everything is connected," and our second simply summarized as, "question authority." Think of them that way if it helps. Or just ask yourself whenever you are interpreting something, "what's going on here?" In short, question *everything*. And one more reminder: Signs are like weather vanes; they point in response to invisible historical winds. We invite you now to start looking at the weather.

PORTFOLIO
September 11, 2001

TIME

SEPTEMBER 11
2001

$4.50

WRITING ABOUT POPULAR CULTURE

Throughout this book, you will find readings on popular culture that you can use as models for your own writing or as subjects to which you may respond, assignments for writing critical essays on popular culture, and semiotic tips to help you analyze a wide variety of cultural phenomena. As you approach these readings and assignments, you may find it helpful to review the following suggestions for writing critical essays — whether on popular culture or on any subject — as well as some examples of student essays written in response to assignments based on *Signs of Life in the U.S.A.* Mastering the skills summarized and exemplified here should prepare you for writing the kinds of papers you will be assigned through the rest of your college career.

As you prepare to write a critical essay on popular culture, remember that you are already an expert in your subject. Being an expert doesn't necessarily mean spending years of studying in a library; simply by actively participating in everyday life, you have accumulated a vast store of knowledge about what makes our culture tick. Just think about all you know about movies, or the thousands on thousands of ads you've seen, or even the many unwritten "rules" governing courtship behavior among your circle of friends. All of these help form the fabric of contemporary American culture — and, if you've ever had to explain to a younger sibling why her latest outfit was inappropriate for work or why his comment to a blind date struck the wrong chord, you've already played the role of expert.

Because popular culture is part of everyday life, however, you may take for granted this knowledge: it might not seem that it can "count" as material for a college-level assignment, and you might not think to include it in an essay. Thus, it can be useful to spend some time, before you start writing, to generate your ideas freely and openly: Your goal at this point is to develop as many ideas as possible, even ones that you might not actually use in your essay. Writing instructors call this process *prewriting,* and it's a step you should take when writing on any subject in any class, not just in your writing class. This textbook includes many suggestions for how you can develop your ideas; even if your instructor doesn't require you to use all of them, you can try them on your own.

Developing Ideas about Popular Culture

The first step in developing your ideas for an essay about any topic is to make sure you understand accurately the reading selections that your instructor has assigned. You want to engage in *active* reading — that is, you want not simply to get the "drift" of a passage but to understand the nuances of how the author constructs his or her argument. With any selection, it can be helpful to read at least twice: first, to gain a general sense of the author's ideas and, second, to study more specifically how those ideas are put together to form an argument. Ask yourself questions, such as the following, that enable you to evaluate the selection:

- What is the author's primary argument? Can you identify a thesis statement, or is the thesis implied?
- What words or key terms are fundamental to that argument? If the fundamental vocabulary of the selection is unfamiliar to you, be sure to check a dictionary or encyclopedia for the word's meaning.
- What evidence does the author provide to support the argument?
- What underlying assumptions shape the author's position? Does the author consider alternative points of view (counterarguments)?
- What style and tone does the author adopt?
- What is the genre of the piece? You need to take into account what kind of writing you are responding to, for different kinds have different purposes and goals. A personal narrative, for instance, expresses the writer's experiences and beliefs, but you shouldn't expect it to present a fully demonstrated argument.
- Who is the intended readership of this selection, and does it affect the author's reasoning or evidence?

Signs of Life in the U.S.A. frequently asks you to respond to a reading selection in your journal, sometimes directly and sometimes indirectly, as in suggestions that you write a letter to the author of a selection. In doing so, you're taking an important first step in articulating your response to the issues and to the author's presentation of them. In asking you to keep a journal or a reading log, your instructor will probably be less concerned with your writing style than with your comprehension of assigned readings and your thoughtful responses to them. Let's say you're asked to write your response to a reading selection; we'll take for an example Emily Prager's "Our Barbies, Ourselves" in Chapter 9. You should first think through exactly what Prager is saying — what her point is — using the questions listed. Then consider how you feel about it. If you agree with Prager's belief that the Barbie doll perpetuates outmoded ideas about women, why do you feel that way? Can you think of other objects (or even people) that seem to exemplify those same ideas? What alternative ways of designing a doll can you imagine? Note that the purpose of imagining your own doll is not so you'll actually produce one; it's so you think through alternatives and explore the implications of Prager's and your own thoughts. Or say you're irritated by Prager's argument: Again, why do you feel that way? What would you say to her in response? What, perhaps in your own experience as a child, might show that she's wrong? Your aim in jotting all this down is not to produce a draft of an essay. It's to play with your own ideas, see where they lead, and even just help you decide what your ideas are in the first place.

Often we or your instructor may ask you to brainstorm ideas or to freewrite in response to an issue. These are both strategies you can use in your journal or on your own as you start working on an essay. Brainstorming is simply amassing as many relevant (and even some irrelevant) ideas as possible. Let's say your instructor asks you to brainstorm a list of popular toys used by girls and boys in preparation for an essay about the gendered designs of children's toys. Try to list your thoughts freely, jotting down whatever comes to mind. Don't censor yourself at this point. That is, don't worry if something is really a toy or a game, or if it is used by both boys and girls, or if it really is an adult toy. Later on you can throw out ideas that don't fit. What you'll be left with is a rich list of examples that you can then study and analyze. Freewriting works much the same way and is particularly useful when you're not sure of how you feel about an issue. Sit down and just start writing or typing, and don't stop until you've written for at least ten or fifteen minutes. Let your ideas wander around your subject, working associatively, following their own path. As with brainstorming, you may produce some irrelevant ideas, but you may also come to a closer understanding of how you really feel about an issue.

Sometimes your instructor may invite you to create your own topic. Where should you start? Let's say you decide to analyze an aspect of the film industry but can't decide on a focus. Here, the Internet might help. You could explore a search engine such as *Yahoo!,* specifically its Movies and Films index. There you'll find dozens of subcategories, such as History, Theory and Criticism, Cultures and Groups, and Trivia. Each of these subcategories has many sites to explore: History, for instance, includes the Archives of Early Lindy Hop as well as the Bill Douglas Centre for the History of Cinema and Popular Culture, a wonderful compendium of 25,000 books, posters, and other movie-related memorabilia. With so many sites to choose from, you're bound to find something that interests you. The Net, in effect, allows you to engage in electronic brainstorming and so arrive at your topic.

One cautionary note: In using the Internet to brainstorm, be sure to evaluate the appropriateness of your sources. Many sites are commercial and therefore are intended more to sell a product or image than to provide reliable information. In addition, since anyone with the technological knowhow can set up a Web site, some sites (especially personal home pages) amount to little more than personal expression and need to be evaluated for their reliability, accuracy, and authenticity. Scrutinize the sites you use carefully: Is the author an authority in the field? Does the site identify the author, at least by name and e-mail address (be wary of fully anonymous sites)? Does the site contain interesting and relevant links? If you find an advocacy site, one that openly advances a special interest, does the site's bias interfere with the accuracy of its information? Asking such questions can help ensure that your electronic brainstorming is fruitful and productive. If you are not sure of the validity of a Web site, you might want to check with your instructor.

Not all prewriting activities need be solitary, of course. In fact, *Signs of Life* includes lots of suggestions that ask you to work with other students, either in your class or from across campus. We do that because much academic work really is collaborative and collegial. When a scientist is conducting research, for instance, he or she often works with a team, may present preliminary findings to colloquia or conferences, and may call or e-mail a colleague at another school to try out some ideas. There's no reason you can't benefit from the social nature of academic thinking as well. But be aware that such in-class group work is by no means "busy work." The goal, rather, is to help you to develop and shape your understanding of the issues and your attitudes toward them. If you're asked to study a men's fashion magazine with three classmates, for instance, you're starting to test Diane Barthel's thesis in "A Gentleman and a Consumer" (Chapter 2), seeing how it applies or doesn't apply and benefiting from your peers' insights.

Let's say you're asked to present to the class a semiotic reading of a childhood toy. By discussing a favorite toy with your class, you are articulating, perhaps for the first time, what it meant (or means) to you and so are taking the first step toward writing a more formal analysis of it in an essay (especially if you receive feedback and comments from your class). Similarly, if you stage an in-class debate over whether Batman is a gay character, you're amassing a wonderful storehouse of arguments, counterarguments, and evidence to consider when you write your own essay that either supports or refutes Andy Medhurst's thesis in "Batman, Deviance, and Camp" (Chapter 9). As with other strategies to develop your ideas, you may not use directly every idea generated in conversation with your classmates, but that's okay. You should find yourself better able to sort through and articulate the ideas that you do find valuable.

Developing Strong Arguments about Popular Culture

We expect that students will write many different sorts of papers in response to the selections in this book. You may write personal experience narratives, opinion pieces, research papers, formal pro-con arguments, and many others. We'd like here to focus on writing analytic essays because the experience of analyzing popular culture may seem different than that of analyzing other subjects. Occasionally we've had students who feel reluctant to analyze popular culture because they think that analysis requires them to trash their subject, and they don't want to write a "negative" essay about what may be their favorite film or TV program. Or a few students may feel uncertain because "it's all subjective." Since most people have opinions about popular culture, they say, how can any one essay be stronger than another?

While these concerns are understandable, they needn't be an obstacle in writing a strong analytic paper — whether on popular culture or any other topic. First, we often suggest that you set aside your own personal tastes when writing an analysis. We do so not because your preferences are not important; recall that we often ask you to explore your beliefs in your journal, and we want you to be aware of your own attitudes and observations about your topic. Rather, we do so because an analysis of, say, *The Mummy* is not the same as a paper that explains "why I like (or dislike) this movie." Instead, an analysis would explain how it works, what cultural beliefs and viewpoints underlie it, what its significance is, and so forth. And such a paper would not necessarily be positive or negative; it would seek to explain how the elements of the film work together to have a particular effect on its audience. If your instructor asks you to write a critical analysis or a critical argument, he or she is requesting neither a hit job nor a celebration of your topic.

As a result, the second concern, about subjectivity, becomes less of a problem. That's because your analysis should center around a clear argument about that movie. You're not simply presenting a personal opinion about it; rather, you're presenting a central insight about how the movie works, and you need to demonstrate it with logical, specific evidence. It's that evidence that will take your essay out of the category of being "merely subjective." You should start with your own opinion, but you want to add to it lots of proof that shows the legitimacy of that opinion. Does that sound familiar? It should, because that's what you need to do in any analytic essay, no matter what your subject matter happens to be.

When writing about popular culture, students sometimes wonder what sort of evidence they can use to support their points. Your instructor will probably give you guidelines for each assignment, but we'll provide some general suggestions here. Start with your subject itself. You'll find it's useful to view your subject — whether it's an ad, a film, or anything else — as a text that you can "read" closely. That's what you would do if you were asked to analyze a poem: you would read it carefully, studying individual words, images, rhythm, and so forth, and those details would support whatever point you wanted to make about the poem. Read your pop culture subject with the same care. Let's say your instructor asks you to analyze an advertisement. Look at the details: Who appears in the ad, and what are their expressions? What props are used, and what is the "story" that the ad tells? Is there anything missing from this scene that you would expect to find? Your answers to such questions could form the basis of the evidence that you use in your essay.

If your instructor has asked you to write a semiotic analysis, you can develop evidence as well by locating your subject within a larger system. Recall that a system is the larger network of related signs to which your subject belongs and that identifying it helps to reveal the significance of your subject. This may sound hard to do, but it is through identifying a system that you can draw on your own vast knowledge of popular culture. And that may sound abstract, but it becomes very specific when applied to a particular example. If you were to analyze platform shoes, for instance, it would help to locate them within the larger fashion system — specifically, other choices of footwear. How do the signals sent by wearing a pair of platforms differ from those sent by wearing, say, a pair of Doc Martens? How does the history of platform shoes, specifically their popularity in the 1970s, affect their current appeal? Can you associate the retro look of platforms with any other fashion and popular cultural trends? Teasing out such differences and associations can help you explain the shoes' social and cultural significance.

You can strengthen your argument as well if you know and use the history of your subject. That might sound like you have to do a lot of library research, but often you don't have to: you may already be familiar with the social and cultural history of your subject. If you know, for instance, that the baggy pants so popular among teens in the mid-1990s were a few years before ubiquitous among street gang members, you know an important historical detail that goes a long way toward explaining their significance. Depending on your assignment, you might want to expand on your own historical knowledge and collect other data about your topic, perhaps through surveys and interviews. If you're analyzing gendered patterns of courtship rituals, for instance, you could interview some people from different age groups, as well as both genders, to get a sense of how such patterns have evolved over time. The material you gather through such an interview will be raw data, and you'll want to do more than just "dump" the information into your essay. See this material instead as an original body of evidence that you'll sort through (you probably won't use every scrap of information), study, and interpret in its own right.

Reading Essays about Popular Culture

In your writing course, it's likely that your instructor will ask you to work in groups with other students, perhaps reviewing each other's rough drafts. You'll find many benefits to this activity. Not only will you receive more feedback on your own in-progress work, but you will see other students' ideas and approaches to an assignment and develop an ability to evaluate academic writing. For the same reasons, we're including three sample student essays that satisfy assignments about popular culture. You may agree or disagree with the authors' views, and you might think you'd respond to the assigned topics differently: that's fine. We've selected these essays because they differ in style, focus, and purpose and thus suggest different approaches to their assignments — approaches that might help you as you write your own essays about popular culture. We've annotated the essays to point out argumentative, organizational, and rhetorical strategies that we found effective. As you read the essays and the annotations, ask why the authors chose these strategies and how you might incorporate some of the same strategies in your own writing.

Essay 1: Personal Experience Essay

Some assignments may allow you to respond to a topic by discussing your own personal experiences and observations. Such assignments enable you to draw on a wealth of details and specific evidence that you have close to hand, and they also enable you to develop your own voice as a writer (because the subject is your own experience, you will want to use the first-person form of address). Dana Mariano, a student at Lehigh University in Bethlehem, Pennsylvannia, wrote the following essay, "Patrons of the Arts," about a recent trend that many young people have embraced despite their parents' disapproval: tattooing and body piercing. Mariano was not required to base her discussion on a close reading of the selections. But notice that she combines her own tale of visiting a tattoo parlor with a full and rich consideration of the system into which her visit can be interpreted — thus fulfilling one of the central tenets of the semiotic approach.

Patrons of the Arts

The glow from Tattoo 46's neon sign reflected onto the dashboard of my car and attracted most of the flies from the surrounding area. As I walked into Tattoo 46, I asked myself a very logical question: "What the hell am I doing here?" I was not a biker, a World War II veteran, or a criminal; I was simply an eighteen-year-old girl who wanted a tattoo. Actually, I had wanted a tattoo since I was in the eighth grade, and now I was finally old enough to get one.

I looked around the waiting room of Tattoo 46 and saw plastered on the walls a potpourri of tattoos that ranged from fire-breathing dragons to roses to cartoon characters. I could hear a faint buzz coming from a room in the back that was shut off with a curtain that looked like a bedspread from the sixties. Luckily, I already knew exactly what tattoo I wanted, so I did not have to search for the perfect one from the plethora of tattoos on the walls. I planned to get my tattoo of a Hawaiian flower and get it tattooed onto my lower stomach.

A burly, gray-haired man, who reminded me so much of Jerry Garcia, walked out from another back room and asked, "So, let me guess. You are here to get your belly-button pierced."

"Actually, I would like it if you could do a tattoo of this," I said as I handed him the picture of the tiny narcissus flower my friend Samantha had drawn for me.

"Yeah, I can do this," he said. "Do you have any ID?"

"Sure, here it is," I said triumphantly as I showed him my driver's license.

"Well, well, well. Happy Birthday. So, are you ready to roll?" he asked.

"As ready as I'll ever be," I replied with a voice that lacked any semblance of confidence.

As I walked into the small room, I saw all over the walls pictures of tattooed and pierced people. Most of these people had body piercings in regions where I had only heard people could get them, but I never thought it was truly physically possible. I heard a man scream from the other room, and once again I asked myself, "What the hell am I doing here?" I was a medium-height, blonde, Abercrombie-wearing, sorority type of girl. Why would I get a tattoo or anything other than my ears pierced?

Looking at society today, one realizes that a variety of people are now getting tattoos and body piercings. These body adornments, which were once an accessory for rebels, punks, bikers, and freaks, are now commonly seen on models, actors, people in the business world, and even teachers. Today, one cannot walk down the street without seeing someone sporting a tattoo, eyebrow ring, tongue ring, or labret (pierced lower lip).

These people are proud to show off their personal artwork. Tattooing and body piercing were once symbols of nonconformity in society; now they almost seem to be a form of conformity. The question is, why have so many decided to pierce their bodies in weird areas and adorn their bodies with tattoos? What exactly has happened to polite society?

Celebrities and rock stars have always influenced the way people believe they should look. With many models, rock icons, sports figures, actors, and actresses getting their bodies tattooed and pierced, the public wants to follow in their footsteps. Even the most feminine and revered actresses and models are tattooing themselves with small flowers and butterflies or getting their belly-buttons pierced as a symbol of sexuality. Sports figures such as Dennis Rodman cannot stop with just one tattoo and body piercing. For many, body piercing and tattooing become a strange addiction. Society has always looked at these types of people as role models. If they can pierce and tattoo, why shouldn't the public?

If one looks at the type of people who are piercing themselves, one sees that many are in their thirties and forties, the baby-boomers who are in the midlife-crisis age range. Many baby-boomers have reached the midlife-crisis age and need something to show a sense of rebellion against society. Also, many baby-boomers did not feel that having a tattoo or body piercing was appropriate until now because of its new appeal in polite society and the mainstream.

My mother is one of the people in this category. She got a tattoo five years ago. One could say that she was going through a midlife crisis. She lost one hundred pounds, grew her once-short hair rather long, and bought a very cute red convertible. The last thing on her agenda of making a new woman was to get a tattoo of a butterfly on her lower stomach. Now she is through her midlife crisis, and she feels a sense of youth from her tattoo. She has even said when she dies she wants there to be a hole in her dress where her tattoo is. She wants everyone to be able to see her personal work of art.

Dana broadens her focus to a general cultural trend.

She analyzes her subject, drawing on popular culture to describe the semiotic system in which tattoos and body piercing exist.

Dana provides an alternative explanation, which adds depth to her analysis.

Another explanation for this trend is the *National Geographic* syndrome. In other parts of the world, tattooing and piercing have been common practices for thousands of years. In many non-Western cultures and societies, body art is an indicator of nobility and the upper class. In India, when a woman gets married, she is covered with patterns in henna, a type of dye. This body art is considered a sacred symbol of beauty for an Indian woman. Since the world is becoming more and more aware of other cultures, we can see other cultures' ways and are far more accepting of them. The globalization of the world has truly opened up society to be more accepting of one another's cultures, views, and even body adornments.

She offers a third explanation and follows it with an extended example.

A compelling reason for the act seems to be to establish identity. This is why many people my age get body piercings and tattoos. Many teenagers are scared of getting lost in the crowd, and that is why they resort to such measures. It is so hard to stand out in a diverse society; teenagers today go to any measure they can to get more attention. My friend Deanna, who is the valedictorian of my class, recently got her eyebrow pierced. She is one of the people who did this as a form of rebellion and to make a departure from her girly, brainy persona. She did this a few days before graduating high school.

"So, do you think all the parents will be thrilled to see my beautiful eyebrow ring?" Deanna asked with a sly grin.

Dialogue dramatizes the point and makes it personal and immediate.

"Oh, you know they are going to love it. I am sure that you will make the school so proud sporting your eyebrow ring," I said in one of my more sarcastic tones.

"Do you know that the principal already asked me to take it out for graduation? He said he doesn't want me to give the school a bad look," Deanna said with a hint of pride.

"You aren't going to take it out, are you?" I asked.

"Are you kidding me? Of course not. I refuse to allow people to remember me as perfect little Deanna. I would look like I was the principal's pet, even though I was at one time. I have worked so hard to move away from the old Deanna. This eyebrow ring represents a new, more independent Deanna," she firmly stated.

Whatever the reason, many people have decided to adorn their bodies with tattoos and piercings. Today's diverse society makes it harder and harder for a person to get noticed, so many have changed their appearance so they can stand out in the crowd. The abundance of body piercing and tattooing has also changed the way society looks at beauty.

It was once considered ugly and manly for a woman to have a tattoo. To-day, it is considered sexy and erotic if a woman has a small, feminine tattoo on her body. The abundance of tattooing and body piercing has certainly changed the way that society views these things that were once considered proper only for freaks.

As I lay on the cold metal table, I tried to decide whether I truly wanted this tattoo or not. I pulled down my pants and watched my tat-too artist get out a new needle. I was going to do this. I had no idea why, but I was going to get the tattoo I always wanted. There is no ra-tional explanation for why I wanted a tattoo; I just did.

"So why are you getting a tattoo?" my tattoo artist asked.

"I don't know," I said. "I just want one."

Dana returns to the intro-duction's dramatic scene, signaling closure to the narrative.

Essay 2: Critical Reading of a Film

Your instructor may ask you to read one of the selections in this text and then to apply the author's general ideas to a new example, either one provided by the assignment or one that you select. Such an assignment asks you to work closely with two "texts" — the reading selection and a pop cultural example — and requires you to articulate the relationship you see between the two. In essence, such an assignment asks you to use the reading selection as a critical framework for analyzing the particular example. In this essay, William Martin-Doyle of Harvard University applies Robert B. Ray's theory of heroic arche-types in American cinema ("The Thematic Paradigm," p. 308) to a film of his own choice, *Cool Hand Luke*. His instructor explained to his class, "A really good essay will not simply say *why* Ray's theory does or does not apply but will go further and speculate what that relevance or irrelevance *means*." As you read Martin-Doyle's essay, look for how the student fulfills both tasks.

William sums up Ray's definition of hero and presents his argument that Cool Hand Luke *(CHL) departs from Ray's archetypal pattern.*

Cool Hand Luke: The Exclusion of the Official Hero in American Cinema

In his article "The Thematic Paradigm," Robert B. Ray contends that the two heroic types of outlaw and official are the stock figures of American cinema. The author implies that by the acceptance of the two characters' juxtaposition in popular culture, Americans are revealing a type of immaturity: "The parallel existence of these two contradictory traditions evinced the general pattern of American mythology: the denial of the necessity for choice" (para. 15). This contention is well rooted: movies such as *Shane,* for example, illustrate Ray's point quite effectively, presenting the viewer with the story of a gunslinger and a farmer joining forces to combat evil and defend the American way. Movies have come a long way since *Shane,* though. Films display their coming-of-age by making choices far more often than they used to. This new decisiveness does not necessarily reflect a responsible adulthood, however; when a choice is made, it is now frequently for the outlaw hero. This trend is easily seen in the movie *Cool Hand Luke* (1967).

The paragraph doesn't just give a plot summary but explains plot details in terms of the ideologies Ray describes.

The movie tells the story of an individualist who is sentenced to two years working on a chain gang for his rebellion against authority. To avoid alienating the viewer with the story of an inhuman criminal, the makers of the movie choose a crime that panders to the audience, in the form of "malicious destruction of municipal property": cutting the heads off parking meters while bored and drunk. In this way, lawbreaking is romanticized as the vice of a man who refuses to conform. Luke's individualism and powerful personality initially alienate the other prisoners, but he soon becomes their idol; through him they live vicariously. After attempting to live in the suffocating atmosphere of the prison camp, Luke begins his escape efforts. He is repeatedly recaptured, with mounting consequences for each attempt. The authorities, as symbolized by the nameless man who supervises the chain gang's work from behind the mask of his sunglasses, attempt to break Luke's spirit. They degrade and beat him for every attempt, and they finally kill him after his third try, but Luke's refusal to conform, expressed through his escapes, is made into a victory for individuality.

Cool Hand Luke's unreserved depiction of the legal system as a brutally unjust entity signals a definite departure from movies that contain both of Ray's stock hero types. Ray asserts that "by customarily portraying the law as the tool of villains . . . this mythology betrayed a profound pessimism about the individual's access to the legal system" (para. 11). The law, confusingly, is also the tool of the official hero. This is a puzzling situation in many movies, as order is the very basis for the character of the official hero. That the support for the "Good Good Boys" (para. 3) should come from an institution that the audience for some reason views with suspicion suggests that the official hero character is only a substitute for the outlaw hero in most people's minds: the renegade is the ideal. The presence of both types in a film might indicate a certain confusion in the viewer about what he or she really values. Ray, however, indicates that American cinema is typified by the presence of the two. *Cool Hand Luke* represents a departure from that "duplicity" (para. 23). There is no confused romanticizing of two conflicting ideals: instead, the clear choice is Newman's outlaw. Everywhere in the movie, the forces of law and order are portrayed as a tool for oppression rather than for the protection of everyday citizens, a group to which one might assume the average audience member belongs.

William presents more fully Ray's definition of heroes and moves to the essay's assertion that CHL fails to fulfill this pattern.

Ray writes of the pervasive theme of the reluctant hero, the man who is eventually forced by outside pressures into promoting the greater good; he is "the private man attempting to keep from being drawn into action on any but his own terms. In this story, the reluctant hero's ultimate willingness to help the community satisfied the official values" (para. 18). In this way, the reluctant hero represents a synthesis of the official and the outlaw hero, rendering a somewhat contradictory picture, almost of a man with a split personality. Once again, *Shane* epitomizes this concept, as the mysterious stranger is drawn into aiding the brave settlers in their struggle against the ranchers, despite his initial desire to lay aside his guns and lead a peaceful life. In contrast, *Cool Hand Luke* presents no such capitulation to the moral pressure of helping others. Luke's only priority is to live his life his own way, not to aid the other prisoners. There is no plot device of the hero righteously leading a rebellion against the armed guards for subjecting them to life in the chain gang. Luke never consciously tries to become a leader, and the other prisoners' admiration for him never fosters a sense of responsibility in him for their well-being. His strong personality induces others to become attached to him, yet he never feels any reciprocal ties. Indeed, the only strong emotional bond that he has during the entire movie is the one to his sickly mother, who comes to visit him at one point. Later in the movie, word of her death arrives, and Luke is cut off from any emotional tie, making him a complete loner. Even this instance is used as an example of the cruelty of the established authority, as Luke is confined

Here and in the next two paragraphs, William analyzes specific cinematic details that demonstrate the kind of hero Luke is.

in a wooden box the size of a closet for several days just so that he won't get any ideas about escaping to go to the funeral. This measure does force Luke to the edge, but his response is not that of Ray's stereotypical hero, who exhibits traits of both the official and the outlaw hero. His response is straightforward, in keeping with his character. He doesn't combat injustice in general, helping the greater good of the other prisoners; instead, he makes his first attempt at escape (a perfectly understandable, yet hardly selfless action). In this way, the character of Luke remains consistent: he begins as an outlaw, and he never strays from that image.

The conspicuous lack of an official hero is accented by George Kennedy's character Dragune, who at first seems like he might play that role. A prisoner who has been serving time for several years, he has become a sort of leader among the prisoners, who listen to him because of his strength and his outspokenness. A bit of a blowhard, he defends the status quo, holding forth on the value of order in the prisoners' lives: "We got rules here. In order to learn 'em, you gotta do more work with your ears than with your mouth." Ray states that the official hero's motto is "You cannot take the law into your own hands" (para. 12), and this is clearly Dragune's own personal opinion. Luke, on the other hand, obviously has no use for society's impositions; during his first night, he says, "I ain't heard that much worth listening to. Just a lot of guys laying down a lot of rules and regulations." When conflict arises between Dragune and Luke, it first appears that the viewpoint of the authority will triumph over Luke's championing of the individual. They box, as is the custom for two prisoners with irreconcilable differences, and Dragune easily beats Luke senseless. This physical triumph of authority quickly turns into a moral victory for Luke, however, as Dragune is forced to leave the ring when he realizes that the only way that Luke will ever stay on the ground after a knockdown is if Dragune kills him. After this turning point, Dragune soon becomes Luke's friend and eventually his disciple.

Luke's tenacity is simultaneously the strong point of his personality, the very trait that makes him worthy of admiration, and his fatal flaw. This character will never give up, no matter the pain he must endure, whether the situation is in the boxing ring against a man who heavily outweighs him, in a bet that he can eat fifty eggs in an hour, or in his repeated attempts at escape, for which he is punished with escalating viciousness. These escape attempts are the main outlet for his rebellion, and they are always initially successful. Despite the fact that he is always later apprehended, he always makes his escapes in grand fashion, confounding the authorities who attempt to chase him. The

William doesn't limit his analysis to Luke; he studies other characters as well.

escapes are therefore victories of a kind against the establishment, symbolic of his death grip on his own identity. After the first recapture, the captain of the camp debases Luke and reflects to the other prisoners: "What we've got here is failure to communicate. Some men, you just can't reach." In this world of polar extremes, there can be no communication between the outlaw hero and the forces of conformity that would normally be wielded by an official hero. It is officialdom's failure to reach Luke, to "get his mind right," that gives the outlaw his victory. His death is imbued with nobility as the car that takes him away, dying, crushes the supervisor's sunglasses that have come to be the recurring metaphor for the rule of the law.

Cool Hand Luke represents a shift away from the standards presented in Ray's article, as illustrated by *Shane,* in which American movies have a conflicting duality of protagonists. *Cool Hand Luke* has instead made the choice for the outlaw hero. This is a definite shift away from earlier movies that emphasized the official hero, such as Jimmy Stewart films, and war movies, which celebrated the triumph of the ultimate official body, the United States government. Despite the fact that the movie was a product of the late 1960s, a time of political and social unrest, *Cool Hand Luke*'s decision still has relevance in this decade. The rejection of society in its present form, as represented by the official hero, is still visible in the progression to modern hits like *Natural Born Killers* and *Pulp Fiction,* which glorify serial killers and organized crime hit men. Ray implies that Americans' failure to make a choice when it comes to their movies is a societal problem. In *Cool Hand Luke,* the choice has been made, but a new problem is reflected in that choice. Any country is based on the idea that there must be rules to govern acceptable and unacceptable behavior; the constant deprecation of those rules therefore signals an extreme dissatisfaction with present society. Such dissatisfaction is a normal reaction against the perceived failure of authority, as exemplified by problems such as the Vietnam War, Watergate, and the national economy. Dissatisfaction isn't necessarily a bad thing, but expressing discontent without hinting at the possibility of a real solution is troubling.

The problem with the choice of the outlaw hero lies in the fact that the outlaw doesn't confront issues and deal with them in a mature fashion. Instead, he runs away as Luke did or uses force until there is nothing left to face. In short, the choice of the outlaw hero exposes the fact that Americans are indulging in a form of moral escapism: they dislike their present circumstances, yet are too scared to face up to them.

William locates CHL in the context of American film history, including films that both predate and postdate CHL.

The essay moves toward its conclusion by suggesting the social implications of the ideology presented in CHL.

William concludes with a sharp statement of his view of those implications.

Essay 3: Open-Ended Analytic Assignment

Your instructor may assign an open-ended topic, one that allows you to select your own focus and subject matter. If you receive such an assignment, first brainstorm possible topics that interest you, for you'll produce the best writing if you're excited about your topic. Many students feel tempted to choose a broad subject (for instance, images of African Americans in modern media), assuming they will have more to say about it, but with such a broad and unwieldy topic you can have trouble deciding where to start. Aim for a more specific topic, preferably one that you discuss with your instructor. The following essay, by Mike Nordberg of Lehigh University, is entitled "Science Fiction: A Mirror to Our Universe," but notice that Mike doesn't attempt to discuss all science fiction; instead, he narrows his focus to the *Star Trek* phenomenon. Note that Mike grounds his argument about science fiction in a rich array of details that constitute the semiotic system in which *Star Trek* and its many spinoffs can be interpreted.

Science Fiction: A Mirror to Our Universe

"Space, the final frontier. These are the voyages of the Starship *Enterprise*. Its continuing mission, to explore strange new worlds. To seek out new life and new civilizations. To boldly go where no man, er . . . um . . . where no one has gone before." This opening monologue to the TV series *Star Trek* and *Star Trek: The Next Generation* is one of the most recognizable in television history. It has existed in nearly the same form since the original series debuted in 1966. However, as one can see above, it has not gone completely unchanged. As the world around *Star Trek* transformed during those thirty years, the program itself adjusted to the changing world around it. And yet this is one of science fiction's great strengths. Behind all the action, technical wizardry, and stunning special effects, there exists an ideal stage to comment on present-day culture. This is because the way we as a society view the future reveals a great deal about how we live in the present. Indeed, science fiction is often a mirror of the real world where present-day issues are discussed in a futuristic setting.

Many controversial issues have been addressed in the four television series — *Star Trek, Star Trek: The Next Generation, Star Trek: Deep Space Nine,* and *Star Trek: Voyager* — and nine movies that make up the *Star Trek* universe. Producer Gene Roddenberry created a fantastic world where humankind has overcome war, greed, and poverty while still leaving room for a moral dilemma or two to creep in. This formula makes for not only interesting and profitable programming but also excellent social commentary when the problems faced in the show have parallels to current events. Take, for example, the original series episode, "Let That Be Your Last Battlefield." In that episode, the crew of the *Enterprise* comes across a species with two distinct races. One is black on the right side of their bodies and white on the left; the other race is the opposite, white on the right and black on the left. The black-and-white race persecutes and enslaves the white-and-black race. The hatred and constant war between the races lead to the destruction of their world. Because this episode was aired in the time of Dr. Martin Luther King Jr.'s work for desegregation, it sent a clear message about the senselessness of racism. Likewise, in the episode "A Private Little War," the evil Klingons supply firearms to one faction of a primitive, usually peaceful, race. To keep the Klingons from gaining control of the planet, Captain Kirk gives guns to the other faction, thus restoring the balance of power. This was a perfect analogy to the Vietnam War that was raging at the time.

Mike grabs the reader's attention with catchy, familiar phrases that are humorously qualified.

Mike states his thesis.

He presents specific supporting evidence.

This tradition of social commentary continued in *Star Trek: The Next Generation*. For instance, the episode "The Outcast" addresses the always delicate topic of homosexuality but with an intriguing twist. In the show, the *Enterprise* travels to a world where all the inhabitants are androgynous. There, the outcasts are the ones who show tendencies toward being female or male and attracted to the opposite sex. Whoever has this "deformity" is dealt with through brainwashing. *Star Trek* has also covered issues such as terrorism, capital punishment, genetic engineering, medical ethics, and drug abuse.

Mike draws additional evidence from the system of sci-fi TV.

Of course, social criticism is not limited solely to *Star Trek*. *Babylon 5*, a science fiction show created by television veteran J. Michael Straczynski, has garnered an audience almost as loyal and fanatical as that of *Star Trek* (Sharkey 20). The show presents a somewhat darker vision of the future than *Star Trek* where humans are not the dominant species in the galaxy. In her article "A Man with a Five-Year Plan," Betsy Sharkey notes, "Set in 2261, the society Straczynski has created allows him to explore the most volatile issues of today — race, culture, life, death, God, religion, truth — outside the boundaries that traditionally define and divide us" (20). Consider the episode "The Geometry of Shadows." Here, a race known as the Drazi begins a ritualistic though seemingly pointless conflict between two groups identified by green and purple scarves. However, the faction that one belongs to is determined simply by what color scarf is pulled out of a barrel. The show makes an obvious correlation to present-day gang violence, where one's affiliation may be determined by nothing more than the color of a bandana, but does so without raising the question of race. In Sharkey's words, "When those at odds are Centauris and Narns, it allows the debate to be conducted without devisiveness" (20). There are countless more examples. *The Terminator* and *2001: A Space Odyssey* comment on our world by describing a society that is increasingly being run by computers. The list goes on and on, with today's issues repeatedly manifesting themselves in our fantasies of the future.

He supports his thesis by citing authoritative sources.

Science fiction not only tells us where we are; it also shows us where we have been. As stated earlier, how society views the future depends on how it functions in the present. Consequently, science fiction programs that deal with the future adapt to the time in which they exist. Just compare the original *Star Trek* series of the 1960s with the *Star Trek* series of the 1980s and 1990s. The repressive gender roles that were still prevalent in the 1960s were quite evident in the original series. In

Mike draws support from the history of science fiction TV programming.

their book *Deep Space and Sacred Time: Star Trek in the American Mythos,* anthropologists Jon G. Wagner and Jan Lundeen note that while women were "usually depicted as twenty-third-century airheads and alien temptresses stuffed into 'tin-foil bikinis' in the original series, a woman finally commands a starship in *Star Trek: Voyager*" (61). The long-awaited female captain was not the only change seen in the politically correct 1990s. While the original series had a racially diverse cast for the time, women and minorities were rarely seen in command decisions. Beginning with *Star Trek: Deep Space Nine* in 1993, that pattern changed. Creators Rick Berman and Michael Piller eventually cast Avery Brooks, an African American, to play the lead character. Said Rick Berman, "Michael Piller and I had discussed at length that we were not going to limit the casting of the lead to a white male. We had decided that we were going to be as open-minded as possible even to the thought of casting a woman" (Dillard 167). A woman was eventually cast in the show's first officer role. As stated earlier, a female captain finally became a reality in *Star Trek: Voyager,* with a Native American first officer to boot. The uniforms worn on the various series also provide a glimpse of society's changing view of women in the workplace. The original series had women wearing miniskirts in the twenty-third century. By the time of *Star Trek: The Next Generation,* women were wearing the same professional outfits as men. In fact, in the first season of *Star Trek: The Next Generation,* many men wore a miniskirt-like tunic as a sort of tongue-in-cheek parody of the original women's uniforms.

He includes more specific details.

So how do they do it? That is to say, how does a television program like *Star Trek* or *Babylon 5* remain so popular while at the same time treating such controversial issues? During the Enlightenment, great philosophers like Voltaire used the art of satire to criticize certain aspects of the world in which they lived. If they had openly expressed their radical ideas, they could have faced serious personal danger. In *Don Quixote,* Cervantes cleverly disguised his views of the Catholic church within the satire of the story. In her book, *Star Trek: "Where No One Has Gone Before,"* author and *Star Trek* enthusiast J. M. Dillard commented,

> In the great tradition of Jonathan Swift and *Gulliver's Travels,* Roddenberry and the many writers who contributed to the *Star Trek* universe were able to attain a level of social commentary that was ahead of its time — all because the series used the trappings of the fantastic as a backdrop. (42)

It would have been nearly impossible for any other kind of television show to air a program that dealt with racism in the way that *Star Trek* did in the turbulent 1960s. As Dillard put it, "This was strong stuff in the sixties. . . . So *Star Trek* used its science-fiction guise to make the statements more palatable" (42). In this way, *Star Trek* and all of science fiction became the twentieth-century version of classic satire.

Mike refers to the history of satire and fantasy writing to contextualize contemporary science fiction's treatment of controversial issues. Mike further contextualizes Star Trek *by relating it to cultural mythologies.*

However, satire does not begin to describe the immense influence that science fiction has had on popular culture. Wagner and Lundeen went so far as to say, "*Star Trek* has become part of the twentieth-century American mythology" (61). They describe myths as "the narratives that structure [a culture's] worldview and give form and meaning to the disconnected data of everyday life" (61). One needs only to look at the over thirty-year history of *Star Trek* and compare that to the three decades of American culture that have gone on around it to see just how much this one television show has structured our worldview. As Dillard commented,

> *Star Trek*'s special spin — born of the volatile era in which it was conceived — was that these morality tales could encourage viewers to think along the lines of such then-radical liberal beliefs as "All men are good, no matter what the color of their skin" and "No good comes of getting involved in other people's internal wars." (42)

Indeed, this is the strength of all kinds of science fiction. No other kind of program is in a more ideal position to comment on our world. Oddly, or perhaps expectedly, science fiction does this from a platform that is usually out of this world.

Sources

Bing, Jonathan, et al. "Deep Space and Sacred Time: *Star Trek* in the American Mythos." *Publishers Weekly*. 2 Nov 1998: 61. Online. ProQuest Direct. Available: http://proquest.umi.com. 25 Nov 1998.

Dillard, J. M. *Star Trek: "Where No One Has Gone Before."* New York: Pocket Books, 1994.

Sharkey, Betsy. "A Man with a Five-Year Plan." *Mediaweek*. 21 Oct 1996: 20, 24, 28. Online. ProQuest Direct. Available: http://proquest.umi .com. 25 Nov 1998.

Wagner, Jon G., and Jan Lundeen. *Deep Space and Sacred Time: Star Trek in the American Mythos*. Westport, Conn.: Praeger, 1998.

CULTURAL PRODUCTIONS

PART ONE

CONSUMING PASSIONS
The Culture of American Consumption

If you were given a blank check to purchase anything — and everything — you wanted, what would you buy? Make a list and then annotate that list with brief explanations for why you want each item. Do your choices say something about yourself that you want others to know? Do they send an image?

Now consider the things you do own. Make another list and annotate it too. Why did you buy this item or that? Which were presents that reflect someone else's tastes and desires? What compromises did you have to make in choosing one item over another? How often did price or quality affect your decisions? How often did style or image? Are the images sent by your actual possessions any different from the ones sent by your ideal ones? Why? Or why not?

Such questions are a good place to begin a semiotic analysis of American consumer culture, for every choice you make in the products you consume, from clothing to furniture to cars to electronics and beyond, is a sign, a signal you are sending to the world about yourself. Those aren't just a pair of shoes you're wearing: They're a statement about your identity. That's not just a collection of CDs: It's a message about your worldview. Indeed, your music collection may say more about you than anything else you own.

To read the signs of American consumption, it is best to start with yourself, because you've already got an angle on the answers. But be careful and be honest. Remember, a cultural sign gets its meaning from the *system,* or *code,* in which it appears. Its significance does not lie in its usefulness but rather in its symbolism, in the image it projects, and that image is socially constructed. You didn't make it by yourself. To decode your own possessions, you've got to ask yourself what you are trying to say with them and what you want other people to think about you. And you've got to remember the difference between fashion and function.

To give you an idea of how to go about analyzing consumer objects and behavior, let's look at a product that on the surface seems completely functional — a tool, not a sign. Let's look at cell phones.

Interpreting the Culture of American Consumption

As you learned in the Introduction to this book, the semiotic interpretation of a cultural sign can usefully begin with a historical survey of the object you are interpreting. Such a survey can reveal how the meaning of an object can change depending on the circumstance in which it is found. This is strikingly true in the case of cell phones, which, while practically ubiquitous today, were once rare and expensive. They first appeared for public use in 1982 and were originally hard-wired into automobiles (often limousines), which is why many people who remember that time still call them "car phones." In such a context, cell phones were potent status symbols, sending an image of unusual wealth and prestige, the exclusive equipment of VIPs.

Something of this meaning lingers when we think of cell phones and their users, but just barely. Because in an era when cell phones can be acquired for free (provided that the consumer also sign up for an activation contract, of course), and when even the latest digitized models cost only a fraction of what the original models cost, the cell phone is so common that it can't send a status message anymore. Everyone seems to have one. But that doesn't mean that cell phones no longer have a semiotic significance or that no image is associated with them. It simply means that the significance of the cell phone has changed as its history has changed.

To interpret the current significance of the cell phone, we need to situate it in its immediate system of related signs and products. One product that is extremely similar to the cell phone, and which thus belongs to the same system, is the pager. The history of the pager is quite similar to that of the cell phone. Once pagers were carried almost exclusively by high-status professionals who needed to be in constant contact with their places of business.

Discussing the Signs of Consumer Culture

On the board, list in categories the fashion styles worn by members of the class. Be sure to note details, such as styles of shoes, jewelry, watches, or sunglasses, as well as broader trends. Then discuss what the clothing choices say about individuals. What messages are people sending about their personal identity? Do individual students agree with the class's interpretations of their clothing choices? Can any distinctions be made by gender, age, or ethnicity? Then discuss what the fashion styles worn by the whole class say: Is a group identity projected by class members?

This was particularly true for physicians, who commonly carried pagers when they were "on call" (this was before the advent of even the earliest cell phones), and so pagers acquired something of the status of their professional users. The image sent by pagers changed radically, however, when they came to be the standard equipment of drug dealers, who would use them to set up clandestine drug deals. The former status image declined as a new one emerged: To carry a pager was to send an image of gangster toughness and, for many American teens, gangster coolness. Once a signifier of professional prestige and responsibility, the pager shifted systems and became part of the code of a bad-assed youth culture.

But now pagers are carried by little children whose parents haven't gotten them cell phones yet, and so they too have changed significance. In fact, as cell phones become more and more common, pagers themselves seem to be dwindling in significance. Not too long ago, pagers were hot stuff. Now, everyone is talking about cell phones.

Of course, one of the reasons cell phones are such a lively conversation topic is purely functional: They are dangerous to use while driving a car and so are coming to be banned in a number of localities. But even here a social semiotic is at work. It isn't likely that cell phones would attract so much controversy if they didn't also send a rather negative image. With almost everyone owning one, it might seem strange to say that cell phones today have a somewhat negative image, but they do — a point that is demonstrated every time someone apologizes for owning one. Have you ever heard someone say, or have said yourself, that "I own a cell phone, but I only use it for emergencies"? Or have you ever seen the bumper sticker that reads, "Hang up and start driving"? We wouldn't make such apologies or post such messages on our cars if we didn't feel that, somehow, there was something wrong with cell phones. And what is wrong lies in their cultural significance, not in the objects themselves.

To see what this significance is, let's look further into the system in which cell phones appear. What often comes to mind when we think of cell phones today is their association with a certain kind of consumer, especially people driving sports utility vehicles (SUVs) and luxury sedans like the Lexus. There is a functional reason for this: Cell phones have become necessary equipment for the sorts of businesspeople, such as real estate professionals, who must spend a great deal of time in their cars and whose business activities make it important (as well as pleasurable) to drive status automobiles. At the same time, many middle-class parents find that cell phones are very good ways of keeping track of their children, and SUVs have become the automotive choice of the middle- and upper-middle-class American mom these days. Indeed, all you need to do is utter the phrase *soccer mom,* and immediately an image of a woman driving a Ford Excursion while chatting on a cell phone may come to mind.

Now, part of the negativity in this image also has something to do with the history of the cell phone, particularly that intermediate era when cell phones were no longer the prerogative of the extremely powerful and wealthy but were still expensive enough to be out of ordinary consumers' reach. At this time, roughly the late 1980s, cell phones were the common possession of the notorious yuppies (an image reinforced by a 1980s song called "Car Phone," a parody of the 1970s hit "Convoy"), and were widely despised accordingly. Ironically, even when millions of non-yuppies and anti-yuppies carry cell phones, the old taint lingers.

But only lingers. For, with the cell phone being such a common possession, its significance is now less a matter of who owns one as how it is used. Here we can look at the behavioral component of the system to which the cell phone belongs. And what we find are not only people who drive dangerously while gabbing on their phones but also compulsive users who chat away in restaurants (causing some eateries to ban cell phone use) and theaters. What all three behaviors share is the way that they reflect a certain privatization of public space, the way, that is, that cell phone users perform in public what was once a highly private act: talking on the phone. Once telephone conversations were conducted in the privacy of one's home or office — or, if in public, with the door to the phone booth shut. Now such conversations, whether for business or for pleasure, take place on the road, in the restaurant or theater, in shops, on the sidewalk, indeed just about everywhere. And here lies a good part of the current negative image of the cell phone, though most people are probably not conscious of it.

For to treat publicly shared space as if it were one's private preserve, annoying or endangering others for one's personal pleasure, is, in essence, antisocial behavior. No one minds when people use their own private space privately, but when public space is treated as if it were private, something is taken away. The sense of a shared, common environment with its own set of rules to govern the social interactions that take place there is lost. And while we may not always be explicitly aware of it, this is one of the reasons we resent cell phone users, even when we use cell phones ourselves.

At this point, as is often the case with a semiotic analysis, we can broaden the scope of our investigation to see what other current cultural phenomena can be associated with the cell phone's privatization of public space. We've already considered one such phenomenon: the SUV. For SUVs are not simply a mode of transportation, or even just status vehicles. Many who purchase them say that they would have preferred another car but feel safer in an SUV. Whether they put it explicitly or not, what they mean is that if they get into an accident, they want to be in the car that "wins." This may seem like perfectly rational behavior, and according to a highly individualistic (perhaps *selfish* would be the better word) code of conduct, it is. But looked at from a more communitarian perspective, the desire to prevail in a car accident, the unconscious decision to kill rather than be killed, is less than social behavior.

Similarly, the increasing number of Americans who withdraw behind the literal gates and figurative moats of gated communities also can be seen to represent a mode of antisocial behavior (it's no accident that they often drive SUVs). In a dangerous world, this behavior too is perfectly rational, but what it signifies is a society that is becoming so mistrustful that it is becoming at-omized into suspicious individuals whose homes and cars are becoming fortresses against everyone else. The cell phone fits neatly into this system in-sofar as many of its users own them for safety purposes, whether it be to keep in touch with children who no longer seem safe in the public realm or with family members. Many women carry them because the streets aren't such a safe place for women anymore.

The September 11 attacks augmented this significance in an especially grim way. Stories of final conversations from passengers and crew on doomed airlines and employees in the World Trade Center lent a new dimen-sion to the image of the cell phone as a safety device. In this sense, it became a signifier within an American system threatened by terrorism, a shift in meaning that undermined, at least for a while, the negative image of the cell phone as the frivolous instrument of inconsiderate people. Once again, we can see from this semiotic adjustment how ordinary objects can be signifiers of changing historical conditions.

The cell phone is such a rich source of semiotic significance that its analy-sis could go on considerably further, investigating, for instance, the way that it can be seen to reflect a workaholic world in which people feel the need to conduct their business anywhere and anytime, or the way that it has con-tributed to a new consciousness that demands constant communication (in both cases, the rise of e-mail is a part of the cultural system behind the mean-ing of the sign). But we'll stop here and leave those analyses to you. The point is that when you interpret a cultural sign, the actual object is not what is meaningful in a semiotic analysis. What matters is the overall cultural system, the social context, in which that object appears. A highly portable, wireless communication box is not a sign in itself. It becomes a sign only when seen in relation to other objects and other signs.

Now, think for yourself of any other current consumer trend and question it. What messages are people sending when they buy the thing? What images do they project? How does the object relate to other objects? Such are the questions that you must ask as a reader of consuming images, probing every-thing that you may find in the marketplace of goods and services, and taking care never to be satisfied with the answer, "because this product is *better* than that" or, more simply, "just because. . . ."

Disposable Decades

When analyzing a consumer sign, you will often find yourself referring to par-ticular decades in which certain popular fads and trends were prominent, for the decade in which a given style appears may be an essential key to the sys-tem that explains it. Have you ever wondered why American cultural trends seem to change with every decade, why it is so easy to speak of the sixties or the seventies or the eighties and immediately recognize the popular styles that dominated each decade? Have you ever looked at the style of a friend and thought, "Oh, she's so seventies"? Can you place an Earth Shoe at the drop of a hat, or a Nehru jacket? A change in the calendar always seems to herald a change in style in a consuming culture. But why?

The decade-to-decade shift in America's pop cultural identity goes back a good number of years. It is still easy, for example, to distinguish F. Scott Fitzgerald's Jazz Age twenties from John Steinbeck's wrathful thirties. The fifties, an especially connotative decade, raise images of ducktail haircuts and poodle skirts, drive-in culture and Elvis, family sitcoms and white-bread innocence, while the sixties are remembered for acid rock, hippies, the student revolution, and back-to-the-land communes. We remember the seventies as a pop cultural era divided between disco, Nashville, and preppiedom, with John Travolta, truckers, and Skippy and Muffy as dominant pop icons. The boom-boom eighties gave us Wall Street glitz and the yuppie invasion. Indeed, each decade since the first World War — which, not accidentally, happens to coincide roughly with the rise of modern advertising and mass production — seems to carry its own consumerist style.

> ## Exploring the Signs of Consumer Culture
>
> "You are what you buy." In your journal, freewrite on the importance of consumer products in your life. How do you respond to being told your identity is equivalent to the products you buy? Do you resist the notion? Do you recall any instances when you have felt lost without a favorite object? How do you communicate your sense of self to others through objects, whether clothing, books, food, home decor, cars, or something else?

It's no accident that the decade-to-decade shift in consumer styles coincides with the advent of modern advertising and mass production because it was mass production that created a need for constant consumer turnover in the first place. Mass production, that is, promotes stylistic change because with so many products being produced, a market must be created to consume all of them, and this means constantly consuming *more*. To get consumers to keep buying all the new stuff, you have to convince them that the stuff they already have has gone out of style. Why else, do you think, do fashion designers completely redesign their lines each year? Why else do car manufacturers annually change their color schemes and body shapes when the old model year seemed good enough? The new designs aren't simply functional improvements (though they are marketed as such); they are inducements to go out and replace what you already have to avoid appearing out of fashion. Just think: If you could afford to buy any car that you want, what would it be? Would your choice a few years ago have been the same?

Mass production, then, creates consumer societies based on the constant production of new products that are intended to be disposed of with the next product year. But something happened along the way to the establishment of our consumer culture: We began to value consumption more than production. Listen to the economic news: consumption, not production, is relied upon to carry America out of its economic downturns. When Americans stop buying, our economy grinds to a halt. Consumption lies at the center of our economic system now, and the result has been a transformation in the very way we view ourselves.

A Tale of Two Cities

It has not always been thus in America, however. Once, Americans prided themselves on their productivity. In 1914, for example, the poet Carl Sandburg boasted of a Chicago that was "Hog butcher for the world, Tool maker, Stacker of Wheat, Player with Railroads and the Nation's Freight Handler." One wonders what Sandburg would think of the place today. From the south shore east to the industrial suburb of Gary, Indiana, Chicago's once-proud mills and factories rust in the winter wind. The broken windows of countless tenements stare blindly at the Amtrak commuter lines that transport the white-collared brokers of the Chicago Mercantile Exchange to the city center, where trade today is in commodity futures, not commodities. Even Michael Jackson, Gary's most famous export, rarely goes home.

Meanwhile, a few hundred miles to the northwest, Bloomington, Minnesota, buzzes with excitement. For there stands the Mall of America, a colossus of consumption so large that it contains within its walls a seven-acre Knott's Berry Farm theme park, with lots of room to spare. You can find almost anything you want in the Mall of America, but most of what you will find won't have been manufactured in America. The proud tag "Made in the USA" is an increasingly rare item.

It's a long way from Sandburg's Chicago to the Mall of America, a trip that traverses America's shift from a producer to a consumer economy. This shift is not simply economic; it is behind a cultural transformation that is shaping a new mythology within which we define ourselves, our hopes, and our desires.

Ask yourself right now what your own goals are in going to college. Do you envision a career in law, medicine, or banking and finance? Do you want to be a teacher, an advertising executive, or a civil servant? Or maybe you are preparing for a career in an Internet-related field. If you've considered any of these career examples, you are contemplating what are known as service jobs. While essential to a society, none of them actually produces anything. If you've given thought to going into some facet of manufacturing, on the other hand, you are unusual because America offers increasingly fewer opportunities in that area and little prestige. The prestige jobs are in law and medicine, and, increasingly, in high-tech marketing operations like Amazon.com, a fact that it is easy to take for granted. But ask yourself: Does it have to be so?

Simply to ask such questions is to begin to reveal the outline of a cultural mythology based in consumption rather than production. For one thing, while law and medicine require specialized training available to only a few, doctors and lawyers also make a lot of money and so are higher up on the scale of consumption. Quite simply, they can buy more than others can. It is easy to presume that this would be the case anywhere, but in the former Soviet Union physicians — most of whom were women — were relatively low on the social scale. Male engineers, on the other hand, were highly valued for their role in facilitating military production. In what was a producer rather than a consumer culture, it was the producers who roosted high on the social ladder.

And as for the Internet, though the road has been a good deal rockier than was originally anticipated, there are still high hopes for the retail potential of the Web. Computer makers and chip manufacturers, who, after all, do produce something, are rivaled by such firms as eBay and America Online, companies that do not produce anything but rather are efficient media for consumption.

To live in a consumer culture is not simply a matter of shopping, however; it is also a matter of *being*. For in a consumer society, you are what you consume, and the entire social and economic order is maintained by the constant encouragement to buy. The ubiquity of television and advertising in America is a direct reflection of this system, for these media deliver the constant stimulus to buy through avalanches of consuming images. Consider how difficult it is to escape the arm of the advertiser. You may turn off your TV set, but a screen awaits you at the checkout counter of your supermarket, displaying incentives to spend your money. If you rush to the rest room to hide, you may find advertisements tacked to the stalls. If you log onto the Internet, advertisements flash on the screen. Resistance is useless. Weren't you planning to do some shopping this weekend anyway?

Reading Consumer Culture on the Net

Log onto one of the many home shopping networks or auction sites. You might try the Internet Shopping Network **(http://www.isn .com)**, Shop at Home **(http://www.shop athome.com),** or e-Bay **(http://www.ebay .com).** Analyze both the products sold and the way they are marketed. Who is the target audience for the network you're studying, and what images and values are used to attract this market? How does the marketing compare with nonelectronic sales pitches, such as displays in shopping malls and magazines or TV advertising? Does the electronic medium affect your own behavior as a consumer? Does the time pressure of an electronic auction affect your behavior as a consumer? How do you account for any differences in electronic and traditional marketing strategies?

When the Going Gets Tough, the Tough Go Shopping

In a cultural system where our identities are displayed in the products we buy, it accordingly behooves us to pay close attention to what we consume and why. From the cars we drive to the clothes we wear, we are enmeshed in a web of consuming images. As students, you are probably freer to choose the particular images you wish to project through the products you consume than most other demographic groups in America. This claim may sound paradoxical: After all, don't working adults have more money than starving students? Yes, generally. But the working world places severe restrictions on the choices employees can make in their clothing and grooming styles, and even automobile choice may be restricted (real estate agents, for example, can't escort their clients around town in VW Beetles). Corporate business wear, for all its variations, still revolves around a central core of necktied and dark-hued sobriety, regardless of the gender of the wearer. And even with the 1990s' return of long hair for men into fashion, few professions outside the entertainment industry allow it on the job. On campus, on the other hand, you can be pretty much whatever you want to be, which is why your own daily lives provide you with a particularly rich field of consumer signs to read and decode.

So go to it. By the time you read this book, a lot will have changed. A new decade is already well underway without yet having achieved a distinctive identity, not to mention a name. What will the "00s" be the decade of? Look around yourself. Start reading the signs.

The Readings

As this chapter's lead essay, Laurence Shames's "The More Factor" provides a mythological background for the discussions of America's consuming behavior that follow. Shames takes a historical approach to American consumerism, relating our frontier history· to our ever-expanding desire for more goods and services. Anne Norton follows with a semiotic analysis of shopping malls, mail-order catalogues, and the Home Shopping Network, focusing on the ways in which they construct a language of consumption tailored to specific consumer groups. John de Graaf, David Wann, and Thomas H. Naylor come next with a scathing indictment of what they see as America's addiction to the material goods that we always seem to want more of, while Rachel Bowlby provides an analysis of the experience of shopping itself. Thomas Hine's interpretation of the packaging that contains America's most commonly consumed products shows how packages constitute complex sign systems intended for consumer "readings," and Fred Davis surveys the history of blue jeans and how they have been transformed from an emblem of labor to one of leisure. Joan Kron follows with a study of the way we use home furnishings to reflect our sense of personal identity, while David Goewey turns to automotive signs in his semiotic analysis of the SUV trend. Damien Cave's sardonic survey of the commodification and commercial exploitation of the September 11 attacks on America is followed by a pair of readings from Benjamin R. Barber and Thomas L. Friedman that, respectively, explore the global dimensions of American consumer culture and offer prescient insights into the cultural conflicts behind the attacks.

LAURENCE SHAMES
THE MORE FACTOR

A bumper sticker popular in the 1980s read, "Whoever dies with the most toys wins." In this selection from The Hunger for More: Searching for Values in an Age of Greed *(1989), Laurence Shames shows how the great American hunger for more — more toys, more land, more opportunities — is an essential part of our history and character, stemming from the frontier era when the horizon alone seemed the only limit to American desire. The author of* The Big Time: The Harvard Business School's Most Successful Class and How It Shaped America *(1986) and the holder of a Harvard M.B.A., Shames is a journalist who has contributed to such publications as* Playboy, Vanity Fair, Manhattan, inc., *and* Esquire. *He currently is working full-time on writing fiction and screenplays, with his most recent publications including* Florida Straits *(1992),* Sunburn *(1995),* Welcome to Paradise *(1999), and* The Naked Detective *(2000).*

1

Americans have always been optimists, and optimists have always liked to speculate. In Texas in the 1880s, the speculative instrument of choice was towns, and there is no tale more American than this.

What people would do was buy up enormous tracts of parched and vacant land, lay out a Main Street, nail together some wooden sidewalks, and start slapping up buildings. One of these buildings would be called the Grand Hotel and would have a saloon complete with swinging doors. Another might be dubbed the New Academy or the Opera House. The developers would erect a flagpole and name a church, and once the workmen had packed up and moved on, the towns would be as empty as the sky.

But no matter. The speculators, next, would hire people to pass out handbills in the Eastern and Midwestern cities, tracts limning the advantages of relocation to "the Athens of the South" or "the new plains Jerusalem." When persuasion failed, the builders might resort to bribery, paying people's moving costs and giving them houses, in exchange for nothing but a pledge to stay until a certain census was taken or a certain inspection made. Once the nose count was completed, people were free to move on, and there was in fact a contingent of folks who made their living by keeping a cabin on skids and dragging it for pay from one town to another.

The speculators' idea, of course, was to lure the railroad. If one could create a convincing semblance of a town, the railroad might come through it, and a real town would develop, making the speculators staggeringly rich. By these devices a man named Sanborn once owned Amarillo.[1]

But railroad tracks are narrow and the state of Texas is very, very wide. For every Wichita Falls or Lubbock there were a dozen College Mounds or Belchervilles,[2] bleached, unpeopled burgs that receded quietly into the dust, taking with them large amounts of speculators' money.

Still, the speculators kept right on bucking the odds and depositing empty towns in the middle of nowhere. Why did they do it? Two reasons — reasons that might be said to summarize the central fact of American economic history and that go a fair way toward explaining what is perhaps the central strand of the national character.

The first reason was simply that the possible returns were so enormous as to partake of the surreal, to create a climate in which ordinary logic and prudence did not seem to apply. In a boom like that of real estate when the railroad barreled through, long shots that might pay one hundred thousand to one seemed worth a bet.

The second reason, more pertinent here, is that there was a presumption that America would *keep on* booming — if not forever, then at least longer than it made sense to worry about. There would always be another gold rush, another Homestead Act, another oil strike. The next generation would always ferret out opportunities that would be still more lavish than any that had gone before. America *was* those opportunities. This was an article not just of faith, but of strategy. You banked on the next windfall, you staked your hopes and even your self-esteem on it, and this led to a national turn of mind that might usefully be thought of as the habit of more.

A century, maybe two centuries, before anyone had heard the term *baby boomer,* much less *yuppie,* the habit of more had been instilled as the operative truth among the economically ambitious. The habit of more seemed to suggest that there was no such thing as getting wiped out in America. A fortune lost in Texas might be recouped in Colorado. Funds frittered away on grazing land where nothing grew might flood back in as silver. There was always a second chance, or always seemed to be, in this land where growth was destiny and where expansion and purpose were the same.

The key was the frontier, not just as a matter of acreage, but as idea. Vast, varied, rough as rocks, America was the place where one never quite came to the end. Ben Franklin explained it to Europe even before the Revolutionary War had finished: America offered new chances to those "who, in their own

---

[1]For a fuller account of railroad-related land speculation in Texas, see F. Stanley, *Story of the Texas Panhandle Railroads* (Borger, Tex.: Hess Publishing Co., 1976).

[2]T. Lindsay Baker, *Ghost Towns of Texas* (Norman, Okla.: University of Oklahoma Press, 1986).

Countries, where all the Lands [were] fully occupied . . . could never [emerge] from the poor Condition wherein they were born."³

So central was this awareness of vacant space and its link to economic promise that Frederick Jackson Turner, the historian who set the tone for much of the twentieth century's understanding of the American past, would write that it was "not the constitution, but free land . . . [that] made the democratic type of society in America."⁴ Good laws mattered; an accountable government mattered; ingenuity and hard work mattered. But those things were, so to speak, an overlay on the natural, geographic America that was simply *there,* and whose vast and beckoning possibilities seemed to generate the ambition and the sometimes reckless liberty that would fill it. First and foremost, it was open space that provided "the freedom of the individual to rise under conditions of social mobility."⁵

Open space generated not just ambition, but metaphor. As early as 1835, Tocqueville was extrapolating from the fact of America's emptiness to the observation that "no natural boundary seems to be set to the efforts of man."⁶ Nor was any limit placed on what he might accomplish, since, in that heyday of the Protestant ethic, a person's rewards were taken to be quite strictly proportionate to his labors.

Frontier; opportunity; more. This has been the American trinity from the very start. The frontier was the backdrop and also the raw material for the streak of economic booms. The booms became the goad and also the justification for the myriad gambles and for Americans' famous optimism. The optimism, in turn, shaped the schemes and visions that were sometimes noble, sometimes appalling, always bold. The frontier, as reality and as symbol, is what has shaped the American way of doing things and the American sense of what's worth doing.

But there has been one further corollary to the legacy of the frontier, with its promise of ever-expanding opportunities: Given that the goal — a realistic goal for most of our history — was *more,* Americans have been somewhat backward in adopting values, hopes, ambitions that have to do with things *other than* more. In America, a sense of quality has lagged far behind a sense of scale. An ideal of contentment has yet to take root in soil traditionally more hospitable to an ideal of restless striving. The ethic of decency has been upstaged by the ethic of success. The concept of growth has been applied almost exclusively to things that can be measured, counted, weighed. And the hunger for those things that are unmeasurable but fine — the sorts of accom-

³Benjamin Franklin, "Information to Those Who Would Remove to America," in *The Autobiography and Other Writings* (New York: Penguin Books, 1986), 242.

⁴Frederick Jackson Turner, *The Frontier in American History* (Melbourne, Fla.: Krieger, 1976 [reprint of 1920 edition]), 293.

⁵Ibid., 266.

⁶Tocqueville, *Democracy in America.*

plishment that cannot be undone by circumstance or a shift in social fashion, the kind of serenity that cannot be shattered by tomorrow's headline — has gone largely unfulfilled, and even unacknowledged.

2

If the supply of more went on forever, perhaps that wouldn't matter very much. Expansion could remain a goal unto itself, and would continue to generate a value system based on bulk rather than on nuance, on quantities of money rather than on quality of life, on "progress" itself rather than on a sense of what the progress was for. But what if, over time, there was less more to be had?

That is the essential situation of America today.

Let's keep things in proportion: The country is not running out of wealth, drive, savvy, or opportunities. We are not facing imminent ruin, and neither panic nor gloom is called for. But there have been ample indications over the past two decades that we are running out of more.

Consider productivity growth — according to many economists, the single most telling and least distortable gauge of changes in real wealth. From 1947 to 1965, productivity in the private sector (adjusted, as are all the following figures, for inflation) was advancing, on average, by an annual 3.3 percent. This means, simply, that each hour of work performed by a specimen American worker contributed 3.3 cents worth or more to every American dollar every year; whether we saved it or spent it, that increment went into a national kitty of ever-enlarging aggregate wealth. Between 1965 and 1972, however, the "more-factor" decreased to 2.4 percent a year, and from 1972 to 1977 it slipped further, to 1.6 percent. By the early 1980s, productivity growth was at a virtual standstill, crawling along at 0.2 percent for the five years ending in 1982.[7] Through the middle years of the 1980s, the numbers rebounded somewhat — but by then the gains were being neutralized by the gargantuan carrying costs on the national debt.[8]

Inevitably, this decline in the national stockpile of more held consequences for the individual wallet.[9] During the 1950s, Americans' average

---

[7]These figures are taken from the Council of Economic Advisers, *Economic Report of the President,* February 1984, 267.

[8]For a lucid and readable account of the meaning and implications of our reservoir of red ink, see Lawrence Malkin, *The National Debt* (New York: Henry Holt and Co., 1987). Through no fault of Malkin's, many of his numbers are already obsolete, but his explanation of who owes what to whom, and what it means, remains sound and even entertaining in a bleak sort of way.

[9]The figures in this paragraph and the next are from "The Average Guy Takes It on the Chin," *New York Times,* 13 July 1986, sec. 3.

hourly earnings were humping ahead at a gratifying 2.5 percent each year. By the late seventies, that figure stood just where productivity growth had come to stand, at a dispiriting 0.2 cents on the dollar. By the first half of the eighties, the Reagan "recovery" notwithstanding, real hourly wages were actually moving backwards — declining at an average annual rate of 0.3 percent.

Compounding the shortage of more was an unfortunate but crucial demo- 20
graphic fact. Real wealth was nearly ceasing to expand just at the moment when the members of that unprecedented population bulge known as the baby boom were entering what should have been their peak years of income expansion. A working man or woman who was thirty years old in 1949 could expect to see his or her real earnings burgeon by 63 percent by age forty. In 1959, a thirty-year-old could still look forward to a gain of 49 percent by his or her fortieth birthday.

But what about the person who turned thirty in 1973? By the time that worker turned forty, his or her real earnings had shrunk by a percentage point. For all the blather about yuppies with their beach houses, BMWs, and radicchio salads, and even factoring in those isolated tens of thousands making ludicrous sums in consulting firms or on Wall Street, the fact is that between 1979 and 1983 real earnings of all Americans between the ages of twenty-five and thirty-four actually declined by 14 percent.[10] The *New York Times,* well before the stock market crash put the kibosh on eighties confidence, summed up the implications of this downturn by observing that "for millions of breadwinners, the American dream is becoming the impossible dream."[11]

Now, it is not our main purpose here to detail the ups and downs of the American economy. Our aim, rather, is to consider the effects of those ups and downs on people's goals, values, sense of their place in the world. What happens at that shadowy juncture where economic prospects meld with personal choice? What sorts of insights and adjustments are called for so that economic ups and downs can be dealt with gracefully?

Fact one in this connection is that, if America's supply of more is in fact diminishing, American values will have to shift and broaden to fill the gap where the expectation of almost automatic gains used to be. Something more durable will have to replace the fat but fragile bubble that had been getting frailer these past two decades and that finally popped — a tentative, partial pop — on October 19, 1987. A different sort of growth — ultimately, a growth in responsibility and happiness — will have to fulfill our need to believe that our possibilities are still expanding.

The transition to that new view of progress will take some fancy stepping, because, at least since the end of World War II, simple economic growth has

[10]See, for example, "The Year of the Yuppie," *Newsweek,* 31 December 1984, 16.
[11]"The Average Guy."

stood, in the American psyche, as the best available substitute for the literal frontier. The economy has *been* the frontier. Instead of more space, we have had more money. Rather than measuring progress in terms of geographical expansion, we have measured it by expansion in our standard of living. Economics has become the metaphor on which we pin our hopes of open space and second chances.

The poignant part is that the literal frontier did not pass yesterday: it   25 has not existed for a hundred years. But the frontier's promise has become so much a part of us that we have not been willing to let the concept die. We have kept the frontier mythology going by invocation, by allusion, by hype.

It is not a coincidence that John F. Kennedy dubbed his political program the New Frontier. It is not mere linguistic accident that makes us speak of Frontiers of Science or of psychedelic drugs as carrying one to Frontiers of Perception. We glorify fads and fashions by calling them Frontiers of Taste. Nuclear energy has been called the Last Frontier; solar energy has been called the Last Frontier. Outer space has been called the Last Frontier; the oceans have been called the Last Frontier. Even the suburbs, those blandest and least adventurous of places, have been wryly described as the crabgrass frontier.[12]

What made all these usages plausible was their being linked to the image of the American economy as an endlessly fertile continent whose boundaries never need be reached, a domain that could expand in perpetuity, a gigantic playing field that would never run out of room and on which the game would get forever bigger and more filled with action. This was the frontier that would not vanish.

It is worth noting that people in other countries (with the possible exception of that other America, Australia) do not talk about frontier this way. In Europe, and in most of Africa and Asia, "frontier" connotes, at worst, a place of barbed wire and men with rifles, and at best, a neutral junction where one changes currency while passing from one fixed system into another. Frontier, for most of the world's people, does not suggest growth, expanse, or opportunity.

For Americans, it does, and always has. This is one of the things that sets America apart from other places and makes American attitudes different from those of other people. It is why, from *Bonanza* to the Sierra Club, the notion or even the fantasy of empty horizons and untapped resources has always evoked in the American heart both passion and wistfulness. And it is why the fear that the economic frontier — our last, best version of the Wild West — may finally be passing creates in us not only money worries but also a crisis of morale and even of purpose.

---

[12]With the suburbs again taking on a sort of fascination, this phrase was resurrected as the title of a 1985 book — *Crabgrass Frontier: The Suburbanization of America*, by Kenneth T. Jackson (Oxford University Press).

3

It might seem strange to call the 1980s an era of nostalgia. The decade, after ₃₀ all, has been more usually described in terms of coolness, pragmatism, and a blithe innocence of history. But the eighties, unawares, were nostalgic for frontiers; and the disappointment of that nostalgia had much to do with the time's greed, narrowness, and strange want of joy. The fear that the world may not be a big enough playground for the full exercise of one's energies and yearnings, and worse, the fear that the playground is being fenced off and will no longer expand — these are real worries and they have had consequences. The eighties were an object lesson in how people play the game when there is an awful and unspoken suspicion that the game is winding down.

It was ironic that the yuppies came to be so reviled for their vaunting ambition and outsized expectations, as if they'd invented the habit of more, when in fact they'd only inherited it the way a fetus picks up an addiction in the womb. The craving was there in the national bloodstream, a remnant of the frontier, and the baby boomers, described in childhood as "the luckiest generation,"[13] found themselves, as young adults, in the melancholy position of wrestling with a two-hundred-year dependency on a drug that was now in short supply.

True, the 1980s raised the clamor for more to new heights of shrillness, insistence, and general obnoxiousness, but this, it can be argued, was in the nature of a final binge, the storm before the calm. America, though fighting the perception every inch of the way, was coming to realize that it was not a preordained part of the natural order that one should be richer every year. If it happened, that was nice. But who had started the flimsy and pernicious rumor that it was normal?

READING THE TEXT

1. Summarize in a paragraph how, according to Shames, the frontier functions as a symbol of American consciousness.
2. What connections does Shames make between America's frontier history and consumer behavior?
3. Why does Shames term the 1980s "an era of nostalgia" (para. 30)?

READING THE SIGNS

1. Shames asserts that Americans have been influenced by the frontier belief "that America would *keep on* booming" (para. 8). Do you feel that this belief continues to be influential into the twenty-first century? Write an essay arguing for your position.

[13]Thomas Hine, *Populuxe* (New York: Alfred A. Knopf, 1986), 15.

2. Shames claims that, because of the desire for more, "the ethic of decency has been upstaged by the ethic of success" (para. 14) in America. In class, form teams that either agree or disagree with this position, and debate the validity of Shames's claim.

3. Read or review Joan Kron's "The Semiotics of Home Decor" (p. 101). How is Martin J. Davidson influenced by the frontier myth that Shames describes?

4. In groups, discuss whether street gang members share the desire for "more" that Shames claims is a distinctly American trait. Then write an essay in which you argue whether you believe gangs can be called "typically American."

ANNE NORTON
THE SIGNS OF SHOPPING

Shopping malls are more than places to shop, just as mail-order catalogues are more than simple lists of goods. Both malls and catalogues are coded systems that not only encourage us to buy but, more profoundly, help us to construct our very sense of identity, as in the J. Peterman catalogue that "constructs the reader as a man of rugged outdoor interests, taste, and money." In this selection from Republic of Signs *(1993), Anne Norton (b. 1954), a professor of political science at the University of Pennsylvania, analyzes the many ways in which malls, catalogues, and home shopping networks sell you what they want by telling you who you are. Norton's other books include* Alternative Americas *(1986) and* Reflections on Political Identity *(1988).*

Shopping at the Mall

The mall has been the subject of innumerable debates. Created out of the modernist impulse for planning and the centralization of public activity, the mall has become the distinguishing sign of suburban decentralization, springing up in unplanned profusion. Intended to restore something of the lost unity of city life to the suburbs, the mall has come to export styles and strategies to stores at the urban center. Deplored by modernists, it is regarded with affection only by their postmodern foes. Ruled more by their content than by their creators' avowed intent, the once sleek futurist shells have taken on a certain aura of postmodern playfulness and popular glitz.

The mall is a favorite subject for the laments of cultural conservatives and others critical of the culture of consumption. It is indisputably the cultural locus of commodity fetishism. It has been noticed, however, by others of a less condemnatory disposition that the mall has something of the mercado, or the agora, about it. It is both a place of meeting for the young and one of the rare places where young and old go together. People of different races and classes, different occupations, different levels of education meet there. As M. Pressdee and John Fiske note, however, though the mall appears to be a public place, it is not. Neither freedom of speech nor freedom of assembly is permitted there. Those who own and manage malls restrict what comes within their confines. Controversial displays, by stores or customers or the plethora of organizations and agencies that present themselves in the open spaces of the mall, are not permitted. These seemingly public spaces conceal a pervasive private authority.

The mall exercises its thorough and discreet authority not only in the regulation of behavior but in the constitution of our visible, inaudible, public discourse. It is the source of those commodities through which we speak of our identities, our opinions, our desires. It is a focus for the discussion of style among peripheral consumers. Adolescents, particularly female adolescents, are inclined to spend a good deal of time at the mall. They spend, indeed, more time than money. They acquire not simple commodities (they may come home with many, few, or none) but a well-developed sense of the significance of those commodities. In prowling the mall they embed themselves in a lexicon of American culture. They find themselves walking through a dictionary. Stores hang a variety of identities on their racks and mannequins. Their window displays provide elaborate scenarios conveying not only what the garment is but what the garment means.

A display in the window of Polo provides an embarrassment of semiotic riches. Everyone, from the architecture critic at the *New York Times* to kids in the hall of a Montana high school, knows what *Ralph Lauren* means. The polo mallet and the saddle, horses and dogs, the broad lawns of Newport, Kennebunkport, old photographs in silver frames, the evocation of age, of ancestry and Anglophilia, of indolence and the Ivy League, evoke the upper class. Indian blankets and buffalo plaids, cowboy hats and Western saddles, evoke a past distinct from England but nevertheless determinedly Anglo. The supposedly arcane and suspect arts of deconstruction are deployed easily, effortlessly, by the readers of these cultural texts.

Walking from one window to another, observing one another, shoppers, 5 especially the astute and observant adolescents, acquire a facility with the language of commodities. They learn not only words but a grammar. Shop windows employ elements of sarcasm and irony, strategies of inversion and allusion. They provide models of elegant, economical, florid, and prosaic expression. They teach composition.

The practice of shopping is, however, more than instructive. It has long been the occasion for women to escape the confines of their homes and enjoy the companionship of other women. The construction of woman's role as one of provision for the needs of the family legitimated her exit. It provided an occasion for women to spend long stretches of time in the company of their friends, without the presence of their husbands. They could exchange information and reflections, ask advice, and receive support. As their daughters grew, they would be brought increasingly within this circle, included in shopping trips and lunches with their mothers. These would form, reproduce, and restructure communities of taste.

The construction of identity and the enjoyment of friendship outside the presence of men was thus effected through a practice that constructed women as consumers and subjected them to the conventions of the marketplace. Insofar as they were dependent on their husbands for money, they were dependent on their husbands for the means to the construction of their identities. They could not represent themselves through commodities without the funds men provided, nor could they, without money, participate in the community of women that was realized in "going shopping." Their identities were made contingent not only on the possession of property but on the recognition of dependence.

Insofar as shopping obliges dependent women to recognize their dependence, it also opens up the possibility of subversion.[1] The housewife who shops for pleasure takes time away from her husband, her family, and her house and claims it for herself. Constantly taught that social order and her private happiness depend on intercourse between men and women, she chooses the company of women instead. She engages with women in an activity marked as feminine, and she enjoys it. When she spends money, she exercises an authority over property that law and custom may deny her. If she has no resources independent of her husband, this may be the only authority over property she is able to exercise. When she buys things her husband does not approve — or does not know of — she further subverts an order that leaves control over property in her husband's hands.[2]

Her choice of feminine company and a feminine pursuit may involve additional subversions. As Fiske and Pressdee recognize, shopping without buying and shopping for bargains have a subversive quality. This is revealed, in a form that gives it additional significance, when a saleswoman leans forward and tells a shopper, "Don't buy that today, it will be on sale on Thursday." Here solidarity of gender (and often of class) overcome, however partially and briefly, the imperatives of the economic order.

Shoppers who look, as most shoppers do, for bargains, and salespeople ₁₀

---

[1]Nuanced and amusing accounts of shopping as subversion are provided in John Fiske's analyses of popular culture, particularly *Reading the Popular* (Boston: Unwin Hyman [now Routledge], 1989), pp. 13–42.

[2]See R. Bowlby, *Just Looking: Consumer Culture in Dreiser, Gissing, and Zola* (London: Methuen, 1985), p. 22, for another discussion and for an example of the recommendation of this strategy by Elizabeth Cady Stanton in the 1850s.

who warn shoppers of impending sales, see choices between commodities as something other than the evidence and the exercise of freedom. They see covert direction and exploitation; they see the withholding of information and the manipulation of knowledge. They recognize that they are on enemy terrain and that their shopping can be, in Michel de Certeau's[3] term, a "guerrilla raid." This recognition in practice of the presence of coercion in choice challenges the liberal conflation of choice and consent.

Shopping at Home

Shopping is an activity that has overcome its geographic limits. One need no longer go to the store to shop. Direct mail catalogues, with their twenty-four-hour phone numbers for ordering, permit people to shop where and when they please. An activity that once obliged one to go out into the public sphere, with its diverse array of semiotic messages, can now be done at home. An activity that once obliged one to be in company, if not in conversation, with one's compatriots can now be conducted in solitude.

The activity of catalogue shopping, and the pursuit of individuality, are not, however, wholly solitary. The catalogues invest their commodities with vivid historical and social references. The J. Peterman catalogue, for example, constructs the reader as a man of rugged outdoor interests, taste, and money.[4] He wears "The Owner's Hat" or "Hemingway's Cap," a leather flight jacket or the classic "Horseman's Duster," and various other garments identified with the military, athletes, and European imperialism. The copy for "The Owner's Hat" naturalizes class distinctions and, covertly, racism:

> Some of us work on the plantation.
> Some of us own the plantation.
> Facts are facts.
> This hat is for those who own the plantation.[5]

Gender roles are strictly delineated. The copy for a skirt captioned "Women's Legs" provides a striking instance of the construction of the gaze as male, of women as the object of the gaze:

---

[3]**Michel de Certeau** (1925–1986) French social scientist and semiologist who played an important role in the development of contemporary cultural studies — Eds.

[4]I have read several of these. I cite *The J. Peterman Company Owner's Manual No. 5*, from the J. Peterman Company, 2444 Palumbo Drive, Lexington, Ky. 40509.

[5]Ibid., p. 5. The hat is also identified with the Canal Zone, "successfully bidding at Beaulieu," intimidation, and LBOs. Quite a hat. It might be argued against my reading that the J. Peterman Company also offers the "Coal Miner's Bag" and a mailbag. However, since the descriptive points of reference on color and texture and experience for these bags are such things as the leather seats of Jaguars, and driving home in a Bentley, I feel fairly confident in my reading.

just when you think you see something, a shape you think you recognize, it's gone and then it begins to return and then it's gone and of course you can't take your eyes off it.

Yes, the long slow motion of women's legs. Whatever happened to those things at carnivals that blew air up into girls' skirts and you could spend hours watching.[6]

"You," of course, are male. There is also the lace blouse captioned "Mystery": "lace says yes at the same time it says no."[7] Finally, there are notes of imperialist nostalgia: the Sheapherd's Hotel (Cairo) bathrobe and white pants for "the bush" and "the humid hell-holes of Bombay and Calcutta."[8]

It may no longer be unforgivable to say that the British left a few good things behind in India and in Kenya, Singapore, Borneo, etc., not the least of which was their Englishness.[9]

As Paul Smith observes, in his reading of their catalogues, the *Banana Republic* has also made capital out of imperial nostalgia.[10]

The communities catalogues create are reinforced by shared mailing lists. The constructed identities are reified and elaborated in an array of semiotically related catalogues. One who orders a spade or a packet of seeds will be constructed as a gardener and receive a deluge of catalogues from plant and garden companies. The companies themselves may expand their commodities to appeal to different manifestations of the identities they respond to and construct. Smith and Hawken, a company that sells gardening supplies with an emphasis on aesthetics and environmental concern, puts out a catalogue in which a group of people diverse in age and in their ethnicity wear the marketed clothes while gardening, painting, or throwing pots. Williams-Sonoma presents its catalogue not as a catalogue of things for cooking but as "A Catalog for Cooks." The catalogue speaks not to need but to the construction of identity.

The Nature Company dedicates its spring 1990 catalogue "to trees," endorses Earth Day, and continues to link itself to the Nature Conservancy through posters and a program in which you buy a tree for a forest restoration project. Here, a not-for-profit agency is itself commodified, adding to the value of the commodities offered in the catalogue.[11] In this catalogue, con-

---

[6]Ibid., p. 3. See also pp. 15 and 17 for instances of women as the object of the male gaze. The identification of the gaze with male sexuality is unambiguous here as well.

[7]Ibid., p. 17.

[8]Ibid., pp. 7, 16, 20, 21, 37, and 50.

[9]Ibid., p. 20.

[10]Paul Smith, "Visiting the Banana Republic," in *Universal Abandon?* ed. Andrew Ross for *Social Text* (Minneapolis: University of Minnesota Press, 1988), pp. 128–48.

[11]*The Nature Company Catalog,* The Nature Company, P.O. Box 2310, Berkeley, Calif. 94702, Spring 1990. See pp. 1–2 and order form insert between pp. 18 and 19. Note also the entailed donation to Designs for Conservation on p. 18.

sumption is not merely a means for the construction and representation of the self, it is also a means for political action. Several commodities are offered as "A Few Things You Can Do" to save the earth: a string shopping bag, a solar battery recharger, a home newspaper recycler. Socially conscious shopping is a liberal practice in every sense. It construes shopping as a form of election, in which one votes for good commodities or refuses one's vote to candidates whose practices are ethically suspect. In this respect, it reveals its adherence to the same ideological presuppositions that structure television's Home Shopping Network and other cable television sales shows.

Both politically informed purchasing and television sales conflate the free market and the electoral process. Dollars are identified with votes, purchases with endorsements. Both offer those who engage in them the possibility to "talk back" to manufacturers. In television sales shows this ability to talk back is both more thoroughly elaborated and more thoroughly exploited. Like the "elections" on MTV that invite viewers to vote for their favorite video by calling a number on their telephones, they permit those who watch to respond, to speak, and to be heard by the television. Their votes, of course, cost money. On MTV, as in the stores, you can buy as much speech as you can afford. On the Home Shopping Network, the purchase of speech becomes complicated by multiple layers and inversions.

Each commodity is introduced. It is invested by the announcer with a number of desirable qualities. The value of these descriptions of the commodities is enhanced by the construction of the announcer as a mediator not only between the commodity and the consumer but between the salespeople and the consumer. The announcer is not, the format suggests, a salesperson (though of course the announcer is). He or she is an announcer, describing goods that others have offered for sale. Television claims to distinguish itself by making objects visible to the eyes, but it is largely through the ears that these commodities are constructed. The consumer, in purchasing the commodity, purchases the commodity, what the commodity signifies, and, as we say, "buys the salesperson's line." The consumer may also acquire the ability to speak on television. Each purchase is recorded and figures as a vote in a rough plebiscite, confirming the desirability of the object. Although the purchase figures are announced as if they were confirming votes, it is, of course, impossible to register one's rejection of the commodity. Certain consumers get a little more (or rather less) for their money. They are invited to explain the virtue of the commodity — and their purchase — to the announcer and the audience. The process of production, of both the consumers and that which they consume, continues in this apology for consumption.

The semiotic identification of consumption as an American activity, indeed, a patriotic one, is made with crude enthusiasm on the Home Shopping Network and other video sales shows. Red, white, and blue figure prominently in set designs and borders framing the television screen. The Home Shopping Network presents its authorities in an office conspicuously adorned with a picture of the Statue of Liberty.[12] Yet the messages that the Home Shopping Network sends its customers — that you can buy as much speech as you can afford, that you are recognized by others in accordance with your capacity to consume — do much to subvert the connection between capitalism and democracy on which this semiotic identification depends.

READING THE TEXT

1. What does Norton mean when she claims that the suburban shopping mall appears to be a public place but in fact is not?

2. What is Norton's interpretation of Ralph Lauren's Polo line?

3. How is shopping a subversive activity for women, according to Norton?

4. How do mail-order catalogues create communities of shoppers, in Norton's view?

5. What are the political messages sent by the Home Shopping Network, as Norton sees them, and how are they communicated?

READING THE SIGNS

1. Visit a local shopping mall, and study the window displays, focusing on stores intended for one group of consumers (teenagers, for instance, or children). Then write an essay in which you analyze how the displays convey what the stores' products "mean."

2. Bring a few product catalogues to class, and then in small groups compare the kind of consumer "constructed" by the catalogues' cultural images and allusions. Do you note any patterns associated with gender, ethnicity, or age group? Report your group's conclusions to the whole class.

3. Interview five women of different age groups on their motivations and activities when they shop in a mall. Then use the results of your interviews as evidence in an essay in which you support, complicate, or refute Norton's assertion that shopping constitutes a subversive activity for women.

4. Watch an episode of the Home Shopping Network (your school's media library may be able to provide you access to cable TV), and write a semiotic analysis of the ways in which products are presented to consumers.

5. Select a single mail-order catalogue, and write a detailed semiotic interpretation of the identity it constructs for its market.

6. Visit the web site for a major store chain (for instance, **http://www.gap.com**), and study how it "moves" the consumer through it. How does the site induce you to consume?

[12]This moment from the Home Shopping Network was generously brought to my attention, on videotape, by Peter Bregman, a student in my American Studies class of fall 1988, at Princeton University.

NINA LEEN

JUST WHAT DO YOU DO ALL DAY?

READING THE SIGNS

1. Nina Leen's photo comes from a June 1947 edition of *Life* magazine, and is intended to present "the material record of one homemaker's weekly toil: 35 beds made, 175 pounds of food prepared, 250 pieces of clothing laundered, 750 items of dishware scrubbed." In the postwar era, when millions of women were leaving factory jobs to raise children and stay at home, this image was intended to show how they were active and productive, even though at home. How well does this image work to convey that message? What elements in the image work against that idea? Be sure to cite specific examples.

2. If you were to compose a photograph showing the kinds of work it takes to sustain a household today, what would you show? What elements of your image would differ from the photo on page 70? What technological innovations have most influenced the work involved in keeping a house?

JOHN DE GRAAF, DAVID WANN, AND THOMAS H. NAYLOR

THE ADDICTIVE VIRUS

Americans are addicted to shopping, and as far as John de Graaf, David Wann, and Thomas Naylor are concerned, they're buying far too much stuff and for all the wrong reasons. Pulling no punches, de Graaf, Wann, and Naylor diagnose a severe case of the "affluenza virus" in contemporary America whose symptoms include an insatiable desire for more and more things coupled with a diminishing sense of satisfaction with the things one already owns. Some sort of twelve-step program is in order, it appears, before we all end up with global positioning system-equipped SUVs. A television writer and producer, John de Graaf (b. 1946) has produced such programs as Running Out of Time, For Earth's Sake: The Life and Times of David Brower, *and* Genetic Time Bomb. *A former employee at the Environmental Protection Agency, David Wann is a writer and video producer whose books include* Biologic: Designing with Nature to Protect the Environment *(1994) and* Deep Design: Pathways to a Livable Future *(1996). And Thomas Naylor is professor emeritus of economics at Duke University and a specialist in international strategic management.*

The urge sweeps over them like a tidal wave. They go into a kind of trance, an addictive high, where what they buy almost doesn't matter.

—Psychotherapist OLIVIA MELLAN

> In my family, money was used to express love, so I later spent money to show myself love.
>
> — Participant in Debtors Anonymous,
> a twelve-step program

You suspect you may be a coffee addict when you start answering the front door *before* the doorbell rings! But when you can't resist buying a coffee mug with a picture of a coffee mug on it . . . it's official. You're hooked. For you and at least thirty-five million other javaholics (four to five cups a day), coffee is life, the rest is only waiting.

But coffee's not the worst of our addictions, not by a long shot. Fourteen million Americans use illegal drugs, twelve million Americans are heavy drinkers, and sixty million are hooked on tobacco. Five million Americans can't stop gambling away incomes and savings. And at least ten million can't stop buying more and more stuff — an addiction that in the long run may be the most destructive of all.[1]

Lianne, a department store publicist in New York City, is a problem shopper. Every year, she uses her employee discount to rack up more than $20,000 in clothing and accessory bills. She finally suspected she might be addicted when she broke up with her boyfriend and moved her stuff out of his apartment. "Some women tend to shop a lot because they live out of two apartments, theirs and their boyfriend's," she explains. "You never look at your wardrobe as one wardrobe. But when I saw how many things I had that were identical, I began to see that maybe I did have a problem."[2]

Addiction to stuff is not easily understood. It's a bubbling cauldron of such traits as anxiety, loneliness, and low self-esteem. "I'd like to think I shop because I don't want to look like everybody else," Lianne confides anonymously, "but the real reason is because I don't want to look like myself. It's easier to buy something new and feel good about yourself than it is to change yourself."

Addicts need to go back for more in order to feel good again. The addictive substance or activity takes away the emotional discomfort of everyday life, and also releases the built-up tensions of craving. The goal is to get back to a place of perceived power and carefree abandonment. The drinker suddenly becomes loose and uninhibited, certain he's the funniest man in the world. The gambler feels the elation of risk and possibility — putting it all on the line so Lady Luck can find him. The addicted shopper seeks the high she felt a few days earlier, when she bought a dress she still hasn't taken out of the box. 5

According to Dr. Ronald Faber, compulsive buyers often report feeling heightened sensations when they shop. Colors and textures are more intense, and extreme levels of focus and concentration are often achieved — literally, altered states of consciousness. Some extreme shoppers compare their highs

[1] National Institute on Drug Abuse, Bethesda, Maryland.
[2] Scott Cohen, "Shopaholics Anonymous," *Elle*, May 1996, p. 120.

to drug experiences, while others have compared the moment of purchase to an orgasm.[3]

"I'm addicted to the smell of suede, the smooth texture of silk, and the rustle of tissue paper," admits one shopping addict. She also loves the captive attention she commands from shopkeepers. And because her credit card is always ready for use, she can shop whenever she wants. Now that's power.

Never Enough

The thrill of shopping is only one aspect of the addiction to stuff. Many Americans are also hooked on building personal fortresses out of their purchases. Whether it's a new set of golf clubs or a walk-in closet full of sweaters and shoes, having the right stuff and sending the right signal somehow reassures addictive buyers. The problem is that the world's signals keep changing, so addicts never reach a point of having enough. The computer never has enough memory, and is never as fast as it should be. The SUV doesn't have a satellite-linked global positioning system, so how do we know where we are? The phone system is obsolete without call waiting and caller ID; the refrigerator doesn't dispense ice cubes; and the big-screen TV is a good six feet narrower than the living-room wall. Deficiencies like these become unacceptable when affluenza sets in.

Economists call it "the law of diminishing marginal utility," jargon that simply means we have to run faster just to stay in place. As social psychologist David Myers phrases it, "The second piece of pie, or the second $100,000, never tastes as good as the first."[4]

Yet, despite diminishing returns that are plain to see, affluenza victims   10 get stuck in the more mode, not knowing when or how to stop. If eating pie ultimately fails to satisfy, we think we need *more* pie to become satisfied. At this point, the affluenza virus has become an addiction. "Consuming becomes pathological because its importance grows larger and larger in direct proportion to our decreasing satisfaction," says economist Herman Daly.[5]

In terms of the social factors that trigger the addictive virus, our thanks go first to the "pusher men" on the supply side. For example, when the highways to which we are addicted become clogged, dealers push *more* highways, which very soon become clogged as well. When we get used to a certain level of sexually explicit advertising, the pusher men push it a step further, and then further, until preteens pose suggestively on network TV ads, in their underwear.

It's the same in restaurants, fast-food outlets, and movie theaters, where portions get bigger, and then get huge. Plates of food become platters, Biggie

[3]"News and Trends," *Psychology Today,* January/February 1995, p. 8.
[4]David G. Myers, "Wealth, Well-Being, and the New American Dream." Center for a New American Dream Web site, July 4, 2000.
[5]Personal interview, August 1997.

burgers become Dino-Burgers, and boxes of popcorn become buckets. What's next, barrels requiring hand trucks? Our stomachs expand to accommodate the larger portion which we soon regard as normal (sixty-four-ounce soft drinks, normal?!).

Sometimes more and bigger are not enough. When we can't maintain our consumer highs with familiar products and activities, we search for new highs. Sports become extreme sports or fantasy sports in which thrill-seekers bungee jump off skyscrapers or gamble in Internet fantasy sports leagues. Even real professional athletes, with fantasy salaries, can never get enough. When a bright young baseball prospect signs for $10 million a year, a veteran who makes only $7 million suddenly feels unsatisfied. This is the plight of the affluenza addict: Even too much is never enough.

Shopping to Fill the Void

Similarities among addictions are alarming. When pathological becomes normal an addict will do whatever is necessary to maintain the habit. Gamblers and overspenders alike bounce checks, borrow from friends, and go deeply in debt to support their habit, often lying to loved ones about their actions. It's not hard to see the connection between addictive behavior and the huge craters in our culture and the environment. Just as gamblers sell family heirlooms to continue gambling, addicted consumers sacrifice priceless natural areas, contentment, and tradition to maintain a steady stream of goods.

Psychologists tell us pathological buying is typically related to a quest for 15
greater recognition and acceptance, an expression of anger, or an escape through fantasy — all connected to shaky self-images. Writes Dr. Ronald Faber,

> One compulsive buyer bought predominantly expensive stereo and television equipment but demonstrated little interest when discussing the types of music or programs he liked. Eventually, it came out that his motivation for buying came mainly from the fact that neighbors recognized him as an expert in electronic equipment and came to him for advice when making their purchases.[6]

Faber reports that anger is often encoded in pathological buying — debt becomes a mechanism for getting back at one's spouse or parent. Or in other cases, extreme shopping is a fleeting getaway from reality:

> Buying provides a way of escaping into a fantasy where the individual can be seen as important and respected. Some people indicated that the possession and use of a charge card made them feel powerful; others found that the attention provided by sales personnel and being known by name at exclusive stores provided feelings of importance and status.[7]

[6]"Money Changes Everything," *American Behavioral Scientist,* July/August 1992. P. 809.
[7]Ibid.

What Are We Thinking

If we could read the minds of the busy, intent shoppers at the region's largest mall, wouldn't we be amazed? Certainly we'd feel a little less abnormal, because we'd see that the mall is packed with shoppers-in-therapy. (We're all crazy!) At least three in ten flee to the mall when things get out of control at home or work. Others come without a particular purchase in mind, just wanting to be around people, to feel less lonely. One woman resents having to buy a present for her son, who recently stole money from her purse. Several teenagers are desperately hoping their new clothes will facilitate sexual conquests that evening. At least six in ten of the shoppers feel a sense of euphoria from all the stimulation, but it's euphoria with a twist of anxiety. Each shopper knows from past experience that guilt, shame, and confusion — consumer regret — lurk right outside the door.

Still, they'll keep coming back, because they're addicted.

That is, unless they find a way to beat the all-consuming bug, as Thomas Monaghan did. In 1991 the founder of Domino's Pizza suddenly began to sell off many of his prized possessions, including three houses designed by Frank Lloyd Wright and thirty antique automobiles, one of which was an $8 million Bugatti Royale. Construction was halted on his multimillion-dollar home, and he even sold his Detroit Tigers baseball team because it was just a "source of excessive pride." He was quoted as saying, "None of the things I've bought, and I mean none of them, have ever really made me happy."[8]

READING THE TEXT

1. What do de Graaf, Wann, and Naylor believe to be America's "most destructive" (para. 2) addiction?

2. What are the costs of compulsive buying, according to de Graaf, Wann, and Naylor?

3. Describe in your own words what the authors mean by "affluenza."

4. What are some of the social and psychological causes of "pathological buying" (para. 15), according to the authors? What is the basis for their assumptions?

READING THE SIGNS

1. Read or reread Laurence Shames's "The More Factor" (p. 56), and write an essay comparing Shames's concept of the "more factor" with the "never enough" principle as described by de Graaf, Wann, and Naylor.

2. Write a journal entry listing some of your recent purchases. Can you attribute any of those purchases to an addiction for stuff? If so, which ones? To what extent does your shopping behavior reflect this article's claims?

[8]Alex Prud'Homme, "Taking the Gospel to the Rich," *New York Times.* February 14, 1999, p. BU 13.

3. Divide the class into work groups, list the products you have bought lately, and then consolidate the lists for the whole class. Discuss whether the lists exemplify the symptoms of addictive buying. If they do, what does that say about the population of the class? If they do not, how do you explain your class's deviation from what the authors claim is normative?

4. Write an essay in which you evaluate the logical validity of the authors' analogy between addictive shopping and physical addictions such as alcoholism. For a definition of addiction, consult an online medical encyclopedia such as **http://www.intelihealth.com** or **http://www.medterms.com**.

RACHEL BOWLBY
The Haunted Superstore

The experience of modern shopping is as complex as the corridors of an IKEA furniture warehouse, at once magical and, as Rachel Bowlby (b. 1957) suggests in this analysis of department stores and supermarkets, insidious. Dazzled by goods, you may feel trapped in an environment for which there is no way out — especially if the computerized cash registers are down. Mixing psychology and history, Bowlby meditates upon the complex, and often contradictory, nature of shopping, exploring its gender implications and its differences when viewed from a European and an American perspective. The author of Just Looking: Consumer Culture in Dreiser, Gissing and Zola *(1985),* Still Crazy After All These Years: Women, Writing, and Psychoanalysis *(1992),* Shopping with Freud *(1992), and* Carried Away: The Invention of Modern Shopping *(2001), from which this selection is taken, Bowlby teaches English, French, and American studies at the University of York.*

Saturday, 21 September 1996;
IKEA, Purley Way, South London

It is late in the afternoon and the lines of wide carts loaded up with flatpacks of future furniture stretch back from the row of checkouts. Back and back, right into the warehouse section, they bump up against the people still trying to pick out their own cardboard packages and happily oblivious, as yet, to the fate in store for them.

But gradually the news is getting through. The computers are down; all the purchase transactions are having to be done manually. The prospect of a handwritten receipt from IKEA seems quaintly unreal. Nobody, nothing moves, forwards or backwards. Nobody protests. Nobody seems to be talking to anyone else, passing the time in complaint or chat. We all stand sullenly by our carts, keeping our places, half-heartedly trying to decode the announcements. And nobody walks out, back through the store or out past the checkouts, leaving their cart behind.

We just can't leave now. These carts bear the tangible results of an afternoon's hard work. It may have been fun at the time, but now the prospect of going home empty-booted obliterates that from view. If we let go of the goods, we would have nothing to show for all this time and effort. And we are attached to these things already. This big brown box contains what a joyous, newly verbal two-year-old, still trailing clouds of consumerly innocence, is already proudly calling "my IKEA bed." Here we are, voluntarily trapped inside a store that we are unable to leave. Why did we come here in the first place? What is keeping us here? Is our behavior perverse, a stubborn refusal to give up? Or is it calmly rational, suffering the short-term frustrations and making the best of a bad situation? In this IKEA world there isn't much to choose between the two, or much to choose at all.

The checkout come to a dead halt is a long-standing nightmare for retailers. For decades, self-service stores of all kinds have sought to ease what they recognize as that difficult moment when customers finally emerge from the dreamier delights of trolley-filling to reach the point of purchase. There, reality intrudes in the form of the monetary transaction, and the trance of the aisles is broken by a slow line at the checkout. For supermarkets, barcode technology was the godsend of the 1980s; but shut down the computers, and chaos — slow despondency — is come again.

IKEA with the computers down might be a comic vision of a late 5 twentieth-century nightmare. We are familiar with tales of shopping as exploitation, addiction, false allure. As we wait, the frame for pondering the experience is already there for us: the store that you can't get out of as a microcosm of this consumer world, where shopping is endless and always, everywhere the same. One IKEA is much like another, each as reproducibly "Swedish" as the next, from Leeds to Groningen and from Paris to New Jersey. For critics of over-consumption, the over-stark contrast between movement and stoppage, dream and reality, that the stores seek to parry is ever present — not the avoidable contingency or the dreaded emergency, but the staple metaphor of shopping as hellish confinement.

Consumer culture lends itself to images of unconscious imprisonment. The deluded are unaware that their desires are for worthless or superfluous things, or that they are shaped — if not entirely created — by the skills and tricks of advertising and other forms of presentation. They do not know that there is a better and freer world than the shopping world in which they find themselves; for them it has no exit, nor do they seek one.

Opposite dark pictures like these stand their mirror images: shopping as freedom of choice, pleasure, material progress. Instead of confinement, darkness, hidden controls, shopping in its positive guise appears as sheer heaven or, more prosaically, as the proud symbol of modern mobility. People are no longer restricted to their traditional horizons, whether geographical, social, or psychological; consumer choice epitomizes their liberty to move away from old constrictions, to indulge the freedom of new desires and demands, and to take on different identities as they wish. This is also the dream world of shopping's own self-images, its beautiful stores and its glossy advertisements, where people's desires are treated as forever open to change and fulfillment. . . .

Supermarket, Anywhere, Around 1999

Here you are in the middle of the things. You are halfway through your list. You steer your way smoothly up and down, putting out your hand to take something at intervals, and placing it in your trolley. You know what you want, what it looks like, whereabouts it will be. You see different categories of product, differences between labels and brands and sizes that enable you to home in quickly on what you are seeking. This, not that. When you have finished, the seventeen items you have expertly selected from among the twenty thousand or so different possibilities are checked through one by one. A job has been efficiently done.

Here you are in the middle of the things. You have been here for quite a while. Twenty minutes, maybe half an hour. You came in to get something for tonight and thought you might as well stock up a bit while you were here. Everywhere around you are colors, letters, figures, pictures, all made to attract you. This and that. There is always something new or something on offer. If something appeals, you'll pick it up, perhaps put it back. But your mind is not really on what you're buying or looking at; you're thinking of other things. You will be here for some time, and eventually you will depart, with the same seventeen things.

What is the difference between the two? None, from the point of view of the receipt, which lists everything both shoppers buy in all-informing detail. To all supermarket intents and purposes, they are one and the same person; and maybe they are. In another life, on another day, the first shopper might easily slip into becoming the second; and the second, when pressed, might find herself or himself acting like the first.

The first shopper thinks of herself as in control, taking what she wants and only what she wants. The second shopper sees herself as comfortably susceptible to all the attractions of the place. The first shopper knows about the second and regards her with a certain affectionate scorn. The second shopper knows about the first and thinks she is missing out on the pleasure of shopping. Both, as well, partly share the other's opinion of them. And the first would also confess that she gets a certain pleasure out of her efficiency, while the second would declare that she also uses the time in the supermarket productively, unwinding the rest of her day as she drifts. Both, at times, when in a particular frame of mind, become the other one. The first is sometimes waylaid by a striking new product, while the second rushes urgently past, blind to everything but the two or three things she came in for.

Both, in one way, are figments or manufactures of the marketing imagination. Once upon a time, in the 1960s, it was principally the second shopper who featured, and she was dim and dazed, a childlike housewife passively picking up brightly colored things she had no thought to resist. Nowadays the shopper is viewed positively, as the rational planner who knows what she wants and competently makes her selection. The upgraded version of the second shopper, meanwhile, is no longer seen as necessarily stupid, but as someone who simply enjoys what others regard as a chore. These characters, and others too, and mixes of all of them, have filtered into shopping consciousness, to become the cartoon versions or templates of how we regard our own behavior. Like the products surrounding us, images of shoppers supply the background to the way that we experience and talk about whatever it might be that we are doing when we shop.

Some may see themselves as more involved or more detached than others, and certainly there is every possible gradation of difference between people's individual consumerly practices and ways of thinking. For what it's worth, shopping seems to be a part of everyday life in which people positively enjoy discussing their own peculiarities, as well as other people's, and often with much more subtlety than is shown by official psychologists of consumer behavior seeking to make predictable sense of shopping. But even when people identify themselves as non-shoppers, or anti-consumers, there is no getting away from the surrounding wash of consumerly ways of representing human choices and feelings, in which we are all immersed.

On the one hand, there is a semi-technical language, derived from the big academic business of consumer psychology, that has entered everyone's vocabulary for describing or experiencing their own behavior. Solemnly or ironically or both, with a knowing mixture of mastery and susceptibility, we refer to "loss-leaders" and describe our "impulse purchases" or avoidance of them. Marketing language may also be applied more widely. The "sell-by date," heralded as an important breakthrough for food retailing in the early 1970s, moved out of the store in the 1990s to be used in relation to anything passé; now the expression has probably passed its own. We can speak the marketing language, we know what is being done to us; but this same language also shapes our understanding.

On the other hand, arguments about shopping and consumption involve 15 much more than the situations in which actual buying takes place. Thirty or forty years ago, the phrase "consumer society" usually suggested a deluded, essentially female population: the unresisting victims of manipulative advertising and vulgar, alluring displays. The implication might have been that too much of their life was shopping; but the consumers of "consumer society" were not represented as being anything other than shoppers. Now, in a remarkable rhetorical turnabout, the consumer has been elevated to a status of exemplary good sense in areas extending far beyond shopping itself, with the name implying not a situation of vulnerability or delusion but quite the contrary. The consumer has ceased to be seen as part of a jellishly susceptible mass, having become instead an individual endowed with rights of which, by implication, his or her previous incarnations had been deprived. She (or he) is no longer a fool, but the model of modern individuality, the one who, as patient or passenger or parent, demands and gets the deal to which, implicitly, she was always entitled but that she was never granted before.

In the course of this process, the consumer has lost her sex. "He or she" is rhetorically removed from the picture of real shopping, where men and women remain readily distinguishable. In terms of perceptions of shopping (and women), the shift is crucial. Ceasing to be seen as passive, exploited, and dim, the consumer has ceased to be seen as female.

The Department Store and the Supermarket

Though it wouldn't be obvious from a glance at the customers in IKEA today, the history of shopping is largely a history of women, who have overwhelmingly been the principal shoppers both in reality and in the multifarious representations of shopping. This history began to gather momentum in the middle of the nineteenth century, when department stores entered the world. Their splendid new buildings and permanent exhibitions of lovely new things brought middle-class women into town to engage in what was historically a new activity: a day's shopping. They were places of leisure and luxury, offering women the image of a life that they could then, in fantasy if not in substance, take home with them. So after the frustrations of IKEA, and before we embark upon the intricacies of the supermarket's many small histories, let us dwell for a moment in the more leisurely spaces of its principal predecessor as a revolutionary new idea in shopping.

The department store offered an experience of aristocratic grandeur to every woman customer. There, she could act the queen and be treated like royalty. Department stores flattered women into seeing themselves as part of a beautiful environment; they fostered a sense of perpetual and limitless desire for things, in a kind of socialized abandonment. Loosened longings blended and unfixed existing social differences: New shopping instincts made no distinction of class, just as anyone might look like a lady.

In the nineteenth century was the department store; in the twentieth century was the supermarket. Department-store shopping was leisured, middle-class, metropolitan. Supermarkets and self-service, the great retailing innovations of the twentieth century, came from the opposite directions. Instead of luxury, they offered functionality and standard products; instead of the plea-sures of being served, consumers could congratulate themselves on saving money by doing the work themselves. Food shopping was associated with ne-cessity and routine, whereas department stores had promoted a sense of goods that engendered new desires and possibilities, out of the ordinary. It was the difference between going shopping — an open-ended, pleasurable, perhaps transgressive experience — and doing the shopping, a regular task to be done with the minimum expenditure of time, labor, and money.

But in many ways, department stores and supermarkets belong together. 20 Both are large-scale institutions, selling a vast range of goods under one roof and making use of modern marketing principles of rapid turnover and low profit margins. Both rely on economies of scale through their large selling ar-eas, and through direct buying in bulk from producers or manufacturers. Both were taken, when they first appeared on the scene, as emblematic of contem-porary developments not only in marketing, but in social life more generally: cities and leisure in one case, suburbs and cars in the other.

Both came to be represented in terms of magic and enchantment, seen as either pleasurable or insidious. Department stores, and supermarkets in their later developments, dazzled with their lighting and displays of goods — so beautiful, or so much. Like the supermarket, the department store pre-sented a new kind of indoor retailing space, which was *open,* with goods on display for looking at, and with no sense that customers had to come in with a definite intention to buy. Both were thought to produce in their female cus-tomers states of mind removed from the normal: the collective ecstasy of the nineteenth-century crowd of women in front of an array of heavenly new fab-rics, or the hypnotic trance of the 1950s housewife numbed by the Muzak as she glides along the aisles.

Yet the differences between the two kinds of store count far more than the similarities in their respective mythologies. First, in what they sell. The department store offered everything and anything, though with a concentra-tion on clothes and furnishings. The supermarket is associated with some-thing the department store did not always sell: food. Whereas the department stores were represented as bringing the glamour of fashion to the middle classes, supermarkets brought cheap food to "the masses." In one case, luxury items are offered to a class aspiring to an image of affluence and a sex aspir-ing to an image of beauty; in the other, necessities are made available to all.

The department store is European; the supermarket is American. The asso-ciation in the first case is false, in the sense that department stores appeared in the United States at more or less the same time as in Paris or London or Berlin. In the second case, it's right; but the contrast functions to reinforce other dis-tinctions. The department store is considered to be feminine, frivolous, French, and fashionable; in its Parisian form, it is one of the emblems of nineteenth-century modernity for Walter Benjamin's retrospect in the first part of the twentieth. The supermarket, massive and materialistic, figures as an American invention subsequently exported to Europe; and it was.

The department store was called (by Emile Zola) "the cathedral of modern commerce,"[1] it was also a "palace" for the middle classes. As a cathedral, it took over from religion; it had its consecrated building, and its own rituals and festive seasons in the form of designated times for sales and events in relation to particular themes and product groups: linens, toys, oriental rugs; autumn and spring fashions; winter and summer sales. The plain checkout visible at the end of each supermarket aisle hardly offers itself as an altar, though the uproar in the early 1990s in England about Sunday opening may suggest that the weekly shopping trip is indeed in some sense a symbolic replacement for the traditional family ritual.

As a palace, the department store offered a spectacle of opulence accessible to anyone who cared to enter and participate in an image of the aristocratic life. In the first American supermarkets, the show was less a planned or beautiful display than a performance or stunt. This was later to appear as a markedly dirty trick. In the 1960s, at the height of consumerist protests against exploitation by the big food corporations, the supermarket took on dramatically negative appearances, as a "jungle" or "trap," both giving titles to influential books of the period.[2] The images imply primitive aggression but also a space of confusion or imprisonment from which you cannot escape. Where the department store invites you in, the supermarket grabs you and won't let you out.

The differences between the images of the two kinds of store are today much less clear than they were. Supermarkets sell many kinds of product apart from food. Like department stores in their heyday, they try to present themselves as places for comfortably spending some time, with refreshments and rest rooms provided. Not the least remarkable feature of IKEA is that it seems to combine, in almost parodically differentiated sequence, the two forms of shopping, in history and experience. It is both department store and supermarket, both leisure and work, the one and then the other as though in artificial textbook separation.

First you walk through the suggestive displays of room settings and pause, looking to your eyes' content, trying out the chairs and pulling open the chests of drawers. There is no buying or selling here; this is shopping as possibility — the sight and feel of things, the embedding of desires and plans. After passing through all the different areas — ending, in true 1990s fashion, with the designer office furniture — you come to the café, where you can stop to gather your strength for the second part. Next, to ease the transition, an area of kitchen goods, plants, bed linen: a conventional, bright, self-service space with lots of small things you can pick up and put on your cart. Then the warehouse area where you find the boxes that contain whatever big-ticket

25

---

[1]Emile Zola, *Au Bonheur des Dames* (1883; Paris: Garnier Flammarion, 1971), p. 258.
[2]See Jennifer Cross, *The Supermarket Trap: The Consumer and the Food Industry* (Bloomington: Indiana UP, 1970), and Marion Giordan, *The Consumer Jungle* (London: Fontana, 1974).

items you have chosen from the room displays earlier on. It is for you to locate them, transport them home, and put them together; by doing the jobs yourself, you are saving costs on distribution and labor. This last lap reminds you in all its functional bareness that IKEA is giving you the best of both worlds, the leisurely indulgence of shopping and then the money-saving minimalism of the work and time you put in yourself.

These two versions of modern shopping, as labor or leisure, the pleasurable or the functional, are installed as co-present orientations in the minds of shoppers, as much as in the layout and self-presentation of shops themselves. At IKEA on that unusual afternoon, it was easy enough for once to pinpoint a moment when shopping shifted its meaning decisively from enjoyment to imposition. But much of the strangeness of shopping and consuming can come from the difficulty of knowing, experientially or otherwise, the difference between shopping's delights and its demands.

READING THE TEXT

1. What are the two kinds of shoppers whom Bowlby describes and marketers imagine?

2. Describe in your own words Bowlby's analytic opposition between the image of the department store and the image of the supermarket. What evidence does she advance to illustrate these images? How adequate do you find that evidence?

3. How has the image of the consumer changed in recent years, according to Bowlby?

4. What support does Bowlby offer to demonstrate her contention that "the consumer has ceased to be seen as female" (para. 16)? Do you find that support to be adequate?

READING THE SIGNS

1. In your journal, discuss whether your behavior resembles that of Bowlby's "first shopper" or that of her "second shopper." What patterns in your upbringing, or in your association with friends, may have led you to fit a particular category? If you resist categorization, why?

2. Bowlby analyzes the shopping experience as a binary set of opposing images: shopping as nightmarish entrapment versus shopping as pleasurable liberation. Write an essay in which you assess the validity of this opposition.

3. Visit a department store, observing both your own behavior and that of other shoppers. To what extent does the store encourage shopping as a form of pleasurable leisure?

4. Write an argumentative essay in which you support, refute, or modify Bowlby's contention that the image of the consumer is no longer female. To develop your

evidence, study images of consumers in advertising (check magazines such as *Better Homes and Gardens*) and in-store video displays.

5. Visit an IKEA store and write your own analysis of how the store's layout and design encourage consumption (for locations of IKEAs, visit **http://www.ikea-usa.com**). To develop your ideas, consult Malcolm Gladwell's "The Science of Shopping" (p. 403). Alternately, visit a local department store, noting its layout and location of stairs and elevators. How easy is it to navigate through the building? What effect does the layout have on your desire or ability to purchase products?

THOMAS HINE

What's in a Package

What's in a package? According to Thomas Hine (b. 1947), a great deal, perhaps even more than what is actually inside the package. From the cereal boxes you find in the supermarket to the perfume bottles sold at Tiffany's, the shape and design of the packages that contain just about every product we consume have been carefully calculated to stimulate consumption. Indeed, as Hine explains in this excerpt from The Total Package: The Evolution and Secret Meanings of Boxes, Bottles, Cans, and Tubes *(1995), "for manufacturers, packaging is the crucial final pay-off to a marketing campaign." A former architecture and design critic for the* Philadelphia Inquirer, *Hine has also published* Populuxe *(1986), on American design and culture;* Facing Tomorrow *(1991), on past and current attitudes toward the future; and* The Rise and Fall of the American Teenager: A New History of the American Adolescent Experience *(1999).*

When you put yourself behind a shopping cart, the world changes. You become an active consumer, and you are moving through environments — the supermarket, the discount store, the warehouse club, the home center — that have been made for you.

During the thirty minutes you spend on an average trip to the supermarket, about thirty thousand different products vie to win your attention and ultimately to make you believe in their promise. When the door opens, automatically, before you, you enter an arena where your emotions and your appetites are in play, and a walk down the aisle is an exercise in self-definition. Are you a good parent, a good provider? Do you have time to do all you think you should, and would you be interested in a shortcut? Are you worried about your health and that of those you love? Do you care about the environment? Do you appreciate the finer things in life? Is your life what you would like it to be? Are you enjoying what you've accomplished? Wouldn't you really like something chocolate?

Few experiences in contemporary life offer the visual intensity of a Safeway, a Krogers, a Pathmark, or a Piggly Wiggly. No marketplace in the world — not Marrakesh or Calcutta or Hong Kong — offers so many different goods with such focused salesmanship as your neighborhood supermarket, where you're exposed to a thousand different products a minute. No wonder it's tiring to shop.

There are, however, some major differences between the supermarket and a traditional marketplace. The cacophony of a traditional market has given way to programmed, innocuous music, punctuated by enthusiastically intoned commercials. A stroll through a traditional market offers an array of sensuous aromas; if you are conscious of smelling something in a supermarket, there is a problem. The life and death matter of eating, expressed in traditional markets by the sale of vegetables with stems and roots and by hanging animal carcasses, is purged from the supermarket, where food is processed somewhere else, or at least trimmed out of sight.

But the most fundamental difference between a traditional market and 5 the places through which you push your cart is that in a modern retail setting nearly all the selling is done without people. The product is totally dissociated from the personality of any particular person selling it — with the possible exception of those who appear in its advertising. The supermarket purges sociability, which slows down sales. It allows manufacturers to control the way they present their products to the world. It replaces people with packages.

Packages are an inescapable part of modern life. They are omnipresent and invisible, deplored and ignored. During most of your waking moments, there are one or more packages within your field of vision. Packages are so ubiquitous that they slip beneath conscious notice, though many packages are designed so that people will respond to them even if they're not paying attention.

Once you begin pushing the shopping cart, it matters little whether you are in a supermarket, a discount store, or a warehouse club. The important thing is that you are among packages: expressive packages intended to engage your emotions, ingenious packages that make a product useful, informative packages that help you understand what you want and what you're getting. Historically, packages are what made self-service retailing possible, and in turn such stores increased the number and variety of items people buy. Now a world without packages is unimaginable.

Packages lead multiple lives. They preserve and protect, allowing people to make use of things that were produced far away, or a while ago. And they are potently expressive. They assure that an item arrives unspoiled, and they help those who use the item feel good about it.

We share our homes with hundreds of packages, mostly in the bathroom and kitchen, the most intimate, body-centered rooms of the house. Some packages — a perfume flacon, a ketchup bottle, a candy wrapper, a beer can —

serve as permanent landmarks in people's lives that outlast homes, careers, or spouses. But packages embody change, not just in their age-old promise that their contents are new and improved, but in their attempt to respond to changing tastes and achieve new standards of convenience. Packages record changing hairstyles and changing life-styles. Even social policy issues are reflected. Nearly unopenable tamperproof seals and other forms of closures testify to the fragility of the social contract, and the susceptibility of the great mass of people to the destructive acts of a very few. It was a mark of rising environmental consciousness when containers recently began to make a novel promise: "less packaging."

For manufacturers, packaging is the crucial final payoff to a marketing cam- 10
paign. Sophisticated packaging is one of the chief ways people find the confidence to buy. It can also give a powerful image to products and commodities that are in themselves characterless. In many cases, the shopper has been prepared for the shopping experience by lush, colorful print advertisements, thirty-second television minidramas, radio jingles, and coupon promotions. But the package makes the final sales pitch, seals the commitment, and gets itself placed in the shopping cart. Advertising leads consumers into temptation. Packaging *is* the temptation. In many cases it is what makes the product possible.

But the package is also useful to the shopper. It is a tool for simplifying and speeding decisions. Packages promise, and usually deliver, predictability. One reason you don't think about packages is that you don't need to. The candy bar, the aspirin, the baking powder, or the beer in the old familiar package may, at times, be touted as new and improved, but it will rarely be very different.

You put the package into your cart, or not, usually without really having focused on the particular product or its many alternatives. But sometimes you do examine the package. You read the label carefully, looking at what the product promises, what it contains, what it warns. You might even look at the package itself and judge whether it will, for example, reseal to keep a product fresh. You might consider how a cosmetic container will look on your dressing table, or you might think about whether someone might have tampered with it or whether it can be easily recycled. The possibility of such scrutiny is one of the things that make each detail of the package so important.

The environment through which you push your shopping cart is extraordinary because of the amount of attention that has been paid to the packages that line the shelves. Most contemporary environments are landscapes of inattention. In housing developments, malls, highways, office buildings, even furniture, design ideas are few and spread very thin. At the supermarket, each box and jar, stand-up pouch and squeeze bottle, each can and bag and tube and spray has been very carefully considered. Designers have worked and reworked the design on their computers and tested mock-ups on the store shelves. Refinements are measured in millimeters.

All sorts of retail establishments have been redefined by packaging. Drugs

and cosmetics were among the earliest packaged products, and most drug-
stores now resemble small supermarkets. Liquor makers use packaging to add
a veneer of style to the intrinsic allure of intoxication, and some sell their
bottle rather than the drink. It is no accident that vodka, the most characterless of spirits, has the highest-profile packages. The local gas station sells
sandwiches and soft drinks rather than tires and motor oil, and in turn, automotive products have been attractively repackaged for sales at supermarkets,
warehouse clubs, and home centers.

With its thousands of images and messages, the supermarket is as visu- 15
ally dense, if not as beautiful, as a Gothic cathedral. It is as complex and as
predatory as a tropical rain forest. It is more than a person can possibly take
in during an ordinary half-hour shopping trip. No wonder a significant percentage of people who need to wear eyeglasses don't wear them when
they're shopping, and some researchers have spoken of the trancelike state
that pushing a cart through this environment induces. The paradox here is
that the visual intensity that overwhelms shoppers is precisely the thing that
makes the design of packages so crucial. Just because you're not looking at a
package doesn't mean you don't see it. Most of the time, you see far more
than a container and a label. You see a personality, an attitude toward life,
perhaps even a set of beliefs.

The shopper's encounter with the product on the shelf is, however, only
the beginning of the emotional life cycle of the package. The package is very
important in the moment when the shopper recognizes it either as an old
friend or a new temptation. Once the product is brought home, the package
seems to disappear, as the quality or usefulness of the product it contains becomes paramount. But in fact, many packages are still selling even at home,
enticing those who have bought them to take them out of the cupboard, the
closet, or the refrigerator and consume their contents. Then once the product
has been used up, and the package is empty, it becomes suddenly visible
once more. This time, though, it is trash that must be discarded or recycled.
This instant of disposal is the time when people are most aware of packages.
It is a negative moment, like the end of a love affair, and what's left seems to
be a horrid waste.

The forces driving package design are not primarily aesthetic. Market researchers have conducted surveys of consumer wants and needs, and consultants have studied photographs of families' kitchen cupboards and medicine
chests to get a sense of how products are used. Test subjects have been tied
into pieces of heavy apparatus that measure their eye movement, their blood
pressure or body temperature, when subjected to different packages. Psychologists get people to talk about the packages in order to get a sense of their innermost feelings about what they want. Government regulators and private
health and safety advocates worry over package design and try to make it
truthful. Stock-market analysts worry about how companies are managing
their "brand equity," that combination of perceived value and consumer loyalty that is expressed in advertising but embodied in packaging. The retailer is

paying attention to the packages in order to weed out the ones that don't sell or aren't sufficiently profitable. The use of supermarket scanners generates information on the profitability of every cubic inch of the store. Space on the supermarket shelf is some of the most valuable real estate in the world, and there are always plenty of new packaged products vying for display.

Packaging performs a series of disparate tasks. It protects its contents from contamination and spoilage. It makes it easier to transport and store goods. It provides uniform measuring of contents. By allowing brands to be created and standardized, it makes advertising meaningful and large-scale distribution possible. Special kinds of packages, with dispensing caps, sprays, and other convenience features, make products more usable. Packages serve as symbols both of their contents and of a way of life. And just as they can very powerfully communicate the satisfaction a product offers, they are equally potent symbols of wastefulness once the product is gone.

Most people use dozens of packages each day and discard hundreds of them each year. The growth of mandatory recycling programs has made people increasingly aware of packages, which account in the United States for about forty-three million tons, or just under 30 percent of all refuse discarded. While forty-three million tons of stuff is hardly insignificant, repeated surveys have shown that the public perceives that far more than 30 percent — indeed, nearly all — their garbage consists of packaging. This perception creates a political problem for the packaging industry, but it also demonstrates the power of packaging. It is symbolic. It creates an emotional relationship. Bones and wasted food (13 million tons), grass clippings and yard waste (thirty-one million tons), or even magazines and newspapers (fourteen million tons) do not feel as wasteful as empty vessels that once contained so much promise.

Packaging is a cultural phenomenon, which means that it works differently in 20
different cultures. The United States has been a good market for packages since it was first settled and has been an important innovator of packaging technology and culture. Moreover, American packaging is part of an international culture of modernity and consumption. At its deepest level, the culture of American packaging deals with the issue of surviving among strangers in a new world. This is an emotion with which anyone who has been touched by modernity can identify. In lives buffeted by change, people seek the safety and reassurance that packaged products offer. American packaging, which has always sought to appeal to large numbers of diverse people, travels better than that of most other cultures.

But the similar appearance of supermarkets throughout the world should not be interpreted as the evidence of a single, global consumer culture. In fact, most companies that do business internationally redesign their packages for each market. This is done partly to satisfy local regulations and adapt to available products and technologies. But the principal reason is that people in different places have different expectations and make different uses of packaging.

The United States and Japan, the world's two leading industrial powers, have almost opposite approaches to packaging. Japan's is far more elaborate

than America's, and it is shaped by rituals of respect and centuries-old traditions of wrapping and presentation. Packaging is explicitly recognized as an
expression of culture in Japan and largely ignored in America. Japanese packaging is designed to be appreciated; American packaging is calculated to be
unthinkingly accepted.

Foods that only Japanese eat — even relatively humble ones like refrigerated prepared fish cakes — have wrappings that resemble handmade paper or
leaves. Even modestly priced refrigerated fish cakes have beautiful wrappings
in which traditional design accommodates a scannable bar code. Such products look Japanese and are unambiguously intended to do so. Products that
are foreign, such as coffee, look foreign, even to the point of having only Roman lettering and no Japanese lettering on the can. American and European
companies are sometimes able to sell their packages in Japan virtually unchanged, because their foreignness is part of their selling power. But Japanese
exporters hire designers in each country to repackage their products. Americans — whose culture is defined not by refinements and distinctions but by
inclusiveness — want to think about the product itself, not its cultural origins.

We speak glibly about global villages and international markets, but problems with packages reveal some unexpected cultural boundaries. Why are
Canadians willing to drink milk out of flexible plastic pouches that fit into
reusable plastic holders, while residents of the United States are believed to
be so resistant to the idea that they have not even been given the opportunity
to do so? Why do Japanese consumers prefer packages that contain two tennis balls and view the standard U.S. pack of three to be cheap and undesir-
able? Why do Germans insist on highly detailed technical specifications on
packages of videotape, while Americans don't? Why do Swedes think that
blue is masculine, while the Dutch see the color as feminine? The answers lie
in unquestioned habits and deep-seated imagery, a culture of containing,
adorning, and understanding that no sharp marketer can change overnight.

There is probably no other field in which designs that are almost a century old — 25
Wrigley's gum, Campbell's soup, Hershey's chocolate bar — remain in production only subtly changed and are understood to be extremely valuable corporate
assets. Yet the culture of packaging, defined by what people are buying and selling every day, keeps evolving, and the role nostalgia plays is very small.

For example, the tall, glass Heinz ketchup bottle has helped define the
American refrigerator skyline for most of the twentieth century (even though
it is generally unnecessary to refrigerate ketchup). Moreover, it provides the
tables of diners and coffee shops with a vertical accent and a token of hospitality, the same qualities projected by candles and vases of flowers in more
upscale eateries. The bottle has remained a fixture of American life, even
though it has always been a nuisance to pour the thick ketchup through the
little hole. It seemed not to matter that you have to shake and shake the
bottle, impotently, until far too much ketchup comes out in one great scarlet
plop. Heinz experimented for years with wide-necked jars and other sorts of
bottles, but they never caught on.

Then in 1992 a survey of consumers indicated that more Americans believed that the plastic squeeze bottle is a better package for ketchup than the glass bottle. The survey did not offer any explanations for this change of preference, which has been evolving for many years as older people for whom the tall bottle is an icon became a less important part of the sample. Could it be that the difficulty of using the tall bottle suddenly became evident to those born after 1960? Perhaps the tall bottle holds too little ketchup. There is a clear trend toward buying things in larger containers, in part because lightweight plastics have made them less costly for manufacturers to ship and easier for consumers to use. This has happened even as the number of people in an average American household has been getting smaller. But houses, like packages, have been getting larger. Culture moves in mysterious ways.

The tall ketchup bottle is still preferred by almost half of consumers, so it is not going to disappear anytime soon. And the squeeze bottle does contain visual echoes of the old bottle. It is certainly not a radical departure. In Japan, ketchup and mayonnaise are sold in cellophane-wrapped plastic bladders that would certainly send Americans into severe culture shock. Still, the tall bottle's loss of absolute authority is a significant change. And its ultimate disappearance would represent a larger change in most people's visual environment than would the razing of nearly any landmark building.

But although some package designs are pleasantly evocative of another time, and a few appear to be unchanging icons in a turbulent world, the reason they still exist is because they still work. Inertia has historically played a role in creating commercial icons. Until quite recently, it was time-consuming and expensive to make new printing plates or to vary the shape or material of a container. Now computerized graphics and rapidly developing technology in the package-manufacturing industries make a packaging change easier than in the past, and a lot cheaper to change than advertising, which seems a far more evanescent medium. There is no constituency of curators or preservationists to protect the endangered package. If a gum wrapper manages to survive nearly unchanged for ninety years, it's not because any expert has determined that it is an important cultural expression. Rather, it's because it still helps sell a lot of gum.

So far, we've been discussing packaging in its most literal sense: designed 30 containers that protect and promote products. Such containers have served as the models for larger types of packaging, such as chain restaurants, supermarkets, theme parks, and festival marketplaces. . . . Still, it is impossible to ignore a broader conception of packaging that is one of the preoccupations of our time. This concerns the ways in which people construct and present their personalities, the ways in which ideas are presented and diffused, the ways in which political candidates are selected and public policies formulated. We must all worry about packaging ourselves and everything we do, because we believe that nobody has time to really pay attention.

Packaging strives at once to offer excitement and reassurance. It promises something newer and better, but not necessarily different. When we talk about a tourist destination, or even a presidential contender, being packaged, that's not really a metaphor. The same projection of intensified ordinariness, the same combination of titillation and reassurance, are used for laundry detergents, theme parks, and candidates alike.

The imperative to package is unavoidable in a society in which people have been encouraged to see themselves as consumers not merely of toothpaste and automobiles, but of such imponderables as lifestyle, government, and health. The marketplace of ideas is not an agora, where people haggle, posture, clash, and come to terms with one another. Rather, it has become a supermarket, where values, aspirations, dreams, and predictions are presented with great sophistication. The individual can choose to buy them, or leave them on the shelf.

In such a packaged culture, the consumer seems to be king. But people cannot be consumers all the time. If nothing else, they must do something to earn the money that allows them to consume. This, in turn, pressures people to package themselves in order to survive. The early 1990s brought economic recession and shrinking opportunities to all the countries of the developed world. Like products fighting for their space on the shelf, individuals have had to re-create, or at least represent, themselves in order to seem both desirable and safe. Moreover, many jobs have been reconceived to depersonalize individuals and to make them part of a packaged service experience.

These phenomena have their own history. For decades, people have spoken of writing resumes in order to package themselves for a specific opportunity. Thomas J. Watson Jr., longtime chairman of IBM, justified his company's famously conservative and inflexible dress code — dark suits, white shirts, and rep ties for all male employees — as "self-packaging," analogous to the celebrated product design, corporate imagery, and packaging done for the company by Elliot Noyes and Paul Rand. You can question whether IBM's employees were packaging themselves or forced into a box by their employer. Still, anyone who has ever dressed for success was doing a packaging job.

Since the 1950s, there have been discussions of packaging a candidate to 35 respond to what voters are telling the pollsters who perform the same tasks as market researchers do for soap or shampoo. More recently, such discussions have dominated American political journalism. The packaged candidate, so he and his handlers hope, projects a message that, like a Diet Pepsi, is stimulating without being threatening. Like a Weight Watchers frozen dessert bar, the candidate's contradictions must be glazed over and, ultimately, comforting. Aspects of the candidate that are confusing or viewed as extraneous are removed, just as stems and sinew are removed from packaged foods. The package is intended to protect the candidate; dirt won't stick. The candidate is uncontaminated, though at a slight remove from the consumer-voter.

People profess to be troubled by this sort of packaging. When we say a person or an experience is "packaged," we are complaining of a sense of excessive calculation and a lack of authenticity. Such a fear of unreality is at least a century old; it arose along with industrialization and rapid communication. Now that the world is more competitive, and we all believe we have less time to consider things, the craft of being instantaneously appealing has taken on more and more importance. We might say, cynically, that the person who appears "packaged" simply doesn't have good packaging.

Still, the sense of uneasiness about encountering packaged people in a packaged world is real, and it shouldn't be dismissed. Indeed, it is a theme of contemporary life, equally evident in politics, entertainment, and the supermarket. Moreover, public uneasiness about the phenomenon of packaging is compounded by confusion over a loss of iconic packages and personalities.

Producers of packaged products have probably never been as nervous as they became during the first half of the 1990s. Many of the world's most famous brands were involved in the merger mania of the 1980s, which produced debt-ridden companies that couldn't afford to wait for results either from their managers or their marketing strategies. At the same time, the feeling was that it was far too risky to produce something really new. The characteristic response was the line extension — "dry" beer, "lite" mayonnaise, "ultra" detergent. New packages have been appearing at a rapid pace, only to be changed whenever a manager gets nervous or a retailer loses patience.

The same skittishness is evident in the projection of public personalities as the clear, if synthetic, images of a few decades ago have lost their sharpness and broken into a spectrum of weaker, reflected apparitions. Marilyn Monroe, for example, had an image that was, Jayne Mansfield notwithstanding, unique and well defined. She was luscious as a Hershey's bar, shapely as a Coke bottle. But in a world where Coke can be sugar free, caffeine free, and cherry flavored (and Pepsi can be clear!), just one image isn't enough for a superstar. Madonna is available as Marilyn or as a brunette, a Catholic schoolgirl, or a bondage devotee. Who knows what brand extension will come next? Likewise, John F. Kennedy and Elvis Presley had clear, carefully projected images. But Bill Clinton is defined largely by evoking memories of both. As our commercial civilization seems to have lost the power to amuse or convince us in new and exciting ways, formerly potent packages are recycled and devalued. That has left the door open for such phenomena as generic cigarettes, President's Choice cola, and H. Ross Perot.

This cultural and personal packaging both fascinates and infuriates. There   40 is something liberating in its promise of aggressive self-creation, and something terrifying in its implication that everything must be subject to the ruthless discipline of the marketplace. People are at once passive consumers of their culture and aggressive packagers of themselves, which can be a stressful and lonely combination.

READING THE TEXT

1. How does Hine compare a supermarket with a traditional marketplace?

2. What does Hine mean when he asserts that modern retailing "replaces people with packages" (para. 5)?

3. How does packaging stimulate the desire to buy, according to Hine?

4. How do American attitudes toward packaging compare with those of the Japanese, according to Hine?

READING THE SIGNS

1. Bring one product package to class, preferably with all students bringing items from the same product category (personal hygiene, say, or snack food or drinks). Give a brief presentation to the class in which you interpret your own package. After all the students have presented, compare the different messages the packages send to consumers.

2. Visit a popular clothing store, such as the Gap or Banana Republic, and study the ways the store uses packaging to create, as Hine puts it, "a personality, an attitude toward life" (para. 15). Be thorough in your investigations, studying everything from the bags in which you carry your purchases to perfume or cologne packages to clothing labels. Use your findings as evidence for an essay in which you analyze the image the store creates for itself and its consumers.

3. In your journal, write an entry in which you explore your motives if you have ever purchased a product because you liked the package. What did you like about the package, and how did it contribute to your sense of identity?

4. Visit a store with an explicit political theme, such as the Body Shop or the Nature Company, and write a semiotic analysis of some of the packaging you see in the store.

5. Study the packages that are visible to a visitor to your home, and then write an analysis of the messages those packages might send to a visitor. To develop your ideas, you might read or reread Joan Kron's "The Semiotics of Home Decor" (p. 101).

FRED DAVIS

BLUE JEANS

Blue jeans are almost certainly America's greatest contribution to fashion history, and in this analysis, which originally appeared in his book Fashion Culture and Identity *(1992), Fred Davis (1925–1992) shows how this staple of the American wardrobe has become a symbol of many of our most enduring, and contradictory, cultural values. At once an emblem of democratic populism and elite status symbol, blue jeans are part of an American dialectic, Davis argues, in which "status and antistatus, democracy and distinction," are in a constant flux, moving with the tides of history itself. A former professor of sociology at the University of California at San Diego, Davis authored such books as* Yearning for

Yesterday: A Sociology of Nostalgia (1979) and Illness, Interaction, and the Self *(1972).*

The new clothes [jeans] express profoundly democratic values. There are no distinctions of wealth or status, no elitism; people confront one another shorn of these distinctions.

— CHARLES A. REICH,
The Greening of America

Throughout the world, the young and their allies are drawn hypnotically to denim's code of hope and solidarity — to an undefined vision of the energetic and fraternal Americanness inherent in them all.

— KENNEDY FRASER,
"That Missing Button"

Karl Lagerfeld for Chanel shapes a classic suit from blue and white denim, $960, with denim bustier, $360, . . . and denim hat, $400. All at Chanel Boutique, Beverly Hills.

— Photograph caption in *Los Angeles Times Magazine*
for article "Dressed-Up Denims," April 19, 1987

Since the dawn of fashion in the West some seven hundred years ago, probably no other article of clothing has in the course of its evolution more fully served as a vehicle for the expression of status ambivalences and ambiguities than blue jeans. Some of the social history supporting this statement is by now generally well known.[1] First fashioned in the mid-nineteenth-century American West by Morris Levi Strauss, a Bavarian Jewish peddler newly arrived in San Francisco, the trousers then as now were made from a sturdy, indigo-dyed cotton cloth said to have originated in Nimes, France. (Hence the anglicized contraction to *denim* from the French *de Nimes*.) A garment similar to that manufactured by Levi Strauss for goldminers and outdoor laborers is said to have been worn earlier in France by sailors and dockworkers from Genoa, Italy, who were referred to as "genes"; hence the term *jeans.* The distinctive copper riveting at the pants pockets and other stress points were the invention of Jacob Davis, a tailor from Carson City, Nevada, who joined the Levi Strauss firm in 1873, some twenty years after the garment's introduction.

More than a century went by, however, before this workingman's garment attained the prominence and near-universal recognition it possesses today. For it was not until the late 1960s that blue jeans, after several failed moves in previous decades into a broader mass market, strikingly crossed over nearly all class, gender, age, regional, national, and ideological lines to become the universally worn and widely accepted item of apparel they are today. And since the crossover, enthusiasm for them has by no means been confined to North America and Western Europe. In former Soviet bloc coun-

---

[1] Excellent, sociologically informed accounts of the origins and social history of blue jeans are to be found in Belasco (n.d.) and Friedmann (1987).

tries and much of the Third World, too, where they have generally been in short supply, they remain highly sought after and hotly bargained over.

A critical feature of this cultural breakthrough is, of course, blue jeans' identity change from a garment associated exclusively with work (and hard work, at that) to one invested with many of the symbolic attributes of leisure: ease, comfort, casualness, sociability, and the outdoors. Or, as the costume historians Jasper and Roach-Higgins (1987) might put it, the garment underwent a process of cultural authentication that led to its acquiring meanings quite different from that with which it began. In bridging the work/leisure divide when it did, it tapped into the new, consumer-goods-oriented, postindustrial affluence of the West on a massive scale. Soon thereafter it penetrated those many other parts of the world that emulate the West.

But this still fails to answer the questions of why so rough-hewn, drably hued, and crudely tailored a piece of clothing should come to exercise the fascination it has for so many diverse societies and peoples, or why within a relatively short time of breaking out of its narrow occupational locus it spread so quickly throughout the world. Even if wholly satisfactory answers elude us, these questions touch intimately on the twists and turns of status symbolism. . . .

To begin with, considering its origins and longtime association with work- 5 ingmen, hard physical labor, the outdoors, and the American West, much of the blue jeans' fundamental mystique seems to emanate from populist sentiments of democracy, independence, equality, freedom, and fraternity. This makes for a sartorial symbolic complex at war, even if rather indifferently for nearly a century following its introduction, with class distinctions, elitism, and snobbism, dispositions extant nearly as much in jeans-originating America as in the Old World. It is not surprising, therefore, that the first non–"working stiffs" to become attached to blue jeans and associated denim wear were painters and other artists, mainly in the southwest United States, in the late 1930s and 1940s (Friedmann 1987). These were soon followed by "hoodlum" motorcycle gangs ("bikers") in the 1950s and by New Left activists and hippies in the 1960s (Belasco n.d.). All these groups (each in its own way, of course) stood strongly in opposition to the dominant conservative, middle-class, consumer-oriented culture of American society. Blue jeans, given their origins and historic associations, offered a visible means for announcing such antiestablishment sentiments. Besides, jeans were cheap, and, at least at first, good fit hardly mattered.

Whereas by the late 1950s one could in some places see jeans worn in outdoor play by middle-class boys, until well into the 1960s a truly ecumenical acceptance of them was inhibited precisely because of their association with (more, perhaps, through media attention than from firsthand experience) such disreputable and deviant groups as bikers and hippies. Major sales and public relations campaigns would be undertaken by jeans manufacturers to break the symbolic linkage with disreputability and to convince consumers that jeans and denim were suitable for one and all and for a wide range of occasions (Belasco n.d.). Apparently such efforts helped; by the late 1960s blue jeans had achieved worldwide popularity and, of greater relevance here, had fully crossed over the occupation, class, gender, and age boundaries that had circumscribed them for over a century.

What was it — and, perhaps, what is it still — about blue jeans? Notwithstanding the symbolic elaborations and revisions (some would say perversions) to which fashion and the mass market have in the intervening years subjected the garment, there can be little doubt that at its crossover phase its underlying symbolic appeal derived from its antifashion significations: its visually persuasive historic allusions to rural democracy, the common man, simplicity, unpretentiousness, and, for many, especially Europeans long captivated by it, the romance of the American West with its figure of the free-spirited, self-reliant cowboy.[2]

But as the history of fashion has demonstrated time and again, no vestmental symbol is inviolable. All can, and usually will be, subjected to the whims of those who wish to convey more or different things about their person than the "pure" symbol in its initial state of signification communicates. Democratic, egalitarian sentiments notwithstanding, social status still counts for too much in Western society to permanently suffer the proletarianization that an unmodified blue-jean declaration of equality and fraternity projected. No sooner, then, had jeans made their way into the mass marketplace than myriad devices were employed for muting and mixing messages, readmitting evicted symbolic allusions, and, in general, promoting invidious distinctions among classes and coteries of jean wearers. Indeed, to the extent that their very acceptance was propelled by fashion as such, it can be said an element of invidiousness was already at play. For, other things being equal and regardless of the "message" a new fashion sends, merely to be "in fashion" is to be one up on those who are not as yet.[3]

---

[2]This is not to put forward some absurd claim to the effect that everyone who donned a pair of jeans was swept up by this imagery. Rather, it is to suggest that it was such imagery that came culturally to be encoded in the wearing of blue jeans (Berger 1984, 80–82), so that whether one wore them indifferently or with calculated symbolic intent, imitatively or in a highly individual manner, they would "on average" be viewed in this light.

[3]From this perspective, assumed by such important French critics as Barthes (1983) and Baudrillard (1984), all fashion, irrespective of the symbolic content that animates one or another manifestation of it, gravitates toward "designification" or the destruction of meaning. That is to say, because it feeds on itself (on its ability to induce others to follow the fashion "regardless"), it soon neutralizes or sterilizes whatever significance its signifiers had before becoming objects of fashion. Sheer display displaces signification; to take the example of blue jeans, even people hostile to their underlying egalitarian message can via fashion's mandate wear them with ease and impunity and, contrary to the garment's symbolic anti-invidious origins, score "status points" by doing so. This argument is powerful but in my view posits, in a manner similar to the claim that fashion is nothing more than change for the sake of change, too complete a break between the symbolic content of culture and the communication processes that embody and reshape it.

Elite vs. Populist Status Markers

Beyond this metacommunicative function, however, the twists, inversions, contradictions, and paradoxes of status symbolism to which blue jeans subsequently lent themselves underscore the subtle identity ambivalences plaguing many of their wearers. In a 1973 piece titled "Denim and the New Conservatives," Kennedy Fraser (1981, 92) noted several such, perhaps the most ironic being this:

> Some of the most expensive versions of the All-American denim theme have come bouncing into our stores from European manufacturers. The irresistible pull of both European fashion and denim means that American customers will pay large sums for, say, French blue jeans despite the galling knowledge that fashionable young people in Saint-Tropez are only imitating young people in America, a country that can and does produce better and cheaper blue jeans than France.

By 1990 a nearly parallel inversion seemed about to occur in regard to the garment's post-1950s image as leisure wear, although for destination other than fields and factories. With the introduction of men's fall fashions for the year featuring "urban denim," a spokesman for the Men's Fashion Association said (Hofmann 1990): "It's not just about cowboys and country and western anymore. It used to be that denim meant play clothes; now men want to wear it to the office the next day." 10

Framing the garment's status dialectic was the contest of polarities, one pole continuing to emphasize and extend blue jeans' "base-line" symbolism of democracy, utility, and classlessness, the other seeking to reintroduce traditional claims to taste, distinction, and hierarchical division. (Any individual wearer, and often the garment itself, might try to meld motifs from both sides in the hope of registering a balanced, yet appropriately ambivalent, statement.)

Conspicuous Poverty: Fading and Fringing

From the "left" symbolic (and not altogether apolitical) pole came the practice of jean fading and fringing. Evocative of a kind of conspicuous poverty, faded blue jeans and those worn to the point of exposing some of the garment's warp and woof were soon more highly prized, particularly by the young, than new, well-blued jeans. Indeed, in some circles worn jeans commanded a higher price than new ones. As with Chanel's little black dress, it cost more to look "truly poor" than just ordinarily so, which new jeans by themselves could easily accomplish. But given the vogue that fading and fringing attained, what ensued in the marketplace was predictable: Jeans manufacturers started producing prefaded, worn-looking, stone- or acid-washed jeans.[4] These obviated, for the average consumer if not for the jeans connoisseur disdainful of such subterfuge, the need for a long break-in period.

Labeling, Ornamentation, and Eroticization

From the "right" symbolic pole emerged a host of stratagems and devices, all of which sought in effect to de-democratize jeans while capitalizing on the ecumenical appeal they had attained: designer jeans, which prominently displayed the label of the designer; jeans bearing factory sewn-in embroidering, nailheads, rhinestones, and other decorative additions; specially cut and sized jeans for women, children, and older persons; in general, jeans combined (with fashion's sanction) with items of clothing standing in sharp symbolic contradiction of them, e.g., sports jackets, furs, dress shoes, spiked heels, ruffled shirts, or silk blouses.

Paralleling the de-democratization of the jean, by the 1970s strong currents toward its eroticization were also evident. These, of course, contravened the unisex, de-gendered associations the garment initially held for many: the relative unconcern for fit and emphasis on comfort; the fly front for both male and female; the coarse denim material, which, though it chafed some, particularly women, was still suffered willingly. Numerous means were found to invest the jean and its associated wear with gender-specific, eroticized meaning. In the instance of women — and this is more salient sociologically since it was they who had been de-feminized by donning the blatantly masculine blue jeans in the first place — these included the fashioning of denim material into skirts, the "jeans for gals" sales pitches of manufacturers, the use of softer materials, cutting jeans so short as to expose the buttocks, and, in general, the transmogrification of jeans from loose-fitting, baggy trousers into pants so snugly pulled over the posterior as to require some women to lie down to get into them. So much for comfort, so much for unisexuality! Interestingly, in the never-ending vestmental dialectic on these matters baggy jeans for women again became fashionable in the mid-1980s.

Designer Jeans

Of all of the modifications wrought upon it, the phenomenon of designer jeans speaks most directly to the garment's encoding of status ambivalences. The very act of affixing a well-known designer's label — and some of the world's leading hautes couturiers in time did so — to the back side of a pair of

---

[4]A yet later variation on the same theme was "shotgun washed" jeans manufactured by a Tennessee company that blasted its garments with a twelve-gauge shotgun (Hochswender 1991).

jeans has to be interpreted, however else it may be seen, along Veblenian lines, as an instance of conspicuous consumption; in effect, a muting of the underlying rough-hewn proletarian connotation of the garment through the introduction of a prominent status marker.[5] True, sewing an exterior designer label onto jeans — a practice designers never resort to with other garments — was facilitated psychologically by the prominent Levi Strauss & Co. label, which had from the beginning been sewn above the right hip pocket of that firm's denim jeans and had over the years become an inseparable part of the garment's image. It could then be argued, as it sometimes was, that the outside sewing of a designer label was consistent with the traditional image of blue jeans. Still, Yves Saint Laurent, Oscar de la Renta, or Gloria Vanderbilt, for that matter, are not names to assimilate easily with Levi Strauss, Lee, or Wrangler, a distinction hardly lost on most consumers.

But as is so characteristic of fashion, every action elicits its reaction. No sooner had the snoblike, status-conscious symbolism of designer jeans made its impact on the market than dress coteries emerged whose sartorial stock-in-trade was a display of disdain for the invidious distinctions registered by so obvious a status ploy. This was accomplished mainly through a demonstration of hyperloyalty to the original, underlying egalitarian message of denim blue jeans. As Kennedy Fraser (1981, 93) was to observe of these countercyclicists in 1973:

> The denim style of the more sensitive enclaves of the Village, the West Side, and SoHo is the style of the purist and neo-ascetic. Unlike the "chic" devotee of blue jeans, this loyalist often wears positively baggy denims, and scorns such travesties as embroideries and nailheads. To underline their association with honesty and toil, the denims of choice are often overalls.

Not long after, the "positively baggy denims" of which Fraser speaks — this antifashion riposte to fashion's prior corruption of denim's 1960s-inspired rejection of status distinctions — were themselves, with that double reflexive irony at which fashion is so adept, assimilated into the fashion cycle. Then those "into" denim styles could by "dressing down" stay ahead of — as had their older, first-time-around denim-clad siblings of the sixties — their more conformist, "properly dressed" alters.

[5]Everyone, without exception, whom I interviewed and spoke with in the course of my research on fashion (designers, apparel manufacturers, buyers, persons from the fashion press, fashion-conscious laypersons) interpreted designer jeans in this light. Most felt that status distinctions were the *only* reason for designer jeans because, except for the display of the designer label, they could detect no significant difference between designer and nondesigner jeans. Not all commentators, however, are of the opinion that the prominent display of an outside label can be attributed solely to invidious status distinctions. Some (Back 1985) find in the phenomenon overtones of a modernist aesthetic akin, for example, to Bauhaus design, exoskeletal building construction, action painting, and certain directions in pop art wherein the identity of the creator and the processual markings of his/her creation are visibly fused with the art work itself.

Conclusion

And so . . . do the dialectics of status and antistatus, democracy and distinction, inclusiveness and exclusiveness pervade fashion's twists and turns; as much, or even more, with the workingman's humble blue jeans as with formal dinner wear and the evening gown.

But such is fashion's way. If it is to thrive it can only feed off the ambiguities and ambivalences we endure in our daily lives and concourse, not only over those marks of social status considered here but equally over such other key identity pegs as age, gender, and sexuality, to mention but the most obvious. Were it the case, as some scholars have maintained, that fashion's sole symbolic end was registering and re-registering invidious distinctions of higher and lower, or better and lesser — that is, distinctions of class and social status — it would hardly have enough "to talk about"; certainly not enough to account for its having thrived in Western society for as long as it has. But, as we have already seen . . . , it does have more to say: about our masculinity and femininity, our youth and age, our sexual scruples or lack thereof, our work and play, our politics, national identity, and religion. This said, one need not take leave of what has engaged us here, that rich symbolic domain that treats of the deference and respect we accord and receive from others (what Max Weber meant by *status*), in order to appreciate that fashion is capable of much greater subtlety, more surprises, more anxious backward glances and searching forward gazes than we credit it with.

WORKS CITED

Back, Kurt W. 1985. "Modernism and Fashion: A Social Psychological Interpretation," in Michael R. Solomon, ed., *The Psychology of Fashion.* Lexington, Mass.: Heath.

Barthes, Roland. 1983. *The Fashion System.* Translated by Matthew Ward and Richard Howard. New York: Hill and Wang.

Baudrillard, Jean. 1984. "La Mode ou la féerie du code." *Traverses* 3 (October): 7–19.

Belasco, Warren A. n.d. "Mainstreaming Blue Jeans: The Ideological Process, 1945–1980." Unpublished.

Berger, Arthur Asa. 1984. *Signs in Contemporary Culture.* New York: Longman.

Fraser, Kennedy. 1981. *The Fashionable Mind.* New York: Knopf.

Friedmann, Daniel. 1987. *Une Histoire du blue jean.* Paris: Ramsay.

Hochswender, Woody. 1991. "Patterns." *New York Times,* Jan. 8.

Hofmann, Deborah. 1990. "New Urbanity for Denim and Chambray." *New York Times,* Sept. 24.

Jasper, Cynthia R., and Mary Ellen Roach-Higgins. 1987. "History of Costume: Theory and Instruction." *Clothing and Textile Research Journal* 5, no. 4 (Summer): 1–6.

Reich, Charles A. 1970. *The Greening of America.* New York: Crown.

READING THE TEXT

1. Why, according to Davis, were jeans linked with "disreputability" (para. 6) until the mid-1960s?

2. In Davis's view, what enabled jeans to "crossover" (para. 2) from being disreputable to fashionable?

3. Summarize in your own words the ambivalence between "democracy and distinction" (para. 17) or "left" (para. 12) and "right" (para. 13) that Davis ascribes to jeans since the 1960s.

4. How does Davis interpret the advent of designer jeans?

READING THE SIGNS

1. Bring to class a current fashion magazine for men or women (such as *Glamour* or *Maxim*), and study the jeans ads in small groups. Do you find that today's jeans ads use the democratizing or dedemocratizing symbolism that Davis describes? How can you account for your observations?

2. This selection, originally published in 1992, takes its analysis through the 1980s. Using Davis's categories of democracy and distinction, write your own update of jeans through today. For evidence of the system in which jeans operate, you can rely on advertisements, videos, film, Web sites of jeans manufacturers, and other popular media.

3. Write an argumentative essay in response to the contention that, rather than having a social or cultural significance as Davis presumes, jeans are worn simply for comfort and budgetary reasons.

4. In your journal, brainstorm a list of brands of jeans, and then note which you currently wear, would like to wear, or would never consider wearing. Reflect on the image associated with each brand. How does image affect your taste in attire?

5. Observe students at your school congregating in a public place (say, the student union building), and note the predominant fashion styles. Then write a semiotic interpretation of the fashion trends you observe.

JOAN KRON

THE SEMIOTICS OF HOME DECOR

Just when you thought it was safe to go back into your living room, here comes Joan Kron with a reminder that your home is a signaling system just as much as your clothing is. In Home-Psych: The Social Psychology of Home and Decoration *(1983), from which this selection is taken, Kron takes a broad look at the significance of interior decoration, showing how home design can reflect both an individual and a group identity. Ranging from a New York entrepreneur to Kwakiutl Indian chiefs, Kron further discusses how different cultures use possessions as a rich symbol system. The author of* High Tech: The Industrial Style and Source Book for the Home *(1978) and of some five hundred articles for American magazines, she is particularly interested in fashion, design, and the social psychology of consumption. Currently an editor-at-large at* Allure *magazine, Kron has also published* Lift: Wanting, Fearing, and Having a Face-Lift *(1998).*

On June 7, 1979, Martin J. Davidson entered the materialism hall of fame. That morning the thirty-four-year-old New York graphic design entrepreneur went to his local newsstand and bought fifty copies of the *New York Times* expecting to read an article about himself in the Home section that would portray him as a man of taste and discrimination. Instead, his loft and his lifestyle, which he shared with singer Dawn Bennett, were given the tongue-in-cheek treatment under the headline: "When Nothing But the Best Will Do."[1]

Davidson, who spent no more money renovating his living quarters than many of the well-to-do folks whose homes are lionized in the *Times*'s Thursday and Sunday design pages — the running ethnographic record of contemporary upper-middle-class life-style — made the unpardonable error of telling reporter Jane Geniesse how much he had paid for his stereo system, among other things. Like many people who have not been on intimate terms with affluence for very long, Davidson is in the habit of price-tagging his possessions. His 69-cent-per-bottle bargain Perrier, his $700 Armani suits from Barney's, his $27,000 cooperative loft and its $150,000 renovation, his sixteen $350-per-section sectionals, and his $11,000 best-of-class stereo. Martin J. Davidson wants the world to know how well he's done. "I live the American dream," he told Mrs. Geniesse, which includes, "being known as one of Barney's best customers."[2]

Davidson even wants the U.S. Census Bureau's computer to know how well he has done. He is furious, in fact, that the 1980 census form did not have a box to check for people who live in cooperatives. "If someone looks at my census form they'll think I must be at the poverty level or lower."[3] No one who read the *Times* article about Martin Davidson would surmise that.

It is hard to remember when a "design" story provoked more outrage. Letters to the editor poured in. Andy Warhol once said that in our fast-paced media world no one could count on being a celebrity for more than fifteen minutes. Martin Davidson was notorious for weeks. "All the Martin Davidsons in New York," wrote one irate reader, "will sit home listening to their $11,000 stereos, while downtown, people go to jail because they ate a meal they

---

[1] Jane Geniesse, "When Nothing But the Best Will Do," *New York Times,* June 7, 1979, p. C1ff.

[2] Ibid.

[3] Author's interview with Martin Davidson.

couldn't pay for."[4] "How can one man embody so many of the ills afflicting our society today?"[5] asked another offended reader. "Thank you for your clever spoof," wrote a third reader. "I was almost convinced that two people as crass as Martin Davidson and Dawn Bennett could exist."[6] Davidson's consumption largesse was even memorialized by Russell Baker, the *Times*'s Pulitzer Prize–winning humorist, who devoted a whole column to him: "While simultaneously consuming yesterday's newspaper," wrote Baker, "I consumed an article about one Martin Davidson, a veritable Ajax of consumption. A man who wants to consume nothing but the best and does."[7] Counting, as usual, Davidson would later tell people, "I was mentioned in the *Times* on three different days."

Davidson, a self-made man whose motto is "I'm not taking it with me 5 and while I'm here I'm going to spend every stinking penny I make," couldn't understand why the *Times* had chosen to make fun of him rather than to glorify his 4,000-square-foot loft complete with bidet, Jacuzzi, professional exercise gear, pool table, pinball machine, sauna, two black-tile bathrooms, circular white Formica cooking island, status-stuffed collections of Steiff animals, pop art (including eleven Warhols), a sound system that could weaken the building's foundations if turned up full blast, and an air-conditioning system that can turn cigarette smoke, which both Davidson and Bennett abhor, into mountain dew — a loft that has everything Martin Davidson ever wanted in a home except a swimming pool and a squash court.

"People were objecting to my life-style," said Davidson. "It's almost as if there were a correlation between the fact that we spend so much on ourselves and other people are starving. No one yells when someone spends $250,000 for a chest of drawers at an auction," he complained. "I just read in the paper that someone paid $650,000 for a stupid stamp. Now it'll be put away in a vault and no one will ever see it."[8]

But Dawn Bennett understood what made Davidson's consumption different. "It's not very fashionable to be an overt consumer and admit it,"[9] she said.

What Are Things For?

As anyone knows who has seen a house turned inside out at a yard sale, furnishing a home entails the acquisition of more objects than there are in a spring housewares catalog. With all the time, money, and space we devote to

---

[4]Richard Moseson, "Letters: Crossroads of Decadence and Destitution," *New York Times*, June 14, 1979, p. A28.

[5]Letter to the Editor, *New York Times*, June 14, 1979, p. C9.

[6]Letter to the Editor, ibid.

[7]Russell Baker, "Observer: Incompleat Consumer," *New York Times*, June 9, 1979, p. 25.

[8]Author's interview with Martin Davidson.

[9]Author's interview with Dawn Bennett.

the acquisition, arrangement, and maintenance of these household possessions, it is curious that we know so little about our relationships to our possessions.

"It is extraordinary to discover that no one knows why people want goods," wrote British anthropologist Mary Douglas in *The World of Goods*.[10] Although no proven or agreed-upon theory of possessiveness in human beings has been arrived at, social scientists are coming up with new insights on our complicated relationships to things. Whether or not it is human nature to be acquisitive, it appears that our household goods have a more meaningful place in our lives than they have been given credit for. What comes across in a wide variety of research is that things matter enormously.

Our possessions give us a sense of security and stability. They make us feel in control. And the more we control an object, the more it is a part of us. If it's *not mine,* it's *not me.*[11] It would probably make sense for everyone on the block to share a lawn mower, but then no one would have control of it. If people are reluctant to share lawn mowers, it should not surprise us that family members are not willing to share TV sets. They want their own sets so they can watch what they please. Apparently, that was why a Chicago woman, furious with her boyfriend for switching from *The Thorn Birds* to basketball, stabbed him to death with a paring knife.[12]

Besides control, we use things to compete. In the late nineteenth century the Kwakiutl Indian chiefs of the Pacific Northwest made war with possessions.[13] Their culture was built on an extravagant festival called the "potlatch," a word that means, roughly, to flatten with gifts. It was not the possession of riches that brought prestige, it was the distribution and destruction of goods. At winter ceremonials that took years to prepare for, rival chiefs would strive to outdo one another with displays of conspicuous waste, heaping on their guests thousands of spoons and blankets, hundreds of gold and silver bracelets, their precious dance masks and coppers (large shields that were their most valuable medium of exchange), and almost impoverishing themselves in the process.

[10]Mary Douglas and Baron Isherwood, *The World of Goods* (New York: Basic Books, 1979), p. 15. A number of other social scientists have mentioned in recent works the lack of attention paid to the human relationship to possessions: See Coleman and Rainwater, *Social Standing,* p. 310. The authors observed that "the role of income in providing a wide range of rewards — consumption — has not received sufficient attention from sociologists." See Carl F. Graumann, "Psychology and the World of Things," *Journal of Phenomenological Psychology,* Vol. 4, 1974–75, pp. 389–404. Graumann accused the field of sociology of being thing-blind.

[11]Lita Furby, "Possessions: Toward a Theory of Their Meaning and Function Throughout the Life Cycle," in Paul B. Baltes (ed.), *Life-Span Development and Behavior,* Vol. 1 (New York: Academic Press, 1978), pp. 297–336.

[12] "'Touch That Dial and You're Dead,'" *New York Post,* March 30, 1983, p. 5.

[13]Ruth Benedict, *Patterns of Culture* (Boston: Houghton Mifflin [1934], 1959); Frederick V. Grunfeld, "Homecoming: The Story of Cultural Outrage," *Connoisseur,* February 1983, pp. 100–106; and Lewis Hyde, *The Gift* (New York: Vintage Books, [1979, 1980], 1983), pp. 25–39.

Today our means of competition is the accumulation and display of symbols of status. Perhaps in Utopia there will be no status, but in this world, every human being is a status seeker on one level or another — and a status reader. "Every member of society," said French anthropologist Claude Lévi-Strauss, "must learn to distinguish his fellow men according to their mutual social status."[14] This discrimination satisfies human needs and has definite survival value. "Status symbols provide the cue that is used in order to discover the status of others, and, from this, the way in which others are to be treated," wrote Erving Goffman in his classic paper, "Symbols of Class Status."[15] Status affects who is invited to share "bed, board, and cult,"[16] said Mary Douglas. Whom we invite to dinner affects who marries whom, which then affects who inherits what, which affects whose children get a head start.

Today what counts is what you eat (gourmet is better than greasy spoon), what you fly (private jet is better than common carrier), what sports you play (sailing is better than bowling), where you matriculate, shop, and vacation, whom you associate with, how you eat (manners count), and most important, where you live. Blue Blood Estates or Hard Scrabble zip codes as one wizard of demographics calls them. He has figured out that "people tend to roost on the same branch as birds of a feather."[17] People also use status symbols to play net worth hide-and-seek. When *Forbes* profiled the 400 richest Americans,[18] its own in-house millionaire Malcolm Forbes refused to disclose his net worth but was delighted to drop clues telling about his status entertainments — his ballooning, his Fabergé egg hunts, his châteaux, and his high life-style. It is up to others to translate those obviously costly perks into dollars.

A high price tag isn't the only attribute that endows an object with status. Status can accrue to something because it's scarce — a one-of-a-kind artwork or a limited edition object. The latest hard-to-get item is Steuben's $27,500 bowl etched with tulips that will be produced in an edition of five — one per year for five years. "Only one bowl will bloom this year,"[19] is the headline on the ad for it. Status is also found in objects made from naturally scarce materials: Hawaii's rare koa wood, lapis lazuli, or moon rock. And even if an object is neither expensive nor rare, status can rub off on something if it is favored by the right people, which explains why celebrities are used to promote coffee, cars, casinos, and credit cards.

If you've been associated with an object long enough you don't even have to retain ownership. Its glory will shine on you retroactively. Perhaps that is

[14]Edmund Leach, *Claude Lévi-Strauss* (New York: Penguin Books, 1980), p. 39.

[15]Erving Goffman, "Symbols of Class Status," *British Journal of Sociology,* Vol. 2, December 1951, pp. 294–304.

[16]Douglas and Isherwood, *World of Goods,* p. 88.

[17]Michael J. Weiss, "By Their Numbers Ye Shall Know Them," *American Way,* February 1983, pp. 102–106 ff. "You tell me someone's zip code," said Jonathan Robbin, "and I can predict what they eat, drink, drive, buy, even think."

[18]"The Forbes 400," *Forbes,* September 13, 1982, pp. 99–186.

[19]Steuben Glass advertisement, *The New Yorker,* April 4, 1983, p. 3.

why a member of Swiss nobility is having two copies made of each of the Old Master paintings in his collection. This way, when he turns his castle into a museum, both his children can still have, so to speak, the complete collection, mnemonics of the pictures that have been in the family for centuries. And the most potent status symbol of all is not the object per se, but the *expertise* that is cultivated over time, such as the appreciation of food, wine, design, or art.

If an object reflects a person *accurately*, it's an index of status. But *symbols* of status are not always good indices of status. They are not official proof of rank in the same way a general's stars are. So clusters of symbols are better than isolated ones. Anyone with $525 to spare can buy one yard of the tiger-patterned silk velvet that Lee Radziwill used to cover her dining chair seats.[20] But one status yard does not a princess make. A taxi driver in Los Angeles gets a superior feeling from owning the same status-initialed luggage that many of her Beverly Hills fares own. "I have the same luggage you have," she tells them. "It blows their minds," she brags. But two status valises do not a glitterati make. Misrepresenting your social status isn't a crime, just "a presumption," said Goffman. Like wearing a $69 copy of a $1,000 watch that the mail-order catalog promises will make you "look like a count or countess on a commoner's salary."[21]

"Signs of status are important ingredients of self. But they do not exhaust all the meanings of objects for people," wrote sociologists Mihaly Csikszentmihalyi and Eugene Rochberg-Halton in *The Meaning of Things: Domestic Symbols of the Self*.[22] The study on which the book was based found that people cherished household objects not for their status-giving properties but especially because they were symbols of the self and one's connections to others.

The idea that possessions are symbols of self is not new. Many people have noticed that *having* is intricately tied up with *being*. "It is clear that between what a man calls *me* and what he simply calls *mine*, the line is difficult to draw," wrote William James in 1890.[23] "Every possession is an extension of the self," said Georg Simmel in 1900.[24] "Humans tend to integrate their selves with objects," observed psychologist Ernest Beaglehole some thirty years later.[25] Eskimos used to *lick* new acquisitions to cement the person/object relationship.[26] We stamp our visual taste on our things making the totality

[20]Paige Rense, "Lee Radziwill," *Celebrity Homes* (New York: Penguin Books, 1979), pp. 172–81.

[21]*Synchronics* catalogue, Hanover, Pennsylvania, Fall 1982.

[22]Mihaly Csikszentmihalyi and Eugene Rochberg-Halton, *The Meaning of Things: Domestic Symbols of the Self* (New York: Cambridge University Press, 1981), p. 18.

[23]William James, *Principles of Psychology*, Vol. 1 (New York: Macmillan, 1890), p. 291.

[24]Georg Simmel, *The Philosophy of Money*, trans. Tom Bottomore and David Frisby (Boston: Routledge & Kegan Paul, 1978), p. 331.

[25]Ernest Beaglehole, *Property: A Study in Social Psychology* (New York: Macmillan, 1932).

[26]Ibid., p. 134.

resemble us. Indeed, theatrical scenic designers would be out of work if Blanche DuBois's boudoir could be furnished with the same props as Hedda Gabler's.

Csikszentmihalyi and Rochberg-Halton discovered that "things are cherished not because of the material comfort they provide but for the information they convey about the owner and his or her ties to others."[27] People didn't value things for their monetary worth, either. A battered toy, a musical instrument, a homemade quilt, they said, provide more meaning than expensive appliances which the respondents had plenty of. "What's amazing is how few of these things really make a difference when you get to the level of what is important in life,"[28] said Csikszentmihalyi. All those expensive furnishings "are required just to keep up with the neighbors or to keep up with what you expect your standard of living should be."

"How else should one relate to the Joneses if not by keeping up with them," asked Mary Douglas provocatively.[29] The principle of reciprocity requires people to consume at the same level as one's friends.[30] If we accept hospitality, we have to offer it in return. And that takes the right equipment and the right setting. But we need things for more than "keeping level" with our friends. We human beings are not only toolmakers but symbol makers as well, and we use our possessions in the same way we use language — the quintessential symbol — to *communicate* with one another. According to Douglas, goods make the universe "more intelligible." They are more than messages to ourselves and others, they are "the hardware and the software . . . of an information system."[31] Possessions speak a language we all understand, and we pay close attention to the inflections, vernacular, and exclamations.

The young husband in the film *Diner* takes his things very seriously. How could his wife be so stupid as to file the Charlie Parker records with his rock 'n' roll records, he wants to know. What's the difference, she wants to know. What's the difference? How will he find them otherwise? Every record is sacred. Different ones remind him of different times in his life. His things *take* him back. Things can also *hold* you back. Perhaps that's why Bing Crosby's widow auctioned off 14,000 of her husband's possessions — including his bed. "'I think my father's belongings have somehow affected her progress in

---

[27]Csikszentmihalyi and Rochberg-Halton, p. 239.

[28]Author's interview with Mihaly Csikszentmihalyi.

[29]Douglas and Isherwood, *World of Goods,* p. 125. Also see Jean Baudrillard, *For a Critique of the Political Economy of the Sign,* trans. Charles Levin (St. Louis, MO: Telos Press, 1981), p. 81. Said Baudrillard: "No one is free to live on raw roots and fresh water. . . . The vital minimum today . . . is the standard package. Beneath this level, you are an outcast." Two classic novels on consumption are (1) Georges Perec, *Les Choses* (New York: Grove Press, [1965], 1967). (2) J. K. Huysmans, *Against the Grain (A Rebours)* (New York: Dover Publications, [1931], 1969).

[30]Douglas and Isherwood, *World of Goods,* p. 124.

[31]Ibid., p. 72.

life,'" said one of Bing's sons.[32] And things can tell you where you stand. Different goods are used to rank occasions and our guests. Costly sets of goods, especially china and porcelain, are "pure rank markers. . . . There will always be luxuries because rank must be marked," said Douglas.[33]

One of the pleasures of goods is "sharing names."[34] We size up people by their expertise in names — sports buffs can converse endlessly about hitters' batting averages, and design buffs want to know whether you speak spongeware, Palladio, Dansk, or Poggenpohl. All names are not equal. We use our special knowledge of them to show solidarity and exclude people.

In fact, the social function of possessions is like the social function of food. Variations in the quality of goods define situations as well as different times of day and seasons. We could survive on a minimum daily allotment of powdered protein mix or grains and berries. But we much prefer going marketing, making choices, learning new recipes. "Next to actually eating food, what devout gastronomes seem to enjoy most is talking about it, planning menus, and remembering meals past," observed food critic Mimi Sheraton.[35] But it's not only experts who thrive on variety. Menu monotony recently drove a Carlsbad, New Mexico, man to shoot the woman he was living with. She served him green beans once too often. "Wouldn't you be mad if you had to eat green beans all the time?" he said.[36] If every meal were the same, and if everyone dressed alike and furnished alike, all meanings in the culture would be wiped out.[37]

The furnishings of a home, the style of a house, and its landscape are all part of a system — a system of symbols. And every item in the system has meaning. Some objects have personal meanings, some have social meanings which change over time. People understand this instinctively and they desire things, not from some mindless greed, but because things are necessary to communicate with. They are the vocabulary of a sign language. To be without things is to be left out of the conversation. When we are "listening" to others we may not necessarily agree with what this person or that "says" with his or her decor, or we may misunderstand what is being said; and when we are doing the "talking" we may not be able to express ourselves as eloquently as we would like. But where there are possessions, there is always a discourse.

And what is truly remarkable is that we are able to comprehend and ma- 25
nipulate all the elements in this rich symbol system as well as we do — for surely the language of the home and its decor is one of the most complex lan-

[32]Maria Wilhelm, "Things Aren't Rosy in the Crosby Clan as Kathryn Sells Bing's Things (and not for a Song)," *People,* May 31, 1982, pp. 31–33.

[33]Douglas and Isherwood, *World of Goods,* p. 118.

[34]Ibid., p. 75.

[35]Mimi Sheraton, "More on Joys of Dining Past," *New York Times,* April 9, 1983, p. 48.

[36]"Green Beans Stir Bad Blood," *New York Times,* March 26, 1983, p. 6.

[37]Douglas and Isherwood, *World of Goods,* p. 66.

guages in the world. But because of that it is also one of the richest and most expressive means of communication.

Decor as Symbol of Self

One aspect of personalization is the big I — Identity. Making distinctions between ourselves and others. "The self can only be known by the signs it gives off in communication," said Eugene Rochberg-Halton.[38] And the language of ornament and decoration communicates particularly well. Perhaps in the future we will be known by our computer communiqués or exotic brainwaves, but until then our rock gardens, tabletop compositions, refrigerator door collages, and other design language will have to do. The Nubian family in Africa with a steamship painted over the front door to indicate that someone in the house works in shipbuilding, and the Shotte family on Long Island who make a visual pun on their name with a rifle for a nameplate, are both decorating their homes to communicate "this is where our territory begins and this is who we are."

Even the most selfless people need a minimum package of identity equipment. One of Pope John Paul I's first acts as pontiff was to send for his own bed. "He didn't like sleeping in strange beds," explained a friend.[39] It hadn't arrived from Venice when he died suddenly.

Without familiar things we feel disoriented. Our identities flicker and fade like ailing light bulbs. "Returning each night to my silent, pictureless apartment, I would look in the bathroom mirror and wonder who I was," wrote D. M. Thomas, author of *The White Hotel,* recalling the sense of detachment he felt while living in a furnished apartment during a stint as author-in-residence at a Washington, D.C., university. "I missed familiar things, familiar ground that would have confirmed my identity."[40]

Wallpaper dealers wouldn't need fifty or sixty sample books filled with assorted geometrics, supergraphics, and peach clamshells on foil backgrounds if everyone were content to have the same roses climbing their walls. Chintz wouldn't come in forty flavors from strawberry to licorice, and Robert Kennedy Jr.'s bride Emily wouldn't have trotted him around from store to store "for ten hours" looking for a china pattern[41] if the home wasn't an elaborate symbol system — as important for the messages it sends to residents and outsiders as for the functions it serves.

---

[38]Eugene Rochberg-Halton, "Where Is the Self: A Semiotic and Pragmatic Theory of Self and the Environment." Paper presented at the 1980 American Sociological Meeting, New York City, 1980, p. 3.

[39]Dora Jane Hamblin, "Brief Record of a Gentle Pope," *Life,* November 1978, p. 103.

[40]D. M. Thomas, "On Literary Celebrity," *The New York Times Magazine,* June 13, 1982, pp. 24–38, citation p. 27.

[41]"Back Home Again in Indiana Emily Black Picks Up a Freighted Name: Mrs. Robert F. Kennedy, Jr.," *People,* April 12, 1982, pp. 121–23, citation p. 123.

In the five-year-long University of Chicago study[42] into how modern 30 Americans relate to their things, investigators Mihaly Csikszentmihalyi and Rochberg-Halton found that we all use possessions to stand for ourselves. "I learned that things can embody self," said Rochberg-Halton. "We create environments that are extensions of ourselves, that serve to tell us who we are, and act as role models for what we can become."[43] But what we cherish and what we use to stand for ourselves, the researchers admitted, seemed to be "scripted by the culture."[44] Even though the roles of men and women are no longer so tightly circumscribed, "it is remarkable how influential sex-stereotyped goals still remain."[45] Men and women "pay attention to different things in the same environment and value the same things for different reasons," said the authors.[46] Men and children cared for action things and tools; women and grandparents cared for objects of contemplation and things that reminded them of family. It was also found that meaning systems are passed down in families from mothers to daughters — not to sons.

Only children and old people cared for a piece of furniture because it was useful. For adults, a specific piece of furniture embodied experiences and memories, or was a symbol of self or family. Photographs which had the power to arouse emotions and preserve memories meant the most to grandparents and the least to children. Stereos were most important to the younger generation, because they provide for the most human and emotional of our needs — release, escape, and venting of emotion. And since music "seems to act as a modulator of emotions," it is particularly important in adolescence "when daily swings of mood are significantly greater than in the middle years and . . . later life."[47] Television sets were cherished more by men than women, more by children than grandparents, more by grandparents than parents. Plants had greater meaning for the lower middle class, and for women, standing for values, especially nurturance and "ecological consciousness."[48] "Plateware," the term used in the study to cover all eating and drinking utensils, was mentioned mostly by women. Of course, "plates" are the tools of the housewife's trade. In many cultures they are the legal possession of the women of the house.

The home is such an important vehicle for the expression of identity that one anthropologist believes "built environments" — houses and settlements —

---

[42]Eugene Rochberg-Halton, "Cultural Signs and Urban Adaptation: The Meaning of Cherished Household Possessions." Ph.D. dissertation, Department of Behavioral Science, Committee on Human Development, University of Chicago, August 1979; and Mihaly Csikszentmihalyi and Eugene Rochberg-Halton, *The Meaning of Things: Domestic Symbols of the Self* (New York: Cambridge University Press, 1981).

[43]Author's interview with Eugene Rochberg-Halton.

[44]Csikszentmihalyi and Rochberg-Halton, *Meaning of Things,* p. 105.

[45]Ibid., p. 112.

[46]Ibid., p. 106.

[47]Ibid., p. 72.

[48]Ibid., p. 79.

were originally developed to "*identify a group*—rather than to provide shelter."[49] But in contemporary Western society, the house more often identifies a person or a family instead of a group. To put no personal stamp on a home is almost pathological in our culture. Fear of attracting attention to themselves constrains people in crime-ridden areas from personalizing, lack of commitment restrains others, and insecurity about decorating skill inhibits still others. But for most people, painting some sort of self-portrait, decoratively, is doing what comes naturally.

All communications, of course, are transactions. The identity we express is subject to interpretation by others. Will it be positive or negative? David Berkowitz, the "Son of Sam" murderer, didn't win any points when it was discovered he had drawn a circle around a hole in the wall in his apartment and written "This is where I live."[50] A person who fails to keep up appearances is stigmatized.

READING THE TEXT

1. Summarize how, according to Kron, our possessions act as signs of our identity.

2. How do our living places work to create group identity?

3. Why did *New York Times* readers object to the consumption habits of Martin J. Davidson?

4. In your own words, explain how possessions give one a sense of "stability" (para. 10).

READING THE SIGNS

1. In a small group, discuss the brand names of possessions that each of you owns. Then interpret the significance of each brand. What do the brands say about each of you? About the group?

2. With your class, brainstorm factors other than possessions that can communicate a person's identity. Then write your own essay in which you compare the relative value of possessions to your own sense of identity with the additional factors your class brainstormed.

3. Write an essay in which you argue for or against Kron's claim that "to put no personal stamp on a home is almost pathological in our culture" (para. 32).

4. Analyze semiotically your own apartment or a room in your house, using Kron's essay as a critical framework. How do your possessions and furnishings act as signs of your identity?

5. Using Kron's essay as a critical framework, analyze the semiotic significance of possessions in Karen Karbo's "The Dining Room" (p. 434)?

[49]Amos Rapoport, "Identity and Environment," in James S. Duncan (ed.), *Housing and Identity: Cross-Cultural Perspectives* (London: Croom Helm, 1981), pp. 6–35, citation p. 18.

[50]Leonard Buder, "Berkowitz Is Described as 'Quiet' and as a Loner," *New York Times,* August 12, 1977, p. 10.

DAVID GOEWEY

"Careful, You May Run Out of Planet":
SUVs and the Exploitation of the American Myth

If you think that a car is just a car and that a sport utility vehicle is just a bigger car, then David Goewey's (b. 1955) semiotic analysis of the SUV craze could be something of an eyeopener for you. Situating America's love affair with the automobile, in general, and the SUV, in particular, within a historical context, Goewey reveals how the sport utility vehicle is a full-fledged myth machine, symbolically incorporating many of America's ideological values and contradictions within its several tons of heavy metal. An actor and teacher, Goewey wrote this essay, which won the Oliver Evans Undergraduate Essay Prize at California State University, Northridge, as a term paper in a class on popular culture.

"For centuries man had fantasized about the glories of independent travel," wrote the thirteenth-century scientist and philosopher Roger Bacon. Although writing during the Middle Ages, Bacon predicted, with uncanny accuracy, that humanity "shall endow chariots with incredible speed, without the aid of any animal" (Pettifer and Turner 9). Bacon's prescient forecast conjured a vision that became a twentieth-century American fact of life: the ubiquitous automobile. By 1872, French inventor Amédée Bollée had developed steam-powered demonstration models (Flink 6), and within the next thirty-five years the United States dominated the world market for gasoline-powered automobiles (Pettifer and Turner 15). In the new century America itself — with a vast geography, scattered settlements, and relatively low population density — seemed best suited to the spread of a romanticized car culture (Flink 43). America, in short, took to the roads with relish.

The automobile quickly entered American popular culture. Tin Pan Alley devoted no fewer than six hundred songs to the pleasures of motoring (Pettifer and Turner 17). The futurist art movement, furthermore, appropriated the automobile as a specific symbol of modernity itself (Wernick 80), representative of speed, progress, and technology. As a token, the car embodied escapist fantasy (Pettifer and Turner 239), allowing the individual to conquer time and space. But it was America's unique values of freedom, individualism, and the pursuit of happiness that became manifested in the automobile — values that imbued the car with definitive mythic significance (Robertson 191).

Now, at the end of the twentieth century, the vehicle that combines the most potent mix of American mythologies is the sport utility vehicle (SUV) — hybrid passenger cars/light trucks with four-wheel drive. With sales expected to exceed one million units in 1998, the SUV is the fastest-growing segment of the automobile market (Storck 79). However, as a social phenomenon, SUVs contain both practical and mythic contradictions. For example, these vehicles are designed for rugged, off-road motoring, yet a mere 10 percent of drivers ever leave surface streets or highways (Storck 99). With their muscular styling and dominant height and weight, SUVs are almost ludicrously masculine in design, yet women account for 40 percent of sales (Storck 79). Furthermore, while SUV advertising campaigns often pose the vehicle in rural settings of woodlands or along lakesides, the SUV is anything but nature-friendly with its thirsty gasoline tank and lower emission standards (Pope 14). In short, the modern SUV represents a preeminent symbol of American popular culture.

A semiotic analysis of the contradictions inherent in the SUV phenomenon, as well as its historical and socioeconomic significance, therefore, reveals the intriguing ironies that underscore America's predominant ideology. American culture's faddish preoccupation with the SUV may be seen as deeply embedded in a national identity. Furthermore, a close look at the SUV trend also reveals America's understanding of reality and fantasy and its conflicting attitude toward human survival and environmental protection. As a cultural signifier, the SUV both reveals and reflects the principal components of America's popular mythology.

The most obvious ironies are perhaps best observed in the SUV model 5 names chosen by the manufacturers. Many vehicle names are directly evocative of America's western frontier mythology, such as the Jeep Wrangler or the

The Mitsubishi Shogun.

Isuzu Rodeo. Others are linked to the Western European tradition of the exploration and settlement of foreign lands, such as the Ford Explorer or the Land Rover Discovery. Indeed, the GMC Yukon blends both American western imagery and the European exploratory drive and thus embodies the American notion of a frontier: remote, extremely wild, and to the average person unknown.

The fascination with the American frontier, which today's automakers so effectively exploit, is directly tied to America's historical beginnings. The idea of the frontier as both sacred and menacing is a principal tenet in the nation's mythology. The first Europeans, after all, encountered a daunting wilderness. *Mayflower* passenger William Bradford described a "hideous and desolate wilderness . . . represent[ing] a wild and savage hue" (Robertson 45). The Europeans, steeped in fairy-tale traditions of the forest as the dark dwelling place of witches and cannibals, therefore considered the woods intrinsically evil (Robertson 49). The forests were godless and had to be tamed before they could be inhabitable, leveled before they could be considered usable. The Native Americans, likewise, were viewed as the personification of this savage wasteland and therefore had to be subjugated along with the wilderness to ensure the spread of civilization (Robertson 50). And the early Americans' religious convictions justified this expansion.

The notion that Americans were on a God-given mission to subdue this newfound jungle and expand Western civilization "into the limitless wilderness" (Robertson 44) became institutionalized in American mythology by the Jacksonian policy of Manifest Destiny. Americans were believed to be ordained by God to carry the noble virtues of democracy, freedom, and civilization westward across the continent (Robertson 72). This relentless expansionism, then, was suffused with religious significance and mission. The frontier was seen as the demarcation between order and disorder, between goodness and evil. To challenge the frontier, therefore, took supreme courage and zeal, and men like Daniel Boone, George Rogers Clark, and Andrew Jackson became outstanding western heroes (Robertson 80).

Corollary to this idea of an expansive frontier was the belief in the ever-abundant opportunities and riches available to whoever was brave and ambitious enough to pursue them. This idea of "more" was contingent on the belief in a limitless frontier and served as a motivating factor in the pursuit of happiness and the drive to succeed. Expansion, in a sense, became an end in itself (Shames 33–34). However, in late twentieth-century America, the concept of more has suffered a practical setback. Diminishing economic expectations from the 1960s through the 1980s, including a shrinking productivity rate, a decrease in real earnings, and a growing national debt, all contributed to challenge the mythic notion of the frontier as fruitful with economic possibilities (Shames 34–36).

It is perhaps not coincidental, then, that the sport utility vehicle craze began in earnest in the early 1980s (Storck 79). In reaction to "the fear that the world may not be . . . big enough" (Shames 37), the decade's penchant for conspicuous consumption can be seen as a challenge to that anxiety. And the introduction of large, powerful vehicles into the mass market, with names like the Ford Bronco and the Chevy Blazer, may represent the reassertion of a courageous American defiance in response to threatened frontiers.

Furthermore, the growth of the SUV market through the 1990s, with this 10 segment comprising 23 percent of total auto sales (Storck 79), suggests the adaptability of the SUV's mythic significance. The expanding economy of the Clinton years — based on the globalization of economic interests and the consequent resurrection of expanding frontiers — recasts the SUV as a celebratory metaphor for power and control. The SUV, in this context, represents the resurgence of the conquering American.

The GMC Yukon, named for a region far from the American mainstream, can be seen to embody the cultural notion of the wild frontier as fearsome and therefore in need of civilization. And the vehicle is certainly well designed for the rugged task of settlement. Weighing in at over 5,300 pounds (with passengers), measuring over $16^{1}/_{2}$ feet in length and just under 6 feet in height, the GMC Yukon is among the largest SUVs on the market (Storck 27). Its massive size arguably manifests the expansive idea of America's western frontier.

However, the GMC Yukon's heftiness necessarily affects its miles-per-gallon ratio. The average rounds off at a measly 13 miles per gallon (Storck 27), less than half what the U.S. government requires for passenger cars. And with a fuel tank capacity of 30 gallons and an estimated full tank mileage of under 400 miles, the GMC Yukon can be seen vehemently to declare the concept of more. Furthermore, juxtaposing the GMC Yukon with its namesake suggests an egregious symmetry. The Yukon Territory, north of British Columbia, Canada, abuts Prudhoe Bay. Exploratory oil drilling there in 1967 uncovered the largest oilfield in North America, with an estimated capacity of about 10 billion barrels (Yergin 571). The American myth of an ever-expansive frontier, then, is powerfully manifested in the heavyweight GMC Yukon, which locates and justifies its own mass production in the fact of a naturally oil-abundant Yukon Territory.

Another popular SUV that contains a doubly potent signifier within the manufacturer's title is the Jeep Cherokee. Considered the original SUV, the Jeep Cherokee dates all the way back to 1948. As a result, owners take a measure of purist's pride, believing their SUV is the one that started it all (Storck 41). But a closer look at this SUV's mythohistorical connections may provide the owners' pride with a deeper significance.

The Jeep Cherokee prototype — the General Purpose Vehicle, which was shortened to Jeep — was introduced during World War II in response to a U.S. Army–sponsored competition among automakers. It was first developed by the Bantam Motor Company, and the design was then completed by the Willys-Overland Company. The Ford Motor Company also assisted in the mass production of what was soon considered the "backbone of all Allied military transport" and the "crowning success of the war" (Flink 276). No doubt drawing on their heroic wartime performance, surplus military jeeps were sold stateside and helped to introduce a market for four-wheel drive recreational vehicles (Flink 276).

The usefulness and durability of four-wheel-drive vehicles, however, was 15 recognized even earlier during World War I, and many automakers, including Packard, Peerless, and Nash motor companies, vied for government contracts. Manufacturers found that luxury car chassis were easily converted to 2 or 3 ton truck bodies (Flink 78) — a literal blending of automobiles and trucks that clearly prefigures the modern SUV. Along with the Jeep's victorious wartime service, then, the SUV conveys such powerful militaristic connotations as morally righteous patriotism, overwhelming industrial ingenuity and might, and the imperative conquest of evil.

An interesting link between automobility and the American frontier was provided approximately forty years earlier by a Civil War hero. On his retirement in 1903, Civil War veteran General Nelson A. Miles, who had successfully hunted Chief Joseph and the Nez Perce to ground in 1877 and to whom the Apache war leader Geronimo surrendered in 1886 (Josephy 416, 429), foresaw the military promise of motor vehicles. He urged Secretary of War Elihu Root to "replace five regiments of calvary" with troops on bicycles and in motor vehicles (Flink 74), believing that the horse was now obsolete. General Miles's foresight was ironic in light of the Jeep Cherokee's double significance.

The Jeep Cherokee's militaristic connotations become oppressive when considering the grotesquely racist misapplication of a Native American tribal name to a motor vehicle. Although the word *Cherokee* is a misnomer derived from the Choctaw definition for cave dwellers and actually has no meaning in the language of those to whom it is applied, it is nevertheless used to designate at least one group of Native Americans, the United Keetoowah Band of Cherokee, in Oklahoma (Josephy 323). This original misnaming indicates the indeterminability of language, especially in the traumatic context of Native American history. And while it may be argued that such indeterminacy freely allows a manufacturer's use of the name to sell a product, the word *Cherokee* nevertheless denotes a group of people still thriving today despite oppression.

In the 1820s, despite the fierce allegiance to tradition held by many Cherokee, a large number of them succumbed to the ongoing proselytizing efforts of Moravian missionaries to become the "most acculturated of southern tribes" (Josephy 320). The Cherokee learned the English alphabet and even innovated a Cherokee alphabet based on the English model. In 1828, this led to the remarkable publication, in English and Cherokee, of a native newspaper (Josephy 320). Cherokee efforts to assimilate into what could be seen even then as a dominant culture, in other words, were vigorous.

Nevertheless, also in 1828, President Andrew Jackson undertook an aggressive campaign of ethnic cleansing against the Cherokee. Capitalizing on white racism to pass anti-Cherokee legislation, and with the discovery of gold on Cherokee territory, Jackson made physical removal of the tribe a national issue (Josephy 325). This culminated in the infamous and tragic Trail of Tears, the forced march west to Oklahoma of eighteen thousand Cherokee men, women, and children under the armed escort of General Winfield Scott and seven thousand U.S. Army troops (Josephy 331).

The manufacturers of the Jeep Cherokee clearly ignore this dismal chap- 20 ter in U.S. history and instead evoke superficially positive components of a mythic American past. Drawing on traditional viewpoints of the western frontier as the border between civilization and wilderness (Robertson 92) and oblivious to the fact that the Cherokee were an enforced western tribe, the Jeep Cherokee manufacturer exploits mythic identifications of Native Americans with the fearsome and violent "imagery and logic of the frontier" (Robertson 106).

The Jeep Cherokee manufacturer also mines the symbol of the quintessential American hero, the cowboy. Pitted against the frontier, the cowboy was directly descended from the backwoodsmen and pathfinders who pioneered west to the Ohio River Valley and beyond to the Northwest Passage. As the frontier pushed on, the continent's western plains and mountains became the wilderness that was next in need of subjugation and control. The cowboy, and his close companions in the American mythic imagination of the Wild West, the U.S. Cavalry, became the defenders of civilization and the champions of progress (Robertson 161–62). As such, they symbolized law and order in a lawless land. Both the cowboy and the U.S. Cavalry were the good guys risking themselves to save civilization from the bad guys, most notably the wildly violent Indians (Robertson 162).

The Jeep Cherokee, then, is a multilayered symbol indeed. This SUV appropriates the token of a victorious American struggle over the frontier, won by American cowboys and cavalrymen, and combines it with the morally righteous conquest over evil achieved during World War II. The modern driver who slips behind the wheel of a Jeep Cherokee assumes the militaristically heroic mantle that is suffused within the vehicle's legend and manifested in the control available in the "tight and precise steering, easy maneuverability . . . and taut overall feel from the firm suspension" (Storck 41). Detached from historical truths, however, the SUV's "excellent visibility all around" and "superior driving position" (Storck 41), qualities essential to success in battle, capitalize on these military/frontier connotations and at the same time sublimate factual battlefield horrors into an aggressive game of on-the-road cowboys and Indians.

The SUV, with its rugged militaristic symbolism, magnifies the traditional association of the automobile as a masculine token. Yet women account for a sizable share of the SUV market (Storck 79). This appeal, in fact, extends and amplifies a traditional relationship between women and motor vehicles. The introduction of the automobile may well have affected the scope of women's societal role more than that of men. Unlike the horse and buggy, for instance, the automobile demanded skill over physical strength to operate, and so women were offered mobility and parity that driving a team of horses denied them (Flink 162).

However, middle-class women by the 1920s were still traditionally tied to the home, for the most part, although electrical household appliances had nevertheless increased leisure time. The refrigerator, for example, permitted the bulk buying of a week's worth of perishable food at one stop, leaving time for socializing or an afternoon movie matinee (Flink 164). The added spare time, combined with automobility's enhanced sense of individual freedom (Robertson 191), afforded women at least temporary escape from the confines of the home that defined their routine (Flink 163).

As the automobile helped to change women's role from that of home-   25
based providers of food and clothing into consumers of mass-produced goods, car designers soon recognized the potential of the female market. Such comfort features as plush upholstery, heaters, and automatic transmissions were planned with women in mind (Flink 163). And advertising executives, quick to determine that women were disproportionately the nation's consumers (Marchand 66), began to target automobile ads at them. One of the most famous advertisements, for the Jordan Motor Company's Playboy automobile, began "Somewhere west of Laramie there's a broncho-busting, steer-roping girl" (Pettifer and Turner 130), clearly utilizing the familiar western imagery of freedom and control.

This relationship between women and their automobiles has grown even more complex in recent years. First, the car didn't so much redefine women's fundamental domestic role as increase the scope of its domain. Also, it is reasonable to assume that the automobile facilitated women's introduction into the workplace by easing transportation between the home and job. And yet in 1997, economic equality still eludes the American workforce: Working women earn less than 75 percent of men's average income (Jones et al. 49). A woman's job, furthermore, may include not only doing outside work but ferrying children to and from school and activities and shopping for the family. A subsequent feeling of disempowerment, then, may find relief behind the wheel of a physically powerful and symbolically potent SUV.

Advertisers evidently think so. They still acknowledge a woman's buying power and capitalize on the appeal SUVs hold for many female drivers. One current SUV advertisement aimed at women, promoting the Subaru Forester, both stresses its inherent power and rugged potential and notes the female-friendly design of this smaller vehicle. The larger photo in a recent two-page spread in *Time* shows the Forester kicking up a dust trail as it barrels down a dirt track. The accompanying smaller picture presents a casually dressed young woman easily tying a kayak to the SUV's roof. The ad's dominant image is a rough and careless strength. And while the woman in the ad is proportionally submissive, she is capably preparing for an exciting outdoor adventure. The double message suggests a sense of diminishment that is compensated for with images of ability, ease, and the casual transference of power.

Perhaps the most logical and disarming association carmakers and advertisers exploit when designing and promoting an SUV is the vehicle's connection to nature. As previously noted, implicit within the SUV's frontier imagery is a confrontational attitude toward the wilderness. Accordingly, automakers design — and advertisers sell — SUVs capable of handling the roughest terrain. And indeed, much of the appeal of SUVs is their promise of providing access to the farthest reaches of the globe. As a marketing gimmick, for instance, Land Rover cosponsors and participates in the annual Camel Trophy relay, pitting various SUVs against the jungle wilds of Borneo and South America. Besides the obvious British imperialistic connotations such a race implies, the challenge of maneuvering a Land Rover Discovery "over garbage can sized rocks" or "through streams where the entire vehicle is submerged" (Storck 6) positions the competitor in a naturally inharmonious contest.

Advertisers take a dual approach when exploiting the adversarial relationship between SUVs and nature. In some print ads this relationship is clothed in benign natural imagery, often with a warning text. The Mitsubishi Montero Sport, for example, pictures a gleaming silver vehicle perched prominently on the rocky shoreline of a wooded lakesite. The tall stand of evergreen trees are at a safe distance; the water surface is without a ripple. The bold black headline proclaims, "It Came to Comfort Earth," and the text goes on to inform the reader that "the planet wasn't exactly designed for your comfort."

So the Montero Sport offers a wondrous solution to an uncomfortable 30 world. The proximity of nature to the vehicle in the photo is remote, suggesting that the mere presence of the Montero Sport is enough to keep nature at bay. Furthermore, the SUV's silver color combines with the headline to imply that the Montero Sport carries an otherworldly salvation. Nature and its uncomfortability, therefore, are controlled by the SUV's omnipresence, and the driver is safe to the vehicle's "car-like . . . civility."

Ads for the luxury Infiniti QX4 portray a similar oppositional message but with a more active approach. A silver SUV is pictured once again, but this time bolting through the shallow water of black-rock lakeshore. The landpoint jutting into the water directly behind the QX4, as though in pursuit, is in silhouette and resembles a large black serpent lagging just behind. The text's message cautions: "careful, you may run out of planet." Although the threat is clear, the presentation is nevertheless one of SUV power in opposition to nature. Indeed, the QX4 appears to be riding atop the water, and the text ends with the admonishment, "resist the urge to circumnavigate the globe."

So while the Infiniti ad sells the promise of adventure, at the same time it positions the SUV's representational power as necessary and inevitable. The QX4 is vigorously slashing through the water on its way to points unknown because it has to; the natural environment is dangerous, hostile to civilization, and quite capable of destroying it if not met with even more superior power. And as if to drive home the point, both the Montero Sport and the Infiniti QX4 ads present a silver SUV as the symbol of modernity, thereby drawing on the traditional American mythology of progress in opposition to a hostile wilderness.

The design and marketing of SUVs are based on traditional American attitudes toward nature and the wilderness. The vehicles are at the same time built for access to the natural world and yet sold by exploiting that relationship as confrontational. The SUV, in other words, makes easily available a world that is threatening to the driver and its occupants. And yet underlying these contradictions, and compounding them, is the very real impact that SUVs make on the environment.

The GMC Suburban, big sister to the aforementioned GMC Yukon, asserts itself with a 42 gallon capacity fuel tank. With a curb-side weight pushing five thousand pounds and amenities like air conditioning, the Suburban's gas mileage is generously estimated at about 16 miles to the gallon (Storck 29). While the GMC Suburban is admittedly the largest SUV model on the market, poor gas mileage ratios are the norm for these vehicles. Where the Environmental Protection Agency has determined that automobiles must meet a fuel economy standard of 27.5 miles a gallon, light trucks, which include all SUVs, currently need only to clear 20.7 miles a gallon. And many don't even achieve that (Bradsher).

The world oil industry may keep billions of barrels in their inventories on   35 any given day (Yergin 686), leading to the understandable public perception that supplies are unlimited. But fossil fuels are still a nonrenewable resource. Moreover, American gasoline use is expected to rise by 33 percent within the next fifteen years, indicating that fuel conservation is not much of an issue with consumers (Bradsher).

But perhaps the more pressing problem, and one that is directly exacerbated by the SUV craze, is the threat of global warming from the increased burning of fossil fuels. Carbon dioxide levels in the atmosphere have risen by about 25 percent in the last century and appear to coincide with a worldwide increase in the use of petroleum. Various cataclysmic effects are predicted as a result, including rising sea levels from melting ice caps, the spread of tropical diseases to normally temperate regions, and extreme weather fluctuations (McKibben 9, 18). Yet the booming SUV market belies any overwhelming concern on the part of American consumers. In fact, the vehicle's popularity in the face of such dire predictions seems the latest manifestation of an established confrontational relationship to nature.

As the world does indeed become more dangerous, the apparent protection that SUVs afford becomes more desirable, and the need to control the uncontrollable becomes more acute. Driving a five thousand pound, resource-devouring behemoth not only justifies the impact on the environment, as a means of revenge against an enemy, but it acts as a means of celebration — the exultation of victory over the savage beast of nature. The SUV, in its design and presentation, seeks to make safely available what it can ultimately dominate; as such, it attempts to reduce the entire world to the state of a drive-through wildlife nature preserve. At the end of the twentieth century, the SUV perfectly embodies an American mythology of conquest and control.

America's love affair with the sport utility vehicle shows the abiding power of traditional beliefs. The expansion of the frontiers continues despite facts that suggest there is nowhere left to go. This joyful faith in "more" feeds on the challenge of less. Indeed, a sport utility vehicle is the triumphant representation of denial — denial of the past, the present, and the future. American mythology is continuously reinvented and thereby endures in this pop cultural symbol.

WORKS CITED

Bradsher, Keith. "Light Trucks Increase Profits But Foul Air More Than Cars." *New York Times* 30 Nov. 1997, national ed., sec. 1:1+.

Flink, James J. *The Automobile Age.* Cambridge: MIT, 1988.

Jones, Barbara, Anita Blair, Barbara Ehrenreich, Arlie Russell Hochschild, Jeanne Lewis, and Elizabeth Perle McKenna. "Giving Women the Business." *Harper's* Dec. 1997: 47–58.

Josephy, Alvin M., Jr. *Five Hundred Nations: An Illustrated History of North American Indians.* New York: Knopf, 1994.

Marchand, Roland. *Advertising the American Dream: Making Way for Modernity 1920–1940.* Berkeley: University of California Press, 1985.

McKibben, Bill. *The End of Nature.* New York: Anchor, 1989.

Pettifer, Julian, and Nigel Turner. *Automania: Man and the Motorcar.* Boston: Little, Brown, 1984.

Pope, Carl. "Car Talks — Motown Walks." *Sierra Magazine* Mar./Apr. 1996: 14+.

Robertson, James Olvier. *American Myth, American Reality.* New York: Hill & Wang, 1980.

Shames, Laurence. "The More Factor." *Signs of Life in the USA: Readings on Popular Culture for Writers.* Ed. Sonia Maasik and Jack Solomon. Boston: Bedford, 1994.

Storck, Bob. *Sport Utility Buyer's Guide '98.* Milwaukee: Pace, 1998.

Wernick, Andrew. "Vehicles for Myth." *Signs of Life in the USA: Readings on Popular Culture for Writers.* Ed. Sonia Maasik and Jack Solomon. Boston: Bedford, 1994.

Yergin, Daniel. *The Prize: The Epic Quest for Oil, Money and Power.* New York: Simon & Schuster, 1991.

READING THE TEXT

1. What significance does Goewey see in the names automakers give to SUVs?

2. In your own words, explain why Goewey considers the popularity of SUVs to be full of "ironies" (para. 5) and "contradictions" (para. 4).

3. How does Goewey account for the SUV's appeal to women?

4. In Goewey's view, why does the imagery associated with SUVs have an adversarial relationship with nature?

5. Chart how Goewey uses the semiotic method. How does he explicate the system to which SUVs belong and the cultural mythologies that such vehicles evoke?

READING THE SIGNS

1. Write a journal entry in which you interpret how your own car (or that of a friend or relative) acts as a sign. What messages does it send about your identity?

2. Using Goewey's approach as a model, interpret a different category of automobile — small two-seaters such as the Mazda Miata or Toyota MR2 Spyder.

3. Collect automobile advertisements from several popular magazines, and analyze how the cars are promoted as signs. What slogans are used to catch your interest? What values and ideologies are linked to particular makes and models?

4. Interview several people who drive SUVs on why they prefer this type of vehicle. Use your findings as a basis for an essay in which you support, refute, or complicate Goewey's thesis. Be sure to keep in mind that Goewey acknowledges that he is analyzing unconscious, not deliberate, motivating factors.

DAMIEN CAVE

THE SPAM SPOILS OF WAR

"The intimate relationship between crises and capitalism has its nausea-inducing moments," Damien Cave (b. 1974) writes in this hard-hitting critique of the post-9/11 flood of new products designed to capitalize on the catastrophe. But before we rush to condemn the purveyors of such products as Osama bin Laden toilet paper and piñatas, we should consider the nature of the American psyche in a consumer culture, whereby grief and frustration are often expressed through the purchase of things. Cave is a senior writer for the online journal Salon.

Rubble from the World Trade Center. Piñatas in the shape of Osama bin Laden. Cipro pills to fight anthrax. "One of a kind patriotic lapel pins!" "Gas masks that are 100 percent certified by the Israeli Army." Mugs, T-shirts, hats, sweatshirts, posters — all with bin Laden's face behind a target or under the label "Wanted: Dead or Alive."

Welcome to the "war on terrorism" shopping mall. Individual Americans may be feeling nearly paralyzed with anthrax paranoia, and unemployment is rising while industrial output continues to fall, but at least one sector of the entrepreneurial American machine is kicking itself back into gear. It's time to cash in on the crisis: Vendors that once focused on celebrity paraphernalia now do a swift business in bin Laden merchandise; volunteers who offered to remove World Trade Center debris now aim to sell it; and once-obscure companies selling security — at home, in airports, online — are suddenly flush with stock-market cash and fully ensconced in the mainstream mind.

The intimate relationship between crises and capitalism has its nausea-inducing moments. It's hard to admire the online scammers pushing the antibiotic ciproflaxicin as a vaccine (which is it not) and it's sickening to see the spate of products spewing hate for all Muslims.

But does that mean that wartime entrepreneurs are all snake oil salesmen? Or are they actually a vital part of the post-Sept. 11 mosaic, a clue to understanding our collective psyche? Every popup ad pushing American flags or e-mail spam offering an anthrax antidote is another piece of the picture. One could even argue that the rush to capitalize on terror's aftermath and the corresponding rush by consumers to purchase goods are quintessentially American: This is how we grieve, how we connect amid catastrophe.

"Analyzing the war-related market is the best way to read the American id," says Robert Thompson, a pop-culture professor at Syracuse University. "It's an entire culture lying down on a couch and spilling out reactions to a worldwide series of Rorschach tests." 5

The post-attacks market still isn't completely mature — bin Laden T-shirts are everywhere, but few antiwar pieces of apparel can be found online or at places like Ralph Nader's recent rally in San Francisco. Of course, that in itself is one indication of where popular sympathies lie. But it is clear that the advent of the Internet, with its low barriers to entry, has made sampling the zeitgeist quicker and easier than ever. Spam is the mirror of our consumer soul.

In the latter half of the twentieth century, war-related products have

Rob Rogers, reprinted by permission of United Features Syndicate.

historically been popular. During World War II, posters of Rosie the Riveter and a stern Uncle Sam declaring "I Want You!" became a common sight.

Subsequent wars — in which popular support was less unified — saw more diverse product lines. During the Vietnam War, private sector T-shirts, buttons, and bumper stickers reflected the public's mood of ambivalence, anger, and disillusionment. Even the short Gulf War, over almost before it started, fostered debate. T-shirts and bumper stickers with phrases like "We Came, We Saw, We Kicked Ass" competed in public with those that called for an end — "No blood for oil!" — to the war.

The response today — flags on cars, spam in inboxes, every other advertisement on television swathed in red, white, and blue — is more dramatic than anything experienced in generations, a fact that shouldn't be surprising, given the unprecedented toll taken by the terrorist attacks.

"People felt anger and a desire for revenge and a frustration that [they] 10 can't do anything about it," says Syracuse's Thompson. "After Pearl Harbor, you could enlist. But here, the dynamic is so different. This terrible thing happened but people feel helpless, like they can't do anything."

David Kirkpatrick, writing in the *New York Times,* pointed out that "we seek connections to the tragedy not to draw it closer but to make it more concrete." Is it possible that the Internet has accelerated our ability to connect to our consumerist emotions — to express our innermost feelings by buying an appropriately sloganed coffee cup?

It took three days for flag vendors to start appearing on New York streets, but CafePress.com — a California company that makes corporate T-shirts and products relating to current events — immediately noticed the urge to market products relating to the attacks.

"We began to see designs [for products] on September 12," says Maheesh Jain, vice president of business development for Café Press. "And on the 13th, things started going crazy."

The company initially placed a ban on attack-related items, but lifted it two weeks later. Now, more than 400 Web sites sell hundreds of war and attack-themed products made by Café Press. All proceeds, according to Jain, are donated to the relief effort.

"So far, we've raised about $75,000," he says.   15

The designs are explicitly noncontroversial. "God Bless America," "God Bless the U.S.A.," "America United" — these are the kinds of phrases you'll find on Café Press products. The most antiwar product includes a peace sign; the most hawkish is one that says "terrorists suck."

But Café Press's merchants represent only a fraction of the overall marketplace. Other vendors, perhaps to express their own emotions, have taken angrier stances. There's the Web site that contains forty-eight different games encouraging players to kill bin Laden, or the surfeit of products that use the Saudi's face as a target. The phrase "Wanted Dead or Alive" is ever popular — and at least one even crosses out the word "alive." Another declares him "guilty until proven dead."

Even as all the major networks accede to White House requests not to show bin Laden's videotaped messages, patriotic-themed spam and other on-line commerce remain uncensored and uncensorable.

Are the entrepreneurs who push these products taking advantage of sud-denly psychologically vulnerable consumers? Should "patriotic scamming" — as Tom Geller, executive director of the anti-spam SpamCon.Foundation, calls it — be a crime? When an advertisement attempts to get worried buyers to purchase Cipro online by pushing a scenario in which you have flu symptoms "and could not get into your doctor for several days because he is totally booked up because of panic," the line between providing a useful service and flat-out fear mongering becomes pretty thin.

And yet, none of these companies are selling into a vacuum. Patients are 20 calling their doctors everywhere, certain they have anthrax and desperate for antibiotics. Security concerns are on everyone's mind and it stands to reason that e-mail spam will reflect that. When Donald Trump reportedly started shopping for a parachute in case he had to jump out of a building that had sustained a terrorist attack, his decision didn't have anything to do with a sug-gestive e-mail. The people buying thousands of T-shirts and rolls of bin Laden toilet paper — more than 6,000 rolls sold so far, according to the manufac-turer — are clearly acting according to their own free will.

Spam, no matter how crass, does reflect reality. The e-mail that declares "confidence is now for sale!" is a clear sign that many Americans are running scared. And it will undoubtedly be difficult to prove false advertising in the case of the spam that cries "Get Cipro NOW! The Threat Is Real; Don't Delay!" Americans, citizens of the world's wealthiest country, may not spend enough time outside the shopping malls and have long been more concerned with who J-Lo is dating than whether our public health infrastructure is appropri-ately robust. But the times are changing, and all you have to do to prove it is check your inbox. Viagra is out, and antibiotics are in. Welcome to the twenty-first century.

READING THE TEXT

1. Why does Cave suggest that "the rush to capitalize on terror's aftermath" (para. 4) is reflective of the American psyche?

2. How has the response of ordinary Americans to the 9/11 terror attacks differed from Americans' response to Pearl Harbor, according to Cave?

3. What does Cave mean when he says that "spam is the mirror of our consumer soul" (para. 6)?

READING THE SIGNS

1. Conduct an in-class debate over marketing critic Tom Geller's proposition that "patriotic scamming" (para. 19) should be a crime. To develop your ideas, con-sult Tom Shales's "Resisting the False Security of TV" (p. 285) and Patrick Goldstein's "The Time to Get Serious Has Come" (p. 384).

2. Search the Internet for remaining offers of post-9/11 products. Use your

findings as the basis of an essay in which you assess the current American psyche. Are consumers still "psychologically vulnerable" (para. 19), as Cave describes them after the attacks, or has the national mood changed? How can you account for any changes?

3. Write an essay agreeing or disagreeing with Cave's contention that wartime entrepreneurship is "quintessentially American" (para. 4).

BENJAMIN R. BARBER

JIHAD VS. MCWORLD

Some books are eerily prescient, and Benjamin R. Barber's (b. 1939) Jihad vs. McWorld *(1995) is certainly one of them. Years before most Americans were aware of the severe fault lines between American-led global capitalism and ethno-religious tribalism, Barber's book analyzed the complex dialectic that would eventually enable jihadic warriors to attack America with the very technologies that American capitalism has made available to the world. Indeed, for Barber, global capitalism and jihadic fanaticism have something in common: Both imperil the traditions of democratic citizenship, the one in the name of individual consumption, the other in the service of "tyrannical paternalism." The Gershon and Carol Kekst Professor of Civil Society and Wilson H. Elkins Professor at the University of Maryland's School of Public Affairs and College of Behavioral and Social Sciences, Barber is the author of fourteen books, which include* Strong Democracy *(1994) and* The Truth of Power: Intellectual Affairs in the Clinton White House *(2001).*

History is not over. Nor are we arrived in the wondrous land of techné promised by the futurologists. The collapse of state communism has not delivered people to a safe democratic haven, and the past, fratricide and civil discord perduring, still clouds the horizon just behind us. Those who look back see all of the horrors of the ancient slaughterbench reenacted in disintegral nations like Bosnia, Sri Lanka, Ossetia, and Rwanda and they declare that nothing has changed. Those who look forward prophesize commercial and technological interdependence — a virtual paradise made possible by spreading markets and global technology — and they proclaim that everything is or soon will be different. The rival observers seem to consult different almanacs drawn from the libraries of contrarian planets.

Yet anyone who reads the daily papers carefully, taking in the front page accounts of civil carnage as well as the business page stories on the mechanics of the information superhighway and the economics of communication mergers, anyone who turns deliberately to take in the whole 360-degree horizon, knows that our world and our lives are caught between what William Butler Yeats called the two eternities of race and soul: that of race reflecting the tribal past, that of soul anticipating the cosmopolitan future. Our secular eternities are corrupted, however, race reduced to an insignia of resentment, and soul sized down to fit the demanding body by which it now measures its needs. Neither race nor soul offers us a future that is other than bleak, neither promises a polity that is remotely democratic.

The first scenario rooted in race holds out the grim prospect of a retribalization of large swaths of humankind by war and bloodshed: a threatened balkanization of nation-states in which culture is pitted against culture, people against people, tribe against tribe, a jihad in the name of a hundred narrowly conceived faiths against every kind of interdependence, every kind of artificial social cooperation and mutuality: against technology, against pop culture, and against integrated markets; against modernity itself as well as the future in which modernity issues. The second paints that future in shimmering pastels, a busy portrait of onrushing economic, technological, and ecological forces that demand integration and uniformity and that mesmerize peoples everywhere with fast music, fast computers, and fast food — MTV, Macintosh, and McDonald's — pressing nations into one homogenous global theme park, one McWorld tied together by communications, information, entertainment, and commerce. Caught between Babel and Disneyland, the planet is falling precipitously apart and coming reluctantly together at the very same moment.

Some stunned observers notice only Babel, complaining about the thousand newly sundered "peoples" who prefer to address their neighbors with sniper rifles and mortars; others — zealots in Disneyland — seize on futurological platitudes and the promise of virtuality, exclaiming "It's a small world after all!" Both are right, but how can that be?

We are compelled to choose between what passes as "the twilight of sovereignty" and an entropic end of all history,[1] or a return to the past's most fractious and demoralizing discord; to "the menace of global anarchy," to Milton's capital of hell, Pandaemonium; to a world totally "out of control."[2]

5

---

[1]Francis Fukuyama, in *The End of History and the Last Man* (New York: Free Press, 1992), although he is far less pleased by his prognosis in his book than he seemed in the original *National Interest* essay that occasioned all the controversy; and Walter B. Wriston, *Twilight of Sovereignty* (New York: Scribner's, 1992).

[2]See Georgie Anne Geyer, "Our Disintegrating World: The Menace of Global Anarchy," *Encyclopaedia Britannica, Book of the Year, 1985* (Chicago: University of Chicago Press, 1985), pp. 11–25. Daniel Patrick Moynihan, *Pandaemonium: Ethnicity in International Politics* (New York: Oxford University Press, 1993); and Zbigniew Brzezinski, *Out of Control: Global Turmoil on the Eve of the Twenty-First Century* (New York: Scribner's, 1993). Also see Tony Judt, "The New Old Nationalisms," *New York Review of Books,* May 26, 1994, pp. 44–51.

The apparent truth, which speaks to the paradox at the core of this book, is that the tendencies of both jihad *and* McWorld are at work, both visible sometimes in the same country at the very same instant. Iranian zealots keep one ear tuned to the mullahs urging holy war and the other cocked to Rupert Murdoch's Star television beaming in *Dynasty, Donahue,* and *The Simpsons* from hovering satellites. Chinese entrepreneurs vie for the attention of party cadres in Beijing and simultaneously pursue KFC franchises in cities like Nanjing, Hangzhou, and Xian where twenty-eight outlets serve over 100,000 customers a day. The Russian Orthodox church, even as it struggles to renew the ancient faith, has entered a joint venture with California businessmen to bottle and sell natural waters under the rubric Saint Springs Water Company. Serbian assassins wear Adidas sneakers and listen to Madonna on Walkman headphones as they take aim through their gunscopes at scurrying Sarajevo civilians looking to fill family watercans. Orthodox Hasids and brooding neo-Nazis have both turned to rock music to get their traditional messages out to the new generation, while fundamentalists plot virtual conspiracies on the Internet.

Now neither jihad nor McWorld is in itself novel. History ending in the triumph of science and reason or some monstrous perversion thereof (Mary Shelley's Doctor Frankenstein) has been the leitmotiv of every philosopher and poet who has regretted the Age of Reason since the Enlightenment. Yeats lamented "the center will not hold, mere anarchy is loosed upon the world," and observers of jihad today have little but historical detail to add. The Christian parable of the Fall and of the possibilities of redemption that it makes possible captures the eighteenth-century ambivalence — and our own — about past and future. I want, however, to do more than dress up the central paradox of human history in modern clothes. It is not jihad and McWorld but the relationship between them that most interests me. For, squeezed between their opposing forces, the world has been sent spinning out of control.[3] Can it be that what jihad and McWorld have in common is anarchy: the absence of common will and that conscious and collective human control under the guidance of law we call democracy?

Progress moves in steps that sometimes lurch backwards; in history's twisting maze, jihad not only revolts against but abets McWorld, while McWorld not only imperils but re-creates and reinforces jihad. They produce their contraries and need one another. . . .

Call it a dialectic of McWorld: a study in the cunning of reason that does

---

[3]Two recent books, the one by Zbigniew Brzezinski cited above about the "global turmoil" of ethnic nationalism (jihad), the other by Kevin Kelly about computers and "the rise of neo-biological civilization [McWorld]" both carry the title "Out of Control." See Brzezinski, *Out of Control;* and Kevin Kelly, *Out of Control: The Rise of Neo-Biological Civilization* (Reading, Mass.: Addison-Wesley, 1994). The metaphor is everywhere: for example, in Andrew Bard Schmookler's *The Illusion of Choice* (Albany: State University of New York at Albany Press, 1993), Part III on runaway markets is also entitled "Out of Control."

Israel's Kosher McDonald's.

honor to the radical differences that distinguish jihad and McWorld yet that acknowledges their powerful and paradoxical interdependence.

There is a crucial difference, however, between my modest attempt at di- 10 alectic and that of the masters of the nineteenth century. Still seduced by the Enlightenment's faith in progress, both Hegel and Marx believed reason's cunning was on the side of progress. But it is harder to believe that the clash of jihad and McWorld will issue in some overriding good. The outcome seems more likely to pervert than to nurture human liberty. The two may, in opposing each other, work to the same ends, work in apparent tension yet in covert harmony, but democracy is not their beneficiary. In East Berlin, tribal communism has yielded to capitalism. In Marx-Engelsplatz, the stolid, overbearing statues of Marx and Engels face east, as if seeking distant solace from Moscow: But now, circling them along the streets that surround the park that is their prison are chain eateries like T.G.I. Friday's, international hotels like the Radisson, and a circle of neon billboards mocking them with brand names like Panasonic, Coke, and GoldStar. New gods, yes, but more liberty?

What then does it mean in concrete terms to view jihad and McWorld dialectically when the tendencies of the two sets of forces initially appear so intractably antithetical? After all, jihad and McWorld operate with equal strength in opposite directions, the one driven by parochial hatreds, the other by

Muslim women in Malaysia.

universalizing markets, the one re-creating ancient subnational and ethnic borders from within, the other making national borders porous from without. Yet jihad and McWorld have this in common: They both make war on the sovereign nation-state and thus undermine the nation-state's democratic institutions. Each eschews civil society and belittles democratic citizenship, neither seeks alternative democratic institutions. Their common thread is indifference to civil liberty. Jihad forges communities of blood rooted in exclusion and hatred, communities that slight democracy in favor of tyrannical paternalism or consensual tribalism. McWorld forges global markets rooted in consumption and profit, leaving to an untrustworthy, if not altogether fictitious, invisible hand issues of public interest and common good that once might have been nurtured by democratic citizenries and their watchful governments. Such governments, intimidated by market ideology, are actually pulling back at the very moment they ought to be aggressively intervening. What was once understood as protecting the public interest is now excoriated as heavy-handed regulatory browbeating.[4] Justice yields to markets, even

---

[4]In its "new tack on technology," writes *New York Times* reporter Edmund L. Andrews, the Clinton administration wants only to avoid doing anything "to spook investors with heavy-handed regulatory brow-beating," hoping rather to reduce "the regulatory barriers that have prevented competition." Edmund L. Andrews, "New Tack on Technology," *New York Times,* January 12, 1994, p. A 1. At the end of the 1994 congressional session, a Communications Bill that would have imposed some controls on the information superhighway expired quietly.

though, as Felix Rohatyn has bluntly confessed, "there is a brutal Darwinian logic to these markets. They are nervous and greedy. They look for stability and transparency, but what they reward is not always our preferred form of democracy."[5] If the traditional conservators of freedom were democratic constitutions and Bills of Rights, "the new temples of liberty," George Steiner suggests, "will be McDonald's and Kentucky Fried Chicken."[6]

In being reduced to a choice between the market's universal church and a retribalizing politics of particularist identities, peoples around the globe are threatened with an atavistic return to medieval politics where local tribes and ambitious emperors together ruled the entire world, women and men united by the universal abstraction of Christianity even as they lived out isolated lives in warring fiefdoms defined by involuntary (ascriptive) forms of identity. This was a world in which princes and kings had little real power until they conceived the ideology of nationalism. Nationalism established government on a scale greater than the tribe yet less cosmopolitan than the universal church and in time gave birth to those intermediate, gradually more democratic institutions that would come to constitute the nation-state. Today, at the far end of this history, we seem intent on re-creating a world in which our only choices are the secular universalism of the cosmopolitan market and the everyday particularism of the fractious tribe.

In the tumult of the confrontation between global commerce and parochial ethnicity, the virtues of the democratic nation are lost and the instrumentalities by which it permitted peoples to transform themselves into nations and seize sovereign power in the name of liberty and the commonweal are put at risk. Neither jihad nor McWorld aspires to re-secure the civic virtues undermined by its denationalizing practices; neither global markets nor blood communities service public goods or pursue equality and justice. Impartial judiciaries and deliberative assemblies play no role in the roving killer bands that speak on behalf of newly liberated "peoples," and such democratic institutions have at best only marginal influence on the roving multinational corporations that speak on behalf of newly liberated markets. Jihad pursues a bloody politics of identity, McWorld a bloodless economics of profit. Belonging by default to McWorld, everyone is a consumer; seeking a repository for identity, everyone belongs to some tribe. But no one is a citizen. Without citizens, how can there be democracy?

---

[5]Rohatyn cited by Thomas L. Friedman, "When Money Talks, Governments Listen," *New York Times,* July 24, 1994, p. E 3.

[6]Steiner writes that the new Eastern European democratic revolutions of recent years were not "inebriate with some abstract passion for freedom, for social justice." Consumer culture, "video cassettes, porno cassettes, American-style cosmetics and fast foods, not editions of Mill, Tocqueville, or Solzhenitsyn, were the prizes snatched from every West[ern] shelf by the liberated." George Steiner, in *Granta,* cited by Anthony Lewis, "A Quake Hits the Summit," *International Herald Tribune,* June 2–3, 1990.

READING THE TEXT

1. Summarize in your own words Barber's definitions of "jihad" and "McWorld."
2. What are the two scenarios for the future as painted by the proponents of what Barber calls "jihad" and "McWorld"? To what extent do you find these scenarios valid?
3. In what ways are jihad and McWorld mutually dependent, according to Barber?
4. How do both jihadic culture and McWorld endanger democracy, in Barber's view?

READING THE SIGNS

1. Barber's book *Jihad vs. McWorld* was written in 1995. To what extent has Barber's argument been verified by recent history, in particular, the September 11, 2001, terrorist attacks?
2. Within the context of global capitalism, America exports vast quantities of its popular cultural output. Write an essay arguing for or against the proposition that the export of American popular culture is beneficial to the rest of the world. To develop your ideas, consult Thomas L. Friedman's "Revolution Is U.S." (p. 132) and Marnie Carroll's "American Television in Europe" (p. 288).
3. America also imports popular cultural products from the rest of the world (recall, for example, the Pokemon phenomenon). Compile a list of recent popular cultural imports, and write an essay in which you analyze the effect of other nations' popular cultures on American culture. To develop your ideas, interview consumers of the products on which you focus.
4. Conduct an in-class debate over the causes of the jihadic hostility to McWorld. To prepare for this debate, each side should consult not only American news sources about recent world events but also international sources (visit **http://www.etown.edu/vl/newsourc.html** for links to international news media).
5. Read Thomas L. Friedman's "Revolution Is U.S." (p. 132), and write an essay that compares and contrasts it to Barber's selection, paying special attention to the tonal differences between the two pieces. How do the authors' tones affect your response to their arguments?

THOMAS L. FRIEDMAN
REVOLUTION IS U.S.

With the downfall of the Soviet Union and the end of the Cold War, a new historical era emerged that replaced superpower competition with a consumer-driven politico-economic dynamic generally referred to as globalization. And though America is not the sole player in this new global system, its domination of the world's consumer and entertainment markets, as Thomas L. Friedman (b. 1953) points out in this selection, is often taken by the rest of the world as a kind of conspiracy to dominate, or American-ize, the world itself. But whether globalization equals Americanization, Friedman suggests, we seem to want a world in which there is "a Web site in every pot, a Pepsi on every lip, [and] Microsoft Windows in every com-puter," for in the end, "globalization is us." The winner of two Pulitzer Prizes for reporting and the winner of a National Book Award for From Beirut to Jerusalem *(1989), Friedman is the foreign affairs columnist for the* New York Times *and the author of* The Lexus and the Olive Tree *(2000), from which this reading is taken.*

I believe in the five gas stations theory of the world.

That's right: I believe you can reduce the world's economies today to basi-cally five different gas stations. First there is the Japanese gas station. Gas is $5 a gallon. Four men in uniforms and white gloves, with lifetime employ-ment contracts, wait on you. They pump your gas. They change your oil. They wash your windows, and they wave at you with a friendly smile as you drive away in peace. Second is the American gas station. Gas costs only $1 a gallon, but you pump it yourself. You wash your own windows. You fill your own tires. And when you drive around the corner four homeless people try to steal your hubcaps. Third is the Western European gas station. Gas there also costs $5 a gallon. There is only one man on duty. He grudgingly pumps your gas and unsmilingly changes your oil, reminding you all the time that his union contract says he only has to pump gas and change oil. He doesn't do win-dows. He works only thirty-five hours a week, with ninety minutes off each day for lunch, during which time the gas station is closed. He also has six weeks' vacation every summer in the south of France. Across the street, his two brothers and uncle, who have not worked in ten years because their state unemployment insurance pays more than their last job, are playing boccie ball. Fourth is the developing-country gas station. Fifteen people work there and they are all cousins. When you drive in, no one pays any attention to you because they are all too busy talking to each other. Gas is only 35 cents a gal-lon because it is subsidized by the government, but only one of the six pumps actually works. The others are broken and they are waiting for the replace-ment parts to be flown in from Europe. The gas station is rather run-down be-cause the absentee owner lives in Zurich and takes all the profits out of the country. The owner doesn't know that half his employees actually sleep in the repair shop at night and use the car wash equipment to shower. Most of the customers at the developing-country gas station either drive the latest-model Mercedes or a motor scooter — nothing in between. The place is al-ways busy, though, because so many people stop in to use the air pump to fill their bicycle tires. Lastly there is the communist gas station. Gas there is only 50 cents a gallon — but there is none, because the four guys working there have sold it all on the black market for $5 a gallon. Just one of the four guys who is employed at the communist gas station is actually there. The other three are working at second jobs in the underground economy and only come around once a week to collect their paychecks.

What is going on in the world today, in the very broadest sense, is that through the process of globalization everyone is being forced toward America's gas station. If you are not an American and don't know how to pump your own gas, I suggest you learn. With the end of the Cold War, globalization is globalizing Anglo-American-style capitalism and the Golden Straitjacket. It is globalizing American culture and cultural icons. It is globalizing the best of America and the worst of America. It is globalizing the American Revolution and it is globalizing the American gas station.

But not everyone likes the American gas station and what it stands for, and you can understand why. Embedded in the Japanese, Western European, and communist gas stations are social contracts very different from the American one, as well as very different attitudes about how markets should operate and be controlled. The Europeans and the Japanese believe in the state exercising power over the people and over markets, while Americans tend to believe more in empowering the people and letting markets be as free as possible to sort out who wins and who loses.

Because the Japanese, Western Europeans, and communists are uncom- 5 fortable with totally unfettered markets and the unequal benefits and punishments they distribute, their gas stations are designed to cushion such inequalities and to equalize rewards. Their gas stations also pay more attention to the distinctive traditions and value preferences of their communities. The Western Europeans do this by employing fewer people, but paying them higher wages and collecting higher taxes to generously support the unemployed and to underwrite a goody bag of other welfare-state handouts. The Japanese do it by paying people a little less but guaranteeing them lifetime employment, and then protecting those lifetime jobs and benefits by restricting foreign competitors from entering the Japanese market. The American gas station, by contrast, is a much more efficient place to drive through: The customer is king; the gas station has no social function; its only purpose is to provide the most gas at the cheapest price. If that can be done with no employees at all — well, all the better. A flexible labor market will find them work somewhere else. Too cruel, you say? Maybe so. But, ready or not, this is the model that the rest of the world is increasingly being pressured to emulate.

America is blamed for this because, in so many ways, globalization is us — or is at least perceived that way by a lot of the world. The three democratizations were mostly nurtured in America. The Golden Straitjacket was made in America and Great Britain. The Electronic Herd is led by American Wall Street bulls. The most powerful agent pressuring other countries to open their markets for free trade and free investment is Uncle Sam, and America's global armed forces keep these markets and sea lanes open for this era of globalization, just as the British navy did for the era of globalization in the nineteenth century. Joseph Nye Jr., dean of the Harvard University Kennedy School, summarized this reality well when he noted: "In its recent incarna-

Street in Lahore, Pakistan.

tion, globalization can be traced in part back to American strategy after World War II and the desire to create an open international economy to forestall another depression and to balance Soviet power and contain communism. The institutional framework and political pressures for opening markets were a product of American power and policy. But they were reinforced by developments in the technology of transportation and communications which made it increasingly costly for states to turn away from global market forces." In other words, even within the Cold War system America was hard at work building out a global economy for its own economic and strategic reasons. As a result, when the information revolution, and the three democratizations, came together at the end of the 1980s, there was a power structure already in place that was very receptive to these trends and technologies and greatly enhanced their spread around the world. As noted earlier, it was this combination of American power and strategic interests, combined with the made-in-America information revolution, that really made this second era of globalization possible, and gave it its distinctly American face.

Today, globalization often wears Mickey Mouse ears, eats Big Macs, drinks Coke or Pepsi, and does its computing on an IBM PC, using Windows 98, with an Intel Pentium II processor, and a network link from Cisco Systems. Therefore, while the distinction between what is globalization and what is Americanization may be clear to most Americans, it is not—unfortunately—to many others around the world. In most societies people cannot distinguish anymore among American power, American exports, American cultural assaults, American cultural exports, and plain vanilla globalization. They are now all wrapped into one. I am not advocating that globalization should be Americanization — but pointing out that that is how it is perceived in many quarters. No wonder the Japanese newspaper *Nihon Keizai Shimbun* carried a headline on June 4, 1999, about a conference in Tokyo on globalization that referred to the phenomenon as "The American-Instigated Globalization." When many people in the developing world look out into this globalization system what they see first is a recruiting poster that reads: UNCLE SAM WANTS YOU (for the Electronic Herd).

Martin Indyk, the former U.S. ambassador to Israel, told me a story that illustrates this point perfectly. As ambassador, he was called upon to open the first McDonald's in Jerusalem. I asked him what he said on the occasion of McDonald's opening in that holy city, and he said, "Fast food for a fast nation." But the best part, he told me later, was that McDonald's gave him a colorful baseball hat with the McDonald's logo on it to wear as he was invited to eat the first ceremonial Big Mac in Jerusalem's first McDonald's — with Israeli television filming every bit for the evening news. The restaurant was packed with young Israelis eager to be on hand for this historic event. While Ambassador Indyk was preparing to eat Jerusalem's first official Big Mac, a young Israeli teenager worked his way through the crowd and walked up to him. The teenager was carrying his own McDonald's hat and he handed it to Ambassador Indyk with a pen and asked, "Are you the ambassador? Can I have your autograph?"

Somewhat sheepishly, Ambassador Indyk replied, "Sure. I've never been asked for my autograph before."

As Ambassador Indyk took the hat and prepared to sign his name on the 10 bill, the teenager said to him, "Wow, what's it like to be the ambassador from McDonald's, going around the world opening McDonald's restaurants everywhere?"

Stunned, Ambassador Indyk looked at the Israeli youth and said, "No, no. I'm the *American* ambassador — not the ambassador from McDonald's!"

The Israeli youth looked totally crestfallen. Ambassador Indyk described what happened next: "I said to him, 'Does this mean you don't want my autograph?' And the kid said, no, I don't want your autograph, and he took his hat back and walked away."

No wonder that the love-hate relationship that has long existed between America and the rest of the world seems to be taking on an even sharper edge these days. For some people Americanization-globalization feels more than ever like a highly attractive, empowering, incredibly tempting pathway to rising living standards. For many others, though, this Americanization-globalization can breed a deep sense of envy and resentment toward the United States — envy because America seems so much better at riding this tiger and resentment because Americanization-globalization so often feels like the United States whipping everyone else to speed up, Web up, downsize, standardize, and march to America's cultural tunes into the Fast World. While I am sure there are still more lovers of America than haters out there, this [essay] is about the haters. It is about the *other* backlash against globalization — the rising resentment of the United States that has been triggered as we move into a globalization system that is so heavily influenced today by American icons, markets, and military might.

As the historian Ronald Steel once pointed out: "It was never the Soviet Union but the United States itself that is the true revolutionary power. We believe that our institutions must confine all others to the ash heap of history. We lead an economic system that has effectively buried every other form of production and distribution — leaving great wealth and sometimes great ruin in its wake. The cultural messages we transmit through Hollywood and McDonald's go out across the world to capture and also undermine other societies. Unlike more traditional conquerors, we are not content merely to subdue others: We insist that they be like us. And of course for their own good. We are the world's most relentless proselytizers. The world must be democratic. It must be capitalistic. It must be tied into the subversive messages of the World Wide Web. No wonder many feel threatened by what we represent."

The classic American self-portrait is Grant Wood's *American Gothic,* the 15 straitlaced couple, pitchfork in hand, expressions controlled, stoically standing watch outside the barn. But to the rest of the world, American Gothic is actually two twentysomething American software engineers who come into your country wearing long hair, beads, and sandals, with rings in their noses and paint on their toes. They kick down your front door, overturn everything in the house, stick a Big Mac in your mouth, fill your kids' heads with ideas you've never had or can't understand, slam a cable box onto your television, lock the channel to MTV, plug an Internet connection into your computer, and tell you: "Download or die."

That's us. We Americans are the apostles of the Fast World, the enemies of tradition, the prophets of the free market, and the high priests of high tech. We want "enlargement" of both our values and our Pizza Huts. We want the world to follow our lead and become democratic, capitalistic, with a Web site in every pot, a Pepsi on every lip, Microsoft Windows in every computer and most of all — most of all — with everyone, everywhere, pumping their own gas.

READING THE TEXT

1. Summarize in your own words Friedman's five gas stations theory of the world. What cultural values are implicit in each variety of station?

2. What did historian Ronald Steel mean when he argued that "it was never the Soviet Union but the United States itself that is the true revolutionary power" (para. 14)?

3. What, to the rest of the world, is the image of "American Gothic" (para. 15), according to Friedman?

4. Characterize Friedman's tone in outlining the five types of gas station. How does his tone affect your response to his piece?

READING THE SIGNS

1. To some of the rest of the world, the United States is responsible for globalization. Conduct an in-class debate arguing whether this assessment is accurate. To develop your team's position, you might interview some international students about the attitudes toward the United States that prevail in their countries.

2. In America there is a great deal of resentment, especially from labor unions, over international trade agreements like the North American Free Trade Agreement (NAFTA) that America has signed in the name of globalization. In the light of this resentment, write an essay arguing for or against the proposition that globalization is beneficial for America. To enhance your argument, research the economic effects of such treaties as NAFTA on the American economy.

3. Evaluate the validity of Friedman's assertion that "we Americans are the apostles of the Fast World, the enemies of tradition, the prophets of the free market, and the high priests of high tech" (para. 16).

4. Write an argumentative essay that analyzes the validity of Friedman's five gas stations theory of the world. To what extent could Friedman be accused of stereotyping cultural patterns? To what extent could his discussion be considered serious or tongue-in-cheek?

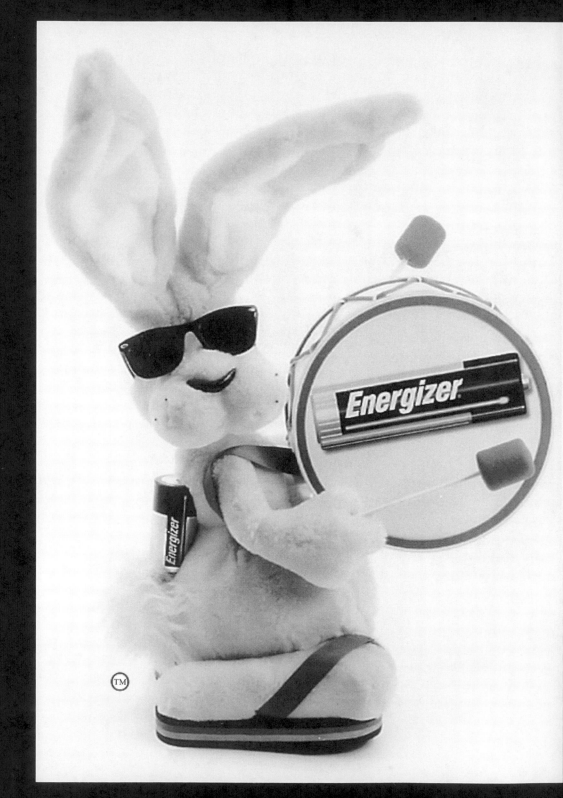

BROUGHT TO YOU B(U)Y
The Signs of Advertising

Do you ever buy batteries? It's not the sort of thing you devote much of your time to thinking about, is it? But when your portable CD player runs down or your flashlight won't shine, you've got to get some. And when you do, you just may find yourself reaching for the Energizers on the store shelf, not because you've given much thought to them as batteries but because a great deal of effort has been made to cause you to unconsciously associate Energizer batteries with the pleasurable sensation of being one cool and clever consumer. That effort was made by advertisers, and whether they are pitching batteries, blue jeans, beer, or a myriad of other products and services, they are more influential in your life than you may realize, filling your head with brand names, jingles, and slogans long after the ads they made may have disappeared.

Advertising: It's not just show and tell. In effect, it's a form of behavior modification, a psychological strategy designed not only to inform you about products but to persuade you to buy them by making associations between the product and certain pleasurable experiences that may have nothing to do with the product at all, like sex or a promise of social superiority, or simply by making you laugh. No one knows for sure just how effective a given ad campaign might be in inducing consumer spending, but no one is taking any chances either, as you can see by the annual increase in advertising costs for the Super Bowl: At last count it was some two million dollars for a thirty-second spot.

With all the advertising out there, it is getting harder and harder for advertisers to get our attention, or keep it, so they are constantly experimenting with new ways of getting us to listen. In recent years, for example, advertisers who are out to snag the youth market have taken to staging their television ads as if they were MTV videos, complete with rapid jump-cut filming techniques, rap or rock background music, and dizzying montage effects. These techniques are used to grab the attention of their target audience and to cause their viewers to associate the product with the pleasures of MTV. Self-conscious irony has also been a popular advertising technique as advertisers strive to overcome the ad-savvy sophistication of generations of consumers who have become skeptical of the claims and techniques of advertising. And goofy humor featuring funny animals has been popular as well, with Budweiser leading the way with a series of ads that began with Spuds MacKenzie in the 1980s and has moved on, respectively, to ants, frogs, lizards, and ferrets. The connection between the product and an unrelated pleasure can be especially striking in this regard. A typical Budweiser ad featuring Louie the lizard and company presents a whole comedy routine without ever mentioning beer until the voiceover at the end says, "Brought to you by the Budweiser Brewing Corporation. Drink responsibly."

The Energizer Bunny campaign, which has been very effective in inducing consumers to choose Energizer batteries, is similar to the Budweiser campaigns not only in its use of a cute animal but also in the way that it has continued year after year as a kind of cultural icon. As such, it merits some close semiotic attention.

Interpreting the Signs of Advertising

The Energizer Bunny campaign, which succeeded a rather lackluster celebrity tie-in pitch featuring Olympic gymnast Mary Lou Retton, introduced a pink mechanical bunny in the late 1980s who beats a toy drum as he storms through a sequence of mock advertisements to show how he "keeps going and going and going" on an Energizer battery. This was just the beginning, but the ad was so successful that it continued to be made in different versions and for different media for over a decade. It was so popular, in fact, that the advertisement itself became a commodity, as the pink bunny joined Spuds MacKenzie and the Claymation Raisins as advertising-figures-turned-toy-store commodities.

Now, let's look at how an ad like this works. Its apparent point, of course, is to tell you how long an Energizer battery lasts, but it could have done that by simply presenting battery test statistics (a dull though still usable advertising strategy). So what is the ad doing under the surface? As with any semiotic analysis, it helps to know the immediate historical context in which the ad appeared. In this case, the pink bunny made his debut after a chief competitor, Duracell, already had been running ads that featured contests between battery-operated toys that "demonstrated" the long-lasting superiority of Duracell products. That's part of the system in which the Energizer ad functions, and it compels us to consider, first, not which is the better *battery* but which is the better *ad*.

That the Energizer ad people wanted us to think more about advertising than about batteries is demonstrated by the fact that the original ads were not only challenges to Duracell; they were also highly entertaining parodies of advertisements for a number of unrelated products. When that bunny suddenly interrupted a startlingly realistic "commercial" for "Chateau Marmoset" wine in the early TV version of the campaign, it reminded viewers of the rather pretentious campaign that Gallo had been pitching to the yuppie market. In spoof after spoof, the Energizer ads invited viewers to relate them to the commercial system as a whole, to the entire terrain of American advertising. Now, why would an advertisement try so hard to make fun of advertisements?

Discussing the Signs of Advertising

Bring to class a print ad from a newspaper or magazine, and in small groups discuss your semiotic reading of it. Be sure to ask, "Why am I being shown this or being told that?" How do the characters in the ad function as signs? What sort of people don't appear as characters? What cultural myths are invoked in this ad? What relationship do you see between those myths and the intended audience of the publication? Which ads do your group members respond to positively and why? Which ads doesn't your group like?

Think about it. When you're sick of something, don't you like to see a good parody of it? That certainly was the thinking of the Energizer advertisers, who calculated that their spoof ads would appeal to a growing disgust in their intended audience, a weariness with Madison Avenue gimmicks. In other words, in a skeptical climate, the Energizer Bunny tells us, really clever advertisers come up with new ways of making us identify with their product. Gladly recognizing spoof ads as reflections of their own frustration with silly and manipulative advertising, viewers find themselves identifying with the creators and sponsors of spoof commercials. And thus they buy a product not because it is better but because they feel good about the way it was presented to them.

About the same time that the Energizer Bunny first appeared, Isuzu ran a somewhat similar campaign of its own, featuring a slick-talking car salesman named Joe Isuzu, who would make extravagant and impossible performance claims for Isuzus as the caption "He's lying" ran across the bottom of the TV screen or billboard. Though wildly popular with both critics and viewers (the actor who played Joe Isuzu was briefly catapulted into his own TV series), the Joe Isuzu campaign didn't succeed in moving many Isuzus, so it was canceled. Still, in 2001, it made a tentative reappearance, proving that extinct ads can be revived just as products can be, a phenomenon we analyzed in the introduction to Chapter 1.

Our analysis of the Energizer Bunny can go further. The campaign can be referred to a larger system beyond the advertising world, to a social complex where citizen-consumers are becoming increasingly fed up with the cynicism of the powerful in America, whether politicians or advertisers. As such, the pink bunny serves as a cultural barometer, pointing towards the same social forces that produced Ross Perot's campaigns for the presidency in 1992 and 1996 and the increasing popularity of registering as an Independent rather than as a Democrat or Republican. But the fact that our barometric reading comes from an *ad* is itself a sign of just how important advertising is in our culture. As the bunny tells us, the powerful are always one step ahead. In response to voter frustration, political incumbents run their campaigns as if they were political "outsiders," while advertisers, detecting a growing consumer immunity to advertising, run anticommercial commercials.

It is likely that in the wake of the September 11 attacks on the United States the widespread skepticism and cynicism that the Energizer Bunny and Joe Isuzu spoke to, and for, will be reversed, or at least suspended. Cynical advertising may disappear for a time. But that won't stop advertisers from trying to get your attention. Indeed, in the immediate aftermath of the attacks, many advertisers tried to capitalize on the newfound patriotism in the land, wrapping their products both literally and figuratively in American flags. As the years pass and the national mood shifts with the tides of history, new advertising techniques will emerge. So look around you and ask yourself as you are bombarded with advertising, "Why am I being shown *that,* or being told *this?*" Or cast yourself as the director of an ad, asking yourself what you would do to pitch a product; then look at what the advertiser has done. Pay attention to the way an ad's imagery is organized. Every detail counts. Why are these colors used, or why is the ad in black and white? Why are cute stuffed animals chosen to pitch toilet paper?

Exploring the Signs of Advertising

Select one of the products advertised in the "Portfolio of Advertisements" (in this chapter), and design in your journal an alternative ad for that product. Consider what different images or cast of characters you could include. What different myths — and thus different values — could you use to pitch this product? Then freewrite on the significance of your alternative ad. If you have any difficulty imagining an alternative image for the product, what does that say about the power of advertising to control our view of the world? What does your choice of imagery and cultural myths say about you?

What are those people *doing* in that perfume commercial? Why the cowboy hat in an ad for jeans? Look too for what the ad *doesn't* include: Is it missing a clear view of the product itself or an ethnically diverse cast of characters? In short, when interpreting an ad, transform it into a text and read it as you would an editorial or any piece of rhetoric, for in its mandate to persuade, advertising constitutes the most potent rhetoric of our times.

The Semiotic Foundation

Having outlined a semiotic analysis of a particular ad campaign, we'll turn now to a semiotic overview of the overall logic of advertising. Indeed, there is perhaps no better field for semiotic analysis than advertising, for ads work characteristically by substituting signs for things, and by reading those signs you can discover the values and desires that advertisers seek to exploit.

It has long been recognized that advertisements substitute images of desire for the actual products, that Coca Cola ads, for example, don't really sell soda: They sell images of fun, or popularity, or of sheer celebrity, promising a gratifying association with the likes of Paula Abdul or Whitney Houston if you'll only drink "The Real Thing." Automobile commercials, for their part, are notorious for selling not transportation but fantasies of power, prestige, sexual potency, or even generational solidarity, as a Mercedes Benz commercial featuring the crooning voice of the late Janis Joplin demonstrates in its appeal to baby-boom consumers most likely to recognize her old song, "Lord, Won't You Buy Me a Mercedes Benz."

By substituting desirable images for concrete needs, modern advertising seeks to transform desire into necessity. You *need* food, for example, but it takes an ad campaign to convince you through attractive images that you need a Big Mac. Your job may require you to have a car, but it's an ad that persuades you that a PT Cruiser is necessary for your happiness. If advertising worked otherwise, it would simply present you with a functional profile of a product and let you decide whether it will do the job.

From the early twentieth century, advertisers have seen their task as the transformation of desire into necessity. In the twenties and thirties, for example, voluminously printed advertisements created elaborate story lines designed to convince readers that they needed this mouthwash to attract a spouse or that caffeine-free breakfast drink to avoid trouble on the job or in the home. In such ads, products were made to appear not only desirable but absolutely necessary. Without them, your very survival as a socially competent being would be in question.

Many ads still work this way, particularly "guilt" ads that prey on your insecurities and fears. Deodorants are typically pitched in such a fashion, playing on our fear of smelling bad in public. Can you think of any other products whose ads play on guilt or shame? Do you find them to be effective?

The Commodification of Desire

Associating a logically unrelated desire with an actual product (as in pitching beer through sexual come-ons) can be called the "commodification" of desire. In other words, desire itself becomes the product that the advertiser is selling. This marketing of desire was recognized as early as the 1950s in Vance Packard's *The Hidden Persuaders* (1957). In that book, Packard points out how by the 1950s America was well along in its historic shift from a producing to a consuming economy. The implications for advertisers were enormous. Since the American economy was increasingly dependent on the constant growth of consumption, as the introduction to Chapter 1 of this text discusses, manufacturers had to find ways to convince people to consume ever more goods.

The Home Shopping Network.

So they turned to the advertising mavens on Madison Avenue, who responded with advertisements that persuaded consumers to replace perfectly serviceable products with "new and improved" substitutions within an overall economy of planned design obsolescence.

America's transformation from a producer to a consumer economy also explains that while advertising is a worldwide phenomenon, it is nowhere so prevalent as it is here. Open a copy of the popular French picture magazine *Paris Match*. You'll find plenty of paparazzi photos of international celebrities but almost no advertisements. Then open a copy of *Vogue*. It is essentially a catalogue, where scarcely a page is without an ad. Indeed, advertisers themselves call this plethora of advertising "clutter" that they must creatively "cut through" each time they design a new ad campaign. The ubiquity of advertising in our lives points to a society in which people are constantly pushed to buy, as opposed to economies like Japan's that emphasize constant increases in production. And desire is what loosens the pocketbook strings.

While the basic logic of advertising may be similar from era to era, the content of an ad, and hence its significance, differs as popular culture changes. Looking at ads from different eras tells the tale. Advertising in the 1920s, for instance, focused especially on its market's desires for improved social status. Ads for elocution and vocabulary lessons, for example, appealed to working- and lower-middle-class consumers who were invited to fantasize that buying the product or service could help them enter the middle class. Meanwhile, middle-class consumers were invited to compare their enjoyment of the sponsor's product with that of the upper-class models shown happily slurping this coffee or purchasing that vacuum cleaner in the ad. Of course, things haven't changed *that* much since the twenties. Can you think of any ads that use this strategy today? How often are glamorous celebrities called in to make you identify with his or her "enjoyment" of a product? Have you heard ads for vocabulary-building programs that promise you a "verbal advantage" in the corporate struggle?

> ### Reading Advertising on the Net
>
> Many viewers watch the Super Bowl as much for the commercials as for the football game; indeed, the Super Bowl ads now have their own pregame public-relations hype and, in many a media outlet, their own postgame analysis and ratings. Visit *Advertising Age*'s report on the most recent Super Bowl (**http://www.adage.com/reports.cms**), and study the ads and their commentary about them. What images and styles predominate, and what do the dominant patterns say about popular taste? What does the public's avid interest in Super Bowl ads say about the power of advertising and its role in American culture?

One particularly amusing ad from the 1920s played on America's fear of communism in the wake of the Bolshevik Revolution in Russia. "Is your washroom breeding Bolsheviks?" asks a print ad from the Scot paper towel company. The ad's lengthy copy explains how it might be doing so: If your company rest room is stocked with inferior paper towels, it says, discontent will proliferate among your employees and lead to subversive activities. RCA Victor and Campbell's Soup, we are assured, are no such breeding grounds of subversion, thanks to their contracts with Scot. You, too, can fight the good fight against communism by buying Scot Towels, the ad suggests. To whom do you think this ad was directed? What did they fear?

Populism vs. Elitism

American advertising tends to swing in a pendulum motion between the status-conscious ads that dominated the 1920s and the more populist approach of decades like the 1970s, when *The Waltons* was a top TV series and country music and truck-driving cowboys lent their popular appeal to Madison Avenue. This swing between elitist and populist approaches in advertising reflects a basic division within the American dream itself, a mythic promise that at once celebrates democratic equality *and* encourages you to rise above the crowd, to be better than anyone else. Sometimes Americans are more attracted to one side than to the other, but there is bound to be a shift back to the other side when the thrill wears off. Thus, the populist appeal of the seventies (even disco had a distinct working-class flavor: recall John Travolta's character in *Saturday Night Fever*) gave way to the elitist eighties, and advertising followed. Products such as Gallo's varietal wines, once considered barely a step up from jug wine, courted an upscale market through ads that featured classy yuppies serving it along with their salmon and asparagus, while Michelob light beer promised its fans that they "could have it all." Status advertising was all the rage in that glitzy, go-for-the-gold decade.

The 1990s brought in a different kind of advertising that was neither populist nor elitist but was characterized by a cutting, edgy sort of humor. This humor was especially common in dot.com ads that typically addressed the sort of young, irreverent, and rather cocky souls who were the backbone of the so-called New Economy. More broadly, edgy advertising appealed to twentysomething consumers who were particularly coveted by the marketers who made possible such youth-oriented television networks as Fox and WB. Raised in the *Saturday Night Live* era, such consumers were accustomed to cutting humor and particularly receptive to anything that smacked of attitude. In the race to get their attention, advertisers followed with attitude-laden advertising.

The collapse of the dot.com era, combined with the aftermath of the September 11 attacks, has created the potential for a new cultural environment. As we write these words, that environment has yet to become clearly identifiable, but when it does, you will be able to see it in the world of advertising, a world that is forever trying to connect to your deepest values and desires. So take a look around. Do the ads reflect a return to populist advertising as America rediscovers patriotism in the wake of 9/11, or has that phase already passed? Is attitude still important, or has a new advertising trend emerged? The answers to such questions are all around you.

The Readings

Our selections in this chapter include interpretations and analyses of the world of advertising, as well as advertisements for you to interpret yourselves. The chapter begins with a historical perspective: Roland Marchand's "The Parable of the Democracy of Goods" shows how advertisers in the 1920s played on the unconscious desires of their market by exploiting the fundamental myths of American culture. Jack Solomon follows with a semiotic analysis of the culture of American advertising, exploring the underlying value systems that cause us to respond to advertisements in the ways that we do. Next, Diane Barthel describes the way that advertisers make use of common gender codes to market to men, especially those kinds of products, like hair spray, that are traditionally associated with women, while Eric Schlosser looks at the world of children's advertising, in which kids are manipulated to manipulate their parents. Gloria Steinem's insider's view of what goes on behind the scenes at women's magazines offers an exposé of the often cozy relationship between magazine content and advertisers' desires. We also include a portfolio of print ads for you to decode for yourselves. James B. Twitchell provides a detailed description of the way that market researchers categorize consumers according to tidy lifestyle stereotypes, while John E. Calfee and Kalle Lasn conclude the readings in this chapter with, respectively, a defense of advertisers as efficient communicators of useful information, and a lament about a society that has become saturated with advertising hype.

ROLAND MARCHAND

The Parable of the Democracy of Goods

*Advertisements do not simply reflect American myths; they create them,
as Roland Marchand (1933–1997) shows in this selection from* Advertising the American Dream *(1985). Focusing on elaborate advertising narratives, he describes "The Parable of the Democracy of Goods," which
pitches a product by convincing middle-class consumers that, by buying
this toilet seat or that brand of coffee, they can share an experience with
the very richest Americans. The advertising strategies Marchand analyzes date from the 1920s to 1940s, and new "parables" have since appeared that reflect more modern times, but even the oldest are still in use
today. A former professor of history at the University of California,
Davis, Marchand was also the author of* The American Peace Movement and Social Reform, 1898–1918 *(1973) and* Creating the Corporate Soul: The Rise of Public Relations and Corporate Imagery in
American Big Business *(1998).*

As they opened their September 1929 issue, readers of the *Ladies' Home Journal*
were treated to an account of the care and feeding of young Livingston Ludlow
Biddle III, scion of the wealthy Biddles of Philadelphia, whose family coat-of-
arms graced the upper right-hand corner of the page. Young Master Biddle,
mounted on his tricycle, fixed a serious, slightly pouting gaze upon the reader,
while the Cream of Wheat Corporation rapturously explained his constant care,
his carefully regulated play and exercise, and the diet prescribed for him by "famous specialists." As master of Sunny Ridge Farm, the Biddles's winter estate
in North Carolina, young Livingston III had "enjoyed every luxury of social position and wealth, since the day he was born." Yet, by the grace of a modern prov-
idence, it happened that Livingston's health was protected by a "simple plan
every mother can use." Mrs. Biddle gave Cream of Wheat to the young heir for
both breakfast and supper. The world's foremost child experts knew of no better diet; great wealth could procure no finer nourishment. As Cream of Wheat's
advertising agency summarized the central point of the campaign that young
Master Biddle initiated, "every mother can give her youngsters the fun and benefits of a Cream of Wheat breakfast just as do the parents of these boys and girls
who have the best that wealth can command."[1]

While enjoying this glimpse of childrearing among the socially distinguished, *Ladies' Home Journal* readers found themselves schooled in one of

[1]*Ladies' Home Journal,* Sept. 1929, second cover; *JWT News Letter,* Oct. 1, 1929, p. 1,
J. Walter Thompson Company (JWT) Archives, New York City.

the most pervasive of all advertising tableaux of the 1920s — the parable of the Democracy of Goods. According to this parable, the wonders of modern mass production and distribution enabled every person to enjoy the society's most significant pleasure, convenience, or benefit. The definition of the particular benefit fluctuated, of course, with each client who employed the parable. But the cumulative effect of the constant reminders that "any woman can" and "every home can afford" was to publicize an image of American society in which concentrated wealth at the top of a hierarchy of social classes restricted no family's opportunity to acquire the most significant products.[2] By implicitly defining "democracy" in terms of equal access to consumer products, and then by depicting the everyday functioning of that "democracy" with regard to one product at a time, these tableaux offered Americans an inviting vision of their society as one of incontestable equality.

In its most common advertising formula, the concept of the Democracy of Goods asserted that although the rich enjoyed a great variety of luxuries, the acquisition of their *one* most significant luxury would provide anyone with the ultimate in satisfaction. For instance, a Chase and Sanborn's Coffee tableau, with an elegant butler serving a family in a dining room with a sixteen-foot ceiling, reminded Chicago families that although "compared with the riches of the more fortunate, your way of life may seem modest indeed," yet no one — "king, prince, statesman, or capitalist" — could enjoy better coffee.[3] The Association of Soap and Glycerine Producers proclaimed that the charm of cleanliness was as readily available to the poor as to the rich, and Ivory Soap reassuringly related how one young housewife, who couldn't afford a $780-a-year maid like her neighbor, still maintained a significant equality in "nice hands" by using Ivory.[4] The C. F. Church Manufacturing Company epitomized this version of the parable of the Democracy of Goods in an ad entitled "a bathroom luxury everyone can afford": "If you lived in one of those palatial apartments on Park Avenue, in New York City, where you have to pay $2,000 to $7,500 a year rent, you still couldn't have a better toilet seat in your bathroom than they have — the Church Sani-white Toilet Seat which you can afford to have right now."[5]

Thus, according to the parable, no discrepancies in wealth could prevent the humblest citizens, provided they chose their purchases wisely, from retiring to a setting in which they could contemplate their essential equality, through possession of an identical product, with the nation's millionaires. In 1929, Howard Dickinson, a contributor to *Printers' Ink,* concisely expressed the social psychology behind Democracy of Goods advertisements: "'With

---

[2]*Saturday Evening Post,* Apr. 3, 1926, pp. 182–83; Nov. 6, 1926, p. 104; Apr. 16, 1927, p. 199; Scrapbook 54 (Brunswick-Balke-Collender), Lord and Thomas Archives, at Foote, Cone and Belding Communications, Inc., Chicago.

[3]*Chicago Tribune,* Nov. 21, 1926, picture section, p. 2.

[4]*Los Angeles Times,* July 14, 1929, part VI, p. 3; *Tide,* July 1928, p. 10; *Photoplay Magazine,* Mar. 1930, p. 1.

[5]*American Magazine,* Mar. 1926, p. 112.

whom do the mass of people think they want to foregather?' asks the psychol-ogist in advertising. 'Why, with the wealthy and socially distinguished, of course!' If we can't get an invitation to tea for our millions of customers, we can at least present the fellowship of using the same brand of merchandise. And it works."[6]

Some advertisers found it more efficacious to employ the parable's nega-tive counterpart — the Democracy of Afflictions. Listerine contributed signifi-cantly to this approach. Most of the unsuspecting victims of halitosis in the mid-1920s possessed wealth and high social position. Other discoverers of new social afflictions soon took up the battle cry of "nobody's immune." "Body Odor plays no favorites," warned Lifebuoy Soap. No one, "banker, baker, or society woman," could count himself safe from B.O.[7] The boss, as well as the employees, might find himself "caught off guard" with dirty hands or cuffs, the Soap and Glycerine Producers assured readers of *True Story*. By 1930, Absorbine Jr. was beginning to document the democratic advance of "athlete's foot" into those rarefied social circles occupied by the "daintiest member of the junior set" and the noted yachtsman who owned "a railroad or two" (Fig. 1).[8]

The central purpose of the Democracy of Afflictions tableaux was to re-mind careless or unsuspecting readers of the universality of the threat from which the product offered protection or relief. Only occasionally did such ads address those of the upper classes who might think that their status and "fas-tidious" attention to personal care made them immune from common social offenses. In 1929 Listerine provided newspaper readers an opportunity to lis-ten while a doctor, whose clientele included those of "the better class," con-fided "what I know about *nice* women."[9] One might have thought that Lis-terine was warning complacent, upper-class women that they were not immune from halitosis — except that the ad appeared in the *Los Angeles Times,* not *Harper's Bazaar.* Similarly, Forhan's toothpaste and the Soap Pro-ducers did not place their Democracy of Afflictions ads in *True Story* in order to reach the social elite. Rather, these tableaux provided enticing glimpses into the lives of the wealthy while suggesting an equalizing "fellowship" in shared susceptibilities to debilitating ailments. The parable of the Democracy of Goods always remained implicit in its negative counterpart. It assured readers that they could be as healthy, as charming, as free from social offense as the very "nicest" (richest) people, simply by using a product that anyone could afford.

Another variation of the parable of the Democracy of Goods employed his-

[6]*Printers' Ink,* Oct. 10, 1929, p. 138.

[7]*Tide,* Sept. 15, 1927, p. 5; *American Magazine,* Aug. 1929, p. 93; *True Story,* June 1929, p. 133; *Chicago Tribune,* Jan. 11, 1928, p. 16; Jan. 18, 1928, p. 15; Jan. 28, 1928, p. 7; *Photo-play Magazine,* Feb. 1929, p. 111.

[8]*True Story,* May 1928, p. 83; June 1929, p. 133; *American Magazine,* Feb. 1930, p. 110; *Saturday Evening Post,* Aug. 23, 1930, p. 124.

[9]*Los Angeles Times,* July 6, 1929, p. 3.

You'd like to be
in this man's shoes
. . . yet he has
"ATHLETE'S
FOOT"

FIGURE 1   A
negative appeal
transformed the
Democracy of
Goods into the
Democracy of Af-
flictions. Com-
mon folk learned
from this parable
that they could
inexpensively
avoid afflictions
that beset even
the yachting set.

torical comparisons to celebrate even the humblest of contemporary Americans as "kings in cottages." "No monarch in all history ever saw the day he could have half as much as you," proclaimed Paramount Pictures. Even reigning sovereigns of the present, Paramount continued, would envy readers for their "luxurious freedom and opportunity" to enter a magnificent, bedazzling "palace for a night," be greeted with fawning bows by liveried attendants, and enjoy modern entertainment for a modest price (Fig. 2). The Fisher Body Corporation coined the phrase "For Kings in Cottages" to compliment ordinary Americans on their freedom from "hardships" that even kings had been forced to endure in the past. Because of a lack of technology, monarchs who traveled in the past had "never enjoyed luxury which even approached that of the present-day automobile." The "American idea," epitomized by the Fisher Body Corporation, was destined to carry the comforts and luxuries conducive to human happiness into "the life of even the humblest cottager."[10]

[10]*Saturday Evening Post,* May 8, 1926, p. 59; *American Magazine,* May 1932, pp. 76–77. See also *Saturday Evening Post,* July 18, 1931, pp. 36–37; Aug. 1, 1931, pp. 30–31; *Better Homes and Gardens,* Mar. 1930, p. 77.

FIGURE 2   Of course, real kings had never shared their status with crowds of other "kings." But the parable of the Democracy of Goods offered a brief, "packaged experience" of luxury and preference.

Even so, many copywriters perceived that equality with past monarchs might not rival the vision of joining the fabled "Four Hundred" that Ward McAllister had marked as America's social elite at the end of the nineteenth century. Americans, in an ostensibly conformist age, hungered for exclusivity. So advertising tableaux celebrated their ascension into this fabled and exclusive American elite. Through mass production and the resulting lower prices, the tableaux explained, the readers could purchase goods formerly available only to the rich — and thus gain admission to a "400" that now numbered millions.

The Simmons Company confessed that inner-coil mattresses had once been a luxury possessed only by the very wealthy. But now (in 1930) they were "priced so everybody in the United States can have one at $19.95." Woodbury's Soap advised the "working girl" readers of *True Story* of their arrival within a select circle. "Yesterday," it recalled, "the skin you love to touch" had been "the privilege of one woman in 65," but today it had become "the beauty right of every woman."[11] If the Democracy of Goods could establish an equal consumer

[11]*Saturday Evening Post,* Nov. 10, 1928, p. 90; *True Story,* Aug. 1934, p. 57. See also *Chicago Tribune,* Oct. 8, 1930, p. 17; *American Magazine,* Aug. 1930, p. 77; *Woman's Home Companion,* May 1927, p. 96.

right to beauty, then perhaps even the ancient religious promise of equality in death might be realized, at least to the extent that material provisions sufficed. In 1927 the Clark Grave Vault Company defined this unique promise: "Not so many years ago the use of a burial vault was confined largely to the rich . . . . Now every family, regardless of its means, may provide absolute protection against the elements of the ground."[12] If it seemed that the residents of Clark vaults had gained equality with the "400" too belatedly for maximum satisfaction, still their loving survivors could now share the same sense of comfort in the "absolute protection" of former loved ones as did the most privileged elites.

The social message of the parable of the Democracy of Goods was clear.   10 Antagonistic envy of the rich was unseemly; programs to redistribute wealth were unnecessary. The best things in life were already available to all at reasonable prices. But the prevalence of the parable of the Democracy of Goods in advertising tableaux did not necessarily betray a concerted conspiracy on the part of advertisers and their agencies to impose a social ideology on the American people. Most advertisers employed the parable of the Democracy of Goods primarily as a narrow, nonideological merchandising tactic. Listerine and Lifebuoy found the parable an obvious, attention-getting strategy for persuading readers that if even society women and bankers were unconsciously guilty of social offenses, the readers themselves were not immune. Simmons Mattresses, Chevrolet, and Clark Grave Vaults chose the parable in an attempt to broaden their market to include lower-income groups. The parable emphasized the affordability of the product to families of modest income while attempting to maintain a "class" image of the product as the preferred choice of their social betters.

Most advertisers found the social message of the parable of the Democracy of Goods a congenial and unexceptionable truism. They also saw it, like the other parables prevalent in advertising tableaux, as an epigrammatic statement of a conventional popular belief. Real income was rising for nearly all Americans during the 1920s, except for some farmers and farmworkers and those in a few depressed industries. Citizens seemed eager for confirmation that they were now driving the same make of car as the wealthy elites and serving their children the same cereal enjoyed by Livingston Ludlow Biddle III. Advertisers did not have to impose the parable of the Democracy of Goods on a contrary-minded public. Theirs was the easier task of subtly substituting this vision of equality, which was certainly satisfying *as a vision,* for broader and more traditional hopes and expectations of an equality of self-sufficiency, personal independence, and social interaction.

Perhaps the most attractive aspect of this parable to advertisers was that it preached the coming of an equalizing democracy without sacrificing those fascinating contrasts of social condition that had long been the touchstone of high drama. Henry James, writing of Hawthorne, had once lamented the obstacles facing the novelist who wrote of an America that lacked such tradition-

---

[12]*American Magazine,* Feb. 1927, p. 130.

laden institutions as a sovereign, a court, an aristocracy, or even a class of country gentlemen. Without castles, manors, and thatched cottages, America lacked those stark juxtapositions of pomp and squalor, nobility and peasantry, wealth and poverty that made Europe so rich a source of social drama.[13] But many versions of the parable of the Democracy of Goods sought to offset that disadvantage without gaining James's desired "complexity of manners." They dressed up America's wealthy as dazzling aristocrats, and then reassured readers that they could easily enjoy an essential equality with such elites in the things that really mattered. The rich were decorative and fun to look at, but in their access to those products most important to comfort and satisfaction, as the magazine *Delineator* put it, "The Four Hundred" had become "the four million."[14] Advertisers left readers to assume that they could gain the same satisfactions of exclusiveness from belonging to the four million as had once been savored by the four hundred.

While parables of consumer democracy frequently used terms like "everyone," "anyone," "any home," or "every woman," these categories were mainly intended to comprise the audience of "consumer-citizens" envisioned by the advertising trade, or families economically among the nation's top 50 percent. Thus the *Delineator* had more in mind than mere alliteration when it chose to contrast the old "400" with the new "four million" rather than a new "one hundred and twenty million." The standard antitheses of the Democracy of Goods parables were "mansion" and "bungalow." Advertising writers rarely took notice of the many millions of Americans whose standard of living fell below that of the cozy bungalow of the advertising tableaux. These millions might overhear the promises of consumer democracy in the newspapers or magazines, but advertising leaders felt no obligation to show how their promises to "everyone" would bring equality to those who lived in the nation's apartment houses and farmhouses without plumbing, let alone those who lived in rural shacks and urban tenements.

In the broadest sense, the parable of the Democracy of Goods may be interpreted as a secularized version of the traditional Christian assurances of ultimate human equality. "Body Odor plays no favorites" might be considered a secular translation of the idea that God "sends rain on the just and on the unjust" (Matt. 5:45). Promises of the essential equality of those possessing the advertised brand recalled the promise of equality of access to God's mercy. Thus the parable recapitulated a familiar, cherished expectation. Far more significant, however, was the parable's insinuation of the capacity of a Democracy of Goods to redeem the already secularized American promise of political equality.

Incessantly and enticingly repeated, advertising visions of fellowship in a Democracy of Goods encouraged Americans to look to similarities in consumption styles rather than to political power or control of wealth for evi- [15]

---

[13]Henry James, *Hawthorne,* rev. ed. (New York, 1967 [c. 1879]), p. 55.
[14]*Printers' Ink,* Nov. 24, 1927, p. 52.

FIGURE 3
Advertising such as this encouraged Americans to pursue consumption-oriented lifestyles.

dence of significant equality. Francesco Nicosia and Robert Mayer describe the result as a "deflection of the success ethic from the sphere of production to that of consumption." Freedom of choice came to be perceived as a freedom more significantly exercised in the marketplace than in the political arena. This process gained momentum in the 1920s; it gained maturity during the 1950s as a sense of class differences was nearly eclipsed by a fascination with the equalities suggested by shared consumption patterns and "freely chosen" consumer "lifestyles."[15]

READING THE TEXT

1. Summarize in your own words what Marchand means by the "parable of the Democracy of Goods" (para. 2).

[15]Francesco M. Nicosia and Robert N. Mayer, "Toward a Sociology of Consumption," *The Journal of Consumer Research* 3 (1976): 73; Roland Marchand, "Visions of Classlessness; Quests for Dominion: American Popular Culture, 1945–1960," in *Reshaping America: Society and Institutions, 1945–1960,* ed. Robert H. Bremner and Gary W. Reichard (Columbus, Ohio, 1982), pp. 165–70.

2. What is the "Democracy of Afflictions" (para. 5), in your own words?

3. In class, brainstorm examples of current ads that illustrate the parable of the democracy of goods and the democracy of afflictions.

READING THE SIGNS

1. Does the parable of the democracy of goods work to make society more egalitarian, or does it reinforce existing power structures? Write an essay arguing for one position or the other, focusing on particular ads for your support.

2. Bring to class a popular magazine of your own choosing. In groups, study your selections. In which magazines is the myth of the democracy of goods most common? Do you find any relationship between the use of this myth and the intended audience of the magazines?

3. Obtain from your college library an issue of *Time* magazine dating from the 1920s, and compare it with a current issue. In what ways, if any, have the social messages communicated in the advertising changed? Try to account for any changes you identify.

4. Compare and contrast the myth of the democracy of goods with the frontier myth that Laurence Shames describes in "The More Factor" (p. 56). Consider how the two myths shape our consuming behavior; you may also want to show how the myths appear in some current ads.

5. Using Marchand's essay as a critical framework, analyze the Devoe paint ad on p. 157.

◀**READING THE SIGNS**

1. The advertisement on page 159 tells a story. What is it? You might start with the title of the ad.

2. To whom is the ad directed? What emotions does it play on? Be sure to provide evidence for your answers. What are the "dearest possessions" the ad refers to?

3. This ad originally appeared in 1914. If you were to update it for a magazine today, what changes would you make? Why?

JACK SOLOMON

MASTERS OF DESIRE: THE CULTURE OF AMERICAN ADVERTISING

Advertising campaigns come and go, as do the products they promote, but what does not change so quickly are the cultural patterns that advertisers rely on to work their magic. For as Jack Solomon (b. 1954) argues in this excerpt from The Signs of Our Time *(1988), advertising does not work in a vacuum: it plays on deeply held cultural values and desires to stimulate consumption. To analyze an ad, then, is to analyze the culture in which it appears. A professor of English at California State University, Northridge, Solomon is also the author of* Discourse and Reference in the Nuclear Age *(1988) and the coeditor (with Sonia Maasik) of* California Dreams and Realities *(1999) and of this textbook.*

Amongst democratic nations, men easily attain a certain equality of condition; but they can never attain as much as they desire.

— ALEXIS DE TOCQUEVILLE

On May 10, 1831, a young French aristocrat named Alexis de Tocqueville arrived in New York City at the start of what would become one of the most famous visits to America in our history. He had come to observe firsthand the institutions of the freest, most egalitarian society of the age, but what he found was a paradox. For behind America's mythic promise of equal opportunity, Tocqueville discovered a desire for *unequal* social rewards, a ferocious competition for privilege and distinction. As he wrote in his monumental study, *Democracy in America*:

> When all privileges of birth and fortune are abolished, when all professions are accessible to all, and a man's own energies may place him at the top of any one of them, an easy and unbounded career seems open to his ambition. . . . But this is an erroneous notion, which is corrected by daily experience. [For when] men are nearly alike, and all follow the same track,

it is very difficult for any one individual to walk quick and cleave a way through the same throng which surrounds and presses him.

Yet walking quick and cleaving a way is precisely what Americans dream of. We Americans dream of rising above the crowd, of attaining a social summit beyond the reach of ordinary citizens. And therein lies the paradox.

The American dream, in other words, has two faces: the one communally egalitarian and the other competitively elitist. This contradiction is no accident; it is fundamental to the structure of American society. Even as America's great myth of equality celebrates the virtues of mom, apple pie, and the girl or boy next door, it also lures us to achieve social distinction, to rise above the crowd and bask alone in the glory. This land is your land and this land is my land, Woody Guthrie's populist anthem tells us, but we keep trying to increase the "my" at the expense of the "your." Rather than fostering contentment, the American dream breeds desire, a longing for a greater share of the pie. It is as if our society were a vast high-school football game, with the bulk of the participants noisily rooting in the stands while, deep down, each of them is wishing he or she could be the star quarterback or head cheerleader.

For the semiotician, the contradictory nature of the American myth of equality is nowhere written so clearly as in the signs that American advertisers use to manipulate us into buying their wares. "Manipulate" is the word here, not "persuade"; for advertising campaigns are not sources of product information, they are exercises in behavior modification. Appealing to our subconscious emotions rather than to our conscious intellects, advertisements are designed to exploit the discontentments fostered by the American dream, the constant desire for social success and the material rewards that accompany it. America's consumer economy runs on desire, and advertising stokes the engines by transforming common objects — from peanut butter to political candidates — into signs of all the things that Americans covet most.

But by semiotically reading the signs that advertising agencies manufacture to stimulate consumption, we can plot the precise state of desire in the audiences to which they are addressed. Let's look at a representative sample of ads and what they say about the emotional climate of the country and the fast-changing trends of American life. Because ours is a highly diverse, pluralistic society, various advertisements may say different things depending on their intended audiences, but in every case they say something about America, about the status of our hopes, fears, desires, and beliefs.

We'll begin with two ad campaigns conducted by the same company that bear out Alexis de Tocqueville's observations about the contradictory nature of American society: General Motors' campaigns for its Cadillac and Chevrolet lines. First, consider an early magazine ad for the Cadillac Allanté. Appearing as a full-color, four-page insert in *Time,* the ad seems to say "I'm special — and so is this car" even before we've begun to read it. Rather than being printed on the ordinary, flimsy pages of the magazine, the Allanté spread appears on glossy coated stock. The unwritten message here is that an extraordinary car deserves an extraordinary advertisement, and that both car and ad are aimed at an extraordinary consumer, or at least one who wishes to appear extraordinary compared to his more ordinary fellow citizens.

Ads of this kind work by creating symbolic associations between their product and what is most coveted by the consumers to whom they are addressed. It is significant, then, that this ad insists that the Allanté is virtually an Italian rather than an American car, an automobile, as its copy runs, "Conceived and Commissioned by America's Luxury Car Leader — Cadillac" but "Designed and Handcrafted by Europe's Renowned Design Leader — Pininfarina, SpA, of Turin, Italy." This is not simply a piece of product information, it's a sign of the prestige that European luxury cars enjoy in today's automotive marketplace. Once the luxury car of choice for America's status drivers, Cadillac has fallen far behind its European competitors in the race for the prestige market. So the Allanté essentially represents Cadillac's decision, after years of resisting the trend toward European cars, to introduce its own European import — whose high cost is clearly printed on the last page of the ad. . . .

American companies manufacture status symbols because American consumers want them. As Alexis de Tocqueville recognized a century and a half ago, the competitive nature of democratic societies breeds a desire for social distinction, a yearning to rise above the crowd. But given the fact that those who do make it to the top in socially mobile societies have often risen from the lower ranks, they still look like everyone else. In the socially immobile societies of aristocratic Europe, generations of fixed social conditions produced subtle class signals. The accent of one's voice, the shape of one's nose, or even the set of one's chin immediately communicated social status. Aside from the nasal bray and uptilted head of the Boston Brahmin, Americans do not have any native sets of personal status signals. If it weren't for his Mercedes-Benz and Manhattan townhouse, the parvenu Wall Street millionaire often couldn't be distinguished from the man who tailors his suits. Hence, the demand for status symbols, for the objects that mark one off as a social success, is particularly strong in democratic nations — stronger even than in aristocratic societies, where the aristocrat so often looks and sounds different from everyone else.

Status symbols, then, are signs that identify their possessors' place in a social hierarchy, markers of rank and prestige. We can all think of any number of status symbols — Rolls-Royces, Beverly Hills mansions, even Shar Pei puppies (whose rareness and expense has rocketed them beyond Russian wolfhounds as status pets and has even inspired whole lines of wrinkle-faced stuffed toys) — but how do we know that something *is* a status symbol? The explanation is quite simple: when an object (or puppy!) either costs a lot of money or requires influential connections to possess, anyone who possesses it must also possess the necessary means and influence to acquire it. The object itself really doesn't matter, since it ultimately disappears behind the presumed social potency of its owner. Semiotically, what matters is the signal it sends, its value as a sign of power. One traditional sign of social distinction is owning a country estate and enjoying the peace and privacy that attend it. Advertisements for Mercedes-Benz, Jaguar, and Audi automobiles thus frequently feature drivers motoring quietly along a country road, presumably on their way to or from their country houses.

Advertisers have been quick to exploit the status signals that belong to body language as well. As Hegel observed in the early nineteenth century, it is an ancient aristocratic prerogative to be seen by the lower orders without having to look at them in return. Tilting his chin high in the air and gazing down at the world under hooded eyelids, the aristocrat invites observation while refusing to look back. We can find such a pose exploited in an advertisement for Cadillac Seville in which we see an elegantly dressed woman out for a drive with her husband in their new Cadillac. If we look closely at the woman's body language, we can see her glance inwardly with a satisfied smile on her face but not outward toward the camera that represents our gaze. She is glad to be seen by us in her Seville, but she isn't interested in looking at *us*!

Ads that are aimed at a broader market take the opposite approach. If the American dream encourages the desire to "arrive," to vault above the mass, it also fosters a desire to be popular, to "belong." Populist commercials accordingly transform products into signs of belonging, utilizing such common icons as country music, small-town life, family picnics, and farmyards. All of these icons are incorporated in GM's "Heartbeat of America" campaign for its Chevrolet line. Unlike the Seville commercial, the faces in the Chevy ads look straight at us and smile. Dress is casual; the mood upbeat. Quick camera cuts take us from rustic to suburban to urban scenes, creating an American montage filmed from sea to shining sea. We all "belong" in a Chevy.

Where price alone doesn't determine the market for a product, advertisers can go either way. Both Johnnie Walker and Jack Daniel's are better-grade whiskies, but where a Johnnie Walker ad appeals to the buyer who wants a mark of aristocratic distinction in his liquor, a Jack Daniel's ad emphasizes the down-home, egalitarian folksiness of its product. Johnnie Walker associates itself with such conventional status symbols as sable coats, Rolls-Royces, and black gold; Jack Daniel's gives us a Good Ol' Boy in overalls. In fact, Jack Daniel's Good Ol' Boy is an icon of backwoods independence, recalling the days of the moonshiner and the Whisky Rebellion of 1794. Evoking emotions quite at odds with those stimulated in Johnnie Walker ads, the advertisers of Jack Daniel's have chosen to transform their product into a sign of America's populist tradition. The fact that both ads successfully sell whisky is itself a sign of the dual nature of the American dream. . . .

Populist advertising is particularly effective in the face of foreign competition. When Americans feel threatened from the outside, they tend to circle the wagons and temporarily forget their class differences. In the face of the Japanese automotive "invasion," Chrysler runs populist commercials in which Lee Iacocca joins the simple folk who buy his cars as the jingle "Born in America" blares in the background. Seeking to capitalize on the popularity of

Bruce Springsteen's *Born in the USA* album, these ads gloss over Springsteen's ironic lyrics in a vast display of flag-waving. Chevrolet's "Heartbeat of America" campaign attempts to woo American motorists away from Japanese automobiles by appealing to their patriotic sentiments.

The patriotic iconography of these campaigns also reflects the general cultural mood of the early to mid-1980s. After a period of national anguish in the wake of the Vietnam War and the Iran hostage crisis, America went on a patriotic binge. American athletic triumphs in the Lake Placid and Los Angeles Olympics introduced a sporting tone into the national celebration, often making international affairs appear like one great Olympiad in which America was always going for the gold. In response, advertisers began to do their own flag-waving.

The mood of advertising during this period was definitely upbeat. Even   15
deodorant commercials, which traditionally work on our self-doubts and fears of social rejection, jumped on the bandwagon. In the guilty sixties, we had ads like the "Ice Blue Secret" campaign with its connotations of guilt and shame. In the feel-good Reagan eighties, "Sure" deodorant commercials featured images of triumphant Americans throwing up their arms in victory to reveal — no wet marks! Deodorant commercials once had the moral echo of Nathaniel Hawthorne's guilt-ridden *The Scarlet Letter;* in the early eighties they had all the moral subtlety of *Rocky IV,* reflecting the emotions of a Vietnam-weary nation eager to embrace the imagery of America Triumphant. . . .

Live the Fantasy

By reading the signs of American advertising, we can conclude that America is a nation of fantasizers, often preferring the sign to the substance and easily enthralled by a veritable Fantasy Island of commercial illusions. Critics of Madison Avenue often complain that advertisers create consumer desire, but semioticians don't think the situation is that simple. Advertisers may give shape to consumer fantasies, but they need raw material to work with, the subconscious dreams and desires of the marketplace. As long as these desires remain unconscious, advertisers will be able to exploit them. But by bringing the fantasies to the surface, you can free yourself from advertising's often hypnotic grasp.

I can think of no company that has more successfully seized upon the subconscious fantasies of the American marketplace — indeed the world marketplace — than McDonald's. By no means the first nor the only hamburger chain in the United States, McDonald's emerged victorious in the "burger wars" by transforming hamburgers into signs of all that was desirable in American life. Other chains like Wendy's, Burger King, and Jack-In-The-Box continue to advertise and sell widely, but no company approaches McDonald's transformation of itself into a symbol of American culture.

McDonald's success can be traced to the precision of its advertising.

Instead of broadcasting a single "one-size-fits-all" campaign at a time, McDonald's pitches its burgers simultaneously at different age groups, different classes, even different races (Budweiser beer, incidentally, has succeeded in the same way). For children, there is the Ronald McDonald campaign, which presents a fantasy world that has little to do with hamburgers in any rational sense but a great deal to do with the emotional desires of kids. Ronald McDonald and his friends are signs that recall the Muppets, *Sesame Street,* the circus, toys, storybook illustrations, even *Alice in Wonderland.* Such signs do not signify hamburgers. Rather, they are displayed in order to prompt in the child's mind an automatic association of fantasy, fun, and McDonald's.

The same approach is taken in ads aimed at older audiences — teens, adults, and senior citizens. In the teen-oriented ads we may catch a fleeting glimpse of a hamburger or two, but what we are really shown is a teenage fantasy: groups of hip and happy adolescents singing, dancing, and cavorting together. Fearing loneliness more than anything else, adolescents quickly respond to the group appeal of such commercials. "Eat a Big Mac," these ads say, "and you won't be stuck home alone on Saturday night."

To appeal to an older and more sophisticated audience no longer so 20 afraid of not belonging and more concerned with finding a place to go out to at night, McDonald's has designed the elaborate "Mac Tonight" commercials, which have for their backdrop a nightlit urban skyline and at their center a cabaret pianist with a moon-shaped head, a glad manner, and Blues Brothers shades. Such signs prompt an association of McDonald's with nightclubs and urban sophistication, persuading us that McDonald's is a place not only for breakfast or lunch but for dinner too, as if it were a popular off-Broadway nightspot, a place to see and be seen. Even the parody of Kurt Weill's "Mack the Knife" theme song that Mac the Pianist performs is a sign, a subtle signal to the sophisticated hamburger eater able to recognize the origin of the tune in Bertolt Brecht's *Threepenny Opera.*

For yet older customers, McDonald's has designed a commercial around the fact that it employs a large number of retirees and seniors. In one such ad, we see an elderly man leaving his pretty little cottage early in the morning to start work as "the new kid" at McDonald's, and then we watch him during his first day on the job. Of course he is a great success, outdoing everyone else with his energy and efficiency, and he returns home in the evening to a loving wife and a happy home. One would almost think that the ad was a kind of moving "help wanted" sign (indeed, McDonald's *was* hiring elderly employees at the time), but it's really just directed at consumers. Older viewers can see themselves wanted and appreciated in the ad — and perhaps be distracted from the rationally uncomfortable fact that many senior citizens take such jobs because of financial need and thus may be unlikely to own the sort of home that one sees in the commercial. But realism isn't the point here. This is fantasyland, a dream world promising instant gratification no matter what the facts of the matter may be.

Practically the only fantasy that McDonald's doesn't exploit is the fantasy of sex. This is understandable, given McDonald's desire to present itself as a family restaurant. But everywhere else, sexual fantasies, which have always had an important place in American advertising, are beginning to dominate the advertising scene. You expect sexual come-ons in ads for perfume or cosmetics or jewelry—after all, that's what they're selling—but for room deodorizers? In a magazine ad for Claire Burke home fragrances, for example, we see a well-dressed couple cavorting about their bedroom in what looks like a cheery preparation for sadomasochistic exercises. Jordache and Calvin Klein pitch blue jeans as props for teenage sexuality. The phallic appeal of automobiles, traditionally an implicit feature in automotive advertising, becomes quite explicit in a Dodge commercial that shifts back and forth from shots of a young man in an automobile to teasing glimpses of a woman—his date—as she dresses in her apartment.

The very language of today's advertisements is charged with sexuality. Products in the more innocent fifties were "new and improved," but everything in the eighties is "hot!"—as in "hot woman," or sexual heat. Cars are "hot." Movies are "hot." An ad for Valvoline pulses to the rhythm of a "heat wave, burning in my car." Sneakers get red hot in a magazine ad for Travel Fox athletic shoes in which we see male and female figures, clad only in Travel Fox shoes, apparently in the act of copulation—an ad that earned one of *Adweek*'s annual "badvertising" awards for shoddy advertising.

The sexual explicitness of contemporary advertising is a sign not so much of American sexual fantasies as of the lengths to which advertisers will go to get attention. Sex never fails as an attention-getter, and in a particularly competitive, and expensive, era for American marketing, advertisers like to bet on a sure thing. Ad people refer to the proliferation of TV, radio, newspaper, magazine, and billboard ads as "clutter," and nothing cuts through the clutter like sex.

By showing the flesh, advertisers work on the deepest, most coercive human emotions of all. Much sexual coercion in advertising, however, is a sign of a desperate need to make certain that clients are getting their money's worth. The appearance of advertisements that refer directly to the prefabricated fantasies of Hollywood is a sign of a different sort of desperation: a desperation for ideas. With the rapid turnover of advertising campaigns mandated by the need to cut through the "clutter," advertisers may be hard pressed for new ad concepts, and so they are more and more frequently turning to already-established models. In the early 1980s, for instance, Pepsi-Cola ran a series of ads broadly alluding to Steven Spielberg's *E.T.* In one such ad, we see a young boy, who, like the hero of *E.T.,* witnesses an extraterrestrial visit. The boy is led to a soft-drink machine where he pauses to drink a can of Pepsi as the spaceship he's spotted flies off into the universe. The relationship between the ad and the movie, accordingly, is a parasitical one, with the ad taking its life from the creative body of the film. . . .

Madison Avenue has also framed ad campaigns around the cultural prestige of high-tech machinery. This is especially the case with sports cars, whose high-tech appeal is so powerful that some people apparently fantasize about *being* sports cars. At least, this is the conclusion one might draw from a Porsche commercial that asked its audience, "If you were a car, what kind of car would you be?" As a candy-red Porsche speeds along a rain-slick forest road, the ad's voice-over describes all the specifications you'd want to have if you *were* a sports car. "If you were a car," the commercial concludes, "you'd be a Porsche."

In his essay "Car Commercials and *Miami Vice*," Todd Gitlin explains the semiotic appeal of such ads as those in the Porsche campaign. Aired at the height of what may be called America's "myth of the entrepreneur," these commercials were aimed at young corporate managers who imaginatively identified with the "lone wolf" image of a Porsche speeding through the woods. Gitlin points out that such images cater to the fantasies of faceless corporate men who dream of entrepreneurial glory, of striking out on their own like John DeLorean and telling the boss to take his job and shove it. But as DeLorean's spectacular failure demonstrates, the life of the entrepreneur can be extremely risky. So rather than having to go it alone and take the risks that accompany entrepreneurial independence, the young executive can substitute fantasy for reality by climbing into his Porsche — or at least that's what Porsche's advertisers wanted him to believe.

But there is more at work in the Porsche ads than the fantasies of corporate America. Ever since Arthur C. Clarke and Stanley Kubrick teamed up to present us with HAL 9000, the demented computer of *2001: A Space Odyssey*, the American imagination has been obsessed with the melding of man and machine. First there was television's *Six Million Dollar Man*, and then movieland's *Star Wars, Blade Runner*, and *Robocop*, fantasy visions of a future dominated by machines. Androids haunt our imaginations as machines seize the initiative. *Time* magazine's "Man of the Year" for 1982 was a computer. Robot-built automobiles appeal to drivers who spend their days in front of computer screens — perhaps designing robots. When so much power and prestige is being given to high-tech machines, wouldn't you rather be a Porsche?

In short, the Porsche campaign is a sign of a new mythology that is emerging before our eyes, a myth of the machine, which is replacing the myth of the human. The iconic figure of the little tramp caught up in the cogs of industrial production in Charlie Chaplin's *Modern Times* signified a humanistic revulsion to the age of the machine. Human beings, such icons said, were superior to machines. Human values should come first in the moral order of things. But as Edith Milton suggests in her essay "The Track of the Mutant," we are now coming to believe that machines are superior to human beings, that mechanical nature is superior to human nature. Rather than being threatened by machines, we long to merge with them. *The Six Million Dollar Man* is one iconic figure in the new mythology; Harrison Ford's sexual coupling with an android is another. In such an age it should come as little wonder that computer-synthesized Max Headroom should be a commercial spokesman for Coca-Cola, or that Federal Express should design a series of TV ads featuring mechanical-looking human beings revolving around strange and powerful machines.

Fear and Trembling in the Marketplace

While advertisers play on and reflect back at us our fantasies about everything from fighter pilots to robots, they also play on darker imaginings. If dream and desire can be exploited in the quest for sales, so can nightmare and fear. 30

The nightmare equivalent of America's populist desire to "belong," for example, is the fear of not belonging, of social rejection, of being different. Advertisements for dandruff shampoos, mouthwashes, deodorants, and laundry detergents ("Ring Around the Collar!") accordingly exploit such fears, bullying us into consumption. Although ads of this type are still around in the 1980s, they were particularly common in the fifties and early sixties, reflecting a society still reeling from the witch-hunts of the McCarthy years. When any sort of social eccentricity or difference could result in a public denunciation and the loss of one's job or even liberty, Americans were keen to conform and be like everyone else. No one wanted to be "guilty" of smelling bad or of having a dirty collar.

"Guilt" ads characteristically work by creating narrative situations in which someone is "accused" of some social "transgression," pronounced guilty, and then offered the sponsor's product as a means of returning to "innocence." Such ads, in essence, are parodies of ancient religious rituals of guilt and atonement, whereby sinning humanity is offered salvation through the agency of priest and church. In the world of advertising, a product takes the place of the priest, but the logic of the situation is quite similar.

In commercials for Wisk detergent, for example, we witness the drama of a hapless housewife and her husband as they are mocked by the jeering voices of children shouting "Ring Around the Collar!" "Oh, those dirty rings!" the housewife groans in despair. It's as if she and her husband were being stoned by an angry crowd. But there's hope, there's help, there's Wisk. Cleansing her soul of sin as well as her husband's, the housewife launders his shirts with Wisk, and behold, his collars are clean. Product salvation is only as far as the supermarket. . . .

If guilt looks backward in time to past transgressions, fear, like desire, faces forward, trembling before the future. In the late 1980s, a new kind of fear commercial appeared, one whose narrative played on the worries of young corporate managers struggling up the ladder of success. Representing the nightmare equivalent of the elitist desire to "arrive," ads of this sort created images of failure, storylines of corporate defeat. In one ad for Apple computers, for example, a group of junior executives sits around a table with the boss as he asks each executive how long it will take his or her department to complete some publishing jobs. "Two or three days," answers one nervous executive. "A week, on overtime," a tight-lipped woman responds. But one young up-and-comer can have everything ready tomorrow, today, or yesterday, because his department uses a Macintosh desktop publishing system. Guess who'll get the next promotion?

For other markets, there are other fears. If McDonald's presents senior citi- 35 zens with bright fantasies of being useful and appreciated beyond retirement, companies like Secure Horizons dramatize senior citizens' fears of being caught short by a major illness. Running its ads in the wake of budgetary cuts in the Medicare system, Secure Horizons designed a series of commercials featuring a pleasant old man named Harry — who looks and sounds rather like Carroll O'Connor — who tells us the story of the scare he got during his wife's recent illness. Fearing that next time Medicare won't cover the bills, he has purchased supplemental health insurance from Secure Horizons and now securely tends his roof-top garden. . . .

The Future of an Illusion

There are some signs in the advertising world that Americans are getting fed up with fantasy advertisements and want to hear some straight talk. Weary of extravagant product claims and irrelevant associations, consumers trained by years of advertising to distrust what they hear seem to be developing an immunity to commercials. At least, this is the semiotic message I read in the "new realism" advertisements of the eighties, ads that attempt to convince you that what you're seeing is the real thing, that the ad is giving you the straight dope, not advertising hype.

You can recognize the "new realism" by its camera techniques. The lighting is usually subdued to give the ad the effect of being filmed without studio lighting or special filters. The scene looks gray, as if the blinds were drawn. The camera shots are jerky and off-angle, often zooming in for sudden and unflattering close-ups, as if the cameraman was an amateur with a home video recorder. In a "realistic" ad for AT&T, for example, we are treated to a monologue by a plump stockbroker — his plumpness intended as a sign that he's for real and not just another actor — who tells us about the problems he's had with his phone system (not AT&T's) as the camera jerks around, generally filming him from below as if the cameraman couldn't quite fit his equipment into the crammed office and had to film the scene on his knees. "This is no fancy advertisement," the ad tries to convince us, "this is sincere."

An ad for Miller draft beer tries the same approach, recreating the effect of an amateur videotape of a wedding celebration. Camera shots shift suddenly from group to group. The picture jumps. Bodies are poorly framed. The color is washed out. Like the beer it is pushing, the ad is supposed to strike us as being "as real as it gets."

Such ads reflect a desire for reality in the marketplace, a weariness with Madison Avenue illusions. But there's no illusion like the illusion of reality. Every special technique that advertisers use to create their "reality effects" is, in fact, more unrealistic than the techniques of "illusory" ads. The world, in reality, doesn't jump around when you look at it. It doesn't appear in subdued gray tones. Our eyes don't have zoom lenses, and we don't look at things with our heads cocked to one side. The irony of the "new realism" is that it is more unrealistic, more artificial, than the ordinary run of television advertising.

But don't expect any truly realistic ads in the future, because a realistic advertisement is a contradiction in terms. The logic of advertising is entirely semiotic: It substitutes signs for things, framed visions of consumer desire for the thing itself. The success of modern advertising, its penetration into every corner of American life, reflects a culture that has itself chosen illusion over reality. At a time when political candidates all have professional image-makers attached to their staffs, and the President of the United States can be an actor who once sold shirt collars, all the cultural signs are pointing to more illusions in our lives rather than fewer — a fecund breeding ground for the world of the advertiser.

READING THE TEXT

1. Describe in your own words the paradox of the American dream, as Solomon sees it.

2. In Solomon's view, why do status symbols work particularly well in manipulating American consumers?

3. What is a "guilt" (para. 32) ad, according to Solomon, and how does it affect consumers?

4. Why, according to Solomon, has McDonald's been so successful in its ad campaigns?

5. What relationship does Solomon see between the "new realism" (para. 37) of some ads and the paradoxes of the American dream?

READING THE SIGNS

1. Bring to class a general-interest magazine, such as *Time* or *Better Homes and Gardens,* and in small groups study the advertising. Do the ads tend to have an elitist or a populist appeal? What relationship do you see between the appeal you identify and the magazine's target readership? Present your findings to the class.

2. Watch an episode of a popular prime-time TV program, such as *ER* or *The West Wing,* focusing your attention on the advertising that sponsors the show. Then write an essay in which you interpret these ads. Do the ads reveal a particular vision of the American dream, and if so, how might the vision be related to the show's audience?

3. Visit your college library, and locate an issue of a popular magazine from earlier decades, such as the 1930s or 1940s. Then write an essay in which you com-

pare and contrast the advertising found in that early issue with that in a current issue of the same publication. What similarities and differences do you find in the myths underlying the advertising, and what is their significance?

4. In class, brainstorm a list of status symbols common in advertising today. Then discuss what groups they appeal to and why. Can you detect any patterns based on gender, ethnicity, or age?

5. The American political scene has changed since the late 1980s, when this essay was first published. In an analytic essay, argue whether you believe the populist/elitist paradox that Solomon describes still affects American advertising and media. Be sure to base your discussion on specific media examples.

DIANE BARTHEL

A GENTLEMAN AND A CONSUMER

It's not only women who are pressured to conform to unattainable standards of physical appearance: men are victims, too. Diane Barthel (b. 1949), in this selection from Putting on Appearances: Gender and Advertising *(1988), surveys the various images men are expected to live up to as presented in advertisements in men's magazines. From the cowboy to the corporate jungle fighter, from the playboy to the polo player, men are urged to adopt traditionally aggressive male gender roles. At the same time, Barthel points out, they are to become obsessed with their appearance — a role that, ironically, is traditionally considered feminine. A professor of sociology at the State University of New York, Stony Brook, Barthel is also the author of* Amana: From Pietist Sect to American Community *(1984) and* Historic Preservation: Collective Memory and Historical Identity *(1996).*

There are no men's beauty and glamour magazines with circulations even approaching those of the women's magazines. The very idea of men's beauty magazines may strike one as odd. In our society men traditionally were supposed to make the right appearance, to be well groomed and neatly tailored. What they were *not* supposed to do was to be overly concerned with their appearance, much less vain about their beauty. That was to be effeminate, and not a "real man." Male beauty was associated with homosexuals, and "real men" had to show how red-blooded they were by maintaining a certain distance from fashion.

Perhaps the best-known male fashion magazine is *GQ* founded in 1957 and with a circulation of 446,000 in 1986. More recently, we have seen the launching of *YMF* and *Young Black Male,* which in 1987 still [had] few advertising pages. *M* magazine, founded in 1983, attracts an audience "a cut above" that of *GQ*.[1]

Esquire magazine, more venerable (founded in 1933), is classified as a general interest magazine. Although it does attract many women readers, many of the columns and features and much of the advertising are definitely directed toward attracting the attention of the male readers, who still make up the overwhelming majority of the readership.

The highest circulations for men's magazines are for magazines specializing either in sex (*Playboy*, circulation 4.1 million; *Penthouse*, circulation nearly 3.8 million; and *Hustler,* circulation 1.5 million) or sports (*Sports Illustrated,* circulation 2.7 million).[2] That these magazines share an emphasis on power — either power over women or over other men on the playing field — should not surprise. In fact, sociologist John Gagnon would argue that sex and sports now represent the major fields in which the male role, as defined by power, is played out, with physical power in work, and even in warfare, being less important than it was before industrialization and technological advance.[3]

If we are looking for comparative evidence as to how advertisements define gender roles for men and women, we should not then see the male role as defined primarily through beauty and fashion. This seems an obvious point, but it is important to emphasize how different cultural attitudes toward both the social person and the physical body shape the gender roles of men and women. These cultural attitudes are changing, and advertisements are helping to legitimate the use of beauty products and an interest in fashion for men, as we shall see. As advertisements directed toward women are beginning to use male imagery, so too advertisements for men occasionally use imagery resembling that found in advertisements directed toward women. We are speaking of two *modes,* then. As Baudrillard[4] writes, these modes "do not result from the differentiated nature of the two sexes, but from the differential logic of the system. The relationship of the Masculine and the Feminine to real men and women is relatively arbitrary."[5] Increasingly today, men and women use both modes. The two great terms of opposition (Masculine and Feminine) still, however, structure the forms that consumption takes; they provide identities for products and consumers.

Baudrillard agrees that the feminine model encourages a woman to please herself, to encourage a certain complacency and even narcissistic solicitude. But by pleasing herself, it is understood that she will also please others,

5

---

[1]Katz and Katz, *Magazines,* pp. 703–5.

[2]Ibid.

[3]John Gagnon, "Physical Strength: Once of Significance," in Joseph H. Pleck and Jack Sawyer, eds., *Men and Masculinity* (Englewood Cliffs, N.J.: Prentice-Hall, 1974), pp. 139–49.

[4]**Jean Baudrillard** (b. 1929) French semiologist. — EDS.

[5]Baudrillard, *La société de consommation,* pp. 144–47.

and that she will be chosen. "She never enters into direct competition. . . . If she is beautiful, that is to say, if this woman is a woman, she will be chosen. If the man is a man, he will choose his woman as he would other objects/signs (HIS car, HIS woman, HIS eau de toilette)."[6]

Whereas the feminine model is based on passivity, complacency, and narcissism, the masculine model is based on exactingness and choice.

> All of masculine advertising insists on rule, on choice, in terms of rigor and inflexible minutiae. He does not neglect a detail. . . . It is not a question of just letting things go, or of taking pleasure in something, but rather of distinguishing himself. To know how to choose, and not to fail at it, is here the equivalent of the military and puritanical virtues: intransigence, decision, "virtus."[7]

This masculine model, these masculine virtues, are best reflected in the many car advertisements. There, the keywords are masculine terms: *power, performance, precision.* Sometimes the car is a woman, responding to the touch and will of her male driver, after attracting him with her sexy body. "Pure shape, pure power, pure Z. It turns you on." But, as the juxtaposition of shape and power in this advertisement suggests, the car is not simply other; it is also an extension of the owner. As he turns it on, he turns himself on. Its power is his power; through it, he will be able to overpower other men and impress and seduce women.

> How well does it perform?
> How well can you drive? (Merkur XR4Ti)

> The 1987 Celica GT-S has the sweeping lines and aggressive stance that promise performance. And Celica keeps its word.

> Renault GTA:
> Zero to sixty to zero in 13.9 sec.
> It's the result of a performance philosophy where acceleration and braking are equally important.
> There's a new Renault sports sedan called GTA. Under its slick monochromatic skin is a road car with a total performance attitude. . . . It's our hot new pocket rocket.

In this last example, the car, like the driver, has a total performance attitude. That is what works. The slick monochromatic skin, like the Bond Street suit, makes a good first impression. But car, like owner, must have what it takes, must be able to go the distance faster and better than the competition. This point is explicitly made in advertisements in which the car becomes a means through which this masculine competition at work is extended in leisure. Some refer directly to the manly sport of auto-racing: "The Mitsubishi Starion ESI-R. Patiently crafted to ignite your imagination. Leaving little else to say

[6]Ibid.
[7]Ibid.

except . . . gentlemen, start your engines." Others refer to competition in the business world: "To move ahead fast in this world, you've got to have connections. The totally new Corolla FX 16 GT-S has the right ones." Or in life in general. "It doesn't take any [Japanese characters] from anyone. It won't stand for any guff from 300ZX. Or RX-7. Introducing Conquest Tsi, the new turbo sport coupe designed and built by Mitsubishi in Japan." Or Ferrari, which says simply, "We are the competition." In this competition between products, the owners become almost superfluous. But the advertisements, of course, suggest that the qualities of the car will reflect the qualities of the owner, as opposed to the purely abstract, apersonal quality of money needed for purchase. Thus, like the would-be owner, the BMW also demonstrates a "relentless refusal to compromise." It is for "those who thrive on a maximum daily requirement of high performance." While the BMW has the business attitude of the old school ("aggression has never been expressed with such dignity"), a Beretta suggests what it takes to survive today in the shark-infested waters of Wall Street. In a glossy three-page cover foldout, a photograph of a shark's fin cutting through indigo waters is accompanied by the legend "Discover a new species from today's Chevrolet." The following two pages show a sleek black Beretta similarly cutting through water and, presumably, through the competition: "Not just a new car, but a new species . . . with a natural instinct for the road . . . Aggressive stance. And a bold tail lamp. See it on the road and you won't soon forget. Drive it, and you never will."

And as with men, so with cars. "Power corrupts. Absolute power corrupts absolutely" (Maserati). Not having the money to pay for a Maserati, to corrupt and be corrupted, is a source of embarrassment. Advertisements reassure the consumer that he need not lose face in this manly battle. Hyundai promises, "It's affordable. (But you'd never know it.)"

> On first impression, the new Hyundai Excel GLS Sedan might seem a trifle beyond most people's means. But that's entirely by design. Sleek European design, to be exact.

Many advertisements suggest sexual pleasure and escape, as in "Pure 10 shape, pure power, pure Z. It turns you on." Or "The all-new Chrysler Le Baron. Beauty . . . with a passion for driving." The Le Baron may initially suggest a beautiful female, with its "image of arresting beauty" and its passion "to drive. And drive it does!" But it *is* "Le Baron," not "La Baronness." And the advertisement continues to emphasize how it "*attacks* [emphasis mine] the road with a high torque, 2.5 fuel-injected engine. And its turbo option can blur the surface of any passing lane." Thus the object of the pleasure hardly has to be female if it is beautiful or sleek. The car is an extension of the male that conquers and tames the (female) road: "Positive-response suspension will calm the most demanding roads." The car becomes the ultimate lover when, like the Honda Prelude, it promises to combine power, "muscle," with finesse. Automobile advertisements thus play with androgyny and sexuality; the pleasure is in the union and confusion of form and movement, sex and speed. As in any sexual union, there is ultimately a merging of identities, rather than rigid maintenance of their separation. Polymorphous perverse? Perhaps. But it sells.

Though power, performance, precision as a complex of traits find their strongest emphasis in automobile advertisements, they also appear as selling points for products as diverse as shoes, stereos, and sunglasses. The car performs on the road, the driver performs for women, even in the parking lot, as Michelin suggests in its two-page spread showing a male from waist down resting on his car and chatting up a curvaceous female: "It performs great. And looks great. So, it not only stands out on the road. But in the parking lot. Which is one more place you're likely to discover how beautifully it can handle the curves" (!).

As media analyst Todd Gitlin points out, most of the drivers shown in advertisements are young white males, loners who become empowered by the car that makes possible their escape from the everyday. Gitlin stresses the advertisements' "emphasis on surface, the blankness of the protagonist; his striving toward self-sufficiency, to the point of displacement from the recognizable world."[8] Even the Chrysler advertisements that coopt Bruce Springsteen's "Born in the USA" for their "Born in America" campaign lose in the process the original political message, "ripping off Springsteen's angry anthem, smoothing it into a Chamber of Commerce ditty as shots of just plain productive-looking folks, black and white . . . whiz by in a montage-made community." As Gitlin comments, "None of Springsteen's losers need apply — or rather, if only they would roll up their sleeves and see what good company they're in, they wouldn't feel like losers any longer."[9]

This is a world of patriarchal order in which the individual male can and must challenge the father. He achieves identity by breaking loose of the structure and breaking free of the pack. In the process he recreates the order and reaffirms the myth of masculine independence. Above all, he demonstrates that he knows what he wants; he is critical, demanding, and free from the constraints of others. What he definitely does not want, and goes to some measure to avoid, is to appear less than masculine, in any way weak, frilly, feminine.

Avoiding the Feminine

Advertisers trying to develop male markets for products previously associated primarily with women must overcome the taboo that only women wear moisturizer, face cream, hair spray, or perfume. They do this by overt reference to masculine symbols, language, and imagery, and sometimes by confronting the problem head-on.

[8]Todd Gitlin, "We Build Excitement," in Todd Gitlin, ed., *Watching Television* (New York: Pantheon, 1986), pp. 139–40.
[9]Ibid.

There is not so much of a problem in selling products to counteract bald- 15
ing — that traditionally has been recognized as a male problem (a bald
woman is a sexual joke that is not particularly amusing to the elderly). But
other hair products are another story, as the March 1987 *GQ* cover asks, "Are
you man enough for mousse?" So the advertisements must make their products seem manly, as with S-Curl's "wave and curl kit" offering "The Manly
Look" on its manly model dressed in business suit and carrying a hard hat (a
nifty social class compromise), and as in college basketball sportscaster Al
McGuire's testimonial for Consort hair spray:

> "Years ago, if someone had said to me, 'Hey Al, do you use hair
> spray?' I would have said, 'No way, baby!'"
> "That was before I tried Consort Pump."
> "Consort adds extra control to my hair without looking stiff or phony.
> Control that lasts clean into overtime and post-game interviews . . ."
> Grooming Gear for Real Guys. *Consort*.

Besides such "grooming gear" as perms and hair sprays, Real Guys use
"skin supplies" and "shaving resources." They adopt a "survival strategy" to
fight balding, and the "Fila philosophy" — "products with a singular purpose:
performance" — for effective "bodycare." If they wear scent, it smells of anything *but* flowers: musk, woods, spices, citrus, and surf are all acceptable. And
the names must be manly, whether symbolizing physical power ("Brut") or financial power ("Giorgio VIP Special Reserve," "The Baron. A distinctive fragrance for men," "Halston — For the privileged few").

As power/precision/performance runs as a theme throughout advertising
to men, so too do references to the business world. Cars, as we have seen,
promise to share their owner's professional attitude and aggressive drive to
beat out the competition. Other products similarly reflect the centrality of
business competition to the male gender role. And at the center of this competition itself, the business suit.

> At the onset of your business day, you choose the suit or sport coat
> that will position you front and center . . .
> The Right Suit can't guarantee he'll see it your way. The wrong suit
> could mean not seeing him at all.

Along with the Right Suit, the right shirt. "You want it every time you reach
across the conference table, or trade on the floor, or just move about. You
want a shirt that truly fits, that is long enough to stay put through the most active day, even for the taller gentleman." The businessman chooses the right
cologne — Grey Flannel, or perhaps Quorum. He wears a Gucci "timepiece" as
he conducts business on a cordless telephone from his poolside — or prefers
the "dignity in styling" promised by Raymond Weil watches, "a beautiful way
to dress for success."

Men's products connect status and success; the right products show that
you have the right stuff, that you're one of them. In the 1950s C. Wright

Mills[10] described what it took to get ahead, to become part of the "power elite":

> The fit survive, and fitness means, not formal competence . . . but confor-mity with the criteria of those who have already succeeded. To be compa-tible with the top men is to act like them, to look like them, to think like them: to be of and for them — or at least to display oneself to them in such a way as to create that impression. This, in fact, is what is meant by "creat-ing" — a well-chosen word — "a good impression." This is what is meant — and nothing else — by being a "sound man," as sound as a dollar.[11]

Today, having what it takes includes knowing "the difference between dressed, and well dressed" (Bally shoes). It is knowing that "what you carry says as much about you as what you put inside it" (Hartmann luggage). It is knowing enough to imitate Doug Fout, "member of one of the foremost equestrian families in the country."

> Because of our adherence to quality and the natural shoulder tradition, Southwick clothing was adopted by the Fout family years ago. Clearly, they have as much appreciation for good lines in a jacket as they do in a thor-oughbred.

There it is, old money. There is no substitute for it, really, in business or in ad-vertising, where appeals to tradition form one of the mainstays guaranteeing men that their choices are not overly fashionable or feminine, not working class or cheap, but, rather, correct, in good form, above criticism. If, when, they achieve this status of gentlemanly perfection, then, the advertisement suggests, they may be invited to join the club.

> When only the best of associations will do

> Recognizing style as the requisite for membership, discerning men prefer the natural shoulder styling of Racquet Club. Meticulously tailored in pure wool, each suit and sportcoat is the ultimate expression of the club-man's classic good taste.

Ralph Lauren has his Polo University Club, and Rolex picks up on the polo theme by sponsoring the Rolex Gold Cup held at the Palm Beach Polo and Country Club, where sixteen teams and sixty-four players competed for "the pure honor of winning, the true glory of victory":

> It has added new lustre to a game so ancient, its history is lost in leg-end. Tamerlane is said to have been its patriarch. Darius's Persian cavalry, we're told, played it. It was the national sport of 16th-century India, Egypt, China, and Japan. The British rediscovered and named it in 1857.

---

[10]**C. Wright Mills** (1916–1962) American sociologist. — Eds.
[11]C. Wright Mills, *The Power Elite* (New York: Oxford University Press, 1956), p. 141.

> The linking of polo and Rolex is uniquely appropriate. Both sponsor and sport personify rugged grace. Each is an arbiter of the art of timing.

In the spring of 1987, there was another interesting club event — or non-event. The prestigious New York University Club was ordered to open its doors to women. This brought the expected protests about freedom of association — and of sanctuary. For that has been one of the points of the men's club. It wasn't open to women. Members knew women had their place, and everyone knew it was not there. In the advertisements, as in the world of reality, there is a place for women in men's lives, one that revolves around: [20]

Sex and Seduction

The growing fascination with appearances, encouraged by advertising, has led to a "feminization" of culture. We are all put in the classic role of the female: manipulable, submissive, seeing ourselves as objects. This "feminization of sexuality" is clearly seen in men's advertisements, where many of the promises made to women are now made to men. If women's advertisements cry, "Buy (this product) and he will notice you," men's advertisements similarly promise that female attention will follow immediately upon purchase, or shortly thereafter. "They can't stay away from Mr. J." "Master the Art of Attracting Attention." She says, "He's wearing my favorite Corbin again." Much as in the advertisements directed at women, the advertisements of men's products promise that they will do the talking for you. "For the look that says come closer." "All the French you'll ever need to know."

Although many advertisements show an admiring and/or dependent female, others depict women in a more active role. "I love him — but life in the fast lane starts at 6 A.M.," says the attractive blonde tying on her jogging shoes, with the "him" in question very handsome and very asleep on the bed in the background. (Does this mean he's in the slow lane?) In another, the man slouches silhouetted against a wall; the woman leans aggressively toward him. He: "Do you always serve Tia Maria . . . or am I special?" She: "Darling, if you weren't special . . . you wouldn't be here."

The masculine role of always being in charge is a tough one. The blunt new honesty about sexually transmitted diseases such as AIDS appears in men's magazines as in women's, in the same "I enjoy sex, but I'm not ready to die for it" condom advertisement. But this new fear is accompanied by old fears of sexual embarrassment and/or rejection. The cartoon shows a man cringing with embarrassment in a pharmacy as the pharmacist yells out, "Hey, there's a guy here wants some information on Trojans." ("Most men would like to know more about Trojan brand condoms. But they're seriously afraid of suffering a spectacular and terminal attack of embarrassment right in the middle of a well-lighted drugstore.") Compared with such agony and responsibility, advertisements promising that women will *want* whatever is on offer, and will even meet the male halfway, must come as blessed relief. Men can finally relax, leaving the courting to the product and seduction to the beguiled woman, which, surely, must seem nice for a change.

Masculine Homilies

A homily is a short sermon, discourse, or informal lecture, often on a moral topic and suggesting a course of conduct. Some of the most intriguing advertisements offer just that, short statements and bits of advice on what masculinity is and on how real men should conduct themselves. As with many short sermons, many of the advertising homilies have a self-congratulatory air about them; after all, you do not want the consumer to feel bad about himself.

What is it, then, to be a man? It is to be *independent*. "There are some 25 things a man will not relinquish." Among them, says the advertisement, his Tretorn tennis shoes.

It is to *savor freedom*. "Dress easy, get away from it all and let Tom Sawyer paint the fence," advises Alexander Julian, the men's designer. "Because man was meant to fly, we gave him wings" (even if only on his sunglasses).

It is to live a life of *adventure*. KL Homme cologne is "for the man who lives on the edge." Prudential Life Insurance preaches, "If you can dream it, you can do it." New Man sportswear tells the reader, "Life is more adventurous when you feel like a New Man."

It is to *keep one's cool*. "J. B. Scotch. A few individuals know how to keep their heads, even when their necks are on the line."

And it is to stay one step *ahead of the competition*. "Altec Lansing. Hear what others only imagine." Alexander Julian again: "Dress up a bit when you dress down. They'll think you know something they don't."

What is it, then, to be a woman? It is to be *dependent*. "A woman needs a 30 man," reads the copy in the Rigolletto advertisement showing a young man changing a tire for a grateful young woman.

The American cowboy as cultural model was not supposed to care for or about appearances. He was what he was, hard-working, straightforward, and honest. He was authentic. Men who cared "too much" about how they looked did not fit this model; the dandy was effete, a European invention, insufficient in masculinity and not red-blooded enough to be a real American. The other cultural model, imported from England, was the gentleman. A gentleman did care about his appearance, in the proper measure and manifestation, attention to tailoring and to quality, understatement rather than exaggeration.[12]

---

[12]See Diane Barthel, "A Gentleman and a Consumer: A Sociological Look at Man at His Best," paper presented at the annual meeting of the Eastern Sociological Society, March 1983, Baltimore.

From the gray flannel suit of the 1950s to the "power look" of the 1980s, clothes made the man fit in with his company's image. Sex appeal and corporate correctness merged in a look that spelled success, that exuded confidence.

Whether or not a man presumed to care about his appearance, he did care about having "the right stuff," as Tom Wolfe and *Esquire* call it, or "men's toys," as in a recent special issue of *M* magazine. Cars, motorcycles, stereos, sports equipment: these are part of the masculine appearance. They allow the man to demonstrate his taste, his special knowledge, his affluence: to extend his control. He can be and is demanding, for only the best will do.

He also wants to be loved, but he does not want to appear needy. Advertisements suggest the magic ability of products ranging from cars to hair creams to attract female attention. With the right products a man can have it all, with no strings attached: no boring marital ties, hefty mortgages, corporate compromises.

According to sociologist Barbara Ehrenreich, *Playboy* magazine did much 35 to legitimate this image of male freedom. The old male ethos, up to the postwar period, required exchanging bachelor irresponsibility for married responsibility, which also symbolized entrance into social adulthood.[13] The perennial bachelor, with his flashy cars and interchangeable women, was the object of both envy and derision; he had fun, but . . . he was not fully grown up. There was something frivolous in his lack of purpose and application.

This old ethos has lost much of its legitimacy. Today's male can, as Baudrillard suggests, operate in both modes: the feminine mode of indulging oneself and being indulged and the masculine mode of exigency and competition. With the right look and the right stuff, he can feel confident and manly in boardroom or suburban backyard. Consumer society thus invites both men and women to live in a world of appearances and to devote ever more attention to them.

READING THE TEXT

1. Define in your own words what Barthel means by the "feminine" (para. 6) and "masculine" (para. 7) modes.

2. Why, according to Barthel, are men's magazines less popular than women's magazines?

3. Summarize what Barthel claims it means "to be a man" (para. 25) in magazine advertising.

4. How are women typically portrayed in men's magazine ads, according to Barthel?

[13]Barbara Ehrenreich, *The Hearts of Men: American Dreams and the Flight from Commitment* (New York: Anchor Books, 1983).

READING THE SIGNS

1. Buy a copy of one of the men's magazines that Barthel mentions in her essay, and study the advertising. Do the ads corroborate Barthel's claim that men today are allowed to demonstrate both their "masculine" and "feminine" sides?

2. Write an essay in which you apply Barthel's analysis of car advertising to an automotive category she doesn't mention — sport utility vehicles. To what extent have the key words "power," "performance," and "precision" influenced the ads you find? To develop your ideas, read or reread David Goewey's "'Careful, You May Run Out of Planet': SUVs and the Exploitation of the American Myth" (p. 112).

3. Have each class member bring a copy of a men's or women's magazine to class. Form same-sex groups, and give each group a few magazines designed for the opposite sex. Analyze the gender roles depicted in the magazines, and report to the class the group's findings.

4. Barthel claims that "the growing fascination with appearances" has led to a "feminization" (para. 21) of our culture. Read or review Holly Devor's "Gender Role Behaviors and Attitudes" (p. 484), and use her essay as a critical framework to critique Barthel's claim.

5. In class, brainstorm images of masculinity and femininity, and write your results on the board. Then compare the class's list to the gender traits that Barthel claims are common in advertising. Discuss with your class the possible origins of your brainstormed images.

ERIC SCHLOSSER

KID KUSTOMERS

Children rarely have much money of their own to spend, but they have a great deal of "pester power," along with the "leverage" to get their parents to buy them what they want. And so, as Eric Schlosser reports in this reading, Madison Avenue has been paying a great deal of attention to "kid kustomers" in recent years, pitching them everything from toys and candy to cell phones and automobiles. With more and more working couples spending more money on their kids to compensate for spending less time with them, Schlosser suggests, we are likely to see only an increase in such advertising in the years to come. Hmmm . . . are preteen dating services next? A correspondent for The Atlantic, *Schlosser is the author of* Fast Food Nation *(2001), from which this selection is taken.*

Twenty-five years ago, only a handful of American companies directed their marketing at children — Disney, McDonald's, candy makers, toy makers, manufacturers of breakfast cereal. Today children are being targeted by phone companies, oil companies, and automobile companies as well as clothing stores and restaurant chains. The explosion in children's advertising occurred during the 1980s. Many working parents, feeling guilty about spending less time with their kids, started spending more money on them. One marketing expert has called the 1980s "the decade of the child consumer." After largely ignoring children for years, Madison Avenue began to scrutinize and pursue them. Major ad agencies now have children's divisions, and a variety of marketing firms focus solely on kids. These groups tend to have sweet-sounding names: Small Talk, Kid Connection, Kid2Kid, the Gepetto Group, Just Kids, Inc. At least three industry publications — *Youth Market Alert, Selling to Kids,* and *Marketing to Kids Report* — cover the latest ad campaigns and market research. The growth in children's advertising has been driven by efforts to increase not just current, but also future, consumption. Hoping that nostalgic childhood memories of a brand will lead to a lifetime of purchases, companies now plan "cradle-to-grave" advertising strategies. They have come to believe what Ray Kroc and Walt Disney realized long ago — a person's "brand loyalty" may begin as early as the age of two. Indeed, market research has found that children often recognize a brand logo before they can recognize their own name.

The discontinued Joe Camel ad campaign, which used a hip cartoon character to sell cigarettes, showed how easily children can be influenced by the right corporate mascot. A 1991 study published in the *Journal of the American Medical Association* found that nearly all of America's six-year-olds could identify Joe Camel, who was just as familiar to them as Mickey Mouse. Another study found that one-third of the cigarettes illegally sold to minors were Camels. More recently, a marketing firm conducted a survey in shopping malls across the country, asking children to describe their favorite TV ads. According to the CME KidCom Ad Traction Study II, released at the 1999 Kids' Marketing Conference in San Antonio, Texas, the Taco Bell commercials featuring a talking chihuahua were the most popular fast food ads. The kids in the survey also like Pepsi and Nike commercials, but their favorite television ad was for Budweiser.

The bulk of the advertising directed at children today has an immediate goal. "It's not just getting kids to whine," one marketer explained in *Selling to Kids,* "it's giving them a specific reason to ask for the product." Years ago sociologist Vance Packard described children as "surrogate salesmen" who had to persuade other people, usually their parents, to buy what they wanted. Marketers now use different terms to explain the intended response to their ads — such as "leverage," "the nudge factor," "pester power." The aim of most children's advertising is straightforward: Get kids to nag their parents and nag them well.

James U. McNeal, a professor of marketing at Texas A&M University, is considered America's leading authority on marketing to children. In his book

Kids As Customers (1992), McNeal provides marketers with a thorough analysis of "children's requesting styles and appeals." He classifies juvenile nagging tactics into seven major categories. A *pleading* nag is one accompanied by repetitions of words like "please" or "mom, mom, mom." A *persistent* nag involves constant requests for the coveted product and may include the phrase "I'm gonna ask just one more time." *Forceful* nags are extremely pushy and may include subtle threats, like "Well, then, I'll go and ask Dad." *Demonstrative* nags are the most high-risk, often characterized by full-blown tantrums in public places, breath-holding, tears, a refusal to leave the store. *Sugar-coated* nags promise affection in return for a purchase and may rely on seemingly heartfelt declarations like "You're the best dad in the world." *Threatening* nags are youthful forms of blackmail, vows of eternal hatred and of running away if something isn't bought. *Pity* nags claim the child will be heartbroken, teased, or socially stunted if the parent refuses to buy a certain item. "All of these appeals and styles may be used in combination," McNeal's research has discovered, "but kids tend to stick to one or two of each that proved most effective . . . for their own parents."

McNeal never advocates turning children into screaming, breath-holding 5 monsters. He has been studying "Kid Kustomers" for more than thirty years and believes in a more traditional marketing approach. "The key is getting children to see a firm . . . in much the same way as [they see] mom or dad, grandma or grandpa," McNeal argues. "Likewise, if a company can ally itself with universal values such as patriotism, national defense, and good health, it is likely to nurture belief in it among children."

Before trying to affect children's behavior, advertisers have to learn about their tastes. Today's market researchers not only conduct surveys of children in shopping malls, they also organize focus groups for kids as young as two or three. They analyze children's artwork, hire children to run focus groups, stage slumber parties and then question children into the night. They send cultural anthropologists into homes, stores, fast food restaurants, and other places where kids like to gather, quietly and surreptitiously observing the behavior of prospective customers. They study the academic literature on child development, seeking insights from the work of theorists such as Erik Erikson and Jean Piaget. They study the fantasy lives of young children, they apply the findings in advertisements and product designs.

Dan S. Acuff — the president of Youth Market System Consulting and the author of *What Kids Buy and Why* (1997) — stresses the importance of dream research. Studies suggest that until the age of six, roughly 80 percent of children's dreams are about animals. Rounded, soft creatures like Barney, Disney's animated characters, and the Teletubbies therefore have an obvious appeal to young children. The Character Lab, a division of Youth Market System Consulting, uses a proprietary technique called Character Appeal Quadrant Analysis to help companies develop new mascots. The technique purports to create imaginary characters who perfectly fit the targeted age group's level of cognitive and neurological development.

Children's clubs have for years been considered an effective means of targeting ads and collecting demographic information; the clubs appeal to a child's fundamental need for status and belonging. Disney's Mickey Mouse Club, formed in 1930, was one of the trailblazers. During the 1980s and 1990s, children's clubs proliferated, as corporations used them to solicit the names, addresses, zip codes, and personal comments of young customers. "Marketing messages sent through a club not only can be personalized," James McNeal advises, "they can be tailored for a certain age or geographical group." A well-designed and well-run children's club can be extremely good for business. According to one Burger King executive, the creation of a Burger King Kids Club in 1991 increased the sales of children's meals as much as 300 percent.

The Internet has become another powerful tool for assembling data about children. In 1998 a federal investigation of Web sites aimed at children found that 89 percent requested personal information from kids; only 1 percent required that children obtain parental approval before supplying the information. A character on the McDonald's Web site told children that Ronald McDonald was "the ultimate authority in everything." The site encouraged kids to send Ronald an e-mail revealing their favorite menu item at McDonald's, their favorite book, their favorite sports team — and their name. Fast food Web sites no longer ask children to provide personal information without first gaining parental approval; to do so is now a violation of federal law, thanks to the Children's Online Privacy Protection Act, which took effect in April of 2000.

Despite the growing importance of the Internet, television remains the   10 primary medium for children's advertising. The effects of these TV ads have long been a subject of controversy. In 1978, the Federal Trade Commission (FTC) tried to ban all television ads directed at children seven years old or younger. Many studies had found that young children often could not tell the difference between television programming and television advertising. They also could not comprehend the real purpose of commercials and trusted that advertising claims were true. Michael Pertschuk, the head of the FTC, argued that children need to be shielded from advertising that preys upon their immaturity. "They cannot protect themselves," he said, "against adults who exploit their present-mindedness."

The FTC's proposed ban was supported by the American Academy of Pediatrics, the National Congress of Parents and Teachers, the Consumers Union, and the Child Welfare League, among others. But it was attacked by the National Association of Broadcasters, the Toy Manufacturers of America, and the Association of National Advertisers. The industry groups lobbied Congress to prevent any restrictions on children's ads and sued in federal court to block Pertschuk from participating in future FTC meetings on the subject. In April of 1981, three months after the inauguration of President Ronald Reagan, an FTC staff report argued that a ban on ads aimed at children would be impractical, effectively killing the proposal. "We are delighted by the FTC's reasonable recommendation," said the head of the National Association of Broadcasters.

The Saturday-morning children's ads that caused angry debates twenty years ago now seem almost quaint. Far from being banned, TV advertising aimed at kids is now broadcast twenty-four hours a day, closed-captioned and in stereo. Nickelodeon, the Disney Channel, the Cartoon Network, and the other children's cable networks are now responsible for about 80 percent of all television viewing by kids. None of these networks existed before 1979. The typical American child now spends about twenty-one hours a week watching television — roughly one and a half months of TV every year. That does not include the time children spend in front of a screen watching videos, playing video games, or using the computer. Outside of school, the typical American child spends more time watching television than doing any other activity except sleeping. During the course of a year, he or she watches more than thirty thousand TV commercials. Even the nation's youngest children are watching a great deal of television. About one-quarter of American children between the ages of two and five have a TV in their room.

READING THE TEXT

1. Why, according to Schlosser, did an "explosion in children's advertising" (para. 1) occur during the 1980s?

2. What is "pester power" (para. 3), and how is it used as a marketing strategy?

3. How has the Internet contributed to the expansion in advertising directed toward children, according to Schlosser?

4. What strategies does Schlosser say marketers use to determine children's tastes in products?

READING THE SIGNS

1. Watch a morning of Saturday cartoon shows on TV, and make a list of all the products that are advertised. What products are directly tied in to the show? Use your observations as the basis for an essay in which you analyze the relationship between children's programming and the advertising that supports it.

2. Perform a semiotic analysis of an advertisement from any medium directed at children. What signifiers in the ad are especially addressed to children? Consider such details as the implied narrative of the ad, its characters and their appearance, colors, music, and voice track.

3. Conduct an in-class debate over whether children's advertising should be more strictly regulated. To develop support for your team's position, watch some TV programs aimed at children and the advertising that accompanies them.

4. Read or reread James Twitchell's "What We Are to Advertisers" (p. 205), and write an essay in which you analyze whether Twitchell's assertion that "mass marketing means the creation of mass stereotypes" (para. 1) applies to child consumers.

GLORIA STEINEM

SEX, LIES, AND ADVERTISING

One of the best-known icons of the women's movement, Gloria Steinem (b. 1934) has been a leader in transforming the image of women in America. As a cofounder of Ms. *magazine, in which this selection first appeared, Steinem has provided a forum for women's voices for more than thirty years, but as her article explains, it has not been easy to keep this forum going. A commercial publication requires commercials, and the needs of advertisers do not always mesh nicely with the goals of a magazine like* Ms. *Steinem ruefully reveals the compromises* Ms. *magazine had to make over the years to satisfy its advertising clients, compromises that came to an end only when* Ms. *ceased to take ads. Steinem's publications include* Revolution from Within *(1992), a personal exploration of the power of self-esteem;* Moving Beyond Words *(1994); and* Outrageous Acts and Everyday Rebellions *(2nd ed., 1995). Currently the president of Voters for Choice and a consulting editor for* Ms., *Steinem continues to combine her passion for writing and activism as an unflagging voice in American feminism.*

Goodbye to cigarette ads where poems should be.
Goodbye to celebrity covers and too little space.
Goodbye to cleaning up language so *Ms.* advertisers won't be boycotted by
    the Moral Majority.
In fact, goodbye to advertisers *and* the Moral Majority.
Goodbye to short articles and short thinking.
Goodbye to "post-feminism" from people who never say "post-
    democracy."
Goodbye to national boundaries and hello to the world.
Welcome to the magazine of the post-patriarchal age.
The turn of the century is *our turn!*

That was my celebratory mood in the summer of 1990 when I finished the original version of the exposé you are about to read. I felt as if I'd been released from a personal, portable Bastille. At least I'd put on paper the ad policies that had been punishing *Ms.* for all the years of its nonconforming life and still were turning more conventional media, especially (but not only) those directed at women, into a dumping ground for fluff.

Those goodbyes were part of a letter inviting readers to try a new, ad-free version of *Ms.* and were also a homage to "Goodbye to All That," a witty and lethal essay in which Robin Morgan bade farewell to the pre-feminist male Left of twenty years before. It seemed the right tone for the birth of a brand-new, reader-supported, more international form of *Ms.*, which Robin was heading as editor-in-chief, and I was serving as consulting editor. Besides, I had a very personal kind of mantra running through my head: *I'll never have to sell another ad as long as I live.*

So I sent the letter off, watched the premiere issue containing my exposé go to press, and then began to have second thoughts: Were ad policies too much of an "inside" concern? Did women readers already know that magazines directed at them were filled with editorial extensions of ads — and not care? Had this deceptive system been in place too long for anyone to have faith in changing it? In other words: Would anybody give a damn?

After almost four years of listening to responses and watching the ripples spread out from this pebble cast upon the waters, I can tell you that, yes, readers do care; and no, most of them were not aware of advertising's control over the words and images around it. Though most people in the publishing industry think this is a practice too deeply embedded ever to be uprooted, a lot of readers are willing to give it a try — even though that's likely to mean paying more for their publications. In any case, as they point out, understanding the nitty-gritty of ad influence has two immediate uses. It strengthens healthy skepticism about what we read, and it keeps us from assuming that other women must want this glamorous, saccharine, unrealistic stuff.

Perhaps that's the worst punishment ad influence has inflicted upon us. 　5 It's made us feel contemptuous of other women. We know we don't need those endless little editorial diagrams of where to put our lipstick or blush — we don't identify with all those airbrushed photos of skeletal women with everything about them credited, *even their perfume* (can you imagine a man's photo airbrushed to perfection, with his shaving lotion credited?) — but we assume there must be women out there somewhere who *do* love it; otherwise, why would it be there?

Well, many don't. Given the sameness of women's magazines resulting from the demands made by makers of women's products that advertise in all of them, we probably don't know yet what a wide variety of women readers want. In any case, we do know it's the advertisers who are determining what women are getting now.

The first wave of response to this exposé came not from readers but from writers and editors for other women's magazines. They phoned to say the pall cast by anticipated or real advertising demands was even more widespread than rebellious *Ms.* had been allowed to know. They told me how brave I was to "burn my bridges" (no critic of advertising would ever be hired as an editor of any of the women's magazines, they said) and generally treated me as if I'd written about organized crime instead of practices that may be unethical but are perfectly legal. After making me promise not to use their names, they offered enough additional horror stories to fill a book, a movie, and maybe a television series. Here is a typical one: when the freelance author of an article on moisturizers observed in print that such products might be less necessary for young women — whose skin tends to be not dry but oily — the article's editor was called on the carpet and denounced by her bosses as "anti-moisturizer." Or how about this: the film critic for a women's magazine asked its top editor, a woman who makes millions for her parent company, whether movies could finally be reviewed critically, since she had so much clout. No, said the editor; if you can't praise a movie, just don't include it; otherwise we'll jeopardize our movie ads. This may sound like surrealism in everyday life, or like our grand-mothers advising, "If you can't say something nice, don't say anything," but such are the forces that control much of our information.

I got few negative responses from insiders, but the ones I did get were bit-ter. Two editors at women's magazines felt I had demeaned them by writing the article. They loved their work, they said, and didn't feel restricted by ads at all. So I would like to make clear in advance that my purpose was and is to change the system, not to blame the people struggling within it. As someone who has written for most women's magazines, I know that many editors work hard to get worthwhile articles into the few pages left over after provid-ing all the "complementary copy" (that is, articles related to and supportive of advertised products). I also know there are editors who sincerely want exactly what the advertisers want, which is why they're so good at their jobs. Nonetheless, criticizing this ad-dominant system is no different from criticiz-ing male-dominant marriage. Both institutions make some people happy, and both seem free as long as your wishes happen to fall within their traditional boundaries. But just as making more equal marital laws alleviates the suffer-ing of many, breaking the link between editorial and advertising will help all media become more honest and diverse.

A second wave of reaction came from advertising executives who were asked to respond by reporters. They attributed all problems to *Ms.* We must have been too controversial or otherwise inappropriate for ads. I saw no sto-ries that asked the next questions: Why had non-women's companies from Johnson & Johnson to IBM found our "controversial" pages fine for their ads? Why did desirable and otherwise unreachable customers read something so "inappropriate"? What were ad policies doing to *other* women's media? To continue my marriage parallel, however, I should note that these executives seemed only mildly annoyed. Just as many women are more dependent than men on the institution of marriage and so are more threatened and angry when it's questioned, editors of women's magazines tended to be more upset than advertisers when questioned about their alliance. . . .

Then came the third wave — reader letters which were smart, thoughtful, 10 innovative, and numbered in the hundreds. Their dominant themes were anger and relief: relief because those vast uncritical oceans of food/fashion/ beauty articles in other women's magazines weren't necessarily what women wanted after all, and also relief because *Ms.* wasn't going to take ads any-more, even those that were accompanied by fewer editorial demands; anger because consumer information, diverse articles, essays, fiction, and poetry could have used the space instead of all those oceans of articles about ad categories that had taken up most of women's magazines for years. . . .

Last and most rewarding was the response that started in the fall. Teachers of journalism, advertising, communications, women's studies, and other contemporary courses asked permission to reprint the exposé as a supplementary text. That's another reason why I've restored cuts, updated information, and added new examples — including this introduction. Getting subversive ideas into classrooms could change the next generation running the media.

The following pages are mostly about women's magazines, but that doesn't mean other media are immune.

Sex, Lies, and Advertising

Toward the end of the 1980s, when glasnost was beginning and *Ms.* magazine seemed to be ending, I was invited to a press lunch for a Soviet official. He entertained us with anecdotes about the new problems of democracy in his country; for instance, local Communist leaders who were being criticized by their own media for the first time, and were angry.

"So I'll have to ask my American friends," he finished pointedly, "how more subtly to control the press."

In the silence that followed, I said: "Advertising."   15

The reporters laughed, but later one of them took me aside angrily: How dare I suggest that freedom of the press was limited in this country? How dare I imply that *his* newsmagazine could be influenced by ads?

I explained that I wasn't trying to lay blame, but to point out advertising's media-wide influence. We can all recite examples of "soft" cover stories that newsmagazines use to sell ads, and self-censorship in articles that should have taken advertised products to task for, say, safety or pollution. Even television news goes "soft" in ratings wars, and other TV shows don't get on the air without advertiser support. But I really had been thinking about women's magazines. There, it isn't just a little content that's designed to attract ads; it's almost all of it. That's why advertisers — not readers — had always been the problem for *Ms.* As the only women's magazine that didn't offer what the ad world euphemistically describes as "supportive editorial atmosphere" or "complementary copy" (for instance, articles that praise food/fashion/beauty subjects in order to "support" and "complement" food/fashion/beauty ads), *Ms.* could never attract enough ads to break even.

"Oh, *women*'s magazines," the journalist said with contempt. "Everybody knows they're catalogs — but who cares? They have nothing to do with journalism."

I can't tell you how many times I've had this argument since I started writing for magazines in the early 1960s, and especially since the current women's movement began. Except as moneymaking machines — "cash cows," as they are so elegantly called in the trade — women's magazines are usually placed beyond the realm of serious consideration. Though societal changes being forged by women have been called more far-reaching than the industrial revolution by such nonfeminist sources as the *Wall Street Journal* — and though women's magazine editors often try hard to reflect these changes in the few pages left after all the ad-related subjects are covered — the magazines serving the female half of this country are still far below the journalistic and ethical standards of news and general-interest counterparts. Most depressing of all, this fact is so taken for granted that it doesn't even rate an exposé.

For instance: If *Time* and *Newsweek,* in order to get automotive and GM 20 ads, had to lavish editorial praise on cars and credit photographs in which newsmakers were driving, say, a Buick from General Motors, there would be a scandal — maybe even a criminal investigation. When women's magazines from *Seventeen* to *Lear's* publish articles lavishing praise on beauty and fashion products, and crediting in text describing cover and other supposedly editorial photographs a particular makeup from Revlon or a dress from Calvin Klein because those companies also advertise, it's just business as usual.

When *Ms.* began, we didn't consider *not* taking ads. The most important reason was to keep the price of a feminist magazine low enough for most women to afford. But the second and almost equal reason was to provide a forum where women and advertisers could talk to each other and experiment with nonstereotyped, informative, imaginative ads. After all, advertising was (and is) as potent a source of information in this country as news or TV or movies. It's where we get not only a big part of our information but also images that shape our dreams.

We decided to proceed in two stages. First, we would convince makers of "people products" that their ads should be placed in a women's magazine: cars, credit cards, insurance, sound equipment, financial services — everything that's used by both men and women but was then advertised only to men. Since those advertisers were accustomed to the division between editorial pages and ads that news and general-interest magazines at least try to maintain, such products would allow our editorial content to be free and diverse. Furthermore, if *Ms.* could prove that women were important purchasers of "people products," just as men were, those advertisers would support other women's magazines, too, and subsidize some pages for articles about something other than the hothouse worlds of food/fashion/beauty. Only in the second phase would we add examples of the best ads for whatever traditional "women's products" (clothes, shampoo, fragrance, food, and so on) that subscriber surveys showed *Ms.* readers actually used. But we would ask those advertisers to come in *without* the usual quid pro quo of editorial features praising their product area; that is, the dreaded "complementary copy."

From the beginning, we knew the second step might be even harder than the first. Clothing advertisers like to be surrounded by editorial fashion spreads (preferably ones that credit their particular labels and designers); food advertisers have always expected women's magazines to publish recipes and articles on entertaining (preferably ones that require their products); and shampoo, fragrance, and beauty products in general insist on positive editorial coverage of beauty aids — a "beauty atmosphere," as they put it — plus photo credits for particular products and nothing too depressing; no bad news. That's why women's magazines look the way they do: saccharine, smiley-faced and product-heavy, with even serious articles presented in a slick and sanitized way.

But if *Ms.* could break this link between ads and editorial content, then we should add "women's products" too. For one thing, publishing ads only for gender-neutral products would give the impression that women have to become "like men" in order to succeed (an impression that *Ms.* ad pages sometimes *did* give when we were still in the first stage). For another, presenting a full circle of products that readers actually need and use would allow us to select the best examples of each category and keep ads from being lost in a sea of similar products. By being part of this realistic but unprecedented mix, products formerly advertised only to men would reach a growth market of women, and good ads for women's products would have a new visibility.

Given the intelligence and leadership of *Ms.* readers, both kinds of products would have unique access to a universe of smart consultants whose response would help them create more effective ads for other media too. Aside from the advertisers themselves, there's nobody who cares as much about the imagery in advertising as those who find themselves stereotyped or rendered invisible by it. And they often have great suggestions for making it better. 25

As you can see, we had all our energy, optimism, and arguments in good working order.

I thought at the time that our main problem would be getting ads with good "creative," as the imagery and text are collectively known. That was where the women's movement had been focusing its efforts, for instance, the National Organization for Women's awards to the best ads, and its "Barefoot and Pregnant" awards for the worst. Needless to say, there were plenty of candidates for the second group. Carmakers were still draping blondes in evening gowns over the hoods like ornaments that could be bought with the car (thus also making clear that car ads weren't directed at women). Even in ads for products that only women used, the authority figures were almost always male, and voice-overs for women's products on television were usually male too. Sadistic, he-man campaigns were winning industry praise; for example, *Advertising Age* hailed the infamous Silva Thin cigarette theme, "How to Get a Woman's Attention: Ignore Her," as "brilliant." Even in medical journals, ads for tranquilizers showed depressed housewives standing next to piles of dirty dishes and promised to get them back to work. As for women's magazines, they seemed to have few guidelines; at least none that excluded even the ads for the fraudulent breast-enlargement or thigh-thinning products for which their back pages were famous.

Obviously, *Ms.* would have to avoid such offensive imagery and seek out the best ads, but this didn't seem impossible. *The New Yorker* had been screening ads for aesthetic reasons for years, a practice that advertisers accepted at the time. *Ebony* and *Essence* were asking for ads with positive black images, and though their struggle was hard, their requests weren't seen as unreasonable. . . .

Let me take you through some of our experiences — greatly condensed, but just as they happened. In fact, if you poured water on any one of these, it would become a novel:

- Cheered on by early support from Volkswagen and one or two other car companies, we finally scrape together time and money to put on a major reception in Detroit. U.S. carmakers firmly believe that women choose the upholstery color, not the car, but we are armed with statistics and reader mail to prove the contrary: A car is an important purchase for women, one that is such a symbol of mobility and freedom that many women will spend a greater percentage of income for a car than will counterpart men. ³⁰

But almost nobody comes. We are left with many pounds of shrimp on the table, and quite a lot of egg on our face. Assuming this near-total boycott is partly because there was a baseball pennant play-off the same day, we blame ourselves for not foreseeing the problem. Executives go out of their way to explain that they wouldn't have come anyway. It's a dramatic beginning for ten years of knocking on resistant or hostile doors, presenting endless documentation of women as car buyers, and hiring a full-time saleswoman in Detroit — all necessary before *Ms.* gets any real results.

This long saga has a semi-happy ending: Foreign carmakers understood better than Detroit that women buy cars, and advertised in *Ms.;* also years of research on the women's market plus door-knocking began to pay off. Eventually, cars became one of our top sources of ad revenue. Even Detroit began to take the women's market seriously enough to put car ads in other women's magazines too, thus freeing a few more of their pages from the food/fashion/beauty hothouse.

But long after figures showed that a third, even half, of many car models were being bought by women, U.S. makers continued to be uncomfortable addressing female buyers. Unlike many foreign carmakers, Detroit never quite learned the secret of creating intelligent ads that exclude no one and then placing them in media that overcome past exclusion. Just as an African American reader may feel more invited by a resort that placed an ad in *Ebony* or *Essence,* even though the same ad appeared in *Newsweek,* women of all races may need to see ads for cars, computers, and other historically "masculine" products in media that are clearly directed at them. Once inclusive ads are well placed, however, there's interest and even gratitude from women. *Ms.* readers were so delighted to be addressed as intelligent consumers by a routine Honda ad with text about rack-and-pinion steering, for example, that they sent fan mail. But even now, Detroit continues to ask: "Should we make special ads for women?" That's probably one reason why foreign cars still have a greater share of the women's market in the United States than of the men's.

- In the *Ms.* Gazette, we do a brief report on a congressional hearing into coal tar derivatives used in hair dyes that are absorbed through the skin and may be carcinogenic. This seems like news of importance: Newspapers and newsmagazines are reporting it too. But Clairol, a Bristol-Myers subsidiary that makes dozens of products, a few of which have just come into our pages as ads *without* the usual quid pro quo of articles on hair and beauty, is outraged. Not at newspapers or newsmagazines, just at us. It's bad enough that *Ms.* is the only women's magazine refusing to provide "supportive editorial" praising beauty products, but to criticize one of their product categories on top of it, however generically or even accurately — well, *that* is going too far.

We offer to publish a letter from Clairol telling its side of the story. In an 35 excess of solicitousness, we even put this letter in the Gazette, not in Letters to the Editors, where it belongs. Eventually, Clairol even changes its hair-coloring formula, apparently in response to those same hearings. But in spite of surveys that show *Ms.* readers to be active women who use more of almost everything Clairol makes than do the readers of other women's magazines, *Ms.* gets almost no ads for those dozens of products for the rest of its natural life.

- Women of color read *Ms.* in disproportionate numbers. This is a source of pride to *Ms.* staffers, who are also more racially representative than the editors of other women's magazines (which may include some beautiful black models but almost no black decisionmakers; Pat Carbine hired the first black editor at *McCall's,* but she left when Pat did). Nonetheless, the reality of *Ms.*'s staff and readership is obscured by ads filled with enough white women to make the casual reader assume *Ms.* is directed at only one part of the population, no matter what the editorial content is.

In fact, those few ads we are able to get that feature women of color — for instance, one made by Max Factor for *Essence* and *Ebony* that Linda Wachner gives us while she is president of Max Factor — are greeted with praise and relief by white readers, too, and make us feel that more inclusive ads should win out in the long run. But there are pathetically few such images. Advertising "creative" also excludes women who are not young, not thin, not conventionally pretty, well-to-do, able-bodied, or heterosexual — which is a hell of a lot of women.

- Our intrepid saleswomen set out early to attract ads for the product category known as consumer electronics: sound equipment, computers, calculators, VCRs, and the like. We know that *Ms.* readers are determined to be part of this technological revolution, not to be left out as women have been in the past. We also know from surveys that readers are buying this kind of stuff in numbers as high as those of readers of magazines like *Playboy* and the "male 18 to 34" market, prime targets of the industry. Moreover, unlike traditional women's products that our readers buy but don't want to read articles about, these are subjects they like to see demystified in our pages. There actually *is* a supportive editorial atmosphere.

"But women don't understand technology," say ad and electronics executives at the end of our presentations. "Maybe not," we respond, "but neither do men — and we all buy it."

"If women *do* buy it," counter the decisionmakers, "it's because they're 40 asking their husbands and boyfriends what to buy first." We produce letters from *Ms.* readers saying how turned off they are when salesmen say things like "Let me know when your husband can come in."

Then the argument turns to why there aren't more women's names sent back on warranties (those much-contested certificates promising repair or replacement if anything goes wrong). We explain that the husband's name may be on the warranty, even if the wife made the purchase. But it's also true that women are experienced enough as consumers to know that such promises are valid only if the item is returned in its original box at midnight in Hong Kong. Sure enough, when we check out hair dryers, curling irons, and other stuff women clearly buy, women don't return those warranties very often either. It isn't the women who are the problem, it's the meaningless warranties.

After several years of this, we get a few ads from companies like JVC and Pioneer for compact sound systems — on the grounds that women can understand compacts, but not sophisticated components. Harry Elias, vice president of JVC, is actually trying to convince his Japanese bosses that there is something called a woman's market. At his invitation, I find myself speaking at trade shows in Chicago and Las Vegas trying to persuade JVC dealers that electronics showrooms don't have to be locker rooms. But as becomes apparent, however, the trade shows are part of the problem. In Las Vegas, the only women working at technology displays are seminude models serving champagne. In Chicago, the big attraction is Marilyn Chambers, a porn star who followed Linda Lovelace of *Deep Throat* fame as Chuck Traynor's captive and/or employee, whose pornographic movies are being used to demonstrate VCRs.

In the end, we get ads for a car stereo now and then, but no VCRs; a welcome breakthrough of some IBM personal computers, but no Apple or no Japanese-made ones. Furthermore, we notice that *Working Woman* and *Savvy,* which are focused on office work, don't benefit as much as they should from ads for office equipment either. . . .

• Then there is the great toy train adventure. Because *Ms.* gets letters from little girls who love toy trains and ask our help in changing ads and box-top photos that show only little boys, we try to talk to Lionel and to get their ads. It turns out that Lionel executives *have* been concerned about little girls. They made a pink train and couldn't understand why it didn't sell.

Eventually, Lionel bows to this consumer pressure by switching to a photograph of a boy *and* a girl — but only on some box tops. If trains are associated with little girls, Lionel executives believe, they will be devalued in the eyes of little boys. Needless to say, *Ms.* gets no train ads. If even 20 percent of little girls wanted trains, they would be a huge growth market, but this remains unexplored. In the many toy stores where displays are still gender divided, the "soft" stuff, even modeling clay, stays on the girls' side, while the "hard" stuff, especially rockets and trains, is displayed for boys — thus depriving both. By 1986, Lionel is put up for sale.

We don't have much luck with other kinds of toys either. A *Ms.* department, Stories for Free Children, edited by Letty Cottin Pogrebin, makes us one of the very few magazines with a regular feature for children. A larger proportion of *Ms.* readers have preschool children than do the readers of any other women's magazine. Nonetheless, the industry can't seem to believe that feminists care about children — much less have them.

• When *Ms.* began, the staff decided not to accept ads for feminine hygiene sprays and cigarettes on the same basis: They are damaging to many women's health but carry no appropriate warnings. We don't think we should tell our readers what to do — if marijuana were legal, for instance, we would carry ads for it along with those for beer and wine — but we should provide facts so readers can decide for themselves. Since we've received letters saying that feminine sprays actually kill cockroaches and take the rust off metal, we give up on those. But antismoking groups have been pressuring for health warnings on cigarette ads as well as packages, so we decide we will accept advertising if the tobacco industry complies.

Philip Morris is among the first to do so. One of its brands, Virginia Slims, is also sponsoring women's tennis tournaments and women's public opinion polls that are historic "firsts." On the other hand, the Virginia Slims theme, "You've come a long way, baby," has more than a "baby" problem. It gives the impression that for women, smoking is a sign of progress.

We explain to the Philip Morris people that this slogan won't do well in our pages. They are convinced that its success with *some* women means it will work with *all* women. No amount of saying that we, like men, are a segmented market, that we don't all think alike, does any good. Finally, we agree to publish a small ad for a Virginia Slims calendar as a test, and to abide by the response of our readers.

The letters from readers are both critical and smart. For instance: Would you show a photo of a black man picking cotton next to one of an African American man in a Cardin suit, and symbolize progress from slavery to civil rights by smoking? Of course not. So why do it for women? But instead of honoring test results, the executives seem angry to have been proved wrong. We refuse Virginia Slims ads, thus annoying tennis players like Billie Jean King as well as incurring a new level of wrath: Philip Morris takes away ads for *all* its many products, costing *Ms.* about $250,000 in the first year. After five years, the damage is so great we can no longer keep track.

Occasionally, a new set of Philip Morris executives listens to *Ms.* saleswomen, or laughs when Pat Carbine points out that even Nixon got pardoned.

I also appeal directly to the chairman of the board, who agrees it is unfair, sends me to another executive — and *he* says no. Because we won't take Virginia Slims, not one other Philip Morris product returns to our pages for the next sixteen years.

Gradually, we also realize our naïveté in thinking we could refuse all cigarette ads, with or without a health warning. They became a disproportionate source of revenue for print media the moment television banned them, and few magazines can compete or survive without them; certainly not *Ms.*, which lacks the support of so many other categories. Though cigarette ads actually inhibit editorial freedom less than ads for food, fashion, and the like — cigarette companies want only to be distant from coverage on the dangers of smoking, and don't require affirmative praise or photo credits of their product — it is still a growing source of sorrow that they are there at all. By the 1980s, when statistics show that women's rate of lung cancer is approaching men's, the necessity of taking cigarette ads has become a kind of prison.

Though I never manage to feel kindly toward groups that protest our ads and pay no attention to magazines and newspapers that can turn them down and still keep their doors open — and though *Ms.* continues to publish new facts about smoking, such as its dangers during pregnancy — I long for the demise of the whole tobacco-related industry. . . .

- General Mills, Pillsbury, Carnation, Del Monte, Dole, Kraft, Stouffer, Hormel, Nabisco: You name the food giant, we try to get its ads. But no matter how desirable the *Ms.* readership, our lack of editorial recipes and traditional homemaking articles proves lethal.

We explain that women flooding into the paid labor force have changed ⁵⁵ the way this country eats; certainly, the boom in convenience foods proves that. We also explain that placing food ads *only* next to recipes and how-to-entertain articles is actually a negative for many women. It associates food with work — in a way that says only women have to cook — or with guilt over *not* cooking and entertaining. Why not advertise food in diverse media that don't always include recipes (thus reaching more men, who have become a third of all supermarket shoppers anyway) and add the recipe interest with specialty magazines like *Gourmet* (a third of whose readers are men)?

These arguments elicit intellectual interest but no ads. No advertising executive wants to be the first to say to a powerful client, "Guess what, I *didn't* get you complementary copy." Except for an occasional hard-won ad for instant coffee, diet drinks, yogurt, or such extras as avocados and almonds, the whole category of food, a mainstay of the publishing industry, remains unavailable to us. Period. . . .

- By the end of 1986, magazine production costs have skyrocketed and postal rates have increased 400 percent. Ad income is flat for the whole magazine industry. The result is more competition, with other magazines offering such "extras" as free golf trips for advertisers or programs for "sampling" their products at parties and other events arranged by the magazine for desirable consumers. We try to compete with the latter by "sampling" at what we certainly have enough of: movement benefits. Thus, little fragrance bottles turn up next to the dinner plates of California women lawyers (who are delighted), or wine samples lower the costs at a reception for political women. A good organizing tactic comes out of this. We hold feminist seminars in shopping centers. They may be to the women's movement what churches were to the civil rights movement in the South—that is, *where people are*. Anyway, shopping center seminars are a great success. Too great. We have to stop doing them in Bloomingdale's up and down the East Coast, because meeting space in the stores is too limited, and too many women are left lined up outside stores. We go on giving out fancy little liquor bottles at store openings, which makes the advertisers happy—but not us.

Mostly, however, we can't compete in this game of "value-added" (the code word for giving the advertisers extras in return for their ads). Neither can many of the other independent magazines. Deep-pocketed corporate parents can offer such extras as reduced rates for ad schedules in a group of magazines, free tie-in spots on radio stations they also own, or vacation junkets on corporate planes.

Meanwhile, higher costs and lowered income have caused the *Ms.* 60/40 preponderance of edit over ads—something we promised to readers—to become 50/50: still a lot better than most women's magazines' goals of 30/70, but not good enough. Children's stories, most poetry, and some fiction are casualties of reduced space. In order to get variety into more limited pages, the length (and sometimes the depth) of articles suffers. Though we don't solicit or accept ads that would look like a parody in our pages, we get so worn down that some slip through. Moreover, we always have the problem of working just as hard to get a single ad as another magazine might for a whole year's schedule of ads.

Still, readers keep right on performing miracles. Though we haven't been 60 able to afford a subscription mailing in two years, they maintain our guaranteed circulation of 450,000 by word of mouth. Some of them also help to make up the advertising deficit by giving *Ms.* a birthday present of $15 on its fifteen anniversary, or contributing $1,000 for a lifetime subscription—even those who can ill afford it.

What's almost as angering as these struggles, however, is the way the media report them. Our financial problems are attributed to lack of reader interest, not an advertising double standard. In the Reagan-Bush era, when "feminism-is-dead" becomes one key on the typewriter, our problems are used to prepare a grave for the whole movement. Clearly, the myth that advertisers go where the readers are—thus, if we had readers, we would have advertisers—is deeply embedded. Even industry reporters rarely mention the editorial demands made by ads for women's products, and if they do, they assume advertisers must be right and *Ms.* must be wrong; we must be too controversial, outrageous, even scatalogical to support. In fact, there's nothing in our pages that couldn't be published in *Time, Esquire,* or *Rolling Stone*—

providing those magazines devoted major space to women — but the media myth often wins out. Though comparable magazines our size (say, *Vanity Fair* or the *Atlantic*) are losing more money in a single year than *Ms.* has lost in sixteen years, *Ms.* is held to a different standard. No matter how much never-to-be-recovered cash is poured into starting a magazine or keeping it going, appearances seem to be all that matter. (Which is why we haven't been able to explain our fragile state in public. Nothing causes ad flight like the smell of nonsuccess.)

My healthy response is anger, but my not-so-healthy one is depression, worry, and an obsession with finding one more rescue. There is hardly a night when I don't wake up with sweaty palms and pounding heart, scared that we won't be able to pay the printer or the post office; scared most of all that closing our doors will be blamed on a lack of readers and thus the movement, instead of the real cause. ("Feminism couldn't even support one magazine," I can hear them saying.)

We're all being flattened by a velvet steamroller. The only difference is that at *Ms.,* we keep standing up again.

Do you think, as I once did, that advertisers make decisions based on rational and uniform criteria? Well, think again. There is clearly a double standard. The same food companies that insist on recipes in women's magazines place ads in *People* where there are no recipes. Cosmetics companies support *The New Yorker,* which has no regular beauty columns, and newspaper pages that have no "beauty atmosphere."

Meanwhile, advertisers' control over the editorial content of women's magazines has become so institutionalized that it is sometimes written into "insertion orders" or dictated to ad salespeople as official policy — whether by the agency, the client, or both. The following are orders given to women's magazines effective in 1990. Try to imagine them being applied to *Time* or *Newsweek*.

65

• Dow's Cleaning Products stipulated that ads for its Vivid and Spray 'n Wash products should be adjacent to "children or fashion editorial"; ads for Bathroom Cleaner should be next to "home furnishing/family" features; with similar requirements for other brands. "If a magazine fails for ½ the brands or more," the Dow order warned, "it will be omitted from further consideration."

• Bristol-Myers, the parent of Clairol, Windex, Drano, Bufferin, and much more, stipulated that ads be placed next to "a full page of compatible editorial."

• S. C. Johnson & Son, makers of Johnson Wax, lawn and laundry products, insect sprays, hair sprays, and so on, insisted that its ads *"should not be opposite extremely controversial features or material antithetical to the nature/ copy of the advertised product."* (Italics theirs.)

• Maidenform, manufacturer of bras and other women's apparel, left a blank for the particular product and stated in its instructions: "The creative concept of the _____ campaign, and the very nature of the product itself appeal to the positive emotions of the reader/consumer. Therefore, it is imperative that all editorial adjacencies reflect that same positive tone. The editorial must not be negative in content or lend itself contrary to the _____ product imagery/message (e.g., *editorial relating to illness, disillusionment, large size fashion, etc.*)." (Italics mine.)

• The De Beers diamond company, a big seller of engagement rings, pro-   70
hibited magazines from placing its ads with "adjacencies to hard news or anti-love/romance themed editorial." . . .

• Kraft/General Foods, a giant with many brands, sent this message with an Instant Pudding ad: "urgently request upbeat parent/child activity editorial, mandatory positioning requirements — opposite full page of positive editorial — right hand page essential for creative — minimum 6 page competitive separation (i.e., all sugar based or sugar free gelatins, puddings, mousses, creames [sic] and pie filling) — Do not back with clippable material. Avoid: controversial/negative topics and any narrow targeted subjects."

• An American Tobacco Company order for a Misty Slims ad noted that the U.S. government warning must be included, but also that there must be: "no adjacency to editorial relating to health, medicine, religion, or death."

• Lorillard's Newport cigarette ad came with similar instructions, plus: "Please be aware that the Nicotine Patch products are competitors. The minimum six page separation is required."

Quite apart from anything else, you can imagine the logistical nightmare this creates when putting a women's magazine together, but the greatest casualty is editorial freedom. Though the ratio of advertising to editorial pages in women's magazines is only about 5 percent more than in *Time* or *Newsweek,* that nothing-to-read feeling comes from all the supposedly editorial pages that are extensions of ads. To find out what we're really getting when we pay our money, I picked up a variety of women's magazines for February 1994, and counted the number of pages in each one (even including table of contents, letters to the editors, horoscopes, and the like) that were not ads and/or copy complementary to ads. Then I compared that number to the total pages. Out of 184 pages, *McCall's* had 49 that were nonad or ad-related. Of 202, *Elle* gave readers 48. *Seventeen* provided its young readers with only 51 nonad or ad-related pages out of 226. *Vogue* had 62 out of 292. *Mirabella* offered readers 45 pages out of a total of 158. *Good Housekeeping* came out on top, though only at about a third, with 60 out of 176 pages. *Martha Stewart Living* offered the least. Even counting her letter to readers, a page devoted to her personal calendar, and another one to a turnip, only seven out of 136 pages had no ads, products, or product mentions. . . .

Within the supposedly editorial text itself, praise for advertisers' products   75
has become so ritualized that fields like "beauty writing" have been invented. One of its practitioners explained to me seriously that "It's a difficult art. How many new adjectives can you find? How much greater can you make a

lipstick sound? The FDA restricts what companies can say on labels, but we create illusion. And ad agencies are on the phone all the time pushing you to get their product in. A lot of them keep the business based on how many editorial clippings they produce every month. The worst are products [whose manufacturers have] their own name involved. It's all ego."

Often, editorial becomes one giant ad. An issue of *Lear's* featured an elegant woman executive on the cover. On the contents page, we learn she is wearing Guerlain makeup and Samsara, a new fragrance by Guerlain. Inside, there just happen to be full-page ads for Samsara, plus a Guerlain antiwrinkle skin cream. In the article about the cover subject, we discover she is Guerlain's director of public relations and is responsible for launching, you guessed it, the new Samsara. . . .

When the *Columbia Journalism Review* cited this example in one of the few articles to include women's magazines in a critique of ad influence, Frances Lear, editor of *Lear's,* was quoted at first saying this was a mistake, and then shifting to the defense that "this kind of thing is done all the time."

She's right. Here's an example with a few more turns of the screw. Martha Stewart, *Family Circle*'s contributing editor, was also "lifestyle and entertaining consultant" for Kmart, the retail chain, which helped to underwrite the renovation of Stewart's country house, using Kmart products; *Family Circle* covered the process in three articles not marked as ads; Kmart bought $4 million worth of ad pages in *Family Circle,* including "advertorials" to introduce a line of Martha Stewart products to be distributed by Kmart; and finally, the "advertorials," which at least are marked and only *look* like editorial pages, were reproduced and distributed in Kmart stores, thus publicizing *Family Circle* (owned by the New York Times Company, which would be unlikely to do this kind of thing in its own news pages) to Kmart customers. This was so lucrative that Martha Stewart now has her own magazine, *Martha Stewart Living* (owned by Time Warner), complete with a television version. Both offer a happy world of cooking, entertaining, and decorating in which nothing critical or negative ever seems to happen.

I don't mean to be a spoilsport, but there are many articles we're very unlikely to get from that or any other women's magazine dependent on food ads. According to Senator Howard Metzenbaum of Ohio, more than half of the chickens we eat (from ConAgra, Tyson, Perdue, and other companies) are contaminated with dangerous bacteria; yet labels haven't yet begun to tell us to scrub the meat and everything it touches — which is our best chance of not getting sick. Nor are we likely to learn about the frequent working conditions of this mostly female work force, standing in water, cutting chickens apart with such repetitive speed that carpal tunnel syndrome is an occupational hazard. Then there's Dole Food, often cited as a company that keeps women in low-level jobs and a target of a lawsuit by Costa Rican workers who were sterilized by contact with pesticides used by Dole — even though Dole must have known these pesticides had been banned in the United States.

The consumerist reporting we're missing sometimes sounds familiar. Remember the *Ms.* episode with Clairol and the article about potential carcino- 80

Portfolio of Advertisements

READING THE SIGNS

Consider these questions as you analyze the advertisements on the following pages.

1. What image of the presumed reader of the advertisement for CBS MarketWatch.com is created by the ad's copy? Does this ad work for you? Why or why not?

2. Implicit in the Eclipse Gum ad is a humorous narrative. Describe in your own words what you think this narrative is. Be sure to interpret what the central figure holding a stick is supposed to represent. Why do you think the advertiser uses humor in this way?

3. Paying close attention to the appearance of the models in the Phoenix Wealth Management advertisement, write a semiotic analysis of the way that the ad plays on cultural stereotypes in its bid to attract clients.

4. Pat Schroeder is a former congressional representative from Colorado. As she poses for this advertisement for the Association of American Publishers, she is surrounded by a wealth of visual detail, including posters, books, a calendar, and other objects. Write a semiotic analysis describing what effect you think these visual images are intended to have on the ad's audience. Be sure to include in your interpretation an analysis of what these images say about Pat Schroeder and how they reinforce the ad's message: "Get caught reading."

5. How does Virgin Atlantic play on reverse expectations to promote its services?

6. Along with the information it conveys about the services it can provide its customers, what further message does American Express want its readers to receive from this ad?

Are you Obsessed?

☐ Do you multi-task in the shower?

☐ Do you have to know everything first, if not sooner?

☐ Do you check your e-mail, and voice mail while you read your snail mail?

☐ Is your microwave oven just "too darn slow?"

We understand this kind of obsession. The kind that means determined—relentless by nature—and just plain not giving up 'til you get what you want. We're obsessed too. About bringing you the hottest financial stories, market data in real-time, and the expert analysis you need to stay ahead of the market.

CBS Marketwatch. The tool to fuel your obsession.

CBS MarketWatch.com

YOUR EYE ON THE MARKET

www.cbsmarketwatch.com
GO. CBS Marketwatch on CompuServe

WHEN WE FIND BAD BREATH, WE KILL IT.

eclipse

LIGHTS OUT BAD BREATH.

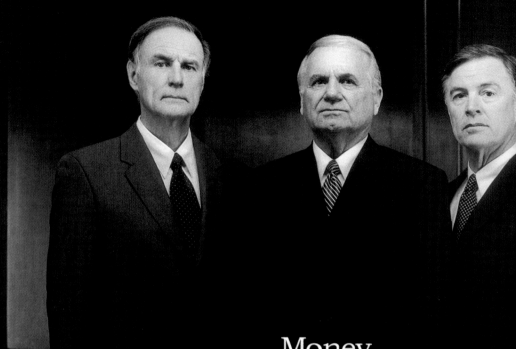

Money.

Investment Management provided by Phoenix Investment Partners through its subsidiaries. Insurance and Annuities issued by Phoenix Life Insurance Company (Statutory Office: East Greenbush, NY) and its insurance subsidiaries. Members of The Phoenix Companies, Inc. ©2000 The Phoenix Companies, Inc.

It's just not what it used to be.

Today the barriers to making it have fallen. Once and for all.

A new generation of entrepreneurs have already made an indelible mark on American business. But where do they go from here? Phoenix has been offering innovative new suggestions for 150 years. We understand that making money– and knowing what to do with it– are two different skills. It's one reason high-net-worth people turn to Phoenix for help. To learn more about how Phoenix could be helping you, contact your financial advisor or visit www.phoenixwm.com.

PHOENIX WEALTH MANAGEMENT℠

NOW YOU CAN TAKE CARE OF THE THREE S's RIGHT AT THE AIRPORT. Y'KNOW, SHOWER, SHAVE, AND SHOESHINE.

Our Upper Class Clubhouse takes care of everything from A to Z. Relax with a soothing massage or manicure. Escape to our private music room, or maybe even browse through our library. And those arriving at Heathrow have our Revivals Lounge for a shower or a bite to eat. As for that other "S" you were thinking of: Yes, you can still play on the Ski Machine in our Clubhouse.

Business Class to London
1-800-862-8621
virgin.com

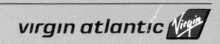

virgin atlantic *Virgin*

"I hand pick the buttons on my coats. I'm not about to leave my cash flow to just anybody."

Maria Barraza
Designer, Owner of Barraza New York
Small Business Services User

After 14 years as a designer, Maria Barraza invested her vision and savings in her own company. And while her focus on detail helps her designs endure, American Express Small Business Services helps make sure her cash flow endures. Her Card gives her maximum flexibility when traveling, a Quarterly Management Report tells her exactly what she spent, while she enjoys 10% savings on many FedEx® delivery services. All of which are always in style.

do more

AMERICAN EXPRESS

Small Business Services

Call 1-800-SUCCESS or visit www.americanexpress.com.

© 1998 American Express. Terms and conditions apply for credits.

gens in hair dye? Well, a similar saga took place with L'Oréal and *Mademoiselle* in 1992, according to an editor at Condé Nast. Now, editors there are supposed to warn publishers of any criticism in advance, a requirement that might well have a chilling effect.

Other penalties are increasing. As older readers will remember, women's magazines used to be a place where new young poets and short story writers could be published. Now, that's very rare. It isn't that advertisers of women's products dislike poetry or fiction, it's just that they pay to be adjacent to articles and features more directly compatible with their products.

Sometimes, advertisers invade editorial pages — literally — by plunging odd-shaped ads into the text, no matter how that increases the difficulty of reading. When Ellen Levine was editor of *Woman's Day,* for instance, a magazine originally founded by a supermarket chain, she admitted, "The day the copy had to rag around a chicken leg was not a happy one."

The question of ad positioning is also decided by important advertisers, a rule that's ignored at a magazine's peril. When Revlon wasn't given the place of the first beauty ad in one Hearst magazine, for instance, it pulled its ads from *all* Hearst magazines. In 1990 Ruth Whitney, editor in chief of *Glamour,* attributed some of this pushiness to "ad agencies wanting to prove to a client that they've squeezed the last drop of blood out of a magazine." She was also "sick and tired of hearing that women's magazines are controlled by cigarette ads." Relatively speaking, she was right. To be as controlling as most advertisers of women's products, tobacco companies would have to demand articles in flat-out praise of smoking, and editorial photos of models smoking a credited brand. As it is, they ask only to be forewarned so they don't advertise in the same issue with an article about the dangers of smoking. But for a magazine like *Essence,* the only national magazine for African American women, even taking them out of one issue may be financially difficult, because other advertisers might neglect its readers. In 1993, a group called Women and Girls Against Tobacco, funded by the California Department of Health Services, prepared an ad headlined "Cigarettes Made Them History." It pictured three black singers — Mary Wells, Eddie Kendricks, and Sarah Vaughan — who died of tobacco-related diseases. *Essence* president Clarence Smith didn't turn the ad down, but he didn't accept it either. When I talked with him in 1994, he said with pain, "the black female market just isn't considered at parity with the white female market; there are too many other categories we don't get." That's in spite of the fact that *Essence* does all the traditional food-fashion-beauty editorial expected by advertisers. According to California statistics, African American women are more addicted to smoking than the female population at large, with all the attendant health problems.

Alexandra Penney, editor of *Self* magazine, feels she has been able to include smoking facts in health articles by warning cigarette advertisers in advance (though smoking is still being advertised in this fitness magazine). On the other hand, up to this writing in 1994, no advertiser has been willing to appear opposite a single-page feature called "Outrage," which is reserved for important controversies, and is very popular with readers. Another women's

magazine publisher told me that to this day Campbell's Soup refuses to advertise because of an article that unfavorably compared the nutritional value of
canned food to that of fresh food — fifteen years ago.

I don't mean to imply that the editors I quote here share my objections to 85
ad demands and/or expectations. Many assume that the women's magazines
at which they work have to be the way they are. Others are justifiably proud
of getting an independent article in under the advertising radar, for instance,
articles on family violence in *Family Circle* or a series on child sexual abuse
and the family courts in *McCall's*. A few insist they would publish exactly the
same editorial, even if there were no ads. But it's also true that it's hard to be
honest while you're still in the job. "Most of the pressure came in the form of
direct product mentions," explained Sey Chassler, who was editor in chief of
Redbook from the sixties to the eighties and is now out of the game. "We got
threats from the big guys, the Revlons, blackmail threats. They wouldn't run
ads unless we credited them."

What could women's magazines be like if they were as editorially free as
good books? as realistic as the best newspaper articles? as creative as poetry
and films? as diverse as women's lives? What if we as women — who are psychic immigrants in a public world rarely constructed by or for us — had the
same kind of watchful, smart, supportive publications on our side that other
immigrant groups have often had?

We'll find out only if we take the media directed at us seriously. If readers
were to act in concert in large numbers for a few years to change the traditional practices of *all* women's magazines and the marketing of *all* women's
products, we could do it. After all, they depend on our consumer dollars —
money we now are more likely to control. If we include all the shopping we
do for families and spouses, women make 85 percent of purchases at point of
sale. You and I could:

- refuse to buy products whose ads have clearly dictated their surroundings, and write to tell the manufacturers why;

- write to editors and publishers (with copies to advertisers) to tell them
that we're willing to pay *more* for magazines with editorial independence,
but will *not* continue to pay for those that are editorial extensions of ads;

- write to advertisers (with copies to editors and publishers) to tell them
that we want fiction, political reporting, consumer reporting, strong opinion, humor, and health coverage that doesn't pull punches, praising them
when their ads support this, and criticizing them when they don't;

- put as much energy and protest into breaking advertising's control over
what's around it as we put into changing the images within it or protesting harmful products like cigarettes;

- support only those women's magazines and products that take us seriously as readers and consumers;

- investigate new laws and regulations to support freedom from advertising
influence. The Center for the Study of Commercialism, a group founded

in 1990 to educate and advocate against "ubiquitous product marketing," recommends whistle-blower laws that protect any members of the media who disclose advertiser and other commercial conflicts of interest, laws that require advertiser influence to be disclosed, Federal Trade Commission involvement, and denial of income tax exemptions for advertising that isn't clearly identified — as well as conferences, citizen watchdog groups, and a national clearinghouse where examples of private censorship can be reported.

Those of us in the magazine world can also use this carrot-and-stick technique. The stick: If magazines were a regulated medium like television, the editorial quid pro quo demanded by advertising would be against the rules of the FCC, and payola and extortion would be penalized. As it is, there are potential illegalities to pursue. For example: A magazine's postal rates are determined by the ratio of ad pages to editorial pages, with the ads being charged at a higher rate than the editorial. Counting up all the pages that are *really* ads could make an interesting legal action. There could be consumer fraud cases lurking in subscriptions that are solicited for a magazine but deliver a catalog.

The carrot is just as important. In twenty years, for instance, I've found no independent, nonproprietary research showing that an ad for, say, fragrance is any more effective placed next to an article about fragrance than it would be when placed next to a good piece of fiction or reporting. As we've seen, there are studies showing that the greatest factor in determining an ad's effectiveness is the credibility and independence of its surroundings. An airtight wall between ads and edit would also shield corporations and agencies from pressures from both ends of the political spectrum and from dozens of pressure groups. Editors would be the only ones responsible for editorial content — which is exactly as it should be.

Unfortunately, few agencies or clients hear such arguments. Editors often 90 maintain the artificial purity of refusing to talk to the people who actually control their lives. Instead, advertisers see salespeople who know little about editorial, are trained in business as usual, and are usually paid on commission. To take on special controversy editors might also band together. That happened once when all the major women's magazines did articles in the same month on the Equal Rights Amendment. It could happen again — and regularly.

Meanwhile, we seem to have a system in which everybody is losing. The reader loses diversity, strong opinion, honest information, access to the arts, and much more. The editor loses pride of work, independence, and freedom from worry about what brand names or other critical words some sincere freelancer is going to come up with. The advertiser loses credibility right along with the ad's surroundings, and gets more and more lost in a sea of similar ads and interchangeable media.

But that's also the good news. Because where there is mutual interest, there is the beginning of change.

If you need one more motive for making it, consider the impact of U.S. media on the rest of the world. The ad policies we tolerate here are invading the lives of women in other cultures — through both the content of U.S. media and the ad practices of multinational corporations imposed on other countries. Look at our women's magazines. Is this what we want to export?

Should *Ms.* have started out with no advertising in the first place? The odd thing is that, in retrospect, I think the struggle was worth it. For all those years, dozens of feminist organizers disguised as *Ms.* ad saleswomen took their courage, research, slide shows, humor, ingenuity, and fresh point of view into every advertising agency, client office, and lion's den in cities where advertising is sold. Not only were sixteen years of *Ms.* sustained in this way, with all the changeful words on those thousands of pages, but some of the advertising industry was affected in its imagery, its practices, and its understanding of the female half of the country. Those dozens of women themselves were affected, for they learned the art of changing a structure from both within and without, and are now rising in crucial publishing positions where women have never been. *Ms.* also helped to open nontraditional categories of ads for women's magazines, thus giving them a little more freedom — not to mention making their changes look reasonable by comparison.

But the world of advertising has a way of reminding us how far there 95 is to go.

Three years ago, as I was finishing this exposé in its first version, I got a call from a writer for *Elle*. She was doing an article on where women parted their hair: Why, she wanted to know, did I part mine in the middle?

It was all so familiar. I could imagine this writer trying to make something out of a nothing assignment. A long-suffering editor laboring to think of new ways to attract ads for shampoo, conditioner, hairdryers, and the like. Readers assuming that other women must want this stuff.

As I was working on this version, I got a letter from Revlon of the sort we disregarded when we took ads. Now, I could appreciate it as a reminder of how much we had to disregard:

> We are delighted to confirm that Lauren Hutton is now under contract to Revlon.
>
> We are very much in favor of her appearing in as much editorial as possible, but it's important that your publication avoid any mention of competitive color cosmetics, beauty treatment, hair care or sun care products in editorial or editorial credits in which she appears.
>
> We would be very appreciative if all concerned are made aware of this.

I could imagine the whole chain of women — Lauren Hutton, preferring to be in the Africa that is her passion; the ad executive who signed the letter, only doing her job; the millions of women readers who would see the resulting artificial images; all of us missing sources of information, insight, creativity, humor, anger, investigation, poetry, confession, outrage, learning, and perhaps most important, a sense of connection to each other; and a gloriously diverse world being flattened by a velvet steamroller.

I ask you: Can't we do better than this?   100

READING THE TEXT

1. What does Steinem mean by "complementary copy" (para. 17)?

2. Summarize the relationship that Steinem sees between editorial content and advertising in women's magazines.

3. According to Steinem, what messages about gender roles does complementary copy send readers of women's magazines?

READING THE SIGNS

1. Steinem asserts that virtually all content in women's magazines is a disguised form of advertising, by what it either says or doesn't say. Test her hypothesis by writing a detailed analysis of a single issue of a magazine such as *Cosmopolitan, Jane,* or *Elle.* Do you find instances of complementary copy? How do you react as a potential reader of such a magazine?

2. Explore whether Steinem's argument holds for men's magazines such as *Maxim* or *GQ.* If you identify differences, how might they be based on different assumptions about gender roles?

3. Have each member of the class bring in a favorite magazine. In small groups, study the relationship between ads and articles. Which magazines have the most complementary copy? How can you account for your findings?

4. Do advertisers infringe on the freedom of the press? Write a journal entry in which you explore this issue.

JAMES B. TWITCHELL

WHAT WE ARE TO ADVERTISERS

Are you a "believer" or a "striver," an "achiever" or a "struggler," an "experiencer" or a "maker"? Or do you have no idea what we're talking about? If you don't, James Twitchell (b. 1943) explains it all to you in this selection in which the psychological profiling schemes of American advertising are laid bare. For like it or not, advertisers have, or think they have, your number, and they will pitch their products according to the personality profile they have concocted for you. And the really spooky thing is that they're often right. A prolific writer on American advertising and culture, Twitchell's most recent books include Adcult USA: The Triumph of Advertising in American Culture *(1996),* Twenty Ads That Shook the World *(2000),* Living It Up: Our Love Affair with Luxury

(2002), and Lead Us Into Temptation: The Triumph of American Materialism *(1999), from which this selection is taken.*

Mass production means mass marketing, and mass marketing means the creation of mass stereotypes. Like objects on shelves, we too cluster in groups.
We find meaning together. As we mature, we move from shelf to shelf, from
aisle to aisle, zip code to zip code, from lifestyle to lifestyle, between what the
historian Daniel Boorstin calls "consumption communities." Finally, as full-
grown consumers, we stabilize in our buying, and hence meaning-making,
patterns. Advertisers soon lose interest in us not just because we stop buying
but because we have stopped changing brands.

The object of advertising is not just to brand parity objects but also to
brand consumers as they move through these various communities. To explain his job, Rosser Reeves, the master of hard-sell advertising like the old
Anacin ads, used to hold up two quarters and claim his job was to make you
believe they were different, and, more importantly, that one was better than
the other. Hence, at the macro level the task of advertising is to convince different sets of consumers — target groups — that the quarter they observe is
somehow different in meaning and value than the same quarter seen by their
across-the-tracks neighbors.

In adspeak, this is called *positioning.* "I could have positioned Dove as a
detergent bar for men with dirty hands," David Ogilvy famously said, "but I
chose to position it as a toilet bar for women with dry skin." Easy to say, hard
to do. But if Anheuser-Busch wants to maximize its sales, the soccer mom driving the shiny Chevy Suburban must feel she drinks a different Budweiser
than the roustabout in the rusted-out Chevy pickup.[1]

The study of audiences goes by any number of names: psychographics,
ethnographics, macrosegmentation, to name a few, but they are all based on
the ineluctable principle that birds of a feather flock together. The object of
much consumer research is not to try to twist their feathers so that they will
flock to your product, but to position your product in such a place that they

---

[1]Cigarette companies were the first to find this out in the 1930s, much to their amazement. Blindfolded smokers couldn't tell what brand they were smoking. Instead of making cigarettes with different tastes, it was easier to make different advertising claims to different audiences. Cigarettes are hardly unique. Ask beer drinkers why they prefer a particular brand
and invariably they tell you: "It's the taste," "This goes down well," "This is light and refresh-
ing," "This is rich and smooth." They will say this about a beer that has been described as
their brand, but is not. Anheuser-Busch, for instance, spent three dollars per barrel in 1980 to
market a barrel of beer; now they spend nine dollars. Since the cost to reach a thousand television households has doubled at the same time the audience has segmented (thanks to cable),
why not go after a particular market segment by tailoring ads emphasizing, in different degrees, the Clydesdales, Ed McMahon, Beechwood aging, the red and white can, dates certify-
ing freshness, the spotted dog, the Eagle, as well as "the crisp, clean taste." While you cannot
be all things to all people, the object of advertising is to be as many things to as many segments as possible. The ultimate object is to convince as many segments as possible that "This
Bud's for you" is a sincere statement.

will have to fly by it and perhaps stop to roost. After roosting, they will eventually think that this is a part of their flyway and return to it again and again.

Since different products have different meanings to different audiences, 5 segmentation studies are crucial. Although agencies have their own systems for naming these groups and their lifestyles, the current supplier of much raw data about them is a not-for-profit organization, the Stanford Research Institute (SRI).

The "psychographic" system of SRI is called acronomically VALS (now VALS2 +), short for Values and Lifestyle System. Essentially this schematic is based on the common-sense view that consumers are motivated "to acquire products, services, and experiences that provide satisfaction and give shape, substance, and character to their identities" in bundles. The more "resources" (namely money, but also health, self-confidence, and energy) each group has, the more likely they will buy "products, services, and experiences" of the group they associate with. But resources are not the only determinant. Customers are also motivated by such ineffables as principles, status, and action. When SRI describes these various audiences they peel apart like this (I have provided them an appropriate car to show their differences):

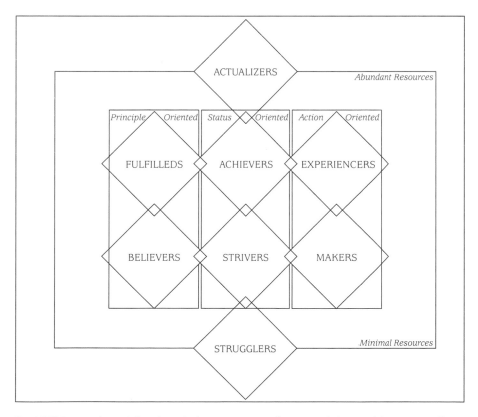

The VALS2 paradigm. Lifestyle styled: a taxonomy of taste and disposable income. (Stanford Research Institute)

- Actualizers: These people at the top of the pyramid are the ideal of every-one but advertisers. They have "it" already, or will soon. They are sophis-ticated, take-charge people interested in independence and character. They don't need new things; in fact, they already have their things. If not, they already know what "the finer things" are and won't be told. They don't need a new car, but if they do they'll read *Consumer Reports*. They do not need a hood ornament on their car.

- Fulfilled: Here are mature, satisfied, comfortable souls who support the sta-tus quo in almost every way. Often they are literally or figuratively retired. They value functionality, durability, and practicality. They drive something called a "town car," which is made by all the big three automakers.

- Believers: As the word expresses, these people support traditional codes of family, church, and community, wearing good Republican cloth coats. As consumers they are predictable, favoring American products and rec-ognizable brands. They regularly attend church and Wal-Mart, and they are transported there in their mid-range automobile like an Oldsmobile. Whether Oldsmobile likes it or not, they do indeed drive "your father's Oldsmobile."

Moving from principle-oriented consumers who look inside to status-driven consumers who look out to others, we find the Achievers and Strivers.

- Achievers: If consumerism has an ideal, here it is. Bingo! Wedded to job as a source of duty, reward, and prestige, these are the people who not only favor the establishment but *are* the establishment. They like the concept of prestige. Not only are they successful, they demonstrate their success by buying such objects as prestigious cars to show it. They like hood orna-ments. They see no contradiction in driving a Land Rover in Manhattan.

- Strivers: A young Striver is fine; he will possibly mature into an achiever. But an old Striver can be nasty; he may well be bitter. Since they are un-sure of themselves, they are eager to be branded as long as the brand is elevating. Money defines success and they don't have enough of it. Being a yuppie is fine as long as the prospect of upward mobility is possible. Strivers like foreign cars even if it means only leasing a BMW.

Again, moving to the right are those driven less by the outside world but by their desire to participate, to be part of a wider world.

- Experiencers: Here is life on the edge — enthusiastic, impulsive, and even reckless. Their energy finds expression in sports, social events, and "do-ing something." Politically and personally uncommitted, experiencers are an advertiser's dream come true as they see consumption as fulfillment and are willing to spend a high percent of their disposable income to at-tain it. When you wonder about who could possibly care how fast a car will accelerate from zero to sixty m.p.h., they care.

- Makers: Here is the practical side of Experiencers; they like to build things and they experience the world by working on it. Conservative, suspicious, respectful, they like to do things in and to their homes, like adding a room, canning vegetables, or changing the oil in their pickup trucks.

- Strugglers: Like Actualizers, these people are outside the pale of material-ism not by choice, but by low income. Strugglers are chronically poor. Their repertoire of things is limited not because they already have it all, but because they have so little. Although they clip coupons like Actualizers, theirs are from the newspaper. Their transportation is usually public, if any. They are the invisible millions.

As one might imagine, these are very fluid categories, and we may move through as many as three of them in our lifetimes. For instance, between ages 18–24 most people (61 percent) are Experiencers in desire or deed, while less than 1 percent are Fulfilled. Between ages 55 to 64, however, the Actualizers, Fulfilled, and Strugglers claim about 15 percent of the population each, while the Believers have settled out at about a fifth. The Achievers, Strivers, and Makers fill about 10 percent apiece, and the remaining 2 percent are Experiencers. The numbers can be broken down at every stage allowing for marital status, education, household size, dependent children, home ownership, household income, and occupation. More interesting still is the ability to accurately predict the appearance of certain goods in each grouping. SRI sells data on precisely who buys single-lens reflex cameras, who owns a laptop computer, who drinks herbal tea, who phones before five o'clock, who reads the *Reader's Digest,* and who watches *Beavis and Butthead.*

When one realizes the fabulous expense of communicating meaning for a product, the simple-mindedness of a system like VALS2+ becomes less risible. When you are spending millions of dollars for a few points of market share for your otherwise indistinguishable product, the idea that you might be able to attract the owners of socket wrenches by shifting ad content around just a bit makes sense. Once you realize that in taste tests consumers cannot tell one brand of cigarettes from another—including their own—nor distinguish such products as soap, gasoline, cola, beer, or what-have-you, it is clear that the product must be overlooked and the audience isolated and sold.

READING THE TEXT

1. What do marketers mean by *"positioning"* (para. 3), and why is it an important strategy to them?

2. What does the acronym VALS stand for, and what is the logic behind this system?

3. Why do marketers believe that the "product must be overlooked and the audience isolated and sold" (para. 9), according to Twitchell?

READING THE SIGNS

1. Consult the VALS2 network chart on page 207, and write a journal entry in which you place yourself on the chart. How neatly do you fit the VALS2 paradigm? What is your attitude toward being stereotyped by marketers?

2. In class, discuss whether the categories of consumers defined by the VALS2 para-
    digm are an accurate predictor of consumer behavior. Use the discussion as the
    basis of an essay in which you argue for against the proposition that stereotyping
    consumer lifestyles is an effective way of marketing goods and services.

3. Study the VALS2 paradigm in terms of the values it presumes. To what extent
    does it presume traditionally American values such as individualism? Use your
    analysis to formulate an argument about whether this marketing tool is an es-
    sentially American phenomenon.

4. Twitchell, Eric Schlosser ("Kid Kustomers," p. 181), and Malcolm Gladwell ("The
    Science of Shopping," p. 403) all describe marketing research strategies. Read
    the three selections, and write an argument that supports, opposes, or modifies
    the proposition that marketers have misappropriated academic research tech-
    niques for manipulative and therefore ethically questionable purposes.

JOHN E. CALFEE

How Advertising Informs to Our Benefit

*Most cultural analysts of advertising don't like it very much, to put it
mildly. George Orwell called it "the rattling of a stick inside a swill
bucket," but John E. Calfee (b. 1947) disagrees. In this article from Consumers' Research Magazine (1998), Calfee argues that advertising performs a valuable public service by providing us with useful information
that we might otherwise not receive. He cites, for example, the Kellogg's
All-Bran campaign that successfully broadcast the heretofore ignored
recommendation from the National Cancer Institute for people to eat
more fiber. Calfee's research interests include advertising, health care
policies, and pharmaceuticals; he is a resident scholar at the American
Enterprise Institute and is the author (with James K. Glassman) of* Fear
of Persuasion: A New Perspective on Advertising and Regulation
(1998) and of Prices, Markets, and the Pharmaceutical Revolution
(2000).

A great truth about advertising is that it is a tool for communicating information and shaping markets. It is one of the forces that compel sellers to cater to
the desires of consumers. Almost everyone knows this because consumers
use advertising every day, and they miss advertising when they cannot get it.
This fact does not keep politicians and opinion leaders from routinely dismissing the value of advertising. But the truth is that people find advertising
very useful indeed.

Of course, advertising primarily seeks to persuade and everyone knows
this, too. The typical ad tries to induce a consumer to do one particular thing —

usually, buy a product — instead of a thousand other things. There is nothing obscure about this purpose or what it means for buyers. Decades of data and centuries of intuition reveal that all consumers everywhere are deeply suspicious of what advertisers say and why they say it. This skepticism is in fact the driving force that makes advertising so effective. The persuasive purpose of advertising and the skepticism with which it is met are two sides of a single process. Persuasion and skepticism work in tandem so advertising can do its job in competitive markets. Hence, ads represent the seller's self-interest, consumers know this, and sellers know that consumers know it.

By understanding this process more fully, we can sort out much of the popular confusion surrounding advertising and how it benefits consumers.

How Useful Is Advertising?

Just how useful is the connection between advertising and information? At first blush, the process sounds rather limited. Volvo ads tell consumers that Volvos have side-impact air bags, people learn a little about the importance of air bags, and Volvo sells a few more cars. This seems to help hardly anyone except Volvo and its customers. But advertising does much more. It routinely provides immense amounts of information that benefits primarily parties other than the advertiser. This may sound odd, but it is a logical result of market forces and the nature of information itself.

The ability to use information to sell products is an incentive to create 5 new information through research. Whether the topic is nutrition, safety, or more mundane matters like how to measure amplifier power, the necessity of achieving credibility with consumers and critics requires much of this research to be placed in the public domain and that it rest upon some academic credentials. That kind of research typically produces results that apply to more than just the brands sold by the firm sponsoring the research. The lack of property rights to such "pure" information ensures that this extra information is available at no charge. Both consumers and competitors may borrow the new information for their own purposes.

Advertising also elicits additional information from other sources. Claims that are striking, original, forceful, or even merely obnoxious will generate news stories about the claims, the controversies they cause, the reactions of competitors (a price war? a splurge of comparison ads?), the reactions of consumers, and the remarks of governments and independent authorities. Probably the most concrete, pervasive, and persistent example of competitive advertising that works for the public good is price advertising. Its effect is invariably to heighten competition and reduce prices, even the prices of firms that assiduously avoid mentioning prices in their own advertising.

There is another area where the public benefits of advertising are less obvious but equally important. The unremitting nature of consumer interest in health, and the eagerness of sellers to cater to consumer desires, guarantee that advertising related to health will provide a storehouse of telling observations on the ways in which the benefits of advertising extend beyond the interests of advertisers to include the interests of the public at large.

A Cascade of Information

Here is probably the best documented example of why advertising is necessary for consumer welfare. In the 1970s, public health experts described compelling evidence that people who eat more fiber are less likely to get cancer, especially cancer of the colon, which happens to be the second leading cause of deaths from cancer in the United States. By 1979, the U.S. Surgeon General was recommending that people eat more fiber in order to prevent cancer. Consumers appeared to take little notice of these recommendations, however. The National Cancer Institute decided that more action was needed. NCI's cancer prevention division undertook to communicate the new information about fiber and cancer to the general public. Their goal was to change consumer diets and reduce the risk of cancer, but they had little hope of success given the tiny advertising budgets of federal agencies like NCI.

Their prospects unexpectedly brightened in 1984. NCI received a call from the Kellogg Corporation, whose All-Bran cereal held a commanding market share of the high-fiber segment. Kellogg proposed to use All-Bran advertising as a vehicle for NCI's public service messages. NCI thought that was an excellent idea. Soon, an agreement was reached in which NCI would review Kellogg's ads and labels for accuracy and value before Kellogg began running their fiber-cancer ads.

The new Kellogg All-Bran campaign opened in October 1984. A typical ad [10] began with the headline, "At last some news about cancer you can live with." The ad continued: "The National Cancer Institute believes a high fiber, low fat diet may reduce your risk of some kinds of cancer. The National Cancer Institute reports some very good health news. There is growing evidence that may link a high fiber, low fat diet to lower incidence of some kinds of cancer. That's why one of their strongest recommendations is to eat high-fiber foods. If you compare, you'll find Kellogg's All-Bran has nine grams of fiber per serving. No other cereal has more. So start your day with a bowl of Kellogg's All-Bran or mix it with your regular cereal."

The campaign quickly achieved two things. One was to create a regulatory crisis between two agencies. The Food and Drug Administration thought that if a food was advertised as a way to prevent cancer, it was being marketed as a drug. Then the FDA's regulations for drug labeling would kick in. The food would be reclassified as a drug and would be removed from the market until the seller either stopped making the health claims or put the product through the clinical testing necessary to obtain formal approval as a drug.

But food advertising is regulated by the Federal Trade Commission, not the FDA. The FTC thought Kellogg's ads were non-deceptive and were therefore perfectly legal. In fact, it thought the ads should be encouraged. The Director of the FTC's Bureau of Consumer Protection declared that "the [Kellogg] ad has presented important public health recommendations in an accurate, useful, and substantiated way. It informs the members of the public that there is a body of data suggesting certain relationships between cancer and diet that they may find important." The FTC won this political battle, and the ads continued.

The second instant effect of the All-Bran campaign was to unleash a flood of health claims. Vegetable oil manufacturers advertised that cholesterol was associated with coronary heart disease, and that vegetable oil does not contain cholesterol. Margarine ads did the same, and added that vitamin A is essential for good vision. Ads for calcium products (such as certain antacids) provided vivid demonstrations of the effects of osteoporosis (which weakens bones in old age), and recounted the advice of experts to increase dietary calcium as a way to prevent osteoporosis. Kellogg's competitors joined in citing the National Cancer Institute dietary recommendations.

Nor did things stop there. In the face of consumer demand for better and fuller information, health claims quickly evolved from a blunt tool to a surprisingly refined mechanism. Cereals were advertised as high in fiber and low in sugar or fat or sodium. Ads for an upscale brand of bread noted: "Well, most high-fiber bran cereals may be high in fiber, but often only one kind: insoluble. It's this kind of fiber that helps promote regularity. But there's also a kind of fiber known as soluble, which most high-fiber bran cereals have in very small amounts, if at all. Yet diets high in this kind of fiber may actually lower your serum cholesterol, a risk factor for some heart diseases." Cereal boxes became convenient sources for a summary of what made for a good diet.

Increased Independent Information

The ads also brought powerful secondary effects. These may have been even more useful than the information that actually appeared in the ads themselves. One effect was an increase in media coverage of diet and health. *Consumer Reports,* a venerable and hugely influential magazine that carries no advertising, revamped its reports on cereals to emphasize fiber and other ingredients (rather than testing the foods to see how well they did at providing a complete diet for laboratory rats). The health-claims phenomenon generated its own press coverage, with articles like "What Has All-Bran Wrought?" and "The Fiber Furor." These stories recounted the ads and the scientific information that prompted the ads; and articles on food and health proliferated. Anyone who lived through these years in the United States can probably remember the unending media attention to health claims and to diet and health generally.

Much of the information on diet and health was new. This was no coincidence. Firms were sponsoring research on their products in the hope of finding results that could provide a basis for persuasive advertising claims. Oat bran manufacturers, for example, funded research on the impact of -

soluble fiber on blood cholesterol. When the results came out "wrong," as they did in a 1990 study published with great fanfare in the *New England Journal of Medicine,* the headline in *Advertising Age* was "Oat Bran Popularity Hitting the Skids," and it did indeed tumble. The manufacturers kept at the research, however, and eventually the best research supported the efficacy of oat bran in reducing cholesterol (even to the satisfaction of the FDA). Thus did pure advertising claims spill over to benefit the information environment at large.

The shift to higher fiber cereals encompassed brands that had never undertaken the effort necessary to construct believable ads about fiber and disease. Two consumer researchers at the FDA reviewed these data and concluded they were "consistent with the successful educational impact of the Kellogg diet and health campaign: consumers seemed to be making an apparently thoughtful discrimination between high- and low-fiber cereals," and that the increased market shares for high-fiber non-advertised products represented "the clearest evidence of a successful consumer education campaign."

Perhaps most dramatic were the changes in consumer awareness of diet and health. An FTC analysis of government surveys showed that when consumers were asked about how they could prevent cancer through their diet, the percentage who mentioned fiber increased from 4 percent before the 1979 Surgeon General's report to 8.5 percent in 1984 (after the report but before the All-Bran campaign) to 32 percent in 1986 after a year and a half or so of health claims (the figure in 1988 was 28 percent). By far the greatest increases in awareness were among women (who do most of the grocery shopping) and the less educated: up from 0 percent for women without a high school education in 1984 to 31 percent for the same group in 1986. For women with incomes of less than $15,000, the increase was from 6 percent to 28 percent.

The health-claims advertising phenomenon achieved what years of effort by government agencies had failed to achieve. With its mastery of the art of brevity, its ability to command attention, and its use of television, brand advertising touched precisely the people the public health community was most desperate to reach. The health claims expanded consumer information along a broad front. The benefits clearly extended far beyond the interests of the relatively few manufacturers who made vigorous use of health claims in advertising.

A Pervasive Phenomenon

Health claims for foods are only one example, however, of a pervasive phenomenon — the use of advertising to provide essential health information with benefits extending beyond the interests of the advertisers themselves. Advertising for soap and detergents, for example, once improved private hygiene and therefore, public health (hygiene being one of the underappreciated triumphs in twentieth century public health). Toothpaste advertising helped to do the same for teeth. When mass advertising for toothpaste and tooth powder began early in this century, tooth brushing was rare. It was common by [20] the 1930s, after which toothpaste sales leveled off even though the advertising, of course, continued. When fluoride toothpastes became available, advertising generated interest in better teeth and professional dental care. Later, a "plaque reduction war" (which first involved mouthwashes, and later toothpastes) brought a new awareness of gum disease and how to prevent it. The financial gains to the toothpaste industry were surely dwarfed by the benefits to consumers in the form of fewer cavities and fewer lost teeth.

Health claims induced changes in foods, in nonfoods such as toothpaste, in publications ranging from university health letters to mainstream newspapers and magazines, and of course, consumer knowledge of diet and health.

These rippling effects from health claims in ads demonstrated the most basic propositions in the economics of information. Useful information initially failed to reach people who needed it because information producers could not charge a price to cover the costs of creating and disseminating pure information. And this problem was alleviated by advertising, sometimes in a most vivid manner.

Other examples of spillover benefits from advertising are far more common than most people realize. Even the much-maligned promotion of expensive new drugs can bring profound health benefits to patients and families, far exceeding what is actually charged for the products themselves. The market processes that produce these benefits bear all the classic features of competitive advertising. We are not analyzing public service announcements here, but old-fashioned profit-seeking brand advertising. Sellers focused on the information that favored their own products. They advertised it in ways that provided a close link with their own brand. It was a purely competitive enterprise, and the benefits to consumers arose from the imperatives of the competitive process.

One might see all this as simply an extended example of the economics of information and greed. And indeed it is, if by greed one means the effort to earn a profit by providing what people are willing to pay for, even if what they want most is information rather than a tangible product. The point is that there is overwhelming evidence that unregulated economic forces dictate that much useful information will be provided by brand advertising, and only by brand advertising. Of course, there is much more to the story. There is the question of how competition does the good I have described without doing even more harm elsewhere. After all, firms want to tell people only what is good about their brands, and people often want to know what is wrong with the brands. It turns out that competition takes care of this problem, too.

Advertising and Context

It is often said that most advertising does not contain very much information. 25 In a way, this is true. Research on the contents of advertising typically finds just a few pieces of concrete information per ad. That's an average, of course. Some ads obviously contain a great deal of information. Still, a lot of ads are mainly images and pleasant talk, with little in the way of what most people would consider hard information. On the whole, information in advertising comes in tiny bits and pieces.

Cost is only one reason. To be sure, cramming more information into ads is expensive. But more to the point is the fact that advertising plays off the information available from outside sources. Hardly anything about advertising is more important than the interplay between what the ad contains and what surrounds it. Sometimes this interplay is a burden for the advertiser because it is beyond his control. But the interchange between advertising and environment is also an invaluable tool for sellers. Ads that work in collaboration with outside information can communicate far more than they ever could on their own.

The upshot is advertising's astonishing ability to communicate a great deal of information in a few words. Economy and vividness of expression almost always rely upon what is in the information environment. The famously concise "Think Small" and "Lemon" ads for the VW "Beetle" in the 1960s and 1970s were highly effective with buyers concerned about fuel economy, repair costs, and extravagant styling in American cars. This was a case where the less said, the better. The ads were more powerful when consumers were free to bring their own ideas about the issues to bear. The same process is repeated over again for all sorts of products. Ads for computer modems once explained what they could be used for. Now a simple reference to the Internet is sufficient to conjure an elaborate mix of equipment and applications. These matters are better left vague so each potential customer can bring to the ad his own idea of what the Internet is really for.

Leaning on information from other sources is also a way to enhance credibility, without which advertising must fail. Much of the most important information in advertising — think of cholesterol and heart disease, antilock brakes and automobile safety — acquires its force from highly credible sources other than the advertiser. To build up this kind of credibility through material actually contained in ads would be cumbersome and inefficient. Far more effective, and far more economical, is the technique of making challenges, raising questions and otherwise making it perfectly clear to the audience that the seller invites comparisons and welcomes the tough questions. Hence the classic slogan, "If you can find a better whiskey, buy it."

Finally, there is the most important point of all. Informational sparseness facilitates competition. It is easier to challenge a competitor through pungent slogans — "Where's the beef?" "Where's the big saving?" — than through a step-by-step recapitulation of what has gone on before. The bits-and-pieces approach makes for quick, unerring attacks and equally quick responses, all under the watchful eye of the consumer over whom the battle is being fought. This is an ideal recipe for competition.

READING THE TEXT

1. Describe in your own words the benefits of advertising according to Calfee.
2. Summarize the history of Kellogg's advertising campaign for All-Bran. What does Calfee see as the significance of this ad campaign?

3. How does Calfee defend the fact that, in his own words, "information in advertising comes in tiny bits and pieces" (para. 25)?

4. According to Calfee, how do competitive market forces help ensure that information in advertising benefits the consumer?

READING THE SIGNS

1. In class, form teams, and debate Calfee's proposition that "Advertising Informs to Our Benefit." To prepare, collect and analyze advertisements that support your team's position.

2. While Calfee focuses on the advertising of health and nutrition products, he implies that all advertising can be beneficial to consumers. Write an essay supporting, refuting, or complicating Calfee's claim that advertising is an efficient medium for transmitting accurate information.

3. Study health- and diet-related ads, which abound in publications such as *Better Homes and Gardens* or *Shape*. Use them as the evidence in an essay that demonstrates, refutes, or modifies Calfee's claim that ads serve the "interests of the public at large" (para. 7).

4. Research the history of cigarette advertising in twentieth-century America. Use your findings as the basis of an argumentative essay on whether the tobacco industry has been a source of beneficial information to consumers.

5. In your journal, reflect on Calfee's claim that consumers "miss advertising when they cannot get it" (para. 1).

KALLE LASN

HYPE

When you hear the Oscar Meyer wiener song when trying instead to remember the opening chords to Beethoven's Ninth Symphony, you know that advertising has been seriously messing with your mind. Or so Kalle Lasn believes, and in this selection from Culture Jam: The Uncooling of America *(1999), Lasn strikes back at the flood of hype that constitutes "the most prevalent and toxic of the mental pollutants." But alas, Lasn concludes, there is no escape, and even he feels that he too has "nowhere to run" in the face of a world that is supersaturated with advertising. A market researcher turned film producer, Lasn is founder and editor of* Adbursts *magazine, the Media Foundation, and the Culture Jammers Network, all projects dedicated to exposing the media's grip on our daily lives.*

Advertisements are the most prevalent and toxic of the mental pollutants. From the moment your radio alarm sounds in the morning to the wee hours of latenight TV, microjolts of commercial pollution flood into your brain at the rate of about three thousand marketing messages per day.[1] Every day, an estimated 12 billion display ads, 3 million radio commercials, and more than 200,000 TV commercials are dumped into North America's collective unconscious.

Corporate advertising (or is it the commercial media?) is the largest single psychological project ever undertaken by the human race. Yet for all of that, its impact on us remains unknown and largely ignored. When I think of the media's influence over years, over decades, I think of those brainwashing experiments conducted by Dr. Ewen Cameron[2] in a Montreal psychiatric hospital in the 1950s. The idea of the CIA-sponsored "depatterning" experiments was to outfit conscious, unconscious, or semiconscious subjects with headphones, and flood their brains with thousands of repetitive "driving" messages that would alter their behavior over time. Sound familiar? Advertising aims to do the same thing. Dr. Cameron's guinea pigs emerged from the Montreal trials with serious psychological damage. It was a great scandal. But no one is saying boo about the ongoing experiment of mass media advertising. In fact, new guinea pigs voluntarily come on board every day.

The proliferation of commercial messages has happened so steadily and relentlessly that we haven't quite woken up to the absurdity of it all. No longer are ads confined to the usual places: buses, billboards, stadiums. Anywhere your eyes can possibly come to rest is now a place that, in corporate America's view, can and ought to be filled with a logo or product message.

You reach down to pull your golf ball out of the hole and there, at the bottom of the cup, is an ad for a brokerage firm. You fill your car with gas, there's an ad on the nozzle. You wait for your bank machine to spit out money and an ad pushing GICs scrolls by in the little window. You drive through the heartland and the view of the wheatfields is broken at intervals by enormous billboards. Your kids watch Pepsi and Snickers ads in the classroom. (The school has made the devil's bargain of accepting free audiovisual equipment in exchange for airing these ads on "Channel One.") You think you've seen it all, but you haven't. An Atlanta-based marketing firm announces plans to send an inflatable billboard filled with corporate logos into geostationary orbit viewable every night like a second moon. British sprinter Linford Christie appears at a press conference with little panthers replacing the pupils of his eyes, where his sponsor's logo has been imprinted on specially made contact lenses. New York software engineers demonstrate a program that turns your cursor into a corporate icon whenever you visit a commercial site. A Japanese schoolboy becomes a neon sign during

---

[1]Mark Landler, Walecia Konrad, Zachary Schiller, and Lois Therrien, "What Happened to Advertising?" *Business Week,* September 23, 1991, page 66. Leslie Savan in *The Sponsored Life* (Temple University Press, 1994), page 1, estimated that "16,000 ads flicker across an individual's consciousness daily." I did an informal survey in March 1995 and found the number to be closer to 1,500 (this included all marketing messages, corporate images, logos, ads, brand names, on TV, radio, billboards, buildings, signs, clothing, appliances, in cyberspace, etc., over a typical twenty-four-hour period in my life).

[2]Bruce Grierson, "Soul Shock," *Adbusters,* Winter 1998, page 18.

his daily two-hour subway commute by wearing a battery-powered vest promoting an electronics giant. Administrators in a Texas school district announce plans to boost revenues by selling ad space on the roofs of the district's seventeen schools — arresting the attention of the fifty-eight million commercial jet passengers who fly into Dallas each year. Kids tattoo their calves with swooshes. Other kids, at raves, begin wearing actual bar codes that other kids can scan, revealing messages such as "I'd like to sleep with you." A boy named David Bentley in Sydney, Australia, literally rents his head to corporate clients, shaving a new ad into his hair every few weeks. ("I know for sure that at least two thousand teenagers at my high school will read my head every day to see what it says," says the young entrepreneur. "I just wish I had a bigger head.") You pick up a banana in the supermarket and there, on a little sticker, is an ad for the new summer blockbuster at the multiplex. ("It's interactive because you have to peel them off," says one ad executive of this new delivery system. "And people look at ten pieces of fruit before they pick one, so we get multiple impressions.") Boy Scouts in the U.K. sell corporate ad space on their merit badges. An Australian radio station dyes its logo on two million eggs. IBM beams its logo onto clouds above San Francisco with a scanning electron microscope and a laser — the millennial equivalent of Commissioner Gordon summoning Batman to the Batcave. (The image is visible from ten miles away.) Bestfoods unveils plans to stamp its Skippy brand of peanut butter onto the crisp tabula rasa of a New Jersey beach each morning at low tide, where it will push peanut butter for a few hours before being washed away by the waves. (The company is widely commended for its environmental responsibility.) Coca-Cola strikes a six-month deal with the Australian postal service for the right to cancel stamps with a Coke ad. A company called VideoCarte installs interactive screens on supermarket carts so that you can see ads while you shop. (A company executive calls the little monitors "the most powerful micromarketing medium available today.")

A few years ago, marketers began installing ad boards in men's washrooms on college campuses, at eye level above the urinals. From their perspective, it was a brilliant coup: Where else is a guy going to look? But when I first heard this was being done, I was incensed. One of the last private acts was being co-opted. "What's been the reaction on campus?" I asked the reporter who told me the story. "Not much reaction," he said. It became apparent, as these ad boards began springing up in bars and restaurants, and just about anywhere men stand to pee, that not only did guys not share my outrage, they actually welcomed a little diversion while nature took its course. 5

This flood of psycho-effluent is spreading all around us, and we love every minute of it. The adspeak means nothing. It means worse than nothing. It is "anti-language"[3] that, whenever it runs into truth and meaning, annihilates it.

There is nowhere to run. No one is exempt and no one will be spared. In the silent moments of my life, I often used to hear the opening movement of

---

[3]"Anti-language," a coinage of social critic George Steiner, was invoked in this context by Jonathon Dee in "But Is It Advertising?" *Harper's,* January 1999, page 66.

Beethoven's Ninth Symphony play in my head. Now I hear that kid singing the Oscar Meyer wiener song.

READING THE TEXT

1. Why does Lasn compare advertising with brainwashing, and what evidence does he advance to support this comparison?

2. What is the effect of Lasn's use of the second-person ("you") address?

3. How do most people's reactions to saturation advertising differ from Lasn's?

4. What tone does Lasn adopt here, and how does the tone affect your response to Lasn's claims?

READING THE SIGNS

1. Conduct a survey of your college campus, and write a report on the ways in which advertisers make their products known on campus. Use your observations as the basis of an argument about whether your school should place restrictions on the number and kind of ads for commercial products that appear on campus.

2. Write an essay supporting, refuting, or complicating Lasn's claim that "advertisements are the most prevalent and toxic of the mental pollutants" (para. 1).

3. Read Vance Packard's *The Hidden Persuaders* (1957), and compare and contrast his view of American advertising with that of Lasn.

4. Spend one day in which you keep an observation log that records all the different places you see advertisements, from clothing logos to license plate frames. Bring your log to class, and compare your results with those of your classmates. What are the implications of your observations? Do they support Lasn's contention in paragraph 7 that "there is nowhere to run"?

Calvin and Hobbes
by WATTERSON

LET'S HURRY DOWN THIS HILL AND GO HOME.

WHAT'S THE RUSH?

THERE'S A TV SHOW ON SLEDDING I WANT TO WATCH.

IN MY OPINION, TELEVISION VALIDATES EXISTENCE.

TAKE THIS SLED RIDE, FOR INSTANCE. THE EXPERIENCE IS FLEETING AND ELUSIVE. BY TOMORROW, WE'LL HAVE FORGOTTEN IT, AND IT MAY AS WELL HAVE NOT EVEN HAPPENED.

BUT IF WE WERE ON TV NOW COUNTLESS VIEWERS WOULD SHARE IN THE EVENT AND CONFIRM IT! THIS RIDE WOULD BECOME A PART OF MASS CONSCIOUSNESS!

AND ON TV, THE IMPACT OF AN EVENT IS DETERMINED BY THE IMAGE, NOT ITS SUBSTANCE.

SO WITH SOME STRONG VISUALS, OUR SLED RIDE COULD CONCEIVABLY MAKE US CULTURAL **ICONS**!

INSTEAD OF BEING BORING OL' CALVIN AND HOBBES, WE'D BE "CALVIN AND HOBBES - *AS SEEN ON TV*"! WOULDN'T THAT BE GREAT? DON'T YOU WISH WE WERE ON TV?

AT THIS MOMENT, I LIKE MY ANONYMITY.

I THINK WE SHOULD GO FOR THE HIGH-BROW PUBLIC TV AUDIENCE, DON'T YOU?

VIDEO DREAMS

Television, Music, and Cultural Forms

Even before the advent of cultural studies, writing about television was a common assignment in American classrooms, so this chapter's topic might be quite familiar to you. Indeed, in high school you may have been asked to write about a favorite TV program or music video, perhaps in a summary writing exercise, a descriptive essay, or an opinion piece on why such-and-such a program is your favorite show, or why you don't like another show. But in college you will be asked to write critical interpretations of television, which is somewhat different from expressing an opinion about how entertaining something is. In interpreting TV, you still need to rely on your skills in description and summary, because you need to describe the show for your reader, but your purpose will be to go beyond these writing tasks towards the construction of interpretive arguments about the cultural significance of your topic.

Interpreting the Televising of America

Television offers an especially rich field of possible writing topics, ranging from a historical analysis of a whole category of TV programming (such as the Western or detective show) to an interpretation of a single episode or video. Some topics, especially if you choose a historical approach, will require research. Let's say, for example, that you want to analyze the roles of women in situation comedies over the years. Comparing the women in *I Love Lucy, Father Knows Best, The Mary Tyler Moore Show, Murphy Brown, Roseanne,* and *Gilmore Girls* will reveal a great deal about the cultural contexts in which those programs appeared and so enable you to construct a thesis about American gender roles over the past fifty years. Such an analysis lends itself particularly well to the semiotic method of establishing a system of related, or associated, signs, and then noting the differences that distinguish your subject. All of the shows from *I Love Lucy* to *Gilmore Girls,* for example, feature funny female leads, but their characters are presented in very different ways. By analyzing those differences and situating each show within its cultural context, you can discover how the cultural perspective on women's roles in society has changed dramatically over the years. Indeed, such shows are particularly striking cultural barometers in this respect.

The interpretation of a single television episode is a lot like interpreting a short story. It is important to consider every potentially significant detail in the episode and subject it to a close reading. As with all semiotic analyses, your first step when preparing to write an analysis of a TV program is to suspend your aesthetic opinions of the show — that is, whether you like it or not. What you are working toward is a critical analysis, what you think a program's underlying cultural significance may be. This process also differs from describing what you think the show's *explicit* message is. Many programs have clearly presented messages, but what you are looking for is the message beyond the message, so to speak, the implicit signals the show is sending — as, for example, the contradiction that emerges when you consider that, while on the surface *Ally McBeal* was the saga of a Harvard-educated lawyer, its heroine was presented as a miniskirted, near-anorexic fashion plate obsessed with babies and romance.

At the same time, you want to situate your episode within an overall television system, first comparing the series your show comes from to other TV series, noting their similarities and differences. If you are analyzing an episode of *Dawson's Creek,* for example, you should associate it with other teen coming-of-age dramas like *Felicity* that were part of the WB network's campaign to attract teen viewers and differentiate it from such other youth-addressed programs as *Roswell, Smallville,* and

---

Discussing the Signs of Television

In class, choose a current television program, and have the entire class watch one episode (either watch the episode as "homework" or ask someone to tape it and then watch it in class). Interpret the episode semiotically. What values and cultural myths does the show project? What do the commercials broadcast during the show say about the presumed audience for it? Go beyond the episode's surface appeal or "message" to look at the particular images it uses to tell its story, always asking, "What is this program *really* saying?"

Buffy the Vampire Slayer, which, while also featuring young and impossibly good-looking protagonists, are dramatically different. If the protagonists on, say, *Dawson's Creek,* play to the desires of their audiences to see their own lives and loves represented on TV, the alien-superheroes of *Roswell* and other such shows reveal different desires. Indeed, their viewers are invited to identify with supernaturally empowered teens and post-teens who are both like everyone else and yet quite different, possibly signifying a fantasy on the part of their teenaged audiences that, while no one may realize it, they too are different from everyone around them in the conformist world of adolescence, as well as playing to a desire to be special in a mass culture in which it is hard to stand out.

Whatever show you choose to analyze, remember why it is on TV in the first place: Television, whether network or cable, is there to make money. It is a major part of our consumer culture, and most of what appears on TV is there because advertisers who want to reach their intended markets sponsor it. The shows that command the highest share of viewers accordingly command the highest advertising rates, and so producers are keen to have their viewers emotionally connect with their shows, which usually involves satisfying viewer fantasies. This is especially striking in teen-address TV shows that feature fashion-model glamorous actors and actresses (often in their twenties) playing adolescents in the awkward years, but it is also true for adult-address shows, which invite their viewers to identify with high-status professionals like doctors (*ER*) and lawyers (*The Practice*). Identifying with the characters on their favorite shows, viewers, or so television sponsors hope, will identify with the products they see associated with them. And buy them.

This is why one of the most revealing features in a TV episode analysis involves the advertising that accompanies the show. Be sure to catalog that advertising to see what it says about the program's intended audience. Why, for example, is the nightly news so often sponsored by over-the-counter pain killers? Why is daytime TV, especially in the morning, so often accompanied by cheesy ads for vocational training purveyors? Why are youth-oriented prime-time shows filled with fast-food commercials, while family programs like *Everyone Loves Raymond* have a lot of car ads?

Your analysis of a single episode of a television program can also usefully include a survey of where it fits within what cultural studies pioneer Raymond Williams called the "flow" of an evening's TV schedule. Flow refers to the sequence of TV programs and advertisements, from, say, the five o'clock news, through the pre-prime time 7:00 to 8:00 slot, through prime time and on through to the 11:00 news and the late-night talk shows. What precedes your program? What follows? Can you determine the strategy behind your show's scheduling?

Reality Bites

In earlier editions of *Signs of Life in the U.S.A.,* we presented an analysis of *Friends* to show how, at least in its early years, it reflected a Gen X ethos in which personal relationships were to be preferred to economic achievement in a McJobs era that seemed to offer few opportunities for financial success in the recession-plagued early 1990s. Twenty-something viewers who had good reason to be worried about their economic prospects in a downsized, restructured America could watch themselves dramatized in *Friends* as happy, emotionally well-connected comrades whose strong bonding appeared as a potent compensation for the prosperity that was denied them.

While at this writing *Friends,* somewhat to our surprise, is still near the top of the Nielsen ratings, it has changed as American culture has changed. The protagonists generally have better jobs, reflecting more prosperous times overall, and their relationships are edgier than they used to be, which in turn reflects a post-Gen X ethos in which edgy humor, especially involving sex, has replaced the mellower romanticism of the pop culture era that also launched *Singles* and *Melrose Place.*

This edginess, in which competitiveness and hostility seem to replace comradeship in much of pop culture (just consider the popularity of performers like Eminem), was dramatically reflected in the explosive rise of a new kind of television programming that for a while seemed to be on the verge of supplanting every other television genre: reality TV. With its relatively low production costs and lack of superstar salary demands to contend with (the stars of *Friends* eventually pulled in three quarters of a million dollars per episode), reality TV was a producer's dream come true, and advertisers loved it (indeed, *Survivor: Outback* became a sort of extended commercial for Mountain Dew).

By the fall of 2001, accordingly, well over a dozen reality programs were scheduled for broadcast. Some of them, like *Survivor: Africa,* were extensions of existing hits, while others, like *The Amazing Race,* were new. Many featured adventure themes, while others focused on greed (*Who Wants to Marry a Multi-Millionaire?*) or lust (*Temptation Island 2*). Several shows, like *The Mole,* went under, however, when actual reality, so to speak, struck back in the wake of the 9/11 terror attacks. Indeed, September 2001 seemed to mark a turning point in the genre as TV viewers began to prefer the gripping realities of the nightly news to the simulated situations of so-called reality programming.

Still, while the tide has apparently turned against reality television, its explosive emergence into American popular culture demands interpretation. Why were so many Americans drawn to such shows? What fantasies and desires did they (and do they) cater to? What do they say about their viewers?

As with any semiotic analysis, a little history is helpful here. One might say that reality television began with Alan Funt's *Candid Camera,* which featured the filming of real people (who didn't know that they were on camera, unlike today's reality contestants) as they reacted to annoying or surprising situations concocted by the show's creators. The show's attraction lay in the humor viewers could enjoy in watching other people get into minor jams. There is a name for this kind of humor that comes from psychoanalytic theory: *schadenfreude,* or taking pleasure in the misfortunes of others. As we shall

Survivor.

see, this early appeal from the history of reality TV is very much a part of the current popularity of the genre.

After *Candid Camera* came the 1970s PBS series *An American Family*. In this program a camera crew moved in with a suburban family named the Louds and filmed them in their day-to-day lives. The Louds were not contestants and there were no prizes to be won. The program was conceived as an experiment to see if it was possible for television to be authentically realistic. The experiment was a bit of a failure, however, as the Loud family members began to act out for the camera. The result was the eventual dissolution of the Louds as a family unit and a general sense of unease about such experiments. There were no sequels. (Though MTV's 2002 hit *The Osbournes* reintroduced the concept in a celebrity format.)

The next, and probably most crucial step, was when MTV launched its *Real World* series in 1992. More like a "real world" anticipation of *Friends* than like its reality predecessors, *Real World* was at once realistic, with its constant camera recording of the actions of a group of people living together in the same house, and a fantasy, insofar as the noncontestant protagonists could offer their viewers the vicarious experience of becoming instant TV stars. That the protagonists of *Real World* are also young and attractive is another part of the show's vicarious fantasy, which enables its viewers to imagine themselves as having the opportunity to live for a while under unusually glamorous and romantic conditions. The fact that, at least in principle, the "characters" on the show are selected from "ordinary" life is a key part of this appeal.

Which takes us to the dawn of the reality revolution. The astounding success of the first versions of *Who Wants to Marry a Multi-Millionaire?* and *Survivor* constituted reality TV's coming of age. In both programs we can see strong traces of what made their pioneering predecessors popular, especially *Real World.* But through their introduction of a game show element into the genre, complete with contestants competing for huge cash prizes, a whole new dimension was added that ultimately differentiates the new reality shows from those of the past and helps establish their significance.

The game show elements of programs like *Who Wants to Marry a Multi-Millionaire?* are obvious enough, and so part of their appeal is just that of the game show: the vicarious chance to imagine oneself as being in the shoes of the contestants (after all, anyone in principle can get on a game show) and winning lots of money. There is also an element of schadenfreude here if one takes pleasure in watching the losers in game show competitions. But by adding the real-life element of actual marriage to the mix, *Who Wants to Marry a Multi-Millionaire?* brought a whole new dimension of humiliation to the genre. It's one thing to be caught on camera during the emotional upheaval of competing for large cash prizes; it's another to be seen competing erotically but losing. The humiliation of not being chosen on the basis of one's erotic power is all the more extreme.

If you don't think that the opportunity to watch other people being sexually humiliated isn't a part of the edgy appeal of *Who Wants to Marry a Multi-Millionaire?,* just consider how soon *Temptation Island,* a show that makes the sexual humiliation of its protagonists the main attraction, was put on the air after *Millionaire?* became a bigger hit than anyone had dreamed of. Here voyeurism meets schadenfreude, and though TV was getting uncomfortably close to violating basic social taboos in broadcasting such fare, the profits to be had overcame any scruples about the matter. *Temptation Island* led to *Temptation Island 2*.

Survivor, for its part, combined a game show element with an action-adventure theme that invited viewers to imagine themselves in exciting outdoor situations that were exaggerated versions of the sort of adventure-safari vacations that had become very popular in the 1990s. With people spending seventy-five thousand dollars and upward to be guided to the top of Mount Everest, a show like *Survivor* was very much a reflection of the fantasies of its viewers. Indeed, *Survivor* presented the ultimate fantasy of enjoying an extreme vacation while becoming a television star overnight as contestants reemerged in civilization on the talk-show circuit and in milk commercials.

Like *Who Wants to Marry a Multi-Millionaire?* and *Temptation Island, Sur-*

vivor also included both voyeurism and schadenfreude in its formula for success, as viewers could watch the weekly humiliation of contestants struggling to stay in the game. But *Survivor* added another dimension to the mix by inviting viewers to identify with some contestants and to despise others (though the creators of the show deny this, there is evidence that contestants are directed to play out specified roles). One need only look at the weekly Internet commentary to see just how much viewers grow to hate the ordinary folk on *Survivor.* The experience of watching them be voted off the show thus brings in a dimension of sadism as viewers take pleasure in the disappointments of the contestants they despise (indeed, some reality programs, like Holland's *Big Brother,* took this element a step further by allowing viewers to participate in voting contestants off).

Finally, while game shows usually feature some competition among the contestants, the *Survivor* series took such competition to a new level in the way it compelled its contestants to engage in backstabbing conspiracies to claw their way towards a million-dollar payoff. It wasn't enough for tribe to compete against tribe; there had to be intratribal backbiting and betrayal as well. Such a subtext constituted a kind of grotesque parody of an American scene that featured cutthroat competition in the economic sphere and a striking lack of loyalty in the realm of romance, where divorce rates continued to soar and dating became an increasingly desperate game that pitted men and women against each other in a competition for sex rather than a search for life-long commitments.

Voyeurism. Schadenfreude. Sadism. Dog-eat-dog competitiveness. No wonder, popular as it was, reality TV made many people uncomfortable. For the creators of such shows seemed to appeal to some of the most primitive and socially disruptive of human instincts, violating taboos in the name of profits. Indeed, in the aftermath of an actual injury suffered by one of the *Survivor: Outback* contestants (he got burned by a fire), commentators wondered whether future installments would have to include the death of a contestant to satisfy their viewers' ever-greater desires for mayhem.

That danger was probably quashed as American TV viewers had the unprecedented, and horrendous, experience of watching real people jump to their deaths from the World Trade Center on September 11, 2001, and this reality check put a serious damper on reality TV. Perhaps the sense of national solidarity that the 9/11 attacks also occasioned may bring an end to the exploitation of such antisocial and alienating emotions as sadism and schadenfreude that reality TV stimulated. As we write these words, the Fall 2002 (and beyond) television seasons are still to come (though we can note that Spring 2002 offered a new series, *The American Embassy,* that looked like it was hustled on the air in the wake of the attacks). Watch the new shows carefully. Do they signify a return to community among Americans? Will they invite us to join each other rather than be entertained by competition and humiliation?

Altered States

We'll leave the answering of such questions to you. Our point is that whether you are considering a show like *Friends* or one like *Survivor,* or any other sort, you can find a cultural message behind the entertaining facade shown on the screen. The facade is the fantasy that distracts its viewers from the ways in which television programmers use their programs to achieve their primary ends — which are, in effect, to get us to go out and buy the products that sponsor the shows. That is why TV shows reflect the attitudes and desires of their core audiences and why interpreting TV reveals what those attitudes and desires are.

Interpreting television programming is especially valuable at a time when TV is blurring the line between fantasy and reality in an ever-more profound manner. Just think of the 1992 presidential election, when Dan Quayle made Murphy Brown a campaign issue because she chose to become a single mother. For months the fictional protagonist of the show, played by Candice Bergen, sparred with the real vice president over the rights of single mothers in a public battle whose most interesting significance was that everyone acted as if Murphy Brown was as real as Dan Quayle.

Such blurring of the line between fiction and reality (a process accelerated by the advent of docudrama-style shows like *America's Most Wanted* and skewered in a film like *Natural Born Killers*) reflects television's profound effect on the very way that we perceive our world. If television were to vanish today — no more shows, no more prime time — its effects would live on in the way it has altered our sense of reality. We expect instant visual access to every corner of the earth because of TV, and we want to get to the point quickly. It is often claimed that our attention spans have been shortened in a universe of televised sound bites, but at the same time our desire for information has been expanded (inquiring minds want to know). Indeed, the television age has equally been an information age.

In semiotic terms, the ubiquity of television and video in our lives represents a shift from one kind of sign system to another. As Marshall McLuhan pointed out almost forty years ago in *The Gutenberg Galaxy* (1962), Western culture since the fifteenth century has defined itself around the printed word — the linear text that in English reads from left to right and top to bottom. The printed word, in the terminology of the American founder of semiotics, Charles Sanders Peirce, is a *symbolic* sign, one whose meaning is entirely arbitrary or conventional. A symbolic sign means what it does because those who use it have decided so. Words don't look like what they mean. Their significance is entirely abstract.

Not so with a visual image like a photograph or TV picture, which does resemble its object and is not entirely arbitrary. Though a photograph is not literally the thing it depicts and often reflects a good deal of staging and manipulation by the photographer, we often respond to it as if it were an innocent reflection of the world. Peirce called such signs *icons,* referring by this term to any sign that resembles what it means. The way you interpret an icon, then, differs from the way you interpret a symbol or word. The interpretation of words involves your cognitive capabilities; the interpretation and reception of icons is far more sensuous, more a matter of vision than cognition. The shift from a civilization governed by the paradigm of the book to one dominated by television accordingly involves a shift in the way we "read" our world, as the symbolic field of the printed page yields to the iconic field of the video screen.

The shift from a symbolic, or word-centered, world to an iconic universe filled with visual images carries profound cultural implications. Such implications are not necessarily negative. The relative accessibility of video technology, for example, has created opportunities for personal expression that never existed before. It is very difficult to publish a book, but anyone can create a widely reproducible video simply by possessing a camcorder. The rapid transmissibility of video images speeds up communication and can bond groups of linguistically and culturally diverse people together, as MTV speaks to millions of people around the nation and world at once in the language of dance and music.

At the same time, video images may be used to stimulate political action. Rappers and their audiences, in particular, view rap and rap videos as subversions of the dominant society, just as baby boomers in the 1960s used rock-and-roll in challenging the "Establishment." Indeed, while many critics of TV deplore the passivity of its viewers, the medium is not inherently passive. Look at it this way: TV has a visceral power that print does not. Words abstractly describe things; television shows concrete images. The world pretty much ignored the famine in sub-Saharan Africa in the early 1980s, for example, until the TV cameras arrived to broadcast its images of starvation. Television, in short, bears the potential to awake the apathetic as written texts cannot.

But there is a price to pay for the new modes of perception that the iconic world of TV stimulates. For while one *can* read the signs of TV and video actively and creatively, and one can be moved to action by a video image, the sheer visibility of icons tempts one to receive them uncritically. Icons look so much like the realities they refer to that it is easy to forget that icons, too, are signs: Images that people construct that carry ideological meanings.

Just think of all those iconic images of the classic fifties-era sitcoms. *Leave It to Beaver, Father Knows Best, The Ozzie and Harriet Show,* and so on have established an American mythology of an idyllic era by the sheer persuasiveness of their images. In fact, the 1950s were not such idyllic years. Along with the McCarthyite hysteria of the cold war and the looming specter of nuclear war and contamination from open-air nuclear testing, there were economic downturns, the Korean War, and a growing sense that American life was becoming sterile, conformist, and materialistic — though it wasn't until the 1960s that this uneasiness broke into the open. Few fathers in the 1950s had the kind of leisure that the sitcom dads had, and the feminist resurgence in the late 1960s demonstrated that not all women were satisfied with the housewifely roles assigned them in every screenplay. And yet, those constructed images of white middle-class contentment and security have become so real in the American imagination that they can be called on in quite concrete ways. *Leave It to Beaver* doesn't simply show up in Trivial Pursuit games: The image of the show has become a potent political weapon. Conservative campaigners point to the classic sitcoms as exemplars of the "family values" that America is losing, but while family dysfunctionality rather than solidarity seems to be the focus of such contemporary sitcoms as *The Simpsons* and *Malcolm in the Middle,* there are still plenty of programs, like *Everyone Loves Raymond* and *The Bernie Mac Show,* in which the old values may still be found, albeit in a culturally updated form.

The Audience Is the Authority

One thing has changed in the relatively brief history of television: the emergence of cable TV. The proliferation of cable channels has fostered a more finely targeted programming schedule by which producers can focus on narrowly defined audiences, from nature lovers to home shoppers. This is referred to as niche marketing, and television today is far more divided into special niches than it was in the early days. For this reason today's Nielsen leaders, which have been designed to appeal to special niche markets, don't get nearly the numbers that 1960s hits like *The Beverly Hillbillies* enjoyed, but they don't need to either. When there was less viewer choice, everyone watched the same shows, but when there is more choice, television producers target the most desirable audiences, those who are perceived as commanding the most disposable income — and thus most prime-time television is aimed at middle- to upper-middle-class viewers between the ages of eighteen and forty-nine.

The fine-tuning of audiences, then, simply reflects a fine-tuning of marketing: specially defined audiences can be targeted for specially defined marketing campaigns. In this sense, the advent of cable repeats the same history as that of traditional commercial television, which became a medium primarily for the pitching of goods and services. But the proliferation of channels bears the potential to upset television's commercial monopoly. When NBC, CBS, ABC, and their affiliates ruled the airwaves, programming decisions for an entire nation were made by a tiny group of executives. Aside from the Nielsen ratings, viewers had little chance to let programmers know what they wanted to see. While certainly no revolution has occurred in the wake of cable, there has been some movement toward audience participation in viewing.

The phenomenal success of MTV provides a good example of the increasing power of the television audience. In TV's early years, rock music appeared in such programs as *American Bandstand* and *The Monkees.* In each case, a

The Simpsons.

rock act had to be toned downed considerably before it could be televised (Elvis was ordered not to bump and grind lest he be banned from the TV screens of the 1950s). What amounted to censorship worked because the venues for the televising of rock were often adult-oriented (consider how the Beatles and the Rolling Stones first appeared to American audiences on the adult variety program *The Ed Sullivan Show*). MTV, on the other hand, is an entirely youth-oriented station. Though it too exists to promote products — through both the videos it displays and the commercials it runs — MTV must conform to the tastes of its audience to succeed. This means that it has to appeal to adolescent fantasies and frustrations in a way that *The Monkees*, for instance, never did. *The Monkees* was a sanitized adventure sitcom whose scripts were written by anonymous professionals. The "scripts" of MTV videos are largely determined by the performers whose popularity among adolescents brought them to the screen in the first place. In other words, while MTV serves establishment corporate sponsors like any other commercial program, it nonetheless derives its authority from its audience more than the three networks do.

Exploring the Signs of Music Videos

In your journal, explore the impact music videos have had on you. How have videos shaped your desires and expectations about life? How were your actions and behavior influenced by MTV? What videos were especially meaningful to you? What did you think about them when you were younger, and how do you see them now? (If you didn't watch MTV, you might focus instead on other types of television programs.)

MTV has also played a hand in what could be called the hip hop revolution, which has effectively made rap music the single most popular youth music in America. For years before the mainstream pop music world was fully aware of it, MTV rap videos were reflecting, and shaping, the tastes of a new generation of fans, helping to transform a genre that had begun on the streets of New York into a entertainment phenomenon that has effectively eclipsed rock-and-roll as the music of young America. Once coded as the music of urban African Americans (which is why white rappers like Vanilla Ice and Marky Mark were regarded as something of a joke), rap has fully "crossed over" to be the preferred pop entertainment of teens of all ethnicities. Thus it isn't his race, one might say, that makes Eminem controversial.

No discussion of MTV is quite complete without a mention of Madonna, whose synthesis of music and video imagery was one of the creative forces behind the emergence of MTV and which has created something of an industry among academic critics eager to interpret her. Some see her as a postmodern feminist heroine who has challenged, through one phase after another, America's sexual mores. Others see her as an irresponsible promoter of teen sexuality whose message to young women is that their bodies are all that matter. Whatever one thinks of her, her preeminent place in American pop culture fairly screams for analysis.

In recent years, Madonna has joined a number of gender-bending pop culture icons — from Marilyn Manson to Dennis Rodman — who challenge the codes that govern sexual identity itself. Thus, where in the past Madonna played with the codes of female sexuality in her impersonations of Marilyn Monroe, she has also adopted the bisexual, cross-dressing persona of Marlene Dietrich — complete with top hat, tux, and tails. "Boys will be girls and girls will be boys" pretty much sums up this phase of Madonna's performance philosophy, but her most recent incarnations, which involve kilts and cowboy

Madonna.

hats, suggest that Madonna has moved on in her unending summer of surfing the waves of popular culture. What do you think her current act reveals about the state of American consciousness?

From MTV to MP3

MTV changed the way American youth culture thinks about music, forging a permanent link between the sound and the imagery of a song. The once-supreme rock act Pearl Jam discovered this when it tried to challenge the video-driven imperatives of contemporary popular music by refusing to make videos and found itself assigned to the sidelines of the pop music world. But even as MTV wedded music to television, a new technological intervention began yet another revolution in the way people consume music. This, of course, was the emergence of technologies that enabled users to download music from the Internet, technologies like MP3 and the music-swapping software of outfits like Napster. Though mired in court battles inaugurated by recording companies and recording artists (Metallica was es-

---

Reading Music on the Net

Many popular musicians and groups boast their own Web site or host special "concert" events on the Internet. Find the site of a favorite artist by using a search engine such as Yahoo! (**http://www.yahoo.com/ Entertainment/Music/Artists**) or trying a commercial site, **http://ubl.artistdirect.com.** Then study your artist's site, and analyze the images created for him or her. How is the artist "packaged" on the Net, and does that packaging differ from that used in other media? What sort of relationship is established between the artist and you, the fan, and how does the electronic medium affect that relationship?

---

pecially prominent in the anti-Napster campaign), the new Internet-based technologies are revolutionizing the traditional buy-a-whole-album mode of music consumption. Now you can put together your own selected music portfolio, picking only those songs that you want, a technological option that makes music consumers more powerful than they ever have been before.

So just as innovations in television technology have rearranged the relationship between content providers and consumers, so too have Internet-based technologies changed the pop music world. As such technologies emerge, our consciousness changes too. For just as the appearance of the first musical recordings and radio broadcasts of a century ago altered the way that we thought about music, causing us to expect the instant and ubiquitous gratification of our desires for musical entertainment, so too is the MTV/MP3 revolution altering our thinking about music. Ask yourself, when you think of a favorite song these days, does an entire set of video images accompany your thoughts? Do you spend more time at your computer than at Tower Records, downloading your own custom-designed musical collection? Just a few years ago you had to go to a store to get the music you wanted. How have your attitudes changed now that you don't have to leave home to get what you want?

The Readings

We begin the readings in this chapter with Todd Davis's analysis of *The West Wing,* an essay in which he suggests that the TV show is so popular precisely because it avoids the controversial and the challenging — a charge likely to upset many of its fans. Similarly analyzing the public response to a hallowed television icon, Steven D. Stark suggests that Oprah Winfrey, and talk-show hosts like her, provide a kind of "group therapy for the masses." A pair of gender-oriented articles follows, with Susan Douglas arguing that behind the progressive surfaces of *NYPD Blue* and *ER* lies a less-than-enlightened ideology, and Amanda Fazzone deconstructing the claim that such postfeminist TV heroines as Felicity actually empower women. Tad Friend comes next with a study of the way that television shows police themselves, making delicate decisions about the language and content that can be allowed on the air. Tricia Rose's semiotic decoding of such "Bad Sistas" as Salt 'N' Pepa and MC Lyte subtly questions whether, when it comes to traditional gender codes, these female rappers are really so bad after all. David Schiff and Robert Hilburn then question the common habit of ranking music, artists, and popular taste: Schiff critiques National Public Radio's choice of the one hundred most significant American musical selections of the twentieth century, and Hilburn exposes the flimsiness of a song's status as "No. 1." Tom Shales provides a candid description of his personal response to the way that television reacted to the September 11 attacks, and Marnie Carroll concludes the chapter with a global perspective on American TV, arguing that European television is no mere appendage of Hollywood.

TODD DAVIS

THE WEST WING *IN AMERICAN CULTURE*

America has already had one actor-president, and Warren Beatty seriously toyed with the idea of running for chief executive in 2000, but with the remarkable success of The West Wing, *America seems to have found its first pretend-president. Because it isn't Martin Sheen whom* West Wing *fans seem to regard as presidential material, it's Josiah Bartlet, a man who doesn't really exist. So what is it that Josiah has that the real politicians don't? Todd Davis provides some telling answers here in his analysis of* The West Wing's *popularity. It helps that while the show dramatizes real-world political issues and controversies, it does so, Davis argues, "in nonthreatening ways," and thus manages to keep just about everyone happy. It even makes us feel good about government, Davis suggests. Now, why can't real politicians do that? Todd Davis is the politics and culture editor at Philly1.com.*

America's living room has moved to *The West Wing.* In less than two years, NBC's political drama has attracted 13 million viewers, won nine Emmys, and resurrected the careers of Martin Sheen and Rob Lowe. Benefiting from series creator Aaron Sorkin's smartly written dialogue, *The West Wing* has become such a mainstay with the American people that national newspapers recently reassured readers that the show would run (one hour earlier than normal) in spite of Al Gore's concession speech. Such notification not only suggests that fiction dominates fact in the contemporary United States. It marks quite an achievement for a drama that — just a short time ago — few network executives wanted to touch. So why is this program so popular and what does that popularity mean?

One reason for the show's appeal is that people like surprises as long as they are not too scary, and, at first blush, *The West Wing* appears to break new ground. Anxious to generate the widest possible audience, television moguls traditionally have eschewed programs with political themes and denigrated shows with controversial viewpoints. According to the entertainment world's cowardly logic, shows that provoke do not generate enough advertising dollars to merit support. This is why having Ellen DeGeneres come out of the closet, why allowing Roseanne Barr to kiss Mariel Hemingway, why witnessing Ed Asner raise money for communist El Salvador has chilled the bones of mustachioed TV elites. Consider these rules: If a show makes Jerry Falwell nervous, it has problems; if it scares Johnson & Johnson, its days are numbered.

Using this thinking, television executives have subjected Americans to a relentless wave of banal programming designed more to generate income than to stimulate thought. Simpleminded reformulations of traditional themes and characters permeate the airwaves: *Big Valley* is *Dallas* is *Titans; Adam-12* is *Hill Street Blues* is *Law & Order; Perry Mason* is *L.A. Law* is *The Practice;* Dave Starsky is Rick Hunter is Andy Sipowitcz; Jim Rockford is Thomas Magnum is *Nash Bridges; Ben Casey* is *Marcus Welby* is *Mark Greene*. In this context, *The West Wing* emerges as a breath of fresh air. Witnessing Martin Sheen's President Josiah Bartlet oppose school vouchers, protect flag burning, denounce religious intolerance, and welcome Chinese immigrants has appealed to millions of people tired of the tedious peccadilloes and melodramas that absorb most television characters. Just as discontented white men wanted to hear Archie Bunker bemoan the decline of civilization during the 1970s, throngs of people want Josiah Bartlet to lead them into the New Millennium. In short, the people craved something new, and Aaron Sorkin delivered.

The West Wing is also well liked because it invokes controversies in nonthreatening ways. Popular shows historically have relied upon appealing actors playing comfortable characters who project traditional values, and Sorkin's creation provides such characters in droves. Although most of the people occupying the Bartlet White House are liberal Democrats, they speak in earnest tones about causes over which reasonable people can disagree. For example, although President Bartlet routinely opposes right-wing efforts to erode the barrier between church and state, he is a deeply religious person able to cite the Bible chapter and verse. Thus, his sorties against the bulwarks of Christian America are not freighted with ideological dynamite. It is assumed that Bartlet, unlike President Clinton, respects the tenets of Christian thought: He is a dissident, not a heretic. Similarly, Sorkin presents the president's deputy chief of staff, Josh Lyman, as a zealous albeit reasonable advocate of civil rights. In one episode, the crusading Lyman meets with an African American lawyer to argue that the federal government should not remunerate the descendants of slaves. By tempering his idealism with a strong dose of pragmatism, Lyman appears more like Hubert Humphrey than Malcom X. He is a happy warrior and someone with whom serious people can transact.

In fact, Aaron Sorkin has filled *The West Wing* with characters who not 5 only temper themselves, but also balance each other's impulses. President Bartlet is an idealistic soul whose political experience has convinced him that effective leaders must practice the art of the possible, and his core values simultaneously inspire and restrain his staff. Moreover, Chief of Staff Leo McGarry is a pragmatist par excellence who routinely reins in the liberal excesses of Communications Director Toby Ziegler and speechwriter Sam Seaborn. This delicate balance springs naturally from Sorkin's corps of highpowered consultants, which has included prominent Democrats like Dee Dee Myers and Lawrence O'Donnell as well as veteran Republicans like Marlin Fitzwater and Peggy Noonan. Therefore, even when *West Wing* characters discuss liberal issues like gun control and environmental legislation, they never stray too far from the political center.

The West Wing's left-leaning bipartisanship enhances the show's popularity because Sorkin uses this quality to suggest that the United States government works. This is a welcome message. Anti-government sentiment has deep roots in American political culture and has become increasingly powerful during the past forty years. Conservatives like Ronald Reagan and, more recently, Newt Gingrich, Tom DeLay, and Trent Lott have attained power by emphasizing the pernicious effects of centralized power and entrenched bureaucracy. Yet the dark side of anti-government thinking has produced so much damage in recent years that people have begun to reject it. Most citizens do not want bullheaded egomaniacs to shut down the government; they do not want paramilitary organizations to blow up federal buildings. In response to this turning worm, the primary vehicle of mainstream antigovernment feeling, the Republican Party, recently decided to proclaim allegiance to more warm-hearted, "compassionate" ideals. The GOP remains a conservative body, but few of its champions still seek to undermine Social Security, pillage Medicare and Medicaid, and abolish the Department of Education. In fact, to the chagrin of paleoconservatives everywhere, Republicans have become consolidators of Franklin Roosevelt's New Deal and Lyndon Johnson's Great Society. Dismantling the welfare state simply exceeds their grasp.

Sorkin's creation capitalizes on this movement away from antigovernment thinking, just as past television executives exploited the movement toward it. Scholar Todd Gitlin, for example, notes that the police drama *Hill Street Blues* became popular during Ronald Reagan's presidency by exploring an urban political infrastructure that repeatedly failed to function. No amount of heroic efforts, *Hill Street*'s creators suggested, could save the Hill from corruption and inefficiency. Sorkin recently inverted this effort by anticipating George W. Bush's call for cooperation in Washington and having the Bartlet administration reach across party lines to shatter government gridlock. Pushed along with the help of Republican counselor Ainsley Hayes, a ratings-friendly, gorgeous woman, this bipartisan advance has captured common imaginations. *The West Wing*'s ratings speak for themselves: Americans like the idea of politicians cooperating with each other to achieve the common good. That President Bartlet has managed to associate liberalism with patriotism as he drags the nation forward makes *The West Wing* especially palatable to Democrats disheartened by the recent "election" of George W. Bush and tortured by President Clinton's tendency to violate conventional morality. Yellow-Dog Democrats finally have true-blue heroes in Josiah Bartlet and his staff.

Furthermore, the complex circumstances surrounding George II's ascension indicate that *The West Wing* will continue to serve a social function (and become more popular as a result) during the next few years. Democrats probably will regard President Bartlet's left-wing presidency as a symbol of hope and possibility—the Gore administration that never was but should have been—and still could be—and Americans of all stripes surely will use Bartlet's demeanor and comportment to evaluate George W. Bush. In a recent edition of the *Philadelphia Inquirer,* editorialist Jane Eisner warned President-elect W.

that watching Bartlet devour important memos, compute abstruse statistics, and convey imperial amiability has influenced public expectations of the president. Americans will not support a president who stumbles over words, takes fishing junkets, and smirks into the camera when they can find a better option on TV every Wednesday night. In order for Bush to win over the millions of Americans who did not vote for him, his life will have to imitate their art.

Yet, although *The West Wing* is an unquestionably first-rate program, it would benefit from fine-tuning. The show's ability to funnel complex issues into an entertaining format has endowed it with an instructive value that escapes most of its competitors. Few other network shows endeavor to discuss how a liberal society can engineer the balance of social justice and law and order. Sorkin, however, could make his creation even more enlightening by showing the darker side of governmental affairs. He currently does little to demystify power politics, allowing his characters to muddle through the political process without falling prey to the innumerable pitfalls awaiting all public officials. *The West Wing* would be better if the self-righteous determination that motivates Bartlet and his followers led them — at least a few steps — down a primrose path. Even the most optimistic of America's constitutional framers understood that virtue can easily become hubris. Sorkin's audience and his actors deserve a treatment of this problem that steers between the rocks of melodrama and the shoals of cynicism.

The West Wing also would serve its audience by discussing the inherently   10 undemocratic nature of modern American government. President Bartlet currently seems deeply concerned with the will of the American people and makes strong efforts to infuse his policies with populist notions. This conception of governance, however, is misleading. The modern world's quicksilver pace forces presidents to act quickly and decisively without considering public moods. If Sorkin forced his characters to cope with more events demanding rapid action — a military coup in the Balkans, an economic collapse in Europe — people might better understand that their leaders must take imperial actions in order to preserve democratic rule. That lesson would be well taken.

Finally, Sorkin should grapple with the Bartlet administration's troubling racial and class imbalance. Although Barlet's White House is supposed to represent a beacon of high-minded thought, the president and most of his advisers are white males from the Ivy League, and the administration's most frequently seen African American is Charlie, a young personal aide who often seems like little more than a manservant. The president treats Charlie like a son, allowing him to date his beloved daughter and giving him the carving knife Paul Revere made for his family during the eighteenth century. However, these actions smack of the white paternalism that still afflicts American society. President Bartlet's National Security Adviser and the Chairman of the Joint Chiefs of Staff are African Americans, and either they should receive more room in the scripts, or the president should come under fire for running a lily-white operation. If George W. Bush's "election" and recent round of cabinet appointments reveal anything, it is that citizens like regular guys who have inner circles that, at least superficially, "look like America."

In the end, *The West Wing* warrants close scrutiny because it could perform an important cultural function during the next few years. Because what people discuss on the airwaves reflects and shapes popular thinking, television touches the lives of almost every citizen and remains, in Todd Gitlin's words, "a hearth of national culture." Therefore, if President Bartlet continues to advance a pragmatically liberal agenda in a manner that impresses and titillates viewers, *The West Wing* not only could increase voter turnout in 2002 and 2004 by keeping people interested in political affairs. By restoring the appeal of liberal government, it could shape the outcomes of those elections. The most important question confronting Americans interested in Aaron Sorkin's creation, then, might not concern the nature of its popularity. People soon might find themselves pondering a puzzling possibility: The United States government might move leftward at the behest of Martin Sheen.

READING THE TEXT

1. Summarize in your own words the reasons Davis believes *The West Wing* is so popular.

2. In Davis's opinion, why are most American television programs banal?

3. What evidence does Davis advance to support his contention that *The West Wing* exploits the trend away from antigovernment thinking?

4. What effect does Davis believe *The West Wing* can have on real-life politics and cultural attitudes, and how convincing do you find his speculations?

READING THE SIGNS

1. Conduct an in-class debate on the efficacy of Josiah Bartlet's "presidency," and then hold a mock election to determine who would win in a 2004 race between Bartlet and George W. Bush.

2. Watch an episode of *The West Wing,* and write an essay that support, refutes, or modifies Davis's contention that the show is "well liked because it invokes controversies in nonthreatening ways" (para. 4). As you develop your argument, pay particular attention to the show's many characters and their interaction. Do they, as Davis claims, "balance each other's impulses" (para. 5)?

3. Write an essay in which you argue for or against the contention that American popular culture champions mainstream and nonthreatening values at the expense of the innovative or challenging. To develop your ideas, consult Sandra Tsing Loh's "The Return of Doris Day" (p. 365). and Benjamin DeMott's "Put on a Happy Face: Masking the Differences between Blacks and Whites" (p. 569).

4. Conduct an informal poll of *The West Wing* fans, asking them not only about their overall response to the show but also to individual characters. Then write a critique of Davis's explanation for the show's success. To what extent is it accurate and complete? Do fans admire the program for additional reasons?

STEVEN D. STARK

THE OPRAH WINFREY SHOW *AND THE* TALK-SHOW FUROR

Oprah Winfrey just might be the most powerful woman in America, and if not, certainly the most influential literary critic. In this selection from Glued to the Set: The Sixty Television Shows and Events That Made Us What We Are Today *(1997), Steven D. Stark (b. 1951) explains how she got that way. Tracing the evolution of daytime talk from Donahue to Jenny Jones, Stark analyzes the social forces behind this much vilified television genre in which Oprah is the reigning monarch. Finding in television a mirror image not of American realities but of American needs and desires, Stark thus provides a model for understanding the cultural significance of the tube. A contributor to such publications as the* Atlantic Monthly *and the* New York Times Magazine, *Stark is also a commentator for National Public Radio.*

Start with these two basic premises:

1. Oprah Winfrey is probably the most celebrated and powerful black woman in U.S. history.
2. Oprah Winfrey is the undisputed leader of a television genre which has been more vehemently attacked by the Establishment than any other in television history.

You don't have to be an Albert Einstein to recognize that these two propositions are related.

The modern daytime talk show — created by Phil Donahue in the late 1960s, revolutionized by Oprah in the 1980s, and then transmogrified in the 1990s by everyone from Ricki Lake to Jenny Jones — is the newest genre to sweep television. On an average mid-nineties weekday, *The Oprah Winfrey Show* was watched by ten million Americans, mostly women, and the 20 or so other daytime talk shows in 1995 had a combined daily audience of around 50 million viewers — though many people undoubtedly watched a whole slew of these shows each day. Though these numbers were high, they pale when compared to those of the combined audiences that watch the violence of prime-time action shows or the local news.

Yet the talk-show genre was absolutely vilified by critics — blamed for everything from the culture's preoccupation with victimization to the general decline of civic discourse. Daytime talk generated a well-publicized crusade (led by two U.S. senators and former Secretary of Education William Bennett) to purify the medium, not to mention a dozen or so critical books and hundreds of negative articles which joined these Washington officials in calling

243

the new genre a "case study of rot" and "the pollution of the human environment."

Admittedly daytime talk shows are not for the squeamish or children — 5
though one hopes that Bennett and his minions were as concerned about the
millions who live full-time in economic and social surroundings far more
squalid than anything on *The Maury Povich Show*. The shows typically involve
from two to six guests talking about their personal experiences, followed by
boos, applause, tears, questions, and shouts from a studio audience modeled
roughly on Howdy Doody's Peanut Gallery. A typical week of mid-nineties
programming on these shows was likely to include such topics as:

    Leathermen Love Triangles
    Bisexuals
    Abusive Boyfriends
    Men Engaged to Three Pregnant Women
    Clueless Men
    Women Who Marry Their Rapists
    Runaway Teens
    Secret Crushes

This was the genre where a man was surprisingly "confronted" with a secret
admirer on *Jenny Jones,* found the admirer was a man, and killed him after
the show for humiliating him on national television. (The show was never
broadcast due to the shooting.) "Rather than being mortified, ashamed, or
trying to hide their stigma," two sociologists wrote of this genre, "guests willingly and eagerly discuss their child-molesting, sexual quirks, and criminal
records in an effort to seek 'understanding' for their particular disease."

These shows obviously offer a distorted vision of America, thrive on feeling rather than thought, and worship the sound-bite rather than the art of
conversation. Yet it's not like television hasn't been walking down these same
paths in other forms every day for the past 50 years. If daytime talk has been
preoccupied with sex, race, and family dysfunction, it may be because there
is still so little discussion of those rather significant topics elsewhere on television, even in the nineties. All movements have their crazies. Yet when Oprah
Winfrey can rank in a poll as the celebrity Americans believe to be most qualified to be president (far more than Bill Bennett, by the way), something significant is going on.

Just as vaudeville was the root of much early American television, the circus and carnival with their freak shows influenced talk shows. Like any new
television genre, these talk shows were a mixture of old programming types —
many of which once dominated the daytime. Morning and afternoon talk,
geared mostly to women, has a long TV history, beginning with Arthur
Godfrey and with Art Linkletter's *People Are Funny.* From the soap opera,
these new shows borrowed a feminine style of disclosure and a focus on issues considered to be of particular relevance to women, like family and relationships. Game shows were a rich source: From programs like *The Price Is*

George W. Bush on *The Oprah Winfrey Show.*

Right the new talk shows learned how to involve an audience of ordinary people. From games like *Strike It Rich* and *Queen for a Day* they learned about the entertainment value of debasing "contestants" who will tell their sob story for money or fleeting fame. And from *Family Feud* they learned that conflict sells in the daytime. Throw in a smattering of TV religion (the televised confession and revelation so prominent on these shows), melodrama (Will the runaway teenager's father take her back?), and the news sensibility of Barbara Walters, once an early-morning mainstay on *Today,* and the pieces were in place for a profitable genre — especially because daytime talk shows are so inexpensive to stage.

Like other popular forms of programming, these shows also mirrored their times. Phil Donahue created the genre because network television wasn't reflecting the serious concerns of many of its women viewers. It began in 1967, at the dawn of the women's movement, when this Midwestern Catholic started a new type of daytime talk show in Dayton, Ohio, hosting for that first show atheist Madalyn Murray O'Hair. Donahue's story was simple: "The average housewife is bright and inquisitive," he said, "but television treats her like a mental midget." His approach was to take TV talk out of its preoccupation with entertainment celebrities, and tackled instead (often with only one guest an hour) "difficult" women's issues that television wasn't addressing — sexism, artificial insemination, impotence, and homosexuality — combined with more-traditional topics, like bathroom fixtures. "He flies in the face of TV tradition, which used to be that you didn't risk offending anyone,"

Steve Allen, former host of *The Tonight Show,* said. Donahue also brilliantly added an active studio audience, usually composed almost entirely of women (though not by design — they're just the ones who showed up), which not only served as a kind of Greek chorus for the guests, but also asked many of the show's most penetrating questions.

For his part, Donahue the rebel frequently bounced about the crowd, microphone in hand, smashing the barrier between host and audience. It didn't hurt the show's populist appeal that it came to stations independently through syndication, rather than from a paternalistic network. In its heyday, *Donahue* also originated from Chicago — in the nation's heartland — rather than among the elites in New York. The more the women's movement progressed, however, the more well-educated women left home for the workplace, and found other outlets for their interests. That left Donahue and his imitators with a growing audience of less-affluent, homebound women who often were full of anger and confusion, ignored as they were by more elite media. The women's movement first made Donahue, and then took away the cream of his audience who were interested in more serious topics.

Still, for over a decade he had the field to himself before along came a 10 certain Oprah Winfrey in 1984. She was an empathetic black woman and former coanchor of the local news in Baltimore. Oprah's advantage over Donahue was that, seeming to resemble her audience, she used that similarity to create a talk show which made the political more personal. Her program was infused with a therapeutic sensibility: Though Oprah did some politics, like her celebrated show in Forsyth County, Georgia, in 1987 (when white racists were on the march), she was more likely to do a show on abusive boyfriends, recovering alcoholics, or competitive sisters. The cause of many of the problems discussed on her show was not so much men, but the so-called rigid confines of traditional family. "What we are witnessing with the proliferating talk show is a social revolution which has at its core the demystification of the family," Michael Arlen, former TV critic for *The New Yorker,* would tell a reporter much later. Say good-bye to Ozzie and Harriet!

Oprah's style was different, too. If Donahue was, at heart, a journalist exposing issues, Oprah ran what she called a "ministry" — the "church" being a branch of pop psychology which held that revealing problems, improving self-esteem, and receiving empathy could cure just about anything, and empower women besides. Oprah hugged her guests, wept openly, and personally said good-bye to each member of the studio audience after a show. Even in 1996, Oprah spoke far more often on her shows than other hosts did. She confessed on the air that she had been sexually abused by relatives as a child, and in later years that she had smoked cocaine. On a show about dieting, she told the audience about the night she ate hot-dog buns drowned in syrup.

Oprah's race and street sass ("Hey, Girl!") also made her more authentically hip, at least to her audience, than almost anyone else on television. Oprah would call her success an alternative to the "Twinkies and Barbie and

Ken dolls" that make up so much of television. "Racism remains the most difficult subject in America, and it is only really on the talk show that the raw hatred and suspicion that the races feel for each other is vented," Arlen had told that reporter. As a host who could walk the narrow line between the races, Oprah offered reassurance which others couldn't hope to match. That cultural bilingualism also allowed her to put together an audience coalition of the sort that Jesse Jackson could only dream about.

With rock-and-roll in the 1950s, black artists had been swept aside so that more-acceptable white singers could "cover" their songs. With daytime talk, the opposite occurred: Oprah's show soon wiped out *Donahue* in the ratings — and everyone else, too. By 1994, *Working Woman* put Oprah's net worth at over $250 million. By then the show itself was grossing almost $200 million a year, had 55 percent more viewers than *Donahue* (its closest competitor), and enjoyed higher ratings on many days than *Today, Good Morning America,* and the *CBS Morning News* combined.

Understandably, Oprah's success bred imitators. Since other hosts couldn't hope to match her in identifying with the audience personally (Ricki Lake was a notable exception, as she went after younger viewers), they tried to win viewers by topping her with their list of sensationalistic topics and revelations. As TV news became ever more tabloid, these shows pushed the envelope even further. By 1992, even Donahue was tackling topics like "Safe Sex Orgies" and "What Happens When Strippers Get Old?" Other shows borrowed from the confrontational style of talk shows once run by Mort Downey Jr. and turned Oprah's group hug into a daily talk riot with topics like "Wives Confront the Other Woman."

By the mid-1990s, an average day on these other shows revealed subjects 15 like "Married Men Who Have Relationships with Their Next-Door Neighbors," "Mothers Who Ran Off with Their Daughter's Fiancé," and "Drag Queens Who Got Makeovers." A 1995 study of these programs, done by a team of researchers at Michigan State University, found that a typical one-hour show had:

> four sexual-activity disclosures, one sexual-orientation disclosure, three abuse disclosures, two embarrassing-situation disclosures, two criminal-activity disclosures and four personal-attribute disclosures, for a total of 16 personal disclosures. . . .

These entertainment programs were selling more, however, than just their guests' disclosures or the "hot" topics which seemed to come straight out of the supermarket tabloids. They also purported to offer group therapy for the masses, at a price everyone could afford. As psychotherapist Murray Nossel once told a reporter, America is "the country that popularized psychoanalysis. Freud's theory of the psyche is that repression brings depression, whereas expression is liberating. Emotionally to cathart in America, to reveal one's darkest secrets, is a desired social good in and of itself." Critics would have a field day pointing out the dangers of trying to provide such "therapy" on television, but that played right into the notion that elites were trying to keep the masses away from something that had once exclusively been available only to the well-to-do. After all, if daytime talk shows thrived on the violation of taboos, that was, in part, to stick a finger in the eye of those members of the Establishment who looked down on a television pursuit favored by the downscale.

The supporters of these shows also felt that they regularly received too little credit for tackling issues which mainstream television had traditionally ignored, like race and family dysfunction. "If people didn't get up there and talk about incest," Lee Fryd, director of media relations for the *Sally Jessy Raphael* show once told a reporter, "it would never come to light." If these shows often presented what many considered a freak parade, others would argue that they had helped bring nonconformists further into the mainstream. Joshua Gamson, a cultural critic, once wrote:

> The story here is not about commercial exploitation but just about how effective the prohibition on asking and telling is in the United States, how stiff the penalties are, how unsafe this place is for people of atypical sexual and gender identities. You know you're in trouble when Sally Jessy Raphael (strained smile and forced tear behind red glasses) seems your best bet for being heard, understood, respected, and protected. That for some of us the loopy, hollow light of talk shows seems a safe, shielding haven should give us all pause.

On the other hand, the values of these talk shows were oddly traditional — one reason why they posted such strong ratings with Bible Belt females who considered themselves conservative. The parade of guests was almost always hooted down by the studio audience, which embodied a rather conventional view of morality (albeit one heavily tempered by empathy for victims). The parade of "trash," to use one critic's words, was also a way for those at home to feel better about themselves, since their lives were rarely as hopeless as what they could find here on the screen. Like so much else on TV, what these shows offered was a form of reassurance.

If these talk shows had a larger political consequence, it came with the administration of Bill Clinton, who accomplished little but empathized with everybody. He ran a kind of talk-show presidency — forged in the 1992 campaign with his appearance on *Donahue,* and continuing in that year into a second debate with George Bush and H. Ross Perot which did away with journalist-questioners and substituted an inquiring studio audience like Oprah's. One of Clinton's principal contributions to our culture was to take the language and zeitgeist of the talk show and bring it into mainstream politics. After all, the "I feel your pain" trademark of his presidency first gained cultural prominence as a talk-show staple: The whole point of talk shows like Oprah's is to encourage "audience-victims" to "feel their pain" as a way of empowering themselves to strike back against those who seem more powerful.

Such a stance was undoubtedly a big reason why women, over time, sup- 20 ported Clinton so strongly. In fact, by 1996, the talk-show style and its celebration of victims was on display throughout both political conventions: There was Liddy Dole's Winfreyesque "among the delegates" talk to the Republican convention, Al Gore's speech recounting his dying sister's final moments, and the endless parade of the disease-afflicted. Our politics had been Opracized.

Yet if the nineties has been a decade tending to elevate feeling over thought and encourage a no-fault approach to behavior, the talk shows were hardly the only culprit, no matter what Bill Bennett thought. Few cultural movements of this magnitude proceed from the bottom up rather than the other way around. As Michiko Kakutani would point out in another context in the *New York Times,* the cult of subjectivity enveloping America came as much from Oliver Stone, with his fantasies about JFK, and from "inventive" biographers like Joe McGinniss, as they came from Ricki Lake. Invective was as much a calling card of CNN's *Crossfire* as it was of Montel and Jerry Springer.

By late 1995, however, in response to criticisms by Bennett and others (and as ratings for the "confrontational" shows dropped by as much as a third), Oprah changed her mix of guests and topics too, moving away from tabloid psychology and toward less-conventional, more-"educational" subjects like anorexia and planning for old age. "She said to us that after 10 years and 2,000 shows of mostly dysfunctional people, she felt it was time to start focusing on solutions," said Tim Bennett, Oprah's production-company president. At the same time, *The Rosie O'Donnell Show* rose to daytime prominence by essentially taking the old fifties' upbeat variety formula, popularized by Arthur Godfrey, and repackaging it with a likable female host, celebrity guests, and a nineties' zeitgeist.

But were even these small shifts something of a betrayal of a large portion of the talk show audience? What was always most striking about this form of "entertainment" — and what made it so different from anything else on television — was its never-ending portrait of despair and alienation. If the downtrodden who populated these shows popularized deviancy or celebrated the cheap confessional, they did it mostly as a plaintive cry for help. Yet Oprah had been there to bless them at the end of every weekday. "They are the people you'd ignore if you saw them in line at the supermarket instead of on TV," Wendy Kaminer, a cultural analyst, once wrote, but that was precisely the point. Talk television was yet another step in the 1990s' trend to democratization of the medium — this time to include the real have-nots. That may be why the elites responded with their usual rejoinder to let them eat cake.

READING THE TEXT

1. What does Stark mean when he says that *The Oprah Winfrey Show* and its imitators "offer group therapy for the masses" (para. 16)?

2. What evidence does Stark provide to support his view that talk shows have had a special appeal to women?

3. Why does Stark say that talk shows are "oddly traditional" (para. 18), despite their often lurid content?

4. Explain what Stark means by saying that Bill Clinton "ran a kind of talk-show presidency" (para. 19).

READING THE SIGNS

1. In your journal, reflect on your responses to talk shows. If you enjoy sensationalized programming, explore why; if you avoid it, discuss the reasons for your distaste.

2. In competing with *The Oprah Winfrey Show,* talk-show hosts such as Jerry Springer and Sally Jessy Raphael have upped the ante with "sensationalistic topics and revelations" (para. 14). In an essay, argue for or against the social value of sensationalized talk shows.

3. Write an argumentative essay supporting, refuting, or complicating Stark's assertion that talk shows have helped to bring about the "democratization" (para. 23) of television.

4. Watch an episode of *The Oprah Winfrey Show,* and write an essay in which you offer your own analysis of its appeal. To develop your support, you might interview some avid fans of the program.

5. Write a letter to talk-show critics such as William Bennett, supporting or refuting their desire to "purify" television.

SUSAN DOUGLAS

SIGNS OF INTELLIGENT LIFE ON TV

Do you look for television programming that reflects an enlightened view of American women? Susan Douglas (b. 1950) does, and in this essay that originally appeared in Ms. *she reports her findings, which are mixed, at best. Although popular TV dramas like* ER *and* NYPD Blue *appear to present characters and plotlines that defy gender stereotypes, Douglas still finds the telltale signs of cultural bias against women in such programs — especially a bias against strong professional women. When not watching TV, Douglas is a professor of communication studies at the University of Michigan and media critic for* The Progressive. *She is the author of* Where the Girls Are: Growing Up Female with the Mass Media *(1994) and* Inventing American Broadcasting, 1899–1922 *(1987).*

When the hospital show *ER* became a surprise hit, the pundits who had de-clared dramatic television "dead" were shocked. But one group wasn't sur-prised at all.

Those of us with jobs, kids, older parents to tend to, backed-up toilets, dog barf on the rug, and friends/partners/husbands we'd like to say more than "hi" to during any diurnal cycle don't have much time to watch televi-sion. And when we do — usually after 9:38 P.M. — we have in recent years been forced to choose between Diane Sawyer interviewing Charles Manson or Connie Chung chasing after Tonya [Harding] and Nancy [Kerrigan]. People like me, who felt that watching the newsmagazines was like exposing yourself to ideological smallpox, were starved for some good escapist drama that takes you somewhere else yet resonates with real life and has ongoing characters you care about.

When *NYPD Blue* premiered in the fall of 1993 with the tough-but-sensitive John Kelly, and featuring strong, accomplished women, great light-ing, bongo drums in the sound track, and male nudity, millions sighed with relief. When *ER* hit the air, we made it one of the tube's highest rated shows. Tagging farther behind, but still cause for hope, is another hospital drama, *Chicago Hope*.

All three shows acknowledge the importance of the adult female audience by featuring women as ongoing characters who work for a living and by fo-cusing on contemporary problems in heterosexual relationships (no, we haven't yet achieved everyday homosexual couples on TV). More to the point, hound-dog-eyed, emotionally wounded yet eager-to-talk-it-through guys are center stage. So what are we getting when we kick back and submerge our-selves in these dramas? And what do they have to say about the ongoing proj-ect of feminism?

For those of you who don't watch these shows regularly, here's a brief 5 précis: *NYPD Blue* is a cop show set in New York City and has producer Steven Bochco's signature style — lots of shaky, hand-held camera work, fast-paced editing (supported by the driving, phallic backbeat in the sound track), and multiple, intersecting plots about various crimes and the personal lives of those who work in the precinct. Last season there were more women in the show; and last season there was John Kelly.

This year, the show is more masculinized. Watching Bobby Simone, played by Jimmy Smits, earn his right to replace Kelly was like witnessing a territorial peeing contest between weimaraners. Bobby had to be as sensi-tive and emotionally ravaged as Johnny, so in an act of New Age male one-upmanship, the scriptwriters made him a widower who had lost his wife to breast cancer. But Bobby had to be one tough customer too, so soon after we learn of his wife's death, we see him throwing some punks up against a fence, warning them that he will be their personal terminator unless they stop deal-ing drugs.

ER has the same kind of simultaneous, intersecting story lines, served up with fast-tracking cameras that sprint down hospital corridors and swirl around operating tables like hawks on speed. And there are the same bongo drums and other percussive sounds when patients are rushed in for treatment. *Chicago Hope* is *ER* on Valium: stationary cameras, slower pace, R&B instead of drumbeats. It's also *ER* on helium or ether, kind of a *Northern Exposure* goes to the hospital, with more offbeat plots and characters, like a patient who eats his hair or a kid whose ear has fallen off.

Whenever I like a show a lot — meaning I am there week in and week out — I figure I have once again embraced a media offering with my best and worst interests at heart. Dramatic TV shows, which seek a big chunk of the middle- and upper-income folks between 18 and 49, need to suck in those women whose lives have been transformed by the women's movement (especially women who work outside the home and have disposable income) while keeping the guys from grabbing the remote. What we get out of these twin desires is a blend of feminism and antifeminism in the plots and in the female characters. And for the male characters we have an updated hybrid of masculinity that crossbreeds decisiveness, technical expertise, and the ability to throw a punch or a basketball, with a soft spot for children and a willingness to cry.

On the surface, these shows seem good for women. We see female cops, lawyers, doctors, and administrators, who are smart, efficient, and successful. But in too many ways, the women take a backseat to the boys. In *NYPD Blue,* for example, we rarely see the women actually doing their jobs. The overall message in the three shows is that, yes, women can be as competent as men, but their entrance into the workforce has wrecked the family and made women so independent and hard-hearted that dealing with them and understanding them is impossible. Despite this, they're still the weaker sex.

In *ER* it is Carol Hathaway (Julianna Margulies), the charge nurse, who   10
tried to commit suicide. It is Dr. Susan Lewis (Sherry Stringfield) who is taken in by an imposter who claims to be a hospital administrator. Dr. Lewis is also the only resident who has trouble standing up to white, male authority figures: She is unable to operate while the head cardiologist watches her. In *Chicago Hope,* a psychiatrist prevails upon a female nurse to dress up like Dorothy (ruby slippers, pigtails, and all) because a patient refusing surgery is a *Wizard of Oz* junkie. Even though she points out that no male doctor would be asked to do anything like it, the shrink insists she continue the masquerade because the patient's life is at stake. Here's the crucial guilt-shifting we've all come to know and love — this patient's illness is somehow more her responsibility than anyone else's. Her humiliation is necessary to save him.

The Ariel Syndrome — Ariel was the name of Walt Disney's little mermaid, who traded her voice for a pair of legs so that she could be with a human prince she'd seen from afar for all of ten seconds — grips many of the women, who have recurring voice problems. Watch out for female characters who "don't want to talk about it," who can't say no, who don't speak up. They make it even harder for the women who do speak their minds, who are, of course, depicted as "bitches."

One major "bitch" is the wife of *ER*'s Dr. Mark Greene (Anthony Edwards). He's a doctor who's barely ever home, she's a lawyer who lands a great job two hours away, and they have a seven-year-old. Those of us constantly negotiating about who will pick up the kids or stay late at work can relate to this. The problem is that *ER* is about *his* efforts to juggle, *his* dreams and ambitions. We know this guy, we like him, we know he's a great doctor who adores his wife and child. Her, we don't know, and there's no comparable female doctor to show the woman's side of this equation. As a result, when conflicts emerge, the audience is primed to want her to compromise (which she's already done, so he can stay at the job he loves). When she insists he quit his job and relocate, she sounds like a spoiled child more wedded to a rigid quid pro quo than to flexibility, love, the family. It's the conservative view of what feminism has turned women into—unfeeling, demanding blocks of granite.

One of the major themes of all three shows is that heterosexual relationships are a national disaster area. And it's the women's fault. Take *NYPD Blue*. Yes, there's the fantasy relationship between Andy Sipowicz (Dennis Franz) and Sylvia Costas (Sharon Lawrence), in which an accomplished woman helps a foul-mouthed, brutality-prone cop with really bad shirts get in touch with his feelings and learn the pleasures of coed showering. While this affair has become the emotional anchor of the show, it is also the lone survivor in the ongoing gender wars.

It looks like splitsville for most of the show's other couples. Greg Medavoy (Gordon Clapp) infuriates Donna Abandando (Gail O'Grady) by his behavior, which includes following her to see whom she's having lunch with. She's absolutely right. But after all the shots of Greg looking at her longingly across the office (again, we're inside his head, not hers), the audience is encouraged to think that she should give the guy a break. By contrast, her explanations of why she's so angry and what she wants have all the depth and emotional warmth of a Morse code message tapped out by an iguana. Of course Greg doesn't understand. She won't help him.

In this world, female friendships are nonexistent or venomous. And there 15 is still worse ideological sludge gumming up these shows. Asian and Latina women are rarely seen, and African American women are also generally absent except as prostitutes, bad welfare moms, and unidentified nurses. In the *ER* emergency room, the black women who are the conscience and much-needed drill sergeants of the show don't get top billing, and are rarely addressed by name. There is also an overabundance of bad mothers of all races: adoptive ones who desert their kids, abusive ones who burn their kids, and hooker ones (ipso facto bad). Since the major female characters—all upper-middle class—don't have kids, we don't see their struggles to manage motherhood and work. And we certainly don't see less privileged moms (the real majority in the United States), like the nurses or office workers, deal with these struggles on a lot less money.

One of the worst things these shows do, under a veneer of liberalism and feminism, is justify the new conservatism in the United States. The suspects brought in for questioning on *NYPD Blue* are frequently threatened and sometimes beaten, but it's O.K. because they all turn out to be guilty, anyway. Legal representation for these witnesses is an unspeakable evil because it hides the truth. After a steady diet of this, one might assume the Fourth Amendment, which prohibits unreasonable search and seizure, is hardly worth preserving.

So why are so many women devoted to these shows? First off, the women we do see are more successful, gutsy, more fully realized than most female TV characters. But as for me, I'm a sucker for the men. I want to believe, despite all the hideous evidence to the contrary, that some men have been humanized by the women's movement, that they have become more nurturing, sensitive, and emotionally responsible. I want to believe that patriarchy is being altered by feminism. Since I get zero evidence of this on the nightly news, I want a few hours a week when I can escape into this fantasy.

Of course, we pay a price for this fantasy. TV depicts "real men" being feminized for the better and women masculinized for the worse. The message from the guys is, "We became the kind of men you feminists said that you wanted, and now you can't appreciate us because you've forgotten how to be a 'real' woman." It's a bizarre twist on the real world, where many women have changed, but too many men have not. Nevertheless, in TV land feminism continues to hoist itself with its own petard. Big surprise.

READING THE TEXT

1. What does Douglas mean by saying that "watching the newsmagazines was like exposing yourself to ideological smallpox" (para. 2), and what attitude toward the media does this comment reveal?

2. Why, according to Douglas, are professional women attracted to programs such as *ER* and *NYPD Blue*?

3. What, according to Douglas, is the overt message about gender roles communicated by the TV shows she discusses? What is the hidden message?

4. How are non-Caucasian women presented in *ER* and *NYPD Blue,* according to Douglas, and what is her opinion about their presentation?

5. How does Douglas view the "new conservatism in the United States" (para. 16)?

READING THE SIGNS

1. Watch an episode of *ER* or *NYPD Blue,* and write an argumentative essay in which you support, refute, or modify Douglas's belief that the show, despite superficial nods at feminism, perpetuates traditional gender roles.

2. In class, brainstorm TV shows that portray women as professionals or in other responsible, intelligent roles. Then, using Douglas's argument as your starting point, discuss whether the shows really adopt a feminist or an antifeminist stance in portraying female characters.

3. In your journal, discuss your favorite prime-time TV show, exploring exactly what you find attractive about the program.

4. Apply Douglas's argument to the films Sandra Tsing Loh discusses in "The Return of Doris Day" (p. 365). To what extent is the good-girl motif that Loh describes symptomatic of the covert antifeminism that Douglas decries?

5. Watch a TV show that focuses on young adult characters. Do you see evidence of the covert antifeminism that Douglas describes? What does the treatment of female characters say about the show's presumed audience? Use your findings as evidence in an analytical essay about how the show depicts women.

6. Do you see any evidence of covert antifeminism in advertising? Write an essay in which you explore the depiction of women in advertising, focusing perhaps on ads in a woman's magazine such as *Elle* or *Vogue*. To develop your argument, consult Gloria Steinem's "Sex, Lies, and Advertising" (p. 186).

AMANDA FAZZONE
BOOB TUBE

> If you think Buffy is a take-charge feminist role model and Felicity a model of female empowerment, then Amanda Fazzone has news for you: "If heroines like Felicity are empowered, it's only because they've decided that what really drives female power is sex." Taking issue with the National Organization for Women's endorsement of such programs as Buffy the Vampire Slayer and Felicity, Fazzone's take-no-prisoners critique of prime-time television implicitly questions the kind of postfeminist perspective that has made Sex and the City a major hit. An assistant managing editor at The New Republic, Fazzone has contributed to such publications as Salon, Time Out New York, and Billboard.com.

Just about everything you need to know about the life and loves of Felicity Porter, a New York City college student played by Keri Russell on the WB's *Felicity,* took place in the show's pilot three years ago. In the pilot, Felicity followed her high school crush to college in the big city. And, three years later, she is still twisting her life around every Wednesday night for the same guy. Elucidates the show's Web site: "She scrapped . . . everything she thought her life would be — all for a guy with a great smile. Well, wouldn't you?"

Evidently the National Organization for Women's answer is yes. Last month, in its "Feminist Primetime Report Update" (the successor to last year's "Feminist Primetime Report"), it ranked *Felicity* as the third-most-feminist of the 59 shows it surveyed, giving it the "NOW Recommends" seal of approval. NOW rated prime-time programs on UPN and the WB, and new prime-time shows on the other four major networks, for gender composition/diversity (the more women and girls, the better!), violence, sexual exploitation, and social responsibility. The shows that did best were those, like *Felicity,* that feature heroines whom NOW called "intelligent," "well-rounded," and able to "break out of the sex object role and portray authentic people." Which would be fine, except that many of the characters NOW praises don't break out of the sex object role at all; they bask in it. If heroines like Felicity are empowered, it's only because they've decided that what really drives female power is sex. Specifically, the power of very attractive, very young women to attract just about any man they want. True, that is power of a sort — just not the sort you'd expect NOW to applaud.

Take *Buffy the Vampire Slayer,* among the shows "NOW Recommends." Starring blond bombshell Sarah Michelle Gellar as a vampire-slaying college coed, *Buffy* receives feminist kudos for depicting a take-charge woman who kicks butts of both genders. But the constant barrage of *Buffy* promo photos featuring the cleavage of a braless and tumescent Gellar makes it difficult to divorce the ass-kicking from the tits and ass. The same goes for *Dawson's Creek,* which makes NOW's list of the ten shows with the least sexual exploitation. But when the show first aired in 1998, even generally lenient TV reviewers were struck that, as the *Los Angeles Times'* Howard Rosenberg put it, "the minors are anatomically fixated, and some of their elders just as genitalia-minded." In the show's pilot, we learn that, as Rosenberg recounts, star Jen "lost her virginity at 12 and went on to 'sleep with half of New York City.'"

Moreover, it's clear that these female leads are being marketed outside their time slots not for their smarts and self-confidence but for their sex appeal. That's why Gellar is selling makeup for Maybelline — that is, when she's not playing silver-screen temptresses in *Cruel Intentions, I Know What You Did Last Summer,* and *Simply Irresistible.* It's why Jessica Biel — star of the WB's *7th Heaven,* which NOW ranked ninth — posed topless in the March 2000 issue of *Gear* magazine. Alexis Bledel, who plays the character NOW dubs the "intelligent daughter" in its top pick, *Gilmore Girls,* is heralded on the show's Web site for having "already spent years in front of the camera as a model." And the Web site for *Charmed,* which NOW ranked high for its gender composition, is hyping a new cast member, Rose McGowan, "who catapulted to stardom as a sexy victim in *Scream.*" In an era of synchronicity, it is clear what these pretty packages are selling, and now they have NOW's endorsement.

Indeed, a trip to the message boards of these programs' Web sites makes it 5 clear that, if NOW thinks these teen-goddess shows smack of feminism, their fans see things rather differently. Hear are some recent snippets from chat among girls on the site for *Dawson's Creek:* "Well I am NOT a lesbian or nothing but personally I think Joey is the prettiest. I so envy her!!" and "Joey is cute, but the sexy one is Jen, she has more attitude." In fact, when Felicity chopped off her trademark tresses, her show's ratings plummeted. Reported a WB spokesman, "When she cut her hair, [women] basically said, 'I don't want to be that person; it ruins the illusion for me.'" But not to fear, ratings grew again, along with actress Russell's locks. "It's grown out," averred Susanne Daniels, the WB's entertainment president, last year. "[S]he looks fabulous . . . the hair crisis has passed." Just to be on the safe side, actresses on NOW's number-one show will not be making the same mistake. Says creator Amy Sherman-Palladino: "No one on *Gilmore Girls* will cut their hair, ever."

To be fair, NOW didn't have much to choose from. Numerous teen shows like *My So-Called Life, The Wonder Years, Party of Five,* and *The Facts of Life* have proved that teen girls need not slay vampires — or be vampy — to handle difficult life situations or to feel empowered. Unfortunately, they've all been canceled. And most of what's on the air has little feminist redeeming value — or any other sort of value, for that matter. *WWF Smackdown!,* for instance, in which breast implants are virtually a requirement for female participation, ranked appropriately poorly. But there is at least one female star who attracts viewers for her smart mouth rather than for her large breasts — Anne Robinson, the surly, whip-smart host of NBC's new hit *Weakest Link.* You'd think that NOW — having complained in last year's report about "male-centered" game shows — would be flush with praise. You'd be wrong. NOW's latest report bashes the show "for its host's nasty demeanor." It adds that Robinson "struck feminist analysts as both a harsh stereotype and a tough ground breaker." Of course, any aggressive, opinionated female host is likely to take flak for not being softer or sexier. But you wouldn't expect it to come from NOW. Perhaps she should grow out her hair.

READING THE TEXT

1. What does Fazzone identify as the criteria for the "NOW Recommends" seal of approval for women-friendly television programming?

2. Why is Fazzone surprised that the National Organization for Women applauded *Felicity* as a feminist series?

3. What sort of evidence does Fazzone present to support her claims, and to what extent do you find it adequate?

4. What sort of empowerment does Fazzone see television giving to women?

READING THE SIGNS

1. HBO's *Sex and the City* is a striking example of the postfeminist tendency in television to display women characters who "bask" in their sexuality. Watch an episode of the program, and write an essay arguing whether it empowers women or confines them to the traditional role as sex objects.

2. Divide the class into groups, and brainstorm a television series concept of which you think Fazzone would approve. Then have the class vote on which would make the best series.

3. Fazzone does not actually analyze an episode of one of the shows she discusses. Select one of the programs, watch an episode, and write an analysis of

the gender roles of the female characters. To develop your ideas, read or reread Susan Douglas, "Signs of Intelligent Life on TV" (p. 250), Holly Devor, "Gender Role Behaviors and Attitudes" (p. 484), or Andre Mayer, "The New Sexual Stone Age" (p. 512).

4. Conduct an in-class debate on the postfeminist tendency to emphasize female sexuality, arguing whether it is an extension of the women's movement's goals or a setback. To develop your ideas, consult the introduction to Chapter 6, "We've Come a Long Way, Maybe: Gender Codes in American Culture" (p. 475).

TAD FRIEND

You Can't Say That

There's a funny disjunction between the language that we routinely use in everyday life and the language that is permitted on television, and in this in-depth report Tad Friend shows just how television censors itself to avoid legal trouble. With every network having a Standards and Practices staff who must approve every "bullshit" or "asshole" and every "controversial" situation or topic ("onscreen lesbian kisses [can] be 'romantic' but not 'passionate'"), creating a realistic TV episode is no easy matter. But as shows like The Sopranos *continue to push the envelope of television language and content, Friend suggests, the line between the permitted and the forbidden will continue to blur. The author of* Lost in Mongolia *(2001), Friend is a staff writer for* The New Yorker.

As a cocreator of the television series *NYPD Blue,* the writer-producer Steven Bochco has done more than his share to broaden the vocabulary promulgated over America's favorite living-room appliance. This season, Bochco has a new legal drama, *Philly,* on ABC, and he decided to use its premiere episode as the occasion for another breakthrough. For the first time, the barnyard epithet of Nixon White House fame would be heard on a network show. In the *Philly* episode, a scrappy defense attorney who has been put in jail for a few hours is told by a fellow-prisoner that one of her clients killed a man. "Bullshit!" she says. "Bullshit?" the prisoner replies. "I saw it happen." Whereupon the network would cut to a commercial and boils would break out on man and beast; and, after the boils, there would be thunder and hail, and, after the hail, swarms of locusts.

That was the plan, anyway. But when I spoke with Bochco shortly before the episode aired, in late September, he'd just got off the phone with Alan

Braverman, ABC's head of legal affairs, who told him that the network's Standards and Practices department considered the word "unacceptably coarse."

Bochco persisted. "I told Alan, 'The audience that watches my *NYPD Blue* and hears "scumbag," "douche bag," and "prick" isn't going to reach for the remote if it hears "bullshit." When you're surrounded by junkies and whores in a jailhouse bullpen, the word just goes by naturally. Furthermore, it's not about this one word; it's about trying to entertain adults at 10 P.M., when they can easily flip to *The Sopranos*.'" According to Bochco, Braverman replied, "We do live in the age of *The Sopranos,* but we also live in the world of restrictions placed by our advertisers and by the government. These are gut calls, but this word crosses a line."

ABC employs twenty-seven Standards and Practices censors, or "editors," and the other broadcast networks have similar staffs. Most Standards editors have experience as lawyers, teachers, and members of the clergy. They scrutinize every show and commercial for vulgarity, sexuality, violence, and subject matter that could violate FCC standards of obscenity, community standards of indecency, and, particularly, corporate standards of comfort. (They also insure that dramas present both sides of controversial subjects like gun control, that game shows are not rigged, and that "reality" shows are more or less unstaged.) A Standards department reports not to the entertainment division but to the corporate executives; it is the superego that shushes the programmers' noisy id. Bryce Zabel, who produced *MANTIS,* a 1995 Fox show about a black superhero, says, "The creative executives would ask me to up the 'action' quotient" — car chases, "run and jumps" (to a helicopter's dangling rope ladder, say), and "sneak and creeps" (gunfights in parking garages) — "and then Standards would question those very things."

Without the approval of the Standards people, nothing goes on the air. 5 They are the ones who insist that onscreen lesbian kisses be "romantic" but not "passionate" (i.e., no tongue); that nasty words be presented in an "empowering" context ("Who you callin' a bitch?"); that guns be aimed at people's heads only in hostage or war situations; that role models do not smoke; that we never see "instructional activities" like rolling a joint or cutting a line of cocaine; and that if someone does take drugs he faces "consequences" — if not arrest, rehab, AIDS, or death, then at least a weepy speech from a concerned friend. Standards departments limit the range of the characters we see — there are few jolly adulterers or lovable anarchists in prime time — and they try to keep stories up-lifting. David Chase, the creator of *The Sopranos,* recalls that when he produced a made-for-television movie called *Off the Minnesota Strip* for ABC, in 1980, Standards wanted him to insert a soupy version of Beethoven's *Ode to Joy* over his ending, in which a fifteen-year-old girl heads off down the Sunset Strip, evidently to become a hooker. "This is a prosocial job," Olivia Cohen-Cutler, the head of ABC's Standards department, told me. "We don't want evil to triumph."

The constantly shifting standards of Hollywood's Standards departments provide a sharper picture of mainstream American mores than any Gallup poll, presidential campaign, or John Irving novel. After the terrorist attacks of September 11th, Standards departments examined every show and commercial for material that could now seem raw or insensitive. Among many other redactions, NBC cancelled a *Law & Order* miniseries about a terrorist attack on New York City; the premiere of *Third Watch,* which dealt with a blackout and subsequent unrest in New York; and a repeat episode of *Will & Grace* which contained a few jokes about airport security. CBS pulled an episode of *The Agency* in which the C.I.A. fights an anthrax threat, and cut an exchange from *The Ellen Show* in which Ellen DeGeneres's character says, "My business collapsed" and her mother replies, "Well, thank your lucky stars you weren't there at the time." Fox snipped a bin Laden joke from a *Family Guy* rerun and cut scenes of a terrorist blowing up a plane from the premiere of a new drama, *24.* Fox's head of Standards, Roland McFarland, told me, "The President has an approval rating of 90 percent. So we won't be taking any more satirical cheap shots at him at this time."

In the last decade, Standards departments have become more tolerant of sex and foul language, but they have cracked down on violence and become more insistent about the politically correct presentation of minorities. Lately, however, they seem to be swinging wildly back and forth between allowing everything and allowing nothing. As recently as 1990, television critics and watchdog groups were outraged when CBS permitted a six-year-old girl on the sitcom *Uncle Buck* to say, "You suck!" Since then, "suck," "fart," "crap" and "friggin'" have all made their way into the network venacular, and on the pilot episodes of this fall's new shows you could see a man and a wolf-woman engage in topless quasi bestiality (the CBS drama *Wolf Lake)*, hear a five-year-old girl announce, "I have a vagina" (the ABC sitcom *According to Jim;* a network spokesman insists that she actually says "bagina"), and even be inadvertently exposed to the NBC comedy *Emeril.*

Yet producers of situation comedies that air at eight o'clock — a time formerly known as "the family hour" — still routinely receive memos from Standards decreeing that "the number of 'hells' and 'damns' must be cut by one-half." Even if only three per cent of a show's audience gets upset by a particular word or image, that's still a population the size of Salt Lake City that's up in arms. (In fact, it usually is Salt Lake City.) The goal of Standards is to make sure nobody's mad, ever.

This confused state of affairs was exemplified on CBS's *The Late Show with David Letterman* in May, when Letterman repeatedly showed a clip from CBS's live broadcast of *On Golden Pond* which featured the word "bullshit." When Letterman used the word nine times himself — to describe his feelings about not being able to use the word — network censors bleeped the second syllable every time. Martin D. Franks, the executive vice-president to whom CBS Program Practices reports, explained to me that "*On Golden Pond* has some classic status, so the term wasn't lazy or exploitative, as it might be if used simply to titillate on one of our eight-o'clock sitcoms." Why, then, couldn't Letterman use the term later at night? "I would say to David, 'Not to use the word in *Golden Pond* would be a compromise of creative freedom, but you haven't convinced me that the word is vital to your creative freedom.'"

As it happens, the tussle between Bochco and ABC over the word "bull-shit" was satirized in advance in June, on a *South Park* episode that used the word "shit" for the first time on Comedy Central — and used it a hundred and sixty-two times. Comedy Central's advertisers weren't bothered by the episode, and programmers at other networks became more eager than ever to do away with Standards departments. The six-year-old UPN is the first modern network not to have such a department, and Dean Valentine, its president and CEO, dismisses his competitors' Standards and Practices guidelines as "the accumulated stupidities of the years."

"There's a huge struggle going on," Jeff Zucker, the president of NBC Entertainment, told me. "I'm not saying we should use 'fuck' and show frontal nudity, but standards shouldn't even be where they were a few years ago. I have weekly discussions with Alan Wurtzel" — the network's head of Standards and Practices — "in which I try to loosen the floodgates and he tries to dam them up. We're now arguing over the word 'asshole' in a pilot. I'm not winning."

"It's a tonnage issue," Wurtzel told me. "Last year, HBO became the creative gold standard, so all our drama guys are saying, 'Why can't we be like *The Sopranos*?' and all our sitcom guys are saying, 'Why can't we be like *Sex and the City*?' One 'asshole' is not going to cause the fall of the republic, but do we want to become known as the 'asshole' network?" On the other hand, Wurtzel acknowledged, Standards has to evolve: "If we're too far behind the culture, viewers will feel *ER* and *Friends* are getting stodgy, and they'll leave. But if we're too far ahead advertisers will get nervous, and they'll leave. Either way, we lose."

In 1953, Rod Serling, who later created *The Twilight Zone,* wrote, "Because TV is a mass medium, you have to be governed by mass medium taboos. Easy on sex. Easy on violence. Nix on religion. Gently does it on controversial themes." Television is to the culture as the seventies was to the sixties — not the locomotive of change but the caboose.

This timidity has its roots in the way television entertainment began. In the early 1950s, most shows, such as *Texaco Star Theatre,* were sponsored by a single advertiser who had enormous power over the program. The Mars Company, which sponsored *Circus Boy,* frowned on references to competing snacks such as cookies and ice cream. When the American Gas Association presented *Judgment at Nuremberg* live on CBS's *Playhouse 90,* in 1959, it insisted that the word "gas" be cut from the script, leading to the suggestion that millions of Jews died in " . . . chambers."

More recently, Standards departments have been affected by a different 15 sort of economic imperative. The most startling show in the past decade has been *NYPD Blue,* which débuted on ABC in 1993, at a time when the network was flailing. After a year of negotiations, Steven Bochco persuaded ABC to let him use vulgarities thirty seven times in each episode, as long as he confined himself to an agreed-upon glossary of such words as "balls," "bastard," "dick-head," "fat ass," "johnson," "prick," "screwing," "scumbag," and "tits." He could show breasts from the side (Standards combed the show's footage frame by frame, looking for a forbidden peep of nipple), and dorsal but not frontal nudity, and he could suggest, but never show, intercourse.

Fifty-seven affiliates refused to air the first episode, and ABC couldn't charge its full ad rate on the show for years. "The networks wouldn't let anyone follow my lead, out of fear," Bochco said. "But fear is also why ABC agreed to make the show — they allowed us latitude because they were getting killed in the ratings. It wasn't an artistic decision; it was an economic decision. It's never an artistic decision."

By watching television carefully, you can almost hear what Standards has taken out of a show, or see why risqué material was left in. A few basic rules clarify how a show's content reveals its place in the network's estimation.

1. The more times you hear "ass," the more successful the show is. "Ass" is the most common vulgarity on network television: According to the Parents Television Council, it can be heard 1.04 times per hour on eight-o'clock shows. When *Martin* first aired, on Fox, in 1992, the sitcom's producers were permitted one "ass" per half-hour episode. As *Martin* became successful, the show's producers were allowed two, then three, then unlimited "ass"es. (On a drama pilot at another network this year, producers were permitted three "ass"es, or 1.5 "ass"es per half hour, which indicates some mild "ass" inflation.)

2. If a show invites you to picture a character's genitalia, it's a proven hit. In the second season of *Friends,* Standards vetoed a story line about the girls fashioning an artificial foreskin for Joey, who was up for an acting role that, for reasons it would be tedious to describe, required an uncircumcised male. This spring, in its seventh season, *Friends* did the foreskin plot. And the "master of your domain" episode on *Seinfeld,* about masturbation, ran in the show's sixth season.

3. A program that shows large expanses of skin makes a lot of money for the network. "When Standards raised a number of wardrobe issues on *Charlie's Angels* in the seventies," Fred Silverman, who was then the president of ABC Entertainment, says, "I'd take them up with my boss, Fred Pierce, and remind him that the show was doing a fifty share. And he'd say, 'Let 'em jiggle!'"

4. If a drama has commercials for Jhirmack shampoo and the Thighmaster, that's a sure indication that its subject was so controversial that the regular advertisers pulled out. A few weeks ago, Sears and Federal Express

withdrew their ads from ABC's *Politically Incorrect* after Bill Maher, the host, suggested that America's long-distance missile attacks were "cowardly." Recent shows ran ads for Trojan condoms and Craftmatic Adjustable Beds.

5. When a long-running drama is short on off-color language or risky topics, you can assume that the Standards people think it's no good. "Last year, we let Aaron Sorkin use the word 'prick' on *The West Wing*," Alan Wurtzel, at NBC, told me, "but only because it is clearly a quality show, and because the characters had been established for two years." A former NBC executive told me, "The producers of *Pretender* and *Profiler*, two extremely pedestrian shows, would always say, 'They used "ballbuster" on *Homicide* — can't we do it?' We'd say politely, 'Your show ain't *Homicide*.'"

Standards departments typically have vague written guidelines but no lists of forbidden words or proscribed scenarios. Theirs is an oral culture, one whose strictures are handed down like Inuit tribal lore. The fiats that emerge from the Standards editors' deliberations are scrupulous, nuanced, and often hilarious. The producers of the CBS drama *Delvecchio* were once told to amend the term "rat doo-doo" to "rat doo"; when a hunchback got knifed on *Get Smart*, the censors decreed that "it would be better if the knife were to go into the part of his back which isn't hunched."

Writers see Standards editors as Emily Posts who cling to archaic rules; the editors see themselves as Emily Dickinsons who strive to preserve a cultural standard. "We're accused of limiting creativity," a Standards editor told me. "But I feel we're challenging creativity. Instead of using 'damn' eleven times, can't you come up with some other word?" Censor-writer colloquies would delight William Safire: does "scumbag" connote a repellent individual, or will older viewers recall that it originally meant a condom? "Schmuck" means a jerk in Los Angeles, but is it still a synonym for "penis" in New York? "Dick" and "pussy" are now sometimes allowed, but only as insults (it may thus be permissible to say "You're a dick," but never "Your dick . . . ").

A few years ago, on a *Mad About You* episode in which Paul filmed a docu- 25 mentary about horses, viewers saw a stallion and a mare coupling. "One horse had a huge erection, and if you're eight years old it's scary to see that," an NBC Standards executive says. "We got a lot of flak, and we deserved it. We'd broken the covenant not to surprise the audience."

That covenant is the one great unspoken standard. In 1997, when Ellen Morgan kissed another woman on *Ellen*, ABC put an "adult content" warning on the episode. An ABC Standards editor maintains, "We put the warning on because Ellen was making a big change. She had been asexual, the crazy single girl, and all of a sudden she became sexual." Yet ABC was clearly skittish about this particular change. The executive producer of *Ellen*, Tim Doyle, says, "I framed the Standards note saying, 'It is unacceptable for Laurie to kiss Ellen here. Please substitute another way for her to express her feeling of togetherness.'"

A forthcoming episode of Fox's *24* also features a gay interlude, and

Standards responded with a memo: "The businessman could be startled with his shirt halfway off, or something similar . . . but we cannot accept any inference that Rogow is/was going down on the guy." Pivoting, with somewhat less concern, to deal with violence, the memo went on to say, "Please use good taste when depicting Bridgit getting hit by the 'long-distance, silenced shot to the head.'"

Standards departments pay particular attention to impiety. Aaron Sorkin, the creator of *The West Wing,* said, "What has surprised me most about television is that Standards and Practices made it very clear that I will be able to say 'mother-fucker' on the air before I can take the Lord's name in vain. They fear that religious groups will aggressively boycott our show." In one episode last year, President Bartlet exploded about being bested by a "damn street gang." "It didn't ring true," Sorkin said. "I originally wrote 'goddamn street gang.' In the movies, it would have been 'fucking street gang.' I'm fighting to get NBC to loosen the reins, and I feel 'bullshit' should be allowed, occasionally — 'That's crap' doesn't play."

The rules of engagement in this routine warfare are understood by everyone involved. Standards editors often tell one another, "Give them seven notes so you can negotiate." The writers, in turn, put "asshole" in the script a few times as "censor bait," knowing they'll have to cut it but hoping to keep two "bitch"es and a "balls" in exchange.

The latest injunction at the networks has been to present minorities as role models. This effort has been so successful that the black boss and the black judge are now clichés. Unfortunately, this "advance" is largely a retreat into safety. In 1994, the producers of the Fox sitcom *Monty* were told that a character in the pilot could not get food poisoning from a Chinese restaurant. He also could not get it from an Italian restaurant. He could, however, get it from a restaurant.

This January, NBC apologized to the National Puerto Rican Coalition for a ³⁰ *Law & Order* episode based on an incident of mayhem during New York City's Puerto Rican Day parade, and said it would not rerun the episode. Six months later, NBC apologized to the Media Action Network for Asian Americans after Sarah Silverman made a joke about "Chinks" on *Late Night with Conan O'Brien,* and said it would cut the word from reruns. Alan Wurtzel, of NBC, says, "We understand that this joke was designed to be a satirical comment on racism. But, to the Asian-American community, 'Chinks' is equivalent to 'niggers' or 'kikes.' Our most difficult Standards issue is racial stereotyping — comedy producers say, 'Don't you have a sense of humor?' and drama producers say, 'But this situation exists in real life!'" Many producers believe that a show like *All in the Family,* in which Archie Bunker inveighed against "spics, spades, Chinks, [and] Hebes" in the first episode, would never make it on the air today.

Television's fundamental internal conflict is played out through the triumphs and defeats of the Standards and Practices departments. That conflict is not between art and commerce but between commerce and commerce. Standards' mandate is to help the network gain viewers (and thus advertisers) without going so far that it loses viewers (and thus advertisers). Fred Silverman, who in his long career helped lead the entertainment division of each of the three major networks, predicts, "If UPN has real success, and it needs to protect what it has, it'll get a Standards department." And yet Standards and Practices' insistence on presenting "commonly accepted values" also helps explain why the networks have lost half of their audience in the last fifteen years. Standards departments throw the baby out with the bathwater. Then the networks wonder why it's so quiet in the tub.

And so Steven Bochco's first episode of *Philly* did not contain the word "bullshit" after all. Instead, the defense attorney said, "No way!" "I'll revisit the matter if the show's a hit," Bochco told me. "Because then the network will be terrified to piss me off. And I guarantee you Aaron Sorkin would win his struggles with NBC if he got a really, really bad case of writer's block. We're going to win the 'bullshit' battle before long, because either I, or Aaron, or someone will be willing to be a real" — he paused, seeking the mot juste — "asshole."

READING THE TEXT

1. Summarize the history of television self-censorship as reported by Friend.

2. According to Friend, what topics are especially subject to censorship on television?

3. Explain how Standards and Practices policies operate as a sign of mainstream American values, in Friend's view.

4. How have race relations affected TV self-censorship according to Friend?

READING THE SIGNS

1. Write an opinion piece in which you support, oppose, or complicate the proposition that television has a responsibility to restrict its language and content in response to cultural sensitivities.

2. Conduct an in-class debate over whether television programs should continue the practice of presenting ethnic minorities as role models. To develop your ideas, study TV programs that include minority characters, and consult Michael Omi's "In Living Color: Race and American Culture" (p. 557) and Benjamin DeMott's "Put on a Happy Face: Masking the Differences between Blacks and Whites" (p. 569).

3. Friend asserts that "writers see Standards editors as Emily Posts who cling to archaic rules; the editors see themselves as Emily Dickinsons who strive to preserve a cultural standard" (para. 24). In an essay, argue which of these two perspectives is the more accurate or propose your own alternative characterization of Standards editors.

4. Friend believes that the patterns of self-censorship by Standards departments reveal a clear picture of "mainstream American mores" (para.6). Write an essay in which you analyze what today's industry standards say about current American cultural values.

TRICIA ROSE
Bad Sistas

Female rappers tell male rappers where to get off when it comes to sexual harassment and exploitation, don't they? Such is the manifest message of rap videos from such performers as Salt 'N' Pepa and MC Lyte. But as Tricia Rose (b. 1962) argues in this selection from Black Noise: Rap Music and Black Culture in Contemporary America *(1994), the tendency of such raps to situate women in the context of sexual courtship rituals undermines their surface meaning. Wouldn't it be even more subversive to perform raps that have nothing to do with sexual relations at all, Rose implies? An associate professor of history and Africana studies at New York University, Rose is coeditor, with Andrew Ross, of* Microphone Fiends: Youth Music and Youth Culture *(1994).*

Courting Disaster

Raps written by women that specifically concern male-female relationships almost always confront the tension between trust and savvy; between vulnerability and control. Some raps celebrate their sisters for "getting over" on men, rather than touting self-reliance and honesty. For example, in Icey Jaye's "It's a Girl Thang," she explains how she and her friends find ways to spend as much of their dates' money as possible and mocks the men who fall for their tricks. Similarly, in the video for Salt 'N' Pepa's "Independent" Salt accepts several expensive gifts from a string of dates who hope to win her affection with diamond necklaces and rings. In raps such as these, women are taking advantage of the logic of heterosexual courtship in which men coax women into submission with trinkets and promises for financial security. Nikki D's "Up the Ante for the Panty" and B. W. P.'s "We Want Money" are more graphic examples of a similar philosophy. However, for the most part, when they choose to rap about male-female relations, women rappers challenge the depictions of women in many male raps as gold diggers and address the fears many women share regarding male dishonesty and infidelity.

MC Lyte and Salt 'N' Pepa have reputations for biting raps that criticize men who manipulate and abuse women. Their lyrics tell the story of men taking advantage of women, cheating on them, taking their money, and leaving them for other unsuspecting female victims. These raps are not mournful ballads about the trials and tribulations of being a heterosexual woman. Similar to women's blues, they are caustic, witty, and aggressive warnings directed at men and at other women who might be seduced by them in the future. By offering a woman's interpretation of the terms of heterosexual courtship, these women's raps cast a new light on male-female sexual power relations and depict women as resistant, aggressive participants. Yet, even the raps that explore and revise women's role in the courtship process often retain the larger patriarchal parameters of heterosexual courtship.

Salt 'N' Pepa's single "Tramp" is strong advice, almost boot camp, for single black women. "Tramp" is not, as Salt 'N' Pepa warn, a "simple rhyme," but a parable about courtship rituals between men and women:

> Homegirls attention you must pay to what I say
> Don't take this as a simple rhyme
> Cause this type of thing happens all the time
> Now what would you do if a stranger said "Hi"
> Would you dis him or would you reply?
> If you'd answer, there is a chance
> That you'd become a victim of circumstance
> Am I right fellas? tell the truth
> Or else I'll have to show and prove
> You are what you are I am what I am
> It just so happens that most men are TRAMPS.[1]

In the absence of any response to "Am I right fellas?" (any number of sampled male replies easily could have been woven in here), Salt 'N' Pepa "show and prove" the trampings of several men who "undress you with their eyeballs," "think you're a dummy, on the first date, had the nerve to tell me he loves me" and of men who always have sex on the mind. Salt 'N' Pepa's parable defines promiscuous *males* as tramps, and thereby inverts the common belief that male sexual promiscuity is a status symbol. This reversal undermines the degrading "woman as tramp" image by stigmatizing male promiscuity. Salt 'N' Pepa suggest that women who respond to sexual advances made by these men are victims of circumstance. In this case, it is predatory, disingenuous men who are the tramps.

The music video for "Tramps" is a comic rendering of a series of social club scenes that highlight tramps on the make, mouth freshener in hand,

[1]Salt 'N' Pepa, "Tramp," *Hot, Cool & Vicious* (Next Plateau Records, 1986).

testing their lines on the nearest woman. Dressed in the then-latest hip hop street gear, Salt 'N' Pepa perform the song on television, on a monitor perched above the bar. Because they appear on the television screen, they seem to be surveying and critiquing the club action, but the club members cannot see them. There are people dancing and talking together (including likeable men who are coded as "nontramps"), who seem unaware of the television monitor. Salt 'N' Pepa are also shown in the club, dressed in very stylish, sexy outfits. Salt 'N' Pepa act as decoys, talking and flirting with the tramps to flesh out the dramatization of tramps on the prowl. They make several knowing gestures at the camera to reassure the viewer that they are unswayed by the tramps' efforts.

The tramps and their victims interact only with body language. The club 5 scenes have no dialogue; we hear only Salt 'N' Pepa lyrics over the musical tracks for "Tramp," which serve respectively as the video's narrative and the club's dance music. Viewing much of the club action from Salt 'N' Pepa's authoritative position — through the television monitor — we can safely observe the playful but cautionary dramatization of heterosexual courtship. One tramp who is rapping to a woman postures and struts, appearing to ask something like the stock pick-up line: "what is your zodiac sign, baby?" When she shows disgust and leaves her seat, he repeats the same body motions and gestures on the next woman who happens to sit down. Near the end of the video, a frustrated "wife" enters the club and drags one of the tramps home, smacking him in the head with her pocketbook. Salt 'N' Pepa are standing next to the wife's tramp in the club, shaking their heads as if to say "what a shame." Simultaneously, they are pointing and laughing at the husband from the television monitor. At the end of the video, a still frame of each man is stamped "tramp," and Salt 'N' Pepa revel in having identified and exposed them. They then leave the club together, without men, seemingly enjoying their skill at exposing the real intentions of these tramps.

Salt 'N' Pepa are "schooling" women about the sexual politics of the club scene, by engaging in and critiquing the drama of heterosexual courtship. The privileged viewer is a woman who is directly addressed in the lyrics and presumably can empathize fully with the visual depiction and interpretation of the scenes. The video's resolution can be interpreted as a warning to both men and women. Women: Don't fall for these men either by talking to them in the clubs or believing the lies they'll tell you when they come home. Men: You will get caught eventually, and you'll be embarrassed. Another message suggested by the video for "Tramp" is that women can go to these clubs, successfully play along with "the game" as long as the power of female sexuality and the terms of male desire are understood and negotiated.

However, "Tramp" does not interrogate "the game" itself. "Tramp" implicitly accepts the larger dynamics and power relationships between men and women. Although the tramps are embarrassed and momentarily contained at the end of the video, in no way can it be suggested that these tramps will stop hustling women and cheating on their wives. More important, what of women's desire? Not only is it presumed that men will continue their dishonest behavior, but women's desire for an idealized monogamous heterosexual relationship is implicitly confirmed as an unrealized (but not unrealizable?) goal. In their quest for an honest man, should not the sobering fact that "most men are tramps" be considered a point of departure for rejecting the current courtship ritual altogether?

Salt 'N' Pepa leave the club together, seemingly pleased by their freedom and by their ability to manipulate men into pursuing them "to no end." But the wife drags her husband home — she is not shocked but rather frustrated by what appears to be frequent dishonest behavior. What conclusion is to be drawn from this lesson? Do not trust tramps, separate the wheat from the tramps, and continue in your quest for an honest, monogamous man. "Tramp" is courtship advice for women who choose to participate in the current configuration of heterosexual courtship, it does not offer an alternative paradigm for such courtship, and in some ways it works inside of the very courtship rules that it highlights and criticizes. At best, "Tramp" is an implicit critique of the club scene as a setting for meeting potential mates as well as of the institution of marriage that permits significant power imbalances clearly weighted in favor of men.

MC Lyte has a far less comedic response to Sam, a boyfriend whom she catches trying to pick up women. MC Lyte's underground hit "Paper Thin" is one of the most scathingly powerful raps about male dishonesty and infidelity and the tensions between trust and vulnerability in heterosexual relations. Lyte has been burned by Sam, but she has turned her experience into a black woman's anthem that sustains an uncomfortable balance between brutal cynicism and honest vulnerability:

> When you say you love me it doesn't matter
> It goes into my head as just chit chatter
> You may think it's egotistical or just very free
> But what you say, I take none of it seriously. . . .
>
> I'm not the kind of girl to try to play a man out
> They take the money and then they break the hell out.
> No that's not my strategy, not the game I play
> I admit I play a game, but it's not done that way.
> Truly when I get involved I give it my heart
>
> I mean my mind, my soul, my body, I mean every part.
> But if it doesn't work out — yo, it just doesn't.
> It wasn't meant to be, you know it just wasn't.
> So, I treat all of you like I treat all of them.
> What you say to me is just paper thin.[2]

Lyte's public acknowledgment that Sam's expressions of love were paper 10 thin is not a source of embarrassment for her but a means of empowerment.

[2]MC Lyte, "Paper Thin," *Lyte as a Rock* (First Priority Records, 1988).

She plays a brutal game of the dozens on Sam while wearing her past commitment to him as a badge of honor and sign of character. Lyte presents commitment, vulnerability, and sensitivity as assets, not indicators of female weakness. In "Paper Thin," emotional and sexual commitment are not romantic, Victorian concepts tied to honorable but dependent women; they are a part of her strategy, part of the game she plays in heterosexual courtship.

"Paper Thin's" high-energy video contains many elements present in hip hop. The video opens with Lyte, dressed in a sweatsuit, chunk jewelry, and sneakers, abandoning her new Jetta hastily because she wants to take the subway to clear her head. A few members of her male posse, shocked at her desire to leave her Jetta on the street for the subway, follow along behind her, down the steps to the subway tracks. (Her sudden decision to leave her new car for the subway and her male posse's surprised reaction seem to establish that Lyte rarely rides the subway anymore.) Lyte enters a subway car with an introspective and distracted expression. Once in the subway car, her DJ K-Rock, doubling as the conductor, announces that the train will be held in the station because of crossed signals. While they wait, Milk Boy (her female but very masculine-looking bodyguard) spots Sam at the other end of the car, rapping heavily to two stylish women, and draws Lyte's attention to him. Lyte, momentarily surprised, begins her rhyme as she stalks toward Sam. Sam's attempts to escape fail; he is left to face MC Lyte's wrath. Eventually, she throws him off the train to the chorus of Ray Charles's R&B classic, "Hit the Road Jack," and locks Sam out of the subway station and out of the action. The subway car is filled with young black teenagers, typical working New Yorkers and street people, many of whom join Lyte in signifying on Sam while they groove on K-Rock's music. MC Lyte's powerful voice and no-nonsense image dominate Sam. The taut, driving music, which is punctuated by sampled guitar and drum sections and an Earth Wind and Fire horn section, complement Lyte's hard, expressive rapping style.

It is important that "Paper Thin" is set in public and on the subway, the quintessential mode of urban transportation. Lyte is drawn to the subway and seems comfortable there. She is also comfortable with the subway riders in her video; they are her community. During musical breaks between raps, we see passengers grooving to her music and responding to the drama. By setting her confrontation with Sam in the subway, in front of their peers, Lyte moves a private problem between lovers into the public arena and effectively dominates both spaces.

When her DJ, the musical and mechanical conductor, announces that crossed signals are holding the train in the station, it frames the video in a moment of communication crisis. The notion of crossed signals represents the inability of Sam and Lyte to communicate with one another, an inability that is primarily the function of the fact that they communicate on different frequencies. Sam thinks he can read Lyte's mind to see what she is thinking and then feed her all the right lines. But what he says carries no weight, no meaning. His discourse is light, it's paper thin. Lyte, who understands courtship as a game, confesses to being a player, yet expresses how she feels directly and in simple language. What she says has integrity, weight, and substance.

After throwing Sam from the train, she nods her head toward a young man standing against the subway door, and he follows her off the train. She will not allow her experiences with Sam to paralyze her but instead continues to participate on revised terms. As she and her new male friend walk down the street, she raps the final stanza for "Paper Thin" that sets down the new courtship ground rules:

> So, now I take precautions when choosing my mate
> I do not touch until the third or fourth date
> Then maybe we'll kiss on the fifth or sixth time that we meet
> Cause a date without a kiss is so incomplete
> And then maybe, I'll let you play with my feet
> You can suck the big toe and play with the middle
> It's so simple unlike a riddle . . .

Lyte has taken control of the process. She has selected her latest companion; he has not pursued her. This is an important move, because it allows her to set the tone of the interaction and subsequently articulates the new ground rules that will protect her from repeating the mistakes she made in her relationship with Sam. Yet, a central revision to her courtship terms involves withholding sexual affection, a familiar strategy in courtship rituals for women that implicitly affirms the process of male pursuit as it forestalls it. Nonetheless, Lyte seems prepared for whatever takes place. Her analysis of courtship seems to acknowledge that there are dishonest men and that she is not interested in negotiating on their terms. Lyte affirms her courtship rules as she identifies and critiques the terms of men such as Sam. In "Paper Thin" she has announced that her desire will govern her behavior and *his* ("you can suck my big toe and then play with the middle") and remains committed to her principles at the same time.

As "products of an ongoing historical conversation," "Paper Thin" and "Tramp" are explicitly dialogic texts that draw on the language and terms imbedded in long-standing struggles over the parameters of heterosexual courtship. These raps are also dialogic in their use of black collective memory via black music. Salt 'N' Pepa's "Tramp" draws its horns and parts of its rhythm section from the 1967 soul song of the same name performed by Otis Redding and Carla Thomas. Otis's and Carla's "Tramp" is a dialogue in which Carla expresses her frustration over Otis's failure in their relationship while he makes excuses and attempts to avoid her accusations.[3] Salt 'N' Pepa's musical

---

[3]See Atlantic Records. *Rhythm and Blues Collection 1966–1969,* vol. 6. In the liner notes for this collection, Robert Pruter refers to "Tramp" as a dialogue between Carla and Otis, in which Carla's "invectives" are insufficiently countered by Otis. It should be pointed out that the Otis and Carla "Tramp" is a remake of (an answer to?) Lowell and Fulsom's version made popular in 1966.

quotation of Otis's and Carla's "Tramp" set a multilayered dialogue in motion. The musical style of Salt 'N' Pepa's "Tramp" carries the blues bar confessional mode of many rhythm and blues songs updated with rap's beats and breaks. Salt 'N' Pepa are testifying to Carla's problems via the music, at the same time providing their contemporary audience with a collective reference to black musical predecessors and the history of black female heterosexual struggles.

Lyte's direct address to Sam ("when you say you love it doesn't matter") is her half of a heated conversation in which Sam is silenced by her, but nonetheless present. Lyte's announcement that she "admits playing a game but it's not done that way" makes it clear that she understands the power relationships that dictate their interaction. Lyte encourages herself and by extension black women to be fearless and self-possessed ("sucker you missed, I know who I am") in the face of significant emotional losses. Her game, her strategy, have a critical sexual difference that lays the groundwork for a black female-centered communal voice that revises and expands the terms of female power in heterosexual courtship.

The dialogic and resistive aspects in "Tramp" and "Paper Thin" are also present in the body of other women rappers' work. Many female rappers address the frustration heterosexual women experience in their desire for intimacy with and commitment from men. The chorus in Neneh Cherry's "Buffalo Stance" tells men not to mess with her, and that money men can't buy her love because it's affection that she's lookin' for; "Say That Then" from West Coast female rappers Oaktown 3-5-7 give no slack to "Finger popping, hip hoppin' wanna be bed rockin'" men; Monie Love's "It's a Shame" is a pep talk for a woman breaking up with a man who apparently needs to be kicked to the curb; Ice Cream Tee's "All Wrong" chastises women who allow men to abuse them; Monie Love's "Just Don't Give a Damn" is a confident and harsh rejection of an emotionally and physically abusive man; and MC Lyte's "I Cram to Understand U," "Please Understand," and "I'm Not Havin' It" are companion pieces to "Paper Thin."

This strategy, in which women square off with men, can be subverted and its power diminished. As Laura Berlant suggests, this mode of confrontational communication can be contained or renamed as the "female complaint." In other words, direct and legitimate criticism is reduced to "bitching" or complaining as a way of containing dissent. Berlant warns that the "female complaint . . . as a mode of expression is an admission and recognition both of privilege and powerlessness . . . circumscribed by a knowledge of woman's inevitable delegitimation within the patriarchal public sphere." Berlant argues that resistance to sexual oppression must take place "in the patriarchal public sphere, the place where significant or momentous exchanges of power are perceived to take place," but that the female complaint is devalued, marginalized, and ineffective in this sphere. Berlant offers an interpretation of "Roxanne's Revenge," an early and popular rap record by black female rapper Roxanne Shante, as an example of the pitfalls of the "female complaint." Attempts were made to contain and humiliate Roxanne on a compilation record that included several other related answer records. Berlant says that "Roxanne's Revenge" is vulnerable to "hystericization by a readily available phallic discourse [which] is immanent in the very genre of her expression."[4]

Berlant is making an important point about the vulnerability of women's voices to devaluation. No doubt women's angry responses have long been made to appear hysterical and irrational or whiny and childlike. I am not sure, though, that we can equate attempts to render women's voices as "complaint" with the voices themselves. To do so may place too much value on the attempts to contain women. "Roxanne's Revenge" gave voice to a young girl's response to real-life street confrontations with men. She entered into black male-dominated public space and drew a great deal of attention away from the UTFO song to which she responded. More importantly, "Roxanne's Revenge" has retained weight and significance in hip hop since 1985 when it was released. This has not been the case for UTFO, the UTFO song, or any of the fabricated responses on the compilation record. Much of the status of the original UTFO song "Roxanne Roxanne" is a result of the power of Roxanne Shante's answer record. What Berlant illustrates is the ways in which Roxanne's "female complaint" needed to be labeled as such and then contained precisely because it was threatening. It did not go unnoticed, because it was a compelling voice in the public domain that captured the attention of male and female hip hop fans. The compilation record is clearly an attempt at containing her voice, but it was in my estimation an unsuccessful attempt. Furthermore, such attempts at circumscription will continue to take place when partial, yet effective, attacks are made, whether in the form of the female complaint or not. Nonetheless, Berlant's larger argument, which calls for substantial female public sphere presence and contestation, is crucial. These public sphere contests must involve more than responses to sexist male speech; they must also entail the development of sustained, strong female voices that stake claim to public space generally.

READING THE TEXT

1. What are the standard themes of female rap videos, according to Rose?

2. How, according to Rose, do many women's rap videos inadvertently subvert the messages of female empowerment that they intend to send?

3. What does Rose believe are the explicit and implicit messages of Salt 'N' Pepa's "Tramp" video, and how does she feel about those messages?

4. In your own words, summarize Rose's interpretation of MC Lyte's "Paper Thin."

READING THE SIGNS

1. Using Rose's article as your critical framework, compare and contrast a male and female rap video. What gender roles do you see in each, and what response is a viewer likely to have to them? To develop your ideas, read or reread Holly Devor's "Gender Role Behaviors and Attitudes" (p. 484).

[4]Laura Berlant, "The Female Complaint," *Social Text,* Fall, 237–59, 1988.

2. In your journal, brainstorm a list of attributes that you would like to give your gender in a video of your own design. Then write a "screenplay" for your own rap video, being sure to incorporate your preferred attributes. Share your screenplay with your class.

3. Watch a current video by either one of the artists Rose discusses or another female rapper. Then write an analysis of your video, examining whether it perpetuates, in Rose's words, "the larger patriarchal parameters of heterosexual courtship" (para. 2).

4. Rose, Susan Douglas ("Signs of Intelligent Life on TV," p. 250), and Andre Mayer ("The New Sexual Stone Age," p. 512) discuss the ways in which popular culture perpetuates traditional gender roles even while it may present a superficially feminist slant. In class, discuss this phenomenon, exploring the reasons behind it. Do you see any evidence that this pattern may change in the twenty-first century? Do you wish to see it change, and why or why not?

DAVID CORIO

SALT 'N' PEPA

READING THE SIGNS

1. What does this photo of Salt 'N' Pepa tell you about rap conventions? That is, based on the evidence in this photo, what does it mean to look like a female rap star? Be sure to examine clothing, hairstyles, jewelry, gestures, and so on.

2. How does this look compare to that of other genres of popular music, such as blues, rock, country, punk, or reggae?

3. The photograph was taken in 1995. How have rap styles changed since then?

DAVID SCHIFF

The Tradition of the Oldie

*When National Public Radio chose to celebrate the millennium with a list
of the "100 most important American musical works of the twentieth
century," over half of its choices, by David Schiff's (b. 1945) estimate,
were popular songs from the period between 1900 and 1979. Aside from
leaving out most of the last twenty years, the NPR 100 also included only
eight classical works (seven if you don't count Ferde Grofé's* Grand
Canyon Suite*). Such an exclusion carries a profound cultural message,
Schiff believes, namely, that the traditional cultural relevance of art music has been supplanted by that most nostalgic of musical compositions:
the oldie. Indeed, in music, as everywhere else in contemporary America,
popular culture is overwhelming elite culture, and it is the song that
speaks to us now, not the symphony. The author of* Gershwin: Rhapsody
in Blue *(1997), Schiff is a composer and professor of music at Reed College.*

Fans of the recent movie *High Fidelity* know that an obsession with top-song
lists is a symptom of male narcissistic personality disorder. The antihero
(played by John Cusack), a used-record dealer, tries to make sense of his serial
disasters with women by ranking and re-ranking popular songs in top-five
lists suited to every emotional crisis. The appearance late in 1999 of National
Public Radio's "100 most important American musical works of the twentieth
century" may be a sign that public radio, too, suffers from neediness, and not
just during pledge drives. Even if I disagree with the list about half the time,
though (and what use is a list if you can't argue with it?), it is reassuring evidence that despite the saturation of our environment with sound fillers,
people still care passionately about music.

The question, of course, is what music and which people. If lists are a guy
thing, as *High Fidelity* would have it, then so are Web surveys, which usually
attract a male, upper-middle-class, lower-middle-aged response. An unspecified group of "NPR staff, critics, and scholars" created a ballot of 300 works
which they posted on the NPR Web site for ten days, attracting 14,000 votes.
Perhaps to lend authority to the final list (available at **http://www.npr.org**),
NPR also invited about twenty musicians, including Wynton Marsalis and
Michael Feinstein, to vote, even though their impact on the totals would be
statistically insignificant. Each of the top 100 works became the subject of a
five-to-fifteen-minute segment presented on NPR news programs such as
Morning Edition and *All Things Considered* over twelve months.

Any list invites skepticism, especially one whose pretentious claims
would be more appropriate coming from the Wizard of Oz than from Susan

Stamberg or Noah Adams. "Here's our definition of 'most important,'" the introduction to the final list on the Web site says.

> By virtue of its achievement, beauty, or excellence, the work is an important milestone of American music in the twentieth century. It significantly changed the musical landscape, opened new horizons, or in itself had a major effect on American culture and civilization.

Good grief! Unlike *Rolling Stone*'s list of top 100 pop songs, the NPR 100 seems contrived, the result of a government-mediated list merger rather than a coherent viewpoint. NPR did not publish the names of its "staff, critics, and scholars" (again unlike *Rolling Stone,* which names the people who compile its list) or the actual tallies. So much for the usual meaning of "public."

No doubt the meetings at which the ballot was determined were rancorous; people at NPR seemed touchy on the subject when I called to ask about it. The carefully orchestrated diversity of the ballot and its knowing combination of popular favorites and cult esoterica has a certain academic whiff — it could be required listening for American Music 101. The ballot wasted nominations on obscurities like Peter Mennin's *Moby Dick* and Spike Jones's "Der Fuehrer's Face" while omitting long-respected classical works such as Edgard Varèse's *Ionisation* and Chales Ives's Symphony no. 4, popular musicals like *Bye Bye Birdie* and *The Sound of Music,* and popular songs like "Mrs. Robinson" and — how soon they forget — Michael Jackson's "Thriller."

Whatever the shortcomings of the process, the result is a fascinating mirror of elite and popular musical taste today. By my estimate, sixteen of the top 100 are popular songs from 1900–1949, fifteen are popular songs from 1950–1959, and twenty-five are popular songs or albums from 1960–1979. Just three are popular recordings from 1980–2000 (the MTV generation does not listen to NPR), and one of these is *Graceland,* which was made by Paul Simon, an artist associated with the sixties as much as with the eighties. Two are religious songs; nine are the scores for stage or film musicals, mostly from the mid-century "golden age"; sixteen are jazz recordings. Six are film scores or "other." Eight are classical works — if you count Ferde Grofé's *Grand Canyon Suite,* a symphonic pops-concert staple, as classical, and Stravinsky's *Symphony of Psalms,* a work composed in Paris in 1930, albeit by a future U.S. citizen, as American.

To a cynic, the overwhelming preponderance of songs — as opposed to extended compositions — on the list might appear to reflect the shortened national attention span more than any musical values. Equating the song genre with American music does, however, represent a growing convergence of popular and critical opinions. Writers on American music have always recognized the existence of highbrow and lowbrow, art and pop, "cultivated" and "vernacular" traditions. Until recently most histories of American music, while recognizing the role of popular song, have emphasized the accomplishments of art composers like Ives and Aaron Copland or elevated jazz to the status of "America's classical music" or musical comedy to "American opera."

In the past decade film scores have begun to attract similar scholarly attention. Although NPR's ballot amply represented these recently exalted genres, the final list, less conditioned by academic fashion, has a distinctive — and, I would say, more honest — profile. The voters rejected the more musicologically correct candidates and overwhelmingly favored a category of music hitherto scorned by scholars: the oldie.

Thirty years ago expert taste and even some popular opinion would have bowed to the shock of the new, assuming that experiment and provocation were signs of artistic accomplishment. Oldies tell us about the way we were, not about the shape of things to come; they satisfy a need for a usable past. Most American cities have a couple of oldies radio stations. Numbingly repeated ads on late-night TV urge us to buy anthologies of the greatest hits from the fifties to the eighties. It is easy to dismiss oldies as the ephemera of the Me Generation. But their transient nature does not negate the importance of a serious aesthetic principle — call it the tradition of the oldie. Let's list the top five components of the oldie aesthetic:

- Oldies are songs, fusions of words and music.
- Oldies (when they were new) marked the passage from adolescence to adulthood, from hormones to heartbreak.
- Oldies are forever linked to their actual historical setting, naming the moment of our fortunate fall into identity and conveying a palpable sense of place and time.
- Oldies are our inner classics. They shape the soundtrack of our lives around indelible emotional moments that remain as vivid as a presidential assassination or an earthquake.
- Oldies, because they are products of mass media, connect the lives of millions, often defining a generation's lifestyle and politics.

Looked at this way, oldies become not just respectable but eminently respectable. In fact, the oldie aesthetic explains the persistent appeal of a lot of classical music, particularly opera, as well as of popular songs. Though we associate the classical category with instrumental music, its prestige is a recent phenomenon, barely a hundred years old and fading fast. Even in the heyday of classical music, symphonies, usually in individual movements, were used to usher people in and out of the theater for concerts that featured operatic favorites. For most of musical history and in most societies music has meant song, with the essential pleasure of music coming from the way a singer, whether a Callas or a Crosby, brings words and music together.

Oldies are mini-operas. You might not suspect a link between Richard Strauss and the Supremes, but doesn't *Der Rosenkavalier* tell the same story as "Where Did Our Love Go" — with a similarly potent blend of nostalgia and eroticism? High-minded listeners might complain that Strauss is second-rate high art, devoid of seriousness, a tragic sense of life, and innovative daring —

a charge that could be leveled against most of the works on the NPR 100. But think of all the musical qualities that oldies, whether by Strauss or by the Supremes, provide instead: the way they link the self and history, psychology and culture; the way they accept the passage of time rather than demanding the timeless status of respectable classics. In her great *scena* in Act I of *Der Rosenkavalier* the Marschallin, a thirty-year-old married woman conducting an affair with a seventeen-year-old boy, describes how she goes through her palace at night stopping all the clocks, to no avail. Listening to "Where Did Our Love Go" lets us, like the Marschallin, play with time or for time, by taking us back to the emotional realities of 1964. Of course, this works only if you were somewhere between the ages of thirteen and twenty-five in 1964. This time-bound state is the essence of oldies: Because they are not universal, because my oldies are not necessarily yours, they are all the more tightly wedded to history. At our house the favorite oldie is Kate and Anna McGarrigle's "First Born," an instant time travel to Manhattan in 1977 — *our* Manhattan in *our* 1977, perhaps not yours.

Seen not as the opposite of classical music but as an aesthetic expression that 10 thrives in classical and pop repertories alike, the oldies may shed some light on the paltry showing of concert music on NPR's list. The minimal appearance of classics is on the face of it harsh evidence of the irrelevance of the concert hall to American culture. Atonal modernist works did not make the final cut (they have gone out of style even in academia), but neither did conservative classics like Roy Harris's Third Symphony, Samuel Barber's *Knoxville: Summer of 1915,* and Gian Carlo Menotti's *Amahl and the Night Visitors,* or postmodern crowd pleasers like George Crumb's *Black Angels,* John Adams's *Nixon in China,* John Corigliano's Symphony no. 1, and even Philip Glass's *Einstein on the Beach.*

According to this list, American composers, no matter what their style, have hardly anything to show for the past century of work — a sobering, if not exactly surprising, message. (When I saw the list, I imagined a *Daily News* headline: "NPR TO COMPOSERS — DROP DEAD!") It would be interesting to know if this absence is a scathing judgment more of American art music than of its European counterpart: is the marginalizing of classical music a local phenomenon — the result of relentless competition from a vital pop scene — or a worldwide reaction against an outmoded form? Not surprisingly, when I showed the list to classical musicians, they were outraged. When I showed it to college students, they didn't even notice the paucity of concert works, though they did protest the absence of their favorite bands — who are recording the oldies of the future.

It's easy to play a blame game about the classical entries — to blame NPR for pandering, classical radio stations for trivializing, and modern composers for alienating audiences. But I think the NPR 100 shows that many kinds of popular music now perform the functions once exclusively associated with art music. Over the century popular songs have expressed patriotism and social protest and love and loss with a conviction that few classical scores — though not as few as the handful on the list — have approached. The landslide victory of popular songs over symphonies and concertos and operas points to one critical failure of classical music over the past century: the failure to fuse living language with music. From "What'll I Do?" to "Let It Be" and beyond, popular songs have echoed and amplified the spoken language, turning its most potent phrases into melodies. Perhaps art composers, following the modernist dictum to "purify the dialect of the tribe," never really learned to speak that language first. It may not be too late to start.

READING THE TEXT

1. What process did National Public Radio use to select the "100 most important American musical works of the twentieth century" (para. 1)?

2. Describe in your own words the kinds of music that made the NPR 100 and those that failed to make the list.

3. What is an "oldie" (para. 6), according to Schiff, and what is the cultural significance of its popularity?

4. How, in Schiff's view, do popular songs "now perform the functions once exclusively associated with art music" (para. 12)?

READING THE SIGNS

1. Break into groups, and have each group prepare a list of top musical compositions in the post–World War II era, then compile the lists to see what kinds of music dominate the class's selections. How do the class's lists compare to the NPR 100, and how do you account for any differences?

2. Consult NPR's Web site (**npr.org**) for a full list of the NPR 100. Study the list, and analyze the pattern of results. Use your observations as the basis for an essay that explains the cultural values of those who voted in the surveys. To what extent does the list reflect Schiff's claim that Web surveys "usually attract a male, upper-middle-class, lower-middle-aged" (para. 2) respondent?

3. Study the NPR 100 list and other lists, such as *Rolling Stone*'s top 100 pop songs or similar lists compiled by a local radio station (check for postings on the station's Web site). Write an essay in which you analyze the validity of such lists. Do they function as accurate measures of an audience's taste? To what extent do you believe that they serve more as a marketing tool for the station or magazine than as a sign of popular taste?

4. Write an essay in which you argue for or against the proposition that commercial forces make it difficult for classical music to thrive in American radio. To develop support for your position, listen to a local classical music station and visit its Web site; you could also interview fans of classical music.

ROBERT HILBURN

The Not-So-Big Hit Single

The year 2001 wasn't the best for Mariah Carey. Her cinematic debut,
Glitter, *was a flop, and Virgin Records canceled her contract. But no one*
could tarnish the luster of her status as the most successful performer of
No. 1 hit singles since the Beatles and Elvis Presley. Or could they? In
this historical analysis of the No. 1 hit single, Robert Hilburn attempts to
do just that, pointing out that the "cultural impact of being No. 1" has
changed a good deal since the golden age of rock-and-roll, and that with
so many categories of music available today an artist can hit No. 1 with
as few as fifteen thousand singles sold. Anyone for a return to the days
when the likes of "I Want to Hold Your Hand" really topped the charts?
Hilburn is the pop music critic for the Los Angeles Times.

Don't cry for Mariah Carey.

Mariah Carey has mastered the art of the No. 1 record in an anonymous
pop age.

The pop diva might have been rudely dumped by Virgin Records, but she
walks away with almost as much money ($49 million) as some of those Enron
executives.

And everyone knows rival labels are lining up to sign the Long Island native with a low-ball offer, knowing that she needs desperately to reestablish
herself after her recent album and movie flops. Billy Crystal scored one of the
biggest laughs of 2001 when he used *Glitter* as the butt of a joke during "The
Concert for New York City," the September 11-related benefit concert.

Setting everyone up by suggesting the country needs to pull together, 5
Crystal said, "Whether we are Christians or Jews or Muslims, we all have to
agree on one thing . . . we can never, ever again let Mariah Carey make another movie."

Truthfully, Crystal would have been just as on target by saying, "We can
never, ever again let Mariah Carey put together another tour."

How bad was the movie *Glitter,* which cast her in the apparently too-
challenging role of a pop diva?

I didn't see *Glitter,* and judging from the box office receipts, neither did
you. But I did see Carey's concert at Staples Center in the spring of 2000, and
it was the most vacuous show by a major pop-music figure I've ever attended.
You'll see more imaginative staging concepts at middle-school talent shows.

The bad movie and the bad tour are no surprise.

For all her record sales, Carey has never been a very satisfying artist. 10
Carey is blessed with one of the great voices in modern pop, with a range that
stretches across octaves, but she has shown little imagination in the use of it.

The only reason record companies are interested in her is that she has sold more than 40 million albums in the United States, but those sales figures shouldn't be used to persuade us that she's a visionary talent, as some of her supporters try to do.

Their favorite figure is that she has more No. 1 singles (15) than anyone since the Beatles (20) and Elvis Presley (18).

On the list of meaningless pop statistics, that's No. 1 with a bullet.

Carey has mastered the art of the No. 1 record in an anonymous pop age — one in which No. 1 records carry only a fraction of the musical character and cultural impact that they did in earlier decades.

Her fans make much of the fact that Carey's teaming with Boyz II Men on "One Sweet Day" in 1995 spent more weeks at No. 1 (16) than any other record in the 1990s. 15

They might not be so quick to suggest that's a sign of excellence if they realized what record had the second-longest run at No. 1 in the 1990s: Los Del Rio's "Macarena."

One way to put the cultural importance of a No. 1 single these days into perspective is to realize that Elvis and the Beatles aren't the leaders in that category. Bing Crosby, the crooner who topped the charts in the 1930s and 1940s, had nearly as many No. 1 pop singles than those two combined: 36.

The reason Crosby's figures aren't counted by record chart researchers to-day is because he recorded in a different era — and the cultural impact of be-ing No. 1 was different.

The "modern" pop era began with the birth of rock 'n' roll in the mid-1950s, and all statistics today pretty much reflect what has happened since then. But one could argue that another dividing line needs to be drawn in terms of pop charts. Conditions in the record business are as different now from the days of Presley and the Beatles as their day was from Crosby's.

Comparing statistics from the different eras is as tricky as trying to compare Babe Ruth's and Barry Bonds's home run marks. 20

During the rock 'n' roll revolution in the 1950s, singles were the main focus of teenage record buyers. They were more affordable — you could buy four or five singles for the price of an album — and it was a lot more fun having all those 45s than an album that might have one hit song and a lot of filler.

The prominence of albums didn't begin in earnest until the arrival of Bob Dylan and the Beatles in the 1960s, when fans started having faith in the artist's ability to deliver an entire album of good work. From that time on, the primary purpose of singles has been to sell albums by exposing the music on radio. The Beatles felt so confident about their music and their popularity by 1967 that they didn't ever release a U.S. single from *Sgt. Pepper's Lonely Hearts Club Band.*

Another change has been radio formats. In the early days of rock, most young music fans listened to Top 40 radio stations that played a broad range of music, picking the strongest cuts from rock and country, R&B, and pop. That meant you could hear Presley, Aretha Franklin, Marvin Gaye, and Frank Sinatra on the same station. Because the stations appealed to such a broad range of fans, it was possible to build a national consensus when it came to No. 1 records. Who alive in 1956 didn't hear "Don't Be Cruel" or "I Want to Hold Your Hand" in 1964 or "Hey Jude" in 1968?

Today, radio formats have been broken into narrow categories — country, urban, adult contemporary, alt/college rock, modern rock, classic rock, and so on. As a result, we don't all hear the same music anymore.

There are still mainstream pop stations, but they don't show nearly the 25 same openness to a broad range of sounds that their forerunners did. Country and hard rock, for instance, are not generally welcome on these mainstream formats. There are many No. 1 records each week, one in each format. But there is no longer that consensus choice for a No. 1 hit that everyone celebrates.

The result: Singles can become No. 1 some weeks by selling as few as 15,000 copies.

Records are ranked on the charts not just by sales, but also by the amount of radio airplay they receive — and record companies spend a fortune trying to influence stations to play their releases.

Between promotional pressure and stations' desperation to hook listeners, the last factor considered is whether the record is any good. You get an idea of how flimsy a No. 1 single can be when you realize Paula Abdul and Milli Vanilli had nine No. 1 singles between them between 1988 and 1991.

Some great records have reached No. 1 in recent years, including Toni Braxton's "UnBreak My Heart," TLC's "Waterfalls," and Sinéad O'Connor's "Nothing Compares 2 U."

Most No. 1 singles, however, have gotten there because they are anony- 30 mous.

Can you even name the performers of these 1990s No. 1 hits? "I'll Be Your Everything" (No.1 for one week in 1990), "Love Takes Time" (two weeks in 1990), "The First Time" (two weeks in 1991), "Here Comes the Hotstepper" (two weeks in 1994), "Always Be My Baby" (two weeks in 1996), and "Too Close" (five weeks in 1998).

One hint: Two of them were by Carey.

Good luck.

Reading the Text

1. How, according to Hilburn, has the history of recording industry and radio station practices altered the significance of a No. 1 hit?

2. How did Bob Dylan and the Beatles change the history of the hit single, in Hilburn's view?

3. Hilburn begins his selection with an extended criticism of singer Mariah Carey. How would you characterize the tone of this opening? What effect does it have on your response to his ideas?

Reading the Signs

1. The history of the hit single, like the history of television, illustrates the effects of niche marketing to ever-more refined audience groups. Research the top prime-time television shows and top No. 1 singles of the 1960s, and compare them to the top shows and singles of the last ten years. Write an essay in which you compare and contrast the status of top-rated shows and records in the two time periods, focusing on the effects of niche marketing.

2. Conduct a poll of music fans of any generation, and ask them whether a record's status as No. 1 has any effect on their listening and album-purchasing habits. Write an essay in which you argue whether No. 1 lists reflect audience taste or whether they serve as a covert form of public relations designed to create a successful image for the artists who make it there.

3. Conduct a class discussion on the effect of downloadable music on the popular music industry. How has the Internet changed the dissemination of music? Do consumers have more choice than they did in the past?

4. Most college and university radio stations are not commercial but are instead funded by student fees, audience donations, or the school's general budget. Interview staff at your school's radio station about their choice of format and the influence that the record industry may have on their playlists. Then write an essay in which you analyze the extent to which noncommercial media have greater creative freedom than commercial media. To develop support for your analysis, listen to the range of music played both on your school's station and on local commercial stations.

TOM SHALES

Resisting the False Security of TV

Americans turn to popular culture, especially television, in times of crisis — a tendency that was dramatically demonstrated in the wake of the September 11 attacks. But was television up to the task? In this darkly comic meditation on post-9/11 TV, Tom Shales (b. 1948) worries that it wasn't, that all TV could do was to abet the profiteers while lulling us "into a false security." Passionately arguing that we can't let that happen, Shales demands that television shake us up in the aftermath of atrocity, not shake us down — even if that makes us uncomfortable. The television editor and chief television critic for The Washington Post, *Shales is a Pulitzer Prize–winning media critic whose books include* On the Air *(1982) and* Legends *(1989).*

Jeez, I'm cranky. Even for me. But I seem to have a lot of company. People are just incredibly ticked off. They're alternately irked and furious. These are times that really try men's souls, and women's too. We've never lived through anything exactly like this before, and so we don't know quite how to behave.

We look to television for cues, but this is new to television, too. As usual, it's easier to carp about what TV is doing than to come up with an alternative course of action. I do think there's an intrinsic reassurance in the fact that TV just keeps going, keeps pouring out the sitcoms and the dramas, the huff and the fluff, the schlock and the slop.

I have referred to this as "the therapeutic effect of banality." It's like: "Oh, look, honey. Kellogg's has a new cereal with strawberries in it." Or "Oh boy, kitty litter that sparkles." These trivial and distracting messages come with trivial and distracting television programs attached: Somebody's pregnant on *Friends,* and somebody's leaving *Judging Amy,* and the brothers are battling again on *Frasier.* If you want to be reminded of the war on terrorism in prime time, you can go to Fox News or CNN or watch one of the network newsmagazines. But do you?

A Jolt to Reality

Frank Rich of the *New York Times* was certainly prescient when he predicted, soon after the tragic events in New York and Washington, that the audience would quickly lose its appetite for the so-called "reality" shows. Seldom has a trend come to so complete and abrupt a halt. *The Mole* is gone. However gorgeous it is to look at, CBS's latest *Survivor* series, shot in Africa, just isn't cutting it. The same thing goes for *The Amazing Race,* which even a nonreality

285

fan like myself thought was pretty damn nifty upon its debut and now never gives it a thought. People are not talking about the characters on these shows, not rooting for anybody, not getting caught up in intrigues or alliances. Everybody might as well pack up and come home.

Very high on the list of things I think everybody is desperate to see are Demonstrations of American Competence. In their way, well-produced TV shows fill that bill, and that may be part of the reassurance factor. We still produce the best commercial TV shows in the world, by God; we've mastered that.

But there are things more profoundly satisfying than a first-rate episode of *ER*. Chief among them, recently, was a short walk taken by the president of the United States — the short walk from the dugout to the pitcher's mound at Yankee Stadium, where George W. Bush threw out the first ball in Game 3 of the World Series.

Taunting the Terrorists

It looked like a good, healthy throw, too — no sissy pitch from Bush. It also looked as though the president were wearing a bulletproof vest under his jacket, because there was an odd bulkiness to it, and he had it zipped up to the top. No one could quibble with the wisdom of taking such precautions. It did nothing to hinder the bracing, bolstering effect of seeing him out there essentially taunting the terrorists, jeering at them, giving a thumbs-up, and hurling that ball.

Of course, Fox had to screw things up a little bit with its enormous electronic billboards in the stadium. In any wide shot with the pitcher on the right, home plate on the left, the screen was dominated by one of these new superimposed banners: "Ally's back, tomorrow night on Fox." This was not only obnoxious, it was apparently ineffective, as Ms. McBeal returned for a new season with ratings that were definitely mediocre, banner or no banner.

During an actual commercial break, viewers saw one terrific spot, part of a campaign called "Live Brave." Tommy Lasorda looked into the camera and said, "You wanna fight terrorism? Go to a ballgame!" And then he barked out a few ways in which going out to the ballpark had the effect of giving the finger to Osama bin Laden.

"Play Ball"

Major League Baseball sponsored another great commercial: "We mourn. We heal. We stand united. We play. But we never forget." The last line was over a photo of the World Trade Center as it stood until the morning of September 11. Up in the stands, meanwhile, fans unfurled a banner: "USA Fears Nobody. Play Ball." You have to be moved. You have to be impressed.

Every network, of course, simply must put a label on its continuing coverage, a superficial way of making that coverage seem distinctive. "America on Guard," "America Fights Back," "America Recovers," whatever. The titles could be more descriptive: "America Gets Sick and Tired of the FBI Telling Us to Be on High Alert While the President Tells Us to Go About Our Business as Usual."

Over on CNN, and probably on other cable networks too, Robert Culp pops up now and then selling something called the American Guardian Homeguard Preparedness Kit. It consists mainly of a videotape ("How to shoot your neighbor if he breaks into your shelter"), plus a "survival pack" that looks like the stuff you find in the bathroom of a good hotel. It sells for $39.95, and dialing the 800 number to order it may be, Mr. Culp solemnly intones, the most important phone call you will ever make. Yes, the practice of cashing in on a crisis is very much with us, and for this crisis has probably only begun.

What should TV do that it isn't doing? I wish I knew. One thing worries me about TV's ability to banish thoughts of the war and the peril we face and the vicious obscenity of the September 11 attacks: Are we going to use television like Prozac to lull us into a false security — perhaps even a tolerance, an acceptance, of an appalling and treacherous evil?

We need to stay angry. We need to remember the horror of that day in 15 September. It was said in the days immediately following that the images of the airplanes crashing into the towers, and of the towers collapsing, and of people leaping from windows to escape the murderous heat, were being cheapened through overexposure, that they were being shown too often. And the networks largely pulled them from the air.

But there's a danger in not showing them, too, isn't there? In pretending it didn't happen? Maybe those images should be replayed every now and then — brought out of the library and shown to us in all their horror, just so there is absolutely no possibility that we might forget.

Of course it will make us uncomfortable. It should. If TV lets us get too comfortable, the war will be over. And we will have lost.

READING THE TEXT

1. What does Shales mean by the phrase "the therapeutic effect of banality" (para. 3)?

2. According to Shales, what was the effect of the 9/11 terror attacks on reality TV?

3. Why is Shales disappointed with television's response to 9/11? What does he like about what he saw on TV in the aftermath of the attacks? What worries him about the future?

READING THE SIGNS

1. In your journal, describe the role television played in your learning about the terrorist attacks on September 11. If you watched television reports, what

impact did the visual images have at the time? What memory do you have of them now, and is your response the same? If you didn't watch TV coverage, do you think your not seeing images of the destruction affected your response to it? How?

2. Shales predicts that, because of the terrorist attacks, reality shows would decline in popularity and audiences would seek programs that demonstrate "American Competence" (para. 5). Study current TV programming schedules. To what extent has Shales's prediction come to pass? How can you account for your observations?

3. One controversial aspect of America's response to the 9/11 attack was the commercial exploitation of it. Write an essay expressing your opinion of the commercial exploitation of the attack on America. To develop your ideas, consult Damien Cave, "The Spam Spoils of War" (p. 122).

4. Because of the power of visual images, television has a strong impact on the national consciousness. Write an essay in which you support, oppose, or complicate Shales's assertion that "maybe those [9/11 attack] images should be replayed every now and then — brought out of the library and shown to us in all their horror, just so there is absolutely no possibility that we might forget" (para. 15).

MARNIE CARROLL

American Television in Europe

America is frequently accused of trying to dominate the world's culture, and, certainly, the products of U.S. popular culture are found virtually everywhere on earth. But as Marnie Carroll (b. 1970), an American living in Switzerland, notes, you can watch MTV in Europe, but it is not the same as American MTV. Have you ever listened to "German fatalism-minimalism-metal"? Or "French rap"? Or "British techno-DJ mixes"? Somehow, a good deal of American popular culture is transformed once it reaches European shores, and the result is distinctly European. And, after all, that fast-food pizza you may be eating right now was invented in Italy, so pop cultural transmissions, Carroll argues, can be a two-way street. Carroll has a Ph.D. in sociology and is interested in researching technology, media, and inequality.

Many Europeans are concerned about the possibility of American culture dominating other cultures. Many Americans believe that their culture is indeed the dominant culture in the world. The increasingly common terms "cultural hegemony" and "monoculturalism" seem by default to refer to American culture and its presence outside of America. In Europe and other places, American culture appears in many forms, such as movies, music, clothing, and television. But does the presence of these kinds of American pop cultural items mean that a cultural takeover is happening, or happening unproblematically?

Obviously, America is an exceedingly powerful country. Its wealthy transnational corporations, its power within international regulatory organizations, and its military might give it a great deal of power in structuring and controlling economic and other interactions all over the globe. But, does it follow from this that cultural items such as American television shows are equally controlling and shaping of other cultures? Does America's economic and political power mean that its pop culture is easily taking over the globe?

I believe that cultural takeover is not so easy, and that many barriers to American cultural hegemony exist. I think it is important to acknowledge and understand these barriers, to look at the interstitial spaces to see just what happens in these sites where two different cultures meet. I myself occupy an interstitial space, as I am not European, and not an American living in America, but an American living in Europe. Speaking from that perspective, I take American television in Europe as a case study to illustrate the barriers and problems involved in the spread of American popular culture. Taking into account various factors that I've observed while living here, I see the notion of the unchecked spread of American pop culture as more problematic than it is often depicted to be.

It is true that American television, movies, and music are all over Europe. Here in Switzerland, at the local theater I can see *Shrek,* at the cafe down the street I can hear Madonna singing about what it feels like to be a girl, and while flipping the channels on my TV I can see *Friends* and *Frasier.* But let's not hastily conclude that all of this equals hegemony. There are a few details to note in this situation, details that may elude the casual observer, especially one observing Europe from across the Atlantic. In my ten months of living here, I have found that the presence of American culture is just not a clear matter of hegemony and monoculture. To understand it, we have to look more deeply at the context and form in which American pop culture appears, how and if it is consumed, and how it is interpreted. Let's wipe off the spectacles and give it a look.

No Blank (or Passive) Slate

First of all, we should acknowledge that American pop cultural imports don't 5
simply land in Europe like Neil Armstrong landing on the moon, placing the first fresh footsteps onto an uninhabited world (and planting the American flag). Europe is not a tabula rasa; far, far, from it. To assume otherwise would really be somewhat imperialistic and shortsighted, wouldn't it? After all, Europeans already have cultures, very long-standing, deeply entrenched, rich, diverse cultures that have long had contact with and influences from many

other cultures, long before the United States even existed. This is nothing new and nothing that Americans have invented.

Second, it's important to understand that Europeans are not simply passive receivers of information. Rather, they choose to receive in certain ways, they alter and interpret what is received, and there is really no one-to-one correspondence between the transmitter and the recipient. Just because American TV shows, channels, or other pop cultural imports appear in another country doesn't mean that they appear just as they are in America. Europeans do have something to say about what is received, how and whether things are received and used (or rejected), and what the things mean in terms of their own definitions and frameworks.

Same Bat Channel, Different Bat Channel

In other words, MTV here isn't MTV in America. CNN here is not CNN in America. Looking at MTV in Europe is a "foreign" experience for an American. The music played is largely different, a lot of it coming from European and other sources around the world. Have you ever heard French rap? How about German fatalism-minimalism-metal? How about British techno-DJ mixes? How about music from India, Africa, and Japan? This is the rude awakening Americans find when they tune in to European MTV: that not all music is sung in English and much American music is not popular here at all. Likewise, most popular music here would be very unpopular in America. Also, the video jockeys (VJs) are not American. They're thoroughly European, representing European cultures, clothing, trends, languages, and so forth. The ads are not American and often aren't in English. And all those fatuous American shows that MTV produces are rarely if ever shown here. Now, I have seen an episode of *Daria* in French, but MTV here mainly just shows music videos.

CNN, another American channel, is available in Europe. However, over here it has many more non-American correspondents and stories. Familiar American faces are replaced by people from all over the globe. The United States and its perspectives are no longer the main focus of "world" news (with the very important exception, of course, of the attacks on the World Trade Center and the Pentagon which now dominate all news here). Watching CNN in Europe, one finds that there are many other stock markets, other influential heads of state, other celebrities, other economies, other political intrigues, other elections, other problems. The United States begins to look like just one among many. In fact, much American news starts to seem much less pressing than, say, news of the recent assassination of Indian civil rights figure Phoolan Devi, or of the terrifying escalations in the Israeli-Palestinian conflict (again, with the very important exception noted above). The point is, just because American television channels are in Europe, it does not mean that they are the same channels that they are in America. Different cultures interpret, shape, and use them in ways that make sense within their own milieus.

Language Barriers

Third, we have to consider the nitty gritty of how television really works in Europe. There are quite a few important differences, the largest of which is language. According to a European Commission report, only 29 percent of Europeans on the continent speak English well enough to hold a conversation. Obviously, most people speak, read, listen, think, and consume in their native language. If you've ever tried to watch (and actually understand) TV or movies in another tongue, even one in which you have some comprehension, you know how utterly exhausting and difficult it is. It's a mammoth feat to acquire a large enough vocabulary to grasp the dialogue in movies and television, which is very rapid, casual, slangy, and accented. And, the topics discussed in movies and television are very diverse and quick-changing, requiring a heck of a lot of cultural knowledge. It's a huge step beyond book-learning, simple conversations or even reading in another language. To think that most Europeans watch American television shows in English, then, would be ludicrous.

Further, the very large variety of languages spoken in Europe really complicates the importation of American television. In Europe, every other channel is in another language. Here in the Lake Geneva area of Switzerland, we get 40-odd channels available via cable. But, unless you're fluent in about 14 languages, most of the channels won't matter to you. This is because they'll be broadcast in various languages depending on whether they're coming from American, British, French, German, Italian, Swiss, Portuguese, Spanish, Turkish, Tunisian, or Croatian stations. And there are more. I've come across a few shows in Romansh, an ancient Latin-based language spoken by about one percent of the Swiss. We occasionally find shows in various Swiss-German dialects (these are completely different from High German and from each other). And, once we found a mystery-language TV show. After about 45 minutes of intense study, we finally distinguished the heavily accented language as English with lots of Scots words. We're still wondering just what "ken" and "bairn" mean.

We have four U.S. channels here (MTV, Turner Classic Movies/The Cartoon Network, CNN, CNBC) out of the 40-odd channels available. However, even the fact that a channel is American in origin does not guarantee that the broadcast will be done in English here. For example, all the movies and cartoons on TCM/TCN are broadcast in foreign languages. You have to buy a special kind of TV if you want to hear the English audio track (if it hasn't been removed completely), and this usually only works on a very few movies and shows. And, even on these American channels, many ads and other bits are in non-English languages.

In American shows and movies seen on television in Europe, the voices have often been changed and replaced by another language. You will see Marilyn Monroe speaking German in *Niagara* and the cast of *Friends* speaking Italian, not English. Sometimes subtitles are present rather than overdubbing, but if you pay attention, you notice that the translations in the subtitles often don't exactly match the meaning of the English being spoken. The translations reflect European kinds of interpretations, humor, expressions, and sometimes the meaning of the translation is quite different from the English. You have to wonder how closely the non-English audio tracks match the original English lines in the case of overdubs. You also have to wonder just how much American culture is really coming through to the European viewer. . . .

Programming Differences

Aside from the language issues, the way that shows are actually scheduled over here is important to note. Rather unlike in America, here there's not much consistency or predictability in television. In America, shows are broadcast on the hour or the half hour, with lots and lots of commercials (groan) set regularly in-between and during the shows. Timeslots are set and religiously adhered to. But, over here, you never quite know what show will be on, when it will start, or whether you'll ever see another episode of it again. We're dealing simultaneously with channels from many different countries, with different policies. Some channels show one program's episodes one after the other for a few hours or over a few days. Other channels seem to choose somewhat randomly when to show an episode. So, though you might see an American show such as *Friends* or *ER* in Europe, the episodes are usually shown out of order, are shown in various languages, and do not appear consistently, making it really hard to get addicted. It's just harder for a show to get entrenched in one's life here, again making it harder for American pop culture to take hold through television.

Another fuzzifying factor involves just what shows actually make it over here. The shows that make it to Europe are not necessarily representative of what's popular or current in American culture. Many of the American shows shown here now weren't even widely popular in America or are now very old and outdated. Oddly, here one can still watch Urkel's silliness (*Family Matters*), but in French. One can find *Murder, She Wrote* and *Columbo* in various foreign languages, and occasionally with an English track (which you need that special TV to hear, of course). One can find Malcolm-Jamal Warner's show *Malcom and Eddie* in French. There is also *Home Improvement* in German (no English track), but the kids are really young and pre-heartthrob, so I guess the episodes are really old. Other than *ER* (George Clooney is still on over here) and *Friends* (Ross's monkey was still on there recently, and without an English track), most of the American shows shown here aren't ones that are wildly popular in America now. Europeans don't know this. Maybe they think Urkel is currently worshipped in America?

Further, what's seen on TCM or the Cartoon Network in the United States [15] may not be what's shown here on those same channels. Local programming can make it onto the U.S.-origin channels. For example, although most of the cartoons shown on the Cartoon Network here are American (with French names and overdubbing), frighteningly, there are a few French-made cartoons shown on TCN. These cartoons would make American children cry. Most of them are about some badly drawn angular birds who live in a world where laws of physics don't seem to work. The world is terrifying, deadly, and looks like the aftermath of a nuclear war. The birds despondently try to survive and they're perpetually depressed. Nothing is ever accomplished and each episode ends on some melancholy note.

Turner Classic Movies here also has some programming that differs from TCM in the United States. Here, there was a well-advertised promotional week called "Allons-y, Gay-ment!" week, meaning, roughly, "Let's go, Gay-ness!" week. They showed great classic movies starring gay men all week long. I spoke to a friend in the United States, a TCM addict, who said that, unsurprisingly, there was no such promotion happening on American TCM. All of these programming differences reflect the fact that American pop culture in Europe just doesn't happen in the same way or form that it happens in America, and it is altered and shaped by European practices, interests, and interpretations. All of this further problematizes the notion of American mono(pop)culture and hegemony.

Cultural Influences Go Both Ways

Growing up in America, I didn't realize how many foreign cultural items were part of American culture. I think many Americans assume that what they grew up with was simply American, or aren't aware of the foreign influences in their midst. For example, try to think of a truly, purely American food. It's difficult. All I could come up with were large steaks and peanut butter. Most of the other seemingly "real" American foods are awfully similar to dishes found in countries from which early settlers to America emigrated. They serve a lovely pot roast in Ireland and England. They also serve great apple pie there and have been for a very long time. Other "American" foods, like Cajun food, barbecue, pizza, hamburgers, hot dogs, pretzels, chips, and so forth also have roots in other cultures. Hmmm, maybe if we count Cheez Whiz as a food?

So, the transmission of cultural influences is not uni-directional, with America simply oozing across the world for all to gather, consume, and imitate. There is a clear two-way (or thousand-way) street in existence. And, just as American cultural items have their own meanings and interpretations in Europe, so do European cultural items in America. Thus, French fries have a wholly different meaning in America than in France where they are called pomme frites and are usually served with fancy fish or meat dinners, not hamburgers, and with Provençal sauce or sauce tartare, not ketchup for goodness sakes.

Or, how about good old Nestle Quik? This American childhood staple is not American at all. The Nestle company can be found in the Swiss Alps among meadows of clover inhabited by dairy cows wearing large bells. In America, Nestle Quik sort of fits in culturally among Saturday morning cartoons in commercials featuring the bunny, and last-ditch efforts to prolong going to bed by insisting on needing a glass of milk. In Switzerland, I've never seen a commercial for Nestle, they don't even have Saturday morning cartoons here, kids already stay up later here, and it seems that people usually make hot chocolate rather than cold chocolate milk.

Thus, Americans have clearly also received, altered, and redefined things [20] from other cultures all along. Just because Americans have French fries, it doesn't mean that France's entire culture(s) was (were) unproblematically plopped down like a dollop of whipped cream onto America. It goes the same way for American culture in other countries. Considering this, why would the presence of some American pop cultural items (such as TV shows) in other countries mean that American culture is easily and clearly taking over other cultures?

U.S. Culture Is Important, But . . .

Now, having said all this, it's also not true that U.S. culture doesn't have an impact on other cultures. It's true that America is a large, highly productive, powerful, populous, monolinguistic mass. And some people are worried about it. In France, they're distressed about English (American, really) words getting into their language. Some countries think that *Friends* is too sexually explicit. But I think that it's a mistake to simply and cleanly assume any of the following: (1) U.S. culture appears exactly in its original form and has exactly the same social meaning in other cultures as it does in America; (2) other cultures really could (or even want to) understand American culture the way it is in America — after all, the United States is 5,000 miles away from Europe; (3) other people don't have an existing culture; (4) other people don't reinterpret, twist, reformulate, alter, and choose (and reject) what (and how) elements of other cultures are received in their culture, how they are integrated, what they mean, and so forth within the context of their own cultural meaning; and (5) Americans are the originators and one-way distributors of culture, and have a pure or purely dominant culture that hasn't been influenced by others.

Conclusion

Television, like anything else we come across in life, is what we make of it, how we interpret it, how we perceive it, how, how much, and in what forms it's accessed, and what meanings it has within a culture already set with its own meanings, traditions, ideas, and innovations. Life is so different here in Europe that Americans just can't imagine it. This is why many Americans who come to visit Europe have rather bad reactions to finding out that they're actually not automatically seen as the best in the world, that they can't just speak English and be understood, that absolutely everything is done differently and thought about differently, and that being American often doesn't work easily over here at all. America is so far away geographically and even philosophically that most Americans are unfortunately rather unaware of the vast numbers of cultures, of completely different ways of doing absolutely everything, that they often have a rather hard time in Europe.

Europeans grow up in an entirely different world, in which many vastly different languages and cultures (not to mention histories) swirl around them continuously. Here is my list of just some of the areas in which I've observed Europeans being simply and utterly NOT American: in approaches to work, to community, to sharing, to views of time, to eating, to drinking, to sex, to nudity, views of space and distance, views of individuals' rights, views of responsibilities, views of community, views of workers and customers, views of logic, views of inconvenience, views of personal space, views of friends, acquaintances, and families, views of independence and individuality, views of leisure and exercise, shopping and consuming, materialism, views of culture, language, art, music, views of being, embodiment, emotions, expression, gender roles, race, class, sexual orientation, views of absolutely everything. These differences comprise something cultural that Americans simply do not know about and just do not get until they've been in Europe for a considerable amount of time (if we can ever truly get it).

We have to balance our views of hegemony and monoculture with a more detailed understanding of cross-cultural interaction. As Americans we can't simply assume that "our" culture is easily dominating the globe, gobbling the world up like a chocolate chip cookie, Americanizing everything in its path. I think that it's almost reassuring in a way to think that that is true. It's kind of an ego-boost for some Americans to think that "our" culture is the most popular, the most sought-after, the one that "rules." Let's face it, it's even a bit of an ego-boost for at least some Americans who are opposed to the global spread of American culture. This still posits America as the originating, dynamic, innovative, powerful country that's taking over all the others. It's still a colonial fantasy (and nightmare) of sorts. And it lacks insight into what it's really like to not be American, and to not live in America.

Europeans should get credit for having their own complexities, ideas, and 25 cultures, and agency as well. And, when we examine those interstices where two cultures meet, we see that there are indeed many obstacles and difficulties in cultural transmission. I value having been yanked out of my original American culture and landing in this interstitial space. Being American, I know how these American cultural items appear in America, and what they mean there. At the same time, being here allows me to see the slippage, the differences in how the same items are located, used, rejected, and altered in another culture. The concept of hegemony is quite complicated and the more I inspect those interstitial spaces, the more problematic they appear.

Now it's time for *Les Supers Nanas* (*The Powerpuff Girls*) in French. Grab the fizzy water, slice up some Gruyere and a baguette, and let's observe.

READING THE TEXT

1. What evidence does Carroll give to support her contention that American popular culture is not taking over the globe?

2. Define in your own words the term "cultural hegemony" (para. 1)

3. How, according to Carroll, do "cultural influences go both ways" (para.17) between America and the rest of the world?

4. What influence do language differences have on European television, according to Carroll?

5. What does Carroll mean by claiming that the belief in American cultural hegemony serves as an "ego-boost" (para. 24) for both those who support it and those who oppose it?

READING THE SIGNS

1. Use the Internet to research the television schedule of a European country of your choice, and study how much of the schedule is made up of American programs or local versions of American programs. Use your observations as evidence in an essay in which you evaluate the accuracy of Carroll's statement that "the notion of the unchecked spread of American pop culture [is] more problematic than it is often depicted to be" (para. 3). Alternately, research the television programming schedule of a non-European country. How do your findings relate to the claims Carroll makes about European TV programming? How can you account for any differences you might find?

2. Conduct an in-class discussion on the topic of why America imports so much of its "high cultural" television programming (most commonly broadcast on PBS) from England.

3. Research the history of rock-and-roll, and write an analysis of cross-cultural influences. To what extent is rock history a tale of American cultural hegemony? Or does it more fully illustrate the two-way street of cultural influence that Carroll describes?

4. Write an essay in which you refute, qualify, or support the contention that American cultural hegemony is responsible for global resentment of the United States To develop your ideas, read or reread Benjamin Barber's "Jihad vs. McWorld" (p. 126) and Thomas Friedman's "Revolution Is U.S." (p. 132).

5. Visit your college or university library and study popular magazines from other countries, paying particular attention to the products advertised. Write an essay, using the advertisements as your evidence, in which you assess Carroll's position that American cultural hegemony is not as unchecked as critics often claim.

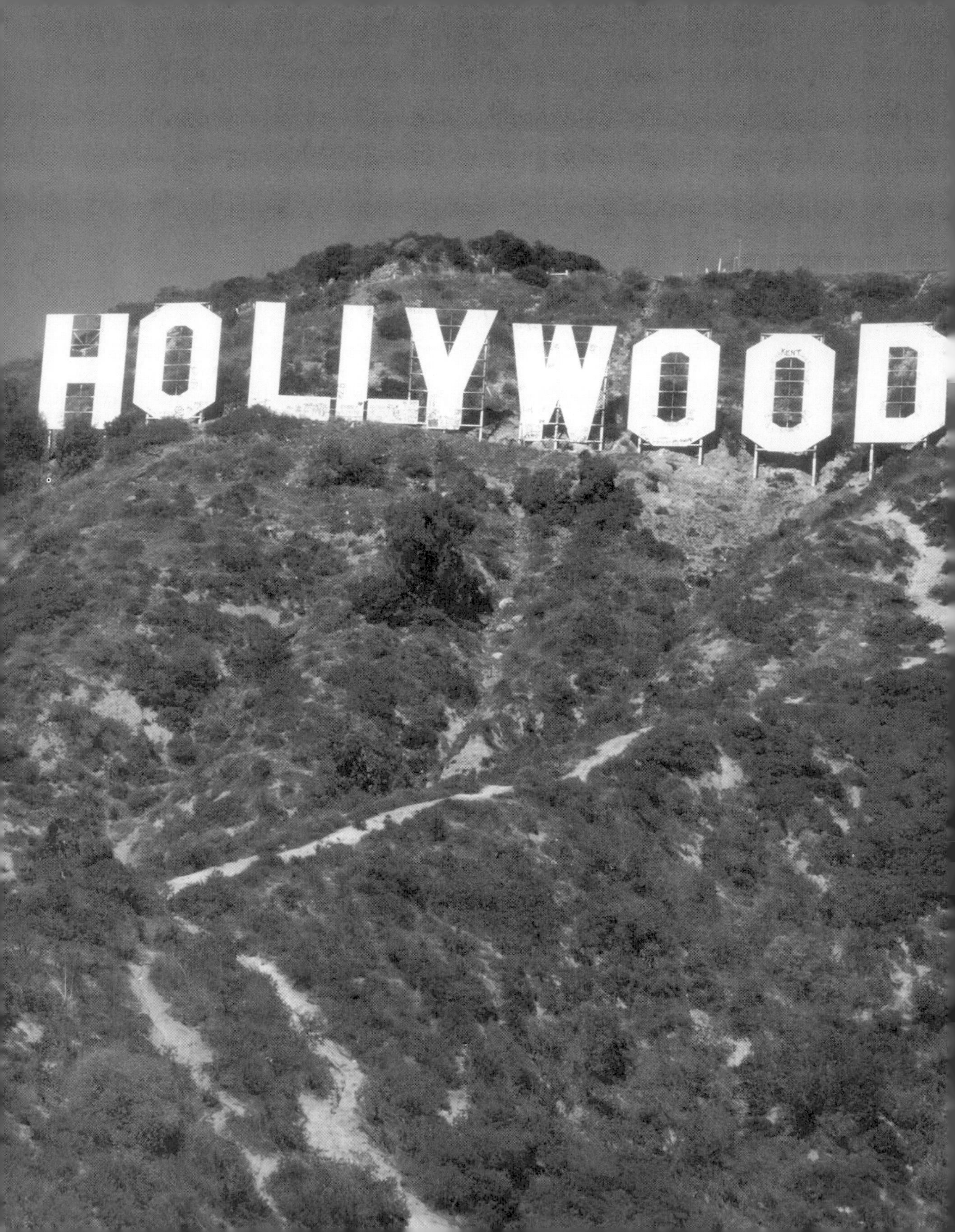
HOLLYWOOD

THE HOLLYWOOD SIGN
The Culture of American Film

Monsters. And wizards. And elves. Oh my. Put them all together and what do you get? The first eight-billion-dollar year in Hollywood history, that's what. For thanks to the box office wizardry of a quartet of fantasy films, which included the animated *Shrek* and *Monsters, Inc.* — and did we mention the first installments of *Harry Potter* and *The Lord of the Rings*? — North American ticket sales passed that magical figure in 2001 with room to spare. With so many people paying record ticket prices to see such movies, they were not merely popular entertainments — they were potent signs of the state of American desire at the beginning of the new millennium.

That a group of fantasy flicks should reflect the dreams and desires of millions of American moviegoers should come as no surprise. Indeed, as the self-styled dream weavers of American culture (Steven Spielberg and company didn't call their new studio DreamWorks for nothing), Hollywood moviemakers have been reflecting and shaping the desires of American audiences for roughly a century now. Long before the advent of TV, the movies were providing their viewers with the glamour, romance, and sheer excitement that modern life seems to deny. So effective have the movies been in molding American consciousness that such early culture critics as Theodor Adorno and Max Horkheimer[1] have accused them of being part of a vast, Hollywood-centered "culture industry" whose products have successfully distracted their audiences

---

[1]**Theodor Adorno** and **Max Horkheimer** Theodor Adorno (1903–1969) and Max Horkheimer (1895–1973), authors of *Dialectic of Enlightenment* (1947), a book whose analyses included a scathing indictment of the culture industry — EDS.

from the inequities of modern life, and so have worked to maintain the social status quo by drawing everyone's attention away from it.

More recent analysts have been far less pessimistic. Indeed, for many cultural studies "populists," the movies, along with the rest of popular culture, can represent a kind of mass resistance to the political dominance — or what is often called the "hegemony" — of the social and economic powers-that-be. For such critics, the movies can provide utopian visions of a better world, stimulating their viewers to imagine how their society might be improved, and so, perhaps, inspiring them to go out and do something about it.

Whether you believe that films distract us from the real world or inspire us to imagine a better one, their central place in contemporary American culture demands interpretation. For the impact of film goes well beyond the movie theater or video screen. Far from being mere entertainments, the movies constitute a profound part of our everyday lives, with every film festival and film award becoming major news stories, and each major release becoming the talk of the country, splashed across the entire terrain of American media from newspapers to television to the Internet. Just think of the pressure you feel to be able to discuss the latest film sensation among your friends. How, if you decide to save a few bucks and wait for the video release, you would lose face and be seriously on the social outs. No, there is nothing frivolous about the movies. You've been watching them all your life: Now's the time to start thinking about them semiotically.

Interpreting the Signs of American Film

Interpreting a movie or a group of movies is not unlike interpreting a television program or group of programs. Here too you must suspend any personal feelings or aesthetic judgments that you may have about your subject. As with any semiotic analysis, your object is to interpret the cultural significance of your topic, not to give it a thumbs up or a thumbs down. Thus, you may find it more rewarding to interpret those films that promise to be culturally meaningful rather than simply choosing your favorite flick. Determining whether a movie is culturally meaningful in the prewriting stage, of course, may be something of a hit-or-miss affair; you may find that your first choice does not present you with any particularly interesting grounds for interpreta-

> ### Exploring the Signs of Film
>
> In your journal, list your favorite movies. Then consider your list: What does it say about you? What cultural myths do the movies tend to reflect, and why do you think those myths appeal to you? What signs particularly appeal to your emotions? What sort of stories about human life do you most respond to?

tion. That's why it can be helpful to consider factors — such as enormous popularity or widespread critical attention — that seem to set off a particular movie as being special. Of course, cult favorites, while often lacking in critical or popular attention, can also be signs pointing toward their more self-selected audiences and so are perfectly good candidates for analysis. Academy Award candidates are also pretty reliable as cultural signs.

As with any other kind of semiotic analysis, your interpretation of a movie should include the establishing of a system whose interplay of similarities and differences can help lead you to your topic's significance. For example, the four movies we have mentioned so far — *Shrek, Monsters, Inc., Harry Potter and the Sorcerer's Stone,* and *The Fellowship of the Ring* — can all be related as children's fantasy films that had widespread adult appeal. In this sense, they can be differentiated from films like *Titanic,* whose box office records *Harry Potter,* in particular, was measured against but that was not a children's fantasy. This difference doesn't tell us why the fantasy films of 2001 were so popular, but it does alert us to search for what made them distinctive and hence significant.

We're Off to See the Wizard

Let's consider further the cultural lesson to be learned from this fantasy foursome from 2001. As is usual in a semiotic analysis, broadening our system to look at some history can be helpful. In the case of these four films, we are looking at what are essentially fairy tales — two of them set in more or less medieval times, two of them contemporary. Accordingly, they can be situated within the history of filmed fairy tales, which began with Walt Disney's 1937 adaptation of that old Grimm's tale, *Snow White and the Seven Dwarfs.* The success of this effort led to further Disney animations from the Brothers Grimm, most notably *Cinderella* and *Sleeping Beauty,* which led to the establishment of the Disney corporation as America's premier provider of children's movies.

Also like Disney's fairy-tale films, our subject movies, with the exception of *Monsters, Inc.,* were based on stories that their audiences could have already read and known. *Grimm's Fairy Tales* has been standard fare for children's reading for generations, and the inevitable success of both *Harry Potter* and *The Fellowship of the Ring* was established by the widespread popularity of the books that they dramatized.

So far, the associations we can make between the beginnings of the fairy-tale film and its latest incarnations tell us that such movies have a secure place in the popular imagination. Generations of American moviegoers have flocked to such films, a cultural phenomenon that can be attributed, in good part, to the highly archetypal nature of fairy tales. An *archetype* is anything that has been repeated in storytelling from ancient times to the present. There are character archetypes — for instance, the ugly duckling, which is behind part of the *Harry Potter* appeal — and plot archetypes — as in the heroic quest, which is the archetypal backbone of *The Lord of the Rings* trilogy. All those male buddy films — from *Butch Cassidy and the Sundance Kid* to *Lethal Weapon* to *Men in Black* — hark back to archetypal male bonding stories as old as *Gilgamesh* (from the third millennium B.C.) and the *Iliad;* while Cruella De Vil from *101 Dalmatians* is sister to the Wicked Witch of the West, Snow White's evil stepmother, and every other witch or crone dreamed up by the patriarchal imagination. All those sea monsters, from Jonah's whale to Moby Dick to Jaws, are part of the same archetypal phylum, and every time a movie hero struggles to return home after a long journey — Dorothy to Kansas, Lassie to Timmy — a story as old as Exodus and the *Odyssey* is retold.

Hollywood is well aware of the enduring appeal of archetypes (see Linda Seger's "Creating the Myth" on page 316 for a how-to description of archetypal script writing). George Lucas's reliance on Joseph Campbell in his creation of the *Star Wars* saga is widely known. But it is not always the case that either creators or consumers are aware of the archetypes before them. Part of a culture's collective unconscious as well as consciousness, archetypal stories can send messages that audiences only subliminally understand. A heavy dosage of male-bonding films in a given Hollywood season, for instance, can send the unspoken cultural message that a man can't really make friends with a woman, that women are simply the sexual reward for manly men. Too many witches can send the message that there are too many bitches (think of *Fatal Attraction* and *Basic Instinct*).

But for all their usefulness in cinematic analysis, archetypes can take us only so far, telling us what certain movies might share but not what makes them different. And there was something different about the fairy tales of 2001 that set them apart from earlier fairy-tale films.

When You Wish upon a Star (War)

This difference could be found in the extraordinary appeal that *Shrek, Monsters, Harry,* and *The Fellowship of the Ring* had for audiences of all ages — not just for small children and their parents, but preteens, teens, twenty-somethings, dating couples, everyone. *Snow White, Cinderella,* and the rest of Disney's classic fairy tale portfolio were children's films that parents might see with their children, but they were hardly date flicks. *The Wizard of Oz* may have become a staple of holiday television, but those fairy tale fantasies that did appear on the big screen prior to the 1970s were definitely kid's stuff.

Star Wars changed all that. Essentially a fairy tale (fledgling warrior-knight rescues princess-in-distress), *Star Wars* was no kid's movie, though children loved it too. Shot through with ironic self-awareness, *Star Wars* made fantasy filmmaking for grown-up audiences not only safe but sensational. But if George Lucas's great breakthrough changed Hollywood history, he didn't do it alone. In fact, he probably couldn't have done it at all without two predecessors named Gene Roddenberry and J. R. R. Tolkien. For it was Tolkien who first brought the grown-up fairy tale to the modern era, and Roddenberry who showed that sci-fi TV could be more sophisticated than *Lost in Space* or *The Jetsons.* Both men, paradoxically enough, were less than successful in their pioneering efforts. When *The Lord of the Rings* was first published in the 1950s, its sales were modest, and *Star Trek* was almost canceled after its first season, and was canceled after its second.

But by the end of the 1960s and the beginning of the 1970s, *The Lord of the Rings* was seized on by the baby-boomer generation as an imaginative alternative to the dreary landscapes of industrial society, presenting virtuous protagonists prevailing in a clear-cut, and successful, struggle against evil. Viewed against the real-world backdrop of the Vietnam War, a war that was neither morally clear-cut nor conclusive, *The Lord of the Rings* satisfied deep desires for a simpler moral universe and heroes with whom readers could identify. As Peter S. Beagle (the author of his own fantasy novel *The Last Unicorn*) informs us in his introduction to the Ballantine edition of *The Lord of the Rings,* "Frodo lives!" was the kind of graffito that one could find in New York subway stations when *Ring* fever was at its peak.

At the same time, *Star Trek,* by now in reruns, was offering an imaginative stage on which the social and moral dilemmas of the time could be dramatized in allegorical form. The conflict between the Klingons and the crew of the *Enterprise* was an obvious metaphor for the cold war conflict between the Soviet Union and the United States, and many of the show's episodes could be seen clearly as thinly disguised dramatizations of many of the racial and cultural controversies of the late sixties (see Mike Nordberg's essay on page 41 in "Writing about Popular Culture" for a fine student paper on this subject). Thus, *Star Trek* made sci-fantasy serious and grown-up, even relevant.

Discussing the Signs of Film

In any given year, one film may dominate the Hollywood box office, becoming a blockbuster that captures that public's cinematic imagination. In class, discuss which film would be your choice as this year's top hit. Then analyze the film semiotically. Why has *this* film so successfully appealed to so many moviegoers?

Taken together, then, Tolkien and Roddenberry opened the door for adult-themed fantasy films. They also helped prepare the ground for the cyber-fantasy craze of the pre-Internet era, the game Dungeons & Dragons, which was the predecessor of many a MUD and MOO virtual adventure. The endurance of such medieval-themed, high-tech fantasies in popular culture demonstrates that the new trend has been no mere fad but has become, as far as we can see, a permanent fixture in the entertainment universe. Thus, even though the 1978 animated version of *The Lord of the Rings* was something of a flop, films like the 1982 *The Dark Crystal* kept the fantasy-quest theme alive,

The Lord of the Rings, 2001.

and it really was only a matter of time before someone would try to film the *Rings* again.

That the first installment of a new *Ring* should appear in the same year as three other fairy-tale blockbusters was itself a historical accident. It takes years to bring a movie from inception to completion, and no one could have predicted in advance that it would have appeared alongside the other films (though the producers of *Monsters, Inc.* did move up the release of their movie a few weeks to avoid colliding with *Harry Potter*). But the fact that so many highly popular fantasy fairy tales did appear virtually all at once shows just how well established grown-up fantasy had become by 2001, so well established that even out-and-out children's films like *Shrek, Monsters,* and *Harry Potter* could be almost as popular among adults as with children — with a little clever marketing. Getting John Goodman and Billy Crystal to voice the leads in

Monsters, Inc., for example, was an important part of its generational crossover appeal, as was securing Eddie Murphy for *Shrek.* Turning the traditional "enchanted frog" fairy-tale archetype on its head, *Shrek* also presented the sort of fractured fairy tale that older audiences could appreciate. Likewise, millions of adult readers and moviegoers, thanks to Tolkien's pioneering efforts, felt no embarrassment in enjoying what was intended, after all, to be a children's tale about a boy wizard.

The enormous popularity of fairy-tale story lines can be seen to signify a desire to be distracted by the images of a simpler, more innocent world. The outlines of a fairy tale are nothing if not clear-cut: They generally feature a virtuous hero, or set of heroes, fighting wickedness successfully. Life is usually a good deal more complicated than that, and at other times in American history the desire for such escapist fare has been regarded as rather, well, childish. But with combined ticket sales somewhere between one and two billion dollars in 2001 alone, our four fairy tales show most people don't see it this way at all anymore. "Life's messy enough as it is," the box office seems to say. "Let us have our distractions and consolations."

That so many grown-ups should be entertained by children's fairy tales is thus a striking sign of our times. And the fact that, through a grim historical coincidence, three of them should have been released in the immediate aftermath of the September 11 attacks on the United States only accentuates their significance. For while all three movies were destined to be successful for the reasons explored above, the need for fantasy distraction and for images of virtue prevailing triumphantly over evil was especially apparent in those shaken weeks and months after the attacks.

Indeed, it can be argued that at least one non–fairy-tale film that appeared immediately after September 11, DreamWorks's *The Last Castle,* suffered from its own moral ambiguities. A movie that was intended to be a patriotic dramatization of good versus evil, presented in the guise of a U.S. military prison uprising against a corrupt prison warden, proved to be a box office disappointment as viewers were apparently confused by the spectacle of American soldier-prisoners (even if led by Robert Redford) combating American soldier-guards. And the promotional poster featuring a U.S. flag waving upside down (the poster was modified immediately after 9/11) didn't help either.

Movies as Metaphors

Our interpretational survey of the fairy-tale phalanx of 2001 is intended to demonstrate how the semiotic analysis of a film (or group of films) can uncover something of cultural significance. But there were any number of films from that year alone that we could have chosen, and even a cheesy joke of a movie can be a cultural signifier. Consider the grade-B horror flicks of the 1950s.

Reading Film on the Net

Most major films now released in the United States receive their own Web site. You can find them listed in print ads for the film (check your local newspaper). Select a current film, find the Web address, log on, and analyze the film's site semiotically. What images are used to attract your interest in the film? What interactive strategies, if any, are used to increase your commitment to the film? If you've seen the movie, how does the Net presentation of it compare with your experience viewing it either in a theater or on video? Alternately, analyze the posters designed to attract attention to a particular film; a useful resource is The Movie Poster Page (**http://www.musicman.com/mp/mp.html**).

Take, for instance, the original *Godzilla*. If we study only its plot, we would see little more than a horror story featuring a reptilian monster that is related archetypally to the dragons of medieval literature. But Godzilla was no mere dragon transported to the modern world. The dragons that populated the world of medieval storytelling were themselves often used as metaphors for the Satanic serpent in the Garden of Eden, but Godzilla was a wholly different sort of metaphor. Created by Japanese filmmakers, Godzilla was originally a metaphor for the nuclear era. A female mutant creation of nuclear poisoning, Godzilla rose over her Japanese audiences like a mushroom cloud, symbolizing the potential for future mushroom clouds both in Japan and around the world in the cold war era.

For their part, American moviemakers in the 1950s had their own metaphors for the nuclear era. Whenever some "blob" threatened to consume New York or some especially toxic slime escaped from a laboratory, the suggestion that science — especially nuclear science — was threatening to destroy the world filled the theater along with the popcorn fumes. And if it wasn't science that was the threat, cold war filmmakers could scare us with communists, as films like *Invasion of the Body Snatchers* metaphorically suggested through its depiction of a town in which everyone looked the same but had really been taken over by aliens. "Beware of your neighbors," the movie warned, "they could be communists."

In such ways, an entire film can be a kind of metaphor, but you can find many smaller metaphors at work in the details of a movie as well. Early filmmakers, for example, used to put a tablecloth on the table in dining scenes to signify that the characters at the table were good, decent people (you can find such a metaphor in Charlie Chaplin's *The Kid,* where an impoverished tramp who can't afford socks or a bathrobe still has a nice tablecloth on the breakfast table). Sometimes a director's metaphors have a broad political significance, as at the end of the James Dean classic *Giant,* where the parting shot presents a tableau of a white baby goat standing next to a black baby goat, which is juxtaposed with the image of a white baby standing in a crib side by side with a brown baby. Since the human babies are both the grandchildren of the film's protagonist (one of whose sons has married a Mexican woman, the other an Anglo), the goats are added to underscore metaphorically the message of racial reconciliation that the director wanted to send.

Reading a film, then, is much like reading a novel. Both are texts filled with intentional and unintentional signs, metaphors, and archetypes. Both are cultural signifiers. The major difference is in their medium of expression. Literary texts are cast entirely in written words; films combine verbal language, visual imagery, and sound effects. Thus, we perceive literary and cinematic texts differently, for the written sign is perceived in a linear fashion that relies on one's cognitive and imaginative powers, while a film primarily targets the senses: One sees and hears (and sometimes even smells!). That film is such a sensory experience often conceals its textuality. One is tempted to sit back and go with the flow, to say that it's only entertainment and doesn't have to "mean" anything at all. But as cinematic forms of storytelling overtake written forms of expression, the study of movies as complex texts bearing cultural messages and values is becoming more and more important. Our "libraries" are increasingly to be found in theaters and mini-malls, where the texts of Hollywood can be read for eight dollars (or so) a view or rented for three dollars a night. There's a lot to read out there.

The Readings

The readings in this chapter address the various myths that pervade Hollywood films, starting with Robert B. Ray's analysis of the ways in which America's "official" and "outlaw" heroes appear both in the cinema and in American history and culture. Linda Seger follows with a screenwriter's how-to-do-it guide for the creation of the kind of archetypal characters that made *Star Wars* one of the most popular movies of all time. Gary Johnson offers a historical survey of the Western, one of the most archetypal and iconographic of Hollywood genres, while Susan Bordo critiques the "just-do-it" culture behind movies like *Braveheart.* The next two selections tackle racial issues, with Todd Boyd situating the "gangsta" film within a history of gangster movies, focusing on the politics of such films as *Boyz N the Hood,* and Jessica Hagedorn surveying a tradition of American filmmaking in which Asian women are presented as either tragic or trivial. Sandra Tsing Loh follows with a tongue-in-cheek report on the return of another mythic figure to American cinema, the Good Girl, exemplified by everyone from that "mother of all modern Good Girls," Doris Day, to that savior of virtual culture, Sandra Bullock. Michael Parenti next provides a class-based approach to the codes of American cinema, noting the social biases inherent in such popular hits as *Pretty Woman,* while Vivian C. Sobchack presents an almost-unflinching analysis of screen violence. Patrick Goldstein concludes with a meditation on how Hollywood should respond in the aftermath of the September 11 attack on America.

ROBERT B. RAY

The Thematic Paradigm

Usually we consider movies to be merely entertainment, but as Robert Ray (b. 1943) demonstrates in this selection from his book A Certain Tendency of the Hollywood Cinema *(1985), American films have long reflected fundamental patterns and contradictions in our society's myths and values. Whether in real life or on the silver screen, Ray explains, Americans have always been ambivalent about the value of civilization, celebrating it through official heroes like George Washington and Jimmy Stewart, while at the same time questioning it through outlaw heroes like Davy Crockett and Jesse James. Especially when presented together in the same film, these two hero types help mediate America's ambivalence, providing a mythic solution. Ray's analyses show how the movies are rich sources for cultural interpretation; they provide a framework for decoding movies as different as* Lethal Weapon *and* Malcolm X. *Ray is a professor and director of film and media studies at the University of Florida at Gainesville. His publications include* The Avant Garde Finds Andy Hardy *(1995) and* How a Film Theory Got Lost and Other Mysteries in Cultural Studies *(2001).*

The dominant tradition of American cinema consistently found ways to overcome dichotomies. Often, the movies' reconciliatory pattern concentrated on a single character magically embodying diametrically opposite traits. A sensitive violinist was also a tough boxer (*Golden Boy*); a boxer was a gentle man who cared for pigeons (*On the Waterfront*). A gangster became a coward because he was brave (*Angels with Dirty Faces*); a soldier became brave because he was a coward (*Lives of a Bengal Lancer*). A war hero was a former pacifist (*Sergeant York*); a pacifist was a former war hero (*Billy Jack*). The ideal was a kind of inclusiveness that would permit all decisions to be undertaken with the knowledge that the alternative was equally available. The attractiveness of Destry's refusal to use guns (*Destry Rides Again*) depended on the tacit understanding that he could shoot with the best of them, Katharine Hepburn's and Claudette Colbert's revolts against conventionality (*Holiday, It Happened One Night*) on their status as aristocrats.

Such two-sided characters seemed particularly designed to appeal to a collective American imagination steeped in myths of inclusiveness. Indeed, in creating such characters, classic Hollywood had connected with what Erik Erikson has described as the fundamental American psychological pattern:

> The functioning American, as the heir of a history of extreme contrasts and abrupt changes, bases his final ego identity on some tentative

combination of dynamic polarities such as migratory and sedentary, individualistic and standardized, competitive and co-operative, pious and free-
thinking, responsible and cynical, etc. . . .

   To leave his choices open, the American, on the whole, lives with two
sets of "truths."[1]

The movies traded on one opposition in particular, American culture's traditional dichotomy of individual and community that had generated the most
significant pair of competing myths: the outlaw hero and the official hero.[2] Embodied in the adventurer, explorer, gunfighter, wanderer, and loner, the outlaw
hero stood for that part of the American imagination valuing self-determination
and freedom from entanglements. By contrast, the official hero, normally portrayed as a teacher, lawyer, politician, farmer, or family man, represented the
American belief in collective action, and the objective legal process that superseded private notions of right and wrong. While the outlaw hero found incarnations in the mythic figures of Davy Crockett, Jesse James, Huck Finn, and all of
Leslie Fiedler's "Good Bad Boys" and Daniel Boorstin's "ring-tailed roarers," the
official hero developed around legends associated with Washington, Jefferson,
Lincoln, Lee, and other "Good Good Boys."

   An extraordinary amount of the traditional American mythology adopted
by Classic Hollywood derived from the variations worked by American ideology around this opposition of natural man versus civilized man. To the extent
that these variations constituted the main tendency of American literature
and legends, Hollywood, in relying on this mythology, committed itself to becoming what Robert Bresson has called "the Cinema."[3] A brief description of
the competing values associated with this outlaw hero–official hero opposition will begin to suggest its pervasiveness in traditional American culture.

   1. *Aging:* The attractiveness of the outlaw hero's childishness and propen-   5
sity to whims, tantrums, and emotional decisions derived from America's cult
of childhood. Fiedler observed that American literature celebrated "the notion
that a mere falling short of adulthood is a guarantee of insight and even innocence." From Huck to Holden Caulfield, children in American literature were
privileged, existing beyond society's confining rules. Often, they set the plot
in motion (e.g., *Intruder in the Dust, To Kill a Mockingbird*), acting for the
adults encumbered by daily affairs. As Fiedler also pointed out, this image of
childhood "has impinged upon adult life itself, has become a 'career' like

---

[1]Erik H. Erikson, *Childhood and Society* (New York: Norton, 1963), p. 286.

   [2]Leading discussions of the individual-community polarity in American culture can be
found in *The Contrapuntal Civilization: Essays Toward a New Understanding of the American Ex-
perience,* ed. Michael Kammen (New York: Crowell, 1971). The most prominent analyses of
American literature's use of this opposition remain Leslie A. Fiedler's *Love and Death in the
American Novel* (New York: Stein and Day, 1966) and A. N. Kaul's *The American Vision* (New
Haven: Yale University Press, 1963).

   [3]Robert Bresson, *Notes on Cinematography,* trans. Jonathan Griffin (New York: Urizen
Books, 1977), p. 12.

everything else in America,"[4] generating stories like *On the Road* or *Easy Rider* in which adults try desperately to postpone responsibilities by clinging to adolescent life-styles.

While the outlaw heroes represented a flight from maturity, the official heroes embodied the best attributes of adulthood: sound reasoning and judgment, wisdom and sympathy based on experience. Franklin's *Autobiography* and *Poor Richard's Almanack* constituted this opposing tradition's basic texts, persuasive enough to appeal even to outsiders (*The Great Gatsby*). Despite the legends surrounding Franklin and the other Founding Fathers, however, the scarcity of mature heroes in American literature and mythology indicated American ideology's fundamental preference for youth, a quality that came to be associated with the country itself. Indeed, American stories often distorted the stock figure of the Wise Old Man, portraying him as mad (Ahab), useless (Rip Van Winkle), or evil (the Godfather).

2. *Society and Women:* The outlaw hero's distrust of civilization, typically represented by women and marriage, constituted a stock motif in American mythology. In his *Studies in Classic American Literature,* D. H. Lawrence detected the recurring pattern of flight, observing that the Founding Fathers had come to America "largely to get *away.* . . . Away from what? In the long run, away from themselves. Away from everything."[5] Sometimes, these heroes undertook this flight alone (Thoreau, *Catcher in the Rye*); more often, they joined ranks with other men: Huck with Jim, Ishmael with Queequeg, Jake Barnes with Bill Gorton. Women were avoided as representing the very entanglements this tradition sought to escape: society, the "settled life," confining responsibilities. The outlaw hero sought only uncompromising relationships, involving either a "bad" woman (whose morals deprived her of all rights to entangling domesticity) or other males (who themselves remained independent). Even the "bad" woman posed a threat, since marriage often uncovered the clinging "good" girl underneath. Typically, therefore, American stories avoided this problem by killing off the "bad" woman before the marriage could transpire (*Destry Rides Again, The Big Heat, The Far Country*). Subsequently, within the all-male group, women became taboo, except as the objects of lust.

The exceptional extent of American outlaw legends suggests an ideological anxiety about civilized life. Often, that anxiety took shape as a romanticizing of the dispossessed, as in the Beat Generation's cult of the bum, or the characters of Huck and "Thoreau," who worked to remain idle, unemployed, and unattached. A passage from Jerzy Kosinski's *Steps* demonstrated the extreme modern version of this romanticizing:

---

[4]Leslie A. Fiedler, *No! In Thunder* (New York: Stein and Day, 1972), pp. 253, 275.

[5]D. H. Lawrence, *Studies in Classic American Literature* (New York: Viking/Compass, 1961), p. 3. See also Fiedler's *Love and Death in the American Novel* and Sam Bluefarb's *The Escape Motif in the American Novel: Mark Twain to Richard Wright* (Columbus: Ohio State University Press, 1972).

I envied those [the poor and the criminals] who lived here and seemed so free, having nothing to regret and nothing to look forward to. In the world of birth certificates, medical examinations, punch cards, and computers, in the world of telephone books, passports, bank accounts, insurance plans, wills, credit cards, pensions, mortgages and loans, they lived unattached.[6]

In contrast to the outlaw heroes, the official heroes were preeminently worldly, comfortable in society, and willing to undertake even those public duties demanding personal sacrifice. Political figures, particularly Washington and Lincoln, provided the principal examples of this tradition, but images of family also persisted in popular literature from *Little Women* to *Life with Father* and *Cheaper by the Dozen*. The most crucial figure in this tradition, however, was Horatio Alger, whose heroes' ambition provided the complement to Huck's disinterest. Alger's characters subscribed fully to the codes of civilization, devoting themselves to proper dress, manners, and behavior, and the attainment of the very things despised by the opposing tradition: the settled life and respectability.[7]

3. *Politics and the Law:* Writing about "The Philosophical Approach of the Americans," Tocqueville noted "a general distaste for accepting any man's word as proof of anything." That distaste took shape as a traditional distrust of politics as collective activity, and of ideology as that activity's. rationale. Such a disavowal of ideology was, of course, itself ideological, a tactic for discouraging systematic political intervention in a nineteenth-century America whose political and economic power remained in the hands of a privileged few. Tocqueville himself noted the results of this mythology of individualism which "disposes each citizen to isolate himself from the mass of his fellows and withdraw into the circle of family and friends; with this little society formed to his taste, he gladly leaves the greater society to look after itself."[8]

This hostility toward political solutions manifested itself further in an ambivalence about the law. The outlaw mythology portrayed the law, the sum of society's standards, as a collective, impersonal ideology imposed on the individual from without. Thus, the law represented the very thing this mythology sought to avoid. In its place, this tradition offered a natural law discovered intuitively by each man. As Tocqueville observed, Americans wanted "To escape from imposed systems . . . to seek by themselves and in themselves for the only reason for things . . . in most mental operations each American relies on individual effort and judgment" (p. 429). This sense of the law's inadequacy to needs detectable only by the heart generated a rich tradition of

---

[6]Jerzy Kosinski, *Steps* (New York: Random House, 1968), p. 133.

[7]See John G. Cawelti, *Apostles of the Self-Made Man: Changing Concepts of Success in America* (Chicago: University of Chicago Press, 1965), pp. 101–23.

[8]Alexis de Tocqueville, *Democracy in America,* ed. J. P. Mayer, trans. George Lawrence (Garden City, N.Y.: Anchor/Doubleday, 1969), pp. 430, 506. Irving Howe has confirmed Tocqueville's point, observing that Americans "make the suspicion of ideology into something approaching a national creed." *Politics and the Novel* (New York: Avon, 1970), p. 337.

legends celebrating legal defiance in the name of some "natural" standard: Thoreau went to jail rather than pay taxes, Huck helped Jim (legally a slave) to escape, Billy the Kid murdered the sheriff's posse that had ambushed his boss, Hester Prynne resisted the community's sexual mores. This mythology transformed all outlaws into Robin Hoods, who "correct" socially unjust laws (Jesse James, Bonnie and Clyde, John Wesley Harding). Furthermore, by customarily portraying the law as the tool of villains (who used it to revoke mining claims, foreclose on mortgages, and disallow election results — all on legal technicalities), this mythology betrayed a profound pessimism about the individual's access to the legal system.

If the outlaw hero's motto was "I don't know what the law says, but I do know what's right and wrong," the official hero's was "We are a nation of laws, not of men," or "No man can place himself above the law." To the outlaw hero's insistence on private standards of right and wrong, the official hero offered the admonition, "You cannot take the law into your own hands." Often, these official heroes were lawyers or politicians, at times (as with Washington and Lincoln), even the executors of the legal system itself. The values accompanying such heroes modified the assurance of Crockett's advice, "Be sure you're right, then go ahead."

In sum, the values associated with these two different sets of heroes contrasted markedly. Clearly, too, each tradition had its good and bad points. If the extreme individualism of the outlaw hero always verged on selfishness, the respectability of the official hero always threatened to involve either blandness or repression. If the outlaw tradition promised adventure and freedom, it also offered danger and loneliness. If the official tradition promised safety and comfort, it also offered entanglements and boredom.

The evident contradiction between these heroes provoked Daniel Boorstin's observation that "Never did a more incongruous pair than Davy Crockett and George Washington live together in a national Valhalla." And yet, as Boorstin admits, "both Crockett and Washington were popular heroes, and both emerged into legendary fame during the first half of the nineteenth century."[9]

The parallel existence of these two contradictory traditions evinced the general pattern of American mythology: the denial of the necessity for choice. In fact, this mythology often portrayed situations requiring decision as temporary aberrations from American life's normal course. By discouraging commitment to any single set of values, this mythology fostered an ideology of improvisation, individualism, and ad hoc solutions for problems depicted as crises. American writers have repeatedly attempted to justify this mythology in terms of material sources. Hence, Irving Howe's "explanation":

> It is when men no longer feel that they have adequate choices in their styles of life, when they conclude that there are no longer possibilities of

---

[9]Daniel J. Boorstin, *The Americans: The National Experience* (New York: Random House, 1965), p. 337.

honorable maneuver and compromise, when they decide that the time has come for "ultimate" social loyalties and political decisions — it is then that ideology begins to flourish. Ideology reflects a hardening of commitment, the freezing of opinion into system. . . . The uniqueness of our history, the freshness of our land, the plenitude of our resources — all these have made possible, and rendered plausible, a style of political improvisation and intellectual free-wheeling.[10]

Despite such an account's pretext of objectivity, its language betrays an acceptance of the mythology it purports to describe: "honorable maneuver and compromise," "hardening," "freezing," "uniqueness," "freshness," and "plenitude" are all assumptive words from an ideology that denies its own status. Furthermore, even granting the legitimacy of the historians' authenticating causes, we are left with a persisting mythology increasingly discredited by historical developments. (In fact, such invalidation began in the early nineteenth century, and perhaps even before.)

The American mythology's refusal to choose between its two heroes went beyond the normal reconciliatory function attributed to myth by Lévi-Strauss. For the American tradition not only overcame binary oppositions; it systematically mythologized the certainty of being able to do so. Part of this process involved blurring the lines between the two sets of heroes. First, legends often brought the solemn official heroes back down to earth, providing the sober Washington with the cherry tree, the prudent Franklin with illegitimate children, and even the upright Jefferson with a slave mistress. On the other side, stories modified the outlaw hero's most potentially damaging quality, his tendency to selfish isolationism, by demonstrating that, however reluctantly, he would act for causes beyond himself. Thus, Huck grudgingly helped Jim escape, and Davy Crockett left the woods for three terms in Congress before dying in the Alamo for Texas independence. In this blurring process, Lincoln, a composite of opposing traits, emerged as the great American figure. His status as president made him an ex officio official hero. But his Western origins, melancholy solitude, and unaided decision-making all qualified him as a member of the other side. Finally, his ambivalent attitude toward the law played the most crucial role in his complex legend. As the chief executive, he inevitably stood for the principle that "we are a nation of laws and not men"; as the Great Emancipator, on the other hand, he provided the prime example of taking the law into one's own hands in the name of some higher standard.

Classic Hollywood's gallery of composite heroes (boxing musicians, rebellious aristocrats, pacifist soldiers) clearly derived from this mythology's rejection of final choices, a tendency whose traces Erikson detected in American psychology:

The process of American identity formation seems to support an individual's ego identity as long as he can preserve a certain element of deliberate tentativeness of autonomous choice. The individual must be able to

---

[10]*Politics and the Novel,* p. 164.

convince himself that the next step is up to him and that no matter where he is staying or going he always had the choice of leaving or turning in the opposite direction if he chooses to do so. In this country the migrant does not want to be told to move on, nor the sedentary man to stay where he is; for the life style (and the family history) of each contains the opposite element as a potential alternative which he wishes to consider his most private and individual decision.[11]

The reconciliatory pattern found its most typical incarnation, however, in one particular narrative: the story of the private man attempting to keep from being drawn into action on any but his own terms. In this story, the reluctant hero's ultimate willingness to help the community satisfied the official values. But by portraying this aid as demanding only a temporary involvement, the story preserved the values of individualism as well.

Like the contrasting heroes' epitomization of basic American dichotomies, the reluctant hero story provided a locus for displacement. Its most famous version, for example, *Adventures of Huckleberry Finn,* offered a typically individualistic solution to the nation's unresolved racial and sectional anxieties, thereby helping to forestall more systematic governmental measures. In adopting this story, Classic Hollywood retained its censoring power, using it, for example, in *Casablanca* to conceal the realistic threats to American self-determination posed by World War II.

Because the reluctant hero story was clearly the basis of the Western, American literature's repeated use of it prompted Leslie Fiedler to call the classic American novels "disguised westerns."[12] In the movies, too, this story appeared in every genre: in Westerns, of course (with *Shane* its most schematic articulation), but also in gangster movies (*Angels with Dirty Faces, Key Largo*), musicals (*Swing Time*), detective stories (*The Thin Man*), war films (*Air Force*), screwball comedy (*The Philadelphia Story*), "problem pictures" (*On the Waterfront*), and even science fiction (the Han Solo character in *Star Wars*). *Gone with the Wind,* in fact, had two selfish heroes who came around at the last moment, Scarlett (taking care of Melanie) and Rhett (running the Union blockade), incompatible only because they were so much alike. The natural culmination of this pattern, perfected by Hollywood in the 1930s and early 1940s, was *Casablanca.* Its version of the outlaw hero–official hero struggle (Rick versus Laszlo) proved stunningly effective, its resolution (their collaboration on the war effort) the prototypical Hollywood ending.

The reluctant hero story's tendency to minimize the official hero's role (by making him dependent on the outsider's intervention) suggested an imbalance basic to the American mythology: Despite the existence of both heroes, the national ideology clearly preferred the outlaw. This ideology strove to make that figure's origins seem spontaneous, concealing the calculated, commercial efforts behind the mythologizing of typical examples like Billy the Kid and Davy Crockett. Its willingness, on the other hand, to allow the official

20

---

[11] *Childhood and Society,* p. 286.
[12] *Love and Death in the American Novel,* p. 355.

hero's traces to show enables Daniel Boorstin to observe of one such myth, "There were elements of spontaneity, of course, in the Washington legend, too, but it was, for the most part, a self-conscious product."[13]

The apparent spontaneity of the outlaw heroes assured their popularity. By contrast, the official values had to rely on a rational allegiance that often wavered. These heroes' different statuses accounted for a structure fundamental to American literature, and assumed by Classic Hollywood: a split between the moral center and the interest center of a story. Thus, while the typical Western contained warnings against violence as a solution, taking the law into one's own hands, and moral isolationism, it simultaneously glamorized the outlaw hero's intense self-possession and willingness to use force to settle what the law could not. In other circumstances, Ishmael's evenhanded philosophy paled beside Ahab's moral vehemence, consciously recognizable as destructive.

D. H. Lawrence called this split the profound "duplicity" at the heart of nineteenth-century American fiction, charging that the classic novels evinced "a tight mental allegiance to a morality which all [the author's] passion goes to destroy." Certainly, too, this "duplicity" involved the mythology's pattern of obscuring the necessity for choosing between contrasting values. Richard Chase has put the matter less pejoratively in an account that applies equally to the American cinema:

> The American novel tends to rest in contradictions and among extreme ranges of experience. When it attempts to resolve contradictions, it does so in oblique, morally equivocal ways. As a general rule it does so either in melodramatic actions or in pastoral idylls, although intermixed with both one may find the stirring instabilities of "American humor."[14]

Or, in other words, when faced with a difficult choice, American stories resolved it either simplistically (by refusing to acknowledge that a choice is necessary), sentimentally (by blurring the differences between the two sides), or by laughing the whole thing off.

READING THE TEXT

1. What are the two basic hero types that Ray describes in American cinema?
2. How do these two hero types relate to America's "psychological pattern" (para. 2)?
3. Explain why, according to Ray, the outlaw hero typically mistrusts women.

READING THE SIGNS

1. Read Gary Engle's "What Makes Superman So Darned American?" (p. 738) and Andy Medhurst's "Batman, Deviance, and Camp" (p. 746), and write an essay

---

[13] *The Americans: The National Experience,* p. 337.

[14] Richard Chase, *The American Novel and Its Tradition* (Garden City, N.Y.: Anchor/Doubleday, 1957), p. 1.

in which you explain which type of heroes Superman and Batman are to their audiences.

2. What sort of hero is Arnold Schwarzenegger in the *Terminator* films? Write an essay in which you apply Ray's categories of hero to the Schwarzenegger character, supporting your argument with specific references to one or more films.

3. In class, brainstorm on the blackboard official and outlaw heroes you've seen in movies. Then categorize these heroes according to characteristics they have in common (such as race, gender, profession, or social class). What patterns emerge in your categories, and what is the significance of those patterns?

4. Rent one of the *Alien* films, and discuss whether Sigourney Weaver fits either of Ray's two categories of hero.

5. Cartoon television series like *The Simpsons* and *South Park* feature characters that don't readily fit Ray's two types of hero. Invent a third type of hero to accommodate such characters.

LINDA SEGER
CREATING THE MYTH

To be a successful screenwriter, Linda Seger suggests in this selection from Making a Good Script Great *(1987), you've got to know your archetypes. Seger reveals the secret behind the success of such Hollywood creations as* Star Wars's *Luke Skywalker and tells you how you can create such heroes yourself. In this "how to" approach to the cinema, Seger echoes the more academic judgments of such semioticians of film as Umberto Eco — the road to popular success in mass culture is paved with cultural myths and clichés. A script consultant and author who has given professional seminars on filmmaking around the world, Seger has also published* When Women Call the Shots: The Developing Power and Influence of Women in Television and Film *(1997).*

All of us have similar experiences. We share in the life journey of growth, development, and transformation. We live the same stories, whether they involve the search for a perfect mate, coming home, the search for fulfillment, going after an ideal, achieving the dream, or hunting for a precious treasure. Whatever our culture, there are universal stories that form the basis for all our particular stories. The trappings might be different, the twists and turns that create suspense might change from culture to culture, the particular characters may take different forms, but underneath it all, it's the same story, drawn from the same experiences.

Many of the most successful films are based on these universal stories. They deal with the basic journey we take in life. We identify with the heroes because we were once heroic (descriptive) or because we wish we could do what the hero does (prescriptive). When Joan Wilder finds the jewel and saves her sister, or James Bond saves the world, or Shane saves the family from the evil ranchers, we identify with the character, and subconsciously recognize the story as having some connection with our own lives. It's the same story as the fairy tales about getting the three golden hairs from the devil, or finding the treasure and winning the princess. And it's not all that different a story from the caveman killing the woolly beast or the Roman slave gaining his freedom through skill and courage. These are our stories — personally and collectively — and the most successful films contain these universal experiences.

Some of these stories are "search" stories. They address our desire to find some kind of rare and wonderful treasure. This might include the search for outer values such as job, relationship, or success; or for inner values such as respect, security, self-expression, love, or home. But it's all a similar search.

Some of these stories are "hero" stories. They come from our own experiences of overcoming adversity, as well as our desire to do great and special acts. We root for the hero and celebrate when he or she achieves the goal because we know that the hero's journey is in many ways similar to our own.

We call these stories *myths*. Myths are the common stories at the root of 5 our universal existence. They're found in all cultures and in all literature, ranging from the Greek myths to fairy tales, legends, and stories drawn from all of the world's religions.

A myth is a story that is "more than true." Many stories are true because one person, somewhere, at some time, lived it. It is based on fact. But a myth is more than true because it is lived by all of us, at some level. It's a story that connects and speaks to us all.

Some myths are true stories that attain mythic significance because the people involved seem larger than life, and seem to live their lives more intensely than common folk. Martin Luther King, Jr., Gandhi, Sir Edmund Hillary, and Lord Mountbatten personify the types of journeys we identify with, because we've taken similar journeys — even if only in a very small way.

Other myths revolve around make-believe characters who might capsulize for us the sum total of many of our journeys. Some of these make-believe characters might seem similar to the characters we meet in our dreams. Or they might be a composite of types of characters we've met.

In both cases, the myth is the "story beneath the story." It's the universal pattern that shows us that Gandhi's journey toward independence and Sir Edmund Hillary's journey to the top of Mount Everest contain many of the same dramatic beats. And these beats are the same beats that Rambo takes to set free the MIAs, that Indiana Jones takes to find the Lost Ark, and that Luke Skywalker takes to defeat the Evil Empire.

In *Hero with a Thousand Faces,* Joseph Campbell traces the elements that form the hero myth. "In their own work with myth, writer Chris Vogler and seminar leader Thomas Schlesinger have applied this criteria to *Star Wars.* The myth within the story helps explain why millions went to see this film again and again."

The hero myth has specific story beats that occur in all hero stories. They show who the hero is, what the hero needs, and how the story and character interact in order to create a transformation. The journey toward heroism is a process. This universal process forms the spine of all the particular stories, such as the *Star Wars* trilogy.

The Hero Myth

1. In most hero stories, the hero is introduced in ordinary surroundings, in a mundane world, doing mundane things. Generally, the hero begins as a non-hero; innocent, young, simple, or humble. In *Star Wars,* the first time we see Luke Skywalker, he's unhappy about having to do his chores, which consists of picking out some new droids for work. He wants to go out and have fun. He wants to leave his planet and go to the Academy, but he's stuck. This is the setup of most myths. This is how we meet the hero before the call to adventure.

Star Wars, 1977.

2. Then something new enters the hero's life. It's a catalyst that sets the story into motion. It might be a telephone call, as in *Romancing the Stone,* or the German attack in *The African Queen,* or the holograph of Princess Leia in *Star Wars.* Whatever form it takes, it's a new ingredient that pushes the hero into an extraordinary adventure. With this call, the stakes are established, and a problem is introduced that demands a solution.

3. Many times, however, the hero doesn't want to leave. He or she is a reluctant hero, afraid of the unknown, uncertain, perhaps, if he or she is up to the challenge. In *Star Wars,* Luke receives a double call to adventure. First, from Princess Leia in the holograph, and then through Obi-Wan Kenobi, who says he needs Luke's help. But Luke is not ready to go. He returns home, only to find that the Imperial Stormtroopers have burned his farmhouse and slaughtered his family. Now he is personally motivated, ready to enter into the adventure.

4. In any journey, the hero usually receives help, and the help often comes from unusual sources. In many fairy tales, an old woman, a dwarf, a witch, or a wizard helps the hero. The hero achieves the goal because of this help, and because the hero is receptive to what this person has to give.

There are a number of fairy tales where the first and second son are sent to complete a task, but they ignore the helpers, often scorning them. Many times they are severely punished for their lack of humility and unwillingness to accept help. Then the third son, the hero, comes along. He receives the help, accomplishes the task, and often wins the princess.

In *Star Wars,* Obi-Wan Kenobi is a perfect example of the "helper" character. He is a kind of mentor to Luke, one who teaches him the Way of the Force and whose teachings continue even after his death. This mentor character appears in most hero stories. He is the person who has special knowledge, special information, and special skills. This might be the prospector in *The Treasure of the Sierra Madre,* or the psychiatrist in *Ordinary People,* or Quint in *Jaws,* who knows all about sharks, or the Good Witch of the North who gives Dorothy the ruby slippers in *The Wizard of Oz.* In *Star Wars,* Obi-Wan gives Luke the light saber that was the special weapon of the Jedi Knight. With this, Luke is ready to move forward and do his training and meet adventure.

5. The hero is now ready to move into the special world where he or she will change from the ordinary into the extraordinary. This starts the hero's transformation, and sets up the obstacles that must be surmounted to reach the goal. Usually, this happens at the first Turning Point of the story, and leads into Act Two development. In *Star Wars,* Obi-Wan and Luke search for a pilot to take them to the planet of Alderaan, so that Obi-Wan can deliver the plans to Princess Leia's father. These plans are essential to the survival of the Rebel Forces. With this action, the adventure is ready to begin.

6. Now begin all the tests and obstacles necessary to overcome the enemy and accomplish the hero's goals. In fairy tales, this often means getting past witches, outwitting the devil, avoiding robbers, or confronting evil. In Homer's *Odyssey,* it means blinding the Cyclops, escaping from the island of

15

the Lotus-Eaters, resisting the temptation of the singing Sirens, and surviving a shipwreck. In *Star Wars,* innumerable adventures confront Luke. He and his cohorts must run to the *Millennium Falcon,* narrowly escaping the Stormtroopers before jumping into hyperspace. They must make it through the meteor shower after Alderaan has been destroyed. They must evade capture on the Death Star, rescue the Princess, and even survive a garbage crusher.

7. At some point in the story, the hero often hits rock bottom. He often 20 has a "death experience," leading to a type of rebirth. In *Star Wars,* Luke seems to have died when the serpent in the garbage-masher pulls him under, but he's saved just in time to ask R2D2 to stop the masher before they're crushed. This is often the "black moment" at the second turning point, the point when the worst is confronted, and the action now moves toward the exciting conclusion.

8. Now, the hero seizes the sword and takes possession of the treasure. He is now in charge, but he still has not completed the journey. Here Luke has the Princess and the plans, but the final confrontation is yet to begin. This starts the third-act escape scene, leading to the final climax.

9. The road back is often the chase scene. In many fairy tales, this is the point where the devil chases the hero and the hero has the last obstacles to overcome before really being free and safe. His challenge is to take what he has learned and integrate it into his daily life. He *must* return to renew the mundane world. In *Star Wars,* Darth Vader is in hot pursuit, planning to blow up the Rebel Planet.

10. Since every hero story is essentially a transformation story, we need to see the hero changed at the end, resurrected into a new type of life. He must face the final ordeal before being "reborn" as the hero, proving his courage and becoming transformed. This is the point, in many fairy tales, where the Miller's Son becomes the Prince or the King and marries the Princess. In *Star Wars,* Luke has survived, becoming quite a different person from the innocent young man he was in Act One.

At this point, the hero returns and is reintegrated into his society. In *Star Wars,* Luke has destroyed the Death Star, and he receives his great reward.

This is the classic "Hero Story." We might call this example a *mission* or *task* 25 *myth,* where the person has to complete a task, but the task itself is not the real treasure. The real reward for Luke is the love of the Princess and the safe, new world he had helped create.

A myth can have many variations. We see variations on this myth in James Bond films (although they lack much of the depth because the hero is not transformed), and in *The African Queen,* where Rose and Allnutt must blow up the *Louisa,* or in *Places in the Heart,* where Edna overcomes obstacles to achieve family stability.

The *treasure myth* is another variation on this theme, as seen in *Romancing the Stone.* In this story, Joan receives a map and a phone call which forces her into the adventure. She is helped by an American birdcatcher and a Mexican pickup truck driver. She overcomes the obstacles of snakes, the jungle, waterfalls, shootouts, and finally receives the treasure, along with the "prince."

Whether the hero's journey is for a treasure or to complete a task, the elements remain the same. The humble, reluctant hero is called to an adventure. The hero is helped by a variety of unique characters. S/he must overcome a series of obstacles that transform him or her in the process, and then faces the final challenge that draws on inner and outer resources.

The Healing Myth

Although the hero myth is the most popular story, many myths involve healing. In these stories, some character is "broken" and must leave home to become whole again.

The universal experience behind these healing stories is our psychological 30 need for rejuvenation, for balance. The journey of the hero into exile is not all that different from the weekend in Palm Springs, or the trip to Hawaii to get away from it all, or lying still in a hospital bed for some weeks to heal. In all cases, something is out of balance and the mythic journey moves toward wholeness.

Being broken can take several forms. It can be physical, emotional, or psychological. Usually, it's all three. In the process of being exiled or hiding out in the forest, the desert, or even the Amish farm in *Witness,* the person becomes whole, balanced, and receptive to love. Love in these stories is both a healing force and a reward.

Think of John Book in *Witness.* In Act One, we see a frenetic, insensitive man, afraid of commitment, critical and unreceptive to the feminine influences in his life. John is suffering from an "inner wound" which he doesn't know about. When he receives an "outer wound" from a gunshot, it forces him into exile, which begins his process of transformation.

At the beginning of Act Two, we see John delirious and close to death. This is a movement into the unconscious, a movement from the rational, active police life of Act One into a mysterious, feminine, more intuitive world. Since John's "inner problem" is the lack of balance with his feminine side, this delirium begins the process of transformation.

Later in Act Two, we see John beginning to change. He moves from his highly independent life-style toward the collective, communal life of his Amish hosts. John now gets up early to milk the cows and to assist with the chores. He uses his carpentry skills to help with the barn building and to complete the birdhouse. Gradually, he begins to develop relationships with Rachel and her son, Samuel. John's life slows down and he becomes more receptive, learning important lessons about love. In Act Three, John finally sees that the feminine is worth saving, and throws down his gun to save Rachel's life. A few beats later, when he has the opportunity to kill Paul, he chooses a nonviolent response instead. Although John doesn't "win" the Princess, he has neverthe- less "won" love and wholeness. By the end of the film, we can see that the John Book of Act Three is a different kind of person from the John Book of Act One. He has a different kind of comradeship with his fellow police officers, he's more relaxed, and we can sense that somehow, this experience has formed a more integrated John Book.

Combination Myths

Many stories are combinations of several different myths. Think of *Ghostbusters,* 35 a simple and rather outrageous comedy about three men saving the city of New York from ghosts. Now think of the story of "Pandora's Box." It's about the woman who let loose all manner of evil upon the earth by opening a box she was told not to touch. In *Ghostbusters,* the EPA man is a Pandora figure. By shut- ting off the power to the containment center, he inadvertently unleashes all the ghosts upon New York City. Combine the story of "Pandora's Box" with a hero story, and notice that we have our three heroes battling the Marshmallow Man. One of them also "gets the Princess" when Dr. Peter Venkman finally receives the affections of Dana Barrett. By looking at these combinations, it is apparent that even *Ghostbusters* is more than "just a comedy."

Tootsie is a type of reworking of many Shakespearean stories where a woman has to dress as a man in order to accomplish a certain task. These Shakespearean stories are reminiscent of many fairy tales where the hero be- comes invisible or takes on another persona, or wears a specific disguise to hide his or her real qualities. In the stories of "The Twelve Dancing Princesses" or "The Man in the Bearskin," disguise is necessary to achieve a goal. Combine these elements with the transformation themes of the hero myth where a hero (such as Michael) must overcome many obstacles to his success as an actor and a human being. It's not difficult to understand why the *Tootsie* story hooks us.

Archetypes

A myth includes certain characters that we see in many stories. These charac- ters are called *archetypes*. They can be thought of as the original "pattern" or "character type" that will be found on the hero's journey. Archetypes take many forms, but they tend to fall within specific categories.

Earlier, we discussed some of the helpers who give advice to help the hero — such as the *wise old man* who possesses special knowledge and often serves as a mentor to the hero.

The female counterpart of the wise old man is the *good mother*. Whereas the wise old man has superior knowledge, the good mother is known for her nurturing qualities, and for her intuition. This figure often gives the hero particular objects to help on the journey. It might be a protective amulet, or the ruby slippers that Dorothy receives in *The Wizard of Oz* from the Good Witch of the North. Sometimes in fairy tales it's a cloak to make the person invisible, or ordinary objects that become extraordinary, as in "The Girl of Courage," an Afghan fairy tale about a maiden who receives a comb, a whetstone, and a mirror to help defeat the devil.

Many myths contain a *shadow figure*. This is a character who is the oppo- 40 site of the hero. Sometimes this figure helps the hero on the journey; other times this figure opposes the hero. The shadow figure can be the negative side of the hero which could be the dark and hostile brother in "Cain and Abel," the stepsisters in "Cinderella," or the Robber Girl in "The Snow Queen." The shadow figure can also help the hero, as the whore with the heart of gold who saves the hero's life, or provides balance to his idealization of woman.

Many myths contain *animal archetypes* that can be positive or negative figures. In "St. George and the Dragon," the dragon is the negative force which is a violent and ravaging animal, not unlike the shark in *Jaws*. But in many stories, animals help the hero. Sometimes there are talking donkeys, or a dolphin which saves the hero, or magical horses or dogs.

The *trickster* is a mischievous archetypical figure who is always causing chaos, disturbing the peace, and generally being an anarchist. The trickster uses wit and cunning to achieve his or her ends. Sometimes the trickster is a harmless prankster or a "bad boy" who is funny and enjoyable. More often, the trickster is a con man, as in *The Sting,* or the devil, as in *The Exorcist,* who demanded all the skills of the priest to outwit him. The "Till Eulenspiegel" stories revolve around the trickster, as do the Spanish picaresque novels. Even the tales of Tom Sawyer have a trickster motif. In all countries, there are stories that revolve around this figure, whose job it is to outwit.

"Mythic" Problems and Solutions

We all grew up with myths. Most of us heard or read fairy tales when we were young. Some of us may have read Bible stories, or stories from other religions or other cultures. These stories are part of us. And the best way to work with them is to let them come out naturally as you write the script.

Of course, some filmmakers are better at this than others. George Lucas and Steven Spielberg have a strong sense of myth and incorporate it into their films. They both have spoken about their love of the stories from childhood, and of their desire to bring these types of stories to audiences. Their stories create some of the same sense of wonder and excitement as myths. Many of the necessary psychological beats are part of their stories, deepening the story beyond the ordinary action-adventure.

Myths bring depth to a hero story. If a filmmaker is thinking only about 45 the action and excitement of a story, audiences might fail to connect with the hero's journey. But if the basic beats of the hero's journey are evident, a film will often inexplicably draw audiences, in spite of critics' responses to the film.

Take *Rambo* for instance. Why was this violent, simple story so popular with audiences? I don't think it was because everyone agreed with its politics. I do think Sylvester Stallone is a master at incorporating the American myth into his filmmaking. That doesn't mean it's done consciously. Somehow he is naturally in sync with the myth, and the myth becomes integrated into his stories.

Clint Eastwood also does hero stories, and gives us the adventure of the myth and the transformation of the myth. Recently Eastwood's films have given more attention to the transformation of the hero, and have been receiving more serious critical attention as a result.

All of these filmmakers — Lucas, Spielberg, Stallone, and Eastwood — dramatize the hero myth in their own particular ways. And all of them prove that myths are marketable.

Application

It is an important part of the writer's or producer's work to continually find opportunities for deepening the themes within a script. Finding the myth beneath the modern story is part of that process.

To find these myths, it's not a bad idea to reread some of Grimm's fairy tales or fairy tales from around the world to begin to get acquainted with various myths. You'll start to see patterns and elements that connect with our own human experience.

Also, read Joseph Campbell and Greek mythology. If you're interested in Jungian psychology, you'll find many rich resources within a number of books on the subject. Since Jungian psychology deals with archetypes, you'll find many new characters to draw on for your own work.

With all of these resources to incorporate, it's important to remember that the myth is not a story to force upon a script. It's more a pattern which you can bring out in your own stories when they seem to be heading in the direction of a myth.

As you work, ask yourself:

Do I have a myth working in my script? If so, what beats am I using of the hero's journey? Which ones seem to be missing?
Am I missing characters? Do I need a mentor type? A wise old man? A wizard? Would one of these characters help dimensionalize the hero's journey?
Could I create new emotional dimensions to the myth by starting my character as reluctant, naive, simple, or decidedly "unheroic"?
Does my character get transformed in the process of the journey?
Have I used a strong three-act structure to support the myth, using

the first turning point to move into the adventure and the second turning point to create a dark moment, or a reversal, or even a "near-death" experience?

Don't be afraid to create variations on the myth, but don't start with the myth itself. Let the myth grow naturally from your story. Developing myths are part of the rewriting process. If you begin with the myth, you'll find your writing becomes rigid, uncreative, and predictable. Working with the myth in the rewriting process will deepen your script, giving it new life as you find the story within the story.

READING THE TEXT

1. How does Seger define the "hero myth" (para. 11)?
2. In your own words, explain what Seger means by "the healing myth" (para. 29).
3. What is an "archetype" (para. 37) in film?

READING THE SIGNS

1. Seger is writing to aspiring screenwriters. How does her status as an industry insider affect her description of heroic archetypes?
2. Compare Seger's formulation of heroes with Robert B. Ray's in "The Thematic Paradigm" (p. 308). To what extent do Seger and Ray adequately explain the role of women in movies?
3. Review Michael Parenti's "Class and Virtue" (p. 373), and then write an essay identifying the myths behind the modern stories *Pretty Woman* and *Indecent Proposal.*
4. Rent a videotape of *Titanic,* and write an essay in which you explain the myths and archetypal characters the film includes. How might archetypal and mythic patterns explain the film's success?
5. Seger recommends that aspiring screenwriters read Grimm's fairy tales for inspiration. Read some Grimm's tales, and then write an argument for or against the suitability of such tales as inspiration for films today.
6. What myths about American history, race, and gender do you see in *Gone with the Wind*? Brainstorm these myths in class, and then use your list of myths to write an essay in which you explain why the film has become an American classic.

GARY JOHNSON
THE WESTERN

If England has King Authur and the Knights of the Round Table, America has John Wayne and the gunslinging cowboys of the Old West. Constituting one of the most popular and enduring of Americans mythologies, the Western — whether inscribed in dime novels, in the cinema, or on TV — reflects the bedrock American belief that, in Richard Schickel's words, "complex moral conflicts [can] be plausibly resolved in clear, clean violent action." In this excerpt from the online magazine ImagesJournal.com, *Gary Johnson offers an overview of the cinematic history and impact of this most American of art forms, explaining why, despite periods of temporary decline, the Western has never vanished into the sunset of popular culture. Johnson is the publisher of* ImagesJournal.com, *a quarterly that focuses on movies, television, videos, and other popular visual arts.*

The Western has left an indelible mark on the world. Thanks to Hollywood, virtually everyone knows the ingredients of the Western — the lassos and the Colt .45s; the long-horned steer and the hanging trees; the stagecoaches and the Stetson hats; the outlaws and the lawmen; the gamblers and the gunfighters. And virtually everyone knows the settings of the Western — the red rock monoliths of Monument Valley; the jagged, snowcapped peaks of the Teton Range; the treeless expanses of the prairie. The iconography of the Western is the largest and richest of all the film genres, and Hollywood has burned it into the minds of moviegoers from Dodge City to Timbuktu.

Part of the allure of the Western was its very simplicity. As critic Richard Schickel said, because "everyone wore a six-shooter, complex moral conflicts could be plausibly resolved in clear, clean violent action" (Buscombe, pg. 11). This decisiveness allowed the West to take on mythical dimensions, to be-

Roy Rogers and Dale Evans.

come a place where great legends could be born. These myths and legends were embodied by Western heroes such as Wyatt Earp, Doc Holliday, Wild Bill Hickok, Buffalo Bill Cody, Calamity Jane, Jesse James, and Billy the Kid.

Equally important, especially in the first half of the twentieth century, was the immediacy of the American West. When Hollywood first set up shop, the last great frontier was so close at hand that gunslingers/lawmen like Wyatt Earp drifted to Hollywood to serve as consultants on movie sets. This closeness to the West made the Western myths tangible and all the more powerful.

At the heart of the Western, and not to be underestimated, was physical action — runaway stagecoaches, Indian raids, bank holdups, posse pursuits, and cattle stampedes. The Western resolved its conflicts through violent brawls and gunplay, reestablishing the moral order with an exhilarating BANG! during the final reel.

Hollywood sold its stories about the West to an eager American public, 5 providing us with a wide range of Westerns, from the series Westerns of Gene Autry and Roy Rogers with their clean-cut stars, fun-loving sidekicks, and guitar strumming singalongs to the obsessed, revenge-bent heroes of Anthony Mann's majestic 1950s Westerns.

The Western provided infinite variety on a relatively small stable of situations and plots, with conflicts often growing out of several archetypal situations: ranchers vs. farmers (*Shane* and *Man without a Star*), Indians vs. settlers (*The Searchers* and *Hondo*), and outlaws vs. civilization (*My Darling Clementine* and *High Noon*). Robert Warshow in his influential essay "Movie Chronicle: The Westerner" described the Western as "an art form for connoisseurs, where the spectator derives his pleasure from the appreciation of minor variations within the working out of a pre-established order" (Warshow, pg. 66).

John Wayne in *The Undefeated*.

Many filmmakers felt at ease with the Western and made their best movies within the genre. In a short speech before the Director's Guild, director John Ford (who had directed movies from many different genres) went on record as saying, "My name's John Ford. I make Westerns." Directors such as Ford, Budd Boetticher, Anthony Mann, and Sam Peckinpah excelled at prying unsuspected complexities and ironies out of well-worn stories of the American West. As a result, in John Ford's *The Searchers* we have much more than a simple quest to find a young girl kidnapped by Indians; we have the story of a quest that will never end, for the story's hero, Ethan Edwards (John Wayne), can never become part of the civilization he strives to restore. And in Anthony Mann's *The Naked Spur,* we have much more than the simple story of a bounty hunter (Jimmy Stewart) bringing home a body; we have a story where vengeance and self-destruction are intertwined. "He's not a man. He's a sack of money."

Some actors became closely identified with the Western, including Tom Mix, W. S. Hart, Roy Rogers, Gene Autry, and Audie Murphy — but for many people, no one epitomized the Western like John Wayne. With a towering stature and a steely gaze, Wayne dominated his movies like a national monument dominates the land. His image has worked its way into the American consciousness as a metaphor for America itself, its strength, its determination, and its reliability. A quick survey of his movies — from *Stagecoach* to *The Man Who Shot Liberty Valance* — is very nearly a list of the greatest Westerns ever made. While Wayne

Clint Eastwood in *Unforgiven.*

owns the top echelon by himself, a host of other actors have made powerful contributions to the genre, including Henry Fonda, James Stewart, Gary Cooper, Joel McCrea, Randolph Scott, and Clint Eastwood.

Hollywood fed us a steady diet of Western myths, legends, and heroes for over five decades. And in the process, the Western myth engulfed American popular culture — from clothes (denim jackets, jeans, and cowboy boots) to children's toys (cap guns, rubber-tipped arrows, and tom toms). Its lexicon entered our language ("round-up," "hog-tied," and "bury the hatchet"). The Western held our interest (with only minor lapses) until postwar cynicism ate away at the American psyche and we started doubting the heroes of the West. Gradually then the West began to fade away, struggling in spasms of violence in *The Wild Bunch* and the Spaghetti Westerns of Italy, until the Western hardly seemed relevant anymore. And not until the 1990s arrived (with films such as *Dances with Wolves* and *Unforgiven*) did it seem possible that the Western could survive in any form other than dewy-eyed nostalgia.

The Western Survives

The Western limped through the 1980s with few hopes for a recovery. *Silver-* 10
ado (1985) attempted to pump up the old clichés and stock situations with rapid-fire editing, larger-than-life images, and a tongue-in-cheek attitude, but for all its verve, the movie wasn't genuine. Its well-rehearsed crescendos car-

Clint Eastwood in *A Fistful of Dollars*.

ried the aura of movie brats gussying up an old form. Audiences largely stayed away. Even Clint Eastwood's *Pale Rider* disappointed with its cloning of *Shane*. *Young Guns* strived to create a teenage audience for the Western by giving us Brat Pack alumni in Western garb. While modestly successful at the box office, *Young Guns* pointed down a dead-end path.

As it struggled into the 1990s, the Western finally discovered salvation in the form of Kevin Costner's *Dances with Wolves*. It packed in audiences and carted away the Academy Award for Best Picture. And soon afterwards, the TV miniseries *Lonesome Dove* (based on Larry McMurtry's Pulitzer Prize-winning novel) attracted a huge following. Eastwood's *Unforgiven* followed in 1992. It's a magnificent meditation on the Old West, filled with bitter ironies and brutal violence meted out by lawmen and outlaws alike. *Unforgiven* took home the Best Picture Academy Award in 1992.

A variety of Westerns then soon appeared, from *The Quick and the Dead,* an inspired but hyperactive fusion of horror movie sensibilities and Spaghetti Western situations, to *Posse,* a black Western with a rap soundtrack. The legendary Gunfight at the OK Corral provided the material for two movies, Lawrence Kasdan's ambitious but stodgy *Wyatt Earp* and George Cosmatos's intermittently dazzling *Tombstone.*

Even with the minor resurgence of the Western in the 1990s, the Western exists in limbo. It still has the power to fan the sparks of imagination, but our distance from the West has weakened its authority. While the West once

Kevin Costner in *Dances with Wolves.*

represented a simpler time in America's history, we now see that the power of the gun (as shown in *Unforgiven* and *Tombstone*) could make lawmen just as dangerous as the outlaws. And although justice may have been swift; it was not necessarily fair and at times it was absolutely deadly. As the myths and heroes of the American West fade away, the Western becomes just another genre, a genre that becomes more remote with each passing year.

WORKS CITED

Buscombe, Edward (ed.) *The BFI Companion to the Western.* New York: Da Capo Press, 1991.
Warshow, Robert. *The Immediate Experience.* New York: Anchor Books, 1964.

READING THE TEXT

1. What, according to Johnson, accounts for the popularity of the Western?

2. What does Johnson say are some of the archetypal situations dramatized by the typical Western?

3. At what point did the Western begin to decline in popularity, in Johnson's view?

READING THE SIGNS

1. Read or reread Robert B. Ray's "The Thematic Paradigm" (p. 308) and use it as a critical framework for an essay in which you analyze a Western movie of your choice. What sorts of hero appear in the movie? What does the choice of hero say about the point of view of the audience?

2. Recently very few Western films have appeared and fewer still, if any, television Westerns. Write an essay offering a cultural explanation for why the Western has fallen out of popular favor.

3. One recent Western, *Wild, Wild West,* was a box office failure, despite the star appeal of its leading actor, Will Smith. Rent a video of this film, and write a semiotic analysis of it. To what extent does the film adhere to — or rewrite — conventions of the Western?

4. Rent a video of one of the classic Westerns that Johnson mentions, and write an essay that supports, refutes, or complicates his claim that such films offer their viewers "dewy-eyed nostalgia" (para. 9).

SUSAN BORDO

BRAVEHEART, BABE, AND THE CONTEMPORARY BODY

"Just do it," Nike commands, and, as Susan Bordo (b. 1947) observes in this selection from Twilight Zones: The Hidden Life of Cultural Images from Plato to O.J. *(1997), a good part of American society has obeyed. Situating movies like Mel Gibson's* Braveheart *in a cultural system in which the "notion that all that is required to succeed . . . is to stop whining, lace up your sneakers, and forge ahead" has become the mantra of a nation of body-mad consumers, Bordo laments the ease with which traditional American self-reliance has been transformed into the freedom to buy what everyone else is buying. Why can't more people be like Babe? Bordo wonders. The little pig can't keep up with the collies but uses his head to come up with a better way to herd sheep—and in so doing, she suggests, offers an allegorical model for our own capacities to change the world. Bordo is the Otis A. Singletary Professor in the Humanities at the University of Kentucky, and the author of many books including* Unbearable Weight: Feminism, Western Culture, and the Body *(1993),* Twilight Zone: The Hidden Life of Cultural Images from Plato to O.J. *(1997), and* The Male Body: A New Look at Men in Public and in Private *(1999).*

Braveheart and "Just Do It"

I was stunned when Mel Gibson's *Braveheart* won the Oscar for best picture of the year. I know Hollywood loves a "sweeping" epic, and I liked the innovative use of mud and the absence of hairbrushes for the men (a commitment to material realism not matched in the commercial-perfect shots of the movie's heroines). But as interesting as it was to see Mel in unkempt cornrows, I didn't think it would add up to an Academy Award. Usually we require at least the semblance of an idea from our award-winning epics. *Braveheart* is a one-liner (actually a one-worder)—and an overworked one. "Your heart is free. Have the courage to follow 'er," the young William Wallace is told by his father's ghost at the start of the film. And he does, leading an animal-house army of howling Scotsmen against the yoke of cruel and effete British tyrants. "Freedom!" he screams, as he is disemboweled in the concluding scene, refusing to declare allegiance to British rule. Between these two scenes, "free," "freedom," and "freemen" were intoned reverently or shrieked passionately. And that was about it for "content."

"Live free or die." That slogan does have historical and ideological resonance for Americans. But it's clearly not the collective fight against political tyranny that counts in the movie; it's the courage to *act* and the triumph of

333

the undauntable, unconquerable action hero. Yes, Gibson makes William Wallace a fluent linguist, educated in Latin, well traveled, a man who uses his brain to plot battle strategy. But this is just a ploy to create the appearance of masculine stereotype busting. It's *doing,* not thinking, that reveals a man's worth in the film, whose notion of heroics is as tough-guy as they come. In the last scene Wallace endures public stretching, racking, and evisceration so that Scotland will know he died without submitting, and Gibson (who directed the film as well as starred in it) makes the torture go on for a long, painful time. Wallace's resistance is really the point of the film. Braveheart has his eyes on a prize, and his will is so strong, so powerful, that he is able to endure anything to achieve it. The man has the right stuff.

This macho model of moral fortitude has a lot of living currency today — and for the first time, we now see it as applying to women as well as men. Undiluted testosterone drives *Braveheart.* Its band of Scottish rebels is described in a voice-over as fighting "like warrior-poets," an unmistakable nod to the mythopoetic men's movement to reclaim masculinity. King Longshank's son is a homosexual, and this is clearly coded in the film as signifying that he lacks the equipment to rule. But the movie's women, within the limits of their social roles, are as rebellious and brave-hearted as the men and enjoy watching a good fight too. (In an early scene Wallace's girl's eyes light up as he and a fellow Scot have sport throwing bricks at each other's heads.) I think this is Gibson's idea of feminism — that one doesn't have to be male in order to be a real man — and it is an idea that is widely shared today, with "power" and "muscle" feminism the culturally approved way of advancing the cause of women.

That women have just as much guts, willpower, and *balls* as men, that they can put their bodies through as much wear and tear, endure as much pain, and remain undaunted, was a major theme of the coverage of the 1996 Summer Olympics. Not since Leni Riefenstahl's *Olympia* of 1936 has there been such a focus on the aesthetics of athletic perfection. But *this* version of beauty, like Riefenstahl's and like those stressed in the numerous photo-articles celebrating the Olympic body, has little to do with looking pretty. It's about strength, yes, and skill, but even more deeply it's about true grit. "Determined, defiant, dominating," the bold caption in the *New York Times Magazine* describes Gwen Torrence. (The same words, applied to rebellious wives or feminist politicos, have not been said so admiringly.) As in *Braveheart,* the ability to rise above the trials of the body is associated with the highest form of courage and commitment. Mary Ellen Clark's bouts of vertigo. Gail Devers's Graves' disease. Gwen Torrence's difficult childbirth. Amy Van Dyken's asthma. *Life* magazine describes these as personal tests of mettle sent by God to weed out the losers from the winners. And when gymnast Kerri Strug performed her second vault on torn tendons, bringing her team to victory in the face of what must have been excruciating pain, she became the unquestionable hero of the games (and set herself up with ten million dollars in endorsement contracts).

It's not the courage of these athletes I'm sniping at here; I admire them 5
enormously. What bothers me is the message that is dramatized by the way
we tell the tales of their success, a message communicated to us mortals too
in commercials and ads. Nike has proven to be the master manipulator and
metaphor maker in this game. Don't moan over life's problems or blame society for holding you back, Nike instructs us. Don't waste your time berating
the "system." Get down to the gym, pick up those free weights, and turn
things around. If it hurts, all the better. No pain, no gain. "Right after Bob
Kempainen qualified for the marathon, he crossed the finish line and puked
all over his Nike running shoes," Nike tells us in a recent advertisement. "We
can't tell you how proud we were." A Nike commercial, shown during the
games: "If you don't lose consciousness at the end, you could have run
faster." Am I the only one who finds this recommendation horrifying in its
implications? But consciousness apparently doesn't figure very much in our
contemporary notion of heroism. What counts, as in *Braveheart,* is action. *Just
Do It.* This is, of course, also what Nike wants us to do when we approach the
cash register. (The call to *act* sends a disturbing political message as well.
Movies like *Braveheart,* as a friend of mine remarked after we'd seen the film,
seem designed to provide inspiration for the militia movement.)

The notion that all that is required to succeed in this culture is to stop
whining, lace up your sneakers, and forge ahead, blasting your way through

Babe, 1995.

social limitations, personal tribulations, and even the laws of nature, is all around us. . . . Commercials and advertisements egg us on: "Go for It!" "Know No Boundaries!" "Take Control!" Pump yourself up with our product — a car, a diet program, hair-coloring, sneakers — and take your destiny into your own hands. The world will open up for you like an oyster. Like the Sector watch advertisement, AT&T urges us to "Imagine a world without limits" in a series of commercials shown during the 1996 Summer Olympics; one graphic depicts a young athlete pole-vaulting over the World Trade Center, another diving down an endless waterfall. And, indeed, in the world of these images, there are no impediments — no genetic disorders, no body-altering accidents, not even any fat — to slow down our progress to the top of the mountain. All that's needed is the power to *buy*.

The worst thing, in the *Braveheart*/Nike universe of values, is to be bossed around, told what to do. This creates a dilemma for advertisers, who somehow must convince hundreds of thousands of people to purchase the same product while assuring them that they are bold and innovative individualists in doing so. The dilemma is compounded because many of these products perform what Foucault and feminist theorists have called "normalization." That is, they function to screen out diversity and perpetuate social norms, often connected to race and gender. This happens not necessarily because advertisers are consciously trying to promote racism or sexism but because in order to sell products they have to either exploit or create a perception of personal *lack* in the consumer (who buys the product in the hope of filling that lack). An effective way to make the consumer feel inadequate is to take advantage of values that are already in place in the culture. For example, in a society where there is a dominant (and racialized) preference for blue-eyed blondes, there is a ready market for blue contact lenses and blonde hair-coloring. The catch is that ad campaigns promoting such products also reglamorize the beauty ideals themselves. Thus, they perpetuate racialized norms.

But people don't like to think that they are pawns of astute advertisers or even that they are responding to social norms. Women who have had or are contemplating cosmetic surgery consistently deny the influence of media images.[1] "I'm doing it for me," they insist. But it's hard to account for most of their choices (breast enlargement and liposuction being the most frequently performed operations) outside the context of current cultural norms. Surgeons help to encourage these mystifications. Plastic surgeon Barbara Hayden claims that breast augmentation today is "as individual as the patient herself"; a moment later in the same article another surgeon adds that the "huge 1980s look is out" and that many stars are trading their old gigantibreasts for the currently stylish smaller models![2]

[1]See Marcene Goodman, "Social, Psychological, and Developmental Factors in Women's Receptivity to Cosmetic Surgery," *Journal of Aging Studies* 8, no. 4 (1994): 375–96.

[2]Quoted in Sally Ogle Davis, "Knifestyles of the Rich and Famous," *Marie Claire*, May 1996, p. 46.

I'm doing it for me. This has become the mantra of the television talk show, and I would gladly accept it if "for me" meant "in order to feel better about myself in this culture that has made me feel inadequate as I am." But people rarely mean this. Most often on these shows, the "for me" answer is produced in defiant refutation of some cultural "argument" (talk-show style, of course) on topics such as "Are Our Beauty Ideals Racist?" or "Are We Obsessed with Youth?" "No, I'm not having my nose (straightened) (narrowed) in order to look less ethnic. I'm doing it *for me.*" "No, I haven't had my breasts enlarged to a 38D in order to be more attractive to men. I did it *for me.*" In these constructions "me" is imagined as a pure and precious inner space, an "authentic" and personal reference point untouched by external values and demands. A place where we live free and won't be pushed around. It's the *Braveheart* place.

But we want to both imagine ourselves as bold, rebellious Bravehearts *and* 10 conform, become what our culture values. Advertisers help us enormously in this self-deception by performing their own sleight-of-hand tricks with rhetoric and image, often invoking, as *Braveheart* does, the metaphor and hype of "political" resistance: "Now it's every woman's right to look good!" declares Pond's (for "age-defying" makeup). "What makes a woman revolutionary?" asks Revlon. "Not wearing makeup for a day!" answers a perfectly made-up Claudia Schiffer (quickly adding, "Just kidding, Revlon!"). A recent Gap ad: "The most defiant act is to be distinguished, singled out, marked. Put our jeans on." The absurdity of suggesting that everyone's donning the same (rather ordinary-looking) jeans can be a "defiant" and individualistic act is visually accompanied by two photos of female models with indistinguishable bodies.

Power as Agency: Masking Reality

From evisceration at the hands of tyrants to defiance through dungarees may seem like a large leap. And in real terms, of course, it is. But we live in a world of commercial rhetoric that brooks no such distinctions. And not only commercial rhetoric. "Just Do It" is an ideology for our time, an idea that bridges the gulf between right and left, grunge and yuppie, chauvinist and feminist. The left wing didn't like "Just Say No," perhaps because it came from Nancy Reagan, perhaps because it was aimed at habits they didn't want to give up themselves. It isn't that easy, they insisted. The neighborhoods, the culture, social despair. . . . But the mind-over-matter message of "Just Do It," with its "neutral" origins (the brain of an ad woman) and associations with jogging, nice bodies, and muscle-lib for women, has roused no protests.

In a recent interview rock star Courtney Love urged "liberals" to "breed" in order to outpopulate the Rush Limbaughs of the world. "It's not that hard," she said. "It's nine months. You know, just do it."[3] But right-wing ideologues like Limbaugh, who celebrate bootstrapping and Horatio Alger and scorn

[3]Interview with Amanda de Cadenet, *Interview,* August 1995.

(what they view as) the liberal's creation of a culture of "victims," also advocate "just doing it."[4] And so too do celebrities like Oprah when they present themselves as proof that "anyone can make it if they want it badly enough and try hard enough." The implication here — which Oprah, I like to believe, would blanch at if she faced it squarely — is that if you *don't* succeed, it's proof that you *didn't* want it badly enough or try hard enough. Racism and sexism? Just so many hurdles to be jumped, personal challenges to be overcome. And what about the fact that in a competitive society someone *always has to lose*? We won't think about that, it's too much of a downer. Actually, in the coverage of the 1996 Olympics, everything short of "getting the gold" was constructed as losing. The men's 4 × 100 relay team, which won the silver medal, was interviewed by NBC after, as the commentator put it, their "defeat"! How can everyone be a winner if "winning" is reserved only for those who make it to the absolute pinnacle?

As far as women's issues go, "power feminists" are telling us that we're past all those tiresome harangues about "the beauty system" and "objectification" and "starving girls." What's so bad about makeup, anyway? Isn't it my right to go for it? Do what I want with my body? Be all that I can be? Just a few years back "third-wave" feminist Naomi Wolf wrote a best-selling book, *The Beauty Myth* (1991), which spoke powerfully and engagingly to young women about a culture that teaches them they are nothing if they are not beautiful. But in a wink of the cultural zeitgeist, she declares in her latest, *Fire with Fire* (1993), that all that bitching and moaning has seen its day. Now, according to the rehabilitated Wolf, we're supposed to stop complaining and — you guessed it — "Just Do It." Wolf, in fact, offers Nike's commercial slogan as her symbol for the new feminism, which as she describes it is about "competition . . . victory . . . self-reliance . . . the desire to win."[5] Wolf is hardly alone in her celebratory mood. Betty Friedan has also said she is "sick of women wallowing in the victim state. We have empowered ourselves." A 1993 *Newsweek* article — most of its authors women — sniffs derisively at an installation of artist Sue Williams, who put a huge piece of plastic vomit on the floor of the Whitney Museum to protest the role of aesthetic ideals in encouraging the development of eating disorders. That kind of action once would have been seen as guerrilla theater. In 1993, *Newsweek* writers sneered: "Tell [the bulimics] to get some therapy and cut it out."[6]

---

[4]Rush Limbaugh, in his tirades against feminists and the academic left, has apparently not noticed that among these groups too the "victim" is *not* politically correct but passé. In the 1990s postmodern academics look around and see not "oppressive" systems (which would be old-fashioned and "totalizing," so very "sixties") but "resistance," "subversion," and "creative negotiation" of the culture. (These academics may balk at being lined up on the side of *Braveheart* and Nike; they might be surprised at how often the trope of cultural "resistance" appears in automobile ads.) In exalting the creative power and efficacy of the individual, the right and left — polarized around so many other issues — seem to be revelers at the same party.

[5]Naomi Wolf, *Fire with Fire* (New York: Random House, 1993), 45.

[6]Friedan quote and "Tell them to get some therapy" in Debra Rosenberg, Stanley Holmes, Martha Brant, Donna Foote, and Nina Biddle, "Sexual Correctness," *Newsweek,* October 25, 1993, p. 56.

Getting one's body in shape, of course, has become the exemplary practice, symbol, and means of empowerment in this culture. "You don't just
shape your body," as Bally Fitness tells us. "You shape your life." As a manufacturer of athletic shoes, Nike — like Reebok and Bally — is dedicated to preserving the connection between having the right stuff and strenuous, physical
activity. "It's about time," they declare disingenuously in a recent ad, "that the
fitness craze that turned into the fashion craze that turned into the marketing
craze turned back into the fitness craze." But despite Nike's emphasis on fitness, in contemporary commercial culture the rhetoric of taking charge of
one's life has been yoked to everything from car purchases to hair-coloring,
with physical effort and discipline often dropping out as a requirement. Even
plastic surgery is continually described today — by patients, surgeons, and
even by some feminist theorists — as *an act* of "taking control," "taking one's
life into one's own hands" (a somewhat odd metaphor, under the circumstances). . . .

Babe: A Real Metaphor for Our Lives . . .

And so I come to *Babe,* which did not win the Academy Award but which   15
moved and haunted me for weeks after I saw it. For a long time I tried to put
my finger on just why that was. As I've said, I generally bristle against the triumphant success story. And *Babe,* like *Braveheart* (and *Rocky*), is a success
story, a tale of individual empowerment and personal triumph against enormous odds, of questing, self-transformation, and, you might even say, transcendence of the body. A little pig, seemingly destined to be dinner, dreams
of becoming a sheepdog — and he succeeds! Crowds cheer and tears flow.
And so did mine (dry at the end of *Braveheart* and *Rocky*).

When I tried to explain to a more cynical friend why I loved the film, I
grasped impotently at the available takes on the film then circulating in magazines and among intellectuals. "Allegory of social prejudice," that sort of thing.
But I knew that wasn't exactly what did it for me, and when my friend
pressed on, amazed that I could be so taken by what she saw as a sentimental
fantasy, I realized that sentimental — in the sense of wrenching emotion while
falsifying reality — was precisely what I found *Babe* not to be and that this was
a large part of the reason why it moved me so powerfully. *Braveheart,* apparently based on real events, seemed like a slick commercial to me from start to
finish. But *Babe* — a fable with talking animals — was for me a moment of reality in a culture dominated by fantasy.

Babe, on the face of it, seems far removed from the land of StairMasters,
liposuction, and face-lifts — and it is certainly nothing like a Nike commercial.
Babe's personal triumph takes place in a world that — as the film never lets us
forget — permits such moments only for a very few. On the farm most of the
animals eke their joy humbly from the circumscribed routines and roles allot-
ted to them — and they are the lucky ones, the safe ones. The others — those
who are destined to be eaten — tremble on little islands of temporary peace,

the vulnerability and perishability of their existence always hovering before them. Death for them will not be accompanied by the dignifying hoopla of the big battle or the knowledge that they have made a statement for history. They will have no control over when death comes, and they will be unable to make the "why" of it more meaningful than the fact that others are luckier and more powerful and more arrogant than they are. This is a world in which those who can "just do it" are a privileged few. A world in which "agency" is real but limited and "empowerment" possible but hardly an everyday affair. A world in which the notion that we are "in charge," "in control," "at the reins" is strictly an illusion. Existence is precarious for the animals on the farm, as it is materially for many people, and as it is existentially for all of us, whether we recognize it or not. We can try to avoid this recognition with illusions of "agency," fantasies of staying young forever, and the distractions of "self-improvement," but it only lies in wait for us.

It is very important to the emotional truth of the film that Babe himself learns about the fragility of his safety. When he decides to go on anyway, it is not as a hopeful hero-to-be, dreaming of glory, but out of the simple fact that despite "the way things are" in the awful world he has learned about, there is still the unanswerable, unbreakable bond between him and the Boss. The men in *Braveheart* are bonded too. But, as Gibson directs it, the relationship amounts to a fraternity handshake, a pledge of affiliation; they're all pumped up, looking out over the grandeur of the countryside, ready to take up arms together. The bond between Babe and the Boss is established in a very different sort of exchange, in which each, in a Kierkegaardian leap of faith, bravely lets down his defenses in a moment of simple caring for and trust in the other. The taciturn and reserved farmer, trying to get depressed Babe to eat and obeying some wild impulse of inspiration, leaps up and performs an unrestrained, goofy hornpipe for him. Babe watches and, although he has heard "the way things are" from Fly, his surrogate-mother (pigs get eaten, even by the Boss and his wife), cedes final authority to the reasons of the heart. He eats.

Babe's world is the one we live in; heroic moments are temporary and connections with others are finally what sustain us. This is a reality we may be inclined to forget as we try to create personal scenarios that will feel like Olympic triumphs and give us the power and "agency" over our bodies and lives that the commercials promise. But we still feel the emotional tug of abandoned dreams of connection and intimacy and relationships that will feed us in the open-hearted way that the Boss feeds little Babe and Babe's eating feeds *him*. My cynical friend disliked the movie for — as she saw it — idealizing parent-child relations through scenes such as this (and Babe's relationship with his surrogate mother, the Border collie Fly). But unlike the Gerber's commercials that feature mother and child ensconced in an immaculate nursery, cocooned together by the accoutrements of cozy furniture, perfectly tended plants, good hair and skin, *Babe*'s images of caring and intimacy do not work through sugarcoating but by keeping the dark realities always on the horizon. They are the reason we need to take care of one another.

Babe is, of course, a success story. But unlike *Rocky, Flashdance, Brave-* 20
heart, and the many other fantasies of empowerment in which socially underprivileged heroes and heroines rise above their circumstances and transform
themselves through discipline, will, and dazzling physical prowess, *Babe* is a
fable about the power of "difference," of nonassimilation. The polite little pig,
who talks to the sheep rather than snap and bark, turns out to be a better
herder than the bossy Border collies! And in a significant way he transforms
the culture and the values of the world he lives in. (It is suggested both at the
beginning and the end of the film that attitudes toward pigs were never
the same after Babe won the competition.) The *Rocky* model of success, like
the "power feminism" model, is one of "making it" in a world that remains
unchanged while the hero or heroine's body transforms itself to meet — and
perhaps even surpass — the requirements of that world. This is what we celebrate when female athletes demonstrate that they can develop the strength
and power of men, when "special" Olympians cross the finish lines in their
competitions, when those who have struggled to lose weight finally squeeze
into those size eight Calvin Kleins; the "outsider" is included by showing that
he or she can "do it" too — on the terms of the culture. When the media celebrates such successes (and I do not deny that they are cause for celebration,
as dramas of individual will, courage, and dedication), it usually leaves those
cultural terms unquestioned.

Babe illustrates a different kind of success, one in which the "it" (of "Just
Do It," "making it," "going for it") is interrogated and challenged. Those collies own the world (their own little world, that is) by virtue of their physical
prowess and aggression, which — until Babe comes along — are the dominant
values of that world. No one could have imagined that sheepherding could be
done in any other way. How many of us have found ourselves struggling to
prove our worth in worlds which do not value us or our contributions? Often,
the pressure to conform is overwhelming. Babe, unable to transform his
waddly little body and unwilling to transform his empathic little soul into a
mean, lean, fighting machine, represents the possibility of resisting that pressure — and transforming "the way things are." In a culture in which people
are shamed for their "defects" and differences and seek safety in conformity,
this may be a fantasy. But it is a precious one, one more worthy of our imaginations and ambitions — and our children's, surely — than "Just Do It!"

Babe is a fable and presents its message through the conventions of that
genre, not through gritty realism. A glorious triumph is the reward for the "alternative" values that the little pig represents. Few of us experience such definitive or resounding validation of our efforts. But it is not necessary to win
the big race in order to transform "the way things are." All of us, in myriad
small ways, have the capacity to do this, because nothing that we do is a self-
contained, disconnected, isolated event. Seemingly minor gestures of resistance to cultural norms can lay deep imprints on the lives of those around us.
Unfortunately, gestures of capitulation do so as well. Consider the message
sent by the mother who anxiously monitors her own weight and ships her

daughter off to Jenny Craig at the first sign that her child's body is less than willowy, or the father who teases his wife (perhaps in front of their daughter) for being "out of shape." I don't mean to sound harsh; these responses may reflect personal insecurity, concern about the social acceptability of loved ones, panic over a child's future. But when we demonstrate seamless solidarity with our culture of images, we make its reign over the lives of those we love just a little bit stronger. And we unwittingly promote for them a life on the cultural treadmill.

I have learned a great deal about the extremes of that treadmill existence from my students' journals and from conversations with them in my office. Yes, my students know that as long as they keep up their daily hours at the gym, they can feel pumped up, look like Madonna, and burn enough calories so perhaps they will not have to throw up after dinner. But how, they wonder, can they possibly keep it up their entire lives? They know there is no equilibrium there, that the conditions of their feeling all right about themselves are *precarious*. Here is where *Babe* does speak to the situation of those who try to stop those breasts from sagging, thighs from spreading, wrinkles from forming. The parable not only makes visible more basic struggles that our obsession with appearance masks but also presents us with a metaphor for the *pathos* of that seemingly "superficial" obsession. The little pig performs in the final competition without any solid assurance of a happy ending. Even as he herds the sheep into the pen, he has not been told, in so many words, that he will be spared the carving knife. He wins the sheepherding trials, and, as is customary, the farmer utters the standard words "real" dogs hear at the end of their runs. "That'll do, Pig. That'll do." A formality usually — but in the context of Babe's long struggle, these words say more, both to Babe and to the viewer. They represent, I believe, an acknowledgment that so many of us fervently long for in our lives — and are so rarely given. So many of us feel like Babe, trying our hardest to become something valued and loved, uncertain about whether we will ever be granted the right to simply exist. "That'll do. That'll do." These are words to break the heart. Enough. You've worked hard enough. I accept you. You can rest.

READING THE TEXT

1. What, according to Bordo, are the different kinds of success dramatized in *Braveheart* and *Babe*?

2. Describe in your own words what Bordo means by "the *Braveheart*/Nike universe of values" (para. 7).

3. What are Bordo's objections to the phrase "Just Do It" (para. 5)?

4. Why does Bordo prefer *Babe* to *Braveheart*?

5. How does Babe represent alternative values, in Bordo's view?

6. Chart Bordo's construction of the *system* in which she analyzes *Braveheart* and *Babe*.

READING THE SIGNS

1. In your journal, reflect on whether you have been influenced by the Just-Do-It philosophy.

2. In class, brainstorm two lists of recent films — those that encourage what Bordo terms the Just-Do-It philosophy and those that encourage viewers to change, not overpower, the world. Analyze your results. Do the lists differ in length or in the commercial success of their titles? Can you account for any differences you find?

3. In an essay, support, refute, or complicate Bordo's criticism of power feminism.

4. Bordo contends that "I'm doing it for me" has become the "mantra of the television talk show" (para. 9). Watch one such show, and write an essay evaluating the validity of Bordo's contention. To develop your ideas, read or reread Steven D. Stark's "*The Oprah Winfrey Show* and the Talk-Show Furor" (p. 243).

TODD BOYD

SO YOU WANNA BE A GANGSTA?

Before there were "gangstas" there were gangsters, and as Todd Boyd points out in this selection from Am I Black Enough for You? Popular Culture from the 'Hood and Beyond *(1997), both have played their part in American and cinematic history. From the Italian gangsters of* Scarface *and the* Godfather *films to the Latino and African American gangstas of* American Me *and* Boyz N the Hood, *the gang movie has provided a dramatic setting for an ongoing contest in which the American underclass both resists and embraces the values of mainstream society. An associate professor of critical studies in the School of Cinema-Television at the University of Southern California, Boyd is coeditor (with Aaron Baker) of* Out of Bounds: Sports, Media, and the Politics of Identity *(1997) and editor of* Basketball Jones: America above the Rim *(2000). He has written for such journals as* Wide Angle, Cinéaste, Filmforum, *and* Public Culture.

The gangster film and the Western are two of the most important genres in the history of Hollywood, especially with respect to articulation of the discourse of American history and masculinity. Whereas the Western concentrated on the mythic settling of the West and a perceived notion of progression, it was primarily concerned with the frontier mentality of the eighteenth through the late nineteenth century. The gangster genre, on the other hand, is about the evolution of American society in the twentieth century into a legitimate entity in the world economy.

Though the Western covertly articulated the politics of oppression against Native Americans during the settling of the West, the gangster genre focused on questions of ethnicity — e.g., Italian, Irish — and how these are transformed over time into questions of race — Black, Latino, etc. This ideological shift provided an interesting representation of the significant position that race has come to occupy in the discourse of American society. We must look at the transformation of the linguistic sign "gangster" and its slow transition to its most recent embodiment as "gangsta" as an instructive historical metaphor. . . .

Americans have always had a fascination with the underworld society populated by those who openly resisted the laws of dominant society and instead created their own world, living by their own rules. Gangsters have in many ways been our version of revolutionaries throughout history. Whereas Europe has always had real-life political revolutionaries, twentieth-century American discourse, upheld by police and government activity, seems to have found ways of perverting for the public the political voices that exist outside the narrow traditions of allowed political expression.

The displacement of these political voices by the forces of oppression has created a renegade space within American culture that allows for the expression of gangster culture. Gangsters indeed function as somewhat revolutionary in comparison to the rest of society, as demonstrated by their open defiance of accepted societal norms and laws, existence in their own environment, and circulation of their own alternative capital. This allows them to remain part of the larger society but to fully exist in their own communities at the same time. This lifestyle has been a consistent media staple throughout the twentieth century, particularly in film.

From as early as D. W. Griffith's *Musketeers of Pig Alley* (1912) and the 5 celebrated studio films of the 1930s — e.g., *Little Caesar* (1930), *Public Enemy* (1931), and *Scarface* (1932) — through the epic treatment rendered in the first two *Godfather* films (1972, 1974), the gangster has enjoyed a vivid screen life. What is important here is that these criminals, as they are deemed by the dominant society, are defined as deviant primarily because of issues of ethnicity, as opposed to issues of race, though to some extent all definitions of ethnicity in this context are inevitably influenced by a subtle definition of race.

This emphasis on ethnicity as it functions in opposition to the standard "white Anglo-Saxon Protestant" is summarized in the first two *Godfather* films. As the United States, both at and immediately after the turn of the century, increasingly became a nation of European immigrants, incoming Italians were consigned to the bottom of the social ladder. In the opening segment of *Godfather II*, Michael Corleone is berated and verbally abused by Senator Geery of Nevada because of his Italian heritage. The word "Italian" is set in opposition to "American" constantly in this segment so as to highlight the ethnic hierarchy which remains a foundational issue in this film. Corleone's ascension to power is complicated by his inability to fully surmount this societal obstacle, at least at this point in the film, and by extension that point in American history — the early 1950s.

It is Francis Ford Coppola's argument that such oppression forced these Italian immigrants into a subversive lifestyle and economy much like that practiced throughout southern Italy, especially in Sicily. Borrowing from their own cultural tradition, some of these new Americans used the underground economy as a vital means of sustenance in the face of ethnic, religious, and cultural oppression. And though their desire, being heavily influenced by the discourse of an "American dream," was to ultimately be fully assimilated into American society, the achievement of this desire was revealed to be at the cost of losing their ethnic and cultural heritage. . . .

At a larger level, the film's historical themes indicate the assimilation of ethnicity into a homogeneous American society, yet foreground the continued rejection of race as a component of the metaphoric "melting pot" — because it is the challenge of race that accelerates the assimilative process of ethnicity.

In the first *Godfather* film, we see this same social dynamic at play regarding ethnicity over race. Near the film's conclusion, we witness the memorable meeting of the "heads of the five families," where the dilemmas of drug trafficking are being discussed by the various Mafia leaders. Vito Corleone is characterized as opposing this potentially lucrative venture for moral reasons, while many of the other members are excited about the possible financial benefits. The chieftain from Kansas City suggests that the Mafia should engage in selling drugs, but only at a distance, leaving the underside of this environment to be experienced by what he describes as the "dark people" because, as he adds, "they're animals anyway, let them lose their souls." His use of the phrase "dark people" and his labeling of them as "animals" clearly reference African Americans, and by extension racialized others in general. This line of dialogue is viewed by many African Americans as prophetic, seeing that the release of *The Godfather* in the early 1970s closely paralleled the upsurge in underworld drug activity throughout African American ghetto communities.

In relation to the assimilation of ethnicity at the expense of race, this line ₁₀ also signifies the way in which the previously mentioned structural hierarchy exists aside from the racial hierarchy, which many African Americans have been unable to transcend because of the difference in skin color. Though Italians through this perverted formulation could be considered inferior to "wasps," those traits that make them different can be easily subsumed when contrasted with the obvious difference of skin color and the history that goes along with being darker. It is in this context that the thematic progression of the *Godfather* films signals the end of the public fascination with the Italian gangster and his ethnically rich underworld.

Furthermore, this line indicates that the drug culture would be an important turning point in the historical discourse specific to the question of race as time moved forward. This line of reasoning has been pursued in numerous texts, most recently through Bill Duke's film *Deep Cover* (1992), which comments on the conspiracy involved in both furnishing and addicting segments of the Black community with drugs as a political maneuver by the government to keep these individuals sedated and oppressed so as to quell any potential political resistance. Mario Van Peebles's film *Panther* (1995) asserts the same theory in connection with the attempted destruction of the Black Panther Party by J. Edgar Hoover and the FBI. In both cases, crime can be seen as affirming capitalism, yet in specifically racial terms.

With this assimilation of ethnicity as signified through the Coppola films, America finds the need to fulfill this otherwise empty space with the next logical descending step on the social ladder, that being race.[1] Two other films from the 1980s effectively mark the shift away from the ethnic gangster to the racialized gangsta. Brian De Palma's remake of *Scarface* (1983) is an obvious rewriting of the genre from the perspective of race. Whereas the main character in the 1932 film was an Italian, in the De Palma version we deal with a racialized Cuban.

Drawing from real political events, De Palma's film begins with the Mariel boat lift of Cuban refugees into south Florida during the latter part of the 1970s, an event which many still consider a lingering legacy of Jimmy Carter's presidency. The film's main character, Tony Montana, is clearly foregrounded as a racialized other. His Cuban identity, broken accent, penchant for garishness, and overall ruthless approach to wealth and human life served as the basis for the popular media representation of Latin American drug dealers that came to dominate the 1980s.

With an increase in drug paranoia from the conservative Reagan and Bush administrations, this form of representation would nearly erase past images of Italian mob figures from the popular memory. While John Gotti was a celebrated folk hero for his stylish media-friendly disposition, individuals such as Carlos Lader Rivas, Pablo Escobar, and Manuel Noriega, who became common sights on the evening news and network news magazine programs, were depicted as threats to the very fabric of our society. To add to this popular

---

[1] The popular 1990 Martin Scorsese film *Goodfellas* is different from the gangster films which preceded it. At the conclusion of this film, the main character, Henry Hill, turns state's evidence on his former colleagues, thus violating one of the most stringent codes of the gangster lifestyle. And though some would argue that this film is a revisionist gangster film, it is sufficiently separated from other examples of the genre so as not to be confused. Scorsese's *Casino* (1995) continues this move to a contemporary gangster epic.

Another example of this revisionist trend would be Barry Levinson's fictional account of the life of Benjamin "Bugsy" Siegel, with its emphasis on Siegel's mistress, Virginia Hill, and the way in which her influence can be read as substantial, though detrimental, to Siegel in the financial decisions that he makes. *Bugsy* (1991) presents a sentimental underworld figure who has been "softened" by this female presence, which goes against the masculinist approach normally associated with the gangster. This rereading of the central character, with an emphasis on the female, adds to my notion of a revisionist trend in the genre, though in this case it is gender, not race, that is the point of transition.

form of representation, NBC's series *Miami Vice* drew many of its story lines and criminal figures from this newly accepted version of racialized representation.[2] . . .

The other major filmic event that reflected this obsession with the drug 15 culture and the question of race was Dennis Hopper's *Colors* (1988). Hopper's film offered an intricate look at the gang culture that existed in both South Central and East Los Angeles. Its main characters were two white Los Angeles police officers who were commissioned with the monumental task of eliminating the urban crime being perpetrated by African American and Latino youth. This film tied in neatly with the increasing commentary presented by national news programs about what had begun as a regional situation and was later argued to have spread throughout the country. Using the police, and by extension the rest of white society, as its victims, the film endorsed the racial paranoia concerning criminality that at this time was in full swing.

Colors, for all intents and purposes, made the gangbanger America's contemporary criminal of choice, turning a localized problem into a national epidemic that once again linked crime with specific notions of race. In many ways, *Colors* served the same function for gangsta culture that *Birth of a Nation* served for the early stages of African American cinema. Both films, through their overt racial paranoia, and in both cases using armed militia as an answer to the perceived Black threat — in one case the Ku Klux Klan, in the other a racist police department — inspired a series of African American cinematic responses. This regressive film engendered a public fascination with the newly defined "gangsta."

With the traditional white ethnic gangster film having all but disappeared, the way was clear for the entrance of a new popular villain to be screened across the mind of American society. The ideological link between crime and race would be made worse, and the image of the African American gangbanger would become not only popular in the sense of repeated representation, but financially lucrative as well. In addition to the changing history of the Hollywood gangster film, several other historical factors specific to African American culture would contribute to the emergence and eventual proliferation of the African American "gangsta."

From the Black Godfather to the Black Guerrilla Family

The late 1960s and early 1970s saw an increase in underworld activity, especially involving drugs, throughout many lower-class Black communities. In many ways more important than the drugs themselves was the culture that

---

[2]For a detailed discussion of the drug trade in Los Angeles, see Mike Davis, "The Political Economy of Crack," in *City of Quartz* (New York: Verso, 1990), and for a larger discussion of the role played by the media, the politics of Reagan/Bush, and the drug culture of the 1980s, see Jimmie Reeves and Richard Campbell, *Cracked Coverage* (Durham: Duke Univ. Press, 1994).

accompanied this underworld lifestyle and the way in which it was represented visually. The garish fashions popularized by Eleganza and Flag Brothers, heavily adorned, ornament-laden Cadillacs, and other materialistic excesses helped to define this cultural terrain as "cool" during this period. . . .

In several of the films that define this period, eventually known as the "Blaxploitation" era of Hollywood (1970–73), the Black protagonist was presented in opposition to a stereotypical white menace who was bent on destroying the African American community, primarily through the influx of drugs and the accompanying culture of violence. For the most part, evil in the films was personified in the form of a corrupt police or mafia figure, if not both at the same time. Thus much of the narrative action appeared in battles between some faction of the white mafia, who had traditionally been in control of the ghetto, albeit from a distance, and the emerging Black underworld figures who were striving to wrest control of this alternative economy from their white counterparts.

It was as if the loosening of societal restrictions gained during the civil [20] rights movement permitted exploitation of the community through control of underworld vices, though the actual control was in the hands of manipulative outsiders, who used the Black gangster as their foil. The Black gangster, whether he was a pimp, dope dealer, or hustler, through these films became a prominent example of what it meant to be an entrepreneur. The tension between outside influence and inside control is represented in many of the films of the period, most notably *Cotton Comes to Harlem, Across 110th Street, Superfly,* and *The Mack.* The African American gangster had become a media staple by the mid-1970s. . . .

Many of the films of this period were based on the dynamics of an African American underworld existence (e.g., *Sweetsweetback's Badass Song, The Mack, Willie Dynamite, Coffy, Cleopatra Jones*), and in conjunction with the popular ghetto literature of Iceberg Slim and Donald Goines, as well as the more esoteric works of author Chester Himes and playwright Charles Gordone, this form of representation remained viable long after this period had passed. In line with Nelson George's argument that "Blaxploitation movies are crucial to the current '70's retro-nuevo phase" (149), this historical period left a series of low-budget films which would eventually be perfect for transfer to the home video format. The "Blaxploitation" films would leave an indelible imprint on African American popular culture as the "gangsta" continued to rise in prominence and position.

A Small Introduction to the "G" Funk Era

With the historical antecedents of the Hollywood gangster film and 1970s Blaxploitation films, along with popular African American literature that explored the culture, the stage was set for the flowering of gangsta culture in the late 1980s and early 1990s. The contemporary manifestation continued to appear in the form of cinema, but also gained increasing visibility in the world of rap music, to the point of establishing its own genre and forming a solid cultural movement. This transition from genre to cultural movement included representations in film, music, and literature, and involved multiple layers of society: communal, political, and corporate. From the regular individuals whose personal narratives drew heavily from gangster culture, to rap artists whose real-life antics coincided with the fictional rhetoric of their lyrics, and finally to the highest levels of government, where questions of moral integrity, community debasement, and freedom of speech were constantly being posed, this cultural movement had a great deal of currency with respect to African Americans in society, especially the African American male. . . .

Though there are glimpses of the gangster lifestyle in a number of films that appeared throughout the late 1980s and especially in the early 1990s, the two films most relevant to an understanding of gangsta culture are John Singleton's *Boyz N the Hood* (1991) and Allen and Albert Hughes's *Menace II Society* (1993). Not to ignore such a popular film as Mario Van Peebles's *New Jack City* (1991) or Abel Ferrera's cult video classic *The King of New York* (1990), but these texts are more directly influenced by the traditional gangster paradigm, in addition to being set in New York City. The filmic representation of gangsta culture draws many of its influences from rap music, and in turn rap music assumes a great deal of identity with the work of Singleton and the Hughes brothers. Contemporary gangsta culture is undoubtedly a West Coast phenomenon.

The other film that holds a vital position in the representation of gangsta culture is Edward James Olmos's *American Me* (1992). This film addresses the culture from a Latino perspective as opposed to an African American one. This is of utmost importance, for while gangsta culture is publicly regarded as an African American entity, much of the culture derives from the close proximity in which African Americans and Latinos coexist in racialized Los Angeles. . . .

Hispanics Causin' Panic

American Me demonstrates that aspects of African American gangsta life and Mexican American gangsta culture are in dialogue with one another, though it can at times be a highly contested dialogue. There are two distinct instances in the film where a potential clash between the races is openly criticized as being counterproductive to someone's coming to consciousness and ultimate cultural empowerment. As the Mexican mafia (La Eme) smuggles drugs into the prison, we witness a Black inmate who steals the cocaine intended for another inmate. Upon revelation of the culprit, Santana, the leader of La Eme, instructs his soldiers to burn the man as an act of punishment. This triggers a cell-block confrontation that borders on a riot between La Eme and the Black Guerrilla Family (BGF). As the prison guards descend, the riot is aborted, but not without critical commentary. Santana informs the leader of the BGF that the situation was not racially motivated, but simply an action of retribution to forestall any future attempts at hindering their drug-trafficking efforts in prison. In other words, "business, never personal." This is a case in which the interest of underground capitalism supersedes any specific racial agenda.

Yet this scene is important as the setup for a similar situation that occurs later in the film. When La Eme attempts to sever its tie with the traditional Italian Mafia, the move is met with much resistance. Scagnelli, the mob boss, refuses to relinquish his end of the drug business in East L.A. As a result, several members of La Eme rape and murder Scagnelli's son while he is in prison. In response, Scagnelli sends uncut heroin into the barrio, causing several overdoses. This creates a chain reaction of retribution, which eventually culminates in Santana's death at the hands of his own men. At a certain point during this series of events, J.D., the only white member of La Eme, who slowly attempts to wrest control of the gang from Santana, orders a hit on the BGF by using the Aryan Brotherhood, the white gang represented in the film. Santana objects to this action and criticizes J.D. for "sending out the wrong message."

Santana's objection is based on his increasing awareness of racial and social consciousness, which has been facilitated by the politically empowered female character Julie. Julie, like the female character of Ronnie in *Menace*, helps Santana to realize the error of his misguided ways. On several occasions she criticizes his violent philosophy in ways that other characters cannot for fear of death. In a pivotal scene late in the film, Julie exposes Santana's position in all its limitations. After a series of extremely critical remarks about Santana's hypocritical use of crime as a way of arguing for *la raza,* he tells her, "If you were a man, I'd . . . " His incomplete sentence is cut short by Julie's own completion of it: "You'd kill me; no, you'd fuck me in the ass." Having witnessed several scenes in which men were raped because of Santana's power over them, in addition to his rape of Julie, we can feel the magnitude of her statement. She not only criticizes his politics, she has criticized his masculinity by alluding to the latent homosexuality of his supposed gestures of power.

Ultimately, she forces Santana to understand that the power struggles which often take place between those who are marginalized permit the continued oppression of their voices by those in power. Santana even says to J.D., "We spend all our time dealing with the miatas [their slang term for Blacks], and the Aryan Brotherhood, only to be dealing with ourselves." In other words, ideological distractions ultimately leave us in the same place, with no advancement in consciousness or power.

These ideas eventually separate Santana's newfound political consciousness from J.D.'s "business as usual" approach to crime and the underlying destruction of the community. It is not coincidental that J.D.'s whiteness, which is endorsed by Santana early in the film, looms as the final authority once he has ordered the killing of Santana and presumably taken control of the gang. At the beginning of the film, as expressed through the American military oppression of the Mexican American citizens, and at the conclusion, with J.D.'s murdering of Santana, thus destroying any possibility for an overall group consciousness, we can see that racism and white supremacy are the root causes of the chaos that permeates much of the present-day urban landscape. It is this fundamental understanding of race, racism, and complicity in one's own oppression that substantiates the importance of *American Me.* *American Me* engages history and politics to subtly yet convincingly argue that the real root of evil in American society as it relates to oppressed minorities is the bondage of systemic and institutionalized racism. This understanding also distinguishes it as a political statement from the rather limited bourgeois politics of *Boyz N the Hood* and the nihilistically apolitical *Menace II Society.* . . .

Boyz Will Be Boyz

> Either they don't know, won't show, or don't care what's going on in the hood.
>
> — DOUGHBOY, *Boyz N the Hood*

While *American Me* serves as an "objective third party" against which to evaluate *Boyz* and *Menace,* the similarities notwithstanding, to engage the culturally specific tenets of Black popular culture we must look at texts which are firmly situated in the domain of African American cinema in order to study the class politics of each film. In this regard, the political position of *Boyz N the Hood* can be defined as either a bourgeois Black nationalist or an Afrocentric model that focuses on the "disappearing" Black male, yet also fits easily into the perceived pathology of the culture in a modernized version of the legendary Moynihan report of the late 1960s. This report regarded the typically broken African American family as a cause of societal dysfunction at the highest level. 30

Singleton's film was integral to the politically charged period of resurgent Black nationalism in the late 1980s and early 1990s. This cultural resurgence of Black nationalism, most closely associated with the work of Public Enemy, KRS-One, and Sister Souljah, also set the tone for the discourse that informed *Do the Right Thing,* as well as many of the debates that emerged after the film's release.

From the outset it is obvious that Singleton's film is conversant with the Afrocentric discourse that permeates much of Black intellectual and cultural life. The film opens by establishing South Central Los Angeles as its geographical, cultural, and political center. Yet the landscape of Los Angeles is a historically specific one. The film begins in 1984, as we quickly spot several campaign posters that support the re-election of President Ronald Reagan — the obvious contradiction of this image being seen in a community such as South Central, which is the type of community most victimized by the racial and class politics of Reagan's first term. Another contradiction is signaled as a young Black male, while looking at an abandoned dead body lying in an alley, gives this political image "the finger." This young character is identified as being closely associated with gang culture. He declares that both of his brothers have been shot, and in turn they are heroic in his mind because they have yet to be killed. His marginal status allows him to recognize at some level that this supreme image of white male authority is in stark contrast to his own existence.

As we enter the classroom, we are presented with another contradiction. The camera pans the student drawings that cover the wall. These pictures contain images of people being shot, police brutality, and other acts that emphasize the daily violence that defines many of the lives in this poor Black community. These images are contradicted by the speech being delivered by the white teacher about the historical importance of the first European "settlers" or "pilgrims" on American soil. Her lecture is on the reasons this country celebrates the Thanksgiving holiday, yet by implication it also articulates the exploitation of America and Native Americans and the ensuing colonization, which was a helpful instrument in establishing the societal hierarchy that we inhabit today.

The ideology that is being discussed is being put into practice through the attitudes and policies of Ronald Reagan. Reagan clearly felt the need to return to some form of these earlier examples of oppression in the course of his

American Me, 1992.

presidential career, as his repeated attacks on affirmative action, his support of states' rights, and his overall embrace of positions consistent with right-wing conservatism about race clearly indicated. In a sense, the actions of those who are being celebrated by the teacher, the "pilgrims," have contributed to the conditions of the people depicted in the children's drawings. The film sets up a binary opposition between the conservative politics of America and African Americans' rejection of these oppressive policies. This scene is one of the few in the film in which racism and white supremacy are directly critiqued.

As the scene develops, Tre, the film's main character, confronts his elementary school teacher, asserting that humankind originated in Africa and not in Europe. Yet in his presentation, Tre is criticized not only by his teacher, but by other students as well. The same student who gave Reagan "the finger" completely dissociates himself from Tre's Afrocentric assertion, "We're all from Africa." In response, this child declares, "I ain't from Africa, I'm from Crenshaw Mafia," further linking himself to gang culture through his identification with the set known as "Crenshaw Mafia." The obvious irony of this scene is that gang affiliation is set in direct conflict with one's racial and cultural identity. It is as if being a gangsta supersedes race, as opposed to being a result of racial and class hierarchies in America.

In this same exchange, we can also hear echoes of Tre's father, Furious, and his lessons on life that recur throughout the film. This is once again set in opposition to the words of the aspiring gangsta's older brothers. This exchange leads to a fight between the two children, underscoring the incompatibility of progressive politics and existence in gangsta culture. Yet through the setting of gangsta culture in opposition to nationalist politics, it becomes clear that this bourgeois understanding ignores the fact that gangsters historically are easily transformed into revolutionaries because of their marginal status in society.

Remarks about the plight of the "Black man" dominate much of Furious's commentary in the film. As critic Michael Dyson has alluded, these comments fit well with the male-centered Afrocentric ideals of thinkers such as Jawanza Kanjufu, Haki Madhabuti, and Molefi Asante. *Boyz* uses gangsta culture as an alluring spectacle, which is underscored by the film's exaggeratedly violent trailer, but this spectacle is used to engage an Afrocentric critique that denounces the routine slaying of Black men, whether by other gang members or by the police. *Boyz* makes interesting use of many of the icons of gangsta culture while conducting its Black nationalist critique. The film straddles both areas, opening the door to the ensuing onslaught of gangsta imagery.

In this sense, *Boyz* is much like the imagery connected with one of its co-stars, Ice Cube. As a rapper, Ice Cube has consistently combined signs of gangsta culture with an ideological perspective that emphasizes a perverted Black nationalist agenda, borrowed primarily from the Nation of Islam. Similarly, *Boyz* combines gangsta icons with Afrocentrism, ultimately privileging the ideological critique over the iconography. This strain of political discourse was popular during the late 1980s and early 1990s, with *Boyz* providing a

35

cinematic counterpart to rap music. Singleton's film, though visualizing gangsta culture on a mass scale, is really more acceptable as a political text than as a thesis on the complex gangsta mentality. In many ways, *Boyz* represents the culmination of this politically resurgent period, as the theme of Black nationalism slowly disappeared from most popular forms shortly thereafter.

Though the film is overtly political, it reflects a bourgeois sense of politics. At the conclusion of the film we see a didactic scroll which tells us that Tre and Brandi, the one utopic Black male/female relationship presented in the film, have ventured off to Morehouse and Spelman College in Atlanta, respectively, to pursue their middle-class dreams far away from South Central L.A. Morehouse and Spelman have often been thought of as the Black equivalent of Harvard or Yale, the historical breeding ground for bourgeois Blackness. The fact that the two colleges are located in Atlanta, the current "mecca" of Black America, underscores the film's flimsy political position. *Boyz N the Hood* demonizes the landscape of Los Angeles while uncritically offering middle-class Atlanta as a metaphoric space where future generations of African Americans can exist free of the obstacles that are depicted in this film.

READING THE TEXT

1. What, according to Boyd, has been the cultural and political significance of the gangster underworld in American history and popular culture?

2. How did Hollywood in the late 1960s and early 1970s respond to the emergence of a drug culture in impoverished black communities, in Boyd's analysis?

3. Why does Boyd believe that *Boyz N the Hood* reflects both black nationalist and conventional bourgeois values?

4. How did *American Me* reflect the conflicts between Mexican American and African American gang subcultures?

5. What is the difference, according to Boyd, between race and ethnicity?

READING THE SIGNS

1. Write an essay supporting, complicating, or refuting the proposition that Hollywood's depiction of gangstas glorifies criminal behavior.

2. Rent a videotape of a film like *Scarface* or *The Godfather,* and write an analysis comparing its treatment of ethnic "others" with the treatment of black gang members in a movie like *Boyz N the Hood.*

3. Write an essay in which you explore the reasons gangsta films and culture are so popular among middle-class white teens. To develop your ideas, consult Nell Bernstein's "Goin' Gangsta, Choosin' Cholita" (p. 599).

4. In class, form teams and debate the proposition that Hollywood exploits the black community in making gang films.

5. Rent a videotape of a film focusing on African Americans that Boyd does not discuss — *Waiting to Exhale.* Then write a response to Boyd in which you address the importance of gender in film analysis.

JESSICA HAGEDORN

ASIAN WOMEN IN FILM: NO JOY, NO LUCK

Why do movies always seem to portray Asian women as tragic victims of history and fate? Jessica Hagedorn (b. 1949) asks in this essay, which originally appeared in Ms. *Even such movies as* The Joy Luck Club, *based on Amy Tan's breakthrough novel that elevated Asian American fiction to best-seller status, reinforce old stereotypes of the powerlessness of Asian and Asian American women. A screenwriter and novelist, Hagedorn calls for a different kind of storytelling that would show Asian women as powerful controllers of their own destinies. Hagedorn's publications include* Dogeaters *(1990) and* The Gangster of Love *(1996), both novels;* Danger and Beauty *(1993), a collection of poems;* Charlie Chan Is Dead: An Anthology of Contemporary Asian American Fiction *(1993); and* Fresh Kill *(1994), a screenplay.*

Pearl of the Orient. Whore. Geisha. Concubine. Whore. Hostess. Bar Girl. Mamasan. Whore. China Doll. Tokyo Rose. Whore. Butterfly. Whore. Miss Saigon. Whore. Dragon Lady. Lotus Blossom. Gook. Whore. Yellow Peril. Whore. Bangkok Bombshell. Whore. Hospitality Girl. Whore. Comfort Woman. Whore. Savage. Whore. Sultry. Whore. Faceless. Whore. Porcelain. Whore. Demure. Whore. Virgin. Whore. Mute. Whore. Model Minority. Whore. Victim. Whore. Woman Warrior. Whore. Mail-Order Bride. Whore. Mother. Wife. Lover. Daughter. Sister.

As I was growing up in the Philippines in the 1950s, my fertile imagination was colonized by thoroughly American fantasies. Yellowface variations on the exotic erotic loomed larger than life on the silver screen. I was mystified and enthralled by Hollywood's skewed representations of Asian women: sleek, evil goddesses with slanted eyes and cunning ways, or smiling, sarong-clad South Seas "maidens" with undulating hips, kinky black hair, and white skin darkened by makeup. Hardly any of the "Asian" characters were played by Asians. White actors like Sidney Toler and Warner Oland played "inscrutable Oriental detective" Charlie Chan with taped eyelids and a singsong, chop suey accent. Jennifer Jones was a Eurasian doctor swept up in a doomed "interracial romance" in *Love Is a Many Splendored Thing*. In my mother's youth, white actor Luise Rainer played the central role of the Patient Chinese Wife in the 1937 film adaptation of Pearl Buck's novel *The Good Earth*. Back then, not many thought to ask why; they were all too busy being grateful to see anyone in the movies remotely like themselves.

Cut to 1960: *The World of Suzie Wong,* another tragic East/West affair. I am now old enough to be impressed. Sexy, sassy Suzie (played by Nancy Kwan) works out of a bar patronized by white sailors, but doesn't seem bothered by any of it. For a hardworking girl turning nightly tricks to support her baby, she manages to parade an astonishing wardrobe in damn near every scene, down to matching handbags and shoes. The sailors are also strictly Hollywood, sanitized and not too menacing. Suzie and all the other prostitutes in this movie are cute, giggling, dancing sex machines with hearts of gold. William Holden plays an earnest, rather prim, Nice Guy painter seeking inspiration in The Other. Of course, Suzie falls madly in love with him. Typically, she tells him, "I not important," and "I'll be with you until you say — Suzie, go away." She also thinks being beaten by a man is a sign of true passion and is terribly disappointed when Mr. Nice Guy refuses to show his true feelings.

Next in Kwan's short-lived but memorable career was the kitschy 1961 musical *Flower Drum Song,* which, like *Suzie Wong,* is a thoroughly American commercial product. The female roles are typical of Hollywood musicals of the times: women are basically airheads, subservient to men. Kwan's counterpart is the Good Chinese Girl, played by Miyoshi Umeki, who was better playing the Loyal Japanese Girl in that other classic Hollywood tale of forbidden love, *Sayonara.* Remember? Umeki was so loyal, she committed double suicide with actor Red Buttons. I instinctively hated *Sayonara* when I first saw it as a child; now I understand why. Contrived tragic resolutions were the only way Hollywood got past the censors in those days. With one or two exceptions, somebody in these movies always had to die to pay for breaking racial and sexual taboos.

Until the recent onslaught of films by both Asian and Asian American 5 filmmakers, Asian Pacific women have generally been perceived by Hollywood with a mixture of fascination, fear, and contempt. Most Hollywood movies either trivialize or exoticize us as people of color and as women. Our intelligence is underestimated, our humanity overlooked, and our diverse cultures treated as interchangeable. If we are "good," we are childlike, submissive, silent, and eager for sex (see France Nuyen's glowing performance as Liat in the film version of *South Pacific*) or else we are tragic victim types (see *Casualties of War,* Brian De Palma's graphic 1989 drama set in Vietnam). And if we are not silent, suffering doormats, we are demonized dragon ladies — cunning, deceitful, sexual provocateurs. Give me the demonic any day — Anna May Wong as a villain slithering around in a slinky gown is at least gratifying to watch, neither servile nor passive. And she steals the show from Marlene Dietrich in Josef von Sternberg's *Shanghai Express.* From the 1920s through the 1930s, Wong was our only female "star." But even she was trapped in limited roles, in what filmmaker Renee Tajima has called the dragon lady/lotus blossom dichotomy.

Cut to 1985: There is a scene toward the end of the terribly dishonest but weirdly compelling Michael Cimino movie *Year of the Dragon* (cowritten by Oliver Stone) that is one of my favorite twisted movie moments of all time. If you ask a lot of my friends who've seen that movie (especially if they're

Michelle Yeoh, *Tomorrow Never Dies,* 1997.

Asian), it's one of their favorites too. The setting is a crowded Chinatown nightclub. There are two very young and very tough Jade Cobra gang girls in a shoot-out with Mickey Rourke, in the role of a demented Polish American cop who, in spite of being Mr. Ugly in the flesh — an arrogant, misogynistic bully devoid of any charm — wins the "good" Asian American anchorwoman in the film's absurd and implausible ending. This is a movie with an actual disclaimer as its lead-in, covering its ass in advance in response to anticipated complaints about "stereotypes."

My pleasure in the hard-edged power of the Chinatown gang girls in *Year of the Dragon* is my small revenge, the answer to all those Suzie Wong "I want to be your slave" female characters. The Jade Cobra girls are mere background to the white male foreground/focus of Cimino's movie. But long after the movie has faded into video-rental heaven, the Jade Cobra girls remain defiant, fabulous images in my memory, flaunting tight metallic dresses and spiky cock's-comb hairdos streaked electric red and blue.

Mickey Rourke looks down with world-weary pity at the unnamed Jade Cobra girl (Doreen Chan) he's just shot who lies sprawled and bleeding on the street: "You look like you're gonna die, beautiful."

JADE COBRA GIRL: "Oh yeah? [blood gushing from her mouth] I'm proud of it."

ROURKE: "You are? You got anything you wanna tell me before you go, sweetheart?"

JADE COBRA GIRL: "Yeah. [pause] Fuck you."

Cut to 1993: I've been told that like many New Yorkers, I watch movies with the right side of my brain on perpetual overdrive. I admit to being grouchy and overcritical, suspicious of sentiment, and cynical. When a critic like Richard Corliss of *Time* magazine gushes about *The Joy Luck Club* being "a fourfold *Terms of Endearment*," my gut instinct is to run the other way. I resent being told how to feel. I went to see the 1993 eight-handkerchief movie version of Amy Tan's best-seller with a group that included my ten-year-old daughter. I was caught between the sincere desire to be swept up by the turbulent mother-daughter sagas and my own stubborn resistance to being so obviously manipulated by the filmmakers. With every flashback came tragedy. The music soared; the voice-overs were solemn or wistful; tears, tears, and more tears flowed onscreen. Daughters were reverent; mothers carried dark secrets.

I was elated by the grandness and strength of the four mothers and the luminous actors who portrayed them, but I was uneasy with the passivity of the Asian American daughters. They seemed to exist solely as receptors for their mothers' amazing life stories. It's almost as if by assimilating so easily into American society, they had lost all sense of self.

In spite of my resistance, my eyes watered as the desperate mother 10 played by Kieu Chinh was forced to abandon her twin baby girls on a country road in war-torn China. (Kieu Chinh resembles my own mother and her twin sister, who suffered through the brutal Japanese occupation of the Philippines.) So far in this movie, an infant son had been deliberately drowned, a mother played by the gravely beautiful France Nuyen had gone catatonic with grief, a concubine had cut her flesh open to save her dying mother, an insecure daughter had been oppressed by her boorish Asian American husband, another insecure daughter had been left by her white husband, and so on. . . . The overall effect was numbing as far as I'm concerned, but a man sitting two rows in front of us broke down sobbing. A Chinese Filipino writer even more grouchy than me later complained, "Must ethnicity only be equated with suffering?"

Because change has been slow, *The Joy Luck Club* carries a lot of cultural baggage. It is a big-budget story about Chinese American women, directed by a Chinese American man, cowritten and coproduced by Chinese American women. That's a lot to be thankful for. And its box office success proves that an immigrant narrative told from female perspectives can have mass appeal. But my cynical side tells me that its success might mean only one thing in Hollywood: more weepy epics about Asian American mother-daughter relationships will be planned.

That the film finally got made was significant. By Hollywood standards (think white male; think money, money, money), a movie about Asian Americans even when adapted from a best-seller was a risky proposition. When I asked a producer I know about the film's rumored delays, he simply said, "It's still an *Asian* movie," surprised I had even asked. Equally interesting was director Wayne Wang's initial reluctance to be involved in the project; he told the *New York Times,* "I didn't want to do another Chinese movie."

Maybe he shouldn't have worried so much. After all, according to the media, the nineties are the decade of "Pacific Overtures" and East Asian chic. Madonna, the pop queen of shameless appropriation, cultivated Japanese high-tech style with her music video "Rain," while Janet Jackson faked kitschy orientalia in hers, titled "If." Critical attention was paid to movies from China, Japan, and Vietnam. But that didn't mean an honest appraisal of women's lives. Even on the art house circuit, filmmakers who should know better took the easy way out. Takehiro Nakajima's 1992 film *Okoge* presents one of the more original film roles for women in recent years. In Japanese, "okoge" means the crust of rice that sticks to the bottom of the rice pot; in pejorative slang, it means fag hag. The way "okoge" is used in the film seems a reappropriation of the term; the portrait Nakajima creates of Sayoko, the so-called fag hag, is clearly an affectionate one. Sayoko is a quirky, self-assured woman in contemporary Tokyo who does voice-overs for cartoons, has a thing for Frida Kahlo paintings, and is drawn to a gentle young gay man named Goh. But the other women's roles are disappointing, stereotypical "hysterical females" and the movie itself turns conventional halfway through. Sayoko sacrifices herself to a macho brute Goh desires, who rapes her as images of Frida Kahlo paintings and her beloved Goh rising from the ocean flash before her. She gives birth to a baby boy and endures a terrible life of poverty with the abusive rapist. This sudden change from spunky survivor to helpless, victimized woman is baffling. Whatever happened to her job? Or that arty little apartment of hers? Didn't her Frida Kahlo obsession teach her anything?

Then there was Tiana Thi Thanh Nga's *From Hollywood to Hanoi,* a self-serving but fascinating documentary. Born in Vietnam to a privileged family that included an uncle who was defense minister in the Thieu government and an idolized father who served as press minister, Nga (a.k.a. Tiana) spent her adolescence in California. A former actor in martial arts movies and fitness teacher ("Karaticize with Tiana"), the vivacious Tiana decided to make a record of her journey back to Vietnam.

From Hollywood to Hanoi is at times unintentionally very funny. Tiana in- 15 cludes a quick scene of herself dancing with a white man at the Metropole hotel in Hanoi, and breathlessly announces: "That's me doing the tango with Oliver Stone!" Then she listens sympathetically to a horrifying account of the My Lai massacre by one of its few female survivors. In another scene, Tiana cheerfully addresses a food vendor on the streets of Hanoi: "Your hairdo is so pretty." The unimpressed, poker-faced woman gives a brusque, deadpan reply: "You want to eat, or what?" Sometimes it is hard to tell the difference between Tiana Thi Thanh Nga and her Hollywood persona: the real Tiana still seems to be playing one of her B-movie roles, which are mainly fun because they're fantasy. The time was certainly right to explore postwar Vietnam from a Vietnamese woman's perspective; it's too bad this film was done by a Valley Girl.

Nineteen ninety-three also brought Tran Anh Hung's *The Scent of Green Papaya,* a different kind of Vietnamese memento — this is a look back at the peaceful, lush country of the director's childhood memories. The film opens in Saigon, in 1951. A willowy ten-year-old girl named Mui comes to work for a troubled family headed by a melancholy musician and his kind, stoic wife. The men of this bourgeois household are idle, pampered types who take naps while the women do all the work. Mui is male fantasy: she is a devoted servant, enduring acts of cruel mischief with patience and dignity; as an adult, she barely speaks. She scrubs floors, shines shoes, and cooks with loving care and never a complaint. When she is sent off to work for another wealthy musician, she ends up being impregnated by him. The movie ends as the camera closes in on Mui's contented face. Languid and precious, *The Scent of Green Papaya* is visually haunting, but it suffers from the director's colonial fantasy of women as docile, domestic creatures. Steeped in highbrow nostalgia, it's the arty Vietnamese version of *My Fair Lady* with the wealthy musician as Professor Higgins, teaching Mui to read and write.

And then there is Ang Lee's tepid 1993 hit, *The Wedding Banquet* — a clever culture-clash farce in which traditional Chinese values collide with contemporary American sexual mores. The somewhat formulaic plot goes like this: Wai-Tung, a yuppie landlord, lives with his white lover, Simon, in a chic Manhattan brownstone. Wai-Tung is an only child and his aging parents in Taiwan long for a grandchild to continue the family legacy. Enter Wei-Wei, an artist who lives in a grungy loft owned by Wai-Tung. She slugs tequila straight

Anna May Wong.

from the bottle as she paints and flirts boldly with her young, uptight land-lord, who brushes her off. "It's my fate. I am always attracted to handsome gay men," she mutters. After this setup, the movie goes downhill, all edges blurred in a cozy nest of happy endings. In a refrain of Sayoko's plight in *Okoge,* a pregnant, suddenly complacent Wei-Wei gives in to family pressures — and never gets her life back.

> "It takes a man to know what it is to be a real woman."
> — Song Liling in *M. Butterfly*

Ironically, two gender-bending films in which men play men playing women reveal more about the mythology of the prized Asian woman and the superficial trappings of gender than most movies that star real women. The slow-moving *M. Butterfly* presents the ultimate object of Western male desire as the spy/opera diva Song Liling, a Suzie Wong/Lotus Blossom played by actor John Lone with a five o'clock shadow and bobbing Adam's apple. The best and most profound of these forays into cross-dressing is the spectacular melodrama *Farewell My Concubine,* directed by Chen Kaige. Banned in China, *Farewell My Concubine* shared the prize for Best Film at the 1993 Cannes Film Festival with Jane Campion's *The Piano.* Sweeping through 50 years of tumultuous history in China, the story revolves around the lives of two male Beijing Opera stars and the woman who marries one of them. The three characters make an unforgettable triangle, struggling over love, art, friendship, and politics against the bloody backdrop of cultural upheaval. They are as capable of casually betraying each other as they are of selfless, heroic acts. The androgynous Dieyi, doomed to play the same female role of concubine over and over again, is portrayed with great vulnerability, wit, and grace by male Hong Kong pop star Leslie Cheung. Dieyi competes with the prostitute Juxian (Gong Li) for the love of his childhood protector and fellow opera star, Duan Xiaolou (Zhang Fengyi).

Cheung's highly stylized performance as the classic concubine-ready-to-die-for-love in the opera within the movie is all about female artifice. His sidelong glances, restrained passion, languid stance, small steps, and delicate, refined gestures say everything about what is considered desirable in Asian women — and are the antithesis of the feisty, outspoken woman played by Gong Li. The characters of Dieyi and Juxian both see suffering as part and parcel of love and life. Juxian matter-of-factly says to Duan Xiaolou before he agrees to marry her: "I'm used to hardship. If you take me in, I'll wait on you hand and foot. If you tire of me, I'll . . . kill myself. No big deal." It's an echo of Suzie Wong's servility, but the context is new. Even with her back to the wall, Juxian is not helpless or whiny. She attempts to manipulate a man while admitting to the harsh reality that is her life.

Dieyi and Juxian are the two sides of the truth of women's lives in most Asian countries. Juxian in particular — wife and ex-prostitute — could be seen as a thankless and stereotypical role. But like the characters Gong Li has played in Chinese director Zhang Yimou's films, *Red Sorghum, Raise the Red Lantern,* and especially *The Story of Qiu Ju,* Juxian is tough, obstinate, sensual, clever, oafish, beautiful, infuriating, cowardly, heroic, and banal. Above all, she is resilient. Gong Li is one of the few Asian Pacific actors whose roles have been drawn with intelligence, honesty, and depth. Nevertheless, the characters she plays are limited by the possibilities that exist for real women in China.

"Let's face it. Women still don't mean shit in China," my friend Meeling reminds me. What she says so bluntly about her culture rings painfully true, but in less obvious fashion for me. In the Philippines, infant girls aren't drowned, nor were their feet bound to make them more desirable. But sons were and are cherished. To this day, men of the bourgeois class are coddled and prized, much like the spoiled men of the elite household in *The Scent of*

Green Papaya. We do not have a geisha tradition like Japan, but physical beauty is overtreasured. Our daughters are protected virgins or primed as potential beauty queens. And many of us have bought into the image of the white man as our handsome savior: G.I. Joe.

Buzz magazine recently featured an article entitled "Asian Women/L.A. Men," a report on a popular hangout that caters to white men's fantasies of nubile Thai women. The lines between movies and real life are blurred. Male screenwriters and cinematographers flock to this bar-restaurant, where the waitresses are eager to "audition" for roles. Many of these men have been to Bangkok while working on film crews for Vietnam War movies. They've come back to L.A., but for them, the movie never ends. In this particular fantasy the boys play G.I. Joe on a rescue mission in the urban jungle, saving the whore from herself. "A scene has developed here, a kind of R-rated *Cheers*," author Alan Rifkin writes. "The waitresses audition for sitcoms. The customers date the waitresses or just keep score."

Colonization of the imagination is a two-way street. And being enshrined on a pedestal as someone's Pearl of the Orient fantasy doesn't seem so demeaning, at first; who wouldn't want to be worshipped? Perhaps that's why Asian women are the ultimate wet dream in most Hollywood movies; it's no secret how well we've been taught to play the role, to take care of our men. In Hollywood vehicles, we are objects of desire or derision; we exist to provide sex, color, and texture in what is essentially a white man's world. It is akin to what Toni Morrison calls "the Africanist presence" in literature. She writes: "Just as entertainers, through or by association with blackface, could render permissible topics that otherwise would have been taboo, so American writers were able to employ an imagined Africanist persona to articulate and imaginatively act out the forbidden in American culture." The same analogy could be made for the often titillating presence of Asian women in movies made by white men.

Movies are still the most seductive and powerful of artistic mediums, manipulating us with ease by a powerful combination of sound and image. In many ways, as females and Asians, as audiences or performers, we have learned to settle for less — to accept the fact that we are either decorative, invisible, or one-dimensional. When there are characters who look like us represented in a movie, we have also learned to view between the lines, or to add what is missing. For many of us, this way of watching has always been a necessity. We fill in the gaps. If a female character is presented as a mute, willowy beauty, we convince ourselves she is an ancestral ghost — so smart she doesn't have to speak at all. If she is a whore with a heart of gold, we claim her as a tough feminist icon. If she is a sexless, sanitized, boring nerd, we embrace her as role model for our daughters, rather than the tragic whore. And if she is presented as an utterly devoted saint suffering nobly in silence, we lie and say she is just like our mothers. Larger than life. Magical and insidious. A movie is never just a movie, after all.

READING THE TEXT

1. Summarize in your own words Hagedorn's view of the traditional images of Asian women as presented in American film.

2. What is the chronology of Asian women in film that Hagedorn presents, and why do you think she gives us a historical overview?

3. Why does Hagedorn say that the film *The Joy Luck Club* "carries a lot of cultural baggage" (para. 11)?

4. What sort of images of Asian women does Hagedorn imply that she would prefer to see?

READING THE SIGNS

1. Rent a videotape of *The Joy Luck Club* (or another film featuring Asian characters), and write an essay in which you support, refute, or modify Hagedorn's interpretation of the film.

2. In class, form teams and debate the proposition that Hollywood writers and directors have a social responsibility to avoid stereotyping ethnic characters. To develop your team's arguments, first brainstorm films that depict various ethnicities, and then discuss whether the portrayals are damaging or benign. You might also consult Michael Omi's "In Living Color: Race and American Culture" (p. 557).

3. Study a magazine that targets Asian American readers, such as *Transpacific* or *Yolk*. Then write an essay in which you discuss the extent to which Asian women fit the stereotypes that Hagedorn describes, keeping in mind the magazine's specific readership (businessmen, twenty-somethings of both sexes, and so forth).

4. In class, compare the stereotyped roles for Asian women that Hagedorn describes with the good and bad girl archetypes that Sandra Tsing Loh discusses in "The Return of Doris Day" (the next selection). What does your comparison suggest for the roles available for female characters of any race?

5. Watch one of the gender-bending films Hagedorn mentions (such as *M. Butterfly*), and write your own analysis of the gender roles portrayed in the film. To develop your ideas, consult Holly Devor's "Gender Role Behaviors and Attitudes" (p. 484).

SANDRA TSING LOH

The Return of Doris Day

Madonna is out and Doris Day is in, according to Sandra Tsing Loh's (b. 1962) pop cultural analysis, first published in Buzz *magazine. Bad girls may have ruled the Hollywood roost in the eighties, Loh observes, but the success of actresses like Sandra Bullock shows that good girls have made a comeback. A journalist with a B.S. in physics from Cal Tech, Loh is a commentator on National Public Radio who writes widely on popular cultural topics. Her publications include* Depth Takes a Holiday: Essays from Lesser Los Angeles *(1996),* Aliens in America *(1997),* If You Lived Here, You'd Be Home by Now *(1997), and* A Year in Van Nuys *(2001).*

The seventies and eighties were tough times for us Good Girls. As polite people, we like to do what's expected of us. Unfortunately, what was expected, in our sexual heyday, was for Girls to be . . . anything but Good.

In junior high, I dutifully grappled with whatever icky senior boy that Spin the Bottle sent me. By college, my sisters and I had graduated to smoking pot and swimming nude in the Sierras, sleeping with men on the first date (or before — you're welcome!), and developing evasive "mumble vaguely and give back rubs" routines if forced into a threesome.

We were lost, I tell you. Lost. But not anymore. Recently I was faced with a Nude Hot Tub Situation. It was a tame one by eighties standards. The tub was vast, the night was dark, and my companions were three platonic male friends — thirtysomethings like me stooped with worry, hardly a threat.

"C'mon!" I heard that inner coach urging me. It was the voice born in 1975, when everyone in my junior high had Chemin de Fer jeans and Candie's sandals. *Don't be a drag,* it said. *Take off your clothes and jump in!*

But then, for the first time, I heard another voice. Clear as a bell, it was 5 the soaring soprano of Mary Martin in *South Pacific,* or perhaps Shirley Jones in *Oklahoma!* It sang:

> I've got a guy!
> A really great guy!
> He makes me as high
> As an elephant's eye!

Or something to that effect. It was like a light bulb going on. Suddenly I felt right with my world — fresh, natural, confident, all the panty-shield adjectives. It was so simple, so clear. The wandering days of these breasts were over.

"If you'd known me in my twenties," I lecture my hot tub companions, as though sharing an amazing story from ancient lore, "you would have seen my boobs and seen them often!" I'm in the water now, but demurely covered in my white cotton T-shirt from Victoria's Secret. (A white cotton T-shirt is typical of what we women actually *buy* there.) "But no more." I lift a teacherly finger. "Today, I feel much more liberated keeping my shirt on. I don't have to prove anything anymore. I can turn the world on with a smile!" I hear myself excitedly half-singing, flashing on Mary Tyler Moore.

My treatise is cut short by the arrival of two 24-year-old modern dancers who rip off towels and flash their naked pink everything. The men's attention snaps away with the zing of taut bungee cords. But I don't feel bad. I know it's only I, Goody Two Shoes, who feels that wonderful glowing specialness inside.

I. Good Girls: A Cleaned and Buffed Thumbnail History

Were our moms actually right way back when? Maybe so. Because like it or not, these days Good Girls are back in. Demure behavior is suddenly clever, fashionable, even attractive.

Who *is* the nineties Good Girl? She is: (a) spunky; (b) virginal; (c) busy $_{10}$ with purposeful activity. But not obsessively so. Her hormones are in balance. Brave chin up, she works within society's rules, finds much to celebrate in her immediate surroundings, makes the best of her lot. Good Girls don't challenge the status quo.

Good Girls have been around a long time in Western culture. The star of the very first novel in English? A Good Girl! We find her in Samuel Richardson's 1740 opus, *Pamela*. In it, Pamela's resistance to sex charges five-hundred-plus pages of narrative tension; it's so effective a gambit that Good Girls (typically poor but beautiful governesses) become the very foundation of the eighteenth- and nineteenth-century novel.

It is in twentieth-century America, however, that we start to see the rowdy Good Girl. She does more than keep her knees crossed. In fact, if so moved, she may even spread her legs boldly akimbo! (If only to punctuate a funny singalong.)

The forties and fifties brought the U.S. Good Girl her two most sacred boons: World War II, and Rodgers & Hammerstein. The former yielded new busy-but-virginal archetypes like Rosie the Riveter, the Andrews Sisters, and the Chipper Navy Nurse. The latter fleshed out the canon via the Feisty Governess of the past (Anna in *The King and I*), the Chipper Navy Nurse of the semipresent (Nellie Forbush in *South Pacific*), even the boldly innovative Frisky Nun of the future (Julie Andrews in *The Sound of Music*). Indeed, Frisky Nun proved so popular she'd soon hop mediums and become TV's *The Flying Nun* (comical ex-Gidget Sally Field). Even *The Mary Tyler Moore Show* — a milestone in the modern Good Girl's progress — almost had Moore playing a version of Frisky Nun. Laugh no more at winged hats: in the past, Frisky Nun was a female star's emancipated alternative!

Doris Day.

　　The quintessential Good Girl of midcentury America — indeed the mother of all modern Good Girls — was Doris Day. We mean, of course, Nubile Doris Day, in her guise as pert, urban, apartment-dwelling career girl (*Pillow Talk*), as opposed to harangued suburban housewife (*Please Don't Eat the Daisies*). Never mind that Doris typically chucked her career at the end of the film for Rock Hudson; what mattered was that while Doris *was* a Good Girl, she was hardly a nun — in fact, she was quite sexy in her spunky purposefulness.

　　It was too bad that Doris stayed mainly in the movies, for the most per- 15
fect form for the American Good Girl remains the musical. Here emerges a unique symbiosis: on the one hand, the musical needs the Good Girl's

soprano, her can-do optimism, the soaring love songs only she can inspire. On the other, not to put too fine a point on it, the Good Girl needs the musical. The musical could *create* Good Girls where there once were none. Example: where, outside the musical, do you find that rarest of beings — the ethnic Good Girl? Sure, ethnic girls can have hearts o' gold, but in the real world they — can we say it? — tend to be a bit sassy. Happily, the musical has the miraculous power to freshen, sanitize, uplift even ethnicities who might feel too irked with society to be Good. We see Jewish Good Girls: Tevye's daughters in *Fiddler on the Roof*. (Imagine "Matchmaker, Matchmaker" done in dialogue on a hot afternoon in Queens — another tale entirely.) It also gave us *Yentl*. Hm. *West Side Story* produces Latina Good Girl Maria (Natalie Wood, but we quibble). *Flower Drum Song* yields that mousy Asian Good Girl whose name no one can remember (not Nancy Kwan, the other one). *The Wiz* even gives us a black Good Girl: Diana Ross (who was never that Good again).

As we move into the late seventies, however, even white Good Girls are hard to come by. There's a general Fall of the Musical (we could discuss Andrew Lloyd Webber, but why?) — and Fall of Filmic Good Girls. We lose our bright, dependable, pony-tailed stars — our June Allysons, Shirley Joneses, Julie Andrewses. We collapse into the nude/seminude group therapy "line" musicals: *Oh! Calcutta!, Pippin,* the exhaustingly confessional *A Chorus Line*. By 1977, we have, God forbid, Liza Minnelli trying to play an ex-WAC in *New York New York*. Liza Minnelli? The eyelashes alone would have scared Our Boys.

And you know why we saw this fall, this demise, this dismal sinking? Because national hope is failing. No one whistles a happy tune. We're moving into bad times for optimism. Bad times for patriotism. Bad times for Good Girls. Forrest Gump drifts out of touch with Jenny . . . and America itself becomes very *dark*.

II. The Enduring Power of Good Girls

If Good Girls are back in the nineties, what does this imply? That we've come full circle? Forgiven Mom and Dad? We're in love with a wonderful guy? More deeply, does the Good Girl's resurgence signal an uplift in national character, a kind of neo-fifties patriotism, a return to what we might call, without irony, American values?

We have no idea — Good Girls are notoriously poor at political analysis. All we know is, we look around and Good Girls seem to be all over the place, winning again.

Look how they flourish, in the very bosom of our society! Good Girls are [20] our great: morning-show hosts (Katie Couric now, Jane Pauley before); figure skaters (Nancy Kerrigan vanquishing Tonya Harding now, Dorothy Hamill vanquishing all those foreigners before); country singers (Reba, Tammy & Co. now; Dolly Parton before); middle-of-the-road pop stars (Whitney Houston,

Paula Abdul now; Linda Ronstadt before); goyische straight gals to nervous Jewish comics (Sally to Harry, Helen Hunt to Paul Reiser now; Diane Keaton to Woody Allen before); Peter Pans (Sandy Duncan now-ish, Mary Martin way before); androgynous gals (Ellen DeGeneres now, Nancy Drew's pal boyish George before); astronauts (Sally Ride); Australians (Olivia Newton-John); MTV newspersons (Tabitha Soren); princesses (Di).

Can a video vixen be Good? Absolutely. Look at ex-Aerosmith girl and rising star Alicia Silverstone. You thought she was Drew Barrymore, but she's not. In Amy Heckerling's surprise summer hit *Clueless* (loosely based on Jane Austen's *Emma*!), Silverstone played Cher, a fashion-obsessed virgin ("You see how picky I am about my shoes, and *they* only go on my feet!"). Alicia the person is very spunky, clean, convincingly virginal, attends Shakespeare camp, takes tap-dancing lessons, and loves animals!

Good Girl accessories are in. Look what Hillary Clinton did for the headband — an astounding semiotic statement. Look how she reinvented cookie baking. Too-thin Nancy Reagan in her let-them-eat-cake Adolfo suit is over. Today, posing as a Good Girl — as clever Hillary does — seems powerfully subversive.

Look how even yesterday's swampy girls are cleaning up. Jane Seymour bounced back from whatever seamy B-stuff she was doing to triumph today as Dr. Quinn, Medicine Woman. Consider post-Donald Ivana, her pertness and brave industry recalling the Czech girl skier of yore. Even Sharon Stone seems downright nice. She makes an effort to dress "up" for press briefings and is so polite, modest, funny! (She showed us her home in *In Style* — the essence of nice! Is a *Redbook* cover in her future?)

And why not? Being a Good Girl pays off. Look how well Meg Ryan/Sandra Bullock films are doing. These girls don't titillate by getting naked. Why? They can turn the world on with a smile!

Even the musical is coming back! Via Disney, we have Belle and the Little 25 Mermaid, even Princess Jasmine and Pocahontas. Look how ethnic! Maybe there *is* a place called Hope.

III. The Nastiest Truth of All

But what is the bottom-line appeal of the Good Girl? Why do we urban nineties women want to *be* her? It's not as uncalculated as one might think. The Good Girl's draw is that she is the opposite of Bad. And Bad is something we no longer want to be.

You remember Bad Girl — she who reigned in the go-go eighties. Bad Girl is very Bad. Ow. She needs a spanking, she wants it, but beware of giving it to her because ironically it is you (or, more likely, Michael Douglas) who will suffer afterward.

Good Girl's opposite, Bad Girl, has out-of-control hormones. Bad Girl comes from a wildly dysfunctional family; her past makes her do strange, erratic things. Bad Girl tells us something is terribly wrong with society. Bad Girl challenges the status quo. Bad Girl uses sex for everything but love and babies: it's power, self-expression, psychosis, hate, revolt, revenge.

What we have in Bad Girl is Power Slut. Like Madonna in, well, ninety percent of her oeuvre. Joan Collins in *Dynasty*. Glenn Close in *Fatal Attraction*. Sharon Stone in *Basic Instinct*. Demi Moore in *Disclosure*. (Sure those last few are technically nineties, but anything written by Joe Eszterhas is really quite eighties, no?)

Good feminists we, we have saluted Bad Girl/Power Slut's right to exist, to 30 demolish, to flourish in her own dark way. But the nagging question remains: Is this a good behavior model for us? Is Bad Girl's life healthy, happy, productive? Does she get enough love? Even more creepily we ask: Is she aging well?

Because the fact is, even we — once-nubile twentysomething gals who gamboled defiantly topless in the mountain streams of yore — feel ourselves gently softening with age each day. The drama in the bathroom no longer centers around the scale. Forget that — we've gained and lost the same fifteen pounds so often that the cycle has become like an old pal, natural as our monthly period. But our skin! Each new wrinkle tells us there's no going back. No wonder our obsessions have become all Oil of Olay, Clinique moisturizer, antiwrinkle cream!

And while we hate to be unsupportive of our Badder sisters, we can't help noticing that, well, Bad Girlhood seems so bad *for* you. Look at Heidi Fleiss — drawn and witchy and actually too thin at 29. Partying, prostitution, cocaine, and, heck, the eighties don't wear well on a gal. And look at spooky seventy-something *Cosmo* girl Helen Gurley Brown, a.k.a. "the Crypt Keeper in capri pants," as she is known to AM-radio wag Peter Tilden.

Even the indestructible Madonna is looking a bit exhausted. Sure she's a zillionaire and superpowerful and has been on top forever. Her *Sex* book broke every boundary, sold tons. But it must be tough, we secretly think, for Madonna to greet her 5,012th weekend with only those girly dancing boys with the weird hair for company. Sean is off having babies with Robin Wright (a Good Girl, if oddly skinny). Geez: Madonna's going to be 40 soon. If she keeps hanging onto Bad Girl, soon she'll be Old Crone girl. Can we women age with dignity? By what strategy will we engineer fabulous forties, fifties, sixties, and beyond? (My God — a healthy woman of 65 today can expect to live to 83! Almost half our life will be spent being 50 or older!)

As we drift past our midthirties, we begin to question the idea of relentlessly pushing the boundaries of society, psychology, and biology. Will we end up like tart-talking Roseanne? We used to love her. We still do, but it's 1995 now and we are confused. She had a hit show, but still she felt the need for plastic surgery, butt tattoos, Tom Arnold tattoos, a Tom Arnold divorce, she hates her family, belched the anthem, lit her farts (or could if she'd wanted), married her bodyguard and has had a new baby, like, surgically implanted . . . where? Is this feminism? Help!

We will not go like that. (Anyway, we can't afford to.) We women are sur- 35 vivors, and we are battening down our hatches . . . for the future.

IV. The Good Girl Manifesto

Herewith, then, a declaration of our principles:

1. We're no longer promiscuous. Diseases suck. And so do noncommittal men our age (often spoiled for commitment by all that free sex we gave them in the sixties, seventies, and eighties). There's really no point. We can do it ourselves.

2. We're tailing down on booze and drugs. Eight glasses of water a day — better for the skin.

3. We're trying not to be anorexic. That seems very eighties. Then again, we don't want to be fat. As a result, we're just a wee bit bulimic. Sorry! We know this is not good.

4. We're *trying* to envision a future without plastic surgery. We try to keep happy, confident, glowing, nonlifted, fortysomething earth mothers Meryl/Cybill/Susan foremost in our minds. (See Nivea wrinkle cream ad: a blond mom in white feels good about her face, baby splashing in the background.)

5. We're trying to love our parents again. Their mortality weighs heavily upon us. When a parent dies, we peruse the photo album, weep while contemplating their jauntily hopeful forties hats, the huge families they came from. We feel suddenly lonely.

6. Were the forties and fifties really so bad? Gee, we feel nostalgic. We yearn for old love songs and old movies. At least our filmic Good Girl heroines do. (See Meg Ryan in *Sleepless in Seattle,* Marisa Tomei in *Only You.*) Although I must tell you: if I hear Harry Connick Jr. singing "It Had to Be You" again on the soundtrack of one more light romantic comedy, I will kill someone.

7. We're drawn to stuff that seems traditional, even if it isn't. Laura Ashley sheets. Coach bags. *Martha Stewart Living.*

8. We're back to white cotton underpants. (And as Victoria's Secret tells us, cotton is sexy again!)

9. We love our pets — our very own Disney familiars. (If we are starring in a movie, we can be expected to talk to our cat or dog in a very cute way. Starlets who need their tawdry images to be cleaned up can be expected to join PETA.)

10. We believe in true love, but we don't expect to find it in Rock Hudson. That's a dream of the past. Urban Lotharios *never* settle down — we've learned that, unlike Doris, we can't domesticate them through interior design.

That's why we're looking for love in all new places. Maybe we find it via a much younger man (a third of today's women already do). Maybe we find it by falling in love again with the family (like Sandra Bullock does in *While You Were Sleeping*). Maybe we find it in our children, postdivorce.

Consider that the template for the female sitcom today is not single newsgal Mary Tyler Moore, but single mom Murphy Brown, divorced mom Brett Butler, divorced mom Cybill. Exhusbands are reduced to comic characters sticking their heads in the door, like Howard the neighbor on the old *Bob Newhart Show*. In these days, when conception's becoming increasingly immaculate, maybe we have a baby without a guy.

Or maybe, hell, we find love for a few beautiful days with a fiftysomething shaman/photographer called Robert Kincaid with a washboard stomach. Maybe we never see him again after that. But today's Good Girl is tough and prudent — a little bit of love and she says, uncomplainingly, "I'm fine. I'm full. I have plenty."

Then goes outside and, into the air, high above her head, throws not her   50
bra . . . but her hat.

READING THE TEXT

1. Why, do you think, does Loh begin her essay with a racy hot tub anecdote?

2. Summarize in your own words what Loh means by "Good Girls" (para. 1).

3. Why do good girls have such an enduring appeal in American culture, according to Loh?

4. What are bad girls, in Loh's view, and why are they a necessary complement to good girls?

5. Why, according to Loh, were the 1980s a decade in which bad girls thrived?

6. What is Loh's tone in this essay, and do you find that her approach to her topic makes the essay more or less persuasive?

READING THE SIGNS

1. If you are female, explore in your journal whether in your childhood you were raised to be a "good girl" and whether that upbringing influences you today. If you are male, explore in your journal whether you believe good girls have a male equivalent: Were you raised to be a "good boy"? If so, what traits were you expected to follow? If not, explore whether you believe our culture values good boys.

2. In class, brainstorm a list of current female film stars and their chief roles, and then discuss whether they are good or bad girls (or neither). Drawing on the class discussion, write an essay in which you challenge, support, or qualify Loh's contention that the 1990s saw a return of good girls to Hollywood.

3. Good girls aren't political enough to explain their return to favor in the 1990s, Loh claims. Write your own interpretation of why the good girl supplanted the bad girl of the 1980s, being sure to base your discussion on specific examples from film.

4. Keeping Loh's discussion of good girls in mind, watch an episode of *ER* or *Dharma and Greg* (or any other "progressive" show), and write an essay that discusses the extent to which the female characters in the show fulfill the good girl archetype. To develop your ideas, read or reread Susan Douglas's "Signs of Intelligent Life on TV" (p. 250).

5. Rent a videotape of one of the Doris Day films that Loh mentions, and write a semiotic analysis of the gender roles portrayed in the film.

6. Study a popular women's fashion magazine such as *Glamour* or *Vogue,* and write an analysis of the way women are portrayed in the advertising. To what extent do advertisers rely on the good-girl archetype that Loh describes? How can you account for your findings?

MICHAEL PARENTI
CLASS AND VIRTUE

In 1993, a movie called Indecent Proposal *presented a story in which a billionaire offers a newly poor middle-class woman a million dollars if she'll sleep with him for one night. In Michael Parenti's (b. 1933) terms, what was really indecent about the movie was the way it showed the woman falling in love with the billionaire, thus making a romance out of a class outrage. But the movie could get away with it, partly because Hollywood has always conditioned audiences to root for the ruling classes and to ignore the inequities of class privilege. In this selection from* Make-Believe Media: The Politics of Entertainment *(1992), Parenti argues that Hollywood has long been in the business of representing the interests of the ruling classes. Whether it is forgiving the classist behavior in* Pretty Woman *or glamorizing the lives of the wealthy, Hollywood makes sure its audiences leave the theater thinking you can't be too rich. Parenti is a writer who lectures widely at university campuses around the country. His publications include* Power and the Powerless *(1978),* Inventing Reality: The Politics of the News Media *(1986),* Democracy for the Few *(1988),* Against Empire *(1995),* Dirty Truths *(1996),* America Besieged *(1998), and* History as Mystery *(1999).*

Class and Virtue

The entertainment media present working people not only as unlettered and uncouth but also as less desirable and less moral than other people. Conversely, virtue is more likely to be ascribed to those characters whose speech and appearance are soundly middle- or upper-middle class.

Even a simple adventure story like *Treasure Island* (1934, 1950, 1972) manifests this implicit class perspective. There are two groups of acquisitive persons searching for a lost treasure. One, headed by a squire, has money enough to hire a ship and crew. The other, led by the rascal Long John Silver, has no money — so they sign up as part of the crew. The narrative implicitly assumes from the beginning that the squire has a moral claim to the treasure, while Long John Silver's gang does not. After all, it is the squire who puts up the venture capital for the ship. Having no investment in the undertaking other than their labor, Long John and his men, by definition, will be "stealing" the treasure, while the squire will be "discovering" it.

To be sure, there are other differences. Long John's men are cutthroats. The squire is not. Yet, one wonders if the difference between a bad pirate and a good squire is itself not preeminently a matter of having the right amount of disposable income. The squire is no less acquisitive than the conspirators. He just does with money what they must achieve with cutlasses. The squire and his associates dress in fine clothes, speak an educated diction, and drink brandy. Long John and his men dress slovenly, speak in guttural accents, and drink rum. From these indications alone, the viewer knows who are the good guys and who are the bad. Virtue is visually measured by one's approximation to proper class appearances.

Sometimes class contrasts are juxtaposed within one person, as in *The Three Faces of Eve* (1957), a movie about a woman who suffers from multiple personalities. When we first meet Eve (Joanne Woodward), she is a disturbed, strongly repressed, puritanically religious person, who speaks with a rural, poor-Southern accent. Her second personality is that of a wild, flirtatious woman who also speaks with a rural, poor-Southern accent. After much treatment by her psychiatrist, she is cured of these schizoid personalities and emerges with a healthy third one, the real Eve, a poised, self-possessed, pleasant woman. What is intriguing is that she now speaks with a cultivated, affluent, Smith College accent, free of any low-income regionalism or ruralism, much like Joanne Woodward herself. This transformation in class style and speech is used to indicate mental health without any awareness of the class bias thusly expressed.

Mental health is also the question in *A Woman under the Influence* (1974), [5] the story of a disturbed woman who is married to a hard-hat husband. He cannot handle — and inadvertently contributes to — her emotional deterioration. She is victimized by a spouse who is nothing more than an insensitive, working-class bull in a china shop. One comes away convinced that every unstable woman needs a kinder, gentler, and above all, more *middle-class* hubby if she wishes to avoid a mental crack-up.

Class prototypes abound in the 1980s television series *The A-Team*. In each episode, a Vietnam-era commando unit helps an underdog, be it a Latino immigrant or a disabled veteran, by vanquishing some menacing force such as organized crime, a business competitor, or corrupt government officials. As always with the make-believe media, the A-Team does good work on an individualized rather than collectively organized basis, helping particular victims by thwarting particular villains. The A-Team's leaders are two white males of privileged background. The lowest ranking members of the team, who do none of the thinking nor the leading, are working-class palookas.

They show they are good with their hands, both by punching out the bad guys and by doing the maintenance work on the team's flying vehicles and cars. One of them, "B.A." (bad ass), played by the African American Mr. T., is visceral, tough, and purposely bad-mannered toward those he doesn't like. He projects an image of crudeness and ignorance and is associated with the physical side of things. In sum, the team has a brain (the intelligent white leaders) and a body with its simpler physical functions (the working-class characters), a hierarchy that corresponds to the social structure itself.[1]

Sometimes class bigotry is interwoven with gender bigotry, as in *Pretty Woman* (1990). A dreamboat millionaire corporate raider finds himself all alone for an extended stay in Hollywood (his girlfriend is unwilling to join him), so he quickly recruits a beautiful prostitute as his playmate of the month. She is paid three thousand dollars a week to wait around his superposh hotel penthouse ready to perform the usual services and accompany him to business dinners at top restaurants. As prostitution goes, it is a dream gig. But there is one cloud on the horizon. She is low-class. She doesn't know which fork to use at those CEO power feasts, and she's bothersomely fidgety, wears tacky clothes, chews gum, and, y'know, doesn't talk so good. But with some tips from the hotel manager, she proves to be a veritable Eliza Doolittle in her class metamorphosis. She dresses in proper attire, sticks the gum away forever, and starts picking the right utensils at dinner. She also figures out how to speak a little more like Joanne Woodward without the benefit of a multiple personality syndrome, and she develops the capacity to sit in a poised, wordless, empty-headed fashion, every inch the expensive female ornament.

She is still a prostitute but a classy one. It is enough of a distinction for the handsome young corporate raider. Having liked her because she was charmingly cheap, he now loves her all the more because she has real polish and is a more suitable companion. So suitable that he decides to do the right thing by her: set her up in an apartment so he can make regular visits at regular prices. But now she wants the better things in life, like marriage, a nice house, and, above all, a different occupation, one that would allow her to use less of herself. She is furious at him for treating her like, well, a prostitute. She decides to give up her profession and get a high-school diploma so that she might make a better life for herself — perhaps as a filing clerk or receptionist or some other of the entry-level jobs awaiting young women with high school diplomas.[2]

After the usual girl-breaks-off-with-boy scenes, the millionaire prince returns. It seems he can't concentrate on making money without her. He even abandons his cutthroat schemes and enters into a less lucrative but supposedly more productive, caring business venture with a struggling old-time entrepreneur. The bad capitalist is transformed into a good capitalist. He then

---

[1]Gina Marchetti, "Class, Ideology and Commercial Television: An Analysis of *The A-Team*," *Journal of Film and Video* 39, Spring 1987, pp. 19–28.

[2]See the excellent review by Lydia Sargent, *Z Magazine,* April 1990, pp. 43–45.

carries off his ex-prostitute for a lifetime of bliss. The moral is a familiar one, updated for post-Reagan yuppiedom: A woman can escape from economic and gender exploitation by winning the love and career advantages offered by a rich male. Sexual allure goes only so far unless it develops a material base and becomes a class act.[3]

READING THE TEXT

1. What characteristics are attributed to working-class and upper-class film characters, according to Parenti?

2. How does Parenti see the relationship between "class bigotry" and "gender bigotry" (para. 7) in *Pretty Woman*?

3. What relationship does Parenti see between mental health and class values in films?

READING THE SIGNS

1. Rent a videotape of *Wall Street,* and analyze the class issues that the movie raises.

2. Using Parenti's argument as a critical framework, interpret the class values implicit in a television show such as *Beverly Hills 90210*. Is the show that you've selected guilty of what Parenti calls "class bigotry" (para. 7)?

3. Do you agree with Parenti's interpretation of *Pretty Woman*? Write an argumentative essay in which you defend, challenge, or complicate his claims.

4. Read or review Holly Devor's "Gender Role Behaviors and Attitudes" (p. 484). How would Devor explain the gender bigotry that Parenti finds in *Pretty Woman*?

5. Rent the 1954 film *On the Waterfront,* and watch it with your class. How are labor unions and working-class characters portrayed in that film? Does the film display the class bigotry that Parenti describes?

6. Read or review Michael Omi's "In Living Color: Race and American Culture" (p. 557). Then write a journal entry in which you create a category of cinematic racial bigotry that corresponds to Parenti's two categories of class and gender bigotry. What films that you have seen illustrate your new category?

[3]Ibid.

VIVIAN C. SOBCHACK

The Postmorbid Condition

When Bonnie and Clyde *shuddered to a spectacular conclusion with the slow-motion machine-gunning of its main characters, the point was that in a society plagued by random and senseless violence Hollywood had a responsibility to make some kind of meaning out of it. But when Quentin Tarantino uses senseless violence for comic effect, the point, Vivian C. Sobchack (b. 1940) argues, is that there is no point at all, or rather, that the human body has lost its meaning in contemporary life and has become little more than a machine whose destruction is on a par with an exploding automobile. Offering a profound and disturbing explanation for the popularity of movies like* Pulp Fiction *and* Natural Born Killers, *Sobchack reveals the forces behind the dehumanization of Hollywood violence. A professor and associate dean in the School of Theater, Film, and Television at UCLA, Sobchack is the author of* Screening Space: The American Science Fiction Film *(1987),* Address of the Eye: A Phenomenology of Film Experience *(1991),* The Persistence of History: Cinema, Television, and the Modern Event *(1995), and* Meta-Morphing: Visual Transformation and the Culture of Quick-Change *(1999).*

In an essay I wrote twenty-five years ago, I argued that screen violence in American films of the late 1960s and early 1970s was new and formally different from earlier "classical" Hollywood representations of violence. This new interest in violence and its new formal treatment not only literally satisfied an intensified cultural desire for "close-up" knowledge about the material fragility of bodies, but also — and more important — made increasingly senseless violence in the "civil" sphere sensible and meaningful by stylizing and aestheticizing it, thus bringing intelligibility and order to both the individual and social body's increasingly random and chaotic destruction. Indeed, I argued that random and senseless violence was elevated to meaning in these then "new" movies, its "transcendence" achieved not only by being up there on the screen, but also through long lingering gazes at carnage and ballets of slow motion that conferred on violence a benediction and the grace of a cinematic "caress."

Today, most American films have more interest in the presence of violence than in its meaning. There are very few attempts to confer order or perform a benediction upon the random and senseless death, the body riddled with bullets, the laying waste of human flesh. (The application of such order, benediction, and transcendental purpose is, perhaps, one of the explicit achievements of Steven Spielberg's high-tech but emotionally anachronistic *Saving Private Ryan,* and it is no accident that its context is a morally intelligible World War II.)

Indeed, in today's films (and whatever happened started happening sometime in the 1980s), there is no transcendence of "senseless" violence: It just *is*. Thus, the camera no longer caresses it or transforms it into something with more significance than its given instance. Instead of caressing violence, the cinema has become increasingly *careless* about it: either merely nonchalant or deeply lacking in care. Unlike medical melodramas, those films that describe violent bodily destruction evoke no tears in the face of mortality and evidence no concern for the fragility of flesh. Samuel L. Jackson's violent role and religious monologues in Quentin Tarantino's *Pulp Fiction* notwithstanding, we see no grace or benediction attached to violence. Indeed, its very intensity seems diminished: we need noise and constant stimulation and quantity to make up for a lack of significant meaning.

Perhaps this change in attitude and treatment of violence is a function of our increasingly *technologized* view of the body and flesh. We see this view dramatized outside the theater in the practices and fantasies of "maintenance" and "repair" represented by the "fitness center" and cosmetic surgery. Inside the theater, we see it dramatized in the "special effects" allowed by new technological developments and in an increasingly hyperbolic and quantified treatment of violence and bodily damage that is as much about "more" as it is about violence. It seems to me that this quantitative move to "more" in relation to violence — more blood, more gore, more characters (they're really not people) blown up or blown away — began with the contemporary horror film, with "slasher" and "splatter" films that hyperbolized violence and its victims in terms of quantity rather than through exaggerations of form. Furthermore, unlike in the "New Hollywood" films of the late 1960s and 1970s (here one thinks of Peckinpah or Penn), excessive violence in these "low" genre films, while eliciting screams also elicited laughter, too much becoming, indeed, "too much": incredible, a "gross-out," so "outrageous" and "over the top" that ironic reflexivity set in (for both films and audiences) and the mounting gore and dead bodies became expected — and funny. (Here *Scream* and its sequel are recent examples.)

This heightened sense of reflexivity and irony that emerges from quantities of violence, from "more," is not necessarily progressive nor does it lead to a "moral" agenda or a critique of violence. (By virtue of its excesses and its emphasis on quantity and despite his intention, Oliver Stone's *Natural Born Killers* is quite ambiguous in this regard.) Indeed, in its present moment, this heightened reflexivity and irony merely leads to a heightened sense of representation: that is, care for the film as experience and text, perhaps, but a lack of any real concern for the bodies blown away (or up) upon the screen. In recent "splatter" films, in Tarantino films like *Reservoir Dogs* and *Pulp Fiction,* and in quite a number of action thrillers, bodies are more carelessly *squandered* than carefully stylized. Except, of course, insofar as excess, and hyperbole, itself constitutes stylization. Thus, most of the violence we see on screen today suggests Grand Guignol rather than Jacobean tragedy. However, in our current cultural moment, tiredly described as "postmodern" but filled with new forms of violence like "road rage," the exaggeration and escalating quantification of violence and gore are a great deal less transgressive than they were — and a great deal more absurd. Thus, Tarantino has said on various occasions that he doesn't take violence "very seriously" and describes it as "funny" and "outrageous."

This hyperbolic escalation and quantification of violence also has become 5 quite common to the action picture and thriller, where the body count only exceeds the number of explosions and neither matters very much to anyone: here violence and the laying waste of bodies seems more "naturalized": that is, it regularly functions to fill up screen space and time in lieu of narrative complexity, and to make the central character look good by "virtue" of his mere survival (see, for example, *Payback*). Again, there seems no moral agenda or critique of violence here — only wisecracks and devaluation uttered out of the sides of a Bruce Willis-type mouth. Indeed, here is the careless violence and laconic commentary of comic books (where the panels crackle with zaps and bullets and explosions and the body count is all that counts).

On a more progressive note, I suppose it is possible to see this new excessive and careless treatment of violence on screen as a satiric form of what Russian literary theorist Mikhail Bakhtin has called "grotesque realism." That is, excessive representations of the body and its messier aspects might be read as containing critical and liberatory potential — this, not only because certain social taboos are broken, but also because these excessive representations of the grotesquerie of being embodied are less "allegorical" and fantastic than they are exaggerations of concrete conditions in the culture of which they are a part. In this regard, and particularly relevant to "indie" crime dramas and the action thriller (a good deal of it science-fictional), much has been written recently about the "crisis of the body" and a related "crisis of masculinity." Both of these crises are no longer of the *Bonnie and Clyde* or *Wild Bunch* variety: They are far too much inflected and informed by *technological* concerns and confusions and a new sense of the body as a technology, altered by technology, enabled by technology, and disabled by technology. Indeed, along with the Fordist assembly line and its increasing production of bodies consumed as they are violently "wasted" on the screen, comes the production of bodies as both technological *subjects* and *subjected to* technology: enhanced and extended, but also extinguished by Ouzis, bombs, whatever the latest in firepower. Thus, we might argue, the excessive violence we see on the screen, the carelessness and devaluation of mere human flesh, is both a recognition of the high-tech, powerful, and uncontrollable subjects we (men, mostly) have become through technology — and an expression of the increasing frustration and rage at what seems a lack of agency and effectiveness as we have become increasingly controlled by and subject to technology.

This new quantification of and carelessness toward violence on the screen also points to other aspects of our contemporary cultural context. We have come both a long way and not so far from the assassins, serial killers, and madmen who made their mass presence visibly felt in the late 1960s and

FIGURE 1   John Travolta and Samuel L. Jackson are buddies and professional killers in *Pulp Fiction*, which takes a cartoonish approach to graphic violence, using a character's exploding head as the basis for an extended comic sketch.

early 1970s. They, like the bodies wasted on the screen, have proliferated at an increasingly faster and decreasingly surprising rate. They and the violence that accompanies them are now a common, omnipresent phenomenon of daily life — so much so that, to an unprecedented degree, we are resigned to living with them in what has become an increasingly uncivil society. "Senseless" and "random" violence pervades our lives and is barely remarkable or specific any longer — and while "road rage" and little children killed by stray bullets of gang bangers do elicit a moral *frisson,* for the most part we live in and suspect the absence of a moral context in this decade of extreme relativism. Violence, like "shit," happens — worth merely a bumper sticker nod that reconciles it with a general sense of helplessness (rather than despair).

No longer elevated through balletic treatment on narrative purpose, violence on the screen is sensed — indeed, appreciated — as senseless. But then so is life under the extremity of such technologized and uncivil conditions. Indeed, what has been called the "postmodern condition" might be more accurately thought of as the "postmortem condition." There's a kind of meta-sensibility at work here: life, death, and the movies are a "joke" or an "illusion" and everyone's in on it. Violence on the screen and in the culture is not related to a moral context, but to a proliferation of images, texts, and spectacle. And, given that we cannot contain or stop this careless proliferation, violence and death both on the street and in *Pulp Fiction* become reduced to the practical — and solvable — problem of cleanup.

Pain, too, drops out of the picture. The spasmodic twitching that ends *Bonnie and Clyde* has become truly lifeless. The bodies now subjected to violence are just "dummies": multiple surfaces devoid of subjectivity and gravity, "straw men," if you will. "Wasting" them doesn't mean much. Hence, the power (both appealing and off-putting) of those few films that remind us that bodily damage hurts, that violently wasting lives has grave consequences. Hence, the immense popularity of *Saving Private Ryan,* a movie in which the massive quantity of graphic physical damage and the violent "squandering" of bodies and lives is "redeemed" to social purpose and meaning, its senselessness made sensible by its (re)insertion in a clearly defined (and clearly past) moral context. Hence, also, the popular neglect of *Beloved* or *Affliction,* movies in which violence is represented "close up" as singularly felt: graphically linked to bodily pain and its destruction of subjectivity. In these films, violence is not dramatized quantitatively or technologically and thus becomes extremely difficult to watch: that is, even though an image, understood by one's own flesh as *real*.

I am not sure how to end this particular postmortem on my original essay. I still can't watch the eyeball being slit in *Un Chien Andalou.* But, as with *Straw Dogs* and *The French Connection,* I could and did watch all the violence in *Pulp Fiction.* Nonetheless, there's been a qualitative change as well as a quantitative one: while I watched those earlier violent films compulsively, with some real need to know what they showed me, I watch the excesses of the current ones casually, aware they won't show me anything real that I don't already know.

READING THE TEXT

1. What was Sobchack's argument in the essay on screen violence that she wrote twenty-five years ago?

2. How does contemporary screen violence differ from that of the 1960s and 1970s, according to Sobchack?

3. What does Sobchack mean by referring to "our increasingly *technologized* view of the body" (para. 3)?

4. In what ways do irony and satire contribute to the desensitizing of contemporary audiences in the face of extreme screen violence, according to Sobchack?

READING THE SIGNS

1. Media violence is one of the most controversial issues in current cultural politics. Referring to a selection of current violent films, write an essay arguing for or against the proposition that screen violence desensitizes viewers to the realities of violence.

2. Write an argumentative essay in which you support, refute, or modify Sobchack's claim that films such as *Beloved* failed to attract audiences because, unlike most violent films, they depict pain and violence as "*real*" (para. 9). To develop support for your position, interview acquaintances who watched such a film and those who chose to avoid it.

3. In class, stage a debate on the proposition that the film industry should restrict its depictions of violence.

4. Rent a video of *Rollerball, Starship Troopers,* or another recent violent film. To what extent does the film illustrate Sobchack's view that "we need noise and constant stimulation and quantity to make up for a lack of significant meaning" (para. 2)?

5. Rent a video of *Boyz N the Hood,* and analyze it semiotically. Use your observations as evidence for an essay in which you argue whether the film's violence is desensitizing, as Sobchack finds to be the case for most contemporary films, or whether it strikes the viewer as "real." How does the film's genre — gangster film — affect your interpretation of the violence? To develop your ideas, read or reread Todd Boyd's "So You Wanna Be a Gangsta?" (p. 343).

6. In class, discuss the reasons many moviegoers find violence entertaining. What does the prevalence of violence say about modern American cultural values?

◀**READING THE SIGNS**

1. Based on the *Reservoir Dogs* poster, how would you characterize the subject matter of this film? Does the poster make you want to see the film? Why or why not? What is the effect of including one figure with part of his face obscured and the other with only his arm visible? What does the image of the four men at the bottom suggest? How do you interpret the splattering on the letters of the title?

2. Who, in your opinion, is the intended audience for this film? Why? What elements in this poster appeal to that intended audience?

3. A version of this poster includes the caption, "Four perfect killers. One perfect crime. Now all they have to fear is each other." In your opinion, is the ad more or less effective with this added text? Why or why not?

4. If you haven't seen *Reservoir Dogs,* rent it (though be warned that parts are quite violent). How well does this poster represent the film? If you had to design your own poster for this movie, what would it look like?

PATRICK GOLDSTEIN

THE TIME TO GET SERIOUS HAS COME

"Hollywood has metamorphosed into a soulless popcorn machine, creating mindless dreck designed to pay off at every stop on the global gravy train," Patrick Goldstein complains in this selection, and in the aftermath of the Pentagon and World Trade Center attacks, some change, he argues, "is overdue." In a more serious era, it is time, in short, for more serious entertainment—if that isn't an oxymoron. But as Goldstein demonstrates, it's been done before, as when Hollywood went to war after Pearl Harbor, and it can be done again. The question is, will Hollywood get serious, or will it be popcorn as usual? Goldstein is a staff writer for the Los Angeles Times, *in which this piece appeared a week after the 9/11 attacks.*

If there's one place where the carnage at the World Trade Center and the Pentagon must have inspired some uncomfortable self-reflection . . . , it was in the executive corridors of this town's studio conglomerates. Summer after summer they have churned out eerily similar fantasy images of planes being hijacked, buildings being blown-up, and cities being reduced to rubble—all under the guise of popular entertainment.

Much has been written . . . about the terrorist attacks' effect on our political and financial institutions. But little has been said about the effect on our pop culture. Yet I suspect that our culture will eventually be transformed as much as any other arena of American life. "When you drop a stone in a pond, it has a ripple effect," says Armyan Bernstein, producer of such films as *13 Days* and *Hurricane*. "Well, this is like dropping a boulder or a meteor. I don't know one person who hasn't had their spirit challenged. People have been changed."

Change is overdue. In the past decade, Hollywood has metamorphosed into a soulless popcorn machine, creating mindless dreck designed to pay off at every stop on the global gravy train, from movie theaters to cable TV to DVDs. The studios have largely abandoned any pretense of grappling with real-life issues of the modern world.

Ask any top screenwriter or producer: It's almost a lost cause to pitch a studio an adult drama or a movie about politics. Unless you've got an A-list movie star in your back pocket — or a project helmed by a director with the pile driver ferocity of an Oliver Stone or Michael Mann — they won't even stamp your parking ticket on the way out. For every *Erin Brokovich* or *Traffic,* there are hundreds of forgettable fantasy thrill rides like *Tomb Raider* or *The Mummy Returns*. If you want to see drama about contemporary issues, you have to turn on your TV and watch *The West Wing,* or *Law and Order,* or *The District*. The movie studios these days are in the celluloid theme-park business.

Hollywood executives argue that they simply make the movies people want to see. So maybe Hollywood will recognize that Americans suddenly view the world as a more serious place. There's a new moral gravity out there. It is a time for soul searching. In Washington, politicians are putting aside petty partisan differences. In hard-boiled New York, there has been an outpouring of good Samaritanism and communal feeling. 5

The terrorist attacks may have brought to a close a decade of enormous frivolity and escapism. No one knows for sure how quickly or enduringly this kind of transformation takes place. Pop culture is largely a province of the subconscious. That's why it's so unpredictable, why it's so hard to tell which movie or CD or TV show will be hit or a flop.

But for years to come, many of us will feel a tiny shiver when we see a bearded Middle Easterner getting on a plane in front of us. So imagine our subconscious reaction to watching a movie where a building full of people is incinerated by a fiery explosion. Will it still feel like "fun"? Will it still be "exciting"? Will studio marketers still cheeringly call it a "spine-tingling thrill ride"?

Hollywood has always been thought of as a pretty silly place; intoxicated by ego and vanity, but in the past, when faced with tragedy, it has sobered up fast. After the Japanese attack on Pearl Harbor, fatuity turned to patriotic fervor overnight.

James Stewart put on enough weight so he could pass an army physical and enlisted as a private — he ended up a bomber pilot. William Holden, using his real name, became army private William F. Beedle Jr. Robert

Dorothy McGuire, Gregory Peck, Sam Jaffe in *Gentleman's Agreement,* a socially conscious hit that won the 1947 Best Picture Oscar.

Mongomery joined the navy and eventually commanded a destroyer during the Normandy invasion. Directors like John Ford, John Huston, and William Wyler went off to war and made combat documentaries, often in life-threatening situations.

After Henry Fonda finished shooting *The Ox-Bow Incident,* he enlisted as a 10 sailor, even though he was 37 with three children. He got as far as San Diego before 20th Century Fox studio chief Darryl Zanuck had the shore patrol send him back to Los Angeles, where Zanuck put him in a film for the war effort. Everyone started shooting war movies, even though the amount of film available was cut by 25 percent because the military needed cellulose to make explosives.

Soon Hollywood was making so many war-in-the-Pacific films that the studios ran out of bad guys, since in the hysteria after Pearl Harbor, the government had rounded up all the Japanese American citizens and put them in internment camps. The studios would have to make do with hastily recruited Chinese actors instead.

So far, today's entertainment giants have reacted to the tragic events with largely cosmetic measures. A few scripts are being tossed out or rewritten.

Warner Bros. has postponed the release of *Collateral Damage,* which opens with a terrorist explosion, while Disney has pulled *Big Trouble,* which features dimwitted criminals hijacking a plane armed with a nuclear weapon. The studios obviously fear that the public will turn away in distaste, especially now that reality is all too interchangeable with special effects.

But how long will our unease last? How would you react today to watching hijackers seize the president's plane in *Air Force One*? Or mercenaries holding an airport hostage in *Die Hard 2*? Or scenes of the White House exploding in *Independence Day*? Will it be too close for comfort to watch this weekend? What about next month or next year? When will gore and mayhem and gung-ho bravado be an acceptable escapist fantasy again?

Zanuck found himself pondering a similar question when he came back from World War II and the army signal corps. As Otto Friedrich writes in "City of Nets," his study of 1940s Hollywood, Zanuck realized that the war had subtly changed America's attitudes about itself. Audiences wanted something different from the cheap westerns and detective stories that had helped keep Hollywood afloat during the Depression-era 1930s.

"When the boys come home you will find they have changed," Zanuck   15
told his production staff. "They have learned in Europe and the Far East. How other people live. How politics can change lives. . . . I recognize there'll always be a market for Betty Grable and Lana Turner and all that [breast] stuff. But they're coming back with new thoughts, new ideas, new hungers.

"We've got to start making movies that entertain, but at the same time match the new climate of the times."

Zanuck followed his instincts by making a string of socially conscious hits, including *The Razor's Edge, Twelve O'Clock High,* and *Gentleman's Agreement,* which won the Oscar for best picture in 1947. Willy Wyler came back from the war and made *The Best Years of Our Lives,* which won the Oscar in 1946. It wasn't just the prestige pictures that sketched a darker, more unsentimental view of the world. The disillusionment and uncertainty of postwar America also spawned a flood of crime thrillers that were so gloomy they became known as film noirs — movies like *The Big Sleep, The Killers, Out of the Past, The Naked City,* and *Force of Evil.* The titles alone tell you what sort of pessimistic tone they had.

It wasn't the only time filmmakers responded to a new audience mood. It now seems clear that the flowering of American film in the late 1960s and early 1970s — the era that produced everything from *Bonnie and Clyde* and *Midnight Cowboy* and *MASH* to *Chinatown* and *The Godfather* — was largely inspired by the tumult of late-1960s anti-Vietnam protests and political assassinations.

Has the suffering we've seen in the past days on TV put a new chill in our lives? We really don't know — it often takes years before anyone can make sense of seismic cultural changes. Obviously some sort of normality will return: Jay Leno will tell jokes again. Britney Spears will be back on MTV. Kids will go see *Monsters, Inc.* But there is a new whiff of melancholy in the air. And our most gifted artists, be they filmmakers or songwriters or poets or painters, will be the first ones to catch the scent. Touched by some tiny spark from this tragedy, they will be the ones to transform our communal sorrow into something that moves us or makes us laugh again.

Art is the community's medicine. As Saul Bellow once wrote: "The artist   20 must be a prophet, not in the sense that he foretells things to come, but that he tells the audience, at the risk of their displeasure, the secrets of their own hearts."

READING THE TEXT

1. Why does Goldstein think that Hollywood needs to change its ways in the aftermath of the September 11 attacks on America?

2. In what ways did Hollywood respond to the Japanese attack on Pearl Harbor, according to Goldstein?

3. Will the new seriousness in America's cultural perspective last, in Goldstein's opinion?

4. What does Goldstein mean by saying that "the movie studios these days are in the celluloid theme-park business" (para. 4)?

READING THE SIGNS

1. By the time this book appears, more than a year will have passed since the 9/11 terrorist attacks. Surveying the current popular cultural scene, especially the movies, write a paper arguing that America has or has not been changed. Has the film industry returned to business as usual? How can you account for the patterns that you see?

2. In the immediate aftermath of the 9/11 attacks, a number of movies that had been scheduled for release were withheld, but after a few months many, like *Collateral Damage,* were released after all. Write an opinion piece arguing for or against the proposition that movies that were deemed unreleasable in September and October 2001 should not have been released.

3. Goldstein claims that "the studios have largely abandoned any pretense of grappling with real-life issues of the modern world" (para. 3). Write an essay in which you defend, repudiate, or modify this claim, supporting your position with specific reference to current films.

4. Goldstein notes that filmmakers respond to a larger cultural mood, citing the post-World War II era and late 1960s as examples. In class, brainstorm films that dominated the 1990s, and discuss the extent to which they reflect the prevailing cultural mood of that decade. Keep in mind that in the 1990s the American economy moved from deep recession to a dot.com-inspired boom.

CULTURAL CONSTRUCTIONS

PART TWO

POPULAR SPACES
Interpreting the Built Environment

The Territorial Imperative

Space. When most of us think about it, if we think about it at all, we think of emptiness, of the nowhere through which we must pass to get somewhere, of sheer distance, or of the starlit reaches of the universe. Time may be money, but space is, well, nothingness, or little more than the empty hollow in which we find ourselves.

And yet, in spite of its apparent blankness, space isn't empty at all, because the spaces in which we conduct our everyday lives are filled with meanings, with visible and invisible codes that govern the way we move and that tell us, quite literally, where we may go and what we may do when we get there. Consider an ordinary street. You may walk down it, but you need to stick to the margins (or sidewalk if there is one), and it's best to stay to the right if there's any oncoming foot traffic. If private houses are on the street, you may approach the front door, but you're not supposed to cut through the yard, and you're certainly not allowed to enter without permission. You *may* enter the public space of a store, shopping center, or post office, but you might need to pay to enter a museum, and you will need to pass through a security checkpoint if you are entering a courthouse or an airline terminal.

The spaces created by the built environment are not the only ones shot through with written and unwritten rules. Take your personal space: What rules govern it? Ask yourself: How close will you allow someone to get to you? It depends upon who it is, doesn't it? Friends can get close, and lovers closer indeed, but what happens when someone who is neither intrudes into those spaces that are reserved only for your closest acquaintances? How does your home signal to others the rules you wish to set for maintaining your personal space?

The spaces of everyday life, both public and private, personal and architectural, are packed, in short, with complex codes that we violate or ignore at our peril. These codes all originate in the way that human beings define their *territories*. A territory is a space that has been given meaning through having been claimed by an individual or group of individuals. Unclaimed, unmarked space is socially meaningless, but put up a building or a fence, and the uncircumscribed landscape becomes a bounded territory, a human habitat with its own rules for permitted and unpermitted behavior. Anyone unaware of those rules can't survive for long in human society.

Human beings, of course, are not alone in living under the territorial imperative. Many animal species mark their territories and so transform empty space into codified environments. Where humans are different is in the complexity of their territorial codes and, more profoundly, in the way that culture has intervened to produce them. To put this another way, the territorial imperative is ours by nature, but the actual codes that govern our territories are socially constructed and thus differ from culture to culture.

To see this, one need only look at the varied ways in which different cultures inscribe space with rules for behavior. Take the way we define the permitted distance between two people who are speaking to one another. The spatial codes of Mediterranean culture, for example, allow you to get very close to the person you are talking to, while those of traditional English society call for quite a generous setback — which is why the English seem cold or standoffish to Italians and why Italians seem pushy or intrusive to the English. Or consider the codes that govern the way you should enter a private home. In traditional Japanese society, the polite move is to take your shoes off first. But how would that look if you do so as you enter a typical American home?

Because the human environment is socially constructed, it is semiotic through and through and thus open to cultural interpretation. By interpreting the spatial rules that govern a culture, you can learn a great deal about that culture. Sometimes what you will learn is not especially earth-shaking (that Italians and the English differ on the rules for proper speaking distance, for instance). But often interpreting spatial codes, especially of the built environment, can be quite eye opening, particularly because public spaces can reflect and reinforce a culture's political ideology and power structure. It is no accident, for example, that the distinctive architecture of Imperial Rome was designed to reflect and convey the massive power of a society that thrived through military conquest. Buildings like the Roman Colosseum and Forum expressed the might of an empire that stretched from North Africa to Britain. While Americans have copied Roman design in their own political architecture (the Capitol Building in Washington, D.C., is Roman in essence), twentieth-century America's contributions to architectural history include the shopping mall and the office tower, buildings that reflect the values of a capitalist society devoted to business and consumption rather than military conquest and empire building.

A culture's spatial codes can reflect its gender codes as well. Consider how Americans tend to regard the private, domestic space of the home as being essentially feminine (if you think not, consider how Martha Stewart targets female consumers or how magazines like *Better Homes and Gardens* are still largely women's publications), while the more public space of a business office is considered to be essentially masculine. Such a division reproduces a cultural ideology that still, after some thirty years of feminist activism, sees the domestic realm as primarily a woman's environment, while men belong in the corporate "jungle," fighting it out with other men for supremacy and power.

The organization of a business office reflects such an ideology of power relations through its distribution of space. Hierarchically patriarchal in its spatial organization, the business office rewards the winner of the fight — the company CEO — with the largest office, the biggest desk, and the best views. Ordinary office workers have to make due with cubicles — nonoffices that spatially communicate their subordinate status in the corporate hierarchy. You could see this pattern rather realistically parodied in the Mike Judge movie *Office Space,* but anyone who has ever worked in a modern office knows all about the semiotics of the cubicle already.

The home, in contrast, is considered a matriarchal space and so reflects the essentially nonhierarchical nature of traditional women's culture (though we should point out that patriarchal privilege intrudes into the domestic space of the home by way of the "master" bedroom, which, as the space where the man of the house sleeps, is usually larger and more luxurious than the other bedrooms in the house). And perhaps no other room in the modern American home better exemplifies the nonhierarchical nature of matriarchal space than the kitchen. Once a place reserved almost exclusively for women, or for servants in richer households, the contemporary kitchen is a space where the whole family can gather together more or less as equals. It is significant, then, that modern homebuyers often regard the size of a home's kitchen as a crucial factor in deciding whether to purchase a house — the bigger, the better. Could this be a sign of a cultural desire, among men as well as women, for a space that is marked by cooperation rather than competition? Or is the size of one's kitchen just another status symbol? Think it over. We'll let you decide.

Home, Home on the Range

Space is of particular importance to Americans, who have made it a part of their national character. From the very beginning of the European settlement of what would become the United States, the availability of land, of open space ("open," of course, to a European: the Native Americans whose

The home as work space.

territory it was didn't consider the land open) has been a crucial factor in the shaping of American identity. Whether officially inscribed in the nineteenth-century notion of Manifest Destiny or simply reflected in a national tendency for itchy-footedness — the restless need to pull up stakes now and then and go on the road — the American desire for an open frontier has never ceased. Indeed, the "open road," which has been celebrated in such literary classics as Walt Whitman's "Song of the Open Road" and Jack Kerouac's *On the Road* (1957), is one of America's most evocative public symbols. Now that the real frontier has long been settled and closed to further free wandering, Americans have turned to a new electronic frontier that is often called, not coincidentally, the "information superhighway."

The American attitude toward space is especially reflected in our preferred housing patterns. Middle-class Europeans tend to live in urban apartments. If they can afford one, a European family may own a country villa, but most have their primary residences in cities. Americans, on the other hand, prefer to live in single-family houses, usually situated in residential suburbs, complete with their own yards and grounds. Those yards, especially when covered with a lawn, are essentially symbolic remnants of the pastures and prairies that once beckoned to restless Americans from the frontier. The frontier has long since disappeared, but its ghost still lingers on the suburban lawn, crabgrass and all.

So important to Americans is the notion of frontier spaciousness that we even give it a moral value. City dwellers are still considered less American than country folk (note how we speak of the agricultural Midwest as the American "heartland": this refers not only to the geographic location of the Midwestern states but to its national significance as the spiritual center of the nation), and the city itself is still often regarded as a corrupt space where you may work or entertain yourself but from which you flee back to the more "wholesome" spaces of a suburb. This national moral preference for rural open space over the tighter city spaces was made explicit in Thomas Jefferson's stated hope that America would remain a nation of small farmers and would not repeat the urban experience of Europe; it continues today in populist political movements that demonize the city (and those who live in it) while celebrating the virtues of country life. Thus, while today America is, despite Jefferson's hopes, largely an urban nation, our ideology is still essentially rural, tied to a vanished frontier that lingers on in our dreams and desires.

Interpreting Popular Spaces

Let's say that you are assigned a paper in which you are to analyze the cultural significance of a public space of your choosing, and you decide to interpret a shopping mall. How would you go about it? You might well begin by visiting one. Now, look around you: What do you see and who do you see? You will want to answer both of these questions carefully, because the answers you come up with will comprise the heart of your analysis.

Let's begin with who you see. Do you see a lot of teenagers? It will be likely that you do. Now ask yourself what they are doing. Are they shopping, or are they walking around in groups and generally hanging out? Some of the

Exploring the Signs of Public Space

In your journal, reflect on your use of public space for recreational or entertainment purposes. Where do you spend most of your time? In fully public parks (include both urban and wilderness parks in your consideration)? Or in commercial spaces such as theme parks or shopping malls? Do you spend time in public libraries or in bookstores such as Borders or Barnes & Noble? In which sort of public spaces do you feel more comfortable, and what is it about the spaces that make you feel this way?

teens will be shopping (we'll get back to them, and other shoppers, in a moment), but many, if not most, will probably be hanging out. Your next question is, "Why here?"

To answer that question, you need to consider some alternatives, some *different* places where teens can hang out. There are many such places, and we'll leave most of them to you to identify and consider, but for the moment we'll look at one alternative: a public park. That would be different, and, what is more, public parks are designed for relaxation, recreation, and socializing. But if you hung out in shopping malls yourself, did you ever consider a park instead?

It is likely that you didn't. Now ask yourself why. Most probably your answer would include one or more of the following responses, depending upon where you grew up. If it was in a large city, you may have considered the local parks to be too dangerous (New York's Central Park, a popular teen hangout, may be an exception here), or there may not have been any parks convenient for the purpose. If you grew up in a suburb, there probably weren't any public parks anyway, beyond a few rather sterile squares of lawn with play equipment designed for young children. And if you spent your hanging-out years in a small town or village, the town center was probably too dull.

All of these possible responses (and any other ones that you may come up with) point to larger cultural issues. Let's look at them one by one. Say that the parks in your city are simply too dangerous for hanging out, that they have been allowed to decay and are now the territories of street gangs, drug dealers, and the homeless. That, of course, isn't what they were built for. America's urban parks are supposed to provide a kind of public garden for city dwellers who otherwise would have little or no access to the pleasures of nature. They are spaces in which all classes of society can gather on terms of relative equality and were once the sites of such public entertainments as band and orchestral concerts. To some extent, urban parks are still used for such purposes, but less and less so in America's most hard-pressed cities, where the public gardens are becoming public nuisances. At the same time, few, if any, parks are being built today on the scale of such urban gardens as San Francisco's Golden Gate Park, the Boston Common, or New York's Central Park, as whatever land is still left for development is reserved for office towers, shopping centers, and condominiums. When new public spaces are developed, as in Baltimore's Harbor Place, they are often tied to commercial projects that favor upscale consumers over the inner-city residents that they frequently displace. Now ask yourself: What shift in values does this neglect of public park construction in favor of commercial development reflect?

But maybe you live in a suburb and the state of the local park isn't an issue. There might not even be any public parks in your neighborhood. So you will have a different set of questions to ask. First, why do you (or your family) live in a suburb? After answering that, ask why your suburb has so few public parks, if any. Are there any substitutes for a park? Does your apartment or condominium complex have recreational facilities, including swimming pools and gyms, reserved for the residents? Do your parents belong to a country club, or do you live in a gated community that has its own exclusive park? Or is your family's yard all the park you need?

The answers to these questions all point to a cultural meaning, from the reasons America has changed from being an urban society (as it was in the 1930s and 1940s) to a suburban society (as it increasingly has been since World War II), to the ways in which spaces tied to private property rights are replacing public parks as places of recreation. These are facts that can be *associated* with some of your conclusions about America's current attitude toward its urban centers, because there is a relation between suburbanization, commercialization, and privatization, on the one hand, and the decay of such public spaces as the urban park, on the other. Can you describe that relation?

Maybe you don't think any of this applies to you because you come from a small town that is neither urban nor suburban. Fine, so ask where teens hang out in your community. Do they choose the town center if a nice new mall has gone up on the interstate? If they are at all typical, it is likely they will prefer the new mall. Why?

The answer seems obvious — because there's more to do at the mall. And there is. A lot more. The same answer could be given by someone from the city or the suburbs. But let's continue to look at what teens are doing at the mall, and, while we're at it, let's now include another group that tends to hang out in modern shopping malls, spending more time sitting and strolling than actually shopping: senior citizens.

Whether teen or senior, we can observe, a lot of people at the mall are using it *as if it was a public park*. Just look at the place. See any park benches, sidewalk-style cafes, trees (artificial or real), even running water? If your local mall is like most contemporary malls, it includes some, if not all, of these features, as well as others that make it resemble, well, what? A public park, right? Which is exactly the way that many of its patrons, who are not, incidentally, spending a lot of money, treat it. It would seem, then, that Americans have not lost the knack of enjoying public parks; it's just that they are looking elsewhere for them and finding them simulated at the local shopping mall. What might this mean?

To answer that question, you should consider what the mall is there for in the first place. It isn't there for the public good, you know. And it isn't owned by the public. Shopping malls are designed and built by corporate interests whose purpose is to make money. Though they resemble, or even actively simulate, nonprofit public spaces like parks, they are not really public; rather, they are quasi-public commercial spaces that wish to attract people into them as potential consumers. And one way of doing that is to offer the kind of park experience that the public sector increasingly fails to offer.

Do you see a pattern emerging here? How might you characterize a society that is investing less and less of its resources in public parks and more and more in what are essentially private parks under corporate control? What does such a society value? What is it losing interest in?

But, you may object, you don't have to spend any money at the mall, and, since anyone can enter and use the facilities, isn't this awfully generous on the part of the private companies that own the malls? Doesn't it save the public sector a lot of money on park construction? A fair enough objection, but consider: Is it true that just anyone can use the mall? Private security patrols are hired to discourage some entrants. And while people are allowed to visit the mall without spending much or any money, malls are not really designed with generosity in mind. As we've just mentioned, the simulated parks found in many modern shopping malls were constructed with the intention of drawing people into the mall. After all, you can't sell anything without having foot traffic. But that's only the beginning, because simulating parks is just the tip of the iceberg when it comes to ways in which shopping malls are designed to encourage consumption. For while the mall does offer a parklike experience to the non-shopping public, the whole structure of the contemporary shopping center, from its spatial arrangement to the "themes" around which modern malls are designed, is addressed to the shopper.

> ### Discussing the Signs of Public Space
>
> Discuss in class the spatial organization of your college or university campus. In what ways does your campus environment encourage—or discourage—communal relations among students, both for socializing and for studying? What styles of learning does classroom space encourage? For instance, are most classrooms large lecture halls or small seminar rooms? Can chairs and desks be moved to facilitate small group work? What message does the campus's architectural style send? Is it monumental and imposing? Cozy and supportive? Sterile and impersonal? Boastful?

To "read" this address, you can turn from asking *who* you see at the mall to *what*. We've already considered the parklike settings, so let's turn to some other features likely to appear in modern malls.

In the past two decades, two thematic styles have tended to dominate mall construction and design. The first, which was especially popular in the 1980s, is the so-called birdcage or atrium mall—like Chicago's Water Tower

Place, Houston's Galleria, and Toronto's Eaton Centre (or probably a mall near you). The second, which has been more popular more recently, especially in large urban areas, is the so-called streetwalk, like Santa Monica's Third Street Promenade. An analysis of these two kinds of mall can reveal a great deal about the ways in which malls are designed to stimulate consumption and so, in effect, pay for themselves. Let's start with the birdcage mall.

Birdcage malls tend to be towers of glass and steel, with vaulting skylights, rocketing glassed-in elevators, cascading stairways, and aerial sidewalks. Though they are often set in urban centers and feature parklike attractions, they tend to shut the real city out by providing no views to the outside save what can be seen of the sky through the skylights. Indeed, with their sprawling food courts and parklike plazas — often filled with carnival-like attractions (especially at Christmastime) — they can look like a mixture of urban park and theme park all rolled into one. So, as always in a semiotic analysis, we need to ask why.

To answer this, consider why birdcage malls would want to shut out any view of the city streets on which they are set. That's not too hard to answer: Many inner cities today are pretty rundown and so can be threatening to the kind of shoppers malls want to attract — middle-class consumers with money to spend. So the birdcage mall insulates them from the grittier realities of the street while offering some of the pleasures of an urban park in a simulated and sanitized form. That's why you're likely to find trees and park benches, fountains and sidewalk cafés, in a birdcage mall. Now, what about the theme park ambience?

To answer this question, just ask yourself how you feel when you enter a real theme park, such as Disney World. Don't you feel like you're on some sort of vacation, happily suspended from the cares of everyday life? Now ask how you spend money in a theme park. Won't you purchase as a souvenir some otherwise useless object that, in other circumstances, you would regard as badly overpriced? Or a snack whose cost might equal the price of several dinners at home? That at least is what most people do when visiting theme parks, because the whole point of the visit is to stop worrying about things like money and just have fun, something that usually translates into a bout of free spending.

How does that explain why birdcage malls are designed to look like theme parks? Are those products you're buying needed purchases or souvenirs? The mall's design is intended to make you forget the difference.

The spatial design of a birdcage mall not only makes you want to spend money, it also controls your itinerary as you walk from one shop to another. Have you ever wondered why it is so difficult to find a stairway that will take you where you want to go in a birdcage mall? That's because the stairways aren't designed to take you where you want: They're designed to take you where the mall designers want, which means past as many shops as possible before you get to your destination. This effect is especially pronounced in the layout of an IKEA furniture warehouse: Visit one if there's one nearby and check it out. Isn't it almost impossible to get out of the store once you've entered it without having to walk past every display in the place? And there's so much nice stuff: Won't you be likely to end up buying something you weren't even looking for?

Streetwalks are different. For one thing, they aren't enclosed. For another, they tend to be as linear as the streets they are set on. And they don't resemble theme parks. But that doesn't make them innocent; streetwalks simply work a different strategy in getting you to buy.

To decode a streetwalk mall, it is useful to consider where it is situated. Usually a streetwalk is located in an area that has been reclaimed from urban blight. Ironically, streetwalk malls often rise on the same streets that once were part of a city's central business district but that decayed as middle-class consumers drifted to the suburbs (and to outlying shopping malls), leaving empty and boarded-up storefronts in their wake, along with a few struggling businesses catering mostly to the poor. As the street is resurrected (or, rather, gentrified) in a streetwalk development, the original look and feel of a nineteenth-century urban business district is often simulated — complete with turn-of-the-century-style streetlamps, brownstone shopfronts, and cobbled streets — but the resulting experience is not authentically urban. For one thing, to make room for the upscale emporia and cappuccino bars that streetwalk malls feature, the lingering businesses that served the poor have to be forced out — usually through the agency of rapidly rising rents. At the same time, to make certain that the clientele that the streetwalk wants to attract — usually younger, affluent consumers — doesn't feel threatened, private security patrols are hired to keep out the sorts of people who might make the streetwalk experience, well, a little too genuine, people like the homeless and street gang members who are very much a part of authentic urban experience these days.

So there's something a little ironic about the streetwalk, isn't there? Designed to re-create an authentic urban shopping experience and so attract shoppers who are tired of the simulations of birdcage and other enclosed malls, the streetwalk creates its own set of simulations. Indeed, as has been made explicit at Universal City's City Walk shopping mall in Los Angeles, which you pay to

---

Reading the Signs of Virtual Space on the Net

With the much-celebrated invention of "virtual space," the Internet has the potential to alter our conceptions and experience of space. Visiting a library, for example, once meant traveling to a large public building; now, with the Internet, you can visit most public and university libraries without leaving your home. Test the effect of this change by visiting online several libraries from around the world, perhaps by conducting a search for information related to a current assignment, and then visit in person your campus library. Then, in a reflective essay, consider the effect that the Internet has on your behavior as a student and on your sense of space. Does the Internet expand your sense of the world or, conversely, shrink it?

enter after parking your car underground so you can shop on a "city street" that has no cars on it, the streetwalk is essentially an urban theme park.

You're now ready to write your analysis. After sifting through all of your observations, and all of the questions and answers that stem from them, you can construct a thesis around the patterns you have discovered. We have seen how the modern shopping mall has replaced the public park as a place to gather and socialize in America, and we have also seen how two contemporary mall styles seek to simulate an urban shopping experience by taking the city out of the city and so, essentially, turn that experience into a commodity itself that can be consumed as the entertainments at a theme park are consumed. These patterns can be further related to America's traditional preference for rural space over urban space — hinting, perhaps, at a certain reversal, or at least modification, of our past attitudes towards the city in the 1980s and 1990s. Which of the two styles of mall characterizes the mall you plan to analyze? Or does your mall use different architectural codes to prompt consumers to buy? We'll leave it to you to put all the pieces together to see what they might mean.

Coda: At Ground Zero

The third edition of *Signs of Life in the U.S.A.* featured a cover on which you could find a variety of spatial signifiers for American life: San Francisco's Transamerica Pyramid, Washington's Capitol Dome and Lincoln Memorial, Seattle's Space Needle, the Hollywood Hills, the Statue of Liberty, the sandstone towers of Monument Valley, a Las Vegas casino, a shot of the open road connecting it all together, and, oh yes, an image of the World Trade Center towers. We didn't give much thought to that last one: It seemed to be just another signifier of American life. Until September 11, 2001.

The destruction of the World Trade Center's twin towers demonstrated, as dramatically as anything can be demonstrated, just how symbolic the built environment can be. Because that's why the WTC towers were destroyed: They were symbols. And when they were destroyed, America rediscovered just how important such symbols can be. Now that they are gone, we realize more fully how the WTC towers were more than just the tallest buildings in New York housing much of the office space of the financial district. The WTC was a symbol of America, and its destruction was a blow to the entire nation, a blow that reinvigorated the symbolism of yet another symbol of American life found on the front cover of the third edition of this book: an American flag.

The Readings

Malcolm Gladwell begins this chapter with a startling revelation of the elaborate research that underlies the design of retail spaces, showing how the most innocent-looking display may be planned in response to detailed studies of the behavior and psychology of the shopping public. Two analyses of commercial spaces dedicated to a single product or service follow, with Anna McCarthy taking us to "the swoosh-branded world" of NikeTown and Susan Willis visiting the synthetic utopia of Disney World. Lucy R. Lippard follows with an analysis of the "alternating current" in the American psyche between the city and the country that pulls us in both directions as we choose our dwelling and work places, while Karen Karbo offers a personal reminiscence on the significance of the family dining room. Daphne Spain's analysis of the gender hierarchies encoded in the typical office space is followed by Rina Swentzell's cultural comparison between a Native American pueblo community and the European American school that was imposed upon it. Next, Camilo José Vergara explores the urban ghetto with his camera and pen, assessing the interactions between human environments and behavior, while Eric Boehlert concludes the chapter with a historical analysis of the World Trade Center, showing how buildings are a great deal more than conglomerations of concrete, glass, and steel, and the price they sometimes have to pay for their deeper significance.

MALCOLM GLADWELL

THE SCIENCE OF SHOPPING

Ever wonder why the season's hottest new styles at stores like the Gap are usually displayed on the right at least fifteen paces in from the front entrance? It's because that's where shoppers are most likely to see them as they enter the store, gear down from the walking pace of a mall corridor, and adjust to the shop's spatial environment. Ever wonder how shop managers know this sort of thing? It's because, as Malcolm Gladwell (b. 1963) reports here, they hire consultants like Paco Underhill, a "retail anthropologist" and "urban geographer" whose studies (often aided by hidden cameras) of shopping behavior have become valuable guides to store managers looking for the best ways to move the goods. Does this feel just a little Orwellian? Read on. A staff writer for The New Yorker, *in which this selection first appeared, Gladwell has also written* The Tipping Point *(2000).*

Human beings walk the way they drive, which is to say that Americans tend to keep to the right when they stroll down shopping-mall concourses or city sidewalks. This is why in a well-designed airport travellers drifting toward their gate will always find the fast-food restaurants on their left and the gift shops on their right: people will readily cross a lane of pedestrian traffic to satisfy their hunger but rarely to make an impulse buy of a T-shirt or a magazine. This is also why Paco Underhill tells his retail clients to make sure that their window displays are canted, preferably to both sides but especially to the left, so that a potential shopper approaching the store on the inside of the sidewalk — the shopper, that is, with the least impeded view of the store window — can see the display from at least twenty-five feet away.

Of course, a lot depends on how fast the potential shopper is walking. Paco, in his previous life, as an urban geographer in Manhattan, spent a great deal of time thinking about walking speeds as he listened in on the great debates of the nineteen-seventies over whether the traffic lights in midtown should be timed to facilitate the movement of cars or to facilitate the movement of pedestrians and so break up the big platoons that move down Manhattan sidewalks. He knows that the faster you walk the more your peripheral vision narrows, so you become unable to pick up visual cues as quickly as someone who is just ambling along. He knows, too, that people who walk fast take a surprising amount of time to slow down — just as it takes a good stretch of road to change gears with a stick-shift automobile. On the basis of his research, Paco estimates the human downshift period to be anywhere from twelve to twenty-five feet, so if you own a store, he says, you never want to be next door to a bank: potential shoppers speed up when they walk past a bank (since there's nothing to look at), and by the time they slow down they've walked right past your business. The downshift factor also means that when potential shoppers enter a store it's going to take them from five to fifteen paces to adjust to the light and refocus and gear down from walking speed to shopping speed — particularly if they've just had to navigate a treacherous parking lot or hurry to make the light at Fifty-seventh and Fifth.

Paco calls that area inside the door the Decompression Zone, and something he tells clients over and over again is never, *ever* put anything of value in that zone — not shopping baskets or tie racks or big promotional displays — because no one is going to see it. Paco believes that, as a rule of thumb, customer interaction with any product or promotional display in the Decompression Zone will increase at least thirty per cent once it's moved to the back edge of the zone, and even more if it's placed to the right, because another of the fundamental rules of how human beings shop is that upon entering a store — whether it's Nordstrom or K Mart, Tiffany or the Gap — the shopper invariably and reflexively turns to the right. Paco believes in the existence of the Invariant Right because he has actually verified it. He has put cameras in stores trained directly on the doorway, and if you go to his office, just above Union Square, where videocassettes and boxes of Super-eight film from all his work over the years are stacked in plastic Tupperware containers practically up to the ceiling, he can show you reel upon reel of grainy entryway video — customers striding in the door, downshifting, refocusing, and then, again and again, making that little half turn.

Paco Underhill is a tall man in his mid-forties, partly bald, with a neatly trimmed beard and an engaging, almost goofy manner. He wears baggy khakis and shirts open at the collar, and generally looks like the academic he might have been if he hadn't been captivated, twenty years ago, by the ideas of the urban anthropologist William Whyte. It was Whyte who pioneered the use of time-lapse photography as a tool of urban planning, putting cameras in parks and the plazas in front of office buildings in midtown Manhattan, in order to determine what distinguished a public space that worked from one that didn't. As a Columbia undergraduate, in 1974, Paco heard a lecture on Whyte's work and, he recalls, left the room "walking on air." He immediately read everything Whyte had written. He emptied his bank account to buy cameras and film and make his own home movie, about a pedestrian mall in Poughkeepsie. He took his "little exercise" to Whyte's advocacy group, the Project for Public Spaces, and was offered a job. Soon, however, it dawned on Paco that Whyte's ideas could be taken a step further — that the same techniques he used to establish why a plaza worked or didn't work could also be used to determine why a store worked or didn't work. Thus was born the field of retail anthropology, and, not long afterward, Paco founded Envirosell, which in just over fifteen years has counselled some of the most familiar names in American retailing, from Levi Strauss to Kinney, Starbucks, McDonald's, Blockbuster, Apple Computer, AT&T, and a number of upscale retailers that Paco would rather not name.

When Paco gets an assignment, he and his staff set up a series of video- 5 cameras throughout the test store and then back the cameras up with Envirosell staffers — trackers, as they're known — armed with clipboards. Where the cameras go and how many trackers Paco deploys depends on exactly what the store wants to know about its shoppers. Typically, though, he might use six cameras and two or three trackers, and let the study run for two or three days, so that at the end he would have pages and pages of carefully annotated tracking sheets and anywhere from a hundred to five hundred hours of film. These days, given the expansion of his business, he might tape fifteen thousand hours in a year, and, given that he has been in operation since the late seventies, he now has well over a hundred thousand hours of tape in his library.

Even in the best of times, this would be a valuable archive. But today, with the retail business in crisis, it is a gold mine. The time per visit that the average American spends in a shopping mall was sixty-six minutes last year — down from seventy-two minutes in 1992 — and is the lowest number ever recorded. The amount of selling space per American shopper is now more than double what it was in the mid-seventies, meaning that profit margins have never been narrower, and the costs of starting a retail business — and of failing — have never been higher. In the past few years, countless dazzling new retailing temples have been built along Fifth and Madison Avenues — Barneys, Calvin Klein, Armani, Valentino, Banana Republic, Prada, Chanel, NikeTown, and on and on — but it is an explosion of growth based on no more than a hunch, a hopeful multimillion-dollar gamble that the way to break through is to provide the shopper with spectacle and more spectacle. "The arrogance is gone," Millard Drexler, the president and C.E.O. of the Gap, told me. "Arrogance makes failure. Once you think you know the answer, it's almost always over." In such a competitive environment, retailers don't just want to know how shoppers behave in their stores. They *have* to know. And who better to ask than Paco Underhill, who in the past decade and a half has analyzed tens of thousands of hours of shopping videotape and, as a result, probably knows more about the strange habits and quirks of the species *Emptor americanus* than anyone else alive?

Paco is considered the originator, for example, of what is known in the trade as the butt-brush theory — or, as Paco calls it, more delicately, *le facteur bousculade* — which holds that the likelihood of a woman's being converted from a browser to a buyer is inversely proportional to the likelihood of her being brushed on her behind while she's examining merchandise. Touch — or brush or bump or jostle — a woman on the behind when she has stopped to look at an item, and she will bolt. Actually, calling this a theory is something of a misnomer, because Paco doesn't offer any explanation for why women react that way, aside from venturing that they are "more sensitive back there." It's really an observation, based on repeated and close analysis of his videotape library, that Paco has transformed into a retailing commandment: a women's product that requires extensive examination should never be placed in a narrow aisle.

Paco approaches the problem of the Invariant Right the same way. Some retail thinkers see this as a subject crying out for interpretation and speculation. The design guru Joseph Weishar, for example, argues, in his magisterial *Design for Effective Selling Space,* that the Invariant Right is a function of the fact that we "absorb and digest information in the left part of the brain" and "assimilate and logically use this information in the right half," the result being that we scan the store from left to right and then fix on an object to the right "essentially at a 45 degree angle from the point that we enter." When I asked Paco about this interpretation, he shrugged, and said he thought the reason was simply that most people are right-handed. Uncovering the fundamentals of "why" is clearly not a pursuit that engages him much. He is not a theoretician but an empiricist, and for him the important thing is that in amassing his huge library of in-store time-lapse photography he has gained enough hard evidence to know how often and under what circumstances the Invariant Right is expressed and how to take advantage of it.

What Paco likes are facts. They come tumbling out when he talks, and, because he speaks with a slight hesitation — lingering over the first syllable in, for example, "re-tail" or "de-sign" — he draws you in, and you find yourself truly hanging on his words. "We have reached a historic point in American history," he told me in our very first conversation. "Men, for the first time, have begun to buy their own underwear." He then paused to let the comment sink in, so that I could absorb its implications, before he elaborated: "Which means that we have to *totally* rethink the way we sell that product." In the parlance of Hollywood scriptwriters, the best endings must be surprising and yet inevitable; and the best of Paco's pronouncements take the same shape. It would never have occurred to me to wonder about the increasingly critical role played by touching — or, as Paco calls it, petting — clothes in the course of making the decision to buy them. But then I went to the Gap and to Banana Republic and saw people touching, and fondling and, one after another, buying shirts and sweaters laid out on big wooden tables, and what Paco told me — which was no doubt based on what he had seen on his videotapes — made perfect sense: that the reason the Gap and Banana Republic have tables is not merely that sweaters and shirts look better there, or that tables fit into the warm and relaxing residential feeling that the Gap and Banana Republic are trying to create in their stores, but that tables invite — indeed, symbolize — touching. "Where do we eat?" Paco asks. "We eat, we pick up food, on tables."

Paco produces for his clients a series of carefully detailed studies, totalling [10] forty to a hundred and fifty pages, filled with product-by-product breakdowns and bright-colored charts and graphs. In one recent case, he was asked by a major clothing retailer to analyze the first of a new chain of stores that the firm planned to open. One of the things the client wanted to know was how successful the store was in drawing people into its depths, since the chances that shoppers will buy something are directly related to how long they spend shopping, and how long they spend shopping is directly related to how deep they get pulled into the store. For this reason, a supermarket will often put dairy products on one side, meat at the back, and fresh produce on the other side, so that the typical shopper can't just do a drive-by but has to make an entire circuit of the store, and be tempted by everything the supermarket has to offer. In the case of the new clothing store, Paco found that ninety-one per cent of all shoppers penetrated as deep as what he called Zone 4, meaning more than three-quarters of the way in, well past the accessories and shirt racks and belts in the front, and little short of the far wall, with the changing rooms and the pants stacked on shelves. Paco regarded this as an extraordinary figure, particularly for a long, narrow store like this one, where it is not unusual for the rate of penetration past, say, Zone 3 to be under fifty per cent. But that didn't mean the store was perfect—far from it. For Paco, all kinds of questions remained.

Purchasers, for example, spent an average of eleven minutes and twenty-seven seconds in the store, nonpurchasers two minutes and thirty-six seconds. It wasn't that the nonpurchasers just cruised in and out: in those two minutes and thirty-six seconds, they went deep into the store and examined an average of 3.42 items. So why didn't they buy? What, exactly, happened to cause some browsers to buy and other browsers to walk out the door?

Then, there was the issue of the number of products examined. The purchasers were looking at an average of 4.81 items but buying only 1.33 items. Paco found this statistic deeply disturbing. As the retail market grows more cutthroat, store owners have come to realize that it's all but impossible to increase the number of customers coming in, and have concentrated instead on getting the customers they do have to buy more. Paco thinks that if you can sell someone a pair of pants you must also be able to sell that person a belt, or a pair of socks, or a pair of underpants, or even do what the Gap does so well: sell a person a complete outfit. To Paco, the figure 1.33 suggested that the store was doing something very wrong, and one day when I visited him in his office he sat me down in front of one of his many VCRs to see how he looked for the 1.33 culprit.

It should be said that sitting next to Paco is a rather strange experience. "My mother says that I'm the best-paid spy in America," he told me. He laughed, but he wasn't entirely joking. As a child, Paco had a nearly debilitating stammer, and, he says, "since I was never that comfortable talking I always relied on my eyes to understand things." That much is obvious from the first moment you meet him: Paco is one of those people who look right at you, soaking up every nuance and detail. It isn't a hostile gaze, because Paco isn't hostile at all. He has a big smile, and he'll call you "chief" and use your first name a lot and generally act as if he knew you well. But that's the awkward thing: He has looked at you so closely that you're sure he does know you well, and you, meanwhile, hardly know him at all.

This kind of asymmetry is even more pronounced when you watch his shopping videos with him, because every movement or gesture means something to Paco—he has spent his adult life deconstructing the shopping experience—but nothing to the outsider, or, at least, not at first. Paco had to keep stopping the video to get me to see things through his eyes before I began to understand. In one sequence, for example, a camera mounted high on the wall outside the changing rooms documented a man and a woman shopping for a pair of pants for what appeared to be their daughter, a girl in her midteens. The tapes are soundless, but the basic steps of the shopping dance are so familiar to Paco that, once I'd grasped the general idea, he was able to provide a running commentary on what was being said and thought. There is the girl emerging from the changing room wearing her first pair. There she is glancing at her reflection in the mirror, then turning to see herself from the back. There is the mother looking on. There is the father — or, as fathers are known in the trade, the "wallet carrier" — stepping forward and pulling up the jeans. There's the girl trying on another pair. There's the primp again. The twirl. The mother. The wallet carrier. And then again, with another pair. The full sequence lasted twenty minutes, and at the end came the take-home lesson, for which Paco called in one of his colleagues, Tom Moseman, who had supervised the project.

"This is a very critical moment," Tom, a young, intense man wearing little   15 round glasses, said, and he pulled up a chair next to mine. "She's saying, 'I don't know whether I should wear a belt.' Now here's the salesclerk. The girl says to him, 'I need a belt,' and he says, 'Take mine.' Now there he is taking her back to the full-length mirror."

A moment later, the girl returns, clearly happy with the purchase. She wants the jeans. The wallet carrier turns to her, and then gestures to the salesclerk. The wallet carrier is telling his daughter to give back the belt. The girl gives back the belt. Tom stops the tape. He's leaning forward now, a finger jabbing at the screen. Beside me, Paco is shaking his head. I don't get it — at least, not at first — and so Tom replays that last segment. The wallet carrier tells the girl to give back the belt. She gives back the belt. And then, finally, it dawns on me why this store has an average purchase number of only 1.33. "Don't you see?" Tom said. "*She wanted the belt.* A great opportunity to make an add-on sale. . . . *lost!*"

Should we be afraid of Paco Underhill? One of the fundamental anxieties of the American consumer, after all, has always been that beneath the pleasure and the frivolity of the shopping experience runs an undercurrent of manipulation, and that anxiety has rarely seemed more justified than today. The practice of prying into the minds and habits of American consumers is now a multibillion-dollar business. Every time a product is pulled across a supermarket checkout scanner, information is recorded, assembled, and sold to a market-research firm for analysis. There are companies that put tiny cameras inside frozen-food cases in supermarket aisles; market-research firms that feed census data and behavioral statistics into algorithms and come out with complicated maps of the American consumer; anthropologists who sift through the garbage of carefully targeted households to analyze their true consumption patterns; and endless rounds of highly organized focus groups and questionnaire takers and phone surveyors. That some people are now tracking our every shopping move with video cameras seems in many respects the last straw: Paco's movies are, after all, creepy. They look like the surveillance videos taken during convenience-store holdups — hazy and soundless and slightly warped by the angle of the lens. When you watch them, you find yourself waiting for something bad to happen, for someone to shoplift or pull a gun on a cashier.

The more time you spend with Paco's videos, though, the less scary they seem. After an hour or so, it's no longer clear whether simply by watching people shop — and analyzing their every move — you can learn how to control them. The shopper that emerges from the videos is not pliable or manipulable. The screen shows people filtering in and out of stores, petting and moving on, abandoning their merchandise because checkout lines are too long, or leaving a store empty-handed because they couldn't fit their stroller into the aisle between two shirt racks. Paco's shoppers are fickle and headstrong, and are quite unwilling to buy anything unless conditions are perfect — unless the belt is presented at *exactly* the right moment. His theories of the butt-brush and petting and the Decompression Zone and the Invariant Right seek not to make shoppers conform to the desires of sellers but to make sellers conform to the desires of shoppers. What Paco is teaching his clients is a kind of slavish devotion to the shopper's every whim. He is teaching them humility.

READING THE TEXT

1. Summarize in your own words the ways that retailers use spatial design to affect the behavior and buying habits of consumers.

2. What is Gladwell's tone in this selection, and what does it reveal about his attitude toward the retail industry's manipulation of customers?

3. What is the effect on the reader of Gladwell's description of Paco Underhill's appearance and background?

4. Why does Paco Underhill's mother say that he is "the best-paid spy in America" (para. 13)?

READING THE SIGNS

1. Write an essay in response to Gladwell's question "Should we be afraid of Paco Underhill?" (para. 17).

2. Visit a local store or supermarket, and study the spatial design. How many of the design strategies that Gladwell describes do you observe, and how do they affect customers' behavior? Use your observations as the basis for an essay interpreting the store's spatial design. To develop your ideas further, consult Anne Norton's "The Signs of Shopping" (63) and Rachel Bowlby's "The Haunted Superstore" (p. 76).

3. In class, form teams and debate the proposition that the surveillance of consumers by retail anthropologists is unethical and manipulative.

4. Visit a Web site of a major retailer (such as **www.eddiebauer.com** or **www.abercrombieandfitch.com**). How is the online "store" designed to encourage consuming behavior?

ANNA McCARTHY

BRAND IDENTITY AT NIKETOWN

Nike cares very deeply about its image, so deeply, Anna McCarthy (b. 1967) suggests in this analysis of NikeTown (Nike's flagship retail outlet), that when you shop there "the store's purpose is not so much the distribution of Nike goods as it is to continually reestablish and reinforce the idea of the brand image as a commodity itself." To put this another way, NikeTown is a kind of cathedral that promotes worship of the great god Nike. Hmmnn — should we just do it, or not? McCarthy is an associate professor of cinema studies at New York University and is the author of Ambient Television: Visual Culture and Public Space *(2001).*

It has become a commonplace in features journalism to describe NikeTown as the architectural touchstone of postmodern "shoppertainment" — it is, after all, a mass-media architecture designed to simulate several structures at once — a museum, a gym, a temple, a theater.[1] However, having photographed so many televisual retail places, I find far more striking the vague and undirected nature of the screen's commercial solicitations within NikeTown. Also, these solicitations *feel* very different from the brand's regular TV ads. Although Nike broke new ground in the linguistic evolution of commercial speech with the intrusive second-person of its famous imperative slogan, "just do it," NikeTown deploys these and other commericals in an architectural form that seems to deliberately *minimize* any suggestion of a personal "message" to the shopper. Compared with installations like the one we saw in Champs [a competitor], an installation that combined several visual, bodily, and rhetorical techniques for orienting and motivating a spectator individually, the screens at NikeTown seem to aim at a sense of *dis*orientation: the production of a collective Nike hallucination.

This unconventional approach to retail aesthetics first became clear to me when I visited the just-opened Chicago NikeTown in 1993. I stood with other viewers in a crowded, dark, and narrow hallway to watch reel after reel of old Nike commercials on a large screen while other shoppers trooped past, blocking the view. This deliberately awkward placement, creating a bottleneck between two areas of the store, violated many of the rules of store architecture — a professional arena governed at times by strict laws of traffic flow and floor plan. Now, in refusing to accommodate its viewers, this screen only made me try to concentrate even more intently on the images. It got my attention. But the motivation for this effect was unclear, for it did not bring me any closer to

---

[1]See Vanderbilt, *Sneaker Book;* "Teach and Sell School"; Laurie MacDonald, "Under Renovation: Entertainment-Oriented Shoe Retail Showcases," *Footwear News,* August 5, 1996, 8.

the merchandise for sale that day. Not only did the commercials feature old "product," but they were also presented in isolation, without any of the featured merchandise nearby or even signs saying where in the store one might pick up the particular products being advertised. This was a noticeable departure from conventional point-of-purchase video techniques. Whereas the latter generally pitch specific merchandise, located within the grasp of the shopper, the reverential, museological display techniques often noted by both critics and celebrants of NikeTown seemed to keep consumer and product at a distance from one another. The brand seemed purposefully out of reach, and NikeTown seemed a monumental and curiously *impersonal* commercial space.

It is striking that NikeTown should feel so different from Champs, given the fact that both use TV to promote what is essentially the same retail

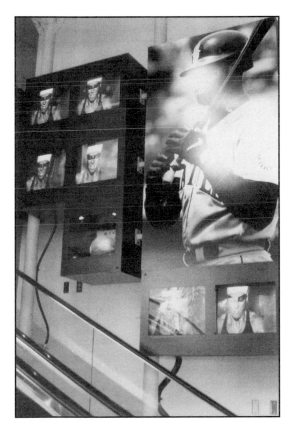

FIGURE 1 At NikeTown in San Francisco merchandise and TV commercials are presented in identical display cases to emphasize that the brand itself is a precious artifact. (Photograph by the author)

FIGURE 2 Celebrity and noncelebrity athletes are hard to tell apart on the synchronized video banks of NikeTown's sales floor. (Photograph by the author)

category — athletic gear (the basketball for sale at Champs is a Nike-brand product, in fact) — and it is worth pursuing the comparison further, with more close reading. Figure 1 shows video monitors, along with some decorative alcoves, on the escalator wall in the San Francisco NikeTown. The cases that display the products are indistinguishable from the ones that house the video screens — a common "theme marketing" technique illustrated in the drawing of the Planet Hollywood gift shop in the following chapter. At NikeTown this visual technique, rendering image and thing indistinguishable, parallels the sculptural technique of Champs's installation. Both blend two-dimensional and three-dimensional forms and combine the *image* of sports with the tactile, material objects of sports participation. However, at NikeTown the objects are removed and set under glass, displayed as much for reverence as for vicarious identification. Here by the escalator and on the main sales floor (Fig. 2) video screens display images of both famous and anonymous athletes. Monitors appear to be programmed separately, although their images occasionally synchronize; these synchronized sequences are followed immediately by the simultaneous appearance of the trademark Nike swoosh. Products and ads are thus made interchangeable; images flow in and out of synch, and anonymity flows into celebrity in this visual environment. The resulting wash of imagery feels like a metaphor for the sports experience of entering "the zone," a state in which all actions feel effortless and successful. However, at NikeTown, unlike Champs, this figuration takes place on a scale of the entire environment. We are always within eyeshot of the video image, and this image, rather than placing us in front of particular displays or asking us to focus on particular products, simply showcases one commodity: the Nike brand image that saturates the space. What is on display at NikeTown is not exchangeable things but the signifier, ownable but unsaleable, that constitutes the brand image itself.

This absence of personal interpellation — nothing, certainly, as personal as Champs's hoop/screen combination — in the display techniques of NikeTown is noteworthy for several reasons. As an example of corporate visual culture on the retail level that seems to deemphasize merchandise while promoting the power of the brand, it conveys the seriousness of organizational anxiety about capitalism's quantum processes. By this I mean simply the indeterminacy of everyday retail practices, from the labor of the clerk displaying the product to the aimless browsing of the shopper. The monumental, elegiac quality of the video at NikeTown suggests that, in contrast to Champs's video, it is not so much the *consumer's* identity as it is the *brand* identity of Nike that must be empowered and rejuvenated in the animated spectacles of its retail flagship store. In this respect, NikeTown's swoosh-branded world tells us a great deal about the broader political economy of name-brand products at the point of purchase. Intense competition among brands on the retail level virtually *requires* that image-based corporations establish single-brand stores of this type. For Nike, as well as for Warner Bros., Reebok, Viacom, and Disney, such stores are sites for the ostentatious recuperation of brand equity in a competition-free and clutter-free environment.[2] The fifteen NikeTowns in North America do not generate particularly large sales figures — indeed, it is a commonplace in journalistic accounts of the store to note how hard it is to actually buy anything there — but they present Nike in an environment unsullied by the clutter of other manufacturers' brand images. Explaining the corporate purpose of NikeTown, one store's public relations executive pointed out that "'mom and pop' stores . . . usually display all the different brands of shoes on the wall and all the clothes on a rail on the floor, and there's no clear connection between Nike shoes and the Nike apparel."[3] As this suggests, the store's purpose is not so much the distribution of Nike goods as it is to continually reestablish and reinforce the idea of the brand image as a commodity itself.

To realize this goal the store at times assumes a rather absolutist, lecturing tone; at the New York branch, for example, "every twenty minutes the building's central atrium is transformed, with screens descending over the windows to dim the light so that visitors' attention is focused on videos about the brand."[4] This commercial address is a hyperbolic pedagogy, lampooning a mythical 1950s model of screen education, and an Orwellian vision of propaganda in which a faceless force compels all shoppers in range of the screen to give it their attention at precisely timed moments. This authoritarian use of video is perhaps only possible in NikeTown, considered the avant-garde of retail design precisely because of its daring use of such ironic techniques. The New York store's ostentatious pedagogical imposition of images might even be interpreted as a lampoon of what many point-of-purchase video installations do routinely — demonstrate products and call shoppers to attention. The joke is that instead of the conventional second-person, expository address that points out benefits of the product to a hypothetical attentive spectator, this screen fills the store's atrium with the elliptical, experimental visual slams that garnered Nike advertisements so much industry praise when they first appeared.

This intrusive imposition of one corporate image style on a space is a highly site-specific technique. It would not be permitted on a regular sales floor, where brand competition is fierce and where the screen's goal is a direct impact on the shopper's decision to make a purchase. In this respect NikeTown exemplifies TV's role in "theme retailing" as opposed to multibrand retailing; it uses TV not to shape behavior in the marketplace but to create a space that, like the brand image in its most idealized representations, exists

[2]British retail and design journalist Julia Thrift defines the architecture of such own-brand flagship stores as "a context which immerses the customer in a brand's imagery, in an environment designed to reinforce every aspect of its core values." Store design, she notes, involves "turning what has previously been a range of products, a logo, and an ad strategy into an attention-grabbing, three-dimensional space, an opportunity for the customers to surround themselves with the brand." Thrift, "What's in Store," 26.

[3]Ibid., 28.

[4]Ibid.

apart from the competition of the market, above the laws governing more routine relations and representations of commerce.

WORKS CITED

Thrift, Julia. "What's in Store for Brands." *Marketing.* February 27, 1997, 25–29.
Vanderbilt, Tom. *The Sneaker Book: An Anatomy of an Industry and an Icon.* New York: New Press, 1998.

READING THE TEXT

1. According to McCarthy, why are the marketing displays in NikeTown "disorient[ing]" (para. 1) and "impersonal" (para. 2)?

2. How does NikeTown make products and ads "interchangeable" (para. 3), according to McCarthy?

3. What does McCarthy mean by claiming that NikeTown's use of images is "ironic" because they "lampoon" (para. 5) point-of-purchase video displays?

4. What is McCarthy's tone and attitude toward her subject?

READING THE SIGNS

1. Media critic Kalle Lasn claims that "advertisements are the most prevalent and toxic of the mental pollutants" ("Hype," p. 217). Read or reread Lasn's selection, and then write a critique of NikeTown as McCarthy describes it. To what extent does NikeTown function as such a "pollutant," or does the store have a different effect on its visitors?

2. If a NikeTown is located in your city, visit it and write your own analysis of its marketing techniques, including store layout and television presentations. For a list of NikeTowns, visit **http://niketown.com.** Alternately, visit another retail store, such as Champs, that relies on mass-media architecture and analyze it. To develop your ideas, you might read or reread Malcolm Gladwell's "The Science of Shopping" (p. 403).

3. McCarthy claims that Nike's marketing techniques work "to continually reestablish and reinforce the idea of the brand image as a commodity itself" (para. 4). In class, brainstorm other companies that may use a similar strategy, and discuss that strategy's effect on consumer behavior. Have you ever, for instance, bought an item of clothing because you wanted to display the brand name? If so, why or why not?

4. McCarthy asserts that NikeTown's marketing strategies constitute an "Orwellian vision of propaganda" (para. 5). In an argumentative essay, support, refute, or complicate this characterization of NikeTown's techniques.

SUSAN WILLIS

DISNEY WORLD: PUBLIC USE/PRIVATE STATE

If your idea of heaven is a place where you need only relax and wait for someone to take care of your every comfort and amusement, and where no unexpected surprises can crop up and destroy your enjoyment, then Disney World is for you. For Susan Willis (b. 1946), on the other hand, such a thoroughly programmed environment falls a good deal short of paradise. In this essay, she explains why. Could it be that Disney World is just another "brave new world"? A professor of English at Duke University, Willis specializes in minority literature and cultural studies and is the author of Specifying: Black Women Writing the American Experience *(1987),* A Primer for Daily Life *(1991), and* Inside the Mouse *(1995).*

At Disney World, the erasure of spontaneity is so great that spontaneity itself has been programmed. On the "Jungle Cruise" khaki-clad tour guides teasingly engage the visitors with their banter, whose apparent spontaneity has been carefully scripted and painstakingly rehearsed. Nothing is left to the imagination or the unforeseen. Even the paths and walkways represent the programmed assimilation of the spontaneous. According to published reports, there were no established walkways laid down for the opening-day crowds at Disneyland.[1] Rather, the Disney Imagineers waited to see where people would walk, then paved over their spontaneous footpaths to make prescribed routes.

The erasure of spontaneity has largely to do with the totality of the built and themed environment. Visitors are inducted into the park's program, their every need predefined and presented to them as a packaged routine and set of choices. "I'm not used to having everything done for me." This is how my companion at Disney World reacted when she checked into a Disney resort hotel and found that she, her suitcase, and her credit card had been turned into the scripted components of a highly orchestrated program. My companion later remarked that while she found it odd not to have to take care of everything herself (as she normally does in order to accomplish her daily tasks), she found it "liberating" to just fall into the proper pattern, knowing that nothing could arise that hadn't already been factored into the system. I have heard my companion's remarks reiterated by many visitors to the park with whom I've talked. Most describe feeling "freed up" ("I didn't have to worry about my kids," "I didn't have to think about anything") by the experience of relinquishing control over the complex problem-solving thoughts and

[1]Scott Bukatman, "There's Always Tomorrowland: Disney and the Hypercinematic Experience," *October* 57 (Summer 1991), pp. 55–78.

Magic Kingdom, Disney World.

operations that otherwise define their lives. Many visitors suspend daily perceptions and judgments altogether, and treat the wonderland environment as more real than real. I saw this happen one morning when walking to breakfast at my Disney resort hotel. Two small children were stooped over a small snake that had crawled out onto the sun-warmed path. "Don't worry, it's rubber," remarked their mother. Clearly only Audio-Animatronic simulacra of the real world can inhabit Disney World. A real snake is an impossibility.

In fact, the entire natural world is subsumed by the primacy of the artificial. The next morning I stepped outside at the end of an early morning shower. The humid atmosphere held the combination of sun and rain. "Oh! Did they turn the sprinklers on?" This is the way my next-door neighbor greeted the day as she emerged from her hotel room. The Disney environment puts visitors inside the world that Philip K. Dick depicted in *Do Androids Dream of Electric Sheep?*— where all animal life has been exterminated, but replaced by the production of simulacra, so real in appearance that people have difficulty recalling that real animals no longer exist. The marvelous effect of science fiction is produced out of a dislocation between two worlds, which the reader apprehends as an estrangement, but the characters inside the novel cannot grasp because they have only the one world: the world of simulacra. The effect of the marvelous cannot be achieved unless the artificial environment is perceived through the retained memory of everyday reality. Total absorption into the Disney environment cancels the possibility for the marvelous and leaves the visitor with the banality of a park-wide sprinkler system. No muggers, no rain, no ants, and no snakes.

Amusement is the commodified negation of play. What is play but the spontaneous coming together of activity and imagination, rendered more pleasurable by the addition of friends? At Disney World, the world's most highly developed private property "state" devoted to amusement, play is all but eliminated by the absolute domination of program over spontaneity. Every ride runs to computerized schedule. There is no possibility of an awful thrill, like being stuck at the top of a ferris wheel. Order prevails particularly in the queues for the rides that zigzag dutifully on a prescribed path created out of stanchions and ropes; and the visitor's assimilation into the queue does not catapult him or her into another universe, as it would if Jorge Luis Borges fabricated the program. The Disney labyrinth is a banal extension of the ride's point of embarkation, which extends into the ride as a hyper-themed continuation of the queue. The "Backstage Movie Tour" has done away with the distinction between the ride and its queue by condemning the visitor to a two-and-a-half-hour-long pedagogical queue that preaches the process of movie production. Guests are mercilessly herded through sound stages and conveyed across endless back lots where one sees the ranch-style houses used in TV commercials and a few wrecked cars from movie chase scenes. Happily, there are a few discreet exit doors, bail-out points for parents with bored children. Even Main Street dictates programmed amusement because it is not a street but a conduit, albeit laden with commodity distractions, that conveys the visitor to the Magic Kingdom's other zones where more queues, rides, and commodities distinguish themselves on the basis of their themes. All historical and cultural references are merely ingredients for decor. Every expectation is met programmatically and in conformity with theme. Mickey as Sorcerer's Apprentice does not appear in the Wild West or the exotic worlds of Jungle and Adventure, the niches for Davy Crockett and Indiana Jones. Just imagine the chaos, a park-wide short circuit, that the mixing of themed ingredients might produce. Amusement areas are identified by a "look," by characters in costume, by the goods on sale: What place — i.e., product — is Snow White promoting if she's arm in arm with an astronaut? The utopian intermingling of thematic opportunities such as occurred at the finale of the movie *Who Framed Roger Rabbit?*, with Warner and Disney "toons" breaking their copyrighted species separation to cavort with each other and the human actors, will not happen at Disney World.

However, now that the costumed embodiment of Roger Rabbit has taken 5 up residence at Disney World, he, too, can expect to have a properly assigned niche in the spectacular Disney parade of characters. These have been augmented with a host of other Disney/Lucas/Spielberg creations, including Michael Jackson of "Captain EO" and C3PO and R2D2 of *Star Wars,* as well as Disney buyouts such as Jim Henson's Muppets and the Saturday morning cartoon heroes, the Teenage Mutant Ninja Turtles. The Disney Corporation's acquisition of the stock-in-trade of popular culture icons facilitates a belief commonly held by young children that every popular childhood figure "lives" at Disney World. In the utopian imagination of children, Disney World may well be a never-ending version of the finale to *Roger Rabbit* where every product of the imagination lives in community. In reality, the products (of adult imaginations) live to sell, to be consumed, to multiply.

What's most interesting about Disney World is what's not there. Intimacy is not in the program even though the architecture includes several secluded nooks, gazebos, and patios. During my five-day stay, I saw only one kiss — and this a husbandly peck on the cheek. Eruptions of imaginative play are just as rare. During the same five-day visit, I observed only one such incident even though there were probably fifty thousand children in the park. What's curious about what's not at Disney is that there is no way of knowing what's not there until an aberrant event occurs and provokes the remembrance of the social forms and behaviors that have been left out. This was the case with the episode of spontaneous play. Until I saw real play, I didn't realize that it was missing. The incident stood out against a humdrum background of uniform amusement: hundreds of kids being pushed from attraction to attraction in their strollers, hundreds more waiting dutifully in the queues or marching about in family groups — all of them abstaining from the loud, jostling, teasing, and rivalrous behaviors that would otherwise characterize many of their activities. Out of this homogenous "amused" mass, two kids snagged a huge sombrero each from an open-air stall at the foot of the Mexico Pavilion's Aztec temple stairway and began their impromptu version of the Mexican hat dance up and down the steps. Their play was clearly counterproductive as it took up most of the stairway, making it difficult for visitors to enter the pavilion. Play negated the function of the stairs as conduit into the attraction. The kids abandoned themselves to their fun, while all around them, the great mass of visitors purposefully kept their activities in line with Disney World's prescribed functions. Everyone but the dancers seemed to have accepted the park's unwritten motto: "If you pay, you shouldn't play." To get your money's worth, you have to do everything and do it in the prescribed manner. Free play is gratuitous and therefore a waste of the family's leisure time expenditure.

Conformity with the park's program upholds the Disney value system. Purposeful consumption — while it costs the consumer a great deal — affirms the value of the consumer. "Don't forget, we drove twenty hours to get here." This is how one father admonished his young son who was squirming about on the floor of EPCOT's Independence Hall, waiting for the amusement to begin. The child's wanton and impatient waste of time was seen as a waste of the family's investment in its amusement. If a family is to realize the value of its leisure time consumptions, then every member must function as a proper consumer.

The success of Disney World as an amusement park has largely to do with the way its use of programming meshes with the economics of consumption as a value system. In a world wholly predicated on consumption, the dominant order need not proscribe those activities that run counter to consumption, such as free play and squirming, because the consuming public largely polices itself against gratuitous acts which would interfere with the production of consumption as a value. Conformity with the practice of consumption is so widespread and deep at Disney World that occasional manifestations of boredom or spontaneity do not influence the compulsively correct behavior of others. Independence Hall did not give way to a seething mass of squirming youngsters even though all had to sit through a twenty-minute wait. Nor did other children on the margins of the hat dance fling themselves into the fun. Such infectious behavior would have indicated communally defined social relations or the desire for such social relations. Outside of Disney World in places of public use, infectious behavior is common. One child squirming about on the library floor breeds others; siblings chasing each other around in a supermarket draw others; one child mischievously poking at a public fountain attracts others; kids freeloading rides on a department store escalator can draw a crowd. These playful, impertinent acts indicate an imperfect mesh between programmed environment and the value system of consumption. Consumers may occasionally reclaim the social, particularly the child consumer who has not yet been fully and properly socialized to accept individuation as the bottom line in the consumer system of value. As an economic factor, the individual exists to maximize consumption — and therefore profits — across the broad mass of consumers. This is the economic maxim most cherished by the fast-food industry, where every burger and order of fries is individually packaged and consumed to preclude consumer pooling and sharing.

At Disney World the basic social unit is the family. This was made particularly clear to me because as a single visitor conducting research, I presented a problem at the point of embarkation for each of the rides. "How many in your group?" "One." The lone occupant of a conveyance invariably constructed to hold the various numerical breakdowns of the nuclear family (two, three, or four) is an anomaly. Perhaps the most family-affirming aspect of Disney World is the way the queues serve as a place where family members negotiate who will ride with whom. Will Mom and Dad separate themselves so as to accompany their two kids on a two-person ride? Will an older sibling assume the responsibility for a younger brother or sister? Every ride asks the family to evaluate each of its member's needs for security and independence. This is probably the only situation in a family's visit to Disney World where the social relations of family materialize as practice. Otherwise and throughout a family's stay, the family as nexus for social relations is subsumed by the primary definition of family as the basic unit of consumption. In consumer society at large, each of us is an atomized consumer. Families are composed of autonomous, individuated consumers, each satisfying his or her age- and gender-differentiated taste in the music, video, food, and pleasure marketplace. In contrast, Disney World puts the family back together. Even teens are integrated in their families and are seldom seen roaming the park in teen groups as they might in shopping malls.

Families at Disney World present themselves as families, like the one I 10 saw one morning on my way to breakfast at a Disney resort hotel: father, mother, and three children small to large, each wearing identical blue Mickey Mouse T-shirts and shorts. As I walked past them, I overheard the middle child say, "We looked better yesterday — in white." Immediately, I envisioned the family in yesterday's matching outfits, and wondered if they had bought identical ensembles for every day of their stay.

All expressions of mass culture include contradictory utopian impulses, which may be buried or depicted in distorted form, but nevertheless generate much of the satisfaction of mass cultural commodities (whether the consumer recognizes them as utopian or not). While the ideology of the family has long functioned to promote conservative — even reactionary — political and social agendas, the structure of the family as a social unit signifies communality rather than individuality and can give impetus to utopian longings for communally defined relations in society at large. However, when the family buys into the look of a family, and appraises itself on the basis of its look ("We looked better yesterday"), it becomes a walking, talking commodity, a packaged unit of consumption stamped with the Mickey logo of approval. The theoretical question that this family poses for me is not whether its representation of itself as family includes utopian possibilities (because it does), but whether such impulses can be expressed and communicated in ways not accessible to commodification.

In its identical dress, the family represents itself as capitalism's version of a democratized unit of consumption. Differences and inequalities among family members are reduced to distinctions in age and size. We have all had occasion to experience the doppelgänger effect in the presence of identical twins who choose (or whose families enforce) identical dress. Whether chosen or imposed, identical twins who practice the art of same dress have the possibility of confounding or subverting social order. In contrast, the heterogeneous family whose members choose to dress identically affirms conformity with social order. The family has cloned itself as a multiple, but identical consumer, thus enabling the maximization of consumption. It is a microcosmic representation of free market democracy where the range of choices is restricted to the series of objects already on the shelf. In this system there is no radical choice. Even the minority of visitors who choose to wear their Rolling Stones and Grateful Dead T-shirts give the impression of having felt constrained not to wear a Disney logo.

Actually, Disney has invented a category of negative consumer choices for those individuals who wish to express nonconformity. This I discovered as I prepared to depart for my Disney research trip, when my daughter Cassie (fifteen years old and "cool" to the max) warned me, "Don't buy me any of that Disney paraphernalia." As it turned out, she was happy to get a pair of boxer shorts emblazoned with the leering images of Disney's villains: two evil queens, the Big Bad Wolf, and Captain Hook. Every area of Disney World includes a Disney Villains Shop, a chain store for bad-guy merchandise. Visitors who harbor anti-Disney sentiments can express their cultural politics by consuming the negative Disney line. There is no possibility of an anticonsumption at Disney World. All visitors are, by definition, consumers, their status conferred with the price of admission.

At Disney World even memories are commodities. How the visitor will remember his or her experience of the park has been programmed and indicated by the thousands of "Kodak Picture Spot" signposts. These position the photographer so as to capture the best views of each and every attraction, so that even the most inept family members can bring home perfect postcard-like photos. To return home from a trip to Disney World with a collection of haphazardly photographed environments or idiosyncratic family shots is tantamount to collecting bad memories. A family album comprised of picture-perfect photo-site images, on the other hand, constitutes the grand narrative of the family's trip to Disney World, the one that can be offered as testimony to money well spent. Meanwhile, all those embarrassing photos, the ones not programmed by the "Picture Spots," that depict babies with ice cream all over their faces or toddlers who burst into tears rather than smiles at the sight of those big-headed costumed characters that crop up all over the park — these are the images that are best left forgotten.

The other commodified form of memory is the souvenir. As long as there has been tourism there have also been souvenirs: objects marketed to concretize the visitor's experience of another place. From a certain point of view, religious pilgrimage includes aspects of tourism, particularly when the culmination of pilgrimage is the acquisition of a transportable relic. Indeed, secular mass culture often imitates the forms and practices of popular religious culture. For many Americans today who make pilgrimages to Graceland and bring home a mass-produced piece of Presley memorabilia, culture and religion collide and mesh.

Of course, the desire to translate meaningful moments into concrete objects need not take commodified form. In Toni Morrison's *Song of Solomon,* Pilate, a larger-than-life earth mother if there ever was one, spent her early vagabondage gathering a stone from every place she visited. Similarly, I know of mountain climbers who mark their ascents by bringing a rock back from each peak they climb. Like Pilate's stones, these tend to be nondescript and embody personal remembrances available only to the collector. In contrast, the commodity souvenir enunciates a single meaning to everyone: "I was there. I bought something." Unlike the souvenirs I remember having seen as a child, seashells painted with seascapes and the name of some picturesque resort town, most souvenirs today are printed with logos (like the Hard Rock Café T-shirt), or renderings of copyrighted material (all the Disney merchandise). The purchase of such a souvenir allows the consumer the illusion of participating in the enterprise as a whole, attaining a piece of the action. This is the consumerist version of small-time buying on the stock exchange. We all trade in logos — buy them, wear them, eat them, and make them the containers of our dreams and memories. Similarly, we may all buy into capital with the purchase of public stock. These consumerist activities give the illusion of democratic participation while denying access to real corporate control which remains intact and autonomous, notwithstanding the mass diffusion of its logos and stock on the public market. Indeed the manipulation of public stock initiated during the Reagan administration, which has facilitated one leveraged buyout after another, gives the lie to whatever wistful remnants of democratic ownership one might once have attached to the notion of "public" stocks.

Disney World is logoland. The merchandise, the costumes, the scenery — all is either stamped with the Disney logo or covered by copyright legislation. In fact, it is impossible to photograph at Disney World without running the risk of infringing a Disney copyright. A family photo in front of Sleeping Beauty's Castle is apt to include dozens of infringements: the castle itself, Uncle Harry's "Goofy" T-shirt, the kids' Donald and Mickey hats, maybe a costumed Chip 'n Dale in the background. The only thing that saves the average family from a lawsuit is that most don't use their vacation photos as a means for making profit. I suspect the staff of "America's Funniest Home Videos" systematically eliminates all family videos shot at Disney World; otherwise prize winners might find themselves having to negotiate the legal difference between prize and profit, and in a larger sense, public use versus private property. As an interesting note, Michael Sorkin, in a recent essay on Disneyland, chose a photo of "[t]he sky above Disney World [as a] substitute for an image of the place itself." Calling Disney World "the first copyrighted urban environment," Sorkin goes on to stress the "litigiousness" of the Disney Corporation.[2] It may be that *Design Quarterly,* where Sorkin published his essay, pays its contributors, thus disqualifying them from "fair use" interpretations of copyright policy.

Logos have become so much a part of our cultural baggage that we hardly notice them. Actually they are the cultural capital of corporations. Pierre Bourdieu invented the notion of cultural capital with reference to individuals. In a nutshell, cultural capital represents the sum total of a person's ability to buy into and trade in the culture. This is circumscribed by the economics of class and, in turn, functions as a means for designating an individual's social standing. Hence people with higher levels of education who distinguish themselves with upscale or trendy consumptions have more cultural capital and can command greater privilege and authority than those who, as Bourdieu put it, are stuck defining themselves by the consumption of necessity. There are no cultural objects or practices that do not constitute capital, no reserves of culture that escape value. Everything that constitutes one's cultural life is a commodity and can be reckoned in terms of capital logic.

In the United States today there is little difference between persons and corporations. Indeed, corporations enjoy many of the legal rights extended to individuals. The market system and its private property state are "peopled" by corporations, which trade in, accumulate, and hoard up logos. These are the cultural signifiers produced by corporations, the impoverished imagery of a wholly rationalized entity. Logos are commodities in the abstract, but they are not so abstracted as to have transcended value. Corporations with lots of logos, particularly upscale, high-tech logos, command more cultural capital than corporations with fewer, more humble logos.

In late twentieth-century America, the cultural capital of corporations has 20 replaced many of the human forms of cultural capital. As we buy, wear, and eat logos, we become the henchmen and admen of the corporations, defining ourselves with respect to the social standing of the various corporations. Some would say that this is a new form of tribalism, that in sporting corpo-

[2]Michael Sorkin, "See You in Disneyland," *Design Quarterly* (Winter 1992), pp. 5–13.

rate logos we ritualize and humanize them, we redefine the cultural capital of the corporations in human social terms. I would say that a state where culture is indistinguishable from logo and where the practice of culture risks infringement of private property is a state that values the corporate over the human.

While at Disney World, I managed to stow away on the behind-the-scenes tour reserved for groups of corporate conventioneers. I had heard about this tour from a friend who is also researching Disney and whose account of underground passageways, conduits for armies of workers and all the necessary materials and services that enable the park to function, had elevated the tour to mythic proportions in my imagination.

But very little of the behind-the-scenes tour was surprising. There was no magic, just a highly rational system built on the compartmentalization of all productive functions and its ensuing division of labor, both aimed at the creation of maximum efficiency. However, instances do arise when the rational infrastructure comes into contradiction with the onstage (park-wide) theatricalized image that the visitor expects to consume. Such is the case with the system that sucks trash collected at street level through unseen pneumatic tubes that transect the backstage area, finally depositing the trash in Disney's own giant compactor site. To the consumer's eyes, trash is never a problem at Disney World. After all, everyone dutifully uses the containers marked "trash," and what little manages to fall to the ground (generally popcorn) is immediately swept up by the French Foreign Legion trash brigade. For the consumer, there is no trash beyond its onstage collection. But there will soon be a problem as environmental pressure groups press Disney to recycle. As my companion on the backstage tour put it, "Why is there no recycling at Disney World — after all, many of the middle-class visitors to the park are already sorting and recycling trash in their homes?" To this the Disney guide pointed out that there is recycling, backstage: bins for workers to toss their Coke cans and other bins for office workers to deposit papers. But recycling onstage would break the magic of themed authenticity. After all, the "real" Cinderella's Castle was not equipped with recycling bins, nor did the denizens of Main Street, U.S.A., circa 1910, foresee the problem of trash. To maintain the image, Disney problem solvers are discussing hiring a minimum-wage workforce to rake, sort, and recycle the trash on back lots that the environmentally aware visitor will never see.

While I have been describing the backstage area as banal, the tour through it was not uneventful. Indeed there was one incident that underscored for me the dramatic collision between people's expectations of public use and the highly controlled nature of Disney's private domain. As I mentioned, the backstage tour took us to the behind-the-scenes staging area for the minute-by-minute servicing of the park and hoopla of its mass spectacles such as firework displays, light shows, and parades. We happened to be in the backstage area just as the parade down Main Street was coming to an end. Elaborate floats and costumed characters descended a ramp behind Cinderella's Castle and began to disassemble before our eyes. The floats were alive with big-headed characters, clambering off the superstructures and out of their heavy, perspiration-drenched costumes. Several "beheaded" characters revealed stocky young men gulping down Gatorade. They walked toward our tour group, bloated Donald and bandy-legged Chip from the neck down, carrying their huge costume heads, while their real heads emerged pea-sized and aberrantly human.

We had been warned *not* to take pictures during the backstage tour, but one of our group, apparently carried away by the spectacle, could not resist. She managed to shoot a couple of photos of the disassembled characters before being approached by one of the tour guides. As if caught in a spy movie, the would-be photographer pried open her camera and ripped out the whole roll of film. The entire tour group stood in stunned amazement; not, I think, at the immediate presence of surveillance, but at the woman's dramatic response. In a situation where control is so omnipresent and conformity with control is taken for granted, any sudden gesture or dramatic response is a surprise.

At the close of the tour, my companion and I lingered behind the rest of the group to talk with our tour guides. As a professional photographer, my companion wanted to know if there is a "normal" procedure for disarming behind-the-scenes photographic spies. The guide explained that the prescribed practice is to impound the cameras, process the film, remove the illicit photos, and return the camera, remaining photos, and complimentary film to the perpetrator. When questioned further, the guide went on to elaborate the Disney rationale for control over the image: the "magic" would be broken if photos of disassembled characters circulated in the public sphere; children might suffer irreparable psychic trauma at the sight of a "beheaded" Mickey; Disney exercises control over the image to safeguard childhood fantasies.

What Disney employees refer to as the "magic" of Disney World has actually to do with the ability to produce fetishized consumptions. The unbroken seamlessness of Disney World, its totality as a consumable artifact, cannot tolerate the revelation of the real work that produces the commodity. There would be no magic if the public should see the entire cast of magicians in various stages of disassembly and fatigue. That selected individuals are permitted to witness the backstage labor facilitates the word-of-mouth affirmation of the tremendous organizational feat that produces Disney World. The interdiction against photography eliminates the possibility of discontinuity at the level of image. There are no images to compete with the copyright-perfect onstage images displayed for public consumption. It's not accidental that our tour guide underscored the fact that Disney costumes are tightly controlled. The character costumes are made at only one production site and this site supplies the costumes used at Tokyo's Disneyland and EuroDisney. There can be no culturally influenced variations on the Disney models. Control over the image ensures the replication of Disney worldwide. The prohibition against photographing disassembled characters is motivated by the same phobia of industrial espionage that runs rampant throughout the high-tech information industry. The woman in our tour group who ripped open her camera and destroyed her film may not have been wrong in acting out a spy melodrama.

Her photos of the disassembled costumes might have revealed the manner of their production — rendering them accessible to non-Disney replication. At Disney World, the magic that resides in the integrity of childhood fantasy is inextricably linked to the fetishism of the commodity and the absolute control over private property as it is registered in the copyrighted image.

As I see it, the individual's right to imagine and to give expression to unique ways of seeing is at stake in struggles against private property. Mickey Mouse, notwithstanding his corporate copyright, exists in our common culture. He is the site for the enactment of childhood wishes and fantasies, for early conceptualizations and renderings of the body, a being who can be imagined as both self and other. If culture is held as private property, then there can be only one correct version of Mickey Mouse, whose logo-like image is the cancellation of creativity. But the multiplicity of quirky versions of Mickey Mouse that children draw can stand as a graphic question to us as adults: Who, indeed, owns Mickey Mouse?

What most distinguishes Disney World from any other amusement park is the way its spatial organization, defined by autonomous "worlds" and wholly themed environments, combines with the homogeneity of its visitors (predominantly white, middle-class families) to produce a sense of community. While Disney World includes an underlying utopian impulse, this is articulated with nostalgia for a small-town, small-business America (Main Street, U.S.A.), and the fantasy of a controllable corporatist world (EPCOT). The illusion of community is enhanced by the longing for community that many visitors bring to the park, which they may feel is unavailable to them in their own careers, daily lives, and neighborhoods, thanks in large part to the systematic erosion of the public sector throughout the Reagan and Bush administrations. In the last decade the inroads of private, for-profit enterprise in areas previously defined by public control, and the hostile aggression of tax backlash coupled with "me first" attitudes have largely defeated the possibility of community in our homes and cities.

Whenever I visit Disney World, I invariably overhear other visitors making comparisons between Disney World and their home towns. They stare out over EPCOT's lake and wonder why developers back home don't produce similar aesthetic spectacles. They talk about botched, abandoned, and misconceived development projects that have wrecked their local landscapes. Others see Disney World as an oasis of social tranquility and security in comparison to their patrolled, but nonetheless deteriorating, maybe even perilous neighborhoods. A recent essay in *Time* captured some of these sentiments: "Do you see anybody [at Disney World] lying on the street or begging for money? Do you see anyone jumping on your car and wanting to clean your windshield — and when you say no, they get abusive?"[3]

Comments such as these do more than betray the class anxiety of the 30 middle strata. They poignantly express the inability of this group to make

[3]"Fantasy's Reality," *Time,* 27 May 1991, p. 54.

distinctions between what necessarily constitutes the public and the private sectors. Do visitors forget that they pay a daily use fee (upwards of $150 for a four-day stay) just to be a citizen of Disney World (not to mention the $100 per night hotel bill)? Maybe so — and maybe it's precisely *forgetting* that visitors pay for.

If there is any distinction to be made between Disney World and our local shopping malls, it would have to do with Disney's successful exclusion of all factors that might put the lie to its uniform social fabric. The occasional Hispanic mother who arrives with extended family and illegal bologna sandwiches is an anomaly. So too is the first-generation Cubana who buys a year-round pass to Disney's nightspot, Pleasure Island, in hopes of meeting a rich and marriageable British tourist. These women testify to the presence of Orlando, Disney World's marginalized "Sister City," whose overflowing cheap labor force and overcrowded and under-funded public institutions are the unseen real world upon which Disney's world depends.

READING THE TEXT

1. In Willis's view, how does Disney World create an artificial, programmed environment, and why does it do this?

2. What does Willis mean when she claims that "amusement is the commodified negation of play" (para. 4)?

3. Why does Willis believe that a theme park such as Disney World "puts the family back together" (para. 9)?

4. How does Disney World appeal to nonconformists?

5. What does Willis mean by saying that "Disney World is logoland" (para. 17)?

6. Summarize in your own words Willis's interpretation of the "magic" of Disney World.

READING THE SIGNS

1. In class, brainstorm a list of Disney products, characters, and movies, and then discuss the impact of the Disney corporation on American consumer life.

2. In an essay, write an argument that defends, refutes, or modifies Willis's assumption that Disney World is too controlling in its "processing" of visitors. If you prefer, you can focus your essay on any other Disney park you may have visited. You may want to refresh your memory of the park by visiting the Disney Web site at **www.disney.go.com**.

3. Visit a local theme park, and study whether it controls the consumer habits of its visitors as Willis claims Disney World does. Then write an essay in which you analyze your park's control over consumer behavior.

4. Write an essay in which you describe how you would design a theme park for the twenty-first century. What themes would you emphasize? What activities and amenities would you provide, and what would they look like? Be sure to explain your choices and what messages you communicate to visitors.

5. At the close of her essay, Willis suggests a comparison between Disney World

and shopping malls. In an essay, compare and contrast the ways that Disney World and a local mall you have visited control consumer spending habits. To develop your ideas, consult Anne Norton's "The Signs of Shopping" (p. 63), Rachel Bowlby's "The Haunted Superstore" (p. 76) or Malcolm Gladwell's "The Science of Shopping" (p. 403).

LUCY R. LIPPARD
Alternating Currents

With three-quarters of the population living in cities or suburbs, America is a thoroughly urbanized nation. But as Lucy Lippard (b. 1937) indicates in this excerpt from The Lure of the Local: Senses of Place in a Multi-centered Society *(1997), you can take an American out of the country, but you can't take the country out of America. Reflecting on the complex interplay between our urban realities and rural mythologies, Lippard meditates here on the role that space plays in the construction of personal and communal consciousness. An art critic and historian whose many books include* Get the Message? A Decade of Art for Social Change *(1984),* Mixed Blessings: New Art in a Multicultural America *(1990),* The Pink Glass Swan: Selected Feminist Essays on Art *(1995), and* White/Red Cesar Paternosto *(2000), Lippard has written as well for the* Village Voice, In These Times, *and* Z Magazine.

The U.S. population today is 75 percent urban/suburban, but there remains an emotional tension between city and country, an alternating current that pulls at most Americans at various times in their lives. If the city represents the high voltage of the new (or at least the novel) and the country represents the calming tradition of the old, we are always looking for ways to balance our needs for both. I lived in Manhattan for my first nine years and returned at age twenty-one for thirty-seven adult years. While my current addresses are rural, my local knowledge of cities is New York–based and New York–biased.

The city has been seen as a field of indifference to the rest of world, as a triumph of objective over subjective, male over female, culture over nature, materialism over spirituality and idealism.[1] The inherited rural kinship systems of ancient cities were replaced with civil communities, which in turn broke down with industrialization (or perhaps before, with the medieval plagues), when cities became increasingly impersonal. The idealized vision of the Puritans' "City on the Hill" (exposed and exemplary to those living

[1] Yi-Fu Tuan's *Topophilia* was an invaluable source for this section.

"below") notwithstanding, most positive American mythologies depend on a rural context. During the nineteenth century, as the colonization of the countryside by capital accelerated, the Jeffersonian ideal of a nation of small towns and farmers waned. Ralph Waldo Emerson's ideal "City of the West" was an attempt to reconcile nature and civilization, intended as a human community with open gates and open arms. Instead, cities, aided by absentee landlords and proto-agribusiness, began to suck up country energy and resources. By 1880, urban populations in the western United States were already growing at four times the rate of the countryside.

Herbert Gans observed in the late sixties that American society gives its allegiance to two poles — the micro-unit of the family and the macro-unit of the nation, while local community falls through the cracks. Today, one of those poles is collapsing: under half of eligible Americans voted in the 1996 presidential election.[2] This decline in participation in social policymaking can be seen as a product of a dehumanized urban ambience, the loss of a sense of local power in places where "neighborliness is often exhausted by a nod of the head."

The clichéd image of the cold, heartless city and the warm, cuddly heartland of small towns has long since been disproved. There is no Eden. But the sheer size of the metropolis can be intimidating as well as exhilarating and seems to belie communal intimacy. What, then, constitutes the lure of the local in this environment presumed to transcend any such effect? How do cities look and feel to those who live in them? And what are their relationships to the land they are built on, to the land people left to come to them?

Cities are enormously complex palimpsests of communal history and   5 memory, a fact that tends to be obscured by their primary identities as sites of immediacy, money, power, and energy concentrated on the present and future. Many people come to the city to escape the "local," the isolation of rural life, the rigidity and constrictions of smaller towns.

> We who live here wear this corner of the city like a comfortable old coat, an extension of our personalities, threadbare yet retaining a beauty of its own. This is the intimacy of cities, made more precious and more secret by our knowledge that it is one of many cells or corners in a great city that is not so much a labyrinth as a web or a shawl. We wrap ourselves in the city as we journey through it. Muffled, we march, "like Juno in a cloud," drawing it around us like a cloak of many colours: a disguise, a refuge, an adventure, a home.
>
> — ELIZABETH WILSON

The urban ego is in fact parochial; New Yorkers (like Parisians or Bostonians) are among the most provincial people in the world. They are often as bound to their own neighborhoods and as ignorant of the rest of the city

---

[2]The League of Women Voters estimates that 49 percent of eligible voters did vote in 1996, some 6 percent less than 1992, but other groups put the figure much lower; I read somewhere that only 39 percent voted in 1992.

(aside from midtown) as any small towner. A city is a center plus the sum of its neighborhoods, a collage created by juxtaposing apples and oranges. When I first lived in New York I would sometimes take the subway to a stop I'd never been to and spend hours walking in new territory, foreign countries. It was always interesting even when it was boring. All those people, all those little rooms. What were they doing in there? What lives were being played out so near and yet so far from my own? I loved my own life and didn't envy the women closed behind those doors; but at the same time I pictured an intimacy, a reassuring monotony that I knew I had surrendered forever.

Women in particular come to the city to break away from family expectations, domestic confinement, or to escape boredom and past mistakes. Some thrive on the crowds and new anonymity; others spend the rest of their lives thinking that someday they'll go "home." My own experience reflects Elizabeth Wilson's contention that the disorder of the city is a woman's medium, implying that it allows us to slip through the cracks of order: "The city is 'masculine' in its triumphal scale, its towers and vistas and arid industrial regions; it is 'feminine' in its enclosing embrace, in its indeterminacy and labyrinthine uncenteredness. We might even go so far as to claim that urban life is actually based on this perpetual struggle between rigid routinized order and pleasurable anarchy, the male-female dichotomy."

Where the citydweller may revel in her daily anonymity and freedom from self within crowded spaces, she also struggles to find an emotional community that will offer the intimacy for which Americans pine, even after we have made the choices that make it less and less likely. In small towns, if you go to the store, you must be prepared for at least minimal social intercourse. In cities, you can go out and float in your own space for hours, expending no more than an occasional monosyllabic request for food or services. You don't even have to say please and thank you if you're in an area where you don't expect to be seen again or where you just want to burn your bridges. However, spaces take on the aura of your interactions in them. There is a hardwon median between idiotically artificial courtesy and complete, even hostile, disregard.

Urban experience, vast and elusive, epitomizes the multicentered experience that fuels such energies. I'd include the arts among them. "One of the most fascinating aspects of place in recent years is that it has become more homogenous in some ways" — through mass culture — "and more heterogeneous in others" (through specialization and ghettoization), according to Sharon Zukin. The city is a social network, a web that entangles everyone who enters it, even the loneliest. Visually articulated by the syncretic cultures it contains, it is defined by a dialectic between the opinions of locals and of outsiders. Looking around in a city is visual overload (whereas looking around in a suburb tips the opposite end of the scale). Impressions are confused and even chaotic. Longtime residents rushing here and there often forget to look at their surroundings while newcomers and visitors get lost and overwhelmed.

The city is the site of delightful and terrifying encounters that could not 10

Times Square, New York City, billboard ads at night.

happen anywhere else. But each city is different, evoking different feelings in its residents and visitors, attractive to individuals at different moods of their lives. The light, the climate, the style, the materials, the flora and fauna (or lack thereof), the spaces and proportions, not to mention the demography and population, make cities and their neighborhoods unique. Cultural geographers have argued about whether the city is a series of reflections of "reality" held as images in the minds of its observers, or whether it is in itself a concrete representation, a collective work of art, a symbolic creation of those who inhabit it or those who control it.

Anne Spirn describes the city as an "infernal machine" with nobody coordinating it, nobody in charge, nobody taking responsibility or understanding the cumulative ecological effect of all the fragmented construction. Yet the city produces spaces and buildings, and even parks, that share its scale and impersonality. Class stratification is one component; especially in midtown New York, where the range of stores, restaurants, and modes of public transportation serves very different clients. Country estates may be inaccessible, and elite suburban neighborhoods guarded, but in cities, rich and poor occupy the same spaces. The habitats of the powerful and the powerless exist within tighter confines, side by side in sharp contrast. (As a child, I had a sitter who often detoured from our culturally determined route to Central Park; she took me to weddings in Fifth Avenue churches, as well as to a German bar in Yorkville where her boyfriend worked.) So long as we behave ourselves, any of us can loiter briefly outside the Plaza Hotel or Park Avenue apartment houses to glimpse the stomping grounds of the rich and famous, and the rich and famous must now and then drive through the Lower East Side or the South Bronx, or the outwardly colorless byways of Forest Hills or Sunnyside. . . .

Nature is fragmented and isolated in the city. Those who have no urge whatsoever to live in the country have houseplants to recall the existence of "nature," or to reassure themselves that nature can be or has been tamed: they go to parks to see trees. The more affluent have rooftop gardens, tiny designer back yards and bucolic weekend retreats. The less affluent cultivate community gardens. Even those who love the city and can live there comfortably look for ways of escaping it periodically, either by the Fresh Air Fund, vacations or, for the more privileged, weekend homes featuring lawns, trees, and other simulacra of small town life — visited, but not committed to. In 1956, Marshall McLuhan wrote that the city was in fact a return to the simultaneity that governed tribal cultures, in which "all experience and all past lives were *now.*" From the Native American historical viewpoint, cities simply replaced civilization. Artist Jimmie Durham decries the deracination of civic centers from their landscapes: "At one time New York was a city *on an island:* it was a city with a location in the physical world. Unlike villages or settlements, cities always establish themselves *against* their environment. . . . Where are we? We are in the European City. The United States is a political/cultural construction *against* the American continent. . . . There have been many, but it is hard for us to imagine a 'great sylvanization,' like a 'great civilization.' Civilizations, cities, build signs and monuments by definition and are then recognized by their signs. The sign of forest dwellers is the absence of monuments."

As soon as we move to a city, we search for our own center in it. In the absence of valid communal centers, cities need artificial symbolic centers like Saint Louis's Arch, Washington's Monument, or particularly obtrusive office buildings that function (only) visually as the church spire once did, marking the place where power is abstracted and institutionalized. Landmarks have to be imposing and/or charged with celebrity status to claim attention. New York's Chrysler and Empire State buildings are classic examples. Like earlier skyscrapers, they were probably inspired to some extent by the "stateliness of the American landscape."[3] [Then] they [were] outgrown but not outclassed by the bland towers of the World Trade Center.[4] Giant complexes like Battery Park City in Lower Manhattan, created by celebrity architects and usually accompanied by large-scale, expensive public art, are "designer" objects "of quality," veiling the reality of social polarization in "real life." Generating ideological vibes of domination through spectacle, such control centers can be seen, Darrel Crilley observes, "not as signs of enduring vitality, but as enormous

---

[3]*Cosmopolitan,* 1875, quoted in Gwendolyn Wright.
[4]This reading was first published in 1997.—Eds.

and cautionary symbols of changes underway in the relationship between property development and aesthetics."

> I view great cities as pestilential to the morals, the health and the liberties of man. True, they nourish some of the elegant arts, but the useful ones can thrive elsewhere, and less perfection in the others, with more health, virtue and freedom, would be my choice.
>
> — THOMAS JEFFERSON (in the midst of a yellow-fever epidemic)

The city's image remains negative, or Un-American, in opposition to the "family values" purportedly nourished outside of these "dens of iniquity." One reason for this bad press is that cities have traditionally been the homes of the sinful arts. Marxists have noted that in order to maintain its dynamism, capitalism must keep destroying and recreating itself, whether through planned obsolescence or a novelty-driven art market. For economic as well as aesthetic and educational reasons, artists are attracted to change.

The city visibly illustrates the dialectic between the heterogenous market, 15 where everything is for sale, and the homogenous place, where people resist the processes of defamiliarization and change. As new ideas and new money-making schemes pop up each day, the most imposing structures can prove short lived. The social cacophony of a big city multiplies exponentially with its diversity and excess of nervous energy. At the same time, the dissolution of its familiar landscapes has the same effect on its inhabitants as slower changes in the countryside. The rug is pulled out from under our sense of self when stores close or switch functions, when vacant lots appear or disappear, or when buildings are remodeled. Even when the changes are for the better, the ghosts remain.

WORKS CITED

Crilley, Darrel. "Megastructures and Urban Change: Aesthetics, Ideology, and Design." In Paul Knox, ed., *The Restless Urban Landscape.* Englewood Cliffs, N.J.: Prentice Hall, 1993.

Durham, Jimmie. *A Certain Lack of Coherence: Writings on Art and Cultural Politics,* ed. Jean Fisher. London: Kala Press, 1993.

Jefferson, Thomas. *Primary Documents,* no. 4, 1995.

McLuhan, Marshall. "The Media Fit the Battle of Jericho." *Explorations Six,* July 1956.

Spirn, Anne W. *The Granite Garden: Urban Nature and Human Design.* New York: Basic Books, 1984.

Tuan, Yi-Fu. *Topophilia: A Study of Environmental Perception, Attitudes and Values.* Englewood Cliffs, N.J.: Prentice Hall, 1974.

Wilson, Elizabeth. *The Sphinx in the City.* Berkeley: University of California Press, 1991.

Wright, Gwendolyn. *Building the Dream: A Social History of Housing in America.* New York: Pantheon Books, 1981.

Zukin, Sharon. *Landscapes of Power: From Detroit to Disney World.* Berkeley: University of California Press, 1991.

READING THE TEXT

1. Define in your own words the "alternating current," as Lippard puts it, "that pulls at most Americans at various times in their lives" (para. 1).

2. According to Lippard, what differential mythological significances do urban and rural areas have?

3. What role does nature play in the cityscape, in Lippard's view?

4. What are the assumptions underlying the common image of the city as "negative, or Un-American" (para. 14)?

5. Why does Lippard assert that women especially find freedom in city life?

READING THE SIGNS

1. Whether you live in a rural or urban environment, reflect in your journal on Lippard's claim that most Americans feel torn between the country and the city at some point in their lives. Have you felt this "alternating current" (para. 1) yourself? Why or why not? If you have, in what way did you resolve the competing desires?

2. Today many Americans live neither in the city nor the country; they live in suburbs. Using Lippard's discussion of the mythologies of the city and country as a model, write an essay in which you analyze the suburb's mythological significance.

3. If you live in a city, conduct a survey of local residents that addresses the "lure" that the urban environment has for them. Use your results to formulate a response to Lippard's question "What . . . constitutes the lure of the local in this environment presumed to transcend any such effect?" (para. 4).

4. Study the landmarks in a city close to you. To what extent do they bear out Lippard's contention that "landmarks have to be imposing and/or charged with celebrity status to claim attention" (para. 13)? Alternately, if you do not live near a city, study the landmarks in a small town or village. What messages do they send to the people who observe them?

5. Write an essay in which you evaluate the validity of Lippard's contention that women can feel more liberated in an urban environment than in a rural community.

KAREN KARBO

The Dining Room

*Real estate agents usually feature the number of bedrooms a house has,
or the view from the deck, but we all know that, for better or for worse,
the family dining room is where the action is. And in this memoir, written in an unusual second-person form, of a life begun in Southern California, Karen Karbo (b. 1956) focuses on the role her family's dining
rooms have had in her life. Here is where "your father never knows what
to say" and you "are not allowed to leave anything on the table." At once
funny and tragic, Karbo's memories assume a near-universal dimension
for just about anyone who has grown up in the United States. A correspondent for* Outside *magazine, Karbo is the author of* Big Girl in the
Middle *(with Gabrielle Reece, 1997),* Motherhood Made a Man Out of
Me *(2000), and* Generation EX: Tales from the Second Wives Club
(2001).

You live with your parents in an apartment building called the Something
Arms in Sherman Oaks, a sun-blasted suburb of Los Angeles. The building is
standard Sun Belt issue, white stucco flecked with gold, a rectangular swimming pool with no diving board, a panel of mailboxes just inside the front
gate. You live in an upstairs apartment overlooking the Dumpsters. Your
dining-room table is a card table, your dining room is the kitchen side of the
living room. They are just starting out, your parents. It is 1962.

Every stuffy apartment has a kid or two in it. All you need to go swimming is one adult sitting poolside. It is usually a mother. It is usually your
mother, who can't swim herself, who is allergic to the sun, but has an itch, always, to be out of the apartment. She is a woman with itches, your mother.
Days before she dies she will admit as much. She will tell you she was born in
the wrong time. She will tell you she should have been you.

One afternoon, when you are five or six, you are showing your mother
how you can swim the entire length of the pool without coming up for air.
Your mother is sitting on a chaise, drinking a beer and clipping articles about
decorating from *Family Circle*. You go under and she is watching you from
over the rim of her glass. When you come up you find her talking to Bernie
the mailman. She is making him laugh with a story about how, in her high
school Senior Will, she bequeathed her thick copper-colored hair to every girl
in the school. How she got on to this subject, you will never know. It is part of
what your mother calls the Gift of Gab, something, along with your mother's
fine hair, you failed to inherit.

The dining-room table, the card table, is the only table in the apartment.
Your mother sews at this table, hemming large squares of floral fabric in the

earth tones of the era — brown, gold, avocado — tablecloths for this very table. You learn cursive writing at this table, your pencil marks pocked and wobbly from writing on the squishy vinyl surface.

At parent-teacher conferences, Mrs. Warnack, your first-grade teacher, tells your mother that your writing resembles the hand of Mrs. Warnack's maiden aunt.

You ask your mother, What's maiden? Your mother says it's what happens when a girl winds up old and unloved.

Mrs. Warnack also tells your mother that while she enjoys having you in class, you need to learn self-control.

You ask your mother, What's self-control? Your mother says not having it is how a girl winds up old and unloved.

When your parents have saved up enough for a down payment, they move to a house in the suburbs, a tract house on the border of Whittier and La Habra, also the border of Los Angeles County and Orange County.

One side of the street has sidewalks but no streetlights (Orange County), the other side has streetlights but no sidewalks (Los Angeles County). Your mother trains you to always say you live in Whittier, on account of it is the hometown of President Nixon, whom your mother worked to help elect. It also has a college, from which President Nixon graduated. La Habra has a lot of Mexicans. Not that we're better than Them, says your mother, but we're Whittier people.

In Whittier, you have a real dining-room table. Your mother calls it a dining-room suite. The suite is made of some heavy wood, ashy brown with little black flecks. The table comes with a couple of leaves, stretching it to seat about eight hundred. The style is Mediterranean, with six matching chairs and a sideboard that, your mother says, nearly gave the furniture delivery man a hernia. She is proud of this fact, her expensive dining-room suite bringing a man to his knees, literally. Now, she says, she can Entertain.

Entertaining means Parties. Your mother likes the minor holidays, Saint Patrick's Day, Memorial Day. One Halloween, the dining-room table is covered with a black paper tablecloth, orange crepe paper streamers twist away from the chandelier, not crystal, but cut glass, bought on time from a furniture store next to the Polar Palace, where you sometimes go ice skating, hoping someone will ask you to skate. Your mother has spent the last two days making Sweet and Sour Meatballs, liver pâté, and a lot of other grown-up food. The night of the party she is dressed in red leotards, black felt tail, and horns.

You ask your mother, Are you a devil, or what?

Your mother says, *The* Devil, sweetheart.

The Whittier dining room is still the kitchen side of the living room, but the living room is bigger than in the Sherman Oaks apartment. It is Fancy. It has burnt orange shag carpeting. On the windows facing the patio are gold brocade curtains that are tied back with thick gold cords with tassels. You like to tickle the dog's nose with the tassel, making him sneeze.

You are not allowed to leave anything on the table. You do your homework on the Formica breakfast bar in the kitchen, where your handwriting improves, and where you eat breakfast and dinner six days a week on all non-Holidays and all non–Other Special Occasions.

The Other Special Occasions include Sunday dinner, birthday dinners, graduation dinners, and the few times you have a boy over to dinner. You can count the number of times you have a boy over to dinner on one hand. You can count the number of boys you actually like who come to dinner on one finger.

Jeff is the summer of eighth grade going into ninth. He is perfect because he is one of three boys in the ninth grade who is taller than you. Together, you make tie-dye T-shirts and make out in the pool when your mother is out at the A&P. Jeff introduces you to hickeys and shoplifting. He knows the meaning of all the lyrics on the soundtrack of *Hair*.

Jeff has hair to his shoulders, streaked with auburn from the sun. Your mother says she doesn't like it, it makes him a hippy pot-smoking flower child, but once you saw her hold it back for him while he was leaning to get a drink of water from the tap at the sink. When you do this you are told to get a glass.

Another time your mother chases Jeff around the kitchen, trying to put his hair in pigtails, while you take pictures with your Instamatic. After you get the pictures back your mother says you shouldn't have taken pictures. You humiliated him. 20

When Jeff eats over, it is always in the dining room. Having what your mother calls a beau is a Special Occasion. You are never sure if Jeff is your beau or just your friend, and neither is Jeff. You worry, because according to your mother, he has to be one or the other. If he kisses you, he is a beau. But what if he also talks about other girls he has kissed? Other *boys* he has kissed? You ask your mother. She says, Just don't let him touch you above your knees or below your shoulders. That's for after you're married. You ask her this while she is sewing you a halter dress, backless, pink gingham. Sexy, you think, but you're not quite sure.

Dinner in the dining room always has beef in it. It is always white, green, and brown — potatoes, vegetables, and the beef. Or it's something that takes forever to cook. Beef Stroganoff, something that needs to simmer. There are Pop 'n' Fresh rolls in a basket, coddled in a cloth napkin that matches the Linen. The Linen is not bought at a department store.

The last time Jeff has dinner at your house he has already found a new girl that he likes, a girl one grade older who, it is rumored, Puts Out. You don't Put Out, you've obeyed your mother. Of all the things you must do to make a boy like you, Putting Out, the one thing he would like you to do above all others, is exactly the thing you must never do. Your mother says it's a little like holding a dog treat just above the dog's nose, so he can smell it but never quite reach it. You say, Yeah, but am I the treat or the person holding the treat? Both, says your mother.

No matter where your family eats, your father never knows what to say. He is an engineer. He can rebuild a sports car from the lug nuts up, but has trouble with simple conversation. No problem, usually, because your mother does all the talking. All the planning, all the shopping, all the cooking, all the table setting, all the serving. On the last night Jeff has dinner at your house, the last night he kisses you, although you will hold a torch for him well into college, where he becomes an art major and the lover of a man ten years his senior, your father attempts a joke.

"What's a wild goose?" 25

"I don't know, Dad, what's a wild goose?"

"About this much off center." He holds up his thumb and forefinger, displaying an invisible inch.

Jeff goes har-har-har. Phony? You can't tell. You don't get it. Jeff is sitting across from you. You catch his eye, mouth the words "I don't get it." He rolls his eyes. He mouths something back, he spells something, three letters, *a-s-s*, partly cupping his hand. You struggle to understand.

You ask your mother, What does an ass have to do with a goose?

Jeff rounds his shoulders, collapsing in on himself like a Halloween pump- 30 kin past its prime. Your mother has a laugh like a machine gun. Your father blushes, mute.

At your birthday dinner, a few months later, there is a present at your place, beside your crystal water glass: *How to Get a Teenage Boy and What to Do with Him When You Get Him*. Not let your father tell jokes, you think, although that seems to be the least of your problems.

When your mother gets the itch to remodel, she has the living room extended to make a real dining room. There are now two steps up and a sliding glass door leading out to the patio. The construction guys arrive a little after seven in the morning and sometimes stay until dinner. Sometimes, you come home from swim team in the afternoon to find the main construction guy having a beer with your mother.

In 1971 there is a huge earthquake, one that will make world news. Most earthquakes are like train rides, but this one feels as if you're standing on a carpet that's being shaken out by unseen hands. You and your mother lunge for the door between the kitchen and the dining room at the same time. You stand there, you two, wedged shoulder to shoulder in the door frame, looking out the sliding glass door, watching while the surface of the swimming pool gathers itself into a tidal wave. You watch while the water slops over the side of the pool, runs down the patio, and sloshes against the sliding glass door, where it seeps beneath the door, drenching the burnt orange shag. Your mother, not a native Californian, worries to the point of insomnia about mildew for weeks. Once, getting up in the middle of the night to use the bathroom, you catch her in her olive green quilted bathrobe, down on her hands and knees, sniffing the carpet.

Senior year, you and most of your friends are not invited to the prom. The Cool Crowd, the soshes, has decided that the prom is only for losers, and as you are in the Second Coolest Crowd, you decide the same thing. You are relieved, since, as your mother says, There is no one Decent on the horizon anyway.

The one boy who she has decided is Decent is Steve, the older brother of 35 one of your friends. Steve has already graduated and gone away to college in Colorado. Your mother buys you special stationery so you can write him letters at his dorm. Steve has had the same girlfriend for years, but she has a terminal disease, so there is hope for you. Steve actually answers your letters. He addresses you Hey Foxy! Your mother put you on Dr. Stillman's diet, hard-boiled eggs and dietetic Jell-O, for when Steve comes home for the summer.

In the meantime, your mother decides you should host a dinner party the night of the prom. She will let each of your guests have a glass of Chablis if you help her plan the menu. You know what this means: cooking. Your mother has forbidden you to take typing in school because, she says, you are destined for Greater things. You secretly feel the same way about cooking.

You and your mother have a fight. You are not going to help plan the menu. You want to know why you can't just eat *food,* why does it always have to be a menu. You don't give a shit about one measly glass of Chablis, you use that word, *shit*. She slaps you across the face. You surprise yourself by slapping her right back. Your fingers leave stripes on her cheek. You say you don't want a dinner party. You say if she's so hot to have a dinner party, she should have one for her own friends and leave yours alone. She says you're an ingrate. You wail, Stop prosecuting me! Your mother's anger dissolves, diluted by amusement.

It's *persecuting*, she says. You're not as smart as you think you are, she says, and I thank the dear Lord for that.

You don't help with the menu, but get your glass of wine anyway. The afternoon of the prom is warm, the evening rose-colored. Even in this stupid suburb (you already know that Whittier, La Habra, whatever you want to call it is a place made for leaving) the evening smells of orange blossoms and possibilities, the kind of evening that, for the rest of your life, for reasons you will never understand, makes you ache. What you will understand is that this kind of evening also made your mother ache, and that's why she cooked.

You have seven friends over. You wear your pink gingham halter dress. Your mother had made lasagna, which she calls la-zag-na, thinking she's funny, a tossed green salad, garlic bread, and Dutch Chocolate Whip 'n' Chill for dessert. You eat off her bone china, use her silver service, then pile into her car, a 1964 Ford Galaxy convertible. You drink sloe gin and 7-Up, you cruise Whittier Boulevard, then cruise the high school, you get so drunk you throw up over the side of your mother's car. You take the car through the all-night, do-it-yourself car wash, spraying chunks of ricotta cheese off the side of the car. You vow to get out of Whittier, La Habra, whatever you want to call it, and never come back.

You go to college, a private college in Los Angeles, thirty minutes away in light traffic. At college, there are many Decent boys on the horizon. More Our Ilk, says your mother.

Your mother keeps track of your boyfriends by their fathers' professions. Mr. Golden West Broadcasting has a father who's the head of production there. Mr. Sunkist's father is vice president. There is also a Mr. Neurosurgeon.

When you talk to your mother on the phone she says, I can't keep your boyfriends straight! She always wants you to bring them home for dinner. You don't, because you can't. Mainly because Mr. Golden West Broadcasting, Mr. Sunkist, and Mr. Neurosurgeon are not your boyfriends. They are boys you know from a class or they are the boyfriends of your new sorority sisters. You pretend they are yours, because you know hearing about them will make your mother happy, and she is.

You should have known something was up when no one was invited to Thanksgiving. Thanksgiving is your mother's favorite holiday. It required days of menu-planning and shopping, getting up in pre-dawn darkness to put in the turkey. It required inviting Family, who drank more than they ate, and were sent stumbling to their cars with paper plates bowed with leftovers.

But this year, it is just you and your father and your mother. Your mother isn't feeling well. She has one of her headaches. She sits at her usual place at the head of the table, trying to slide a mound of stuffing onto her fork, then working to bring the fork to her mouth. She makes it look as difficult as a party trick. If you were either a child or an adult, you would notice that she is not right. But you are seventeen, and only have eyes for yourself.

Twenty minutes after you arrive at your dorm your father calls to tell you what he couldn't bring himself to tell you at the dining-room table: in a week, your mother will have exploratory brain surgery.

You ask your father, Will she be okay?

Your father says, Of course.

After the surgery, the surgeon comes out in his greens. He looks at you, but he talks to your father. The surgeon says, "How old is she?"

Your mother doesn't die right away, but her personality does. The tumor was shaped like a plate of spaghetti minus the plate. To remove as much of it as possible, they needed to take a goodly amount of healthy brain tissue. *Goodly* is the surgeon's word. You ask your father, in the car on the way home, What does he mean by goodly? A sound comes out of your father, like someone gasping for air.

Your mother comes home from the hospital. She stops cooking, but she refuses to stop smoking. You do not have Friday classes, so you come home every weekend on Thursday afternoon. You come home every Thursday afternoon to find her sitting in the kitchen, at the Formica breakfast bar, trying to get the cigarette to stay between her fingers. She wraps a rubber band around the top of her index and middle fingers to keep them closed.

You drive her to chemo on Friday. Afterward, you stop for a box of glazed doughnuts, her lunch. She sits at the dining-room table while you tell her about your boyfriends. It doesn't matter that this is not an Occasion. The way you make it sound, a marriage proposal is just around the corner.

You do have a date with a boy from your oceanography class. He is Mr. Head Lettuce; his father owns a corporate farm in Bakersfield. You don't tell your mother about Mr. Head Lettuce. You don't know why. You have the feeling she won't understand that his father isn't a hick with manure beneath his fingernails; also, you make Mr. Head Lettuce cry, telling him how your mother is dying, only she doesn't really know it. She knows it, then she forgets it.

You and Mr. Head Lettuce stand in line for six hours to see *The Exorcist*. It gives you a lot of time to talk.

You tell him how, just last week, your mother told you she wanted Fun Mom 55
put on her headstone. You were sitting at the dining-room table. She was eating
her glazed doughnuts straight from the box, flecks of glaze on her chin.

Your mother says, Aren't I the Funnest Mom you know?

You say, You are.

Your mother says, Don't humor me because I look like a plucked chicken.
Do I look like a plucked chicken?

In the first days after her surgery, your mother gamely bought a wardrobe
of turbans, all in shades of orange — apricot, squash, and tangerine. Now, she
doesn't bother. Her hair is gone. On one side of her head is the scar, scabby, a
rusty croquet wicket. Scratching it has become a bad habit, something she
does when she isn't smoking or eating.

Mr. Head Lettuce whispers, Are you close to her, your mother I mean?   60

You say, I don't know. Sure.

You mean, Yes. You mean, No. You mean, N/A. It's like asking if your left
leg is close to your right leg.

You never go out with Mr. Head Lettuce again. No one is touching you
above your knees or below your shoulders. Your mother should be relieved,
but you know this is not what she had in mind. No one is touching you at all.

Then, a miracle happens.

Suddenly, there is a Boy, Mr. Orthodontist from Palos Verdes. His name is 65
also Jeff. You meet him at a fraternity mixer and you hear through the
grapevine that he is going to ask you out, and — this is the miracle — the
grapevine was right, he does ask you out. He asks you out for the night of
your eighteenth birthday.

You are expected home for your birthday, which falls on a Saturday that
year. You come home in the afternoon to find the dining-room table already
set. The gold brocade curtains are open, sun filters through the dark pink
bougainvillea that covers the trellis over the patio. The table is covered with a
gold tablecloth, the cut crystal is out, two glasses at each place, one for water,
one for wine.

At your place, oddly, there is a stack of identical envelopes. Birthday cards
that came in the mail? You don't think you know that many people.

Your mother shuffles in with another card for the pile. She is supposed to
be getting better, your mother, but something in you knows that you don't get
better from this; the most you can hope for is not getting worse.

You flip through the cards, recognizing her palsied handwriting on each
envelope. You and your mother understand what has happened at the same
moment. Apparently, she couldn't remember whether she'd gotten you a
card or not.

Your mother says, They are all from me.   70

Dinner is prime rib with baked potato. Sour cream and chives, only your
mother brings out Cool Whip and chives. You look at your father over the table.
He will not meet your gaze. He slices open his potato, then leaves it empty. Your
mother bypasses her potato, spooning Cool Whip directly into her mouth.

You, like your mother, are a woman with itches. Suddenly, you itch to get away. Away from this dining-room table, away from this tract house, this suburb, this life. You stand up, in the middle of your birthday dinner and say, I have a date. I have to go.

Your father says, Your mother worked for a week on this meal.

Your mother says, Let her go.

It is the last thing your mother ever says to you.   75

You date Mr. Orthodontist twice, then set him up with a sorority sister he eventually marries. Six days after your birthday, your father calls, crying incoherently — you think it's an obscene phone call — to say that your mother has gone into a coma. She lives like that for a day and a night. A month after your mother's death, your father sells her dining-room suite. You note he sells it at a loss.

READING THE TEXT

1. Karbo uses the second-person address ("you") in this selection, even though, as a memoir, it describes her own experiences. How does the second person affect your reading of this selection?

2. Karbo elects to capitalize some words that normally do not require capitalization (for instance, "Entertain," "Fancy"). What message does she communicate by using such capitalization?

3. Characterize Karbo's and her mother's relationships to the male characters, including Karbo's father, her boyfriends, and visitors to the house. How do they compare?

4. Why does Karbo's father sells the dining-room suite after her mother dies?

5. In class, write on the board passages from "The Dining Room" you find humorous. Discuss why you think Karbo includes such humor and its effect on the reader.

READING THE SIGNS

1. Write an essay in which you analyze the ways in which the various dining tables and rooms that Karbo describes symbolize her relationship with her mother. What connection do you see in the differences in physical spaces and in the evolution of the daughter-mother relationship as Karbo grows up?

2. Karbo describes her mother from her point of view. Study the selection, looking for clues that would allow you to infer her mother's attitudes throughout the piece. Then try some role-playing: assume the role of Karbo's mother, and write her remembrance of the dining rooms that this selection describes.

3. In a journal entry, write a memoir of a physical place, whether in your own home or elsewhere, that symbolizes your relationship with family members or others important in your life.

4. Chart Karbo's characterization of her mother before and after she develops a brain tumor. How does that characterization evolve, both in content and in tone? Use your observations as evidence for a stylistic analysis of this selection.

RICHARD HUTCHINGS

ARGUMENT AT DINNER

1. What evidence in the photo supports the idea that this group of people is a family? How would you characterize their relationships? What event is taking place?

2. Assume that this scene has been staged for the camera. Why has the photographer chosen to position the people as they are? Describe how each character contributes to the overall effect of the scene.

3. Write a scene in which you imagine dialogue for the characters in the photograph.

DAPHNE SPAIN

Spatial Segregation and Gender Stratification in the Workplace

> *In the spatial hierarchy of the American workplace, having a private office all to yourself is one of the most visible signifiers of status within the organization. But as Daphne Spain reveals, the spatial arrangement of the ordinary workplace is often a marker of gender relations as well. With most women working in "open-floor" (such as secretarial) occupations, and most men frequently enjoying "closed-door" (or managerial) positions, a certain level of gender segregation is to be found in the typical American workplace. Analyzing the social implications of this stratification of working space, Spain shows how the architecture of the workplace not only reflects but reinforces existing gender hierarchies. Daphne Spain teaches in the School of Architecture at the University of Virginia and is the author of* Gendered Spaces *(1992), from which this selection is taken, and co-author, with Suzanne M. Bianchi, of* Balancing Act: Motherhood, Marriage, and Employment among American Women *(1996).*

To what extent do women and men who work in different occupations also work in different spaces? Baran and Teegarden (1987, 206) propose that occupational segregation in the insurance industry is "tantamount to spatial segregation by gender" since managers are overwhelmingly male and clerical staff are predominantly female. This essay examines the spatial conditions of women's work and men's work and proposes that working women and men come into daily contact with one another very infrequently. Further, women's jobs can be classified as "open floor," but men's jobs are more likely to be "closed door." That is, women work in a more public environment with less control of their space than men. This lack of spatial control both reflects and contributes to women's lower occupational status by limiting opportunities for the transfer of knowledge from men to women.

It bears repeating that my argument concerning space and status deals with structural workplace arrangements of women as a group and men as a group, *not* with occupational mobility for individual men and women. Extraordinary people always escape the statistical norm and experience upward mobility under a variety of circumstances. The emphasis here is on the ways in which workplaces are structured to provide different spatial arrangements for the typical working woman and the typical working man and how those arrangements contribute to gender stratification. . . .

443

Typical Women's Work: "Open-Floor Jobs"

A significant proportion of women are employed in just three occupations: teaching, nursing, and secretarial work. In 1990 these three categories alone accounted for 16.5 million women, or 31 percent of all women in the labor force (U.S. Department of Labor 1991, 163, 183). Aside from being concentrated in occupations that bring them primarily into contact with other women, women are also concentrated spatially in jobs that limit their access to knowledge. The work of elementary schoolteachers, for example, brings them into daily contact with children, but with few other adults. When not dealing with patients, nurses spend their time in a lounge separate from the doctors' lounge. Nursing and teaching share common spatial characteristics with the third major "women's job" — that of secretary.

Secretarial/clerical work is the single largest job category for American women. In 1990, 14.9 million women, or more than one of every four employed women, were classified as "administrative support, including clerical"; 98 percent of all secretaries are female (U.S. Department of Labor 1991, 163, 183). Secretarial and clerical occupations account for over three-quarters of this category and epitomize the typical "woman's job." It is similar to teaching and nursing in terms of the spatial context in which it occurs.

Two spatial aspects of secretarial work operate to reduce women's status. 5 One is the concentration of many women together in one place (the secretarial "pool") that removes them from observation of and/or input into the decision-making processes of the organization. Those decisions occur behind the "closed doors" of the managers' offices. Second, paradoxically, is the very public nature of the space in which secretaries work. The lack of privacy, repeated interruptions, and potential for surveillance contribute to an inability to turn valuable knowledge into human capital that might advance careers or improve women's salaries relative to men's.

Like teachers and nurses, secretaries process knowledge, but seldom in a way beneficial to their own status. In fact, secretaries may wield considerable informal power in an organization, because they control the information flow. Management, however, has very clear expectations about how secretaries are to handle office information. Drawing from their successful experience with grid theory, business consultants Robert Blake, Jane Mouton, and Artie Stockton have outlined the ideal boss-secretary relationship for effective office teamwork. In the first chapter of *The Secretary Grid,* an American Management Association publication, the following advice is offered:

> The secretary's position at the center of the information network raises the issue of privileged communications and how best to handle it. Privileged communication is information the secretary is not free to divulge, no matter how helpful it might be to others. And the key to handling it is the answer to the question "Who owns the information?" The answer is, "The

boss does." . . . The secretary's position with regard to this information is that of the hotel desk clerk to the contents of the safety deposit box that stores the guest's valuables. She doesn't own it, but she knows what it is and what is in it. The root of the word *secretary* is, after all, *secret:* something kept from the knowledge of others. (Blake, Mouton, and Stockton 1983, 4–5; emphasis in original)

In other words, secretaries are paid *not* to use their knowledge for personal gain, but only for their employers' gain. The workplace arrangements that separate secretaries from managers within the same office reinforce status differences by exposing the secretary mainly to other secretaries bound by the same rules of confidentiality. Lack of access to and interaction with managers inherently limits the status women can achieve within the organization.

The executive secretary is an exception to the rule of gendered spatial segregation in the workplace. The executive secretary may have her own office, and she has access to more aspects of the managerial process than other secretaries. According to another American Management Association publication titled *The Successful Secretary:* "Probably no person gets to observe and see management principles in operation on a more practical basis than an executive secretary. She is privy to nearly every decision the executive makes. She has the opportunity to witness the gathering of information and the elements that are considered before major decisions are made and implemented" (Belker 1981, 191).

Yet instructions to the successful executive secretary suggest that those with the closest access to power are subject to the strictest guidelines regarding confidentiality. When physical barriers are breached and secretaries spend a great deal of time with the managers, rules governing the secretary's use of information become more important. The executive secretary is cautioned to hide shorthand notes, remove partially typed letters from the typewriter, lock files, and personally deliver interoffice memos to prevent unauthorized persons from gaining confidential information from the boss's office (Belker 1981, 66).

The executive secretary has access to substantial information about the company, but the highest compliment that can be paid her is that she does not divulge it to anyone or use it for personal gain. Comparing the importance of confidentiality to the seal of the confessional, Belker counsels secretaries that "the importance of confidentiality can't be over-emphasized. Your company can be involved in some delicate business matters or negotiations, and the wrong thing leaked to the wrong person could have an adverse effect on the result. . . . Years ago, executive secretaries were sometimes referred to as confidential secretaries. It's a shame that title fell out of popular usage, because it's an accurate description of the job" (Belker 1981, 73–74).

Typical Men's Work: "Closed-Door Jobs"

The largest occupational category for men is that of manager. In 1990, 8.9 million men were classified as "executive, administrative, and managerial." This group constituted 14 percent of all employed men (U.S. Department of Labor 1991, 163, 183). Thus, more than one in ten men works in a supervisory position.

Spatial arrangements in the workplace reinforce these status distinctions, partially by providing more "closed door" potential to managers than to those they supervise. Although sales and production supervisors may circulate among their employees, their higher status within the organization is reflected by the private offices to which they can withdraw. The expectation is that privacy is required for making decisions that affect the organization. Rather than sharing this privacy, the secretary is often in charge of "gatekeeping" — protecting the boss from interruptions.

Just as there are professional manuals for the successful secretary, there are also numerous guidelines for the aspiring manager. Harry Levinson's widely read *Executive* (1981) (a revision of his 1968 *The Exceptional Executive*) stresses the importance of managerial knowledge of the entire organization. A survey of large American companies asking presidents about suitable qualities in their successors revealed the following profile: "A desirable successor is a person with a general knowledge and an understanding of the whole organization, capable of fitting specialized contributions into profitable patterns. . . . The person needs a wide range of liberal arts knowledge together with a fundamental knowledge of business. . . . A leader will be able to view the business in global historical and technical perspective. Such a perspective is itself the basis for the most important requisite, what one might call 'feel' — a certain intuitive sensitivity for the right action and for handling relationships with people" (Levinson 1981, 136).

The importance of knowledge is stressed repeatedly in this description. The successful manager needs knowledge of the organization, of liberal arts, and of business in general. But equally important is the intuitive ability to carry out actions. This "feel" is not truly intuitive, of course, but is developed through observation and emulation of successful executives. Levinson identifies managerial leadership as "an art to be cultivated and developed," which is why it cannot be learned by the book; rather, "it must be learned in a relationship, through identification with a teacher" (Levinson 1981, 145).

Because the transfer of knowledge and the ability to use it are so crucial 15 to leadership, Levinson devotes a chapter to "The Executive as Teacher." He advises that there is no prescription an executive can follow in acting as a teacher. The best strategy is the "shine and show them" approach — the manager carries out the duties of office as effectively as possible and thereby demonstrates to subordinates how decisions are made. There are no formal conditions under which teaching takes place; it is incorporated as part of the routine of the business day. In Levinson's words, "The process of example-setting goes on all the time. Executives behave in certain ways, sizing up problems, considering the resources . . . that can be utilized to meet them, and making decisions about procedure. Subordinates, likewise, watch what they are doing and how they do it" (Levinson 1981, 154).

Just as in the ceremonial men's huts of nonindustrial societies, constant contact between elders and initiates is necessary for the transmission of knowledge. Levinson implies that it should be frequent contact to transfer most effectively formal and informal knowledge. Such frequent and significant contact is missing from the interaction between managers and secretaries. Given the spatial distance between the closed doors of managers and the open floors of secretaries, it is highly unlikely that sufficient contact between the two groups could occur for secretaries to alter their positions within the organization.

In addition to giving subordinates an opportunity to learn from the boss, spatial proximity provides opportunities for subordinates to be seen by the boss. This opportunity has been labeled "visiposure" by the author of *Routes to the Executive Suite* (Jennings 1971, 113). A combination of "visibility" and "exposure," visiposure refers to the opportunity to "see and be seen by the right people" (Jennings 1971, 113). Jennings counsels the rising executive that "the abilities to see and copy those who can influence his career and to keep himself in view of those who might promote him are all-important to success." The ultimate form of visiposure is for the subordinate's manager to be seen by the right managers as well. Such "serial visiposure" is the "sine qua non of fast upward mobility" and is facilitated by face-to-face interaction among several levels of managers and subordinates (Jennings 1971, 113–14).

Both Levinson and Jennings acknowledge the importance of physical proximity to achieving power within an organization, yet neither pursues the assumptions underlying the transactions they discuss — that is, the spatial context within which such interactions occur. To the extent women are segregated from men, the transfer of knowledge — with the potential for improving women's status — is limited.

Office Design and Gender Stratification

Contemporary office design clearly reflects the spatial segregation separating women and men. Secretaries (almost all of whom are women) and managers (nearly two-thirds of whom are men) have designated areas assigned within the organization. . . .

Privacy can be a scarce resource in the modern office. Empirical studies [20] have shown that privacy in the office involves "the ability to control access to one's self or group, particularly the ability to *limit others' access to one's workspace*" (Sundstrom 1986, 178; emphasis added). Business executives commonly define privacy as the ability to control information and space. In other words, privacy is connected in people's minds with the spatial reinforcement of secrecy. Studies of executives, managers, technicians, and clerical employees have found a high correlation between enclosure of the work space (walls and doors) and perceptions of privacy; the greater the privacy, the greater the satisfaction with work. Employees perceive spatial control as a resource in the workplace that affects their job satisfaction and performance (Sundstrom, Burt, and Kemp 1980; Sundstrom 1986).

Not surprisingly, higher status within an organization is accompanied by greater control of space. In the Sundstrom study, most secretaries (75 percent) reported sharing an office; about one-half (55 percent) of bookkeepers and accountants shared an office; and only 18 percent of managers and administrators shared space. Secretaries had the least physical separation from other workers, while executives had the most (Sundstrom 1986, 184).

Two aspects of the work environment are striking when the spatial features of the workplaces for secretaries and executives are compared: the low number of walls or partitions surrounding secretaries (an average of 2.1), compared with executives (an average of 3.5), and the greater surveillance that accompanies the public space of secretaries. Three-quarters of all secretaries were visible to their supervisors, compared with only one-tenth of executives. As one would expect given the physical description of their respective offices, executives report the greatest sense of privacy and secretaries the least (Sundstrom 1986, 185). Doors do not necessarily have to be closed or locked in order to convey the message of differential power; they merely have to be available for closing and be seen as controlled at the executive's discretion (Steele 1986, 46).

The spatial distribution of employees in an office highlights the complex ways in which spatial segregation contributes to gender stratification. Workers obviously are not assigned space on the basis of sex, but on the basis of their positions within the organization. Theoretically, managers have the most complex jobs and secretaries have the least complex, yet research on secretaries and managers with equal degrees of office enclosure suggests that women's space is still considered more public than men's space. Sundstrom found that "in the workspaces with equivalent enclosure — private offices — [respondents] showed differential ratings of privacy, with lowest ratings by secretaries. This could reflect social norms. Secretaries have low ranks, and co-workers or visitors may feel free to walk unannounced into their workspaces. However, they may knock respectfully at the entrance of the workspaces of managers. . . . *Perhaps a private office is more private when occupied by a manager than when occupied by a secretary*" (Sundstrom 1986, 191; emphasis added). This passage suggests that even walls and a door do not insure privacy for the typical working woman in the same way they do for the typical working man. Features that should allow control of workspace do not operate for secretaries as they do for managers.

WORKS CITED

Baran, Barbara, and Suzanne Teegarden. 1987. "Women's Labor in the Office of the Future: A Case Study of the Insurance Industry." In *Women, Households, and the Economy,* edited by Lourdes Beneria and Catharine R. Stimpson, pp. 201–24. New Brunswick, N.J.: Rutgers University Press.

Belker, Loren. 1981. *The Successful Secretary.* New York: American Management Association.

Blake, Robert, Jane S. Mouton, and Artie Stockton. 1983. *The Secretary Grid.* New York: American Management Association.

Jennings, Eugene Emerson. 1971. *Routes to the Executive Suite.* New York: McGraw-Hill.

Levinson, Harry. 1981. *Executive.* Cambridge: Harvard University Press.

Steele, Fritz. 1986. "The Dynamics of Power and Influence in Workplace Design and Management." In *Behavioral Issues in Office Design,* edited by Jean D. Wineman, pp. 43–64. New York: Van Nostrand Reinhold.

Sundstrom, Eric. 1986. "Privacy in the Office." In *Behavioral Issues in Office Design,* edited by Jean Wineman, pp. 177–202. New York: Van Nostrand Reinhold.

Sundstrom, Eric, Robert Burt, and Douglas Kemp. 1980. "Privacy at Work: Architectural Correlates of Job Satisfaction and Job Performance." *Academy of Management Journal* 23 (March): 101–17.

U.S. Department of Labor. 1991. *Employment and Earnings* 38 (January). Washington, D.C.: Bureau of Labor Statistics.

READING THE TEXT

1. Summarize in your own words how traditional office design can be considered "'tantamount to spatial segregation by gender'" (para. 1).

2. Define the differences between "open-floor" and "closed-door" (para. 1) jobs. What are the spatial arrangements that signal those differences?

3. According to Spain, how is the executive secretary "an exception to the rule of gendered spatial segregation in the workplace" (para. 8)?

4. What sort of evidence does Spain present to demonstrate her claim that the workplace exhibits gender segregation?

5. In Spain's view, how does office design restrict or enhance the privacy of employees?

READING THE SIGNS

1. In class, form small groups, and design an office space that is not hierarchically organized. Have the groups present the design to the class, explaining the reasoning behind their design choices.

2. If you work in an office environment, write an analysis of the spatial design of your workplace. To what extent does it follow the gendered patterns that Spain describes? Alternately, survey the faculty and staff offices at your college or university. Do they reflect Spain's analysis?

3. Interview at least five women about their jobs and work environment. To what extent do their experiences support Spain's claim that "women are . . . concentrated spatially in jobs that limit their access to knowledge" (para. 3)?

4. Write a letter to business consultants Robert Blake, Jane Mouton, and Artie Stockton in which you respond to their description of the ideal boss-secretary relationship, published in the American Management Association's *The Secretary Grid* (para. 6).

RINA SWENTZELL

CONFLICTING LANDSCAPE VALUES: THE SANTA CLARA PUEBLO AND DAY SCHOOL

For the European American builders of the Bureau of Indian Affairs day school for the Santa Clara Pueblo community, a building was a kind of triumph over nature, a way of organizing and controlling space for specifically human purposes. For the Pueblo Indians who were compelled to go to school there, a building must exist in a harmonious relationship with the land it is on to reflect the larger bond between human beings and the earth. Thus, the effect of educating Pueblo children in a European building, as Rina Swentzell (b. 1939) suggests in this selection, is, at best, to confuse them, and, at worst, to destroy the traditional basis of their culture. The results, Swentzell reveals, are not heartening. Trained in architecture and American studies, Swentzell actively promotes the traditional Pueblo way of life as well as environmental communication through architecture.

Two very different relationships to the land are represented by the Santa Clara Pueblo, in New Mexico and the Bureau of Indian Affairs (BIA) day school established next to it. These relationships reflect the divergent world views of two cultures, as well as their differing methods and content of education.

Pueblo people believe that the primary and most important relationship for humans is with the land, the natural environment, and the cosmos, which in the pueblo world are synonymous. Humans exist within the cosmos and are an integral part of the functioning of the earth community.

The mystical nature of the land, the earth, is recognized and honored. Direct contact and interaction with the land, the natural environment, is sought. In the pueblo, there are no manipulated outdoor areas that serve to distinguish humans from nature. There are no outdoor areas that attest to human control over nature, no areas where nature is domesticated.

Santa Clara, where I was born, is a typical Tewa pueblo with myths that connect it to the nearby prehistoric sites and that also inextricably weave the

FIGURE 1   Santa Clara Pueblo, 1879. Photo by J. K. Hillers. Courtesy Smithsonian Institution, National Anthropological Archives.

human place into a union with the land whence the people emerged. The people dwell at the center, around the *nansipu*, the "emergence place" or "breathing place." The breath flows through the center as it does through other breathing places in the low hills and far mountains. These symbolic places remind the people of the vital, breathing earth and their specific locations are where the people can feel the strongest connection to the flow of energy, or the creation of the universe. The plants, rocks, land, and people are part of an entity that is sacred because it breathes the creative energy of the universe.

The physical location of Santa Clara Pueblo is of great importance — the Rio Grande snakes along the east of the pueblo; the mysterious Black Mesa, where the mask whippers emerge, is to the south; the surrounding low hills contain shrines and special ceremonial areas; and the far mountains define the valley where humans live.

This world, for me as a child, was very comfortable and secure because it gave a sense of containment. We roamed in the fields and nearby hills. At an early age we learned an intimacy with the natural environment and other living creatures. We learned of their connectedness to rocks, plants, and other animals through physical interaction and verbal communication. We gained tremendous confidence and an unquestioning sense of belonging within the natural

FIGURE 2   Kiva at Santa Clara Pueblo, 1930. Photo by Fayette W. Van Zile. Courtesy Smithsonian Institution, National Anthropological Archives.

ordering of the cosmos. Learning happened easily. It was about living. In fact, the word for learning in Tewa is *haa-pu-weh*, which translates as "to have breath." To breathe or to be alive is to learn.

Within the pueblo, outdoor and indoor spaces flowed freely and were hardly distinguishable. One moved in bare feet from interior dirt floors enclosed by mud walls to the well-packed dirt smoothness of the pueblo plaza. In this movement, all senses were utilized. Each of the various dirt surfaces (interior walls, outdoor walls, plaza floor) was touched, smelled, and tasted. Special rocks were carried in the mouth so that their energy would flow into us. Everything was touchable, knowable, and accessible.

There was consistency in that world because the colors, textures, and movements of the natural landscape were reflected everywhere in the human-made landscape. Reflection on the cosmos was encouraged. Separation of natural and human-made spaces was minimal, so conscious beautification of either outdoor or indoor spaces was not necessary. Landscaping—bringing in trees, shrubs, and grass for aesthetic reasons—was thought to be totally unnecessary. The mobility of humans and animals was accepted, but the mobility of plants rooted in their earth places was inconceivable.

The pueblo plaza was almost always full. People cooked outdoors, husked corn, dried food, and sat in the sun. The scale of the pueblo plaza was such that I never felt lost in it even when I was the only person there.

The form and organization of the pueblo house reinforced the sense of se-   10
curity and importance of place. One sat on and played on the center of the
world (the *nansipu*) and thereby derived a sense of significance. Houses were
climbed on, jumped on, slept on, and cooked on. They were not material
symbols of wealth but were rather, in Thoreau's terminology, a most direct
and elegantly simple expression of meeting the human need for shelter.

Construction methods and materials were uncomplicated. The most direct methods were combined with the most accessible materials. Everyone
participated, without exception — children, men, women, and elders. Anybody could build a house or any necessary structure. Designers and architects
were unnecessary since there was no conscious aesthetic striving or stylistic
interest.

Crucial elements of the house interiors were the low ceilings; rounded
and hand-plastered walls; small, dark areas; tiny, sparse windows, and doors;
and multiple-use rooms. All interior spaces were shared by everybody, as
were the exterior spaces. The need for individual privacy was not important
enough to affect the plan of pueblo houses. Privacy was viewed in a different
way; it was carried around within the individual and walls and physical space
were not needed to defend it. Sharing was crucial.

Within the house, as without, spirits moved freely. Members of families
were sometimes buried in the dirt floor and their spirits became a part of the
house environment. Besides those spirits there were others who had special

FIGURE 3 Santa Clara Pueblo: view from roof of Pueblo Church, 1899. Photo by
Vroman. Courtesy Smithsonian Institution, National Anthropological Archives.

FIGURE 4   Santa Clara Pueblo: view from roof of Pueblo Church, 1899. Photo by Vromen. Courtesy Smithsonian Institution, National Anthropological Archives.

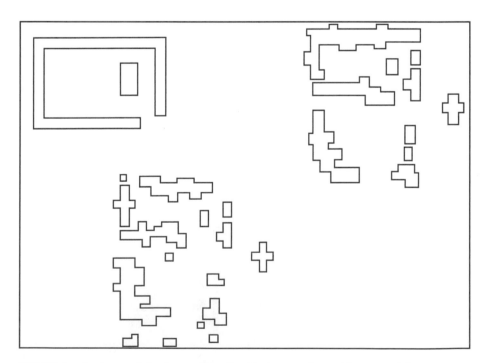

FIGURE 5   Evolution of the Santa Clara Pueblo from traditional form (top left) to recent years (bottom). Drawing by Rina Swentzell.

FIGURE 6 Typical pueblo interior room arrangements: (a) traditional, (b) 1940s, (c) 1970s. Drawing by Rina Swentzell.

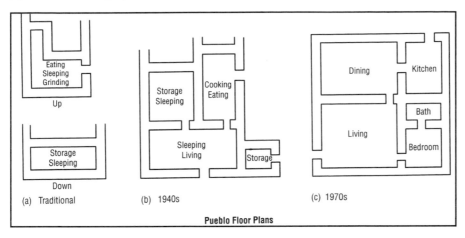

connections with the house structure because they assisted in its construction or because they were born or died in it. Since houses survived many generations, the spirits were many. Houses were blessed with a special ceremony similar to the ritual performed for a baby at birth. There was also an easy acceptance of the deterioration of a house. Houses, like people's bodies, came from and went back into the earth.

Ideas that characterize the pueblo human-made and natural environments, then, are that humans and nature are inseparable, that human environments emulate and reflect the cosmos, that creative energy flows through the natural environment (of which every aspect, including rocks, trees, clouds, and people, is alive), and that aesthetics and the cosmos are synonymous.

How Western Education Shaped the BIA Day School Landscape

"The goal, from the beginning of attempts at formal education of the American Indian, has been not so much to educate him as to change him."[1]

Santa Clara Day School was introduced to such a world in the early 1890s during the BIA's golden age of constructing schools for Native Americans. In the very early years of European settlement in America, various religious groups attempted to civilize and Christianize Native Americans. In 1832, that responsibility was assumed by the Commissioner of Indian Affairs and the focus narrowed to civilizing Native Americans.

[1]Committee on Labor and Public Welfare, *Indian Education: A National Tragedy — A National Challenge* (Washington: U.S. Government Printing Office, 1969), 10.

FIGURE 7   Santa Clara Bureau of Indian Affairs school grounds: plan. Drawing by Rina Swentzell.

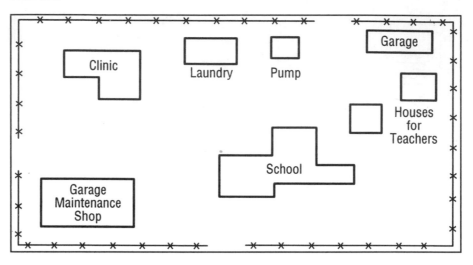

From 1890 to 1928, the goal was to assimilate Native Americans; the tactics were dissolving their social structure through Western education and destroying their land base. After 1928, when an influential government study asked for "a change in point of view" in how Native Americans should be educated, programs in bilingual education, adult basic education, training of Native American teachers, Native American culture, and in-service teacher training were initiated across the country. But these programs were halted almost as quickly, and certainly before the ideas reached the Santa Clara Day School.

The years after 1944 saw a new determination to terminate Native American reservations and abolish the special relationships between Native Americans and the federal government, relationships that had been guaranteed by centuries of law and treaties.[2] It was during this time, from 1945 to 1951, that I attended Santa Clara Pueblo Day School.

The government school grounds and buildings, built during the 1920s, not only reflected that attitude of changing and civilizing Native Americans but also characterized the general Western European attitude of human control that seems to stem from the Renaissance glorification of human capabilities. Everything had to be changed to make it accord with the Western way of thinking and being. The BIA school compounds reflected a foreign world view that opposed the pueblo world and its physical organization.

At Santa Clara, the BIA school complex was located a quarter of a mile from the center of the pueblo and had a barbed-wire fence around its periphery. That fence defined the complex and effectively kept the two worlds separate. The cattle guards and the double-stiled ladders built over the fence pro-

20

[2]Ibid., 13.

vided the only openings into the compound. They kept out both animals and old people. All large rocks and natural trees had been removed a long time before I was a student and there were but a few foreign elm trees in the barren, isolated landscape.

The loss of trust that occurred when people moved from the pueblo to the school setting was most striking. Within the pueblo, preschool-aged children were allowed enormous freedom of activity and choice; to a great extent they were trusted as capable of being in charge of themselves. This liberal assumption created its own self-fulfilling prophecy. Since pueblo children were expected to care for themselves in an adequate, responsible way, they generally did.

But within the BIA school, there was a different attitude: The overall atmosphere was one of skepticism. The fence was an expression of the lack of respect and trust in others. Although the formal reason given for the fence was that it kept out animals, everyone in the pueblo knew its purpose was also to keep people out. It was unsettling to know that other people had to protect themselves physically from community.

As the school grounds were separated from the life and environment around them, so were the various structures located within the compound separate from each other. There were separate laundry and shower buildings — as part of the civilizing effort, everybody, including adults, was supposed to take showers. Also included in the compound were a health clinic, a maintenance shop, the main school building, and small separate houses for the teachers. All of them were scattered seemingly randomly in the approximately five-acre compound.

Within the school building, children were grouped into rooms according to grade level. Inside the various classrooms, the divisions continued. Those who could read well were separated from those who could not. Individual desks and mats were assigned. Individual achievement was praised. Concentration on the individual, or the parts, which has become the hallmark of modern American society, was strongly emphasized. This was in contrast to the holistic concepts of the pueblo, which emphasized togetherness and cooperation and which were expressed in connected and multiple-function structures.

The floor plan of the school was efficient and designed to create an aspiration of moving up — the good old American attitude of upward mobility — from one room and grade level to the next. The move, however, was always disappointing because there were expectations that something special would happen in the next room, but it never did. The whole system had a way of making people unhappy with the present situation. Again, this was totally foreign to pueblo thinking, which worked toward a settling into the earth and, consequently, into being more satisfied with the moment and the present.

Inside the schoolhouse the ceilings were very high. The proportions of the rooms were discomforting — the walls were very tall relative to the small floor space. The Catholic church in the pueblo also had high ceilings, for Spanish

FIGURE 8   Santa Clara Pueblo Day School: plan. Drawing by Rina Swentzell.

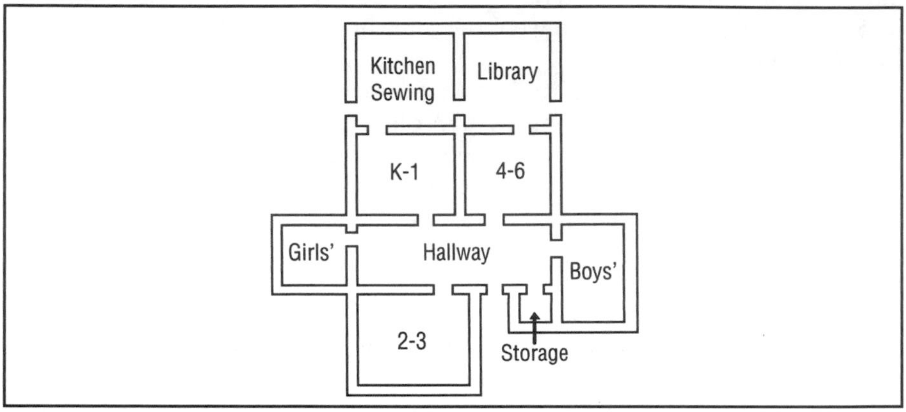

priests sought to maximize both interior and exterior height in the missions they built. But in the church there was no sense of overhead, top-heavy space. It had heavy, soft walls at eye level to balance its height, as well as dark interiors that made the height less obvious.

Although there were plenty of buildings on the school grounds, it seemed that there were never enough people to make the spaces within the grounds feel comfortable. Everything seemed at a distance. The message was, Don't touch, don't interact. The exterior formality of the structures, as well as the materials used, discouraged climbing on them, scratching them, tasting them, or otherwise affecting them. There was no way to be part of the place, the buildings, or the lives of teachers who lived there.

The creation of artificial play areas on the school grounds within the pueblo context and community was ironic. The total environment (natural as well as human-created) was included in the pueblo world of play. Play and work were barely distinguishable. Every activity was something to be done and done as well as possible; the relaxation or joy that play gives was to be found in submerging oneself in the activity at hand.

Play and work were distinguished from one another in the BIA school, and specific time was assigned for both. There were recesses from work, yet play was constantly supervised so that the children could not discover the world for themselves. Every possible danger was guarded against. Lack of trust was evident in the playground as opposed to the pueblo setting, where we roamed the fields and hills.

It was apparent that the Anglo teachers preferred indoor and human-made spaces over the outdoors, and they tried to instill this preference in us. In the pueblo, the outdoors was unquestionably preferred. 30

The saddest aspect of the entire school complex was the ground. There was no centering, no thought, no respect given to the ground. The native plants and rocks had been disturbed a long time ago and the land had lost all the variety

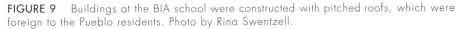

FIGURE 9   Buildings at the BIA school were constructed with pitched roofs, which were foreign to the Pueblo residents. Photo by Rina Swentzell.

one finds in small places created by bushes, rocks or rises, and falls of the ground. The ground has been scraped and leveled, and metal play equipment was set upon it. It was also a gray color, which was puzzling because the ground in the pueblo plaza, only a quarter of a mile away, was a warm brown.

The sensation of being in the pueblo was very different from that of being on the school grounds. The pueblo plaza had soulfulness. It was endowed with spirit. The emergence place of the people from the underground was located within the plaza and the breath of the cosmos flowed in and out of it. The land, the ground, breathed there; it was alive. The school grounds were imbued with sadness because the spirit of the place, the land, was not recognized. Nothing flowed naturally. The vitality of the school came from faraway worlds, from lands described in books. Appreciation of the immediate landscape was impossible.

The Legacy of Conflicting Landscape Values

The pueblo and the school grounds were imbued with different cultural values, attitudes, and perceptions, and the students who moved from one setting to the other were deeply affected by those differences.

The school was part of a world that was whole unto itself and its orientation toward the future, time assignments, specialized buildings, artificial playgrounds, and overall concern with segmentation were elements of a conscious world view that was not concerned with harmony and acceptance of spirituality in the landscape.

The government did not come to Santa Clara Pueblo out of inner kind- 35
ness or benevolence. Rather, the government was dealing with Native Americans in what it considered to be the most efficient manner. This efficiency,
which was so apparent in the structures, took away human interaction and
dignity. We had to give ourselves totally to this order.

BIA authoritarianism assured the absence of any human-to-human or
human-to-nature interaction. The monumental structures and sterile outdoor
spaces in no manner stimulated the community to enter and exchange communications at any time or at any level of equality. In that people-proof environment, the natural curiosity that children have about their world was dulled
and respect for teachers far exceeded respect for the larger forces in the
world.

Santa Clara Day School was a typical American school of its era — isolated
and authoritatively emphatic. Its visual landscape read accordingly with the
surrounding fence, the barren land, and the tall, pitched-roof structures scattered within the compound.

But the longest-lasting impact may not be visual. The two physical settings taught different types of behavior to pueblo children. Consequently, lack
of confidence and feelings of inadequacy have become characteristic traits of
children who lived in the pueblo and went to the BIA school.

READING THE TEXT

1. Summarize in your own words the Pueblo community's relationship to the
   land.
2. In class, list on the board the typical architectural features of a Pueblo village.
   Then, discuss how those features reflect the Pueblo worldview. What underlying
   cultural values, in other words, are expressed in Pueblo building and community design?
3. List the architectural features of the BIA day school. How does this list compare
   with your list of the Pueblo's traditionally preferred architectural design?
4. Summarize in your own words the traditional Pueblo and the BIA methods of
   education.
5. Swentzell reveals that she grew up in the Santa Clara Pueblo. In what ways does
   her inclusion of personal experience affect the persuasiveness of her argument?

READING THE SIGNS

1. Study the physical design of your composition classroom. Does it have movable
   chairs, or are the seats bolted to the floor? Does the design enable small group
   work to occur, or is it more conducive to lectures? Of what materials is the furniture constructed? Use the details of your observations as evidence for an essay in which you argue whether the room's physical layout enhances or im-
   pedes learning as your instructor has designed the course.

2. Write an essay in which you argue to what extent the BIA day school architecture reflects the American myth of Manifest Destiny, or the belief that it was plainly God's plan that Anglo Americans should dominate North America from the Atlantic to the Pacific oceans. You might consult your history text or the Internet for an overview of this belief.

3. Both Swentzell and Fan Shen ("The Classroom and the Wider Culture: Identity as a Key to Learning English Composition," p. 613) describe non-Western approaches to education. Study the two selections, noting the educational methods that the authors describe as non-Western. Write an argumentative essay in which you evaluate those methods. To what extent would American education benefit from including approaches it traditionally has not emphasized?

4. Swentzell describes Pueblo educational philosophy as valuing hands-on learning that could stimulate students' curiosity in the world around them. In class, debate whether you believe that philosophy could benefit education at the university level. Use your class discussion as a springboard for your own argumentative essay about this question.

CAMILO JOSÉ VERGARA

THE GHETTO CITYSCAPE

What happens when a society abandons its central-city residential districts (better known as urban ghettos) to the forces of poverty and decay? Usually those who take an interest in these matters focus on the people left behind in such neighborhoods, but Camilo José Vergara (b. 1944) feels that something has been left out of the sociology of urban poverty: an examination of the ghetto environment itself and its effects on the people who live there. So packing camera and notebook, Vergara has spent years visiting the places that much of America would like to forget — the "green ghettos," the "institutional ghettos," and the "new immigrant ghettos," as he defines them — that lie beyond the gaze of most Americans. A photographer, Vergara has written for many publications, including the New York Times, *the* Nation, *the* Atlantic, *and* Architectural Record, *and has published* Silent Cities: The Evolution of the American Cemetery *and* The New American Ghetto *(1995), from which this selection was taken.*

If you were among the nearly eleven thousand people who lived in two-story row houses in North Camden in the 1960s, you could walk to work at

Esterbrook Pen, at Knox Gelatin, at RCA, or at J. R. Evans Leather. You could shop on Broadway, a busy three-mile-long commercial thoroughfare, nicknamed the "Street of Lights" because of its five first-run movie theaters with their bright neon signs.

After J. R. Evans Leather was abandoned and almost completely demolished, its smokestack stood alone in a vast field by the Delaware River, a symbol of the demise of industry in Camden. Hundreds of row houses — once counted among the best ordinary urban dwellings in America — have been scooped up by bulldozers, their debris carted to a dump in Delaware. Walking along North Camden's narrow streets, one passes entire blocks without a single structure, the empty land crisscrossed by footpaths. The scattered dwellings that remain are faced with iron bars, so that they resemble cages.

With nearly half of its overwhelmingly Latino population on some form of public assistance, this once thriving working-class neighborhood is now the poorest urban community in New Jersey. In 1986, former mayor Alfred Pierce called Camden a reservation for the destitute. The north section of the city has become the drug center for South Jersey, and it hosts a large state prison.

North Camden is not unique. Since the riots of the 1960s, American cities have experienced profound transformations, best revealed in the spatial restructuring of their ghettos and in the emergence of new urban forms. During the past decade, however, the "underclass" and homelessness have dominated the study of urban poverty. Meanwhile, the power of the physical surroundings to shape lives, to mirror people's existence, and to symbolize social relations has been ignored. When scholars from across the political spectrum discuss the factors that account for the persistence of poverty, they fail to consider its living environments. And when prescribing solutions, they overlook the very elements that define the new ghettos: the ruins and the semi-ruins; the medical, warehousing, and behavior-modification institutions; the various NIMBYs, fortresses, and walls; and, not least, the bitterness and anger resulting from living in these places.

Dismissing the value of information received through sight, taste, and 5 smell, or through the emotional overtones in an informant's voice, or from the sensation of moving through the spaces studied, has led to the creation of constructs without character, individuality, or a sense of place. And although the limitations of statistical data — particularly when dealing with very poor populations — are widely acknowledged, our great dependency on numbers is fiercely defended. Other approaches are dismissed as impressionistic, anecdotal, as poetry, or "windshield surveys."

Yet today's ghettos are diverse, rich in public and private responses to the environment, in expressions of cultural identity, and in reminders of history. These communities are uncharted territory; to be understood, their forms need to be identified, described, inventoried, and mapped.

An examination of scores of ghettos across the nation reveals three types: "green ghettos," characterized by depopulation, vacant land overgrown by nature, and ruins; "institutional ghettos," publicly financed places of confinement designed mainly for the native-born; and "new immigrant ghettos," deriving their character from an influx of immigrants, mainly Latino and West Indian. Some of these communities have continued to lose population; others have emerged where a quarter-century ago there were white ethnic blue-collar neighborhoods; and sections of older ghettos have remained stable, working neighborhoods or have been rebuilt.

The Green Ghetto: Return to Wilderness?

Green ghettos, where little has been done to counter the effect of disinvestment, abandonment, depopulation, and dependency, are the leftovers of a society. Best exemplified by North Camden, Detroit's East Side, Chicago's Lawndale, and East St. Louis in Illinois, they are expanding outward to include poor suburbs of large cities such as Robbins, Illinois, and are even found in small cities such as Benton Harbor, Michigan.

Residents, remembering the businesses that moved to suburban malls, the closed factories, the fires, complain of living in a threatening place bereft of jobs and stores and neglected by City Hall. In many sections of these ghettos, pheasants and rabbits have regained the space once occupied by humans, yet these are not wilderness retreats in the heart of the city. "Nothing but weeds are growing there" is a frequent complaint about vacant lots, expressing no mere distaste for the vegetation, but moral outrage at the neglect that produces these anomalies. Plants grow wildly on and around the vestiges of the former International Harvester Component Plant in West Pullman, Chicago. Derelict industrial buildings here and in other ghettos have long ago been stripped of anything of value. Large parcels of land lie unkempt or paved over, subtracted from the life of the city. Contradicting a long-held vision of our country as a place of endless progress, ruins, once unforeseen, are now ignored.

Institutional Ghettos: The New Poorhouses

In New York City, Newark, and Chicago, large and expensive habitats — institutional ghettos — have been created for the weakest and most vulnerable members of our society. Institution by institution, facility by facility, these environments have been assembled in the most drug-infested and destitute parts of cities. They are the complex poorhouses of the twenty-first century, places to store a growing marginal population officially certified as "not employable." Residents are selected from the entire population of the municipal-

Sterling Street, Newark, 1980.

ity for their lack of money or home, for their addictions, for their diseases and other afflictions. Nonresidents come to these institutions to pick up medications, surplus food, used clothes; to get counseling or training; or to do a stint in prison. Other visitors buy drugs and sex.

As Greg Turner, the manager of a day shelter on the Near West Side of Chicago, puts it: "They say, 'Let's get them off the streets and put them together in groups.' It is like the zoo: we are going to put the birds over here; we are going to put the reptiles over there; we are going to put the buffalo over here; we are going to put the seals by the pool. It is doing nothing to work with the root of the problem, just like they do nothing to work with the children, to teach them things so they don't grow up and become more homeless people or substance abusers."

Although the need for individual components — for instance, a homeless shelter or a waste incinerator — may be subject to public debate, the overall consequences of creating such "campuses" of institutions are dismissed. The most important barrier to their growth is the cost to the taxpayers of building and maintaining them.

Such sections of the city are not neighborhoods. The streets surrounding Lincoln Park in south Newark, for example, an area that includes landmark houses, grand public buildings, and a once-elegant hotel, were chosen by two drug treatment programs because six of its large mansions would provide inexpensive housing for a residential treatment program. On the northwest corner of the park, a shelter for battered women just opened in another mansion, and a block north in a former garage is a men's shelter and

Sterling Street replaced by a parking lot, 1994.

soup kitchen. The largest structures overlooking the park, the hotel and a former federal office building, house the elderly, who fear going out by themselves. No children play in the park; no parents come home from work. This is a no-man's-land devoted to the contradictory goals of selling drugs and getting high, on the one hand, and becoming clean and employed on the other.

New Immigrant Ghettos: Dynamic and Fluid

In other parts of New York and Chicago a community of recent immigrants is growing up, but this type of ghetto is most visible in South Central Los Angeles and Compton, where the built environment is more intimate than in older ghettos, the physical structures are more adaptable, and it is easier for newcomers to imprint their identity. Here paint goes a long way to transform the appearance of the street.

The new immigrant ghettos are characterized by tiny offices providing 15 services such as driving instruction, insurance, and immigration assistance; by stores that sell imported beer, produce, and canned goods; and by restaurants offering home cooking. Notable are the businesses that reflect the busy exchange between the local population and their native country: money transfers, travel agencies, even funeral homes that arrange to have bodies shipped home.

To get by, most residents are forced to resort to exploitative jobs paying minimum wage or less and usually lacking health benefits. For housing they crowd together in small, badly maintained apartments, in cinder-block garages, or in trailers.

Not being eligible for public or city-owned housing may in the long run prove to be a blessing for the newcomers. Although forced to pay high rents, immigrants tend to concentrate in neighborhoods that are part of the urban economy, thus avoiding the extreme social disorganization, isolation, and violence that characterize other types of ghettos. Because of the huge influx of young people with expectations that life will be better for their children and grandchildren, these ghettos are more dynamic and fluid, resembling the foreign-born communities of a century ago.

READING THE TEXT

1. Why does Vergara see North Camden, New Jersey, as exemplary of city life?
2. According to Vergara, what realities of city life have scholars overlooked, and what explanation does he give for their oversights?
3. Summarize in your own words the three categories of cityscape that Vergara proposes.

READING THE SIGNS

1. If you live in or near an inner-city area, analyze it in terms of the three categories Vergara proposes in this selection. Which category does it best fit, and why? If it doesn't fit any of Vergara's categories, propose one of your own, and explain why it best fits your area.
2. Adopting Vergara's perspective, write a response to Lucy R. Lippard ("Alternating Currents," p. 427) in which you critique her analysis of city life. Consider both her interpretations and the scope of her selection.
3. In a reflective essay, discuss the symbolic meaning of nature in urban life. In addition to Vergara's selection, read or reread Lucy R. Lippard's "Alternating Currents" (p. 427) and Rina Swentzell's "Conflicting Landscape Values: The Santa Clara Pueblo and Day School" (p. 450).
4. In an essay, support, challenge, or modify Vergara's suggestion that "the power of the physical surroundings to shape lives, to mirror people's existence, and to symbolize social relations" (para. 4) is at least equivalent to economic conditions.

ERIC BOEHLERT

New York's Most Disliked Building?

*When we lost them, it was hard to remember that the World Trade Cen-
ter towers were not quite thirty years old and had never really been popular among architectural critics. But as Eric Boehlert (b. 1965) shows in
this historical survey of the WTC written less than a week after its destruction, the enormous towers were always a source of fascination, lur-
ing high-wire daredevils and parachutists, eventually becoming a symbol
of the American way of life, and so drawing to themselves in the end
those who dreamed of destroying America itself. With the surviving WTC
flag having become one of the most poignant symbols in American history, the twin towers, whether they are rebuilt or not, promise to join the
Statue of Liberty and the Washington Monument as emblems of our
country. Boehlert is a senior writer for Salon.com.*

They jeered when they went up. They cried when it crashed down.

During its nearly thirty year residence at the southern tip of Manhattan,
the World Trade Center's twin towers lived an unusual, contradictory city life.

Built, according to its chief architect Minoru Yamasaki, "as a living symbol
of man's dedication to world peace," the World Trade Center was destroyed
by terrorists in a devastating act of war.

The towers were acknowledged as a wonder of modern engineering, yet
were riddled with quirks, like the way pencils rolled off desktops on the top
floors when the wind began to gust. Real estate developers in the 1960s and
1970s derided the World Trade Center as government-sponsored folly. Yet in
summer 2001, the twin towers morphed into the most valuable piece of privately run real estate in New York. And while the twin towers were embraced
worldwide as *the* symbol of New York's grandeur and prowess, locals, not to
mention merciless critics, were cool to the sprawling complex, if not outright
contemptuous of the "dreary" creation. Instead, they more often pointed to
the Empire State and Chrysler buildings as structures that best echoed the
city's aspirations.

From the time the two towers opened for business in 1972, New Yorkers 5
were fascinated by their sheer size and oddity. Daredevils parachuted off the
roofs, scaled up windows, and walked tightropes between the towers. Movie
directors sent mechanical apes to the side (*King Kong*), and staged extravagant dance numbers in the plaza (*The Wiz*). Everyone wanted to touch the
new towers, to prod them, to see if the glistening giants had a heart or a soul.
The towers, though, never seemed to look down, to notice the commotion below. "The towers kept you at a distance. They said you are divided from me.
It was a weird message," says Eric Darton, author of *Divided We Stand: A*

Biography of New York's World Trade Center. "They never cohered as a symbolic value like the Statue of Liberty or the Brooklyn Bridge."

Few want to contemplate what the towers' rubble may symbolize today. Instead, the question is how the buildings will be remembered. "The thing we're going to miss the most is the skyline," says Angus Kress Gillespie, professor of American studies at Rutgers and author of *Twin Towers: The Life of New York City's World Trade Center*. "I don't want to minimize the loss of life or the financial loss. But a year from now what we'll miss is the beautiful outline in the sky." "Even though New Yorkers didn't necessarily love the buildings, they will be remembered with such pain," says Carol Willis, founding director of New York's Skyscraper Museum. "They were always there [looking south to] the bottom of Fifth Avenue. Now you keep looking at this fractured skyline and there's this constant reminder they aren't there anymore."

The World Trade Center, despite its eventual role as a concrete symbol of New York's financial prowess, was not originally intended to be one of the world's great landmarks. Instead, it was simply a way for business leaders to clean up the neighborhood and boost rents. In the 1950s David Rockefeller, co-chairman for Chase Manhattan Bank, had recently opened up headquarters downtown and wanted to stimulate the surrounding real estate market. Concerned that most businesses flocked to midtown, and even financial professionals deserted downtown after work, Rockefeller envisioned a world-class complex that would be the center of international trade. With his brother Nelson serving as New York's governor, Rockefeller lined up support from the bi-state, New York/New Jersey Port Authority agency. A wealthy, quasi-public commission (voting members are appointed by each state's governor), the Port Authority was created at the turn of last century and given "full power and authority to purchase, construct, lease and operate terminal, transportation and other facilities of commerce." For the most part, that meant operating Hudson River crossings as well as Newark's airport. But at the urging of the Rockefeller brothers, the Port Authority agreed to build the World Trade Center. In the 1970s, critics suggested the towers No. 1 and No. 2 be called by their true names, David and Nelson.

Midtown's real estate developers adamantly opposed the project, afraid the new complex would glut the market with too much new office space and open the floodgates to a downtown migration. Displaced local businesses located along a now-forgotten downtown section of the city known as Radio Row also protested. But the Port Authority enjoyed the power of eminent domain, giving it free rein to raze buildings for construction. (This was at a time when neighborhood objections to construction were routinely ignored by the government-sponsored developers.)

By the time construction began, the Port Authority had upped to 10 million square feet the amount of office space it needed in order to make the deal economically viable. According to author Darton, Yamasaki, who had settled on a twin tower approach, then heeded the advice he received from a chief Port Authority planner: "Do a project that will get noticed."

The World Trade Center towers and the Statue of Liberty.

When the towers were officially opened in 1972, New York Governor ₁₀
Rockefeller again came to the towers' aid, solving a widespread vacancy problem by housing tens of thousands of state employees in the building. The
state paid just $10 per square foot in rent. When vacancies began to shrink in
the mid 1980s and new tenants were paying office rents in the $30–$40
range, New York State opted to move its employees out, conveniently freeing
up valuable space for the Port Authority to lease. Although the twin towers
were never seen as one of the city's most prestigious addresses, by the 1990s
early shipping and merchant marine tenants from the 1970s had been largely
replaced by multinational banks and investment brokers such as Morgan
Stanley Dean Witter. At the time of the attack the towers' occupancy rate was
a robust 98 percent. Few if any of its remaining tenants had any real connection to port trade.

How best to remember the World Trade Center? The irony is that over the
years many critics wished the towers were never there to begin with. Writing for
the *New York Times*, architectural commentator Paul Goldberger often referred
to the twin towers as "banal," and once suggested the World Trade Center represented "New York's most disliked building." (*New York* magazine eventually
came up with just such a list; the Pan-Am building actually topped it.)

"Banal to me implies cliché and it's been done all over the world, so I
wouldn't use that word," says noted New York architect Hugh Hardy, who
oversaw the restoration of the World Trade Center's Windows on the World
restaurant following the 1993 bombing. Hardy instead opts for "arrogant." Arrogant in the way the bullying, flat-top towers "gave no recognition to the skyline" around them; "arrogant in their placement." Hardy suggests it wasn't
until the nearby Cesar Pelli-designed World Financial Center office complex
was constructed in 1985 that the lower Manhattan skyline again began to jell.
(Post-twin towers, it is now Pelli's building that looks strangely out of place.)

The World Trade Center's off-putting, five-acre concrete plaza, created to
set the towers off as two jewels, also never made much sense. "The plaza has
always been alienating," says skyscraper historian Willis. "It's so vast, so out
of scale with human beings. They would try to populate it during the
lunchtime hour with outdoor dance performers and set up a stage. But inevitably the stage would look like a toy. Plus, there was always heavy wind
swirling around. It was not an oasis, but more like a tundra. It was not the
type of place that drew people to it."

And then there were the unusually narrow office windows that robbed
tower inhabitants of what should have been an indisputable perk: the view.
Yamasaki was afraid of heights and decided in order to make everyone feel
secure while they worked in the offices, the windows, set between columns,
would be just 18 inches across, narrower than Yamasaki's own shoulder span.
The height-sensitive architect also designed a special window rig for Roko
Camaj, who'd been washing tower windows since 1975. Days after the attack
Camaj's son was seen on a local New York television newscast, going from

hospital to hospital searching for his father, who called moments after the first explosions but days later was still missing.

The problem with Yamasaki's window design, says Willis, is the towers of- 15 fered "no sense of the spectacular panorama" for the workers inside, which is why she, like many professionals, declares the towers' interior "a failure, aesthetically." (The exception, of course, was the exclusive Windows on the World located on the 107th floor; thanks to the demands of the restaurant's creator, Joseph Baum, the spectacular room boasted enormous windows and peerless views of the city.) The irony is that one of the tower's selling points was its unique floor construction of prefabricated trussed steel, only 33 inches in depth. That allowed everyone a chance to look out the windows because the massive office space was uninterrupted by columns, a modernist ideal of the day. In the end, the views, due to poor design, were a bust. But no other office complex before or after the towers ever boasted as much room. "It was a shrewd, intelligent way to house a wide-open space," says architect Hardy.

Not only were the towers obscenely tall, but massively wide as well. The towers' floors were 40,000 square feet, offering up an acre of space per floor; 220 acres between the twin towers. Together, they boasted 10 million square feet in office space. That's larger than the Pentagon and more space than some entire American downtown business districts, such as St. Louis, Miami, and San Diego. Record-breaking skyscrapers built today, many of them in Southeast Asia, are taller than the twin towers, but much narrower and nowhere near as massive all the way around.

"The professional critics of architecture were never really brought around. They say the towers were boring and unadorned," says Gillespie, who can't point to a single prominent critic or architect who over the years came forward to defend the twin towers. "Journalists and the man on the street will say nice things about it. But architectural critics are cemented in their positions. I think they did miss the beauty, the way the towers were offset, not side-by-side, and how when you're on a boat on the Hudson River you can see shapes shift between the two [tower] forms. Or how at sunset at Jersey City's Liberty State Park [across the Hudson], the towers' polished aluminum reflected the golden sunshine."

Architect Hardy recalls a favorite image of looking down West Broadway, a street lined with small-scale shops, only to be greeted at the end with the sight of the obscenely large twin towers hovering over it all. "It's a classic photograph of the city because of the absurdity, which was quite wonderful," he says. Historian Willis cites another classic World Trade Center photo she saw tourists take time and time again; walking to the base of a tower and just pointing their camera straight up in the air, following the tower's contour to the sky. "That view couldn't help but impress people," she says.

But while tourists over the years snatched up twin tower postcards by the millions, and New Yorkers did marvel at their dimensions, they never seemed to see themselves in the towers. That changed in part on February 26, 1993, when Islamic terrorists tried to blow up the World Trade Center by detonating bombs in the underground parking garage. The brazen attack left six dead, more than 1,000 injured and a science fiction-sized crater beneath the twin towers. But the building, and the city, did not bend. "We were the *Titanic* that hit the iceberg, but we kept going," says Darton.

Following "Operation Spit and Polish," the towers reopened for business 20 just in time for the runaway financial bull market that lifted New York City to unmatched prosperity. "They were a metaphor: the height of the tower and the heights of the markets," says the author.

The World Trade Center reached its financial summit in summer 2001 when the Port Authority privatized the complex, selling a 99-year lease to local developer Larry Silverstein for $3.2 billion, the most expensive real estate deal of its kind.

Preparing to take over the lease this summer, Silverstein, suddenly New York's largest commercial landlord, told the *New York Times,* "I've been looking at the Trade Center for years, thinking what a great piece of real estate, what a thrill it would be to own it. There's nothing like it in the world."

And there may never be anything quite like it again in New York.

READING THE SIGNS

1. What, according to Boehlert, was the contradictory response New Yorkers had to the World Trade Center? How did the history of the towers' construction contribute to that response?

2. What was the critique of the World Trade Center by professional architects?

3. Why did the World Trade Center lack a coherent symbolic significance, according to this selection?

READING THE TEXT

1. Boehlert quotes author Eric Darton as claiming the World Trade Center "never cohered as a symbolic value like the Statue of Liberty or the Brooklyn Bridge" (para. 5). Write an essay in which you argue the extent to which the twin towers' destruction in an act of terrorism has, given them, in effect, a posthumous symbolic value that they did not have when they stood.

2. Select a public building in your city that has monumental or symbolic status, and visit it. Study not only its architectural design but also how it stands in relation to the neighborhood surrounding it. Then write an analysis of the building in which you explain why it has earned this symbolic status.

3. Study images of the World Trade Center (see pg. 469 or visit **http://www .constantreader.org/wtcgallery.html**). Then write an essay in which you support, oppose, or modify architect Hugh Hardy's contention that the WTC was "arrogant" (para. 12).

WE'VE COME A LONG WAY, MAYBE

Gender Codes in American Culture

6

Once upon a time, an unmarried woman in America was an object of commiseration, even pity. A Miss, not a Ms., she was someone for whom her married sisters felt responsible, someone to arrange dates for, someone in need of a man. And unlike her unmarried equivalent on the other side of the gender divide — the bachelor whose swinging image often connoted freedom and pleasure — she was stuck with the stuffiest of images, one that connoted drab clothing and sensible shoes, bunned hair and eyeglasses. She was, alas, a *spinster*.

But that was then and things have changed. The image of the unmarried woman has undergone a profound transformation in American culture, a transformation that has been dramatically reflected in one of the most popular and talked about television programs of the new millennium. You have probably already guessed the show we mean — HBO's *Sex and the City* — a TV series that may well have banished the image of the spinster once and for all, replacing her with the swinging "singleton," the sexy new unmarried woman for a new era.

Interpreting American Gender Codes

Not yet ready for network TV but one of the hottest hits of the cable lineup, *Sex and the City* was the first television series to take the *Cosmo* philosophy to prime time. Hardly the first TV series to feature single women as protagonists — single women starred on television as far back as the 1950s' *Our Miss Brooks* and continued to be featured in such other hits as *The Mary Tyler*

Moore Show, Laverne and Shirley, and *Murphy Brown* — *Sex and the City* still broke ground for its edgy, postfeminist take on the sexual mores of the single life. But while the popularity among women viewers of these four straight-talking New York singletons (singletons, that is to say, in the inaugural episodes of the series) has been without question, the ideological significance of its postfeminist message is far more complicated. For while the show presents itself, and is often viewed, as a revolutionary challenge to the gender codes that govern American life, a semiotic reading of the program can reveal a striking contradiction that may well undermine its claims to gender subversion.

To see how, we must first consider what, exactly, a gender code is. Whether you have ever heard the term, you are already familiar with what it constitutes, because a gender code is a culturally constructed belief system that defines and dictates the appropriate roles and behavior for men and women in society. Whether you are a woman or a man, one has been guiding your life since you were born. It is a gender code, for example, that impels parents to give their female children dolls to prepare them for their adult lives as mothers while giving male children sports equipment and violent video games to prepare them for the active and aggressive roles that men are supposed to take in society. It is a gender code that tells girls that their primary concern should be with their appearance and with attracting boys, while telling boys that it's not their appearance that counts but how many times they "score." And it is a gender code that tells girls that they aren't good at math (one talking Barbie doll exclaimed just this), while leading boys to math-savvy careers in science and technology.

Since gender codes are often justified on the basis of appeals to the "natural" differences between the two sexes, they are especially difficult to contest, and those women and men who do challenge them are often denounced accordingly as being "unnatural." But one of the key arguments of the feminist movement as it emerged in the 1970s was that gender codes are socially, not naturally, constructed, and usually reflect cultural values rather than natural facts. Take, for example, the huge national controversy that erupted in the early 1990s when a young woman named Shannon Faulkner had to go all the way to the Supreme Court to gain entrance to the Citadel Military Academy. Although by that time women regularly were being admitted to academies like West Point, the Citadel's admissions policy maintained a lingering cultural belief that women don't really belong in the military. This belief continues to be encoded in the fact that women who *are* in the armed services are not allowed to serve in combat units (former Speaker of the House Newt Gingrich justified this ban by insisting that women couldn't fight in the field because they "got infections" — a classic appeal to nature). By contesting the Citadel's admissions policy, Shannon Faulkner was challenging, in effect, a deeply held gender code, and the fuss made about the whole matter illustrates just how emotional such codes can be. When Faulkner finally won her court case and entered the Citadel, she was followed around by hordes of reporters (who

carefully reported on everything from her pushup performance to her weight), and when she finally succumbed to the pressure and left, the campus erupted in an ecstatic celebration.

In the Faulkner incident, then, we find the gender code that holds that it is the role of men, not of women, to be warriors: men are the protectors, women are the ones to be protected (women and children first, as they said on the *Titanic*). This code is reinforced by the traditional belief that men are the aggressive sex, while women are passive. In sexual matters, men, accordingly, are expected to be the pursuers (he calls), while women are the pursued (she waits by the phone). Men gaze (upon women), and women are gazed upon (a gender belief that has been made much of in contemporary film analysis, which considers the way a movie camera represents the gaze of a male viewer).

We could go on and on. Note, though, how in each case gender roles are arrayed across a system of binary oppositions (men are this, women are the opposite). Indeed, these oppositions are so deeply encoded in our culture that you may find yourself protesting that men *are* aggressive, women *are* passive, men (as the bestseller has it) *are* from Mars, women *are* from Venus. But the fact that these roles can be reversed — indeed, they are being reversed more and more often these days — shows that they reflect cultural values rather than natural facts.

Sex and the Singleton Girl

What made *Sex and the City* subversive (at least on the surface), then, was the way in which it challenged the gender codes that govern traditional American sexuality. Independent, sexually forthright, aggressive, and unsentimental, the four lead characters of the original episodes seemed to reverse the old codes that called for women to be sexual shrinking violets. If the old codes defined it to be the role of men to be sexually exploitative, cynical, and crude, well, Samantha and Carrie reversed all that, out-guying the guys with plenty of backchat of their own. And all four women had their own careers — writer, lawyer, PR executive, art gallery director — to keep them well heeled (in both a financial and fashion sense) and independent.

Exploring the Signs of Gender

In your journal, explore the expectations about gender roles that you grew up with. What gender norms were you taught by your family, either overtly or implicitly? Have you ever had any conflicts with your parents over "natural" gender roles? If so, how did you resolve them? Do you think your gender-related expectations today are the same as those you had when you were a child?

The freedom with which Carrie, Charlotte, Miranda, and Samantha practiced and discussed their sex lives made them postfeminist heroines for millions of women viewers who identified with them and their problems. But there's something a little funny going on here. If *Sex and the City* heralds a new era in which women can take charge of the sexual gender code and use it for their own ends, why is it that the women of the show seem to be obsessed with exactly those things that the traditional gender codes tell them they should be concerned with: good looks, fashion, and sexual love? Why does the HBO Web site for *Sex and the City* breathlessly describe the fashion sense of each of the protagonists? Why is Charlotte, now married, desperately trying to conceive a child? Why didn't Miranda, in an era when "choice" is a rallying cry for the women's movement, go ahead with her planned abortion? Why is Carrie, at this writing, contemplating marriage? Why, finally, are all four protagonists rich and beautiful?

Such questions probe to the heart of the debate over what has come to be called postfeminism. Proponents of the postfeminist perspective hold that using her body to get what she wants is part of a woman's empowerment, that having a child out of wedlock is a statement of female independence, and that being beautiful is part of being a woman. Feminists who are less persuaded by this position point out, however, that the traditional gender chart tells women that their primary concern is with their bodies, while men are identified with intellect, and so, by focusing their attention upon their bodies and what they can do, and get, with them, the women of *Sex and the City* seem to be quite traditional after all. And at least three of them (Samantha is the apparent exception) are quite concerned with those goals that the traditional gender codes tell them they should be concerned with: marriage and motherhood. Couldn't just one of them be interested in math?

The Myths of Gender

If you still find yourself feeling uneasy about analyzing gender roles, you are not alone. For this uneasiness is rooted in the fact that our gender codes, like any cultural mythology, provide a framework through which we can understand and experience our world. If that framework is disrupted, our world suffers a dislocation and we feel threatened. You may think this isn't so, believing, for instance, that women *shouldn't* be in the military. If that's the case, ask yourself why you feel that way. If you're concerned about women getting unfair advantages in the feminist era (one reason some Americans rooted for the Citadel), wouldn't it seem that allowing them to share the dangerous duty of military combat would actually be the opposite of a privilege?

That many Americans, women as well as men, don't always see it this way shows just how durable our gender codes are. It thus is one of the major tasks of cultural semiotics to expose the outlines of gender myths to reveal just how deeply they influence our lives. Think of how these myths may shape your own behavior. Traditionally, for instance, the myths that govern courtship in America dictate that the man pays the expenses on a date and is responsible for all the logistics, even providing transportation and a destination. But there is no natural reason for this to be so; it's just a cultural expectation, one that has been changing for some time. Ask yourself: Who pays when you date? Who drives? Do you even care? Your answers will help you find your place in today's shifting terrain of gender myths.

In examining the gender myths that influence your own life, you should recognize the difference between the biological category of *sex* and the cultural category of *gender*. Your sex is determined by your chromosomes, but your gender goes beyond your sex to the roles that society has determined are appropriate for you. Your sex, in other words, is your birthright, but the roles you play in society are largely determined by your culture. In everyday life, however, this distinction between the natural category of sex and the cultural category of gender is blurred because socially determined gender roles are regarded as naturally dictated sexual necessities.

> ### Discussing the Signs of Gender
>
> Bring to class a magazine that targets one gender (such as *Maxim* or *Marie Claire*). In small groups, study both the articles and the advertising in your sample magazines, focusing on the gender roles assumed for men and women. List the major roles on the board by magazine title. What patterns do you find? Do some magazines adhere to traditional roles, while others depart from them? How can you account for your findings?

Even the standards of beauty that men as well as women are held to are culturally determined. The ideal medieval woman, for example, was short, slender, high-waisted, small-breasted, and boasted a high, domed forehead whose effect she enhanced by shaving her hairline. By the Renaissance, she had filled out considerably, and in the paintings of Peter Paul Rubens could appear positively pudgy by contemporary standards (we even have an adjective, *Rubenesque,* for well-padded feminine beauty). In more recent times, we have seen a shift from the hour-glass figures of the 1950s to the aerobically muscled hard bodies of the 1990s. You may assume that this is it, the last stop, the one truly beautiful body, but stick around. Wait to see what's fashionable in bodies in the years to come.

Men, too, have seen their bodily ideals change over time. The ideal man of the eighteenth century, for example, was a rather heavyset fellow, rounded in appearance, and with a hint of a double chin, while today's ideal (especially in the corporate world) has square-hewn features and a jutting jaw (cleft if possible: Just look at some ads for business-oriented services to see what today's businessman wants to look like). Now think for a moment: what would you look like if you had the choice? Would you look like the ideal of the 1950s or 1960s? Would you be long and lean, or buff, courtesy of Nautilus?

Iron John

It is important to realize, then, that men, too, are influenced by gender myths. Men, as we've seen, are supposed to be warriors (he who flinches is a coward) and studs (have you ever said "What a stud" to mean "What a great guy"?).

Just think of the typical Big Man On Campus. Is he not likely to be an athlete (the warrior role on a school campus) and a sexual star? What do you think of the guy who avoids athletics and doesn't "score"? How popular is he? With whom?

The men's movement in America, currently led by such writers as Robert Bly, has arisen alongside the women's movement to challenge the traditional masculine gender roles that require men to be aggressive, competitive, and unemotional. In his bestseller *Iron John: A Book about Men* (1990), Bly calls for an exploration of both the masculine and the feminine side of male being. Thus, Bly's drum-beating warrior has a sensitive side, which distinguishes him from the sort of Conan the Barbarian hero America's popular culture continues to admire. How else could we explain the rise of Arnold Schwarzenegger to the top of the Hollywood heap?

Indeed, the images that are shaping your own sense of gender identity are playing now at a theater near you. Start there, or with TV or MTV. What are you being told about your sexual identity? What stars are you supposed to emulate? What images do you avoid? What does a "real man" look like on screen? How about a "real woman"? Do you ever wish that they would just "get real"?

Gender Bending

Probably the most deeply held gender codes in our culture are those that define our sexual orientation. So fundamental are such codes to our sense of personal and social identity that it is still somewhat controversial to analyze them. Surely, you may believe, sexual orientation is determined by nature. What has culture to do with it?

But a growing number of scholars engaged in gender studies are questioning the natural determination of sexual orientation. This is especially true for those involved in queer theory, a movement that deliberately takes a once-pejorative term and subverts it to signify the dismantling of traditional gender norms. For such scholars, the categories of human sexuality, too, are social constructions, inscribing cultural rather than natural divisions. For example, what counts as homosexual behavior in American culture is not necessarily considered homosexual in other cultures, as could be seen when in the early 1980s many of the Haitian men who contracted AIDS denied being homosexual (they were bisexual), because in their cultural code bisexuality and homosexuality are clearly distinguished from each other, which they are not in the United States.

The most dramatic signs that America's codes governing sexual orientation are shifting can be seen not in the scholarly publications of queer theorists, however, but in the products of popular culture. When *Newsweek* ran a cover story on the new bisexuality in the early 1990s, few protested. Similarly, no great fuss was made when an episode of *Friends* dramatized a lesbian marriage in 1996 (a greater fuss occurred a few years earlier when *Roseanne* featured a lesbian kiss). In popular music, Marilyn Manson has attracted a huge following through his gender-bending antics. And the coming out of Ellen DeGeneres on her sitcom *Ellen* was one of the most-watched television programs in history, an episode that prompted a lot of clucking from the religious right but that was more remarkable for the fact that it aired at all.

Reading Gender on the Net

Use search engines such as *Yahoo!* or *Google* to research what issues are considered "male" and "female" territory on the Internet. Focus your search on a comparison of specific topics, such as "men's rights" and "women's rights." Compare your findings with those of your classmates.

We aren't telling you to applaud or to condemn these signifiers of change in American gender codes: We are simply drawing your attention to them. The fact that you may feel strongly about the matter is itself a signifier of the powerful hold our value systems have upon us. Gender values take us to the core of our sense of ourselves as individual and social beings and involve religious and moral beliefs that have recently become a central component of our country's political system, as in the "family values" movement. And this too is a sign of the essentially political nature of our social codes or mythologies, for if our values weren't political, they wouldn't be entered into the electoral process. So the analysis of gender codes in America isn't simply an academic exercise: It is a social and political activity that will affect you well beyond the classroom.

The Readings

Our chapter begins with Holly Devor's analysis of gender roles and the ways in which men and women manipulate the signs by which we traditionally communicate our gender identity. Kevin Jennings follows with a personal memoir that chronicles his struggles with growing up gay in conflict with the traditional construction of male heterosexuality. Deborah Blum is next with an article suggesting that biology *does* play a role in gender identity and that we can best understand the gender gap by looking at both the cultural and the physiological determinants of human behavior. Jennifer Scanlon looks at the way that children's board games help construct the gender identities of adolescent girls. Next, Andre Mayer examines the messages sent by pop culture superstars like Britney Spears and Kid Rock who, despite their hip and cool images, assume strikingly traditional gender roles. Naomi Wolf's indictment of the "beauty myth" that forces otherwise liberated women to feel trapped inside their own bodies follows. Deborah Tannen then looks at the way women are always "marked" in our society: no detail of a woman's appearance, from her hair to her shoes to her name, fails to send a gender-coded message about her, Tannen argues. James William Gibson's analysis of the warrior fantasies that have arisen in the wake of the Vietnam War and the rise of feminism sounds a warning note in the politics of gender identity, and Laura Miller concludes the chapter with a challenge to the widespread assumption that women are second-class citizens on the Net who need special protection against sexual harassment.

HOLLY DEVOR

GENDER ROLE BEHAVIORS AND ATTITUDES

"Boys will be boys, and girls will be girls": few of our cultural mytholo-
gies seem as natural as this one. But in this exploration of the gender
signals that traditionally tell what a "boy" or "girl" is supposed to look
and act like, Holly Devor (b. 1951) shows how these signals are not "nat-
ural" at all but instead are cultural constructs. While the classic cues of
masculinity — aggressive posture, self-confidence, a tough appearance —
and the traditional signs of femininity — gentleness, passivity, strong
nurturing instincts — are often considered "normal," Devor explains that
they are by no means biological or psychological necessities. Indeed, she
suggests, they can be richly mixed and varied, or to paraphrase the old
Kinks song, "Lola," "Boys can be girls and girls can be boys." Devor is
associate dean of social sciences at the University of Victoria and is the
author of Gender Blending: Confronting the Limits of Duality *(1989),*
from which this selection is excerpted, and FTM: Female-to-Male Transsexuals in Society *(1997).*

Gender Role Behaviors and Attitudes

The clusters of social definitions used to identify persons by gender are collectively known as "femininity" and "masculinity." Masculine characteristics are
used to identify persons as males, while feminine ones are used as signifiers for
femaleness. People use femininity or masculinity to claim and communicate
their membership in their assigned, or chosen, sex or gender. Others recognize
our sex or gender more on the basis of these characteristics than on the basis of
sex characteristics, which are usually largely covered by clothing in daily life.

These two clusters of attributes are most commonly seen as mirror images of one another with masculinity usually characterized by dominance and
aggression, and femininity by passivity and submission. A more evenhanded
description of the social qualities subsumed by femininity and masculinity
might be to label masculinity as generally concerned with egoistic dominance
and femininity as striving for cooperation or communion.[1] Characterizing
femininity and masculinity in such a way does not portray the two clusters of
characteristics as being in a hierarchical relationship to one another but rather

---

[1]Eleanor Maccoby, *Social Development: Psychological Growth and the Parent-Child Relation-*
ship (New York: Harcourt, Brace, Jovanovich, 1980), p. 217. Egoistic dominance is a striving
for superior rewards for oneself or a competitive striving to reduce the rewards for one's competitors even if such action will not increase one's own rewards. Persons who are motivated by
desires for egoistic dominance not only wish the best for themselves but also wish to diminish
the advantages of others whom they may perceive as competing with them.

as being two different approaches to the same question, that question being centrally concerned with the goals, means, and use of power. Such an alternative conception of gender roles captures the hierarchical and competitive masculine thirst for power, which can, but need not, lead to aggression, and the feminine quest for harmony and communal well-being, which can, but need not, result in passivity and dependence.

Many activities and modes of expression are recognized by most members of society as feminine. Any of these can be, and often are, displayed by persons of either gender. In some cases, cross-gender behaviors are ignored by observers, and therefore do not compromise the integrity of a person's gender display. In other cases, they are labeled as inappropriate gender role behaviors. Although these behaviors are closely linked to sexual status in the minds and experiences of most people, research shows that dominant persons of either gender tend to use influence tactics and verbal styles usually associated with men and masculinity, while subordinate persons, of either gender, tend to use those considered to be the province of women.[2] Thus it seems likely that many aspects of masculinity and femininity are the result, rather than the cause, of status inequalities.

Popular conceptions of femininity and masculinity instead revolve around hierarchical appraisals of the "natural" roles of males and females. Members of both genders are believed to share many of the same human characteristics, although in different relative proportions; both males and females are popularly thought to be able to do many of the same things, but most activities are divided into suitable and unsuitable categories for each gender class. Persons who perform the activities considered appropriate for another gender will be expected to perform them poorly; if they succeed adequately, or even well, at their endeavors, they may be rewarded with ridicule or scorn for blurring the gender dividing line.

The patriarchal gender schema currently in use in mainstream North   5 American society reserves highly valued attributes for males and actively supports the high evaluation of any characteristics which might inadvertently become associated with maleness. The ideology underlying the schema postulates that the cultural superiority of males is a natural outgrowth of the innate predisposition of males toward aggression and dominance, which is assumed to flow inevitably from evolutionary and biological sources. Female attributes are likewise postulated to find their source in innate predispositions acquired in the evolution of the species. Feminine characteristics are thought to be intrinsic to the female facility for childbirth and breastfeeding. Hence, it is popularly believed that the social position of females is biologically mandated to be intertwined with the care of children and a "natural" dependency on

---

[2]Judith Howard, Philip Blumstein, and Pepper Schwartz, "Sex, Power, and Influence Tactics in Intimate Relationships," *Journal of Personality and Social Psychology* 51 (1986), pp. 102–109; Peter Kollock, Philip Blumstein, and Pepper Schwartz, "Sex and Power in Interaction: Conversational Privileges and Duties," *American Sociological Review* 50 (1985), pp. 34–46.

men for the maintenance of mother-child units. Thus the goals of femininity and, by implication, of all biological females are presumed to revolve around heterosexuality and maternity.[3]

Femininity, according to this traditional formulation, "would result in warm and continued relationships with men, a sense of maternity, interest in caring for children, and the capacity to work productively and continuously in female occupations."[4] This recipe translates into a vast number of proscriptions and prescriptions. Warm and continued relations with men and an interest in maternity require that females be heterosexually oriented. A heterosexual orientation requires women to dress, move, speak, and act in ways that men will find attractive. As patriarchy has reserved active expressions of power as a masculine attribute, femininity must be expressed through modes of dress, movement, speech, and action which communicate weakness, dependency, ineffectualness, availability for sexual or emotional service, and sensitivity to the needs of others.

Some, but not all, of these modes of interrelation also serve the demands of maternity and many female job ghettos. In many cases, though, femininity is not particularly useful in maternity or employment. Both mothers and workers often need to be strong, independent, and effectual in order to do their jobs well. Thus femininity, as a role, is best suited to satisfying a masculine vision of heterosexual attractiveness.

Body postures and demeanors which communicate subordinate status and vulnerability to trespass through a message of "no threat" make people appear to be feminine. They demonstrate subordination through a minimizing of spatial use: People appear feminine when they keep their arms closer to their bodies, their legs closer together, and their torsos and heads less vertical than do masculine-looking individuals. People also look feminine when they point their toes inward and use their hands in small or childlike gestures. Other people also tend to stand closer to people they see as feminine, often invading their personal space, while people who make frequent appeasement gestures, such as smiling, also give the appearance of femininity. Perhaps as an outgrowth of a subordinate status and the need to avoid conflict with more socially powerful people, women tend to excel over men at the ability to correctly interpret, and effectively display, nonverbal communication cues.[5]

Speech characterized by inflections, intonations, and phrases that convey

---

[3]Nancy Chodorow, *The Reproduction of Mothering: Psychoanalysis and the Reproduction of Mothering* (Berkeley: University of California Press, 1978), p. 134.

[4]Jon K. Meyer and John E. Hoopes, "The Gender Dysphoria Syndromes: A Position Statement on So-Called 'Transsexualism,'" *Plastic and Reconstructive Surgery* 54 (Oct. 1974), pp. 444–51.

[5]Erving Goffman, *Gender Advertisements* (New York: Harper Colophon Books, 1976); Judith A. Hall, *Non-Verbal Sex Differences: Communication Accuracy and Expressive Style* (Baltimore: Johns Hopkins University Press, 1984); Nancy M. Henley, *Body Politics: Power, Sex and Non-Verbal Communication* (Englewood Cliffs, N.J.: Prentice-Hall, 1979); Marianne Wex, *"Let's Take Back Our Space": "Female" and "Male" Body Language as a Result of Patriarchal Structures* (Berlin: Frauenliteraturverlag Hermine Fees, 1979).

nonaggression and subordinate status also make a speaker appear more feminine. Subordinate speakers who use more polite expressions and ask more questions in conversation seem more feminine. Speech characterized by sounds of higher frequencies are often interpreted by listeners as feminine, childlike, and ineffectual.[6] Feminine styles of dress likewise display subordinate status through greater restriction of the free movement of the body, greater exposure of the bare skin, and an emphasis on sexual characteristics. The more gender distinct the dress, the more this is the case.

Masculinity, like femininity, can be demonstrated through a wide variety 10 of cues. Pleck has argued that it is commonly expressed in North American society through the attainment of some level of proficiency at some, or all, of the following four main attitudes of masculinity. Persons who display success and high status in their social group, who exhibit "a manly air of toughness, confidence, and self-reliance" and "the aura of aggression, violence, and daring," and who conscientiously avoid anything associated with femininity are seen as exuding masculinity.[7] These requirements reflect the patriarchal ideology that masculinity results from an excess of testosterone, the assumption being that androgens supply a natural impetus toward aggression, which in turn impels males toward achievement and success. This vision of masculinity also reflects the ideological stance that ideal maleness (masculinity) must remain untainted by female (feminine) pollutants.

Masculinity, then, requires of its actors that they organize themselves and their society in a hierarchical manner so as to be able to explicitly quantify the achievement of success. The achievement of high status in one's social group requires competitive and aggressive behavior from those who wish to obtain it. Competition which is motivated by a goal of individual achievement, or egoistic dominance, also requires of its participants a degree of emotional insensitivity to feelings of hurt and loss in defeated others, and a measure of emotional insularity to protect oneself from becoming vulnerable to manipulation by others. Such values lead those who subscribe to them to view feminine persons as "born losers" and to strive to eliminate any similarities to feminine people from their own personalities. In patriarchally organized societies, masculine values become the ideological structure of the society as a whole. Masculinity thus becomes "innately" valuable and femininity serves a contrapuntal function to delineate and magnify the hierarchical dominance of masculinity.

Body postures, speech patterns, and styles of dress which demonstrate and support the assumption of dominance and authority convey an impression of masculinity. Typical masculine body postures tend to be expansive and aggressive. People who hold their arms and hands in positions away from their bodies, and who stand, sit, or lie with their legs apart — thus maximizing the amount of

---

[6]Karen L. Adams, "Sexism and the English Language: The Linguistic Implications of Being a Woman," in *Women: A Feminist Perspective*, 3rd ed., ed. Jo Freeman (Palo Alto, Calif.: Mayfield, 1984), pp. 478–91; Hall, pp. 37, 130–37.

[7]Joseph H. Pleck, *The Myth of Masculinity* (Cambridge, Mass.: MIT Press, 1981), p. 139.

space that they physically occupy — appear most physically masculine. Persons who communicate an air of authority or a readiness for aggression by standing erect and moving forcefully also tend to appear more masculine. Movements that are abrupt and stiff, communicating force and threat rather than flexibility and cooperation, make an actor look masculine. Masculinity can also be conveyed by stern or serious facial expressions that suggest minimal receptivity to the influence of others, a characteristic which is an important element in the attainment and maintenance of egoistic dominance.[8]

Speech and dress which likewise demonstrate or claim superior status are also seen as characteristically masculine behavior patterns. Masculine speech patterns display a tendency toward expansiveness similar to that found in masculine body postures. People who attempt to control the direction of conversations seem more masculine. Those who tend to speak more loudly, use less polite and more assertive forms, and tend to interrupt the conversations of others more often also communicate masculinity to others. Styles of dress which emphasize the size of upper body musculature, allow freedom of movement, and encourage an illusion of physical power and a look of easy physicality all suggest masculinity. Such appearances of strength and readiness to action serve to create or enhance an aura of aggressiveness and intimidation central to an appearance of masculinity. Expansive postures and gestures combine with these qualities to insinuate that a position of secure dominance is a masculine one.

Gender role characteristics reflect the ideological contentions underlying the dominant gender schema in North American society. That schema leads us to believe that female and male behaviors are the result of socially directed hormonal instructions which specify that females will want to have children and will therefore find themselves relatively helpless and dependent on males for support and protection. The schema claims that males are innately aggressive and competitive and therefore will dominate over females. The social hegemony of this ideology ensures that we are all raised to practice gender roles which will confirm this vision of the nature of the sexes. Fortunately, our training to gender roles is neither complete nor uniform. As a result, it is possible to point to multitudinous exceptions to, and variations on, these themes. Biological evidence is equivocal about the source of gender roles; psychological androgyny is a widely accepted concept. It seems most likely that gender roles are the result of systematic power imbalances based on gender discrimination.[9]

Reading the Text

1. List the characteristics that Devor describes as being traditional conceptions of "masculinity" and "femininity" (para. 1).

[8]Goffman; Hall; Henley; Wex.
[9]Howard, Blumstein, and Schwartz; Kollock, Blumstein, and Schwartz.

2. What relationship does Devor see between characteristics considered masculine and feminine?

3. How does Devor explain the cultural belief in the "superiority" (para. 5) of males?

4. How, according to Devor, do speech and dress communicate gender roles?

READING THE SIGNS

1. In small same-sex groups, brainstorm lists of traits that you consider masculine and feminine, and then have each group write its list on the board. Compare the lists produced by male and female groups. What patterns of differences or similarities do you see? To what extent do the traits presume a heterosexual orientation? How do you account for your results?

2. Study the speech patterns, styles of dress, and other nonverbal cues communicated by your friends during a social occasion, such as a party, trying not to reveal that you are observing them for an assignment. Then write an essay in which you analyze these cues used by your friends. To what extent do your friends enact the traditional gender roles Devor describes?

3. Look through a popular magazine such as *Vogue, Rolling Stone,* or *Maxim* for advertisements that depict men and women interacting with each other. Then write an essay in which you interpret the body postures of the models, using Devor's selection as your framework for analysis. How do males and females typically stand? To what extent do the models enact stereotypically masculine or feminine stances? To develop your essay, consult Diane Barthel, "A Gentleman and a Consumer" (p. 171).

4. Devor argues that female fashion traditionally has restricted body movement while male styles of dress have commonly allowed freedom of movement. In class, discuss whether this gender division is still true today, being sure to consider a range of clothing types (e.g., athletic wear, corporate dress, party fashion, and so forth). To develop your ideas, consult Deborah Tannen, "There Is No Unmarked Woman" (p. 525).

KEVIN JENNINGS

AMERICAN DREAMS

When Ellen DeGeneres became the first television star to come out of the closet on prime-time TV, gay men and lesbians around the country celebrated what appeared to be a major step forward for one of America's most marginalized communities. But the firestorm of protest that also attended Ellen's coming out equally demonstrated just how far homosex-

uals have to go before winning full acceptance into American society. In this personal narrative of what it means to grow up gay in America, Kevin Jennings (b. 1963) reveals the torment endured by a child forced to conceal his difference from everyone around him, especially his own parents. With years of self-denial and one suicide attempt behind him, Jennings shows how he eventually came to accept himself as he is and in so doing achieved his own version of the American dream.

When I was little, I honestly thought I would grow up to be the president. After all, I lived in a land of opportunity where anyone, with enough determination and hard work, could aspire to the highest office in the land. I planned to live out the American Dream.

I realized, however, that something was amiss from an early age. I grew up in the rural community of Lewisville, North Carolina, just outside the city of Winston-Salem. As you might guess from the city's name, Winston-Salem, Winston-Salem makes its living from the tobacco industry: It was cigarettes that propelled local conglomerate RJR-Nabisco to its status as one of the world's largest multinational corporations. Somehow this rising tide of prosperity never lapped at our doors, and the Jennings family was a bitter family indeed. Poor whites descended from Confederate veterans, we eagerly sought out scapegoats for our inexplicable failure to "make it" in the land of opportunity. My uncles and cousins joined the Ku Klux Klan, while my father, a fundamentalist minister, used religion to excuse his prejudices — against blacks, against Jews, against Catholics, against Yankees, against Communists and liberals (basically the same thing, as far as he was concerned), and, of course, against gays. Somehow the golden rule of "Do unto others as you would have them do unto you" never made it into his gospel. Instead, I remember church services filled with outbursts of paranoia, as we were warned about the evils of those whom we (incorrectly) held responsible for our very real oppression. I grew up believing that there was a Communist plot undermining our nation, a Jewish conspiracy controlling the banks and the media, and that black men — whom I unselfconsciously referred to as "niggers" — spent their days plotting to rape white women. In case this seems like a history lesson on the Stone Age, please consider that I was born in 1963 and graduated from high school in 1981. Hardly the ancient past!

My father's profession as a traveling minister never left much money for luxuries like college tuition. Nevertheless, my mother was determined that I, her last chance, was going to make good on the Dream that had been denied to her and to my four older siblings. Not that it was going to be easy: my father died when I was eight, and my mother went to work at McDonald's (the only job she could get with her limited credentials). Every penny was watched carefully; dinner was often leftover quarter-pounders that she didn't have to pay for. I'm the only person I know who sees the Golden Arches, takes a bite, and thinks, "Mmm, just like Mom used to make!"

Seniors march for gay rights.

Throughout high school, I was determined to make it, determined to show my mother — and myself — that the American Dream really could come true. I worked hard and got ahead, earning a scholarship to Harvard after I had remade myself into the image of what I was told a successful person was like. Little did I realize at that point the price I was paying to fit in.

The first thing to go was any sign of my Southern heritage. As I came into   5 contact with mainstream America, through high school "gifted and talented" programs and, later, at college in Massachusetts, I began to realize that we Southerners were different. Our home-cooked meals — grits, turnip greens, red-eye gravy — never seemed to show up in frozen dinners, and if a character on television spoke with a Southern accent, that immediately identified him or her as stupid or as comic relief. As the lesbian writer Blanche Boyd put it:

> When television programs appeared, a dreadful truth came clear to me: Southerners were not normal people. We did not sound like normal people . . . [and] what we chose to talk about seemed peculiarly different also. I began to realize we were hicks. Television took away my faith in my surroundings. I didn't want to be a hick. I decided to go North, where people talked fast, walked fast, and acted cool. I practiced talking like the people on television. . . . I became desperate to leave the South.

Like Blanche Boyd, I deliberately erased my accent and aped the false mono-tone of television newscasters. I never invited college friends home to North

Carolina for fear they might meet my family and realize they were worthless, ignorant hicks — which is how I'd come to view those whom I loved. I applied to colleges on the sole criterion that they not be in the South. I ran as far from Lewisville, North Carolina, as I could.

But there were some things about myself I could not escape from or change, no matter how hard I tried — among them the fact that I am gay.

I had always known I was gay, even before I had heard the word or knew what it meant. I remember that at age six or seven, the "adult" magazines that so fascinated my older brothers simply didn't interest me at all, and I somehow knew that I'd better hide this feeling from them. As I grew older and began to understand what my feelings meant, I recoiled in horror from myself. After all, my religious upbringing as a Southern Baptist had taught me that gay people were twisted perverts destined for a lifetime of eternal damnation.

Being as set as I was on achieving the American Dream, I was not about to accept the fact that I was gay. Here is where I paid the heaviest price for my Dream. I pursued what I thought was "normal" with a vengeance in high school, determined that, if the spirit was weak, the flesh would be more willing at the prospect of heterosexuality. I dated every girl I could literally get my hands on, earning a well-deserved reputation as a jerk who tried to see how far he could get on the first date. I attacked anyone who suggested that gay people might be entitled to some rights, too, and was the biggest teller of fag jokes at Radford High. But what I really hated was myself, and this I couldn't escape from, no matter how drunk or stoned I got, which I was doing on an almost daily basis by senior year.

That was also the year I fell in love for the first time, with another boy in my class. It turned out he was gay, too, and we made love one night in late May. I woke up the next morning and realized that it was true — I really was a fag after all. I spent that day trying to figure out how I was going to live the American Dream, which seemed impossible if I was homosexual. By nightfall I decided it *was* impossible, and without my Dream I couldn't see a reason why I'd want to be alive at all. I went to my family's medicine cabinet, took the new bottle of aspirin out, and proceeded to wash down 140 pills with a glass of gin. I remember the exact number — 140 — because I figured I could only get down about ten at one swallow, so I carefully counted out fourteen little stacks before I began. Thanks to a friend who got to me in time, I didn't die that night. My story has a happy ending — but a lot of them don't. Those moments of desperation helped me understand why one out of every three gay teens tries to commit suicide.

At Harvard, the most important lessons I learned had little to do with Latin 10 American or European history, which were my majors. Instead, I learned the importance of taking control of my own destiny. I met a great professor who taught me that as long as I stayed in the closet, I was accepting the idea that there was something wrong with me, something that I needed to hide. After all, as my favorite bisexual, Eleanor Roosevelt, once said, "No one can make you feel inferior without your consent." By staying closeted, I was consenting to my own inferiority. I realized that for years, I had let a Dream — a beautiful, seductive, but ultimately false Dream — rule my life. I had agreed to pay its price, which was the rejection of my family, my culture, and eventually myself. I came to understand that the costs of the Dream far outweighed its rewards. I learned that true freedom would be mine only when I was able to make my own decisions about what I wanted out of life instead of accepting those thrust upon me by the Dream. Since I made that realization, I have followed my own path instead of the one I had been taught was "right" all my life.

Once I started down this new path, I began to make some discoveries about the society in which I was raised, and about its notions of right and wrong. I began to ask many questions, and the answers to these questions were not always pleasant. Why, for example, did my mother always earn less than men who did the same exact work? Why did I learn as a child that to cheat someone was to "Jew" them? Why was my brother ostracized when he fell in love with and later married a black woman? Why did everyone in my family work so hard and yet have so little? I realized that these inequalities were part of the game, the rules of which were such that gays, blacks, poor people, women, and many others would always lose to the wealthy white heterosexual Christian men who have won the Presidency forty-two out of forty-two times. Those odds — 100 percent — are pretty good ones to bet on. No, I discovered that true freedom could not be achieved by a Dream that calls on us to give up who we are in order to fit in and become "worthy" of power. Holding power means little if women have to become masculine "iron ladies" to get it, if Jews have to "Americanize" their names, if blacks have to learn to speak so-called Standard English (though we never acknowledge *whose* standard it is), or if gays and lesbians have to hide what everyone else gets to celebrate — the loves of their lives.

Real freedom will be ours when the people around us — and when we ourselves — accept that we, too, are "real" Americans, and that we shouldn't have to change to meet anyone else's standards. In 1924, at age twenty-two, the gay African-American poet Langston Hughes said it best, in his poem "I, Too":

> Tomorrow,
> I'll be at the table
> When company comes.
> Nobody'll dare
> Say to me,
> "Eat in the kitchen,"
> Then.
> Besides,
> They'll see how beautiful I am
> And be ashamed —
> I, too, am America.

By coming out as a gay man and demanding my freedom, I realize that I have done the most American thing of all. And while I have come a long way since the days when I dreamed of living in the White House, I have discovered that what I'm fighting for now is the very thing I thought I'd be fighting for if I ever became President — "liberty and justice for all."

READING THE TEXT

1. According to Jennings, how did his Southern upbringing influence his goals for the future?

2. Why did Jennings feel he had to eschew his Southern heritage?

3. In what ways did Jennings deny to himself his sexual orientation, and why did he do so?

4. In your own words, trace the evolution of Jennings's understanding of the American dream as he grew up.

5. What is the relationship between the excerpt from Langston Hughes's "I, Too" and Jennings's story?

READING THE SIGNS

1. In your journal, write your own account of how you responded to normative gender codes as a high school student. To what extent did you feel pressure to conform or to renounce traditional expectations — or to do both?

2. Jennings describes his early attempts to deny his sexual orientation. In class, discuss how other minority or underprivileged groups — ethnic minorities, women, the disabled — sometimes try to erase their own identity. What social and cultural forces motivate such self-denial? Use the discussion as the basis for an essay in which you explore why one might be motivated to treat oneself as an "other."

3. In class, brainstorm two lists: films or TV shows that reinforce heterosexuality as normative and those that present homosexuality in a positive light. Then compare your lists. What conclusions do you draw about popular culture's influence on American gender codes?

4. Compare and contrast Jennings's arrival at a confident sense of identity with that of Melissa Algranati ("Being an Other," p. 608). How do you explain any differences you observe?

DEBORAH BLUM

THE GENDER BLUR: WHERE DOES BIOLOGY END AND SOCIETY TAKE OVER?

There's an old argument over whether nature or nurture is more impor-tant in determining human behavior. Nowhere is this argument more in-tense than in gender studies, where proponents of the social construc-tion of gender identities are currently exploring the many ways in which our upbringing shapes our behavior. But after watching her two-year-old son emphatically choose to play only with carnivorous dinosaur toys and disdainfully reject the "wimpy" vegetarian variety, Deborah Blum decided that nurture couldn't be all that there was to it. Exploring the role of bi-ology in the determination of human behavior, Blum argues that both na-ture and nurture have to be taken into account if we are to understand gender differences. A Pulitzer Prize–winning professor of journalism at the University of Wisconsin at Madison, Blum is the author of Sex on the Brain: The Biological Differences between Men and Women *(1997).*

I was raised in one of those university-based, liberal elite families that politi-cians like to ridicule. In my childhood, every human being — regardless of gender — was exactly alike under the skin, and I mean exactly, barring his or her different opportunities. My parents wasted no opportunity to bring this point home. One Christmas, I received a Barbie doll and a softball glove. An-other brought a green enamel stove, which baked tiny cakes by the heat of a lightbulb, and also a set of steel-tipped darts and competition-quality dart-board. Did I mention the year of the chemistry set and the ballerina doll?

It wasn't until I became a parent — I should say, a parent of two boys — that I realized I had been fed a line and swallowed it like a sucker (barring the part about opportunities, which I still believe). This dawned on me during my older son's dinosaur phase, which began when he was about two-and-a-half. Oh, he loved dinosaurs, all right, but only the blood-swilling carnivores. Plant-eaters were wimps and losers, and he refused to wear a T-shirt marred by a picture of a stegosaur. I looked down at him one day, as he was snarling around my feet and doing his toddler best to gnaw off my right leg, and I thought: This goes a lot deeper than culture.

Raising children tends to bring on this kind of politically incorrect reac-tion. Another friend came to the same conclusion watching a son deter-minedly bite his breakfast toast into the shape of a pistol he hoped would blow away — or at least terrify — his younger brother. Once you get past the guilt part — Did I do this? Should I have bought him that plastic allosaur with

495

the oversized teeth? — such revelations can lead you to consider the far more interesting field of gender biology, where the questions take a different shape: Does love of carnage begin in culture or genetics, and which drives which? Do the gender roles of our culture reflect an underlying biology, and, in turn, does the way we behave influence that biology?

The point I'm leading up to — through the example of my son's innocent love of predatory dinosaurs — is actually one of the most straightforward in this debate. One of the reasons we're so fascinated by childhood behaviors is that, as the old saying goes, the child becomes the man (or woman, of course). Most girls don't spend their preschool years snarling around the house and pretending to chew off their companion's legs. And they — mostly — don't grow up to be as aggressive as men. Do the ways that we amplify those early differences in childhood shape the adults we become? Absolutely. But it's worth exploring the starting place — the faint signal that somehow gets amplified.

"There's plenty of room in society to influence sex differences," says 5 Marc Breedlove, a behavioral endocrinologist at the University of California at Berkeley and a pioneer in defining how hormones can help build sexually different nervous systems. "Yes, we're born with predispositions, but it's society that amplifies them, exaggerates them. I believe that — except for the sex differences in aggression. Those [differences] are too massive to be explained simply by society."

Aggression does allow a straightforward look at the issue. Consider the following statistics: Crime reports in both the United States and Europe record between 10 and 15 robberies committed by men for every one by a woman. At one point, people argued that this was explained by size difference. Women weren't big enough to intimidate, but that would change, they predicted, with the availability of compact weapons. But just as little girls don't routinely make weapons out of toast, women — even criminal ones — don't seem drawn to weaponry in the same way that men are. Almost twice as many male thieves and robbers use guns as their female counterparts do.

Or you can look at more personal crimes: domestic partner murders. Three-fourths of men use guns in those killings; 50 percent of women do. Here's more from the domestic front: In conflicts in which a woman killed a man, he tended to be the one who had started the fight — in 51.8 percent of the cases, to be exact. When the man was the killer, he again was the likely first aggressor, and by an even more dramatic margin. In fights in which women died, they had started the argument only 12.5 percent of the time.

Enough. You can parade endless similar statistics but the point is this: Males are more aggressive, not just among humans but among almost all species on earth. Male chimpanzees, for instance, declare war on neighboring troops, and one of their strategies is a warning strike: They kill females and infants to terrorize and intimidate. In terms of simple, reproductive genetics, it's an advantage of males to be aggressive: You can muscle your way into dominance, winning more sexual encounters, more offspring, more genetic future. For the female — especially in a species like ours, with time for just one successful pregnancy a year — what's the genetic advantage in brawling?

Thus the issue becomes not whether there is a biologically influenced sex difference in aggression — the answer being a solid, technical "You betcha" — but rather how rigid that difference is. The best science, in my opinion, tends to align with basic common sense. We all know that there are extraordinarily gentle men and murderous women. Sex differences are always generalizations: they refer to a behavior, with some evolutionary rationale behind it. They never define, entirely, an individual. And that fact alone should tell us that there's always — even in the most biologically dominated traits — some flexibility, an instinctive ability to respond, for better and worse, to the world around us.

This is true even with physical characteristics that we've often assumed 10 are nailed down by genetics. Scientists now believe height, for instance, is only about 90 percent heritable. A person's genes might code for a six-foot-tall body, but malnutrition could literally cut that short. And there's also some evidence, in girls anyway, that children with stressful childhoods tend to become shorter adults. So while some factors are predetermined, there's evidence that the prototypical male/female body design can be readily altered.

It's a given that humans, like most other species — bananas, spiders, sharks, ducks, any rabbit you pull out of a hat — rely on two sexes for reproduction. So basic is that requirement that we have chromosomes whose primary purpose is to deliver the genes that order up a male or a female. All other chromosomes are numbered, but we label the sex chromosomes with the letters X and Y. We get one each from our mother and our father, and the basic combinations are these: XX makes female, XY makes male.

There are two important — and little known — points about these chromosomal matches. One is that even with this apparently precise system, there's nothing precise — or guaranteed — about the physical construction of male and female. The other point makes that possible. It appears that sex doesn't matter in the early stages of embryonic development. We are unisex at the point of conception.

If you examine an embryo at about six weeks, you see that it has the ability to develop in either direction. The fledgling embryo has two sets of ducts — Wolffian for male, Muellerian for female — an either/or structure, held in readiness for further development. If testosterone and other androgens are released by hormone-producing cells, then the Wolffian ducts develop into the channel that connects penis to testes, and the female ducts wither away.

Without testosterone, the embryo takes on a female form; the male ducts vanish and the Muellerian ducts expand into oviducts, uterus, and vagina. In other words, in humans, anyways (the opposite is true in birds), the female is the default sex. Back in the 1950s, the famed biologist Alfred Jost showed that if you castrate a male rabbit fetus, choking off testosterone, you produce a completely feminized rabbit.

We don't do these experiments in humans — for obvious reasons — but 15 there are naturally occurring instances that prove the same point. For instance: In the fetal testes are a group of cells, called Leydig cells, that make testosterone. In rare cases, the fetus doesn't make enough of these cells (a defect known as Leydig cell hypoplasia). In this circumstance we see the limited power of the XY chromosome. These boys have the right chromosomes and the right genes to be boys; they just don't grow a penis. Obstetricians and parents often think they see a baby girl, and these children are routinely raised as daughters. Usually, the "mistake" is caught about the time of puberty, when menstruation doesn't start. A doctor's examination shows the child to be internally male; there are usually small testes, often tucked within the abdomen. As the researchers put it, if the condition had been known from the beginning, "the sisters would have been born as brothers."

Just to emphasize how tricky all this body-building can get, there's a peculiar genetic defect that seems to be clustered by heredity in a small group of villages in the Dominican Republic. The result of the defect is a failure to produce an enzyme that concentrates testosterone, specifically for building the genitals. One obscure little enzyme only, but here's what happens without it: You get a boy with undescended testes and a penis so short and stubby that it resembles an oversized clitoris.

In the mountain villages of this Caribbean nation, people are used to it. The children are usually raised as "conditional" girls. At puberty, the secondary tide of androgens rises and is apparently enough to finish the construction project. The scrotum suddenly descends, the phallus grows, and the child develops a distinctly male body — narrow hips, muscular build, and even slight beard growth. At that point, the family shifts the child over from daughter to son. The dresses are thrown out. He begins to wear male clothes and starts dating girls. People in the Dominican Republic are so familiar with this condition that there's a colloquial name for it: *guevedoces,* meaning "eggs (or testes) at 12."

It's the comfort level with this slip-slide of sexual identity that's so remarkable and, I imagine, so comforting to the children involved. I'm positive that the sexual transition of these children is less traumatic than the abrupt awareness of the "sisters who would have been brothers." There's a message of tolerance there, well worth repeating, and there are some other key lessons too.

These defects are rare and don't alter the basic male-female division of our species. They do emphasize how fragile those divisions can be. Biology allows flexibility, room to change, to vary and grow. With that comes room for error as well. That it's possible to live with these genetic defects, that they don't merely kill us off, is a reminder that we, male and female alike, exist on a continuum of biological possibilities that can overlap and sustain either sex.

Marc Breedlove points out that the most difficult task may be separating [20] how the brain responds to hormones from how the brain responds to the *results* of hormones. Which brings us back, briefly, below the belt: In this context, the penis is just a result, the product of androgens at work before birth.

"And after birth," says Breedlove, "virtually everyone who interacts with that individual will note that he has a penis, and will, in many instances, behave differently than if the individual was a female."

Do the ways that we amplify physical and behavioral differences in childhood shape who we become as adults? Absolutely. But to understand that, you have to understand the differences themselves — their beginning and the very real biochemistry that may lie behind them.

Here is a good place to focus on testosterone — a hormone that is both well-studied and generally underrated. First, however, I want to acknowledge that there are many other hormones and neurotransmitters that appear to influence behavior. Preliminary work shows that fetal boys are a little more active than fetal girls. It's pretty difficult to argue socialization at that point. There's a strong suspicion that testosterone may create the difference.

And there are a couple of relevant animal models to emphasize the point. Back in the 1960s, Robert Goy, a psychologist at the University of Wisconsin at Madison, first documented that young male monkeys play much more roughly than young females. Goy went on to show that if you manipulate testosterone level — raising it in females, damping it down in males — you can reverse those effects, creating sweet little male monkeys and rowdy young females.

Is testosterone the only factor at work here? I don't think so. But clearly we can argue a strong influence, and, interestingly, studies have found that girls with congenital adrenal hypoplasia — who run high in testosterone — tend to be far more fascinated by trucks and toy weaponry than most little girls are. They lean toward rough-and-tumble play, too. As it turns out, the strongest influence on this "abnormal" behavior is not parental disapproval, but the company of other little girls, who tone them down and direct them toward more routine girl games.

And that reinforces an early point: If there is indeed a biology to sex differences, we amplify it. At some point — when it is still up for debate — we gain a sense of our gender, and with it a sense of "gender-appropriate" behavior. 25

Some scientists argue for some evidence of gender awareness in infancy, perhaps by the age of 12 months. The consensus seems to be that full-blown "I'm a girl" or "I'm a boy" instincts arrive between the ages of 2 and 3. Research shows that if a family operates in a very traditional, Beaver Cleaver kind of environment, filled with awareness of and association with "proper" gender behaviors, the "boys do trucks, girls do dolls" attitude seems to come very early. If a child grows up in a less traditional family, with an emphasis on partnership and sharing — "We all do the dishes, Joshua" — children maintain a more flexible sense of gender roles until about age 6.

In this period, too, relationships between boys and girls tend to fall into remarkably strict lines. Interviews with children find that 3-year-olds say that about half their friendships are with the opposite sex. By the age of 5, that drops to 20 percent. By 7, almost no boys or girls have, or will admit to having, best friends of the opposite sex. They still hang out on the same playground, play on the same soccer teams. They may be friendly, but the real friendships tend to be boy-to-boy or girl-to-girl.

There's some interesting science that suggests that the space between boys and girls is a normal part of development; there are periods during which children may thrive and learn from hanging out with peers of the same sex. Do we, as parents, as a culture at large, reinforce such separations? Is the pope Catholic? One of my favorite studies looked at little boys who asked for toys. If they asked for a heavily armed action figure, they got the soldier about 70 percent of the time. If they asked for a "girl" toy, like a baby doll or a Barbie, their parents purchased it maybe 40 percent of the time. Name a child who won't figure out how to work *that* system.

How does all this fit together — toys and testosterone, biology and behavior, the development of the child into the adult, the way that men and women relate to one another?

Let me make a cautious statement about testosterone: It not only has some body-building functions, it influences some behaviors as well. Let's make that a little less cautious: These behaviors include rowdy play, sex drive, competitiveness, and an in-your-face attitude. Males tend to have a higher baseline of testosterone than females — in our species, about seven to ten times as much — and therefore you would predict (correctly, I think) that all of those behaviors would be more generally found in men than in women.

But testosterone is also one of my favorite examples of how responsive biology is, how attuned it is to the way we live our lives. Testosterone, it turns out, rises in response to competition and threat. In the days of our ancestors, this might have been hand-to-hand combat or high-risk hunting endeavors. Today, scientists have measured testosterone rise in athletes preparing for a game, in chess players awaiting a match, in spectators following a soccer competition.

If a person — or even just a person's favored team — wins, testosterone continues to rise. It falls with a loss. (This also makes sense in an evolutionary perspective. If one was being clobbered with a club, it would be extremely unhelpful to have a hormone urging one to battle on.) Testosterone also rises in the competitive world of dating, settles down with a stable and supportive relationship, climbs again if the relationship starts to falter.

It's been known for years that men in high-stress professions — say, police work or corporate law — have higher testosterone levels than men in the ministry. It turns out that women in the same kind of strong-attitude professions have higher testosterone than women who choose to stay home. What I like about this is the chicken-or-egg aspect. If you argue that testosterone influenced the behavior of those women, which came first? Did they have high testosterone and choose the law? Or did they choose the law, and the competitive environment ratcheted them up on the androgen scale? Or could both be at work?

And, returning to children for a moment, there's an ongoing study by Pennsylvania researchers, tracking that question in adolescent girls, who are being encouraged by their parents to engage in competitive activities that were once for boys only. As they do so, the researchers are monitoring, regularly, two hormones: testosterone and cortisol, a stress hormone. Will these hormones rise in response to this new, more traditionally male environment? What if more girls choose the competitive path; more boys choose the other? Will female testosterone levels rise, male levels fall? Will that wonderful, unpredictable, flexible biology that we've been given allow a shift, so that one day, we will literally be far more alike?

We may not have answers to all those questions, but we can ask them,   35 and we can expect that the answers will come someday, because science clearly shows us that such possibilities exist. In this most important sense, sex differences offer us a paradox. It is only through exploring and understanding what makes us different that we can begin to understand what binds us together.

READING THE TEXT

1. What effect do Blum's opening personal-experience anecdotes have on the persuasiveness of her argument?

2. What evidence does Blum offer to support her contention that males are naturally more aggressive than females?

3. How does testosterone affect human behavior, according to Blum's research?

4. In Blum's view, how do the cultural choices that humans make, such as engaging in sports or other competitive activities, affect hormonal balances?

READING THE SIGNS

1. In your journal, reflect on the way your upbringing shaped your sense of appropriate gender behavior.

2. Blum's selection challenges the common cultural studies position that gender behavior is socially constructed. Write an essay in which you defend, qualify, or reject Blum's point of view. To develop your ideas, consult Holly Devor's "Gender Role Behaviors and Attitudes" (p. 484).

3. Write an essay describing how you would raise a boy to counteract his tendencies to aggressive behavior. To develop your ideas, consult James William Gibson, "Warrior Dreams" (p. 530).

4. Visit the library, and investigate recent research on the possible genetic basis for homosexuality. Then write an essay in which you extend Blum's argument for the biological basis of gendered behavior to sexual orientation.

ROGER RESSMEYER

Babies in a Cart

READING THE SIGNS

1. Describe the scene in the photo. What is taking place? How are the genders of the babies indicated? Why is the bird in the photo?

2. What are the implications of placing a pair of children in a shopping cart? On what aspects of contemporary society do you think this image comments?

JENNIFER SCANLON

BOYS-R-US: BOARD GAMES AND THE SOCIALIZATION OF YOUNG ADOLESCENT GIRLS

Heart-Throb: The Dream Date Game. Sweet Valley High: Can You Find a Boyfriend in Time for the Big Date? No, these aren't the titles of romance novels: They're box games for girls, ages eight and up, and as Jennifer Scanlon argues in this analysis of games for young girls, they aren't innocent. For games like these help shape the consciousness of young girls, telling them what should matter to them (boys) and what shouldn't (things like intellectual achievement), and that, Scanlon suggests, isn't child's play. An associate professor and director of women's studies at Plattsburgh State University, Scanlon is the author of Inarticulate Longings: The Ladies' Home Journal, Gender, and the Promises of Consumer Culture *(1995) and editor of* Significant Contemporary American Feminists *(1999) and of* Gender and Consumer Culture Reader *(2000).*

In a 1973 volume of *Ms.* magazine, Letty Cottin Pogrebin introduced a checklist for parents who wanted to buy nonsexist toys for their children. An acceptable toy would be "respectful of the child's intellect and creativity, nonracist, moral in terms of the values it engenders, and nonsexist in the way it is packaged, conceived, and planned for play" (48). One of the board games she recommended was Life, a Milton Bradley product, as it encouraged all players to pursue lives of their own, money of their own, careers of their own.

Now, readers, as the instructions on a game might tell you, advance twenty years. Enter the 1990s, a mall, Anytown U.S.A. A parent looking for nonsexist toys for children might, at a Toys Я Us store, find a few toys and games that Pogrebin would approve of. The game of Life remains popular, and consumers can find numerous trivia games, memory games, and games of skill on the shelves. Unfortunately, however, mall toy stores rely heavily on gender stereotypes for their displays, layout, advertising, and most importantly, products. This essay looks at four gender-specific board games directed at young adolescent girls, examines their messages in light of Pogrebin's now twenty-five-year-old suggestions, and brings to light issues about a much-neglected period in girls' lives, early adolescence, and a much-neglected area of popular culture or leisure studies, gender-specific games.

The least gender-specific toys and games in the stores are, arguably, those in the baby and toddler section. Primary colors predominate in these toys, and customers purchase chunky trains and boats for baby girls or boys. Sex-typing occurs quickly as you move either down the aisle or up in age, as trucks become masculinized, dolls feminized. Pastels replace primary colors in girls' toys, and the packaging, game boards and pieces, even the cover photographs become feminized. For boys' toys, camouflage greens and browns replace soft colors, and war toys and sports equipment fill the shelves. And now you arrive at these four games for young adolescent girls, where the players featured on the game boxes, girls only, dress in feminine clothing and wear heavy make-up and jewelry, even though the suggested starting age for the games is eight.

Heart-Throb: The Dream Date Game, and Sweet Valley High: Can You Find a Boyfriend in Time for the Big Date? are both produced by Milton Bradley, subsidiary of Hasbro, a company with $410 million in annual sales. Hasbro, with no women on its board of directors, produces board games for children and adults as well as a range of other products from teething rings to women's undergarments, baby pacifiers to girls' nightwear. The second two games, Girl Talk: A Game of Truth or Dare, and Girl Talk: Date Line, are produced by Western Publishing Company, which has annual sales of $495 million and produces, among other things, board games for children and adults, gift wrap and novelties, stationery, and books (Dun and Bradstreet 813, 1831).

Not surprisingly, these four games invite girls to enter the consumer marketplace by encouraging players to use products such as clothing and make-up to enhance their looks. Another game for young adolescent girls, Meet Me at the Mall, more blatantly emphasizes the consumer side of things; players run around the mall, visiting stores like the Gap and Benetton, trying to out-buy the competition. For the four games discussed in this [essay], though, players must obtain boyfriends rather than consumer goods. Whether a girl steals one from a friend, wins one through her own matchmaking skills, or reads one in her future, a boyfriend rather than a career or a life remains the player's central goal. . . . 5

Of course, gender is a crucial element in adolescent development for girls and boys. In no other period of life except infancy do so many biological changes occur so quickly, and many of those biological changes are sex-specific (Montemayor et al. 9). Those who study adolescence, however, argue that social expectations, even more than physical changes, shape gender roles (Huston and Alvarez 158). When young people respond to peers and television as socializing influences, they often become increasingly intolerant of deviations from traditional sex role norms; surprisingly enough, peers often promote more traditional roles than do parents. Stereotypical attitudes about girls and boys, while not born in adolescence, often solidify at this age into hard and fast rules rather than simple observations (Montemayor et al. 13; Coleman and Hendry 123; Chandler 150).

The implications of this rigid agenda for girls are dramatic. Studies show that girls' academic and career ambitions actually decline in early adolescence when they internalize the notion that females should achieve less than males. During this period females and males both come to view math, science, and computer skills as male domains (Huston and Alvarez 158, 169). Teachers and educational programs as well as the family encourage such messages. Girls also learn by early adolescence that in order to be defined as successful they must please others, putting the needs of others first. Girls have few illusions about how this translates into real life experiences. Sadly, while cognitive developments that take place in early adolescence can encourage children to look at roles, including gender roles, in a flexible way, social constraints encourage them to limit their thinking and conceptualize gender roles in highly conformist and predictable ways (Huston and Alvarez 173). For girls this translates to the rule that they must get a boyfriend, keep a boyfriend, and learn dependence on males to be successful in life (McRobbie xvii; Newman and Newman 150–51; Chandler x).

While young children repeatedly get these messages at home and in school, they get them from popular culture as well. Widely documented studies of television's influence on gender role socialization reveal the connections between television watching and the likelihood that children and teenagers will have stereotypical beliefs about gender roles (Comstock 160–75). Adolescence heightens sensitivity about gender, and numerous studies demonstrate the extent of gender stereotyping on contemporary television. Males are overrepresented two or three to one in commercial television, and the voice-over in commercials remains male 90 percent of the time. This is significant, of course, as children in the United States watch an average of 40,000 commercials per year (Comstock 188). In addition to television, magazines and fiction addressed to pre-adolescent and adolescent girls stress traditional gender roles, the importance of girls' bodies, and the overwhelming and incessant need to find a boy. Magazines, for example, provide constant reminders that a girl must consciously and continuously cultivate sexual attractiveness, her greatest asset. Magazines, teen formula romance fiction, and other commercial enterprises replay the messages that come, in other forms, through the family and school.

However, unlike family or school, leisure pursuits like reading magazines or playing games do not appear to be coercive. Simply because of this, they demand attention. Associated with freedom, leisure activities for girls often carry heavy ideological messages wrapped in the context of an escape from limits (McRobbie 88). These activities define girlhood in class-, race-, and behavior-specific ways. Three out of four teen fashion magazines in the United States, with a combined circulation of almost four million, portray young American women as white, very feminine, carefree, boy-crazy virgins. A recent issue of *Teen* featured liposuction and plastic surgery as options for those readers dissatisfied with their bodies. *Sassy,* noted for its initial frank discussions of adolescent sexuality, bent to pressure and omitted much of what made it controversial and, not coincidentally, a favorite among many young women craving honest discussion of their needs. These forms of popular culture, rather than an escape from limitations, provide clear and limited definitions of what it means to be a girl.

Board games, another form of popular culture, are a significant aspect of 10 same-sex play for girls. Girls do not play them with boys, nor do they play them to get boys' attention. As the back covers of the games illustrate, girls play in the company of other girls, often in the privacy of one of their bedrooms. The picture on the back of Heart-Throb is typical: four girls in a bedroom, one of them on the bed, the others lounging on the carpeted floor. The game board sits on the floor, and the background features a telephone, a radio/tape player, and a bowl of popcorn. In fact, three of these four covers show a telephone, a radio/tape player, and popcorn, which is, of course, a low-calorie snack. In this sacred space girls learn to define themselves. Real boys do not invade this very feminine scene, but the idea of boys takes up a good deal of space, as each game encourages girls to think about themselves in relation to boys. By playing these board games, girls learn a central rule: they need boys to complete their self-definition.

The four games featured here offer young adolescent girls a wide variety of messages, all of them gender specific. From the uniformly "pretty" boxes to the uniform goal of getting a guy, the games promote traditional gender role behaviors, emphasize clear messages about race, class, and sexual orientation, and encourage play that is decidedly humdrum if not outright insulting to any young adolescent's intelligence. They clearly fail Letty Pogrebin's test for nonsexist toys, but the ways in which they do so and fail young women in the process is worth examining further.

All of these board games promote the idea that the central object in a girl's life is to get a guy. In Sweet Valley High, girls literally race around the school trying to retrieve a boyfriend, a teacher chaperon, and all the accessories needed for a big date. In the process of trying to get it all done first, girls can steal other girls' boyfriends or fight over boyfriends; such behaviors receive rewards.

In Heart-Throb, each player chooses which boy she would like to have ask her out and guesses which boys her competitors will choose. The game pieces include 60 boyfriend cards, each picturing a different boy, and 162 personality cards, which reveal both good and bad qualities of boys. In Girl Talk: Date Line, players match up girl and boy cards they hold in their hands in order to create successful dates. While they travel around the board, trying to set up a date, the players date as well; if they do not secure a date for the imaginary characters they hold in their hands, they themselves must go stag or settle for a blind date.

In Girl Talk: A Game of Truth or Dare, the initial focus seems different. Girls spin a wheel and then must reveal a secret or do a stunt. Many of the stunts are unrelated to getting a boyfriend and include doing situps or sucking a lemon. Others, however, clearly promote the overall gender-enforcing plan and include pretending to put on make-up, calling a boy and telling him a joke, rating your looks from one to ten, or revealing what you would like to change about your looks. Anytime a girl does not complete the required stunt, she must peel off a red zit sticker and wear it on her face for the rest of the game. The game's instructions warn that the zit sticker must be visible: It cannot go under the chin or behind the ear.

The end goal of this game is to collect one of each of the fortune cards, 15 which fit into four categories: Marriage, Children, Career, and Special Moments. However, dependency on boys or men dictates girls' experiences in each of the four categories except Children. Under Marriage, two possible fortunes are "You will marry _____'s boyfriend" or "You will meet your future husband while working together at _____ fast-food restaurant." Under Career, you could receive "After three weeks on your first job as a _____ (profession), you will meet the man that you will eventually marry," or "You will take a job as a carhop just to get a date with a certain boy who drives a _____." Finally, under Special Moments, fortunes include "A tall, dark, and handsome policeman will stop you for speeding and give you a ticket, but will make up for it by asking you for a date," or "While visiting a dude ranch, your horse will bolt and you will be rescued by a ranch hand who looks just like _____ (actor)." In the category of Special Moments, with twenty-four possible cards, seven are specifically about boys, but only one portrays a girl having a special moment with a girlfriend.

Each of these four games portrays girls in strictly feminine terms and boys in strictly masculine terms, with little overlap in traditional definitions. In the Sweet Valley High game, for example, students vote Jessica Most Popular Girl in the school; she is also, not coincidentally, co-captain of the cheerleading squad. Elizabeth, Jessica's sister, receives an award for her newspaper column, a gossip column called "Eyes and Ears." The names used in the Sweet Valley game indicate which girls and boys are popular and which are not. The nerdy and nonmasculine boy is called Winston Egbert; Winston prefers feminine activities like talking and being gentle to masculine qualities like playing football and being aloof. The desirable boys in Sweet Valley, Todd Wilkins and Bruce Patman, do masculine things like skiing and driving expensive sports cars.

Names are used as indicators of appropriate levels of feminine or masculine qualities in Girl Talk: Date Line as well. When players land on a date space, they choose two of the character cards in their hand and set them up for a date. When they put the cards together in a microphone machine, girls discover whether or not the date they choreographed went well. The characters Gert and Homer stand out as nerds in appearance, name, and behavior. Both Gert and Homer wear glasses, but none of the many popular characters wear glasses, and the popular people have names like Nicole and Drew, Stephanie and Matt.

In Girl Talk: Date Line, Homer's personality profile reveals that he loves the computer club and collecting bugs but hates sports and school dances. Boys clearly should love sports, including the sport of pursuing girls at dances, whether or not they actually like to dance. Gert, the girl without make-up and hence without much personality, loves Latin and algebra, hates rock music and gym class. Obviously girls should not have academic aspirations. The attributes of the popular people in Girl Talk: Date Line confirm clear rules about what it means to be a girl or boy. Stacie loves talking on the phone and shopping but hates greasy hair and book reports. Tina loves pizza and make-up but hates computers and report cards. Eric, on the other hand, loves tennis and water skiing, hates shopping malls. Matt loves math and football, hates double-dating (wants to be in control?) and haircuts.

In Heart-Throb, girls and boys behave in gender-specific ways in dating. When the players choose which of the boys in the boyfriend cards they would like to date and which they think the other players will choose, it seems that at last girls are making choices. In actuality, though, the rules state that three boys from the boyfriend cards ask the girls first to dance, then to go on a date, then to go steady. The girls must choose from among the three boys. Players have some very limited choices: They can choose which boy they want, but they cannot choose not to accept a dance, a date, or a steady boyfriend. Refusing the advances of all three boys is not an option, regardless of how uninviting they appear in their personality cards.

These board games clearly promote male privilege, then; they also promote the privileges of race, wealth, and heterosexuality. In the four games, virtually all of the characters are white. In Sweet Valley High, located in California, all of the students are fair-skinned, and the only ones with names that deviate from the most popular or trendy, which include Ken — who does in fact look like Barbie's counterpart — are the names of the nerdy characters, but Winston remains, nevertheless, a Waspy nerd. In Heart-Throb, a game with sixty boyfriend cards, not one of the boys even has an ethnic-sounding name. The only feature that distinguishes a few, and makes them appear somewhat "different," is the appearance of dark sunglasses. In Girl Talk: Date Line, the trendy names include, for the girls, Danielle, Tina, Allison, and Stephanie, and for the boys, Drew, Trent, Eric, and Brad. This game, interestingly enough, features one African American boy but no African American girls; one wonders who players match him up with for a date.

In addition to the privilege of race, the characters in these games have the privilege of social class. The Sweet Valley High game goes the furthest with this: One character gets rewarded for giving her housekeeper the day off and making her own bed, another for donating a large sum to charity, a third for taking everyone for a ride in her new sports car. In each of the other games, the girls shown playing the games or the character pieces in the games dress well, have access to income to buy clothing and make-up, and have private space all their

20

own. No apartment living for these girls; they relax in their suburban bedrooms with plush carpet or scoot around town in their very own vehicles.

These board games promote the social control of girls' sexuality as well, with heterosexuality consistently privileged. In three of the four games, the only object is either to secure a boyfriend for oneself or secure one for others. The fourth clearly favors marriage and children as the end goal in life. Each game encourages competition among girls for boys, as girls steal others' boyfriends or find warnings in the instructions, as they do in the Sweet Valley game, that they need to keep an eye on their thieving girlfriends. Girls play these games together, but rather than promoting positive female culture or solidarity, the games teach girls that they cannot trust each other when it comes to their primary life definition: boys. The directions in the Sweet Valley game specify that girls can never have more than one boyfriend at a time; if they pick up a second, they must discard one. In Girl Talk: Date Line, the directions actually state in writing that players should not attempt to match up a girl with a girl or a boy with a boy for a date. According to these games, all girls, even the nerdy ones, can look forward to a shared future. What the games encourage players to share, however, is not the ability to laugh, intelligence, or even stereotypical nurturing qualities; instead, players share a future that must, apparently at any cost, include a man.

These four games rely on stereotypes about girls that stray far from the goal of promoting more egalitarian, difference-respecting play experiences. The games suggest that their characters represent the "ordinary" adolescent in the United States. Virtually all young adolescents, the games would have us believe, are white, long-haired, fair-haired, blemish-free, wealthy, heterosexual, and well dressed. The overall message does not necessarily suggest that all adolescent girls think the same way, because aside from their desire to secure a boyfriend we or the players learn little about what interests girls. What ties young adolescent girls together, through these games, is simply that they must acquire a boyfriend.

Interestingly enough, the stars of these games, the girls featured on the covers and on the boards and playing pieces, do not closely resemble the voluptuous and flashy young women of the teen magazines. In fact, they seem far closer to the "average" than that. It would be a mistake to think for a moment, though, that they represent anything but a carefully crafted version of the ideal, of the "average" ideal. Perhaps girls read fashion magazines and wish they could have the beautiful looks of the models. Perhaps when they play the board games they wish they could be the average girl, fit easily into developing peer norms, and blend into their settings as easily as the girls on the game boxes seem to blend into theirs. The games present a message just as damaging as that of the magazines, though, because if the game characters represent the norm, the average, they must represent the attainable. The truth remains that white wealthy heterosexuality is not the norm, not what young girls have in common. Unfortunately, however, most adolescents share a strong desire to meet the established, if largely unattainable, norm.

The final way in which these games fail Letty Pogrebin's test and, in so 25 doing, fail real girls' needs, is that they completely fail to challenge girls' intellects or inspire their creativity. Researchers have revealed that girls' games often provide fewer intellectual challenges than do boys' games. Girls, more restricted in their play than boys in terms of movement and noise, learn to appreciate indoor activities, in smaller groups, and at lower skill levels (Rivers et al. 105–7). The few board games we have focused on match those findings.

The most insulting of the four games is Girl Talk: Date Line. Girls match couples up and then hope that the date takes place. In fact, though, the individual qualities players match up do not determine whether or not the date takes place. Instead, a continuously running cassette tape determines everything. While the game instructs players that if the two individuals seem compatible the date will happen, sheer luck actually determines the course of action. If a player is fortunate enough to put her two characters in the microphone machine when the tape is about to play a successful date scenario, she wins. If not, she loses.

The next two games provide little more of a challenge. In Heart-Throb girls choose which boy they prefer, then they guess which boy their friends will prefer. A simple guessing game, Heart-Throb is packaged as though it contains something of consequence. Girls could easily play the same game, if they wished, using a magazine with pictures of boys in it; they hardly need the game board or pieces. Sweet Valley High is essentially a memory game. Girls have to remember in which classroom the corsage card sits, in which classroom their boyfriend sits. This game hardly differs from any matching game with cards played by young children, except for the ideological messages reinforcing gender and other stereotypes.

Girl Talk: A Game of Truth or Dare is the most sophisticated and potentially challenging of these board games. Girls actually do things in this game; they move around, they talk to each other, they share secrets. Were the end goals not so blatantly sexist, the packaging not so stereotypically feminine, and the zit stickers not so offensive, this might not be a bad game.

Games encourage players to develop particular skills. By encouraging large group play in a variety of settings, many boys' games urge them to achieve success in the world at large. Most girls' games, however, prepare girls for a life in one setting, the home, by emphasizing verbal skills in small groups rather than large ones, and by taking place indoors. Interestingly enough, although the object of many of the girls' games is to secure a boyfriend, the verbal skills emphasized do not apply to him. In other words, girls learn to talk to each other about boys, but they do not learn to communicate with those boys.

Further research may reveal that girls use these games in subversive as 30 well as stereotypical ways or that, like the latest fashions, these trendy games spend more time in closets than they do in the center of girls' play areas. For the many girls who do play them as designated, however, these sex-stereotyped games promote damaging stereotypes, passive rather than active play, and skills that fall short of girls' cognitive abilities. The games assume that all girls share a common future of domestic work, subservience to men, and limited life experience. They also further the likelihood of such a future by failing to encourage intellectual growth. In an advice book for girls published in 1936, Mary Brockman wrote that "boys don't want girls to talk too much or try to appear too wise. . . . [T]hey want girls to know when to sit back and look interested" (173). Apparently, the lesson lives on. These board games, as much a part of the toy-store world of the 1990s as they were of the 1970s, frame a world of limited possibilities for girls.

WORKS CITED

Brockman, Mary. *What Is She Like? A Personality Book for Girls.* New York: Scribner's, 1936.

Chandler, E. M. *Educating Adolescent Girls.* London: Allen, 1980.

Coleman, John C., and Leo Hendry. *The Nature of Adolescence.* New York: Routledge, 1990.

Comstock, George. *Television and the American Child.* San Diego: Academic, 1991.

Dun and Bradstreet. *America's Corporate Families.* Parsippany: Dun and Bradstreet, 1992.

Huston, Aletha, and Mildred Alvarez. "The Socialization Context of Gender Role Development in Early Adolescence." *From Childhood to Adolescence: A Transitional Period?* Ed. Raymond Montemayor, Gerald Adams, and Thomas Gullotta. Newbury Park: Sage, 1990. 156–79.

McRobbie, Angela. *Feminism and Youth Culture: From "Jackie" to "Just Seventeen."* Boston: Unwin Hyman, 1991.

Montemayor, Raymond, Gerald Adams, and Thomas Gullotta, eds. *From Childhood to Adolescence: A Transitional Period?* Introduction. Newbury Park: Sage, 1990.

Newman, Barbara, and Philip Newman. *Adolescent Development.* Columbus: Merrill, 1986.

Pogrebin, Letty Cottin. "Toys for Free Children." *Ms.* Dec. 1973: 48+.

Rivers, Caryl, Rosalind Barnett, and Brace Baruch. *Beyond Sugar and Spice: How Women Grow, Learn, and Thrive.* New York: Putnam, 1979.

READING THE TEXT

1. What gender values do games like Heart-Throb: The Dream Date Game and Girl Talk: Date Line teach the girls who play them, according to Scanlon?

2. How do race and class figure in the board games that Scanlon analyzes?

3. What is an "ordinary" (para. 23) American adolescent, according to the images projected by board games?

4. How are male identities constructed in the board games Scanlon discusses?

READING THE SIGNS

1. As a child, did you play with one of the games Scanlon discusses (or with one like them)? If so, write a journal entry reflecting on their influence on you. Did you play with them subversively, or did you follow the rules? If you didn't play such games, reflect on the ways the games you did play may have socialized you.

2. As a class project, design a game that would counteract the gender constructions that Scanlon identifies in her essay.

3. Read or reread Naomi Wolf's "The Beauty Myth" (p. 515), and compare the role of board games in constructing young girls' gender identities with that of the advertising and the beauty industries.

4. Adopting Scanlon's perspective, write a response to Deborah Blum's argument for the biological basis of gender behaviors ("The Gender Blur: Where Does Biology End and Society Take Over?" p. 495).

ANDRE MAYER

THE NEW SEXUAL STONE AGE

More than thirty years after the beginning of the modern women's movement, the traditional codes that govern gender behavior and identity are being replaced by new notions of what it means to be a man or woman. But you wouldn't know it by listening to contemporary pop music, especially rap-metallists like Kid Rock and Limp Bizkit, who, Andre Mayer argues in this selection from the online magazine Shift.com, *have returned "to an age of rampant chauvinism, where men swagger about in a testosterone rage and women are reduced to sexual ornaments." Suddenly, it's "pimp culture" time on the pop airwaves, where men are men and women are, well — maybe you should watch a videotape of the Britney Spears Pepsi commercial run during Super Bowl XXXVI. Mayer is a columnist for* Shift.com *magazine.*

Everywhere you look, people are taking a more open-minded stance on gender roles. In October 2000, the Dutch parliament implemented legislation that would make it the first country in the world to recognize gay marriages. Ohio University announced it would designate thirty campus bathrooms "unisex" to accommodate transgendered students. The number of male nurses is rising, as is the overall viewership of women's sports. Outmoded notions about the roles of men and women are relaxing; except, that is, in pop music, where quite the opposite is true. Glance at magazine covers, at videos, at lyric sheets: We've returned to an age of rampant chauvinism, where men swagger about in a testosterone rage and women are reduced to sexual ornaments.

The most visible advocates are artists like Kid Rock, Limp Bizkit, and Crazy Town, who not only resemble eighties hair metal in their thudding guitar assault, but in their celebration of male debauchery and female subservience. In song, females are oppugned; in videos, they're totted up like bimbos and objectified. Limp Bizkit's "Nookie" does both: The track is a misogynistic kiss-off to a girlfriend, and when singer Fred Durst shouts "I did it all for the nookie," he's blatantly admitting that he exploited her for sex. Critics have long reproved hip hop for its too-enthusiastic use of words like "bitches" and "hos," but rappers could always deflect accountability for claiming that their lyrics were a stark reflection of ghetto reality. With the advent of rap-metal, however, artists like Kid Rock and Limp Bizkit have taken the gritty argot of their hip hop heroes and are passing it off as their own. With widespread use, such hateful language becomes more accepted.

The same can be said for the current prevalence of pimp iconography. Echoing rappers like the Notorious B.I.G. and Too $hort, Kid Rock fancies himself an "American pimp," but he's part of a greater trend that includes apparel (Phat Pimp Clothing, Pimpdaddy.com), movies (the Hughes brothers' documentary *American Pimp* and the upcoming comedy *Lil' Pimp,* about a nine-year-old procurer), and staged events, like Boston's annual "Pimps and Hos Ball." It stems from the general nostalgia for blaxploitation flicks like *Cleopatra Jones* and *The Mack,* in which pimps are the pinnacle of camp, dressing in garish attire and spouting comical jive. Real pimps are far less cuddly — as we know, they insult, abuse, and unscrupulously lord over their female charges. Most people would agree that pimping is abhorrent, but the image has become so widespread — and in many cases, sentimentalized — that a new generation of pop culture consumers blithely embraces it.

Unfortunately, the current contingent of female stars is doing little to correct these primitive attitudes. Many of them — the Britneys, the Christinas, the Jessicas — dress like prostitutes, or at the very least, extras in a Van Halen video. When these chirpy, vacuous singers swept into vogue, they knocked more intelligent and progressive gals like Tori Amos and Alanis Morrissette off the charts. Every new video or awards show is an opportunity for immodest types like Mariah Carey and Toni Braxton to set new standards for libidinous spectacle, and while they pay lip service to positive messages, the only thing they offer their distaff fans is an unattainable image of female sexuality.

So what's the cause of this retrograde sexism? Many critics have pointed 5 to the feelings described by Susan Faludi in her book *Stiffed: The Betrayal of the American Man,* in which she claims that feelings of emasculation (due to a number of factors, including joblessness and feminism) have spurred many men to reassert their manhood. The most glaring consequence of this may be the popularity of so-called "lad mags," of which *Maxim* was arguably the catalyst. Started in the mid-nineties, *Maxim* captured an immense demographic of horny males by offering *Playboy*-type titillation (stopping just short of pornography) and insolent commentary. The effect inevitably snowballed into other media — while pop has always used sex to help sell albums, record executives undoubtedly felt that increasing the T&A in the marketing of female artists would also satisfy the booming *Maxim* niche.

The music press seems eerily complicit with the problem. While some writers have commented on the inherent virgin-whore complex in Britney Spears's image, for example, many seem only too happy to defend it, or at the very least excuse it. The Spears profile in the September 13th issue of *Rolling Stone* typifies the music press's soft treatment of gender. The cover features Spears with trademark bared midriff and salacious leer and carries the kicker "Britney talks back: Don't treat me like a little girl." Like most Spears interviews, it's a shameless red herring. The story is punctuated with Spears's cheerily oblivious musings on the nature of her appeal, and in lieu of any remotely revealing quotes, writer Jenny Eliscu comes to the shrugging conclusion that "Britney and her image are one and the same — she is as much of a delightful contradiction as she seems." The title of Spears' single, "I'm a Slave 4 U," suggests that her provocative image shows no signs of flagging.

Meanwhile, those females who assert their strength often seem misguided. The catchphrase "independent women" is as hollow as the shrieks of "girl power!" back in 1997.

Destiny's Child equate self-sufficiency with having the wherewithal to buy their own clothes, shoes, and cars. Then again, any assertion of dignity seems practical at a time when Eminem protégés D12 spout, "Independent women in the house / Show us your tits and shut your motherfucking mouth" ("Ain't Nuttin' But Music").

This prevailing machismo not only denigrates women, but inherently scorns anyone whom it deems less than "manly" (i.e., impervious to sensitivity and militantly hetero). Barring gender benders like Marilyn Manson and Placebo's Brian Molko, few artists seem interested in exploring the androgyny of David Bowie and Freddie Mercury. And why would they? Right now, pop seems not only unreceptive but hostile to such liberalism.

The easiest qualification of music's current homophobia is taking a tally   10 of the number of openly gay stars. There are few beyond Elton John, k.d. lang, Melissa Etheridge, and Rufus Wainwright. Has anyone heard from George Michael lately? He's probably wary of returning to this increasingly homophobic milieu. Given the current indication for close-mindedness, sitting out until pop emerges from the Stone Age seems like a sound idea.

READING THE TEXT

1. What contradiction does Mayer see in the evolution of gender roles and the content and style of contemporary pop music?

2. What does Mayer mean by "pimp iconography" (para. 3)?

3. Characterize Mayer's tone in this selection. How does it affect your response to his argument?

4. According to Mayer, what is the significance of the relative dirth of gay performers in today's pop music world?

READING THE SIGNS

1. Write an essay in which you defend, refute, or modify Mayer's argument that much of popular music reinforces outmoded notions about gender roles.

2. Mayer describes a trend he sees in popular music, but he does not offer his own explanation for it. Write an essay in which you present your thesis for why so much modern pop music is sexist. To develop support for your argument, you might analyze current videos on MTV, paying attention to both lyrics and the personal style of the artists you watch.

3. Mayer cites *Maxim* as a current magazine that exploits the desire of "many men to reassert their manhood" (para. 5). Analyze an issue of *Maxim,* and write an essay that disputes or supports Mayer's characterization of it. To develop your argument, you might interview some men who are regular readers of the publication and some men who find no interest in it.

4. Write an essay in which you analyze the style of female rappers. To what extent do they share the "primitive" (para. 4) attitudes that Mayer ascribes to such stars as Britney Spears and Mariah Carey? How do you account for any differences that you may observe? To develop your ideas, consult Tricia Rose's "Bad Sistas" (p. 266).

5. Form teams and conduct an in-class debate on whether the patterns Mayer sees in pop music are indeed chauvinistic and dangerous or, instead, a sign of liberation. Use the debate to generate ideas for an essay in which you formulate your own argument about this question.

NAOMI WOLF

THE BEAUTY MYTH

Before Kate Moss there was Twiggy, and before Twiggy, well, women weren't expected to look so slim — not, at least, if we judge by Marilyn Monroe. And for Naomi Wolf (b. 1962), that's exactly the problem. Contemporary standards of feminine beauty have devolved to a point that can only be described as anorexic, and America's young women are paying the price through a near-epidemic of bulimia and anorexia. The most effective way to combat this epidemic, Wolf argues, is to show how what we call "beautiful" is a cultural myth that has been framed for certain purposes — essentially, Wolf believes, to keep women under control by imprisoning them in their bodies. A prominent figure in feminist and neofeminist circles, Wolf is the author of The Beauty Myth *(1991), from which this selection is excerpted,* Fire with Fire *(1993),* Promiscuities

(1997), and Misconceptions: Truth, Lies, and the Unexpected on the Journey to Motherhood *(2001).*

At last, after a long silence, women took to the streets. In the two decades of radical action that followed the rebirth of feminism in the early 1970s, Western women gained legal and reproductive rights, pursued higher education, entered the trades and the professions, and overturned ancient and revered beliefs about their social role. A generation on, do women feel free?

The affluent, educated, liberated women of the First World, who can enjoy freedoms unavailable to any woman ever before, do not feel as free as they want to. And they can no longer restrict to the subconscious their sense that this lack of freedom has something to do with — with apparently frivolous issues, things that really should not matter. Many are ashamed to admit that such trivial concerns — to do with physical appearance, bodies, faces, hair, clothes — matter so much. But in spite of shame, guilt, and denial, more and more women are wondering if it isn't that they are entirely neurotic and alone but rather that something important is indeed at stake that has to do with the relationship between female liberation and female beauty.

The more legal and material hindrances women have broken through, the more strictly and heavily and cruelly images of female beauty have come to weigh upon us. Many women sense that women's collective progress has stalled; compared with the heady momentum of earlier days, there is a dispiriting climate of confusion, division, cynicism, and above all, exhaustion. After years of much struggle and little recognition, many older women feel burned out; after years of taking its light for granted, many younger women show little interest in touching new fire to the torch.

During the past decade, women breached the power structure; meanwhile, eating disorders rose exponentially and cosmetic surgery became the fastest-growing medical specialty. During the past five years, consumer spending doubled, pornography became the main media category, ahead of legitimate films and records combined, and thirty-three thousand American women told researchers that they would rather lose ten to fifteen pounds than achieve any other goal. More women have more money and power and scope and legal recognition than we have ever had before; but in terms of how we feel about ourselves *physically,* we may actually be worse off than our unliberated grandmothers. Recent research consistently shows that inside the majority of the West's controlled, attractive, successful working women, there is a secret "underlife" poisoning our freedom; infused with notions of beauty, it is a dark vein of self-hatred, physical obsessions, terror of aging, and dread of lost control.

It is no accident that so many potentially powerful women feel this way. 5 We are in the midst of a violent backlash against feminism that uses images of female beauty as a political weapon against women's advancement: the beauty myth. It is the modern version of a social reflex that has been in force since the Industrial Revolution. As women released themselves from the feminine mystique of domesticity, the beauty myth took over its lost ground, expanding as it waned to carry on its work of social control.

The contemporary backlash is so violent because the ideology of beauty is the last one remaining of the old feminine ideologies that still has the power to control those women whom second-wave feminism would have otherwise made relatively uncontrollable: It has grown stronger to take over the work of social coercion that myths about motherhood, domesticity, chastity, and passivity no longer can manage. It is seeking right now to undo psychologically and covertly all the good things that feminism did for women materially and overtly.

This counterforce is operating to checkmate the inheritance of feminism on every level in the lives of Western women. Feminism gave us laws against job discrimination based on gender; immediately case law evolved in Britain and the United States that institutionalized job discrimination based on women's appearances. Patriarchal religion declined; new religious dogma, using some of the mind-altering techniques of older cults and sects, arose around age and weight to functionally supplant traditional ritual. Feminists, inspired by Betty Friedan, broke the stranglehold on the women's popular press of advertisers for household products, who were promoting the feminine mystique; at once, the diet and skin care industries became the new cultural censors of women's intellectual space, and because of their pressure, the gaunt, youthful model supplanted the happy housewife as the arbiter of successful womanhood. The sexual revolution promoted the discovery of female sexuality; "beauty pornography" — which for the first time in women's history artificially links a commodified "beauty" directly and explicitly to sexuality — invaded the mainstream to undermine women's new and vulnerable sense of sexual self-worth. Reproductive rights gave Western women control over our own bodies; the weight of fashion models plummeted to 23 percent below that of ordinary women, eating disorders rose exponentially, and a mass neurosis was promoted that used food and weight to strip women of that sense of control. Women insisted on politicizing health; new technologies of invasive, potentially deadly "cosmetic" surgeries developed apace to re-exert old forms of medical control of women.

Every generation since about 1830 has had to fight its version of the beauty myth. "It is very little to me," said the suffragist Lucy Stone in 1855, "to have the right to vote, to own property, etcetera, if I may not keep my body, and its uses, in my absolute right." Eighty years later, after women had won the vote, and the first wave of the organized women's movement had subsided, Virginia Woolf wrote that it would still be decades before women could tell the truth about their bodies. In 1962, Betty Friedan quoted a young woman trapped in the Feminine Mystique: "Lately, I look in the mirror, and I'm so afraid that I'm going to look like my mother." Eight years after that, heralding the cataclysmic second wave of feminism, Germaine Greer described "the Stereotype": "To her belongs all that is beautiful, even the very word beauty itself . . . she is a doll . . . I'm sick of the masquerade." In spite of the great revolution of the second wave, we are not exempt. Now we can look out over ruined barricades: A revolution has come upon us and changed everything in its path, enough time has passed since then for babies to have grown into women, but there still remains a final right not fully claimed.

The beauty myth tells a story: The quality called "beauty" objectively and universally exists. Women must want to embody it and men must want to possess women who embody it. This embodiment is an imperative for women and not for men, which situation is necessary and natural because it is biological, sexual, and evolutionary: Strong men battle for beautiful women, and beautiful women are more reproductively successful. Women's beauty must correlate to their fertility, and since this system is based on sexual selection, it is inevitable and changeless.

None of this is true. "Beauty" is a currency system like the gold standard. 10 Like any economy, it is determined by politics, and in the modern age in the West it is the last, best belief system that keeps male dominance intact. In assigning value to women in a vertical hierarchy according to a culturally imposed physical standard, it is an expression of power relations in which women must unnaturally compete for resources that men have appropriated for themselves.

"Beauty" is not universal or changeless, though the West pretends that all ideals of female beauty stem from one Platonic Ideal Woman; the Maori admire a fat vulva, and the Padung, droopy breasts. Nor is "beauty" a function of evolution: Its ideals change at a pace far more rapid than that of the evolution of species, and Charles Darwin was himself unconvinced by his own explanation that "beauty" resulted from a "sexual selection" that deviated from the rule of natural selection; for women to compete with women through "beauty" is a reversal of the way in which natural selection affects all other mammals. Anthropology has overturned the notion that females must be "beautiful" to be selected to mate: Evelyn Reed, Elaine Morgan, and others have dismissed sociobiological assertions of innate male polygamy and female monogamy. Female higher primates are the sexual initiators; not only do they seek out and enjoy sex with many partners, but "every nonpregnant female takes her turn at being the most desirable of all her troop. And that cycle keeps turning as long as she lives." The inflamed pink sexual organs of primates are often cited by male sociobiologists as analogous to human arrangements relating to female "beauty," when in fact that is a universal, nonhierarchical female primate characteristic.

Nor has the beauty myth always been this way. Though the pairing of the older rich men with young, "beautiful" women is taken to be somehow inevitable, in the matriarchal Goddess religions that dominated the Mediterranean from about 25,000 B.C.E. to about 700 B.C.E., the situation was reversed: "In every culture, the Goddess has many lovers. . . .The clear pattern is of an older woman with a beautiful but expendable youth—Ishtar and

Tammuz, Venus and Adonis, Cybele and Attis, Isis and Osiris . . . their only function the service of the divine 'womb.'" Nor is it something only women do and only men watch: among the Nigerian Wodaabes, the women hold economic power and the tribe is obsessed with male beauty; Wodaabe men spend hours together in elaborate makeup sessions, and compete — provocatively painted and dressed, with swaying hips and seductive expressions — in beauty contests judged by women. There is no legitimate historical or biological justification for the beauty myth; what it is doing to women today is a result of nothing more exalted than the need of today's power structure, economy, and culture to mount a counteroffensive against women.

If the beauty myth is not based on evolution, sex, gender, aesthetics, or God, on what is it based? It claims to be about intimacy and sex and life, a celebration of women. It is actually composed of emotional distance, politics, finance, and sexual repression. The beauty myth is not about women at all. It is about men's institutions and institutional power.

The qualities that a given period calls beautiful in women are merely symbols of the female behavior that that period considers desirable: *The beauty myth is always actually prescribing behavior and not appearance.* Competition between women has been made part of the myth so that women will be divided from one another. Youth and (until recently) virginity have been "beautiful" in women since they stand for experiential and sexual ignorance. Aging in women is "unbeautiful" since women grow more powerful with time, and since the links between generations of women must always be newly broken: Older women fear young ones, young women fear old, and the beauty myth truncates for all the female life span. Most urgently, women's identity must be premised upon our "beauty" so that we will remain vulnerable to outside approval, carrying the vital sensitive organ of self-esteem exposed to the air.

Though there has, of course, been a beauty myth in some form for as 15 long as there has been patriarchy, the beauty myth in its modern form is a fairly recent invention. The myth flourishes when material constraints on women are dangerously loosened. Before the Industrial Revolution, the average woman could not have had the same feelings about "beauty" that modern women do who experience the myth as continual comparison to a mass-disseminated physical ideal. Before the development of technologies of mass production — daguerreotypes, photographs, etc. — an ordinary woman was exposed to few such images outside the Church. Since the family was a productive unit and women's work complemented men's, the value of women who were not aristocrats or prostitutes lay in their work skills, economic shrewdness, physical strength, and fertility. Physical attraction, obviously, played its part; but "beauty" as we understand it was not, for ordinary women, a serious issue in the marriage marketplace. The beauty myth in its modern form gained ground after the upheavals of industrialization, as the work unit of the family was destroyed, and urbanization and the emerging factory system demanded what social engineers of the time termed the

At the beauty parlor: a "trivial" concern?

"separate sphere" of domesticity, which supported the new labor category of the "breadwinner" who left home for the workplace during the day. The middle class expanded, the standards of living and of literacy rose, the size of families shrank; a new class of literate, idle women developed, on whose submission to enforced domesticity the evolving system of industrial capitalism depended. Most of our assumptions about the way women have always thought about "beauty" date from no earlier than the 1830s, when the cult of domesticity was first consolidated and the beauty index invented.

For the first time new technologies could reproduce — in fashion plates, daguerreotypes, tintypes, and rotogravures — images of how women should look. In the 1840s the first nude photographs of prostitutes were taken; advertisements using images of "beautiful" women first appeared in mid-century. Copies of classical artworks, postcards of society beauties and royal mistresses, Currier and Ives prints, and porcelain figurines flooded the separate sphere to which middle-class women were confined.

Since the Industrial Revolution, middle-class Western women have been controlled by ideals and stereotypes as much as by material constraints. This situation, unique to this group, means that analyses that trace "cultural con-spiracies" are uniquely plausible in relation to them. The rise of the beauty myth was just one of several emerging social fictions that masqueraded as natural components of the feminine sphere, the better to enclose those women inside it. Other such fictions arose contemporaneously: a version of childhood that required continual maternal supervision; a concept of female biology that required middle-class women to act out the roles of hysterics and hypochondriacs; a conviction that respectable women were sexually anes-thetic; and a definition of women's work that occupied them with repetitive, time-consuming, and painstaking tasks such as needlepoint and lacemaking. All such Victorian inventions as these served a double function—that is, though they were encouraged as a means to expend female energy and intel-ligence in harmless ways, women often used them to express genuine creativ-ity and passion.

But in spite of middle-class women's creativity with fashion and embroi-dery and child rearing, and, a century later, with the role of the suburban housewife that devolved from these social fictions, the fictions' main purpose was served: During a century and a half of unprecedented feminist agitation, they effectively counteracted middle-class women's dangerous new leisure, literacy, and relative freedom from material constraints.

Though these time- and mind-consuming fictions about women's natural role adapted themselves to resurface in the postwar Feminine Mystique, when the second wave of the women's movement took apart what women's maga-zines had portrayed as the "romance," "science," and "adventure" of home-making and suburban family life, they temporarily failed. The cloying domes-tic fiction of "togetherness" lost its meaning and middle-class women walked out of their front doors in masses.

So the fictions simply transformed themselves once more: Since the 20 women's movement had successfully taken apart most other necessary fictions of femininity, all the work of social control once spread out over the whole net-work of these fictions had to be reassigned to the only strand left intact, which action consequently strengthened it a hundredfold. This reimposed onto liber-ated women's faces and bodies all the limitations, taboos, and punishments of the repressive laws, religious injunctions and reproductive enslavement that no longer carried sufficient force. Inexhaustible but ephemeral beauty work took over from inexhaustible but ephemeral housework. As the economy, law, reli-gion, sexual mores, education, and culture were forcibly opened up to include women more fairly, a private reality colonized female consciousness. By using ideas about "beauty," it reconstructed an alternative female world with its own laws, economy, religion, sexuality, education, and culture, each element as re-pressive as any that had gone before.

Since middle-class Western women can best be weakened psychologi-cally now that we are stronger materially, the beauty myth, as it has resur-faced in the last generation, has had to draw on more technological sophisti-cation and reactionary fervor than ever before. The modern arsenal of the myth is a dissemination of millions of images of the current ideal; although this barrage is generally seen as a collective sexual fantasy, there is in fact little that is sexual about it. It is summoned out of political fear on the part of male-dominated institutions threatened by women's freedom, and it exploits female guilt and apprehension about our own liberation — latent fears that we might be going too far. This frantic aggregation of imagery is a collective reactionary hallucination willed into being by both men and women stunned and disoriented by the rapidity with which gender relations have been transformed: a bulwark of reassurance against the flood of change. The mass depiction of the modern woman as a "beauty" is a contradiction: Where modern women are growing, moving, and expressing their individuality, as the myth has it, "beauty" is by definition inert, timeless, and generic. That this hallucination is necessary and deliberate is evident in the way "beauty" so directly contradicts women's real situation.

And the unconscious hallucination grows ever more influential and pervasive because of what is now conscious market manipulation: powerful industries — the $33-billion-a-year diet industry, the $20-billion cosmetics industry, the $300-million cosmetic surgery industry, and the $7-billion pornography industry — have arisen from the capital made out of unconscious anxieties, and are in turn able, through their influence on mass culture, to use, stimulate, and reinforce the hallucination in a rising economic spiral.

This is not a conspiracy theory; it doesn't have to be. Societies tell themselves necessary fictions in the same way that individuals and families do. Henrik Ibsen called them "vital lies," and psychologist Daniel Goleman describes them working the same way on the social level that they do within families: "The collusion is maintained by directing attention away from the fearsome fact, or by repackaging its meaning in an acceptable format." The costs of these social blind spots, he writes, are destructive communal illusions. Possibilities for women have become so open-ended that they threaten to destabilize the institutions on which a male-dominated culture has depended, and a collective panic reaction on the part of both sexes has forced a demand for counter-images.

The resulting hallucination materializes, for women, as something all too real. No longer just an idea, it becomes three-dimensional, incorporating within itself how women live and how they do not live: It becomes the Iron Maiden. The original Iron Maiden was a medieval German instrument of torture, a body-shaped casket painted with the limbs and features of a lovely, smiling young woman. The unlucky victim was slowly enclosed inside her; the lid fell shut to immobilize the victim, who died either of starvation or, less cruelly, of the metal spikes embedded in her interior. The modern hallucination in which women are trapped or trap themselves is similarly rigid, cruel, and euphemistically painted. Contemporary culture directs attention to imagery of the Iron Maiden, while censoring real women's faces and bodies.

Why does the social order feel the need to defend itself by evading the [25] fact of real women, our faces and voices and bodies, and reducing the meaning of women to these formulaic and endlessly reproduced "beautiful" images? Though unconscious personal anxieties can be a powerful force in the creation of a vital lie, economic necessity practically guarantees it. An economy that depends on slavery needs to promote images of slaves that "justify" the institution of slavery. Western economics are absolutely dependent now on the continued underpayment of women. An ideology that makes women feel "worth less" was urgently needed to counteract the way feminism had begun to make us feel worth more. This does not require a conspiracy; merely an atmosphere. The contemporary economy depends right now on the representation of women within the beauty myth. Economist John Kenneth Galbraith offers an economic explanation for "the persistence of the view of homemaking as a 'higher calling'": the concept of women as naturally trapped within the Feminine Mystique, he feels, "has been forced on us by popular sociology, by magazines, and by fiction to disguise the fact that woman in her role of consumer has been essential to the development of our industrial society. . . . Behavior that is essential for economic reasons is transformed into a social virtue." As soon as a woman's primary social value could no longer be defined as the attainment of virtuous domesticity, the beauty myth redefined it as the attainment of virtuous beauty. It did so to substitute both a new consumer imperative and a new justification for economic unfairness in the workplace where the old ones had lost their hold over newly liberated women.

Another hallucination arose to accompany that of the Iron Maiden: The caricature of the Ugly Feminist was resurrected to dog the steps of the women's movement. The caricature is unoriginal; it was coined to ridicule the feminists of the nineteenth century. Lucy Stone herself, whom supporters saw as "a prototype of womanly grace . . . fresh and fair as the morning," was derided by detractors with "the usual report" about Victorian feminists: "a big masculine woman, wearing boots, smoking a cigar, swearing like a trooper." As Betty Friedan put it presciently in 1960, even before the savage revamping of that old caricature: "The unpleasant image of feminists today resembles less the feminists themselves than the image fostered by the interests who so bitterly opposed the vote for women in state after state." Thirty years on, her conclusion is more true than ever: That resurrected caricature, which sought to punish women for their public acts by going after their private sense of self, became the paradigm for new limits placed on aspiring women everywhere. After the success of the women's movement's second wave, the beauty myth was perfected to checkmate power at every level in individual women's lives. The modern neuroses of life in the female body spread to woman after woman at epidemic rates. The myth is undermining — slowly, imperceptibly, without our being aware of the real forces of erosion — the ground women have gained through long, hard, honorable struggle.

The beauty myth of the present is more insidious than any mystique of femininity yet: A century ago, Nora slammed the door of the doll's house; a generation ago, women turned their backs on the consumer heaven of the isolated multi-applianced home; but where women are trapped today, there is no door to slam. The contemporary ravages of the beauty backlash are destroying women physically and depleting us psychologically. If we are to free ourselves from the dead weight that has once again been made out of femaleness, it is not ballots or lobbyists or placards that women will need first; it is a new way to see.

READING THE TEXT

1. What is the "secret 'underlife' poisoning" (para. 4) modern women's lives, according to Wolf?
2. Summarize in your own words what Wolf means by "the beauty myth" (para. 5).
3. What relationship does Wolf see between the beauty myth and feminism?
4. How has the beauty myth replaced the myth of "virtuous domesticity" (para. 25), in Wolf's opinion?
5. What are the behaviors that Wolf believes the beauty myth forces women to adopt, and why?
6. What does Wolf see as the significance of the Iron Maiden, both historically and today?

READING THE SIGNS

1. Discuss in your journal your attitudes toward your own body. To what extent have your attitudes been shaped by contemporary standards of physical attractiveness for your gender?
2. Visit a local art museum (or consult a volume of art reproductions), and study the different ways in which women's bodies are represented. How do the images reflect the history of the beauty myth that Wolf presents? Use your findings to support an analytical essay about how women are represented in art.
3. Bring to class a women's fashion magazine such as *Elle* or *Vogue* and in small groups examine the ways in which both advertising and fashion displays portray women. Discuss what the ideal image of female beauty is in your publications.
4. Write an essay in which you support, challenge, or qualify Wolf's belief that the beauty myth constitutes an "Iron Maiden" (para. 24) that torments the lives of modern women.
5. Implicit in Wolf's argument is the assumption that men are not bound by their own version of the beauty myth. In class, form teams, and debate whether men are as trapped by standards of ideal physical attractiveness as women. To develop your ideas, consult Diane Barthel, "A Gentleman and a Consumer" (p. 171), and Mariah Burton Nelson, "I Won. I'm Sorry." (p. 679).

DEBORAH TANNEN

There Is No Unmarked Woman

If you use the pronoun "s/he" when writing, or write "women and men" rather than "men and women," you are not just writing words: You are making a statement that may "mark" you as being a "feminist." In this analysis of the way everything a woman does marks her in some way or other—from writing and speaking to the way she dresses and styles her hair—Deborah Tannen (b. 1945) reveals the asymmetrical nature of gender semiotics in our culture. Wearing makeup or not wearing makeup sends a signal about a woman, whereas a man without makeup sends no signal at all. Tannen's analysis shows how what men do is implicitly considered the norm in society, and so is relatively neutral, while women's difference inevitably marks them, "because there is no unmarked woman." University Professor in Linguistics at Georgetown University, Tannen is the author of many books, including the best-selling You Just Don't Understand: Women and Men in Conversation *(1986),* Talking from 9 to 5 *(1994),* Gender and Discourse *(1994),* The Argument Culture *(1998), and* I Only Say This Because I Love You: How the Way We Talk Can Make or Break Family Relationships Throughout Our Lives *(2001).*

Some years ago I was at a small working conference of four women and eight men. Instead of concentrating on the discussion I found myself looking at the three other women at the table, thinking how each had a different style and how each style was coherent.

One woman had dark brown hair in a classic style, a cross between Cleopatra and Plain Jane. The severity of her straight hair was softened by wavy bangs and ends that turned under. Because she was beautiful, the effect was more Cleopatra than plain.

The second woman was older, full of dignity and composure. Her hair was cut in a fashionable style that left her with only one eye, thanks to a side part that let a curtain of hair fall across half her face. As she looked down to read her prepared paper, the hair robbed her of bifocal vision and created a barrier between her and the listeners.

The third woman's hair was wild, a frosted blond avalanche falling over and beyond her shoulders. When she spoke she frequently tossed her head, calling attention to her hair and away from her lecture.

Then there was makeup. The first woman wore facial cover that made her 5 skin smooth and pale, a black line under each eye and mascara that darkened already dark lashes. The second wore only a light gloss on her lips and a hint of shadow on her eyes. The third had blue bands under her eyes, dark blue shadow, mascara, bright red lipstick, and rouge; her fingernails flashed red.

I considered the clothes each woman had worn during the three days of the conference: In the first case, man-tailored suits in primary colors with solid-color blouses. In the second, casual but stylish black T-shirts, a floppy collarless jacket and baggy slacks or a skirt in neutral colors. The third wore a sexy jumpsuit; tight sleeveless jersey and tight yellow slacks; a dress with gaping armholes and an indulged tendency to fall off one shoulder.

Shoes? No. 1 wore string sandals with medium heels; No. 2, sensible, comfortable walking shoes; No. 3, pumps with spike heels. You can fill in the jewelry, scarves, shawls, sweaters — or lack of them.

As I amused myself finding coherence in these styles, I suddenly wondered why I was scrutinizing only the women. I scanned the eight men at the table. And then I knew why I wasn't studying them. The men's styles were unmarked.

The term "marked" is a staple of linguistic theory. It refers to the way language alters the base meaning of a word by adding a linguistic particle that has no meaning on its own. The unmarked form of a word carries the meaning that goes without saying — what you think of when you're not thinking anything special.

The unmarked tense of verbs in English is the present — for example, *visit*. To indicate past, you mark the verb by adding *ed* to yield *visited*. For future, you add a word: *will visit*. Nouns are presumed to be singular until marked for plural, typically by adding *s* or *es,* so *visit* becomes *visits* and *dish* becomes *dishes*. 10

The unmarked forms of most English words also convey "male." Being male is the unmarked case. Endings like *ess* and *ette* mark words as "female." Unfortunately, they also tend to mark them for frivolousness. Would you feel safe entrusting your life to a doctorette? Alfre Woodard, who was an Oscar nominee for best supporting actress, says she identifies herself as an actor because "actresses worry about eyelashes and cellulite, and women who are actors worry about the characters we are playing." Gender markers pick up extra meanings that reflect common associations with the female gender: not quite serious, often sexual.

Each of the women at the conference had to make decisions about hair, clothing, makeup and accessories, and each decision carried meaning. Every style available to us was marked. The men in our group had made decisions, too, but the range from which they chose was incomparably narrower. Men can choose styles that are marked, but they don't have to, and in this group none did. Unlike the women, they had the option of being unmarked.

Take the men's hair styles. There was no marine crew cut or oily longish hair falling into eyes, no asymmetrical, two-tiered construction to swirl over a bald top. One man was unabashedly bald; the others had hair of standard length, parted on one side, in natural shades of brown or gray or graying.

Their hair obstructed no views, left little to toss or push back or run fingers through and, consequently, needed and attracted no attention. A few men had beards. In a business setting, beards might be marked. In this academic gathering, they weren't.

There could have been a cowboy shirt with string tie or a three-piece suit or a necklaced hippie in jeans. But there wasn't. All eight men wore brown or blue slacks and nondescript shirts of light colors. No man wore sandals or boots; their shoes were dark, closed, comfortable, and flat. In short, unmarked.

Although no man wore makeup, you couldn't say the men didn't wear   15 makeup in the sense that you could say a woman didn't wear makeup. For men, no makeup is unmarked.

I asked myself what style we women could have adopted that would have been unmarked, like the men's. The answer was none. There is no unmarked woman.

There is no woman's hairstyle that can be called standard, that says nothing about her. The range of women's hairstyles is staggering, but a woman whose hair has no particular style is perceived as not caring about how she looks, which can disqualify her from many positions, and will subtly diminish her as a person in the eyes of some.

Women must choose between attractive shoes and comfortable shoes. When our group made an unexpected trek, the woman who wore flat, laced shoes arrived first. Last to arrive was the woman in spike heels, shoes in hand and a handful of men around her.

If a woman's clothing is tight or revealing (in other words, sexy), it sends a message — an intended one of wanting to be attractive, but also a possibly unintended one of availability. If her clothes are not sexy, that too sends a message, lent meaning by the knowledge that they could have been. There are thousands of cosmetic products from which women can choose and myriad ways of applying them. Yet no makeup at all is anything but unmarked. Some men see it as a hostile refusal to please them.

Women can't even fill out a form without telling stories about themselves.   20 Most forms give four titles to choose from. "Mr." carries no meaning other than that the respondent is male. But a woman who checks "Mrs." or "Miss" communicates not only whether she has been married but also whether she has conservative tastes in forms of address — and probably other conservative values as well. Checking "Ms." declines to let on about marriage (checking "Mr." declines nothing since nothing was asked), but it also marks her as either liberated or rebellious, depending on the observer's attitudes and assumptions.

I sometimes try to duck these variously marked choices by giving my title as "Dr." — and in so doing risk marking myself as either uppity (hence sarcastic responses like "Excuse *me*!") or an overachiever (hence reactions of congratulatory surprise like "Good for you!").

All married women's surnames are marked. If a woman takes her husband's name, she announces to the world that she is married and has traditional values. To some it will indicate that she is less herself, more identified by her husband's identity. If she does not take her husband's name, this too is marked, seen as worthy of comment: She has *done* something; she has "kept her own name." A man is never said to have "kept his own name" because it never occurs to anyone that he might have given it up. For him using his own name is unmarked.

A married woman who wants to have her cake and eat it too may use her surname plus his, with or without a hyphen. But this too announces her marital status and often results in a tongue-tying string. In a list (Harvey O'Donovan, Jonathan Feldman, Stephanie Woodbury McGillicutty), the woman's multiple name stands out. It is marked.

I have never been inclined toward biological explanations of gender differences in language, but I was intrigued to see Ralph Fasold bring biological phenomena to bear on the question of linguistic marking in his book *The Sociolinguistics of Language*. Fasold stresses that language and culture are particularly unfair in treating women as the marked case because biologically it is the male that is marked. While two X chromosomes make a female, two Y chromosomes make nothing. Like the linguistic markers *s, es,* or *ess,* the Y chromosome doesn't "mean" anything unless it is attached to a root form — an X chromosome.

Developing this idea elsewhere Fasold points out that girls are born with 25 fully female bodies, while boys are born with modified female bodies. He invites men who doubt this to lift up their shirts and contemplate why they have nipples.

In his book, Fasold notes "a wide range of facts which demonstrates that female is the unmarked sex." For example, he observes that there are a few species that produce only females, like the whiptail lizard. Thanks to parthenogenesis, they have no trouble having as many daughters as they like. There are no species, however, that produce only males. This is no surprise, since any such species would become extinct in its first generation.

Fasold is also intrigued by species that produce individuals not involved in reproduction, like honeybees and leaf-cutter ants. Reproduction is handled by the queen and a relatively few males; the workers are sterile females. "Since they do not reproduce," Fasold said, "there is no reason for them to be one sex or the other, so they default, so to speak, to female."

Fasold ends his discussion of these matters by pointing out that if language reflected biology, grammar books would direct us to use "she" to include males and females and "he" only for specifically male referents. But they don't. They tell us that "he" means "he or she," and that "she" is used only if the referent is specifically female. This use of "he" as the sex-indefinite pronoun is an innovation introduced into English by grammarians in the eighteenth and nineteenth centuries, according to Peter Mühlhäusler and Rom Harré in *Pronouns and People*. From at least about 1500, the correct sex-indefinite pronoun was "they," as it still is in casual spoken English. In other words, the female was declared by grammarians to be the marked case.

Writing this article may mark me not as a writer, not as a linguist, not as an analyst of human behavior, but as a feminist — which will have positive or negative, but in any case powerful, connotations for readers. Yet I doubt that anyone reading Ralph Fasold's book would put that label on him.

I discovered the markedness inherent in the very topic of gender after 30 writing a book on differences in conversational style based on geographical region, ethnicity, class, age, and gender. When I was interviewed, the vast majority of journalists wanted to talk about the differences between women and men. While I thought I was simply describing what I observed — something I had learned to do as a researcher — merely mentioning women and men marked me as a feminist for some.

When I wrote a book devoted to gender differences in ways of speaking, I sent the manuscript to five male colleagues, asking them to alert me to any interpretation, phrasing, or wording that might seem unfairly negative toward men. Even so, when the book came out, I encountered responses like that of the television talk show host who, after interviewing me, turned to the audience and asked if they thought I was male-bashing.

Leaping upon a poor fellow who affably nodded in agreement, she made him stand and asked, "Did what she say accurately describe you?" "Oh, yes," he answered. "That's me exactly." "And what she said about women — does that sound like your wife?" "Oh yes," he responded. "That's her exactly." "Then why do you think she's male-bashing?" He answered, with disarming honesty, "Because she's a woman and she's saying things about men."

To say anything about women and men without marking oneself as either feminist or anti-feminist, male-basher or apologist for men seems as impossible for a woman as trying to get dressed in the morning without inviting interpretations of her character.

Sitting at the conference table musing on these matters, I felt sad to think that we women didn't have the freedom to be unmarked that the men sitting next to us had. Some days you just want to get dressed and go about your business. But if you're a woman, you can't, because there is no unmarked woman.

READING THE TEXT

1. Explain in your own words what Tannen means by "marked" (para. 9).

2. Why does Tannen say that men have the option of being "unmarked" (para. 9)?

3. What significance does Tannen see in Ralph Fasold's biological explanations of linguistic gender differences?

READING THE SIGNS

1. Do you agree with Tannen's assumption that men have the luxury of remaining "unmarked" (para. 9) in our society? Do you think it's possible to be purely unmarked? To develop your essay, you might interview some men, particularly those who elect to have an unconventional appearance, and read James William Gibson's "Warrior Dreams" (p. 530).

2. In class, survey the extent to which the males and females in your class are "marked" or "unmarked," in Tannen's terms, studying such signs as clothing and hair style. Do the males tend to have unmarked styles, while the women tend to send a message by their choices? Discuss the results of your survey, and reflect on the validity of Tannen's claims.

3. Interview at least five women who are married, and ask them about their choice of names: Did they keep their "own" name, adopt their husband's, or opt for a hyphenated version? What signals do they want to send about their identity through their names? Use the results of your interviews to write a reflective essay on how our names function as signs, particularly as gender-related signs.

4. What would an unmarked appearance for women be like? Write a speculative essay in which you imagine the features of an unmarked female appearance. If you have difficulty imagining such an appearance, try to explain why.

JAMES WILLIAM GIBSON
WARRIOR DREAMS

If you think that Rambo was a joke, James William Gibson has news for you: his popularity was a symptom of an identity crisis that has afflicted American men since the advent of feminism and the U.S. defeat in Vietnam more than a quarter of a century ago. Feeling unmanned by a war lost and by the rewriting of gender codes in the wake of the sexual revolution, millions of American men, as Gibson puts it, "began to dream, to fantasize about the powers and features of another kind of man who could retake and reorder the world." Such fantasy warriors include Rambo, Dirty Harry, and Jack Ryan, fictional role models for the gun-toting legions of a new paramilitary subculture that is quite real, and growing. Paintball, anyone? A professor of sociology at California State University, Long Beach, Gibson is also the author of The Perfect War: Technowar in Vietnam *(1986).*

We couldn't see them, but we could hear their bugles sound the call. The Communist battalions were organizing for a predawn assault. Captain Kokalis smiled wickedly; he'd been through this before. A "human wave" assault composed of thousands of enemy soldiers was headed our way. The captain ordered the remaining soldiers in his command to check their .30- and .50-caliber machine guns. Earlier in the night, the demolitions squad attached to our unit had planted mines and explosive charges for hundreds of meters in front of our position.

And then it began. At a thousand meters, the soldiers emerged screaming from the gray-blue fog. "Fire!" yelled Captain Kokalis. The gun crews opened up with short bursts of three to seven rounds; their bullets struck meat. Everywhere I could see, clusters of Communist troops were falling by the second. But the wave still surged forward. At five hundred meters, Kokalis passed the word to his gunners to increase their rate of fire to longer strings of ten to twenty rounds. Sergeant Donovan, the demolitions squad leader, began to reap the harvest from the night's planting. Massive explosions ripped through the Communist troops. Fire and smoke blasted into the dawn sky. It was as if the human wave had hit a submerged reef; as the dying fell, wide gaps appeared in the line where casualties could no longer be replaced.

But still they kept coming, hundreds of men, each and every one bent on taking the American position and wiping us out. As the Communists reached one hundred meters, Kokalis gave one more command. Every machine gun in our platoon went to its maximum rate of sustained full-automatic frenzy, sounding like chain saws that just keep cutting and cutting.

And then it was over. The attack subsided into a flat sea of Communist dead. No Americans had been killed or wounded. We were happy to be alive, proud of our victory. We only wondered if our ears would ever stop ringing and if we would ever again smell anything other than the bittersweet aroma of burning gunpowder. . . .

Although an astonishing triumph was achieved that day, no historian will 5 ever find a record of this battle in the hundreds of volumes and thousands of official reports written about the Korean or Vietnam wars. Nor was the blood spilt part of a covert operation in Afghanistan or some unnamed country in Africa, Asia, or Latin America.

No, this battle was fought inside the United States, a few miles north of Las Vegas, in September 1986. It was a purely *imaginary* battle, a dream of victory staged as part of the *Soldier of Fortune* magazine's annual convention. The audience of several hundred men, women, and children, together with reporters and a camera crew from *CBS News,* sat in bleachers behind half a dozen medium and heavy machine guns owned by civilians. Peter G. Kokalis, *SOF*'s firearms editor, set the scene for the audience and asked them to imagine that the sandy brushland of the Desert Sportsman Rifle and Pistol Club was really a killing zone for incoming Communist troops. Kokalis was a seasoned storyteller; he'd given this performance before. When the fantasy battle was over, the fans went wild with applause. Kokalis picked up a microphone, praised Donovan (another *SOF* staff member) — "He was responsible for that whole damn Communist bunker that went up" — and told the parents in the audience to buy "claymores [antipersonnel land mines] and other good shit for the kids." A marvelous actor who knew what his audience wanted, Kokalis sneered, "Did you get that, CBS, on your videocam? Screw you knee-jerk liberals."[1]

[1]Peter G. Kokalis, speaking at the *Soldier of Fortune* firepower demonstration at the Desert Sportsman Rifle and Pistol Club, Las Vegas, Nev., September 20, 1986.

The shoot-out and victory over Communist forces conducted at the Desert Sportsman Rifle and Pistol Club was but one battle in a cultural or imaginary "New War" that had been going on since the late 1960s and early 1970s. The bitter controversies surrounding the Vietnam War had discredited the old American ideal of the masculine warrior hero for much of the public. But in 1971, when Clint Eastwood made the transition from playing cowboys in old *Rawhide* reruns and spaghetti westerns to portraying San Francisco police detective Harry Callahan in *Dirty Harry,* the warrior hero returned in full force. His backup arrived in 1974 when Charles Bronson appeared in *Death Wish,* the story of a mild-mannered, middle-aged architect in New York City who, after his wife is murdered and his daughter is raped and driven insane, finds new meaning in life through an endless war of revenge against street punks.

In the 1980s, Rambo and his friends made their assault. The experience of John Rambo, a former Green Beret, was the paradigmatic story of the decade. In *First Blood* (1982), he burns down a small Oregon town while suffering hallucinatory flashbacks to his service in Vietnam. Three years later, in *Rambo: First Blood, Part 2,* he is taken off a prison chain gang by his former commanding officer in Vietnam and asked to perform a special reconnaissance mission to find suspected American POWs in Laos, in exchange for a Presidential pardon. His only question: "Do we get to win this time?" And indeed, Rambo does win. Betrayed by the CIA bureaucrat in charge of the mission, Rambo fights the Russians and Vietnamese by himself and brings the POWs back home.

Hundreds of similar films celebrating the victory of good men over bad through armed combat were made during the late 1970s and 1980s. Many were directed by major Hollywood directors and starred well-known actors. Elaborate special effects and exotic film locations added tens of millions to production costs. And for every large-budget film, there were scores of cheaper formula films employing lesser-known actors and production crews. Often these "action-adventure" films had only brief theatrical releases in major markets. Instead, they made their money in smaller cities and towns, in sales to Europe and the Third World, and most of all, in the sale of videocassettes to rental stores. Movie producers could even turn a profit on "video-only" releases; action-adventure films were the largest category of video rentals in the 1980s.

At the same time, Tom Clancy became a star in the publishing world. His 10 book *The Hunt for Red October* (1984) told the story of the Soviet Navy's most erudite submarine commander, Captain Markus Ramius, and his effort to defect to the United States with the Soviets' premier missile-firing submarine. *Red Storm Rising* (1986) followed, an epic of World War III framed as a high-tech conventional war against the Soviet Union. Clancy's novels all featured Jack Ryan, Ph.D., a former Marine captain in Vietnam turned academic naval historian who returns to duty as a CIA analyst and repeatedly stumbles into life-and-death struggles in which the fate of the world rests on his prowess. All were bestsellers.

President Reagan, Secretary of the Navy John Lehman, and many other high officials applauded Clancy and his hero. Soon the author had a multimillion-dollar contract for a whole series of novels, movie deals with Paramount, and a new part-time job as a foreign-policy expert writing op-ed pieces for the *Washington Post,* the *Los Angeles Times,* and other influential newspapers around the country. His success motivated dozens of authors, mostly active-duty or retired military men, to take up the genre. The "techno-thriller" was born.

At a slightly lower level in the literary establishment, the same publishing houses that marketed women's romance novels on grocery and drugstore paperback racks rapidly expanded their collections of pulp fiction for men. Most were written like hard-core pornography, except that inch-by-inch descriptions of penises entering vaginas were replaced by equally graphic portrayals of bullets, grenade fragments, and knives shredding flesh: "He tried to grab the handle of the commando knife, but the terrorist pushed down on the butt, raised the point and yanked the knife upward through the muscle tissue and guts. It ripped intestines, spilling blood and gore."[2] A minimum of 20 but sometimes as many as 120 such graphically described killings occurred in each 200- to 250-page paperback. Most series came out four times a year with domestic print runs of 60,000 to 250,000 copies. More than a dozen different comic books with titles like *Punisher, Vigilante,* and *Scout* followed suit with clones of the novels.

Along with the novels and comics came a new kind of periodical which replaced the older adventure magazines for men, such as *True* and *Argosy,* that had folded in the 1960s. Robert K. Brown, a former captain in the U.S. Army Special Forces during the Vietnam War, founded *Soldier of Fortune: The Journal of Professional Adventurers* in the spring of 1975, just before the fall of Saigon. *SOF*'s position was explicit from the start: the independent warrior must step in to fill the dangerous void created by the American failure in Vietnam. By the mid-1980s *SOF* was reaching 35,000 subscribers, had newsstand sales of another 150,000, and was being passed around to at least twice as many readers.[3]

Half a dozen new warrior magazines soon entered the market. Some, like *Eagle, New Breed,* and *Gung-Ho,* tried to copy the *SOF* editorial package — a strategy that ultimately failed. But most developed their own particular pitch. *Combat Handguns* focused on pistols for would-be gunfighters. *American*

---

[2]Gar Wilson, *The Fury Bombs,* vol. 5 of *Phoenix Force* (Toronto: Worldwide Library, 1983), 30.

[3]*SOF* regularly hired the firm of Starch, Inra, Hopper to study their readership. A condensed version of their 1986 report, from which these figures were taken, was made available to the press at the September 1986 *SOF* convention in Las Vegas.

Survival Guide advertised and reviewed everything needed for "the good life" after the end of civilization (except birth control devices — too many Mormon subscribers, the editor said), while *S.W.A.T.* found its way to men who idealized these elite police teams and who were worried about home defense against "multiple intruders."

During the same period, sales of military weapons took off. Colt offered two semiautomatic versions of the M16 used by U.S. soldiers in Vietnam (a full-size rifle and a shorter-barreled carbine with collapsible stock). European armories exported their latest products, accompanied by sophisticated advertising campaigns in *SOF* and the more mainstream gun magazines. Israeli Defense Industries put a longer, 16-inch barrel on the Uzi submachine gun (to make it legal) and sold it as a semiautomatic carbine. And the Communist countries of Eastern Europe, together with the People's Republic of China, jumped into the market with the devil's own favorite hardware, the infamous AK47. The AK sold in the United States was the semiautomatic version of the assault rifle used by the victorious Communists in Vietnam and by all kinds of radical movements and terrorist organizations around the world. It retailed for $300 to $400, half the price of an Uzi or an AR-15; complete with three 30-round magazines, cleaning kit, and bayonet, it was truly a bargain.

To feed these hungry guns, munitions manufacturers packaged new "generic" brands of military ammo at discount prices, often selling them in cases of 500 or 1,000 rounds. New lines of aftermarket accessories offered parts for full-automatic conversions, improved flash-hiders, scopes, folding stocks, and scores of other goodies. In 1989, the U.S. Bureau of Alcohol, Tobacco and Firearms (ATF) estimated that two to three million military-style rifles had been sold in this country since the Vietnam War. The Bureau released these figures in response to the public outcry over a series of mass murders committed by psychotics armed with assault rifles.

But the Bureau's statistics tell only part of the story. In less than two decades, millions of American men had purchased combat rifles, pistols, and shotguns and begun training to fight their own personal wars. Elite combat shooting schools teaching the most modern techniques and often costing $500 to over $1,000 in tuition alone were attended not only by soldiers and police but by increasing numbers of civilians as well. Hundreds of new indoor pistol-shooting ranges opened for business in old warehouses and shopping malls around the country, locations ideal for city dwellers and suburbanites.

A new game of "tag" blurred the line between play and actual violence: men got the opportunity to hunt and shoot other men without killing them or risking death themselves. The National Survival Game was invented in 1981 by two old friends, one a screenwriter for the weight-lifting sagas that gave Arnold Schwarzenegger his first starring roles, and the other a former member of the Army's Long Range Reconnaissance Patrol (LRRP) in Vietnam.[4]

---

[4]Lionel Atwill, *Survival Game: Airgun National Manual* (New London, N.H.: The National Survival Game, Inc., 1987), 22–30.

Later called paintball because it utilized guns firing balls of watercolor paint, by 1987 the game was being played by at least fifty thousand people (mostly men) each weekend on both outdoor and indoor battlefields scattered across the nation. Players wore hard-plastic face masks intended to resemble those of ancient tribal warriors and dressed from head to toe in camouflage clothes imported by specialty stores from military outfitters around the world. The object of the game was to capture the opposing team's flag, inflicting the highest possible body count along the way.

One major park out in the Mojave Desert seventy miles southeast of Los Angeles was named Sat Cong Village. *Sat Cong* is a slang Vietnamese phrase meaning "Kill Communists" that had been popularized by the CIA as part of its psychological-warfare program. Sat Cong Village employed an attractive Asian woman to rent the guns, sell the paintballs, and collect the twenty-dollar entrance fee. Players had their choice of playing fields: Vietnam, Cambodia, or Nicaragua. On the Nicaragua field, the owner built a full-size facsimile of the crashed C-47 cargo plane contracted by Lieutenant Colonel Oliver North to supply the Contras. The scene even had three parachutes hanging from trees; the only thing missing was the sole survivor of the crash, Eugene Hasenfus.

The 1980s, then, saw the emergence of a highly energized culture of war and 20 the warrior. For all its varied manifestations, a few common features stood out. The New War culture was not so much military as paramilitary. The new warrior hero was only occasionally portrayed as a member of a conventional military or law enforcement unit; typically, he fought alone or with a small, elite group of fellow warriors. Moreover, by separating the warrior from his traditional state-sanctioned occupations — policeman or soldier — the New War culture presented the warrior roles as the ideal identity for *all* men. Bankers, professors, factory workers, and postal clerks could all transcend their regular stations in life and prepare for heroic battle against the enemies of society.

To many people, this new fascination with warriors and weapons seemed a terribly bad joke. The major newspapers and magazines that arbitrate what is to be taken seriously in American society scoffed at the attempts to resurrect the warrior hero. Movie critics were particularly disdainful of Stallone's Rambo films. *Rambo: First Blood, Part 2* was called "narcissistic jingoism" by *The New Yorker* and "hare-brained" by the *Wall Street Journal*. The *Washington Post* even intoned that "Sly's body looks fine. Now can't you come up with a workout for his soul?"

But in dismissing Rambo so quickly and contemptuously, commentators failed to notice the true significance of the emerging paramilitary culture. They missed the fact that quite a few people were not writing Rambo off as a complete joke; behind the Indian bandanna, necklace, and bulging muscles, a new culture hero affirmed such traditional American values as self-reliance, honesty, courage, and concern for fellow citizens. Rambo was a worker and a former enlisted man, not a smooth-talking professional. That so many seemingly well-to-do, sophisticated liberals hated him for both his politics and his uncouthness only added to his glory. Further, in their emphasis on Stallone's clownishness the commentators failed to see not only how widespread paramilitary culture had become but also its relation to the historical moment in which it arose.

Indeed, paramilitary culture can be understood only when it is placed in relation to the Vietnam War. America's failure to win that war was a truly profound blow. The nation's long, proud tradition of military victories, from the Revolutionary War through the century-long battles against the Indians to World Wars I and II, had finally come to an end. Politically, the defeat in Vietnam meant that the post–World War II era of overwhelming American political and military power in international affairs, the era that in 1945 *Time* magazine publisher Henry Luce had prophesied would be the "American Century," was over after only thirty years. No longer could U.S. diplomacy wield the big stick of military intervention as a ready threat — a significant part of the American public would no longer support such interventions, and the rest of the world knew it.

Moreover, besides eroding U.S. influence internationally, the defeat had subtle but serious effects on the American psyche. America has always celebrated war and the warrior. Our long, unbroken record of military victories has been crucially important both to the national identity and to the personal identity of many Americans — particularly men. The historian Richard Slotkin locates a primary "cultural archetype" of the nation in the story of a heroic warrior whose victories over the enemy symbolically affirm the country's fundamental goodness and power; we win our wars because, morally, we deserve to win. Clearly, the archetypical pattern Slotkin calls "regeneration through violence" was broken with the defeat in Vietnam.[5] The result was a massive disjunction in American culture, a crisis of self-image: If Americans were no longer winners, then who were they?

This disruption of cultural identity was amplified by other social transformations. During the 1960s, the civil rights and ethnic pride movements won many victories in their challenges to racial oppression. Also, during the 1970s and 1980s, the United States experienced massive waves of immigration from Mexico, Central America, Vietnam, Cambodia, Korea, and Taiwan. Whites, no longer secure in their power abroad, also lost their unquestionable dominance at home; for the first time, many began to feel that they too were just another hyphenated ethnic group, the Anglo-Americans.

Extraordinary economic changes also marked the 1970s and 1980s. U.S. manufacturing strength declined substantially; staggering trade deficits with other countries and the chronic federal budget deficits shifted the United States from creditor to debtor nation. The post–World War II American

25

[5]Richard Slotkin, *Regeneration through Violence: The Mythology of the American Frontier, 1660–1860* (Middletown, Conn.: Wesleyan University Press, 1973).

Dream — which promised a combination of technological progress and social reforms, together with high employment rates, rising wages, widespread home ownership, and ever increasing consumer options — no longer seemed a likely prospect for the great majority. At the same time, the rise in crime rates, particularly because of drug abuse and its accompanying violence, made people feel more powerless than ever.

While the public world dominated by men seemed to come apart, the private world of family life also felt the shocks. The feminist movement challenged formerly exclusive male domains, not only in the labor market and in many areas of political and social life but in the home as well. Customary male behavior was no longer acceptable in either private relationships or public policy. Feminism was widely experienced by men as a profound threat to their identity. Men had to change, but to what? No one knew for sure what a "good man" was anymore.

It is hardly surprising, then, that American men — lacking confidence in the government and the economy, troubled by the changing relations between the sexes, uncertain of their identity or their future — began to *dream,* to fantasize about the powers and features of another kind of man who could retake and reorder the world. And the hero of all these dreams was the paramilitary warrior. In the New War he fights the battles of Vietnam a thousand times, each time winning decisively. Terrorists and drug dealers are blasted into oblivion. Illegal aliens inside the United States and the hordes of nonwhites in the Third World are returned by force to their proper place. Women are revealed as dangerous temptresses who have to be mastered, avoided, or terminated.

Obviously these dreams represented a flight from the present and a rejection and denial of events of the preceding twenty years. But they also indicated a more profound and severe distress. The whole modern world was damned as unacceptable. Unable to find a rational way to face the tasks of rebuilding society and reinventing themselves, men instead sought refuge in myths from both America's frontier past and ancient times. Indeed, the fundamental narratives that shape paramilitary culture and its New War fantasies are often nothing but reinterpretations or reworkings of archaic warrior myths.

In ancient societies, the most important stories a people told about them- 30 selves concerned how the physical universe came into existence, how their ancestors first came to live in this universe, and how the gods, the universe, and society were related to one another. These cosmogonic, or creation, myths frequently posit a violent conflict between the good forces of order and the evil forces dedicated to the perpetuation of primordial chaos.[6] After the war in which the gods defeat the evil ones, they establish the "sacred order," in which all of the society's most important values are fully embodied. Some

[6]Mircea Eliade, *Myth and Reality,* trans. Willard R. Trask (New York: Harper and Row, 1963).

creation myths focus primarily on the sacred order and on the deeds of the gods and goddesses in paradise. Other myths, however, focus on the battles between the heroes and villains that lead up to the founding.[7] In these myths it is war and the warrior that are most sacred. American paramilitary culture borrows from both kinds of stories, but mostly from this second, more violent, type.

In either case, the presence, if not the outright predominance, of archaic male myths at the moment of crisis indicates just how far American men jumped psychically when faced with the declining power of their identities and organizations. The always-precarious balance in modern society between secular institutions and ways of thinking on the one hand and older patterns of belief informed by myth and ritual on the other tilted decisively in the direction of myth. The crisis revealed that at some deep, unconscious level these ancient male creation myths live on in the psyche of many men and that the images and tales from this mythic world of warriors and war still shape men's fantasies about who they are as men, their commitments to each other and to women, and their relationships to society and the state.

READING THE TEXT

1. How, according to Gibson, did the American defeat in Vietnam lead to the construction of a new kind of "warrior" (para. 20) identity for men?

2. Outline how popular culture helped to shape the warrior image, in Gibson's view.

3. What role does Gibson believe the women's movement played in constructing a new male identity?

4. Explain in your own words how today's "warrior" (para. 20) dreams relate to ancient mythologies.

5. Why does Gibson believe that *Rambo* should be taken seriously?

READING THE SIGNS

1. Read or reread Michael A. Messner's "Power at Play: Sport and Gender Relations" (p. 668), and compare Messner's argument about the role of sports in the construction of masculine identity with Gibson's analysis of warrior dreams.

2. Gibson suggests that the warrior fantasies found throughout political and popular culture have dangerous real-world implications. Write a critical essay in which you support, complicate, or challenge this suggestion. As you develop your argument, consider incidents such as the 1999 Columbine High School massacre and the 2001 murders of two Dartmouth college professors, both committed by teenage boys.

[7]Richard Stivers, *Evil in Modern Myth and Ritual* (Athens: University of Georgia Press, 1982).

3. Using Gibson's argument as your critical framework, write an analysis of the attractions of professional wrestling as described in Henry Jenkins's "'Never Trust a Snake': WWF Wrestling as Masculine Melodrama" (p. 688).

4. In class, brainstorm current films, TV shows, and video games that are targeted to a male audience. Then discuss the extent to which the warrior dreams that Gibson describes still influence popular culture.

LAURA MILLER

WOMEN AND CHILDREN FIRST: GENDER AND THE SETTLING OF THE ELECTRONIC FRONTIER

The Web is often considered a masculine space into which women enter at their peril. Sexual harassment and outright intimidation of women are legion on the Web, right? Wrong, says Laura Miller (b. 1960), in this response to a Newsweek *feature that dwelt on the danger women faced on the Internet. An avid and experienced Internet participant, Miller feels she, and the many women like her who also spend a lot of time in cyberspace, can take care of themselves very well, thank you, and have no need for special protections. Senior editor at* Salon, *an Internet magazine, Miller has published in the* San Francisco Examiner, Wired, Harper's Bazaar, *and the* New York Times Book Review *and is the editor of* The Salon Readers' Guide to Contemporary Authors *(2000).*

When *Newsweek* (May 16, 1994) ran an article entitled "Men, Women, and Computers," all hell broke out on the Net, particularly on the online service I've participated in for six years, the WELL (Whole Earth 'Lectronic Link). "Cyberspace, it turns out," declared *Newsweek*'s Nancy Kantrowitz, "isn't much of an Eden after all. It's marred by just as many sexist ruts and gender conflicts as the Real World. . . . Women often feel about as welcome as a system crash." "It was horrible. Awful, poorly researched, unsubstantiated drivel," one member wrote, a sentiment echoed throughout some 480 postings.

However egregious the errors in the article (some sources maintain that they were incorrectly quoted), it's only one of several mainstream media depictions of the Net as an environment hostile to women. Even women who had been complaining about online gender relations found themselves increasingly annoyed by what one WELL member termed the "cyberbabe harassment" angle that seems to typify media coverage of the issue. Reified in the pages of *Newsweek* and other journals, what had once been the topic of discussions by insiders — online commentary is informal, conversational, and often spontaneous — became a journalistic "fact" about the Net known by complete strangers and novices. In a matter of months, the airy stuff of bitch sessions became widespread, hardened stereotypes.

At the same time, the Internet has come under increasing scrutiny as it mutates from an obscure, freewheeling web of computer networks used by a small elite of academics, scientists, and hobbyists to . . . well, nobody seems to know exactly what. But the business press prints vague, fevered prophecies of fabulous wealth, and a bonanza mentality has blossomed. With it comes big business and the government, intent on regulating this amorphous medium into a manageable and profitable industry. The Net's history of informal self-regulation and its wide libertarian streak guarantee that battles like the one over the Clipper chip (a mandatory decoding device that would make all encrypted data readable by federal agents) will be only the first among many.

Yet the threat of regulation is built into the very mythos used to conceptualize the Net by its defenders — and gender plays a crucial role in that threat. However revolutionary the technologized interactions of online communities may seem, we understand them by deploying a set of very familiar metaphors from the rich figurative soup of American culture. Would different metaphors have allowed the Net a different, better historical trajectory? Perhaps not, but the way we choose to describe the Net now encourages us to see regulation as its inevitable fate. And, by examining how gender roles provide a foundation for the intensification of such social controls, we can illuminate the way those roles proscribe the freedoms of men as well as women.

For months I mistakenly referred to the EFF (an organization founded by ₅ John Perry Barlow and Lotus 1-2-3 designer Mitch Kapor to foster access to, and further the discursive freedom of, online communications) as "The Electronic Freedom Foundation," instead of by its actual name, "The Electronic Frontier Foundation." Once corrected, I was struck by how intimately related the ideas "frontier" and "freedom" are in the Western mythos. The *frontier,* as a realm of limitless possibilities and few social controls, hovers, grail-like, in the American psyche, the dream our national identity is based on, but a dream that's always, somehow, just vanishing away.

Once made, the choice to see the Net as a frontier feels unavoidable, but it's actually quite problematic. The word "frontier" has traditionally described a place, if not land then the limitless "final frontier" of space. The Net, on the other hand, occupies precisely no physical space (although the computers and phone lines that make it possible do). It is a completely bodiless, symbolic thing with no discernable boundaries or location. The land of the American frontier did not become a "frontier" until Europeans determined to conquer it, but the continent existed before the intention to settle it. Unlike land, the Net was created by its pioneers.

Most peculiar, then, is the choice of the word "frontier" to describe an artifact so humanly constructed that it only exists as ideas or information. For central to the idea of the frontier is that it contains no (or very few) other people — fewer than two per square mile according to the nineteenth-century historian Frederick Turner. The freedom the frontier promises is a liberation from the demands of society, while the Net (I'm thinking now of Usenet) has nothing but society to offer. Without other people, news groups, mailing lists, and files simply wouldn't exist and e-mail would be purposeless. Unlike real space, cyberspace must be shared.

Nevertheless, the choice of a spatial metaphor (credited to the science-fiction novelist William Gibson, who coined the term "cyberspace"), however awkward, isn't surprising. Psychologist Julian Jaynes has pointed out that geographical analogies have long predominated humanity's efforts to conceptualize — map out — consciousness. Unfortunately, these analogies bring with them a heavy load of baggage comparable to Pandora's box: open it and a complex series of problems have come to stay.

The frontier exists beyond the edge of settled or owned land. As the land that doesn't belong to anybody (or to people who "don't count," like Native Americans), it is on the verge of being acquired; currently unowned, but still ownable. Just as the idea of chastity makes virginity sexually provocative, so does the unclaimed territory invite settlers, irresistibly so. Americans regard the lost geographical frontier with a melancholy, voluptuous fatalism — we had no choice but to advance upon it and it had no alternative but to submit. When an EFF member compares the Clipper chip to barbed wire encroaching on the prairie, doesn't he realize the surrender implied in his metaphor?

The psychosexual undercurrents (if anyone still thinks of them as "under") in the idea of civilization's phallic intrusion into nature's passive, feminine space have been observed, exhaustively, elsewhere. The classic Western narrative is actually far more concerned with social relationships than conflicts between man and nature. In these stories, the frontier is a lawless society of men, a milieu in which physical strength, courage, and personal charisma supplant institutional authority and violent conflict is the accepted means of settling disputes. The Western narrative connects pleasurably with the American romance of individualistic masculinity; small wonder that the predominantly male founders of the Net's culture found it so appealing.

When civilization arrives on the frontier, it comes dressed in skirts and short pants. In the archetypal 1939 movie *Dodge City,* Wade Hatton (Errol Flynn) refuses to accept the position of marshal because he prefers the footloose life of a trail driver. Abbie Irving (Olivia de Haviland), a recent arrival from the civilized East, scolds him for his unwillingness to accept and advance the cause of law; she can't function (in her job as crusading journalist) in a town governed by brute force. It takes the accidental killing of a child in a street brawl for Hatton to realize that he must pin on the badge and clean up Dodge City.

In the Western mythos, civilization is necessary because women and children are victimized in conditions of freedom. Introduce women and children into a frontier town and the law must follow because women and children must be protected. Women, in fact, are usually the most vocal proponents of the conversion from frontier justice to civil society.

The imperiled women and children of the Western narrative make their appearance today in newspaper and magazine articles that focus on the intimidation and sexual harassment of women online and reports of pedophiles trolling for victims in computerized chat rooms. If online women successfully contest these attempts to depict them as the beleaguered prey of brutish men, expect the pedophile to assume a larger profile in arguments that the Net is out of control.

In the meantime, the media prefer to cast women as the victims, probably because many women actively participate in the call for greater regulation of online interactions, just as Abbie Irving urges Wade Hatton to bring the rule of law to Dodge City. These requests have a long cultural tradition, based on the idea that women, like children, constitute a peculiarly vulnerable class of people who require special protection from the elements of society men are expected to confront alone. In an insufficiently civilized society like the frontier, women, by virtue of this childlike vulnerability, are thought to live under the constant threat of kidnap, abuse, murder, and especially rape.

Women, who have every right to expect that crimes against their person 15 will be rigorously prosecuted, should nevertheless regard the notion of special protections (chivalry, by another name) with suspicion. Based as it is on the idea that women are inherently weak and incapable of self-defense and that men are innately predatory, it actually reinforces the power imbalance between the sexes, with its roots in the concept of women as property, constantly under siege and requiring the vigilant protection of their male owners. If the romance of the frontier arises from the promise of vast stretches of unowned land, an escape from the restrictions of a society based on private property, the introduction of women spoils that dream by reintroducing the imperative of property in their own persons.

How does any of this relate to online interactions, which occur not on a desert landscape but in a complex, technological society where women are supposed to command equal status with men? It accompanies us as a set of unexamined assumptions about what it means to be male or female, assumptions that we believe are rooted in the imperatives of our bodies. These assumptions follow us into the bodiless realm of cyberspace, a forum where, as one scholar puts it "participants are washed clean of the stigmata of their real 'selves' and are free to invent new ones to their tastes." Perhaps some observers feel that the replication of gender roles in a context where the absence of bodies supposedly makes them superfluous proves exactly how innate those roles are. Instead, I see in the relentless attempts to interpret online interactions as highly gendered, an intimation of just how artificial, how created, our gender system is. If it comes "naturally," why does it need to be perpetually defended and reasserted?

Complaints about the treatment of women online fall into three categories: that women are subjected to excessive, unwanted sexual attention, that the prevailing style of online discussion turns women off, and that women are singled out by male participants for exceptionally dismissive or hostile treatment. In making these assertions, the *Newsweek* article and other stories on the issue do echo grievances that some online women have made for years. And, without a doubt, people have encountered sexual come-ons, aggressive debating tactics, and ad hominem attacks on the Net. However, individual users interpret such events in widely different ways, and to generalize from those interpretations to describe the experiences of women and men as a whole is a rash leap indeed.

I am one of many women who don't recognize their own experience of the Net in the misogynist gauntlet described above. In researching this essay, I joined America Online and spent an hour or two "hanging out" in the real-time chat rooms reputed to be rife with sexual harassment. I received several "instant messages" from men, initiating private conversations with innocuous questions about my hometown and tenure on the service. One man politely inquired if I was interested in "hot phone talk" and just as politely bowed out when I declined. At no point did I feel harassed or treated with disrespect. If I ever want to find a phone-sex partner, I now know where to look but until then I probably won't frequent certain chat rooms.

Other women may experience a request for phone sex or even those tame instant messages as both intrusive and insulting (while still others maintain that they have received much more explicit messages and inquiries completely out of the blue). My point isn't that my reactions are the more correct, but rather that both are the reactions of women, and no journalist has any reason to believe that mine are the exception rather than the rule.

For me, the menace in sexual harassment comes from the underlying 20 threat of rape or physical violence. I see my body as the site of my heightened vulnerability as a woman. But online—where I have no body and neither does anyone else—I consider rape to be impossible. Not everyone agrees. Julian Dibble, in an article for the *Village Voice,* describes the repercussions of a "rape" in a multiuser dimension, or MUD, in which one user employed a subprogram called a "voodoo doll" to cause the personae of other users to perform sexual acts. Citing the "conflation of speech and act that's inevitable in any computer-mediated world," he moved toward the conclusion that "since rape can occur without any physical pain or damage, then it must be classified as a crime against the mind." Therefore, the offending user had committed something on the same "conceptual continuum" as rape. Tellingly, the incident led to the formation of the first governmental entity on the MUD.

No doubt the cyber-rapist (who went by the nom de guerre Mr. Bungle) appreciated the elevation of his mischief-making to the rank of virtual felony: all of the outlaw glamour and none of the prison time (he was exiled from the MUD). Mr. Bungle limited his victims to personae created by women users, a choice that, in its obedience to prevailing gender roles, shaped the debate that followed his crimes. For, in accordance with the real-world understanding that women's smaller, physically weaker bodies and lower social status make them subject to violation by men, there's a troubling notion in the real and virtual worlds that women's minds are also more vulnerable to invasion, degradation, and abuse.

This sense of fragility extends beyond interactions with sexual overtones. The *Newsweek* article reports that women participants can't tolerate the harsh, contentious quality of online discussions, that they prefer mutual support to heated debate, and are retreating wholesale to women-only conferences and newsgroups. As someone who values online forums precisely because they mandate equal time for each user who chooses to take it and forestall various "alpha male" rhetorical tactics like interrupting, loudness, or exploiting the psychosocial advantages of greater size or a deeper voice, I find this perplexing and disturbing. In these laments I hear the reluctance of women to enter into the kind of robust debate that characterizes healthy public life, a willingness to let men bully us even when they've been relieved of most of their traditional advantages. Withdrawing into an electronic purdah where one will never be challenged or provoked, allowing the ludicrous ritual chest-thumping of some users to intimidate us into silence — surely women can come up with a more spirited response than this.

And of course they can, because besides being riddled with reductive stereotypes, media analyses like *Newsweek*'s simply aren't accurate. While the online population is predominantly male, a significant and vocal minority of women contribute regularly and more than manage to hold their own. Some of the WELL's most bombastic participants are women, just as there are many tactful and conciliatory men. At least, I think there are, because, ultimately, it's impossible to be sure of anyone's biological gender online. "Transpostites," people who pose as members of the opposite gender, are an established element of Net society, most famously a man who, pretending to be a disabled lesbian, built warm and intimate friendships with women on several CompuServe forums.

Perhaps what we should be examining is not the triumph of gender differences on the Net, but their potential blurring. In this light, *Newsweek*'s stout assertion that in cyberspace "the gender gap is real" begins to seem less objective than defensive, an insistence that online culture is "the same" as real life because the idea that it might be different, when it comes to gender, is too scary. If gender roles can be cast off so easily, they may be less deeply rooted, less "natural" than we believe. There may not actually be a "masculine" or "feminine" mind or outlook, but simply a conventional way of interpreting individuals that recognizes behavior seen as in accordance with their biological gender and ignores behavior that isn't.

For example, John Seabury wrote in *The New Yorker* (June 6, 1994) of his stricken reaction to his first "flame," a colorful slice of adolescent invective sent to him by an unnamed technology journalist. Reading it, he begins to "shiver" like a burn victim, an effect that worsens with repeated readings. He writes that "the technology greased the words . . . with a kind of immediacy

Protesters march for safety.

that allowed them to slide easily into my brain." He tells his friends, his coworkers, his partner — even his mother — and, predictably, appeals to CompuServe's management for recourse — to no avail. Soon enough, he's talking about civilization and anarchy, how the liberating "lack of social barriers is also what is appalling about the Net," and calling for regulation.

As a newcomer, Seabury was chided for brooding over a missive that most Net veterans would have dismissed and forgotten as the crude potshot of an envious jerk. (I can't help wondering if my fellow journalist never received hate mail in response to his other writings; this bit of e-mail seems comparable, par for the course when one assumes a public profile.) What nobody did was observe that Seabury's reaction — the shock, the feelings of violation, the appeals to his family and support network, the bootless complaints to the authorities — reads exactly like many horror stories about women's trials on the Net. Yet, because Seabury is a man, no one attributes the attack to his gender or suggests that the Net has proven an environment hostile to men. Furthermore, the idea that the Net must be more strictly governed to prevent the abuse of guys who write for *The New Yorker* seems laughable — though who's to say that Seabury's pain is less than any woman's? Who can doubt that, were he a woman, his tribulations would be seen as compelling evidence of Internet sexism?

The idea that women merit special protections in an environment as incorporeal as the Net is intimately bound up with the idea that women's minds are weak, fragile, and unsuited to the rough and tumble of public discourse. It's an argument that women should recognize with profound mistrust and resist, especially when we are used as rhetorical pawns in a battle to regulate a rare (if elite) space of gender ambiguity. When the mainstream media generalize about women's experiences on line in ways that just happen to uphold the most conventional and pernicious gender stereotypes, they can expect to be greeted with howls of disapproval from women who refuse to acquiesce in these roles and pass them on to other women.

And there are plenty of us, as the WELL's response to the *Newsweek* article indicates. Women have always participated in online communications, women whose chosen careers in technology and the sciences have already marked them as gender-role resisters. As the schoolmarms arrive on the electronic frontier, their female predecessors find themselves cast in the role of saloon girls, their willingness to engage in "masculine" activities like verbal aggression, debate, or sexual experimentation marking them as insufficiently feminine, or "bad" women. "If that's what women online are like, I must be a Martian," one WELL woman wrote in response to the shrinking female technophobes depicted in the *Newsweek* article. Rather than relegating so many people to the status of gender aliens, we ought to reconsider how adequate those roles are to the task of describing real human beings.

READING THE TEXT

1. What images of women on the Net do the mainstream media construct, according to Miller?

2. What does Miller see as the significance of the word "frontier" (para. 5), and how does she relate that word to the Internet?

3. Summarize in your own words the charges that critics make about the gender bias and harassment on the Internet and Miller's response to those charges.

4. Why does Miller state that women should "regard the notion of special protections . . . with suspicion" (para. 15)?

READING THE SIGNS

1. Log onto a chat room, and see for yourself how gender roles are depicted on the Net. To what extent do you find traditional roles perpetuated or ignored? Use your findings to support an argument for or against Miller's position that women should not be granted special protections on the Internet.

2. Form teams and debate whether regulation should be established to protect Internet users, whether male or female, from harassment, intimidation, or other sorts of abusive language.

3. Read or reread Laurence Shames's "The More Factor" (p. 56). Using his argument as your starting point, write an essay in which you explain the extent to which the Internet appeals to Americans' desire for "more."

4. In your journal, reflect on the controversy Miller mentions over whether online rape is possible. How might one change the traditional definition of rape to include electronic assaults?

5. Interview four or five women on campus who are avid Internet users, asking them about their experiences online. To what extent have they faced the gender-based problems that Miller describes? Use your findings as the basis for an argument about how gender roles are constructed online.

CONSTRUCTING RACE

Readings in Multicultural Semiotics

Michael Jordan. Michael Jackson. Miles Davis. Duke Ellington. Ella Fitzgerald. Oprah Winfrey. Whitney Houston. Serena Williams. Venus Williams. Tiger Woods. Tupac Shakur. Barry Bonds. Bill Cosby. Eddie Murphy. Will Smith. Denzel Washington. Muhammad Ali. Shaquille O'Neal. Naomi Campbell. Mariah Carey. Alicia Keys. Halle Berry.

The list could go on, of course, but in naming just this partial roster of African American popular cultural superstars we mean to point to a multicultural phenomenon that can make one think twice about what is meant by the words *dominant culture*. For while Caucasians remain the dominant ethnic group in America, and European culture remains our dominant culture, when it comes to popular culture, African Americans enjoy an especially prominent status. Indeed, given that African Americans are the originators of America's most popular musical forms today — hip hop, rhythm and blues, rock-and-roll, and jazz — and are the stars of America's most popular professional sports, it is impossible to imagine modern culture without them. You may even already object that our brief list of African American icons is far too short to do justice to their place in the current cultural pantheon.

It has not always been this way, of course. Jazz was once denounced as "jungle music" by white critics, and rock-and-roll was regarded as the "devil's music." Black athletes were barred from participation in mainstream professional sports (the Harlem Globe Trotters were created because blacks weren't allowed in the early NBA), and black actors and actresses often had to accept demeaning roles to get any work in Hollywood at all (think of *Amos 'n' Andy* or of Prissy in *Gone with the Wind*). Even today, the National Association for the Advancement of Colored People (NAACP) can point every year to a new television season that once again underrepresents African Americans.

Still, when it comes to popular culture, the multicultural nature of American society is especially striking. Multiculturalism refers to that scholarly, political, and educational movement that contests the traditional monocultural perspective on America. That perspective regards American culture as a product of European history, the extension of a tradition that began in Greece and Rome and which was brought to America by the English. Multiculturalists challenge that perspective by exploring the contributions of such historically marginalized Americans as Africans, Asians, Latins, and Native Americans in the creation of American culture. And nowhere has this contribution been more prominent than in the realm of popular culture.

Interpreting Multicultural Semiotics

Until recently, the multicultural nature of American popular culture has been most visible in binary terms: that is, black and white. But with the emerging Ñ generation, whose pop superstars include Ricky Martin, Marc Anthony, and Jennifer Lopez, along with the increasing number of Dominican stars in professional baseball, the Latino and Latina contribution to popular culture is no longer in the shadows. The Asian contribution, which has tended to be restricted to a certain stereotyping of Asians as experts in the martial arts, includes such performers as Bruce Lee and Jackie Chan (who, to be precise, is not an American), but as one of the fastest growing demographic groups in America, Asians will continue to increase their presence in popular culture. Native Americans, for their part, are still struggling with a dominant cultural tendency either to view them through the eye of a gunsight (the most common perspective of midcentury cinema and TV) or to sentimentalize them as New Age Noble Savages (consider Oliver Stone's use of Native American characters in *The Doors* and *Natural Born Killers*). But as multicultural awareness continues to grow, the roster of Native American popular cultural stars will certainly go well beyond Buffy Ste. Marie.

The special place that African Americans enjoy in popular culture was underscored in 2001 with the making of *Ali,* a movie that brought together two of the defining icons of contemporary American popular culture: Muhammad Ali and Will Smith. Commanding the highest box office gross ever for a Christmas-day release, the movie was a potent signifier of the way that, at least within popular culture, the racial polarities of American history are receding. Once, Muhammad Ali was an outlaw, whose change of name and religion, along with his high-profile refusal to be drafted into the armed services, made him a symbol of racial resistance. In his famous showdown with Joe Frazier — the historic "thrilla in Manilla" — he was widely regarded as black America's champion in a confrontation in which he denounced his op-

Alicia Keys performing at Radio City Music Hall.

ponent as an Uncle Tom in the service of white America — an aspersion that it took Ali thirty years to apologize for to the wounded Frazier. But now, Muhammad Ali is a national symbol like Martin Luther King Jr. Indeed, in the wake of the September 11, 2001, attacks, he was asked to make a public service address, to be broadcast throughout the Islamic world, explaining that America's war on terrorism is not a war on Islam.

As a cultural signifier, *Ali* can be related to Spike Lee's *Malcolm X,* a film that also marked the culmination of a historical process by which a symbol of racial resistance has been transformed into a national hero who has even been featured on his own postage stamp. Such an association can show us how *Ali*'s release is no isolated event: It is a signifier of a change in American cultural relations that has seen the emergence of black heroes who are as important, for many, as such traditional heroes as George Washington and Abraham Lincoln. Indeed, a related signifier in this context is the fact

---

Exploring the Signs of Race

In your journal, reflect on the question, "Who are you?" How does your ethnicity contribute to your sense of self? Are there other factors that contribute to your identity? If so, what are they, and how do they relate to your ethnicity? If you don't perceive yourself in ethnic terms, why do you think that's the case?

---

that both Washington's and Lincoln's birthdays, once celebrated as separate national holidays, have been consolidated into a single, somewhat anonymous President's Day.

The careers of the actors who played Ali and Malcolm X in these two films are also culturally significant. Before Denzel Washington was picked to play Malcolm X in Lee's movie, he had already established himself as one of Hollywood's leading men. By playing Malcolm X, one of the most powerful icons in African American history, Washington, who was certainly aware of the historic mantle that was being cast across his shoulders, fully emerged as another such icon. A later signifier of Washington's iconic status was his portrayal of a corrupt cop in *Training Day.* Prior to this film, Washington always played the good guy. By playing Alonzo in *Training Day,* Washington demonstrated not only that he had a wider range than that but that his place in pop culture was so secure that he could be cast as a villain without exacerbating sensitivities to negative stereotyping. At a time when Hollywood is trying to live down a history of portraying black men as criminals and callous womanizers, few black actors can safely be cast in such roles. But Denzel Washington's heroic status ensured that his casting in this role would be seen as a star branching out and not as a denigrating stereotype, which was demonstrated when he was rewarded with an Oscar for the role in 2002.

Will Smith's playing of Muhammad Ali, for its part, is semiotically related to Washington's Malcolm X. For by the time he took this role, Smith, too, had become one of Hollywood's leading men. By playing Ali — indeed, as *Entertainment Weekly* has noted, by *becoming* Ali — Smith signified his ascension into the ranks of certified cultural icons. It is interesting to note how Smith began his career as a rapper, before rap had fully crossed over to become young America's favorite form of musical entertainment, moved to prime-time TV in *The Fresh Prince of Bel Air,* and then turned to Hollywood in such films as *Men in Black* and *Wild Wild West.* Playing Ali, then, gave Will Smith a chance not only to aim for full cultural superstardom but also to become involved, at least imaginatively, in professional sports, a career move that, in effect, placed him in a starring role in all four of America's leading entertainment venues. Keep your eye out: He may soon be playing a black president — whether on the silver screen or in the White House remains to be seen.

Who Are We?

Whether in the realm of popular or political culture, multicultural semiotics always involves the question of cultural identity, because from the semiotic point of view, value systems and mythologies are culturally constructed. To put this another way, *what* you value depends upon *who* you are. So, ask yourself a simple question: "Who am I?" Ask a classmate, "Who are you?" What's the answer? Did your classmate give her name? Did you? Or did each of you answer differently? Did you say "I am an American"? Or did you say "I am an African American," or an "Asian American," or a "Latino," or a "Native American"? Would you answer "I am a European American" or a "Jewish American"? However you answered the question, can you say why you answered as you did?

To ask how you identify yourself and why is to probe further into the semiotics of race and culture in America's multicultural society. Some of you may believe that there is a right answer to our question, that it is essential that all Americans think of themselves as *Americans* first and foremost. Others of you may believe just as strongly that your ethnic and cultural identity comes first. In either case, your beliefs reflect a worldview, or cultural mythology, that guides you in your most fundamental thoughts about your identity. Let's look at those myths for a moment.

> ### Discussing the Signs of Race
>
> Demographers predict that, by the middle of the twenty-first century, America will no longer have any racial or ethnic majority population. In class, discuss what effects this may have on Americans' sense of this country's history, culture, and identity.

Say that you feel that all American citizens should view themselves simply as Americans. If so, your feelings reflect a basic cultural mythology best known as the myth of the American "melting pot." This is the belief that America offers all of its citizens the opportunity to blend together into one harmonious whole that will erase the many differences among us on behalf of a new, distinctly American, identity. This belief has led many immigrants to seek to assimilate into what they perceive as the dominant American culture, shedding the specific cultural characteristics that may distinguish them from what they see as the American norm. And it is a belief that stands behind some of the most generous impulses in our culture — at least ideally.

But what if you don't buy this belief? What if, as far as you're concerned, you're proud to belong to a different community, one that differs from the basically Anglo-Saxon culture that has become the dominant and normative culture for assimilation? Or what if you and your people have found that you were never really allowed to blend in anyway, that in spite of the promise, the melting pot was never meant for you? If so, how does the myth of the melting pot look to you? Does it look the same as it would to someone who never had any trouble assimilating, or never needed to, because he or she already belonged to the dominant culture?

To see that the myth of the melting pot looks different depending upon who is looking at it is to see why it is so precious to some Americans and so irrelevant to others. It is to realize again the fundamental semiotic precept that our social values are culturally determined rather than inscribed in the marble of absolute truth. This may be difficult to accept, especially if you and your classmates all come from the same culture and hence all hold the same values. But if you know people who are different, you might want to ask them how the myth of the melting pot looks from their perspective. Does it look like an ideal that our nation should strive to achieve? Or does it look like an invitation to cultural submission? It all depends on who's looking.

The failure to recognize that different people view the melting pot differently is one of the major sources of racial misunderstanding and, thus, conflict in America today. On the one hand, we need to realize that many Americans, particularly nonwhites, have felt excluded from full economic and cultural participation in American life and may deeply resent the view that we all should just see ourselves as Americans. But on the other hand, we also need to realize that many of today's Americans descend from non–Anglo-Saxon European immigrants who embraced the image of the melting pot, prospered, and passed their gratitude on to their descendants. For such Americans, the myth of the melting pot appears to be so benevolent that it doesn't seem right to attack it. A debate that acknowledges the historical reasons for this difference in viewpoint has a better chance to result in some consensus than one that presumes that one side's affection for the melting pot is "racist" or that the other's resentment is "petty" or "un-American."

Such a recognition is difficult to achieve, of course, because of the way that cultural worldviews tend to present themselves in absolute terms. We don't look at our belief systems and say "this is our belief system"; we say "this is the truth." All cultures do this. Even the way cultures form their sense of identity involves a certain reliance on absolutes by assuming that their culture is normative, the right way to be. It's not just Anglo-Saxon America that presumes its centrality in the order of things. We can see how groups of people implicitly believe in their privileged place in the world by looking at the names with which they identify themselves. Take the members of the largest Native American tribe in the United States. To the rest of the world, they are known as the Navajos. This is not the name the Navajos use among themselves, however, for the word *Navajo* does not come from their language.

> ### Reading Race on the Net
>
> Many Internet sites are devoted to the culture of a particular ethnicity, such as Afronet (**http://www.afronet.com**). Visit several such sites, and survey the breadth of information available about different ethnic groups. To what extent can a researcher learn about various ethnicities on the Net? Is there any information that you wish would appear on the Net but could not find? Do you find any material problematic?

In all likelihood, the name was given to them by neighboring Pueblo Indians, for whom the term *Navahu* means "large area of cultivated lands." But in the language of the Navajo, which is quite different from that of the Pueblo, they are not the people of the tilled fields. They are, quite simply, the People, the most common English translation of the word *diné,* the name by which the Navajo know themselves.

Or take the Hmong of Southeast Asia. *Hmong* simply means "person," and so to say "I am a Hmong" implicitly states "I am a person." And even the names of such different nations as Ireland and Iran harbor an ancient sense of normative "peoplehood," for both names are derived from the word *Aryan,* which itself once bore the simple meaning "the people." To be sure, when someone says "I am diné," or "I am Hmong," or "I am Irish," he or she does not mean "I am a human being and the rest of you aren't." Nonetheless, we find inscribed within the unconscious history of these ancient tribal names the trace of a belief found within many a tribal name: the sense that one's own tribe comes first in the order of things.

The terrorist attacks of 2001, which were an assault on all Americans, made no such tribal distinctions, however. In the post-9/11 world, which has caused many Americans to experience their common national and cultural identity, a new kind of multiculturalism may be emerging. Rather than exploring cultural differences alone, we may also come to explore the multicultural identity that is modern America. Leaving behind the melting pot metaphor that assumed the assimilation of many-into-one, we may discover a new metaphor for a culture that the many have constructed. Then, it would be time to rephrase our question, no longer asking "Who are you?" but "Who are we?"

The Readings

This chapter looks at the social construction of racial identity in America, beginning with Michael Omi's survey of how race works as a sign in popular American culture. Benjamin DeMott indicts Hollywood's tendency to mask the grim realities of America's racial history behind "happy faced" images of black-white friendship and solidarity. Paul C. Taylor, Jack Lopez, and Nell

Bernstein next offer a trio of readings on popular cultural "crossovers," with Taylor focusing on white performers who excel in black-identified cultural activities like basketball and the blues, Lopez offering a personal memoir of what it was like to be a wannabe surfer in the Mexican American community of East Los Angeles, and Bernstein reporting on the phenomenon of "claiming" — white teens choosing to identify themselves with nonwhite ethnic groups. An autobiographical reflection by bell hooks on her childhood preference for brown dolls over white follows, after which Melissa Algranati offers a college student's perspective on what it's like to be a Puerto Rican-Egyptian-American Jew in a country that demands clear ethnic identifications. Fan Shen analyzes the role his Chinese heritage has played in his experience both as a student and as a professor of freshman composition, while LynNell Hancock explores the social and economic implications of online access, or lack thereof, for race relations in America. Finally, Randall Kennedy concludes the chapter with a provocative look at the controversy over racial profiling.

MICHAEL OMI

In Living Color: Race and American Culture

Though many like to think that racism in America is a thing of the past, Michael Omi argues that racism is a pervasive feature in our lives, one that is both overt and inferential. Using race as a sign by which we judge a person's character, inferential racism invokes deep-rooted stereotypes, and as Omi shows in his survey of American film, television, and music, our popular culture is hardly immune from such stereotyping. Indeed, when ostensibly "progressive" programs like Saturday Night Live *can win the National Ethnic Coalition of Organizations' "Platinum Pit Award" for racist stereotyping in television, and shock jocks such as Howard Stern command big audiences and salaries, one can see popular culture has a way to go before it becomes colorblind. The author of* Racial Formation in the United States: From the 1960s to the 1980s *(with Howard Winant, 1986, 1994), Omi is a professor of comparative ethnic studies at the University of California, Berkeley. His most recent project is a survey of antiracist organizations and initiatives.*

In February 1987, Assistant Attorney General William Bradford Reynolds, the nation's chief civil rights enforcer, declared that the recent death of a black man in Howard Beach, New York and the Ku Klux Klan attack on civil rights marchers in Forsyth County, Georgia were "isolated" racial incidences. He emphasized that the places where racial conflict could potentially flare up were "far fewer now than ever before in our history," and concluded that such a diminishment of racism stood as "a powerful testament to how far we have come in the civil rights struggle."[1]

Events in the months following his remarks raise the question as to whether we have come quite so far. They suggest that dramatic instances of racial tension and violence merely constitute the surface manifestations of a deeper racial organization of American society — a system of inequality which has shaped, and in turn been shaped by, our popular culture.

In March, the NAACP released a report on blacks in the record industry entitled "The Discordant Sound of Music." It found that despite the revenues generated by black performers, blacks remain "grossly underrepresented" in the business, marketing, and A&R (Artists and Repertoire) departments of major record labels. In addition, few blacks are employed as managers, agents, concert promoters, distributors, and retailers. The report concluded that:

---

[1]Reynolds's remarks were made at a conference on equal opportunity held by the bar association in Orlando, Florida. *The San Francisco Chronicle* (7 February 1987).

> The record industry is overwhelmingly segregated and discrimination is rampant. No other industry in America so openly classifies its operations on a racial basis. At every level of the industry, beginning with the separation of black artists into a special category, barriers exist that severely limit opportunities for blacks.[2]

Decades after the passage of civil rights legislation and the affirmation of the principle of "equal opportunity," patterns of racial segregation and exclusion, it seems, continue to characterize the production of popular music.

The enduring logic of Jim Crow is also present in professional sports. In April, Al Campanis, vice president of player personnel for the Los Angeles Dodgers, explained to Ted Koppel on ABC's *Nightline* about the paucity of blacks in baseball front offices and as managers. "I truly believe," Campanis said, "that [blacks] may not have some of the necessities to be, let's say, a field manager or perhaps a general manager." When pressed for a reason, Campanis offered an explanation which had little to do with the structure of opportunity of institutional discrimination within professional sports:

> [W]hy are black men or black people not good swimmers? Because they don't have the buoyancy. . . . They are gifted with great musculature and various other things. They're fleet of foot. And this is why there are a lot of black major league ballplayers. Now as far as having the background to become club presidents, or presidents of a bank, I don't know.[3]

Black exclusion from the front office, therefore, was justified on the basis of biological "difference."

The issue of race, of course, is not confined to the institutional arrange- 5
ments of popular culture production. Since popular culture deals with the symbolic realm of social life, the images which it creates, represents, and disseminates contribute to the overall racial climate. They become the subject of analysis and political scrutiny. In August, the National Ethnic Coalition of Organizations bestowed the "Golden Pit Awards" on television programs, commercials, and movies that were deemed offensive to racial and ethnic groups. *Saturday Night Live,* regarded by many media critics as a politically "progressive" show, was singled out for the "Platinum Pit Award" for its comedy skit "Ching Chang" which depicted a Chinese storeowner and his family in a derogatory manner.[4]

These examples highlight the *overt* manifestations of racism in popular culture — institutional forms of discrimination which keep racial minorities out

---

[2]Economic Development Department of the NAACP, "The Discordant Sound of Music (A Report on the Record Industry)," (Baltimore, Maryland: The NAACP, 1987), pp. 16–17.

[3]Campanis's remarks on *Nightline* were reprinted in *The San Francisco Chronicle* (April 9, 1987).

[4]Ellen Wulfhorst, "TV Stereotyping: It's the 'Pits,'" *The San Francisco Chronicle* (August 24, 1987).

of the production and organization of popular culture, and the crude racial caricatures by which these groups are portrayed. Yet racism in popular culture is often conveyed in a variety of implicit, and at times invisible, ways. Political theorist Stuart Hall makes an important distinction between *overt* racism, the elaboration of an explicitly racist argument, policy, or view, and *inferential* racism which refers to "those apparently naturalized representations of events and situations relating to race, whether 'factual' or 'fictional,' which have racist premises and propositions inscribed in them as a set of *unquestioned assumptions.*" He argues that inferential racism is more widespread, common, and indeed insidious since "it is largely *invisible* even to those who formulate the world in its terms."[5]

Race itself is a slippery social concept which is paradoxically both "obvious" and "invisible." In our society, one of the first things we notice about people when we encounter them (along with their sex/gender) is their *race*. We utilize race to provide clues about *who* a person is and *how* we should relate to her/him. Our perception of race determines our "presentation of *self,*" distinctions in status, and appropriate modes of conduct in daily and institutional life. This process is often unconscious; we tend to operate off of an unexamined set of *racial beliefs*.

Racial beliefs account for and explain variations in "human nature." Differences in skin color and other obvious physical characteristics supposedly provide visible clues to more substantive differences lurking underneath. Among other qualities, temperament, sexuality, intelligence, and artistic and athletic ability are presumed to be fixed and discernible from the palpable mark of race. Such diverse questions as our confidence and trust in others (as salespeople, neighbors, media figures); our sexual preferences and romantic images; our tastes in music, film, dance, or sports; indeed our very ways of walking and talking are ineluctably shaped by notions of race.

Ideas about race, therefore, have become "common sense" — a way of comprehending, explaining, and acting in the world. This is made painfully obvious when someone disrupts our common sense understandings. An encounter with someone who is, for example, racially "mixed" or of a racial/ethnic group we are unfamiliar with becomes a source of discomfort for us, and momentarily creates a crisis of racial meaning. We also become disoriented when people do not act "black," "Latino," or indeed "white." The content of such stereotypes reveals a series of unsubstantiated beliefs about who these groups are, what they are like, and how they behave.

The existence of such racial consciousness should hardly be surprising. 10 Even prior to the inception of the republic, the United States was a society shaped by racial conflict. The establishment of the Southern plantation economy, Western expansion, and the emergence of the labor movement, among

---

[5]Stuart Hall, "The Whites of Their Eyes: Racist Ideologies and the Media," in George Bridges and Rosalind Brunt, eds., *Silver Linings* (London: Lawrence and Wishart, 1981), pp. 36–37.

other significant historical developments, have all involved conflicts over the definition and nature of the *color line*. The historical results have been distinct and different groups have encountered unique forms of racial oppression — Native Americans faced genocide, blacks were subjected to slavery, Mexicans were invaded and colonized, and Asians faced exclusion. What is common to the experiences of these groups is that their particular "fate" was linked to historically specific ideas about the significance and meaning of race.[6] Whites defined them as separate "species," ones inferior to Northern European cultural stocks, and thereby rationalized the conditions of their subordination in the economy, in political life, and in the realm of culture.

A crucial dimension of racial oppression in the United States is the elaboration of an ideology of difference or "otherness." This involves defining "us" (i.e., white Americans) in opposition to "them," an important task when distinct racial groups are first encountered, or in historically specific periods where preexisting racial boundaries are threatened or crumbling.

Political struggles over the very definition of who an "American" is illustrate this process. The Naturalization Law of 1790 declared that only free *white* immigrants could qualify, reflecting the initial desire among Congress to create and maintain a racially homogeneous society. The extension of eligibility to all racial groups has been a long and protracted process. Japanese, for example, were finally eligible to become naturalized citizens after the passage of the Walter-McCarran Act of 1952. The ideological residue of these restrictions in naturalization and citizenship laws is the equation within popular parlance of the term "American" with "white," while other "Americans" are described as black, Mexican, "Oriental," etc.

Popular culture has been an important realm within which racial ideologies have been created, reproduced, and sustained. Such ideologies provide a framework of symbols, concepts, and images through which we understand, interpret, and represent aspects of our "racial" existence.

Race has often formed the central themes of American popular culture. Historian W. L. Rose notes that it is a "curious coincidence" that four of the "most popular reading-viewing events in all American history" have in some manner dealt with race, specifically black/white relations in the south.[7] Harriet Beecher Stowe's *Uncle Tom's Cabin*, Thomas Ryan Dixon's *The Clansman* (the inspiration for D. W. Griffith's *The Birth of a Nation*), Margaret Mitchell's *Gone with the Wind* (as a book and film), and Alex Haley's *Roots* (as a book and television miniseries), each appeared at a critical juncture in American race relations and helped to shape new understandings of race.

Emerging social definitions of race and the "real American" were reflected in American popular culture of the nineteenth century. Racial and eth-   15

---

[6]For an excellent survey of racial beliefs see Thomas F. Gossett, *Race: The History of an Idea in America* (New York: Shocken Books, 1965).

[7]W. L. Rose, *Race and Region in American Historical Fiction: Four Episodes in Popular Culture* (Oxford: Clarendon Press, 1979).

nic stereotypes were shaped and reinforced in the newspapers, magazines, and pulp fiction of the period. But the evolution and ever-increasing sophistication of visual mass communications throughout the twentieth century provided, and continue to provide, the most dramatic means by which racial images are generated and reproduced.

Film and television have been notorious in disseminating images of racial minorities which establish for audiences what these groups look like, how they behave, and, in essence, "who they are." The power of the media lies not only in their ability to reflect the dominant racial ideology, but in their capacity to shape that ideology in the first place. D. W. Griffith's aforementioned epic *Birth of a Nation,* a sympathetic treatment of the rise of the Ku Klux Klan during Reconstruction, helped to generate, consolidate, and "nationalize" images of blacks which had been more disparate (more regionally specific, for example) prior to the film's appearance.[8]

In television and film, the necessity to define characters in the briefest and most condensed manner has led to the perpetuation of racial caricatures, as racial stereotypes serve as shorthand for scriptwriters, directors, and actors. Television's tendency to address the "lowest common denominator" in order to render programs "familiar" to an enormous and diverse audience leads it regularly to assign and reassign racial characteristics to particular groups, both minority and majority.

Many of the earliest American films deal with racial and ethnic "difference." The large influx of "new immigrants" at the turn of the century led to a proliferation of negative images of Jews, Italians, and Irish which were assimilated and adapted by such films as Thomas Edison's *Cohen's Advertising Scheme* (1904). Based on an old vaudeville routine, the film featured a scheming Jewish merchant, aggressively hawking his wares. Though stereotypes of these groups persist to this day,[9] by the 1940s many of the earlier ethnic stereotypes had disappeared from Hollywood. But, as historian Michael Winston observes, the "outsiders" of the 1890s remained: "the ever-popular Indian of the Westerns; the inscrutable or sinister Oriental; the sly, but colorful Mexican; and the clowning or submissive Negro."[10]

In many respects the "Western" as a genre has been paradigmatic in establishing images of racial minorities in film and television. The classic scenario involves the encircled wagon train or surrounded fort from which whites bravely fight off fierce bands of Native American Indians. The point of

---

[8]Melanie Martindale-Sikes, "Nationalizing 'Nigger' Imagery Through *Birth of a Nation,*" paper prepared for the 73rd Annual Meeting of the American Sociological Association (September 4–8, 1978) in San Francisco.

[9]For a discussion of Italian, Irish, Jewish, Slavic, and German stereotypes in film, see Randall M. Miller, ed., *The Kaleidoscopic Lens: How Hollywood Views Ethnic Groups* (Englewood, N.J.: Jerome S. Ozer, 1980).

[10]Michael R. Winston, "Racial Consciousness and the Evolution of Mass Communications in the United States," *Daedalus,* vol. III, No. 4 (Fall 1982).

reference and viewer identification lies with those huddled within the circle — the representatives of "civilization" who valiantly attempt to ward off the forces of barbarism. In the classic Western, as writer Tom Engelhardt observes, "the viewer is forced behind the barrel of a repeating rifle and it is from that position, through its gun sights, that he receives a picture history of Western colonialism and imperialism."[11]

Westerns have indeed become the prototype for European and American 20 excursions throughout the Third World. The cast of characters may change, but the story remains the same. The "humanity" of whites is contrasted with the brutality and treachery of nonwhites; brave (i.e., white) souls are pitted against the merciless hordes in conflicts ranging from Indians against the British Lancers to Zulus against the Boers. What Stuart Hall refers to as the imperializing "white eye" provides the framework for these films, lurking outside the frame and yet seeing and positioning everything within; it is "the unmarked position from which . . . 'observations' are made and from which, alone, they make sense."[12]

Our "common sense" assumptions about race and racial minorities in the United States are both generated and reflected in the stereotypes presented by the visual media. In the crudest sense, it could be said that such stereotypes underscore white "superiority" by reinforcing the traits, habits, and predispositions of nonwhites which demonstrate their "inferiority." Yet a more careful assessment of racial stereotypes reveals intriguing trends and seemingly contradictory themes.

While all racial minorities have been portrayed as "less than human," there are significant differences in the images of different groups. Specific racial minority groups, in spite of their often interchangeable presence in films steeped in the "Western" paradigm, have distinct and often unique qualities assigned to them. Latinos are portrayed as being prone toward violent outbursts of anger; blacks as physically strong, but dim-witted; while Asians are seen as sneaky and cunningly evil. Such differences are crucial to observe and analyze. Race in the United States is not reducible to black/white relations. These differences are significant for a broader understanding of the patterns of race in America, and the unique experience of specific racial minority groups.

It is somewhat ironic that *real* differences which exist within a racially defined minority group are minimized, distorted, or obliterated by the media. "All Asians look alike," the saying goes, and indeed there has been little or no attention given to the vast differences which exist between, say, the Chinese and Japanese with respect to food, dress, language, and culture. This blurring within popular culture has given us supposedly Chinese characters who wear kimonos; it is also the reason why the fast-food restaurant McDonald's can of-

[11]Tom Engelhardt, "Ambush at Kamikaze Pass," in Emma Gee, ed., *Counterpoint: Perspectives on Asian America* (Los Angeles: Asian American Studies Center, UCLA, 1976), p. 270.
[12]Hall, "Whites of Their Eyes," p. 38.

fer "Shanghai McNuggets" with teriyaki sauce. Other groups suffer a similar fate. Professor Gretchen Bataille and Charles Silet find the cinematic Native American of the Northeast wearing the clothing of the Plains Indians, while living in the dwellings of Southwestern tribes:

> The movie men did what thousands of years of social evolution could not do, even what the threat of the encroaching white man could not do; Hollywood produced the homogenized Native American, devoid of tribal characteristics or regional differences.[13]

The need to paint in broad racial strokes has thus rendered "internal" differences invisible. This has been exacerbated by the tendency for screenwriters to "invent" mythical Asian, Latin American, and African countries. Ostensibly done to avoid offending particular nations and peoples, such a subterfuge reinforces the notion that all the countries and cultures of a specific region are the same. European countries retain their distinctiveness, while the Third World is presented as one homogeneous mass riddled with poverty and governed by ruthless and corrupt regimes.

While rendering specific groups in a monolithic fashion, the popular cultural imagination simultaneously reveals a compelling need to distinguish and articulate "bad" and "good" variants of particular racial groups and individuals. Thus each stereotypic image is filled with contradictions: The bloodthirsty Indian is tempered with the image of the noble savage; the *bandido* exists along with the loyal sidekick; and Fu Manchu is offset by Charlie Chan. The existence of such contradictions, however, does not negate the one-dimensionality of these images, nor does it challenge the explicit subservient role of racial minorities. Even the "good" person of color usually exists as a foil in novels and films to underscore the intelligence, courage, and virility of the white male hero.

Another important, perhaps central, dimension of racial minority stereo- 25 types is sex/gender differentiation. The connection between race and sex has traditionally been an explosive and controversial one. For most of American history, sexual and marital relations between whites and nonwhites were forbidden by social custom and by legal restrictions. It was not until 1967, for example, that the U.S. Supreme Court ruled that antimiscegenation laws were unconstitutional. Beginning in the 1920s, the notorious Hays Office, Hollywood's attempt at self-censorship, prohibited scenes and subjects which dealt with miscegenation. The prohibition, however, was not evenly applied in practice. White men could seduce racial minority women, but white women were not to be romantically or sexually linked to racial minority men.

Women of color were sometimes treated as exotic sex objects. The sultry Latin temptress–such as Dolores Del Rio and Lupe Velez — invariably had boyfriends who were white North Americans; their Latino suitors were

---

[13]Gretchen Bataille and Charles Silet, "The Entertaining Anachronism: Indians in American Film," in Randall M. Miller, ed., *Kaleidoscopic Lens,* p. 40.

portrayed as being unable to keep up with the Anglo-American competition. From Mary Pickford as Cho-Cho San in *Madame Butterfly* (1915) to Nancy Kwan in *The World of Suzie Wong* (1961), Asian women have often been seen as the gracious "geisha girl" or the prostitute with a "heart of gold," willing to do anything to please her man.

By contrast, Asian men, whether cast in the role of villain, servant, side-kick, or kung fu master, are seen as asexual or, at least, romantically undesir-able. As Asian American studies professor Elaine Kim notes, even a hero such as Bruce Lee played characters whose "single-minded focus on perfecting his fighting skills precludes all other interests, including an interest in women, friendship, or a social life."[14]

The shifting trajectory of black images over time reveals an interesting dynamic with respect to sex and gender. The black male characters in *The Birth of a Nation* were clearly presented as sexual threats to "white woman-hood." For decades afterwards, however, Hollywood consciously avoided por-traying black men as assertive or sexually aggressive in order to minimize controversy. Black men were instead cast as comic, harmless, and nonthreat-ening figures exemplified by such stars as Bill "Bojangles" Robinson, Stepin Fetchit, and Eddie "Rochester" Anderson. Black women, by contrast, were di-vided into two broad character types based on color categories. Dark black women such as Hattie McDaniel and Louise Beavers were cast as "dowdy, frumpy, dumpy, overweight mammy figures"; while those "close to the white ideal," such as Lena Horne and Dorothy Dandridge, became "Hollywood's treasured mulattoes" in roles emphasizing the tragedy of being of mixed blood.[15]

It was not until the early 1970s that tough, aggressive, sexually assertive black characters, both male and female, appeared. The "blaxploitation" films of the period provided new heroes (e.g., *Shaft, Superfly, Coffy,* and *Cleopatra Jones*) in sharp contrast to the submissive and subservient images of the past. Unfortunately, most of these films were shoddy productions which did little to create more enduring "positive" images of blacks, either male or female.

In contemporary television and film, there is a tendency to present and equate racial minority groups and individuals with specific social problems. Blacks are associated with drugs and urban crime, Latinos with "illegal" immi-gration, while Native Americans cope with alcoholism and tribal conflicts. Rarely do we see racial minorities "out of character," in situations removed from the stereotypic arenas in which scriptwriters have traditionally embedded them. Nearly the only time we see young Asians and Latinos of either sex, for example, is when they are members of youth gangs, as *Boulevard Nights* (1979), *Year of the Dragon* (1985), and countless TV cop shows can attest to.

30

---

[14]Elaine Kim, "Asian Americans and American Popular Culture" in Hyung-Chan Kim, ed., *Dictionary of Asian American History* (New York: Greenwood Press, 1986), p. 107.

[15]Donald Bogle, "A Familiar Plot (A Look at the History of Blacks in American Movies)," *The Crisis,* Vol. 90, No. 1 (January 1983), p. 15.

Racial minority actors have continually bemoaned the fact that the roles assigned them on stage and screen are often one-dimensional and imbued with stereotypic assumptions. In theater, the movement toward "blind casting" (i.e., casting actors for roles without regard to race) is a progressive step, but it remains to be seen whether large numbers of audiences can suspend their "beliefs" and deal with a Latino King Lear or an Asian Stanley Kowalski. By contrast, white actors are allowed to play anybody. Though the use of white actors to play blacks in "black face" is clearly unacceptable in the contemporary period, white actors continue to portray Asian, Latino, and Native American characters on stage and screen.

Scores of Charlie Chan films, for example, have been made with white leads (the last one was the 1981 *Charlie Chan and the Curse of the Dragon Queen*). Roland Winters, who played Chan in six features, was once asked to explain the logic of casting a white man in the role of Charlie Chan: "The only thing I can think of is, if you want to cast a homosexual in a show, and you get a homosexual, it'll be awful. It won't be funny . . . and maybe there's something there."[16]

Such a comment reveals an interesting aspect about myth and reality in popular culture. Michael Winston argues that stereotypic images in the visual media were not originally conceived as representations of reality, nor were they initially understood to be "real" by audiences. They were, he suggests, ways of "coding and rationalizing" the racial hierarchy and interracial behavior. Over time, however, "a complex interactive relationship between myth and reality developed, so that images originally understood to be unreal, through constant repetition began to *seem* real."[17]

Such a process consolidated, among other things, our "common sense" understandings of what we think various groups should look like. Such presumptions have led to tragicomical results. Latinos auditioning for a role in a television soap opera, for example, did not fit the Hollywood image of "real Mexicans" and had their faces bronzed with powder before filming because they looked too white. Model Aurora Garza said, "I'm a real Mexican and very dark anyway. I'm even darker right now because I have a tan. But they kept wanting to make my face darker and darker."[18]

Historically in Hollywood, the fact of having "dark skin" made an actor or actress potentially adaptable for numerous "racial" roles. Actress Lupe Velez once commented that she had portrayed "Chinese, Eskimos, Japs, squaws, Hindus, Swedes, Malays, and Japanese."[19] Dorothy Dandridge, who was the first black woman teamed romantically with white actors, presented a   35

[16]Frank Chin, "Confessions of the Chinatown Cowboy," *Bulletin of Concerned Asian Scholars,* Vol. 4, No. 3 (Fall 1972).

[17]Winston, "Racial Consciousness," p. 176.

[18]*The San Francisco Chronicle,* September 21, 1984.

[19]Quoted in Allen L. Woll, "Bandits and Lovers: Hispanic Images in American Film," in Miller, ed., *Kaleidoscopic Lens,* p. 60.

quandary for studio executives who weren't sure what race and nationality to make her. They debated whether she should be a "foreigner," an island girl, or a West Indian.[20] Ironically, what they refused to entertain as a possibility was to present her as what she really was, a black American woman.

The importance of race in popular culture is not restricted to the visual media. In popular music, race and race consciousness have defined, and continue to define, formats, musical communities, and tastes. In the mid-1950s, the secretary of the North Alabama White Citizens Council declared that "Rock and roll is a means of pulling the white man down to the level of the Negro."[21] While rock may no longer be popularly regarded as a racially subversive musical form, the very genres of contemporary popular music remain, in essence, thinly veiled racial categories. "R & B" (Rhythm and Blues) and "soul" music are clearly references to *black* music, while Country & Western or heavy metal music are viewed, in the popular imagination, as *white* music. Black performers who want to break out of this artistic ghettoization must "cross over," a contemporary form of "passing" in which their music is seen as acceptable to white audiences.

The airwaves themselves are segregated. The designation "urban contemporary" is merely radio lingo for a "black" musical format. Such categorization affects playlists, advertising accounts, and shares of the listening market. On cable television, black music videos rarely receive airplay on MTV, but are confined instead to the more marginal BET (Black Entertainment Television) network.

In spite of such segregation, many performing artists have been able to garner a racially diverse group of fans. And yet, racially integrated concert audiences are extremely rare. Curiously, this "perverse phenomenon" of racially homogeneous crowds takes place despite the color of the performer. Lionel Richie's concert audiences, for example, are virtually all-white, while Teena Marie's are all-black.[22]

Racial symbols and images are omnipresent in popular culture. Commonplace household objects such as cookie jars, salt and pepper shakers, and ashtrays have frequently been designed and fashioned in the form of racial caricatures. Sociologist Steve Dublin in an analysis of these objects found that former tasks of domestic service were symbolically transferred onto these commodities.[23] An Aunt Jemima-type character, for example, is used to hold a roll of paper towels, her outstretched hands supporting the item to be dis-

[20]Bogle, "Familiar Plot," p. 17.

[21]Dave Marsh and Kevin Stein, *The Book of Rock Lists* (New York: Dell Publishing Co., 1981), p. 8.

[22]*Rock & Roll Confidential,* No. 44 (February 1987), p. 2.

[23]Steven C. Dublin, "Symbolic Slavery: Black Representations in Popular Culture," *Social Problems,* Vol. 34, No. 2 (April 1987).

pensed. "Sprinkle Plenty," a sprinkle bottle in the shape of an Asian man, was used to wet clothes in preparation for ironing. Simple commodities, the household implements which help us perform everyday tasks, may reveal, therefore, a deep structure of racial meaning.

A crucial dimension for discerning the meaning of particular stereotypes and 40 images is the *situation context* for the creation and consumption of popular culture. For example, the setting in which "racist" jokes are told determines the function of humor. Jokes about blacks where the teller and audience are black constitute a form of self-awareness; they allow blacks to cope and "take the edge off" of oppressive aspects of the social order which they commonly confront. The meaning of these same jokes, however, is dramatically transformed when told across the "color line." If a white, or even black, person tells these jokes to a white audience, it will, despite its "purely" humorous intent, serve to reinforce stereotypes and rationalize the existing relations of racial inequality.

Concepts of race and racial images are both overt and implicit within popular culture — the organization of cultural production, the products themselves, and the manner in which they are consumed are deeply structured by race. Particular racial meanings, stereotypes, and myths can change, but the presence of a *system* of racial meanings and stereotypes, of racial ideology, seems to be an enduring aspect of American popular culture.

The era of Reaganism and the overall rightward drift of American politics and culture has added a new twist to the question of racial images and meanings. Increasingly, the problem for racial minorities is not that of misportrayal, but of "invisibility." Instead of celebrating racial and cultural diversity, we are witnessing an attempt by the right to define, once again, who the "real" American is, and what "correct" American values, mores, and political beliefs are. In such a context, racial minorities are no longer the focus of sustained media attention; when they do appear, they are cast as colored versions of essentially "white" characters.

The possibilities for change — for transforming racial stereotypes and challenging institutional inequities — nonetheless exist. Historically, strategies have involved the mobilization of political pressure against an offending institution(s). In the late 1950s, for instance, "Nigger Hair" tobacco changed its name to "Bigger Hare" due to concerted NAACP pressure on the manufacturer. In the early 1970s, Asian American community groups successfully fought NBC's attempt to resurrect Charlie Chan as a television series with white actor Ross Martin. Amidst the furor generated by Al Campanis's remarks cited at the beginning of this essay, Jesse Jackson suggested that a boycott of major league games be initiated in order to push for a restructuring of hiring and promotion practices.

Partially in response to such action, Baseball Commissioner Peter Ueberroth announced plans in June 1987 to help put more racial minorities in management roles. "The challenge we have," Ueberroth said, "is to manage change without losing tradition."[24] The problem with respect to the issue of race and popular culture, however, is that the *tradition* itself may need to be thoroughly examined, its "common sense" assumptions unearthed and challenged, and its racial images contested and transformed.

READING THE TEXT

1. Describe in your own words the difference between "overt" and "inferential racism" (para. 6).

2. Why, according to Omi, is popular culture so powerful in shaping America's attitudes toward race?

3. What relationship does Omi see between gender and racial stereotypes?

4. How did racial relations change in America during the 1980s, in Omi's view?

READING THE SIGNS

1. In class, brainstorm on the blackboard stereotypes, both "good" and "bad," attributed to specific racial groups. Then discuss the possible sources of these stereotypes. In what ways have they been perpetuated in popular culture, including movies, television, advertising, music, and consumer products? What does your discussion reveal about popular culture's influence on our most basic ways of seeing the world?

2. Rent a videotape of *Gone with the Wind,* and view the film. Write a semiotic essay in which you analyze how race operates as a sign in this movie. How, to use Omi's terms, does the film create, reproduce, and sustain racial ideologies in America? What does its racial ideology reveal about its status as a "classic" American film?

3. Rent a videotape of *Malcolm X* or another film that addresses race relations, such as *Mi Familia,* and view the film. Using Omi's essay as your critical framework, write an essay in which you explore how this film may reflect or redefine American attitudes toward racial identity and race relations.

4. Buy an issue of a magazine targeted to a specific ethnic readership, such as *Hispanic, Ebony,* or *A.,* and study both its advertising and its articles. Then write an essay in which you explore the extent to which the magazine accurately reflects that ethnicity or, in Omi's words, appeals to readers as "colored versions of essentially 'white' characters" (para. 42).

[24]*The San Francisco Chronicle* (June 13, 1987).

BENJAMIN DeMOTT

PUT ON A HAPPY FACE: MASKING THE DIFFERENCES BETWEEN BLACKS AND WHITES

By looking at the movies, you'd think that race relations in the United States were in splendid shape. Just look at Danny Glover and Mel Gibson in the Lethal Weapon *movies, or consider* Driving Miss Daisy. *But according to Benjamin DeMott (b. 1924), things are not so rosy. In fact, DeMott argues in this essay that Hollywood has effectively concealed the true state of American racial politics behind a pleasing façade of black and white happy-faces, and so has inadvertently worked to distract movie audiences from the pressing need to improve our racial climate. A writer whose interests include the media and American racial and class politics, DeMott's books include* Created Equal: Reading and Writing about Class in America *(1985),* The Imperial Middle: Why Americans Can't Think Straight about Class *(1990),* The Trouble with Friendship: Why Americans Can't Think Straight about Race *(1995), and* Killer Woman Blues: Why Americans Can't Think Straight about Gender and Power *(2000).*

At the movies these days, questions about racial injustice have been amicably resolved. Watch *Pulp Fiction* or *Congo* or *A Little Princess* or any other recent film in which both blacks and whites are primary characters and you can, if you want, forget about race. Whites and blacks greet one another on the screen with loving candor, revealing their common humanity. In *Pulp Fiction,* an armed black mobster (played by Samuel L. Jackson) looks deep into the eyes of an armed white thief in the middle of a holdup (played by Tim Roth) and shares his version of God's word in Ezekiel, whereupon the two men lay aside their weapons, both more or less redeemed. The moment inverts an earlier scene in which a white boxer (played by Bruce Willis) risks his life to save another black mobster (played by Ving Rhames), who is being sexually tortured as a prelude to his execution.

Pulp Fiction (gross through July [1995]: $107 million) is one of a series of films suggesting that the beast of American racism is tamed and harmless. Close to the start of *Die Hard with a Vengeance* (gross through July [1995]: $95 million) the camera finds a white man wearing sandwich boards on the corner of Amsterdam Avenue and 138th Street in Harlem. The boards carry a horrific legend: I HATE NIGGERS. A group of young blacks approach the man with murderous intent, bearing guns and knives. They are figures straight out of a national nightmare — ugly, enraged, terrifying. No problem. A black man, again played by Jackson, appears and rescues the white man, played by

Willis. The black man and white man come to know each other well. In time the white man declares flatly to the black, "I need you more than you need me." A moment later he charges the black with being a racist — with not liking whites as much as the white man likes blacks — and the two talk frankly about their racial prejudices. Near the end of the film, the men have grown so close that each volunteers to die for the other.

Pulp Fiction and *Die Hard with a Vengeance* follow the pattern of *Lethal Weapon 1, 2,* and *3,* the Danny Glover/Mel Gibson buddy vehicles that collectively grossed $357 million, and *White Men Can't Jump,* which, in the year of the L.A. riots, grossed $76 million. In *White Men Can't Jump,* a white dropout, played by Woody Harrelson, ekes out a living on black-dominated basketball courts in Los Angeles. He's arrogant and aggressive but never in danger because he has a black protector and friend, played by Wesley Snipes. At the movie's end, the white, flying above the hoop like a stereotypical black player, scores the winning basket in a two-on-two pickup game on an alley-oop pass from his black chum, whereupon the two men fall into each other's arms in joy. Later, the black friend agrees to find work for the white at the store he manages.

> WHITE (helpless): I gotta get a job. Can you get me a job?
> BLACK (affectionately teasing): Got any references?
> WHITE (shy grin): You.

Such dialogue is the stuff of romance. What's dreamed of and gained is a place where whites are unafraid of blacks, where blacks ask for and need nothing from whites, and where the sameness of the races creates a common fund of sweet content.[1] The details of the dream matter less than the force that makes it come true for both races, eliminating the constraints of objective reality and redistributing resources, status, and capabilities. That cleansing social force supersedes political and economic fact or policy; that force, improbably enough, is friendship.

Watching the beaming white men who know how to jump, we do well to remind ourselves of what the camera shot leaves out. Black infants die in America at twice the rate of white infants. (Despite the increased numbers of middle-class blacks, the rates are diverging, with black rates actually rising.) One out of every two black children lives below the poverty line (as compared with one out of seven white children). Nearly four times as many black fami- 5

---

[1] I could go on with examples of movies that deliver the good news of friendship: *Regarding Henry, Driving Miss Daisy, Forrest Gump, The Shawshank Redemption, Philadelphia, The Last Boy Scout, 48 Hours I–II, Rising Sun, Iron Eagle I–II, Rudy, Sister Act, Hearts of Dixie, Betrayed, The Power of One, White Nights, Clara's Heart, Doc Hollywood, Cool Runnings, Places in the Heart, Trading Places, Fried Green Tomatoes, Q & A, Platoon, A Mother's Courage: The Mary Thomas Story, The Unforgiven, The Air Up There, The Pelican Brief, Losing Isaiah, Smoke, Searching for Bobby Fischer, An Officer and a Gentleman, Speed,* etc.

lies exist below the poverty line as white families. More than 50 percent of African American families have incomes below $25,000. Among black youths under age twenty, death by murder occurs nearly ten times as often as among whites. Over 60 percent of births to black mothers occur out of wedlock, more than four times the rate for white mothers. The net worth of the typical white household is ten times that of the typical black household. In many states, five to ten times as many blacks as whites age eighteen to thirty are in prison.

The good news at the movies obscures the bad news in the streets and confirms the Supreme Court's recent decisions on busing, affirmative action, and redistricting. Like the plot of *White Men Can't Jump,* the Court postulates the existence of a society no longer troubled by racism. Because black-white friendship is now understood to be the rule, there is no need for integrated schools or a congressional Black Caucus or affirmative action. The Congress and state governors can guiltlessly cut welfare, food assistance, fuel assistance, Head Start, housing money, fellowship money, vaccine money. Justice Anthony Kennedy can declare, speaking for the Supreme Court majority last June, that creating a world of genuine equality and sameness requires only that "our political system and our society cleanse themselves . . . of discrimination."

The deep logic runs as follows: *Yesterday white people didn't like black people, and accordingly suffered guilt, knowing that the dislike was racist and knowing also that as moral persons they would have to atone for the guilt. They would have to ante up for welfare and Head Start and halfway houses and free vaccine and midnight basketball and summer jobs for schoolkids and graduate fellowships for promising scholars and craft-union apprenticeships and so on, endlessly. A considerable and wasteful expense. But at length came the realization that by ending dislike or hatred it would be possible to end guilt, which in turn would mean an end to redress: no more wasteful ransom money. There would be but one requirement: the regular production and continuous showing forth of evidence indisputably proving that hatred has totally vanished from the land.*

I cannot tell the reader how much I would like to believe in this sunshine world. After the theater lights brighten and I've found coins for a black beggar on the way to my car and am driving home through downtown Springfield, Massachusetts, the world invented by *Die Hard with a Vengeance* and America's highest court gives way only slowly to the familiar urban vision in my windshield — homeless blacks on trash-strewn streets, black prostitutes staked out on a corner, and signs of a not very furtive drug trade. I know perfectly well that most African Americans don't commit crimes or live in alleys. I also know that for somebody like myself, downtown Springfield in the late evening is not a good place to be.

The movies reflect the larger dynamic of wish and dream. Day after day the nation's corporate ministries of culture churn out images of racial harmony. Millions awaken each morning to the friendly sight of Katie Couric nudging a perky elbow into good buddy Bryant Gumbel's side. My mailbox and millions of demographically similar others are choked with flyers from companies (Wal-Mart, Victoria's Secret) bent on publicizing both their wares and their social bona fides by displaying black and white models at cordial ease with one another. A torrent of goodwill messages about race arrives daily — revelations of corporate largesse, commercials, news features, TV specials, all proclaiming that whites like me feel strongly positive impulses of friendship for blacks and that those same admirable impulses are effectively eradicating racial differences, rendering blacks and whites the same. BellSouth TV commercials present children singing "I am the keeper of the world" — first a white child, then a black child, then a white child, then a black child. Because Dow Chemical likes black America, it recruits young black college grads for its research division and dramatizes, in TV commercials, their tearful-joyful partings from home. ("Son, show 'em what you got," says a black lad's father.) American Express shows an elegant black couple and an elegant white couple sitting together in a theater, happy in one another's company. (The couples share the box with an oversized Gold Card.) During the evening news I watch a black mom offer Robitussin to a miserably coughing white mom. Here's *People* magazine promoting itself under a photo of John Lee Hooker, the black bluesman. "We're these kinds of people, too," *People* claims in the caption. In [a recent] production of *Hamlet* on Broadway, Horatio [was] played by a black actor. On *The 700 Club,* Pat Robertson joshes Ben Kinchlow, his black sidekick, about Ben's far-out ties.

What counts here is not the saccharine clumsiness of the interchanges 10 but the bulk of them — the ceaseless, self-validating gestures of friendship, the humming, buzzing background theme: *All decent Americans extend the hand of friendship to African Americans; nothing but nothing is more auspicious for the African American future than this extended hand.* Faith in the miracle cure of racism by change-of-heart turns out to be so familiar as to have become unnoticeable. And yes, the faith has its benign aspect. Even as they nudge me and others toward belief in magic (instant pals and no-money-down equality), the images and messages of devoted relationships between blacks and whites do exert a humanizing influence.

Nonetheless, through these same images and messages the comfortable majority tells itself a fatuous untruth. Promoting the fantasy of painless answers, inspiring groundless self-approval among whites, joining the Supreme Court in treating "cleansing" as *inevitable,* the new orthodoxy of friendship incites culture-wide evasion, justifies one political step backward after another, and greases the skids along which, tomorrow, welfare block grants will slide into state highway-resurfacing budgets. Whites are part of the solution, says this orthodoxy, if we break out of the prison of our skin color, say hello, as equals, one-on-one, to a black stranger, and make a black friend. We're part of the problem if we have an aversion to black people or are frightened of them, or if we feel that the more distance we put between them and us the better, or if we're in the habit of asserting our superiority rather than acknowledging our common humanity. Thus we shift the problem away from politics — from black experience and the history of slavery — and perceive it as a matter of the suspicion and fear found within the white heart; solving the problem asks no more of us than that we work on ourselves, scrubbing off the dirt of ill will.

The approach miniaturizes, personalizes, and moralizes; it removes the large and complex dilemmas of race from the public sphere. It tempts audiences to see history as irrelevant and to regard feelings as decisive — to believe that the fate of black Americans is shaped mainly by events occurring in the hearts and minds of the privileged. And let's be frank: the orthodoxy of friendship feels *nice*. It practically *consecrates* self-flattery. The "good" Bill Clinton who attends black churches and talks with likable ease to fellow worshipers was campaigning when Los Angeles rioted in '92. "White Americans," he said, "are gripped by the isolation of their own experience. Too many still simply have no friends of other races and do not know any differently." Few black youths of working age in South-Central L.A. had been near enough to the idea of a job even to think of looking for work before the Rodney King verdict, but the problem, according to Clinton, was that whites need black friends.

Most of the country's leading voices of journalistic conscience (editorial writers, television anchorpersons, syndicated columnists) roundly endorse the doctrine of black-white friendship as a means of redressing the inequalities between the races. Roger Rosenblatt, editor of the *Columbia Journalism Review* and an especially deft supplier of warm and fuzzy sentiment, published an essay in *Family Circle* arguing that white friendship and sympathy for blacks simultaneously make power differentials vanish and create interracial identity between us, one by one. The author finds his *exemplum* in an episode revealing the personal sensitivity, to injured blacks, of one of his children.

"When our oldest child, Carl, was in high school," he writes, "he and two black friends were standing on a street corner in New York City one spring evening, trying to hail a taxi. The three boys were dressed decently and were doing nothing wild or threatening. Still, no taxi would pick them up. If a driver spotted Carl first, he might slow down, but he would take off again when he saw the others. Carl's two companions were familiar with this sort of abuse. Carl, who had never observed it firsthand before, burned with anger and embarrassment that he was the color of a world that would so mistreat his friends."

Rosenblatt notes that when his son "was applying to colleges, he wrote   15
his essay on that taxi incident with his two black friends. . . . He was able to articulate what he could not say at the time — how ashamed and impotent he felt. He also wrote of the power of their friendship, which has lasted to this day and has carried all three young men into the country that belongs to them. To all of us."

In this homily white sympathy begets interracial sameness in several ways. The three classmates are said to react identically to the cabdrivers' snub; i.e., they feel humiliated. "[Carl] could not find the words to express his humiliation and his friends *would* not express theirs."

The anger that inspires the younger Rosenblatt's college-admission essay on racism is seen as identical with black anger. Friendship brings the classmates together as joint, equal owners of the land of their birth ("the country that belongs to [all of] them"). And Rosenblatt supplies a still larger vision of essential black-white sameness near the end of his essay: "Our proper hearts tell the truth," he declares, "which is that we are all in the same boat, rich and poor, black and white. We are helpless, wicked, heroic, terrified, and we need one another. We need to give rides to one another."

Thus do acts of private piety substitute for public policy while the possibility of urgent political action disappears into a sentimental haze. "If we're looking for a formula to ease the tensions between the races," Rosenblatt observes, then we should "attack the disintegration of the black community" and "the desperation of the poor." Without overtly mocking civil rights activists who look toward the political arena "to erase the tensions," Rosenblatt alludes to them in a throwaway manner, implying that properly adjusted whites look elsewhere, that there was a time for politicking for "equal rights" but we've passed through it. Now is a time in which we should listen to our hearts at moments of epiphany and allow sympathy to work its wizardry, cleansing and floating us, blacks and whites "all in the same boat," on a mystical undercurrent of the New Age.

Blacks themselves aren't necessarily proof against this theme, as witness a recent essay by James Alan McPherson in the Harvard journal *Reconstruction*. McPherson, who received the 1977 Pulitzer Prize for fiction for his collection of stories *Elbow Room,* says that "the only possible steps, the safest steps . . . small ones" in the movement "toward a universal culture" will be those built not on "ideologies and formulas and programs" but on experiences of personal connectedness.

"Just this past spring," he writes, "when I was leaving a restaurant after [20] taking a [white] former student to dinner, a black [woman on the sidewalk] said to my friend, in a rasping voice, 'Hello, girlfriend. Have you got anything to spare?'" The person speaking was a female crack addict with a child who was also addicted. "But," writes McPherson, when the addict made her pitch to his dinner companion, "I saw in my friend's face an understanding and sympathy and a shining which transcended race and class. Her face reflected one human soul's connection with another. The magnetic field between the two women was charged with spiritual energy."

The writer points the path to progress through interpersonal gestures by people who "insist on remaining human, and having human responses. . . . Perhaps the best that can be done, now, is the offering of understanding and support to the few out of many who are capable of such gestures, rather than devising another plan to engineer the many into one."

The elevated vocabulary ("soul," "spiritual") beatifies the impulse to turn away from the real-life agenda of actions capable of reducing racial injustice. Wherever that impulse dominates, the rhetoric of racial sameness thrives, diminishing historical catastrophes affecting millions over centuries and inflating the significance of tremors of tenderness briefly troubling the heart or conscience of a single individual — the boy waiting for a cab, the woman leaving the restaurant. People forget the theoretically unforgettable — the caste history of American blacks, the connection between no schools for longer than a century and bad school performance now, between hateful social attitudes and zero employment opportunities, between minority anguish and majority fear.

How could this way of seeing have become conventional so swiftly? How did the dogmas of instant equality insinuate themselves so effortlessly into courts and mass audiences alike? How can a white man like myself, who taught Southern blacks in the 1960s, find himself seduced — as I have been more than once — by the orthodoxy of friendship? In the civil rights era, the experience for many millions of Americans was one of discovery. A hitherto unimagined continent of human reality and history came into view, inducing genuine concern and at least a temporary setting aside of self-importance. I remember with utter clarity what I felt at Mary Holmes College in West Point, Mississippi, when a black student of mine was killed by tailgating rednecks; my fellow tutors and I were overwhelmed with how shamefully wrong a wrong could be. For a time, we were released from the prisons of moral weakness and ambiguity. In the year or two that followed — the mid-Sixties — the notion that some humans are more human than others, whites more human than blacks, appeared to have been overturned. The next step seemed obvious: society would have to admit that when one race deprives another of its humanity for centuries, those who have done the depriving are obligated to do what they can to restore the humanity of the deprived. The obligation clearly entailed the mounting of comprehensive *long-term* programs of developmental assistance — not guilt-money handouts — for nearly the entire black population. The path forward was unavoidable.

It was avoided. Shortly after the award of civil rights and the institution, in 1966, of limited preferential treatment to remedy employment and educational discrimination against African Americans, a measure of economic progress for blacks did appear in census reports. Not much, but enough to stimulate glowing tales of universal black advance and to launch the good-news barrage that continues to this day (headline in the *New York Times,* June 18, 1995: "Moving On Up: The Greening of America's Black Middle Class").

After Ronald Reagan was elected to his first term, the new dogma of black-white sameness found ideological support in the form of criticism of so-called coddling. Liberal activists of both races were berated by critics of both races for fostering an allegedly enfeebling psychology of dependency that discouraged African Americans from committing themselves to individual self-development. In 1988, the charge was passionately voiced in an essay in these pages, "I'm Black, You're White, Who's Innocent?" by Shelby Steele, who attributed the difference between black rates of advance and those of other minority groups to white folks' pampering. Most blacks, Steele claimed, 25 could make it on their own — as voluntary immigrants have done — were they not held back by devitalizing programs that presented them, to themselves and others, as somehow dissimilar to and weaker than other Americans. This argument was all-in-the-same-boatism in a different key; the claim remained that progress depends upon recognition of black-white sameness. Let us see through superficial differences to the underlying, equally distributed gift for success. Let us teach ourselves — in the words of the Garth Brooks tune — to ignore "the color of skin" and "look for . . . the beauty within."

Still further support for the policy once known as "do-nothingism" came from points-of-light barkers, who held that a little something might perhaps be done *if* accompanied by enough publicity. Nearly every broadcaster and publisher in America moves a bale of reportage on pro bono efforts by white Americans to speed the advance of black Americans. Example: McDonald's and the National Basketball Association distribute balloons when they announce they are addressing the dropout problem with an annual "Stay in School" scheme that gives schoolkids who don't miss a January school day a ticket to an all-star exhibition. The publicity strengthens the idea that these initiatives will nullify the social context — the city I see through my windshield. Reports of white philanthropy suggest that the troubles of this block and the next should be understood as phenomena in transition. The condition of American blacks need not be read as the fixed, unchanging consequence of generations of bottom-caste existence. Edging discreetly past a beggar posted near the entrance to Zabar's or H&H Bagels, or, while walking the dog, stepping politely around black men asleep on the sidewalk, we need not see ourselves and our fellows as uncaring accomplices in the acts of social injustice.

Yet more powerful has been the ceaseless assault, over the past generation, on our knowledge of the historical situation of black Americans. On the face of things it seems improbable that the cumulative weight of documented historical injury to African Americans could ever be lightly assessed. Gifted black writers continue to show, in scene after scene — in their studies of middle-class blacks interacting with whites — how historical realities shape the lives of their black characters. In *Killer of Sheep,* the brilliant black filmmaker Charles Burnett dramatizes the daily encounters that suck poor blacks into will-lessness and contempt for white fairy tales of interracial harmony; he quickens his historical themes with images of faceless black meat processors gutting undifferentiated, unchoosing animal life. Here, say these images, as though talking back to Clarence Thomas, here is a basic level of black life unchanged over generations. Where there's work, it's miserably paid and ugly. Space allotments at home and at work cramp body and mind. Positive expectation withers in infancy. People fall into the habit of jeering at aspiration as though at the bidding of physical law. Obstacles at every hand prevent people from loving and being loved in decent ways, prevent children from believing their parents, prevent parents from believing they themselves know anything worth knowing. The only true self, now as in the long past, is the one mocked by one's own race. "Shit on you, nigger," says a voice in *Killer of Sheep*. "Nothing you say matters a good goddamn."

For whites, these words produce guilt, and for blacks, I can only assume, pain and despair. The audience for tragedy remains small, while at the multiplex the popular enthusiasm for historical romance remains constant and vast. During the last two decades, the entertainment industry has conducted a siege on the pertinent past, systematically excising knowledge of the consequences of the historical exploitation of African Americans. Factitious renderings of the American past blur the outlines of black-white conflict, redefine the ground of black grievances for the purpose of diminishing the grievances, restage black life in accordance with the illusory conventions of American success mythology, and present the operative influences on race history as the same as those implied to be pivotal in *White Men Can't Jump* or a Bell-South advertisement.

Although there was scant popular awareness of it at the time (1977), the television miniseries *Roots* introduced the figure of the Unscathed Slave. To an enthralled audience of more than 80 million the series intimated that the damage resulting from generations of birth-ascribed, semianimal status was largely temporary, that slavery was a product of motiveless malignity on the social margins rather than of respectable rationality, and that the ultimate significance of the institution lay in the demonstration, by freed slaves, that no force on earth can best the energies of American Individualism. ("Much like the Waltons confronting the depression," writes historian Eric Foner, a widely respected authority on American slavery, "the family in *Roots* neither seeks nor requires outside help; individual or family effort is always sufficient.") Ken Burns's much applauded PBS documentary *The Civil War* (1990) went even further than *Roots* in downscaling black injury; the series treated slavery, birth-ascribed inferiority, and the centuries-old denial of dignity as matters of slight consequence. (By "implicitly denying the brutal reality of slavery," writes historian Jeanie Attie, Burns's programs crossed "a dangerous moral threshold." To a group of historians who asked him why slavery had been so slighted, Burns said that any discussion of slavery "would have been lengthy and boring.")

Mass media treatments of the civil rights protest years carried forward   30
the process, contributing to the "positive" erasure of difference. Big-budget films like *Mississippi Burning,* together with an array of TV biographical specials on Dr. Martin Luther King and others, presented the long-running struggle between disenfranchised blacks and the majority white culture as a heartwarming episode of interracial unity; the speed and caringness of white response to the oppression of blacks demonstrated that broadscale race conflict or race difference was inconceivable.

A consciousness that ingests either a part or the whole of this revisionism loses touch with the two fundamental truths of race in America; namely, that because of what happened in the past, blacks and whites cannot yet be the same; and that because what happened in the past was no mere matter of ill will or insult but the outcome of an established caste structure that has only very recently begun to be dismantled, it is not reparable by one-on-one goodwill. The word "slavery" comes to induce stock responses with no vital sense of a grinding devastation of mind visited upon generation after generation. Hoodwinked by the orthodoxy of friendship, the nation either ignores the past, summons for it a detached, correct "compassion," or gazes at it as though it were a set of aesthetic conventions, like twisted trees and fragmented rocks in nineteenth-century picturesque painting — lifeless phenomena without bearing on the present. The chance of striking through the mask of corporate-underwritten, feel-good, ahistorical racism grows daily more remote. The trade-off — whites promise friendship, blacks accept the status quo — begins to seem like a good deal.

Cosseted by Hollywood's magic lantern and soothed by press releases from Washington and the American Enterprise Institute, we should never forget what we see and hear for ourselves. Broken out by race, the results of every social tabulation from unemployment to life expectancy add up to a chronicle of atrocity. The history of black America fully explains — to anyone who approaches it honestly — how the disaster happened and why neither guilt money nor lectures on personal responsibility can, in and of themselves, repair the damage. The vision of friendship and sympathy placing blacks and whites "all in the same boat," rendering them equally able to do each other favors, "to give rides to one another," is a smiling but monstrous lie.

READING THE TEXT

1. How does DeMott view current race relations in America, and how have recent Hollywood films presented a distorted view of those relations?

2. How, in DeMott's view, do films represent the wish fulfillment of mainstream America?

3. What does DeMott see as the social effect of fantasy-laden images of happy race relations?

4. What does DeMott mean when he says that "acts of private piety substitute for public policy while the possibility of urgent political action disappears into a sentimental haze" (para. 18)?

5. How does DeMott interpret the depiction of slavery in productions such as *Roots* and *The Civil War*?

READING THE SIGNS

1. Rent a videotape of one of the films that DeMott discusses in his essay. Then write your own analysis of the race relations depicted in the film. To what extent do you find his claim that the film sugarcoats race relations to be valid?

2. DeMott focuses on black-white relations in this essay. In class, discuss how other ethnicities, such as Latinos or Asian Americans, fit his argument. To develop your ideas, consult the introduction to this chapter.

3. DeMott is critical of the unrealistic portrayal of race relations in film. In your journal, explore whether you believe this lack of realism has a positive or negative impact on Americans' attitudes toward race.

4. DeMott contends that we can see the same unrealistic friendships between the races in product catalogues and advertising. Select a favorite catalogue or magazine and study the models populating the pages. Then write an essay in which you support, refute, or modify his contention.

5. If you were to produce a film that depicts current race relations in America, what sort of film would you create? Write a creative essay describing your ideal film, then share it with your classmates.

PAUL C. TAYLOR

FUNKY WHITE BOYS AND HONORARY SOUL SISTERS

Can white boys really sing the blues? Or is Eric Clapton just a wannabe who's never paid his dues? For some black critics, the only way that Clapton, and other white performers of black cultural forms, could pay their dues would be to become black, but Paul C. Taylor (b. 1967) isn't so sure. Reflecting on his own youthful identification with white musicians and athletes whose mastery of black cultural activities qualified them for membership in what he called "The Funky White Boys Club," Taylor explains why many blacks are uncomfortable with funky white boys (and honorary white soul sisters). Taylor is an assistant professor of philosophy at the University of Washington, where he also teaches courses in American ethnic studies.

Question: What do Stevie Ray Vaughan, Larry Bird, and Phil Woods have in common? Answer: All were charter members of a club that I created when I was growing up. They didn't know this, of course; and the existence of the club says at least as much about me as it does about its members. It speaks, for example, to the existence of an impulse that found expression in other ways — in, for example, the all-star bands that I imagined to unite the likes of Louis Armstrong and Wynton Marsalis, Bird and Branford Marsalis; as well as in my attachment to comic books like *The Justice League of America,* featuring super-groups composed of heroes who otherwise flew solo. But the club I created wasn't just about me and my need to foster cooperation among my idols and heroes. It was also about something that its members had in common, a commonality indicated by the name they collectively bore: The Funky White Boys Club.

One became eligible for admission to the FWB by being a white person who excelled in a cultural practice that might plausibly be considered part of, or disproportionately shaped by or linked to, black culture. So the late bluesman Vaughan gained entry for his faithful extension of the guitar artistry of Albert King and Jimi Hendrix, Woods was honored for his reverent appropriation of Charlie Parker, and Larry Bird got in just because he was so damn *good* at basketball, never mind his stereotypically "white" playing style and overwhelmingly white team (tellingly, the *Celtics* of Boston). Creating the FWB was my way of marking and celebrating what seemed to me that most anomalous of circumstances: the existence of white people who violated the core assumptions of commonsense racial logic and dared to do things white people weren't supposed to be capable of.

Eventually noticing that the FWB was indeed a boys club, I created a companion female group and inducted Bonnie Raitt and Martina Navratilova as charter members. But due either to a dearth of imagination or a loss of interest, I neglected to name the female group and soon neglected the whole project. That may have been the year when video killed the radio star and MTV was born, giving me more pleasantly mind-numbing ways to spend my time.

The clubs languished in the depths of my memory until fairly recently, when an article in *Vibe* magazine called them to my attention once again.[1] The article was an update on the R&B singer/bassist Teena Marie, a white woman who at one time was the protégée of Rick James. (James is the man who gave us — and, unfortunately, M. C. Hammer — the song "Superfreak" and then acted out the song in a series of encounters with the law. Luckily his, well, eccentricities form no part of our story here and won't be mentioned again.) The text of the piece was arrayed around a series of moody photographs of Marie, one of which bore the caption "honorary soul sister." When I saw this my mind made one of those instant and unmotivated associations that keep psychoanalysts in business and I realized that that should have been the name of the female funky white boys: the honorary soul sisters.

I found the name appropriate not only because, as I then remembered, 5 Marie was one of the early members of the group, but also because the title laid bare the curious nature of the venture I'd undertaken all those years ago, exposing assumptions that the expression "funky white boys" leaves submerged. Why is Teena Marie only an *honorary* soul sister? Why can't she be a real one? Clearly the answer lies in the other title. According to the dominant assumptions of commonsense racial logic, white boys aren't *supposed* to be funky, and white women aren't supposed to be soulful. Teena Marie is just honorary because she's white, and Stevie Ray Vaughan was funky despite being white. There is rather widespread agreement on these assumptions, as evidenced by the frequency with which one still encounters references to the stereotypical white person without rhythm. But it's much less clear what's behind the assumptions. Just what does race have to do with being soulful?

---

[1] Chuck Eddy, "Teena in Wonderland," *Vibe* magazine, November 1994.

The *Vibe* article inspired these sorts of questions for me because I read it shortly after concluding an unsatisfactory print debate with another philosopher on a related topic, the question of whether white people can play the blues.[2] His position was that they can, despite claims to the contrary; my position was, and is, that *of course* they can, and that perhaps we'd be better served by looking into the motivation one might have for claiming the contrary. That debate put me in the habit of examining issues of race, culture, and authenticity, so I started to wonder about my youthful conviction that Stevie Ray Vaughan's status as a bluesman was merely honorary. In effect, the issue we'd pursued in the earlier debate was focused and narrowed into this question: What was I doing in those younger days when I created the clubs? Or: What is it about Teena Marie's whiteness that makes her only an *honorary* soul sister?

I'd like to share my thoughts on that topic, as well as on one other. I want to consider also what we should say about the urge to create Funky White Boys clubs. Is it a simple and indefensible racist impulse, relying on essentialist notions of racial characteristics and traits? Or is it something else?

1. Metaphysical Nationalism and the FWB

My clubs started with some rough but fairly reliable generalizations about race and culture. Here's one: By and large, black people tend to participate jointly in distinctive forms of life. This is a claim that sociology can bear out and that history can explain. More important, it is a claim that is neither contradicted nor undermined by the remarkable variety of lives and styles that black people can inhabit. People always say that no two snowflakes are alike, but if they had nothing in common we wouldn't call them both snowflakes. Both are tiny bits of crystalized water, a fact which is prior to all of the very real differences between them. They differ widely within a certain sphere of commonality: there is unity underlying the diversity. The same is true of black people — by which I mean "African-descended peoples in the Americas." Or, alternatively, to paraphrase a definition from W. E. B. Du Bois, "those people who would have had to ride the Jim Crow car in Georgia had they been there in 1940."[3]

By and large, black people speak or at least understand cognate cultural and experiential languages, whatever our many regional, political, religious, ethnic, or individual differences. This is what struck me as a youth. I knew that my black friends differed from my white friends, that they listened to different music and ate different foods and spoke differently: I had seen it and

---

[2]" . . . So Black and Blue: Response to Rudinow," *Journal of Aesthetics and Art Criticism* 53:3, 313–16, 1995.

[3]See W. E. B. Du Bois, *Dusk of Dawn* (1940; New Brunswick: Transaction Press, 1984), 153.

heard it myself. I knew they aspired to different styles of play on the basketball court after school; I knew that this Bud Powell fellow I'd started listening to was playing in a way that my white piano teachers never mentioned, much less demonstrated.

Knowing these things I drew a conclusion: white people who do things the way we do must have a special status, because most white people don't, or can't. And this conclusion led me to another rough but reliable generalization: By and large, white people are unable to participate in or appreciate black cultural practices. So in the same way that John Turturro's character in Spike Lee's *Do the Right Thing* exempts Magic Johnson and Prince from blackness because they're somehow special, my young mind exempted from whiteness the white people who could participate in black culture. They became honorary black folk, almost. No longer just white boys, but *funky* white boys.

Now, rough but reliable generalizations may suffer one of two fates when stored in an active and curious mind. On the one hand, they may be complicated by additional conditions and have the limits of their reliability precisely marked. This is what happened in my case. When I learned about class differences within and across races, about regional cultural variation and so forth, I realized that whatever I said about The Race was going to be riddled with exceptions and conditions except at a very lofty level of abstraction, and that whatever I said was going to have to answer to the evidence of history and sociology.

On the other hand, the generalizations may be rigidified into necessary truths and the observations which motivate them rendered inevitable. This happens to the points I started with when they are taken up into the framework of a certain kind of cultural nationalism. Cultural nationalism is in part the view that all black people participate in a common form of life, that we share a disposition to enjoy and create the same cultural forms, the same modes of speech and movement, expression and performance. For a cultural nationalist, the possibility of both a vibrant black community and a sane, settled individual black identity rest principally upon one thing: the existence of a coherent, identifiable, *distinct* set of black cultural practices. For the nationalist, "black English" and "black art" and "black music" have to be meaningful expressions, marking some important boundaries. And the behaviors inside the boundaries have to add up to a distinctive culture.

So far the nationalist position is consistent with the mindset that motivated my clubs. But a truly committed nationalist goes farther. A committed nationalist on the model of Molefi Asante hardens my rough generalizations into metaphysical and ethical principles in his search for something deeper and more reliable than the contingencies of history to underwrite the unity of black culture. The metaphysical principle is *essentialism,* which in this context entails that *it is of the nature* of black people, completely apart from considerations of history and sociology, to produce certain forms of life. The list of adjectives used in describing that life ought to be familiar. We favor rhythm over melody, it says; organic unities over dualist bifurcations, blues scales over Greek modes, improvisation over scripting, and so forth and so on. On this view black people naturally and *necessarily* gravitate toward certain cultural forms simply because that's what it is to be black.

The ethical principle has to do with *authenticity,* and like the metaphysical principle from which it follows, hardens a rough generalization into dogma. The generalization, you'll recall, was that white people tend not to be able to participate in or enjoy black cultural practices. Essentialism rigidifies this generalization about how capacities *tend* to be distributed into an airtight claim of necessity, the claim that all black people and only black people can participate in black culture because black cultural practices express the nature of black people. The authenticity principle takes the claim about capacity, about what certain people *can* do, and turns it into a claim about permission, about what certain people *may* do. Not only, it turns out, are white people not able to take part in black culture; they are not even allowed to try. (Perhaps this is the sort of slip that English teachers are trying to help us avoid with their fussiness about the distinction between "may" and "can.")

There is another element to the ethics of committed nationalism, the idea   15
of racial *obligation.* This idea follows also from a plausible generalization, this time the point that if the people who created a culture don't maintain it by continued participation, chances are it will die out. The committed nationalist takes this simple point and turns it into a moral imperative. Black people, he argues, should participate in their culture; those who don't are shirking an obligation to the race. As an added incentive, the nationalist I have in mind is likely to point out that the moral error of opting out of the culture carries with it the prospect of psychological ruin, as the unscrupulous negro loses touch with her true identity and, on Asante's version of this account, "loses her center." The notion of cultural-racial obligation provides some additional support for the exclusionary rhetoric of authenticity: white people are in the same position with regard to their own culture, facing the same psychological and moral dangers, and so should worry about their own ways of life instead of dabbling elsewhere. Instead of interfering with our culture they should be contributing to their own.

Let's get clear on the plausible claims behind (way behind) what I've been calling committed cultural nationalism. For one thing, there are regularities in the practices of black diaspora cultures. For another, it does seem to be a good thing for black people to participate in these cultures, good, that is, for both the people and the practices. The individual participants are able to draw existential sustenance from and take shelter in the symbolic and meaningful practices of their cultures, while the cultures themselves are able to persist and proliferate. (Although in this age of pluralism and global consumer culture there is less danger of a cultural form dying out if its original participants neglect it. Blues music, for example, is more likely to die out these days if white people start to neglect it, since many blacks have already consigned it to the dustbin of history.) The difficulty with committed cultural nationalism is that it tries to find some otherworldly support for these plausible ideas.

In particular, this nationalism tries to find some basis for black cultural continuity that's deeper than culture, than history, than the empirical striving and effort of concrete human beings, and as a result culture turns out not to be very important after all. Perhaps a better name for the view would be *metaphysical nationalism,* because it requires invoking an elaborate and unnecessary metaphysical apparatus to make sense of perfectly natural facts. Sociology, anthropology, history, and politics are more than adequate to account for the continuities that interest the nationalist. We just don't *need* to conjure up an elaborate metaphysics to explain the extent to which black people are, culturally and otherwise, *a* people. To do so is a bit like using an atom bomb to kill a housefly. But questions of explanatory adequacy aside, it is simply more interesting to point out the concrete, historical linkages that connect santeria to West Africa, King Sunny Ade to James Brown, than to trace them all to a single transhistorical essence. It is far more impressive for people to remember their roots themselves and create *themselves* despite the fetters of oppression and forced forgetfulness than it is for them to serve as the vehicles of a transcendent racial essence.

As we saw above, metaphysical nationalism also provides an ontological grounding for racial exclusivism, for the claim that all and *only* black people can participate in black culture. From this perspective Teena Marie is an honorary soul sister because she gets close to the core styles and conventions of R&B. The same holds true for Stevie Ray Vaughan and blues performance. But these performers will never be more than honorary because they're not truly expressing their deepest essences. That is to say, to participate truly and fully in the practice is to express the essence that manifests itself in the practice, and white people simply don't have the essence to express. On this view Vaughan is just imitating Albert King; Phil Woods is just imitating Charlie Parker. And if you listen closely, some people say, you can tell the difference. Never mind that white performers in black idioms or styles are not always mimics, or the possibility that any alleged categorical difference between white and black performances may simply be an overzealous interpretation of stylistic differences between individual performers. And never mind that we could account for any discernible categorical difference that *did* arise by referring to culture, to the lower probability that a white person will be socialized into the communities where the conventions of performance are taught and learned.

As we also saw above, the ethical dimensions of metaphysical nationalism can lead to an exclusivist posture by supporting the claim that even if white people can participate in black styles, they *shouldn't* do so. From this perspective Teena Marie is honorary because she's treading on what is by rights someone else's cultural turf. The honor of (almost-) soul sister status is

Blues legend Stevie Ray Vaughan.

extended as a grant of permission, and participation without it is immoral. But the frailty of nationalist metaphysics undermines this point as well. Without the metaphysics that link the racial essence to its cultural manifestation there is no reason to assume that the boundaries of culture and the boundaries of race are coextensive. Without the metaphysics there is no reason not to let Bonnie Raitt or Eric Clapton carry on the blues aspect of black culture. And even apart from the historical and sociological considerations I've mentioned above, there seems to be little reason to accept the metaphysics of racial essences. That is, on the evidence of the biological sciences alone, evidence that has been steadily mounting for some time, especially in this century, the idea that race membership as a matter of physiology somehow carries with it interesting moral and cultural traits seems to be a pernicious fiction.

2. Aesthetics Instead of Authenticity

I want to distance both my present self and my thirteen-year-old self from meta- 20 physical nationalism and its excesses. All those years ago I hadn't yet thought out the possible theoretical extensions of the commonsense racial logic I'd accepted. Having done so now, I reject them. Metaphysical nationalism is too timid and narrow; it downplays the wonderful diversity and creativity of African diaspora cultures — with an "s" — and of the concrete, historically located people who've created reggae, R&B, hard bop, and hip-hop. And worst of all for our present purposes, it stands in the way of explaining how we can reasonably make judgments like the ones behind the title of "honorary soul sister." The metaphysical nationalist approach makes these judgments just as inappropriate and ungrounded as any other racist exclusion. Either whites are just naturally incapable or black culture is just naturally off limits.

But having rejected the metaphysical/ethical route to racial exclusivism, I need to offer some other motivation for the urge that led to my imagined clubs. I do this not just to defend myself (although that's always fun) but also, and more importantly, because I want to displace and decenter the dialectic of essentialism-cum-racism. That is, I want to mark off a conceptual space within which we can examine assertions like "white people can't play the blues" without recourse to the vocabularies of essentialism *or* racism. I want us to be able to say something more interesting about the roots of these assertions than that the speaker is a racial essentialist and therefore a racist. This is important to me because I think relatively few of the people who make or presuppose assertions of the sort I have in mind are essentialists or racists. I don't think the FWB was a racist venture, nor do I think that of *Vibe* magazine's decision to use the expression "honorary soul sister." Luckily, there is a way to understand what I was up to, what the *Vibe* magazine people were up to, without slipping into the paralogisms of racial essences. There is a way to explain the urge to withhold or confer the status of funkiness and soulfulness without relying on the bare fact of race.

The approach I have in mind proceeds from yet another plausible and probably familiar idea, especially familiar when it comes to black music, that I'll call *the Elvis Effect*. When white participation in traditionally black avenues of cultural production produces feelings of unease, this is the Elvis Effect. I could as easily call it the Benny Goodman, the Dave Brubeck, or the Vanilla Ice effect, because all follow the same pattern. Black people participate almost exclusively in a cultural practice, mostly untouched by the interest, interference, or acclaim of the white community. A white person finds his or her way into the practice, becomes proficient, and is "discovered" by the white community. The community embraces the practice, but only in the person of the white "pioneer" who introduced it. It snaps up his records or copies his arrangements (or flocks to get cornrows, or lets its jeans sag around its knees), all the while oblivious to the fact that the true pioneers are probably still toiling in obscurity and poverty, and that the black community has probably moved on to something else that has yet to be "discovered."

Of course my brief description of phenomena that produce the Elvis Effect is a crude and over-simple rendering of complex historical events. For one thing it overlooks issues like the extent to which "white" country music and "black" blues grow from common southern roots that grew into people like Elvis as naturally as it did into, say, Muddy Waters; for another, it passes completely over the role of white record companies in preserving and promulgating black musical culture. But it isn't too crude to make the point. How else can we explain the fact that Benny Goodman gets movies made about him, gigs at Carnegie Hall, and the title of the king of swing, while we're still waiting for the movies — the *big* movies — about Duke Ellington and Fletcher Henderson? How else can we account for the fact that Maynard Ferguson and Chet Baker could, decades ago, beat out Dizzy Gillespie, Miles, *and* Clifford Brown in *Downbeat* polls for best trumpeter? (Baker, maybe. But Ferguson?) How else can we explain the phenomenal sales of Vanilla Ice and New Kids on the Block, not to mention Dave Koz?

The Elvis Effect isn't hard to explain. When we talk about black music in the twentieth century we're talking about commodities, market phenomena, so the relative weakness of black consumer power, as a function both of community size and individual wealth and income, is certainly a factor. And then there's the industrial side, the cynical marketing side, of the music business, which gave us Terence Trent D'Arby in much the same way that it gave us Vanilla Ice (the relative merits of each I'll leave up to you). But the most important factor is *the historically racist trajectory* of white American appetites for cultural commodities. That's why in the early days of the blues-based pop styles (soul, rock, and R&B) black musicians often heard their songs on the radio being covered by white performers, or found their pictures effaced from their own album covers to avoid repulsing white consumers. (Both of which are well rendered in Robert Townsend's film, *The Five Heartbeats.*) That's why the Beatles and the rest of the 1960s British invaders were surprised that no one here seemed to understand the homegrown roots of this new rock and roll: that's why we need Eric Clapton to explain Muddy Waters to us — or one reason, anyway. It is too easy for too many people here to assume that nothing of cultural value can come from black folks, or to concede the point but limit the damage by treating the black origins as raw material to be refined by sophisticated whites.

The Elvis Effect is not new. I've just given the name to a phenomenon 25 with which we're all familiar. I bring it up now to make two points. The first is that the familiarity of the Elvis Effect allows it to provide a backdrop for the experience of art in traditionally black idioms. The second is that this backdrop, and the way it mediates the aesthetic experience, can explain what I've been calling the funky white boys urge, the impulse to distinguish white contributions to traditionally black cultural practices.

When I talk about an aesthetic experience I mean an event, the collection of related perceptions and appraisals that emerges from a certain kind of interaction between an observer and an object. On some conceptions of aesthetic experience, like the one John Dewey articulates in his book, *Art as Experience,* the aesthetic experience is more appropriately considered the work of art than the art object itself. The aesthetic experience brings the object to life in what you do with the sounds D'Angelo has recorded for you, what you do with the figures and hues that Picasso has kindly left you — and what they do with, and to, you.

The art object, the painting or the recorded sounds or the novel, is the focus of an aesthetic experience, which — and here we reach the crucial point — works very much like an experience of visual perception and recognition. When you focus your eyes on something, all around the central point of clarity you see a vast fringe that's fuzzy and out of focus. You usually don't notice this fringe, this periphery; that is, after all, what being focused means. But the fringe is there, and it is essential to the coherence of what you see. If you didn't have peripheral vision the objects in plain sight would seem disconnected and isolated, floating free from the rest of the world. Much like this perceptual fringe there is a theoretical fringe that helps us make sense of the sensations that arise from the encounter with the object. The sensations become organized into an experience of a certain *kind* of object, say, a cow, only if you have the concept "cow" available in your cognitive repertoire. Otherwise you've simply encountered a big, smelly beast that makes weird sounds. Perhaps more clearly, you can experience something as a baseball bat only if the right theoretical background is in place to support your perceptual encounter with the stick of wood. If it isn't, if, say, you're from a pre-industrial culture and don't know how to distinguish a baseball from Bisquick, then you've simply encountered a funny stick.

The experience of an artwork follows the same pattern. The work itself is surrounded by a vast range of peripheral experience which stretches out and makes connections with the rest of the world. You may not think about this fringe, this backdrop to experience, but without it the art object doesn't make sense as the kind of thing it's supposed to be, and it can't contribute to the right kind of aesthetic experience. Unless one internalizes the conventions of western painterly representation, one will see only splashes of paint where an art critic sees angels or receding horizons or bowls of fruit. And unless one understands that the conventions of artistic practice undergird the experience of painterly representation, one treats the painting as nothing more than a *picture* when it is so much more, a commentary on a tradition, a manipulation and rejection of themes and approaches created and perfected over time. Unless one can read these in the work, see them along with the work, the work remains opaque. This history is the fringe, the penumbra that makes the experience coherent and complete.

Similarly, unless we appreciate the narrative of the development of jazz composition and improvisation, Ornette Coleman sounds like he never quite finished learning how to play the saxophone. But when we know the history, when we can notice the periphery of the experience, we can hear his interpretation and critique of the techniques of jazz performance. Or: until you can hear the echoes of Marvin Gaye and Prince and southern gospel *and* hip-hop on D'Angelo's album *Brown Sugar,* until you feel the incredible syncretism of the church organ grounded by a thundering jeep beat on the song "Higher," you'll miss the point and miss out on the most satisfying aspects of the experiences promised by encounters with the album — which, incidentally, is precisely what some hip-hop obsessed reviewers did before the album's sales showed them that maybe this guy was onto something.

My claim here is that the Elvis Effect can serve as the periphery for the reception and experience of white performances in black expressive traditions. In the same way that knowing a bit of art history changes the way we appreciate, the way we *see,* a painting, knowing the historically racist trajectory of white American appetites for cultural commodities can change the way one hears Eric Clapton — or the Canadian dancehall dj Snow. Knowledge of the historically racist trajectory of white American appetites for cultural commodities can erect affective obstacles to the reception and enjoyment of otherwise impeccable arrangements of sounds; that knowledge can interfere with and frustrate the pattern of response that would otherwise attend the perception of the music, just as knowing a little more about the context for Picasso's work can and should frustrate the pattern of response that would otherwise lead one to say "my little sister can do *that.*"

My point is that the urge to keep Teena Marie at arm's length, to invite her in conditionally as an honorary participant, can be an aesthetic response rather than a moral or a metaphysical one. It can proceed from the realization that "I've heard of Eric Clapton only because he's white," the realization that the dollars I spend on a ticket to his show or to buy his CD will fuel the machine which perhaps without racist intent produces racist outcomes: the realization that if I participate in this process, I'll be partially responsible for the next sister who toils in poverty while the white woman with her style gets the big record deal.

3. Conclusion

What, then, does race have to do with funkiness and soulfulness? Simply this: Race is the principal dynamic in an historical drama that shapes the possibilities for aesthetic experience of traditionally black cultural practices. Less concisely but more simply: Most of us share or are at least acquainted with a cluster of moderately plausible intuitions linking race to cultural production. I've been concerned here with three in particular. One says that there is something answering to the title "black culture," or that there are some things answering to that title. Another says that it is good for black people to perpetuate these cultures. And the last says that white people are either unwilling or unable to participate in these cultures, and that the ones who are willing and who are able differ somehow from the rest. These intuitions, when ossified into a metaphysical nationalism, can support a project something like my honorary soul sisters club, but a project predicated on the view that white people have neither the proper nature nor the moral standing to participate in black culture. This approach can lead to the urge to create funky white boys clubs, but it does so while leaving the undeniable fact of white participation utterly inexplicable, making black and white participants immoral and neurotic, and subordinating history to the dictates of a transcendent racial essence. I've explained these consequences of metaphysical nationalism already, so I'll introduce one more for good measure: it plays into the hands of racism. After all, even if the metaphysical nationalist denies that she's a racist, she has given plenty of ammunition to the white racist. While she's saying that the black essence is linked to rhythm and the like, the white racist can say "You're right, we don't have rhythm; our essence is concerned with other things, like rationality and cognitive powers."

I propose avoiding, instead of inviting, this debate with the racist. Instead of invoking nationalist metaphysics, let's take history and culture seriously. On the view I propose, the three plausible intuitions regarding the existence and worth of black culture and the relation between white participants and the culture are joined by a fourth, which says that white participation tends to exploit and thereby to imperil black culture and its main proponents. This intuition leads to the Elvis Effect, and recognizing that fact enables us to link the other intuitions to the funky white boys club impulse *without* inciting the racist or engaging in an act of metaphysical conjuring. History reports that the fate of black expressive innovation has too often been cooptation without compensation, and it supports the prediction that white participation portends dilution, commercialization, and decay for the culture. Awareness of this history seeps into the reception of white performances and makes a qualitative difference in the aesthetic experience — it seeps in, incidentally, not to distract but to inform, the way the history of painting informs one's appreciation of Picasso's *Les Demoiselles D'Avignon*.

This appeal to what we might call a problematized aesthetic response motivates the claim that Stevie Ray Vaughan and Stan Getz are merely honorary. The background to the aesthetic experience is such that what would otherwise be heard as a blues performance is instead experienced as the performance of an honorary bluesman. Teena Marie is honorary not because she lacks the right nature or the moral entitlement to participate in the culture of black music, but because the listener's encounter with the sounds that Marie produces is complicated by the background of commonsense theory that informs the perception and recognition of the sounds.

Some disclaimers are in order. First of all, I am not claiming that the way to understand my particular adolescent urge to designate funky white boys 35 and honorary soul sisters proceeded from an awareness of the historically racist trajectory of white cultural consumption. In the same way that my FWB project didn't rise to the level of definiteness necessary to become metaphysical nationalism, it certainly wasn't definite or politically astute enough to be motivated by the Elvis Effect. It was simply what it was: a youthful effort to occupy an idle mind by following out the consequences of certain familiar and prominent generalizations about race and culture. I am claiming, however, that just as my FWB-urge was neither racist nor essentialist, other similar positions can be neither racist nor essentialist, and that one way to account for such positions is by appeal to the Elvis Effect and the long shadow it can cast over aesthetic experiences.

Second, I don't mean to endorse the claim that white people can only be honorary participants in black culture. I mean only to explain it, or some versions of it. My aim has been to point out only that one can make such claims without being a racist or an essentialist, largely on the basis of certain rough but plausible generalizations about race and culture. Of course, such claims and generalizations are much less plausible now than they were even ten years ago, now that hip-hop culture has penetrated into the deepest and palest recesses of America. And, as it happens, they weren't terribly plausible even then, standing as they did in a tense relationship to the long history of white contribution to and participation in allegedly "black" forms like blues and jazz. But their validity aside, the claims and generalizations are familiar, and as such can be expected to serve as the backdrop to aesthetic experience.

I have a final comment about one of those generalizations, the one concerning what I've labeled "the Elvis Effect." Focusing on the racism of the processes by which black cultural forms have historically found their way into the broader culture moves us past the dialectic of essentialism and authenticity. It shows that there may be concrete political concerns that make racial solidarity an attractive mode of political and cultural practice. It reminds us that anything validly claiming the title "black culture" comes from the concrete strivings of black people rather than from some essence outside of culture. And it reminds us that the strivings of those people take place not in the sociological and historical vacuum often assumed in discussions of racial justice, but in the context of a rich historical drama that is shaped by power relations, by economics and politics. Furthermore, linking judgments like the ones behind the FWB to the background material of economics, history, and politics reminds us that aesthetic experience has a context, one that is as much cultural and political as it is theoretical and art-historical.

READING THE TEXT

1. What were the criteria for inclusion in Paul C. Taylor's "Funky White Boys Club" (para. 1)?

2. Why did *Vibe* call Teena Marie an "honorary soul sister" (para. 4) rather than a real one?

3. What is the difference between "cultural nationalism" (para. 16) and "meta-physical nationalism" (para. 17)?

4. Define the "Elvis Effect" (para. 22) in your own words.

READING THE SIGNS

1. Conduct a class debate on whether whites can be authentic performers of African American cultural activities. Be sure to base your arguments on the work of specific artists and performers.

2. Taylor suggests that metaphysical nationalism "plays into the hands of racism" (para. 32) and thus rejects it. Write an essay in which you argue your position on racial exclusivity in popular entertainment and sports.

3. As rap and hip-hop win mainstream acceptance, more white performers are adopting their styles and rhythms. Write an essay comparing the history of rap and hip-hop with that of rock-and-roll. To what extent do you believe history will repeat itself?

4. Write an essay arguing for or against the value of preserving one's biological ethnic heritage. To develop your ideas, consult Nell Bernstein ("Goin' Gangsta, Choosin' Cholita," p. 599), bell hooks ("Baby," p. 605), or Jack Lopez ("Of Cholos and Surfers," below).

JACK LOPEZ
OF CHOLOS AND SURFERS

If you want to be a surfer, L.A.'s the place to be, but things can get complicated if you come from East Los Angeles, which is not only miles from the beach but is also the home turf for many a cholo street gangster who may not look kindly on a Mexican American kid carrying a copy of Surfer Quarterly *and wearing Bermuda shorts. This is exactly what happened to Jack Lopez (b. 1950), as he tells it in this memoir of growing up Latino in the 1960s—but not to worry, the beach and the barrio are not mutually exclusive, and, in the end, Lopez was able to have "the best of both worlds." A professor of English at California State University, Northridge, Lopez is a short-story writer and essayist whose books include* Cholos and Surfers: A Latino Family Album *(1998) and* Snapping Lines *(2001).*

The only store around that had this new magazine was a Food Giant on Vermont Avenue, just off Imperial. *Surfer Quarterly,* it was then called. Now it's

Surfer Magazine and they've celebrated their thirtieth anniversary. Sheldon made the discovery by chance when he'd gone shopping with his mother, who needed something found only at Food Giant. Normally we didn't go that far east to shop; we went west toward Crenshaw, to the nicer part of town.

We all wanted to be surfers, in fact called ourselves surfers even though we never made it to the beach, though it was less than ten miles away. One of the ways you could become a surfer was to own an issue of *Surfer Quarterly.* Since there had been only one prior issue, I was hot to get the new one. To be a surfer you also had to wear baggy shorts, large Penney's Towncraft T-shirts, and go barefoot, no matter how much the hot sidewalks burned your soles.

That summer in the early sixties I was doing all sorts of odd jobs around the house for my parents: weeding, painting the eaves, baby-sitting during the daytime. I was earning money so that I could buy Lenny Muelich's surfboard, another way to be a surfer. It was a Velzy-Jacobs, ten feet six inches long, twenty-four inches wide, and it had the coolest red oval decal. Lenny was my across-the-street neighbor, two years older than I, the kid who'd taught me the facts of life, the kid who'd taught me how to wrestle, the kid who'd played army with me when we were children, still playing in the dirt.

Now we no longer saw much of each other, though he still looked out for me. A strange thing happened to Lenny the previous school year. He grew. Like the Green Giant or something. He was over six feet tall and the older guys would let him hang out with them. So Lenny had become sort of a hood, wearing huge Sir Guy wool shirts, baggy khaki pants with the cuffs rolled, and French-toed black shoes. He drank wine, even getting drunk in the daytime with his hoodlum friends. Lenny was now respected, feared, even, by some of the parents, and no longer needed or desired to own a surfboard — he was going in the opposite direction. There were two distinct paths in my neighborhood: hood or surfer.

I was entering junior high school in a month, and my best friends were   5 Sheldon Cohen and Tom Gheridelli. They lived by Morningside Heights, and their fathers were the only ones to work, and their houses were more expensive than mine, and they'd both been surfers before I'd aspired toward such a life. Sheldon and Tom wore their hair long, constantly cranking their heads back to keep their bangs out of their eyes. They were thirteen years old. I was twelve. My parents wouldn't let hair grow over my ears no matter how much I argued with them. But I was the one buying a surfboard. Lenny was holding it for me. My parents would match any money I saved over the summer.

Yet *Surfer Quarterly* was more tangible since it only cost one dollar. Lenny's Velzy Jacobs was forty-five dollars, quite a large sum for the time. The issue then became one of how to obtain the object of desire. The Food Giant on Vermont was reachable by bike, but I was no longer allowed to ride up there. Not since my older brother had gone to the Southside Theatre one Saturday and had seen a boy get knifed because he wasn't colored. Vermont was a tough area, though some of the kids I went to school with lived up there and they weren't any different from us. Yet none of them wished to be surfers, I don't think.

What was needed was for me to include my father in the negotiation. I wasn't allowed to ride my bike to Vermont, I reasoned with him. Therefore, he should drive me. He agreed with me and that was that. Except I had to wait until the following Friday when he didn't have to work.

My father was a printer by trade. He worked the graveyard shift. I watched my younger brother and sister during the day (my older brother, who was fifteen years old, was around in case anything of consequence should arise, but we mostly left him alone) until my mother returned from work — Reaganomics had hit my family decades before the rest of the country. Watching my younger sister and bother consisted of keeping them quiet so my father could sleep.

In the late afternoons I'd go to Sportsman's Park, where I'd virtually grown up. I made the all-stars in baseball, basketball, and football. Our first opponent on the path to the city championships was always Will Rogers Park in Watts. Sheldon and Tom and I had been on the same teams. Sometimes I'd see them in the afternoons before we'd all have to return home for dinner. We'd pore over Sheldon's issue of *Surfer* while sitting in the bleachers next to the baseball diamond. If it was too hot we'd go in the wading pool, though we were getting too old for that scene, since mostly women and kids used it.

When Friday afternoon arrived and my father had showered and my 10 mother had returned from work, I reminded my father of our agreement. We drove the neighborhood streets up to Vermont, passing Washington High School, Normandie Avenue, Woodcrest Elementary School, and so on. We spoke mostly of me. Was I looking forward to attending Henry Clay Junior High? Would I still be in accelerated classes? My teachers and the principal had talked with my parents about my skipping a grade but my parents said no.

Just as my father had exhausted his repertoire of school questions, we arrived at the Food Giant. After parking in the back lot, we entered the store and made for the liquor section, where the magazines were housed. I stood in front of the rack, butterflies of expectation overtaking my stomach while my father bought himself some beer. I knew immediately when I found the magazine. It looked like a square of water was floating in the air. An ocean-blue cover of a huge wave completely engulfing a surfer with the headline BANZAI PIPELINE. I held the magazine with great reverence, as if I were holding something of spiritual value, which it was.

"Is that it?" my father asked. He held a quart of Hamm's in each hand, his Friday night allotment.

"Yes." I beamed.

At the counter my father took the magazine from me, leafing through it much too casually, I thought. I could see the bulging veins in his powerful forearms, and saw too the solid bumps that were his biceps.

"Looks like a crazy thing to do," he said, finally placing the magazine on 15 the counter next to the beer. My father, the practical provider, the person whose closet was pristine for lack of clothes — although the ones he did own were stylish, yet not expensive. This was why he drank beer from quart bottles — it was cheaper that way. I know now how difficult it must have been raising four children on the hourly wages my parents made.

The man at the counter rang up the purchases, stopping for a moment to look at the *Surfer.* He smiled.

"*¿Eres mexicano?*" my father asked him.

"*Sí, ¿cómo no?*" the man answered.

Then my father and the store clerk began poking fun at my magazine in Spanish, nothing too mean, but ranking it as silly adolescent nonsense.

When we got back in the car I asked my father why he always asked cer- 20
tain people if they were Mexican. He only asked men who obviously were, thus knowing in advance their answers. He shrugged his shoulders and said he didn't know. It was a way of initiating conversation, he said. Well, it was embarrassing for me, I told him. Because I held the magazine in my lap, I let my father off the hook. It was more important that I give it a quick thumb-through as we drove home. The *Surfer* was far more interesting for me as a twelve-year-old than larger issues of race.

I spent the entire Friday evening holed up in my room, poring over the magazine, not even interested in eating popcorn or watching *77 Sunset Strip,* our familial Friday-night ritual. By the next morning I had almost memorized every photo caption and their sequence. I spoke with Sheldon on the phone and he and Tom were meeting me later at Sportsman's Park. I did my chores in a self-absorbed trance, waiting for the time when I could share my treasure with my friends. My mother made me eat lunch before I was finally able to leave.

Walking the long walk along Western Avenue toward Century and glancing at the photos in the magazine, I didn't pay attention to the cholo whom I passed on the sidewalk. I should have been more aware, but was too preoccupied. So there I was, in a street confrontation before I knew what had happened.

"You a surfer?" he said with disdain. He said it the way you start to say *chocolate. Ch,* like in *choc — churfer.* But that didn't quite capture it, either.

I stopped and turned to face him. He wore a wool watch cap pulled down onto his eyebrows, a long Sir Guy wool shirt with the top button buttoned and all the rest unbuttoned, khaki pants so long they were frayed at the bottoms and so baggy I couldn't see his shoes. I wore Bermuda shorts and a large Towncraft T-shirt. I was barefoot. My parents wouldn't let hair grow over my ears. Cholo meets surfer. Not a good thing. As he clenched his fists I saw a black cross tattooed onto the fleshy part of his hand.

His question was *not* like my father's. My father, I now sensed, wanted a 25
common bond upon which to get closer to strangers. This guy was Mexican American, and he wanted to fight me because I wore the outfit of a surfer.

I rolled the magazine in a futile attempt to hide it, but the cholo viewed this action as an escalation with a perceived weapon. It wasn't that I was overly afraid of him, though fear can work to your advantage if used correctly. I was big for my age, athletic, and had been in many fights. The problem was this: I was hurrying off to see my friends, to share something important with them, walking on a summer day, and I didn't feel like rolling on the ground with some stranger because *he'd* decided we must do so. Why did he get to dictate when or where you would fight? There was another consideration, one more utilitarian: Who knew what sort of weapons he had under all that baggy clothing? A rattail comb, at the least. More likely a knife, because in those days guns weren't that common.

At Woodcrest Elementary School there was a recently arrived Dutch Indonesian immigrant population. One of the most vicious fights I had ever seen was the one when Victor VerHagen fought his own cousin. And the toughest fight I'd ever been in was against Julio, something during a baseball game. There must be some element of self-loathing that propels us to fight those of our own ethnicity with a particular ferocity.

Just before the cholo was going to initiate the fight, I said, "I'm Mexican." American of Mexican descent, actually.

He seemed unable to process this new information. How could someone be Mexican and dress like a surfer? He looked at me again, this time seeing beyond the clothes I wore. He nodded slightly.

This revelation, this recognition verbalized, molded me in the years to 30 come. A surfer with a peeled nose and a Karmann Ghia with surf racks driving down Whittier Boulevard in East L.A. to visit my grandparents. The charmed life of a surfer in the midst of cholos.

When I began attending junior high school, there was a boy nicknamed Niño, who limped around the school yard one day. I discovered the reason for his limp when I went to the bathroom and he had a rifle pointed at boys and was taking their money. I fell in love with a girl named Shirley Pelland, the younger sister of a local surfboard maker. I saw her in her brother's shop after school, but she had no idea I loved her. That fall the gang escalation in my neighborhood became so pronounced my parents decided to move. We sold our house very quickly and moved to Huntington Beach, and none of us could sleep at night for the quiet. We were surrounded by cornfields and strawberry fields and tomato fields. As a bribe for our sudden move my parents chipped in much more than matching funds so I could buy Lenny Muelich's surfboard. I almost drowned in the big waves of a late-autumn south swell, the first time I went out on the Velzy-Jacobs. But later, after I'd surfed for a few years, I expertly rode the waves next to the pier, surfing with new friends.

But I've got ahead of myself. I must return to the cholo who is about to attack. But there isn't any more to tell about the incident. We didn't fight that summer's day over thirty years ago. In fact, I never fought another of my own race and don't know if this was a conscious decision or if circumstances dictated it. As luck would have it, I fought only a few more times during my adolescence and did so only when attacked.

My father's question, which he'd asked numerous people so long ago, taught me these things: The reason he had to ask was because he and my mother had left the safe confines of their Boyle Heights upbringing. They had thrust themselves and their children into what was called at the time the melting pot of Los Angeles. They bought the post–World War II American dream of assimilation. I was a pioneer in the sociological sense that I had no distinct ethnic piece of geography on which my pride and honor depended. Cast adrift in the city streets. Something gained, something lost. I couldn't return to my ethnic neighborhood, but I could be a surfer. And I didn't have to fight for ethnic pride over my city street. The neighborhood kids did, however, stick together, though this was not based upon race. It was a necessity. The older guys would step forward to protect the younger ones. That was how it was done.

The most important thing I learned was that I could do just about anything I wished, within reason. I could be a surfer, if I chose, and even cholos would respect my decision. During my adolescence I went to my grandparents' house for all the holidays. They lived in East Los Angeles. When I was old enough to drive I went on my own, sometimes with a girlfriend, I was able to observe my Los Angeles Mexican heritage, taking a date to the *placita* for Easter service and then having lunch at Olvera Street. An Orange County girl who had no idea this part of Los Angeles existed. I was lucky; I got the best of both worlds.

READING THE TEXT

1. What symbolic significance did being a surfer have for Lopez and his friends?

2. How did Lopez's attitude toward his Mexican heritage compare with that of his father, and how do you explain any difference?

3. Why does the cholo object to Lopez's surfer clothing?

4. How did Lopez eventually reconcile his surfer and his Mexican American identities?

5. Characterize Lopez's tone and persona in this selection. How do they affect your response as a reader?

READING THE SIGNS

1. In your journal, write your own account of how, in your childhood, you developed a sense of ethnic identity. Use Lopez's article as a model that pinpoints concrete, specific events as being significant.

2. Compare and contrast Lopez's development of a sense of ethnic identity with that of Melissa Algranati ("Being an Other," p. 608). How can you account for any differences you might see?

3. A generational gap separated Lopez's and his father's attitudes toward assimilation. Interview several friends, preferably of different ethnicities, and their parents about their sense of ethnic identity. Write an essay in which you explore the extent to which one's age can influence one's attitudes toward ethnicity.

4. In class, discuss the extent to which your community is characterized by "distinct ethnic piece[s] of geography" (para. 33). Do people of different ethnicities interact frequently? Or do people tend to associate primarily with those of the same background? Use your discussion as the basis of an essay in which you evaluate the race relations in your community, taking care to suggest causes for the patterns that you see.

JIM WHITMER
Four Teens

READING THE SIGNS

1. Describe this photograph. What is taking place? How would you characterize the attitudes of the four youths in this photo? Examine them one by one. You might comment on their facial and body expressions, for instance.

2. What do you think is the relationship among these four youths? What evidence do you have for your answers? Assume that the photographer has deliberately placed each subject in the photograph. Speculate on the motives of his placement and the effect he has achieved.

3. How would you characterize the clothing, hair, and jewelry — the styles — of the figures in the photo? That is, what do their styles say about them? Would you be willing to adopt their styles? Why or why not?

NELL BERNSTEIN

GOIN' GANGSTA, CHOOSIN' CHOLITA

Ever wonder about wannabes — white suburban teenagers who dress and act like nonwhite inner-city gangsters? In this report on the phenomenon of "claiming," Nell Bernstein (b. 1965) probes some of the feelings and motives of teens who are "goin' gangsta" or "choosin' cholita" — kids who try on a racial identity not their own. Their reasons may surprise you. Bernstein is editor of YO!, *a San Francisco area journal of teen life published by the Pacific News Service, and she has published in* Glamour, Woman's Day, Salon, *and* Mother Jones.

Her lipstick is dark, the lip liner even darker, nearly black. In baggy pants, a blue plaid Pendleton, her bangs pulled back tight off her forehead, 15-year-old April is a perfect cholita, a Mexican gangsta girl.

But April Miller is Anglo. "And I don't like it!" she complains. "I'd rather be Mexican."

April's father wanders into the family room of their home in San Leandro, California, a suburb near Oakland. "Hey, cholita," he teases. "Go get a suntan. We'll put you in a barrio and see how much you like it."

A large, sandy-haired man with "April" tattooed on one arm and "Kelly" — the name of his older daughter — on the other, Miller spent 21 years working in a San Leandro glass factory that shut down and moved to Mexico a couple of years ago. He recently got a job in another factory, but he expects NAFTA to swallow that one, too.

"Sooner or later we'll all get nailed," he says. "Just another stab in the 5 back of the American middle class."

Later, April gets her revenge: "Hey, Mr. White Man's Last Stand," she teases. "Wait till you see how well I manage my welfare check. You'll be asking me for money."

A once almost exclusively white, now increasingly Latin and black working-class suburb, San Leandro borders on predominantly black East Oakland. For decades, the boundary was strictly policed and practically impermeable. In 1970 April Miller's hometown was 97 percent white. By 1990 San Leandro was 65 percent white, 6 percent black, 15 percent Hispanic, and 13 percent Asian or Pacific Islander. With minorities moving into suburbs in growing numbers and cities becoming ever more diverse, the boundary between city and suburb is dissolving, and suburban teenagers are changing with the times.

In April's bedroom, her past and present selves lie in layers, the pink walls of girlhood almost obscured, Guns N' Roses and Pearl Jam posters overlaid by rappers Paris and Ice Cube. "I don't have a big enough attitude to be a black girl," says April, explaining her current choice of ethnic identification.

What matters is that she thinks the choice is hers. For April and her friends, identity is not a matter of where you come from, what you were born into, what color your skin is. It's what you wear, the music you listen to, the words you use — everything to which you pledge allegiance, no matter how fleetingly.

The hybridization of American teens has become talk show fodder, with 10 "wiggers" — white kids who dress and talk "black" — appearing on TV in full gangsta regalia. In Indiana a group of white high school girls raised a national stir when they triggered an imitation race war at their virtually all-white high school last fall simply by dressing "black."

In many parts of the country, it's television and radio, not neighbors, that introduce teens to the allure of ethnic difference. But in California, which demographers predict will be the first state with no racial majority by the year 2000, the influences are more immediate. The California public schools are the most diverse in the country: 42 percent white, 36 percent Hispanic, 9 percent black, 8 percent Asian.

Sometimes young people fight over their differences. Students at virtually any school in the Bay Area can recount the details of at least one "race riot" in which a conflict between individuals escalated into a battle between their clans. More often, though, teens would rather join than fight. Adolescence, after all, is the period when you're most inclined to mimic the power closest at hand, from stealing your older sister's clothes to copying the ruling clique at school.

White skaters and Mexican would-be gangbangers listen to gangsta rap and call each other "nigga" as a term of endearment; white girls sometimes affect Spanish accents; blond cheerleaders claim Cherokee ancestors.

"Claiming" is the central concept here. A Vietnamese teen in Hayward, another Oakland suburb, "claims" Oakland — and by implication blackness — because he lived there as a child. A law-abiding white kid "claims" a Mexican gang he says he hangs with. A brown-skinned girl with a Mexican father and a white mother "claims" her Mexican side, while her fair-skinned sister "claims" white. The word comes up over and over, as if identity were territory, the self a kind of turf.

At a restaurant in a minimall in Hayward, Nicole Huffstutler, 13, sits with her 15 friends and describes herself as "Indian, German, French, Welsh, and, um . . . American": "If somebody says anything like 'Yeah, you're just a peckerwood,' I'll walk up and I'll say 'white pride!' 'Cause I'm proud of my race, and I wouldn't wanna be any other race."

"Claiming" white has become a matter of principle for Heather, too, who says she's "sick of the majority looking at us like we're less than them." (Hayward schools were 51 percent white in 1990, down from 77 percent in 1980, and whites are now the minority in many schools.)

Asked if she knows that nonwhites have not traditionally been referred to as "the majority" in America, Heather gets exasperated: "I hear that all the time, every day. They say, 'Well, you guys controlled us for many years, and it's time for us to control you.' Every day."

When Jennifer Vargas — a small, brown-skinned girl in purple jeans who quietly eats her salad while Heather talks — softly announces that she's "mostly Mexican," she gets in trouble with her friends.

"No, you're not!" scolds Heather.

"I'm mostly Indian and Mexican," Jennifer continues flatly. "I'm very little . . . I'm mostly . . . " 20

"Your mom's white!" Nicole reminds her sharply. "She has blond hair."

"That's what I mean," Nicole adds. "People think that white is a bad thing. They think that white is a bad race. So she's trying to claim more Mexican than white."

"I have very little white in me," Jennifer repeats. "I have mostly my dad's side, 'cause I look like him and stuff. And most of my friends think that me and my brother and sister aren't related, 'cause they look more like my mom."

"But you guys are all the same race, you just look different," Nicole insists. She stops eating and frowns. "OK, you're half and half each what your parents have. So you're equal as your brother and sister, you just look different. And you should be proud of what you are — every little piece and bit of what you are. Even if you were Afghan or whatever, you should be proud of it."

Will Mosley, Heather's 17-year-old brother, says he and his friends listen to rap 25 groups like Compton's Most Wanted, NWA, and Above the Law because they "sing about life" — that is, what happens in Oakland, Los Angeles, anyplace but where Will is sitting today, an empty Round Table Pizza in a minimall.

"No matter what race you are," Will says, "if you live like we do, then that's the kind of music you like."

And how do they live?

"We don't live bad or anything," Will admits. "We live in a pretty good neighborhood, there's no violence or crime. I was just . . . we're just city people, I guess."

Will and his friend Adolfo Garcia, 16, say they've outgrown trying to be something they're not. "When I was 11 or 12," Will says, "I thought I was becoming a big gangsta and stuff. Because I liked that music, and thought it was the coolest, I wanted to become that. I wore big clothes, like you wear in jail. But then I kind of woke up. I looked at myself and thought, 'Who am I trying to be?'"

They may have outgrown blatant mimicry, but Will and his friends re- 30 main convinced that they can live in a suburban tract house with a well-kept lawn on a tree-lined street in "not a bad neighborhood" and still call themselves "city" people on the basis of musical tastes. "City" for these young people means crime, graffiti, drugs. The kids are law-abiding, but these activities connote what Will admiringly calls "action." With pride in his voice, Will predicts that "in a couple of years, Hayward will be like Oakland. It's starting to get more known, because of crime and things. I think it'll be bigger, more things happening, more crime, more graffiti, stealing cars."

"That's good," chimes in 15-year-old Matt Jenkins, whose new beeper — an item that once connoted gangsta chic but now means little more than an active social life — goes off periodically. "More fun."

The three young men imagine with disdain life in a gangsta-free zone. "Too bland, too boring," Adolfo says. "You have to have something going on. You can't just have everyday life."

"Mowing your lawn," Matt sneers.

"Like Beaver Cleaver's house," Adolfo adds. "It's too clean out here."

Not only white kids believe that identity is a matter of choice or taste, or 35 that the power of "claiming" can transcend ethnicity. The Manor Park Locos — a group of mostly Mexican-Americans who hang out in San Leandro's Manor Park — say they descend from the Manor Lords, tough white guys who ruled the neighborhood a generation ago.

They "are like our . . . uncles and dads, the older generation," says Jesse Martinez, 14. "We're what they were when they were around, except we're Mexican."

"There's three generations," says Oso, Jesse's younger brother. "There's Manor Lords, Manor Park Locos, and Manor Park Pee Wees." The Pee Wees consist mainly of the Locos' younger brothers, eager kids who circle the older boys on bikes and brag about "punking people."

Unlike Will Mosley, the Locos find little glamour in city life. They survey the changing suburban landscape and see not "action" or "more fun" but frightening decline. Though most of them are not yet 18, the Locos are already nostalgic, longing for a Beaver Cleaver past that white kids who mimic them would scoff at.

Walking through nearly empty Manor Park, with its eucalyptus stands, its softball diamond and tennis courts, Jesse's friend Alex, the only Asian in the group, waves his arms in a gesture of futility. "A few years ago, every bench was filled," he says. "Now no one comes here. I guess it's because of everything that's going on. My parents paid a lot for this house, and I want it to be nice for them. I just hope this doesn't turn into Oakland."

Glancing across the park at April Miller's street, Jesse says he knows what 40 the white cholitas are about. "It's not a racial thing," he explains. "It's just all the most popular people out here are Mexican. We're just the gangstas that everyone knows. I guess those girls wanna be known."

Not every young Californian embraces the new racial hybridism. Andrea Jones, 20, an African American who grew up in the Bay Area suburbs of Union City and Hayward, is unimpressed by what she sees mainly as shallow mimicry. "It's full of posers out here," she says. "When *Boyz N the Hood* came out on video, it was sold out for weeks. The boys all wanna be black, the girls all wanna be Mexican. It's the glamour."

Driving down the quiet, shaded streets of her old neighborhood in Union City, Andrea spots two white preteen boys in Raiders jackets and hugely baggy pants strutting erratically down the empty sidewalk. "Look at them," she says. "Dislocated."

She knows why. "In a lot of these schools out here, it's hard being white," she says. "I don't think these kids were prepared for the backlash that is going on, all the pride now in people of color's ethnicity, and our boldness with it. They have nothing like that, no identity, nothing they can say they're proud of.

"So they latch onto their great-grandmother who's a Cherokee, or they take on the most stereotypical aspects of being black or Mexican. It's beautiful to appreciate different aspects of other people's culture — that's like the dream of what the 21st century should be. But to garnish yourself with pop culture stereotypes just to blend — that's really sad."

Roland Krevocheza, 18, graduated last year from Arroyo High School in   45
San Leandro. He is Mexican on his mother's side, Eastern European on his father's. In the new hierarchies, it may be mixed kids like Roland who have the hardest time finding their place, even as their numbers grow. (One in five marriages in California is between people of different races.) They can always be called "wannabes," no matter what they claim.

"I'll state all my nationalities," Roland says. But he takes a greater interest in his father's side, his Ukrainian, Romanian, and Czech ancestors. "It's more unique," he explains. "Mexican culture is all around me. We eat Mexican food all the time, I hear stories from my grandmother. I see the low-riders and stuff. I'm already part of it. I'm not trying to be; I am."

His darker-skinned brother "says he's not proud to be white," Roland adds. "He calls me 'Mr. Nazi.'" In the room the two share, the American flags and the reproduction of the Bill of Rights are Roland's; the Public Enemy poster belongs to his brother.

Roland has good reason to mistrust gangsta attitudes. In his junior year in high school, he was one of several Arroyo students who were beaten up outside the school at lunchtime by a group of Samoans who came in cars from Oakland. Roland wound up with a split lip, a concussion, and a broken tailbone. Later he was told that the assault was "gang-related" — that the Samoans were beating up anyone wearing red.

"Rappers, I don't like them," Roland says. "I think they're a bad influence on kids. It makes kids think they're all tough and bad."

Those who, like Roland, dismiss the gangsta and cholo styles as affecta-   50
tions can point to the fact that several companies market overpriced knockoffs of "ghetto wear" targeted at teens.

But there's also something going on out here that transcends adolescent faddishness and pop culture exoticism. When white kids call their parents "racist" for nagging them about their baggy pants; when they learn Spanish to talk to their boyfriends; when Mexican-American boys feel themselves descended in spirit from white "uncles"; when children of mixed marriages insist that they are whatever race they say they are, all of them are more than just confused.

They're inching toward what Andrea Jones calls "the dream of what the

21st century should be." In the ever more diverse communities of Northern California, they're also facing the complicated reality of what their 21st century will be.

Meanwhile, in the living room of the Miller family's San Leandro home, the argument continues unabated. "You don't know what you are," April's father has told her more than once. But she just keeps on telling him he doesn't know what time it is.

READING THE TEXT

1. How do teens like April Miller define their identity, according to Bernstein?

2. Describe in your own words what "claiming" (para. 14) an ethnic identity means. Why do so many teens "claim" a new ethnicity, according to Bernstein?

3. What relationship does Bernstein see between claiming and the mass media?

4. What does being white mean to many of the kids who claim a nonwhite identity?

5. What does the city signify to the young people whom Bernstein describes?

READING THE SIGNS

1. In class, stage a conversation between April Miller and her father on her adoption of a Mexican identity, with April defending her choice and her father repudiating it.

2. Write an essay in which you support, challenge, or modify Andrea Jones's assumption that it is media-generated "glamour" that prompts young people to claim a new ethnic identity.

3. Write an argumentative essay in which you explain whether the claiming fad is an expression of racial tolerance or racial stereotyping.

4. Bernstein describes teens claiming the identities of ethnic minorities, but she provides few instances of claiming a white identity. In class, discuss what being white signifies to these teens.

5. Assuming the perspective of Jack Lopez ("Of Cholos and Surfers," p. 592), write an analysis of the social and cultural pressures that prompt these teens' desire to "claim" an ethnicity. Do they desire to "have the best of both worlds," as Lopez does, or are other forces at work?

BELL HOOKS

BABY

Dolls are among the oldest of toys, traditionally given to little girls to help model their future behavior as wives and mothers. But what is a child to think about a doll that isn't of her own race? This dilemma is faced by millions of American girls who aren't white when they are given dolls like white Barbie. Faced with a similar dilemma as a little girl when given a Barbie doll, bell hooks (b. 1952) describes in this personal reminiscence how she chose to give her loyalty instead to a brown doll named Baby, who looked a lot more like her. bell hooks (the pen name of Gloria Watkins) is Distinguished Professor of English at City College of New York and the author of numerous books of cultural criticism, including Black Looks: Race and Representation *(1992),* Killing Rage: Ending Racism *(1995),* All About Love: New Visions *(2001),* Communion: The Female Search for Love *(2002), and* Bone Black *(1996), from which this selection is taken.*

We learn early that it is important for a woman to marry. We are always marrying our dolls to someone. He of course is always invisible, that is until they made the Ken doll to go with Barbie. One of us has been given a Barbie doll for Christmas. Her skin is not white white but almost brown from the tan they have painted on her. We know she is white because of her blond hair. The newest Barbie is bald, with many wigs of all different colors. We spend hours dressing and undressing her, pretending she is going somewhere important. We want to make new clothes for her. We want to buy the outfits made just for her that we see in the store but they are too expensive. Some of them cost as much as real clothes for real people. Barbie is anything but real, that is why we like her. She never does housework, washes dishes, or has children to care for. She is free to spend all day dreaming about the Kens of the world. Mama laughs when we tell her there should be more than one Ken for Barbie, there should be Joe, Sam, Charlie, men in all shapes and sizes. We do not think that Barbie should have a girlfriend. We know that Barbie was born to be alone — that the fantasy woman, the soap opera girl, the girl of *True Confessions,* the Miss America girl was born to be alone. We know that she is not us.

My favorite doll is brown, brown like light milk chocolate. She is a baby doll and I give her a baby doll name, Baby. She is almost the same size as a real baby. She comes with no clothes, only a pink diaper, fastened with tiny gold pins and a plastic bottle. She has a red mouth the color of lipstick slightly open so that we can stick the bottle in it. We fill the bottle with water and wait for it to come through the tiny hole in Baby's bottom. We make her many new diapers, but we

"I demanded a brown doll, one that would look like me."

are soon bored with changing them. We lose the bottle and Baby can no longer drink. We still love her. She is the only doll we will not destroy. We have lost Barbie. We have broken the leg of another doll. We have cracked open the head of an antique doll to see what makes the crying sound. The little thing inside is not interesting. We are sorry but nothing can be done — not even mama can put the pieces together again. She tells us that if this is the way we intend to treat our babies she hopes we do not have any. She laughs at our careless parenting. Sometimes she takes a minute to show us the right thing to do. She too is terribly fond of Baby. She says that she looks so much like a real newborn. Once she came upstairs, saw Baby under the covers, and wanted to know who had brought the real baby from downstairs.

She loves to tell the story of how Baby was born. She tells us that I, her problem child, decided out of nowhere that I did not want a white doll to play with, I demanded a brown doll, one that would look like me. Only grown-ups think that the things children say come out of nowhere. We know they come from the deepest parts of ourselves. Deep within myself I had begun to worry that all this loving care we gave to the pink and white flesh-colored dolls meant that somewhere left high on the shelves were boxes of unwanted, unloved brown dolls covered in dust. I thought that they would remain there forever, orphaned and alone, unless someone began to want them, to want to give them love and care, to want them more than anything. At first they ignored my wanting. They complained. They pointed out that white dolls were easier to find, cheaper. They never said where they found Baby but I know. She was always there high on the shelf, covered in dust — waiting.

READING THE TEXT

1. What does hooks mean when she says "we know that Barbie was born to be alone" (para. 1)?

2. Why has Baby received more care and protection than other dolls and toys that were in her family?

3. What is the purpose of giving little girls dolls, according to hooks?

4. Describe hooks's style and personal voice in this selection. How do they affect your response to her ideas?

READING THE SIGNS

1. If you played with dolls as a child, reflect in your journal on the extent to which the ethnicity of the dolls made a difference to you.

2. Read Jennifer Scanlon's "Boys-R-Us: Board Games and the Socialization of Young Adolescent Girls" (p. 503). Write an essay comparing the ways that dolls and board games construct gender roles for girls. You might consult as well Emily Prager's "Our Barbies, Ourselves" (p. 766).

3. Visit a toy store, and study the ethnic identities of the dolls you see there. How many ethnicities are represented? How do you account for your observations?

4. Investigate the ethnic patterns in other forms of children's entertainment and play, such as video games. Then write an essay analyzing the racial ideologies you discover. To develop your ideas, consult Michael Omi's "In Living Color: Race and American Culture" (p. 557).

MELISSA ALGRANATI

BEING AN OTHER

In a country as obsessed with racial identification as America is, Melissa Algranati poses a dilemma. As she puts it, "there are not too many Puerto Rican, Egyptian Jews out there," so the only category left for her on the census form is "other." In this personal essay, Algranati tells the story of how she came to be an "other," a saga of two immigrant families from different continents who eventually came together in a "marriage that only a country like America could create." Algranati is a graduate of the State University of New York at Binghamton and has a master's degree from Columbia University.

Throughout my whole life, people have mistaken me for other ethnic backgrounds rather than for what I really am. I learned at a young age that there are not too many Puerto Rican, Egyptian Jews out there. For most of my life I have been living in two worlds, and at the same time I have been living in neither. When I was young I did not realize that I was unique, because my family brought me up with a healthy balance of Puerto Rican and Sephardic customs. It was not until I took the standardized PSAT exam that I was confronted with the question: "Who am I?" I remember the feeling of confusion as I struggled to find the right answer. I was faced with a bad multiple-choice question in which there was only supposed to be one right answer, but more than one answer seemed to be correct. I did not understand how a country built on the concept of diversity could forget about its most diverse group, inter-ethnic children. I felt lost in a world of classification. The only way for me to take pride in who I am was to proclaim myself as an other, yet that leaves out so much. As a product of a marriage only a country like America could create, I would now try to help people understand what it is like to be a member of the most underrepresented group in the country, the "others."

My father, Jacques Algranati, was born in Alexandria, Egypt. As a Sephardic Jew, my father was a minority in a predominantly Arab world. Although in the minority, socially my father was a member of the upper middle class and lived a very comfortable life. As a result of strong French influence in the Middle Eastern Jewish world, my father attended a French private school. Since Arabic was the language of the lower class, the Algranati family spoke French as their first language. My whole family is polyglot, speaking languages from the traditional Sephardic tongue of Ladino to Turkish and Greek. My grandfather spoke seven languages. Basically, my father grew up in a close-knit Sephardic community surrounded by family and friends.

However, in 1960 my father's world came to a halt when he was faced with persecution on an institutional level. As a result of the Egyptian-Israeli

An extended American family.

conflict, in 1956 an edict was issued forcing all foreign-born citizens and Jews out of Egypt. Although my father was a native-born citizen of the country, because of a very strong anti-Jewish sentiment, his citizenship meant nothing. So in 1960 when my family got their exit visas, as Jews had done since the time of the Inquisition, they packed up and left the country as one large family group.

Unable to take many possessions or much money with them, my father's family, like many Egyptian Jews, immigrated to France. They proceeded to France because they had family who were able to sponsor them. Also, once in France my family hoped to be able to receive a visa to America much sooner, since French immigration quotas to the United States were much higher than those in Egypt. Once in France my family relied on the generosity of a Jewish organization, the United Jewish Appeal. For nine months my father lived in a hotel sponsored by the United Jewish Appeal and attended French school until the family was granted a visa to the United States.

Since my father's oldest brother came to the United States first with his 5 wife, they were able to sponsor the rest of the family's passage over. The Algranati family eventually settled in Forest Hills, Queens. Like most immigrants, my family settled in a neighborhood filled with immigrants of the same background. Once in the United States, my father rejoined many of his old friends from Egypt, since most Egyptian Jewish refugees followed a similar immigration path. At the age of fourteen my father and his group of friends were once again forced to adjust to life in a new country, but this time they had to learn a new language in order to survive. Like many of his friends, my father was forced to leave the comforts and luxuries of his world for the hardships of a new world. But as he eloquently puts it, once his family and friends were forced to leave, there was really nothing to stay for.

Like my father, my mother is also an immigrant; however my parents come from very different parts of the world. Born in Maniti, Puerto Rico, my mom spent the first five years of her life in a small town outside of San Juan. Since my grandfather had attended private school in the United States when he was younger, he was relatively proficient in English. Like many immigrants, my grandfather came to the United States first, in order to help establish the family. After securing a job and an apartment, he sent for my grandmother, and three weeks later my mother and her fourteen-year-old sister came.

Puerto Ricans are different from many other people who come to this country, in the sense that legally they are not considered immigrants. Because Puerto Rico is a commonwealth of the United States, Puerto Ricans are granted automatic U.S. citizenship. So unlike most, from the day my mother and her family stepped on U.S. soil they were considered citizens. The only problem was that the difference in language and social status led "real" Americans not to consider them citizens.

As a result of this unique status, my mother faced many hardships in this new country. From the day my mother entered first grade, her process of Americanization had begun. Her identity was transformed. She went from being Maria Louisa Pinto to becoming Mary L. Pinto. Not only was my mother given a new name when she began school, but a new language was forced upon her as well. Confronted by an Irish teacher, Mrs. Walsh, who was determined to Americanize her, my mother began her uphill battle with the English language. Even until this day my mother recalls her traumatic experience when she learned how to pronounce the word "run":

"Repeat after me, run."

"Rrrrrrrrrun."   10

"No, Mary, run."

"Rrrrrrrrrun."

No matter how hard my mother tried she could not stop rolling her "r's." After several similar exchanges Mrs. Walsh, with a look of anger on her face, grabbed my mother's cheeks in her hand and squeezed as she repeated in a stern voice, "RUN!" Suffice it to say my mother learned how to speak English without a Spanish accent. It was because of these experiences that my mother made sure the only language spoken in the house or to me and my sister was English. My parents never wanted their children to experience the pain my mother went through just to learn how to say the word "run."

My mother was confronted with discrimination not only from American - society but also from her community. While in the United States, my mother lived in a predominantly Spanish community. On first coming to this country her family lived in a tenement in the Bronx. At the age of twelve my mother was once more uprooted and moved to the projects on the Lower East Side. As one of the first families in a predominantly Jewish building, it was a step up for her family.

It was not her environment that posed the biggest conflict for her; it was   15 her appearance. My mother is what people call a "white Hispanic." With her blond hair and blue eyes my mother was taken for everything but a Puerto Rican. Once my mother perfected her English, no one suspected her ethnicity unless she told them. Since she was raised to be above the ghetto, never picking up typical "Hispanic mannerisms," she was able to exist in American society with very little difficulty. Because of a very strong and protective mother and the positive influence and assistance received from the Henry Street Settlement, my mother was able to escape the ghetto. As a result of organizations like Henry Street, my mother was given opportunities such as fresh air camps and jobs in good areas of the city, where she was able to rise above the drugs, alcohol, and violence that consumed so many of her peers.

As a result of her appearance and her upbringing, my mother left her people and the ghetto to enter American society. It was here as an attractive "white" female that my mother and father's two very different worlds merged. My parents, both working on Wall Street at the time, were introduced by a mutual friend. Since both had developed a rather liberal view, the differences in their backgrounds did not seem to be a major factor. After a year of dating my parents decided to get engaged.

Although they were from two different worlds, their engagement seemed to bring them together. Growing up in the midst of the Jewish community of the Lower East Side, my mother was constantly influenced by the beauty of Judaism. Therefore, since my mother never had much connection with Catholicism and had never been baptized, she decided to convert to Judaism and raise her children as Jews. The beauty of the conversion was that no one in my father's family forced her to convert; they accepted her whether she converted or not. As for my mother's family, they too had no real objections to the wedding or conversion. To them the only thing that mattered was that my father was a nice guy who made my mom happy. The most amusing part of the union of these two different families came when they tried to communicate. My father's family is descended from Spanish Jewry where many of them spoke an old Castilian-style Spanish, while my mother's family spoke a very modern Caribbean-style Spanish. To watch them try to communicate in any language other than English was like watching a session of the United Nations.

It was this new world, that of Puerto Rican Jewry, my parents created for me and my sister, Danielle. Resembling both my parents, having my mother's coloring with my father's features, I have often been mistaken for various ethnicities. Possessing light hair and blue eyes, I am generally perceived as the "all-American" girl. Occasionally I have been mistaken for Italian since my last name, Algranati, although Sephardic, has a very Italian flair to it. I have basically lived a chameleon-like existence for most of my life.

As a result of my "otherness," I have gained "acceptance" in many different crowds. From this acceptance I have learned the harsh reality behind my "otherness." I will never forget the time I learned about how the parents of one of my Asian friends perceived me. From very early on, I gained acceptance with the parents of one of my Korean friends. Not only did they respect me as a person and a student, but her father even went so far as to consider me like "one of his daughters." I will always remember how I felt when I heard they made one of their daughters cancel a party because she had invited Hispanics. Even when my friend pointed out that I, the one they loved, was Hispanic they refused to accept it. Even today to them, I will always be Jewish and not Puerto Rican because to them it is unacceptable to "love" a Puerto Rican.

Regardless of community, Jewish or Puerto Rican, I am always confronted 20 by bigots. Often I am forced to sit in silence while friends utter in ignorance stereotypical responses like: "It was probably some spic who stole it," or "You're just like a Jew, always cheap."

For the past three years I have worked on the Lower East Side of Manhattan at the Henry Street Settlement. Basically my mother wanted me to support the organization that helped her get out of the ghetto. Unlike when my mother was there, the population is mostly black and Hispanic. So one day during work I had one of my fellow workers say to me "that is such a collegian white thing to say." I responded by saying that his assumption was only partially correct and asked him if he considered Puerto Rican to be white. Of course he doubted I was any part Hispanic until he met my cousin who "looks" Puerto Rican. At times like these I really feel for my mother, because I know how it feels not to be recognized by society for who you are.

Throughout my life I do not think I have really felt completely a part of any group. I have gone through phases of hanging out with different crowds trying in a sense to find myself. Basically, I have kept my life diverse by attending both Catholic-sponsored camps and Hebrew school at the same time. Similar to my parents, my main goal is to live within American society. I choose my battles carefully. By being diverse I have learned that in a society that is obsessed with classification the only way I will find my place is within myself. Unfortunately, society has not come to terms with a fast-growing population, the "others." Therefore when asked the infamous question: "Who are you?" I respond with a smile, "a Puerto Rican Egyptian Jew." Contrary to what society may think, I know that I am somebody.

READING THE TEXT

1. Summarize in your own words why Algranati feels like one of the "others" (para. 1).

2. How did the childhood experiences of Algranati's parents differ?

3. How does physical appearance affect strangers' perceptions of ethnic identity, according to Algranati?

4. Why does Algranati say she has never "really felt completely a part of any group" (para. 22)?

READING THE SIGNS

1. In your journal, reflect on your answer to the question "Who are you?"

2. Write an essay in which you defend or oppose the practice of asking individuals to identify their ethnicity in official documents such as census forms and school applications.

3. Algranati's background includes racial, cultural, and religious differences. Write an essay explaining how you would identify yourself if you were in her shoes.

4. Do you think Algranati would be sympathetic or hostile to people who "try on" different ethnic identities? Writing as if you were Algranati, write a letter to one of the teens who claims a new ethnic identity in Nell Bernstein's "Goin' Gangsta, Choosin' Cholita" (p. 599).

5. In class, brainstorm names of biracial actors, musicians, or models. Then discuss the extent to which the mass media presume that people fit neatly into ethnic categories. What is the effect of such a presumption?

FAN SHEN

THE CLASSROOM AND THE WIDER CULTURE: IDENTITY AS A KEY TO LEARNING ENGLISH COMPOSITION

Writing conventions involve more cultural presuppositions and mythologies than we ordinarily recognize. Take the current practice of using the first-person singular pronoun "I" when writing an essay. Such a convention presumes an individualistic worldview, which can appear very strange to someone coming from a communal culture, as Fan Shen relates in this analysis of the relation between culture and composition. Hailing from the People's Republic of China, where the group comes before the individual in social consciousness, Shen describes what it was like to move to the United States and have to learn a whole new worldview to master the writing conventions that he himself now teaches as a professor of English at Rochester Community and Technical College. A writer as well as a teacher, Shen has translated three books from English into Chinese and has written numerous articles for both English and Chinese publications.

One day in June 1975, when I walked into the aircraft factory where I was working as an electrician, I saw many large-letter posters on the walls and many people parading around the workshops shouting slogans like "Down with the word 'I'!" and "Trust in masses and the Party!" I then remembered that a new political campaign called "Against Individualism" was scheduled to begin that day. Ten years later, I got back my first English composition paper at the University of Nebraska–Lincoln. The professor's first comments were: "Why did you always use 'we' instead of 'I'?" and "Your paper would be stronger if you eliminated some sentences in the passive voice." The clashes between my Chinese background and the requirements of English composition had begun. At the center of this mental struggle, which has lasted several years and is still not completely over, is the prolonged, uphill battle to recapture "myself."

In this paper I will try to describe and explore this experience of reconciling my Chinese identity with an English identity dictated by the rules of English composition. I want to show how my cultural background shaped — and shapes — my approaches to my writing in English and how writing in English redefined — and redefines — my *ideological* and *logical* identities. By "ideological identity" I mean the system of values that I acquired (consciously and unconsciously) from my social and cultural background. And by "logical identity" I mean the natural (or Oriental) way I organize and express my thoughts in writing. Both had to be modified or redefined in learning English composition. Becoming aware of the process of redefinition of these different identities is a mode of learning that has helped me in my efforts to write in English, and, I hope, will be of help to teachers of English composition in this country. In presenting my case for this view, I will use examples from both my composition courses and literature courses, for I believe that writing papers for both kinds of courses contributed to the development of my "English identity." Although what I will describe is based on personal experience, many Chinese students whom I talked to said that they had had the same or similar experiences in their initial stages of learning to write in English.

Identity of the Self: Ideological and Cultural

Starting with the first English paper I wrote, I found that learning to compose in English is not an isolated classroom activity, but a social and cultural experience. The rules of English composition encapsulate values that are absent in, or sometimes contradictory to, the values of other societies (in my case, China). Therefore, learning the rules of English composition is, to a certain extent, learning the values of Anglo-American society. In writing classes in the United States I found that I had to reprogram my mind, to redefine some of the basic concepts and values that I had about myself, about society, and about the universe, values that had been imprinted and reinforced in my mind by my cultural background, and that had been part of me all my life.

Rule number one in English composition is: Be yourself. (More than one composition instructor has told me, "Just write what *you* think.") The values behind this rule, it seems to me, are based on the principle of protecting and promoting individuality (and private property) in this country. The instruction was probably crystal clear to students raised on these values, but, as a guideline of composition, it was not very clear or useful to me when I first heard it. First of all, the image or meaning that I attached to the word "I" or "myself" was, as I found out, different from that of my English teacher. In China, "I" is always subordinated to "We" — be it the working class, the Party, the country, or some other collective body. Both political pressure and literary tradition require that "I" be somewhat hidden or buried in writings and speeches; presenting the "self" too obviously would give people the impression of being disrespectful of the Communist Party in political writings and boastful in scholarly writings. The word "I" has often been identified with another "bad" word, "individualism," which has become a synonym for selfishness in China. For a long time the words "self" and "individualism" have had negative connotations in my mind, and the negative force of the words naturally extended to the field of literary studies. As a result, even if I had brilliant ideas, the "I" in my papers always had to show some modesty by not competing with or trying to stand above the names of ancient and modern authoritative figures. Appealing to Mao or other Marxist authorities became the required way (as well as the most "forceful" or "persuasive" way) to prove one's point in written discourse. I remember that in China I had even committed what I can call "reversed plagiarism" — here, I suppose it would be called "forgery" — when I was in middle school: willfully attributing some of my thoughts to "experts" when I needed some arguments but could not find a suitable quotation from a literary or political "giant."

Now, in America, I had to learn to accept the words "I" and "self" as 5 something glorious (as Whitman did), or at least something not to be ashamed of or embarrassed about. It was the first and probably biggest step I took into English composition and critical writing. Acting upon my professor's suggestion, I intentionally tried to show my "individuality" and to "glorify" "I" in my papers by using as many "I's" as possible — "I think," "I believe," "I see" — and deliberately cut out quotations from authorities. It was rather painful to hand in such "pompous" (I mean immodest) papers to my instructors. But to an extent it worked. After a while I became more comfortable with only "the shadow of myself." I felt more at ease to put down *my* thoughts without looking over my shoulder to worry about the attitudes of my teachers or the reactions of the Party secretaries, and to speak out as "bluntly" and "immodestly" as my American instructors demanded.

But writing many "I's" was only the beginning of the process of redefining myself. Speaking of redefining myself is, in an important sense, speaking of redefining the word "I." By such a redefinition I mean not only the change in how I envisioned myself, but also the change in how *I* perceived the world. The old "I" used to embody only one set of values, but now it had to embody multiple sets of values. To be truly "myself," which I knew was a key to my success in learning English composition, meant *not to be my Chinese self* at all. That is to say, when I write in English I have to wrestle with and abandon (at least temporarily) the whole system of ideology which previously defined me in myself.

I had to forget Marxist doctrines (even though I do not see myself as a Marxist by choice) and the Party lines imprinted in my mind and familiarize myself with a system of capitalist/bourgeois values. I had to put aside an ideology of collectivism and adopt the values of individualism. In composition as well as in literature classes, I had to make a fundamental adjustment: If I used to examine society and literary materials through the microscopes of Marxist dialectical materialism and historical materialism, I now had to learn to look through the microscopes the other way around, i.e., to learn to look at and understand the world from the point of view of "idealism." (I must add here that there are American professors who use a Marxist approach in their teaching.)

The word "idealism," which affects my view of both myself and the universe, is loaded with social connotations, and can serve as a good example of how redefining a key word can be a pivotal part of redefining my ideological identity as a whole.

To me, idealism is the philosophical foundation of the dictum of English composition: "Be yourself." In order to write good English, I knew that I had to be myself, which actually meant not to be my Chinese self. It meant that I had to create an English self and be *that* self. And to be that English self, I felt, I had to understand and accept idealism the way a Westerner does. That is to say, I had to accept the way a Westerner sees himself in relation to the universe and society. On the one hand, I knew a lot about idealism. But on the other hand, I knew nothing about it. I mean I knew a lot about idealism through the propaganda and objections of its opponent, Marxism, but I knew little about it from its own point of view. When I thought of the word "materialism" — which is a major part of Marxism and in China has repeatedly been "shown" to be the absolute truth — there were always positive connotations, and words like "right," "true," etc., flashed in my mind. On the other hand, the word "idealism" always came to me with the dark connotations that surround words like "absurd," "illogical," "wrong," etc. In China "idealism" is depicted as a ferocious and ridiculous enemy of Marxist philosophy. Idealism, as the simplified definition imprinted in my mind had it, is the view that the material world does not exist; that all that exists is the mind and its ideas. It is just the opposite of Marxist dialectical materialism which sees the mind as a product of the material world. It is not too difficult to see that idealism, with its idea that mind is of primary importance, provides a philosophical foundation for the Western emphasis on the value of individual human minds, and hence individual human beings. Therefore, my final acceptance of myself as of primary importance — an importance that overshadowed that of authority figures in English composition — was, I decided, dependent on an acceptance of idealism.

My struggle with idealism came mainly from my efforts to understand and to write about works such as Coleridge's *Biographia Literaria* and Emerson's "Over-Soul." For a long time I was frustrated and puzzled by the idealism expressed by Coleridge and Emerson — given their ideas, such as "I think, therefore I am" (Coleridge obviously borrowed from Descartes) and "the transparent eyeball" (Emerson's view of himself) — because in my mind, drenched as it was in dialectical materialism, there was always a little voice whispering in my ear "You are, therefore you think." I could not see how human consciousness, which is not material, could create apples and trees. My intellectual conscience refused to let me believe that the human mind is the primary world and the material world secondary. Finally, I had to imagine that I was looking at a world with my head upside down. When I imagined that I was in a new body (born with the head upside down) it was easier to forget biases imprinted in my subconsciousness about idealism, the mind, and my former self. Starting from scratch, the new inverted self — which I called my "English Self" and into which I have transformed myself — could understand and *accept,* with ease, idealism as "the truth" and "himself" (i.e., my English Self) as the "creator" of the world.

Here is how I created my new "English Self." I played a "game" similar to   10 ones played by mental therapists. First I made a list of (simplified) features about writing associated with my old identity (the Chinese Self), both ideological and logical, and then beside the first list I added a column of features about writing associated with my new identity (the English Self). After that I pictured myself getting out of my old identity, the timid, humble, modest Chinese "I," and creeping into my new identity (often in the form of a new skin or a mask), the confident, assertive, and aggressive English "I." The new "Self" helped me to remember and accept the different rules of Chinese and English composition and the values that underpin these rules. In a sense, creating an English Self is a way of reconciling my old cultural values with the new values required by English writing, without losing the former.

An interesting structural but not material parallel to my experiences in this regard has been well described by Min-zhan Lu in her important article, "From Silence to Words: Writing as Struggle" (*College English* 49 [April 1987]: 437–48). Min-zhan Lu talks about struggles between two selves, an open self and a secret self, and between two discourses, a mainstream Marxist discourse and a bourgeois discourse her parents wanted her to learn. But her struggle was different from mine. Her Chinese self was severely constrained and suppressed by mainstream cultural discourse, but never interfused with it. Her experiences, then, were not representative of those of the majority of the younger generation who, like me, were brought up on only one discourse. I came to English composition as a Chinese person, in the fullest sense of the term, with a Chinese identity already fully formed.

Identity of the Mind: Illogical and Alogical

In learning to write in English, besides wrestling with a different ideological system, I found that I had to wrestle with a logical system very different from the blueprint of logic at the back of my mind. By "logical system" I mean two things: the Chinese way of thinking I used to approach my theme or topic in written discourse, and the Chinese critical/logical way to develop a theme or topic. By English rules, the first is illogical, for it is the opposite of the English way of approaching a topic; the second is alogical (nonlogical), for it mainly uses mental pictures instead of words as a critical vehicle.

THE ILLOGICAL PATTERN

In English composition, an essential rule for the logical organization of a piece of writing is the use of a "topic sentence." In Chinese composition, "from surface to core" is an essential rule, a rule which means that one ought to reach a topic gradually and "systematically" instead of "abruptly."

The concept of a topic sentence, it seems to me, is symbolic of the values of a busy people in an industrialized society, rushing to get things done, hoping to attract and satisfy the busy reader very quickly. Thinking back, I realized that I did not fully understand the virtue of the concept until my life began to rush at the speed of everyone else's in this country. Chinese composition, on the other hand, seems to embody the values of a leisurely paced rural society whose inhabitants have the time to chew and taste a topic slowly. In Chinese composition, an introduction explaining how and why one chooses this topic is not only acceptable, but often regarded as necessary. It arouses the reader's interest in the topic little by little (and this is seen as a virtue of composition) and gives him/her a sense of refinement. The famous Robert B. Kaplan "noodles" contrasting a spiral Oriental thought process with a straight-line Western approach ("Cultural Thought Patterns in Inter-Cultural Education," *Readings on English as a Second Language,* Ed. Kenneth Croft, 2nd ed., Winthrop, 1980, 403–10) may be too simplistic to capture the preferred pattern of writing in English, but I think they still express some truth about Oriental writing. A Chinese writer often clears the surrounding bushes before attacking the real target. This bush-clearing pattern in Chinese writing goes back two thousand years to Kong Fuzi (Confucius). Before doing anything, Kong says in his *Luen Yu (Analects),* one first needs to call things by their proper names (expressed by his phrase "Zheng Ming" 正名). In other words, before touching one's main thesis, one should first state the "conditions" of composition: how, why, and when the piece is being composed. All of this will serve as a proper foundation on which to build the "house" of the piece. In the two thousand years after Kong, this principle of composition was gradually formalized (especially through the formal essays required by imperial examinations) and became known as "Ba Gu," or the eight-legged essay. The logic of Chinese composition, exemplified by the eight-legged essay, is like the peeling of an onion: Layer after layer is removed until the reader finally arrives at the central point, the core.

Ba Gu still influences modern Chinese writing. Carolyn Matalene has an 15 excellent discussion of this logical (or illogical) structure and its influence on her Chinese students' efforts to write in English ("Contrastive Rhetoric: An American Writing Teacher in China," *College English* 47 [November 1985]:

789–808). A recent Chinese textbook for composition lists six essential steps (factors) for writing a narrative essay, steps to be taken in this order: time, place, character, event, cause, and consequence (*Yuwen Jichu Zhishi Liushi Jiang* [*Sixty Lessons on the Basics of the Chinese Language*], Ed. Beijing Research Institute of Education, Beijing Publishing House, 1981, 525–609). Most Chinese students (including me) are taught to follow this sequence in composition.

The straightforward approach to composition in English seemed to me, at first, illogical. One could not jump to the topic. One had to walk step by step to reach the topic. In several of my early papers I found that the Chinese approach — the bush-clearing approach — persisted, and I had considerable difficulty writing (and in fact understanding) topic sentences. In what I deemed to be topic sentences, I grudgingly gave out themes. Today, those papers look to me like Chinese papers with forced or false English openings. For example, in a narrative paper on a trip to New York, I wrote the forced/false topic sentence, "A trip to New York in winter is boring." In the next few paragraphs, I talked about the weather, the people who went with me, and so on, before I talked about what I learned from the trip. My real thesis was that one could always learn something even on a boring trip.

THE ALOGICAL PATTERN

In learning English composition, I found that there was yet another cultural blueprint affecting my logical thinking. I found from my early papers that very often I was unconsciously under the influence of a Chinese critical approach called the creation of "yijing," which is totally non-Western. The direct translation of the word "yijing" is: yi, "mind or consciousness," and jing, "environment." An ancient approach which has existed in China for many centuries and is still the subject of much discussion, yijing is a complicated concept that defies a universal definition. But most critics in China nowadays seem to agree on one point, that yijing is the critical approach that separates Chinese literature and criticism from Western literature and criticism. Roughly speaking, yijing is the process of creating a pictorial environment while reading a piece of literature. Many critics in China believe that yijing is a creative process of inducing oneself, while reading a piece of literature or looking at a piece of art, to create mental pictures, in order to reach a unity of nature, the author, and the reader. Therefore, it is by its very nature both creative and critical. According to the theory, this nonverbal, pictorial process leads directly to a higher ground of beauty and morality. Almost all critics in China agree that yijing is not a process of logical thinking — it is not a process of moving from the premises of an argument to its conclusion, which is the foundation of Western criticism. According to yijing, the process of criticizing a piece of art or literary work has to involve the process of creation on the reader's part. In yijing, verbal thoughts and pictorial thoughts are one. Thinking is conducted largely in pictures and then "transcribed" into words. (Ezra

Pound once tried to capture the creative aspect of yijing in poems such as "In a Station of the Metro." He also tried to capture the critical aspect of it in his theory of imagism and vorticism, even though he did not know the term "yijing.") One characteristic of the yijing approach to criticism, therefore, is that it often includes a description of the created mental pictures on the part of the reader/critic and his/her mental attempt to bridge (unite) the literary work, the pictures, with ultimate beauty and peace.

In looking back at my critical papers for various classes, I discovered that I unconsciously used the approach of yijing, especially in some of my earlier papers when I seemed not yet to have been in the grip of Western logical critical approaches. I wrote, for instance, an essay entitled "Wordsworth's Sound and Imagination: The Snowdon Episode." In the major part of the essay I described the pictures that flashed in my mind while I was reading passages in Wordsworth's long poem, *The Prelude.*

> I saw three climbers (myself among them) winding up the mountain in silence "at the dead of night," absorbed in their "private thoughts." The sky was full of blocks of clouds of different colors, freely changing their shapes, like oily pigments disturbed in a bucket of water. All of a sudden, the moonlight broke the darkness "like a flash," lighting up the mountain tops. Under the "naked moon," the band saw a vast sea of mist and vapor, a silent ocean. Then the silence was abruptly broken, and we heard the "roaring of waters, torrents, streams/Innumerable, roaring with one voice" from a "blue chasm," a fracture in the vapor of the sea. It was a joyful revelation of divine truth to the human mind: the bright, "naked" moon sheds the light of "higher reasons" and "spiritual love" upon us; the vast ocean of mist looked like a thin curtain through which we vaguely saw the infinity of nature beyond; and the sounds of roaring waters coming out of the chasm of vapor cast us into the boundless spring of imagination from the depth of the human heart. Evoked by the divine light from above, the human spring of imagination is joined by the natural spring and becomes a sustaining source of energy, feeding "upon infinity" while transcending infinity at the same time. . . .

Here I was describing my own experience more than Wordsworth's. The picture described by the poet is taken over and developed by the reader. The imagination of the author and the imagination of the reader are thus joined together. There was no "because" or "therefore" in the paper. There was little *logic*. And I thought it was (and it is) criticism. This seems to me a typical (but simplified) example of the yijing approach. (Incidentally, the instructor, a kind professor, found the paper interesting, though a bit "strange.")

I am not saying that such a pattern of "alogical" thinking is wrong — in fact some English instructors find it interesting and acceptable — but it is very non-Western. Since I was in this country to learn the English language and English literature, I had to abandon Chinese "pictorial logic," and to learn Western "verbal logic."

If I Had to Start Again

The change is profound: Through my understanding of new meanings of words like "individualism," "idealism," and "I," I began to accept the underlying concepts and values of American writing, and by learning to use "topic sentences" I began to accept a new logic. Thus, when I write papers in English, I am able to obey all the general rules of English composition. In doing this I feel that I am writing through, with, and because of a new identity. I welcome the change, for it has added a new dimension to me and to my view of the world. I am not saying that I have entirely lost my Chinese identity. In fact I feel that I will never lose it. Any time I write in Chinese, I resume my old identity, and obey the rules of Chinese composition such as "Make the 'I' modest," and "Beat around the bush before attacking the central topic." It is necessary for me to have such a Chinese identity in order to write authentic Chinese. (I have seen people who, after learning to write in English, use English logic and sentence patterning to write Chinese. They produce very awkward Chinese texts.) But when I write in English, I imagine myself slipping into a new "skin," and I let the "I" behave much more aggressively and knock the topic right on the head. Being conscious of these different identities has helped me to reconcile different systems of values and logic, and has played a pivotal role in my learning to compose in English.

Looking back, I realize that the process of learning to write in English is in fact a process of creating and defining a new identity and balancing it with the old identity. The process of learning English composition would have been easier if I had realized this earlier and consciously sought to compare the two different identities required by the two writing systems from two different cultures. It is fine and perhaps even necessary for American composition teachers to teach about topic sentences, paragraphs, the use of punctuation, documentation, and so on, but can anyone design exercises sensitive to the ideological and logical differences that students like me experience — and design them so they can be introduced at an early stage of an English composition class? As I pointed out earlier, the traditional advice "Just be yourself" is not clear and helpful to students from Korea, China, Vietnam, or India. From "Be yourself" we are likely to hear either "Forget your cultural habit of writing" or "Write as you would write in your own language." But neither of the two is what the instructor meant or what we want to do. It would be helpful if he or she pointed out the different cultural/ideological connotations of the word "I," the connotations that exist in a group-centered culture and an individual-centered culture. To sharpen the contrast, it might be useful to design papers on topics like "The Individual vs. The Group: China vs. America" or "Different 'I's' in Different Cultures."

Carolyn Matalene mentioned in her article (789) an incident concerning American businessmen who presented their Chinese hosts with gifts of cheddar cheese, not knowing that the Chinese generally do not like cheese. Liking cheddar cheese may not be essential to writing English prose, but being truly accustomed to the social norms that stand behind ideas such as the English "I" and the logical pattern of English composition — call it "compositional cheddar cheese" — is essential to writing in English. Matalene does not provide an "elixir" to help her Chinese students like English "compositional cheese," but rather recommends, as do I, that composition teachers not be afraid to give foreign students English "cheese," but to make sure to hand it out slowly, sympathetically, and fully realizing that it tastes very peculiar in the mouths of those used to a very different cuisine.

READING THE TEXT

1. Why does Shen say English composition is "a social and cultural experience" (para. 3)?

2. What are the differences between Western and Chinese views of the self, according to Shen?

3. What does Shen mean by the "yijing" (para. 17) approach to writing?

4. In a paragraph, summarize the process by which Shen learned to write English composition essays.

READING THE SIGNS

1. In your journal, brainstorm ways in which you were brought up either to assert your individuality or to subordinate yourself to group interests (you might consider involvement in sports or school activities). Then stand back, and consider your brainstormed list. To what extent were you raised with a "Western" concept of self? How do your ethnic background and gender affect your sense of self-identity?

2. Compare and contrast Shen's experience in his composition class with your own experiences. How do ethnicity and gender shape a writer's experiences?

3. In class, discuss the extent to which your classes, including your writing class, assume Western styles of learning and discourse. Then write an essay describing the results of your discussion, using the "yijing" approach that Shen describes. Read your essay aloud in class.

4. Has anything you have learned in your writing class felt "foreign" to you? Write a list, as Shen did, in which you name features about writing that come "naturally" to you, and then list those that seem "unnatural." Study your lists. Which features seem culturally determined, and which seem linked to your own personality and way of thinking? Can you make such a distinction? How can these lists help you as a writer?

LynNell HANCOCK

THE HAVES AND THE HAVE-NOTS

As the world gets wired, it gets more and more important to go online if you're going to keep up in a competitive environment. That's why an increasing number of schools are hooking up to the Internet, thus giving their students the earliest possible advantage in the race through cyberspace. As LynNell Hancock (b. 1953) points out, however, not every school can afford the price of admission. If our already economically divided society is not to become even more divided between those who have and those who don't, measures will have to be taken to be sure that everyone has access to the Web. An assistant professor of journalism and director of the Prudential Fellowship for Children and the News at Columbia University, Hancock is also a freelance writer who specializes in public education. Her publications include Hands to Work: The Stories of Three Families Racing the Welfare Clock *(2002).*

Aaron Smith is a teenager on the techno track. In America's breathless race to achieve information nirvana, the senior from Issaqua, a middle-class district east of Seattle, has the hardware and hookups to run the route. Aaron and 600 of his fellow students at Liberty High School have their own electronic-mail addresses. They can log on to the Internet every day, joining only about 15 percent of America's schoolchildren who can now forage on their own for documents in European libraries or chat with experts around the world. At home, the 18-year-old e-mails his teachers, when he is not prowling the World Wide Web to track down snowboarding conditions on his favorite Cascade mountain passes. "We have the newest, greatest thing," Aaron says.

On the opposite coast, in Boston's South End, Marilee Colon scoots a mouse along a grimy Apple pad, playing a Kid Pix game on an old black-and-white terminal. It's Wednesday at a neighborhood center, Marilee's only chance to poke around on a computer. Her mom, a secretary at the center, can't afford one in their home. Marilee's public-school classroom doesn't have any either. The 10-year-old from Roxbury depends on the United South End Settlement Center and its less than state-of-the-art Macs and IBMs perched on mismatched desks. Marilee has never heard of the Internet. She is thrilled to double-click on the stick of dynamite and watch her teddy-bear creation fly off the screen. "It's fun blowing it up," says the delicate fifth grader, twisting a brown ponytail around her finger.

Certainly Aaron was born with a stack of statistical advantages over Marilee. He is white and middle class and lives with two working parents who both have higher degrees. Economists say the swift pace of high-tech advances will only drive a further wedge between these youngsters. To have an edge in America's job search, it used to be enough to be well educated. Now, say the experts, it's critical to be digital. Employees who are adept at technology "earn roughly 10 to 15 percent higher pay," according to Alan Krueger, chief economist for the U.S. Labor Department. Some argue that this pay gap has less to do with technology than with industries' efforts to streamline their work forces during the recession. . . . Still, nearly every American business from Wall Street to McDonald's requires some computer knowledge. Taco Bell is modeling its cash registers after Nintendo controls, according to Rosabeth Moss Kanter. The "haves," says the Harvard Business School professor, will be able to communicate around the globe. The "have-nots" will be consigned to the "rural backwater of the information society."

Like it or not, America is a land of inequities. And technology, despite its potential to level the social landscape, is not yet blind to race, wealth, and age. The richer the family, the more likely it is to own and use a computer, according to 1993 census data. White families are three times as likely as blacks or Hispanics to have computers at home. Seventy-four percent of Americans making more than $75,000 own at least one terminal, but not even one third of all Americans own computers. A small fraction — only about 7 percent — of students' families subscribe to online services that transform the plastic terminal into a telecommunications port.

At least in public schools, the computer gap is closing. More than half the students have some kind of computer, even if it's obsolete. But schools with the biggest concentration of poor children have the least equipment, according to Jeanne Hayes of Quality Education Data. Ten years ago schools had one computer for every 125 children, according to Hayes. Today that figure is one for 12. 5

Though the gap is slowly closing, technology is advancing so fast, and at such huge costs, that it's nearly impossible for cash-strapped municipalities to catch up. Seattle is taking bids for one company to wire each ZIP code with fiber optics, so everyone — rich or poor — can hook up to video, audio and other multimedia services. Estimated cost: $500 million. Prosperous Montgomery County, Md., has an $81 million plan to put every classroom online. Next door, the District of Columbia public schools have the same ambitious plan but less than $1 million in the budget to accomplish it.

New ideas — and demands — for the schools are announced every week. The '90s populist slogan is no longer "A chicken in every pot" but "A computer on every desk." Vice President Al Gore has appealed to the telecommunications industry to cut costs and wire all schools, a task Education Secretary Richard Riley estimates will cost $10 billion. House Speaker Newt Gingrich stumbled into the discussion with a suggestion that every poor family get a laptop from Uncle Sam. Rep. Ed Markey wants a computer sitting on every school desk within 10 years. "The opportunities are enormous," Markey says.

Enormous, yes, but who is going to pay for them? Some successful school projects have relied heavily on the kindness of strangers. In Union City, N.J., school officials renovated the guts of a 100-year-old building five years ago,

Closing the gap? A student works on a nearly obsolete computer.

overhauling the curriculum and wiring every classroom in Christopher Columbus Middle School for high tech. Bell Atlantic provided wiring free and agreed to give each student in last year's seventh-grade class a computer to take home. Even parents, most of whom are South American immigrants, can use their children's computers to e-mail the principal in Spanish. He uses translation software and answers them electronically. The results have shown up in test scores. In a school where 80 percent of the children are poor, reading, math, attendance and writing scores are now the best in the district. "We believe that technology will improve our everyday life," says principal Bob Fazio. "And that other schools will piggyback and learn from us."

Still, for every Christopher Columbus, there are far more schools like Jordan High School in South-Central Los Angeles. Only 30 computers in the school's lab, most of them 12 to 15 years old, are available for Jordan's 2,000 students, many of whom live in the nearby Jordan Downs housing project. "I am teaching these kids on a system that will do them no good in the real world when they get out there," says Robert Doornbos, Jordan's computer-science instructor. "The school system has not made these kids' getting on the Information Highway a priority."

Having enough terminals to go around is one problem. But another 10 important question is what the equipment is used for. Not much beyond rote drills and word processing, according to Linda Roberts, a technology consultant for the U.S. Department of Education. A 1992 National Assessment of Educational Progress survey found that most fourth-grade math students were using computers to play games, "like Donkey Kong." By the eighth grade, most math students weren't using them at all.

Many school officials think that access to the Internet could become the most effective equalizer in the educational lives of students. With a modem attached, even most ancient terminals can connect children in rural Mississippi to universities in Asia. A Department of Education report last week found that 35 percent of schools have at least one computer with a modem. But only half the schools let students use it. Apparently administrators and teachers are hogging the Info Highway for themselves.

There is another gap to be considered. Not just between rich and poor, but between the young and the used-to-be-young. Of the 100 million Americans who use computers at home, school or work, nearly 60 percent are 17 or younger, according to the census. Children, for the most part, rule cyberspace, leaving the over-40 set to browse through the almanac.

The gap between the generations may be the most important, says MIT guru Nicholas Negroponte, author of the new book "Being Digital." Adults are the true "digitally homeless, the needy," he says. In other words, adults like Debbie Needleman, 43, an office manager at Wallpaper Warehouse in Natick, Mass., are wary of the digital age. "I really don't mind that the rest of the world passes me by as long as I can still earn a living," she says.

These aging choose-nots become a more serious issue when they are teachers in schools. Even if schools manage to acquire state-of-the-art equipment, there is no guarantee that trained adults will be available to understand them. This is something that tries Aaron Smith's patience. "A lot of my teachers are quite illiterate," says Aaron, the fully equipped Issaqua teenager. "You have to explain it to them real slow to make sure they understand everything." Fast or slow, Marilee Colon, Roxbury's fifth-grade computer lover, would like her chance to understand everything too.

READING THE TEXT

1. Why does Hancock begin her essay by contrasting Aaron Smith with Marilee Colon, and what effect does that contrast have on her reader?

2. What evidence does Hancock advance to demonstrate that "technology . . . is not yet blind to race, wealth, and age" (para. 4)?

3. According to Hancock, what are some of the problems that impoverished school districts face in trying to bring their students online?

4. Why does MIT professor Nicholas Negroponte say that adults are the "digitally homeless, the needy" (para. 13) in cyberspace?

READING THE SIGNS

1. In class, propose answers to the question that Hancock raises in her selection: Who is going to pay for making access to the Internet socioeconomically equal?

2. Laura Miller ("Women and Children First," p. 539) accuses mainstream media of insisting "that online culture is 'the same' as real life" (para. 24). In an essay, discuss the extent to which that accusation applies to Hancock's selection, which first appeared in *Newsweek*.

3. Read through a cybermagazine such as *Wired*, studying how genders, ethnicities, and age groups are portrayed in both advertising and articles. Then write a semiotic analysis of the publication, explaining the extent to which it portrays a world of "inequalities." To develop your ideas, consult Laura Miller's "Women and Children First" (p. 539).

4. Write an essay in which you support, refute, or complicate the contention "that access to the Internet could become the most effective equalizer in the educational lives of students" (para. 11). You might gather evidence for your position by interviewing students of varying ethnic or socioeconomic backgrounds on their access to cyberspace prior to attending college.

RANDALL KENNEDY

BLIND SPOT

Racial profiling has been a hot-button issue recently, eliciting such condemnations as the claim that for many Americans it has become a crime to be caught "driving while black." Randall Kennedy (b. 1955), a professor of law at Harvard Law School, enters the controversy from an unusual angle, arguing that supporters and opponents of racial profiling alike face an inconsistency when arguing about affirmative action, which Kennedy regards as the "alter ego" of racial profiling. With supporters of racial profiling asserting the rights of the community over those of the individual, while at the same time endorsing the rights of the individual over those of the community when it comes to affirmative action, and opponents of racial profiling doing just the reverse, it is time, Kennedy suggests, for both sides to listen to what the other has to say. Kennedy is the author of Race, Crime, and the Law *(1997) and* Nigger: The Strange Career of a Troublesome Word *(2002).*

What is one to think about "racial profiling"? Confusion abounds about what the term even means. It should be defined as the policy or practice of using race as a factor in selecting whom to place under special surveillance: if police officers at an airport decide to search Passenger A because he is twenty-five to forty years old, bought a first-class ticket with cash, is flying cross-country, and is apparently of Arab ancestry, Passenger A has been subjected to racial profiling. But officials often prefer to define racial profiling as being based *solely* on race; and in doing so they are often seeking to preserve their authority to act against a person *partly* on the basis of race. Civil-rights activists, too, often define racial profiling as solely race-based; but their aim is to arouse their followers and to portray law-enforcement officials in as menacing a light as possible.

The problem with defining racial profiling in the narrow manner of these strange bedfellows is that doing so obfuscates the real issue confronting Americans. Exceedingly few police officers, airport screeners, or other authorities charged with the task of foiling or apprehending criminals act solely on the basis of race. Many, however, act on the basis of intuition, using race along with other indicators (sex, age, patterns of past conduct) as a guide. The difficult question, then, is not whether the authorities ought to be allowed to act against individuals on the basis of race alone; almost everyone would disapprove of that. The difficult question is whether they ought to be allowed to use race *at all* in schemes of surveillance. If, indeed, it is used, the action amounts to racial discrimination. The extent of the discrimination may be relatively small when race is only one factor among many, but even a little racial discrimination should require lots of justification.

The key argument in favor of racial profiling, essentially, is that taking race into account enables the authorities to screen carefully and at less expense those sectors of the population that are more likely than others to contain the criminals for whom officials are searching. Proponents of this theory stress that resources for surveillance are scarce, that the dangers to be avoided are grave, and that reducing these dangers helps everyone — including, sometimes especially, those in the groups subjected to special scrutiny. Proponents also assert that it makes good sense to consider whiteness if the search is for Ku Klux Klan assassins, blackness if the search is for drug couriers in certain locales, and Arab nationality or ethnicity if the search is for agents of al Qaeda.

Some commentators embrace this position as if it were unassailable, but under U.S. law racial discrimination backed by state power is presumptively illicit. This means that supporters of racial profiling carry a heavy burden of persuasion. Opponents rightly argue, however, that not much rigorous empirical proof supports the idea of racial profiling as an effective tool of law enforcement. Opponents rightly contend, also, that alternatives to racial profiling have not been much studied or pursued. Stressing that racial profiling generates clear harm (for example, the fear, resentment, and alienation felt by innocent people in the profiled group), opponents of racial profiling sensibly question whether compromising our hard-earned principle of antidiscrimination is worth merely speculative gains in overall security.

A notable feature of this conflict is that champions of each position fre-   5 quently embrace rhetoric, attitudes, and value systems that are completely at odds with those they adopt when confronting another controversial instance of racial discrimination — namely, affirmative action. Vocal supporters of racial profiling who trumpet the urgency of communal needs when discussing law enforcement all of a sudden become fanatical individualists when condemning affirmative action in college admissions and the labor market. Supporters of profiling, who are willing to impose what amounts to a racial tax on profiled groups, denounce as betrayals of "color blindness" programs that require racial diversity. A similar turnabout can be seen on the part of many of those who support affirmative action. Impatient with talk of communal needs in assessing racial profiling, they very often have no difficulty with subordinating the interests of individual white candidates to the purported good of the whole. Opposed to race consciousness in policing, they demand race consciousness in deciding whom to admit to college or select for a job.

The racial-profiling controversy — like the conflict over affirmative action — will not end soon. For one thing, in both cases many of the contestants are animated by decent but contending sentiments. Although exasperating, this is actually good for our society; and it would be even better if participants in the debates acknowledged the simple truth that their adversaries have something useful to say.

READING THE TEXT

1. Why does Kennedy say that "confusion abounds" when we try to define the term "racial profiling" (para. 1)?

2. Why does Kennedy see opponents and supporters of racial profiling as "strange bedfellows" (para. 2)?

3. Summarize in your own words the relationship Kennedy finds in the controversies over racial profiling and affirmative action.

4. Why do you think that Kennedy finds "the decent but contending sentiments" at the heart of the racial profiling controversy to be "good for our society" (para. 6)?

READING THE SIGNS

1. Write a journal entry in which you reflect on an experience in which you believe you were singled out because of your appearance, ethnicity, gender, or other physically obvious characteristic. How did you respond at the time, and would you respond the same way today? Alternately, write about an acquaintance who had such an experience.

2. Kennedy contends that there is a contradiction between opposing racial profiling and promoting affirmative action. Write an essay in which you support, refute, or complicate his position.

3. Form teams and conduct an in-class debate over the proposition that racial profiling is necessary to both individual and national security in the post–September 11 era.

4. Write an essay in which you explore the relative claims of the rights of the individual and the rights of the community in modern American culture.

5. In the debates over both racial profiling and affirmative action, the discussions tend to presume that determining ethnic identity is a simple matter. Read or reread Jack Lopez's "Of Cholos and Surfers" (p. 592), Nell Bernstein's "Goin' Gangsta, Choosin' Cholita" (p. 599), and Melissa Algranati's "Being an Other" (p. 608), and write an essay in which you explore the implications that mixed-race backgrounds and cultural practices such as claiming may have for these debates.

IT'S NOT JUST A GAME

Sports and American Culture

First they lowered the pitcher's mound. Then they widened the strike zone. They split the difference on the designated hitter, and they set back the goalposts ten yards. They introduced the three-point basket and professionalized the Olympics. And on January 1, 2002, they scheduled something called the Tostitos Fiesta Bowl.

When it comes to athletics in America, Toto, we aren't in Kansas anymore. Once a largely leisure-time recreational activity for unpaid participants, sport has become a major component of what we might call, with apologies to Dwight David Eisenhower, America's "sports-and-entertainment-postindustrial complex," that vast array of commercial entertainments that comes to us from an ever-expanding culture industry. Athletic contests that were once governed by the purity of the amateur ideal and a devotion to tradition are now being retailored to suit advertisers and corporate sponsors who need to be assured of a sufficient market to justify their investments.

That's why, thanks to such dominating pitchers as Sandy Koufax and Bob Gibson, when in the late 1960s and early 1970s too many baseball games ended with boring 2-1 or 1-0 scores, professional baseball lowered the mound. It gave batters an advantage — as did a reputed livening up of the baseball — so that fans would be entertained with more hits and homeruns. And when, a generation later, careful pitchers who took plenty of time between pitches were messing up television schedules by extending the length of ballgames, a time clock between pitches was introduced to speed up the game, and the strike zone was widened to encourage batters to swing at more pitches.

And that's why when the Miami Dolphins won three straight Super Bowls in the 1970s through a dull strategy of grinding out yards on the ground till they could get near enough for a field goal, the goal posts were moved back. Before too long, the Bob Griese era came to an end and Dan Marino's aerial circus began. Similarly, when professional basketball threatened to become a boringly predictable game in which players simply got the ball to some giant in the lane who would dunk it, the three-point basket was invented.

Though athletic purists complain that such crowd-pleasing rule adjustments are ruining the game, their voices have been drowned out by the swelling tide of a new reality: American sport, thanks largely to the influence of TV, is becoming just another form of entertainment. Where it was once easy to distinguish between such obviously entertainment-oriented pseudosports as professional wrestling and the real thing, the line between athletic competition and popular entertainment is fast eroding. Baseball may have been the only game in town in Mighty Casey's Mudville, but now it must compete not only with football and basketball and hockey, but also with the movies, television, the Internet, and every other form of universally available entertainment. The real competition in sports now is the competition for markets, and to reach those markets, American sport has been compelled to behave like all those other competing entertainments in an entertainment-saturated society.

It can't afford not to. To pay all those astronomical salaries, professional sports leagues have to secure lucrative television contracts, and they can't get those contracts unless the networks can secure lucrative advertising contracts. A thirty-second television spot for Super Bowl XXXVI, for example, cost advertisers some two million dollars, so advertisers want to make sure they're getting their money's worth. This is why the halftime show gets ever more elaborate, and why gimmicks like a Victoria's Secret fashion show are tied in via the Internet. Neither has anything to do with football, but they grab viewers, and that is the new name of the game.

Exploring the Signs of Sports in American Culture

Write a journal entry in which you reflect upon the role of sports in your life as you were growing up. Were you directly involved in sports as a participant, or were you an avid fan? Conversely, did you have little or no interest in sports at all? Whatever your experience, reflect upon how your relationship to sports affected you socially and personally. What cultural and social pressures did you experience to participate in sports either as an athlete or a spectator?

Indeed, advertising has become such an integral part of the Super Bowl that it is now a significant participant in the pregame hyping rituals. In the weeks prior to Super Bowl XXXVI, for example, Levi's jeans ran its own parallel to the playoffs with its Super-Vote campaign, an Internet-based scheme that offered fans a chance to vote for one of three possible TV ads to be run during the game (the guy with the funny walk won). Through abundant PR, Pepsi made certain that everyone would know that Britney Spears would appear in an elaborate retro spot in which she would cruise through five decades of American popular culture. For its part, E-trade concocted an ad that comically referred to the way that postgame run-downs now include an analysis of the *ads* as well as the game (a chimpanzee is "fired" by E-trade's CEO after getting a postgame thumbs down from the critics for a Busby Berkeley-style musical revue) — but maybe you had to see it.

In short, sports are no different from any other popular entertainment in our consumer society and so offer a rich field for cultural analysis. In this chapter you will have the opportunity to read a number of pieces that explore various aspects of the cultural significance of American sport, from controversies in collegiate athletics to the relations between sport and the politics of gender. To help you further situate sports within the system of American culture, we will look in the next section at the changing significance of sports in the context of our social class system.

Interpreting the Signs of American Sports

It is difficult to imagine in these days when the NFL draws so many of its players from impoverished rural and inner-city neighborhoods that the original stars of the game were helmetless student athletes from such upper-crust universities as Harvard, Princeton, and Yale, amateurs drawn largely from the upper classes (it's important to note that it has only been in the post–World War II era that professional football has surpassed the college game in popularity). With golfers like Tiger Woods earning multimillions, it is difficult to grasp why Bobby Jones, the golfing sensation who won thirteen major championships between 1923 and 1930, chose to compete as an amateur when he had professional options, or why Wimbledon, the crown jewel of tennis tournaments, excluded professionals until 1968 and so prevented tennis legends like Rod Laver from competing there in their prime. And how can anyone today fully understand, now that the Olympic Games have been fully professionalized, how the International Olympic Committee could have stripped Jim Thorpe of all his medals for the "crime" of competing in a semiprofessional baseball league — and how it still won't give them back?

It is difficult to imagine all this because the cultural significance of sports has changed dramatically over the years. In the nineteenth and early twentieth centuries, certain sports — especially golf, tennis, swimming, sailing, and collegiate football — were regarded as the recreational prerogatives of upper-class life, leisure-time activities for a leisure class. They could help build character, but not bank accounts. To play for money was declassé, something that the lower orders might do, but not the inheriting classes. Professional boxing — which has offered a way out of poverty for generations of working-class immigrant-athletes (from the Irish, Polish, Jewish, and Italian fighters of the late nineteenth and early twentieth centuries to the Latinos of the present) and which has been a way out of the ghetto since Jack Johnson became the first black heavyweight champion in 1908—was the epitome of everything that the upper-class amateur ideal sought to avoid. You can see something of this attitude in *Chariots of Fire,* a film that dramatizes the early-twentieth-century English version of the code of athletic amateurism.

The amateur ideal lingers on today in the realm of collegiate athletics, where, while it is not defended along social class lines, it has still kindled a firestorm of controversy at a time when every other athletic venue—from the Olympics to Wimbledon—has opened its gates to professional athletes. With top Division I teams earning their campuses substantial television and ticket revenues, an increasing number of collegiate athletes are demanding a piece of the pie. There are good arguments on both sides of the debate (see Frank Deford's essay in this chapter for a strong "pro" argument), and it's hard to guess just now how it is all going to come out. Significantly, however, collegiate baseball isn't much caught up in the controversy both because baseball brings in much less revenue than football and basketball and because professional baseball maintains its own minor league teams, which deflects a lot of attention from the college players (by contrast, the NBA and the NFL use the NCAA as a breeding ground for future professionals). But there is a semiotic angle to consider here as well that relates to the social class issues we have been discussing so far.

Discussing the Signs of Sports in American Culture

In class, discuss the cultural image of such sports as basketball, baseball, football, and hockey, as well as track and field, long-distance running, skiing, golf, and tennis (as well as any other sports you choose to consider). Include in your discussions the images of those classmates who participate in sports, whether in your high school years or at college. If you are an athlete, share with your class the image you think others have of you and whether it corresponds with your own personal image. If you are not an athlete, describe your experience of the social status of athletes on school campuses.

Think about it: What are the class connotations of baseball? It's hard to give a definite answer, isn't it, certainly harder than determining the class connotations of, say, golf or tennis. Unlike football, with its Ivy League origins and upper-class amateurs, baseball has a long and highly popular professional history. Many of its early stars were ordinary farm boys, and sandlot and stickball games are a poignant part of the memories of immigrant children struggling to assimilate to the ways of their new country from the beginning of the twentieth century on. Certainly, then, baseball lacks upper-class connotations.

But while baseball has most definitely been a game of the working classes, it does not bear the same working-class connotations that, say, box-ing and wrestling do. Baseball, rather, has a more democratic connotation, and by *democratic* we mean more universal. In addition to triggering memo-ries of stickball-playing immigrants, it also reminds us of generations of sub-urban Little Leaguers. It has been a game of the farm and of the city, and everything in between. That's why, in a country whose ideology is so proudly democratic, it has become such a symbol for America itself and is called "the national pastime." Baseball, then, is rather like the Statue of Liberty: a symbol that belongs to all Americans.

The Color Barrier

But like so many other symbols, there is a gap between the meaning of baseball and the realities surrounding it. The most profound of those realities is the fact that, even as it was celebrated as the national pastime of a proud democracy, its professional ranks once excluded African Americans. This exclusion, along with exclusions in the other professional sports leagues, has left a racial edge to the semiotics of sport that parallels the profound racial issues that still lurk beneath the surface of much of America's social and political life.

In the era that baseball's Jackie Robinson helped to open up — an era when black athletes dominate the NBA, while the NFL and MLB would be unimaginable without them, when they enable America to preserve its com-manding leadership in international track and field, and when athletes like Michael Jordan, Tiger Woods, and Shaquille O'Neal have assumed super-iconic status — it might seem that sports are the one area where race is no longer an issue. Indeed, if one were to listen only to NFL, NBA, and MLB PR-talk, or to the sports journalists found in every medium from old-time sports pages in the newspaper to the Internet, one might get the impression that race *is* no longer an issue.

But you don't really need to recall the image of Tommie Smith and John Carlos making their black power salute during the Mexico City Olympics in 1968, or the "free Spre" controversy of the 1990s when NBA star Lawrence Sprewell got into trouble for assaulting his white coach, to see that there is still a racial edge to American sports. Part of the problem is that while most of the players in professional sports are black these days, most of the coaches, general managers, and team owners are white. But it goes further than that.

An important element of the racial semiotics of sports has precisely to do with their professionalization. In an era when athletes are, in effect, highly paid entertainers who perform for passive, nonparticipating audiences, the fact that so many of those entertainers are African American has created cer-tain self-perpetuating stereotypes. That is, while once black athletes were for-bidden to perform alongside white ones, black athletic superiority is now something of a social stereotype. Similar to the image of the tough, cool, and violent black urban gangster that the entertainment industry sells to

---

Reading Sports on the Net

Visit the Yahoo! (**http://www.yahoo.com**) or Netscape (**http://www. netscape.com**) home pages on the Internet, and follow the links you find there to sports information. How do marketing, sports information, and celebrity-athlete gossip blend together in the construction of a "sports-and-entertainment-postindustrial complex"? Compare what you find on the Net to what can be found in the sports pages of a daily newspaper. What similarities do you find? What differences?

---

audiences of all ethnicities, professional sports defines the black male as an athlete and sells that image back not only to white fans but also to young black males. This is often presented as a "positive" message for inner-city youth (professional sports are the wholesome way out of poverty), but it is doubly problematic, first because only the tiniest fraction of even Division I starters ever attains a professional career, and second, because it distracts black males from other, more intellectual careers even as it conforms to a history of treating the black male as little more than a powerful body.

This analysis may shock you, especially if you are a sports fan. After all, sports are so much fun, and aren't all those athletes happy with all the money they've got? And, of course, the answer to such a question is yes. It is also quite true that sports have enabled many an African American, from Magic Johnson to Michael Jordan, to graduate from athletic competition to entrepreneurial competition, and in the process sports have given hope and inspiration to generations of inner-city kids. The problem has to do with the way it all works. For while the *image* of successful white athletes may inspire many white kids to pursue athletic careers (from the little boys who want to be the next Joe Montana to the little girls who want to be the next Tara Lipinski or Mary Lou Retton), that is not the only image that white children are sent in our society. With plenty of social images to choose from, most ambitious white kids want to become doctors, or lawyers, or dot.commers, or whatever. Many ambitious black kids want these careers too, but it's harder to stay focused when you are inundated with images of spectacularly successful athletes whose covert message is that your body is all that you should count on.

Girls Just Want to Have Fun

So, as with every other segment of American popular culture, sport too has a serious political and ideological significance that is subject to semiotic analysis. And no discussion of the ideological significance of sports can be complete without a look at its place in constructing gender identities.

Until the advent of Title IX, the legislation that requires college campuses

An athlete competes at the Paralympics.

to spend equal amounts of money on their men's and women's athletic programs, girls weren't even supposed to get involved in sports. Oh, the more aristocratic sports like tennis and golf had their women's stars, and the elegant ones like figure skating, gymnastics, and synchronized swimming were considered appropriate women's activities. Of course, women could join softball, basketball, and swim teams on college campuses, but these sports received neither much money nor much attention. As for little girls, who had no Little League and (believe it or not) no soccer, their aspirations, society told them, should be to become cheerleaders.

For sport was regarded not simply as a recreational activity *for* boys and men; it was regarded as the shaping activity *of* boys and men. Little League baseball, Pop Warner football, and the myriad of other athletic venues open to little boys were, and to some degree still are, regarded as essential male initiation rituals. Competitive team sports particularly (the more violent the better), with their close resemblance to (and probable origin in) warfare (the Olympic games originally included spear throwing and shield-carrying contests), are part of the aggressive socializing of the American male. For women to be mixed up in such things seemed to threaten the whole point of the enterprise. Thus, even today, over twenty years after the introduction of Title IX there is still resistance to women's athletics that go beyond the still mostly amateur, and single competitor, competitions of the Olympic games (there are no professional swimming or gymnastic leagues, for example) or the genteel traditions of tennis and golf.

But America's reaction to the victory of the national women's soccer

Brandi Chastain celebrating after scoring the goal that won the 1999 Women's World Cup championship for the U.S. national team.

team over the Chinese in 1999 was a striking sign that such attitudes are beginning to change. It wasn't the victory that was significant, however; it was the reaction. Everyone went nuts, rather like the way they did when the men's hockey team beat the Soviets at the Lake Placid Olympics in 1980. That athletic team victories should be celebrated as surrogate military victories over hostile nations (which is essentially what both the celebrations of the hockey and soccer victories constituted) is not only nothing new, it is one of the reasons that international athletics were created in the first place: as a substitute for war. But that a team of women athletes should be so celebrated was a breakthrough, the culmination of a decades-long process by which young American girls, especially through the creation of girls soccer leagues, have been allowed entrance into the hallowed corridors of team sport. Heck, even the WNBA is finally getting some respect.

The Readings

D. Stanley Eitzen begins this chapter with an analysis of the contradictions that big-time, big-money Division I sports present to America's college campuses. Frank Deford follows with an opinion piece calling for a revision of NCAA eligibility rules to allow for collegiate professionalism, while David Kamp explores the history of soccer in America. In a trio of gender analyses, Michael Messner explores the role that sport takes in the construction of masculine identity in America, Mariah Burton Nelson critiques the codes that drive women athletes to be as concerned about their makeup as their performance, and Henry Jenkins interprets the WWF as a kind of soap opera for working-class men. E. M. Swift and Don Yaeger report on the current state of, and possible future for, genetic engineering in sports medicine, anticipating the eventual advent of the bionic athlete. Gary Smith concludes the chapter with a personal reminiscence of a man who, having devoted his life to sports, wonders what it all might mean in the aftermath of the September 11, 2001, terror attacks.

D. STANLEY EITZEN

The Contradictions of Big-Time College Sport

D. Stanley Eitzen (b. 1934) loves college sports, but as a sociologist he has had a chance to see firsthand the effects that big-time athletics can have on a college campus. Run along the lines of big-business enterprises, NCAA Division I athletic programs threaten to compromise the educational missions of the universities that maintain them, Eitzen believes, bringing academically ill-prepared athlete-students to campus who often have little chance of making it to graduation. And the irony of it all is that in spite of the big-bucks contracts that top programs can arrange with television networks and companies like Nike, most of them still lose money. Can anyone spell "amateur athletics"? Professor emeritus at Colorado State University, Eitzen is the author of over a dozen books, including Sociology of North American Sport *(1998) and* Fair and Foul: Beyond the Myths and Paradoxes of Sport *(1999).*

A few years ago, after Duke was eliminated from the NCAA Division I men's basketball tournament, its highly successful and esteemed coach, Mike Krzyzewski, made an emotional speech. Coach K, as he is affectionately known, extolled the virtues of big-time college sport — the camaraderie, the shared sacrifice, the commitment to excellence, collective responsibility, and integrity. He said, "All this stuff where people talk about college sports and things as bad, you have no idea. I want to whack everybody who says that. College sports are great. They're O.K. when you yell at each other, when you hug each other, when you live."[1]

Contrast Coach Krzyzewski's statement with sportswriter Mike Littwin's comment: "It's a dirty business, big-time college sports. The best way to watch is with blinders and to pretend what you're seeing smells like school spirit."[2]

I love sports. As sportswriter John Feinstein says, "As in life, [sport] is really about competition and teamwork and succeeding — or failing — after a worthy struggle."[3] College sport intensifies those feelings for me. Although I truly love college sport, I believe that big-time college sport compromises the val-

---

[1]Mike Krzyzewski, "Despite Loss, Krzyzewski Lauds His Team," *New York Times,* March 28, 1993, sec. 8, p. 9.

[2]Mike Littwin, "The Dean Comes Clean in Dirty Business," *Rocky Mountain News,* October 12, 1997, p. 2C.

[3]John Feinstein, "Why the Ryder Cup Makes Legs Shake," *USA Today,* September 25, 1997, p. 15A.

ues of higher education. I am one of those critics that Coach K wants to "whack." Coach K acknowledges that there are abuses in college sports — cheating and other unethical practices. In his view, these are behaviors by bad people "who have lost sight of the true purpose of college sport and let the pursuit of winning override the pursuit of teaching."[4] I do not question Coach K's genuine affection for his players or his sincerity about the glories of big-time college sport. I do question his perception and analysis. Coach K takes an individualistic perspective, which means that he does not see — and this is the crucial sociological point — the wrongs that occur because of the way big-time college sport is organized.

Is big-time college sport compatible with higher education? Clearly, it has entertainment value, unites supporters of a given school, provides free publicity for the schools, gives good athletes from economically disadvantaged backgrounds the chance for a college education, and serves as a training ground for the relatively few future professional athletes. But does big-time college sport[5] complement or promote the educational goals of colleges and universities? Put another way, are the athletic programs at big-time schools consistent with the educational mission of U.S. colleges and universities? To answer this question, I shall, as is my sociological inclination, examine the dark side of big-time college sport as well as the "big picture." . . .

The Education of Athletes

The education of inadequately prepared athletes is a daunting task. The latest 5 data show that athletes in big-time programs are more than two hundred points behind the average student on the SAT. At Clemson the average SAT score of the football squad trails the average of all students at that university by 271 points; at Duke, 304 points; at Colorado, 216 points; at Rice, 382 points; at Michigan, 364 points; at UCLA, 229 points; at Stanford, 298 points; at Arizona, 213 points; and at Florida, 319 points.[6] How do the schools deal with these discrepancies? The athletic departments hire tutors for their athletes. Typically, there are mandatory study sessions for freshmen and for nonfreshmen whose grades are in jeopardy. That's the good news. The bad news is that the athletic role, in the eyes of many coaches and athletes, supersedes the student role. A statement by the late Paul "Bear" Bryant, legendary football coach at the University of Alabama, illustrates a fundamental contradiction that big-time sport brings to academe:

---

[4]Ibid.

[5]Big-time college sport refers exclusively to men's football in the 106 Division I-A schools and the 305 men's basketball programs in NCAA Division I.

[6]Gary Mihoces, "Football Programs Try Settling Score," *USA Today,* December 22, 1993, pp. 1C–2C; 6C.

> I used to go along with the idea that football players on scholarship were "student-athletes," which is what the NCAA calls them. Meaning a student first, an athlete second. We were kidding ourselves, trying to make it more palatable to the academicians. We don't have to say that and we shouldn't. At the level we play, the boy is really an athlete first and a student second.[7]

Coaches who concur with this sentiment, coupled with the pressure to win, tend to diminish the student role by counseling their students to take easy courses, to choose easy majors, and to sign up for courses from cooperative faculty members who are willing to give athletes "special" considerations in the classroom. Or they may steer them toward correspondence courses with few or no requirements. To accentuate the athlete role, the coaches demand incredible amounts of time (practices, meetings, travel, studying videotape and playbooks). Athletes are required to lift weights and engage in other forms of conditioning as well as "informal" practices during the off-season. The NCAA has attempted to control the excesses of these demands but has met with little success.

In addition to the time constraints of big-time college sport, the athletes must also cope with physical exhaustion, mental fatigue, media attention, and demanding coaches. Athletes in these commercialized, professionalized programs have trouble reconciling the roles associated with their dual status of athlete and student. This problem is especially acute for those who were poorly prepared for higher education. Academically challenged athletes, research has shown, are most likely to take easy courses, cheat on exams, hire surrogate test takers, take phantom courses, and otherwise do the minimum.[8] A study of one basketball program by sociologists Patricia and Peter Adler found that the pressures of big-time sport and academic demands resulted in the gradual disengagement of the athletes from their academic roles.[9] The researchers found that most athletes entered the university feeling idealistic about the academic side of their college performance. This idealism lasted about one year and was replaced by disappointment and a growing cynicism as they realized how difficult it was to keep up with their schoolwork. The athletic role came to dominate all facets of their existence. The athletes received greater positive reinforcement for their athletic performance than for their academic performance. They became increasingly isolated from the student body as a result of segregated living arrangements, and their racial and socioeconomic differences isolated them culturally from the rest of the students. They were even isolated socially from other students by their physical size, which many found intimidating. They interacted primarily with other ath-

---

[7]Paul W. Bryant and John Underwood, *Bear: The Hard Life and Good Times of Alabama's Coach Bryant* (Boston: Little, Brown, 1974), p. 325.

[8]See, for example, Allen L. Sack and Robert Thiel, "College Basketball and Role Conflict: A National Survey," *Sociology of Sport Journal* 2, no. 3 (1985): 195–209.

[9]Patricia A. Adler and Peter Adler, *Backboards and Blackboards: College Athletics and Role Engulfment* (New York: Columbia University Press, 1991).

letes, and these peers tended to put down academics. First-year athletes took courses from "sympathetic" professors, but this changed as they moved through the university curriculum. The athletes were unprepared for escalating academic expectations. The typical response of these athletes was role distancing, that is, they distanced themselves from the student role. The Adlers say that for these athletes, "it was better not to try than to try and not succeed."[10] This attitude was reinforced by the peer subculture. Thus the structure of big-time programs works to maximize the athlete role and minimize the academic role — clearly opposite the goals of higher education.

Poor preparation for college and depreciation of the role of student result in a lower graduation rate for big-time college athletes compared to their nonathlete peers. This is contrary to the NCAA media spin. Its 1997 report on graduation rates noted that 58 percent of the more than 13,000 scholarship athletes who entered Division I schools as freshmen in 1990 had earned degrees by the summer of 1996. That exceeds the 56 percent graduation rate for the general student body at the same schools. This relatively high rate of 58 percent is attributable to female athletes' graduating at a much higher rate (68 percent) than male athletes (53 percent). Race is also an important variable to consider, since African Americans are overrepresented in the revenue-producing sports. The graduation rate for white athletes in football was 61 percent and in men's basketball, 45 percent. For African American athletes, the graduation rate in football was 53 percent and in men's basketball, 39 percent.

Although some schools have superior graduation rates for their athletes, many of the top athletic programs have low rates. Consider, for example, the top men's basketball programs. In 1996, seven of the season's final top ten teams had four-year graduation rates below the Division I average, including first-ranked Arizona (25 percent), second-ranked Kentucky (27 percent), and third-ranked Minnesota (29 percent). Cincinnati had a 0 percent graduation rate and Louisville had a 15 percent rate.[11]

There are at least three probable explanations for these low rates among basketball powers. First, the best programs have the best athletes, some of whom leave their schools prior to graduation to become professionals. Second, the most successful programs may recruit academically marginal players to stay on top, and, third, about 50 percent of the players in Division I men's basketball are African Americans, and they are much more likely than whites to come from economically and educationally deprived backgrounds.

In every study African Americans, when compared to their white counterparts, are less prepared for college. They enter as marginal students and, in general, leave that way. Sociologist Harry Edwards, an African American, has argued that the black "dumb jock" is a social creation. "Dumb jocks are not

10

[10]Ibid., p. 247.
[11]Steve Wieberg, "Grad Rates for Scholarship Athletes Hold Steady," *USA Today,* June 27, 1997, p. 10C; Marc Ethier, "Male Basketball Players Continue to Lag in Graduation Rates," *Chronicle of Higher Education,* July 3, 1997, 39A.

born; they are systematically created."[12] This social construction results from several factors. First, African American athlete-students must contend with two negative labels: the dumb athlete caricature and the dumb black stereotype. This double negative tends to result in a self-fulfilling prophecy as professors, fellow students, and the athletes themselves assume low academic performance.

Moreover, as soon as African American youngsters are labeled as potential athletic superstars, many teachers, administrators, and parents lower their academic demands, believing that athletic stardom will be the ticket out of the ghetto. In junior high school and high school little is demanded of them academically. The reduced academic expectations continue in college (or in community college if they do not qualify for college). With professors who "give" grades, occasional altered transcripts, surrogate test takers, and phantom courses, there is, as Harry Edwards has said, "little wonder that so many black scholarship student-athletes manage to go through four years of college enrollment virtually unscathed by education."[13]

The inescapable conclusion is that providing a free education to athletes while expecting more from them as athletes than as students, as well as creating a situation that moves them away from academic pursuits, is contrary to the lofty goals of higher education.

College Sport as Big Business

Big-time college sport is organized in such a way that separating the business aspects from the play on the field is impossible. The intrusion of money into collegiate sport is evident in the following representative examples:

1. Some university athletic budgets are now as much as $33 million.
2. Each school in the 1999 Rose Bowl received $12.6 million, which it divided with other schools in its conference.
3. A number of bowls have corporate tie-ins. For example, for an annual contribution of $2 million, USF&G sponsors the Sugar Bowl. At the university level, a school such as San Diego State has corporate sponsors that pay, collectively, $2 million a year to the athletic department. Coors Brewing Company paid $5 million to the University of Colorado when the university agreed to name the new field house Coors Events Center.
4. Notre Dame has a $45 million contract to televise its football games for several years. The sale of Notre Dame merchandise brings the school another $1 million in royalties, and an appearance in a bowl game raises more millions.
5. An estimated $2.5 billion a year in college merchandise is sold under li-

---

[12]Harry Edwards, "The Black 'Dumb Jock': An American Sports Tragedy," *College Board Review,* Spring 1984, p. 8.
[13]Ibid., p. 9.

cense, generating about $100 million to the schools in royalties. The University of Michigan receives the most income from this source — about $6 million annually. After Kentucky won the NCAA men's basketball tournament in 1996, it received about $3 million in royalties from the sale of basketball-related merchandise.[14]

6. The University of Colorado will receive $5.6 million (in shoes, apparel, and cash) over six years from Nike. In addition, CU will receive a $100,000 bonus from Nike if its football team ends the season with a number-one ranking (only $5,000 for a number-five ranking). If CU wins the NCAA men's basketball tournament, it receives $200,000 in bonuses ($50,000 for a Final Four appearance).[15] Nike has similar contracts with other top programs, including Florida State, Ohio State, Penn State, Miami, Michigan, North Carolina, and Southern California. Nike's competitor, Reebok, has contracts with four major schools: Georgia Tech, UCLA, Texas, and Wisconsin. Wisconsin, for example, has a five-year contract with Reebok worth $9.1 million.[16]

7. Each school in the Big Twelve receives $4.25 million annually from the conference distribution of television, bowl money, and basketball tournament payoffs.

8. In 1994 CBS agreed to pay the NCAA $1.725 billion ($215.6 million a year) for the rights to televise the men's basketball tournament through 2002.

9. When Kentucky basketball coach Rick Pitino was being sought by the pros in 1996, he was offered a $3 million deal to stay (three times more than any other college basketball coach at the time). But he turned the offer down, and his replacement, Tubby Smith, signed a deal worth $1.2 million. The highest-paid college football coach is Steve Spurrier of Florida, who has a contract through the 2002 season that averages $2 million a season in salary, bonuses, and extras.

These illustrations have serious implications for institutions of higher education. First, the system creates economic imperatives that lead college administrators, athletic directors, and coaches to make business decisions that supersede educational considerations. Tulane law professor Gary Roberts argues that this emphasis results in what he calls an "athletic arms race" among the schools: 15

> The careers of key policy-makers [in sport] depend on the program's ability to produce and sell an entertainment product that will be attractive to consumers only if it spends enough money to be consistently competitive with

[14]Goldie Blumenstyk, "Money-Making Champs," *Chronicle of Higher Education,* April 19, 1996, p. 49A.

[15]Jim Armstrong, "Just Don't Over Do It: Money Talks, Nike Walks Fine Line with Tradition," *Denver Post,* July 6, 1997, pp. 1C, 10C.

[16]Jim Naughton, "Exclusive Deal with Reebok Brings U. of Wisconsin Millions of Dollars and Unexpected Criticism," *Chronicle of Higher Education,* September 6, 1996, p. 65A.

other institutions that are constantly increasing their expenditures. So the desperate pressure to generate increasingly large amounts of revenue inevitably leads to business, not academic decisions.

What else could explain why schools have special admits for the most unprepared students, go to all great lengths to keep them eligible, schedule as many games as allowed and play them at absurd times of the week and night to accommodate television? Division I programs are, first and foremost, market-driven revenue producers, and their professed commitment to academics and the welfare of the student-athlete must be accommodated within and compromised by the limits that each institution's minimum-revenue requirements dictate.[17]

Thus to make money, an athletic department must spend money on, for example, increasing the recruiting budget, hiring more fund raisers, improving practice facilities, adding new seating in the stadiums and arenas (especially skyboxes), purchasing the latest equipment, and building expensive new sports annexes with state-of-the-art locker rooms, weight rooms, training rooms, meeting rooms, and offices for the coaches and athletic administrators.

Nevertheless, except for a few schools, athletic programs lose money. About fifty out of the NCAA's eight hundred member institutions make more money on their athletic programs than they spend. The losses are covered by their schools' general revenue funds.[18] It is commonly believed that men's basketball and especially football bring in the funds that pay for the rest of the athletic budget. But, for the most part, this is a fiction. The NCAA reported that only 17 percent of its member institutions made money on their football programs in 1995, with a majority of Division I programs reporting a deficit and 45 percent losing an average of $628,000 in 1995.[19] These deficits would be much greater, however, if the accounting procedures were more appropriate. That is, the football teams play in stadiums paid for by taxpayers, contributors, and, more typically, bonds being paid off by students *at no expense to the athletic departments.* As John Silber, president of Boston University, said of his former employer, the University of Texas: "They've got a $50 million to $60 million capital investment in their football plant at U.T. Try amortizing that at 5 or 6 percent and you will see the program is actually losing money."[20] Moreover, a large proportion of student fees are automatically turned over to the athletic departments, as are subsidies from state legislatures and school administrators to pay for the athletes' scholarships. Using the University of Colorado as an example, the 1995 athletic budget included $900,000 in presidential support, $1,064,331 in chancellor's support, and

---

[17]Gary R. Roberts, "Financial Incentives Wrong for College Athletics," *NCAA News,* November 4, 1991, p. 4.

[18]Sperber, *College Sport Inc.;* Ben Brown, "Most Schools Losing Money on Athletics," *USA Today,* November 9, 1993, pp. 1C–2C.

[19]Robert Brustad, "Title IX Unfairly Blamed for Sports Cuts," *Fort Collins Coloradoan,* September 14, 1997, p. 2C.

[20]John Silber, quoted in Sperber, *College Sports Inc.,* p. 65.

"*I'm glad we won, and I hope that someday we'll have a university that our football team can be proud of.*"

$1,254,000 in support from mandatory student fees.[21] These student fees and university subsidies (in the case of Colorado totaling $3.218 million) artificially inflate athletic department income. At Colorado State University (a school with a budget $13 million below that of the University of Colorado), more than one-third of the budget comes from within the university — university support and student fees.[22]

These subsidies also show how universities make business decisions concerning athletics that override educational considerations. In 1996 Tulane's governing board announced that it would increase its subsidy to the athletic

---

[21]B. G. Brooks, "CU, Boosters Help Neuheisel Purchase $1.5 Million Home," *Rocky Mountain News,* July 10, 1997, p. 3C.

[22]Tony Phifer, "More Than They Bargained For," *Fort Collins Coloradoan,* July 26, 1998, p. 4D.

department sixfold, from $550,000 to $3.4 million. This action by the board occurred just as it approved trimming $8.5 million from the university's budget while raising the tuition by 4 percent, freezing most faculty and staff salaries for one year, cutting fifty staff positions, and reducing funds for undergraduate student financial aid and graduate student stipends.[23] Clearly, in this situation moneys are being transferred from the educational function of the universities to the entertainment function — a questionable transfer of wealth to say the least.

Successful programs (mostly in football) do generate donations to the university but almost exclusively to the athletic programs rather than to the general operating budget of the university.[24] And if an athletic department happens to generate a surplus, the money almost always stays with it and is not distributed to the academic budgets. There are several reasons for the red ink generated by big-time athletic departments. I have already mentioned the continuing perception that programs must be upgraded with costly improvements to stay even or ahead of competitors. Another reason is that employees in athletic departments tend to be better paid than other university employees. Travel budgets for the teams and recruiters are generous. A common practice, for example, is for the football team and coaches to stay in a local hotel the night before *home* games. Deficits are also generated by the costs associated with pregame football parties given by the athletic departments for influential alumni, boosters, and legislators. At the University of Colorado the annual cost of brunches and game tickets for important supporters of the athletic program is about $100,000.

A third consequence of an athletic department's quest for money is that decision making tends to leave the university and flow toward the sources of revenue. Television money dictates schedules. Booster organizations that supply funds may influence the hiring and firing of coaches. At the University of Colorado twenty-five boosters pledged $40,000 each toward the purchase of a new house for football coach Rick Neuheisel.[25] What kind of power will these twenty-five big spenders have over the University of Colorado's athletic program? Similarly, who has the power when a football coach makes over eight times more money than the university president (as is the case at the University of Florida) and when the coach has a powerful constituency outside the university? On numerous occasions public opinion, governors, and boards of regents have sided with the coach when the university president and a popular coach clashed.[26] For

20

[23]Debra E. Blum, "Faculty Is Furious over Six-Fold Budget Increase for Athletics," *Chronicle of Higher Education,* February 16, 1996, p. 40A.

[24]Douglas Lederman, "Do Winning Teams Spur Contributions? Scholars and Fund Raisers Are Skeptical," *Chronicle of Higher Education,* January 13, 1988, pp. 1A, 32A–33A; Barbara R. Bergmann, "Do Sports Really Make Money for the University?" *Academe* 77 (January–February, 1991): 28–30.

[25]Curtis Eichelberger. "The Party May Be Over at CU," *Rocky Mountain News,* April 9, 1995, p. 28B.

[26]Jim Naughton, "Who Runs College Sports? A Million-Dollar Contract for a Football Coach in Florida Raises That Question," *Chronicle of Higher Education,* November 22, 1996, pp. 37A–38A.

example, John DiBiaggio resigned as president of Michigan State University when its board of trustees twice circumvented his authority, extending the contract of the head football coach and then making that coach, George Perles, interim director of athletics. The point of these examples is that the athletic "tail" is wagging the university "dog." As Murray Sperber says, these practices "undermine one of the fundamental tenets of colleges and universities — their independence."[27] . . .

Winning begets money, which increases the pressure to win, which, when the pressure becomes too great, may result in cheating. Cheating takes several forms. Most common is the offer of special inducements outside the rules by coaches and/or boosters to lure athletes to the school and to keep them there. Cheating may also involve unethical means to ensure the scholastic eligibility of the athletes. According to a recent expose by *Sports Illustrated,* test fraud on the SAT examination is common, promoted by recruiters, high school coaches, middlemen, agents, and college coaches.[28] Scandals also involve altering transcripts, fraudulent courses from diploma mills, the use of surrogate test takers, and the like. In one celebrated case, a federal jury indicted Baylor University's head basketball coach and three of his assistants, two junior college coaches, and two junior college administrators on charges of violating federal mail fraud, wire fraud, and conspiracy statutes. In effect, Baylor had faxed a term paper to a junior college player it was recruiting so that the player could use that paper in an English composition class he was taking at Westark Community College. Moreover, another Baylor recruit was instructed to take a correspondence course on the Old Testament from Southeastern College of the Assemblies of God because the Baylor coaches had a copy of the final exam for this course and others.[29] Finally, an athlete wanting to enroll at Baylor was provided with a fraudulent transcript by two administrators at his school, Shelton State Community College.[30]

There are many examples of scandal in big-time programs. In most instances school administrators, students, and supporters do not demand that guilty coaches be fired for their transgressions — if they win. As *Sports Illustrated* writer John Underwood has characterized the situation, "We've told them that it doesn't matter how clean they keep their programs. It doesn't matter what percentage of their athletes graduate or take a useful place in society. It doesn't even matter how well the coaches teach their sports. All that matters are the flashing scoreboard lights."[31]

[27]Sperber, *College Sports Inc.,* p. 65.

[28]Don Yaeger and Alexander Wolff, "Troubling Questions," *Sports Illustrated,* July 7, 1997, pp. 70–79.

[29]For an expose on how a Bible college, Southeastern College, was used by various colleges and junior colleges for bogus academic credits, see Alexander Wolff and Don Yaeger, "Credit Risk," *Sports Illustrated,* August 7, 1995, pp. 47–55.

[30]Jack McCallum, "Paper Trail," *Sports Illustrated,* November 28, 1994, pp. 45–48. See also Wolff and Yaeger, "Credit Risk," pp. 46–55.

[31]John Underwood, "A Game Plan for America," *Sports Illustrated,* February 23, 1981, p. 81.

The pursuit of money has prostituted the university, demeaning the education of the athletes and fostering immorality. In this milieu winning and the money that is generated by winning are paramount. Thus the evil that results is not due to the malevolent personalities of coaches but to a perverse system. In this regard Philip Taubman has said:

> [Big-time college sport] has become a big business, completely disconnected from the fundamental purposes of academic institutions. The goal of college ball is no longer for young men to test and strengthen their bodies, to learn about teamwork, and to have a good time. All that matters is winning, moving up in the national rankings, and grabbing a bigger share of the TV dollar. . . . To achieve these aims, schools and coaches not only bend and break the National Collegiate Athletic Association (NCAA) rules governing college football but, far more destructively, violate the intellectual integrity and principles of the American university system. . . .[32]

The Dominance of Male Elite Sport

Title IX, which Congress passed in 1972, mandated gender equity in school sports programs. Women's intercollegiate sports programs have made tremendous strides toward that goal in the intervening years. Participation in intercollegiate sports has risen from 30,000 women in 1971 to more than 116,272 (43,712 in Division I) in 1996. In 1971 only about 7 percent of the athletic budget went to women, whereas now it is 27 percent. Athletic scholarships for women were virtually unknown in 1972, whereas now women athletes receive 35 percent of the athletic scholarship money that is distributed. These increases in a generation represent the good news concerning gender equity in collegiate sport. The bad news, however, is quite significant. An assessment of the situation at big-time schools for 1995–1996 discloses the following disparities by gender:

1. Head coaches of women's teams were paid 63 cents for every dollar earned by coaches of men's teams[33] (not including the many more extras the coaches of men's teams receive).
2. Only seven schools met the proportionality test for equity (if the percentage of women athletes in a school is within 5 percent of the proportion of women undergraduates enrolled, the school meets the proportionality test). The average negative gap was 16 percent between the numbers of women participating in sports with the numbers of women enrolled.

---

[32]Philip Taubman, "Oklahoma Football: A Powerhouse That Barry Built," *Esquire* 90 (December 1978): 91.

[33]*USA Today,* "Women's Group Grades Colleges," June 19, 1997, p. 3C; R. Vivian Acosta and Linda Jean Carpenter, "Women in Intercollegiate Sport: 1977–1996" (manuscript, Department of Physical Education, Brooklyn College, 1996).

3. The average athletic department had 292 male athletes and 163 female athletes[34] (65 percent male and 35 percent female), with a similarly disproportionate distribution of scholarships.
4. Spending for recruiting was skewed 76 percent to 24 percent in favor of males.

Operational expenditures were distributed even more unevenly at 78 percent to 22 percent in favor of males.[35] And, most telling, it was not uncommon for a school with a big-time football program to spend *twice as much on its football team as it spent on all women's sports.* In 1993, for example, 85 Division I-A schools spent an average of $4 million on men's football while spending an average of $1.8 million on *all* women's sports.[36]

Clearly, gender equity is not part of big-time college sports programs. To move from its current 65 percent-35 percent split toward gender balance, athletic administrations have three choices: spend more on women's sports, reduce or eliminate nonrevenue men's sports, or constrict football. If recent history is a guide, athletic departments will continue to add low-cost women's sports such as soccer and crew and cut low-profile men's sports such as wrestling, gymnastics, and baseball. Adding women's sports increases their participation, but it does not move them much closer to gender parity in scholarships or in other forms of economic assistance. Cutting men's programs is unfair to men because it reduces their participation and opportunities in the so-called minor sports. College sport, it seems to me, should enhance opportunities for participation, not limit them. Athletic departments achieve high male participation, but they do this with disproportionate participation opportunities for men in football. Division I-A programs are allowed to have 85 scholarship players, and squads include as many as 130 players. Thus football is a huge drain on the athletic budget and forms the basis for gender inequality in college athletics.

The rationale advanced to justify this unequal largesse to one sport is that football underwrites women's sport. *This is a myth.* Only about one-third of Division I-A football programs make a profit; one-third of them run an annual deficit that averages more than $1 million.[37] The truth is that at most schools students pay for football through mandatory student fees and university subsidies.

Another myth is that football has already been cut to the bone. The NCAA a few years back did institute some cost-cutting reforms for football, such as reducing the number of scholarships to eighty-five and limiting the number of coaches. But some incredibly spendthrift practices remain, such as quartering

[34]Carol Slezak, "Colleges Still Lag on Title IX," *Chicago Sun-Times,* March 2, 1997, p. 3A.
[35]Steve Wieberg, "NCAA Finds Too Little Progress," *USA Today,* June 20, 1997, p. 11C.
[36]John C. Weistart, "Can Gender Equity Find a Place in Commercialized College Sports?" *Duke Journal of Gender Law and Policy* 3 (Spring 1996): 193.
[37]Alexander Wolff and Richard O'Brien, "The Third Sex," *Sports Illustrated,* February 6, 1995, p. 15.

entire squads in off-campus hotels on the night before home games, buying out the lucrative contracts for coaches no longer in favor and replacing them with even more expensive coaches, and building ever more palatial football annexes and arenas.[38]

The law requires that women receive the same opportunities to play sports as men. Football, "the overfed sacred cow of college sports," stands in the way of gender equity, however. Football does bring in more money than any other sport and generates a profit for a relatively few schools. Football and men's basketball do bring in the deals from shoe and apparel companies that provide a good share of the equipment for athletes in all sports, but only at the most successful programs. But with football considered sacred, men's so-called minor sports have been cut and women's sports underfunded. The answer, I believe, is to reduce the outlay for football without reducing the quality of the product. This can be easily achieved by reducing football squads to sixty scholarship athletes (the pros have squads of fifty without sacrificing quality). This reduction in numbers decreases the cost of scholarships, equipment, training supplies, and the like. Accompanying this reduction would be a proportionate decrease in the number of coaches. Does a football team really need an interior offensive line coach or an outside linebacker coach? Such a plan cannot be enacted unilaterally and must be accomplished by the NCAA. This plan can also bring more balance to big-time football, as it would prevent the major powers from stockpiling talented benchwarmers.[39]

Another solution to the gender equity bind is for women's sports to gener- 30
ate more revenue. In 1995–1996 men's sports teams generated $13 for every $1 from women's sports at the Division I level.[40] Women's sports programs are at a disadvantage in producing significant revenues for several reasons:

1. Men's intercollegiate sport had a hundred-year head start in building tradition and fan support.
2. It takes money to make money, and women's sports programs have not been given anything approaching parity in resource allocation.
3. Women's sports are relatively ignored by university sports publicity and promotion staff, local and national newspapers, magazines, and television.
4. Women's sports continue to be trivialized by the schools in the naming of their teams (e.g., Wildkittens),[41] as well as by the emphasis on the looks and nonathletic side of women athletes rather than their performance.

Granted, some of these obstacles to gender equity are changing slowly, with more television time being devoted to women's play, better promotions

---

[38]Ibid.

[39]Ibid.

[40]Tanya Albert, "Women's Programs Show Revenue Gains," *USA Today,* March 4, 1997, p. 6C.

[41]D. Stanley Eitzen and Maxine Baca Zinn, "The De-athleticization of Women: The Naming and Gender Marking of Collegiate Sport Teams," *Sociology of Sport Journal* 6 (1989): 362–370.

by the athletic departments, and the success of U.S. women athletes in international competition. Some women's basketball programs are profitable (the national champion Connecticut women's basketball team showed a profit of nearly a half million dollars in 1995–1996). But with success, women's budgets increase just as men's do. For example, Pat Summitt, coach of the women's basketball team at Tennessee (1997 NCAA champions), received about $400,000 in base salary and extras for the 1997–1998 season. The problem with women's programs focusing on revenue is that in time they are likely to replicate all of the problems that money has brought to men's collegiate programs. Women's programs need more money, but at what point will money taint the women's game?

Finally, with regard to gender, universities must address the following question: Is it appropriate for a college or university to deny women the opportunities that it provides men? Shouldn't our daughters have the same opportunities that our sons have in all aspects of higher education? Women represent slightly more than half of the undergraduates in U.S. higher education. They receive half of all master's degrees. Should they be second-class participants in any aspect of the university's activities? The present unequal state of affairs in sport is not inevitable. Choices made in the past have given men an advantage in university sports. As Duke law professor John Weistart has put it, "Just as the existing tensions between genders in sport are the product of choice, they can be unchosen."[42] University administrators could implement true gender equity if they wished. Why do they continue to drag their collective feet on gender equity?. . .

Contradictions

Big-time college sport confronts us with a fundamental dilemma. Positively, college football and basketball offer entertainment, spectacle, excitement, festival, and excellence. Negatively, the commercial entertainment function of big-time college sport has severely compromised academia. Educational goals have been superseded by the quest for big money. Because winning programs receive huge revenues from television, gate receipts, bowl and tournament appearances, boosters, and even legislatures, many sports programs are guided by a win-at-any-costs philosophy.

The enormous pressures to win result sometimes in scandalous behaviors. Sometimes there are illegal payments to athletes. Education is mocked by recruiting athletes unprepared for college studies, by altering transcripts, by having surrogate test-takers, by providing phantom courses, and by not moving the athletes toward graduation. William Reed of *Sports Illustrated* made the following comment about college basketball, but it is relevant to college football as well:

[42]Weistart, "Gender Equity," p. 264.

Every fan knows that underneath its shiny veneer of color, fun and excitement, college basketball is a sewer full of rats. Lift the manhole cover on the street of gold, and the odor will knock you down. . . . The misdeeds allegedly committed by college basketball programs today are the same stuff that has plagued the game for decades — buying players, cheating in academics, shaving points, etc. And the NCAA is powerless to stop it. Make a statement by coming down hard on a Kentucky or a Maryland, and what happens? Nothing, really. The filth merely oozes from another crack.[43]

To this ugly mix can be added problems associated with the exploitation of athletes, gender inequality, and the maintenance of a male-segregated athletic subculture that, when compared to its nonathletic counterpart, tends to be more anti-intellectual, sexist, aggressive, and criminal. How can any university defend and promote this hypocritical, scandal-laden activity?

Several contradictions further delineate the dilemma that big-time college sport presents. The overarching contradiction is that we have organized a commercial entertainment activity within an educational environment, and in the process we have compromised educational goals. Ernest L. Boyer, former president of the Carnegie Foundation for the Advancement for Teaching, put it this way: "I believe that the college sports system is one of the most corrupting and destructive influences on higher education. It is obscene, and there is no way to put an educational gloss on this enterprise."[44] In short, as currently structured, big-time sport is not compatible with education.

A fundamental problem is that athletes are recruited as students. Yet demanding coaches, as well as the athletic subculture, work against the student role. At the heart of this contradiction is the fact that institutions of higher learning allow the enrollment and subsidization of ill-prepared and uninterested students solely for the purpose of winning games, enhancing the visibility of the university, and producing revenue. Sometimes these universities recruit known thugs for the same purposes.

The third contradiction is that although big-time sports are revenue producing, for most schools they actually drain money away from academics. As I have demonstrated, athletic budgets are supplemented with generous sums from student fees and subsidies from the academic budgets.

The fourth contradiction is that although the marketing/sales side of big-time sport is big business, the production side is an amateur extracurricular activity in which athletes are "paid" only with an "education."[45] Meanwhile, individuals and organizations make huge amounts of money.

A final contradiction involves the issue of whether or not participation in sport is educational. University administrators often advance this as a rationale for college sport. But such administrators are caught in a contradiction

---

[43]William F. Reed, "Absolutely Incredible!" *Sports Illustrated,* March 26, 1990, p. 66.

[44]Quoted in Michael Goodwin, "When the Cash Register Is the Scoreboard," *New York Times,* June 8, 1986, pp. 27–28.

[45]Gary Roberts, "Should College Athletes Be Paid? Yes: Trends Make Changes Inevitable," *USA Today,* June 8, 1994, p. 2C.

because most of them willingly accept the present maldistribution of resources, scholarships, and opportunities for women's sport. Sociologist Allen Sack argues:

> If one accepts the notion that student athletes are the prime beneficiaries of college sport, how in the world can women's programs receive less financial support than men's? If sport is educational, what possible academic justification can there be for denying this aspect of education for women? Wouldn't the denial of equal athletic opportunities be tantamount to saying that men should have more microscopes, laboratory facilities and library privileges than women?[46]

And, I would add, if sport is a useful, educational activity, why limit these benefits to the athletic elite? Why should the best athletic facilities be reserved for their exclusive use? Why are we limited to one team in each sport, rather than several teams based on differences in size and skill? If sport is justifiable as an educational experience, why limit the number of men's so-called minor sports? Should they not be expanded to meet the wishes of the student body? In my view, participation in sport is good and we should maximize it instead of limiting its benefits to the few. . . .

The dilemma is this: We like (I like) big-time college sport — the festival, the pageantry, the exuberance, the excitement, and the excellence. But are we then willing to accept the hypocrisy that goes with it? I long for a more pristine sports system for our schools such as the one that exists at the NCAA Division III level or among the NAIA level schools. Here the athletic programs are in harmony with what college sport, in my view, should be. That is, athletic scholarships would be regional in scope. There would be a full complement of minor sports for men and the absolute implementation of Title IX, financed by student fees and discretionary funds from the administration, as well as from legislatures. I like this part of the scenario. Here college sport is in balance with other activities and academics; participation opportunities are maximized. This would truly eliminate the sham and the shame from college sports. If academic institutions really stand for educational values, they would move to this lower level of sports programming. In doing so, they would leave the professional level to the professional leagues, which would fund minor league systems that are outside the school system.

READING THE TEXT

1. Summarize in your own words what Eitzen describes as "the dark side of big-time college sport" (para. 4).
2. What special problems does big-time college sport pose for African American athletes, according to Eitzen?

---

[46]Allen L. Sack, "College Sports Must Choose: Amateur or Pro?" *New York Times,* May 3, 1981, p. 2S.

3. What economic incentives exist to maintain the status quo in big-time college sport, in Eitzen's view?

4. Examine the evidence Eitzen advances to support his claims. From what fields does he draw his evidence? How comprehensive and persuasive do you find his support?

5. Why does Eitzen characterize the education of athletes as "a daunting task" (para. 5)?

READING THE SIGNS

1. Research the economics of the sports program on your campus, and write an argumentative essay in which you support, oppose, or complicate Eitzen's claim that "the pursuit of money has prostituted the university" (para. 23). To develop support for your position, you might consult your school's Web site for information about the size of the athletic program, its costs, and the revenue it may generate.

2. Write an essay in which you write your own answer to Eitzen's question, "are the athletic programs at big-time schools consistent with the educational mission of U.S. colleges and universities?" (para. 4). To develop support for your argument, you might interview students, both athletes and nonathletes, coaches, and faculty.

3. Read or reread Michael Messner's "Power at Play" (p. 668) and Mariah Burton Nelson's "I Won. I'm Sorry." (p. 679), and write an essay supporting, refuting, or complicating the proposition that big-time college sport reinforces traditional male gender codes.

4. Conduct an in-class debate over whether Title IX's attempts to establish gender equity in college sports is a reasonable mandate. To develop support for your position, interview both male and female athletes and study the size and range of your school's sports program.

5. In class, outline how Eitzen's concluding suggestions for a more "pristine" (para. 42) sports program, if applied to your campus, would change your school's sports program. Then write your own essay in which you argue for or against the implementation of such changes at your school.

FRANK DEFORD

ATHLETICS 101: A CHANGE IN ELIGIBILITY RULES IS LONG OVERDUE

Add it all up and "amateur" college sport is a multibillion-dollar industry, so isn't it time for its "workers" to share in the wealth? That, at least, is the opinion of many college athletes themselves, and of Frank Deford (b. 1938), who thinks that it is high time that the NCAA give up the nine-teenth-century amateur ideal, which was designed to protect British upper-class athletes from working-class competition. What's the differ-ence between playing in a professional dance band and getting paid to sink hoops? Do they throw the band member off the college glee club for making a few bucks on the weekend, Deford asks? Of course not, so why not let the athlete get paid, too? A member of the Hall of Fame of the Na-tional Association of Sportscasters and Sportswriters, Deford is a long-time writer for Sports Illustrated, *a commentator for HBO and NPR, and the author of twelve books, the latest of which is entitled* The Other Ado-nis: A Novel of Reincarnation *(2001).*

As the NBA draft approaches, there is, anew, a great deal of weeping and wail-ing and gnashing of teeth about the poor basketball players who will be de-prived of more higher education if they opt to turn pro after high school or af-ter only a year or two of college.

Curiously, no one seemed very upset about Tiger Woods's educational loss when he departed Stanford early. There were no cries of academic an-guish when Pete Sampras, Andre Agassi, and Venus and Serena Williams went on tour instead of on campus — and never is anybody disturbed by the hundreds of baseball prospects who abandon schooling every year for the mi-nor leagues. But, of course, deeply concerned educators do care about the minds of basketball and football players because those just happen to be the only two sports that draw big-ticket crowds and rich television contracts for the universities. Similarly, the NFL and NBA want prospects to play in college so they build up their box-office appeal before moving up to the pros.

The answer to this cynical dilemma is very simple, of course. Throw out all the antiquated amateur rules. After a player is drafted, he should be al-lowed to stay in school and play college basketball or football for up to four seasons. Who cares whether he's been paid money? Who cares whether his daddy, the school's athletic scholarship program, or the Indiana Pacers is pay-ing his tuition?

Look at it this way: A student who wants a career in radio is praised if he gets a summer internship at a radio station. When he comes back to college in the fall nobody says *well, son, you can't work at the college radio station anymore because you're a radio pro.* Are sports professionals any different from that — or any different from the kid who makes money singing in a dance band on weekends and then is allowed to sing for free in the college glee club on weekdays? Does he soil the other members of the chorus who aren't good enough to get paid?

There's a student at Princeton named Chris Young who was signed to   5 play in the Pittsburgh Pirates's farm system during the summer. As a result, he is not only banned from playing on his school's baseball team in the spring, but because he is a summer *baseball* intern, he is banned from playing *basketball* for Princeton in the winter. This is like prohibiting a published student poet from writing for the college newspaper.

But these nutty rules are affirmed by the Ivy League presidents, some of our brightest educators. When it comes to sports, though, even our smartest people go bonkers.

To be sure, some athletes who come to college with great sums of bonus money will goof off and do nothing but play their sport. So what? That's already all too often the case. But then, some kids with huge trust funds go to college and play video games. And some make Phi Beta Kappa.

It's time we admitted that this idiotic system of amateur athletic eligibility is nothing but a vestige of a nineteenth century arrangement from a class system in another country. It was created in the 1800s by the English swells to restrict young working men from competing against the leisure classes. It has no relevance in twenty-first century America.

Open up college sports to all eligible students. Stop caring about who's paying the bills, and everybody — pro leagues and colleges alike — will be happier, nobody will be hurt, and a great deal of the sham and hypocrisy of sport will be instantly eliminated.

READING THE TEXT

1. What is Deford's explanation for the reason colleges, the NFL, and the NBA prefer that star athletes remain in school rather than turn professional after high school or after their freshman year in college?

2. What are the historical origins of current amateur athletic eligibility rules, according to Deford?

3. What hypocrisies does Deford find in the way colleges treat students who earn money while in college?

READING THE SIGNS

1. Write an opinion piece arguing for or against Deford's proposal to "throw out all the antiquated amateur rules" (para. 3).

2. Research the history of amateur athletics, and write a paper supporting, qualifying, or refuting Deford's contention that the amateur athletics codes were de-

signed "to restrict young working men from competing against the leisure classes" (para. 8).

3. Read or reread D. Stanley Eitzen's "The Contradictions of Big-Time College Sport" (p. 642), and write an essay arguing for or against the proposition that professionalizing college athletics will worsen the negative effects that Eitzen believes college sports programs have on college campuses.

4. Compare and contrast Deford's and D. Stanley Eitzen's ("The Contradictions of Big-Time College Sport," p. 642) assessments of the hypocrisies in college sports. Be sure to consider not only their definitions of what constitutes these hypocrisies but also their visions of how college sports should be reformed.

DAVID KAMP

AMERICA'S SPAZ-TIME

What on earth happened to soccer ("football" to the rest of the world) when it finally caught on in America, David Kamp asks in this cultural analysis of his favorite sport. How did this game that inspires soccer hooliganism and explosive violence everywhere turn into a feel-good icon of suburban soccer moms and dads who regard it as being "at the roots of . . . good parent[ing]"? Sports should provide a "bumpy, harrowing, exhausting" ride for its enthusiasts, Kamp believes, not a bunch of "pseudoinspirational hooey." So why does U.S. soccer feel like something out of The Care Bears? *When not participating as a "crazed, tortured, [and] obsessed" sports fan, Kamp is a contributing editor at* Vanity Fair *and* GQ *magazines.*

In the 1970s, the American soccer revolution was one of those things that were forever just around the corner, like the gasless electromobile and our imminent conversion to the metric system. It wouldn't be long before we, too, embraced the rest of the world's favorite sport and became international citizens who followed the World Cup, purchased Umbro jerseys, and knew what FIFA was. Certainly, I felt this rush of inevitability as I stood with the rest of the crowd in Giants Stadium on October 1, 1977, to watch Pelé, the world's biggest soccer star, participate in his final pro game: a novelty exhibition in which he played the first half with his current team, the New York Cosmos of the North American Soccer League, and the second half with his old team (and the Cosmos's opponent that day), Santos of Brazil. It was the third or fourth Cosmos game I'd attended that year, a year in which the team had won the NASL championship and routinely pulled in home crowds of 20,000 to 40,000; as a matter of fact, the June game to which I was taken for my eleventh birthday, against the Tampa Bay Rowdies, had drawn a boffo 62,394 spectators, at the time the largest crowd ever to assemble in the United States for a soccer match. The Cosmos were a glammed-up, well-capitalized outfit, owned by Warner Communications and run by Ahmet and Neshui Ertegun, the boulevardier brothers who founded Atlantic Records. They had cheerleaders, a theme song, and an imposing lineup of slightly past-it international all-stars: Pelé from Brazil, Giorgio Chinaglia from Italy, Franz Beckenbauer from Germany, Steve Hunt from England. Appropriately, the Pelé-fest had an air of jet-set swank and giddy globalism about it; I remember the scoreboard flashing the names of the celebrities in attendance (MICK AND BIANCA JAGGER . . .), and Pelé's pregame address to the crowd, in which he made us all, in unison, intone the word *love* three times in a row. Who could argue with such a juggernaut?

Yet a few years later, the Cosmos and the rest of the NASL had fizzled out. The 1970s soccer boomlet was like an organ transplant that didn't take; though it initially appeared a success, it was ultimately rejected for what it was: foreign. The lesson learned: If soccer was ever to take hold in America, it would have to do so as a grassroots phenomenon rather than as a top-down one, with kids learning and watching the sport from an early age instead of abruptly accepting it into their lives mid-puberty. Soccer was already a part of almost every town's athletics program by the time I reached high school, in the early 1980s, but there was still a certain otherness to it, a sense that it existed outside the canon of the "normal" sports — baseball, football, and basketball. To our dads and granddads, who couldn't teach us the game because they hadn't experienced it, soccer was downright exotic, and borderline insidious. My hometown's athletics director, a banty old codger with Bear Bryant pretensions who, in his coaching days, had willed our small school into a perennial local football power (through pure biliousness, it seemed), could not process soccer as anything but a threat. One afternoon he flagged down our junior-varsity soccer team's bus as it was pulling out of the parking lot for an away game, stormed onto the bus, and launched into a profane tirade in which he accused his shocked audience of engaging in what he called a "fuckin' Communist sport."

A generation later, we can laugh about such outmoded attitudes the way we laugh about the discredited, heirloom-hocking ex-Soviets, for we are now a serene nation of soccer moms and dads; watching the tykes kick around the ball is as American as slidin' shut a minivan door. Though Major League Soccer, the latest American pro-soccer league, has yet to approach the new-dawn delirium of its predecessor's late-1970s, Cosmos-driven hey-day, it begins its sixth season stocked with more homegrown stars than ever, and with corporate America enthusiastically on board. (MasterCard, in literature detailing its sponsorship of MLS, used the catchphrase "Soccer, apple pie, and hot dogs!") The New York

Soccer: Not just for hooligans?

Yankees have just entered into a formal alliance with their soccer-world equivalent, the perpetually triumphant Manchester United of England's Premier League, ostensibly as a means of establishing a marketing beachhead in the UK, but realistically as leverage for that anticipated time when pro soccer finally goes mega in the United States. Meanwhile, down at the grass roots, things are really flourishing. Kids' soccer leagues dominate the public swards the way peewee baseball games used to, and if advertising and TV programming are anything to go by, soccer is now the de facto official sport of America's very young. The little blond boy smiling through his snack-time idyll on the back of a bag of Pepperidge Farm Goldfish crackers wears cleats and sits beside a soccer ball, not the mitt and bat he'd have had fifteen, twenty years ago. On morning kids' shows such as *Arthur* and *Clifford the Big Red Dog* — compulsory viewing for the preschool set — the feel-good, you-can-do-it coed soccer game is a plot staple, having all but replaced the chaotic baseball contests reliably bungled by the Bad News Bears and Charlie Brown's team.

Soccer has at last arrived as an American sport, a circumstance that, in anticipation, I could have regarded only as a good thing. So why doesn't it feel right? Why do I find myself resenting the game's ascendancy rather than welcoming soccer to our A-list of national pastimes? Well, because this isn't the soccer I bargained for. It's soccer-as-cult, a creepy perversion of a fun game by the twaddly adults who control it in America, adults who have either forgotten or never understood why people are hooked on sports.

Whether as amateurs or professionals, spectators or participants, we love 5 sports for the sense of thrill and competition they provide, for the relatively safe way they allow us to experience both vertiginous highs and black troughs of despair — emotional states that in real life would get us into serious trouble. It's bumpy, harrowing, exhausting terrain, and we're up for it, even as kids, *especially* as kids. But the tenor of soccer in the United States is, to use an inelegant but nevertheless appropriate word, *spazzy.* It's all hugs and stroking and everybody-wins and no-one-loses and camcorder dads in Dockers going "Yaaaay!" US Youth Soccer, the kid-oriented branch of the United States Soccer Federation, the governing body for soccer in this country, offers a manifesto on its Web site that states "At US YOUTH SOCCER, we provide a fun, safe and healthy game for ALL KIDS . . . big kids, little kids, tall kids, short kids, young kids, older kids. . . . Kids are different, and because they are different, their physical, social, and psychological needs are different. We at US YOUTH SOCCER recognize this and our programs are aimed at meeting the different needs of ALL KIDS. . . . [Our] programs emphasize FUN, and de-emphasize winning at all costs. Every child is guaranteed playing time and the game is taught in a fun and enjoyable atmosphere."

Forgive me this heresy, but my natural instinct is to shield my children from any sports organization that right off the bat wants to address my kids' "social and psychological needs." Obviously, the gang at US Youth Soccer is well-intentioned, but its desire to plane off the rough edges of the sporting experience is presumptuous, wrongheaded and, alas, all too typical of the mentality that pervades organized soccer in this country. In the big chain bookstores, the Soccer shelves groan with inspirational tomes and manuals, virtually all of recent vintage and icky sentiment. One book I picked up, *Goal! The Ultimate Guide for Soccer Moms and Dads,* by Gloria Averbuch and Ashley Michael Hammond, comes emblazoned with a "Recommended by US Youth Soccer" seal and features an introduction by Averbuch in which she eyebrow-raisingly asserts, "At its most basic, soccer is at the roots of being a complete parent." Come again? "Through this seemingly simple yet complex activity," she continues, "we can learn how best to support, protect, love, and encourage our children. We can take pleasure in developing their physical health and social development and cheer their personal accomplishments." Later, recounting how she worked with her child's coach to iron out a kink in the kid's game, Averbuch notes that she learned "an invaluable lesson in parent-child communication." Meanwhile, the incomplete, nonsoccer parents of the world flail on, utterly at loose ends. Right next to *Goal!* at my local Barnes & Noble was Jonathan Littman's *The Beautiful Game,* a suffocatingly thorough nonfiction chronicle of a girls'-league soccer team in California ("Kim was Naomi's opposite in appearance and skill. Her turquoise eyes blazed as intently as the scowls she tossed around like darts . . . ") as the team morphs from a ragtag band of underachievers to fine-tuned league champion. Naturally, declares the jacket copy, the gals emerge "not just as powerful athletes, but as strong, confident, emotionally healthy human beings — champions in the game of soccer, and in the game of life."

Now, every major sport inspires more than its share of pseudoinspirational hooey, what with the Gipper and the field of dreams and all, but we recognize these narratives as sentimental glosses on a muddy reality; we dig the myth, but we're hip to the psychopathology and violence of sports, too. Only in American soccer is the gloss enforced as the prevailing reality. No other game in modern sports history has been so burdened with the responsibility of being edifying and nurturing. It really is extraordinary — imagine if part of football's credo were to address the "needs" of its players, or if some mom or dad had the cheek to assert publicly that enrolling one's child in league basketball is integral to good parenting. Imagine if Bill Parcells spoke in the language of "empowerment" and "esteem" and if an appreciative nation nodded its approval.

The weird thing is, there's nothing inherently Stuart Smalley-ish about the game of soccer. In Europe and South America, there's nothing "nice" about it at all — it's an insane passion in the same way our major team sports are insane passions, with no cuddly overlay of self-esteeminess. One reason Nick Hornby's very English soccer-fan memoir, *Fever Pitch,* connected with a surprisingly large American audience is that it is, stripped of its details, an astute encapsulation of every sports obsessive's deranged yet sated psyche. "The natural state of the football fan," he writes, using the English term for soccer, "is bitter disappointment, no matter what the score." A few years ago, I had the good fortune to break bread with Hornby, and we had an easy rapport — his social-life-crippling fandom of Arsenal, the Premier League team to which he has been devoted since childhood, mirrored my lifelong devotion to the National Football League's New York Giants. We both grew up rooting for bad-to-mediocre teams that didn't get good until we became adults. We were both spectacularly unqualified to play the sports we love, yet we enjoyed a pickup game now and then with similarly athletically challenged friends. (Hornby writes with scary accuracy of the secret joy of pantomiming the pros' tics: "the high-fives when you score, the clenched fists and hand-clasps when your teammates require encouragement, the open arms and upturned palms indicating your superior positioning and your teammate's greed.") We both felt our childhoods had been shaped by multiple episodes of abject sports-related despair, but that we weren't necessarily the worse for it. We were both, in other words, typical sports nut jobs; that Hornby's sport was soccer didn't make him any more enlightened or "emotionally healthy."

More recently, I took in a UEFA Cup game between Liverpool and AS Roma at one of New York City's expats' sports bars and was again reminded of soccer's intrinsic normality. I had a good time — I remembered that I actually enjoy pro soccer when I make a point of watching it — and the urgings, oaths, and roars around me were the usual conditioned responses to a professional sports contest; but for the funny accents, it could have been the Knicks versus the Lakers. The only out-of-the-ordinary part of the experience was a blip of a moment in which the two soccer cultures, American and Euro, briefly collided and sparked. Fox Sports World, the satellite service these bars carry, overdubs the European video feed with audio commentary from American announcers. One of the guys calling our game was especially inane and Kevin Costner-ish of vocal timbre, and after a Liverpool player had just missed on a perfect scoring opportunity, the announcer offered up the particularly US Youth Soccer-ish observation that the fans were nevertheless "applauding the effort, as well they should." To which the blokey Liverpool supporter sitting in front of me responded, *"Faaack awfffff!"*

I don't quite understand how the meaning of soccer changed as it crossed   10 the Atlantic, how we ended up with soccer moms whereas the Europeans got soccer hooligans. Maybe it's because when the U.S. soccer movement was first reaching critical mass, in the 1960s and early 1970s, a lot of its adherents regarded the sport as a less violent alternative to football, which in those Nixonian years was viewed by student protesters as an extension of the military-industrial complex. Maybe soccer got caught up in the polarizations and definitions of that era and wound up in the custody of people who thought it should be egalitarian and gentle — a rebuke to the coldly meritocratic, winner-take-all mentality of football and other popular U.S. sports.

Also, soccer is inextricably linked in American minds to Title IX, the federal statute that prohibits discrimination against girls and women in education and athletics programs. The law, passed by Congress in 1972 (and signed by Richard Nixon, of all people), paved the way for the establishment of thousands of new women's sports teams at the high school and college levels, and it's common today for athletes such as Mia Hamm, the star of the World Cup-winning 1999 team, to be referred to as "Title IX babies." It's easy to understand why women's soccer would have taken off in the wake of Title IX, since the game hadn't acquired a high enough profile in this country to be defined primarily as a man's sport (like football and baseball) and didn't require constrictive padding or expensive equipment. It's also easy to understand why women's sports inherently have a greater "inspirational" component than men's, since the whole idea of a girl's growing up to be a famous athlete is still relatively new.

But none of these circumstances make women's soccer any kinder, gentler, or softer-focus than any other sport, which brings us back to the 1999 Cup victory. I was as thrilled as anyone else that our team won, but, like a lot of women and men with whom I've discussed this subject, I was put off by the cloying terms in which the women's success was sold to us — not so much as a rip-roaring athletic triumph as a Hallmark movie of the week crossed with a patronizing self-help lesson in goal fulfillment. *Sports Illustrated*'s Rick Reilly, a columnist who so aggressively cultivates his lovable public image that one can't help but suspect he's a hateful diva offstage, led the charge by dubbing the team the "Goal-Goal Girls" and a "Thrillith Fair," and he skin-crawlingly asserted, "You figured when a U.S. women's team finally broke through . . . it would be a bunch of women with Bronko Nagurski shoulders and five o'clock shadows. Well, the revolution is here, and it has bright-red toenails. And it shops. And it carries diaper bags. The U.S. women's soccer team is towing the country around by the heart in this Women's World Cup, and just look at the players. They've got ponytails! They've got kids! They've got (gulp) curves!" What is it about soccer that invites this shit? The comparable achievements of Rebecca Lobo and Chamique Holdsclaw in college basketball never got this treatment, fortunately, and the WNBA for which they now play is, first and foremost, an exciting sports league, not an encounter group.

A new women's pro-soccer league, the Women's United Soccer Association, has just begun its inaugural season, boasting a TV deal with Turner Network Television and many of the players from the World Cup team: Mia Hamm, Brandi Chastain, Michelle Akers, Carla Overbeck. Right now the league has a bit of a rinky-dink feel to it (a mere eight teams, one of which is tragically named the Bay Area CyberRays), but it's only a matter of time, I think, before soccer finally catches on permanently in the United States as a first-tier professional sport, fulfilling the failed promise of the Cosmos. The little soccer sprouts currently playing at the peewee level have never known their sport to be in any way "other," and as they grow and improve, they will simultaneously provide a corps of elite players and a dedicated fan base.

My fantasy of a thriving U.S. soccer scene involves all the things we love and hate about baseball, football, and basketball in this country: heroic captains; villainous defenders; hothead coaches; headcase rookies; network overpayments for TV rights; late-season matchups fraught with prime-time tension; controversial calls; fantastic finishes; crazed, tortured, obsessed fans — the parameters of an all-American sport. If I close my eyes and dream real hard, I can see it: Mia Hamm holding out from training camp because she wants her contract renegotiated, coming back just in time for the season opener, saying it "wasn't about the money, but respect," scoring three spectacular goals and blowing off Rick Reilly and the rest of the press in the postgame locker room.

READING THE TEXT

1. Why, according to Kamp, did the North American Soccer League ultimately fail?
2. Summarize Kamp's objections to the current cultural status of soccer in America.

3. How does Kamp say the cultural attitudes towards soccer in America and the rest of the world differ?

4. What benefits should we gain from sports, according to Kamp? How, in his view, do current youth soccer programs fail to provide these benefits?

5. What is Kamp's fantasy for the future of soccer in America?

READING THE SIGNS

1. Read or reread Mariah Burton Nelson's "I Won. I'm Sorry." (p. 679), and write an analysis of Rick Reilly's response to the American women's team victory in the 1999 World Cup (para. 12). In what ways was his response a reflection of traditional gender codes?

2. Write a journal entry describing what soccer, or any other sport, meant to you as a child — whether you participated in sports or not. To what extent did it influence your sense of personal identity?

3. Write an essay in which you agree, disagree, or modify Kamp's claim that soccer in America is "a creepy perversion of a fun game" (para. 4).

4. Write a semiotic analysis of the profile of soccer in American popular culture. How does the sport's cultural significance compare to others in the system of sports? Alternately, compare soccer's cultural significance in America to that in other nations, such as Brazil or England.

MICHAEL A. MESSNER

POWER AT PLAY: SPORT AND GENDER RELATIONS

Every little boy should play Little League, right? Sports help to build character, right? Perhaps, but according to Michael A. Messner (b. 1952), the games men play are more than that: They are rituals designed to maintain the ideology and values of a competitive and hierarchical culture. Because masculine identity is rooted in the need to win, athletic competition, according to Messner, causes "men to experience their own bodies as machines . . . and to see other people's bodies as objects of their power and domination." Author of Power at Play: Sports and the Problem of Masculinity *(1992), from which this selection is excerpted, Messner is associate professor in the Department of Sociology and the Program for the Study of Women and Men in Society at the University of Southern California. He is also coeditor of* Men's Lives *(1995) and* Sport, Men, and the Gender Order: Critical Feminist Perspectives *(1990) and coauthor of* Sex, Violence, and Power in Sports: Rethinking Masculinity *(1994).*

The closer we come to uncovering some form of exemplary masculinity, a masculinity which is solid and sure of itself, the clearer it becomes that masculinity is structured through contradiction: the more it asserts itself, the more it calls itself into question.

— LYNN SEGAL, *Slow Motion*

In 1973, conservative writer George Gilder, later to become a central theorist of the antifeminist family policies of the Reagan administration, was among the first to sound the alarm that the contemporary explosion of female athletic participation might threaten the very fabric of civilization. "Sports," Gilder wrote, "are possibly the single most important male rite in modern society." The woman athlete "reduces the game from a religious male rite to a mere physical exercise, with some treacherous danger of psychic effect." Athletic performance, for males, embodies "an ideal of beauty and truth," while women's participation represents a "disgusting perversion" of this truth.[1] In 1986, over a decade later, a similar view was expressed by John Carroll in a respected academic journal. Carroll lauded the masculine "virtue and grace" of sport, and defended it against its critics, especially feminists. He concluded that in order to preserve sport's "naturally conserving and creating" tendencies, especially in the realms of "the moral and the religious, . . . women should once again be prohibited from sport: They are the true defenders of the humanist values that emanate from the household, the values of tenderness, nurture and compassion, and this most important role must not be confused by the military and political values inherent in sport. Likewise, sport should not be muzzled by humanist values: it is the living arena for the great virtue of manliness."[2]

The key to Gilder's and Carroll's chest-beating about the importance of maintaining sport as a "male rite" is their neo-Victorian belief that male-female biological differences predispose men to aggressively dominate public life, while females are naturally suited to serve as the nurturant guardians of home and hearth. As Gilder put it, "The tendency to bond with other males in intensely purposeful and dangerous activity is said to come from the collective demands of pursuing large animals. The female body, on the other hand, more closely resembles the body of nonhunting primates. A woman throws, for example, very like a male chimpanzee."[3] This perspective

---

[1]G. Gilder, *Sexual Suicide* (New York: Bantam Books, 1973), pp. 216, 218.

[2]J. Carroll, "Sport: Virtue and Grace," *Theory, Culture and Society* 3 (1986), pp. 91–98. Jennifer Hargreaves delivers a brilliant feminist rebuttal to Carroll's masculinist defense of sport in the same issue of the journal. See J. Hargreaves, "Where's the Virtue? Where's the Grace? A Discussion of the Social Production of Gender through Sport," pp. 109–121.

[3]G. Gilder, p. 221.

ignores a wealth of historical, anthropological, and biological data that suggest that the equation of males with domination of public life and females with the care of the domestic sphere is a cultural and historical construction.[4] In fact, Gilder's and Carroll's belief that sport, *a socially constructed institution,* is needed to sustain male-female difference contradicts their assumption that these differences are "natural." As R. W. Connell has argued, social practices that exaggerate male-female difference (such as dress, adornment, and sport) "are part of a continuing effort to sustain a social definition of gender, an effort that is necessary precisely *because the biological logic . . . cannot sustain the gender categories.*"[5]

Indeed, I must argue against the view that sees sport as a natural realm within which some essence of masculinity unfolds. Rather, sport is a social institution that, in its dominant forms, was created by and for men. It should not be surprising, then, that my research with male athletes reveals an affinity between the institution of sport and men's developing identities. As the young males in my study became committed to athletic careers, the gendered values of the institution of sport made it extremely unlikely that they would construct anything but the kinds of personalities and relationships that were consistent with the dominant values and power relations of the larger gender order. The competitive hierarchy of athletic careers encouraged the development of masculine identities based on very narrow definitions of public success. Homophobia and misogyny were the key bonding agents among male athletes, serving to construct a masculine personality that disparaged anything considered "feminine" in women, in other men, or in oneself. The fact that winning was premised on physical power, strength, discipline, and willingness to take, ignore, or deaden pain inclined men to experience their own bodies as machines, as instruments of power and domination—and to see other peoples' bodies as objects of their power and domination. . . .

The Costs of Athletic Masculinity

As boys, the men in my study were initially attracted to playing sport because it was a primary means to connect with other people—especially fathers, brothers, and male peers. But as these young males became committed to

---

[4]For a critical overview of the biological research on male-female difference, see A. Fausto-Sterling, *Myths of Gender: Biological Theories about Men and Women* (New York: Basic Books, 1985). For an overview of the historical basis of male domination, see R. Lee and R. Daly, "Man's Domination and Woman's Oppression: The Question of Origins," in M. Kaufman, ed., *Beyond Patriarchy: Essays by Men on Pleasure, Power, and Change* (Toronto: Oxford University Press, 1987), pp. 30–44.

[5]R. W. Connell, *Gender and Power* (Stanford: Stanford University Press, 1987), p. 81 (emphasis in original text).

athletic careers, their identities became directly tied to continued public success. Increasingly, it was not just "being there with the guys" but beating the other guys that mattered most. As their need for connection with others became defined more abstractly, through their relationships with "the crowd," their actual relationships with other people tended to become distorted. Other individuals were increasingly likely to be viewed as (male) objects to be defeated or (female) objects to be manipulated and sexually conquered. As a result, the socially learned means through which they constructed their identities (public achievement within competitive hierarchies) did not deliver what was most craved and needed: intimate connection and unity with other people. More often than not, athletic careers have exacerbated existing insecurities and ambivalences in young men's developing identities, thus further diminishing their capacity for intimate relationships with others.

In addition to relational costs, many athletes — especially those in "combat sports" such as football — paid a heavy price in terms of health. While the successful operation of the male body-as-weapon may have led, for a time, to victories on the athletic field, it also led to injuries and other health problems that lasted far beyond the end of the athletic career. 5

It is extremely unlikely that a public illumination of the relational and health costs paid by male athletes will lead to a widespread rejection of sport by young males. There are three reasons for this. First, the continued affinity between sport and developing masculine identities suggests that many boys will continue to be attracted to athletic careers for the same reasons they have in the past. Second, since the successful athlete often basks in the limelight of public adoration, the relational costs of athletic masculinity are often not apparent until after the athletic career ends, and he suddenly loses his connection to the crowd. Third, though athletes may recognize the present and future health costs of their athletic careers, they are likely to view them as dues willingly paid. In short, there is a neat enough fit between the psychological and emotional tendencies of young males and the institution of sport that these costs — if they are recognized at all — will be considered "necessary evils," the price men pay for the promise of "being on top."[6]

[6]Indeed, "men's liberationists" of the 1970s were overly optimistic in believing that a public illumination of the "costs of masculinity" would induce men to "reject the male role." See, for instance, W. Farrell, *The Liberated Man* (New York: Bantam Books, 1975); J. Nichols, *Men's Liberation: A New Definition of Masculinity* (New York: Penguin Books, 1975). These men's liberationists underestimated the extent to which the costs of masculinity are linked to the promise of power and privilege. One commentator went so far as to argue that the privileges of masculinity were a "myth" perpetrated by women to keep men in destructive success-object roles. See H. Goldberg, *The Hazards of Being Male: Surviving the Myth of Masculine Privilege* (New York: Signet, 1976). For more recent discussions of the need to analyze both the "costs" and the "privileges" of dominant conceptions of masculinity, see M. E. Kann, "The Costs of Being on Top," *Journal of the National Association for Women Deans, Administrators, and Counselors* 49 (1986): 29–37; and M. A. Messner, "Men Studying Masculinity: Some Epistemological Questions in Sport Sociology," *Sociology of Sport Journal* 7 (1990): 136–153.

Competing Masculinities

Boys' emerging identities may influence them to be attracted to sport, but they nevertheless tend to experience athletic careers differently, based upon variations in class, race, and sexual orientation. Despite their similarities, boys and young men bring different problems, anxieties, hopes, and dreams to their athletic experiences, and thus tend to draw different meanings from, and make different choices about, their athletic careers.

RACE, CLASS, AND THE CONSTRUCTION OF ATHLETIC MASCULINITY

My interviews reveal that within a social context stratified by class and by race, the choice to pursue — or not to pursue — an athletic career is determined by the individual's rational assessment of the available means to construct a respected masculine identity. White middle-class men were likely to reject athletic careers and shift their masculine strivings to education and nonsport careers. Conversely, men from poor and blue-collar backgrounds, especially blacks, often perceived athletic careers to be their best chance for success in the public sphere. For nearly all of the men from lower-class backgrounds, the status and respect that they received through sport was temporary — it did not translate into upward mobility.

One might conclude from this that the United States should adopt a public policy of encouraging young lower-class black males to "just say no" to sport. This strategy would be doomed to failure, because poor young black men's decisions to pursue athletic careers can be viewed as rational, given the constraints that they continue to face. Despite the increased number of black role models in nonsport professions, employment opportunities for young black males actually deteriorated in the 1980s, and nonathletic opportunities in higher education also declined. By 1985, blacks constituted 14 percent of the college-aged (18–24 years) U.S. population, but as a proportion of students in four-year colleges and universities, they had dropped to 8 percent. By contrast, black men constituted 49 percent of male college basketball players, and 61 percent of male basketball players in institutions that grant athletic scholarships.[7] For young black men, then, organized sport appears to be more likely to get them to college than their own efforts in nonathletic activities.

In addition to viewing athletic careers as an arena for career success, there is considerable evidence that black male athletes have used sport as a cultural space within which to forge a uniquely expressive style of masculinity, a "cool pose." As Richard Majors puts it,

[7]W. J. Wilson and K. M. Neckerman, "Poverty and Family Structure: The Widening Gap between Evidence and Public Policy Issues," in S. H. Danzinger and D. H. Weinberg, eds., *Fighting Poverty* (Cambridge: Harvard University Press, 1986), pp. 232–259; F. J. Berghorn et al., "Racial Participation in Men's and Women's Intercollegiate Basketball: Continuity and Change, 1958–1985." *Sociology of Sport Journal* 5 (1988), 107–124.

Due to structural limitations, a black man may be impotent in the intellectual, political, and corporate world, but he can nevertheless display a potent personal style from the pulpit, in entertainment, and in athletic competition, with a verve that borders on the spectacular. Through the virtuosity of a performance, he tips the socially imbalanced scales in his favor and sends the subliminal message: "See me, touch me, hear me, but, white man, you can't copy me!"[8]

In particular, black men have put their "stamp" on the game of basketball. There is considerable pride in U.S. black communities in the fact that black men have come to dominate the higher levels of basketball — and in the expressive style with which they have come to do so. The often aggressive "cool pose" of black male athletes can thus be interpreted as a form of masculinity that symbolically challenges the class constraints and the institutionalized racism that so many young black males face.

SEXUAL ORIENTATION AND THE CONSTRUCTION OF ATHLETIC MASCULINITY

Until very recently, it was widely believed that gay men did not play organized sports. Nongay people tended to stereotype gay men as "too effeminate" to be athletic. This belief revealed a confusion between sexual orientation and gender. We now know that there is no neat fit between how "masculine" or "feminine" a man is, and whether or not he is sexually attracted to women, to men, to both, or to neither.[9] Interestingly, some gay writers also believed that gay men were not active in sport. For instance, Dennis Altman wrote in 1982 that most gay men were not interested in sport, since they tended to reject the sexual repression, homophobia, and misogyny that are built into the sportsworld.[10]

The belief that gay men are not interested or involved in sport has proven to be wrong. People who made this assumption were observing the overtly masculine and heterosexual culture of sport and then falsely concluding that all of the people within that culture must be heterosexual. My interview with Mike T. and biographies of gay athletes such as David Kopay suggest that young gay males are often attracted to sport because they are just as concerned as heterosexual boys and young men with constructing masculine identities.[11] Indeed, a young closeted gay male like Mike T. may view the projection of an unambiguous masculinity as even more critical than his nongay counterparts do. As Mike told me, "There are a *lot* of gay men in sports," but they are almost all closeted and thus not visible to public view.

[8]R. Majors, "'Cool Pose': Black Masculinity and Sports," in M. A. Messner and D. F. Sabo, *Sport, Men, and the Gender Order: Critical Feminist Perspectives* (Champaign, Ill.: Human Kinetics Publishers, 1990), p. 111.

[9]See S. Kleinberg, "The New Masculinity of Gay Men, and Beyond," in Kaufman, *Beyond Patriarchy,* pp. 120–138.

[10]D. Altman, *The Homosexualization of America* (Boston: Beacon Press, 1982).

[11]See D. Kopay and P. D. Young, *The Dave Kopay Story* (New York: Arbor House, 1977).

As Mike's story illustrates, gay male athletes often share similar motivations and experiences with nongay athletes. This suggests that as long as gay athletes stay closeted, they are contributing to the construction of culturally dominant conceptions of masculinity. However, Brian Pronger's recent research suggests that many gay male athletes experience organized sport in unique ways. In particular, Pronger's interviews with gay male athletes indicate that they have a "paradoxical" relationship to the male athletic culture. Though the institution itself is built largely on the denial (or sublimation) of any erotic bond between men, Pronger argues, many (but not all) gay athletes experience life in the locker room, as well as the excitement of athletic competition, as highly erotic. Since their secret desires (and, at times, secret actions) run counter to the heterosexist culture of the male locker room, closeted gay male athletes develop ironic sensibilities about themselves, their bodies, and the sporting activity itself.[12] Gay men are sexually oppressed through sport, Pronger argues, but the ironic ways they often redefine the athletic context can be interpreted as a form of resistance with the potential to undermine and transform the heterosexist culture of sport.

THE LIMITS OF MASCULINE RESISTANCES

Men's experience of athletic careers — and the meanings they assign to these experiences — are contextualized by class, race, and sexual orientation. My research, and that of other social scientists, suggests that black male athletes construct and draw on an expressive and "cool" masculinity in order to resist racial oppression. Gay male athletes sometimes construct and draw on an "ironic" masculinity in order to resist sexual oppression. In other words, poor, black, and gay men have often found sport to be an arena in which they can build a masculinity that is, in some ways, resistant to the oppressions they face within hierarchies of intermale dominance.

But how real is the challenge these resistant masculinities pose to the role that sport has historically played in perpetuating existing differences and inequalities? A feminist perspective reveals the limited extent to which we can interpret black and gay athletic masculinities as liberating. Through a feminist lens, we can see that in adopting as their expressive vehicle many of the dominant aspects of athletic masculinity (narrow definitions of public success; aggressive, sometimes violent competition; glorification of the athletic male body-as-machine; verbal misogyny and homophobia), poor, black, and gay male athletes contribute to the continued subordination of women, as well as to the circumscription of their own relationships and development.

Tim Carrigan, Bob Connell, and John Lee assert that rather than under-

---

[12]B. Pronger, "Gay Jocks: A Phenomenology of Gay Men in Athletics," in Messner and Sabo, *Sport, Men, and the Gender Order,* pp. 141–152; and *The Arena of Masculinity: Sports, Homosexuality, and the Meaning of Sex* (New York: St. Martin's Press, 1990).

mining social inequality, men's struggles within class, racial, and sexual hierarchies of intermale dominance serve to reinforce men's global subordination of women. Although strains caused by differences and inequalities among men represent potential avenues for social change, ultimately, "the fissuring of the categories 'men' and 'women' is one of the central facts about a patriarchal power and the way it works. In the case of men, the crucial division is between hegemonic masculinity and various subordinated masculinities."[13] Hegemonic masculinity is thus defined in relation to various subordinated masculinities as well as in relation to femininities. This is a key insight for the contemporary meaning of sport. Utilizing the concept of "multiple masculinities," we can begin to understand how race, class, age, and sexual hierarchies among men help to construct and legitimize men's overall power and privilege over women. In addition, the false promise of sharing in the fruits of hegemonic masculinity often ties black, working-class, or gay men into their marginalized and subordinate status. For instance, my research suggests that while black men's development of "cool pose" within sport can be interpreted as creative resistance against one form of social domination (racism), it also demonstrates the limits of an agency that adopts other forms of social domination (athletic masculinity) as its vehicle.

My research also suggests how homophobia within athletic masculine cultures tends to lock men — whether gay or not — into narrowly defined heterosexual identities and relationships. Within the athletic context, homophobia is closely linked with misogyny in ways that ultimately serve to bond men together as superior to women. Given the extremely oppressive levels of homophobia within organized sport, it is understandable why the vast majority of gay male athletes would decide to remain closeted. But the public construction of a heterosexual/masculine status requires that a closeted gay athlete actively participate in (or at the very least, tolerate) the ongoing group expressions of homophobia and misogyny — what Mike T. called "locker room garbage." Thus, though he may feel a sense of irony, and may even confidentially express that sense of irony to gay male friends or to researchers, the public face that the closeted gay male athlete presents to the world is really no different from that of his nongay teammates. As long as he is successful in this public presentation-of-self as heterosexual/masculine, he will continue to contribute to (and benefit from) men's power over women.

SPORT IN GAY COMMUNITIES

The fissuring of the category "men," then, as it is played out within the dominant institution of sport, does little to threaten — indeed, may be a central mechanism in — the reconstruction of existing class, racial, sexual, and gen-

[13]T. Carrigan, B. Connell, and J. Lee, "Hard and Heavy: Toward a New Sociology of Masculinity," *Theory and Society* 14 (1985): 551–603.

der inequalities.[14] Nevertheless, since the outset of the gay liberation movement in the early 1970s, organized sport has become an integral part of developing gay and lesbian communities. The ways that "gay" sports have been
defined and organized are sometimes different — even radically different —
than the dominant institution of sport in society.

The most public sign of the growing interest in athletics in gay communities was the rapid growth and popularity of bodybuilding among many young,
urban gay men in the 1970s and early 1980s. The meanings of gay male
bodybuilding are multiple and contradictory.[15] On the one hand, gay male
bodybuilding overtly eroticizes the muscular male body, thus potentially dis-
rupting the tendency of sport to eroticize male bodies under the guise of aggression and competition. On the other hand, the building of muscular bodies
is often motivated by a conscious need by gay men to prove to the world that
they are "real men." Gay bodybuilding thus undermines cultural stereotypes
of homosexual men as "nelly," effeminate, and womanlike. But it also tends
to adopt and promote a very conventional equation of masculinity with
physical strength and muscularity.[16] In effect, then, as gay bodybuilders attempt to sever the cultural link between masculinity and heterosexuality, they
uncritically affirm a conventional dichotomization of masculinity/male vs.
femininity/female.

By contrast, some gay athletes have initiated alternative athletic institutions that aim to challenge conventional views of sexuality and gender. Origi-

[14]One potentially important, but largely unexplored, fissure among men is that between
athletes and nonathletes. There are tens of millions of boys who do *not* pursue athletic careers.
Many boys dislike sport. Others may yearn to be athletes, but may not have the body size,
strength, physical capabilities, coordination, emotional predisposition, or health that is necessary to successfully compete in sports. What happens to these boys and young men? What
kinds of adult masculine identities and relationships do they eventually develop? Does the fact
of not having been an athlete play any significant role in their masculine identities, goals, self-
images, and relationships? The answers to these questions, of course, lie outside the purview
of my study. But they are key to understanding the contemporary role that sport plays in constructions of gender.

[15]For interesting discussions of bodybuilding, gender, and sexuality, see B. Glassner, *Bodies: Why We Look the Way We Do (and How We Feel about It)* (New York: G. P. Putnam's Sons,
1988); A. M. Klein, "Little Big Man: Hustling, Gender Narcissism, and Homophobia in Bodybuilding," in Messner and Sabo, *Sport, Men, and the Gender Order,* pp. 127–140.

[16]Alan Klein's research revealed that nongay male bodybuilders are also commonly motivated by a need to make a public statement with their muscular bodies that they are indeed
"masculine." To the nongay bodybuilder, muscles are the ultimate sign of heterosexual masculinity. But, ironically, as one nongay male bodybuilder put it, "We're everything the U.S. is
supposed to stand for: strength, determination, everything to be admired. But it's not the girls
that like us, it's the fags!" Interestingly, Klein found that many male bodybuilders who defined
themselves as "straight" (including the one quoted above) made a living by prostituting themselves to gay men. See Klein, "Little Big Man," p. 135.

For a thought-provoking feminist analysis of the contradictory relationship between gay
male sexuality and masculinity, see T. Edwards, "Beyond Sex and Gender: Masculinity, Homosexuality, and Social Theory, in J. Hearn and D. Morgan, eds., *Men, Masculinities, and Social
Theory* (London: Unwin Hyman, 1990), pp. 110–123.

nally Mike T. had gone into sport to prove that he was "male," and cover up the fact that he was gay. When his career as an Olympic athlete finally ended, he came out publicly, and soon was a very active member of the San Francisco Bay Area gay community. He rekindled his interest in the arts and dance. He also remained very active in athletics, and he increasingly imagined how wonderful it would be to blend the beauty and exhilaration of sport, as he had experienced it, with the emergent, liberating values of the feminist, gay, and lesbian communities of which he was a part. In 1982, his dream became a reality, as 1,300 athletes from twelve different nations gathered in San Francisco to participate in the first ever Gay Games.[17]

Though many of the events in the Gay Games are "conventional" sports (track and field, swimming, etc.), and a number of "serious athletes" compete in the events, overall the Games reflect a value system and a vision based on feminist and gay liberationist ideals of equality and universal participation. As Mike T. said,

> You don't win by beating someone else. We defined winning as doing your very best. That way, everyone is a winner. And we have age-group competition, so all ages are involved. We have parity: If there's a men's sport, there's a women's sport to complement it. And we go out and recruit in Third World and minority areas. All of these people are gonna get together for a week, they're gonna march in together, they're gonna hold hands, and they'll say, "Jesus Christ! This is wonderful!" There's this *discovery*: "I had no idea women were such fun!" and, "God! Blacks are okay — I didn't do anything to offend him, and we became *friends*!" and, "God, that guy over there is in his sixties, and I had no *idea* they were so sexually *active*!" — [laughs].

This emphasis on bridging differences, overcoming prejudices, and building relationships definitely enhanced the athletic experience for one participant I interviewed. This man said that he loved to swim, and even loved to compete, because it "pushed" him to swim "a whole lot better." Yet in past competitions, he had always come in last place. As he put it, "The Gay Games were just wonderful in many respects. One of them was that people who came in second, or third, and *last* got standing ovations from the crowd — the crowd genuinely recognized the thrill of giving a damn good shot, regardless of where you came in, and gave support to that. Among the competitors, there was a whole lot of joking and supportiveness."

---

[17]The Gay Games were originally called the "Gay Olympics," but the U.S. Olympic Committee went to court to see that the word "Olympics" was not used to denote this event. Despite the existence of "Police Olympics," "Special Olympics," "Senior Olympics," "Xerox Olympics," "Armenian Olympics," even "Crab Cooking Olympics," the U.S.O.C. chose to enforce their control legally over the term "Olympics" when it came to the "Gay Olympics." For further discussion of the politics of the Gay Games, see M. A. Messner, "Gay Athletes and the Gay Games: An Interview with Tom Waddell," *M: Gentle Men for Gender Justice* 13 (1984): 13–14.

In 1986, 3,482 athletes participated in Gay Games II in San Francisco. In 1990, at Gay Games III in Vancouver, 7,200 athletes continued the vision of building, partly through sport, an "exemplary community" that eliminates sexism, homophobia, and racism. Mike T. described what the Gay Games mean to him:

> To me, it's one of those steps in a thousand-mile journey to try and raise consciousness and enlighten people — *not* just people outside the gay community, but within the gay community as well, [because] we're just as racist, ageist, nationalistic, and chauvinistic as anybody else. Maybe it's simplistic to some people, you know, but why does it have to be complicated? Put people in a position where they can experience this process of discovery, and here it is! I just hope that this is something that'll take hold and a lot of people will get the idea.

The Gay Games represent a radical break from past and current conceptions of the role of sport in society. But they do not represent a major challenge to sport as an institution. Alternative athletic venues like the Gay Games, since they exist outside of the dominant sports institution, do not directly confront or change the dominant structure. On the other hand, these experiments are valuable in terms of demonstrating the fact that alternative value systems and structures are possible.[18]

READING THE TEXT

1. Why, in Messner's view, did conservatives such as George Gilder and John Carroll want to prohibit women from competing in athletic competitions?

2. What does Messner mean when he says that "sports is a social institution that . . . was created by and for men" (para. 3)?

3. What roles do class, race, and sexual orientation play in the construction of athletic masculinity, according to Messner?

4. In what ways, according to Messner, do the Gay Games differ from the Olympic Games?

---

[18]During the 1982 Gay Games in San Francisco, the major local newspapers tended to cover the Games mostly in the "lifestyle" sections of the paper, not in the sports pages. Alternative sports demonstrate the difficulties of attempting to change sport in the absence of larger institutional transformations. For instance, the European sport of korfball was developed explicitly as a sex-egalitarian sport. The rules of korfball aim to neutralize male-female biological differences that may translate into different levels of ability. But recent research shows that old patterns show up, even among the relatively "enlightened" korfball players. Korfball league officials are more likely to be male than female. More important, the more "key" roles within the game appear to be dominated by men, while women are partially marginalized. See D. Summerfield and A. White, "Korfball: A Model of Egalitarianism?" *Sociology of Sport Journal* 6 (1989): 144–151.

READING THE SIGNS

1. In your journal, explore what athletic participation, whether in organized sports such as Little League or in informal activities such as jogging or hiking, has meant to you. Do you believe that the participation has shaped your attitudes about gender roles? If you haven't participated much in sports, what is your attitude toward athletic competition?

2. Write an argumentative essay challenging or supporting George Gilder's position that the female athlete "reduces the game from a religious male rite to a mere physical exercise, with some treacherous danger of psychic effect" (para. 1).

3. In class, outline the racial and gender coding of professional sports. Which ethnicities dominate which sports? In which sports, if any, have women received social acceptance? Then discuss the reasons for the ethnic and gender patterns you have found.

4. Study a magazine such as *Sports Illustrated,* and write an essay in which you explain the extent to which the magazine perpetuates the traditional attitudes toward gender roles that Messner claims sports encourage.

5. In class, form mixed-gender teams and debate Messner's contention that sports encourage homophobia and misogyny. To develop your ideas, consult Mariah Burton Nelson's "I Won. I'm Sorry." (below) and Henry Jenkins's "'Never Trust a Snake': WWF Wrestling as Masculine Melodrama" (p. 688).

MARIAH BURTON NELSON
I WON. I'M SORRY.

Athletic competition, when you come right down to it, is about winning, which is no problem for men, whose gender codes tell them that aggression and domination are admirable male traits. But "how can you win, if you're female?" Mariah Burton asks, when the same gender codes insist that women must be "feminine," "not aggressive, not victorious." And so women athletes, even when they do win, go out of their way to signal their femininity by dolling themselves up and smiling a lot. Beauty and vulnerability seem to be as important to today's female athlete as brawn and gold medals, Nelson complains, paradoxically contradicting the apparent feminist gains that women athletes have made in recent years. Nelson is a former Stanford University and professional basketball player and is author of four books, including Embracing Victory *(1998) and* The Unburdened Heart *(2000).*

When Sylvia Plath's husband, Ted Hughes, published his first book of poems, Sylvia wrote to her mother: "I am so happy that HIS book is accepted FIRST. It will make it so much easier for me when mine is accepted. . . . "

After Sylvia killed herself, her mother published a collection of Sylvia's letters. In her explanatory notes, Aurelia Plath commented that from the time she was very young, Sylvia "catered to the male of any age so as to bolster his sense of superiority." In seventh grade, Aurelia Plath noted, Sylvia was pleased to finish second in a spelling contest. "It was nicer, she felt, to have a boy first."

How many women still collude in the myth of male superiority, believing it's "nicer" when boys and men finish first? How many of us achieve but only in a lesser, smaller, feminine way, a manner consciously or unconsciously designed to be as nonthreatening as possible?

Since I'm tall, women often talk to me about height. Short women tell me, "I've always wanted to be tall — but not as tall as you!" I find this amusing, but also curious. Why not? Why not be six-two?

Tall women tell me that they won't wear heels because they don't want to appear taller than their husbands or boyfriends, even by an inch. What are these women telling me — and their male companions? Why do women regulate their height in relation to men's height? Why is it still rare to see a woman who is taller than her husband? 5

Women want to be tall enough to feel elegant and attractive, like models. They want to feel respected and looked up to. But they don't want to be so tall that their height threatens men. They want to win — to achieve, to reach new heights — but without exceeding male heights.

How can you win, if you're female? Can you just do it? No. You have to play the femininity game. Femininity by definition is not large, not imposing, not competitive. Feminine women are not ruthless, not aggressive, not victorious. It's not feminine to have a killer instinct, to want with all your heart and soul to win — neither tennis matches nor elected office nor feminist victories such as abortion rights. It's not feminine to know exactly what you want, then go for it.

Femininity is about appearing beautiful and vulnerable and small. It's about winning male approval.

One downhill skier who asked not to be identified told me the following story: "I love male approval. Most women skiers do. We talk about it often. There's only one thing more satisfying than one of the top male skiers saying, 'Wow, you are a great skier. You rip. You're awesome.'

"But it's so fun leaving 99 percent of the world's guys in the dust — oops," she laughs. "I try not to gloat. I've learned something: If I kick guys' butts and lord it over them, they don't like me. If, however, I kick guys' butts then act 'like a girl,' there is no problem. And I do mean girl, not woman. Nonthreatening." 10

Femininity is also about accommodating men, allowing them to feel bigger than and stronger than and superior to women; not emasculated by them.

Femininity is unhealthy, obviously. It would be unhealthy for men to act passive, dainty, obsessed with their physical appearance, and dedicated to bolstering the sense of superiority in the other gender, so it's unhealthy for women too. These days, some women are redefining femininity as strong, as athletic, as however a female happens to be, so that "feminine" becomes synonymous with "female." Other women reject both feminine and masculine terms and stereotypes, selecting from the entire range of human behaviors instead of limiting themselves to the "gender-appropriate" ones. These women smile only when they're happy, act angry when they're angry, dress how they want to. They cling to their self-respect and dignity like a life raft.

But most female winners play the femininity game to some extent, using femininity as a defense, a shield against accusations such as bitch, man-hater, lesbian. Feminine behavior and attire mitigate against the affront of female

Serena Williams at Wimbledon.

victory, soften the hard edges of winning. Women who want to win without losing male approval temper their victories with beauty, with softness, with smallness, with smiles.

In the fifties, at each of the Amateur Athletic Union's women's basketball championships, one of the players was crowned a beauty queen. (This still happens at Russian women's ice hockey tournaments.) Athletes in the All-American Girls Baseball League of the forties and fifties slid into base wearing skirts. In 1979, professional basketball players with the California Dreams were sent to John Robert Powers' charm school. Ed Temple, the legendary coach of the Tennessee State Tigerbelles, the team that produced Wilma Rudolph, Wyomia Tyus, Willye White, Madeline Manning, and countless other champions, enforced a dress code and stressed that his athletes should be "young ladies first, track girls second."

Makeup, jewelry, dress, and demeanor were often dictated by the male coaches and owners in these leagues, but to some extent the players played along, understanding the tradeoff: in order to be "allowed" to compete, they had to demonstrate that they were, despite their "masculine" strivings, real ("feminine") women.   15

Today, both men and women wear earrings, notes Felshin, "but the media is still selling heterosexism and 'feminine' beauty. And if you listen carefully, in almost every interview" female athletes still express apologetic behavior through feminine dress, behavior, and values.

Florence Griffith-Joyner, Gail Devers, and other track stars of this modern era dedicate considerable attention to portraying a feminine appearance. Basketball star Lisa Leslie has received more attention for being a model than for leading the Americans to Olympic victory. Steffi Graf posed in bikinis for the 1997 *Sports Illustrated* swimsuit issue. In a Sears commercial, Olympic basketball players apply lipstick, paint their toenails, rock babies, lounge in bed, and pose and dance in their underwear. Lisa Leslie says, "Everybody's allowed to be themselves. Me, for example, I'm very feminine."

In an Avon commercial, Jackie Joyner Kersee is shown running on a beach while the camera lingers on her buttocks and breasts. She tells us that she can bench-press 150 pounds and brags that she can jump farther than "all but 128 men." Then she says: "And I have red toenails." Words flash on the screen: "Just another Avon lady." Graf, Mary Pierce, Monica Seles, and Mary Jo Fernandez have all played in dresses. They are "so much more comfortable" than skirts, Fernandez explained. "You don't have to worry about the shirt coming up or the skirt being too tight. It's cooler, and it's so feminine."

"When I put on a dress I feel different — more feminine, more elegant, more ladylike — and that's nice," added Australia's Nicole Bradtke: "We're in a sport where we're throwing ourselves around, so it's a real asset to the game to be able to look pretty at the same time."

Athletes have become gorgeous, flirtatious, elegant, angelic, darling — and   20 the skating commentators' favorite term: "vulnerable." Some think this is good news: proof that femininity and sports are compatible. "There doesn't have to be such a complete division between 'You're beautiful and sexy' and 'you're athletic and strong,'" says Linda Hanley, a pro beach volleyball player who also appeared in a bikini in the 1997 *Sports Illustrated* swimsuit issue.

Athletes and advertisers reassure viewers that women who compete are still willing to play the femininity game, to be cheerleaders. Don't worry about us, the commercials imply. We're winners but we'll still look pretty for you. We're acting in ways that only men used to act but we'll still act how you want women to act. We're not threatening. We're not lesbians. We're not ugly, not bad marriage material. We're strong but feminine. Linguists note that the word "but" negates the part of the sentence that precedes it.

There are some recent examples of the media emphasizing female power in an unambiguous way. "Women Muscle In," the *New York Times Magazine* proclaimed in a headline. The *Washington Post* wrote, "At Olympics, Women Show Their Strength." And a new genre of commercials protests that female athletes are NOT cheerleaders, and don't have to be. Olympic and pro basketball star Dawn Staley says in a Nike commercial that she plays basketball "for the competitiveness" of it. "I need some place to release it. It just builds up, and sports is a great outlet for it. I started out playing with the guys. I wasn't always accepted. You get criticized, like: 'You need to be in the kitchen. Go put on a skirt.' I just got mad and angry and went out to show them that I belong here as much as they do."

Other commercials tell us that women can compete like conquerors. A Nike ad called "Wolves" shows girls leaping and spiking volleyballs while a voice says, "They are not sisters. They are not classmates. They are not friends. They are not even the girls' team. They are a pack of wolves. Tend to your sheep." Though the athletes look serious, the message sounds absurd. When I show this commercial to audiences, they laugh. Still, the images do depict the power of the volleyball players: their intensity, their ability to pound the ball almost through the floor. The script gives the players (and viewers) permission not to be ladylike, not to worry about whether their toenails are red.

But in an American Basketball League commercial, the Philadelphia Rage's female basketball players are playing rough; their bodies collide. Maurice Chevalier sings, "Thank heaven for little girls." The tag line: "Thank heaven, they're on our side."

Doesn't all this talk about girls and ladies simply focus our attention on femaleness, femininity, and ladylike behavior? The lady issue is always there in the equation: something to redefine, to rebel against. It's always present, like sneakers, so every time you hear the word athlete you also hear the word lady — or feminine, or unfeminine. It reminds me of a beer magazine ad from the eighties that featured a photo of Olympic track star Valerie Brisco-Hooks. "Funny, she doesn't look like the weaker sex," said the print. You could see her impressive muscles. Clearly the intent of the ad was to contrast an old stereotype with the reality of female strength and ability. But Brisco-Hooks was seated, her legs twisted pretzel style, arms covering her chest. But in that position, Brisco-Hooks didn't look very strong or able. In the line, "Funny, she doesn't look like the weaker sex," the most eye-catching words are funny, look, weaker, and sex. Looking at the pretzel that is Valerie, you begin to think that she looks funny. You think about weakness. And you think about sex.

When she was young, Nancy Kerrigan wanted to play ice hockey with her older brothers. Her mother told her, "You're a girl. Do girl things."

Figure skating is a girl thing. Athletes in sequins and "sheer illusion sleeves" glide and dance, their tiny skirts flapping in the breeze. They achieve, but without touching or pushing anyone else. They win, but without visible signs of sweat. They compete, but not directly. Their success is measured not by confrontation with an opponent, nor even by a clock or a scoreboard. Rather, they are judged as beauty contestants are judged: by a panel of people who interpret the success of the routines. Prettiness is mandatory. Petite and groomed and gracious, figure skaters — like cheerleaders, gymnasts, and aerobic dancers — camouflage their competitiveness with niceness and prettiness until it no longer seems male or aggressive or unseemly.

The most popular sport for high school and college women is basketball. More than a million fans shelled out an average of $15 per ticket in 1997, the inaugural summer of the Women's National Basketball Association. But the most televised women's sport is figure skating. In 1995 revenue from skating shows and competitions topped six hundred million dollars. In the seven months between October 1996 and March 1997, ABC, CBS, NBC, Fox, ESPN, TBS, and USA dedicated 162.5 hours of programming to figure skating, half of it in prime time. Kerrigan earns up to three hundred thousand dollars for a single performance.

Nearly 75 percent of the viewers of televised skating are women. The average age is between twenty-five and forty-five years old, with a household income of more than fifty thousand dollars. What are these women watching? What are they seeing? What's the appeal?

Like golf, tennis, and gymnastics, figure skating is an individual sport favored by white people from the upper classes. The skaters wear cosmetics, frozen smiles, and revealing dresses. Behind the scenes they lift weights and sweat like any serious athlete but figure skating seems more dance than sport, more grace than guts, more art than athleticism. Figure skating allows women to compete like champions while dressed like cheerleaders.

In women's figure skating, smiling is part of "artistic expression." In the final round, if the competitors are of equal merit, artistry weighs more heavily than technique. Midori Ito, the best jumper in the history of women's skating, explained a weak showing at the 1995 world championships this way: "I wasn't 100 percent satisfied. . . . I probably wasn't smiling enough."

The media portray female figure skaters as "little girl dancers" or "fairy tale princesses" (NBC commentator John Tesh); as "elegant" (Dick Button); as "little angels" (Peggy Fleming); as "ice beauties" and "ladies who lutz" (*People* magazine). Commentators frame skaters as small, young, and decorative creatures, not superwomen but fairy-tale figments of someone's imagination.

After Kerrigan was assaulted by a member of Tonya Harding's entourage, she was featured on a *Sports Illustrated* cover crying "Why me?" When she recovered to win a silver medal at the Olympics that year, she became "America's sweetheart" and rich to boot. But the princess turned pumpkin shortly after midnight, as soon as the ball was over and she stopped smiling and started speaking. Growing impatient during the Olympic medal ceremony while everyone waited for Baiul, Kerrigan grumbled, "Oh, give me a break, she's just going to cry out there again. What's the difference?"

What were Kerrigan's crimes? She felt too old to cavort with cartoon characters. Isn't she? She expressed anger and disappointment — even bitterness and bad sportsmanship — about losing the gold. But wasn't she supposed to want to win? What happens to baseball players who, disappointed about a loss, hit each other or spit on umpires? What happens to basketball players and football players and hockey players who fight? Men can't tumble from a princess palace because we don't expect them to be princesses in the first place, only athletes.

Americans fell out of love with Kerrigan not because they couldn't adore   35
an athlete who lacked grace in defeat, but because they couldn't adore a female athlete who lacked grace in defeat.

Female politicians, lawyers, and businesswomen of all ethnic groups also play the femininity game. Like tennis players in short dresses, working women seem to believe it's an asset to look pretty (but not too pretty) while throwing themselves around. The female apologetic is alive and well in corporate board rooms, where women say "I'm sorry, maybe someone else already stated this idea, but . . . " and smile while they say it.

When Newt Gingrich's mother revealed on television that Newt had referred to Hillary Clinton as a bitch, how did Hillary respond? She donned a pink suit and met with female reporters to ask how she could "soften her image." She seemed to think that her competitiveness was the problem and femininity the solution.

So if you want to be a winner and you're female, you'll feel pressured to play by special, female rules. Like men, you'll have to be smart and industrious, but in addition you'll have to be "like women": kind, nurturing, accommodating, nonthreatening, placating, pretty, and small. You'll have to smile. And not act angry. And wear skirts. Nail polish and makeup help, too.

READING THE TEXT

1. Nelson begins her article by relating an anecdote about poet Sylvia Plath. How does this opening frame her argument about women in sports?

2. What is the "femininity game" (para. 7), according to Nelson?

3. How do the media contribute to the perpetuation of the femininity game?

4. What sports are coded as "feminine," according to Nelson, and why?

READING THE SIGNS

1. Watch a women's sports event on television, such as an LPGA match, analyzing the behavior and appearance of the athletes. Use your observations as evidence in an essay in which you assess the extent to which Nelson's claims about the femininity game are valid.

2. If you are a female athlete, write a journal entry discussing whether you are pressured to act feminine and your responses to that pressure. If you are not a female athlete, reflect on the behavior and appearance of women athletes on your campus. Do you see signs that they are affected by the femininity game?

3. Obtain a copy of a magazine that focuses on women's sports, such as *Sports Illustrated Woman*. Analyze the articles and ads in the magazine, noting models' and athletes' clothing, physical appearance, and speech patterns. Using Nelson's argument as a critical framework, write an essay in which you analyze the extent to which the magazine perpetuates traditional gender codes.

4. Write an argumentative essay that supports, refutes, or complicates the proposition that sports dictate heterosexual gender norms for both men and women athletes. To develop your ideas, consult Michael A. Messner's "Power at Play: Sport and Gender Relations" (p. 668) and Henry Jenkins's "'Never Trust a Snake': WWF Wrestling as Masculine Melodrama" (p. 688).

5. Interview women athletes at your campus and ask them about the extent to which they are pressured by the femininity game. Have they been accused of being lesbians or bitches simply because they are athletes? Do they feel pressure to be physically attractive or charming? Do you see any correlation between an athlete's sport and her responses? Use your observations as the basis of an argument about the influence of traditional gender codes on women's sports at your school.

Two Girls Playing Golf, 1903

◀ **READING THE SIGNS**

1. Imagine that the image on page 687 is an argument. To whom is it aimed? What claims does it make? What is the significance of the letters U and P?

2. This image was first produced in 1903. What has changed in women's golf since then, based on your analysis of this image and your knowledge of golf today?

HENRY JENKINS

"Never Trust a Snake": WWF Wrestling as Masculine Melodrama

When Big Boss Man goes up against Repo Man, he is not only filling a slot in the World Wrestling Federation lineup: He's providing cathartic relief for every working-class Joe who's ever had his truck repossessed, Henry Jenkins (b. 1958) suggests in this social analysis of the WWF. Falling further and further behind in a postindustrial economy, working-class men turn to professional wrestling for fantasies of empowerment. And the WWF gladly complies, offering elaborately staged "morality plays" that can make a man feel like, well, a man *again in a world in which physical might always makes right. Think of it as a muscle-bound soap opera. The director of the Comparative Media Studies Program at MIT, Jenkins is the editor of* The Children's Culture Reader *(1998) and the coeditor of* Classical Hollywood Comedy *(with Kristine B. Karnick, 1994),* Science Fiction Audiences: Doctor Who, Star Trek and Their Followers *(with John Tulloch, 1995), and* From Barbie to Mortal Kombat: Gender and Computer Games *(with Justine Cassell, 1998).*

See, your problem is that you're looking at this as a *wrestling* battle — two guys getting into the ring together to see who's the better athlete. But it goes so much deeper than that. Yes, wrestling's involved. Yes, we're going to pound each other's flesh, slam each other's bodies and hurt each other really bad. But there's more at stake than just wrestling, my man. There's a morality play. Randy Savage thinks he represents the light of righteousness. But, you know, it takes an awful lot of light to illuminate a dark kingdom.

—JAKE "THE SNAKE" ROBERTS[1]

[1]"WWF Interview: A Talk with Jake 'the Snake' Roberts," *WWF Magazine,* February 1992, p. 17.

> There are people who think that wrestling is an ignoble sport. Wrestling is not a sport, it is a spectacle, and it is no more ignoble to attend a wrestled performance of Suffering than a performance of the sorrows of Arnolphe or Andromaque.
>
> — ROLAND BARTHES[2]

Like World Wrestling Federation superstar Jake "the Snake" Roberts, Roland Barthes saw wrestling as a "morality play," a curious hybrid of sports and theater. For Barthes, wrestling was at once a "spectacle of excess," evoking the pleasure of grandiloquent gestures and violent contact, and a lower form of tragedy, where issues of morality, ethics, and politics were staged. Wrestling enthusiasts have no interest in seeing a fair fight but rather hope for a satisfying restaging of the ageless struggle between the "perfect bastard" and the suffering hero.[3] What wrestling offers its spectators, Barthes tells us, is a story of treachery and revenge, "the intolerable spectacle of powerlessness" and the exhilaration of the hero's victorious return from near-collapse. Wrestling, like conventional melodrama, externalizes emotion, mapping it onto the combatants' bodies and transforming their physical competition into a search for a moral order. Restraint or subtlety has little place in such a world. Everything that matters must be displayed, publicly, unambiguously, and mercilessly.

Barthes's account focuses entirely upon the one-on-one match as an isolated event within which each gesture must be instantly legible apart from any larger context of expectations and associations: "One must always understand everything on the spot."[4] Barthes could not have predicted how this focus upon the discrete event or the isolated gesture would be transformed through the narrative mechanisms of television. On television, where wrestling comes with a cast of continuing characters, no single match is self-enclosed; rather, personal conflicts unfold across a number of fights, interviews, and enacted encounters. Television wrestling offers its viewers complexly plotted, ongoing narratives of professional ambition, personal suffering, friendship and alliance, betrayal and reversal of fortune. Matches still offer their share of acrobatic spectacle, snake handling, fire eating, and colorful costumes. They are, as such, immediately accessible to the casual viewer, yet they reward the informed spectator for whom each body slam and double-arm suplex bears specific narrative consequences. A demand for closure is satisfied at the level of individual events, but those matches are always contained within a larger narrative trajectory which is itself fluid and open.

The WWF broadcast provides us with multiple sources of identification,

[2]Roland Barthes, "The World of Wrestling," in Susan Sontag, ed., *A Barthes Reader* (New York: Hill and Wang, 1982), p. 23.

[3]Ibid., p. 25.

[4]Ibid., p. 29.

multiple protagonists locked in their own moral struggles against the forces of evil. The proliferation of champion titles — the WWF World Champion belt, the Million Dollar belt, the Tag Team champion belt, the Intercontinental champion belt — allows for multiple lines of narrative development, each centering around its own cluster of affiliations and antagonisms. The resolution of one title competition at a major event does little to stabilize the program universe, since there are always more belts to be won and lost, and in any case, each match can always be followed by a rematch which reopens old issues. Outcomes may be inconclusive because of count-outs or disqualifications, requiring future rematches. Accidents may result in surprising shifts in moral and paradigmatic alignment. Good guys betray their comrades and form uneasy alliances with the forces of evil; rule-breakers undergo redemption after suffering crushing defeats.

The economic rationale for this constant "buildup" and deferral of narrative interests is obvious. The World Wrestling Federation (WWF) knows how to use its five weekly television series and its glossy monthly magazine to ensure subscription to its four annual pay-per-view events and occasional pay-per-view specials.[5] Enigmas are raised during the free broadcasts which will be resolved only for a paying audience. Much of the weekly broadcast consists of interviews with the wrestlers about their forthcoming bouts, staged scenes providing background on their antagonisms, and in-the-ring encounters between WWF stars and sparring partners which provide a backdrop for speculations about forthcoming plot developments. Read cynically, the broadcast consists purely of commercial exploitation. Yet this promotion also has important aesthetic consequences, heightening the melodramatic dimensions of the staged fights and transforming televised wrestling into a form of serial fiction for men. . . .

Playing with Our Feelings

Norbert Elias and Eric Dunning's pathbreaking study *The Quest for Excitement: Sport and Leisure in the Civilizing Process* invites us to reconsider the affective dimensions of athletic competition. According to their account, modern civilization demands restraint on instinctive and affective experience, a process of repression and sublimation which they call the "civilizing process." Elias has spent much of his intellectual life tracing the gradual process by which Western civilization has intensified its demands for bodily and emotional control, rejecting the emotional volatility and bodily abandon that characterized Europe during the Middle Ages:

[5]For useful background on the historical development of television wrestling, as well as for an alternative reading of its narrative structures, see Michael R. Ball, *Professional Wrestling as Ritual Drama in American Popular Culture* (Lewiston: Edwin Mellen Press, 1990). For a performance-centered account of WWF Wrestling, see Sharon Mazer, "The Doggie Doggie World of Professional Wrestling," *The Drama Review,* Winter 1990, pp. 96–122.

> Social survival and success in these [contemporary] societies depend . . .
> on a reliable armour, not too strong and not too weak, of individual self-
> restraint. In such societies, there is only a comparatively limited scope for
> the show of strong feelings, of strong antipathies towards and dislike of
> other people, let alone of hot anger, wild hatred or the urge to hit someone
> over the head.[6]

Such feelings do not disappear, but they are contained by social expectations:

> To see grown-up men and women shaken by tears and abandon them-
> selves to their bitter sorrow in public . . . or beat each other savagely under
> the impact of their violent excitement [experiences more common during
> the Middle Ages] has ceased to be regarded as normal. It is usually a mat-
> ter of embarrassment for the onlooker and often a matter of shame or re-
> gret for those who have allowed themselves to be carried away by their ex-
> citement.[7]

What is at stake here is not the intensity of feeling but our discomfort about
its spectacular display. Emotion may be strongly felt, but it must be rendered
invisible, private, personal; emotion must not be allowed to have a decisive
impact upon social interactions. Emotional openness is read as a sign of vulnerability, while emotional restraint is the marker of social integration. Leaders are to master emotions rather than to be mastered by them. Yet, as Elias
writes, "We do not stop feeling. We only prevent or delay our acting in accordance with it."[8] Elias traces the process by which this emotional control has
moved from being outwardly imposed by rules of conduct to an internalized
and largely unconscious aspect of our personalities. The totality of this restraint exacts its own social costs, creating psychic tensions which somehow
must be redirected and released within socially approved limitations.

Sports, he argues, constitute one of many institutions which society
creates for the production and expression of affective excitement.[9] Sports
must somehow reconcile two contradictory functions — "the pleasurable de-
controlling of human feelings, the full evocation of an enjoyable excitement
on the one hand and on the other the maintenance of a set of checks to keep
the pleasantly de-controlled emotions under control."[10] These two functions
are never fully resolved, resulting in occasional hooliganism as excitement
outstrips social control. Yet the conventionality of sports and the removal of
the real-world consequences of physical combat (in short, sport's status as
adult play) facilitate a controlled and sanctioned release from ordinary affective restraints. The ability to resolve conflicts through a prespecified moment

---

[6]Norbert Elias and Eric Dunning, *The Quest for Excitement: Sport and Leisure in the Civilizing Process* (New York: Basil Blackwell, 1986), p. 41.

[7]Ibid., pp. 64–65.

[8]Ibid., p. 111.

[9]Ibid., p. 49.

[10]Ibid.

A curious hybrid of sports and theater.

of arbitrary closure delimits the spectator's emotional experience. Perhaps most important, sports offer a shared emotional experience, one which reasserts the desirability of belonging to a community.

Elias and Dunning are sensitive to the class implications of this argument: the "civilizing process" began at the center of "court society" with the aristocracy and spread outward to merchants wishing access to the realms of social and economic power and to the servants who must become unintrusive participants in their masters' lives. Elias and Dunning argue that these class distinctions still surface in the very different forms of emotional display tolerated at the legitimate theater (which provides an emotional outlet for bourgeois spectators) and the sports arena (which provides a space for working-class excitement): the theater audience is to "be moved without moving," to restrain emotional display until the conclusion, when it may be indicated through their applause; while for the sports audience, "motion and emotion are intimately linked," and emotional display is immediate and uncensored.[11] These

[11] Ibid., p. 50.

same distinctions separate upper-class sports (tennis, polo, golf) which allow minimal emotional expression from lower-class sports (boxing, wrestling, soccer) which demand more overt affective display. Of course, such spectacles also allow the possibility for upper- or middle-class patrons to "slum it," to adopt working-class attitudes and sensibilities while engaging with the earthy spectacle of the wrestling match. They can play at being working-class (with working-class norms experienced as a remasculinization of yuppie minds and bodies), can imagine themselves as down to earth, with the people, safe in the knowledge that they can go back to the office the next morning without too much embarrassment at what is a ritualized release of repressed emotions.

Oddly absent from their account is any acknowledgment of the gender-specificity of the rules governing emotional display. Social conventions have traditionally restricted the public expression of sorrow or affection by men and of anger or laughter by women. Men stereotypically learn to translate their softer feelings into physical aggressiveness, while women convert their rage into the shedding of tears. Such a culture provides gender-specific spaces for emotional release which are consistent with dominant constructions of masculinity and femininity — melodrama (and its various manifestations in soap opera or romance) for women, sports for men. Elias and Dunning's emphasis upon the affective dimensions of sports allows us to more accurately (albeit schematically) map the similarities and differences between sports and melodrama. Melodrama links female affect to domesticity, sentimentality, and vulnerability, while sports links male affect to physical prowess, competition, and mastery. Melodrama explores the concerns of the private sphere, sports those of the public. Melodrama announces its fictional status, while sports claims for itself the status of reality. Melodrama allows for the shedding of tears, while sports solicits shouts, cheers, and boos. Crying, a characteristically feminine form of emotional display, embodies internalized emotion; tears are quiet and passive. Shouting, the preferred outlet for male affect, embodies externalized emotion; it is aggressive and noisy. Women cry from a position of emotional (and often social) vulnerability; men shout from a position of physical and social strength (however illusory).

WWF wrestling, as a form which bridges the gap between sport and melodrama, allows for the spectacle of male physical prowess (a display which is greeted by shouts and boos) but also for the exploration of the emotional and moral life of its combatants. WWF wrestling focuses on both the public and the private, links nonfictional forms with fictional content, and embeds the competitive dimensions of sports within a larger narrative framework which emphasizes the personal consequences of that competition. The "sports entertainment" of WWF wrestling adopts the narrative and thematic structures implicit within traditional sports and heightens them to ensure the maximum emotional impact. At the same time, WWF wrestling adopts the personal, social, and moral conflicts that characterized nineteenth-century theatrical melodrama and enacts them in terms of physical combat between male athletes. In doing so, it foregrounds aspects of masculine mythology which have a particular significance for its predominantly working-class male audience — the experience of vulnerability, the possibilities of male trust and intimacy, and the populist myth of the national community. . . .

Might Makes Right

Within traditional sports, competition is impersonal, the product of pre- 10
scribed rules which assign competitors on the basis of their standings or on some prespecified form of rotation. Rivalries do, of course, arise within this system and are the stuff of the daily sports page, but many games do not carry this added affective significance. Within the WWF, however, all competition depends upon intense rivalry. Each fight requires the creation of a social and moral opposition and often stems from a personal grievance. Irwin R. Schyster (IRS) falsely accuses the Big Boss Man's mother of tax evasion and threatens to throw her in jail. Sid Justice betrays Hulk Hogan's friendship, turning his back on his tag team partner in the middle of a major match and allowing him to be beaten to a pulp by his opponents, Ric Flair and the Undertaker. Fisticuffs break out between Bret Hart and his brother, "Rocket," during a special "Family Feud" match which awakens long-simmering sibling rivalries. Such offenses require retribution within a world which sees trial by combat as the preferred means of resolving all disputes. Someone has to "pay" for these outrages, and the exacting of payment will occur in the squared ring.

The core myth of WWF wrestling is a fascistic one: ultimately, might makes right; moral authority is linked directly to the possession of physical strength, while evil operates through stealth or craftiness (mental rather than physical sources of power). The appeal of such a myth to a working-class audience should be obvious. In the realm of their everyday experience, strength often gets subordinated into alienated labor. Powerful bodies become the means of their economic exploitation rather than a resource for bettering their lot. In WWF wrestling, physical strength reemerges as a tool for personal empowerment, a means of striking back against personal and moral injustices. Valerie Walkerdine argues that the *Rocky* films, which display a similar appeal, offer "fantasies of omnipotence, heroism and salvation . . . a counterpoint to the experience of oppression and powerlessness."[12] Images of fighting, Walkerdine argues, embody "a class-specific and gendered use of the body," which ennobles the physical skills possessed by the working-class spectator: "Physical violence is presented as the only way open to those whose lot is manual and not intellectual labor. . . . The fantasy of the fighter is

[12]Valerie Walkerdine, "Video Replay: Families, Films and Fantasy," in Victor Burgin, James Donald, and Cora Kaplan, eds., *Formations of Fantasy* (London: Methuen, 1986), pp. 172–74.

the fantasy of a working-class male omnipotence over the forces of humiliating oppression which mutilate and break the body in manual labor."[13]

A central concern within wrestling, then, is how physical strength can ensure triumph over one's abusers, how one can rise from defeat and regain dignity through hand-to-hand combat. Bad guys cheat to win. They manipulate the system and step outside the rules. They use deception, misdirection, subterfuge, and trickery. Rarely do they win fairly. They smuggle weapons into the ring to attack their opponents while their managers distract the referees. They unwrap the turnbuckle pads and slam their foes' heads into metal posts. They adopt choke holds to suffocate them or zap them with cattle prods. Million Dollar Man purposefully focuses his force upon Roddy Piper's wounded knee, doing everything he can to injure him permanently. Such atrocities require rematches to ensure justice; the underdog heroes return next month and, through sheer determination and willpower, battle their antagonists into submission.

Such plots allow for the serialization of the WWF narrative, forestalling its resolution, intensifying its emotional impact. Yet at the same time, the individual match must be made narratively satisfying on its own terms, and so, in practice, such injustices do not stand. Even though the match is over and its official outcome determined, the hero shoves the referee aside and, with renewed energy, bests his opponent in a fair (if nonbonding) fight. Whatever the outcome, most fights end with the protagonist standing proudly in the center of the ring, while his badly beaten antagonist retreats shamefully to his dressing room. Justice triumphs both in the long run and in the short run. For the casual viewer, it is the immediate presentation of triumphant innocence that matters, that satisfactorily resolves the drama. Yet for the WWF fan, what matters is the ultimate pursuit of justice as it unfolds through the complexly intertwined stories of the many different wrestlers.

Body Doubles

Melodramatic wrestling allows working-class men to confront their own feelings of vulnerability, their own frustrations at a world which promises them patriarchal authority but which is experienced through relations of economic subordination. Gender identities are most rigidly policed in working-class male culture, since unable to act *as* men, they are forced to act *like* men, with a failure to assume the proper role the source of added humiliation. WWF wrestling offers a utopian alternative to this situation, allowing a movement from victimization toward mastery. Such a scenario requires both the creation and the constant rearticulation of moral distinctions. Morality is defined, first and foremost, through personal antagonisms. As Christine Gledhill has

[13]Ibid., p. 173.

written of traditional melodrama, "Innocence and villainy construct each other: while the villain is necessary to the production and revelation of innocence, innocence defines the boundaries of the forbidden which the villain breaks."[14] In the most aesthetically pleasing and emotionally gripping matches, these personal antagonisms reflect much deeper mythological oppositions — the struggles between rich and poor, white and black, urban and rural, America and the world. Each character stands for something, draws symbolic meaning by borrowing stereotypes already in broader circulation. An important role played by color commentary is to inscribe and reinscribe the basic mythic oppositions at play within a given match. Here, the moral dualism of masculine melodrama finds its voice through the exchanges between two announcers, one (Mean Jean Okerlund) articulating the protagonist's virtues, the other (Bobby "the Brain" Heenan) justifying the rule-breaker's transgressions.

Wrestlers are often cast as doppelgängers, similar yet morally opposite figures. Consider, for example, how *WWF Magazine* characterizes a contest between the evil Mountie and the heroic Big Boss Man: "In conflict are Big Boss Man's and the Mountie's personal philosophies: the enforcement of the law vs. taking the law into one's own hands, the nightstick vs. the cattle prod, weakening a foe with the spike slam vs. disabling him with the nerve-crushing carotid control technique."[15] The Canadian Mountie stands on one page, dressed in his bright red uniform, clutching his cattle prod and snarling. The former Georgia prison guard, Big Boss Man, stands on the other, dressed in his pale blue uniform, clutching an open pair of handcuffs, with a look of quiet earnestness. At this moment the two opponents seem to be made for each other, as if no other possible contest could bear so much meaning, though the Big Boss Man and the Mountie will pair off against other challengers in the next major event.

The most successful wrestlers are those who provoke immediate emotional commitments (either positive or negative) and are open to constant rearticulation, who can be fit into a number of different conflicts and retain semiotic value. Hulk Hogan may stand as the defender of freedom in his feud with Sgt. Slaughter, as innocence betrayed by an ambitious friend in his contest against Sid Justice, and as an aging athlete confronting and overcoming the threat of death in his battle with the Undertaker. Big Boss Man may defend the interests of the economically depressed against the Repo Man, make the streets safe from the Nasty Boys, and assert honest law enforcement in the face of the Mountie's bad example.

The introduction of new characters requires their careful integration into the WWF's moral universe before their first match can be fought. We need to

---

[14]Christine Gledhill, "The Melodramatic Field: An Investigation," in Christine Gledhill, ed., *Home Is Where the Heart Is: Studies in Melodrama and the Woman's Film* (London: BFI, 1987), p. 21.

[15]Keith Elliot Greenberg, "One Step Too Far: Boss Man and Mountie Clash over Meaning of Justice," *WWF Magazine,* May 1991, p. 40.

know where they will stand in relation to the other protagonists and antago-nists. The arrival of Tatanka on the WWF roster was preceded by a series of segments showing the Native American hero visiting the tribal elders, under-going rites of initiation, explaining the meaning of his haircut, makeup, cos-tume, and war shout. His ridicule by the fashion-minded Rick "the Model" Martel introduced his first antagonism and ensured the viewer's recognition of his essential goodness.

Much of the weekly broadcasts centers on the manufacturing of these moral distinctions and the creation of these basic antagonisms. A classic ex-ample might be the breakup of the Rockers. A series of accidents and minor disagreements sparked a public showdown on Brutus "the Barber" Beefcake's Barber Shop, a special program segment. Shawn Michaels appeared at the in-terview, dressed in black leather and wearing sunglasses (already adopting iconography signaling his shift toward the dark side). After a pretense of rec-onciliation and a series of clips reviewing their past together, Michaels shoved his partner, Marty Jannetty, through the barber-shop window, amid Brutus's impotent protests.[16] The decision to feature the two team members as inde-pendent combatants required the creation of moral difference, while the dis-integration of their partnership fit perfectly within the program's familiar dop-pelgänger structure. *WWF Magazine* portrayed the events in terms of the biblical story of Cain and Abel, as the rivalry of two "brothers":

> [The Rockers] were as close as brothers. They did everything together, in and out of the ring. But Michaels grew jealous of Jannetty and became im-patient to succeed. While Jannetty was content to bide his time, work to steadily improve with the knowledge that championships don't come eas-ily in the WWF, Michaels decided he wanted it all now — and all for him-self.[17]

If an earlier profile had questioned whether the two had "separate identities," this reporter has no trouble making moral distinctions between the patient Jannetty and the impatient Michaels, the self-sacrificing Jannetty and the self-centered Michaels. Subsequent broadcasts would link Michaels professionally and romantically with Sensational Sherri, a woman whose seductive charms have been the downfall of many WWF champs. As a manager, Sherri is noted for her habit of smuggling foreign objects to ringside in her purse and interfer-ing in the matches to ensure her man's victory. Sherri, who had previously been romantically involved with Million Dollar Man Ted Dibiase, announced that she would use her "Teddy Bear's" money to back Michaels's solo career,

---

[16]Brutus was injured in a motorcycle accident several years ago and had his skull recon-structed; he is no longer able to fight but has come to represent the voice of aged wisdom within the WWF universe. Brutus constantly articulates the values of fairness and loyalty in the face of their abuse by the rule-breaking characters, pushing for reconciliations that might re-solve old feuds, and watching as these disputes erupt and destroy his barber shop.

[17]"The Mark of Cain: Shawn Michaels Betrays His Tag Team Brother," *WWF Magazine,* March 1992, p. 41.

linking his betrayal of his partner to her own greedy and adulterous impulses. All of these plot twists differentiate Jannetty and Michaels, aligning spectator identification with the morally superior partner. Michaels's paramount moral failing is his all-consuming ambition, his desire to dominate rather than work alongside his long-time partner.

The Rockers' story points to the contradictory status of personal advancement within the WWF narrative: these stories hinge upon fantasies of upward mobility, yet ambition is just as often regarded in negative terms, as ultimately corrupting. Such a view of ambition reflects the experience of people who have worked hard all of their lives without much advancement and therefore remain profoundly suspicious of those on top. Wrestling speaks to those who recognize that upward mobility often has little to do with personal merit and a lot to do with a willingness to stomp on those who get in your way. Virtue, in the WWF moral universe, is often defined by a willingness to temper ambition through personal loyalties, through affiliation with others, while vice comes from putting self-interest ahead of everything else. This distrust of self-gain was vividly illustrated during a bout between Rowdy Roddy Piper and Bret "the Hitman" Hart at the 1992 Wrestlemania. This competition uncharacteristically centered on two good guys. As a result, most viewers suspected that one fighter would ultimately be driven to base conduct by personal desire for the Intercontinental Championship belt. Such speculations were encouraged by ambiguous signs from the combatants during "buildup" interviews and exploited during the match through a number of gestures which indicate moral indecision: Rowdy stood ready to club Hart with an illegal foreign object; the camera cut repeatedly to close-ups of his face as he struggled with his conscience before casting the object aside and continuing a fair fight. In the end, however, the two long-time friends embraced each other as Piper congratulated Hart on a more or less fairly won fight. The program situated this bout as a sharp contrast to the feud between Hulk Hogan and Sid Justice, the major attraction at this pay-per-view event. Their budding friendship had been totally destroyed by Justice's overriding desire to dominate the WWF: "I'm gonna crack the head of somebody big in the WWF. . . . No longer is this Farmboy from Arkansas gonna take a back seat to anybody."[18] Rowdy and Hart value their friendship over their ambition; Justice lets nothing stand in the way of his quest for power.

Perfect Bastards

WWF wrestlers are not rounded characters; the spectacle has little room for the novelistic, and here the form may push the melodramatic imagination to its logical extremes. WWF wrestlers experience no internal conflicts which might blur their moral distinctiveness. Rather, they often display the "undivid-

20

[18]"WWF Superstars Talk about Wrestlemania," *WWF Magazine,* March 1992, p. 18.

edness" that Robert Heilman sees as a defining aspect of nineteenth-century melodramatic characters:

> [The melodramatic character displays] oneness of feeling as competitor, crusader, aggressor; as defender, counterattacker, fighter for survival; he may be assertive or compelled, questing or resistant, obsessed or desperate; he may triumph or lose, be victor or victim, exert pressure or be pressed. Always he is undivided, unperplexed by alternatives, untorn by divergent impulses; all of his strength or weakness faces in one direction.[19]

The WWF athletes sketch their moral failings in broad profile: The Mountie pounds on his chest and roars, "I am the Mountie," convinced that no one can contest his superiority, yet as soon as the match gets rough, he slides under the ropes and tries to hide behind his scrawny manager. The Million Dollar Man shoves hundred-dollar bills into the mouths of his defeated opponents, while Sherri paints her face with gilded dollar signs to mark her possession by the highest bidder. Ravishing Rick Rude wears pictures of his opponents on his arse, relishing his own vulgarity. Virtue similarly displays itself without fear of misrecognition. Hacksaw Jim Duggan clutches an American flag in one hand and a two-by-four in the other.

The need for a constant recombination of a fixed number of characters requires occasional shifts in moral allegiances (as occurred with the breakup of the Rockers). Characters may undergo redemption or seduction, but these shifts typically occur quickly and without much ambiguity. There is rarely any lingering doubt or moral fence-straddling. Such characters are good one week and evil the next. Jake "the Snake" Roberts, a long-time hero — albeit one who enjoys his distance from the other protagonists — uncharacteristically offered to help the Ultimate Warrior prepare for his fight against the Undertaker. Their grim preparations unfolded over several weeks, with Jake forcing the Warrior to undergo progressively more twisted rituals — locking him into a coffin, burying him alive — until finally Jake shoved him into a room full of venomous snakes. Bitten by Jake's cobra, Lucifer, the Ultimate Warrior staggered toward his friend, who simply brushed him aside. As the camera pulled back to show the Undertaker standing side by side with Jake, the turncoat laughed, "Never trust a snake." From that moment forward, Jake was portrayed as totally evil, Barthes's perfect bastard. Jake attacks Macho Man Randy Savage's bride, Elizabeth, on their wedding day and terrorizes the couple every chance he gets.

The program provides no motivation for such outrages, though commentary both in the broadcasts and in the pages of the wrestling magazines constantly invites such speculation: "What makes Jake hate Savage and his bride so fiercely? Why does he get his jollies — as he admits — from tormenting her?" What Peter Brooks said about the villains of traditional melodrama holds

---

[19]Robert Bechtold Heilman, *The Iceman, the Arsonist and the Troubled Agent: Tragedy and Melodrama on the Modern Stage* (Seattle: University of Washington Press, 1973), p. 53.

equally well here: "Evil in the world of melodrama does not need justification; it exists, simply. . . . And the less it is adequately motivated, the more this evil appears simply volitional, the product of pure will."[20] Jake is evil because he is a snake; it's in his character and nothing can change him, even though in this case, less than a year ago, Jake was as essentially good as he is now totally demented. We know Jake is evil without redemption, because he tells us so, over and over:

> I'm not really sure I have any soul at all. . . . Once I get involved in something — no matter how demented, no matter how treacherous, no matter how far off the mark it is from normal standards — I never back down. I just keep on going, deeper and deeper into the blackness, far past the point where any sensible person would venture. You see, a person with a conscience — a person with a soul — would be frightened by the sordid world I frequent. But Jake the Snake isn't scared at all. To tell you the truth, I can't get enough of it.[21]

Jake recognizes and acknowledges his villainy; he names it publicly and unrepentantly.

Peter Brooks sees such a process of "self-nomination" as an essential feature of the melodramatic imagination: "Nothing is spared because nothing is left unsaid; the characters stand on stage and utter the unspeakable, give voice to their deepest feelings, dramatize through their heightened and polarized words and gestures the whole lesson of their relationship."[22] The soliloquy, that stock device of the traditional melodrama, is alive and well in WWF wrestling. Wrestlers look directly into the audience and shove their fists toward the camera; they proclaim their personal credos and describe their sufferings. Tag team partners repeat their dedication to each other and their plans to dominate their challengers. Villains profess their evil intentions and vow to perform various forms of mayhem upon their opponents. Their rhetoric is excessively metaphoric, transforming every fight into a life-and-death struggle. Much as nineteenth-century theatrical melodrama used denotative music to define the characters' moral stances, the wrestlers' entry into the arena is preceded by theme songs which encapsulate their personalities. Hulk's song describes him as "a real American hero" who "fights for the rights of every man." The Million Dollar Man's jingle proclaims his compelling interest in "money, money, money," while Jake's song repeats "trust me, trust me, trust me."

This public declaration ensures the constant moral legibility of the WWF narrative and thereby maximizes the audience's own emotional response. Spectators come to the arena or turn on the program to express intense emotion — to cheer the hero, to boo and jeer the villain — without moral ambiguity or

---

[20]Brooks, p. 34.
[21]"WWF Interview: A Talk with Jake 'the Snake' Roberts," p. 17.
[22]Brooks, p. 4.

emotional complexity. (Wrestling fans sometimes choose to root for the villains, taking pleasure in their self-conscious inversion of the WWF's moral universe, yet even this perverse pleasure requires moral legibility.) Operating within a world of absolutes, WWF wrestlers wear their hearts on their sleeves (or, in Ravishing Rick Rude's case, on the seat of their pants) and project their emotions from every inch of their bodies. Much as in classic melodrama, external actions reveal internal states; moral disagreements demand physical expressions. As Brooks writes, "Emotions are given a full acting-out, a full representation before our eyes. . . . Nothing is *under*stated, all is *over*stated."[23] The Million Dollar Man cowers, covering his face and retreating, crawling on hands and knees backward across the ring. Sherri shouts at the top of her ample lungs and pounds the floor with her high-heel shoe. Rowdy Roddy Piper gets his dander up and charges into the ring. With a burst of furious energy, he swings madly at his opponents, forcing them to scatter right and left. Roddy spits in the Million Dollar Man's eyes, flings his sweaty shirt in his face, or grabs Sherri, rips off her dress, throws her over his knee, and spanks her. Such characters embody the shameful spectacle of emotional display, acting as focal points for the audience's own expression of otherwise repressed affect.

Invincible Victims

Fans eagerly anticipate these excessive gestures as the most appropriate   25 means of conveying the characters' moral attitudes. Through a process of simplification, the wrestler's body has been reduced to a series of iconic surfaces and stock attitudes. We know not only how the performer is apt to respond to a given situation but what bodily means will be adopted to express that response. Wrestlers perform less with their eyes and hands than with their arms and legs and with their deep, resounding voices. Earthquake's bass rumble and Roddy's fiery outbursts, Ric Flair's vicious laughter and Macho Man's red-faced indignation are "too much" for the small screen, yet they articulate feelings that are too intense to be contained.

This process of simplification and exaggeration transforms the wrestlers into cartoonish figures who may slam each other's heads into iron steps, throw each other onto wooden floors, smash each other with steel chairs, land with their full weight on the other's prone stomach, and emerge without a scratch, ready to fight again. Moral conflict will continue unabated; no defeat can be final within a world where the characters are omnipotent. If traditional melodrama foregrounded long-suffering women's endurance of whatever injustices the world might throw against them, WWF wrestling centers around male victims who ultimately refuse to accept any more abuse and fight back against the aggressors.

[23]Ibid., p. 41.

Such a scenario allows men to acknowledge their own vulnerability, safe in the knowledge that their masculine potency will ultimately be restored and that they will be strong enough to overcome the forces which subordinate them. Hulk Hogan has perfected the image of the martyred hero who somehow captures victory from the closing jaws of defeat. Badly beaten in a fight, Hulk lies in a crumpled heap. The referee lifts his limp arms up, once, twice, ready to call the fight, when the crowd begins to clap and stomp. The mighty hero rises slowly, painfully to his feet, rejuvenated by the crowd's response. Blood streams through his blond hair and drips across his face, but he whips it aside with a broad swing of his mighty arms. Hulk turns to face his now-terrified assailant.

"Seeing Is Believing"

Such broad theatricality cuts against wrestling's tradition of pseudorealism; the programs' formats mimic the structures and visual style of nonfiction television, of sports coverage, news broadcasts, and talk shows. The fiction is, of course, that all of this fighting is authentic, spontaneous, unscripted. The WWF narrative preserves that illusion at all costs. There is no stepping outside the fiction, no acknowledgment of the production process or the act of authorship. When the performers are featured in *WWF Magazine,* they are profiled in character. Story segments are told in the form of late-breaking news reports or framed as interviews. The commentators are taken by surprise, interrupted by seemingly unplanned occurrences. During one broadcast, Jake the Snake captured Macho Man, dragging him into the ring. Jake tied him to the ropes and menaced him with a cobra which sprang and bit him on the forearm. The camera was jostled from side to side by people racing to Macho's assistance and panned abruptly trying to follow his hysterical wife as she ran in horror to ringside. A reaction shot shows a child in the audience reduced to tears by this brutal spectacle. Yet, at the same time, the camera refused to show us an image "too shocking" for broadcast. Macho Man's arm and the snake's gaping mouth were censored, blocked by white bars, not unlike the blue dot that covered the witness's face at the William Kennedy Smith rape trial that same week. (A few weeks later, the "uncensored" footage was at last shown, during a prime-time broadcast, so that viewers could see "what really happened.") The plot lines are thus told through public moments where a camera could plausibly be present, though such moments allow us insight into the characters' private motivations.

As Ric Flair often asserted during his brief stay in the WWF, "Pictures don't lie; seeing is believing," and yet it is precisely seeing and not believing that is a central pleasure in watching television wrestling. What audiences see is completely "unbelievable," as ring commentators frequently proclaim — unbelievable because these human bodies are unnaturally proportioned and monstrously large, because these figures who leap through the air seem to defy all natural laws, and, most important, because these characters participate within the corny and timeworn plots of the nineteenth-century melodrama. The pleasure comes in seeing what cannot be believed, yet is constantly asserted to us as undeniably true. Fans elbow each other in the ribs, "Look how fake," taking great pride in their ability to see through a deception that was never intended to convince.

Such campy self-acknowledgment may be part of what makes male spectators' affective engagement with this melodramatic form safe and acceptable within a traditionally masculine culture which otherwise backs away from overt emotional display. Whenever the emotions become too intense, there is always a way of pulling back, laughing at what might otherwise provoke tears. WWF wrestling, at another level, provokes authentic pain and rage, particularly when it embraces populist myths of economic exploitation and class solidarity, feeds a hunger for homosocial bonding, or speaks to utopian fantasies of empowerment. The gap between the campy and the earnest reception of wrestling may reflect the double role which Elias and Dunning ascribe to traditional sports: the need to allow for the de-controlling of powerful affects while at the same time regulating their expression and ensuring their ultimate containment. The melodramatic aspects are what trigger emotional release, while the campy aspects contain it within safe bounds. The plots of wrestling cut close to the bone, inciting racial and class antagonisms that rarely surface this overtly elsewhere in popular culture, while comic exaggeration ensures that such images can never fully be taken seriously.

READING THE TEXT

1. What are the similarities between Roland Barthes's and Jake "the Snake" Roberts's attitudes towards professional wrestling?

2. What is the "core myth" (para. 11) of the WWF, according to Jenkins? What evidence does he give for his contention?

3. How does professional wrestling allow "working-class men to confront their own feelings of vulnerability" (para. 14)?

4. How does the WWF maintain its fiction that its contests are "authentic, spontaneous, unscripted" (para. 28)?

5. In what sense is the WWF a source of melodrama for men, according to Jenkins?

READING THE SIGNS

1. Watch some WWF contests, and write an analysis interpreting the viewer fantasies to which they appeal.

2. Read or reread Michael Messner's "Power at Play: Sport and Gender Relations" (p. 668) and write an essay analyzing the ways in which the WWF reinforces traditional masculine gender codes. To develop your ideas, consult Holly Devor's "Gender Role Behaviors and Attitudes" (p. 484).

3. Write a journal entry describing your attraction to WWF events if you are a fan. Conversely, explain why you never watch the WWF if you are not a fan.

4. For many fans of the WWF, the attraction is campy irony rather than literal belief. Write an essay comparing and contrasting the social class differences that divide those fans who believe in the fictions of the WWF and those who don't. For a discussion of camp, consult Andy Medhurst's "Batman, Deviance, and Camp" (p. 746).

5. Write an essay in which you explore the extent to which Jenkins's claim that sports "reasserts the desirability of belonging to a community" (para. 6) is valid. Be sure to use as evidence sports other than wrestling.

E. M. SWIFT AND DON YAEGER
UNNATURAL SELECTION

If you think that steroids and blood doping are medical outrages that are ruining international sports, just wait until the first genetically engineered athlete appears. And as E. M. Swift and Don Yaeger report in this Sports Illustrated *exposé, the time is not far off when this will happen. For with the Human Genome Project finally completed, scientists now have the data they need to determine just what genes need to be tweaked to improve such biological functions as muscle development and oxygen transport. And there won't be any urine analyses to distinguish the genetically engineered competitor from the unenhanced, except one of them will be able to high-jump ten feet or run a sub-three-minute mile. A senior writer at* Sports Illustrated, *E. M. Swift has published* Each Thief Passing By *(1981), and* Eleven Seconds *(1998). Don Yaeger is an associate editor for* Sports Illustrated. *He has written eleven books, including* Under the Tarnished Dome *(1993) and* Pros and Cons: The Criminals Who Play in the NFL *(1998).*

In an unmarked cage in the bowels of the University of Pennsylvania's Department of Physiology crawls the future of sport. It is a genetically altered mouse. We'll call him He-man because a creature of such import should be known by a name, not a number.

Soon after He-man was born, a team of Penn researchers led by Dr. H. Lee Sweeney injected its muscles with a synthetic gene that instructed its muscle cells to produce more IGF-1 (insulin-like growth factor-1). IGF-1 is a protein that, in a nutshell, makes muscles grow and helps them repair themselves when they've been damaged. It is indispensable to the formation and maintenance of strong physiques. For the most part, when those of us under thirty exercise vigorously, our bodies start producing lots of IGF-1. Our muscles get bigger, and we get stronger.

As we age, the muscles stop producing IGF-1 in the quantities we need to keep our muscles looking as they did when we were younger. They sag, and they don't repair themselves as effectively as they used to. We get slower and weaker. "Even if you train," says Sweeney, "you lose speed."

It happened to Carl Lewis, Wayne Gretzky and Jerry Rice, among others. But it hasn't happened to He-man. Because of the gene that was injected two years ago, the mouse grew exceptionally large muscles, and those muscles keep producing IGF-1. He-man, in the throes of mouse old age, remains as mighty as he ever was, an Arnold Schwarzenegger of mice. His muscle mass is 60 percent greater than that of a normal mouse. He effortlessly climbs a ladder with 120 grams of weights — equal to three times his body weight — strapped on his back.

"We showed that with a onetime injection of this gene we can get bigger muscles in young animals and that, as they get older, the muscles never change," says Sweeney, whose research is funded by the National Institutes of Health. "The muscles maintain their size through the whole life of the animal."

The implications for athletes are not lost on Sweeney. Implant this IGF-1 gene into the proper muscles and Olympic sprint champion Maurice Greene might be as fast at 48 as he is at 24. Randy Moss might still outrun and outjump defensive backs in 2020. Pavel Bure might be skating as fast thirty years from now as he does today.

Fanciful? Don't bet against it. Whether in one year, three years or five years — the last of those being the prediction of most experts — the first genetically engineered athlete will be secretly competing. "It's not rocket science," says Theodore Friedmann, director of the gene-therapy program at UC San Diego and a member of the medical-research committee of the World Anti-Doping Agency (WADA). "If you asked any molecular biologist, or even his students, how he would implant genes to change muscle function, within half an hour he could write down three or four ways to do it. The same would apply if you asked him, How would you improve oxygen transport? How would you change athletes so they could jump higher and run faster? Be taller, stronger, whatever? Because of the whole Human Genome Project [a federally funded effort to identify the estimated 100,000 genes in human DNA], synthetic genes are available, and putting genes into people to express new functions is becoming reality."

"If this is being done on mice and rats, humans aren't far behind," says Bengt Saltin, a Swedish professor of human physiology at the University of Copenhagen and a member of WADA's special committee on gene doping. "The only thing keeping it from happening today is the control problem. For example, you can insert a gene to increase EPO production" — EPO is a hormone some athletes inject to illicitly boost the production of red blood cells, thus enhancing their endurance — "but you can't shut [that production] off when you want to." When the technology is developed that will enable us to turn hormone production on and off at will, says Saltin, we'll "have real problems."

Sweeney believes the IGF-1-inducing gene will slow the muscle deterioration brought on by muscular dystrophy, and he had hoped to have a clinical trial on humans under way by this spring. But he has delayed seeking approval from the Food and Drug Administration (FDA) because of the 1999 death of a patient in a different gene-therapy trial at Penn. If approval is granted, as is expected, and the synthetic IGF-1 gene proves safe in the muscular dystrophy trial, the next step would be to conduct a trial of the gene's ability to maintain a person's muscle strength as that person ages. "All this is being driven by our aging population," Sweeney says. "As people get old, they get weak, and if they have an injury, [the muscle involved] doesn't repair itself, so they lose even more muscle. They lose their mobility. The ability to maintain muscle mass is [hugely important] for an aging society."

"When [Sweeney's work] is done, it will decrease the incidence of hip 10 fractures in the elderly," says Gary Wadler, associate professor at the New York University School of Medicine and an adviser to the White House Office of National Drug Control Policy. "But you'd better start inventorying the genes because athletes will be trying to get them. That's the plain truth. His work has the potential to be misused. It won't be long before someone does a kinesiologic study of a pitcher's motion, say, to determine which muscles should be enhanced for throwing a baseball. Then with the injection of the IGF-1 gene you create a superpitcher. The only way you'll be able to prove an athlete is cheating is through a muscle biopsy, and that's not going to happen."

WADA, a two-year-old organization that was founded by the International Olympic Committee (IOC), is so worried about the possible impact of genetic research on sport that it's hosting a symposium on gene manipulation in September in Cold Spring Harbor, N.Y. The purpose is to discuss the ethics of the matter. Is gene *therapy,* the medical use of genes to repair an illness or injury, acceptable for Olympic athletes? Is gene *enhancement,* the implantation of genes to increase the performance of a perfectly healthy body, unacceptable? Are there gray areas somewhere in between?

"I am very clear on this," says IOC Medical Commission vice chairman Jacques Rogge of Belgium, an orthopedic surgeon who may succeed Juan Antonio Samaranch later this year as head of the Olympic movement. "Genetic manipulation is there to treat people who have ailments, not there to treat a healthy person."

However, the IGF-1 gene repairs *and* enhances muscle tissue. It also keeps the muscles churning out insulin-like growth factor-1 indefinitely, which theoretically could allow the athlete to perform at an optimal level years past what is now considered his prime. Is WADA going to forbid the injured athlete from using that particular form of gene therapy — one that may well be available to the public — on the grounds it might fix him better than new?

In fact, there's a tremendous upside to these forays into the genetic mine-field that even the naysayers see. "This gene manipulation is not all bad," says WADA's secretary general, Harri Syvasalmi of Finland. "We have to accept that some of these enhancements will be wonderful, especially for athletes who are injured."

It isn't only professional athletes who stand to benefit. Weekend warriors   15
could see a marked improvement in the quality of their lives and athletic per-formances. More than 100,000 anterior cruciate ligaments are torn annually in the U.S. Damage to knee cartilage is also common. Stress fractures account for 15% of all injuries to runners. These statistics are cited in a February 2000 report published by three researchers from the University of Pittsburgh, Dr. Freddie H. Fu, Dr. Johnny Huard, and Vladimir Martinek, who write that their early findings show recovery from sports-related injuries involving slow-healing tissues can be significantly sped up and enhanced through gene ther-apy — specifically, by introducing genes, like the synthetic IGF-1 gene, that ex-press growth factors. "One day injured tendons, cartilage or ligaments will be repaired through an injection," says Wadler. "It will be like a salamander re-growing a tail."

Bobby Orr, his knees crippled from six operations, would not have had to retire at age 30. Joe Namath would not have limped off the field for the last time at 34. His elbow pain gone, Sandy Koufax could have pitched past 30. Tantalizing, yes? A little frightening too. As at the dawn of any age, man's ven-ture into genetic engineering will have its champions and its detractors. But it won't be stopped. Time will tell whether we are on the brink of enrichment or the brink of disaster.

"The sports world was not prepared for anabolic steroids," says Syvasalmi. "We can't get behind [on a doping trend] again. By looking at gene enhancement now, we hope to raise the ethical issues and appeal to the ethics of athletes."

The ethics of athletes? That's a good one. If history has taught us any-thing, it's that athletes will do anything, try anything and risk everything to win. "Go all the way back to the ancient Greek Olympics and you'll find sto-ries," says Saltin. "Man has always believed there was something he could put in his mouth to help him win. Gene manipulation is only the next step. I guess I'm naïve, but I hope that ethics will win out. If I'm wrong, it's the end of sport as we know it. Sport will be a circus of unbelievable performances."

Norwegian speed skater Johann Olav Koss, a triple Olympic gold medalist in 1994, knows something about both unbelievable performances and the na-ture of athletes. A recent graduate of the University of Queensland medical school in Australia and an athlete's representative to both the IOC and WADA, Koss doesn't know whether to be more frightened of gene manipulation from an athlete's perspective or a doctor's. "Athletes should realize the research that's been done in this field is absolutely not good enough to know the risk of long-term damage," he says. "Don't let the doctors tell you differently. There is no knowledge about the potentially damaging side effects of genetic changes. Saying that, we also know some athletes don't care about long-term risk.

"This is an ethical question, not only for sport, but for the human race," 20 Koss continues. "You are tinkering with nature. How far are you going to go? What is acceptable? What will be the effect long term? Why shouldn't we create something genetically that is much smarter, stronger and better than a human? Why shouldn't we put wings on a human? Why shouldn't we give humans the eyes of a fly? Then we are no longer human, we are something else. You could eliminate the human race."

There are many reasons that we should not go down that road. Trouble is, world-class athletes, even without genetic enhancement, are a different breed. "An atmosphere has been created in which it doesn't matter if you cheat," says Koss, "as long as you win."

Over the years sports officials from many countries have proved they're as prone to embrace that mentality as the athletes they oversee. East Germany's state-run steroid program, which has come to light in the last couple of years, exacted a terrible physical and psychological toll from a generation of that country's athletes. No nation's ruling sports bodies are above suspicion, including those from the U.S. Small wonder, then, that among WADA's long-term fears is state-sponsored cloning. "It's a real issue for sport," says Saltin. "If you're a country, why not take the chance and clone Pelé — or 25 Pelés — and engineer an entire team?"

A Quebec company called Clonaid may have already begun human cloning experiments. Using the DNA of a dead infant, the company is supposedly trying to clone another child for the bereaved parents for $500,000. Since DNA can be obtained from a strand of hair, the imagination races with visions of molecular biology students of an entrepreneurial bent swooping in to gather hair after Tiger Woods leaves a barbershop and then selling the strands for underground cloning experiments.

"I honestly believe that if the Soviet Union hadn't fallen apart, it would be genetically altering humans by now," Sweeney says. "The Soviets were always more willing to push the envelope than we're allowed to here. And the next step would be to pick mothers and fathers of the next generation of athletes, give their children altered genes to determine all kinds of talents, then watch them grow. Who knows where it would go?"

No one. Athletes, though, are sure to step forward for many of the experi- 25 ments. Even after knowing the potentially damaging, sometimes fatal, side effects of the performance-enhancing drugs now available, athletes of all cultures have not hesitated to experiment with steroids, EPO, human growth hormone, blood doping and God knows what else. They're 21st-century Fausts, willing to bargain future health for present glory.

Sweeney has certainly discovered that. He has already been contacted by several athletes, most of them weightlifters, who have heard about his research and wonder if he's looking for human volunteers on whom to test the IGF-1 gene. "They wanted to know what I thought it would do for them and what the safety issues were," Sweeney says. "Then the main question was how they could get it. I told them I had no safety data on humans whatsoever, but based on the mice, I didn't think it was a big risk. They were fine with that. Safety data didn't mean anything to them. They basically said they were willing to do it right now. I told them the FDA wouldn't be fine with that and I could go to jail if I helped them."

What are the risks of genetic engineering? The theories range from Koss's worries about the elimination of the human race as we know it, to only slightly less apocalyptic scenarios involving genetically altered viruses running amok and genes spinning out of control. Right now the preferred delivery vehicle for a gene like the one Sweeney implanted in He-man is a common virus. Essentially, the virus is denuded of its illness-causing characteristics and all genes, then stuffed with a synthetic gene and injected into a particular muscle or organ. If all goes well, the new gene will live harmoniously within the host for the rest of the host's life, reproducing itself in the new cells it helps create and merrily expressing whatever function it was selected to express.

If things go badly, the gene could sit sullenly in its new home and refuse to express. Far worse, the body's natural defense mechanisms could kick into gear and attack the virus or the synthetic gene, as happened in the gene-therapy trial at Penn two years ago, when a young patient who'd had a gene injected into his hepatic artery died after his body's immune system shut down his liver.

Then there are the control issues to which Saltin referred. Who's calling the shots, you or your new gene? What if in its enthusiasm, your new gene overdoes it and gives you too much of a good thing? Be careful of what you wish for. Visions of 12-foot-tall basketball players come to mind, and football players with muscles so immense and powerful that they can't be supported by the surrounding tendons and skeletal structure.

Genetically altered houseflies demonstrated a variation of the latter problem. Researchers found that they could genetically enhance a fly's flight muscles so that they were 300 percent stronger than normal. That was the good news. The bad news was that the fly couldn't get off the ground. "The fly actually lost power because it couldn't make its wings move fast enough," explains Sweeney. "It's a good example of why we need to learn more about how muscle groups work and interact." 30

Try to explain that to a college lineman yearning to be drafted by the NFL, who learns that with one injection of something called growth-hormone-releasing hormone (GHRH) he could gain 70 to 80 pounds of muscle. "If athletes are willing to take hGH [human growth hormone]," says Sweeney, referring to a banned substance believed to be widely used among Olympic athletes, "this is, in my opinion, safer, cheaper and probably gets better results. GHRH will be the next great problem for athletics."

In research conducted by Dr. Robert Schwartz of Baylor College of Medicine, piglets injected with GHRH grew 37 percent heavier than their siblings and had 10 percent less fat. The pigs were stronger and leaner. GHRH is different from hGH in that it sends a signal to the pituitary gland to start cranking out growth hormones. And keep cranking. The growth hormones aren't introduced externally, so the body tends to accept them. "This has got the pig farmers all excited, but I know that athletes read many of these scientific journals," says Sweeney. "So I'm sure some out there are already looking into it. The only thing I'd advise is to be sure to put it into a muscle you're not too fond of, in case one day you want to stop growing, you could just cut that muscle out."

One thing is clear. We'll all share an interest in genetic *enhancement,* whether for something as simple as a hair-growth gene to end our baldness or as potentially life-changing as the ability to remain mobile, even spry, in our dotage. "The public will accept genetic interventions because it will want them," says Sweeney. "I see a day when this is going to be commonly used in the population because the population does not like getting old and weak and ending up in a wheelchair. Once society accepts it, the Olympic committee is going to have to deal with it. The days that it can try to stop it are numbered."

READING THE TEXT

1. What is IGF-1, and what is its significance to the future of sports?

2. How might the Human Genome Project one day affect athletics, in the authors' view? What evidence do the authors present to support their predictions, and how persuasive do you find it?

3. What ethical concerns about the future of sports are raised by Johann Olav Koss, a triple Olympic gold medalist?

4. What are some of the dangers associated with gene therapy, according to the authors?

READING THE SIGNS

1. Swift and Yaeger report that genetically engineered athletes should begin to appear within the next five years or so. Write an opinion piece arguing whether legal measures should be taken to prevent this scientific development.

2. Write a journal entry discussing whether you would allow yourself to be modified by genetic engineering techniques if it would improve your athletic performance. What ethical or practical considerations would affect your position?

3. While this article says nothing about the possibility, imagine that scientists are on the verge of introducing genetically engineered intelligence. Conduct a class discussion on whether this development would have the same ethical implications as it does in athletics. Would you want to attend school with students who have what might be called "artificial intelligence"? Why or why not?

4. Write an essay in which you analyze the significance of using genetic engineering to enhance athletic performance. What does this use of sophisticated technology for sports suggest about American cultural values?

5. The authors refer to the common use of the banned substance hGH by athletes, and how the use of performance-enhancing drugs has marred the most recent Olympic games. Write an essay in which you analyze the social, cultural, and competitive pressures that may lead athletes to use such substances.

GARY SMITH

THE BOYS ON THE BUS

Immediately after the September 11, 2001, terror attacks, a lot of sports-writers, sports fans, and athletes alike started "wondering why the hell games mattered anymore," as Gary Smith puts it in this personal ac-count of his own post-9/11 reassessment. So instead of going to the Braves/Phillies game as planned, he took his son to a high school football game, traveling on the bus with the players themselves to see how they were handling it all. One boy's father had narrowly escaped death in the World Trade Center; a classmate's dad wasn't so lucky. So was the game worth going on with? Yes, Smith answers, a bit uneasily, because coming to the game enabled its viewers "to come together and show that they cared about their kids, their country, and the families who'd lost so much." Which is basically the way that the whole country has responded in much bigger contests, from the World Series to the Super Bowl.

Everything in the little town came to a halt at dusk on the day America mourned. Five police cars, blinking blue as they wove in escort, sealed off traffic and froze pedestrians in their paths. Drivers peeled to the shoulder of the road and stopped, waved and craned their necks to glimpse the passing procession.

In Paris on that same day, last Friday, the Métro had gone still so passen-gers could pray, and the bells of Notre Dame had tolled for an hour in mem-ory of thousands of people feared dead. In Berlin 200,000 had gathered be-fore the Brandenburg Gate to reflect at the place where the wall between democracy and communism had stood. In Dublin commerce and drinking had both been called off, shops and pubs shut tight, and in England the Queen had broken off her holiday to return home and grieve. In America, where the mass murder had occurred, four busloads of kids were leaving Summerville, South Carolina, to play a high school football game.

I was in the fourth row, left side, lead bus. Weeks earlier I'd promised my 11-year-old son, Noah, that we'd play hooky last week and make the five-hour drive to Atlanta to watch the Braves and the Philadelphia Phillies decide a pennant race. A nightmare had intervened, so here we were instead.

It was an odd thing to do — to go to a game — on a day when you walked around wondering why the hell games mattered anymore. But I wanted to know what a game felt and smelled like at a moment like this, why people bothered playing and watching, and even more so, what it all smelled like to my son. Sports, thanks to me, had already taken firm grip of Noah's life, but now and then I'd get this uneasy feeling about where it all might be leading, a feeling I'd never spoken of with him. Now that the earth had shaken and the whole deck of cards had spilled on the floor, it made no sense to hide what I'd been holding.

Already the stink of sweat filled the bus, the smell of teenage boys look- 5 ing inside themselves to see if what they would need, just an hour later, was there. The Green Wave of Summerville High was leaving its flag-festooned town and heading to its biggest game of the season, at Stratford High in nearby Goose Creek, against the team ranked No. 2 in the state. However, the Summerville boys, too, were a perennial power; in two of the last three seasons, the winner of this game had gone on to win the state championship.

Noah flipped and spun a football in his hands. That had been the first thing he'd thought of when I told him we were going to a ball game on the day of mourning. "Can we go on the field?" he asked. "Can we play catch?"

"Well, I . . . guess so," I'd said.

Hell, what had I expected? I'd flung him, back and forth, between two worlds. He'd played on a baseball team in Australia, where parents applauded and cooed, "Awwww, bad *luck,* mate," whenever a boy or girl on his team swung and missed by a foot — and he'd played on a traveling AAU baseball team in the United States, where parents stormed the dugout and seethed at coaches for pulling their sons out of games so benchwarmers could have a chance. He'd lived for a year in an old fishing village in Spain, where adoring grandmothers stroked his head each day on their daily shopping strolls — and he'd practiced for a year under a coach who nailed him in the head with a basketball from 20 feet away when his attention lapsed.

As his dad, I'd assigned him to ladle cabbage to the homeless in soup kitchens, and as his coach, to break the press in the last second of one-point, double-overtime championship games. He'd lived out *my* ambivalence, spent some years thousands of miles removed from box scores and title chases, spent others high-fiving me over touchdowns and slam dunks, slurping down *SportsCenter* and sports pages first thing every morning along with cereal and milk. Only a month ago my wife and I had argued over whether Noah should play baseball on the travel team again this fall, only a month after his all-star tournament had ended; argued over how much competition was too much in the making of a kid. She'd won.

Now, with a kickoff scheduled to rise into the air at eight o'clock and join 10 the smoke and human ashes riding in the wind, with sports and suffering suddenly teetering on the scales of a national debate over who we are, I too was craning for a glimpse. A sideways look to see which world's values had taken stronger hold of my son; to see what ruled in his heart when people were suffering; to see what I had wrought.

In whispers I asked the boy seated in front of me on the bus if our police escort was unusual, related to the tragedy and the day of prayer. No, he murmured, it happened every time the Green Wave hit the road. I started there with Noah, on the edges of what I wanted to learn. "What do you think," I asked, "of 86 kids getting a police escort to play a high school game?"

His eyes squinched. "They don't even do this for big league players," he said. "Must be nothing to do here."

I gazed around the bus, wondering which boys really wanted to play and which had just been swept along. The pros had shut down. The colleges had fallen silent. Why not the high school kids?

I laid that question in the lap of a legend, the Summerville coach, who had won more football games than any other coach in history. I wanted Noah to hear the opinion of John McKissick, a 74-year-old grandfather who had stayed for 50 years at one school, where he'd won 483 games, 10 state titles and 25 conference championships. A man who'd gone shoeless growing up in a two-bedroom shack after his daddy went bankrupt during the Depression, and then found his calling in a town that once postponed Halloween because it fell on a game night, and molded the lives of 1,700 of its kids because he never cut a player. A man who would've dropped from the sky as a paratrooper in the 82d Airborne during the invasion of Japan had two atomic bombs not dropped from the sky first.

Never in those five decades in Summerville had McKissick gone a week in 15 autumn without coaching a football game, not even when a heart attack killed his father the day before a game. But hadn't he wondered, when even some of the townspeople started calling in and saying the game should be postponed, whether it was time, finally, to let people sit still, to think and to feel?

"No," he said. "I don't think these kids should be home watching TV. I think they've seen enough. To be honest, I don't think they'd be home watching it anyway if we didn't play. Look, everybody has mourned. We've had moments of silence, prayers, talked about it in school. I called the team together the day it happened and said, 'Keep the people who died in your prayers, but we can't let it interfere with our schoolwork and our goals here on the football field. We've got to not dwell on it. We've got to keep moving on.'"

He noticed the bump on Noah's football where our dog's teeth had broken the skin and let the bladder push through, and he got him a replacement. "Kid on our team's daddy worked at the Pentagon," McKissick said. "Name's Ryan Snipes."

Noah was silent, unreadable. I went looking for Ryan, a sophomore tight end with big hands and heartful eyes. On the morning of the attacks Ryan had watched a classmate — a girl whose father had called her that morning on his way to a meeting in one of the World Trade Center towers — faint when she saw the towers implode. That shook him, hard. Suddenly flashing before him were pictures of the Pentagon in flames, the building where his dad, an air force lieutenant colonel, had meetings nearly every day. Everything inside Ryan, level by level, collapsed. He bolted for the classroom door, and then fell to tears in front of everyone in the school lobby the moment he saw his sister and mom. For the next three hours, every 30 seconds, they called five phone numbers: nothing.

"There aren't words for the emptiness I felt inside," Ryan said. "Finally around two o'clock my sister called again, and I heard her say, *'Dad,'* and I knew he was alive. I cried again. He'd gotten a call on his way to the Pentagon to turn back, just after the planes hit the World Trade Center."

Ryan's sister and mother persuaded him to swallow his embarrassment 20 over the tears and to return to school that day for practice, and to play this week to celebrate life, to show the terrorists that Americans can't be cowed. However, the girl who'd fainted didn't return to school on Wednesday, Thursday, Friday, her empty seat filling the classroom with dread, and the locker room was quieter than it had ever been, and Ryan's sports heroes kept saying no, no way they'd play ball at a time like this.

Now game time was nearing, and the guilt was sawing away. "I don't know how I feel about playing this game," Ryan said. "Where I'd like to be right now is up there digging up the rubble. I think a lot of the guys haven't been sure how they felt about this. Then we decided yesterday, Let's win it for the people up there."

The buses rolled into the parking lot at Stratford High. Noah carried his ball as we followed the players out. From the opposite direction came the Stratford Knights, heading toward the field for calisthenics. The two squads passed each other in single file, inches apart. On the day of national unity, no two players exchanged a glance.

Me? I had my notions on the subject, but I hadn't said a word yet to Noah — I didn't want to stack the deck.

He'd never been in a football locker room. He'd never seen kids prowl and pace and pee before a game. Comp McCurry, the Green Wave's hard-muscled, hard-jawed young assistant coach, worked his way through the locker room, popping players with forearm shivers and chucks on the chin: "Woooooo! Ready to play a *ball* game! Ready to strap it *on!* Ready to bust some *chops!*" The boys strapped on their equipment and filed out in silent platoons — offense, defense, special teams — accompanied by McKissick's sergeants, steeling themselves one last time for what was about to come. I looked at Noah. No, 11 years old was too young. He couldn't be watching those kids and seeing what I was seeing, future soldiers being readied for an unimaginably treacherous war.

The stands were packed, 8,000 strong, wearing patriotic ribbons and 25 waving flags. The bands from the two schools joined on the field and played "God Bless America." Eyes filled with tears. Coach McKissick kept his team behind the stands, speaking softly to the players, fighting the tide. "Gonna do what we've done for 50 years," he said. "Nothing different. Get your mind on the football game."

The P.A. announcer began a tribute to those lost and those still searching for them. His voice crackled, then cracked, then choked with sobs. The flag was raised, and a minister said a prayer. I turned to Noah. "Have you prayed?" I asked as Stratford students sent balloons into the air.

"We had 15 minutes of silence at school today," he said.

"What happened during those 15 minutes?" I asked.

"I heard Sidra sniffling, so I think she was crying, and Laura Jett's mouth was moving, so I think she was praying."

"But you — what about you?"   30

"Yeah. I did. And I prayed in bed the other night for all the families."

"Was that the first time you've ever prayed — not at dinner with us, I mean, but on your own?"

"Uh . . . I guess."

"Might want to try that again."

"Yeah."   35

The metal stands beneath us began to shake from the stomping feet. The kickoff sailed through the night, and the crowd, as crowds are wont to do, roared. The Summerville offense quickly stalled. "Do you think we should go to war?" I asked Noah.

"No," he said. "I don't want to worry about getting bombed every night. I don't want to end up right dab in the middle of a war."

I loved that *dab*. I looked out as cheerleaders for the black-clad Knights cartwheeled and flipped before us, and somehow I saw my high horse. I couldn't resist climbing on. "You know," I said to Noah, "a lot of people say we should have games right away so we can get back to normal as soon as possible. But maybe we shouldn't be in such a hurry for normal. Maybe we should stop for a while and think about whether we could do better than that. What if we started spending, say, only a quarter of the time we spend on sports and did something good for some of those families we saw on TV?"

He said nothing for a while. Then he asked, "Is that called a reverse?"

I glanced at the field, where the Stratford quarterback had passed the ball   40
to the wide receiver, who was passing it right back to the quarterback.

"No," I said. "That's a flea-flicker."

Stratford was leading 7-0 in the second quarter. I sat there watching fans cheer and groan, parents pass out burgers, tuba players blare the *Rocky* theme song. I had been to only one Summerville game in my life, so I couldn't quite gauge whether it was me or if the air really was lacking a certain charge. Ryan Snipes's mom sure noticed it. Then a Stratford kid fumbled, players dived for the bouncing ball . . . and the stadium went black.

Stone cold black, lights out, all four stanchions. A gasp went up. My heart clawed its way into my throat. A girl cried, "They're gonna bomb us!"

A teenager called, "What should we do?"

"Quiet!" men shouted. *"Quiet!"*   45

"Dad, look!" said Noah. "There's a plane up there!"

"It's O.K.," I said. All eyes were fixed on the blinking light. "It's just the electricity. The power went out."

On the field silhouettes stampeded here, then there. "Dad," said Noah, "don't you think we should go?"

"No," I lied.

A few people began to exit. "Ladies and gentlemen!" the P.A. announcer   50
called out. "Please limit your movements!"

The plane had nearly passed. "They wouldn't know about a little thing like a Summerville football game . . . would they?" Noah asked.

I hated that *they*. We sat through 12 minutes of silence and darkness during a football game on the day America mourned.

He wanted to play catch at halftime behind the stands, so we did, running down each other's spirals as a trumpeter on the field played taps. He wanted to eat funnel cake buried in sugar, so we did that, too, as we talked to the piccolo player whose 42-year-old dad spoke of reenlisting. She was scared and thought we shouldn't be there.

We settled back into our seats and watched Stratford score on a one-yard burst to take a 14-0 lead. The crowd roared. I looked at Noah and stumbled around for words.

"So, what do you think about games?" I asked.   55

"Huh?"

"You know, what do they *mean* to you? I mean, when a game you're playing in is about to start, what's it feel like to you, how important is it to you. . . . I mean, *really?*"

I waited. Had I gone too far, drilling him on the stop-and-go move under the driveway hoop, hitting him grounder after grounder in Shortstop Showdowns between Jeter and A-Rod? Had I pulled the rope back the other way often enough, hard enough? Then again, how far would my heart sink if he said, You know, Dad, winning, losing — I don't really give a hoot.

"I try my hardest to win games," Noah said. "I'll dive on any court for a ball except the one at our school — it's just too hard. I don't like losing. I think about what I could've done better."

"And how about that championship game against Charleston Catholic, the   60
double-overtime loss?"

"That bothered me awhile. I pretended it was that game a couple of days later when I was playing alone, and I made all kinds of baskets, and we killed 'em, and the announcer kept saying, 'Look at Noah Smith! He's going wild!' I didn't think about it much more after that. That's only one game. If I make the pros, I kinda think I won't remember that."

We rode back to Summerville with the Green Wave, another half hour of silence, after its 21-0 loss. Coach McKissick said his boys had looked confused out there, and that maybe events had made them lose focus. Ryan Snipes said his game face had sure gone to pieces during that pregame prayer and tribute. Coach McCurry exploded, stepping over bodies and shoulder pads in the bus to scream, "Nothing's damn funny!" at a couple of players who'd pulled down a window and exchanged giggles with a girl.

We left the bus and got into our car to head home. Now that it was over, I told him what I really thought: that there was nothing terrible, or even remotely disrespectful, about playing a game or watching one. That most of the fans out there seemed to enjoy the chance to come together and show that they cared about their kids, their country and the families who'd lost so much. And that, God knows, no matter the individual price down the road, we needed folks now who didn't dwell, who turned anguish into action, lickety-split.

However, something, I said, was still off about that game. I'd played in and watched too many games not to know it. Because when games are right, they're like pulling a blanket over your head when you're a kid — suddenly the world goes away and nothing outside that little space even exists; it's delicious.

Yep, it's like playing a trick on yourself, and for it all to work right, it has 65 to start with the players believing that the outcome *really* matters, then spread out over the crowd and the viewers at home and cover them too, get them screaming and jumping and throwing pillows at the screen. Only a few athletes, or maybe a handful of fans, not losing themselves in the game can start lifting the edge of the blanket, start making everyone see that the game doesn't mean a thing. So how can we possibly expect the pretense to hold up three days after a mass murder, and why would we even ask it to? But, I said, when it does work, it's a thing of such beauty that I want him always to treasure the trick, on one condition: that some part of him, when he isn't playing in a game, knows it's just that — a trick. O.K., Noah? *Noah?*

I took my eyes off the road and sneaked a look in the backseat. It was nearly midnight on the national day of mourning, and the kid was fast asleep.

READING THE TEXT

1. Why did Smith take his son Noah on a bus trip to see a high school football game so soon after the September 11 terrorist attacks?

2. Summarize the personal September 11 story of Noah Smith. How is this the story of more than one family?

3. What is Smith's final opinion about the football game he attended? What is Noah's?

READING THE SIGNS

1. Throughout America, people had to decide whether to go on with whatever they had planned to do in the immediate aftermath of the September 11 attacks. Write a journal entry in which you discuss those activities that you found

difficult, and perhaps even inappropriate, to take part in after the attacks. What social and ethical values affected your choices?

2. Within a few weeks of the attacks, most of American popular culture, including sports, had returned to its normal schedule. Write a paper arguing whether returning to "normal" (para. 38) was an appropriate response.

3. The NFL and collegiate football leagues canceled their weekend schedules just after the September 11 attacks, but many high school football games, as Smith relates, went ahead as scheduled. Taking Smith's own conclusions into consideration, write an essay arguing whether it was appropriate for athletics to continue in the immediate aftermath of the attack.

4. In addition to Smith's article, consult Damien Cave's "The Spam Spoils of War" (p. 122), Tom Shales's "Resisting the False Security of TV" (p. 285), Patrick Goldstein's "The Time to Get Serious Has Come" (p. 384), and Tim Layden's "A Patriot's Tale" (p. 795). What patterns do you see in their descriptions of Americans' responses to the September 11 attacks? Would you describe these responses as revealing essentially "American" values and habits?

AMERICAN ICONS
The Mythic Characters of Popular Culture

In the fall of 2001, Michael Jordan came out of retirement for the second time to return to active play in the NBA. After months of speculation, the build-up to Jordan's reappearance was enormous, promising to make it one of the media events of the year. But then, literally overnight, the national mood changed, and by the time Jordan soared towards his first postretirement slam dunk, America had rediscovered a different kind of national hero, one who prompted us to reappraise just what heroism means. And so, at least for the time, Michael Jordan's preeminent stature as an American icon was redefined as a new set of icons suddenly emerged.

In this chapter, you will read about America's cultural icons, about those figures — some entirely fictional and others quite real — who have been mythologized into larger-than-life symbols that capture our imagination by embodying our deepest values and desires. An icon is not simply a popular figure or celebrity (though he or she often *is* in our entertainment culture); an icon is someone, or something, that has a *meaning,* a cultural significance that goes beyond any particular qualities he, she, or it might have. Which is why it was particularly significant that America's new icons in the fall of 2001 weren't celebrities at all. They were the firefighters and police officers of the Port Authority and the New York City police departments, the men and women who entered the maelstrom of the World Trade Center even as the towers came crashing down upon them.

Interpreting American Icons

The dramatic emergence of the firefighter and police officer as American icons was underscored in the immediate aftermath of the September 11, 2001, attacks by the way that they became the central figures at such celebrity-led benefits as the Concert for New York. Though the headliners for the event included such pop culture icons as Paul McCartney, the Who, David Bowie, and Destiny's Child, the real heroes for the night were the firefighters, police officers, and other emergency workers who came to represent their colleagues who were still sifting through the rubble of the towers, searching for remains. FDNY replaced Prada and Versace as the fashion logo of the evening.

Everywhere in the country, police and firefighter action figures flew off the shelves of toy stores, while police and firefighter costumes became *de rigeur* that Halloween. For the first time, even leading figures within the entertainment industry began to question America's fascination with the glitter and glamour of the sports-and-entertainment celebrity pantheon in light of the heroic self-sacrifice of the humble cops and firefighters who were demonstrating through their deeds, not their publicists, what heroism is really all about. A profound reassessment of what, and whom, Americans ought to value began.

It is easy to take this reassessment for granted; after all, the traumatic events of September 11 were bound to trigger a sobering appraisal of a society that seemed driven primarily by the pleasure principle. But that it took such a trauma to awaken Americans to the drift of their culture away from the sterner values that they once had held is itself significant. For America's traditional heroes and cultural icons weren't entertainers at all: they were men like George Washington and Abraham Lincoln, who dedicated their lives to building and preserving their country, or like Frederick Douglass and Martin Luther King Jr., who struggled to win for their people the rights that their country promised. And they were women like Susan B. Anthony and Eleanor Roosevelt, who helped redefine the place of women in American political life. It has only been in the era of mass culture that entertainers have come to replace such traditional icons, beginning with the Golden Age of Hollywood and of baseball, when names like Clark Gable, Greta Garbo, and Babe Ruth came to represent the emerging center of American desire.

When we situate the reemergence of the firefighter and police officer as heroes within this historical context, its significance becomes especially apparent. For the trend of American life had been, until that awful morning in September, strongly towards celebrity worship. From the huge circulations of such celebrity-oriented publications as *People* and *The National Enquirer*, to the elaborate cultural rituals surrounding the Emmy, Oscar, and Grammy awards — not to mention the Super Bowl and the NBA Finals (with Jack Nicholson and company highlighted in every crowd shot) — the signs were all pointing to an American culture dedicated to the celebration of wealth, fame, and entertainment. Few Americans even seemed to notice or care that these weren't the values that their country had been founded upon.

That is what made so striking the guilt-edged reappraisal after September 11. A number of celebrities, feeling that they had become irrelevant (or fearing they might appear irrelevant) cancelled their public appearances, some even deciding to pass up the rescheduled Emmys — rescheduled due to the fear that they would look especially frivolous in the light cast by the burning towers of the World Trade Center. Sports stars found it difficult to concentrate at a time when their efforts looked to be almost ludicrously pointless. Everything, everyone said, was different, and the difference was that for the first time the Emperor of Entertainment, so to speak, was seen to be wearing no clothes.

There was another crucial difference that helped establish the cultural significance of the new heroism. This was the fact that until September 11, the cultural image of America's police departments was at, or near, a historical nadir. Police scandals in New York and Los Angeles had strongly contributed to a cultural drift in which police officers, who had once been regarded as what Robert B. Ray calls "official heroes" (see Ray's selection in Chapter 4), were not only losing their heroic status but were coming to be widely regarded as cultural villains. Official heroes in general — that is, those figures who work from within society to protect it — were falling out of favor everywhere, as politicians, the FBI, CIA, and every other institution signifying governmental authority came to be objects of suspicion, or even hatred, across the spectrum of American political belief.

> ### Exploring the Signs of American Characters
>
> Children's television is filled with characters, from Winnie the Pooh to G.I. Joe, from the Muppets to the Mighty Morphin Power Rangers. Choose a character with whom you grew up, and explore in your journal what role that character played in your life. Did you simply watch the character on TV, or did you play-act games with it? Did you ever buy — or want to buy — any products related to that character? Why? Does that character mean anything to you today?

All of that changed after the attacks. Not only the police but politicians too suddenly came to be regarded as necessary public servants dedicated to our protection. College students announced that they would pursue careers in the FBI and CIA (an almost unheard-of cultural shift), and even once-despised ROTC programs came to be regarded with benevolence. Indeed, it could be said that, far from shaking America to its foundations, the terrorist assault only strengthened it. And should this continue to be the case, that would be the most profound semiotic lesson of all.

The More Things Change, the More They Stay the Same

The emergence of firefighters and police officers as popular cultural icons, important as it is, still did not change everything. Part of the normalcy that Americans were encouraged to return to included the entertainment world and its icons. It is significant, after all, that the Concert for New York, along with similar benefits in Washington, D.C., and Nashville, were celebrity-led events. It is significant that the Emmys, after a second postponement, went ahead in the end. It is significant that the World Series not only was played but that its playing was regarded as a sign of American resilience and defiance. And it is significant that the combination of *Harry Potter, The Fellowship of the Ring,* and *Monsters, Inc.* produced a record-breaking Hollywood box office tally even as emergency workers continued to pick through the WTC debris.

All this is significant because it indicates just how profoundly an entertainment culture we have become, and while the attacks may have made this more apparent, they could not alter the fact that it was to entertainment and its icons that many Americans turned for consolation in the aftermath of the catastrophe. The breakup of Tom and Nicole was still a big story in the weeks after the disaster (the fact that we can presume that you know which Tom and Nicole we mean is itself significant); Michael Jordan's return to the NBA became a pretty big story after all when his Wizards went over .500; and Charles Barkley's much-repeated naysaying seemed to be so much sour grapes.

To see just how important our cultural icons — especially those drawn from popular culture — are to us, try to imagine how things would be without them. And we don't only mean such living icons as Michael Jordan, Tom Cruise, or Nicole Kidman, but such even larger-than-life figures as Elvis and Marilyn. Again, it is significant that we can assume that you know which Elvis and which Marilyn we mean.

Forever Elvis

Elvis Presley is one of our most popular and enduring cultural icons, a man who, more in death than in life, has become the object of an almost cultlike veneration. Though his significance is not precisely the same to everyone, his cultural status is such that Paul Simon could make him a symbol for American life in his 1980s hit "Graceland," and the word *Elvis* has seemed to assume a life of its own. But what is it that has enabled this humble southern truck driver to become such a potent American icon? What does Elvis mean to us?

The fact that Elvis Presley began his life as a humble southern truck driver is an important part of his iconic significance. After all, in his rise to the peak of early rock-and-roll stardom, Elvis exemplified, in an especially glamorous way, the mythic promise of the American dream. Few American mythologies are more important to us than this one, and Elvis Presley's life has been particularly inspiring to those rural and small-town southern working-class youth who can most closely identify with it (the identification of working-class fans from New Jersey with Bruce Springsteen is a closely related phenomenon: indeed, Springsteen's nickname, the Boss, is a signifier of his cultural connection to the King).

But that is not the end of Elvis Presley's iconic significance, not by a long shot. After all, a lot of other figures in the entertainment world have exemplified the American dream, but none quite stands up to Elvis. There is something different about Elvis, a difference that helps explain just what is so special about him.

That difference lies, in part, in his pioneering role in the invention of rock-and-roll. It is important to note in this regard that Elvis Presley did not actually invent rock-and-roll. The credit for that has been given to such figures as Chuck Berry, Bill Haley, and Carl Perkins. Nor was Elvis alone in popularizing the new music, though he became its biggest star. What made Presley so special had less to do with the music than with what the music signified, and to see what that was we need only consider such well-known historical facts as the one that his performances were so sexually suggestive that when he first appeared on *The Ed Sullivan Show* he was filmed from the waist up.

Bumping and grinding to the beat, Elvis Presley brought to the stage the raw sexual energy that lay at the heart of the blues, boogie, and bop — those African American musical forms that Chuck Berry combined with country music in his invention of rock music. It was this sexual energy, combined with the racist climate of the Jim Crow South, that caused rock-and-roll to be denounced as the devil's music and that led to a musical segregation in which rhythm and blues, with all of its original sexual energy intact, was socially marginalized as "black music." Meanwhile rock, often in a sanitized form, came to be appropriated by such squeaky clean white performers as Pat Boone, Ricky Nelson, and Connie Francis.

But sex was too important a part of rock's essential appeal to be so neatly suppressed, and while, in the segregated America of the 1950s, a black performer could not deliver it, a white boy who "sounded black" could. By making sex such an explicit part of his act, Elvis Presley, in effect, released the erotic energies of a generation that was gearing up for a sexual revolution.

In doing so, Elvis became a kind of modern Dionysus. The mythic center of a cult that swept through Greece over two thousand years ago, Dionysus was a godlike figure — usually depicted as a young man — whose rituals included the violent release of sexual energy. Dionysus has since become an enduring symbol of sexual expression, an archetypal figure whose universal appeal has been reflected in American popular culture through such male sex symbols as Rudolph Valentino and Elvis Presley, men who are not simply good-looking or sexy but who seem to embody sexuality itself.

Indeed, Dionysus offers us a clue into the origin of all those stories about Elvis's "survival." That is, part of the cult of Dionysus included his ritual murder, but he always came back to life, refusing to die. Now think of Elvis's death, and all those funny denials, the rumors: that he did not really die, that he is working as a grocery checkout clerk in Minneapolis, that he was just spotted at the 7 Eleven down the street. Refusing to stay dead, Elvis completes his mythic circuit, becoming archetypal through the never-dying, ever-potent figure of Dionysus. Such a man can never die.

Like a Candle in the Wind

If all this sounds like a lot for one man to symbolize, don't worry, Elvis isn't America's only sex symbol, nor even its most prominent. That honor belongs to Marilyn Monroe.

In many ways, the iconic significance of Marilyn Monroe resembles that of Elvis. The rise of factory worker Norma Jean Dougherty to superstardom, for example, also exemplifies the American dream in its gaudiest aspects. And like Elvis, Marilyn functions as a potent sex symbol in a society ever on the lookout for sex symbols. Again like Elvis, Marilyn died young and thus enjoys the legendary status of those other popular American characters who died early (have you seen her with Elvis and James Dean in that poster where they are all sitting together at a fifties-style coffee shop counter?). And, of course, like Elvis, Marilyn has her own postage stamp. But still Marilyn Monroe is different. She's no female Dionysus, for example. Her appeal is more subtle than that, less violent and ecstatic. But it has proven just as enduring.

> ### Discussing the Signs of American Characters
>
> In class, brainstorm a list of your favorite pop cultural icons. Then analyze your list. What mythological significance can you attach to the characters on your list? Do any rival the stature of an Elvis or a Marilyn? If so, what's their appeal; if not, why do you think they don't? What does the list say about the class's collective interests, concerns, and values?

So what does Marilyn Monroe mean to you? Is she just another sex symbol? But then, why do some women still identify with her today, women who can hardly be said to be sexists in their response to her? And men too: Is the enduring popularity of Marilyn Monroe among American men simply a sexual thing? Why is she such a popular icon among gays?

As you ponder such questions, you might consider the system of American sex symbols to which Marilyn Monroe belongs. Each decade seems to have its dominant figure. In the 1930s, for example, there was Jean Harlow, a platinum-blonde sex goddess who is best remembered through a photograph in which she is posed lying seductively on a bear skin rug. In the 1940s, there was Rita Hayworth, whose most famous image shows her posed crouching in her lingerie on a bed. But then there's Monroe in *The Seven Year Itch,* playing a gentle if airheaded sex toy who displays her sexuality without fully being aware of it. Probably her most famous image comes from that film, when an updraft of air blows her skirts around her waist as she walks over a subway vent. She laughs as she tries to hold her skirts down. And that's how she's most often remembered, laughing and innocent, even vulnerable.

Now consider the difference between these three images: Harlow's and Hayworth's, seductive, challenging poses, and Monroe's childlike laughter and vulnerability. It's that laughter and that innocence that sets Monroe apart, the vulnerability that distinguishes her from the other sex goddesses of American popular culture. As the song goes, Marilyn is remembered "like a candle in the wind," as a fragile flame unable to endure the gales of popular attention. What can you make of that vulnerability, of the way that Marilyn signifies today more as a victim of her own fame than as a sex symbol? Does this indicate any uneasiness on America's part about its tendency to worship, and so sometimes destroy, its entertainers?

Pitching the Product

By analyzing such cultural icons as Elvis Presley and Marilyn Monroe — real people who came to embody their society's most basic desires — we can thus learn a great deal about American culture. But there are many other kinds of American icons — from social heroes like Martin Luther King Jr., to scientific icons like Albert Einstein — who represent the best in a culture. The trouble is that such heroes, at least up to 9/11, are getting harder to find. For one thing, many of them — like Thomas Jefferson, and, to a lesser extent, George Washington and Abraham Lincoln — are being pulled off their pedestals. And for another, they are getting crowded out by another kind of cultural character, one that is constructed not from the stuff of America's social and political history but from its nature as a consumer culture. For these icons, whether they are real-life people or pure inventions, are constructed for one purpose: to pitch the product.

Reading Characters on the Net

One important component in American popular culture is the cult of the celebrity. What role has the Internet played in fostering a celebrity's status? Select a celebrity who interests you, and visit the Web sites, both offical and fan-sponsored, associated with that person. How does the official site construct an image for the celebrity, and how does it create a community of fans? In what ways are the fan-generated sites responses to the celebrity's image?

Note how whenever anyone achieves widespread popularity, or even notoriety, in America, the measure of their success is made by how many product endorsements they get. Tiger Woods is the current king of the endorsers, but consider how one gymnastic leap in the 1996 Summer Olympics turned into a multimillion dollar endorsement bonanza for Keri Strug. And when the heretofore shy and un-mediagenic Mark McGwire shattered baseball's single season home run record in 1998, everyone started talking about the endorsements he would soon be lining up (now, we can wonder about Barry Bonds's future in the same way). Indeed, sometimes it seems that no American success story is complete without a product endorsement.

Wherever you look, you can find such commercial icons, and some of them aren't even real. How much beer has Louie the Lizard sold, and what were Joe Camel's sales figures before antismoking legislation forced him to "retire"? How many flashlights has the Energizer Bunny lit up? And how's the Taco Bell chihuahua doing? Advertisers are constantly creating such figures in order to appeal to specifically targetted markets (Joe Camel, for instance, was accused of being created to sell cigarettes to children), and they often become much admired in their own right (Spuds MacKenzie was quite a hero in the late 1980s).

That so many of America's cultural icons have been subsumed, or even created, to serve commercial interests is a sign of just how profoundly America has embraced the values of a consumer culture. And few icons have been left out of the consumer stampede. Martin Luther King Jr. has been appropriated for a telecommunications pitch, and Albert Einstein's image has been splashed across more ad campaigns than we can count. For their part, George Washington and Abraham Lincoln are the names of sales events. Very little, it seems, is too sacred not to be used for commercial purposes. Or is it that consumerism itself has become sacred?

The Readings

The readings in this chapter analyze a range of American characters, some of whom have been used for marketing purposes and others who function as American heroes, real and fictional. Michael Eric Dyson starts with an interpretation of the cultural significance of Michael Jordan, a reading of a real-world superman. Gary Engle follows with an analysis of the original Superman, a cartoon hero who, Engle argues, is very much a symbol of the American way. Andy Medhurst's interpretation of Batman from a gay perspective provides some clues as to why Robin was excluded from Tim Burton's *Batman,* while N'Gai Croal and Jane Hughes present a profile of Lara Croft, an icon of the cyberset who doesn't have to wear tights. Emily Prager and Gary Cross come next with analyses of two of America's favorite characters, Barbie and G.I. Joe — iconic toys that continue to shape American childhoods. Mark Caldwell takes a look at Martha Stewart and her not uncontroversial role as an icon of American domestic life, while Roy Rivenburg offers a tongue-in-cheek celebrity profile of some of America's favorite product pitchmen, like Tony the Tiger and Mr. Clean. Jenny Lyn Bader's nostalgic essay on the place of heroes within her own generation — twentysomethings who have seen the old heroes topple and who wonder whether America has any room for any new ones — is followed by Tim Layden's sketch of precisely the kind of hero that Bader misses: a family of New York City firefighters.

MICHAEL ERIC DYSON

BE LIKE MIKE? MICHAEL JORDAN AND THE PEDAGOGY OF DESIRE

It's hard to keep up with Michael Jordan. Not only is it impossible to beat him on the court, but you can't even figure out what to call him these days. A former NBA megastar? Well, he's retired twice and has now come back for the second time, which is an appropriate addition to the legend that Michael Eric Dyson (b. 1958) analyzes in this selection. Situating Jordan within the context of American social and cultural history, Dyson shows what basketball, and everything that goes with it, means in America, especially for African American youth. And it isn't just air time. A professor of religious studies at DePaul University, Dyson is author of Reflecting Black: African-American Cultural Criticism *(1993), from which this essay is taken,* Making Malcolm: The Myth and Meaning of Malcolm X *(1995),* Between God and Gangsta Rap: Bearing Witness to Black Culture *(1996), and* Holler If You Hear Me: Searching for Tupac Shakur *(2001).*

Michael Jordan is perhaps the best, and best-known, athlete in the world today. He has attained unparalleled cultural status because of his extraordinary physical gifts, his marketing as an icon of race-transcending American athletic and moral excellence, and his mastery of a sport that has become the metaphoric center of black cultural imagination. But the Olympian sum of Jordan's cultural meaning is greater than the fluent parts of his persona as athlete, family man, and marketing creation. There is hardly cultural precedence for the character of his unique fame, which has blurred the line between private and public, between personality and celebrity, and between substance and symbol. Michael Jordan stands at the breach between perception and intuition, his cultural meaning perennially deferred from closure because his career symbolizes possibility itself, gathering into its unfolding narrative the shattered remnants of previous incarnations of fame and yet transcending their reach.

Jordan has been called "the new DiMaggio" (Boers 1990, 30) and "Elvis in high-tops," indications of the herculean cultural heroism he has come to embody. There is even a religious element to the near worship of Jordan as a cultural icon of invincibility, as he has been called a "savior of sorts," "basketball's high priest" (Bradley 1991–92, 60), and "more popular than Jesus," except with "better endorsement deals" (Vancil 1992, 51). But the quickly developing cultural canonization of Michael Jordan provokes reflection about the contradictory uses to which Jordan's body is put as a seminal cultural text and ambiguous symbol of fantasy, and the avenues of agency and resistance available especially to black youth who make symbolic investment in Jordan's body as a means of cultural and personal possibility, creativity, and desire.

I understand Jordan in the broadest sense of the term to be a public pedagogue, a figure of estimable public moral authority whose career educates us
about productive and disenabling forms of knowledge, desire, interest, consumption, and culture in three spheres: the culture of athletics that thrives on
skill and performance; the specific expression of elements of African American culture; and the market forces and processes of commodification expressed by, and produced in, advanced capitalism. By probing these dimensions of Jordan's cultural importance, we may gain a clearer understanding of
his function in American society.

Athletic activity has shaped and reflected important sectors of American
society. First, it produced communities of common athletic interest organized
around the development of highly skilled performance. The development of
norms of athletic excellence evidenced in sports activities cemented communities of participants who valorized rigorous sorts of physical discipline in
preparation for athletic competition and in expressing the highest degree of
athletic skill. Second, it produced potent subcultures that inculcated in their
participants norms of individual and team accomplishment. Such norms
tapped into the bipolar structures of competition and cooperation that pervade American culture. Third, it provided a means of reinscribing Western
frontier myths of exploration and discovery-as-conquest onto a vital sphere of
American culture. Sports activities can be viewed in part as the attempt to
symbolically ritualize and metaphorically extend the ongoing quest for mastery of environment and vanquishing of opponents within the limits of physical contest.

Fourth, athletic activity has served to reinforce habits and virtues cen-   5
tered in collective pursuit of communal goals that are intimately connected to
the common good, usually characterized within athletic circles as "team
spirit." The culture of sport has physically captured and athletically articulated
the mores, folkways, and dominant visions of American society, and at its
best it has been conceived as a means of symbolically embracing and equi-
tably pursuing the just, the good, the true, and the beautiful. And finally, the
culture of athletics has provided an acceptable and widely accessible means
of white male bonding. For much of its history, American sports activity has
reflected white patriarchal privilege, and it has been rigidly defined and socially shaped by rules that restricted the equitable participation of women and
people of color.

Black participation in sports in mainstream society, therefore, is a relatively recent phenomenon. Of course, there have existed venerable traditions
of black sports, such as the Negro (baseball) Leagues, which countered the exclusion of black bodies from white sports. The prohibition of athletic activity
by black men in mainstream society severely limited publicly acceptable
forms of displaying black physical prowess, an issue that had been politicized
during slavery and whose legacy extended into the middle of the twentieth
century. Hence, the potentially superior physical prowess of black men, vali-

dated for many by the long tradition of slave labor that built American society, helped reinforce racist arguments about the racial regimentation of social space and the denigration of the black body as an inappropriate presence in traditions of American sport.

Coupled with this fear of superior black physical prowess was the notion that inferior black intelligence limited the ability of blacks to perform excellently in those sports activities that required mental concentration and agility. These two forces — the presumed lack of sophisticated black cognitive skills and the fear of superior black physical prowess — restricted black sports participation to thriving but financially handicapped subcultures of black athletic activity. Later, of course, the physical prowess of the black body would be acknowledged and exploited as a supremely fertile zone of profit as mainstream athletic society literally cashed in on the symbolic danger of black sports excellence.

Because of its marginalized status within the regime of American sports, black athletic activity often acquired a social significance that transcended the internal dimensions of game, sport, and skill. Black sport became an arena not only for testing the limits of physical endurance and forms of athletic excellence — while reproducing or repudiating ideals of American justice, goodness, truth, and beauty — but it also became a way of ritualizing racial achievement against socially imposed barriers to cultural performance.

In short, black sport activity often acquired a heroic dimension, as viewed in the careers of figures such as Joe Louis, Jackie Robinson, Althea Gibson, Wilma Rudolph, Muhammad Ali, and Arthur Ashe. Black sports heroes transcended the narrow boundaries of specific sports activities and garnered importance as icons of cultural excellence, symbolic figures who embodied social possibilities of success denied to other people of color. But they also captured and catalyzed the black cultural fetishization of sport as a means of expressing black cultural style, as a means of valorizing craft as a marker of racial and self-expression, and as a means of pursuing social and economic mobility.

It is this culture of black athletics, created against the background of social and historical forces that shaped American athletic activity, that helped produce Jordan and help explain the craft that he practices. Craft is the honing of skill by the application of discipline, time, talent, and energy toward the realization of a particular cultural or personal goal. American folk cultures are pervaded by craft, from the production of cultural artifacts that express particular ethnic histories and traditions to the development of styles of life and work that reflect and symbolize a community's values, virtues, and goals. Michael Jordan's skills within basketball are clearly phenomenal, but his game can only be sufficiently explained by understanding its link to the fusion of African American cultural norms and practices, and the idealization of skill and performance that characterize important aspects of American sport. I will identify three defining characteristics of Jordan's game that reflect the influence of African American culture on his style of play.

First, Jordan's style of basketball reflects the *will to spontaneity*. I mean here the way in which historical accidence is transformed into cultural advantage, and the way acts of apparently random occurrence are spontaneously and imaginatively employed by Africans and African Americans in a variety of forms of cultural expression. When examining Jordan's game, this feature of African American culture clearly functions in his unpredictable eruptions of basketball creativity. It was apparent, for instance, during game two of the National Basketball Association 1991 championship series between Jordan's Chicago Bulls and the Los Angeles Lakers, in a shot that even Jordan ranked in his all-time top ten (McCallum 1991, 32). Jordan made a drive toward the lane, gesturing with his hands and body that he was about to complete a patent Jordan dunk shot with his right hand. But when he spied defender Sam Perkins slipping over to oppose his shot, he switched the ball in midair to his left hand to make an underhanded scoop shot instead, which immediately became known as the "levitation" shot. Such improvisation, a staple of the will to spontaneity, allows Jordan to expand his vocabulary of athletic spectacle, which is the stimulation of a desire to bear witness to the revelation of truth and beauty compressed into acts of athletic creativity.

Second, Jordan's game reflects the *stylization of the performed self*. This is the creation and projection of a sport persona that is an identifying mark of diverse African American creative enterprises, from the complexly layered jazz experimentation of John Coltrane, the trickstering and signifying comedic routines of Richard Pryor, and the rhetorical ripostes and oral significations of rapper Kool Moe Dee. Jordan's whole game persona is a graphic depiction of the performed self as flying acrobat, resulting in his famous moniker "Air Jordan." Jordan's performed self is rife with the language of physical expressiveness: head moving, arms extending, hands waving, tongue wagging, and legs spreading.

He has also developed a resourceful repertoire of dazzling dunk shots that further express his performed self and that have garnered him a special niche within the folklore of the game: the cradle jam, rock-a-baby, kiss the rim, lean in, and the tomahawk. In Jordan's game, the stylization of a performed self has allowed him to create a distinct sports persona that has athletic as well as economic consequences, while mastering sophisticated levels of physical expression and redefining the possibilities of athletic achievement within basketball.

Finally, there is the subversion of perceived limits through the use of *edifying deception,* which in Jordan's case centers around the space/time continuum. This moment in African American cultural practice is the ability to flout widely understood boundaries through mesmerization and alchemy, a subversion of common perceptions of the culturally or physically possible through the creative and deceptive manipulation of appearance. Jordan is perhaps most famous for his alleged "hang time," the uncanny ability to remain suspended in midair longer than other basketball players while executing his stunning array of improvised moves. But Jordan's "hang time" is technically a misnomer and can be more accurately attributed to Jordan's skillful athletic deception, his acrobatic leaping ability, and his intellectual toughness in projecting an aura of uniqueness around his craft than to his defiance of gravity and the laws of physics.

No human being, including Michael Jordan, can successfully defy the law of gravity and achieve relatively sustained altitude without the benefit of machines. As Douglas Kirkpatrick points out, the equation for altitude is $1/2g \times t2 = VO \times t$ ("How Does Michael Fly?"). However, Jordan appears to hang by *stylistically* relativizing the fixed coordinates of space and time through the skillful management and manipulation of his body in midair. For basketball players, hang time is the velocity and speed with which a player takes off combined with the path the player's center of gravity follows on the way up. At the peak of a player's vertical jump, the velocity and speed is close to, or at, zero; hanging motionless in the air is the work of masterful skill and illusion ("How Does Michael Fly?"). Michael Jordan, through the consummate skill and style of his game, only appears to be hanging in space for more than the one second that human beings are capable of remaining airborne.

But the African American aspects of Jordan's game are indissolubly linked to the culture of consumption and the commodification of black culture.[1] Because of Jordan's supreme mastery of basketball, his squeaky-clean image, and his youthful vigor in pursuit of the American Dream, he has become, along with Bill Cosby, the quintessential pitchman in American society. Even his highly publicized troubles with gambling, his refusal to visit the White House after the Bulls' championship season, and a book that purports to expose the underside of his heroic myth have barely tarnished his All-American image.[2] Jordan eats Wheaties, drives Chevrolets, wears Hanes, drinks Coca-Cola, consumes McDonald's, guzzles Gatorade, and, of course, wears Nikes. He and his shrewd handlers have successfully produced, packaged, marketed, and distributed his image and commodified his symbolic worth, transforming cultural capital into cash, influence, prestige, status, and wealth. To that degree, at least, Jordan repudiates the sorry tradition of the black athlete as the naif who loses his money to piranha-like financial wizards, investors, and hangers-on. He represents the new-age athletic entrepreneur who understands that American sport is ensconced in the cultural practices associated with business, and that it demands particular forms of intelligence, perception, and representation to prevent abuse and maximize profit.

From the very beginning of his professional career, Jordan was consciously marketed by his agency Pro-Serv as a peripatetic vehicle of American

---

[1] I do not mean here a theory of commodification that does not accentuate the forms of agency that can function even within restrictive and hegemonic cultural practices. Rather, I think that, contrary to elitist and overly pessimistic Frankfurt School readings of the spectacle of commodity within mass cultures, common people can exercise "everyday forms of resistance" to hegemonic forms of cultural knowledge and practice. For an explication of the function of everyday forms of resistance, see Scott, *Domination and the Arts of Resistance*.

[2] For a critical look at Jordan behind the myth, see Smith, *The Jordan Rules*.

fantasies of capital accumulation and material consumption tied to Jordan's personal modesty and moral probity. In so doing, they skillfully avoided attaching to Jordan the image of questionable ethics and lethal excess that plagued inside traders and corporate raiders on Wall Street during the mid-eighties, as Jordan began to emerge as a cultural icon. But Jordan is also the symbol of the spectacle-laden black athletic body as the site of commodified black cultural imagination. Ironically, the black male body, which has been historically viewed as threatening and inappropriate in American society (and remains so outside of sports and entertainment), is made an object of white desires to domesticate and dilute its more ominous and subversive uses, even symbolically reducing Jordan's body to dead meat (McDonald's McJordan hamburger), which can be consumed and expelled as waste.

Jordan's body is also the screen upon which is projected black desires to emulate his athletic excellence and replicate his entry into reaches of unimaginable wealth and fame. But there is more than vicarious substitution and the projection of fantasy onto Jordan's body that is occurring in the circulation and reproduction of black cultural desire. There is also the creative use of desire and fantasy by young blacks to counter, and capitulate to, the forces of cultural dominance that attempt to reduce the black body to a commodity and text that is employed for entertainment, titillation, or financial gain. Simply said, there is no easy correlation between the commodification of black youth culture and the evidences of a completely dominated consciousness.

Even within the dominant cultural practices that seek to turn the black body into pure profit, disruptions of capital are embodied, for instance, in messages circulated in black communities by public moralists who criticize the exploitation of black cultural creativity by casual footwear companies. In short, there are instances of both black complicity and resistance in the commodification of black cultural imagination, and the ideological criticism of exploitative cultural practices must always be linked to the language of possibility and agency in rendering a complex picture of the black cultural situation. As Henry Giroux observes:

> The power of complicity and the complicity of power are not exhausted simply by registering how people are positioned and located through the production of particular ideologies structured through particular discourses. . . .
> It is important to see that an overreliance on ideology critique has limited our ability to understand how people actively participate in the dominant culture through processes of accommodation, negotiation, and even resistance. (Giroux 1992, 194–95)

In making judgments about the various uses of the black body, especially Jordan's symbolic corporeality, we must specify how both consent and opposition to exploitation are often signaled in expressions of cultural creativity.

In examining his reactions to the racial ordering of athletic and cultural life, the ominous specificity of the black body creates anxieties for Jordan. His encounters with the limits of culturally mediated symbols of race and racial identity have occasionally mocked his desire to live beyond race, to be "neither black nor white" (Patton 1986, 52), to be "viewed as a person" (Vancil 1992, 57). While Jordan chafes under indictment by black critics who claim that he is not "black enough," he has perhaps not clearly understood the differences between enabling versions of human experience that transcend the exclusive gaze of race and disenabling visions of human community that seek race neutrality.

The former is the attempt to expand the perimeters of human experience beyond racial determinism, to nuance and deepen our understanding of the constituent elements of racial identity, and to understand how race, along with class, gender, geography, and sexual preference, shape and constrain human experience. The latter is the belief in an intangible, amorphous, nonhistorical, and raceless category of "person," existing in a zone beyond not simply the negative consequences of race, but beyond the specific patterns of cultural and racial identity that constitute and help shape human experience. Jordan's unclarity is consequential, weighing heavily on his apolitical bearing and his refusal to acknowledge the public character of his private beliefs about American society and the responsibility of his role as a public pedagogue.

Indeed it is the potency of black cultural expressions that not only have helped influence his style of play, but have also made the sneaker industry he lucratively participates in a multi-billion-dollar business. Michael Jordan has helped seize upon the commercial consequences of black cultural preoccupation with style and the commodification of the black juvenile imagination at the site of the sneaker. At the juncture of the sneaker, a host of cultural, political, and economic forces and meanings meet, collide, shatter, and are reassembled to symbolize the situation of contemporary black culture.

The sneaker reflects at once the projection and stylization of black urban realities linked in our contemporary historical moment to rap culture and the underground political economy of crack, and reigns as the universal icon for the culture of consumption. The sneaker symbolizes the ingenious manner in which black cultural nuances of cool, hip, and chic have influenced the broader American cultural landscape. It was black street culture that influenced sneaker companies' aggressive invasion of the black juvenile market in taking advantage of the increasing amounts of disposable income of young black men as a result of legitimate and illegitimate forms of work.

Problematically, though, the sneaker also epitomizes the worst features of the social production of desire and represents the ways in which moral energies of social conscience about material values are drained by the messages of undisciplined acquisitiveness promoted by corporate dimensions of the culture of consumption. These messages, of rapacious consumerism supported by cultural and personal narcissism, are articulated on Wall Street and are related to the expanding inner-city juvenocracy, where young black men rule over black urban space in the culture of crack and illicit criminal activity, fed by desires to "live large" and to reproduce capitalism's excesses on their own terrain. Also, sneaker companies make significant sums of money from the illicit gains of drug dealers.

Moreover, while sneaker companies have exploited black cultural expressions of cool, hip, chic, and style, they rarely benefit the people who both consume the largest quantity of products and whose culture redefined the sneaker companies' raison d'être. This situation is more severely compounded by the presence of spokespeople like Jordan, Spike Lee, and Bo Jackson, who are either ineffectual or defensive about or indifferent to the lethal consequences (especially in urban black-on-black violence over sneaker company products) of black juvenile acquisition of products that these figures have helped make culturally desirable and economically marketable.

Basketball is the metaphoric center of black juvenile culture, a major means by which even temporary forms of cultural and personal transcendence of personal limits are experienced. Michael Jordan is at the center of this black athletic culture, the supreme symbol of black cultural creativity in a society of diminishing tolerance for the black youth whose fascination with Jordan has helped sustain him. But Jordan is also the iconic fixture of broader segments of American society, who see in him the ideal figure: a black man of extraordinary genius on the court and before the cameras, who by virtue of his magical skills and godlike talents symbolizes the meaning of human possibility, while refusing to root it in the specific forms of culture and race in which it must inevitably make sense or fade to ultimate irrelevance.

Jordan also represents the contradictory impulses of the contemporary culture of consumption, where the black athletic body is deified, reified, and rearticulated within the narrow meanings of capital and commodity. But there is both resistance and consent to the exploitation of black bodies in Jordan's explicit cultural symbolism, as he provides brilliant glimpses of black culture's ingenuity of improvisation as a means of cultural expression and survival. It is also partially this element of black culture that has created in American society a desire to dream Jordan, to "be like Mike."

This pedagogy of desire that Jordan embodies, although at points immobilized by its depoliticized cultural contexts, is nevertheless a remarkable achievement in contemporary American culture: a six-foot-six American man of obvious African descent is the dominant presence and central cause of athletic fantasy in a sport that twenty years ago was denigrated as a black man's game and hence deemed unworthy of wide attention or support. Jordan is therefore the bearer of meanings about black culture larger than his individual life, the symbol of a pedagogy of style, presence, and desire that is immediately communicated by the sight of his black body before it can be contravened by reflection.

In the final analysis, his big black body — graceful and powerful, elegant and dark — symbolizes the possibilities of other black bodies to remain safe long enough to survive within the limited but significant sphere of sport, since Jordan's achievements have furthered the cultural acceptance of at least the athletic black body. In that sense, Jordan's powerful cultural capital has not been exhausted by narrow understandings of his symbolic absorption by the demands of capital and consumption. His body is still the symbolic carrier of racial and cultural desires to fly beyond limits and obstacles, a fluid metaphor of mobility and ascent to heights of excellence secured by genius and industry. It is this power to embody the often conflicting desires of so many that makes Michael Jordan a supremely instructive figure for our times.

WORKS CITED

Boers, Terry. "Getting Better All the Time." *Inside Sports,* May 1990, pp. 30–33.

Bradley, Michael. "Air Everything." *Basketball Forecast,* 1991–92, pp. 60–67.

Giroux, Henry. *Border Crossings: Cultural Workers and the Politics of Education.* New York: Routledge, 1992.

"How Does Michael Fly?" *Chicago Tribune,* February 27, 1990, p. 28.

McCallum, Jack. "His Highness." *Sports Illustrated,* June 17, 1991, pp. 28–33.

Patton, Paul. "The Selling of Michael Jordan." *New York Times Magazine,* November 9, 1986, pp. 48–58.

Scott, James. *Domination and the Arts of Resistance.* New Haven, Conn.: Yale University Press, 1990.

Smith, Sam. *The Jordan Rules.* New York: Simon and Schuster, 1992.

Vancil, Mark. "*Playboy* Interview: Michael Jordan." *Playboy,* May 1992, pp. 51–64.

READING THE TEXT

1. What does Dyson mean by the term "public pedagogue" (para. 3)?

2. What social forces have caused black athletes to assume "a heroic dimension" (para. 9) in American life, according to Dyson?

3. What evidence does Dyson provide to show that Jordan's skills express African American "cultural norms and practices" (para. 10)?

4. What connection does Dyson make between Jordan's athletic skills and America's "culture of consumption" (para. 16)?

5. Why, in Dyson's view, was Jordan especially effective in promoting the sneaker industry?

READING THE SIGNS

1. Dyson observes that some critics have complained that Jordan is not "black enough" (para. 20). Write an essay in which you support or repudiate this criticism, being sure to discuss the underlying assumptions about the role of a hero or role model.

2. Write an argumentative essay in response to the proposition that basketball is primarily a black form of cultural expression. To develop your ideas, read Paul C. Taylor's "Funky White Boys and Honorary Soul Sisters" (p. 579).

3. In class, brainstorm athletic heroes, both male and female. Then discuss the reasons these athletes appeal to the public. Use the class discussion as a basis for an essay in which you analyze why Americans so often turn to athletes for heroes and role models.

4. Write an essay in which you support or refute Dyson's contention that "the culture of athletics has provided an acceptable and widely accessible means of white male bonding" (para. 5). To develop your ideas, consult Michael A. Messner, "Power at Play: Sport and Gender Relations" (p. 668).

GARY ENGLE

WHAT MAKES SUPERMAN SO DARNED AMERICAN?

Since his initial appearance in a June 1938 comic book, and through countless more radio serials, books, toys, Web sites, video games, movies, and television shows—including his latest incarnation in the hit WB show Smallville—*Superman has fought for "truth, justice, and the American way." In this semiotic analysis of the enduring appeal of Superman, Gary Engle (b. 1947) argues why the Man of Steel—whom Engle views as the ultimate immigrant—has dominated the pantheon of American characters for so many years. Of all our heroes, Engle claims, Superman alone "achieves truly mythic stature, interweaving a pattern of beliefs, literary conventions, and cultural traditions of the American people more powerfully and more accessibly than any other cultural symbol of the twentieth century, perhaps of any period in our history." A specialist in popular culture, Engle is an associate professor of English at Cleveland State University. In addition to over two hundred magazine and journal articles, he has written* The Grotesque Essence: Plays from American Minstrel Style *(1978).*

When I was young I spent a lot of time arguing with myself about who would win in a fight between John Wayne and Superman. On days when I wore my cowboy hat and cap guns, I knew the Duke would win because of his pronounced superiority in the all-important matter of swagger. There were days, though, when a frayed army blanket tied cape-fashion around my neck signalled a young man's need to believe there could be no end to the potency of his being. Then the Man of Steel was the odds-on favorite to knock the Duke for a cosmic loop. My greatest childhood problem was that the question could never be resolved because no such battle could ever take place. I mean, how would a fight start between the only two Americans who never started anything, who always fought only to defend their rights and the American way?

Now that I'm older and able to look with reason on the mysteries of childhood, I've finally resolved the dilemma. John Wayne was the best older brother any kid could ever hope to have, but he was no Superman.

Superman is *the* great American hero. We are a nation rich with legendary figures. But among the Davy Crocketts and Paul Bunyans and Mike Finks and Pecos Bills and all the rest who speak for various regional identities in the pantheon of American folklore, only Superman achieves truly mythic stature, interweaving a pattern of beliefs, literary conventions, and cultural traditions of the American people more powerfully and more accessibly than any other cultural symbol of the twentieth century, perhaps of any period in our history.

The core of the American myth in *Superman* consists of a few basic facts that remain unchanged throughout the infinitely varied ways in which the myth is told — facts with which everyone is familiar, however marginal their knowledge of the story. Superman is an orphan rocketed to Earth when his native planet Krypton explodes; he lands near Smallville and is adopted by Jonathan and Martha Kent, who inculcate in him their American middle-class ethic; as an adult he migrates to Metropolis where he defends America — no, the world! no, the Universe! — from all evil and harm while playing a romantic game in which, as Clark Kent, he hopelessly pursues Lois Lane, who hopelessly pursues Superman, who remains aloof until such time as Lois proves worthy of him by falling in love with his feigned identity as a weakling. That's it. Every narrative thread in the mythology, each one of the thousands of plots in the fifty-year stream of comics and films and TV shows, all the tales involving the demigods of the Superman pantheon — Superboy, Supergirl, even Krypto the Superdog — every single one reinforces by never contradicting this basic set of facts. That's the myth, and that's where one looks to understand America.

It is impossible to imagine Superman being as popular as he is and 5 speaking as deeply to the American character were he not an immigrant and an orphan. Immigration, of course, is the overwhelming fact in American history. Except for the Indians, all Americans have an immediate sense of their origins elsewhere. No nation on Earth has so deeply embedded in its social consciousness the imagery of passage from one social identity to another: the *Mayflower* of the New England separatists, the slave ships from Africa and the subsequent underground railroads toward freedom in the North, the sailing ships and steamers running shuttles across two oceans in the nineteenth century, the freedom airlifts in the twentieth. Somehow the picture just isn't complete without Superman's rocketship.

Like the peoples of the nation whose values he defends, Superman is an alien, but not just any alien. He's the consummate and totally uncompromised alien, an immigrant whose visible difference from the norm is underscored by his decision to wear a costume of bold primary colors so tight as to be his very skin. Moreover, Superman the alien is real. He stands out among the hosts of comic book characters (Batman is a good example) for whom the superhero role is like a mask assumed when needed, a costume worn over their real identities as normal Americans. Superman's powers — strength, mobility, x-ray vision and the like — are the comic-book equivalents of ethnic characteristics, and they protect and preserve the vitality of the foster community in which he lives in the same way that immigrant ethnicity has sustained American culture linguistically, artistically, economically, politically, and spiritually. The myth of Superman asserts with total confidence and a childlike innocence the value of the immigrant in American culture.

From this nation's beginnings Americans have looked for ways of coming to terms with the immigrant experience. This is why, for example, so much of American literature and popular culture deals with the theme of dislocation, generally focused in characters devoted or doomed to constant physical movement. Daniel Boone became an American legend in part as a result of apocryphal stories that he moved every time his neighbors got close enough for him to see the smoke of their cabin fires. James Fenimore Cooper's Natty Bumppo spent the five long novels of the Leatherstocking saga drifting ever westward, like the pioneers who were his spiritual offspring, from the Mohawk valley of upstate New York to the Great Plains where he died. Huck Finn sailed through the moral heart of America on a raft. Melville's Ishmael, Wister's Virginian, Shane, Gatsby, the entire Lost Generation, Steinbeck's Okies, Little Orphan Annie, a thousand fiddlefooted cowboy heroes of dime novels and films and television — all in motion, searching for the American dream or stubbornly refusing to give up their innocence by growing old, all symptomatic of a national sense of rootlessness stemming from an identity founded on the experience of immigration.

Individual mobility is an integral part of America's dreamwork. Is it any wonder, then, that our greatest hero can take to the air at will? Superman's ability to fly does more than place him in a tradition of mythic figures going back to the Greek messenger god Hermes or Zetes the flying Argonaut. It makes him an exemplar in the American dream. Take away a young man's wheels and you take away his manhood. Jack Kerouac and Charles Kuralt go on the road; William Least Heat Moon looks for himself in a van exploring the veins of America in its system of blue highways; legions of gray-haired retirees turn Air Stream trailers and Winnebagos into proof positive that you can, in the end, take it with you. On a human scale, the American need to keep moving suggests a neurotic aimlessness under the surface of adventure. But take the human restraints off, let Superman fly unencumbered when and wherever he will, and the meaning of mobility in the American consciousness begins to reveal itself. Superman's incredible speed allows him to be as close to everywhere at once as it is physically possible to be. Displacement is, therefore, impossible. His sense of self is not dispersed by his life's migration but rather enhanced by all the universe that he is able to occupy. What American, whether an immigrant in spirit or in fact, could resist the appeal of one with such an ironclad immunity to the anxiety of dislocation?

In America, physical dislocation serves as a symbol of social and psychological movement. When our immigrant ancestors arrived on America's shores they hit the ground running, some to homestead on the Great Plains, others to claw their way up the socioeconomic ladder in coastal ghettos. Upward mobility, westward migration, Sunbelt relocation — the wisdom in America is that people don't, can't, mustn't end up where they begin. This belief has the moral force of religious doctrine. Thus the American identity is ordered around the psychological experience of forsaking or losing the past for the opportunity of reinventing oneself in the future. This makes the orphan a potent symbol of the American character. Orphans aren't merely free to reinvent themselves. They are obliged to do so.

When Superman reinvents himself, he becomes the bumbling Clark Kent, 10 a figure as immobile as Superman is mobile, as weak as his alter ego is strong. Over the years commentators have been fond of stressing how Clark Kent provides an illusory image of wimpiness onto which children can project their insecurities about their own potential (and, hopefully, equally illusory) weaknesses. But I think the role of Clark Kent is far more complex than that.

During my childhood, Kent contributed nothing to my love for the Man of Steel. If left to contemplate him for too long, I found myself changing from cape back into cowboy hat and guns. John Wayne, at least, was no sissy that I could ever see. Of course, in all the Westerns that the Duke came to stand for in my mind, there were elements that left me as confused as the paradox between Kent and Superman. For example, I could never seem to figure out why cowboys so often fell in love when there were obviously better options: horses to ride, guns to shoot, outlaws to chase, and savages to kill. Even on the days when I became John Wayne, I could fall victim to a never-articulated anxiety about the potential for poor judgment in my cowboy heroes. Then, I generally drifted back into a worship of Superman. With him, at least, the mysterious communion of opposites was honest and on the surface of things.

What disturbed me as a child is what I now think makes the myth of Superman so appealing to an immigrant sensibility. The shape-shifting between Clark Kent and Superman is the means by which this mid-twentieth-century, urban story — like the pastoral, nineteenth-century Western before it — addresses in dramatic terms the theme of cultural assimilation.

At its most basic level, the Western was an imaginative record of the American experience of westward migration and settlement. By bringing the forces of civilization and savagery together on a mythical frontier, the Western addressed the problem of conflict between apparently mutually exclusive identities and explored options for negotiating between them. In terms that a boy could comprehend, the myth explored the dilemma of assimilation — marry the school marm and start wearing Eastern clothes or saddle up and drift further westward with the boys.

The Western was never a myth of stark moral simplicity. Pioneers fled civilization by migrating west, but their purpose in the wilderness was to rebuild civilization. So civilization was both good and bad, what Americans fled from and journeyed toward. A similar moral ambiguity rested at the heart of the wilderness. It was an Eden in which innocence could be achieved through spiritual rebirth, but it was also the anarchic force that most directly threatened the civilized values America wanted to impose on the frontier. So the dilemma arose: In negotiating between civilization and the wilderness, between the old order and the new, between the identity the pioneers carried with them from wherever they came and the identity they sought to invent, Americans faced an impossible choice. Either they pushed into the New World wilderness and forsook the ideals that motivated them or they clung to their origins and polluted Eden.

The myth of the Western responded to this dilemma by inventing the idea of the frontier in which civilized ideals embodied in the institutions of family, church, law, and education are revitalized by the virtues of savagery: independence, self-reliance, personal honor, sympathy with nature, and ethical uses of violence. In effect, the mythical frontier represented an attempt to embody the perfect degree of assimilation in which both the old and new identities came together, if not in a single self-image, then at least in idealized relationships, like the symbolic marriage of reformed cowboy and displaced school marm that ended Owen Wister's prototypical *The Virginian,* or the mystical masculine bonding between representatives of an ascendant and a vanishing America — Natty Bumppo and Chingachgook, the Lone Ranger and Tonto. On the Western frontier, both the old and new identities equally mattered.

As powerful a myth as the Western was, however, there were certain limits to its ability to speak directly to an increasingly common twentieth-century immigrant sensibility. First, it was pastoral. Its imagery of dusty frontier towns and breathtaking mountainous desolation spoke most affectingly to those who conceived of the American dream in terms of the nineteenth-century immigrant experience of rural settlement. As the twentieth century wore on, more immigrants were, like Superman, moving from rural or small-town backgrounds to metropolitan environments. Moreover, the Western was historical, often elegiacally so. Underlying the air of celebration in even the most epic and romantic of Westerns — the films of John Ford, say, in which John Wayne stood tall for all that any good American boy could ever want to be — was an awareness that the frontier was less a place than a state of mind represented in historic terms by a fleeting moment glimpsed imperfectly in the rapid wave of westward migration and settlement. Implicitly, then, whatever balance of past and future identities the frontier could offer was itself tenuous or illusory.

Twentieth-century immigrants, particularly the Eastern European Jews who came to America after 1880 and who settled in the industrial and mercantile centers of the Northeast — cities like Cleveland where Jerry Siegel and Joe Shuster grew up and created Superman — could be entertained by the Western, but they developed a separate literary tradition that addressed the theme of assimilation in terms closer to their personal experience. In this tradition issues were clear-cut: Clinging to an Old World identity meant isolation in ghettos, confrontation with a prejudiced mainstream culture, second-class social status, and impoverishment. On the other hand, forsaking the past in favor of total absorption into the mainstream, while it could result in socioeconomic progress, meant a loss of the religious, linguistic, even culinary traditions that provided a foundation for psychological well-being. Such loss was particularly tragic for the Jews because of the fundamental role played by history in Jewish culture.

Writers who worked in this tradition — Abraham Cahan, Daniel Fuchs, Henry Roth, and Delmore Schwarz, among others — generally found little reason to view the experience of assimilation with joy or optimism. Typical of the tradition was Cahan's early novel *Yekl,* on which Joan Micklin Silver's film *Hester Street* was based. A young married couple, Jake and Gitl, clash over his need to be absorbed as quickly as possible into the American mainstream and her obsessive preservation of their Russian-Jewish heritage. In symbolic terms, their confrontation is as simple as their choice of headgear — a derby for him, a babushka for her. That the story ends with their divorce, even in the context of their gradual movement toward mutual understanding of one another's point of view, suggests the divisive nature of the pressures at work in the immigrant communities.

Where the pressures were perhaps most keenly felt was in the schools. Educational theory of the period stressed the benefits of rapid assimilation. In the first decades of this century, for example, New York schools flatly rejected bilingual education — a common response to the plight of non–English-speaking immigrants even today — and there were conscientious efforts to indoctrinate the children of immigrants with American values, often at the expense of traditions within the ethnic community. What resulted was a generational rift in which children were openly embarrassed by and even contemptuous of their parents' values, setting a pattern in American life in which second-generation immigrants migrate psychologically if not physically from their parents, leaving it up to the third generation and beyond to rediscover their ethnic roots.

Under such circumstances, finding a believable and inspiring balance be- 20 tween the old identity and the new, like that implicit in the myth of the frontier, was next to impossible. The images and characters that did emerge from the immigrant communities were often comic. Seen over and over in the fiction and popular theater of the day was the figure of the *yiddische Yankee,* a jingoistic optimist who spoke heavily accented American slang, talked baseball like an addict without understanding the game, and dressed like a Broadway dandy on a budget — in short, one who didn't understand America well enough to distinguish between image and substance and who paid for the mistake by becoming the butt of a style of comedy bordering on pathos. So engrained was this stereotype in popular culture that it echoes today in TV situation comedy. . . .

Throughout American popular culture between 1880 and the Second World War the story was the same. Oxlike Swedish farmers, German brewers, Jewish merchants, corrupt Irish ward healers, Italian gangsters — there was a parade of images that reflected in terms often comic, sometimes tragic, the humiliation, pain, and cultural insecurity of people in a state of transition.

Even in the comics, a medium intimately connected with immigrant culture, there simply was no image that presented a blending of identities in the assimilation process in a way that stressed pride, self-confidence, integrity, and psychological well-being. None, that is, until Superman.

The brilliant stroke in the conception of Superman — the sine qua non that makes the whole myth work — is the fact that he has two identities. The myth simply wouldn't work without Clark Kent, mild-mannered newspaper reporter and later, as the myth evolved, bland TV newsman. Adopting the white-bread image of a wimp is first and foremost a moral act for the Man of Steel. He does it to protect his parents from nefarious sorts who might use them to gain an edge over the powerful alien. Moreover, Kent adds to Superman's powers the moral guidance of a Smallville upbringing. It is Jonathan Kent, fans remember, who instructs the alien that his powers must always be used for good. Thus does the myth add a mainstream white Anglo-Saxon Protestant ingredient to the American stew. Clark Kent is the clearest stereotype of a self-effacing, hesitant, doubting, middle-class weakling ever invented. He is the epitome of visible invisibility, someone whose extraordinary ordinariness makes him disappear in a crowd. In a phrase, he is the consummate figure of total cultural assimilation, and significantly, he is not real. Implicit in this is the notion that mainstream cultural norms, however useful, are illusions.

Though a disguise, Kent is necessary for the myth to work. This uniquely American hero has two identities, one based on where he comes from in life's journey, one on where he is going. One is real, one an illusion, and both are necessary for the myth of balance in the assimilation process to be complete. Superman's powers make the hero capable of saving humanity; Kent's total immersion in the American heartland makes him want to do it. The result is an improvement on the Western: an optimistic myth of assimilation but with an urban, technocratic setting.

One must never underestimate the importance to a myth of the most minute elements which do not change over time and by which we recognize the story. Take Superman's cape, for example. When Joe Shuster inked the first Superman stories, in the early thirties when he was still a student at Cleveland's Glenville High School, Superman was strictly beefcake in tights, looking more like a circus acrobat than the ultimate Man of Steel. By June of 1938 when *Action Comics* no. 1 was issued, the image had been altered to include a cape, ostensibly to make flight easier to render in the pictures. But it wasn't the cape of Victorian melodrama and adventure fiction, the kind worn with a clasp around the neck. In fact, one is hard-pressed to find any precedent in popular culture for the kind of cape Superman wears. His emerges in a seamless line from either side of the front yoke of his tunic. It is a veritable growth from behind his pectorals and hangs, when he stands at ease, in a line that doesn't so much drape his shoulders as stand apart from them and echo their curve, like an angel's wings.

In light of this graphic detail, it seems hardly coincidental that Super- 25 man's real, Kryptonic name is Kal-El, an apparent neologism by George Lowther, the author who novelized the comic strip in 1942. In Hebrew, *el* can be both root and affix. As a root, it is the masculine singular word for God. Angels in Hebrew mythology are called *benei Elohim* (literally, sons of the Gods), or *Elyonim* (higher beings). As an affix, *el* is most often translated as "of God," as in the plenitude of Old Testament given names: Ishma-el, Dani-el, Ezeki-el, Samu-el, etc. It is also a common form for named angels in most Semitic mythologies: Israf-el, Aza-el, Uri-el, Yo-el, Rapha-el, Gabri-el and — the one perhaps most like Superman — Micha-el, the warrior angel and Satan's principal adversary.

The morpheme *Kal* bears a linguistic relation to two Hebrew roots. The first, *kal,* means "with lightness" or "swiftness" (faster than a speeding bullet in Hebrew?). It also bears a connection to the root *hal,* where *h* is the guttural *ch* of *chutzpah. Hal* translates roughly as "everything" or "all." *Kal-el,* then, can be read as "all that is God," or perhaps more in the spirit of the myth of Superman, "all that God is." And while we're at it, *Kent* is a form of the Hebrew *kana.* In its *k-n-t* form, the word appears in the Bible, meaning "I have found a son."

I'm suggesting that Superman raises the American immigrant experience to the level of religious myth. And why not? He's not just some immigrant from across the waters like all our ancestors, but a real alien, an extraterrestrial, a visitor from heaven if you will, which fact lends an element of the supernatural to the myth. America has no national religious icons nor any pilgrimage shrines. The idea of a patron saint is ludicrous in a nation whose Founding Fathers wrote into the founding documents the fundamental if not eternal separation of church and state. America, though, is pretty much as religious as other industrialized countries. It's just that our tradition of religious diversity precludes the nation's religious character from being embodied in objects or persons recognizably religious, for such are immediately identified by their attachment to specific sectarian traditions and thus contradict the eclecticism of the American religious spirit.

In America, cultural icons that manage to tap the national religious spirit are of necessity secular on the surface and sufficiently generalized to incorporate the diversity of American religious traditions. Superman doesn't have to be seen as an angel to be appreciated, but in the absence of a tradition of national religious iconography, he can serve as a safe, nonsectarian focus for essentially religious sentiments, particularly among the young.

In the last analysis, Superman is like nothing so much as an American boy's fantasy of a messiah. He is the male, heroic match for the Statue of Liberty, come like an immigrant from heaven to deliver humankind by sacrificing himself in the service of others. He protects the weak and defends truth and justice and all the other moral virtues inherent in the Judeo-Christian tradition, remaining ever vigilant and ever chaste. What purer or stronger vision could there possibly be for a child? Now that I put my mind to it, I see that John Wayne never had a chance.

READING THE TEXT

1. Why does Superman's status as "an immigrant and an orphan" (para. 5) make him deeply American, according to Engle?
2. What is the significance of Superman's ability to fly?
3. Why does Engle see physical dislocation as being so typically American?
4. What is the significance of Superman's two identities, according to Engle?

READING THE SIGNS

1. Interview three classmates or friends whose families are immigrants to this country. Then compare their experience with that of the mythological character, Superman. To what extent does the Superman character reflect real-life immigrant experience? What does his story leave out? Try to account for any differences you may find.
2. Do you agree with Engle's suggestion "that Superman raises the American immigrant experience to the level of religious myth" (para. 27)?
3. How would Superman fit the definitions of hero that Robert B. Ray ("The Thematic Paradigm," p. 308) outlines?
4. Engle claims that Superman is a more authentically American hero than is John Wayne. Write an argument supporting or refuting this claim, basing your argument on specific roles that Wayne has played in film.
5. Engle only briefly discusses the fact that Superman happens to be both male and Caucasian. What is the significance of his gender and race? How do you think they may have influenced his status as an American mythological hero? For a discussion of race and gender, consult Michael Omi's "In Living Color: Race and American Culture" (p. 557) and Holly Devor's "Gender Role Behaviors and Attitudes" (p. 484).
6. Rent a videotape of one of the *Superman* movies, and write an essay in which you explore whether the cinematic depiction of this character either perpetuates or alters his mythological status.

ANDY MEDHURST

BATMAN, DEVIANCE, AND CAMP

Have you ever wondered what happened to Robin in the recent Batman movies? In this analysis of the history of the Batman, excerpted from
The Many Lives of the Batman *(1991), Andy Medhurst (b. 1959) explains why Robin had to disappear. Arguing that Batman has been "re-heterosexualized" in the wake of the insinuatingly homoerotic TV series of the 1960s, Medhurst indicts the homophobia of Batfans whose "Bat-*

Platonic Ideal of how Batman should really be" holds no place for the "camped crusader." Andy Medhurst teaches media studies, popular culture, and lesbian and gay studies at the University of Sussex, England. His current research interests include British popular culture and autobiography. He has coedited, with Sally Munt, *Lesian and Gay Studies: A Critical Introduction (1997).*

Only someone ignorant of the fundamentals of psychiatry and of the psychopathology of sex can fail to realize a subtle atmosphere of homoeroticism which pervades the adventure of the mature "Batman" and his young friend "Robin."

—FREDRIC WERTHAM[1]

It's embarrassing to be solemn and treatise-like about Camp. One runs the risk of having, oneself, produced a very inferior piece of Camp.

—SUSAN SONTAG[2]

I'm not sure how qualified I am to write this essay. Batman hasn't been particularly important in my life since I was seven years old. Back then he was crucial, paramount, unmissable as I sat twice weekly to watch the latest episode on TV. Pure pleasure, except for the annoying fact that my parents didn't seem to appreciate the thrills on offer. Worse than that, they actually laughed. How could anyone laugh when the Dynamic Duo were about to be turned into Frostie Freezies (pineapple for the Caped Crusader, lime for his chum) by the evil Mr. Freeze?

Batman and I drifted apart after those early days. Every now and then I'd see a repeated episode and I soon began to understand and share that once infuriating parental hilarity, but this aside I hardly thought about the man in the cape at all. I knew about the subculture of comic freaks, and the new and alarmingly pretentious phrase "graphic novel" made itself known to me, but I still regarded (with the confidence of distant ignorance) such texts as violent, macho, adolescent and, well, silly.

That's when the warning bells rang. The word "silly" reeks of the complacent condescension that has at various times been bestowed on all the cultural forms that matter most to me (Hollywood musicals, British melodramas, pop music, soap operas), so what right had I to apply it to someone else's part of the popular cultural playground? I had to rethink my disdain, and 1989 has been a very good year in which to do so, because in terms of popular culture 1989 has been the Year of the Bat.

This essay, then, is not written by a devotee of Batman, someone steeped in every last twist of the mythology. I come to these texts as an interested outsider, armed with a particular perspective. That perspective is homosexual-

---

[1]Fredric Wertham, *Seduction of the Innocent* (London: Museum Press, 1955), p. 190.
[2]Susan Sontag, "Notes on Camp," in *A Susan Sontag Reader* (Harmondsworth: Penguin Books), p. 106.

ity, and what I want to try and do here is to offer a gay reading of the whole Bat-business. It has no pretension to definitiveness, I don't presume to speak for all gay people everywhere. I'm male, white, British, thirty years old (at the time of writing) and all of those factors need to be taken into account. Nonetheless, I'd argue that Batman is especially interesting to gay audiences for three reasons.

Firstly, he was one of the first fictional characters to be attacked on the grounds of presumed homosexuality, by Fredric Wertham in his book *Seduction of the Innocent*. Secondly, the 1960s TV series was and remains a touchstone of camp (a banal attempt to define the meaning of camp might well start with "like the sixties' *Batman* series"). Thirdly, as a recurring hero figure for the last fifty years, Batman merits analysis as a notably successful construction of masculinity.

Nightmare on Psychiatry Street: Freddy's Obsession

Seduction of the Innocent is an extraordinary book. It is a gripping, flamboyant melodrama masquerading as social psychology. Fredric Wertham is, like Senator McCarthy,[3] like Batman, a crusader, a man with a mission, an evangelist. He wants to save the youth of America from its own worst impulses, from its id, from comic books. His attack on comic books is founded on an astonishingly crude stimulus-and-response model of reading, in which the child (the child, for Wertham, seems an unusually innocent, blank slate waiting to be written on) reads, absorbs, and feels compelled to copy, if only in fantasy terms, the content of the comics. It is a model, in other words, which takes for granted extreme audience passivity.

This is not the place to go into a detailed refutation of Wertham's work, besides which such a refutation has already been done in Martin Barker's excellent *A Haunt of Fears*.[4] The central point of audience passivity needs stressing, however, because it is crucial to the celebrated passage where Wertham points his shrill, witch-hunting finger at the Dynamic Duo and cries "queer."

Such language is not present on the page, of course, but in some ways *Seduction of the Innocent* (a film title crying out for either D. W. Griffith or Cecil B. DeMille) would be easier to stomach if it were. Instead, Wertham writes with anguished concern about the potential harm that Batman might do to vulnerable children, innocents who might be turned into deviants. He employs what was then conventional psychiatric wisdom about the idea of homosexuality as a "phase":

> Many pre-adolescent boys pass through a phase of disdain for girls. Some comic books tend to fix that attitude and instill the idea that girls are only good for being banged around or used as decoys. A homoerotic attitude is

---

[3]**Senator McCarthy** United States Senator Joseph R. McCarthy (1908–1957), who in the 1950s hunted and persecuted suspected Communists and Communist sympathizers. — EDS.

[4]Martin Barker, *A Haunt of Fears* (London: Pluto Press, 1984).

also suggested by the presentation of masculine, bad, witch-like or violent women. In such comics women are depicted in a definitely anti-erotic light, while the young male heroes have pronounced erotic overtones. The muscular male supertype, whose primary sex characteristics are usually well emphasized, is in the setting of certain stories the object of homo-erotic sexual curiosity and stimulation.[5]

The implications of this are breathtaking. Homosexuality, for Wertham, is synonymous with misogyny. Men love other men because they hate women. The sight of women being "banged around" is liable to appeal to repressed homoerotic desires (this, I think, would be news to the thousands of women who are systematically physically abused by heterosexual men). Women who do not conform to existing stereotypes of femininity are another incitement to homosexuality.

Having mapped out his terms of reference, Wertham goes on to peel the 10 lid from Wayne Manor:

> Sometimes Batman ends up in bed injured and young Robin is shown sit-ting next to him. At home they lead an idyllic life. They are Bruce Wayne and "Dick" Grayson. Bruce Wayne is described as a "socialite" and the offi-cial relationship is that Dick is Bruce's ward. They live in sumptuous quar-ters, with beautiful flowers in large vases, and have a butler, Alfred. Batman is sometimes shown in a dressing gown. . . . It is like a wish dream of two homosexuals living together. Sometimes they are shown on a couch, Bruce reclining and Dick sitting next to him, jacket off, collar open, and his hand on his friend's arm.[6]

So, Wertham's assumptions of homosexuality are fabricated out of his in-terpretation of certain visual signs. To avoid being thought queer by Wertham, Bruce and Dick should have done the following: Never show concern if the other is hurt, live in a shack, only have ugly flowers in small vases, call the butler "Chip" or "Joe" if you have to have one at all, never share a couch, keep your collar buttoned up, keep your jacket on, and never, ever wear a dressing gown. After all, didn't Noel Coward[7] wear a dressing gown?

Wertham is easy to mock, but the identification of homosexuals through dress codes has a long history.[8] Moreover, such codes originate as semiotic systems adopted by gay people themselves, as a way of signalling the otherwise invisible fact of sexual preference. There is a difference, though, be-tween sporting the secret symbols of a subculture if you form part of that sub-culture and the elephantine spot-the-homo routine that Wertham performs.

Bat-fans have always responded angrily to Wertham's accusation. One

---

[5]Wertham, p. 188.

[6]Wertham, p. 190.

[7]**Noel Coward** (1899–1973) British playwright, actor, and composer known for witty, so-phisticated comedies. — EDS.

[8]See, for example, the newspaper stories on "how to spot" homosexuals printed in Britain in the fifties and sixties, and discussed in Jeffrey Weeks, *Coming Out: Homosexual Politics in Britain* (London: Quartet, 1979).

calls it "one of the most incredible charges . . . unfounded rumours . . . sly sneers"[9] and the general response has been to reassert the masculinity of the two heroes, mixed with a little indignation: "If they had been actual men they could have won a libel suit."[10] This seems to me not only to miss the point, but also to *reinforce* Wertham's homophobia — it is only possible to win a libel suit over an "accusation" of homosexuality in a culture where homosexuality is deemed categorically inferior to heterosexuality.

Thus the rush to "protect" Batman and Robin from Wertham is simply the other side to the coin of his bigotry. It may reject Wertham, cast him in the role of dirty-minded old man, but its view of homosexuality is identical. Mark Cotta Vaz thus describes the imputed homosexual relationship as "licentious" while claiming that in fact Bruce Wayne "regularly squired the most beautiful women in Gotham City and presumably had a healthy sex life."[11] Licentious versus healthy — Dr. Wertham himself could not have bettered this homophobic opposition.

Despite the passions aroused on both sides (or rather the two facets of the same side), there is something comic at the heart of this dispute. It is, simply, that Bruce and Dick are *not* real people but fictional constructions, and hence to squabble over their "real" sex life is to take things a little too far. What is at stake here is the question of reading, of what readers do with the raw material that they are given. Readers are at liberty to construct whatever fantasy lives they like with the characters of the fiction they read (within the limits of generic and narrative credibility, that is). This returns us to the unfortunate patients of Dr. Wertham: 15

> One young homosexual during psychotherapy brought us a copy of *Detective* comic, with a Batman story. He pointed out a picture of "The Home of Bruce and Dick," a house beautifully landscaped, warmly lighted and showing the devoted pair side by side, looking out a picture window. When he was eight this boy had realized from fantasies about comic book pictures that he was aroused by men. At the age of ten or eleven, "I found my liking, my sexual desires, in comic books. I think I put myself in the position of Robin. I did want to have relations with Batman . . . I remember the first time I came across the page mentioning the 'secret batcave.' The thought of Batman and Robin living together and possibly having sex relations came to my mind. . . . "[12]

Wertham quotes this to shock us, to impel us to tear the pages of *Detective* away before little Tommy grows up and moves to Greenwich Village, but reading it as a gay man today I find it rather moving and also highly recognizable.

[9]Phrases taken from Chapters 5 and 6 of Mark Cotta Vaz, *Tales of the Dark Knight: Batman's First Fifty Years* (London: Futura, 1989).

[10]Les Daniels, *Comix: A History of Comic Books in America* (New York: Bonanza Books, 1971), p. 87.

[11]Cotta Vaz, pp. 47 and 53.

[12]Wertham, p. 192.

What this anonymous gay man did was to practice that form of brico-lage[13] which Richard Dyer has identified as a characteristic reading strategy of gay audiences.[14] Denied even the remotest possibility of supportive images of homosexuality within the dominant heterosexual culture, gay people have had to fashion what we could out of the imageries of dominance, to snatch il-licit meanings from the fabric of normality, to undertake a corrupt decoding for the purposes of satisfying marginalized desires.[15] This may not be as nec-essary as it once was, given the greater visibility of gay representations, but it is still an important practice. Wertham's patient evokes in me an admiration, that in a period of American history even more homophobic than most, there he was, raiding the citadels of masculinity, weaving fantasies of oppositional desire. What effect the dread Wertham had on him is hard to predict, but I profoundly hope that he wasn't "cured."

It wasn't only Batman who was subjected to Dr. Doom's bizarre ideas about human sexuality. Hence:

> The homosexual connotation of the Wonder Woman type of story is psycho-logically unmistakable. . . . For boys, Wonder Woman is a frightening image. For girls she is a morbid ideal. Where Batman is anti-feminine, the attractive Wonder Woman and her counterparts are definitely anti-masculine. Wonder Woman has her own female following. . . . Her followers are the "Holiday girls," i.e. the holiday girls, the gay party girls, the gay girls.[16]

Just how much elision can be covered with one "i.e."? Wertham's view of homosexuality is not, at least, inconsistent. Strong, admirable women will turn little girls into dykes — such a heroine can only be seen as a "morbid ideal."

Crazed as Wertham's ideas were, their effectiveness is not in doubt. The mid-fifties saw a moral panic about the assumed dangers of comic books. In the United States companies were driven out of business, careers wrecked, and the Comics Code introduced. This had distinct shades of the Hays Code[17] that had been brought in to clamp down on Hollywood in the 1930s, and un-der its jurisdiction comics opted for the bland, the safe, and the reactionary. In Britain there was government legislation to prohibit the importing of Amer-ican comics, as the comics panic slotted neatly into a whole series of anxi-eties about the effects on British youth of American popular culture.[18]

---

[13]**bricolage** A new object created by reassembling bits and pieces of other objects; here, gay-identified readings produced from classic texts. — EDS.

[14]Richard Dyer, ed., *Gays and Film,* 2nd edition (New York: Zoetrope, 1984), p. 1.

[15]See Richard Dyer, "Judy Garland and Gay Men," in Dyer, *Heavenly Bodies* (London: BFI, 1987), and Claire Whitaker, "Hollywood Transformed: Interviews with Lesbian Viewers," in Peter Steven, ed., *Jump Cut: Hollywood, Politics and Counter-Cinema* (Toronto: Between the Lines, 1985).

[16]Wertham, pp. 192–93.

[17]**Hays Code** The 1930 Motion Picture Production Code, which described in detail what was morally acceptable in films. — EDS.

[18]See Barker.

And in all of this, what happened to Batman? He turned into Fred [20] MacMurray from *My Three Sons.* He lost any remaining edge of the shadowy vigilante of his earliest years, and became an upholder of the most stifling small-town American values. Batwoman and Batgirl appeared (June Allyson and Bat-Gidget) to take away any lingering doubts about the Dynamic Duo's sex lives. A 1963 story called "The Great Clayface-Joker Feud" has some especially choice examples of the new, squeaky-clean sexuality of the assembled Bats.

Batgirl says to Robin, "I can hardly wait to get into my Batgirl costume again! Won't it be terrific if we could go on a crime case together like the last time? (sigh)." Robin replies, "It sure would, Betty (sigh)." The elder Bats look on approvingly. Batgirl is Batwoman's niece — to make her a daughter would have implied that Batwoman had had (gulp) sexual intercourse, and that would never do. This is the era of Troy Donohue and Pat Boone,[19] and Batman as ever serves as a cultural thermometer, taking the temperature of the times.

The Clayface/Joker business is wrapped up (the villains of this period are wacky conjurors, nothing more, with no menace or violence about them) and the episode concludes with another tableau of terrifying heterosexual contentment. "Oh Robin," simpers Batgirl, "I'm afraid you'll just have to hold me! I'm still so shaky after fighting Clayface . . . and you're so strong!" Robin: "Gosh Batgirl, it was swell of you to calm me down when I was worried about Batman tackling Clayface alone." (One feels a distinct Wertham influence here: If Robin shows concern about Batman, wheel on a supportive female, the very opposite of a "morbid ideal," to minister in a suitably self-effacing way.) Batwoman here seizes her chance and tackles Batman: "You look worried about Clayface, Batman . . . so why don't you follow Robin's example and let me soothe you?" Batman can only reply "Gulp."

Gulp indeed. While it's easy simply to laugh at strips like these, knowing as we do the way in which such straight-faced material would be mercilessly shredded by the sixties' TV series, they do reveal the retreat into coziness forced on comics by the Wertham onslaught and its repercussions. There no doubt were still subversive readers of *Batman,* erasing Batgirl on her every preposterous appearance and reworking the Duo's capers to leave some room for homoerotic speculation, but such a reading would have had to work so much harder than before. The *Batman* of this era was such a closed text, so immune to polysemic interpretation, that its interest today is only as a symptom — or, more productively, as camp. "The Great Clayface-Joker Feud" may have been published in 1963, but in every other respect it is a fifties' text. If the 1960s began for the world in general with the Beatles, the 1960s for Batman began with the TV series in 1966. If the Caped Crusader had been all but Werthamed out of existence, he was about to be camped back into life.

[19]**Troy Donohue and Pat Boone** Clean-cut, all-American-boy stars from the 1950s and 1960s. — EDS.

The Camped Crusader and the Boys Wondered

Trying to define "camp" is like attempting to sit in the corner of a circular room. It can't be done, which only adds to the quixotic appeal of the attempt. Try these:

> To be camp is to present oneself as being committed to the marginal with a commitment greater than the marginal merits.[20]
>
> Camp sees everything in quotation marks. It's not a lamp but a "lamp"; not a woman but a "woman." . . . It is the farthest extension, in sensibility, of the metaphor of life as theatre.[21]
>
> Camp is . . . a way of poking fun at the whole cosmology of restrictive sex roles and sexual identifications which our society uses to oppress its women and repress its men.[22]
>
> Camp was and is a way for gay men to re-imagine the world around them . . . by exaggerating, stylizing and remaking what is usually thought to be average or normal.[23]
>
> Camp was a prison for an illegal minority; now it is a holiday for consenting adults.[24]

All true, in their way, but all inadequate. The problem with camp is that it is primarily an experiential rather than an analytical discourse. Camp is a set of attitudes, a gallery of snapshots, an inventory of postures, a modus vivendi, a shop-full of frocks, an arch of eyebrows, a great big pink butterfly that just won't be pinned down. Camp is primarily an adjective, occasionally a verb, but never anything as prosaic, as earthbound, as a noun.

Yet if I propose to use this adjective as a way of describing one or more of the guises of Batman, I need to arrive at some sort of working definition. So, for the purposes of this analysis, I intend the term "camp" to refer to a playful, knowing, self-reflexive theatricality. *Batman,* the sixties' TV series, was nothing if not knowing. It employed the codes of camp in an unusually public and heavily signaled way. This makes it different from those people or texts who are taken up by camp audiences without ever consciously putting camp into practice. The difference may be very briefly spelled out by reference to Hollywood films. If *Mildred Pierce*[25] and *The Letter*[26] were taken up *as* camp, teased by primarily gay male audiences into yielding meaning not intended

[20]Mark Booth, *Camp* (London: Quartet, 1983), p. 18.

[21]Sontag, p. 109.

[22]Jack Babuscio, "Camp and the Gay Sensibility," in Dyer, ed., *Gays and Film,* p. 46.

[23]Michael Bronski, *Culture Clash: The Making of Gay Sensibility* (Boston: South End Press), p. 42.

[24]Philip Core, *Camp: The Lie That Tells the Truth* (London: Plexus), p. 7.

[25]***Mildred Pierce*** 1945 murder mystery film that traces the fortunes of a homemaker who breaks with her husband. — EDS.

[26]***The Letter*** 1940 murder movie whose ending was changed to satisfy moral standards of the time. — EDS.

by their makers, then *Whatever Happened to Baby Jane?*[27] is a piece of self-conscious camp, capitalizing on certain attitudinal and stylistic tendencies known to exist in audiences. *Baby Jane* is also, significantly, a 1960s' film, and the 1960s were the decade in which camp swished out of the ghetto and up into the scarcely prepared mainstream.

A number of key events and texts reinforced this. Susan Sontag wrote her *Notes on Camp,* which remains the starting point for researchers even now. Pop Art[28] was in vogue (and in *Vogue*) and whatever the more elevated claims of Lichtenstein,[29] Warhol,[30] and the rest, their artworks were on one level a new inflection of camp. The growing intellectual respectability of pop music displayed very clearly that the old barriers that once rigidly separated high and low culture were no longer in force. The James Bond films, and even more so their successors like *Modesty Blaise,* popularized a dry, self-mocking wit that makes up one part of the multifaceted diamond of camp. And on television there were *The Avengers, The Man from UNCLE, Thunderbirds,* and *Batman.*

To quote the inevitable Sontag, "The whole point of Camp is to dethrone the serious. . . . More precisely, Camp involves a new, more complex relation to 'the serious.' One can be serious about the frivolous, frivolous about the serious."[31]

The problem with Batman in those terms is that there was never anything truly serious to begin with (unless one swallows that whole portentous Dark Knight charade, more of which in the next section). Batman in its comic book form had, unwittingly, always been camp — it was serious (the tone, the moral homilies) about the frivolous (a man in a stupid suit). He was camp in the way that classic Hollywood was camp, but what the sixties' TV series and film did was to overlay this "innocent" camp with a thick layer of ironic distance, the self-mockery version of camp. And given the long associations of camp with the homosexual male subculture, Batman was a particular gift on the grounds of his relationship with Robin. As George Melly put it, "The real Batman series were beautiful because of their unselfconscious absurdity. The remakes, too, at first worked on a double level. Over the absorbed children's heads we winked and nudged, but in the end what were we laughing at? The fact they didn't know that Batman had it off with Robin."[32]

---

[27]***Whatever Happened to Baby Jane?*** Macabre 1962 film about a former child movie star living in an old Hollywood mansion. — EDS.

[28]**Pop Art** Art movement, begun in the 1950s, that borrowed images and symbols from popular culture, particularly from commercial products and mass media, as a critique of traditional fine art. — EDS.

[29]**Lichtenstein** Roy Lichtenstein (1923–1997), American artist at the center of the Pop Art movement, best known for melodramatic comic-book scenes. — EDS.

[30]**Warhol** Andy Warhol (1930?–1987), pioneering Pop artist known for reproducing stereotyped images of famous people, such as Marilyn Monroe, and of commercial products, such as Campbell's Soup cans. — EDS.

[31]Sontag, p. 116.

[32]George Melly, *Revolt into Style: The Pop Arts in the 50s and 60s* (Oxford: Oxford University Press, 1989 [first published 1970]), p. 193.

It was as if Wertham's fears were being vindicated at last, but his 1950s' bigot's anguish had been supplanted by a self-consciously hip 1960s' playfulness. What adult audiences laughed at in the sixties' *Batman* was a camped-up version of the fifties they had just left behind.

Batman's lessons in good citizenship ("We'd like to feel that our efforts may help every youngster to grow up into an honest, useful citizen"[33]) were another part of the character ripe for ridiculing deconstruction — "Let's go, Robin, we've set another youth on the road to a brighter tomorrow" (the episode "It's How You Play the Game"). Everything the Adam West Batman said was a parody of seriousness, and how could it be otherwise? How could anyone take genuinely seriously the words of a man dressed like that?

The Batman/Robin relationship is never referred to directly; more fun can be had by presenting it "straight," in other words, screamingly camp. Wertham's reading of the Dubious Duo had been so extensively aired as to pass into the general consciousness (in George Melly's words, "We all knew Robin and Batman were pouves"[34]), it was part of the fabric of *Batman,* and the makers of the TV series proceeded accordingly.

Consider the Duo's encounter with Marsha, Queen of Diamonds. The threat she embodies is nothing less than heterosexuality itself, the deadliest threat to the domestic bliss of the Bat-couple. She is even about to marry Batman before Alfred intervenes to save the day. He and Batman flee the church, but have to do so in the already decorated Batmobile, festooned with wedding paraphernalia including a large "Just Married" sign. "We'll have to drive it as it is," says Batman, while somewhere in the audience a Dr. Wertham takes feverish notes. Robin, Commissioner Gordon, and Chief O'Hara have all been drugged with Marsha's "Cupid Dart," but it is of course the Boy Wonder who Batman saves first. The dart, he tells Robin, "contains some secret ingredient by which your sense and your will were affected," and it isn't hard to read that ingredient as heterosexual desire, since its result, seen in the previous episode, was to turn Robin into Marsha's slobbering slave.

We can tell with relief now, though, as Robin is "back in fighting form" (with impeccable timing, Batman clasps Robin's shoulder on the word "fighting"). Marsha has one last attempt to destroy the duo, but naturally she fails. The female temptress, the seductress, the enchantress must be vanquished. None of this is in the least subtle (Marsha's cat, for example, is called Circe) but this type of mass-market camp can't afford the luxury of subtlety. The threat of heterosexuality is similarly mobilized in the 1966 feature film, where it is Bruce Wayne's infatuation with Kitka (Catwoman in disguise) that causes all manner of problems.

A more interesting employment of camp comes in the episodes where the Duo battle the Black Widow, played by Tallulah Bankhead. The major camp coup here, of course, is the casting. Bankhead was one of the supreme icons of camp, one of its goddesses: "Too intelligent not to be self-conscious, too ambitious to

---

[33]"The Batman Says," *Batman* #3 (1940), quoted in Cotta Vaz, p. 15.
[34]Melly, p. 192.

bother about her self-consciousness, too insecure ever to be content, but too arrogant ever to admit insecurity, Tallulah personified camp."[35]

A heady claim, but perhaps justified, because the Black Widow episodes are, against stiff competition, the campiest slices of Batman of them all. The stories about Bankhead are legendary — the time when on finding no toilet paper in her cubicle she slipped a ten dollar bill under the partition and asked the woman next door for two fives, or her whispered remark to a priest conducting a particularly elaborate service and swinging a censor of smoking incense, "Darling, I love the drag, but your purse is on fire" — and casting her in Batman was the final demonstration of the series' commitment to camp.

The plot is unremarkable, the usual Bat-shenanigans; the pleasure lies in the detail. Details like the elderly Bankhead crammed into her Super-Villainess costume, or like the way in which (through a plot detail I won't go into) she impersonates Robin, so we see Burt Ward miming to Bankhead's voice, giving the unforgettable image of Robin flirting with burly traffic cops. Best of all, and Bankhead isn't even in this scene but the thrill of having her involved clearly spurred the writer to new heights of camp, Batman has to sing a song to break free of the Black Widow's spell. Does he choose to sing "God Bless America"? Nothing so rugged. He clutches a flower to his Bat chest and sings Gilbert and Sullivan's "I'm Just a Little Buttercup." It is this single image, more than any other, that prevents me from taking the post–Adam West Dark Knight at all seriously.

The fundamental camp trick which the series pulls is to make the comics speak. What was acceptable on the page, in speech balloons, stands revealed as ridiculous once given audible voice. The famous visualized sound effects (URKKK! KA-SPLOOSH!) that are for many the fondest memory of the series work along similar lines. Camp often makes its point by transposing the codes of one cultural form into the inappropriate codes of another. It thrives on mischievous incongruity.

The incongruities, the absurdities, the sheer ludicrousness of Batman were brought out so well by the sixties' version that for some audiences there will never be another credible approach. I have to include myself here. I've recently read widely in postsixties Bat-lore, and I can appreciate what the writers and artists are trying to do, but my Batman will always be Adam West. It's impossible to be somber or pompous about Batman because if you try the ghost of West will come Bat-climbing into your mind, fortune cookie wisdom on his lips and keen young Dick by his side. It's significant, I think, that the letters I received from the editors of this book began "Dear Bat-Contributor."[36] Writers preparing chapters about James Joyce or Ingmar Bergman do not, I suspect, receive analogous greetings. To deny the large camp component of Batman is to blind oneself to one of the richest parts of his history.

[35]Core, p. 25.

[36]This essay originally appeared in an anthology, *The Many Lives of the Batman: Critical Approaches to a Superhero and His Media.* — EDS.

Is There Bat-Life after Bat-Camp?

The international success of the Adam West incarnation left Batman high and 40 dry. The camping around had been fun while it lasted, but it hadn't lasted very long. Most camp humor has a relatively short life span, new targets are always needed, and the camp aspect of Batman had been squeezed dry. The mass public had moved on to other heroes, other genres, other acres of merchandising, but there was still a hard Bat-core of fans to satisfy. Where could the Bat go next? Clearly there was no possibility of returning to the caped Eisenhower, the benevolent patriarch of the 1950s. That option had been well and truly closed down by the TV show. Batman needed to be given his dignity back, and this entailed a return to his roots.

This, in any case, is the official version. For the unreconstructed devotee of the Batman (that is, people who insist on giving him the definite article before the name), the West years had been hell — a tricksy travesty, an effeminizing of the cowled avenger. There's a scene in *Midnight Cowboy* where Dustin Hoffman tells Jon Voight that the only audience liable to be receptive to his cowboy clothes are gay men looking for rough trade. Voight is appalled — "You mean to tell me John Wayne was a fag?" (quoted, roughly, from memory). This outrage, this horror at shattered illusions, comes close to encapsulating the loathing and dread the campy Batman has received from the old guard of Gotham City and the younger born-again Bat-fans.

So what has happened since the 1960s has been the painstaking re-heterosexualization of Batman. I apologize for coining such a clumsy word, but no other quite gets the sense that I mean. This strategy has worked, too, for large audiences, reaching its peak with the 1989 film. To watch this and then come home to see a video of the 1966 movie is to grasp how complete the transformation has been. What I want to do in this section is to trace some of the crucial moments in that change, written from the standpoint of someone still unashamedly committed to Bat-camp.

If one wants to take Batman as a Real Man, the biggest stumbling block has always been Robin. There have been disingenuous claims that "Batman and Robin had a blood-brother closeness. Theirs was a spiritual intimacy forged from the stress of countless battles fought side by side"[37] (one can imagine what Tallulah Bankhead might say to *that*), but we know otherwise. The Wertham lobby and the acolytes of camp alike have ensured that any Batman/Robin relationship is guaranteed to bring on the sniggers. Besides which, in the late 1960s, Robin was getting to be a big boy, too big for any shreds of credibility to attach themselves to all that father-son smokescreen. So in 1969 Dick Grayson was packed off to college and the Bat was solitary once more.

This was a shrewd move. It's impossible to conceive of the recent, obsessive, sturm-und-drang Batman with a chirpy little Robin getting in the

[37]Cotta Vaz, p. 53.

way.[38] A text of the disturbing power of *The Killing Joke*[39] could not have functioned with Robin to rupture the grim dualism of its Batman/Joker struggle. There was, however, a post-Dick Robin, but he was killed off by fans in that infamous telephone poll.[40]

It's intriguing to speculate how much latent (or blatant) homophobia lay [45] behind that vote. Did the fans decide to kill off Jason Todd so as to redeem Batman for unproblematic heterosexuality? Impossible to say. There are other factors to take into account, such as Jason's apparent failure to live up to the expectations of what a Robin should be like. The sequence of issues in which Jason/Robin died, *A Death in the Family,* is worth looking at in some detail, however, in order to see whether the camp connotations of Bruce and Dick had been fully purged.

The depressing answer is that they had. This is very much the Batman of the 1980s, his endless feud with the Joker this time uneasily stretched over a framework involving the Middle East and Ethiopia. Little to be camp about there, though the presence of the Joker guarantees a quota of sick jokes. The sickest of all is the introduction of the Ayatollah Khomeini, a real and important political figure, into this fantasy world of THUNK! and THER-ACKK! and grown men dressed as bats. (As someone who lived in the part of England from which Reagan's planes took off on their murderous mission to bomb Libya, I fail to see the humor in this cartoon version of American foreign policy: It's too near the real thing.)

Jason dies at the Joker's hands because he becomes involved in a search for his own origins, a clear parallel to Batman's endless returns to *his* Oedipal scenario. Families, in the Bat-mythology, are dark and troubled things, one more reason why the introduction of the fifties versions of Batwoman and Batgirl seemed so inappropriate. This applies only to real, biological families, though; the true familial bond is between Batman and Robin, hence the title of these issues. Whether one chooses to read Robin as Batman's ward (official version), son (approved fantasy), or lover (forbidden fantasy), the sense of loss at his death is bound to be devastating. Batman finds Robin's body and, in the time-honored tradition of Hollywood cinema, is at least able to give him a loving embrace. Good guys hug their dead buddies, only queers smooch when still alive.

If the word "camp" is applied at all to the eighties' Batman, it is a label for the Joker. This sly displacement is the cleverest method yet devised of pre-

---

[38]A female Robin is introduced in the *Dark Knight Returns* series, which, while raising interesting questions about the sexuality of Batman, which I don't here have the space to address, seems significant in that the Dark Knight cannot run the risk of reader speculation that a traditionally male Robin might provoke.

[39]***The Killing Joke*** Graphic novel by Alan Moore, Brian Bolland, and John Higgins (New York: DC Comics 1988). — Eds.

[40]**telephone poll** In a 1988 issue of the *Batman* comic, a "post-Dick Robin," Jason Todd, was badly injured in an explosion, and readers were allowed to phone the publisher to vote on whether he should be allowed to survive. — Eds.

serving Bat-heterosexuality. The play that the texts regularly make with the concept of Batman and the Joker as mirror images now takes a new twist. The Joker is Batman's "bad twin," and part of that badness is, increasingly, an implied homosexuality. This is certainly present in the 1989 film, a generally glum and portentous affair except for Jack Nicholson's Joker, a characterization enacted with venomous camp. The only moment when this dour film comes to life is when the Joker and his gang raid the Art Gallery, spraying the paintings and generally camping up a storm.

The film strives and strains to make us forget the Adam West Batman, to the point of giving us Vicki Vale as Bruce Wayne's lover, and certainly Michael Keaton's existential agonizing (variations on the theme of why-did-I-have-to-be-a-Bat) is a world away from West's gleeful subversion of truth, justice and the American Way. This is the same species of Batman celebrated by Frank Miller: "If your only memory of Batman is that of Adam West and Burt Ward exchanging camped-out quips while clobbering slumming guest-stars Vincent Price and Cesar Romero, I hope this book will come as a surprise. . . . For me, Batman was never funny. . . ."[41]

The most recent linkage of the Joker with homosexuality comes in 50 *Arkham Asylum,* the darkest image of the Bat-world yet. Here the Joker has become a parody of a screaming queen, calling Batman "honey pie," given to exclamations like "oooh!" (one of the oldest homophobic clichés in the book), and pinching Batman's behind with the advice, "Loosen up, tight ass." He also, having no doubt read his Wertham, follows the pinching by asking, "What's the matter? Have I touched a nerve? How is the Boy Wonder? Started shaving yet?" The Bat-response is unequivocal: "Take your filthy hands off me . . . Filthy degenerate!"

Arkham Asylum is a highly complex reworking of certain key aspects of the mythology, of which the sexual tension between Batman and the Joker is only one small part. Nonetheless the Joker's question "Have I touched a nerve?" seems a crucial one, as revealed by the homophobic ferocity of Batman's reply. After all, the dominant cultural construction of gay men at the end of the 1980s is as plague carriers, and the word "degenerate" is not far removed from some of the labels affixed to us in the age of AIDS.

Batman: Is He or Isn't He?

The one constant factor through all of the transformations of Batman has been the devotion of his admirers. They will defend him against what they see as negative interpretations, and they carry around in their heads a kind of essence of batness, a Bat-Platonic Ideal of how Batman should really be. The Titan Books reissue of key comics from the 1970s each carry a preface by a

---

[41] Frank Miller, "Introduction," *Batman: Year One* (London: Titan, 1988).

noted fan, and most of them contain claims such as "This, I feel, is Batman as he was meant to be."[42]

Where a negative construction is specifically targeted, no prizes for guessing which one it is: "you . . . are probably also fond of the TV show he appeared in. But then maybe you prefer Elvis Presley's Vegas years or the later Jerry Lewis movies over their early stuff . . . for me, the definitive Batman was then and always will be the one portrayed in these pages."[43]

The sixties' TV show remains anathema to the serious Bat-fan precisely because it heaps ridicule on the very notion of a serious Batman. *Batman* the series revealed the man in the cape as a pompous fool, an embodiment of superseded ethics, and a closet queen. As Marsha, Queen of Diamonds, put it, "Oh Batman, darling, you're so divinely square." Perhaps the enormous success of the 1989 film will help to advance the cause of the rival Bat-archetype, the grim, vengeful Dark Knight whose heterosexuality is rarely called into question (his humorlessness, fondness for violence, and obsessive monomania seem to me exemplary qualities for a heterosexual man). The answer, surely, is that they needn't be mutually exclusive.

If I might be permitted a rather camp comparison, each generation 55 has its definitive Hamlet, so why not the same for Batman? I'm prepared to admit the validity, for some people, of the swooping eighties' vigilante, so why are they so concerned to trash my sixties' camped crusader? Why do they insist so vehemently that Adam West was a faggy aberration, a blot on the otherwise impeccably butch Bat-landscape? What *are* they trying to hide?

If I had a suspicious frame of mind, I might think that they were protesting too much, that maybe Dr. Wertham was on to something when he targeted these narratives as incitements to homosexual fantasy. And if I want Batman to be gay, then, for me, he is. After all, outside of the minds of his writers and readers, he doesn't really exist.

READING THE TEXT

1. Summarize the objections Fredric Wertham makes to Batman in *Seduction of the Innocent*.

2. In a paragraph, write your own explanation of what Medhurst means by "camp" (para. 24).

3. What evidence does Medhurst supply to demonstrate that Batman is a gay character?

4. Explain what Medhurst means by his closing comment: "And if I want Batman to be gay, then, for me, he is. After all, outside of the minds of his writers and readers, he doesn't really exist" (para. 56).

[42]Kim Newman, "Introduction," *Batman: The Demon Awakes* (London: Titan, 1989).
[43]Jonathan Ross, "Introduction," *Batman: Vow from the Grave* (London: Titan, 1989).

READING THE SIGNS

1. Do you agree with Medhurst's argument that the Batman and Robin duo were really a covert homosexual couple? Write an essay arguing for or challenging his position, being sure to study his evidence closely. You may want to visit your campus's media library to see if they have file tapes of old *Batman* shows, or read contemporary reviews of *Batman,* to gather evidence for your own essay.

2. Check your college library for a copy of Fredric Wertham's *Seduction of the Innocent.* Then write your own critique of Wertham's attack on Batman.

3. Buy a few copies of the current *Batman* comic book, and write an essay in which you explain Batman's current sexual orientation.

4. Visit your college library, and obtain a copy of Susan Sontag's "Notes on Camp" (included in Sontag's collections *Against Interpretation* and *The Susan Sontag Reader*). How would Sontag interpret the character of Batman?

N'GAI CROAL AND JANE HUGHES

LARA CROFT, THE BIT GIRL

She's toured with U2, modeled for Gucci, recorded her own single, inspired a feature film, and has been called "the perfect fantasy girl for the digital generation." No, we're not talking about Jennifer Lopez; this is the profile of Lara Croft, the Tomb Raider *star who has taken virtual celebrity into a dimension that Max Headroom could only dream of. The center of a multimillion dollar videogame empire, Croft is a sort of evolutionary successor to the "toon," an icon of virtual reality who may only be the harbinger of things to come. Will there someday be an Oscar award for Best Virtual Actress? Virtual celebs fleeing virtual paparazzi on the pages of a virtual* Enquirer? *Virtual minds want to know. N'Gai Croal and Jane Hughes are writers for* Newsweek, *where this selection originally appeared.*

It's not easy being Lara Croft. After the British aristocrat and adventure-seeking archeologist starred in last year's hit Tomb Raider, she appeared on the cover of 40 magazines, toured with U2, modeled Gucci fashions, and recorded a single with ex-Eurythmics guitarist Dave Stewart. All the while, she's been in China, Tibet, and Venice working on the sequel. But you won't hear Lara whine about her hectic schedule. When you're a woman made of more than 540 polygons, part of your job is making it all look easy.

Lara Croft: pinup girl of the twenty-first century.

Equal parts Pamela Anderson and Indiana Jones with a dash of *La Femme Nikita,* Lara Croft is the computer-generated action heroine at the center of one of the hottest PC and console videogames on the market. To date nearly 8 million copies have been sold worldwide, putting it in the same company as the best-selling adventure game Myst.

Along the way, Lara became an icon as recognizable to gamers as Mario and Sonic the Hedgehog. U2 got the game makers at Core Design in England to create custom footage of Lara for the video wall in its current PopMart world tour. Some fans, convinced or praying that she's real, have bombarded Core with e-mail requesting info on her boyfriends and favorite pop bands. There are more than 100 Web sites devoted to her glory, ranging from nice, like the well-written *Croft Times* newsletter **www.cubeit.com/ctimes,** to naughty, like *Nude Raider,* for fans who think Lara's a bit overdressed in her skintight vest and Daisy Duke shorts.

Like Lara, the folks at Core haven't had much time to enjoy their success; plans for a sequel were underway two months before the first game came out. Since then it's been nothing but takeout food and catnaps on inflatable beds at the company's funky offices in a converted mansion on the outskirts of the northern English town of Derby for the designers as they scramble to get Tomb Raider 2 in stores.

The folks at Core are still a bit surprised at the Tomb Raider phenome- 5 non. "Lara has had an awful lot more media attention than the game itself because people like to lead on the sex angle, the size of her chest, and whether she takes her clothes off," says Core managing director Jeremy Smith. Yet he's shocked, shocked, to hear that U.S. parent company Eidos is pushing the pinup angle by listing her measurements as 38-24-34. Core insists that, in Lara's native England at least, she is a more modest 34D. "We have never really got hung up on that sort of thing," Smith sniffs. "When people ask what she would be like if you took her clothes off, the team simply says she would be a wire mesh. I am sure a lot of people enjoy ogling her, but she was never designed with the marketing in mind."

J. C. Herz, the author of *Joystick Nation,* a book on the history of videogames, isn't buying it. "Female characters are the rage because boys like to look at them. They're the pinup girls of the twenty-first century." But she thinks it was smart of Eidos to build the game around Lara. "If you can create a great character, what you've got is a franchise. It's like making a blockbuster movie and knowing that before anyone says a word you can make $100 million."

There's so much software on store shelves these days that simply creating a good game isn't enough to break out of the pack. With Lara, Eidos has created a star. "And the character belongs to you," Herz adds. "It doesn't pout in a trailer or ask you for $20 million for its next videogame. You own it. It's like minting money."

It all seems obvious now that Tomb Raider would go over big with lads of all ages, but when Core prodigy Toby Gard who later left to start his own company created a game around his vision of the perfect woman, he was violating several unspoken rules of 3-D gaming. Unlike with popular first-person-perspective games like Doom and Duke Nukem, players see the action over Lara's shoulder, like a movie. It's a single-player game with no options for Internet play. And, as Core's reps in France and Germany warned, who's going to play a game where the hero is a girl?

They shouldn't have worried. When the first version hit the stores in November 1996, it sold 500,000 copies in two months. Any good videogame is as much about the experience of watching as it is playing, and it was quite a corneal treat for players to see Lara run fluidly through caves and tunnels, turning cartwheels like Dominique Dawes and diving off ledges like Fu Mingxia. But unlike most action games, TR balances shooting and butt-kicking with exploration and puzzle-solving. So a female character — smart, strong, and supadupa fly — fit in perfectly with Core's vision for the game.

"A man," says designer Adrian Smith, "would have changed what the 10 game's about. But it wouldn't have mattered how gorgeous Lara was if the game itself wasn't any good." When Lara caps her foes, both guns blazing like Chow-Yun Fat in a John Woo action flick, Lara takes the slogan "Girl Power" to the next level. Call her Shotgun Spice; right in front of you, yet always just out of reach, she's the perfect fantasy girl for the digital generation.

Tomb Raider 2 is more ambitious and complex than its predecessor, so there are also more opportunities for error. At Core HQ, six testers play the game over and over — each runthrough takes about 11 hours — hunting down stray bugs. Smith was playing the game an hour before the PlayStation version went to Sony, when Lara fell off a ledge, and he couldn't get her back up. "If Sony found a bug, it would be nuclear here, but we're almost there." Then they found that they'd sent out thousands of demo CD-ROMs with the copy-protection timers already expired, making them unplayable. Then they went nuclear. Fortunately, someone came up with a patch, and they recalled the discs to make the fix. That's par for the course in the high-stakes world of game design, says Adrian's brother and managing director Jeremy Smith. "You're working under pressure to meet deadlines, and somehow you forget to take out one line of code. Still, it could have been worse. It could have gone out to the whole game," he laughs.

Core hasn't changed the formula much for the sequel, but the team of four artists and three programmers have crammed in a bunch of ideas that they didn't have time to put in the original. Gameplay is smoother and more detailed, with impressive lighting effects, such as flares illuminating a corridor as they fly through the air. Where the first game had mostly animal opponents, the sequel has several human villains as well as new beasties. There are new puzzles, new locations, outdoor as well as indoor, new weapons, new moves. See Lara climb. See Lara drive. And Lara herself has had a digital make-over to give her what Eidos calls "a more shapely and life-like look," including 46 polygons alone for her fully animated ponytail. But what fans really want are new form-fitting outfits, and Core has obliged with a wet suit, a flight jacket and, for those who finish the game, a nightie.

How long Tomb Raider will be able to preserve its unique qualities remains to be seen. Eidos CEO Mike McGarvey acknowledges that there's tremendous pressure to bring multiplayer and Internet play to the Tomb Raider franchise. The designers at Core aren't convinced that they should go that route. "We know from the success of Tomb Raider that the combination of different elements — exploration, puzzles, and combat — works really well as it stands," says Adrian Smith. "The interaction is between the player and

Lara; it's a very personal experience. Having seven or eight Laras running around on screen would detract from the whole atmosphere of the game."

Eidos is now the house that Lara built; sales of Tomb Raider helped turn a 1996 pretax loss of $2.6 million into a $14.5 million profit. So the company is proceeding aggressively in its efforts to leverage her appeal into other areas. The action figure is already in stores, and you can order jackets at the Web site **www.tombraider.com.** The single performed by Rhona Mitra, who serves as Lara's flesh-and-flesh incarnation at trade shows, has been postponed so it won't interfere with the movie deal that Eidos hopes to finalize [soon]. The designers — and most fans — hope that it will be a computer-animated movie, but McGarvey says it will probably be live action. For now, fans will have to content themselves with the ad blitz on MTV, ESPN, and the syndicated show *Xena: Warrior Princess.* The tag line? "Lara's Back. Where the Boys Are."

READING THE TEXT

1. Why did some Core employees believe at first that the Tomb Raider video game would be a commercial failure?

2. According to Croal and Hughes, what are the reasons for the extraordinary success of Tomb Raider?

3. Why did Lara Croft become a 1990s cultural icon, according to the authors?

READING THE SIGNS

1. In your journal, reflect on the success of Lara Croft. If you play video games, are you a fan of Lara, and if so, why? If you are not a fan, what is your explanation for her appeal?

2. This selection originally was published in *Newsweek*'s Focus on Technology section. In what ways do the style and content reflect the article's journalistic origins?

3. As an independent and powerful female character, Lara Croft could be seen as a potentially feminist icon, but her physical appearance could be seen as sexist. Write an essay arguing whether Lara Croft is a feminist or counterfeminist character.

4. Select a male video game character, and write a semiotic analysis of him. In what ways does he embody traditional male gender codes? To develop your ideas, consult Holly Devor's "Gender Role Behaviors and Attitudes" (p. 484) or James William Gibson's "Warrior Dreams" (p. 530).

5. Rent a videotape of *Tomb Raider*. Write an essay in which you analyze the depiction of Lara Croft. To what extent does the character reproduce traditional gender roles?

EMILY PRAGER

Our Barbies, Ourselves

Little girls throughout America should know that Barbie is not drawn to scale. In this tongue-in-cheek essay on the role Barbie has played in her life, Emily Prager (b. 1952) reveals the damaging effect of a doll that establishes such an impossible standard of physical perfection for little girls — and for little boys who grow up expecting their girlfriends to look like Barbie. When not contemplating what Barbie has done to her, Prager is a columnist with the New York Times *and an essayist and fiction writer who has published for* The National Lampoon, *the* Village Voice, *and* Penthouse, *among other magazines. Her books include a work of historical fiction for children,* World War II Resistance Stories; *a book of humor,* The Official I Hate Videogames Handbook; *and works of fiction such as* Eve's Tattoo *(1991) and* Clea and Zeus Divorce *(1987). Her most recent book is* Wuhu Diary: On Taking My Adopted Daughter Back to Her Hometown in China *(2001).*

I read an astounding obituary in the *New York Times* not too long ago. It concerned the death of one Jack Ryan. A former husband of Zsa Zsa Gabor, it said, Mr. Ryan had been an inventor and designer during his lifetime. A man of eclectic creativity, he designed Sparrow and Hawk missiles when he worked for the Raytheon Company, and, the notice said, when he consulted for Mattel he designed Barbie.

If Barbie was designed by a man, suddenly a lot of things made sense to me, things I'd wondered about for years. I used to look at Barbie and wonder, What's wrong with this picture? What kind of woman designed this doll? Let's be honest: Barbie looks like someone who got her start at the Playboy Mansion. She could be a regular guest on *The Howard Stern Show*. It is a fact of Barbie's design that her breasts are so out of proportion to the rest of her body that if she were a human woman, she'd fall flat on her face.

If it's true that a woman didn't design Barbie, you don't know how much saner that makes me feel. Of course, that doesn't ameliorate the damage. There are millions of women who are subliminally sure that a thirty-nine-inch bust and a twenty-three-inch waist are the epitome of lovability. Could this account for the popularity of breast implant surgery?

I don't mean to step on anyone's toes here. I loved my Barbie. Secretly, I still believe that neon pink and turquoise blue are the only colors in which to decorate a duplex condo. And like many others of my generation, I've never married, simply because I cannot find a man who looks as good in clam diggers as Ken.

The question that comes to mind is, of course, Did Mr. Ryan design Barbie 5 as a weapon? Because it *is* odd that Barbie appeared about the same time in my

Got Barbie?

consciousness as the feminist movement — a time when women sought equality and small breasts were king. Or is Barbie the dream date of weapons designers? Or perhaps it's simpler than that: Perhaps Barbie is Zsa Zsa if she were eleven inches tall. No matter what, my discovery of Jack Ryan confirms what I have always felt: There is something indescribably masculine about Barbie — dare I say it, phallic. For all her giant breasts and high-heeled feet, she lacks a certain softness. If you asked a little girl what kind of doll she wanted for Christmas, I just don't think she'd reply, "Please, Santa, I want a hard-body."

On the other hand, you could say that Barbie, in feminist terms, is definitely her own person. With her condos and fashion plazas and pools and beauty salons, she is definitely a liberated woman, a gal on the move. And she has always been sexual, even totemic. Before Barbie, American dolls were flat-footed and breastless, and ineffably dignified. They were created in the image of little girls or babies. Madame Alexander was the queen of doll makers in the fifties, and her dollies looked like Elizabeth Taylor in *National Velvet*. They represented the kind of girls who looked perfect in jodhpurs, whose hair was never out of place, who grew up to be Jackie Kennedy — before she married Onassis. Her dolls' boyfriends were figments of the imagination, figments with large portfolios and three-piece suits and presidential aspirations, figments who could keep dolly in the style to which little girls of the fifties were programmed to become accustomed, a style that spasm-ed with the sixties and the appearance of Barbie. And perhaps what accounts for Barbie's vast popularity is that she was also a sixties woman: into free love and fun colors, anticlass, and possessed of real, molded boyfriend, Ken, with whom she could chant a mantra.

But there were problems with Ken. I always felt weird about him. He had no genitals, and, even at age ten, I found that ominous. I mean, here was Barbie with these humongous breasts, and that was OK with the toy company. And then, there was Ken with that truncated, unidentifiable lump at his groin. I sensed injustice at work. Why, I wondered, was Barbie designed with such obvious sexual equipment and Ken not? Why was his treated as if it were more mysterious than hers? Did the fact that it was treated as such indicate that somehow his equipment, his essential maleness, was considered more powerful than hers, more worthy of the dignity of concealment? And if the issue in the mind of the toy company was obscenity and its possible damage to children, I still object. How do they think I felt, knowing that no matter how many water beds they slept in, or hot tubs they romped in, or swimming pools they lounged by under the stars, Barbie and Ken could never make love? No matter how much sexuality Barbie possessed, she would never turn Ken on. He would be forever withholding, forever detached. There was a loneliness about Barbie's situation that was always disturbing. And twenty-five years later, movies and videos are still filled with topless women and covered men. As if we're all trapped in Barbie's world and can never escape.

God, it certainly has cheered me up to think that Barbie was designed by Jack Ryan. . . .

READING THE TEXT

1. Why does Prager say "a lot of things made sense" (para. 2) to her after she learned Barbie was designed by a man?
2. What is Prager's attitude toward Ken?
3. How do Madame Alexander dolls differ from Barbies?

READING THE SIGNS

1. Bring a toy to class, and, in same-sex groups, discuss its semiotic significance; you may want to focus particularly on how the toys may be intended for one

gender or another. Then have each group select one toy and present your interpretation of it to the whole class. What gender-related patterns do you find in
the presentations?

2. Think of a toy you played with as a child, and write a semiotic interpretation of
it, using Prager's essay as a model. Be sure to consider differences between
your childhood response to the toy and your current response.

3. Did you have a Barbie doll when you were a child? If so, write a journal entry in
which you explore what the doll meant to you when you were young and how
Prager's essay has caused you to rethink your attitudes.

4. Consider how Jack Ryan, the creator of Barbie, would defend his design. Write a
letter, as if you were Ryan, addressed to Prager in which you justify Barbie's
appearance and refute Prager's analysis.

5. Barbie can be seen as embodying not only America's traditional gender roles
but also its consumerist ethos. Visit a toy store to learn what "accessories" one
can buy for Barbie, and then write an essay in which you explore the extent to
which she illustrates the "hunger for more" described by Laurence Shames
("The More Factor," p. 56).

GARY CROSS

BARBIE, G.I. JOE, AND PLAY IN THE 1960S

Toys aren't only toys. For as Gary Cross observes in this excerpt from
Kid's Stuff: Toys and the Changing World of American Childhood
*(1997), toys are signifiers of the shifting terrain of American culture and
belief. So it is revealing that Barbie, who was designed to be the ultimate
consumer, has stayed that way for more than forty years, while G.I. Joe
mutated from an ordinary infantryman into a high-tech action-adventure
hero and finally disappeared. Consumption, it seems, never goes out of
style, but not everything we consume stays in fashion. So who says that
toys aren't signs of our times? Cross is a professor of history at Pennsylvania State University who specializes in analyzing the roles that toys
play in the shaping of American childhood. He is author of* Money: The
Making of Consumer Culture *(1993) and coauthor of* Technology and
American Society, A History *(1995).*

Television and the new business climate in the toy industry alone did not
transform the meaning of play. Toys were changing because American society
was changing. By looking at the two most important trend-setting toys we can
find clues to these changes. Much has been written about Barbie and G.I. Joe

as icons of popular culture. But Barbie and G.I. Joe were also toys, and like other toys they were mostly given to children by adults.

Barbie began her career as a stiff plastic dress-up figure. Ruth Handler often claimed that she invented Barbie to fill a void in girls' play. Girls wanted a less cumbersome and more fun version of the fashion paper doll. In using paper dolls as a model Mattel was in effect redirecting doll play away from the friendship and nurturing themes of the companion and baby dolls that had predominated since the 1900s. In the nineteenth century paper dolls were used to display the latest styles and to portray royalty and famous actresses, especially in magazines devoted to fashion. They were associated with an adult world of quasi-aristocratic consumption. They had little to do with domestic or friendship themes. Paper dolls and their focus on fashion were an important part of girls' play in the first half of the twentieth century, but they were only a minor part of the toy business.[1]

Mattel, however, put fashion doll play at the center of the industry. The idea of making the paper fashion doll three dimensional was hardly new. Even the association of doll play with consumption was not innovative. It had been built into the concepts of dolls from Patsy to Toni. But Barbie was not a child doll dressed in children's fashions. Rather Barbie was in the shape of a young woman with very long legs and an exaggerated hourglass figure. She looked neither like the little girl who owned her nor like the little girl's mother. She was neither a baby, a child, nor a mother but a liberated teenager, almost a young woman. Handler admitted that even in this her creation was not so original. She "borrowed" the look from a German dress-up doll she and her daughter Barbara had noticed on a vacation in Switzerland. But she marketed it on a grand scale at a perfect point in the history of American childhood: at the end of the 1950s.[2]

Barbie was an early rebel against the domesticity that dominated the lives of baby-boom mothers. It may not be surprising that some of the first generation of Barbie owners became feminists in the late 1960s and 1970s. The revolt against, at least, the momism of the feminine mystique was played out with Barbie, who never cared for babies or children. But Mattel's doll was also an autonomous teenager with no visible ties to parents in a time when the earliest of the baby-boom generation were just entering their teens. This crop of teenagers, coming of age in a more affluent United States, had more choices than their parents had had and were freer of adult control. To the eight-year-old of 1960, Barbie represented a hoped-for future of teenage freedom. It was this attraction of Barbie that long survived the maturation of the

---

[1]Ruth Handler, *Dream Doll* (Stamford, Conn.: Longmeadow Press, 1994), chs. 4–5; Rebecca Harnmell, "To Educate and Amuse: Paper Dolls and Toys, 1640–1900" (M.A. thesis, University of Delaware, 1988, University Microforms International, Ann Arbor, 1989).

[2]Handler, *Dream Doll;* A. Glen Mandeville, *Doll Fashion Anthology and Price Guide,* 4th ed. (Cumberland, Md.: Hobby House, 1993), 1–33; K. Westenhouser, *The Story of Barbie* (Paducah, Ky.: Collector Books, 1994), 5–15; Billy Boy, *Barbie: Her Life and Times* (New York: Crown, 1987), 17–28, 40–44.

baby-boom generation. It is also not surprising that when Mattel market-tested Barbie it found that mothers were not nearly so positive about the doll as were their daughters. Mothers recognized that this doll was a break from the tradition of nurturing and companion play and that girls apparently welcomed it.

Despite all this, Barbie hardly "taught" girls to shed female stereotypes. 5 Rather she prompted them to associate the freedom of being an adult with carefree consumption. With her breasts and slender waist, Barbie came literally to embody the little girl's image of what it meant to be grown up. At the same time, in her contemporary fashions, she represented the up-to-date. Barbie did not invite children to be Mommy, nor was she the child's friend in a secret garden of caring and sharing. She was what the little girl was not and, even more important, what her mother was not. She was a fashion model with a large wardrobe designed to attract attention. Instead of teaching girls how to diaper a baby or use floor cleaners, Barbie play was an education in consumption — going to the hairdresser and shopping for that perfect evening gown for the big dance. Even when she had a job (model, stewardess, or later even a doctor), her work and life had nothing to do with the jobs of most women. Barbie was never a cashier at Wal-Mart or a homemaker.

If Barbie taught that freedom meant consumption, the Barbie line was designed to maximize parents' real spending. Playing consumer required that Barbie have a constantly changing wardrobe of coordinated clothing and accessories. Clothing sets were often much more expensive than the "hook," the doll itself. The first Barbie advertising brochure featured, for example, a Barbie-Q Outfit, Suburban Shopper, Picnic Set (with fishing pole), Evening Splendor (complete with strapless sheath), and even a Wedding Day Set. By the early 1960s Barbie had play environments, for example the Barbie Fashion Shop and Barbie's Dream House.[3]

Barbie's glamour required constant purchases of dolls and accessories. Playing grown up meant that Barbie had to have a boy friend, Ken (introduced in 1961). Because Barbie seemed to be six to seven years older than her owners, Mattel introduced in 1964 a little sister, Skipper, with whom the children could identify. Naturally Skipper developed her own entourage of "friends." In 1975 Mattel carried the transition doll to its logical conclusion with "Growing Up Skipper." Six-year-olds could mechanically reenact their growing-up fantasy: when her arm was rotated, Skipper grew taller and developed breasts.

Barbie also needed "friends" to shop and have fun with. Mattel manufactured an endless array of Midge, Francie, and Stacey dolls, all "sold separately." Like Barbie's clothing, they changed with the times. While Midge (1963) was the "freckled-faced and impish" girl next door, Francie (1966) and

---

[3]Mattel, "Barbie, Teen-Age Fashion Model," "Barbie, Teen-Age Fashion Model, and Ken, Barbie's Boy Friend (He's a Doll)," "Exclusive Fashions by Mattel," book 3 (Hawthorne, Calif.: Mattel, 1958, 1960, 1963). All in the Strong Museum.

Stacey (1968) reflected the impact of English styles and music in the age of the Beatles. In 1968 Christie, a black friend for Barbie, was introduced, reflecting changing American race relations. Ken vanished suddenly in 1969 (apparently too stodgy an image to fit the long-haired Vietnam era) only to reappear two years later looking much more husky and hip.[4]

Mattel tapped into a young girl's fantasy life to create a demand for possessions. Company researchers watched girls play and noted that they enjoyed hair and dress-up games as well as acting out shopping, travel, and dating. They designed accessories to provide props for these play activities. And if the child did not immediately know what the story lines were to be, Mattel provided them on the back of the packages.

Barbie's impact on the traditional doll industry was enormous. Only [10] 60 doll companies remained in 1969 of the more than 200 that existed when Barbie appeared in 1959. Barbie helped reduce the share of baby dolls from 80 percent of dolls in 1959 to only 38 percent in 1975. Barbie's success inevitably prompted much imitation. Ideal produced Tammy (who conceded the existence of parents with Mom and Dad dolls). American Character offered Tressy, with "hair that really grows." Topper's Penny Brite and the "perfectly proportioned" Tina of Ross Products were others. None survived long in a field dominated by Barbie.[5]

Mattel succeeded [in] keeping successive generations of little girls wanting Barbie and not some other fashion doll. Ruth Handler resisted the temptation to give Barbie a fixed personality or even a "look." Handler liked to say this allowed girls to imagine what Barbie was really like. But from a marketing standpoint this made Barbie a fixture, even a "clothes hanger," upon which accessories could be draped. Partly because she came first, Barbie became the trademark fashion doll. All others were imitations. And Barbie never grew old or out of date as did the dolls made in the image of ephemeral glamour queens like Farah Fawcett-Majors. Barbie was the eternal star — despite her changeable hair and skin color. Barbie was still Barbie.

Mattel even succeeded in persuading little girls to "trade in" their old Barbies for a discount on a new look in 1967. Adults found this strange — voluntarily parting with a "loved" doll. But the girls saw it differently: they were simply trading in an old model for a new, much as their parents traded in their flashy 1959 Chevys for the more sedate look of 1960s models. Barbie's environment — clothes, hair, playsets, and friends — changed with adult fashion. But Barbie's face and shape remained a constant symbol of growing up. Thus Mattel created that elusive and contradictory prize — an ephemeral classic — and in doing so reshaped the play of American girls. A doll that mothers at first disliked became the doll that mothers had to give to their daughters.[6]

---

[4]"The Origins of the Barbie Doll (and Her 'Family')," Mattel Press Kit, Please Touch Museum, Toy Fair Collection (hereafter TFC), Box 5.

[5]"Inside the Doll Market," *Toys,* March 1975, 23–25.

[6]Billy Boy, *Barbie,* 92; Mandeville, *Fashion Anthology,* 41–43, 69–71; Ron Goulart, *The Assault on Childhood* (Los Angeles: Sherbourne, 1969), 26.

Hasbro's G.I. Joe mirrored the success of Barbie by becoming a perennial fad. It achieved this feat, at first, not by challenging expectations of fathers as Barbie broke with the doll culture of mothers, but by affirming the values and experiences of many fathers. Like so many other contemporary toys, G.I. Joe was inspired by a TV series, an action-adventure show, *The Lieutenant* (1963), that was supposed to appeal to adult men. But the program failed even before the toy appeared. G.I. Joe was not tied to any specific media personality or story. He represented the average soldier, evoking memories of fathers' experience in World War II and the Korean War. The original G.I. Joe of 1964 shared with Barbie the critical feature of being a dress-up doll, although marketed as "America's Moveable Fighting Man." At twelve inches, half an inch taller than Barbie, G.I. Joe was suitable for costuming in the uniforms of the four American military services (sold separately). Again like Barbie, G.I. Joe was accessorized. Hasbro adopted what was often called the "razor and razor blade" principle of marketing. Once the boy had the doll he needed accessories — multiple sets of uniforms, jeeps, tents, and weaponry.[7]

Still, Joe was not simply a boys' version of Barbie. The obvious historical precedent was the cast-metal soldier, very different from the paper doll. Miniature soldiers had been part of boy's play for centuries. The object was to reenact the drama of present and past battles. G.I. Joe added to this traditional game by giving boys articulated figures with a man's shape and musculature. The Joes were a major improvement over cheap and impersonal plastic soldiers that stood on bases. Joe took the play beyond the traditional deployment of infantry, cannon, and cavalry. Detailed "Manuals," accompanying the doll, marched "Joe through basic training up to combat readiness," showing the boy how to pose his toy to crouch in a trench or throw a grenade. Joe changed war games from the pleasure of acting the general — arranging soldiers and weapons on a field of battle — to playing the soldier, the G.I. whom the boy dressed and posed. This probably made war play far more appealing to young children because they could identify with the individual soldier. Joe may have contributed to the decline of other forms of boys' play, at least temporarily, insofar as erector sets almost disappeared and Tinkertoys and Lincoln Logs were relegated to preschoolers in the G.I. Joe era.[8]

Nevertheless, the early G.I. Joe did not challenge traditional war play as Barbie displaced baby doll and companion doll play. G.I. Joe's success was based on a boy's identity with the all-male world of heroic action aided by modern military equipment and gadgetry. The play was conventional, featuring males bonding in adventure. This was a womanless world. Boys rejected the idea of a female nurse when it was introduced to the G.I. Joe line in 1965. These boys could play war the way their fathers might have fought it in World War II or in Korea.

15

[7]"Fact Sheet: Hasbro's G.I. Joe, A Real American Hero," Hasbro Press Kit, Feb. 1993, TFC, Box 3; Susan Manos and Paris Manos, *Collectible Male Action Figures* (Paducah, Ky.: Collector Books, 1990), 8–9.

[8]"G.I. Joe, Action Soldiers: America's Moveable Fighting Man" (Pawtucket, R.I.: Hasbro, 1964), Strong Museum.

And they could dress their Joes in battle gear similar to that worn by conscripted uncles or older brothers serving their two-year stints in the army of the mid-1960s. The object was not the clash of enemies (as would be the case with later action figures). Even though boys made their Joe dolls fight each other, Hasbro offered soldiers from only one side. The point was to imitate the real world of adults in the military. G.I. Joe still connected fathers with sons.

Again in contrast to Barbie, G.I. Joe went through major changes. By 1967 as the Vietnam war heated up and adults such as Benjamin Spock attacked war toys, sales decreased. Beginning in 1970 Hasbro responded by transforming the "fighting" Joes into an "Adventure Team." Joes searched for sunken treasure and captured wild animals. As the Vietnam war wound down to its bitter end in 1975, it was awkward to sell military toys glorifying contemporary jungle warfare. While veterans of World War II and even Korea might enjoy giving their sons toys that memorialized their own youth, the situation for fathers who had reached manhood during the Vietnam era was very different. Most of these men wanted to forget the Vietnam war (whether they fought in it or opposed it), not to give their sons toys recalling this military disaster or any real war.

In 1976, with the Vietnam War in the past, G.I. Joe became "Super Joe" and shrunk to eight inches (because of higher costs for plastic). He no longer could be dressed. He returned to the role of a fighter, but he did not rejoin the ranks of enlisted men. He no longer was part of a world that fathers, uncles, or older brothers had ever experienced. Instead he was a high-tech hero, no longer connected to a troublesome reality. His laser beams and rocket command vehicles helped him fight off aliens, the Intruders. Added to his team was Bullet Man, the first of a long line of superhumans. The object of play was to pit good guys against bad guys, not to imitate real military life. But even these changes could not save Joe. From 1978 to 1981 the "Great American Hero" disappeared from store shelves to be pushed aside by an even more fantasyful line of toys based on George Lucas's *Star Wars.*[9]

With Barbie little girls combined growing up with feminine consumerism. This gave Barbie a permanent aisle of hot-pink packages in every serious toy store. G.I. Joe began as a celebration of an all-male world of realistic combat. But Joe encountered deeper contradictions in the 1960s than did Barbie and was forced to flee into fantasy. Still, both toys became models for toy play and consumption that still prevail today. They did so by breaking away from the worlds of parents.

READING THE TEXT

1. According to Cross, how was the creation of Barbie related to the fashion paper doll?

[9]Manos and Manos, *Male Action Figures,* 20–33, 38–43; Vincent Santelmo, *The Official 30th Anniversary Salute to G.I. Joe* (Iola, Wis.: Kreuse, 1994), 17–18, 66–72, 75–97, 325, 343, 412–413.

2. How did Barbie assist, in Cross's words, in the "revolt against . . . the momism of the feminine mystique" (para. 4)?

3. Why did the G.I. Joe doll undergo more profound design changes in its history than did Barbie?

4. In Cross's view, what were the ingredients for the G.I. Joe doll's success?

READING THE SIGNS

1. What sort of doll would you design for girls or boys? Sketch your proposed doll, and write an essay explaining the rationale for your design. Share your sketch with your class.

2. Visit a toy store, and study the action-adventure dolls that now share shelf space with G.I. Joe. Then write an essay in which you analyze the extent to which the dolls reflect the "warrior dreams" that James William Gibson describes ("Warrior Dreams," p. 530).

3. Write an essay in which you explain your own view of how toys and games socialize children to cultural norms and expectations. To develop your ideas, read or reread Jennifer Scanlon ("Boys-R-Us: Board Games and the Socialization of Young Adolescent Girls," p. 503), bell hooks ("Baby," p. 605), and Emily Prager ("Our Barbies, Ourselves," p. 766).

4. Divide the blackboard into two sections: male and female. Have the class write on the board, in the gender-appropriate section, the name of a favorite childhood toy. Then study the results. Do you find any gender patterns? How many of the toys could be classified as "gender-neutral"?

MARK CALDWELL

THE ASSAULT ON MARTHA STEWART

> *You learn something new every day on "Ask Martha," or at least, that's what Martha Stewart will tell you at the end of her daily radio commentary, and in this selection Mark Caldwell (b. 1946) analyzes the rise of Martha Stewart to her current "institutional status." If you've ever turned on Martha Stewart to discover whether the toilet paper flap should hang over or under the roll, this is a must read, whether or not Kmart ever emerges from bankruptcy. Caldwell teaches at Fordham University and is the author of* The Last Crusade *(1988).*

Martha Stewart began her ascent to fame as a Connecticut caterer. But by 1990 she had become an institution, both a national symbol of the epidemic

American infatuation with gracious living and the scapegoat of a nascent backlash. Miss Manners, at present probably our most influential etiquette authority, has a widely syndicated newspaper column and a number of books in general circulation. But Martha Stewart represents an altogether different order of fame, with dozens of titles in print, her own monthly magazine, *Martha Stewart Living*, a daily syndicated half-hour TV program, an interactive World Wide Web site, a mail-order shopping service, an eponymous home products department in Kmart stores, even an umbrella corporation with a suitable business-octopus name: Martha Stewart Living Omnimedia, Inc.

Stewart is only the most visible figure in a thriving lifestyle industry that churns out books, magazines, and exemplars of every other medium from television to CD-ROMs. It has mirrored the growth of retail chains like Crate and Barrel, Pottery Barn, the Gap, and Williams-Sonoma, which sell the trappings of designer-anointed home life in mall outlets and mail-order catalogues. Stewart stands out because of her relentless drive; also because her audience is so large and devoted. She has even achieved the dubious apotheosis of academic attention (a cultural studies anthology is in the works, to be titled *The Martha Stewart Collection*).[1] And, in the culminating proof of her ascent to institutional status, she recently provoked a best-selling unauthorized biography, Jerry Oppenheimer's *Martha Stewart—Just Desserts*. Both her popularity and the negative reaction it has inspired warrant a closer look.

Oppenheimer dwells relentlessly on what he sees as Stewart's pathological ambition and cutthroat business competitiveness, but — hostile though his portrait is — he never questions the sincerity of her dedication to raising the aesthetic tone of American domestic life. Stewart has a reputation for fussy and expensive elegance, but her interests span cooking, gardening, decorating, entertaining, even family relations and finance. And her dominant theme is not costly luxury, but rather studious care — taking pains to make one's daily life pleasant, artful, dignified. The acutest pleasure, in Stewart's world, lies not in buying elegance (though she offers multiple shopping opportunities), but in achieving it through skill and thoughtfulness. In early 1997, she and Kmart inaugurated a new "Everyday" collection, cornerstone of a design-it-yourself department for the budget-minded devotee of good taste. There are no carriage-trade pretensions in these store displays, no attempts to ape the moneyed ambiance of expensive retail stores like Bergdorf Goodman or ABC Carpet and Home.

At Kmart, a near-life-sized cardboard Martha stands at the main entrance, directing customers to the home furnishings department. At the Astor Square branch in Manhattan (a recent immigrant from the suburbs), in the fall of 1997, Martha Stewart Everyday abutted a pre-Halloween display of plastic pumpkins, Reese's Peanut Butter cups, vinyl trash cans, and zebra-stripped polyester rugs.

---

[1] This project, to be undertaken by Linda Robertson and Jodi Dean of Hobart & William Smith colleges, was announced in a September 15, 1997, posting in the online magazine *Slate*.

Stewart's wares were well made, subdued in color, simply designed, and unpretentious: a line of trademarked paints, some terrycloth bathrobes (modeled by Stewart with a matching towel wrapped around her head), table linens, bedsheets. Amidst it all stood a TV monitor reeling out a promotional video loop in which Stewart, smiling and husky voiced, touted her merchandise: not, however, with a hard sell, but a characteristic emphasis on technique. "Our fitted sheets," Stewart purred, "have extra-deep pockets. . . . Do you know the secret of folding a fitted sheet? I learned this from my mom. . . ."[2]

Martha Stewart Living, her monthly magazine, conjures a colorful yet   5 gauzy panorama of amiable, sun-dappled home life, a blend of casual, sentimental, and elegant. Longer established home life magazines like *Architectural Digest* or *House Beautiful* tend to embody their visions of the lush life in detailed spreads of aggressively "done" rooms and distinctive, almost always expensive houses, more or less exhaustively documented in photographs, often accompanied by floor plans and replete with tips about where to buy the furniture and accessories pictured. Artful touches, often contributed by a stylist, suggest human occupancy — a just-this-side-of-slovenly heap of books and magazines on the night stand, or a dining-room table with candles ablaze and one chair casually pulled aside, as if drawing the reader to fantasize himself into the scene. With Stewart, it's usually not the design concept that draws the reader or viewer in, but rather Stewart's presence, sometimes in a photo but always hovering in the text and offering hints about how to create an atmosphere of elegance. Her advice is on the whole heavier on labor than expense: instructions for how to make miniature hamburgers for parties, or for donning dust mask and rubber gloves to color linen napkins with natural dyes like fustic and madder root (two projects included in the September 1997 issue of *Martha Stewart Living*). Her message is that beyond a merely passable way of doing things glimmers a classy and distinguished way, discoverable if one pursues it with the dedicated perfectionism of the artist.

Stationery, for example. The undiscriminating may buy it off the drug or convenience store shelf; the more ambitious may splurge on the expensive formal letter papers ready boxed at a stationery store; the still more *raffiné* can have them printed or engraved. But all these upward increments in taste leave one short of the Stewart standard.

> Martha Stewart looked for years for just the right emblem for her stationery. Last year, she found an image she liked: a cornucopia engraved onto the frontispiece of a rare seventeenth-century book called *Worlidge's Husbandry*. She brought it to Joy Lewis, who recognized the drawing as a banknote-style engraving. Lewis hired a retired employee of the bureau that engraves United States banknotes to recreate the design. Martha's monogram was blind-embossed, or impressed onto the paper without

---

[2]Transcribed at Kmart, 8th Street and Broadway, New York, September 25, 1997.

color, in classic Roman type. The cornucopia was engraved and inked in "van Dyck Brown," the color black fades to after a hundred years.[3]

Snobbery and materialism? That has certainly become a major theme in the attack on Martha Stewart that began in the early 1990s. Oppenheimer's *Just Desserts*, for example, juxtaposes Stewart's unremarkable Polish American childhood in Nutley, New Jersey, against her supposed pretensions, implying that the determination with which she climbed out of it and her obsession with style constitute an attempt to hide sordid beginnings, break out the humble sphere she belongs in by right, and elbow her way in among the wealthy elite.

But this exaggerates Stewart's snobbery and ignores her attentiveness to the hard work behind good taste. The distinguishing characteristic of her stationery, after all, lies not in its cost but rather in the ingenuity and painstaking research that went into its design, as well as in its rejection of the mass-produced. And nowhere does Stewart try to conceal either her lower-middle-class origins, or painful events in her adult life, like her 1990 divorce.[4] Indeed, she writes quite candidly about them in the "Letter from Martha" that opens, and the "Remembering" column that closes, every issue of *Martha Stewart Living*. In one such column, she recalls a childhood memory of her family poring longingly through Sears and Montgomery Ward catalogues,[5] which at the time seemed the utmost reach of upward-aspiring fantasy. Oppenheimer, with an air of having discovered a closely guarded secret, reveals that Stewart's parents shopped at Two Guys from Harrison, a now defunct and decidedly low-rent New Jersey discount outlet; but Stewart herself has reminisced almost nostalgically about Two Guys in "Remembering."[6] Stewart's agenda seems not to imitate upper-class manner, but rather to *separate* the art of civilized living from class; to relocate it . . . from a sense of belonging to a particular status group to a schooling in good taste that anybody might acquire with thought and careful study.

Stewart's stationery is described — and readers seem to take it — not as a possession to drool jealously over but rather as an illustration of the forethought, care, and discrimination everyday life deserves. When Stewart photographs a house, she usually emphasizes not the likely-to-be-intimidating whole, but rather a nook, a corner in the garden, a space small and intimate enough for anyone to imitate no matter how unprepossessing the property or how unexceptional one's means. Her locations exude a leisure and luxury that encourage imitation, and don't remove the reader to an envying distance. Like Emily Post before her, Stewart tries to universalize rather than

[3]*Martha Stewart Living* (May 1996), p. 118.
[4]See Jerry Oppenheimer, *Martha Stewart — Just Desserts: The Unauthorized Biography* (New York: Morrow, 1997), p. 318.
[5]*Martha Stewart Living* (June 1996), p. 156.
[6]*Martha Stewart Living* (September 1997), p. 216.

restrict the accomplishments of class. Post's difficulty lay in never being quite able to explain or decide who the "Best People" were, even though she believed in their existence. Stewart, however, represents a contemporary effort to solve this difficulty. Her criterion for admission among the Best People is a readily learnable ability to appreciate and create what she likes to call "Good Things," an approach more apt to break down social barriers than fortify them. One recent feature in *Martha Stewart Living* covered an impeccable soul-food luncheon served in a Harlem apartment.[7] Good taste and an appreciation for "Good Things" are, as Stewart presents them, meant to cross cultural, ethnic, and class lines, becoming accessible to everybody everywhere.

The democratizing of good taste has been decried: Pottery Barn, for example, has been taxed by critics for offering mass-produced good design at bargain prices to mail-order customers in the hinterlands as well as to well-heeled urbanites. The implication — rather unflattering to design considered as a serious pursuit — is that a beautiful object loses it aesthetic value as soon as it gains wide appreciation. Beauty, in other words, is a quality conferred by an elite rather than created by an artist, and the patina vanishes as soon as the masses admire it. Stewart, I suspect, would disagree. Do her critics mistrust her because she encourages snobbery or because she undercuts it? 10

READING THE TEXT

1. What evidence does Caldwell provide to demonstrate Martha Stewart's status as an icon of the "lifestyle industry" (para. 2)?

2. What are the ingredients of Stewart's appeal to the consumers who turn to her for advice on domestic design, according to Caldwell?

3. What does Caldwell suggest is the basis for the criticism that Stewart encourages snobbery and materialism?

4. Explain in your own words what Caldwell means by the "democratizing of good taste" (para. 10).

READING THE SIGNS

1. Buy an issue of *Martha Stewart Living* and analyze it, studying the text, the photographs, and the advertising. Use your observations as evidence for an essay in which you evaluate whether the magazine does "cross cultural, ethnic, and class lines" (para. 9).

2. Interview some fans of Martha Stewart's empire, asking them about their attraction to her products and the ways in which they use them. Do they, for instance, follow her instructions on making their own decorative objects? Use your results to formulate an argument about whether Stewart's appeal really is the "democratizing of good taste" (para 10).

[7]*Martha Stewart Living* (May 1996), p. 104.

3. Visit a Martha Stewart display in a local Kmart store, and study the layout and marketing features of this part of the store. Write a semiotic analysis of the display, focusing on how its design works to encourage consumption and to create brand loyalty. To develop your ideas, consult Anne Norton, "The Signs of Shopping" (p. 63), and Malcolm Gladwell, "The Science of Shopping" (p. 403).

4. Consult "The Addictive Virus" by John de Graaf, David Wann, and Thomas N. Naylor (p. 71), and write an essay in which you argue whether the Martha Stewart empire is predicated on Americans' increasing tendency to be addicted to "stuff."

ROY RIVENBURG

Snap! Crackle! Plot!

In this age of insatiable curiosity about the private lives of American celebrities, why don't we know more about the love life of Tony the Tiger or the Energizer Bunny? After all, these product mascots, and dozens like them, both human and humanoid, are as familiar to us, thanks to advertising, as most Hollywood stars. So in this tongue-in-cheek feature that originally appeared in the Los Angeles Times *in 1999, Roy Rivenburg sets out on a journalistic mission to find out whatever he can about the personal "lives" of the commercial characters who sell us everything from toilet paper to green beans. And while Rivenburg's article is meant to be a joke, the fact that the product mascots he "researches" are so well known to us is not, signifying just how ad-saturated a culture we are. Rivenburg is a staff writer for the* Los Angeles Times *who specializes in humorous features and columns.*

Now that it's open season on the warped personal lives of presidents and politicians, we decided to investigate a few other American icons, such as the Pillsbury Doughboy, Betty Crocker, and Count Chocula.

What we uncovered is shocking.

For example, when the Jolly Green Giant first appeared in 1925, he was neither green nor jolly. He wore a bearskin outfit and scowled. It wasn't until the 1930s that someone in marketing apparently realized that "Angry White Endocrine Freak" probably wouldn't sell very many frozen peas. So the giant donned a suit of leaves, started reading Dale Carnegie, and had his skin surgically altered to green (which also came in handy for affirmative-action programs).

And that's just the beginning.

Consider the case of Mrs. Butterworth and Mrs. Paul. When we phoned 5
Aurora Foods for biographical information on the mascots' husbands, a
spokesman confessed that both characters had never been married. He acknowledged that the "Mrs." title is misleading but said it is legally accurate
and not impeachable.

Next we called Quaker Oats to ask about Aunt Jemima. Whose aunt is
she, exactly? Answer: nobody's. Corporate genealogists could produce no evidence of nephews, nieces, or relatives of any kind.

In fact, someone should open a dating service for product mascots be-
cause none seems to have a spouse. A few possible exceptions are at General
Mills, home of the Trix rabbit, the Lucky Charms leprechaun, Betty Crocker,
Frankenberry, Count Chocula, and Sonny the CooCoo for Cocoa Puffs bird.
When asked about the marital status of those characters, spokeswoman Pam
Becker said, "I don't know. We don't delve into their personal lives."

But nearly every other mascot we scrutinized — from the Ty-D-Bol man to
Charlie the Tuna (sorry, Charlie) — is single. The Energizer bunny's official biography, for example, says he is "interested in a long-term relationship but
too busy at the moment." No wonder the divorce rate in this country is so
high, with role models like these. About the closest we came to a nuclear family was 46-year-old Tony the Tiger and his son, Tony Jr.

Is there a Mrs. Tony?

"Uh, no," admitted a Kellogg publicist. 10

Wait. How can that be?

Good point, said the publicist. "We can't have Tony fathering children out
of wedlock. Let me look into this." About a week later, Kellogg called back to
report that Tony Jr.'s mother, who has no name, once appeared in a TV commercial on an unspecified date. The publicist also discovered that in 1974,
which was the Chinese year of the tiger, Tony briefly had a daughter,
Antoinette.

Another suspicious family history involves Jack in the Box's clown mascot, Jack, who had a near-death experience in 1980 (when his own company
blew him up) and remained in hiding until 1995. The new Jack, who lives in
La Jolla and wears Armani suits, has a look-alike son and a human wife. Company officials say Jack Jr.'s physique "proves that the gene for large white plastic heads is passed on the male side of the family." Maybe so, but it's still a biological miracle. That's because Jack Jr. is actually older than his mother, who
wasn't created by the company's ad agency until July 31. Perhaps that also
explains why Jack's corporate associates are tight-lipped about the woman's
background, identifying her only as "Mrs. Box."

Of course, being related to a product mascot can be hazardous.

The Chicken of the Sea mermaid originally had an older sister, but the 15
sibling must've been rammed by a Russian fishing trawler or something because company officials cannot account for her whereabouts now. Nor can

they provide a name or exact birth date for the mermaid herself. "She's a very mysterious person," a company spokesman said. "We think she's about 45 years old."

Likewise, the Pillsbury Doughboy — who has been poked in the gut an estimated 57,000 times during his 33 years of existence — once fraternized with a doughgirl and a doughdog, but they also vanished quickly and mysteriously. (Perhaps in a baking accident?)

Even Toucan Sam's innocent young nephews were given the Jimmy Hoffa treatment shortly after they hatched.

Sam must have known too much about that incident because, in the early 1970s, he underwent a Witness Protection Program-style identity change. He had a "beak job" to shorten his nose, cosmetic surgery to brighten his feathers, and he was ordered to stop speaking Toucanese (a variation of Pig Latin) and dump the towering Carmen Miranda–style fruit hat worn in his 1963 debut.

Other mascot make-overs include the Brawny paper towel man (who recently moved the part in his hair and discarded his Lizzie Borden-esque ax), the smiling Kool-Aid pitcher (which in 1975 inexplicably sprouted legs, arms, and a torso) and Kellogg's Snap, Crackle, and Pop (who began life as gnomes with huge noses, floppy ears, and oversized hats but in 1949 adopted boyish haircuts, new uniforms, and smaller facial features).

But sometimes cosmetic surgery can backfire. According to the *Wall* [20] *Street Journal,* Kellogg is so convinced that the Exxon tiger is becoming a Tony the Tiger copycat that it recently sued for trademark infringement, alleging in court papers that Exxon's "whimsical tiger" illegally emulates Tony because he "walks or runs on his two hind legs and acts in a friendly manner."

Other mascot facts and figures:

- Little Sprout is no relation to the Jolly Green Giant.
- The Keebler elves insist they are "not leprechauns, gnomes, dryads, shoemakers, fairies, or sprites. We're American elves, and our job is to bake uncommonly good cookies and crackers."
- The name of the Kellogg's Corn Flakes mascot is Cornelius. Although he is mute, company officials describe him as "a happy-go-lucky, confident rooster."
- The diameter of Jack in the Box's plastic head is 2 feet. There's also a fan inside it, according to *Restaurant and Institutions* magazine.
- Mr. Clean is not gay, despite the earring. Also, his full name is Mr. Veritably Clean.
- Cap'n Crunch's Crunchberry Beast was developed by Jay Ward and Bill Scott, who also created Rocky and Bullwinkle. Ditto for Quisp, the pink-fleshed space alien whose cereal vanished in the 1970s but is staging a comeback. Quisp also recently broke up with his human girlfriend, Sandy Rosenbaum, citing "cross-species dating obstacles."

- The filmstrip character who appears in previews at AMC movie theaters is named Clip. He is 7 years old.

- Mr. Goodwrench, the Ty-D-Bol man, the Ajax white knight, the politically incorrect Frito Bandito, Quisp's muscleman rival Quake, and Mr. Whipple are described by their corporate slave masters as "no longer active," a euphemism for comatose or deceased.

- The oldest mascots in our survey are Aunt Jemima and the Michelin tire man, who are 109 and 100, respectively. Perhaps they'd make a good couple if someone ever starts a mascot matchmaker service.

READING THE TEXT

1. In Rivenburg's view, why are "the warped personal lives of presidents and politicians" (para. 1) a context for interpreting advertising characters?

2. What evidence does Rivenburg advance for his statement that "someone should open a dating service for product mascots" (para. 7)?

3. Explain in your own words why "being related to a product mascot can be hazardous" (para. 14).

4. Characterize Rivenburg's tone in this selection: To what audience do you think he is appealing?

READING THE SIGNS

1. In class, brainstorm on the blackboard as many advertising characters as you can, drawing both from Rivenburg's essay and your own experience. With your class, categorize the characters, perhaps according to gender, ethnicity, or profession. Then discuss the significance of your categories. How do the different groups appeal to consumers to buy their products? What do they reveal about American values?

2. Visit your college library and research the controversy surrounding Joe Camel. What was his appeal, and to whom and why? Do you believe that this character's influence was as great as cigarette-industry critics claimed?

3. Select one of the products from the "Portfolio of Ads" in Chapter 2 and sketch a new character that could serve as an advertising representative of that product. Then write an essay in which you explain how your character would act as a sign. How would it sell the product? What values would it project?

4. Write a semiotic analysis of the Taco Bell chihuahua. How do you explain the appeal of this advertising character? To develop your ideas, consult Michael Omi, "In Living Color: Race and American Culture" (p. 557).

GO AHEAD. MAKE MY SPRAY.

Why buy so many cleaners? Mix your own spray!

Ultra Mr. Clean's concentrated, and stronger than ever. Mix him in a spray bottle, and watch him cut greasy dirt on contact!

Put his muscle to work in a bucket, on a sponge or even in a spray. One powerful cleaner. One easy way to clean it all!

READING THE SIGNS

1. What particular product does this advertisement promote? What argument does it make in the text at the lower left? How persuasive is this ad, in your opinion? How do the images contribute to the effectiveness of the ad?

2. Describe "Mr. Clean." (For additional images of Mr. Clean — including the Mr. Clean action figure — log onto **www.homemadesimple.com/mrclean**.) What physical characteristics make him a good pitchman for a cleaning product?

3. What is the significance of the text "Go Ahead. Make My Spray."? Why would the makers of Mr. Clean want to include this text when advertising their product? Do you think its use is effective? Why or why not?

JENNY LYN BADER

LARGER THAN LIFE

Do you have any heroes? Or does the very concept of heroism seem passé in today's irony-rich, self-conscious era? In this essay that first appeared in Next: Young American Writers on the New Generation *(1994), Jenny Lyn Bader (b. 1968) surveys the role of heroes for her generation, comparing her point of view with those of past generations. Maybe heroes are obsolete, Bader suggests; maybe we'd just be better off with role models who, while not providing the commanding presence of the full-fledged hero, can at least provide some guidance to an often confused Generation X. A New York–based playwright, Bader has published numerous essays on language and culture, specializing in artistic, spiritual, and moral issues. She is coauthor of* He Meant, She Meant: The Definitive Male-Female Dictionary *(1997).*

When my grandmother was young, she would sometimes spot the emperor Franz Josef riding down the cobbled roads of the Austro-Hungarian Empire.

She came of age so long ago that the few surviving photographs are colored cream and chestnut. Early on, she saw cars replace horses and carriages. When she got older, she marveled at the first televisions. Near the end of her life, she grew accustomed to remote control and could spot prime ministers on color TV. By the time she died, the world was freshly populated by gadgetry and myth. Her generation bore witness to the rise of new machinery created by visionaries. My generation has seen machinery break down and visionaries come under fire.

As children, we enjoyed collecting visionaries, the way we collected toys or baseball cards. When I was a kid, I first met Patrick Henry and Eleanor Roosevelt, Abraham Lincoln and Albert Einstein. They could always be summoned by the imagination and so were never late for play dates. I thought heroes figured in any decent childhood. I knew their stats.

Nathan Hale. Nelson Mandela. Heroes have guts.

Michelangelo. Shakespeare. Heroes have imagination.   5

They fight. Alexander the Great. Joan of Arc.

They fight for what they believe in. Susan B. Anthony. Martin Luther King.

Heroes overcome massive obstacles. Beethoven, while deaf, still managed to carry an unforgettable tune. Homer, while blind, never failed to give an excellent description. Helen Keller, both deaf and blind, still spoke to the world. FDR, despite his polio, became president. Moses, despite his speech impediment, held productive discussions with God.

They inspire three-hour movies. They make us weepy. They do the right thing while enduring attractive amounts of suffering. They tend to be self-employed. They are often killed off. They sense the future. They lead lives that make us question our own. They are our ideals, but not our friends.

They don't have to be real. Some of them live in books and legends. They 10 don't have to be famous. There are lower-profile heroes who get resurrected by ambitious biographers. There are collective heroes: firefighters and astronauts, unsung homemakers, persecuted peoples. There are those whose names we can't remember, only their deeds: "you know, that woman who swam the English Channel," "the guy who died running the first marathon," "the student who threw himself in front of the tank at Tiananmen Square." There are those whose names we'll never find out: the anonymous benefactor, the masked man, the undercover agent, the inventor of the wheel, the unknown soldier. The one who did the thing so gutsy and terrific that no one will ever know what it was.

Unlike icons (Marilyn, Elvis) heroes are not only sexy but noble, too. Unlike idols (Gretzky, Streisand), who vary from fan to fan, they are almost universally beloved. Unlike icons and idols, heroes lack irony. And unlike icons and idols, heroes are no longer in style.

As centuries end, so do visions of faith — maybe because the faithful get nervous as the double zeroes approach and question what they've been worshipping. Kings and queens got roughed up at the end of the eighteenth century; God took a beating at the end of the nineteenth; and as the twentieth century draws to a close, outstanding human beings are the casualties of the moment. In the 1970s and 1980s, Americans started feeling queasy about heroism. Those of us born in the sixties found ourselves on the cusp of that change. A sweep of new beliefs, priorities, and headlines has conspired to take our pantheon away from us.

Members of my generation believed in heroes when they were younger but now find themselves grasping for them. Even the word *hero* sounds awkward. I find myself embarrassed to ask people who their heroes are, because the word just doesn't trip off the tongue. My friend Katrin sounded irritated when I asked for hers. She said, "Oh, Jesus . . . Do people still have heroes?"

We don't. Certainly not in the traditional sense of adoring perfect people. Frequently not at all. "I'm sort of intrigued by the fact that I don't have heroes right off the top of my head," said a colleague, Peter. "Can I get back to you?"

Some of us are more upset about this than others. It's easy to tell which 15 of us miss the heroic age. We are moved by schmaltzy political speeches, we warm up to stories of pets saving their owners, we even get misty-eyed watching the Olympics. We mope when model citizens fail us. My college roommate, Linda, remembers a seventh-grade class called "Heroes and She-roes." The first assignment was to write about a personal hero or she-ro. "I came home," Linda told me, "and cried and cried because I didn't have one. . . . Carter had screwed up in Iran and given the malaise speech. Gerald Ford was a nothing and Nixon was evil. My parents told me to write about Jane Fonda the political activist and I just kept crying."

Not everyone feels sentimental about it. A twentyish émigré raised in the former Soviet Union told me: "It's kind of anticlimactic to look for heroes when you've been brought up in a culture that insists on so many heroes. . . . What do you want me to say? Lenin? Trotsky?" Even though I grew up in the relatively propaganda-free United States, I understood. The America of my childhood insisted on heroes, too.

Of all the myths I happily ate for breakfast, the most powerful one was our story of revolution. I sang about it as early as kindergarten and read about it long after. The story goes, a few guys in wigs skipped town on some grumpy church leaders and spurned a loopy king to branch out on their own. The children who hear the story realize they don't have to believe in old-fangled clergy or a rusty crown — but they had better believe in those guys with the wigs.

I sure did. I loved a set of books known as the "Meet" series: *Meet George Washington, Meet Andrew Jackson, Meet the Men Who Sailed the Seas,* and many more. I remember one picture of an inspired Thomas Jefferson, his auburn ponytail tied in a black ribbon, penning words with a feather as a battle of banners and cannon fire raged behind him.

A favorite "Meet" book starred Christopher Columbus. His resistance to the flat-earth society of his day was engrossing, especially to a kid like me who had trouble trying new foods let alone seeking new land masses. I identified with his yearning for a new world and his difficulty with finding investors. Standing up to the king and queen of Spain was like convincing your parents to let you do stuff they thought was idiotic. Now, my allowance was only thirty-five cents a week, but that didn't mean I wasn't going to ask for three ships at some later date.

This is pretty embarrassing: I adored those guys. The ones in the white 20 powder and ponytails, the voluptuous hats, the little breeches and cuffs. They were funny-looking, but lovable. They did outrageous things without asking for permission. They invented the pursuit of happiness.

I had a special fondness for Ben Franklin, statesman and eccentric inventor. Inventions, like heroes, made me feel as though I lived in a dull era. If I'd grown up at the end of the nineteenth century, I could have spoken on early telephones. A few decades later, I could have heard the new sounds of radio. In the sixties, I could have watched black-and-white TVs graduate to color.

Instead, I saw my colorful heroes demoted to black and white. Mostly white. By the time I finished high school, it was no longer hip to look up to the paternalistic dead white males who launched our country, kept slaves and mistresses, and massacred native peoples. Suddenly they weren't visionaries but oppressors, or worse — objects. Samuel Adams became a beer, John Hancock became a building, and the rest of the guys in wigs were knocked off one by one, in a whodunit that couldn't be explained away by the fact of growing up.

The flag-waving of my youth, epitomized by America's bicentennial, was a more loving homage than I know today. The year 1976 rolled in while Washington was still reeling from Saigon, but the irony was lost on me and my second-grade classmates. The idea of losing seemed miles away. We celebrated July Fourth with wide eyes and patriotic parties. Grown-ups had yet to tell themselves (so why should they tell us?) that the young nation on its birthday had suffered a tragic defeat.

Historians soon filled us in about that loss, and of others. Discovering America was nothing compared to discovering the flaws of its discoverers, now cast as imperialist sleaze, racist and sexist and genocidal. All things heroic — human potential, spiritual fervor, moral resplendence — soon became suspect. With the possible exception of bodybuilding, epic qualities went out of fashion. Some will remember 1992 as the year Superman died. Literally, the writers and illustrators at D.C. Comics decided the guy was too old to keep leaping buildings and rescuing an aging damsel in distress. When rumors circulated that he would be resurrected, readers protested via calls to radio shows, letters to editors, and complaints to stores that they were in no mood for such an event.

A monster named Doomsday killed Superman, overcoming him not with 25 Kryptonite but with brute force. Who killed the others? I blame improved modes of character assassination, media hype artists, and scholars. The experts told me that Columbus had destroyed cultures and ravaged the environment. They also broke the news that the cowboys had brazenly taken land that wasn't theirs. In a way, I'm glad I didn't know that earlier; dressing up as a cowgirl for Halloween wouldn't have felt right. In a more urgent way, I wish I had known it then so I wouldn't have had to learn it later.

Just fifteen years after America's bicentennial came Columbus's quincentennial, when several towns canceled their annual parades in protest of his sins. Soon other festivities started to feel funny. When my aunt served corn pudding last Thanksgiving, my cousin took a spoonful, then said drily that the dish was made in honor of the Indians who taught us to use corn before we eliminated them. Uncomfortable chuckles followed. Actually, neither "we" nor my personal ancestors had come to America in time to kill any Native Americans. Yet the holiday put us in the same boat with the pilgrims and anchored us in the white man's domain.

I am fascinated by how we become "we" and "they." It's as if siding with the establishment is the Alka-Seltzer that helps us stomach the past. To swallow history lessons, we turn into "we": one nation under God of proud but remorseful Indian killers. We also identify with people who look like us. For example, white northerners studying the Civil War identify both with white slaveholders and with northern abolitionists, aligning with both race and place. Transsexuals empathize with men and women. Immigrants identify with their homeland and their adopted country. Historians proposing a black Athena and a black Jesus have inspired more of such bonding.

I'll admit that these empathies can be empowering. I always understood the idea of feeling stranded by unlikely role models but never emotionally grasped it until I watched Penny Marshall's movie *A League of Their Own*. For the first time, I appreciated why so many women complain that sports bore them. I had enjoyed baseball before but never as intensely as I enjoyed the games in that film. The players were people like me. Lori Petty, petite, chirpy, wearing a skirt, commanded the pitcher's mound with such aplomb that I was moved. There's something to be said for identifying with people who remind us of ourselves, though Thomas Jefferson and Lori Petty look more like each other than either of them looks like me. I'll never know if I would've read the "Meet" books with more zeal if they'd described our founding mothers. I liked them as they were.

Despite the thrill of dames batting something on the big screen besides their eyelashes, the fixation on look-alike idols is disturbing for those who get left out. In the movie *White Men Can't Jump*, Wesley Snipes tells Woody Harrelson not to listen to Jimi Hendrix, because "White people can't hear Jimi." Does this joke imply that black people can't hear Mozart? That I can admire Geena Davis's batting but never appreciate Carlton Fisk? Besides dividing us from one another, these emotional allegiances divide us from potential heroes too, causing us to empathize with, say, General Custer and his last stand instead of with Sitting Bull and the victorious Sioux.

Rejecting heroes for having the wrong ethnic credentials or sex organs 30 says less about our multicultural vision than our lack of imagination. By focusing on what we are instead of who we can become, by typecasting and miscasting our ideals — that's how we become "we" and "they." If heroes are those we'd like to emulate, it does make sense that they resemble us. But the focus on physical resemblance seems limited and racist.

Heroes should be judged on their deeds, and there are those with plenty in common heroically but not much in terms of ethnicity, nationality, or gender. Just look at Harriet Tubman and Moses; George Washington and Simón Bolívar; Mahatma Gandhi and Martin Luther King; Murasaki and Milton; Cicero and Ann Richards. Real paragons transcend nationality. It didn't matter to me that Robin Hood was English — as long as he did good, he was as

American as a barbecue. It didn't matter to Queen Isabella that Columbus was Italian as long as he sailed for Spain and sprinkled her flags about. The British epic warrior Beowulf was actually Swedish. Both the German hero Etzel and the Scandinavian hero Atli were really Attila, king of the Huns. With all this borrowing going on, we shouldn't have to check the passports of our luminaries; the idea that we can be like them not literally but spiritually is what's uplifting in the first place.

The idea that we can never be like them has led to what I call jealousy journalism. You know, we're not remotely heroic so let's tear down anyone who is. It's become hard to remember which papers are tabloids. Tell-all articles promise us the "real story" — implying that greatness can't be real. The safe thing about *Meet George Washington* was that you couldn't actually meet him. Today's stories and pictures bring us closer. And actually meeting your heroes isn't the best idea. Who wants to learn that a favorite saint is really just an egomaniac with a publicist?

Media maestros have not only knocked public figures off their pedestals, they've also lowered heroism standards by idealizing just about everyone. Oprah, Geraldo, and the rest turn their guests into heroes of the afternoon because they overcame abusive roommates, childhood disfigurement, deranged spouses, multiple genitalia, cheerleading practice, or zany sexual predilections. In under an hour, a studio audience can hear their epic sagas told.

While TV and magazine producers helped lead heroes to their graves, the academic community gave the final push. Just as my peers and I made our way through college, curriculum reformers were promoting "P.C." agendas at the expense of humanistic absolutes. Scholars invented their own tabloidism, investigating and maligning both dead professors and trusty historical figures. Even literary theory helped, when deconstructionists made it trendy to look for questions instead of answers, for circular logic instead of linear sense, for defects, contradictions, and the ironic instead of meaning, absolutes, and the heroic.

It was the generations that preceded ours who killed off our heroes. And 35 like everyone who crucified a superstar, these people thought they were doing a good thing. The professors and journalists consciously moved in a positive direction — toward greater tolerance, openness, and realism — eliminating our inspirations in the process. The death of an era of hero worship was not the result of the cynical, clinical materialism too often identified with my generation. It was the side effect of a complicated cultural surgery, of an operation that may have been necessary and that many prescribed.

So with the best of intentions, these storytellers destroyed bedtime stories. Which is too bad for the kids, because stories make great teachers. Children glean by example. You can't tell a child "Be ingenious," or "Do productive things." You can tell them, "This Paul Revere person jumped on a horse at midnight, rode wildly through the dark, figured out where the mean British troops were coming to attack the warm, fuzzy, sweet, great-looking colonists, and sent messages by code, igniting our fight for freedom," and they'll get the idea. America's rugged values come gift wrapped in the frontier tales of Paul Bunyan, Daniel Boone, Davy Crockett — fables of independence and natural resources. Kids understand that Johnny Appleseed or Laura Ingalls Wilder would never need a Cuisinart. Pioneer and prairie stories convey the fun of roughing it, showing kids how to be self-reliant, or at least less spoiled.

Children catch on to the idea of imitating qualities, not literal feats. After returning his storybook to the shelf, little Billy doesn't look around for a dragon to slay. Far-off stories capture the imagination in an abstract but compelling way, different from, say, the more immediate action-adventure flick. After watching a James Bond film festival, I might fantasize about killing the five people in front of me on line at the supermarket, while legends are remote enough that Columbus might inspire one to be original, but not necessarily to study Portuguese or enlist in the navy. In tales about conquerors and cavaliers, I first flirted with the idea of ideas.

Even Saturday-morning cartoons served me as parables, when I woke up early enough to watch the classy Superfriends do good deeds. Sure, the gender ratio between Wonder Woman and the gaggle of men in capes seemed unfair, but I was rapt. I wonder whether I glued myself to my television and my high expectations with too much trust, and helped to set my own heroes up for a fall.

Some heroes have literally been sentenced to death by their own followers. *Batman* subscribers, for example, were responsible for getting rid of Batman's sidekick, Robin. At the end of one issue, the Joker threatened to kill the Boy Wonder, and readers could decide whether Robin lived or died by calling one of two "900" numbers. The public voted overwhelmingly for his murder. I understand the impulse of those who dialed for death. At a certain point, eternal invincibility grows as dull and predictable as wearing a yellow cape and red tights every day of the year. It's not human. We get fed up.

My generation helped to kill off heroism as teenagers, with our language. 40 We used heroic words that once described brave deeds — *excellent, amazing, awesome* — to describe a good slice of pizza or a sunny day. In our everyday speech, *bad* meant good. *Hot* meant cool. In the sarcastic slang of street gangs in Los Angeles, *hero* currently means traitor, specifically someone who snitches on a graffiti artist.

Even those of us who lived by them helped shatter our own myths, which wasn't all negative. We discovered that even the superhero meets his match. Every Achilles needs a podiatrist. Every rhapsodically handsome leader has a mistress or a moment of moral ambiguity. We injected a dose of reality into our expectations. We even saw a viable presidential candidate under a heap of slung mud, a few imperfections, an alleged tryst or two.

We're used to trysts in a way our elders aren't. Our parents and grandparents behave as if they miss the good old days when adulterers wore letter sweaters. They feign shock at the extramarital exploits of Thomas Jefferson, Frank Sinatra, JFK, Princess Di. Their hero worship is a romance that falters when beloved knights end up unfaithful to their own spouses. People my age aren't amazed by betrayal. We are suspicious of shining armor. Even so, tabloid sales escalate when a Lancelot gives in to temptation — maybe because the jerk who cheats on you somehow becomes more attractive. Other generations have gossiped many of our heroes into philanderers. The presumptuous hero who breaks your heart is the most compelling reason not to get involved in the first place.

Seeing your legends discredited is like ending a romance with someone you loved but ultimately didn't like. However much you longed to trust that person, it just makes more sense not to. Why pine away for an aloof godlet who proves unstable, erratic, and a rotten lover besides? It's sad to give up fantasies but mature to trade them in for healthier relationships grounded in reality.

We require a new pantheon: a set of heroes upon whom we can rely, who will not desert us when the winds change, and whom we will not desert. It's unsettling, if not downright depressing, to go through life embarrassed about the identity of one's childhood idols.

Maybe we should stick to role models instead. Heroes have become 45 quaint, as old-fashioned as gas-guzzlers — and as unwieldy, requiring too much investment and energy. Role models are more like compact cars, less glam and roomy but easier to handle. They take up less parking space in the imagination. Role models have a certain degree of consciousness about their job. The cast members of *Beverly Hills 90210,* for example, have acknowledged that they serve as role models for adolescents, and their characters behave accordingly: they refrain from committing major crimes; they overcome inclinations toward substance abuse; they see through adult hypocrisy; and any misdemeanors they do perpetrate are punished. For moral mediators we could do better, but at least the prime-time writing staff is aware of the burden of having teen groupies.

Heroes don't have the luxury of staff writers or the opportunity to endorse designer jeans. Hercules can't go on *Nightline* and pledge to stop taking steroids. Prometheus can't get a presidential pardon. Columbus won't have a chance to weep to Barbara Walters that he didn't mean to endanger leatherback turtles or monk seals or the tribes of the Lucayas. Elizabeth I never wrote a best-seller about how she did it her way.

Role models can go on talk shows, or even host them. Role models may live next door. While a hero might be a courageous head of state, a saint, a leader of armies, a role model might be someone who put in a three-day presidential bid, your local minister, your boss. They don't need their planes to go down in flames to earn respect. Role models have a job, accomplishment, or hairstyle worth emulating.

Rather than encompassing that vast kit and caboodle of ideals, role models can perform a little neat division of labor. One could wish to give orders like Norman Schwarzkopf but perform psychoanalysis like Lucy Van Pelt, to chair a round-table meeting as well as King Arthur but negotiate as well as

Queen Esther,[1] to eat like Orson Welles but look like Helen of Troy, and so forth. It was General Schwarzkopf, the most tangible military hero for anyone my age, who vied instead for role-model status by claiming on the cover of his book: *It Doesn't Take a Hero*. With this title he modestly implies that anyone with some smarts and élan could strategize and storm as well as he has.

Role models are admirable individuals who haven't given up their lives or livelihoods and may even have a few hangups. They don't have to be prone to excessive self-sacrifice. They don't go on hunger strikes; they diet. They are therefore more likely than heroes to be free for lunch, and they are oftener still alive.

Heroism is a living thing for many of my contemporaries. In my informal poll, I not only heard sob stories about the decline of heroes, I also discovered something surprising: the ascent of parents. While the founding fathers may be passé, actual mothers, fathers, grands, and great-grands are undeniably "in." An overwhelming number of those I polled named their household fore-bears as those they most admired. By choosing their own relatives as ideals, people in their twenties have replaced impersonal heroes with the most personal role models of all. Members of my purportedly lost generation have not only realized that it's time to stop believing in Santa Claus, they have chosen to believe instead in their families — the actual tooth fairy, the real Mr. and Mrs. Claus. They have stopped needing the folks from the North Pole, the guys with the wigs, the studs and studettes in tights and capes.

In a way it bodes well that Superman and the rest could be killed or re-ported missing. They were needed to quash the most villainous folks of all: in-sane communists bearing nuclear weapons, heinous war criminals, monsters named Doomsday. The good news about Superman bleeding to death was that Doomsday died in the struggle.

If the good guys are gone, so is the world that divides down the middle into good guys and bad guys. A world without heroes is a rigorous, demand-ing place, where things don't boil down to black and white but are rich with shades of gray; where faith in lofty, dead personages can be replaced by faith in ourselves and one another; where we must summon the strength to imag-ine a five-dimensional future in colors not yet invented. My generation grew up to see our world shift, so it's up to us to steer a course between naiveté and nihilism, to reshape vintage stories, to create stories of spirit without apologies.

I've heard a few. There was one about the woman who taught Shake-speare to inner-city fourth graders in Chicago who were previously thought to be retarded or hopeless. There was a college groundskeeper and night watch-man, a black man with a seventh-grade education, who became a contracts expert, wrote poetry and memoirs, and invested his salary so wisely that he bequeathed 450 acres of mountainous parkland to the university when he

50

---

[1]**Queen Esther** Jewish heroine of the biblical Book of Esther. — EDS.

died. There was the motorcyclist who slid under an eighteen-wheeler at full speed, survived his physical therapy only to wind up in a plane crash, recovered, and as a disfigured quadriplegic started a business, got happily married, and ran for public office; his campaign button bore a caption that said "Send me to Congress and I won't be just another pretty face. . . ."

When asked for her heroes, a colleague of mine spoke of her great-grandmother, a woman whose husband left her with three kids in Galicia, near Poland, and went to the United States. He meant to send for her, but the First World War broke out. When she made it to America, her husband soon died, and she supported her family; at one point she even ran a nightclub. According to the great-granddaughter, "When she was ninety she would tell me she was going to volunteer at the hospital. I would ask how and she'd say, 'Oh, I just go over there to read to the old folks.' The 'old folks' were probably seventy. She was a great lady."

My grandmother saved her family, too, in the next great war. She did not ₅₅ live to see the age of the fax, but she did see something remarkable in her time, more remarkable even than the emperor riding down the street: she saw him walking down the street. I used to ask her, "Did you really see the emperor Franz Josef walking down the street?"

She would say, "Ya. Walking down the street." I would laugh, and though she'd repeat it to amuse me, she did not see what was so funny. To me, the emperor was someone you met in history books, not on the streets of Vienna. He was larger than life, a surprising pedestrian. He was probably just getting some air, but he was also laying the groundwork for my nostalgia of that time when it would be natural for him to take an evening stroll, when those who were larger than life roamed cobblestones.

Today, life is larger.

READING THE TEXT

1. Why do you think Bader begins and ends her essay with an anecdote regarding her grandmother, and what effect does that anecdote have on the reader?

2. How does Bader define *hero, icon,* and *role model,* and what is her attitude toward each?

3. What are the heroes and myths that Bader grew up with, and how does she feel about them now?

4. In your own words, explain Bader's attitude toward political correctness.

5. How does Bader characterize her generation of twentysomethings?

READING THE SIGNS

1. In your journal, brainstorm a list of heroes that you admired as a child, and then compare your list with the traditional heroes whom Bader mentions. How do you account for any differences or similarities?

2. Write an argumentative essay that supports, challenges, or modifies Bader's central contention that her generation needs role models, not heroes.

3. In class, discuss how a writer might, as Bader suggests, "reshape vintage stories, . . . create stories of spirit without apologies" (para. 52). Then, in a creative essay, write your own "story of spirit."

4. In class, brainstorm a list of traditional American heroes, and then discuss whether they have lost their luster and, if so, why.

5. Assume Bader's perspective on heroes, and write an analytic essay in which you explain why Michael Jordan remains so admired by today's twentysomething generation. To develop your ideas, read or reread Michael Eric Dyson's "Be Like Mike? Michael Jordan and the Pedagogy of Desire" (p. 729).

6. In class, discuss the extent to which the September 11 attacks have altered Americans' conceptions of heroism. Use the discussion as the basis of an essay in which you propose your own definition of what constitutes a hero today. You might consult Tim Layden's "A Patriot's Tale" (below).

TIM LAYDEN
A PATRIOT'S TALE

NFL stars may pull in more money for one football game than a firefighter may make in an entire career. Is something wrong with this picture? Few people really thought so until September 11, 2001, when the fire crews of the New York City fire department became America's newest heroes. And for one NFL starter, New England Patriot right guard Joe Andruzzi, whose three brothers are all NYC firefighters, the irony is especially keen. In this profile of the Andruzzi brothers — Joe, Marc, Billy, and Jimmy, who was in Tower 1 of the World Trade Center just before it collapsed — Tim Layden invites us to reconsider just who our real heroes should be. A senior writer for Sports Illustrated, *Layden specializes in college football commentary.*

The Andruzzis grew up the best kind of brothers, four boys wedged into two small bedrooms in their Staten Island home, loving and fighting, best friends and worst enemies. They spent long Saturday afternoons at the little league field and Sundays at home, eating their mother's ritual macaroni and meatballs. They handed down paper routes and school clothes through four mini-generations. They were the sons of a New York City cop who sometimes worked three jobs at once to keep them all in parochial school, and their neighborhood was filled with the children of policemen and firefighters. Fathers were sometimes hurt or lost in the line of duty; that was part of life. Many sons would follow the same path.

Three of the Andruzzi boys became New York City firemen. Jimmy, 30, was first, graduating from the academy in October 1995. Billy, the oldest, at 32, first worked as a case manager for the New York City welfare department, but when he saw how much Jimmy loved his job, he joined the firefighting ranks in the summer of '99. The baby, Marc, 24, finished eight weeks of academy training in early September and is a "probie," beginning the probationary period that precedes graduation. "Their father was a cop, and now three sons are in the fire department," says their mother, Mary Ann, with a look of pride in her eyes. "My boys love to help people."

Joe, 26, would be the odd one. He kept growing long after his 200-pound brothers stopped, played football as an offensive lineman at Southern Connecticut State and clawed his way into the NFL as an undrafted free agent in 1997, making the roster of the Super Bowl champion Green Bay Packers. Despite three knee surgeries, he is the starting right guard for the New England Patriots, a 6' 3", 315-pound contradiction of weekday calm and Sunday mayhem. "If I didn't play football, I would be teaching special education," says Joe. "I'm the black sheep, I guess. I wouldn't be a firefighter."

Still, he admires his brothers as much as they do him. "What's important is that my brothers are happy in what they do, and I know they are," says Joe. "A lot of people hate their jobs. I know my brothers are excited when they go to work. I'm excited when I get up on Sunday morning and know I've got a game to play. And I know they're excited when they go into a building to put out a fire." Nonetheless, he fights guilt over the opulence made possible by his profession. "I see them driving old cars, scrounging for second jobs," says Joe of his siblings. "The wage difference, it doesn't feel right for what they do."

Joe was in a dentist's chair on the morning of Tuesday, September 11, 5 when he heard a radio report of a fire at the World Trade Center. He rushed back to his house in North Attleboro, Massachusetts, with his wife, Jen, and their children, Hunter, 3, and Breanna, 17 months, and they watched coverage of the attacks. Both towers were still standing but soon would fall. Joe knew that Jimmy was stationed in lower Manhattan (Engine 5, on East 14th Street). "I was thinking Jimmy could be in the middle of all that," says Joe. "I knew he had to be close. My heart was in my throat." Five hours passed before Joe learned that his brothers were all safe and that Jimmy had, indeed, been terrifyingly close to death.

On the day after the disaster, Joe sleepwalked through meetings and practice in preparation for a game at Carolina that he hoped would not take place. "I was there, but not really there," he says. When the NFL announced the next day that its games were canceled, Joe drove to Staten Island. Late last Friday afternoon he was sitting in the living room of his parents' modest split-level house when Jimmy walked through the door and stopped at the entrance to

Police and firefighters at the World Trade Center on September 11, 2001.

the room. He raised his right hand and held his thumb and index finger less than an inch apart, wordlessly demonstrating the margin of his survival as his lip trembled and his eyes watered. Both men began to cry, and they embraced in the center of the room, sobbing for longer than either could ever remember.

On the morning of the attack, Jimmy was scheduled to work a nine-to-six shift, but firefighters all know that means showing up at eight. Just after 8:30 Jimmy and his squad were called to a smoky apartment on East 19th Street. Food left on a stove. They put out the fire and, as they climbed back on to the truck, heard a jet screaming overhead. Awfully low, they said to one another. Seconds later, the engine radio sounded. *Engine 10, Ladder 10, a plane has hit Tower 1 of the World Trade Center*. Engine 10 is in the shadow of the twin towers; firefighters from that company saw the first plane hit. Engine 5, fresh from the kitchen fire, was not far away. Within minutes the two companies were at the base of Tower 1, the first building that was struck.

Five days later Jimmy Andruzzi sat on a couch in his parents' living room, unshaven, wearing denim shorts and a white T-shirt. His brothers, Joe and Billy, sat nearby. Their father, Bill, thirteen years retired from the police force, was on his way home from his sales job. Their mother was in the kitchen, making the Sunday macaroni and meatballs, seeking blessed routine even as a newspaper lay open on a table showing pictures of dozens of the missing, many of them friends of the Andruzzis.

In a soft voice Jimmy described the events of September 11.

"We're on the rig, and we look up and see the first tower burning, and my buddy, Derek Brogan, says to me, 'We're going to the biggest disaster in the history of New York City.' Once we're there, we're thinking about the protocol for a high-rise: command post in the lobby, another command post three floors below the fire. They told us the bottom of the fire was on the 79th floor. We're in the lobby when we hear another huge explosion. I figured out later that was the second plane hitting. I'm thinking, When we practice terrorist scenarios, they always tell us, 'First responders will be casualties.' The building is shaking, and nobody wants to go up now. They tell us, 'Engine 5, go with Engine 10 to 79. Put that fire out.' So we go up the stairs, me and Derek and Manny Delvalle and Gerard Gorman and Eddie Mecner and Lieutenant Bob Bohak. That's what we do. We put out fires.

"People are coming down the stairs. They're saying, 'You guys are so brave, ₁₀ thank you, thank you.' The stairwell is narrow — one line going up, another line going down. At the ninth floor Derek's getting chest pains. The lieutenant tells him to stop, but he keeps going. We're carrying 160 pounds of equipment, and it's hot. We get to the 23rd floor, and Derek is worse. The lieutenant radios for oxygen and tells the cops who bring up the oxygen to bring Derek back down. We start up again, maybe four more floors before we hear the biggest, loudest, most intense sound I've ever heard in my life. I didn't know at the time, but that was Tower 2 coming down. We thought it was our building coming down or a huge bomb. I figured I was dead right there. That's it.

"Lieutenant Bohak says, 'Drop your hoses and get out! Right now! Out!' We start running down the stairs, and it's all black smoke. [Here Jimmy begins to sob loudly.] We're leaving all those firemen behind, and they're still going up. All those guys, those guys, going up, but we had to leave. Those poor guys. . . . [He pauses to compose himself.] We get to the fourth floor, and the door out of the stairwell to the lobby is locked. I feel this rumble, like thunder, and the walls start cracking and the beams are bending. Some guy, not a firefighter — God bless him, he was an angel — points out another door, we got through that into the lobby. I ran out into the street and kept going, and the whole building came down, maybe 45 seconds behind me. All those firemen got killed, and I'm alive because Derek got chest pains and because my lieutenant told us to get out and that guy was on the fourth floor. [Long pause as he begins crying again.] It's not supposed to happen. Terrorists aren't supposed to fly jet planes into a building full of innocent people, and the World Trade Center isn't supposed to fall down. It's just not supposed to happen."

Firefighters have two families: one at home, one at the station house. "My brothers, they're blood," says Jimmy. "But the guys in the station house, they're my brothers too. Everybody knows everything about everybody else. You know who's got a new girlfriend, you know whose kids are sick. The guys with seniority, they get all the respect. The probies, they get their balls broken a lot. Thin skin doesn't play in the station house."

When Jimmy exited onto the street that Tuesday morning, he found that among his group from the stairwell, only Delvalle was missing. Five days later he was still missing, along with Engine 5 lieutenant Paul Mitchell, who was off duty at the time of the crash but rushed to the site to help. They were two of the more than 300 New York City firefighters lost in the disaster, equal to more than a third of all previous casualties in the department's history. "Probably 100 of them were friends of mine," says Jimmy, who has worked at four station houses in his six-plus years with the department. "That's true of a lot of guys."

At the core of this immeasurable disaster, the missing firefighters were at once heroes and victims, symbols of bravery and tragedy. It will be years before their ranks fully recover the experience and skill that was lost. Two days after the towers fell, Jimmy joined the thousands of firemen and other volunteers searching through the rubble for survivors and bodies. Standing atop a pile of twisted steel and compacted concrete, he felt another rumble, similar to what he had felt forty-eight hours earlier. He ran from the pile in terror and promised not to return soon.

His brothers Billy and Marc have done multiple shifts on what rescue and 15 recovery workers have come to call "the mountain," their name for the pile of rubble that had been the tallest buildings in the city. "I hate to say that it's hard to appreciate what it's like down there," said Billy on Sunday, "but television does not do justice to how terrible it is."

The previous evening he had held a fellow firefighter's ankles as the man reached deep into the wreckage and scooped intestines out of a detached torso for DNA identification. In another place he picked up a single tooth. "By the end of my shift down there, I smelled like death," he said, and then he too began to cry.

On a cool, crystal-clear Sunday morning, Joe went with Jimmy to the Engine 5 station house, a three-story building that is one of the oldest firehouses in the city. He found tough men, scarred but battling for their sanity. "There were guys there who said they'd been crying for three days and it was time to stop," Joe said later. They were also worried about Jimmy, who had taken things harder than most. "They said he's not back yet," said Joe. "They said he needs more time. I hope it helps him to talk about it."

Joe sat on the steps of his mom and dad's home. A soft breeze ruffled the American flag on the front of the house. Inside, the table was set for dinner. Soon Joe would return to Massachusetts to begin preparing for this Sunday's game against the New York Jets in Foxboro. Football business. "Regular game week," said Joe.

Normalcy beckons, but reaching it will take longest for those survivors who were closest to the flame.

READING THE TEXT

1. How does Joe Andruzzi characterize himself in comparison to his brothers?

2. Describe the organization and narration of events of this article. To what extent do they work to create an emotional impact on the reader?

3. Layden begins the article not by describing his main subject, the firefighter heroes, but by focusing on their football-player brother. What effect does this opening have on you as reader?

4. In your own words, why does Layden see the firefighters missing in the wreckage as having symbolic status?

READING THE SIGNS

1. Time has passed since the September 11 attacks, and less press coverage is devoted to the police, firefighters, and others who worked to save victims. In class, discuss whether these workers still have the heroic status they were granted in the immediate aftermath of the attacks. Reflect on your class discussion, and write an essay in which you explore whether America's devotion to its heroes is deep-rooted and genuine or, alternately, subject to trends.

2. This article was first published in *Sports Illustrated*. Study its organization and rhetorical strategies. To what extent do you find it designed for a mass-market readership? To what extent is the message tailored for such a readership?

3. After the September 11 attacks, many Americans talked about the need to redefine our notions of heroism. Read or reread Jenny Lyn Bader's "Larger Than Life" (p. 785). To what extent would the Andruzzi brothers, and other rescue personnel, fulfill her call for "a new pantheon" (para. 44) of heroes? Would she see them, and their deeds, as a return to a world when some stand "larger than life" (para. 56)?

GLOSSARY

archetype (n.) A recurring character type or plot pattern found in literature, mythology, and popular culture. Sea monsters like Jonah's whale and Moby Dick are archetypes, as are stories that involve long sea journeys or descents into the underworld.

canon (n.) Books or works that are considered essential to a literary tradition, as the plays of Shakespeare are part of the canon of English literature.

class (n.) A group of related objects or people. Those who share the same economic status in a society are said to be of the same social class: for example, working class, middle class, upper class. Members of a social class tend to share the same interests and political viewpoints.

code (n.) A system of **signs** or values that assigns meanings to the elements that belong to it. Thus, a traffic code defines a red light as a "stop" signal and a green light as a "go," while a fashion code determines whether an article of clothing is stylish. To *decode* a system is to figure out its meanings, as in interpreting the tattooing and body-piercing fads.

connotation (n.) The meaning suggested by a word, as opposed to its objective reference, or **denotation.** Thus, the word *flag* might connote (or suggest) feelings of patriotism, while it literally denotes (or refers to) a pennantlike object.

consumption (n.) The use of products and services, as opposed to their production. A *consumer culture* is one that consumes more than it produces. As a consumer culture, for example, America uses more goods such as TV sets and stereos than it manufactures, which results in a trade deficit with those *producer cultures* (such as Japan) with which America trades.

context (n.)   The environment in which a **sign** can be interpreted. In the context of a college classroom, for example, T-shirts, jeans, and sneakers are interpreted as ordinary casual dress. Wearing the same outfit in the context of a job interview at IBM would be interpreted as meaning that you're not serious about wanting the job.

cultural studies (n.)   The academic study of ordinary, everyday culture rather than **high culture**. See also **culture; culture industry; mass culture; popular culture.**

culture (n.)   The overall system of values and traditions shared by a group of people. Not exactly synonymous with *society,* which can include numerous cultures within its boundaries, a culture encompasses the worldviews of those who belong to it. Thus, the United States, which is a **multicultural** society, includes the differing worldviews of people of African, Asian, Native American, and European descent. See also **cultural studies; culture industry; high culture; mass culture; popular culture.**

culture industry (n.)   The commercial forces behind the production of **mass culture** or entertainment. See also **culture; cultural studies; high culture; mass culture; popular culture.**

denotation (n.)   The particular object or class of objects to which a word refers. Contrast with **connotation**.

discourse (n.)   The words, concepts, and presuppositions that constitute the knowledge and understanding of a particular community, often academic or professional.

dominant culture (n.)   The group within a **multicultural** society whose traditions, values, and beliefs are held to be normative, as the European tradition·is the dominant culture in the United States.

Eurocentric (adj.)   Related to a worldview founded on the traditions and history of European culture, usually at the expense of non-European cultures.

function (n.)   The utility of an object, as opposed to its cultural meaning. Spandex or lycra shorts, for example, have a functional value for cyclists because they're lightweight and aerodynamic. On the other hand, such shorts have become a general fashion item for both men and women because of their cultural meaning, not their function. Many noncyclists wear spandex to project an image of hard-bodied fitness, sexiness, or just plain trendiness, for instance.

gender (n.)   One's sexual identity and the roles that follow from it, as determined by the norms of one's culture rather than by biology or genetics. The assumption that women should be foremost in the nurturing of children is a gender norm; the fact that only women can give birth is a biological phenomenon.

hacker (n.)   A person who "breaks into" another person's or an institution's computer system without permission, either for entertainment or criminal purposes.

high culture (n.)   The products of the elite arts, including classical music, literature, drama, opera, painting, and sculpture. See also **cultural studies; culture; culture industry; mass culture; popular culture.**

icon (n.), **iconic** (adj.)   In **semiotics,** a **sign** that visibly resembles its referent, as a photograph looks like the thing it represents. More broadly, an icon is someone (often a celebrity) who enjoys a commanding or representative place in popular culture. Michael Jackson and Madonna are music video icons. Contrast with **symbol.**

ideology (n.)   The beliefs, interests, and values that determine one's interpretations or judgments and that are often associated with one's social class. For example, in the ideology of modern business, a business is designed to produce profits, not social benefits.

image (n.)   Literally, a pictorial representation; more generally, the identity that one projects to others through such things as clothing, grooming, speech, and behavior.

Internet, the (n.)   An electronic network, originally developed for military purposes, that links millions of computers around the world. Also called *the Net, World Wide Web,* or *Web.*

mass culture (n.)   A subset of **popular culture** that includes the popular entertainments that are commercially produced for widespread consumption. See also **cultural studies; culture; culture industry; high culture.**

mass media (n. pl.)   The means of communication, often controlled by the **culture industry,** that include newspapers, popular magazines, radio, television, film, and the Internet.

multiculturalism (n.), **multicultural** (adj.)   In American education, the movement to incorporate the traditions, history, and beliefs of the United States' non-European cultures into a traditionally *monocultural* (or single-culture) curriculum dominated by European thought and history.

mythology (n.)   The overall framework of values and beliefs incorporated in a given cultural system or worldview. Any given belief within such a structure — like the belief that "a woman's place is in the home" — is called a *myth.*

politics (n.)   Essentially, the practice of promoting one's interests in a competitive social environment. Not restricted to electioneering; there may be office politics, classroom politics, academic politics, and sexual politics.

popular culture (n.)   That segment of a **culture** that incorporates the activities of everyday life, including the consumption of consumer goods and the production and enjoyment of mass-produced entertainments. See also **cultural studies; culture industry; high culture; mass culture.**

postmodernism (n.), **postmodern** (adj.)   The worldview behind contemporary literature, art, music, architecture, and philosophy that rejects traditional attempts to make meaning out of human history and experience. For the *postmodern* artist, art does not attempt to create new explanatory myths or **symbols** but rather recycles or repeats existing images, as does the art of Andy Warhol.

semiotics (n.)   In short, the study of **signs.** Synonymous with *semiology,* semiotics is concerned with both the theory and practice of interpreting linguistic, cultural, and behavioral sign systems. One who practices *semiotic analysis* is called a *semiotician* or *semiologist.*

sign (n.)   Anything that bears a meaning. Words, objects, images, and forms of behavior are all signs whose meanings are determined by the particular **codes,** or **systems,** in which they appear.

symbol (n.), **symbolic** (adj.)   A **sign,** according to semiotician C. S. Peirce, whose significance is arbitrary. The meaning of the word *bear,* for example, is arbitrarily determined by those who use it. Contrast with **icon.**

system (n.)   The **code,** or network, within which a **sign** functions and so achieves its meaning through its associational and differential relations with other signs. The English language is a sign system, as is a fashion code.

text (n.)   A complex of **signs,** which may be linguistic, imagistic, behavioral, or musical, that can be read or interpreted.

virtual reality (n.)   A simulated world that is created using computer technology.

CITING SOURCES

When you write an essay and use another author's work — whether you use the author's exact words or his or her ideas — you need to cite that source for your readers. In most humanities courses, writers use the system of documentation developed by the Modern Language Association (MLA). This system indicates a source in two ways: (1) notations that briefly identify the sources in the body of your essay and (2) notations that give fuller bibliographic information about the sources at the end of your essay. The notations for some commonly used types of sources are illustrated below. For documenting other sources, consult a writing handbook or Joseph Gibaldi's *MLA Handbook for Writers of Research Papers,* Fifth edition (New York: Modern Language Association of America, 1999).

In-Text Citations

In the body of your essay, you should signal to your reader that you've used a source and indicate, in parentheses, where your reader can find the source in your list of works cited. You don't need to repeat the author's name in both your writing and in the parenthetical note.

SOURCE WITH ONE AUTHOR

Patrick Goldstein asserts that "Talk radio has pumped up the volume of our public discourse and created a whole new political language — perhaps the prevailing political language" (16).

SOURCE WITH TWO OR THREE AUTHORS

Researchers have found it difficult to study biker subcultures because, as one team describes the problem, "it was too dangerous to take issue with outlaws on their own turf" (Hooper and Moore 368).

INDIRECT SOURCE

In discussing the baby mania trend, *Time* claimed that "Career women are opting for pregnancy and they are doing it in style" (qtd. in Faludi 106).

List of Works Cited

At the end of your essay, include a list of all the sources you have cited in parenthetical notations. This list, alphabetized by author, should provide full publishing information for each source; you should indicate the date you accessed any online sources.

    The first line of each entry should begin flush left. Subsequent lines should be indented half an inch (or five spaces) from the left margin. Double space the entire list, both between and within entries.

Non-Electronic Sources

BOOK BY ONE AUTHOR

Faludi, Susan. *Backlash: The Undeclared War against American Women.* New York: Crown, 1991.

BOOK BY TWO OR MORE AUTHORS

Collins, Ronald K. L., and David M. Skover. *The Death of Discourse.* New York: Westview Press, 1996.

    (Note that only the first author's name is reversed.)

WORK IN AN ANTHOLOGY

Prager, Emily. "Our Barbies, Ourselves." *Signs of Life in the U.S.A.: Readings on Popular Culture for Writers.* 4th ed. Ed. Sonia Maasik and Jack Solomon. Boston: Bedford/St. Martin's, 2003.

ARTICLE IN A WEEKLY MAGAZINE

Goldstein, Patrick. "Yakety-Yak, Please Talk Back." *Los Angeles Times Magazine* 16 July 1995: 16+.

    (A plus sign is used to indicate that the article is not printed on consecutive pages; otherwise, a page range should be given: 16–25, for example.)

ARTICLE IN A MONTHLY MAGAZINE

Smith, Gina. "Worlds without End." *Buzz* Sept. 1995: 46–48.

ARTICLE IN A JOURNAL

Hooper, Columbus B., and Johnny Moore. "Women in Outlaw Motorcycle Gangs." *Journal of Contemporary Ethnography* 18 (1990): 363–87.

FILM OR VIDEOTAPE

The English Patient. Dir. Anthony Minghella. Perf. Willem Dafoe, Juliette Binoche, Ralph Fiennes, and Kristin Scott Thomas. Miramax, 1996.

TELEVISION PROGRAM

Ally McBeal. Perf. Calista Flockhart. KBFX, Bakersfield. 2 Aug. 1999.

PERSONAL INTERVIEW

Chese, Charlie. Personal interview. 28 Sept. 2003.

Electronic Sources

E-MAIL

Katt, Susie. "Interpreting the Mall." E-mail to the author. 29 Sept. 2003.

ARTICLE IN AN ONLINE REFERENCE BOOK

"Gender." *Britannica Online.* 31 July 2002. Encyclopaedia Britannica. 30 May 2003 <http://www.britannica.com/eb/article?eu=37051>.

(Note that the first date indicates when the information was posted; the second indicates date of access.)

ARTICLE IN AN ONLINE JOURNAL

Schaffer, Scott. "Disney and the Imagineering of History." *Postmodern Culture* 6.3 (1996): 62 pars. 12 Aug. 2003 <http://jefferson.village.virginia.edu/pmc/backissues/contents.596.html>.

ARTICLE IN AN ONLINE MAGAZINE

Rosenberg, Scott. "Don't Link or I'll Sue!" *Salon* 12 Aug. 1999. 13 Aug. 2003 <http://www.salon.com/tech/col/rose/1999/08/12/deep_links/index.html>.

ONLINE BOOK

James, Henry. *The Bostonians*. London and New York, 1886. *The Henry James Scholar's Guide to Web Sites*. Ed. Richard Hathaway. Aug. 1999. SUNY New Paltz. 13 Aug. 2003 <http://www.newpaltz.edu/~hathaway/bostonians1.html>.

ONLINE POEM

Frost, Robert. "The Road Not Taken." *Mountain Interval*. New York, 1915. *Project Bartleby Archive*. Ed. Steven van Leeuwen. Mar. 1995. 13 Aug. 2003 <http://www.bartleby.com/119/1.html>.

PROFESSIONAL WEB SITE

National Council of Teachers of English. Urbana, IL. Jan. 2002. 1 May 2003 <http://www.ncte.org>.

PERSONAL HOME PAGE

Rochelle, James. Home page. May 2003. 13 Aug. 2003 <http://www.homestead.com/jamestheviking>.

POSTING TO A DISCUSSION LIST

Diaz, Joanne. "Poetic Expressions." Online posting. 29 Apr. 2003. Conference on College Composition and Communication. 4 Jul. 2003 <http://www.ncte.org/cccc/03>.

ONLINE SCHOLARLY PROJECT

Corpus Linguistics. Ed. Michael Barlow. Apr. 1998. Rice U. 13 Aug. 2003 <http//www.ruf.rice.edu/~barlow/corpus.html>.

WORK FROM AN ONLINE SUBSCRIPTION SERVICE

"Race." *Compton's Encyclopedia Online*. Vers. 3.5. 1999. America Online. 30 Jul. 2003. Keyword: Compton's.

Acknowledgments (continued from page iv)

Jenny Lyn Bader, "Larger Than Life" by Jenny Lyn Bader. Copyright © 1994 by Jenny Lyn Bader, from *Next: Young American Writers of the New Generation*, edited by Eric Liu. Used by permission of the author and W. W. Norton & Company, Inc.

Benjamin R. Barber, excerpt from *Jihad vs. McWorld* by Benjamin R. Barber, copyright © 1995 by Benjamin R. Barber. Used by permission of Times Books, a division of Random House, Inc.

Diane Barthel, from "A Gentleman and a Consumer," which appears in *Putting on Appearances: Gender and Advertising*, by Diane Barthel, pages 169–183. Reprinted by permission of Temple University Press. Copyright © 1988 by Temple University. All rights reserved.

Nell Bernstein, "Goin' Gangsta, Choosin' Cholita," from *The Utne Reader*, March–April 1995. Reprinted by permission of the author.

Deborah Blum, "The Gender Blur: Where Does Biology End and Society Take Over?" Reprinted by permission of International Creative Management, Inc. Copyright © 1998 by Deborah Blum.

Eric Boehlert, "New York's Most Disliked Building." This article first appeared in *Salon.com*, at < http://www.Salon.com >. An online version remains in the *Salon* archives. Reprinted with permission.

Susan Bordo, "*Braveheart, Babe*, and the Contemporary Body," from *Twilight Zones: The Hidden Life of Cultural Images from Plato to O.J.* Copyright © 1997. Reprinted by permission of the University of California Press.

Rachel Bowlby, "The Haunted Superstore," from *Carried Away: The Invention of Modern Shopping* by Rachel Bowlby. Copyright © 2000 by Columbia University Press. Reprinted with the permission of the publisher.

Todd Boyd, excerpt from *Am I Black Enough for You? Popular Culture from the 'Hood and Beyond* (edited version). Copyright © 1997 by Todd Boyd. Reprinted by permission of the Indiana University Press.

Mark Caldwell, "The Assault on Martha Stewart." From: *A Short History of Rudeness* by Mark Caldwell. Copyright © 1999 by Mark Caldwell. Reprinted by permission of St. Martin's Press, LLC.

John E. Calfee, "How Advertising Informs to Our Benefit," from *Consumers' Research Magazine*, April 1998 as adapted from *Fear of Persuasion: A New Perspective on Advertising and Regulation* (American Enterprise Institute, 1997). Copyright © 1997 by John E. Calfee. Reprinted by permission of the author.

Marnie Carroll, "American Television in Europe," from *Bad Subjects*, October 2001. Reprinted by permission of the author.

Damien Cave, "The Spam Spoils of War." This article first appeared in *Salon.com*, at < http://www.Salon.com >. An online version remains in the *Salon* archives. Reprinted with permission.

N'Gai Croal and Jane Hughes, "Lara Croft, the Bit Girl," from *Newsweek*, November 10, 1997. Copyright © 1997 Newsweek, Inc. All rights reserved. Reprinted by permission.

Gary Cross, "Barbie, G.I. Joe, and Play in the 1960s." Reprinted by permission of the publisher from "The Boomer's Box of Toys: Barbie, G.I. Joe, and Play in the 1960s" in *Kid's Stuff: Toys and the Changing World of American Childhood* by Gary Cross, pp. 171–177, Cambridge, MA: Harvard University Press, Copyright © 1997 by the President and Fellows of Harvard College.

Fred Davis, "Blue Jeans." Originally titled "Of Maids' Uniforms and Blue Jeans: The Drama of Status Ambivalence in Clothing and Fashion." First appeared in *Qualitative Sociology* 12, no. 4 (Winter 1989). Copyright © 1989. Reprinted by permission of Kluwer Academic/Human Sciences Press.

Todd J. Davis, "*The West Wing* in Popular Culture: Will Josiah Bartlet Run in 2004?", from *Philly1.com*. Reprinted by permission of the author.

Frank Deford, "Athletics 101: A Change in Eligibility Rules Is Long Overdue," as originally broadcast on National Public Radio. Reprinted by permission of the author.

John de Graaf, David Wann, and Thomas H. Naylor, "The Addictive Virus." Reprinted with permission of the publisher. From *Affluenza*, copyright © 2001 by John de Graaf, David Wann, and

Thomas H. Naylor. Berrett-Koehler Publishers, Inc., San Francisco, CA. All rights reserved. < www.bkconnection.com >

Benjamin DeMott, "Put on a Happy Face." Appeared in the September 1995 issue of *Harper's* magazine. Copyright © 1995 by *Harper's* magazine. All rights reserved. Reproduced by special permission.

Holly Devor, "Gender Role Behaviors and Attitudes," from *Gender Blending* by Holly Devor. Copyright © 1989 by Holly Devor. Reprinted by permission of Indiana University Press

Susan Douglas, "Signs of Intelligent Life on TV." Appeared in the May–June 1995 issue of *Ms.* Copyright © 1995 by *Ms.* magazine. Reprinted by permission of *Ms.* Magazine

Michael Eric Dyson, "Be Like Mike? Michael Jordan and the Pedagogy of Desire," from *Cultural Studies*, vol. 6, 1993. Reprinted by permission of Taylor & Francis Ltd. < http://www.tandf .co.uk/journals > and Michael Eric Dyson.

D. Stanley Eitzen, "The Contradictions of Big-Time College Sport," from *Fair and Foul: Beyond the Myths and Paradoxes of Sport*. Copyright © 1999 by Rowman & Littlefield Publishers, Inc. Reprinted by permission of Rowman & Littlefield Publishers, Inc.

Gary Engle, "What Makes Superman So Darned American?" from *Superman at Fifty: The Persistence of a Legend*, Gary Engle and Dennis Dooley, eds. Copyright © 1987 by Octavia Press. Reprinted by permission of Octavia Press.

Amanda Fazzone, "Boob Tube," from *The New Republic*, July 30, 2001. Reprinted by permission of *The New Republic*, copyright © 2001 by The New Republic, Inc.

Thomas Friedman, approximately 5⅓ pages from "Revolution Is U.S." from *The Lexus and the Olive Tree: Understanding Globalization* by Thomas Friedman. Copyright © 1999, 2000 by Thomas L. Friedman. Reprinted by permission of Farrar, Straus and Giroux, LLC.

Tad Friend, "You Can't Say That." Reprinted by permission of International Creative Management, Inc. Copyright © 2001 by Tad Friend. First appeared in *The New Yorker*.

James William Gibson, "Post Vietnam Blues," from *Warrior Dreams: Paramilitary Culture in a Post-Vietnam America* by James William Gibson. Copyright © 1994 by James William Gibson. Reprinted by permission of Hill and Wang, a division of Farrar, Straus and Giroux, LLC.

Malcolm Gladwell, "The Science of Shopping," from *The New Yorker*, November 4, 1996. Reprinted with permission.

David Goewey, "'Careful, You May Run Out of Planet': SUVs and the Exploitation of American Myth." Copyright 1999. Used with permission.

Patrick Goldstein, "The Time to Get Serious Has Come," from the *Los Angeles Times*, September 18, 2001. Reprinted by permission of *The Los Angeles Times*.

Jessica Hagedorn, "Asian Women in Film: No Joy, No Luck." Appeared in the January–February 1994 issue of *Ms.* magazine. Copyright © 1994 by Jessica Hagedorn. Reprinted by permission of the author and her agents, Harold Schmidt Literary Agency.

LynNell Hancock, "The Haves and the Have-Nots," from *Newsweek*, February 17, 1995. Copyright © 1995 Newsweek, Inc. All rights reserved. Reprinted by permission.

Robert Hilburn, "The Not-So-Big Hit Single," from the *Los Angeles Times*, February 17, 2001. Reprinted by permission of *The Los Angeles Times*.

Thomas Hine, "What's in a Package" From *The Total Package* by Thomas Hine. Copyright © 1995 by Thomas Hine. By permission of Little, Brown and Company (Inc.).

bell hooks, Chapter 8 from *Bone Black* by bell hooks, © 1996 by Gloria Watkins. Reprinted by permission of Henry Holt and Company, LLC.

Langston Hughes, "I, Too," from *The Collected Poems of Langston Hughes* by Langston Hughes, copyright © 1994 by The Estate of Langston Hughes. Used by permission of Alfred A. Knopf, a division of Random House, Inc.

Henry Jenkins, "'Never Trust a Snake': WWF Wrestling as Masculine Melodrama," from *Out of Bounds*, edited by Aaron Baker and Todd Boyd. Reprinted by permission of Indiana University Press.

Kevin Jennings, "American Dreams." Copyright © 1994 *Growing Up Gay / Growing Up Lesbian: A Literary Anthology* edited by Bennett L. Singer. Reprinted by permission of The New Press. (800) 233-4830

Gary Johnson, "The Western," from < www.imagesjournal.com >, October 23, 2001. Reprinted by permission of the author.

David Kamp, "America's Spaz-Time," from *GQ*. Reprinted by permission of the author.

Karen Karbo, "The Dining Room." Copyright © 1995 by Karen Karbo, from *Home: American Writers Remember Rooms of Their Own*, edited by Sharon Sloan Fiffer and Steve Fiffer, copyright © 1995 by Sharon Sloan Fiffer and Steve Fiffer. Used by permission of Pantheon Books, a division of Random House, Inc.

Randall Kennedy, "Blind Spot," from *The Atlantic Monthly*, April 2002. Reprinted by permission of the author.

Joan Kron, "The Semiotics of Home Décor," from *Home Psych: The Social Psychology of Home and Decoration*. Copyright © 1983 by Joan Kron. Reprinted by arrangement with Joan Kron and The Barbara Hogensen Agency. All rights reserved.

Kalle Lasn, "Hype," from *Culture Jam: The Uncooling of America* by Kalle Lasn [pp. 18–21]. Copyright © 1997 by Kalle Lasn. Reprinted by permission of HarperCollins Publishers, Inc.

Tim Layden, "A Patriot's Tale," *Sports Illustrated*, September 24, 2001. Copyright © 2001, Time, Inc. All rights reserved.

Lucy R. Lippard, "Alternating Currents." Copyright © 1997 *The Lure of the Local: Senses of Place in a Multicentered Society* by Lucy L. Lippard. Reprinted by permission of The New Press. (800) 233-4830

Sandra Tsing Loh, "The Return of Doris Day." Appeared in the September 1995 issue of *Buzz* magazine. Copyright © 1995 by Buzz, Inc. All rights reserved. Reprinted by permission.

Jack Lopez, "Of Cholos and Surfers," from *California Dreaming: Myths of the Golden Land*. Reprinted by permission of the author.

Roland Marchand, "The Parable of the Democracy of Goods," from *Advertising the American Dream: Making Way for Modernity, 1920–1940* by Roland Marchand. Copyright © 1985 by The Regents of the University of California. Reprinted by permission of The Regents of the University of California.

Andre Mayer, "The New Sexual Stone Age," from *Shift.com*. Reprinted courtesy of *Shift* magazine < www.shift.com >, copyright © 2001.

Anna McCarthy, "Brand Identity at NikeTown," from *Ambient Television: Visual Culture and Public Space*. Copyright © 2001 by Duke University Press. All rights reserved. Reprinted with permission.

Andy Medhurst, "Batman, Deviance, and Camp," from *Many Lives of the Batman*, edited by Roberta E. Pearson and William Uricchio. Reprinted by permission of Andy Medhurst.

Michael Messner, "Power at Play," from *Power at Play* by Michael Messner. Copyright © 1992 by Michael A. Messner. Reprinted by permission of Beacon Press, Boston.

Laura Miller, "Women and Children First: Gender and the Setting of the Electronic Frontier," from *Resisting the Virtual Life: The Culture and Politics of Information*, edited by James Brook and Ian A. Babel. Reprinted by permission of City Lights Books. Copyright © 1995 by Laura Miller.

Mariah Burton Nelson, "I Won. I'm Sorry," from *Self* magazine, March 1998. Copyright © 1998 by Mariah Burton Nelson. Reprinted by permission of the author.

Anne Norton, "The Signs of Shopping," from *Republic of Signs*, by Anne Norton, pp. 68–75. Copyright © 1993 by The University of Chicago Press. Reprinted with the permission of The University of Chicago Press.

Michael Omi, "In Living Color: Race and American Culture," from *Culture Politics in Contemporary America*, edited by Ian Angus and Sut Jhally, Routledge, New York. Copyright © 1989 by the author. Reprinted by permission of the author.

Michael Parenti, "Class and Virtue," from *Make-Believe Media*, First Edition, by Michael Parenti. Copyright © 1992. Reprinted with permission of Wadsworth, an imprint of the Wadsworth Group, a division of Thomson Learning. Fax: 800-730-2215.

Emily Prager, "Our Barbies, Ourselves." Originally published in *Interview* magazine, Brant Publications, Inc., December 1991. Reprinted by permission of Interview, Inc.

Robert B. Ray, "The Thematic Paradigm," from *A Certain Tendency of the Hollywood Cinema*,

1997, v 36, n 2. Copyright © 1997 by Paul C. Taylor. Reprinted by permission of Paul C. Taylor.

James B. Twitchell, "What We Are to Advertisers," from *Lead Us Into Temptation: The Triumph of American Materialism*, by James B. Twitchell. Copyright © 1999 Columbia University Press. Reprinted with the permission of the publisher.

Camilo José Vergara, "The Ghetto Cityscape," from *The New American Ghetto*, copyright © 1995 by Camilo Vergara. Reprinted by permission of Rutgers University Press.

Susan Willis, "Public Use / Private State," from *Inside the Mouse: Work and Play at Disney World* by Susan Willis. Copyright © 1993 by Duke University Press. All rights reserved. Reprinted with permission.

Naomi Wolf, "The Beauty Myth," extracted from *The Beauty Myth* by Naomi Wolf. Copyright © 1990 by Naomi Wolf. Reprinted by permission of Random House Canada, a division of Random House of Canada Limited.

ARTWORK

Chapter 1

Photo of Starbucks, Baltimore, appears by permission of Lauren Goodsmith/ The Image Works.

Photo of Seiji Ozawa with Boston Symphony Orchestra appears by permission of Miro Vintoniv, Stock Boston.

Barnum & Bailey Circus Poster appears by permission of the Granger Collection.

VW Beetle photograph courtesy of Jack Solomon and Sonia Maasik.

"Destruction of 9/11" *Time* magazine cover appears by permission of TimePix.

Rescue dog at Ground Zero photograph appears by permission of Alan Diaz–AP/World Wide Photos.

Rubble at Ground Zero photograph appears by permission of Monika Graff/The Image Works.

Image of World Financial Center and rubble appears by permission of Roberto Borea–AP/World Wide Photos.

Photo of high school football players with American flag appears by permission of Nick Falzarano/Nicholas Studios.

"The Economy Doctor" appears by permission of the New Yorker Collection/Roz Chast.

"Just what do you do all day?" appears by permission of Nina Leen–*Life*.

Mitsubishi SUV photo courtesy of Martyn Goddard/Getty Images.

"I'm sick of advertisers cashing in on consumer patriotism." Appears by permission of Rob Rogers/United Features Sydicate.

Image of Israel's Kosher McDonald's appears by permission of A. Ramey/Woodfin Camp and Associates.

Photo of Muslim women using computers appears by permission of Chris Brown/Stock Boston.

Lahore Street, Pakistan, photo appears by permission of Sean Sprague/Stock Boston.

Chapter 2

Energizer Bunny: Used by permission of Eveready Battery Co., Inc. Eveready® is a registered trademark of Eveready Battery Co.

Image of Home Shopping Network from TV screen appears by permission of Jeff Greenberg/ Photo Edit.

Portfolio of Advertisements:

CBS Marketwatch ad courtesy of CBS Marketwatch.com.

Eclipse gum advertisement courtesy of Wm. Wrigley Jr. Company.

Phoenix Wealth Management ad used with permission from The Phoenix Companies, Inc.

Association of American Publishing used with permission of the Association of American Publishers, Inc.

Virgin Atlantic ad used with permission of Virgin Atlantic.

American Express ad used with permission of American Express.

Chapter 3

Calvin and Hobbes cartoon appears by permission of Universal Press Syndicate.

Survivor photograph appears by permission of Monty Brighton/CBS Photo Archive.

Simpsons appears by permission of TM & 20th Century Fox Film Corporation.

Madonna photograph appears by permission of Fitzroy Barret/Retna.

Oprah Winfrey and George Bush photograph appears by permission of Tannen Maury/The Image Works.

Salt 'n' Pepa photograph appears by permission of David Corio/Retna.

Photo of Rock concert "Up In Smoke" appears by permission of Michael Schreiber/Retna.

Chapter 4

Hollywood Sign photo appears by permission of Landau/Corbis.

Photo of Ian McKellan in *Lord of the Rings* appears by permission of Photofest.

Image from Star Wars appears by permission of Photofest.

Stagecoach and riders photo appears by permission of Culver Pictures.

Photo of Roy Rogers and Dale Evans appears by permission of Photofest.

Clint Eastwood in *The Unforgiven* appears by permission of Photofest.

Clint Eastwood in *Fistful of Dollars* appears by permission of Photofest.

Kevin Costner in *Dances with Wolves* appears by permission of Photofest.

Babe appears by permission of Photofest.

American Me appears by permission of Photofest.

Michelle Yeoh in *Tomorrow Never Dies* appears by permission of Photofest.

Photo of Anna May Wong appears by permission of Photofest.

Doris Day photograph appears by permission of Archive Photos/Getty Images.

Image from *Pulp Fiction* appears by permission of Photofest.

Image from *Gentleman's Agreement* appears by permission of Photofest.

Chapter 5

Photo of Eaton Centre Mall, Toronto appears by permission of Mike Mazzaschi/Stock Boston.

Photo of couple working in split-level house appears by permission of Stephen Simpson/Getty Images.

Two San Francisco "NikeTown" photographs appear by permission of Anna McCarthy/Duke University Press.

Disney World photograph appears by permission of Dagmar Fabricius/Stock Boston.

Times Square photograph appears by permission of Joel Gordon.

Father and teens at dinner photograph appears by permission of Richard Hutchings/Photo Researchers.

Santa Clara Pueblo J. K. Hillers, 1879, appears by permission of the Smithsonian Institution, National Anthropological Archives.

Santa Clara Pueblo Fayette W. Van Zile, 1930, appears by permission of the Smithsonian Institution, National Anthropological Archives.

Santa Clara Pueblo Vroman, 1899 (Hillers), appears by permission of the Smithsonian Institution, National Anthropological Archives.

Santa Clara Pueblo Vroman, 1899, appears by permission of the Smithsonian Institution, National Anthropological Archives.

Drawings of layouts of Santa Clara appear by permission of Rina Swentzell.

Photo of BIA School at Santa Clara appears by permission of Rina Swentzell.

Camilo José Vergara, "Sterling Street, Newark, 1980." Copyright © 1995 by Camilo José Vergara. By permission of the author.

Camilo José Vergara, "Sterling Street replaced by a parking lot, 1994." Copyright © 1995 by Camilo José Vergara. By permission of the author.

World Trade Center Towers photograph appears by permission of Jack Pottle/Design Conceptions.

Chapter 6

Hennessey advertisement, "appropriately complex," appears by permission of Schieffelin & Somerset, Company.

Photo of female soldier with gun appears by permission of N. R. Rowan/Stock Boston.

"Senior Action in a Gay Environment" photograph appears by permission of Joel Gordon.

Stork on shopping cart with babies photograph appears by permission of Roger Ressmeyer/ Corbis.

Woman in a beauty parlor photo appears by permission of Joel Gordon.

Take Back the Night photograph appears by permission of Joel Gordon.

Chapter 7

Photo of Native American family with dog appears by permission of Joel Gordon.

Photo of Alicia Keys at piano appears by permission of Robert Spencer/Retna.

Stevie Ray Vaughan photo appears by permission of Andrea Laubach/Retna.

Four teenagers photograph appears by permission of Jim Whitmer/Stock Boston.

Photo of African American girl with black doll appears by permission of Jean-Claude LeJeune/ Stock Boston.

Extended Hispanic family photograph appears by permission of Joel Gordon.

African American child at computer photograph appears by permission of Joel Gordon.

Chapter 8

Photo of Carl Lewis winning the gold medal at the Barcelona Olympics appears by permission of Bill Frakes/Sports Illustrated.

Photo of woman in wheelchair at Para-Olympics, Atlanta, appears by permission of Robert Ginn/Photo Edit.

Photo of soccer player Brandi Chastain appears by permission of Robert Beck/Sports Illustrated.

"I'm Glad We Won . . . " cartoon appears by permission of the New Yorker Collection, 1997.

High school soccer team photograph appears by permission of Bob Daemmrich/Stock Boston.

Serena Williams photograph appears by permission of Alastair Grant/AP/World Wide Photos.

Two women playing golf (1903) appears by permission of Bettmann/Corbis.

Images of wrestlers at professional school appear by permission of Co Rentmeester.

Chapter 9

Photograph of Elvis Presley performing appears by permission of AP/World Wide Photos.

Lara Croft image appears by permission of Eidos Interactive.

Barbie "Got Milk?" photograph by Greg Mancuso. Appears by permission of Stock Boston.

Mr. Clean advertisement. Copyright © The Procter & Gamble Company. Used by permission.

Firefighters and police at World Trade Center photograph appears by permission of Fabian Falcon/Stock Boston.

Index of Authors and Titles

FOURTH EDITION

SIGNS OF LIFE

IN THE USA

Readings on Popular Culture for Writers

Sonia Maasik   Jack Solomon

We realize that few instructors sit down and read an entire text cover-to-cover before designing their syllabi. You simply don't have the time, and doing so would likely interfere with your ability to adjust your course to your students' interests and needs. And we also realize that most instructors roam around in the texts they use, jumping from chapter to chapter and selecting some readings while skipping others. Accordingly, we've designed this instructor's manual to make it easier for you to plan your course. We suggest possible ways to combine chapters to form a coherent unit and ways to abbreviate chapters should you not have time to cover all the readings in each. We suggest thematic links that run throughout *Signs of Life*, links that may not always be apparent in the selections' titles. And we suggest ways to sequence your discussion of the readings so your students can build on their experience addressing other topics.

But the manual doesn't just organize the material in the text; we've also designed it to suggest how you can use *Signs of Life* in the classroom. Perhaps most important, we explain why we've chosen to make a theoretical approach explicit in a reader for composition students and why we've adopted semiotics as that approach. We also anticipate students' responses to the issues raised in *Signs of Life*. This text is based on widespread classroom experience, as we've received ample feedback from instructors across the nation who've used the previous three editions of *Signs of Life*. In addition, we've assigned many of the readings ourselves, and we've both adopted a semiotic approach in teaching students at different levels. Thus, by identifying which essays are likely to anger or excite students, which selections are relatively difficult or easy to read, which topics are perfect for personal reflection, and so forth, we can help you to devise a class plan that will work for *your* students.

In addition, we suggest activities beyond essay writing that will enhance students' understanding of the issues the text raises. These activities range from journal writing and prewriting exercises to classroom activities, such as debates and small group work, that encourage lively student involvement. We firmly believe that one of the best things a teacher can do is organize a class such that the students take charge of their own learning. Particularly in a writing class (but also in discipline-specific courses), students need to be active participants in their education. We've designed *Signs of Life* to allow students to do that. It is based on the premise that students come to college with a high level of expertise in popular culture that you can rely on to generate lively class discussion, inspire a commitment to learning, and create a community of writers within your class.

So what doesn't the manual do? It doesn't "give the answers" to the comprehension and writing/activity questions that follow each selection. We realize that some manuals take the instructor through answers step by step, but we haven't done that, for both practical and philosophical reasons. As is appropriate for a composition textbook, there are no readings here that you would have difficulty understanding, so we don't need to outline answers for the comprehension questions, although we do address cases where authors raise unusually thorny or problematic points. And even with comprehension questions, you may feel it appropriate for your students to emphasize one angle or another. The writing/activity questions don't have "right" or "wrong" responses, and they don't invite single correct answers. That's not to say that the questions are hard or that some responses might not be stronger than others. And we do provide suggestions for how you can use these questions with your students. It's just that we believe that critical thinking is nurtured if students explore an issue, sort out the evidence from several alternative sources that would best support a thesis, and consider what contrary positions might be held on an issue. In other words, the questions are intended to encourage students to *think* about an issue — to think thoroughly, specifically, and carefully. With that preparation, we believe, students are well on their way to becoming strong academic writers.

A word on the manual's organization is in order. We first provide an overview to using *Signs of Life* in your class, suggesting how to create thematic units, abbreviate chapters, or combine chapters, and giving hints on how to encourage student involvement. We also explain why we've used a semiotic approach and give you a little background history of semiotics. Next are two essays from instructors who have used *Signs of Life*, offering their advice to teachers new to the book. The bulk of the manual takes you through the readings, suggesting ways to use them in class and anticipating likely student reactions, creating links between selections and chapters, and providing hints on how you can have a lively discussion and assign successful writing topics based on the selections.

CONTENTS

USING POPULAR CULTURE AND SEMIOTICS IN THE COMPOSITION COURSE

Why Popular Culture?

We decided to focus this text on popular culture because we are convinced that students think and write at their best when they are in command of their subject matter. This is crucial when students are learning university-level writing strategies, for the newness of a subject can make students lack confidence as writers or lead them to adopt ineffective writing habits. Sometimes, for instance, students may oversummarize an issue because they are just learning about it and, essentially, are explaining it to themselves. *Signs of Life* is designed to take advantage of students' literacy in popular culture to generate sharp analysis and insightful interpretations. This is not to say that we assume all students are voracious consumers of popular culture in the same way. On the contrary: we assume that our readers will come to the book from a variety of backgrounds and with a variety of interests and experiences. The book, and particularly the apparatus, should allow students to share that variety through class and group activities.

In keeping with the increasing academic interest in cultural studies, we also assume an inclusive definition of popular culture. We address topics like advertising that traditionally have been considered part of popular culture, but we also include issues such as race that form part of America's social and cultural fabric. This notion of popular culture differs from the one that reigned when we began teaching twenty-five years ago. We recall a textbook that, as its nod to "popular culture," asked students to compare and contrast a Volkswagen and a Porsche, with no attention to the cars' social or cultural significance. This text used popular culture as an occasion for teaching rhetorical modes; in contrast, *Signs of Life* addresses the way broader issues, such as gender and ethnicity, affect cultural values and ideologies. As a result, we hope that your students will find the materials in *Signs of Life* to be both personally engaging and intellectually stimulating — among the two most important ingredients for a successful writing class.

In our experience, students respond to the materials in *Signs of Life* with delight, a little surprise, and great enthusiasm. Indeed, instructors who used the first three editions report that their students complete reading assignments and come to class eager to discuss and debate the issues. You'll find that your students often will be the experts on a subject, knowing more about, say, the latest band than you do. For some instructors that may be a discomforting role reversal. But we encourage you to let your students enjoy the role of expert, for that may well be their first step on the road to enjoying the role of writer.

Why Semiotics?

By making our choice of a semiotic approach explicit, we've departed from some textbook conventions. Traditionally, textbook authors assume a neutral stance toward their material, playing the role of objective compiler. Students then read the text, their task being to argue about or analyze it. But we see problems in this formulation of the roles of both author and student. As a comparison of textbooks can easily show, no textbook author is a mere compiler: the choices of what to include or exclude can reveal the author's values, philosophies, and ideologies. This point is hardly new (witness the many recent critiques of the canon), but our semiotic approach is designed to put this point into practice.

Discussed less often is the role of the student. It has long struck us that textbooks invite students to analyze, but textbooks authors hardly ever say what that means. There's the old "break up into constituent parts" definition, but that often remains a mystery to students: we're not even sure what it means when applied to real issues that don't have distinct parts. Essentially, analysis remains a pure category, with theoretical assumptions and ideological positions unexplored and undefined. But we don't believe there's such a thing as pure analysis, even for students. Indeed, it's likely that, in their discipline-specific courses, students will be asked to use various approaches or theories in their essays. In a sociology class, for instance, students may be asked to perform a Marxist analysis of a social problem; in an economics class, they may be assigned to assess tax-cutting proposals from a supply-side perspective. Being self-conscious about one's point of view is essential to academic writing; we can think of no better place for students to learn that lesson than in a writing class, and the semiotic approach is especially suited to this purpose.

Our own experience has borne this out. As an analytic method, semiotics teaches students to formulate cogent, well-supported interpretations. It emphasizes the examination of assumptions and beliefs and the way language shapes our apprehension of the world. Most students feel comfortable with semiotics: since one of its precepts is that its job is to *reveal* interests and ideologies, not to *judge* them, students are less likely to feel that you are peddling a single point of view on a topic if you adopt a semiotic approach. Semiotics also makes it easier for a class to discuss sensitive or politically charged issues: the goal is not to judge individuals' beliefs but to locate those beliefs within a social and cultural context.

Using semiotics in a writing class makes sense, too, because of things our students have told us. Much to our delight, students sometimes report that they're covering semiotics in another class. That shouldn't be too surprising, for semiotics also has the benefit of being a cross-disciplinary approach. A wing of critical theory in literature departments, semiotics also has been influential in film and media studies, anthropology, law, pyschology, sociology, political science, and even management studies. Although we can't guarantee that all students will revisit semiotics in their academic future, we feel its cross-disciplinary nature makes it suitable for a writing class made up of students who are studying a variety of majors and disciplines. Finally, our students have told us that they enjoy semiotics. In fact, we've had students say that they appreciate learning something entirely *new* in our classes, and what's new extends beyond the topics covered to a way of looking at the world.

With all that said, we recognize that a semiotics approach may be new to some instructors. We've accordingly designed the book to allow you to be as "semiotic" with your class as you choose. We'll be delighted if you discuss semiotics with your students, try out semiotic readings in class, and assign semiotic essay topics. But if you prefer to use the approach with a lighter touch, that's fine, too. Indeed, colleagues have told us that they appreciate the fact that the text does not obligate them to spend a lot of time with semiotics or to involve the class in technical definitions (we've avoided the technical jargon that makes much semiotics research seem turgid). Your class may be content knowing that semiotics means the interpretation of popular culture — and that can be your focus.

Some Background in Semiotics

Students often become intrigued by semiotics, asking about its history and wondering how they can learn about it. We'll anticipate their most common questions here, but don't worry, you don't have to be an expert to answer their questions. Their first question may well be: "Semi what? How do you pronounce it?" Well, it's simple: /semiótiks/. The word might seem unfamiliar because it was coined a little more than a century ago by Charles Sanders Peirce, who derived it from the Greek word for sign, or meaning — *semeiotikos*. The fact that Peirce, who founded the modern study of semiotics in the last third of the nineteenth century, could adopt an ancient Greek term so readily testifies to the long heritage of reading signs. From Plato and Aristotle to the Stoics, ancient philosophers speculated on the nature of signs; indeed, the Stoic philosophers anticipated contemporary semiotic theory by arguing that the meaning of a sign lies in a concept, not in a thing or referent.

Despite its antiquity, semiotics may be unfamiliar because unlike linguistics, which is a regular part of the university curriculum, relatively few colleges have programs or departments in semiotics. Most semiotic study takes place within disciplines such as literary and film studies and anthropology; here, the emphasis tends to be on semiotic theory — which, like any theoretical study, can be technical and forbidding. But just as you don't need to master transformational generative linguistics to decode a sentence, you don't need to master theoretical semiotics to perform semiotic analyses. In fact, we do just that every day, especially in regard to popular culture — and that's why students are perfectly capable of using a semiotic approach.

Students really need only a few basic principles to conduct a semiotic analysis. The first is that the meaning of a sign — whether it is a linguistic symbol, an artifact, a belief, or a form of behavior — is to be found within the system to which it belongs, not in some absolute realm of nature or reality. In semiotic terms, the meaning of a linguistic sign, for example, lies in its place within a system of culturally constituted concepts, not in a "real" object to which it refers. Similarly, in popular culture, a BMW gets its significance from its place in the system of automotive status symbols, not from its reference to any sort of concrete referent. It can at once be *associated* with other status symbols (like Land Rovers) and *differentiated* from non-status cars like Hyundais. Through such differential and associational relations, the meaning of a popular sign is constructed. Your students may want to insist that BMWs are popular because they're built well, that they refer to some objective measure of quality, but that functional answer fails to account for the many well-built cars that do not carry the status value of a "beamer." Just ask them to compare a BMW to an Oldsmobile. The difference between the two cars as they appear within the system is where the meaning lies, in the images that they project, not in the materials with which they are constructed. If your students doubt this, ask them to consider why Oldsmobile tried so hard to change its products' image among youthful consumers in its rather futile "This Is Not Your Father's Oldsmobile" campaign.

In technical terms, the systematic interpretation of a popular sign represents an adaptation of Ferdinand de Saussure's semiological principle that the meaning of a linguistic sign lies in its differences with respect to all the other signs in a linguistic system. Because structural semiology is a formalistic method that tends to ignore history and politics, we have expanded upon Saussure to add both Peircean and Marxist semiotic insights. From Peirce we take the principle that signs are situated in history and that their meanings shift as our knowledge or experience shifts. From Marxism we take the principle that cultural signs bear ideological weight. Thus, when we speak of the system to which a sign belongs, we refer to historical and ideological (or mythological) systems as well as formal ones. One could say that, in a broad sense, the semiotic method we propose resembles that found in Roland Barthes's *Mythologies*.

The ability to interpret something by locating it within an overall system is fundamental to any analytic writing, not just the interpretation of popular signs. As a result, teaching your students to see things like cars within their cultural contexts is a step toward helping them to see how, say, understanding Shakespeare in their literature classes requires a knowledge of the cultural system within which his plays appeared. The difference is that, with Shakespeare, the cultural system is historically alien to our time and must be learned. In our own time, the systems are well known; they simply need to be made explicit.

This should help you when, after interpreting the status value of something like a BMW, a student says, "Well, isn't all that obvious?" And, yes, semiotic analyses of popular culture sometimes may appear obvious, precisely because the systems within which popular signs appear are familiar. But ask your students if the meanings, say, of their clothing styles are obvious to their parents or to someone from a different culture who may have no knowledge of the fashion system to which American youth styles belong.

The key to teaching your students how to conduct semiotic analyses of popular culture is to cue them in to the social environments within which signs appear. In one sense, this involves the teaching of present history, which is rather different from the teaching of "current events." Current events tend to be the larger-than-life events — usually crises — that make headlines. Present history includes everything that we think and do on a day-to-day basis. Current events are macrofocused and have relatively little bearing on the conduct of our lives (unless we are in the center of them). Present history is microfocused, and part of semiotics is simply bringing to light the small things with which we live.

Thus, one need not be an expert in semiotic theory to be adept at semiotic interpretation. You may have studied semiotics in graduate school or as part of your postgraduate training, and though you may have found stimulating the writings of such semiotic masters as Ferdinand de Saussure, Charles Sanders Peirce, Roland Barthes, Umberto Eco, and Jean Baudrillard, you may still wonder how your composition students will fare in the realm of semiotics. You needn't worry. Just as one can write a syntactically flawless essay without knowing linguistic theory, one can go right to the heart of a cultural sign without bothering with whether Saussure or Peirce should be your guide. The secret is in the system, and that can be your focus.

Responding to Questions about Semiotics

The corollary to our fundamental semiotic precept, that the meaning of a sign is to be found in the system to which it belongs, is that meaning is a social construct, not a simple reflection of truth or reality. The systems within which our values and beliefs function are mythologies, not absolute revelations. This semiotic principle — that meaning is mythological (or ideological) in origin — may well raise the most challenging of your students' questions, questions that are likely to be of two sorts: scientific and moral. Here are some ways to cope with such questions.

Let's start with the scientific objections. We live in an empirical culture that believes in the truth of observation: If you want to get to the heart of something, all you need to do is look at it. European culture was not always like this, of course. In the Middle Ages, for example, the truths of faith were held to be higher than the truths of observation — so Galileo was ordered to retract what he said about what his telescope showed him. But since our society now believes in empirical observation, some students may be shaken by the semiotic suggestion that when we speak of "reality," and of the names we give to our experience of reality, we are speaking of the system of concepts within which we operate, a system that determines what it is possible for us to know.

For the semiotician, our knowledge reflects not ultimate realities but systems of values that can be called *worldviews* or *cultural myths*. Myths are not legends and stories in the semiotic view; they are value and belief systems that frame the very way we perceive and define reality. From a semiotic perspective, reality is not something waiting passively out there for us to discover: it is the product of our own interpretive decisions. There is always a semiotic frame, a mythology, that mediates between our consciousness and the reality we interpret, and therefore construct, because of that frame. This is one of the most profound, and disturbing, principles of semiotic understanding — disturbing because it flies in the face of our cultural belief in the sanctity of "objective" knowledge. For that reason, it is probably the most difficult obstacle to overcome in learning to think semiotically.

But a little history, read in the light of semiotic understanding, shows that our very belief in scientific objectivity is itself a form of interpretation, not an absolute fact. Fundamentally, your students will probably take a more or less positivistic approach if they object to semiotic principles. Positivism, a nineteenth-century philosophical movement that held that "truth" is revealed through the clear gaze of objective observation, is the ideology of most laypersons today when it comes to scientific interpretation. However, positivism is no longer in force among contemporary scientists. Modern scientists themselves take the position that the "truths" of science are fundamentally interpretations that are themselves made possible by what Thomas Kuhn, a scientific historian and philosopher, called the "paradigms" of "normal science." (Kuhn's book, *The Structure of Scientific Revolutions*, revolutionized the philosophy of science.) At any given time, according to Kuhn, a scientist pursues the research programs that the state of understanding at the moment permits. In an era of relativity, for example, physicists work within a relativistic paradigm of understanding. If relativity theory is ever overthrown, a new paradigm of understanding will emerge to govern future research. The object of study is reality, but it is the paradigm that determines what the researcher will look for and how it will be interpreted.

The profound effect our cultural mythologies have on the way we view reality can be seen by looking at the different ways that different cultures regard language itself. In European American culture, for example, the myth holds that the purpose of language is to communicate one's intentions, emotions, or meanings. Language, in short, is regarded as a transparent medium whose primary purpose is to convey information. The natural ground for language is considered to be logic and truth, the projection of objective facts, not persuasion and purpose. Thus, language is considered essentially apolitical, something that cannot ethically be manipulated. We even invent stories to support this mythology, taking America's most successful politician, George Washington, and glorifying him as an apolitical man who never told a lie. (Note how the myth stresses his reluctance when drafted as the first president.)

Things were not always thus in Western culture, however. In ancient Athens, wealthy men sent their sons to school primarily to learn the art of rhetoric, which was understood as the art of making political speeches. The Sophists, who ran the schools, specialized in rhetoric — teaching how to manipulate linguistic tropes to achieve one's ends. But it is not the Sophists whom we remember today (except negatively — the word *sophistical* now refers to an argument that can't be trusted). Rather, we remember Socrates, Plato's teacher, who hated the Sophists — among other things, he didn't like their habit of accepting tuition fees — and who believed that the purpose of language was to lead one objectively to absolute philosophical truth. Socrates' philosophical predilection to regard language logically and objectively eventually triumphed as the dominant language mythology of European culture. The Sophists' rhetorically based, political attitude toward language was defeated, and the philosophical view of language as an objective bearer of the truth became the now-invisible (because it is so widely embraced) linguistic myth of Western civilization.

Modern rhetoricians and semioticians, however, can point out just how many rhetorical tricks Plato used in his own writings to attack the rhetoricians of ancient Athens. (There is another irony here: Plato, the first great writer of secular prose in European history, despised and condemned writing as being too prone to trickiness and misinterpretation.) In other words, Western culture's embrace of an antirhetorical mythology of language is based, at least in part, upon some pretty fancy rhetoric. Plato, after all, got his way, which is what persuasive argumentation is meant to allow one to do.

Students may also raise a moral objection to semiotics; the approach can raise the specter of relativism. We think it is fair for students to ask, "If semiotics argues that values are culturally relative, then what's the point in having values?" Since such questions are difficult to answer, they may be either ignored or dismissed in a manner that suggests that some semioticians are eager enough to expose the ideological underpinnings of their opponents' values but that they consider their own values unassailable. We do not believe that this is a good way to teach semiotic thinking, so we will address the issue of ethical relativism that semiotics raises in a more tentative way. We intend to open up the question for further debate — perhaps the first debate you may engage in with your class.

Our first response to the "What's the point, then?" question is that every attempt to come up with an absolute standard of values is going to run into trouble anyway. Most commonly, people rely on religious teachings to provide moral guidance, but it doesn't take long to see how ambiguous things can get even when we can agree on the same guide. American moral culture, for example, is founded on the injunctions of the Bible, whose commandment on killing seems clear enough. "Thou shalt not kill," the commandment says, but then the interpretation begins. Killing nonhumans is rarely included in the injunction (though in Buddhist culture, the ideal is to kill no animal at all), but what about war, capital punishment, euthanasia, and that most intractable of controversies, abortion? If your students begin to pronounce judgment on such matters, let the class discussion reveal the sources of their judgments. Likely as not there will be disagreement, and when students probe the ground for their opinions, they will discover that many such grounds are possible. Ask your class, then, who gets to decide which ground is paramount, and the ensuing discussion should reveal just how political our values are.

The point, then, is not whether value systems are possible; it is how convincing we can be when presenting our values. Often, the mere challenge to justify one's opinions can illuminate their ideological foundations. Semiotic thinking teaches us to probe our values, not to give them up, and such probing can help us — especially as writers — find better ways of persuading others to adopt our point of view. Simply denouncing the opposition gets one nowhere: a writer has to find the terms that make most sense to a reader who may not share his or her perspective at first. Indeed, as semioticians, we have written this text with the understanding that the semiotic point of view is hardly universal but that if it is thoughtfully, even considerately, presented, it can contribute to anyone's intellectual growth.

Further Readings in Semiotics

If you want to pursue semiotics further, we suggest the following books as a place to start. Some are introductions to the field (and would also be suitable for student readers), while others are technical and theoretical.

Barthes, Roland. *The Fashion System*. Berkeley: Univ. of California Press, 1990. A classic semiotic reading of clothing styles.

———. *Mythologies*, trans. Annette Lavers. New York: Hill and Wang, 1972. One of the first applications of semiotic theory to the interpretation of popular culture. Barthes's wide-ranging analyses take in everything from the cultural significance of plastic and strip tease to professional wrestling and Einstein's brain.

Baudrillard, Jean. *America*. London: Verso, 1988. A classic reading of American culture, focusing on New York and Los Angeles, by the world's preeminent postmodern semiologist.

Berger, Asa. *Signs in Contemporary Culture: An Introduction to Semiotics*. New York: Longman, 1984. A popular introduction to semiotics, applying semiotic insights to the interpretation of Shakespeare, Sherlock Holmes, pop art, the comics, digital watches, baseball, and much more.

_____. *Cultural Criticism: A Primer of Key Concepts*. Thousand Oaks, CA: Sage, 1995.

Blonsky, Marshall. *American Mythologies*. New York: Oxford, 1992. A reading of American popular culture.

_____. *On Signs*. Baltimore: Johns Hopkins Univ. Press, 1985. An anthology of essays written by leading semioticians from Umberto Eco to Jacques Derrida. Essays range from technical expositions on semiotic theory to cultural and literary criticism.

Bondanella, Peter. *Umberto Eco and the Open Text: Semiotics, Fiction, Popular Culture*. Cambridge: Cambridge Univ. Press, 1997.

Clarke, D.S., Jr. *Sources of Semiotic: Readings With Commentary from Antiquity to the Present*. Carbondale: Southern Illinois Univ. Press, 1990. An anthology of semiotic writings from Aristotle to the present, with each selection annotated by Clarke.

Deely, John. *Basics of Semiotics*. Bloomington: Indiana Univ. Press, 1990. A primer in semiotic theory from one of the major figures in the Semiotic Society of America.

Eco, Umberto. *A Theory of Semiotics*. Bloomington: Indiana Univ. Press, 1979. A magisterial summation of semiotic theory from the world's leading semiotician, establishing a theoretical grounding for the connection between signs and culture.

_____. *Travels in Hyperreality*. New York: Harcourt, Brace, 1990. A collection of essays that interpret American and Italian popular culture.

Hawkes, Terence. *Structuralism and Semiotics*. Berkeley: Univ. of California Press, 1977. A primer in structural semiology and deconstruction written for students of literary criticism and theory.

Hodge, Bob. *Social Semiotics*. Cambridge: Polity Press with Basil Blackwell, 1988.

Holbrook, Morris B., and Elizabeth C. Hirshman. *The Semiotics of Consumption*. New York: Mouton de Gruyter, 1993.

Nöth, Winfried. *Handbook of Semiotics*. Bloomington: Indiana Univ. Press, 1989. An encyclopedic dictionary of major semiotic terms and concepts.

Peirce, Charles Sanders. *Collected Papers*. 8 vols. Ed. Charles Hartshorne and Paul Weiss. Cambridge: Cambridge Univ. Press, 1931–66. Eight volumes of the original essays, papers, and random jottings that inaugurated the modern study of semiotics in America.

Saussure, Ferdinand de. *Course in General Linguistics*. Ed. Charles Bally and Albert Sechehage. Trans. Roy Harris. London: Duckworth, 1983. A transcription of the pioneering lectures that led to the development of semiology and structuralism.

Scholes, Robert. *Semiotics and Interpretation*. New Haven: Yale Univ. Press, 1982. An introduction to semiotics for students of literary theory and criticism.

Sebeok, Thomas, ed. *Encyclopedic Dictionary of Semiotics*. Berlin and New York: Mouton de Gruyter, 1986. A guide to semiotic terms and concepts, edited by the dean of American semiotics and the founder of the Semiotic Society of America.

Sebeok, Thomas, and Smith, Iris. *American Signatures: Semiotic Inquiry and Method*. Norman: Univ. of Oklahoma Press Project for Discourse and Theory, 1990. A collection of essays on problems in semiotics, including a historical overview of the growth of the semiotic enterprise in the United States.

Silverman, Kaja. *The Subject of Semiotics*. New York: Oxford Univ. Press, 1983. A psychoanalytic and feminist approach to semiotics, especially applied to films.

Solomon, Jack. *The Signs of Our Times: The Secret Meanings of Everyday Life*. New York: Harper/Collins Perennial Library, 1990. A nonacademic introduction to semiotics, focusing on its application to popular culture. Essays range from interpretations of TV shows and advertisements to toys, food, clothing, architecture, and postmodernism. This book has been used as a class text for college writing classes across the nation.

Umiker-Sebeok, Jean, ed. *Marketing and Semiotics: New Directions in the Study of Signs for Sale*. Berlin: Mouton de Gruyter, 1987. A collection of papers devoted to the semiotics of marketing goods and services.

Wollen, Peter. *Signs and Meaning in the Cinema*. Bloomington: Indiana Univ. Press, 1972. A semiotic approach to the interpretation of films.

Using *Signs of Life in the U.S.A.*

THE TEXT'S ORGANIZATION

We have divided *Signs of Life* into two major sections, both to enhance the text's flexibility and to highlight the essential cultural connection between the things we consume and the things we believe. Part One, Cultural Productions, focuses on the marketing and consumption of cultural products, particularly the objects we buy, the ads that sell us those objects, and the TV shows, videos, and films that shape and express our consuming passions. Your students will take to such topics immediately — they form the core of their cultural literacy — and your class ought to have a lot of fun with your assignments. Part Two, Cultural Constructions, may seem more sobering, but the issues presented there should be just as familiar to your students as are those of Part One. This half of the book encourages students to see that popular culture is a serious thing, shaped by beliefs and values that are often ignored when one considers only the gaudy imagery of the culture industry. Is *Pretty Woman* your students' favorite movie? Well, Chapter Six, on gender, can help them see the social undercurrents that made the film such a hit. Do some wonder why they feel out of place in an office environment, while others thrive in that setting? Both groups can connect with Chapter Five, "Popular Spaces: Interpreting the Built Environment." In short, behind every cultural production is ideology. What we do, whether at work at or play, is linked to what we believe, and the twofold division of *Signs of Life* is intended to emphasize graphically and thematically this fundamental semiotic connection.

ALTERNATIVE THEMATIC ARRANGEMENTS

You're not likely to march through *Signs of Life* chapter by chapter, assigning your students every selection; even if you want to do that, you probably wouldn't have time. You'll probably need to abbreviate the text to accommodate the length of your school term and the skill level of your students. There are better and worse ways to do that. One way, of course, is by covering the entire text but eliminating readings from each chapter. We advise against that simply because your students may feel frustrated by what can seem a whirlwind tour of topics (the "if it's Tuesday, it must be gender" feeling). Some instructors might choose to cover just one half of the book. Although that's a workable approach that would score points for focus, we'd be sorry to have students lose the deliberate cross-pollination of issues that occurs throughout the text. Here's a brief example. The images perpetuated by the media (Part One) are shaped by our culture's assumptions about race (Chapter Seven); similarly, prevailing beliefs about gender (Chapter Six) are reinforced and given legitimacy through advertising (Chapter Two), television (Chapter Three), and film (Chapter Four). If you emphasize just one half of the book, we urge you to include in your syllabus at least one chapter from the other half.

So what do we recommend? We strongly suggest beginning with the general introduction so that students can gain an overview of the book, understand the semiotic approach, and learn why they're covering popular culture in their writing class. At this point, you might ask them for their ideas on which selections they'd like to cover. Although it may seem scary to begin the course without everything mapped out in detail, you may win greater class involvement if you allow your students some say in what they have to read. Together you could pick and choose among all the selections, creating your own themes as you go along. As an alternative, you could plan out the first half of the course, then solicit student suggestions for what to cover during the second half. If you prefer more structure, we see two possible approaches: (1) organizing your course around one broad theme or (2) creating several small units, each with its own theme.

1. *Organizing your course around one broad theme.* Three of the chapters — "Consuming Passions: The Culture of American Consumption" (Chapter One), "We've Come a Long Way, Maybe: Gender Codes in American Culture" (Chapter Six), and "Constructing Race: Readings in Multicultural Semiotics" (Chapter Seven) — address themes far-ranging enough that you could select one and focus your entire course on the single theme it introduces. After beginning with one of these chapters and covering it entirely, you could pick among other chapters that contain readings related to the theme and select those that would most usefully enhance your approach to the overall topic. The following possibilities would work if you plan to cover five additional chapters, although you certainly can adapt these schemes or invent your own.

> *Theme:* Consuming Behavior in America
> Begin with: "Consuming Passions" (Chapter One)
> Do: "Brought to You B(u)y" (Chapter Two)
> Pick three: "Video Dreams" (Chapter Three), "The Hollywood Sign" (Chapter Four), "Popular Spaces" (Chapter Five), "We've Come a Long Way, Maybe" (Chapter Six), "American Icons" (Chapter Nine)
>
> *Theme:* Multiculturalism/Ethnicity
> Begin with: "Constructing Race" (Chapter Seven)
> Pick four: "Brought to You B(u)y" (Chapter Two), "Video Dreams" (Chapter Three), "The Hollywood Sign" (Chapter Four), "We've Come a Long Way, Maybe" (Chapter Six), "American Icons" (Chapter Nine)
>
> *Theme:* Gender
> Begin with: "We've Come a Long Way, Maybe" (Chapter Six)
> Pick four: "Brought to You B(u)y" (Chapter Two), "Video Dreams" (Chapter Three), "The Hollywood Sign" (Chapter Four), "Popular Spaces" (Chapter Five), "American Icons" (Chapter Nine)

2. *Creating several small units, each with its own theme.* Because the selections cover many interrelated themes, you could organize your course around several smaller issues. You'll probably spot such units as you skim through the book; we suggest some here that we find especially appealing. We also suggest possible readings from throughout the book, but by no means should this be read as a definitive list, nor should you feel obligated to cover all the readings suggested for each theme.

Ethnicity
Do: "Constructing Race" (Chapter Seven)
Pick from: Rose (Chapter Three); Boyd, Hagedorn, Loh (Chapter Four); Swentzell (Chapter Five); Eitzen (Chapter Eight); Dyson (Chapter Nine)

Consumerism/Commodification
Do: "Consuming Passions" (Chapter One)
Pick from: Marchand, Solomon, Schlosser, Steinem, Twitchell (Chapter Two); Hilburn (Chapter Three); Gladwell, McCarthy, Willis (Chapter Five); Omi, Hancock (Chapter Seven); Dyson, Prager, Cross, Caldwell, Rivenburg (Chapter Nine)

Gender
Do: "We've Come a Long Way, Maybe" (Chapter Six)
Pick from: Bowlby (Chapter One); Barthel, Steinem (Chapter Two); Stark, Douglas, Fazzone, Rose (Chapter Three); Bordo, Hagedorn, Loh, Sobchack (Chapter Four); Lippard, Karbo, Spain (Chapter Five); Messner, Nelson, Jenkins (Chapter Eight); Medhurst, Croal and Hughes, Prager, Cross (Chapter Nine)

The Formation of Personal Identity
Begin with Kron (Chapter One)
Pick from: de Graaf et al., Hine, Davis, Goewey (Chapter One); Twitchell (Chapter Two); Bordo (Chapter Four); Devor, Jennings, Blum, Scanlon, Wolf, Gibson (Chapter Six); Lopez, Bernstein, Algranati, Shen (Chapter Seven); Messner, Nelson (Chapter Eight); Bader (Chapter Nine)

Interpreting Signs and Images
Do: "American Icons" (Chapter Nine); cover, frontispieces, images, and photos throughout the text
Pick from: Norton, Hine, Davis, Kron, Goewey (Chapter One); Solomon, Barthel, Portfolio of Ads (Chapter Two); Davis, Stark, Douglas (Chapter Three); Bordo, Boyd, Hagedorn, Loh, Parenti (Chapter Four); Willis, Karbo, Vergara, Boehlert (Chapter Five); Devor, Scanlon, Mayer, Wolf, Tannen, Gibson (Chapter Six); Omi, Bernstein, hooks, Kennedy (Chapter Seven); Kamp, Nelson (Chapter Eight)

Cultural Implications of the September 11, 2001, Terrorist Attacks
Do: September 11 Portfolio
Pick from: Cave, Barber, Friedman (Chapter One); Shales (Chapter Three); Goldstein (Chapter Four); Boehlert (Chapter Five); Kennedy (Chapter Seven); Smith (Chapter Eight); Layden (Chapter Nine)

ENCOURAGING STUDENT RESPONSE AND INVOLVEMENT

Signs of Life presumes a class with active students. It calls on their knowledge of popular culture and encourages them to participate in their writing class. We've built into the apparatus suggestions for a variety of ways students can respond to readings, reflect on them alone, and discuss them with others. We've tried to suggest responses that are appropriate to each reading. For instance, we include at least one reflective journal topic for selections that might disturb readers. But our suggestions are meant to be flexible: that we frame a topic as an essay question, for instance, doesn't mean that you can't rewrite it as a journal prompt. We'll summarize for you the major strategies we've relied on to trigger students' response, and we'll offer whatever hints we can for ensuring their success.

Cover   On the first day of class, you might start by asking students to interpret the cover. What's the significance of the Rubik's cube? What does its inclusion suggest about the text's approach to popular culture? And ask your students to study the images on the cube as well. How do they function as signs of American culture? Should there be any dispute about what the images are, here's a quick run-down. The top panel: the Statue of Liberty, hamburger, stop sign, laptop, ice cream cone, shopping cart, dustbroom and pan, "sale" sign, U.S. flag. The left panel: handgun, cell phone, outlet, White House, bar code, soccer ball, basketball, mailbox, cloudy earth. The right panel: earth as a map, jeans, computer circuits, coffee cup, firefighter ladder, baseball, airplane, hotdog, computer keyboard.

Frontispieces and Images   We feel that it's essential for a semiotics-based reader to include both images and text, so each chapter begins with a frontispiece that presents an image related to the chapter's topic, and throughout the book appear photos and images ripe for analysis. Do discuss these images with your students, perhaps as a way to begin class discussion of a new topic. Some, such as the Calvin and Hobbes frontispiece (Chapter Three), offer critical commentary of their own. Some illustrate points mentioned in the chapter introductions or articles (the frontispiece showing the Eaton Centre Mall, for instance, demonstrates the discussion in Chapter Five's introduction). Others coordinate with adjacent articles (the photograph of Salt 'N' Pepa meshes with the Rose selection in Chapter Three, for instance, just as the photo of Serena Williams accompanies the Nelson piece in Chapter Eight). Some extend the issues raised in adjacent articles (such as the babies in the cart in Chapter Six). Discuss with your students both the immediate impact the images have on them — their gut reponses — and the images' cultural and social significance. To get your students thinking about an issue, ask them to brainstorm alternative images and then to debate which ones they would or would not want to see in a text. Not only would such a discussion reveal much about their own worldview, it would enable students to see that they've already been semioticians all along.

In addition, we've included a Portfolio of September 11 photographs. Not only does it serve as a memorial to those who lost their lives and a recognition of those who struggled to save the victims; in addition, we include it as a reminder of the enormity of the events of that terrible day. The September 11 attacks have been compared to other landmark historical moments — Pearl Harbor, the assassination of John F. Kennedy — that have altered the course of American history and culture. Ask your students about their responses to watching images of the attacks as they happened. How do they compare the responses they had then with those they have today? In what way do the events of September 11 serve as a defining moment of their generation?

Introduction   We consider the general introduction essential if you plan to use the semiotic approach, for that's where we not only explain the method and our rationale for using it but also walk students through sample interpretations that can serve as models for their own analyses. Notice that often we stop short of completing an analysis. We've deliberately not provided definitive readings of the topics raised; instead, we try to give just enough so that students will be excited and encouraged to pursue their own interpretations. Thus, often we stop in the middle of an analysis and turn to the students. Use such moments as a way to stimulate class discussion. Ask your students to finish the job — to amplify and extend, or even to contradict, the analyses that we've started. Even if you don't use semiotics, the introduction explains why their textbook focuses on popular culture as its topic.

Writing about Popular Culture   We recognize that many students, even early in their writing process, may want to see what a "real" essay looks like as a model to guide their own revision and thinking. We've thus included in our introduction suggestions for writing on popular culture as well as student-written essays on topics prompted by this text. Of course, you may wish to supplement this material with sample essays written by your own students. But these sample essays are particularly useful if you want to review student work early in the term before your own students have produced any final drafts, or you may prefer the diplomatically easier choice of critiquing an essay not written by someone sitting in class.

This section has two parts: an introduction to writing about popular culture and three sample students essays. You can assign the introductory comments with or without the subsequent essays — the two can exist independently if you like. The introductory material would be best assigned early in the term, perhaps even before students start their first writing assignment. Here we emphasize prewriting strategies, especially invention techniques, and offer suggestions for writing arguments about popular culture. Specifically, we emphasize constructing a strong argument with specific evidence — one of the most common need of students, even at varying levels and abilities, is to learn how to translate their personal reactions and private opinions into a defensible argument that can stand up in the court of public discussion. Our comments are intended not to be exhaustive but rather to suggest to your students how academic discourse demands that writers be responsible to their readership, in addition to their own ideas.

The second part presents three student essays, chosen because they represent a range of styles and topics, with brief marginal annotations. Although we believe each writer is effective in achieving his or her goals, be aware that, as with any student writing, there's always room for improvement. So we suggest that you describe these essays not as "ideal" models — that might intimidate some students, anyway — but as interesting and effective responses to some of the issues *Signs of Life* raises. If your students can suggest revisions to strengthen the essays, great!

The first essay, by William Martin-Doyle of Harvard University, is a strong semiotic reading of *Cool Hand Luke*. This essay is particularly useful if you're emphasizing text-based arguments, as Martin-Doyle draws on Robert B. Ray's "The Thematic Paradigm" in Chapter Four for his critical framework. Interestingly, Martin-Doyle departs from Ray in his argument, showing a spirit of intellectual independence that we think is worth promoting. In addition, the argument is supported with a good, close reading of the film. We recognize that some students may not have seen *Cool Hand Luke*. That shouldn't be a problem, because students can focus on how Martin-Doyle draws on both Ray's essay and the film to construct his own interpretation. If curious, students can rent the video (or you may wish to do that yourself).

The second essay, by Dana Mariano of Lehigh University, is based on her experience with a recent popular trend: tattooing and body piercing. This is a fully accessible essay that we selected because Mariano goes beyond simply narrating her visit to the tattoo parlor to interpret the appeal of the fad itself — a nice blend of the personal and the broader social context. We include the third essay, by Mike Nordberg of Lehigh University, because students often receive open-ended assignments but don't quite know where to go with them. Mike's essay provides a good model of how to focus a topic and how to ground it in lots of specific, relevent details.

Chapter Introductions and Boxed Questions   A crucial part of the book, the chapter introductions suggest ways to analyze the chapter's subject and provide a critical framework for reading and understanding the essays that follow. Such a framework is vital for a popular-culture textbook, for the students' strengths can become their weaknesses. Because students know so much about the culture around them, it's sometimes hard for them to adopt a critical stance toward it; guiding students toward that critical stance is one of the introductions' main tasks. The introductions suggest ways to read a subject, model interpretations of examples, link the various issues raised by the selections, and (as with the general introduction) create opportunities for students to explore an issue further. You can also trigger discussion by assigning the boxed questions included with each introduction. "The Exploring the Signs" questions are all journal or prewriting topics, intended to stimulate a student's thinking on a topic even before you discuss it in class. Most relate the chapter's subject to the student's personal experience, and they're meant to lead students to see how a broad or abstract topic can apply to their own lives. The "Discussing the Signs" boxes suggest in-class activities such as debates, discussions, or small-group work. You could try these tasks either on the day you discuss the chapter introduction or any time when you're covering the chapter readings. The "Reading on the Net" exercises suggest ways to investigate a topic on the Internet. Some Net exercises send students online to research a topic, while others ask them to interpret what they find at a given Web site. In some cases, we've given specific Internet addresses, but be aware that the Net is always changing — your students may find alternative sites that are as interesting as the ones we've suggested.

"Reading the Text" Questions   All selections are accompanied first by questions we've dubbed "Reading the Text," essentially comprehension questions designed to ensure careful, accurate reading. They ask students to identify the selections' key concepts, to explain difficult terms, and to articulate how the selections' main ideas relate to each other and to the evidence the authors present. These questions are ideal for readings logs or journals. You could routinely assign them whenever you give a reading assignment, or you could assign them just for selections you anticipate may be difficult for your students. We suggest that you create some mechanism whereby your students can share their responses with others. You might begin discussion of a reading by asking some students to read their responses to the class; that will enable you to see quickly whether your students had any trouble understanding the selection. Alternatively, your students could share their responses in small groups, or they might write brief responses on the board at the beginning of class.

"Reading the Signs" Questions   Each selection is also accompanied by various writing and activity questions designed to produce clear analytic thinking and strong student writing. You'll see that most "Reading the Signs" questions call for a written response to the text. Some we've framed as journal topics; we find it valuable pedagogically for students to be able to link the sometimes abstract or theoretical concepts to their own lives. Seeing that their schoolwork doesn't have to exist independently of their home culture can prove a tremendous motivation for students. Journal entries can also be particularly useful for selections that might disturb your students; writing in their journals allows them a chance to explore their responses before they get to class. Occasionally, you might ask students to read their entries aloud in small groups or before the entire class (for sensitive topics, you might read the entries to the class yourself, without revealing the students' names). But be sure to let your class know at the beginning of the term whether the journal is to be public (shared with other students) or private (shared with just you), or both.

The essay questions range from fairly simple and straightforward to challenging and controversial, calling for different modes of response (argumentation, comparison, and so forth). Some topics focus on a single selection, while others ask students to consider two or more selections in relation to each other. You'll find that some questions ask students to conduct nontraditional research, such as interviews. We've found that students become excited when doing such work and that they often produce their best writing when they can generate their own primary evidence. To ensure successful interviews, you should provide them with some guidelines ahead of time. You might discuss with your class the difference between questions that are open-ended and those that prompt yes-no responses. You could ask students to prepare interview questions for your review. Particularly if students will be asking about sensitive topics, they can benefit from role-playing an interview in small groups. Role-playing can also help students with timing; they usually underestimate how long it will take to cover a set of issues.

A number of questions invite other in-class activities, such as group work, debates, and hypothetical conversations. We encourage you to try these to stimulate all your students to participate. We've found small groups can work for almost any sort of class activity, from discussing a selection to writing a collaborative research paper. Small groups often allow students to be more honest, and being in a group can make it easier for quiet students to participate in the class. We particularly like to use groups to create a different class dynamic than exists during a whole-class discussion. In addressing gender issues, for instance, you can create same-sex groups to discuss an issue and then have the groups report to the whole class. That way not only will students benefit from their group discussion, but they can stand back and examine the groups themselves for evidence of gender-based patterns. One kind of group work that can yield surprising results is a hypothetical conversation between two authors or characters from the readings. We like these conversations because students must first discuss among themselves the likely positions each author would take on an issue (*what* the author would say); then they must consider the manner of presentation appropriate for each author (*how* the author would say it). If you ask your students to stage such a conversation, be sure to give them plenty of time for planning it — that's when half the learning takes place!

Debates are particularly valuable for teaching argumentative strategies: students must generate logical arguments, amass compelling evidence, and anticipate opposing viewpoints. When creating debating teams, we've found it works best to mix students of various viewpoints — in other words, it's not necessary for everyone on a team to hold the same opinion of an issue. If the group members have different opinions, students will be exposed to alternative positions when planning their presentations.

Some questions call for nonanalytic assignments, such as designing an advertisement. Do give these a try; they provide students with a chance to put the analytical and theoretical material to practical use. Students may see such assignments as just fun, so we suggest that you create some mechanism whereby they reflect on or analyze their creations. They might present their work to the class, explaining the rationale behind it; or, in an essay, they could describe their goals and discuss the extent to which their creation fulfilled those goals.

Glossary of Key Terms   We include a glossary of key words and concepts drawn from the chapter introductions to provide a ready reference for you and your students.

Citing Sources   On the end pages appears a brief guide to citing sources, including on-line and media sources, for your students' quick reference.

Companion Web Site   For supplementary material, consult the Web site that accompanies this text at **www.bedfordstmartins.com/signsoflife.** This Web site offers a rich array of links, from manufacturers' sites that are ripe for analysis and interpretation to critical sites, such as one for Ken Burns's PBS documentary *The West*, to archives such as the American Advertising Museum. You can search our companion Web site either by chapter or by subject.

Advice from Experienced Instructors

Since we began working on the first edition of *Signs of Life* several years ago, we have benefited from the fresh ideas and innovative teaching techniques of our friends and colleagues. For this version of the instructor's manual, we thought we should share some of this helpful advice with you. Meredith Kurz of California State University, Northridge, provides suggestions for an array of pedagogical issues, ranging from sequencing assignments throughout the term to preventing plagiarism. Next, Deborah Banner of UCLA describes an imaginative class project that involves group work, student presentations, the collaborative creation of an ad, and individual student essays. We find their ideas striking and believe you will as well, whether you're new to *Signs of Life* or a veteran.

MEREDITH KURZ

SIGNS OF LIFE IN THE COMPOSITION CLASS

My title's obviously pilfered wordplay echoes what I believe to be the spirit of this textbook and its perhaps secondary or tertiary message — that a somewhat less than deadly serious approach to the subject of composition and composition pedagogy is not undesirable. When all is said and done, to write is to play, and to teach writing also is to play — to play with ideas, writing techniques, grammar, and words. The problem I faced in teaching my early semesters was that I had not yet found my own way to that realization; consequently, there was no way that I could help my students find their own way there. But since lately I have made some modest progress in that respect, I submit my roadmap for perusal by both novice and seasoned instructors. It is marked with concepts, directions, tips, and other miscellanea that I have picked up along the way from professorial mentors, collegial colleagues, and anyone else who had something to offer and did.

During the first of my university's two teaching assistant training semesters, my composition director gave our class some very useful advice: "Get a good textbook, and let it support you," she said. With this idea in mind, we TAs set about finding the most supportive book available and chose for our first-teaching-semester textbook a reader-rhetoric-handbook combination. We were motivated to select such a text for three reasons:

- For our students' sakes (having everything included in one book would lower course costs for them);

- By our own insecurities (this textbook was so complete that it could teach the course all by itself; then we would be able to relax and cruise right through our first semester because "we had a good textbook, and we were going to let it support us"); and

- Because our instructor advised us to choose that particular textbook.

That first semester, I cleaved to that book with religious fervor, presenting the text to my students, chapter and verse, rigidly following the order of the textbook from Chapter One and forward. Then, somewhere around midsemester, I realized that I was losing my class's interest and my own energy. My undeviating progress through the textbook was boring me to death, and I seemed to be taking my students with me. Certainly, none of us was turning out any deathless prose. This complete textbook dependence on my part fostered a rigidity that worked to stifle almost all the original ideas anyone might have had, to abort any innovative writing styles that may have been gestating in my students' minds, and to suffocate whatever creative teaching I might have attempted.

Fortunately, at about that time, my composition director gave our TA class (many of whom found themselves in a similar situation) a second very useful bit of advice: "Don't allow your textbook to control you," she said. At first, this new useful advice seemed to contradict the old useful advice, until I realized that support and control are two entirely different concepts. At that point, I decided to change to a less prescriptive textbook format so that I wouldn't be tempted to lean so heavily on it. Accordingly, I set about finding a book that would afford my students and me a greater degree of flexibility, offer some not unwanted guidance, and yet not encourage dependence. Please forgive me if I sound like a textbook commercial here, but it was just about then that *Signs of Life in the U.S.A.* (hereinafter affectionately referred to as *SOL*) came into my life — just in time to breathe some life into my teaching. A reader with something extra, *SOL* provided both the readings and the "way" for my class and for me. *SOL* is a textbook that offers instructive but not pedantic readings and that provides a flexible and dynamic analytical methodology for reading and for writing. Additionally, the sheer number and diversity of essays make the textbook adaptable to many different types of semester formats, allowing room for instructor creativity and providing enough material for a multitude of assignment focuses.

I also welcomed the move from division by modes — to my mind, a rather outmoded and useless structure — to this text's focus on popular culture, semiotic methodology, and subject-oriented organization. The textbook's content, approach, and arrangement are such that anyone from anywhere can find material of interest and a way to write about it. Equally important, however, I also found in *SOL* room to play and flexible rules to play by. Although it may have been too late to resurrect my first semester, I had found a way to infuse life into my second.

Here ends the testimonial for *SOL* and begins some (I hope) useful suggestions for its application.

My Choice: The Assignment-Driven Semester

Some colleges and universities supply to their composition faculty a departmentally mandated textbook and require that the composition course follow its, usually, prescriptive text. I have been fortunate enough never to have worked in such circumstances except in my first TA semester. The English departments for which I have taught generally have given me a wide choice of textbooks as well as the discretion to formulate my semester as I see fit. Each has supplied me with only a very general course outline that allows for a great deal of creativity on my part. These course outlines vary little from school to school and seem to adhere to the following broad assignment pattern: (1) the narrative essay, (2) the analysis essay, (3) the argument essay, and (4) the research essay. Making semester planning a bit more complex, at California State University, Northridge, where I did my TA training and teaching, the department required, in addition to the class textbook, a full-text nonfiction work as well.

My first semester's semidisaster served me well in helping me to devise my second. I learned a lot from that experience, and one important lesson involved that first essay assignment — the narrative. In that first semester, most students turned in narratives that were exclusive rather than inclusive. These essays could not have been of interest to anyone but the writer herself and maybe, just maybe, her best friend. The writing was far too personal and, unfortunately, set a tone for the semester that I found difficult to dislodge. Subsequent essays, no matter what their purpose, always seemed to emerge from a too-personal point of view and consequently spoke only to an exclusive audience, no matter what purpose and audience directives I had supplied. I realized that the problem had a great deal to do with the students' rhetorical maturity and that it was my job to move them from their writing adolescence into a writing adulthood. Clearly, I needed to set up a model that would move them from "I" to "we" and finally to "they" — from subjective to intersubjective to objective, the academic objective being the writing style that they needed to acquire. My goal would be to achieve a synthesis between the four types of essays required and the three rhetorical stances I wished to move them through.

My Unit I: Narrative (The Inclusive "I")

My whole text, Mike Rose's excellent autobiographical narrative *Lives on the Boundary* (New York: Penguin, 1990), provided a perfect jumping off point for the semester. Rose writes an autobiographical narrative that is "I" oriented but also discusses many other issues, literacy among them, and literacy, after all, is what we are after in our classes. After two weeks spent reading, discussing, and writing about the Rose narrative, it was an easy segue into *SOL,* where I began by assigning a personal literacy narrative. Fan Shen's "The Classroom and the Wider Culture: Identity as a Key to Learning English Composition" (Chapter Seven) chronicles the author's rhetorical journey from his own culture's composition form to our Western academic approach. In so doing, he explores the differences in form and style and the cultural and ideological reasons behind those differences. Most freshman composition students have no idea that writing form and style varies from culture to culture, so interacting with Shen's essay is a real eye opener for them. From studying Shen's "I" (more than just personal) narratives, the students glean new and interesting information and perspectives from content and at the same time gain a more sophisticated understanding of personal narrative form. They learn that each of them can universalize the "I" and that their "I" can signify something beyond themselves. With this preparation, the students attempted their first essay, the "I" narrative. The assignment asked them to write either a cultural autobiography, a cultural biography, or a literacy narrative and, like the authors of their textbook models, to write inclusively rather than exclusively.

My Unit II: Analysis (The Cultural "We")

In the second unit, students moved from a subjective to an intersubjective point of view, focusing on how we construct and know ourselves as individuals within our own cultures and how we relate as members of or visitors to American culture, in particular. We all need to understand the worldview within which we must operate. To begin, I assigned the general introduction to SOL so that students could apprehend the central focus and critical methodology that would support their reading and writing in Units II, III, and IV of the course. At this point, I began really to "let my textbook support me." I made good use of the boxed questions imbedded in the text of the introduction for freewriting and journal writing. I also encouraged students to question the text itself and then attempt to answer their own questions either in group discussions or in individual journal entries. Since the introduction informs the reader of the constructed mythological underpinnings of all they know and believe, I consider it fitting that students question any possible mythological bases for the textbook authors' stance, as well. I want them to question everything!

Next, we read the introductions to Chapter One, "Consuming Passions: The Culture of American Consumption," and Chapter Two, "Brought to You B(u)y: The Signs of Advertising," along with selected essays from each of these chapters, to learn how "we" come to be products of our shared cultures. I found Laurence Shames's "The More Factor" (Chapter One) to be a real eye opener to the basic American myth and its all-pervasive influence on our national psyche. I then moved from the general principals of the myth to some of the manifestations. Finally, selections in Chapter Two, such as Roland Marchand's "The Parable of the Democracy of Goods" and Jack Solomon's "Masters of Desire: The Culture of American Advertising," helped all of us to understand some of the ways in which we disseminate and perpetuate that myth.

Working through these first two chapters prepared the students to write their second essay of the semester, an analysis for which I gave them a rather broad directive;

they could analyze a trend, a style, a fad, or an advertisement. Then, with Units I and II under our belts, we were ready to go on to my Units III and IV and *SOL,* "Part Two: Cultural Constructions."

My Unit III: Argument (The Position Paper)

About halfway through the semester we made the giant leap from subjective to objective writing, understanding that writing, either from "I" or "we," never allows us to be wholly objective. Moving to Part Two, "Cultural Constructions," focused our discussions and writing exercises outside of ourselves as we examined some of the issues featured in the textbook as well as some too new to have made it to the latest edition. Once we had worked through one issue chapter, reading the introduction and then at least three or four essays, the students acquired a basic understanding of how to address an issue. The textbook essays modeled for them how to examine an issue by presenting and interpreting data and then taking a position and supporting it. Chapter Six, "We've Come A Long Way, Maybe: Gender Codes in American Culture," and Chapter Seven, "Constructing Race: Readings in Multicultural Semiotics," generally are of interest to students because the readings deal with concerns that touch or have touched their lives. The readings in these chapters stimulated very active classroom discussion and some intense freewriting and journaling. Since students had by now liberated their writing from self, it seemed appropriate that their third essay assignment allow them a greater degree of latitude. Accordingly, for this assignment, they had the freedom to interact with any essay or essays from either one of the issue chapters we'd covered or to select an essay from one of the other issue chapters.

In addition, while we were working in this unit, students had the opportunity to begin integrating information from source texts into their writing (a skill that they would need to develop for their fourth major essay assignment). Furthermore, by interacting with one or more of the textbook essays, they learned not only to interact with other writers (by including a voice or voices other than their own in their writing) but also to work with the conventions of integrating and citing sources according to MLA guidelines. After that, it was onward to the final assignment of the semester.

My Unit IV: Research (The Academic Objective)

Now that my students had experienced taking a supported position using textual evidence in the argument essay, they were ready for the final challenge of the semester, the research paper. I never have been in favor of pointless research essays that are nothing more than information dumps; therefore, I required that the research essay make some kind of point and express a thesis, whether stated or implied. At this point, I made good use of SOL's model student essays located in "Writing about Popular Culture." The students had already read this section before writing their first essay, but I encouraged them to reread it each time they began to a new assignment.

For this assignment, even more than the previous one, I also relied on the textbook to supply the subject bases for the students' papers and to act as the primary research resource, as well. I did this with good reason.

Reason 1: To Plagiarism-Proof the Paper (well, almost)

Unfortunately, the plagiarism problem continues to exist, exacerbated by one of our best new research tools, the Internet. Not only do students turn in papers borrowed from friends or culled from sorority or fraternity files, but they also download papers from cyberfiles full of essays for sale. One way of circumventing the problem is to construct a research essay assignment that, like the argument paper, bounces off a textbook essay, thereby helping to ensure that students will not be able to submit a borrowed or purchased paper. I find that requiring my students to integrate two SOL essays in with their other sources to create the finished product allows little opportunity for plagiarism. This is another example of how allowing my textbook to support me helps me to maintain control in a critical area.

Reason 2: Creating Interesting Concept Connections and Facilitating Research

One thought-provoking way to construct the research assignment is to have the students not only address the issue itself but also examine the ways that media present it. Taking this approach, students can make use of both the textbook issue section they've chosen and one or more of the media-focused chapters back in Part One. With the textbook as their primary research resource, they have access to a number of essays from which to draw, and of course they can and must move outside of it to find additional material in the university's library and on the Internet. (I do limit the number of allowable Internet sources to two.) My students have turned out some extremely successful research papers using the textbook in this way.

I have continued to use *SOL* in subsequent semesters, always finding new ways to use its content and method. It's just like the mythical magic purse: each time I spend some of it, the expenditure increases rather than decreases its content for me.

Still More Support

Throughout the semester, the students can enhance their active, critical reading skills using the questions headed "Reading the Text" for reading journal entries. These questions encourage students not simply to read but to interact critically with the text to formulate their answers. I save the questions listed under the "Reading the Signs" heading for in-class work: freewriting, group discussions, group exercises, and other productive activities I otherwise would have to invent. These questions engage students in evaluating and analyzing the material content of the essay and their own points of view in relation to the material.

Here, again, I allow the textbook to support me. It is awfully hard work to come up with interesting writing prompts, whether for journal entries, freewrites, group activities, or formal essay assignments. Instructors spend many hours devising these kinds of questions, as did I during my first TA semester. It's a wonderful relief to let the textbook do more of that work so that I have the time, energy, and freedom to enjoy my job and to teach my students that writing need not be drudgery but an interesting, involving, and immensely enjoyable and rewarding pastime.

Finally, I want to reemphasize the point that accepting this kind of support does not amount to allowing the textbook to control my semester or me. I still make all the major decisions. I construct my semester, select the essays I want my students to read, make the assignments, and decide exactly how semiotic I want us to be. The choices are all mine. *SOL* allows me that degree of latitude. And what of the rhethorical art: invention, form, and style? In my experience so far, students learn more from reading good, interesting writing and then writing, writing, writing, themselves than they ever will learn from reading the dry passages found in many rhetorics and handbooks. What extra information I think they need concerning invention, form, and style I can supply from my own education and experience as a college reader and writer. We all can. We've made it this far: we must know something!

DEBORAH BANNER

Undergraduates in Grey Flannel Suits: Advertising in the Composition Classroom

On one unusually crisp Monday afternoon in November, a corporate behemoth took over my English composition classroom. Five creative teams vied for financial and administrative support as they presented advertising strategies for new consumer products to their supervisors. Each team unveiled a new product, discussed marketing plans, and debuted original print and video ads. Unlike most marketing meetings, however, this one ended in an awards ceremony, at which each group received certificates of achievement and rousing ovations. Also unlike most meetings, every participant submitted a five-page paper to the "Executive Vice President" — actually, me — at the end of the session.

It sounds elaborate, but to my students, that Monday was just another deadline for their fall class in composition, rhetoric, and language. They were used to odd pedagogical shenanigans — I had already impersonated a talk-show host, a fitness instructor, and an appellate judge — and my assumption of executive power over a fictitious conglomerate was, to them, the least quirky aspect of their assignment. For this project, I had required them to participate in the charade: each student took on a distinct role within his or her group, so that their presentations and papers were "reports" to the company's management from the "creative executive" or the "art director" of each campaign. Following the presentations, each student team submitted its ads along with individually written and revised papers; each student ultimately received a grade that combined the collaborative and the individual elements of the project. Without a doubt, this was a labor-intensive assignment for all of us. It was also one of the most successful class projects in which I've participated.

The assignment was inspired by Chapter Two, "Brought to You B(u)y: The Signs of Advertising" of *Signs of Life,* particularly several articles that I had taught before. Ads are great material for composition classes for many reasons, not least of which are their familiarity to students and the ways in which ads themselves can be examined for a visual "thesis" and "examples." I had assigned earlier classes Roland Marchand's "The Parable of the Democracy of Goods"; Jack Solomon's "Masters of Desire: The Culture of American Advertising"; and Diane Barthel's "A Gentleman and a Consumer" (all in Chapter Two). These three articles are excellent models for the mechanics of semiotic analysis, as well as for their presentation of arguments supported by reference to multiple specific examples. In particular, Solomon's article is helpful to students writing papers on advertising. Thomas Hine's "What's in a Package" (from Chapter One, "Consuming Passions: The Culture of American Consumption") is another article that supports this assignment well, and having students read Roy Rivenburg's "Snap! Crackle! Plot!" (from Chapter Nine, "American Icons: The Mythic Characters of Popular Culture") might be helpful as they design their own ads.

My earlier classes had discussed these essays in small groups and as a class; we had analyzed ads in small groups and as a class; and eventually, students wrote a paper on ad analysis. This approach was successful, but I had grown tired of my old plan. This time, once my students were familiar with the semiotic approach, I asked them to become ad executives. In groups of five, they were responsible for inventing a consumer product or service and designing a marketing strategy, complete with print and video ads. Along with the ads, each student was to write a five-page paper that referenced the articles in *Signs of Life* to examine his or her particular role in the group project. While I designed the individual job titles and separated the class into groups of five, students were responsible for assigning each role according to their own interests. This was more than a concession to my love of role-playing assignments; individual paper assignments were determined according to a student's position in the group. Each group had a Creative Executive, who coordinated the presentation and the advertisements with one other; organized students self-selected for this job within minutes of receiving the assignment. The Marketing Manager — usually a budding business major — was responsible for analyzing the target markets of the product and the target audiences of the ads. Public Relations Gurus examined the correspondence among the images of the company as a whole and those projected through the product and the ad campaign. Finally, the Art Director and Video Director took primary responsibility for analyzing the print ad and the video ad, respectively. Most students assumed their roles with great panache: one Marketing Manager promised in his paper that his team's product would "become the flagship brand for the corporation in the twenty-first century," while one Video Director requested my help in lobbying the campus media lab for permission to use their digital editing equipment, above and beyond the assignment's requirements. (The lab approved her request, and the resulting ad for a state-of-the-art health club was stunningly professional.)

I realize that the above constitutes a lot of work for two weeks. Then again, I work at an institution with remarkable technological resources for instructors and undergraduates. My students had free access to video cameras, viewing monitors, analog and digital editing booths, networked computers, color printers, and several different desktop publishing and photo editing applications, as well as university employees whose job it is to train and assist undergraduates in using these resources. With hindsight, however, a modified version of this assignment would work, with few adjustments, for students whose multimedia resources extend to a box of magic markers and a piece of paper. The assignment stipulated that no points would be added or subtracted for technological prowess or the lack thereof, and team grades were determined by the creativity and coherence of the ideas behind the advertising campaign rather than by any advanced graphics in the ads themselves. I received an assortment of print ads, including a construction paper and crayon collage, a computer-generated blend of text and scanned images, and one hand-lettered, hand-colored posterboard.

I had two goals for this project. Primarily, I hoped to help strengthen students' critical thinking, reading, and writing skills. By putting them in the role of producers, rather than consumers, of popular culture, I hoped that my students would take a more active critical stance toward their subject matter. By requiring a significant amount of teamwork, I multiplied the occasions on which students would examine, critique, or simply discuss their own writing and how to improve it. Beyond merely drilling students in criticism, however, I tried to engage those critical skills on a terrain where the class felt more at ease and more invested than they do with traditional academic analysis. Using *Signs of Life* gave me a head start here: students are already impressed and excited to be analyzing popular culture — a field that they often feel more authorized to critique than they do others. I deliberately structured the assignment as a "professional" project that employed several different media, in the hope that students might think of composition as more than a dull, academic rite of passage and see that clear writing skills have valuable applications in the rest of the world.

In previous composition classes, my students had examined popular culture as critical consumers but consumers nonetheless. Often, students felt so close to the objects under scrutiny that they had difficulty suspending personal judgments: for example, students who attend class bedecked in Calvin Klein logo attire rarely want to consider the semiotic subtexts of CK advertisements. They want reassurance that they look cool. Alternatively, out of a naive belief that "criticism" as such is inherently negative, some students resist imputing any motive to advertising other than genuine desire to communicate a product's virtues. By imagining themselves as advertisers, my students gained a crucial detachment from their material. Indeed, this is one of the reasons that the editors of *Signs of Life* suggest putting students in the role of advertisers for a day. Not only did my students take advantage of multiple possibilities for building signs into advertisements, but the depth of their subsequent analyses improved once they had recognized how far those signs and sign systems could extend. Because they were responsible for every editorial decision in creating the ads, students quickly dispensed with the obvious images — a smiling trio of women, for example — to focus on countless subtle signals working alongside the obvious. During one class period given over to team strategy, I overheard students arguing about the semiotic importance of the size and color of different typefaces, longer or shorter words in a slogan, the ethnic backgrounds of the people depicted in each ad, and the placement of each element in relation to the others.

Thus the smiling trio of women in one group's print advertisement was meant to signal feminist independence, appropriately enough for the product, which was marketed to women. Yet in the final analysis, the trio was also deliberately multicultural, dressed in casual clothes that bore insignias from prestigious universities, depicted in black and white, seated on comfortable couches, smiling at each other rather than at the camera, in a home and not outdoors or in a bar, surrounded by signs of professional success such as briefcases, cellular phones, and computers, and, finally, accompanied by a minimum of discreet advertising copy. Another group, selling sports sunglasses to the college market, designed their ad so that the sunglasses appeared in the center of the page, lit with a spotlight. Through the lighting, which they intended to connote museum exhibits or stage performance, they suggested the elitism, prestige, and attention-getting qualities of their product without including any text to that effect. Once students understood from experience that such signals are at least as important to a successful ad's composition as the depiction of the commodity itself, they ceased making the single most common undergraduate objection to pop culture analysis. In other words, they stopped saying, "It's just an ad. Aren't we reading too much into this?" and directed their energies at designing advertisements and writing their papers.

My students had fun designing their products and advertisements, and they zeroed in on some great marketing opportunities: one group dreamed up "the Air Executive," a comfortable shoe for businessmen, while another spotted an opening in the beverage market and created Belmont Beer for Women, named for Portia's hometown in *The Merchant of Venice*. Their general enthusiasm for the project carried over to their papers, which helped to motivate some extremely productive individual and peer writing conferences. While I have used several forms of peer review in previous courses, I sometimes fear that it can be a one-sided process. Peer editors have little invested in the outcome of their reviews, other than their desire that a conscientious reading will elicit an equally careful review from their partners. Yet my students tended to grow complacent with or tired of the peer review process over the term, giving cursory attention to the papers of their peers. With this assignment, though, each student's paper was linked to the group's final project. Every student thus had a vested interest in improving his or her teammates' papers, inasmuch as each member's understanding of the team's goals directly affected the group's success. Each student's paper was reviewed by two other teammates, doubling the amount of constructive criticism for each paper and ensuring that the group was in accord regarding the strategy behind the ad campaign.

Without exception, the quality of my students' writing shot up on these papers. Of course, not everyone received an A, but I was able to give the first A that term. Also, for the first time that term, every student received a passing grade on the paper. This was in part due to a significant amount of class time spent discussing the papers and the group project as a whole. During four different class meetings, at least thirty minutes were devoted to team meetings, so that students could plan projects and talk about papers, and we spent one entire class peer reviewing drafts. I discovered that students conceived of the project as a whole: during meetings that were technically scheduled for planning presentations, I overheard students brainstorming paper ideas; similarly, students used some of the time intended for essay review to work on video scripts or to discuss the layout of print ads. Because I required every team to meet me at least once during the planning stages, I could keep track of their progress and offer help wherever needed. Unexpectedly, these mandatory group meetings increased the number of individual student appointments: while reviewing their team project with me, many students signed up for additional one-on-one conferences to discuss their papers. Several students commented to me or on final evaluations that they had never before considered English classes to be that interesting. Such positive feedback was a real thrill on its own but also a gratifying indication that I was successful in achieving my less measurable goals for the project: generating interest in a field that students considered dull or irrelevant and applying student strengths in other fields to composition.

Most of my students were neither English nor humanities majors, and many felt alienated by writing and reading critical essays. Their levels of intimidation ranged from some students' vehement dislike of composition as a practice to the mental block that writing was a born gift and not a teachable skill that improves with practice. By requiring students to work with graphics and video as well as writing, I hoped to tap their creative sides and to uncover dormant talents for alternative forms of composition. One of the great strengths of *Signs of Life* is in its modeling of sophisticated written analysis with everyday objects and media, a feature that tends to make students feel more authorized to critique the material under consideration. I hoped to complement this strategy by combining writing, a skill with which my students did not feel comfortable, with related creative fields where they might feel more at home. Among other things, I discovered that my students excelled at creative multimedia composition, something I wouldn't have known had I assigned only written papers.

Discovering creativity in one area proved helpful in coaching students through other areas. Several students proved to be superb video directors, with a natural visual sense of narrative that they were not able to match in their writing. So we started discussing writing on their terms, comparing thesis statements to visual exposition, specific examples to shot composition, and revision to dubbing and editing. I stressed to students that writing, too, is a creative act, even when it is done for academic purposes. Composition skills are not only translatable across different media — from graphic design to written text, say — but are of equal importance in different media for the professional futures of many students. For example, a strong writer will design a web site better than someone who cannot support a general argument with specific examples. One student, whose level of academic motivation seemed exemplified by his confession (intended, no doubt, as a compliment) that mine was the only class in his schedule that he attended on a regular basis, turned out to be an absolute whiz at video and Web design. His paper, a semiotic analysis of the video ad by the sunglasses group, showcased a previously hidden ability to organize a convincing argument. Like many students, once he wrote about a subject of genuine interest, his writing improved. His argument was an analysis of the episodic nature of the group's ad, which was designed to mimic MTV videos, capitalizing on the short attention spans of the young target market as well as the aura of coolness and sex appeal that MTV projects. His discussion of and evidence for these claims were among the most entertaining, intelligent written work submitted that term.

Along with all of my lofty goals, though, I hoped that this project would help me do what every teacher wants: I wanted to have fun with my class. In this regard, the assignment was an unqualified success. Student presentations and ads were consistently entertaining and intelligent, regardless of the teams' technical prowess. Even the students who borrowed an existing commercial strategy were remarkably canny about the way they chose to do so. By reconfiguring a popular sales pitch to their own product, the student teams were able to reason out the mechanics of how and why particular pitches work. For example, one memorable ad campaign borrowed the "Got Milk?" ad format to sell a college-age dating service. The team was able both to defend the copycat style as a means of investing their service with an aura of wholesomeness, as well as to examine the applicability of the original ad series' signs to their own service, such as the implied urgency in the brief question, the tactic of coming right to the point, and the association of dating with an essential life function. Much more gratifying than the entertainment afforded by such presentations, however, was this project's unexpected effect of forging solidarity among my students, via productive, mutually supportive team relationships that lasted throughout the term. Of course, there was a dysfunctional moment or two — such as a group in which a student defaulted on his or her work or one in which an individual tried to impose his or her personal agenda on the rest of the team. Yet these kinds of glitches, inevitable with any classroom situation involving more than one student, were by far the exception. In each case, difficulty with one individual had the effect of bonding the other members of the team more solidly. With five members to each student team, this still left four people to execute a project, more than enough for successful group work.

I solicited student feedback at all stages of the assignment, reminding them that they were free to offer critiques and make suggestions for improvement, just as I would eventually critique their work. I'd use some of their suggestions if I taught this class again. For one thing, this project was more time-consuming than I had anticipated, for me and for the class. One student suggested simply allowing more than two weeks from start to finish, while another suggested that the video assignment could be modified into a skit forming part of the class presentation, thus saving the time otherwise spent filming and editing. Instead of submitting a video, student groups would turn in their scripts and stage directions. Students also observed that organizing meetings outside of class was difficult for anyone living far from campus. I had randomly assigned students to teams without considering the logistics of their meeting schedules; next time, I'd allow students to organize themselves by geography if that would enable meetings after hours. Finally, it's hard to grade individual students on a group project. Each student justifiably wanted a grade that reflected the work of the individual student, but it can be difficult to separate individual contributions to a group effort. Also justifiably, no student wanted anybody to take credit for work that others had done. My solution was to give each student an average of the group's grade for the project and the individual's grade for the paper. Of course, this had the effect of raising some students' final project grades and lowering others, but there was no case where a student who received a failing grade on the paper received a passing grade for the project. This was the result of luck, not careful planning: nobody failed the paper. Next time, I'd stipulate that a failing grade on the paper meant a failing grade for that individual on the assignment.

Overall, the advertising project was productive as well as entertaining. I learned along with my students and enjoyed the opportunity to work more closely with them than I usually do: I attended video training sessions with them and held many, many extra office hours to strategize ad campaigns with the different teams or to discuss papers with different students. My one caveat to instructors considering some form of this assignment would be to outdo yourself in offering positive reinforcement. At every stage of the project, I praised the work and the effort that my students were exerting, and our final presentations were followed by a small "Class Clio" ceremony, at which every group and every student received silly awards and certificates for achievements in "coolest name for a new product," "most likely to turn a huge profit," "ads so hip they're worth taping," and so on. Approximately half of my class were first-year students, and the rest were split fairly evenly among the upperclassmen, but all of them responded equally well to steady cheerleading.

Ultimately, the true test of a classroom project is the question of whether it is worth repeating. I don't need to think about that one. I'd do it again in a heartbeat — but I'd have to change at least one thing. Next time, I will dispense with the fiction of being Executive Vice President. Next time, I will be CEO.

Cultural Productions

CONSUMING PASSIONS
The Culture of American Consumption

We've made consuming behavior the subject of our first chapter because of the essential role that consumption plays in shaping American popular culture. The culture of consumption is linked most obviously to the topics covered in the first part of *Signs of Life* — that is, cultural products such as advertising, television, and film — but it affects as well issues such as gender and race that are raised in the book's second half. Thus, Chapter One serves as a useful starting point for a course, no matter which other chapters you include in your syllabus. You'll also find that consuming behavior is an ideal topic for beginning your course because it's a part of every student's life. This is true whether your students hail from wealthy suburbs and have lots of disposable income or are working single mothers struggling to make a life for themselves and their families. And it's true for traditional students and nontraditional students alike, those entering college straight from high school and those returning after a hiatus. The constant pressure to buy is an unavoidable part of their lives, even if not all are able or willing to respond to that pressure. If you like to start your course by concentrating on personal experience writing, begin with this chapter.

This chapter is also a fine place to start if you plan to adopt in an explicit fashion the semiotic approach that underlies this text. We've found that semiotics makes immediate sense to students when it's presented in the context of their own behavior. They know, for instance, that they are sending messages to others by their choice of clothing — and they're likely to admit it. Just ask them about the different messages they send when they dress for work, for school, or for a party. Or ask them how their friends would "read" them differently if they showed up driving a Miata or, conversely, a Hummer. The chapter's introduction emphasizes the link between consumer behavior and one's sense of personal identity to enable students to see that, in a sense, they've been semioticians all along.

The Discussing the Signs of Consumer Culture exercise, which asks the class to list and interpret their own clothing styles, is a great ice-breaker for the first few days of the term, when students may not know each other and may be a bit shy about talking in class. Note that the exercise forces students to distinguish between their own interpretations of their clothing and those of others. In addition, this distinction between personal and public meaning is important as students learn that academic writing is not simply an assertion of opinion but an expression of opinion through socially constituted conventions of discourse. In addition, this exercise can raise the distinction between a functional and a cultural meaning of an object. Students often are willing to challenge another student's claim that, for instance, she wears her ripped blue jeans "just because they're comfortable." Someone in the class inevitably will point out that jeans can be purchased ripped for fifty dollars, or that they project a cool image, and so on.

Students may be somewhat more resistant to the issue raised in the "Exploring the Signs of Consumer Culture" question, which asks them to reflect on the importance of consumer products in their lives. Because Americans still cling to the belief that one's identity is a highly individualized matter of soul and spirit, it's understandable that students may feel uncomfortable with the claim, made explicitly in the introduction and implicitly in many of the readings, that "you are what you consume." Ask students to volunteer to share their responses in class, and use them to trigger a discussion of the relative importance of consumer objects and other matters in their lives. You might want to return to this issue later in the term, especially after covering some of the chapters from the second half of the book, which show how even serious issues can be commodified in American culture. It would be particularly interesting to revisit the issue after discussing Chapter Seven, "Constructing Race: Readings in Multicultural Semiotics." Race is deeply connected to one's sense of personal identity and selfhood, and it is increasingly being appropriated to peddle everything from clothing to universities (check your college catalog for calculated images of multiculturalism).

The "Reading Consumer Culture on the Net" exercise should allow your students to have some fun in interpreting the mythology of American consumerism. You can ask your students to explore home-shopping networks and auction Web sites either individually or in small groups; they can visit the addresses suggested in the exercise, but by all means invite them to explore other sites as well. Students may not be instinctively analytical when visiting these sites because shopping is such a common behavior; you might prepare them by asking them to look at the products advertised (are they necessities? luxuries?), the images used to make those products seem desirable, and, particularly, the target market (typically women). If you ask your whole class to complete this exercise, try assigning small groups a different site and then ask your students to compare their findings in class. One final note: this exercise works perfectly with the Anne Norton selection.

The chapter covers a range of consumer objects and behaviors, and if pressed for time you could focus on the ones you feel your students could easily relate to. The selections by Laurence Shames and by John de Graaf, David Wann, and Thomas H. Naylor provide a general framework for analyzing consumerism — the former relates American frontier history to our desire for more goods and services, while the latter sees Americans as pathologically addicted to shopping. For two selections that focus more particularly on consumers' behavior, assign Anne Norton, who argues that shopping malls and catalogues operate as sign systems designed to stimulate consumption, and Rachel Bowlby, who analyzes the shopping experience as a binary set of images (nightmare versus liberation). A suite of four selections addresses different categories of consumer objects — objects that are all semiotically rich in significance. Thomas Hine studies a part of everyday life that's often overlooked in academic study — the semiotics of packages — while Fred Davis turns his attention to the packaging used to adorn our bodies, clothing; his focus on blue jeans should appeal to students of any demographic group. Joan Kron analyzes how home decor works as a sign of personal and group identity, and David Goewey examines the current taste for SUVs as an indicator of a cultural ethos. We conclude the chapter with a broader, more international perspective on American consumer culture: Damien Cave looks at the way marketers have turned terrorism, and Americans' renewed patriotism after September 11, into a source of profit; Benjamin R. Barber compares global capitalism and jihadic fanaticism; and Thomas L. Friedman reflects on the concerns often expressed on college campuses about globalization and the supposed Americanization of international culture. It's important for students to realize, we believe, that consumerism is not just about shopping and buying; it has serious implications for economic and political stability throughout the world, as the September 11 attacks so dramatically revealed.

LAURENCE SHAMES
THE MORE FACTOR (p. 56)

Shames attacks a cherished American myth — that the United States is a land of endless opportunity — so be prepared for some real opposition to his thesis. Because many students are attending college precisely so that they can expand their opportunities, they hardly want to hear that their hunger for more may not be nourished. Their response may also be complicated if they are recent immigrants whose lives have been directly shaped by this myth. In class, you may want to focus initially on the first part of Shames's essay, his discussion of the frontier myth of limitless opportunity. Your students are likely to be familiar with this myth from popular media; they could brainstorm examples of TV shows and films that perpetuate this myth. You might ask them to analyze as well the "Just What Do You Do All Day?" photo on page 70. Appearing first in a 1947 edition of *Life* magazine, the photo presents "the material record of one homemaker's weekly toil," thus making an interesting equivalence between domestic labor and consumption. Then move to the more troubling of Shames's assertions, his claim that America is "running out of more." This selection was published in 1989, so you could ask your class whether the current recession and drop in the stock market have altered the "hunger for more." If you have adults in your class, try sparking a debate between them and their younger counterparts, who may have had less experience in the working world. Politically conservative students might object that Shames questions the efficacy of a free- market economy, and they'd be right: it's just that Shames would see the free-market ideology as problematic. The essay could also be complicated by introducing issues of race and gender; the opportunities Shames describes have not always been equally available to everyone in our society.

The selection is particularly good for teaching critical reading and summarizing skills. The three Reading the Text questions ask students to identify some of the key concepts in Shames's essay; you could use these exercises to gauge quickly how well your students have grasped Shames's ideas. The first Reading the Signs question asks students to extend Shames's thesis into the twenty-first century; you might invite students to generate evidence both from personal experience and observation and from current political events. Because question 2 points to what is perhaps Shames's most controversial claim — that ethical standards have been destroyed by the hunger for more — it's ideal for staging an in-class debate. In preparing for a debate, students will need to anticipate counterarguments and develop specific evidence; be sure to allot sufficient class time for them to do this in groups. You may also want to combine a debate with a discussion of library research techniques (students could investigate, for instance, some of the recent scandals surrounding Enron and Arthur Andersen). Question 2, of course, could be adapted to an at-home essay as well. The remaining questions ask students to relate Shames's selection to other issues raised in the text. Question 3 is straightforward, asking students to apply Shames's argument to the Kron essay found in this chapter. Question 4 is more challenging and open-ended, for it asks students whether gangs share the hunger for more and thus can be considered typically American. You might ask students first to explore in their journal their assumptions about gang members; those assumptions are likely to shape their responses. Although often seen as countercultural groups, gangs also display a strong sense of territory and acquire consumer objects, particularly clothing, as badges of identity — characteristics that, in Shames's terms, can be seen as evidence of a desire for more.

ANNE NORTON
THE SIGNS OF SHOPPING (p. 63)

You can have a lot of fun with Norton's essay: it's a rich analysis of something most people take for granted — shopping malls and catalogues. The article begins in a somewhat dense academic style, but that style diminishes as the article progresses. Whatever your students' economic background, you can assume they're familiar with some sort of mall and occasionally peruse catalogues. Norton's selection works well early in a term, for it provides a wonderful opportunity for combining discussion of personal experience with an analytic interpretation of an accessible topic. Some students may resist Norton's claim that one's behavior can be so thoroughly manipulated by marketers, but ask them to consider specific examples that are close to their own experiences. Why do Victoria's Secret shops feature gilded and lacy touches? What's the image projected by that slick Gap storefront? Your students may balk at Norton's suggestion that malls appeal to women's desire for independence and escape from home; ask them to test her assertion empirically by performing a rough demographic survey at a local mall. What do their results suggest about the gender patterns in malls?

The Reading the Text questions will enable you to see if students grasp Norton's central concepts or if they have difficulty with her occasionally academic style; they will also reveal if your students hesitate to accept her premise that an everyday activity such as shopping can be constrained by political ideologies and cultural mythologies. If they do resist this premise, ask them whether they respond differently when visiting, say, a Banana Republic outlet and a Target store — and why. In varying ways, the Reading the Signs questions ask students to apply or extend Norton's argument about shopping. Question 1 asks them to apply Norton's claims to window displays in a local mall; this question works especially well if they study the displays of at least two shops, preferably shops intended for the same market. Question 2 should trigger a great in-class discussion, with students comparing catalogues in small groups. (For variety, you might bring in some catalogues you receive; expect many students to bring in Victoria's Secret or Abercrombie and Fitch.) Question 5 is an at-home companion question that invites students to analyze closely one catalogue. For questions 2 and 5, encourage your students to focus on details. Why does the L. L. Bean catalogue include a golden retriever, not a rottweiler? Question 3 is ambitious, for it invites students to test Norton's gender-based argument by interviewing women of different ages. For this question, you might first want to discuss interviewing strategies — and the importance of interpreting an interviewee's comments. Questions 4 and 6 turn to the Internet, with 4 asking students to study the Home Shopping Network and 6 focusing their attention on a commercial Web site.

JOHN DE GRAAF, DAVID WANN, AND THOMAS H. NAYLOR
THE ADDICTIVE VIRUS (p. 71)

A brief and accessible selection, "The Addictive Virus" presents a slightly audacious but nonetheless compelling argument about Americans' "addiction" to shopping. Students can have fun with this piece. You might jump-start class discussion by asking students about their own behaviors as shoppers: Do they ever feel a "high" after a successful shopping trip? Do they develop "heightened sensations" while at a mall? Do they find themselves building what the authors call "personal fortresses" with their purchases? (Before discussing the article, consider assigning Reading the Signs question 2, which invites a journal entry in which students reflect on their own purchases.) To prompt honest responses, encourage students to think about product categories that mean something to them. Some students might initially balk at the notion of being addicted to shopping but then reconsider when they think about all the computer gadgets and upgrades that they constantly buy. Others may not care about technology but go ga-ga when visiting a store such as Aahs! that sells an endless array of trinkets, cute knick-knacks and stuffed toys, cards, and even some soft-porn doo-dads. For a lively class activity, try the exercise suggested in Reading the Signs question 3, which has the class brainstorm lists of products they have bought recently, then assess the lists for signs of addictive buying. We suggest this exercise so students can gain a collective sense of their shopping behavior and not be limited by their individual habits. You should discuss as well the authors' tone, which is sprightly, a bit tongue-in-cheek (to wit: "We're all crazy!"). How does the tone affect students' response to the article's argument?

After discussing shopping behavior, you can move to the authors' more debatable point, their analogy between "affluenza" and physical addictions. Expect students to accept shopping addiction with a small *a*; in other words, they may agree that it can be a compulsive, emotionally satisfying experience but disagree with the authors' analogy with conditions such as alcoholism and addictive gambling. This analogy is the focus of Reading the Signs question 4, which prompts students to evaluate the logical validity of this analogy. We suggest that students consult a medical encyclopedia for a definition of *addiction*; we're sure they understand that, although addiction is commonly seen as an abuse of a physical substance (alcohol, drugs), some behaviors can also be considered clinically as addictive (gambling). For a challenging essay assignment, try question 1, which asks students to compare Laurence Shames's concept of the "more factor" with the "never enough" principle described in "The Addictive Virus." Alternately, you could ask students to critique the two articles' presentations of fundamentally similar concepts. How do the authors' rather different styles, attempts at contextualizing the issues, and evidence affect the relative persuasiveness of their arguments?

RACHEL BOWLBY

The Haunted Superstore (p. 76)

Bowlby's selection can serve as a useful companion to "The Addictive Virus," for while she acknowledges that shopping trips can be addictive, she complicates that depiction by analyzing shopping trips as sets of opposing experiences, nightmare versus liberation. But you may want to take some time working through this selection in class, because Bowlby's discussion tends to meander and the selection lacks an up-front statement of thesis. Indeed, you might sketch on the board a chart of the several sets of binary oppositions that, she claims, share a parallel logic. She starts by describing a visit to an IKEA that encapsulates her binary opposition: with the computers down, customers who formerly enjoyed the thrill of fulfilling material desires feel trapped and imprisoned. This binary opposition, Bowlby suggests, extends to images of shoppers that are perpetuated by marketers and that affect our behavior as consumers. Ask your students about these two images: the methodical, rational shopper and the more impulsive shopper who is susceptible to marketing ploys. To what extent are store designs geared for one or the other? In which category do students locate themselves? (To prepare students to answer this question, assign in advance of your class discussion Reading the Signs question 1.) Is the first kind of shopper really less vulnerable to marketing ploys, or is that perception, in itself, a form of flattery designed to encourage one to buy? Are they really distinct images? (Bowlby herself claims that an individual shopper can easily assume both identities depending on the circumstance.) You then should move to a parallel set of opposites, Bowlby's distinction between the department store (which she links to leisure, luxury, pleasure) and the supermarket (which is related to functionality, work, even entrapment). To make her discussion more concrete, you might look at magazines from several decades ago and examine the advertising: How are the two sorts of stores presented? What images are attached to them, and how do those images promote different patterns of consumption? We find her oppositions to be most interesting, and persuasive, in her concluding discussion of IKEA as a combination of the two forms of stores. Ask your students if they, too, have experienced both "leisure" and "work" in an IKEA. If no IKEA is located in your area, you can ask them about their experiences in a local shopping mall. To what extent is the mall set up to appeal both to pleasure and to function?

A basic analysis assignment, Reading the Signs question 2 asks students to assess Bowlby's view of shopping as a series of binary oppositions; you should encourage students to generate evidence drawn from specific stores that they have frequented. For assignments based on field observations, consider question 3, which has students visit and analyze a department store, or question 5, which asks them to visit an IKEA. If your class is emphasizing gender issues, you'll be interested in question 4, which asks students to assess Bowlby's contention that the image of the consumer is no longer exclusively female. For evidence, students could study media examples (magazine and television advertising would provide lots to analyze) and in-store and in-mall displays.

THOMAS HINE

WHAT'S IN A PACKAGE (p. 84)

At first students may view packages as purely functional: we need them to hold toothpaste, or deodorant, or whatever. But Hine should open their eyes to the images packages create for their products. His selection is easy to read, and students are likely to be persuaded by his discussion both of the marketing decision-making behind package design (why are billions spent on packaging, anyway?) and of the cultural differences in packaging. Ask your students about trends in packaging design. Why, for instance, is Oral-B dental floss now sold in a translucent aqua package reminiscent of an iMac? Why does Pepsi seem to change its cans every few months? Whether or not your students accept Hine's notions, you can plan a great session by assigning Reading the Signs question 1, which asks students to bring a product to class. We've suggested that students all bring items from the same product category to allow for comparison of design choices. As an alternative, you might identify four or five categories and have small groups of students sign up for each. If you ask students to give brief presentations of their object, be sure to give them a strict time limit (probably just a few minutes), or else some students may not to have a chance to present. Questions 2 and 4 are similar in that they invite students to analyze the packaging of one retail outlet (with the latter question specifying an outlet with an explicit political theme). You can stage in-class activities similar to those called for in question 1 by asking your students to bring to class samples of the packaging from their store. Questions 3 and 5 relate the issue to students' own consuming behaviors. Number 3 calls for a journal entry on the appeal of packaging, while 5 asks students to interpret, through a stranger's eyes, the packages visible in their own home. Joan Kron's essay in this chapter is a natural complement to Hine's selection and can help students respond to this question.

FRED DAVIS
BLUE JEANS (p. 93)

You'll probably find that students accept the notion that clothing is a sign system: Just ask them about the different meanings clothing can have in the context of the office or school — or a date at a club. Were any styles banned from their high school, and if so, why? What did the forbidden styles mean to students and to parents and administrators? Fred Davis focuses on one of the most ubiquitous articles of clothing in American culture: blue jeans. Davis's selection is accessible, but be sure students don't overlook his central argument that jeans have occupied two contradictory sets of symbolic significance in American society: values that he terms "democratic" and "left" wing compared to values he dubs "dedemocratizing" and "right" wing. Note that this distinction is roughly parallel to that articulated in Jack Solomon's selection in Chapter Two, a nice companion piece to the Davis essay.

    Students will enjoy Reading the Signs question 1, which asks them to bring a current fashion magazine to class, but be forewarned that they may have some difficulty applying the democratizing/dedemocratizing concepts. To help them, you might start with an issue of *Vogue*, which is likely to contain many examples of high fashion, and then move to the other magazines that your students bring to class. Question 2 calls for an update of Davis's essay through an analysis of current trends in the blue jean industry; students should take into account the current taste for ultra-faded, bizarrely cut jeans that seem to outdo each other in looking dirty. Question 3 is ideal if you are emphasizing the semiotic method, for it asks students to weigh the relative value of function and cultural significance in clothing choices. The last two questions invite students to study real people's fashion tastes, with 4 calling for a journal entry in which students reflect on their own preferences and 5 asking them to interpret the styles predominant on your campus (this last question could work nicely as a group project).

JOAN KRON
THE SEMIOTICS OF HOME DECOR (p. 101)

We consider Kron's essay one of the best in the chapter, both for its clear, lively writing and for its insightful exploration of how home decor works as a sign of one's identity. And students respond positively to her argument. Like most people, they probably have never considered the issues she raises but are quick to recognize the validity of her claims. Students may quarrel with Kron's implied criticism of materialism in our lives — especially if they stop reading after the Martin J. Davidson anecdote — but be sure they notice that she does not limit her discussion to American culture and that she is not entirely critical of people's use of objects and decor as a symbol system. Indeed, Kron believes that the use of material symbols and signs is intrinsically human. If your class includes students from a variety of ethnicities or nationalities, you might ask them to do a sort of cross-cultural survey of domestic decor and furnishings to see how different cultures make, in Kron's terms, "distinctions between ourselves and others."

This essay lends itself to questions and exercises that invite students to use personal experience; Reading the Signs questions 1, 2, and 4 all do this in various ways. Question 3 invites students to argue with or modify one of Kron's more extreme claims, that "To put no personal stamp on a home is almost pathological in our culture." The last question may be the most challenging. It directs students to Karen Karbo's "The Dining Room" in Chapter Five; the link between Kron's and Karbo's selections involves the way possessions can serve as signs of relationships, and you'll want to be sure your class discusses that topic.

DAVID GOEWEY

"CAREFUL, YOU MAY RUN OUT OF PLANET": SUVs AND THE EXPLOITATION OF THE AMERICAN MYTH (p. 112)

If you're emphasizing a semiotic approach, this selection is a sure bet for your syllabus, for Goewey provides a model semiotic reading of the most popular current trend in the automotive world. Not only does Goewey discuss the broad cultural significance of SUVs, but he clearly and effectively outlines the larger system in which they appear. A profitable class exercise would be to dissect Goewey's methodology — and to study the ways in which his inclusion of abundant specific details works to make his argument both vivid and logical. Even if you're not using semiotics explicitly, this selection is likely to trigger a lively response from students. Although some may balk at Goewey's historical analysis, few would claim that image and cultural association have nothing to do with one's automotive preferences. Ask your students: What sorts of vehicle would they like to be seen driving, and why? Why is it that some people identify totally with their cars? Note that, in its discussion of American frontier myth, this selection pairs well with the Laurence Shames selection in this chapter.

This selection is ideal for both personal and analytic assignments. A journal entry topic, Reading the Signs question 1 invites students to interpret the significance of their own car (or that of an acquaintance); this topic could be suitable for a personal essay as well. For straightforward analytic topics, consider question 2, which calls for a Goewey-style analysis of a different category of vehicles (sporty two-seaters, pick-up trucks, retro cars like the PT Cruiser, and luxury sedans all would be good choices because they have clearly recognizable cultural associations), or question 3, which sends students to automobile advertising for signs of the values and ideologies associated with particular car models. In working with students on such assignments, you'll want to make sure they see beyond the functional appeal of a particular vehicle (for example, an ad's performance claims) to the values the ad connotes. For an argumentative assignment, assign question 4, which suggests that students use interview evidence as support in a response to Goewey's thesis about the motivations behind SUV ownership.

DAMIEN CAVE

THE SPAM SPOILS OF WAR (p. 122)

You'll want to make sure students grasp the more significant points made in this very accessible article. Cave describes the flood of post–September 11 merchandise, from flags to terrorist hex dolls, and the ludicrousness of some of these products makes it easy to dismiss the phenomenon as just another cheap way to make a buck (see as well the political cartoon on p. 000). And although it's certainly fair to do that, you'll want your students to grasp Cave's more profound claim that the rush to produce and buy war-related merchandise is "quintessentially American." Ask your students to debate this point; for help in outlining the American consumerist psyche, suggest that they consult Laurence Shames's "The More Factor." In addition, they might interview people who, long after the attacks, continue to sport flag-related paraphernalia and ask them about their motivations and desires; see Reading the Signs question 3, an essay topic that could also serve as an in-class debate. Another debate topic is suggested by question 1, which addresses the proposal that patriotic scamming should be a crime. If you assign this topic, expect lots of discussion of the relative values of the right to free speech, the need for national security, and simple decency and good taste. To update Cave's references and argument, you could assign question 2, which sends students to the Internet to discover the current availability of post–9/11 products. Encourage your students not simply to report on their findings but to analyze them as well. What do their results say about the current national mood? What recent political and social events may explain any changes that they discover?

BENJAMIN R. BARBER

JIHAD VS. McWORLD (p. 126)

The global dimensions of American popular culture have become increasingly apparent in recent years, with works like George Ritzer's *The McDonaldization Thesis* (1998) exploring the profound influence of American-style consumer culture within and beyond our own borders. In the aftermath of the September 11, 2001, attacks, Benjamin R. Barber's pioneering analysis of some of the ramifications of this influence have assumed a special urgency, and your students should respond with great interest to his observations. Be sure that they understand that Barber critiques rather than endorses the common tendency to see international politics in the form of a simple us-versus-them dichotomy, a war between tribalism and technological modernity, for though he does introduce such a polarity into his discussion (especially through his provocative title), his point is to complicate, not propound, it. You might begin class discussion by asking students to describe in their own words what Barber dubs "jihad" and "McWorld"; this is an important first step because, although Barber's terms can refer to Islamist fundamentalism and to the McDonalds chain, they encompass much more than that. Indeed, the terms refer to a whole constellation of values, attitudes, and cultural practices, which, though typically seen as oppositional, are, according to Barber, interdependent and share an essentially antidemocratic core. This point is one you may need to spend some time reviewing with your students, because Barber's presentation of it is general and theoretical, not grounded in specifics. You can expect that most students would more easily grasp how jihad can be antidemocratic (they may know, for instance, that countries such as Iran and Saudi Arabia are run by repressive regimes, and the war in Afghanistan spurred a flood of new stories about that nation's tyranny), but some students may be puzzled by the claim that McWorld is antidemocratic as well. To illustrate how the marketing and advertising forces of modern capitalism can also have an antidemocratic effect, assign James B. Twitchell's "What We Are to Advertisers" (p. 205) as a companion piece.

Barber alludes briefly to some instances of corporate America's global reach, but some students may not be that familiar with this phenomenon. You might draw their attention to the photo of Muslim women using computers on p. 130 and to the photo of the Lahore, Pakistan, street scene on p. 135. In addition, students might do some Internet research on globalization; in June, 2002, for instance, the McDonalds Web site (**www.mcdonalds.com**) boasted outlets in 121 countries, with a link to each country that promotes how the host nation benefits from all those golden arches. Indeed, this Web site can be studied rhetorically, because it definitely shows signs of defensiveness about engaging in cultural domination (students should keep in mind that the Web site is a marketing device, and so corporate claims should be read critically). Should students want an alternative perspective, they can consult **www.mcspotlight.org,** which claims it's the most popular anti-McDonalds group in the world.

Barber's selection lends itself to thought-provoking assignments. Reading the Signs question 1 is straightforward but challenging: it asks students to view Barber's argument in the light of the September 11, 2001, attacks. Question 2 has students take on the question of whether globalization benefits the rest of the world (Web sites such as the two mentioned in the previous paragraph can provide students with specific evidence), and question 3 turns the issue around, asking students to consider the effect of other nations' popular culture on American culture. Perhaps the most heated issues are raised by question 4, which has the class stage a debate over the causes of jihadic hostility toward McWorld. To defuse possible tensions in class, we suggest that you assign students to groups arbitrarily, so it's clear that individuals are not necessarily arguing their heart and soul. For a textual analysis assignment, try question 5, which calls for a comparison and contrast between Barber's essay and Thomas L. Friedman's "Revolution Is U.S." (p. 132), an article that addresses similar issues but that has marked tonal and rhetorical differences than the Barber piece.

THOMAS L. FRIEDMAN
REVOLUTION IS U.S. (p. 132)

With its focus on globalization, Friedman's selection makes a handy companion piece to Benjamin R. Barber's "Jihad vs. McWorld," but it's hardly a repeat. Friedman draws his own distinction between globalization, which once had a nationally complex dynamic, and Americanization, which is unidirectional. (You might look at the photo of the Lahore, Pakistan, street on p. 135 in this regard, for it illustrates simultaneously old globalization, in the Imperial Book Depot, and the new Americanization, in the Coca-Cola advertisement.) Because of various political changes, such as the end of the cold war, that distinction is rapidly fading, with Americanization supplanting globalization. Indeed, for Friedman, what's significant is not simply the influence of American corporations across the world but the inevitable exportation of American cultural values and ideologies that are carried by those corporations. That's why he opens with his "five gas stations theory of the world," an amusing analogy that rather wickedly caricatures the cultural values and social practices inherent in five different economic systems. You might start your discussion here, asking students first to outline, perhaps on the board, those economies and the values and practices common to each. (We enjoy Friedman's sardonic humor here, but some students may object that he is stereotyping cultural patterns. If they do, that's a good opportunity to address the relationship between stereotypes and generalizations and to discuss Friedman's rhetorical strategy in beginning with this rather flamboyant "theory." And such students might enjoy responding to Reading the Signs question 4, which invites them to assess the validity of Friedman's theory.) Then move to his larger concerns about how the tendency to adopt American practices essentially violates "social contracts" (para. 4) that are very different than our own. What are the consequences of this tendency? What does Friedman's anecdote about an Israeli youth's desire for a McDonalds' autograph from former U.S. Ambassador Martin Indyk say about the love-hate response to American culture?

Like the Barber selection, the Friedman essay is ripe for thought-provoking assignments. Reading the Signs question 1 has the class debate the extent to which America is responsible for globalization. We suggest that students interview international students about American corporate impact in their home countries; in addition, they might consult the Barber selection in this chapter and the Marnie Carroll piece in Chapter Three. Question 2 shifts the perspective and asks students to evaluate the benefits of globalization to America. Encourage them to consider both apparent advantages (more markets in which to peddle goods) and disadvantages (job loss for American workers). The last two questions allow students to take issue with or support Friedman, with number 3 focusing on a claim he makes about American values and 4 addressing his five gas stations theory of the world.

Chapter Two
BROUGHT TO YOU B(U)Y
The Signs of Advertising

Advertising has long been a favorite topic in composition classes, and with good reason. Students can write critically about visual texts that affect their everyday lives and that therefore may seem more accessible than written texts. In this chapter, we hope to enable students to go beyond the usual evaluative criticism of advertising to an assessment of how ads not only reflect but shape American society. We've chosen readings that do not simply interpret ads but that address the ways advertising uses the fundamental myths of American culture to shape a consumerist ideology. It's unlikely that students have encountered such a perspective in high school (where they may also have discussed advertising), so you can look forward to introducing them to a fresh angle on the subject. If you're emphasizing a semiotic approach, we strongly recommend including this chapter in your syllabus, for ads are a natural for semiotic analysis. If you're skirting the semiotics, you can still use these selections, for they can trigger careful, close readings of advertising texts no matter what the methodology. We've seen that students take to analyzing advertising quite readily, so you should encounter little or no resistance to this topic. Indeed, you and your class should have some fun with it!

Your students will need little preparation for discussing advertising, but because it's such a familiar part of their lives, they may need some guidance in talking critically and precisely about it. Providing such guidance is the aim of the Discussing the Signs of Advertising exercise, which asks that students each bring an ad to class and discuss their interpretations of it in small groups. You may want to review first the follow-up questions in the exercise, for they are intended to help students move beyond evaluative judgments to a critical analysis of how ads work. We suggest that, as students discuss their ads, you move from group to group, pushing them to be ever more precise and analytic. If you have time, ask each group to select one ad and present their interpretation to the whole class. The Exploring the Signs of Advertising exercise stimulates students' critical thinking in a different way: it asks them to create their own alternative ad and then assess their creation. Putting students in the advertisers' seat, we hope, will enable them to see how the complex rhetoric of advertising is constituted. It would work best if you suggest that students redesign an ad they don't like because of its ideology. We don't see it as a problem if students have trouble coming up with a new design, for they could then reflect on the tenacious power advertising images have on our imaginations and worldviews. We've made this a journal topic, but it certainly could be a more formal assignment. The Reading Advertising on the Net exercise asks students to visit *Advertising Age's* Web site for its compendium of Super Bowl ads. This question is meant to inspire consideration of how advertising has become a source of entertainment in its own right; after all, many a viewer turns on the Super Bowl to check out the ads, not the football game, and many ads, such as 2002's Britney Spears Pepsi ad, come with their own pre-broadcast media hype. If your students do not all have access to the Internet, try downloading the text and images for class discussion.

Here are a few tips on constructing assignments involving advertising. Be sure to require students to attach copies of print ads they may be interpreting to their essays; otherwise, you'll have trouble evaluating their work. Students can benefit if, early in the drafting stage, you review a few simple, precise terms. Words such as *copy* and *layout* would enable students to avoid such clunky phrasing as "the words that appear in the advertisement" or "the way the images are arranged in the ad."

　　　This chapter approaches advertising from a wide range of perspectives. Several selections take a broad view, and we recommend that you include at least one of them in your syllabus. Roland Marchand is essential for a historical sense of how the mythologies exploited by American advertising have evolved, Jack Solomon argues that a fundamental American ideology is revealed in advertising's paradoxical adoption of elitist and populist appeals, and John E. Calfee offers an alternative voice that defends the advertising industry. We include inside looks at how the advertising business operates: Gloria Steinem exposes the surprisingly cozy relationship between advertising and journalism in the magazine industry, and James B. Twitchell reveals how marketers categorize and stereotype consumers. Two selections focus on particular consumer groups: Diane Barthel addresses male-oriented advertising, and Eric Schlosser studies the strategies used to get kids to want more goodies. The final reading, by Kalle Lasn, laments the ubiquity of advertising in our lives; closing the chapter, the Portfolio of Ads presents sample ads that you could use for class discussion or essay assignments. If you plan to use just a few selections, many of them pair up well with other chapters and themes. If your course focuses on gender, the Diane Barthel and the Gloria Steinem essays are essential readings. The Marchand, Solomon, and Schlosser pieces complement Chapter One, "Consuming Passions." If you're interested in critiquing the behind-the-scenes techniques used to stimulate consumer desire, Schlosser, Steinem, and Twitchell can be read in conjunction with Malcolm Gladwell in Chapter Five.

ROLAND MARCHAND

THE PARABLE OF THE DEMOCRACY OF GOODS (p. 150)

Students can't help but be experts in advertising, for they're surrounded by it in their daily lives, but they may know little about advertising's early history. The Marchand selection provides some of this history, but it's not just background: Marchand reveals the surprising continuity of ploys used from advertising's infancy to today. Although early advertising looks dated and old-fashioned — often amusingly so — the images it projects and the myths it exploits are still around. One way to make sure that your students understand what Marchand means by the "democracy of goods" and the "democracy of afflictions" (the point of the first two Reading the Text questions) is to compare the 1920s ads he discusses with their present-day descendents. Today ads peddling everything from Internet access to wine suggest that you, too, can live the good life, and ads promoting personal care products still invoke the democracy of afflictions (even the wealthiest eligible bachelor can have dandruff). To prepare your students for class discussion, ask them to bring some modern candidates to class (see Reading the Signs question 2); you'll want to be sure to discuss how the ads' use of these myths may have changed since the 1920s and what those changes reveal about American values and culture.

　　　Reading the Signs question 5 asks students to apply Marchand's ideas to the Devoe paint ad on p. 157, while questions 2 and 3 ask them to do the same with ads they themselves have collected; they should have little difficulty with such assignments. You might preface such an assignment with an in-class discussion of the Pyrene fire extinguisher ad on p. 159; be sure students note who the "you" in the ad's title refers to. Questions 1 and 4 are more challenging because they ask students to grapple with more abstract concepts. To prepare students for them, you might first brainstorm in class (either in whole group or in small group discussion) possible responses and, particularly, possible specific evidence students can bring to bear on the topics.

JACK SOLOMON

MASTERS OF DESIRE: THE CULTURE OF AMERICAN ADVERTISING (p. 160)

This selection is particularly useful for its examination of the mythologies underlying American advertising; if you're emphasizing semiotics, it's a must. Solomon identifies two basic appeals used in advertising — the populist and the elitist appeals — and illustrates them with abundant specific examples. You should find that students easily grasp the clear paradox that Solomon outlines; for that reason, this reading is ideal for analytic essays in which students apply this paradox to advertising that they have selected. If your students complain that some of the ads are dated (this essay was first published in 1988), challenge them to come up with their own examples (the task required by Reading the Signs question 1). We've noticed that these appeals are most commonly used in media that target a wide audience (not surprisingly, since such an audience is more likely to hold mainstream American values); a twist to this question would ask students to compare ads in general interest magazines and those intended for more specialized readerships. Reading the Signs question 2 shifts from print to electronic media, asking students to analyze the advertising that accompanies a popular TV show in terms of its vision of the American dream. If you're encouraging your students to take a historical view, assign question 3, which asks them to compare advertising appeals from earlier decades with those used today. As you explain this topic to your students, be sure to encourage them to go beyond describing the differences and similarities they see to analyzing the values and mythologies that underly the ads. A broader issue is addressed in question 4, which asks the class to brainstorm a list of status symbols and then study the nature of their appeals; this topic would make a successful essay assignment as well. Perhaps the most challenging question is number 5, which asks students to argue whether the populist/elitist paradox still affects American media. For this one, you might suggest that students work inductively — that is, they should study particular media examples first, then arrive at an argument — for what they discover may be surprising.

DIANE BARTHEL

A GENTLEMAN AND A CONSUMER (p. 171)

Gender too often is construed as a "women's issue," and to combat that misconception we include Barthel's essay. While occasionally addressing the gender roles that advertising imposes on women, Barthel concentrates on the images that ads encourage men to emulate. If your class is focusing on gender issues, Barthel's selection is a must. Expect her essay to stimulate a lively discussion: students probably will accept her readings of individual ads, but some may resist her larger argument about gender roles. Borrowing from Baudrillard (don't worry — she keeps the diction accessible), Barthel speaks of the "feminine" and "masculine" modes, concepts that warrant some class review. You'll want to make sure students understand that when she says "the feminine model is based on passivity," for instance, she's talking about social norms, not biological necessity (see the first Reading the Text question). Her striking conclusion, that men increasingly are allowed to adopt both modes in advertising and in life, is good debate fodder. In fact, we recommend that you encourage debate by, for instance, dividing your class into teams debating the validity of Barthel's conclusion and asking each team to collect evidence from magazines to support their position. As part of the debate, students could present their own interpretations of ads.

Students should both enjoy and be challenged by the Reading the Signs questions. Perhaps the most straightforward questions are number 1, which asks students to test Barthel's claims against a current men's magazine; number 2, which focuses more narrowly on Barthel's views of car advertising; and number 3, which asks them to analyze the gender roles in a magazine designed for either men or women. We've made the latter question a small-group exercise, where you can take advantage of gender dynamics by forming same-sex groups; if you have time, have each group report their conclusions to the whole class, and then interpret any gender-based patterns in the groups' reports. Question 4 sends students to Holly Devor's "Gender Role Behaviors and Attitudes" (Chapter Six) to extend or reflect on Barthel's argument; students should be able to detect direct links between the essays. Finally, question 5 is deliberately speculative, intended to suggest the power advertising has on our understanding of an issue as basic as gender. It would work well either before or after you've discussed the essay.

If you like to include audiovisual material in your course, a dated but still relevant film titled *Killing Us Softly* (1979) is an ideal companion to the Barthel essay. Addressing the ways women function as signs (of sexuality, passivity, even stupidity) in advertising, this film shows lots of sample ads and delivers a lively, accurate interpretation of them. It's never failed to trigger a strong response from our students, and you can compensate for its age by asking students to test its claims on current advertising. A sequel, *Killing Us Softly Again* (1987), is also available, though it's similar to the first; it's worth checking to see if your school's film library has either film.

ERIC SCHLOSSER

KID KUSTOMERS (p. 181)

Students often assume that they are impervious to advertising, because they cherish a self-perception of being logical, independent-minded consumers. And thus they sometimes dismiss as much ado about nothing critiques of advertising, such as the one by Kalle Lasn in this chapter, that skewer the industry. But Schlosser's exposé of the techniques marketers use to attract children may give them pause, especially his discussion of "pester power" and the use of focus groups as young as two or three that are intended to provide insight into children's tastes. Ask your students about the ethical implications of such strategies. What are the implications of encouraging kids to manipulate their parents so that Mom and Dad buy the latest toy or video game? What values are advertisers implicitly inspiring in children? Should two-year-olds be considered the same as adult participants in a focus group? An interesting class project could have small groups visit Web sites for children's clubs or product lines designed for children; students should study both the pitches and claims for the products and the extent to which the sites ask users for personal information (indeed, it would be revealing if students discover Web sites that violate the Children's Online Privacy Protection Act). Be sure to extend your discussion to some of the larger ramifications of hard-sell advertising to kids. What are advertisers teaching children about the value of material goods? Do students see any connection between such advertising practices and the "addiction to stuff" described in "The Addictive Virus" (Chapter One)? As you discuss these matters, keep in mind that, as Schlosser points out, children's advertising exploded during the 1980s — precisely the decade when eighteen- and nineteen-year-olds were themselves kids. Ask your students to recall their own experiences: Did they use "pester power"? Did their parents impose restrictions on their consuming behavior? What was their attitude toward consumption at the time, and how does it compare to their current attitudes and behavior as consumers?

It's a natural to ask students to analyze children's advertising based on this selection. Reading the Signs question 1 asks students to analyze the advertising that accompanies Saturday cartoon shows, encouraging them to see the relationship between the advertising and the shows (you'll find that often the two are indistinguishable). For a more focused analysis, number 2 limits students to interpreting a single ad. As is likely to emerge in class discussion, children's advertising, especially in its more manipulative forms, often triggers calls for more regulation to protect these youngest (and most vulnerable) of consumers. Question 3 has the class debate whether such regulation is warranted; we suggest that teams work energetically to amass examples from print and broadcast media and from the Internet and to use them as evidence for their position. Implicit in Schlosser's discussion is an approach to market research that parallels the techniques described by James B. Twitchell in "What We Are to Advertisers." Perhaps the most challenging question, number 4 asks students whether Twitchell's claim that marketing relies on mass stereotypes applies to children. We say this question may be challenging because we've seen that kid's advertising often appeals to a sense of individualism — "You're special!" — and students need to be skeptical when such claims go out to millions of kids.

GLORIA STEINEM

Sex, Lies, and Advertising (p. 186)

No, we didn't include this selection just for its great title! This is a long essay, but a must for any class that addresses either advertising or gender issues. Steinem exposes the compromises magazines — particularly women's magazines — must make when soliciting advertising. Forget about freedom of the press: the advertising industry makes tremendous demands related not only to its ads, as one might expect, but to editorial content as well. And Steinem documents these demands thoroughly. Some of our students have been shocked by this essay, claiming that their eyes have been opened to a practice they never realized existed. Some, insulted at being conned by advertising disguised as "journalism," have vowed that they'll now think twice about buying popular magazines. If you want your students to cover something fresh in your class, this essay is for you.

Note that this is an updated version of Steinem's now-classic essay. The major change is a preface, in which Steinem describes the many reactions to the original publication of "Sex, Lies, and Advertising," reactions that ranged from bitter sneering to outright celebration. You'll find this preface extremely useful for its creation of a historical context and for its documentation of actual readers' responses to a text. Be sure to notice that Steinem dubs as the "most rewarding response" the inclusion of her essay on college reading lists!

We've never had trouble generating lively discussion about the Steinem essay. Her writing is clear, concrete, and accessible, so your students should be able to handle the selection's length. A few students may be puzzled by the term "complementary copy," but you can ask their peers to help explain it. When assigning the essay, you might also ask students to look through magazines they have at home to see whether Steinem's argument about complementary copy applies to them (Reading the Signs questions 1,

2, and 3 encourage and structure such explorations). We urge you to ask your students to bring in one of their magazines and present their findings to the class. Be fore-warned that some students have trouble distinguishing between copy and advertising. That difficulty actually proves Steinem's point, but it also means that you may need to spend some time covering the difference between the two. We've found that Steinem's claims hold for most magazines — certainly for all women's magazines, but for men's and special interest magazines as well (*Car and Driver, Shape, Cat Fancy* — the list is virtually endless). It holds true the least for general-interest magazines such as *Time* and *Newsweek*, but even there you'll see some complementary copy, and students could develop Steinem's discussion of why these magazines' content seems less influenced by the ad industry. Finally, question 4 asks students to explore the First Amendment implications of Steinem's revelations. We've made it a journal topic, but it could be adapted to a formal essay assignment as well.

JAMES B. TWITCHELL

What We Are to Advertisers (p. 205)

Twitchell's selection should raise more than a few eyebrows, for he exposes the schemes that advertisers use to categorize the interests and needs of different market segments. You can initially have some fun with Twitchell, because many readers will instinctively be prompted to see where they would be slotted in the Values and Lifestyle System, a scheme marketers use to correlate consumer taste, personality profile, and financial resources so that they tailor their campaigns for their target groups. In which slots do most of your students (or their families, if they don't see themselves as having enough disposable income to find their profile) fit? Are there any patterns in the class's responses? Note that because students may have to reveal financial background, you'd do well to keep your survey informal and anonymous. (Reading the Signs question 1 has students write a journal entry in which they place themselves on the VALS chart and respond to their doing so.) But you'll want to move quickly from your testing of the VALS paradigm to the larger issues it raises. What are its limitations: Are there consumer groups that are not accounted for? VALS does not make explicit ethnicity or gender as criteria, but are ethnic and gender identities presumed? If so, what difference does that make? VALS essentially relies on stereotypes of consumer behavior. Do students see larger consequences in a multibillion-dollar industry relying heavily on narrowly drawn social stereotypes? And you should raise one counterquestion as well: As Twitchell himself acknowledges, such categorization of consumers seems to be an effective marketing tool. What does that suggest about the power of marketing campaigns not simply to get us to buy but also to adjust our behaviors, even values, to social norms?

Because Twitchell makes unambiguous claims here, students should have no problem responding to his essay. Reading the Signs question 2 allows students to address the question of whether the VALS paradigm accurately predicts consumer behavior; to generate evidence for this topic, they might conduct surveys of acquaintances' habits as consumers. Questions 3 and 4 solicit argumentative essays: number 3 invites students to analyze the values implicit in VALS itself, while the more philosophical number 4 sends them to the Eric Schlosser selection in this chapter and the Malcolm Gladwell essay in Chapter Five to argue whether the research techniques described in these selections are ethical.

JOHN E. CALFEE

How Advertising Informs to Our Benefit (p. 210)

Are you looking for a counterpoint to the generally critical view of advertising that appears elsewhere in this chapter? If so, Calfee's easy-to-read selection is for you. Treating advertising as a competitive tool in free-market capitalism, Calfee argues that ads help consumers by providing a "cascade of information" about not only products but also serious issues such as health and nutrition. Most students are likely to be skeptical of Calfee's attribution of essentially altruistic motives to advertisers. But expect some students, particularly those who resist academic criticism of the media, to embrace warmly Calfee's claims (indeed, some who resist interpreting ads may echo this essay in their claims that "advertising doesn't affect me; it just tells me about what products are out there"). If you hear this claim often, you may wish to return to our distinction between an object's *function* and its *cultural significance.* For an illuminating in-class activity, ask students to bring to class ads that they believe do inform to the consumer's benefit; break them into groups and have them evaluate the extent to which the ads offer only useful information, not alluring images or empty promises. You might have each group select the ad in their group that best matches Calfee's claims, and then discuss the group's results with the whole class (if groups have trouble selecting beneficial ads, make a point of discussing why that would be so).

Although we don't buy Calfee's claims ourselves, his selection is useful for its alternative perspective on advertising; as such, it is ideal for pro-con arguments or in-class debates. Reading the Signs question 1 calls on students to debate on Calfee's central thesis, question 3 asks them to study current health- and diet-related ads to test his claim that ads serve the public interest, and question 2 broadens the issue to advertising in general. Given Calfee's emphasis on the health-related information that advertising supposedly provides, we couldn't resist asking question 4, which suggests that students research the history of cigarette advertising. Before the 1960s, the claims for the health benefits of cigarettes were explicit — a point raised in the few lawsuits against the tobacco industry that have been successful. If you wish to ground these issues in your students' own lives, assign question 5, which has students reflect on Calfee's claim that consumers "miss advertising when they cannot get it." If you prefer to make this an essay topic, you might assign Kalle Lasn's "Hype" in this chapter as well.

KALLE LASN

Hype (p. 217)

Do you have skeptics who proclaim that advertising doesn't really have much effect on them anyway? Or that people really don't notice advertising? If you do, you'll want to assign Lasn's strident condemnation of, in his words, "the most prevalent and toxic of the mental pollutants" (para. 1). Strong words, yes, but they are why we like his piece: he offers a brief, vigorous illustration of the ubiquity of advertising in our daily lives. Expect some students to scoff at the force of his language ("toxic," "no one will be spared," "the absurdity of it all"). But you should ask students why Lasn is so vehement, and why he uses the second person so often. And you should challenge them to address his examples of ridiculous ads and their larger implications. What does the proliferation of advertising suggest about cultural values? What does it suggest about the separation of public and private space (a question raised by the ads above the urinals Lasn describes in paragraph 5)?

The clarity of Lasn's position makes for a variety of straightforward essay assignments. Because Lasn describes the inappropriate placement of ads on a college campus, we thought a productive assignment (Reading the Signs question 1) would ask students to survey their own campus for the range of advertisements and to use their results in an argument about whether on-campus ads should be restricted. Because campus ads are so common, you might brainstorm in class categories of ads, both formal and informal, that they might find, being sure to not ignore unlikely places (restrooms, elevators, water fountains). As a warm-up or a stand-alone assignment, question 4 asks students to keep an observation log that records all the different marketing devices they see in a day (this question doesn't limit students to the campus environment). You can use their results to trigger discussion of the Lasn essay and as the basis for their own essays. If you want your students to gain a historical sense of advertising's impact, assign question 3, which asks them to compare Lasn's piece with Vance Packard's exposé *The Hidden Persuaders* (New York: Pocket, 1980) — a classic unveiling of the power advertising has on our daily lives.

PORTFOLIO OF ADVERTISEMENTS *(color insert)*

We felt that it was essential to include some ads that your entire class could share. You'll find that the ads are ideal for semiotic readings, as well as for discussion of audience, purpose, and style. And they relate to some of the broader themes, such as gender, that emerge throughout *Signs of Life*. You can use the portfolio in a number of ways. It's perfect for class discussion, because every student will have the ads in his or her text and can refer easily to details. You might break the class into small groups, and have each interpret an ad of their own choosing; as the first Reading the Signs question suggests, you might have the class vote on the ads they consider most and least effective, and then discuss the significance of the results. If students find any of the ads problematic or offensive, ask them what alternative appeals they'd suggest. How would they redesign the ads?

Chapter Three
VIDEO DREAMS
Television, Music, and Cultural Forms

Your students will be the experts when you cover this chapter. We've had students claim that their arrival at full "adult" consciousness dates from August 1, 1981 (the day MTV began broadcasting). We've had students proudly assert that they've watched every episode of *The Sopranos*. And we've had students narrate with exact precision the labyrinthine plot of the most confusing *X-Files* episodes. Although not all your students will be TV junkies, many will be (or were, in their early teen years), and they may be far more familiar with current music and TV programming than you are. Take advantage of their expertise by asking them to shape your class discussion. Your students are likely to know which current shows are the best ones to consider in light of Susan Douglas's essay about women's roles on television, for instance, or they'll be able to tell you whether today's female rappers follow the trends that Tricia Rose outlines. Your job will be to steer them toward writing careful critical analyses of the shows and videos they watch and the music that they enjoy. That may not always be easy. We've found that some students identify closely with their favorite TV programs or bands, and they can resist critical discussion of them because they may feel their own tastes are under attack. (The Exploring the Signs of Music Videos questions, accordingly, allow students to explore the impact that music videos have had on them.) Be sure your students understand that asking *why* this image or this story appears in a video or TV program is not the same as evaluating their worth as individuals. Indeed, you should expect the argument against analysis that claims, "But it's just entertainment." You might respond with the central semiotic insight that nothing is innocent. In fact, media products are designed precisely to appeal to a culture's dreams and desires — that's what makes them entertaining — and what you're doing is studying the nature and social significance of such appeals. You could study the images included in the chapter introduction — a scene from the first *Survivor* (p. 227), a shot of the Simpsons watching TV (p. 233), and a photo of Madonna in performance (p. 235) — and ask them how, in different ways, the three are constructed to appeal to their audience. Are any of them "*just* entertainment"? If any students think so, they are more likely to feel that way about *The Simpsons*; you may need to remind them that the cartoon's originator, Matt Groening, began it as a self-conscious skewering of mainstream American culture. And, for light-hearted prodding to view mass entertainment critically, discuss the Calvin and Hobbes frontispiece, which is dead-on in revealing the power of TV to create iconic status when otherwise none would exist.

The Discussing the Signs of Television question is further intended to nurture such a critical approach by asking students to go beyond a show's surface appeal to ask, "What is the program really saying?" The Reading Music on the Net question has a similar goal. By asking students to explore how their favorite artists are "packaged" on the Net, the question not only prompts them to engage in some semiotic interpretation but also encourages them to see the ubiquity of promotion and image creation in American culture. In addition, you could ask your students to visit MTV's site (**http://www.mtv.com.**) and interpret what they find there.

To facilitate class discussion, you'll want to ensure that students all have seen the same videos or programs. Although more than 99 percent of American families own at least one TV set, some students might not be able to watch assigned programs, either because of work schedules or because some dorm residents don't have their own television. We highly recommend that, if your school can provide the necessary technology, you tape videos or TV programs and view them in class before analyzing them. That way, you can stop and study details or go back and watch significant scenes a second time. You'll find that useful because students won't always remember details, or the details they recall won't necessarily be the most significant ones. Don't worry about using all your class time. Videos are usually short (four or five minutes), you could focus on particular scenes in long shows, and single segments of TV programs usually provide plenty to analyze (a half-hour show typically translates into about twenty-two minutes, sans commercials). You should feel free to zap those commercials — unless, of course, you want to study the significance of what products are pitched to which audiences and how they relate to the programs they sponsor.

The chapter addresses both television and music, and if you need to cut the chapter, you might focus on one or the other. The first two selections, by Todd Davis and Steven D. Stark, offer cultural interpretations of two very popular shows (*The West Wing* and *The Oprah Winfrey Show*, respectively) and are ideal if you are emphasizing a semiotic approach. The next two selections, Susan Douglas's feminist reading of women's roles in three supposedly "enlightened" programs and Amanda Fazzone's attack on programs that supposedly "empower" women, form a gender-themed duet. Tricia Rose's analysis of female rappers could easily make this a gender-themed trio. Tad Friend's discussion of the tolerance for foul-mouthed language on TV raises serious questions about cultural values and tastes — and the conditions that make them change from decade to decade. Two selections address TV programming from a broader political perspective: Tom Shales reflects on TV's ability to respond to the September 11 attacks, and Marnie Carroll counters the common critique of American cultural imperialism by pointing out that, at least in Europe, American TV's influence isn't nearly as extensive as many American culture critics would have us believe. Rose's selection, with its focus on music, also works well with David Schiff's and Robert Hilburn's articles, which both raise questions about the common practice of ranking popular music, artists, and trends.

TODD DAVIS

THE WEST WING *IN AMERICAN CULTURE (p. 238)*

We lead the chapter with Davis's essay because it's a fine piece of cultural analysis. Davis's argument is that one of today's most popular TV shows is so popular precisely because, on one hand, it seems to address "important" issues but, on the other, it does so in nonthreatening ways. In a sense, Davis is arguing that *The West Wing* fits into a long American tradition of diluting the controversial and the pungent, of turning sharp Wensleydale cheddar into Velveeta. You'll find this a tidy, admirably clear essay: Stark raises his central question of why the show is so popular; he suggests various reasons, locating the show within both the system of "serious" TV programming and the real-life political context; he concludes with his own recommendations for improving the show. Most students should be familiar with this show, so before you assign this essay, you might ask them to freewrite on why it is so popular. Collect their freewrites; then, to stimulate discussion of the essay, ask the class to compare their freewrites with Davis's analysis: Are there points of overlap and deviation? How might students account for any differences in their responses? Then you can move to a discussion of Davis's argument, perhaps comparing *The West Wing*'s handling of political and social issues with that of other programs, such as *The Practice*. The selection also raises questions about the increasingly blurry relationship between media and reality, because the show stars a popular make-believe president at the same time that the real-life president used one of the most highly rated TV shows as part of his campaign (see the photo of George W. Bush on *The Oprah Winfrey Show*, p. 245).

Because Davis's argument is clear and direct, it provides a good analytic framework for class activities and essay assignments. Reading the Signs question 1 may be the most provocative in having students consider the blurring of reality and fantasy: it asks the class to debate Josiah Bartlett's presidency and then to hold a mock election between Bartlett and the real-life George W. Bush. If students start talking about Bartlett as if he is real, be sure to discuss that after they've held their election. A straightforward question that triggers an argumentative essay, number 2 has students evaluate Davis's central argument, while number 3 broadens the issue by asking students to assess whether American popular culture in general has the impulse to champion the banal and the bland (Sandra Tsing Loh's selection in Chapter Four and Benjamin DeMott's in Chapter Seven offer complementary arguments and could be assigned to supplement Davis). If you'd like an assignment that asks students to generate their own investigation, try question 4, which has them poll *West Wing* viewers about their response to the show and then use the results as evidence for a critique of Davis's argument. For this topic, you might have students submit survey questions to you in draft form (you'll want to warn them about leading or overly ambiguous questions); you might also discuss with them the likelihood that viewers will initially have noncritical responses ("I just like the show") and strategies for generating more revealing responses (viewers might be asked to rank their preferences for individual characters, for instance, and then students could analyze the pattern of responses they see).

STEVEN D. STARK

THE OPRAH WINFREY SHOW AND THE TALK-SHOW FUROR (p. 243)

Expect this selection to test your students' ability to separate personal tastes from analytic judgment. Though some of your students are likely to have never thought twice about Oprah Winfrey, many may be avid fans — the sort who who eat the foods she says she likes or who read the books she recommends because, well, she recommends them. It will be important for both groups to see that, in this selection, Stark isn't making an aesthetic or even a personal judgment about the Oprah Winfrey empire. Rather, he situates her program in the context of the system of talk shows and teases out the differences in an attempt to explain why her program achieved a stature the others didn't quite manage. If your students are tempted to respond in only a personal way to the show (and not to Stark's argument), assign Reading the Signs question 1, a journal topic, to get that out of their systems.

This selection is ideal for argumentative topics, particularly those that address the value and appropriate content of television. Reading the Signs question 2 allows for a traditional pro-con argument on sensationalism in talk shows; for a more difficult topic, consider assigning question 3, which focuses on Stark's central assertion that talk shows have had a democratizing influence on television. A more narrow-gauge question, number 4 has students watch an episode of *The Oprah Winfrey Show* and write their own explanation of its appeal (you can prevent simple restatements of Stark's position by asking students to consider as well whether the show and its appeal have evolved since Stark published this essay). For a topic that engages current debate, try number 5, which asks students to respond to media critics who wish to "purify" TV. Be sure that students recognize an interesting political twist here: Whereas Stark cites conservative critic William Bennett as exemplary of this position, liberals have it on their agenda as well.

SUSAN DOUGLAS

SIGNS OF INTELLIGENT LIFE ON TV (p. 250)

We include this selection not just because Douglas's title echoes our own! We like Douglas because she offers an insightful interpretation of some of today's most popular TV programs — and she explores the mythologies that underlie them as well. If you're emphasizing gender issues in your class, be sure to include Douglas in your syllabus; this selection pairs particularly well with Amanda Fazzone's "Boob Tube" in this chapter and Sandra Tsing Loh's "The Return of Doris Day" in Chapter Four. Your students should have little trouble with Douglas's clear, accessible style, but expect a few students to complain that she's making a mountain out of a very little molehill. If some students do so complain, discuss with your class the personal spin Douglas adds to her essay: She's critiquing programs she *likes,* not those she hates. (Such students may appreciate answering Reading the Signs question 3, which invites them to explore their response to their favorite TV show.) To ensure a specific discussion of the programs, try supplementing the class's reading of her essay by taping a segment of one of the programs that she discusses; to save class time, you could watch only the parts in which male and female characters interact or display what Douglas considers stereotypical behavior. Such viewing would prepare students for the first Reading the Signs question, which asks them to support or oppose Douglas's thesis using evidence from the shows she discusses. You'll find that her thesis can easily be applied to other shows and even other media — her essay allows for great flexibility in assignment creation. Reading the Signs question 2 invites students to extend Douglas's concerns to other shows that portray women as professionals (*Sex and the City* is a natural for this question, but others would work as well), and question 5 asks them extend it to young adult shows. Films also invite an analysis à la Douglas; question 4 thus sends students to Sandra Tsing Loh's essay. Question 6 moves to advertising, where students are likely to find lots of instances of covert (and overt) antifeminism.

AMANDA FAZZONE

BOOB TUBE (p. 255)

Expect some students to be unhappy with Fazzone's selection, because she takes issue with some TV programs that, despite low ratings, have been favorites among young audiences, particularly female viewers. *Felicity,* for instance, drew much of its fandom from college-age women, and *Buffy the Vampire Slayer* became something of a cult classic among the twentysomething set. To gauge the lay of the land, you might begin discussion of this piece by polling your students about their familiarity with the shows she discusses and their responses to them. If you have some die-hard fans, you could remind them that cultural analysis isn't the same as personal appreciation. Indeed, as you discuss Fazzone's argument, you might ask what her real object of attack is here: Is it primarily the depiction of women on these programs, or is it assumption by groups like NOW that such characters represent empowered women? Expect some students to focus on only part of the evidence (for example, "What's wrong with Buffy's being pretty and sexy? She's in charge!"). Here you might discuss the traditional positioning of female characters as sex objects and encourage the class to tease out any differences between those portrayals and the ones Fazzone describes (to our mind, the differences are largely superficial). As a companion piece, Andre Meyer's "The New Sexual Stone Age" in Chapter Six provides additional evidence, drawn from other media, of female stars whose ostensibly empowered surfaces cover an essentially retrograde core. In addition, Fazzone's selection pairs well with Susan Douglas's essay, with Douglas decrying the undercutting of the professional roles sometimes accorded women characters on prime-time TV and Fazzone lambasting ostensibly strong female characters who have been championed as feminist role models. To discuss both essays, you might have the class first brainstorm on the board shows that feature prominent female lead characters; then ask the class to categorize the characters who exemplify Fazzone's or Douglas's arguments, as well as those who don't illustrate either position. Then ask the class to analyze their results: What do they say about trends in the depiction of women on TV? Have there been changes since these articles were written?

Fazzone's essay allows for focused, straightforward analysis and argumentative topics. Reading the Signs question 1 asks students to apply Fazzone's argument to the very popular *Sex and the City* (you might refer students to the discussion of that program in the introduction to Chapter Six, "We've Come a Long Way, Maybe: Gender Codes in American Culture"), while number 3 invites them to select one of the shows Fazzone discusses and to analyze it. For a mind-stretching exercise, number 2 asks small groups of students to devise a show that Fazzone would approve of; we suggest that groups present their concept to the class, being sure to make explicit exactly what criteria they believe Fazzone would support (she doesn't directly say in the article, and identifying these criteria accurately would make for a test in close reading and interpretation). A broader question, number 4 has the class debate the postfeminist tendency to emphasize female sexuality; this could be an essay assignment as well. In either case, students might research both traditional feminist and postfeminist writers to learn their positions on this issue.

TAD FRIEND

You Can't Say That (p. 258)

It's been more than thirty years since George Carlin made audiences howl with laughter with his classic routine "The Seven Words You Can't Say on Radio," but while ordinary American language today is freer — or more expletive-filled — than ever before, network television is still rather nervous about the matter. Your class is bound to be amused by Tad Friend's slightly arch, but definitely serious, report on the way the networks police the language on their shows in the age of *The Sopranos* and other cable programs in which the dialogue goes where NBC, ABC, and CBS fear to tread. Friend's article reveals a far more profound point, however, than the more superficial matter of whether someone is going to say "bullshit" on TV; the real issue here, as Michel Foucault would have put it, is the power to restrict discourse in general. Most Americans, and especially your students, believe that they have absolute freedom of speech, but point out, even as they discuss Friend's piece, just how reluctant they may be to use certain words in class that they may use all the time at home or with their friends. (We've had students write "s*?@#" when quoting from an assigned reading that didn't hesitate to write out the word.) Someone may even say something like "pardon my French" before or after using a common expletive; if so, have the class analyze why they may feel it necessary to apologize for using certain words.

It might be helpful to instruct your class about the historical nature of restricted speech. In the Middle Ages, the blasphemous invocation of the Lord's name by Christians was particularly forbidden; this led to such curse-dodging neologisms as "zounds" (short for "by God's wounds") and "bloody" (short for "by my Lady), which are still popular today. References to body parts and farting were not so taboo then (think of Chaucer's "The Miller's Tale") and became taboo only in the Reformation era. "Damn" and "hell," once taboo words (they still were in our childhoods, at least), are now quite acceptable, while other once acceptable words, especially those that refer to groups of people, are not. Though you may not want anyone in your class to actually utter such words aloud (they really are quite forbidden), you may want to raise the point to demonstrate that discourse is always being policed, but we tend to be most aware of the fact with words that are on the verge of breaking out of confinement — like the ones Tony Soprano uses with abandon.

Reading the Signs question 1 gives your students a chance to write an op-ed spiece expressing their opinions about linguistic censorship when it comes to television programming. Question 2 looks at the broader issue of content, inviting your class to debate whether television should be obliged to represent ethnic minorities in certain socially approved ways. Number 3 calls for a critical essay analyzing the nature of the television standards departments on which Friend reports, asking your students to decode whether such operations are cultural archaisms or preservers of important cultural values. And question 4 asks your students to think about the broader field of American values that television's contortions over acceptable diction illuminate.

TRICIA ROSE

Bad Sistas (p. 266)

Your students are likely to be quite familiar with the controversies surrounding male rappers, and many may have full defenses ready for their favorite rap stars. But often overlooked in the debates about rap are the female rappers — which is precisely why we've included this selection. You'll find Tricia Rose's "Bad Sistas" useful for a number of reasons. Her analysis of several female raps is implicitly semiotic, and you could use her essay as a model of how to defend an argument by citing specific details from an imagistic and musical text. She also asserts a clear, though controversial, argument, and that alone can trigger lots of debate about the gender roles represented in both female and male rap songs (Reading the Signs question 1 prompts a comparison of the two). As you discuss gender roles, you should turn your students' attention to the photo of Salt 'N' Pepa on p. 275. How do clothing, expression, and body language combine to create an image for the group? Be aware that some sensitive issues may be raised in class discussion: Rose sees female rap artists as challenging the depictions of women perpetuated in male raps, and this position points to both gender and ethnic tensions. If discussion gets heated, try to defuse things by narrowing the discussion, perhaps to one of the raps Rose describes. You might also ask students to share with the class their responses to Reading the Signs question 2, which invites students to write a "screenplay" for a video that depicts their gender in a way that they like. We've made this question a journal topic, but it's workable as an essay or even as a group assignment.

Rose's essay lends itself to straightforward analysis topics as well. Question 3 asks students to analyze a video of their own choice using Rose's argument. A more philosophical question, number 4 asks the class to discuss why popular culture tends to disguise traditional gender roles with a superficial feminist slant. Your students' comments will necessarily be speculative, but a discussion of the appeal of particular pop culture examples may move them closer to a real understanding of American values and attitudes toward gender.

DAVID SCHIFF

The Tradition of the Oldie (p. 276)

If you're considering skipping this essay because you don't feel your students know or care about the oldies, think again, for Schiff raises broader, meaty questions about both elite and popular taste and ways *popular* came to be defined. In his analysis of National Public Radio's top 100 musical compositions of the twentieth century, he finds, to some surprise, that it is the oldie, that rules the list. Before you assign this selection, you might poll the class for their own choices, then compare your results with NPR's (they will likely be quite different). Ask your students about the legitimacy of NPR's ballotting process, which Schiff describes in some detail. To what extent did the process itself lead the results in one direction? You might also ask about the legitimacy of any top 100 list, which tends to be based on not random samples but on self-selected participants who have an avid fan's stake in the outcome. You might point out to students that these lists are, in part, a marketing tool for their creators: radio stations know, for example, that they will gain a larger listenership when they broadcast the top ten (or whatever), and they also know that the process of voting increases listeners' identification with a certain station — they become personally invested in what is broadcast. Do your students participate in creating such lists, whether on the Internet, in magazines, or on the radio? What is their motivation? What effect does the list have on their consumption of popular music: Does it broaden the range or does it conversely tend to narrow it (because radio stations so often play music that will be a "sure bet" with their particular listenership)? What difference, especially in the era of MP3, does such list creation make?

As Schiff notes, it's likely that college students would have a different response to the NPR list than he does, since they may be unfamiliar with many of the oldies on the list and are likely to be less sensitive to the relative absence of classical compositions. To prepare for discussion, you might download some of the oldies that won and play them in class. Ask your students whether they illustrate the appeal to nostalgia and emotionalism that Schiff claims characterizes them — and, if so, why such an appeal would be so influential. Such an exercise could be good preparation for Reading the Signs question 2, which has students examine the NPR 100 (available online) and to analyze the cultural values implicit in the results. (Alternatively, you might put a selection of songs on reserve in your school's music library.) Schiff's article lends itself to being revised by a different generation; students are likely to enjoy question 1, which has small groups brainstorm their lists of top post-war musical compositions (note that we specify this time period but fully expect many students to start with the 1990s). Have the groups compare their lists, both with NPR's and with classmates'. How can they account for changes in musical taste? In differences within the class? Question 3 asks students to address whether such lists are valid; to develop their responses, they might study not only NPR's methodology but that of magazines or other radio stations. Finally, question 4 has students to consider whether commercial forces are responsible for displacing classical music from America's airwaves. To prevent a simplistic response (for example, "Classical music isn't played because people don't like it"), we suggest that students spend some time listening to a classical station, visiting its Web site, and interviewing classical music fans (you may have some in your class). Students may be surprised to see the passion that devotees have for this form of music.

ROBERT HILBURN
THE NOT-SO-BIG HIT SINGLE (p. 281)

Hilburn's selection pairs well with David Schiff's "The Tradition of the Oldie," for both authors consider how it is that the popular becomes popular. Schiff take the long view in discussing NPR's top 100 of the twentieth century; Hilburn takes a shorter view, considering how it is that this week's No. 1 single gains that status. He argues that changes in the record industry — singles are no longer snapped up by listeners as they were in the 1960s, for instance — and the movement to ultrasegmentation of the radio audience have rendered the No. 1 status virtually meaningless. To make sure your students understand why this is so, ask them to name all the formats of music that they know, then have them compare their list with that from the 1960s (they could visit the school library's microfiche archive and look for the Saturday or Sunday entertainment section of a local or national newspaper, which is where the top ten singles were listed as news). In this era of crossover artists — an appelation given to musicians who appear in anything but their "home" formats — they may be surprised that Gladys Knight could share the same space as Tom Jones and the Who. You might also discuss why we consider No. 1 to be important anyway — and the extent to which such ratings serve a marketing purpose for the record industry.

Hilburn's selection is ripe for assignments that go beyond the immediate range that he establishes. Reading the Signs question 1 asks students to research a parallel phenomenon, the history of TV broadcasting, that is marked by a similar trend toward niche marketing. Be sure your students consider the impact of cable in responding to this question. Question 2 shifts students' attention to the effect of No. 1 status, asking them to poll music fans about the role the ratings game has in their consumption of music. Question 3 has students assess a change in the music industry that Hilburn neglects — the advent of downloadable music from the Internet — while number 4 invites students to consider whether noncommercial radio stations, such as your university's station, have greater freedom in programming than do commercial stations.

One warning: students might bristle at Hilburn's opening salvo, directed at Mariah Carey, but ask them what his point is. He's not simply attacking her ability (in fact, he does lob some praise her way), but he is using her as an illustration of the changing patterns in the music industry that he is assailing.

TOM SHALES
RESISTING THE FALSE SECURITY OF TV (p. 285)

Tom Shales's tone in this brief selection is sarcastic, even flip at times, but don't let that get in the way of addressing the more serious questions that he is raising. Essentially Shales is speculating on the range of functions television can serve in modern American culture. Entertainment, of course. But while Shales doesn't articulate alternate functions precisely, he implicitly would like to see TV serve as a social and political conscience as well, as a medium that can keep public attention directed to the "uncomfortable" as it allows for the profusion of the banal and the trivial. Ask your students: Is this is a laudable purpose of television? More problematically, is it possible for this to happen? If so, what changes in media business practices — and in audience taste and values — would have to occur?

Shales's piece is useful for assignments that address the place of television in American culture. Reading the Signs question 1 allows for a personal response to Shales's focus on TV's coverage of the September 11 attacks, while number 2 asks them to respond more analytically, this time assessing Shales's prediction that TV programming may get a bit more serious after the attacks. To demonstrate their arguments, students should base their essays on a careful consideration of current programming trends. Question 3 sends students to Damien Cave's selection in Chapter One to address the commercial exploitation of the 9/11 attacks (TV participated in it along with the Internet sources Cave describes). Perhaps the most challenging question, number 4 has students reflect on the power of visual images, especially in light of the events of 9/11. To develop their ideas, students might revisit the September 11 portfolio starting on p. 19. Many of those images will be familiar to students; how does their response to them now compare to seeing such images in the fall of 2001?

MARNIE CARROLL

AMERICAN TELEVISION IN EUROPE (p. 288)

It's a bit of a cliché that America's strongest export is its popular culture: McDonalds and Coca-Cola, blue jeans and Madonna. And there's a tendency among culture critics to see that ability to export popular culture as omnipotent: the world is being taken over by MTV, the argument goes, and other cultures and ways of life are being annihilated in the process. Although there's certainly some truth to that charge, it can be overstated, as Marnie Carroll points out in this interesting article from the online journal *Bad Subjects*. Carroll does not deny that American popular culture has been highly influential abroad; it's just that such influence does not necessitate erasure of native culture. Be sure your students note one of the strengths of her selection: the abundance of specific, telling details that demonstrate that European culture is surviving despite the onslaught of *Friends* and *Frasier*. To contextualize Carroll's discussion, you might assign her selection along with Benjamin R. Barber's "Jihad vs. McWorld" and Thomas L. Friedman's "Revolution Is U.S.," both in Chapter One. As your students discuss the influence of popular culture on their own lives, encourage them to extend the discussion to its effect on other nations. What are the drawbacks and advantages of cross-cultural exchange? Is it really as unidirectional as some critics fear? What are the larger political ramifications (Barber in particular can provide context for this question). Reading the Signs question 4 calls for an argumentative essay about these questions and has students refer to both Barber and Friedman.

You'll find that Carroll's selection yields lots of provocative assignments that can focus on a range of cultural issues. Reading the Signs question 1 asks students to evaluate the validity of Carroll's argument by having them analyze the TV programming schedule of another country (they can find one on the Internet), while question 5 asks them to perform the same task, this time by studying popular magazines from other countries (a selection should be available in your school's library). Another research question, number 3, asks them to argue whether rock 'n' roll is an example of the American cultural hegemony that critics so often decry (be sure students don't forget about the British invasion of the 1960s as they respond to this question). We've framed number 2, about why so much TV programming imported from Britain is "high cultural," as a discussion topic, but that could make a good essay topic as well.

Chapter Four

THE HOLLYWOOD SIGN
The Culture of American Film

It's not surprising that writing instructors have long used films as texts for student analysis, for the best films can offer the complexity, narrative structures, characters, and symbol systems of a novel or story. Film has also been a favorite subject of semiotic analysis, and with good reason. Movies are rich sign systems, deliberately designed to appeal to an audience's values and desires, both reflecting and shaping a society's dreams. We find that using a semiotic approach can help students make the leap from writing simply their judgments of movies — why they like a particular film — to writing critical analyses of them. Because movies are so much a part of their lives, it's sometimes difficult for students to interpret them critically. By providing an analytic framework, this chapter is designed to help them do just that. The Exploring the Signs of Film question asks students to examine their favorite films, reflecting on what their personal preferences reveal about their own tastes, values, and beliefs. In essence, students will explore how their cinematic tastes serve as signs of their individual identity. The Discussing the Signs of Film question looks at film as a broader social phenomenon, this time asking them to consider why blockbuster hits achieve such a status. For this question, have your class identify the most recent megahits, locate the films in the context of other popular fads, and consider the social values and ideologies that the films manipulate. It's worth asking students to consider how Hollywood's image-making machine works its magic on its own products; accordingly, the Reading Film on the Net exercise invites students to study the Web site of a recent film or the posters that advertise films. Students should consider this question: How does the packaging of a film affect a viewer's understanding of its meaning?

As with Chapter Three on television and music, it's useful to structure class discussion around a common text but given time constraints, you might find it trickier to watch an entire feature film in class. Some movies are ninety minutes long, so if your class runs in a two-hour block you probably can watch one movie in class. If that's not an option, consider assigning a current film for homework, or check to see if your campus has a film series that would enable the class to see the same film (usually at a discounted rate). Your students are likely to possess a tremendously high level of cinematic literacy — so high that it may pose a problem. When discussing a movie, you may find it necessary to steer students away from celebrity worship. Among themselves, they're used to talking about what film a particular actress has appeared in recently or what a certain actor earned for a film; at times, we've just had to say that celebrity gossip isn't the same as a critical discussion. You may also have to remind students that a public relations spin on a movie isn't the same as an objective analysis of it. The fact that Madonna says she is "telling all" in *Truth or Dare* (1991), for example, doesn't mean that it's the case. You'll be able to keep students on track if you remind them of that semiotic question "Why?" Keep at them to ask why this plot twist, or why a male rather than a female character, or why a black actor for this role: you'll have them on their way to writing sharp analytic papers.

Because the readings in the chapter address various myths that influence films, you'll find the chapter easy to adapt to your course's focus and students' interests. Robert B. Ray provides a broad framework for examining Hollywood archetypes, so we strongly recommend that you include his essay in your syllabus. Alternately, Linda Seger's selection outlines the "universal" story lines that give shape to the mythologies underlying many popular films. If you need to cut the chapter, you can do so according to the themes you're emphasizing. Gary Johnson focuses on the iconography of the

Western, the Sandra Tsing Loh and Jessica Hagedorn selections focus on gender issues, and the Michael Parenti selection examines social class. Susan Bordo and Vivian C. Sobchack provide cultural analysis (their selections are valuable for a semiotically centered course); the Hagedorn and Todd Boyd selections are perfect for a class addressing multicultural issues. Patrick Goldstein concludes the chapter with a reflection on whether it's time Hollywood got serious after the devastation of September 11.

ROBERT B. RAY
THE THEMATIC PARADIGM (p. 308)

Ray's selection has been one of the most frequently assigned in the earlier editions of this text — and that's no surprise. It's useful no matter what films your class analyzes, and whether or not you emphasize semiotics, because it focuses on an essential pattern of protagonists in American films: the outlaw and the official heroes. This pattern is by no means limited to Westerns. These protagonists are found in action-adventure, mystery, political, and even romance movies. Ray thus provides your students with a clear, accessible paradigm for interpreting characters from almost any film. Students should have little trouble identifying the paradigm, but be sure, in class, to review the ideological significance of the two character types — a more abstract point that students may overlook. Ask, for instance, why Americans tend to prefer the outlaw hero. What does that reveal about the American character? To encourage students to consider the significance of Ray's categories, we strongly suggest that you do Reading the Signs question 3, which asks the class to brainstorm examples of outlaw and official heroes, then to categorize them according to shared traits (such as race or gender). Consider as well assigning William Martin-Doyle's "*Cool Hand Luke*: The Exclusion of the Official Hero in American Cinema" (p. 36), one of the student essays in the Writing about Popular Culture section. Although not all students will be familiar with *Cool Hand Luke*, Martin-Doyle provides a sufficient summary and uses Ray effectively to interpret the film.

Ray's selection provides an ideal framework for analyzing not only films but other media. Not all heroes need be real, of course; question 1 has students consult Gary Engle's and Andy Medhurst's selections in Chapter Nine and consider which type of hero Superman and Batman are to their audiences (for a simpler question, ask students to analyze just one hero). Questions 2 and 4 are similar, asking students to apply Ray's paradigm to the central characters in the *Terminator* and *Alien* films, respectively; in discussing the *Alien* films, students should consider gender issues as well, for the protagonist is female, and American heroes traditionally have been male. Finally, question 5 is speculative, asking students to create a third category of hero to accommodate the characters in such cartoons as *The Simpsons* and *South Park*. To prepare students for writing about this topic, you might assign the introduction to Chapter Nine, "American Icons: The Mythic Characters of Popular Culture."

LINDA SEGER

CREATING THE MYTH (p. 316)

You'll find that you use Seger's selection clear, accessible discussion in a number of ways. This essay can introduce your students to cultural myths; it provides a critical framework for analyzing a broad range of films; its central argument, that successful films employ archetypes which tap into universal human desires, is open to debate and modification. This essay complements Ray's in that Seger focuses on heroic myths, but unlike Ray she traces classic hero patterns through a single film, *Star Wars*, that should be familiar to most students (be sure to draw their attention to the *Star Wars* photo on p. 318). She also complicates the heroic myth by examining what she calls "broken" characters and combination myths; this examination will give you great flexibility in class discussion, as most films fit her scheme somehow. Seger also raises some interesting open-ended questions (for instance, why the *Rambo* films were so successful). Herself a screenwriter, Seger wrote this selection for a readership of aspiring screenwriters, and that shapes her tone and attitudes. Her status as an industry insider helps to explain her apparent endorsement of using existing myths in film — she doesn't recommend originality in screenplays. You may want to discuss that essentially conservative viewpoint with your class. (Reading the Signs question 1 addresses this issue; question 5 calls for an evaluation of Seger's suggestion that screenwriters use Grimm's fairy tales for inspiration.)

If you're covering both the Ray and the Seger selections, consider assigning question 2, which calls for a gender-based comparison of the two approaches to heroes. Question 3 sends students to Michael Parenti's essay for help in analyzing *Pretty Woman* and *Indecent Proposal*, while question 4 asks them to examine the archetype-filled *Titanic*. Perhaps the most challenging question (and our favorite) is the last, which asks students to explore the myths about American history, race, and gender underlying *Gone with the Wind*. (Remember: The film runs more than three hours and thus is difficult to show in class.) After doing this assignment, some of our students have lamented that they will never view the movie the same way again — proof to us that the assignment works.

GARY JOHNSON

THE WESTERN (p. 326)

In focusing on the iconography of the Western, Johnson's selection is ideal paired with the Ray or the Seger selections in this chapter. Your students may not be fans of this film genre, but see that as an advantage. Because they won't be tempted to champion their favorite movies or stars, students may be more inclined to adopt a critical perspective. You might begin discussion by asking the class to brainstorm all associations they have with Westerns; then turn to Johnson and compare his discussion with your students' list. It's likely that there will be considerable overlap, and you could discuss why, in an era when Westerns have fallen out of cinematic favor, students are so familiar with the conventions. You could also ask students to consider why the Western was so dominant in the early part of the twentieth century. What myths and ideologies did it presume? How might those cultural values have changed, and along with them, the popularity of the genre? Given that some students may not have seen many Westerns, you might rent a few of the classic Westerns that Johnson names and show selected archetypically rich scenes in class; ask whether some of Johnson's broader assertions, such as the claim that John Wayne serves as "a metaphor for America itself," are borne out by the scenes. Direct students' attention to the photo of Clint Eastwood in *Fistful of Dollars* (p. 330): Does Eastwood exemplify any of the character traits that Johnson describes? Alternatively, you might show in class or put on reserve in your school's film library one of the more recent Westerns, such as *Dances with Wolves* or *Unforgiven*. To what extent does the film replicate — or ring changes on — the classic Western iconography?

This selection lends itself to assignments that ask students to interpret particular films. Reading the Signs question 1 sends them to Ray's "The Thematic Paradigm" for help in analyzing the hero of a Western of their choice; alternatively, you can assign students to write about a film that you select and show in class. Students who prefer more contemporary movies might enjoy question 3, which has them interpret a recent Western, *Wild, Wild West*; the film's box-office failure is particularly interesting given the star value of its lead, Will Smith. This question prompts students to consider both the evolution of the genre's popularity and the conventions governing ethnic roles in Westerns. A focused analytic question, number 4 invites students to critique one of Johnson's explanations for the Western's appeal; the broadest, and perhaps most challenging, question is number 2, which asks students to account for the Western's fading popularity at the box office. Be sure they realize that, thanks to video and DVD, Westerns do retain an audience; students might do some Internet research to determine the profile of Western fans, and their results might push them to consider the generational complexities of movie audiences.

SUSAN BORDO

BRAVEHEART, BABE, *AND THE* CONTEMPORARY BODY *(p. 333)*

We like Bordo's selection because it provides an excellent analysis of the cultural beliefs that underlie the success of a film like *Braveheart*, beliefs that she sees as dramatically different than those that animate a movie like *Babe*. Bordo masterfully blends discussion of the film with details drawn from the larger cultural system in which it exists, including advertising, the 1996 Summer Olympics, and the fitness industry. That might sound like the essay is diffuse and rambling, but it's anything but that: throughout, Bordo maintains a steady focus on how what she calls the Just-Do-It philosophy dominates both personal self-image and pop culture products. Your students should have little trouble understanding her, but expect some resistance to her critique of the Just-Do-It philosophy. They may ask, what's wrong with self-reliance? Send your students back to Bordo for an answer: she doesn't oppose self-reliance but finds the ideology of success and empowerment to be a deceptive distortion of real-life struggles. (Reading the Signs question 1 allows students to reflect on the influence this philosophy has had on their own lives.) In addition, you might want to direct your students' attention to Bordo's style. Although this is an academic piece, Bordo allows her personal voice to emerge (note the frequent use of the first person and occasional autobiographical details), displays a sense of humor, and moves gracefully and seamlessly from one concrete detail to the next — a good model for students addicted to stuffy academese to emulate.

You'll find that this selection creates opportunies for a creative variety of analytic and argumentative essays. A natural choice would be to ask students to argue for or against Bordo's interpretation of either *Braveheart* or *Babe*. Question 2 invites the class to extend Bordo's analysis to current films; we predict that your students will find that those reflecting the *Braveheart* ideology will outnumber those in the *Babe* vein. The more challenging questions are the last two. Number 3 has students respond to Bordo's criticism of power feminism; you could make this a research topic, with students investigating further this brand of feminism. Finally, number 4 asks students to apply Bordo's argument to an episode of a television talk show; as preparation for this topic, you might assign as well the Steven D. Stark essay on Oprah Winfrey in Chapter Three.

TODD BOYD
So You Wanna Be a Gangsta? (p. 343)

This selection is essential if your course emphasizes ethnic issues; it's also ideal if you like to emphasize the historical context in which pop culture products should be interpreted. Boyd outlines a full and rich history of the gangster genre of film, starting with the good, old-fashioned American Western, moving to ethnic white gangster films such as the *Godfather* series and then the Blaxploitation flicks, and concluding with analyses of *American Me* and *Boyz N the Hood*. You'll find that this historical approach can head off simple evaluative judgments of recent black gangsta films and help prevent unproductive digressions into social issues that are only tangentially related (whether gangsters face a bum rap by society, for instance). Even though both *American Me* and *Boyz N the Hood* are now quite a few years old, we find most first-year students have seen at least one (usually *Boyz*) and often both. Students sometimes see *Boyz* as an "alternative" film; expect some to bristle at Boyd's suggestion that the film reflects a "bourgeois sense of politics." Boyd's writing should be accessible to most students; the one section that may be more difficult is his discussion of black nationalist politics. Determine early in class discussion whether students grasp Boyd's point, since missing it can mean missing his overall argument about *Boyz*.

If you assign this selection, try to arrange an in-class viewing of *Boyz* or place it and *American Me* on reserve in your college's media library: that will allow for a richer discussion of Boyd's readings of these films. A natural assignment based on Boyd's essay is to ask students to view one of the films and either respond to his argument about it or write their own interpretations of it. For a somewhat more complicated topic, try Reading the Signs question 2, which invites students to compare the representation of ethnic "others" in a film such as *Scarface* with that of black gang members in a movie like *Boyz N the Hood*. Two questions allow students to explore the implications raised in Boyd's essay: number 1 asks whether Hollywood glorifies criminal behavior (if you're interested in this angle, you could assign Vivian C. Sobchack's "The Postmorbid Condition" in this chapter as a companion piece), and number 4 asks whether gangsta films exploit the black community. Both questions would make good research paper topics. Question 3 asks students to consider why gangsta culture is so popular among middle-class teens; you could organize your class into teams and have them interview adolescents as a means of gathering primary evidence for their papers. Finally, question 5 extends the issues to gender by asking students to interpret a film that Boyd does not address, *Waiting to Exhale*. Boyd focuses largely on films that feature the black male underclass; you may find it useful to have your students interpret a film with African American characters who are both female and middle-class — a departure from usual cinematic conventions.

JESSICA HAGEDORN

ASIAN WOMEN IN FILM: NO JOY, NO LUCK (p. 355)

Hagedorn's selection fits well into courses that focus on either gender or ethnic issues. Although you're not likely to be surprised by her argument — that films tend to relegate Asian women to the traditional whore/angel dichotomy — your students may not have considered this issue at all. If you've read Sandra Tsing Loh's selection in this chapter, you could ask your students to relate the dichotomy Hagedorn describes to Loh's taxonomy of "good " and "bad" girls — the two authors are basically talking about the same gender steretotypes, though Hagedorn adds a racial spin to her treatment of them (see Reading the Signs question 4). Ask them as well to interpret the photos of Michelle Yeoh (p. 357) and Anna May Wong (p. 361): To what extent do these actresses illustrate Hagedorn's point? (Yeoh is best known as Jackie Chan's costar in *Supercop*, and in this photo she plays a Chinese secret agent in *Tomorrow Never Dies*; Wong was an early twentieth-century actress who appeared in *The Thief of Baghdad* [1924] and played a prostitute in *Shanghai Express* [1932].) We should warn you that students may be unhappy with Hagedorn's criticism of *The Joy Luck Club*, a film that we've discovered is a sentimental favorite among many students, both male and female and of all ethnic backgrounds. Since many students have seen this film, you might want to combine your discussion of this essay with a viewing of the film, to allow your students to test Hagedorn's thesis (see Reading the Signs question 1).

A basic analysis assignment is to ask students to view one of the films that Hagedorn mentions (or any other with Asian characters) and interpret the depiction of women in the film. Question 5 is similar, but it has students focus on one of the gender-bending films, such as *M. Butterfly*, that Hagedorn mentions (note that some conservative students may feel uncomfortable watching this film). You can broaden the issues that Hagedorn raises by addressing more generally Hollywood's tendency to stereotype different ethnicities. Question 2 invites the class to stage a debate on this issue; students could prepare for the debate by reading Michael Omi's essay in Chapter Seven. These issues apply to other media as well; question 3 invites students to analyze a magazine that targets Asian American readers. As an alternative to an essay assignment, consider bringing to class some such magazine for small groups to study.

SANDRA TSING LOH

THE RETURN OF DORIS DAY (p. 365)

If your class is emphasizing gender issues, this selection will make a lively and relevant addition to your syllabus. Loh provides a taxonomy of female archetypes in American film (and in popular culture more broadly), arguing that in the mid-1990s the "good girl" archetype triumphed over the "bad girl." You might begin your discussion of this selection by asking your students to complete Reading the Signs question 1, which asks them to explore in a journal entry the extent to which the gender archetypes Loh describes affected them in their childhood. This question should prompt students to consider how traditional gender roles have shaped their own attitudes and beliefs. In addition, Loh's taxonomy creates lots of opportunities for in-class activities. You could have students brainstorm their own updated list of good and bad girls in film, and then explain whatever trends they happen to find (see Reading the Signs question 2). Or ask them to trace in detail the career of one of the figures Loh mentions: Has this figure evolved? If so, how, and, more important, why? For a different perspective, apply Loh's thesis to male characters: Do your students find a predominance of good or bad boys? And what's the significance of their findings? As you discuss this selection, be sure students move from slotting characters and stars into Loh's pigeonholes to contemplating the larger significance of the patterns that they find. (Question 3 urges students to consider the reasons for these patterns.)

Your students will have little trouble understanding this selection, but be aware that Loh's style is decidedly nonacademic. You could discuss her style directly, asking your students what Loh gains — and perhaps loses — by writing in such a resolutely tongue-in-cheek manner. Because Loh provides a paradigm for studying gender roles, this selection is ideal for interpreting particular examples from the media. Questions 4, 5, and 6 ask students to use Loh's essay in analyzing "progressive" TV shows, a Doris Day film, and a women's fashion magazine, respectively. But you can tailor the question to your students' interests by asking them to focus on any film, show, or other media text in which female characters play a significant role.

MICHAEL PARENTI
CLASS AND VIRTUE (p. 373)

We decided to include this selection after hearing the umpteenth student proclaim that *Pretty Woman* is her favorite movie of all time. At least in our classes, most of the film's avid fans have been female — and, to our surprise, most consider themselves feminists. Such students are likely to be irked by Parenti, who finds the film objectionable on many grounds. He concentrates on the class issues implicit in this film and in others; we've found it interesting that many students respond, "Well, of course, one has to get of rid of low-class habits." And we've had students argue that the film doesn't really show prostitution because the rich guy is Prince Charming. The film's fans will relish responding to Reading the Signs question 3, which invites them to argue with Parenti's interpretation. Be sure your students ask "why are we shown *this*?" when offering a counterinterpretation. Parenti mentions briefly the gender bigotry in the film; question 4 sends students to Holly Devor's essay in Chapter Six for help in analyzing the film's gender roles.

Parenti's comments about class can be applied to examples from other media. It works well when applied to other films such as *Wall Street* (see question 1) or to television shows such as *Beverly Hills 90210* (see question 2); it can also be used to illuminate films such as *On the Waterfront* (see question 5). An exploratory topic, question 6 asks students to create a category of "racial bigotry" to parallel Parenti's two categories of class and gender bigotry. For this question, we strongly suggest that students first read Michael Omi's "In Living Color" (Chapter Seven); Omi comments on the ways the media reinforce ethnic biases.

VIVIAN C. SOBCHACK
The Postmorbid Condition (p. 377)

We like Sobchack's selection because she offers a cultural explanation for the current spate of violent films — a fresh angle that goes beyond the usual debate of the effect of media violence on our culture. Her writing is accessible but on the theoretical side, so you might want to walk your students through her essay. She begins by describing succinctly an article she had written twenty-five years earlier on violence in film; at that time, she saw the violence as being aestheticized. To demonstrate what she means by this, you might show in class a short clip from *Bonnie and Clyde* or another film from the era. Then your students will be better prepared for her indictment of more recent violent movies, ones that she feels do quite the opposite: rather than aestheticizing violence, she claims, current films are "careless" about it. The blasted bodies are just that, bodies, not people; the technologizing and escalation of violence becomes the object of interest, not pain and suffering; and the violence becomes an illusory joke, not a moral offense. While she finds the depiction of modern culture as postmodern to be tiresome, nonetheless you might get your class to appreciate the connotations of her title, for "postmorbid" echoes *postmodern,* and she essentially is critiquing a postmodern tendency to substitute image and effect for substance and the real. A effective way to get to the heart of her essay is to tease out the reasons she distinguishes overtly violent films like *Saving Private Ryan* and *Beloved* from overtly violent films like *Pulp Fiction* and *Reservoir Dogs.* Ask your students how they responded to the violent scenes in the first two films: Did they laugh? Or did they squirm, turn their heads, or feel disgusted? If the latter, that's because the violence is made to seem real and carries with it a moral burden. It's likely students didn't react that way watching the second pair of films, because, as Sobchack points out, the violence is hyperbolic and over the top. And that, she finds, is exactly what's wrong with it. Students might analyze the poster for *Reservoir Dogs* (p. 383) to analyze what sort of violence it depicts.

Once students grasp her point, they're likely to want to debate it. Many students have grown up watching violent films and may see nothing wrong with unreal violence; in fact, they may argue that it's superior in that everyone knows it's "just entertainment." You might ask your class what that says about cultural values and attitudes. Reading the Signs question 6 invites the class to discuss this issue, though you could make it an essay topic; the next selection in the chapter, Patrick Goldstein's "The Time to Get Serious Has Come," can shed some light on this matter as well. You might also get your students to talk about the gendered patterns of responding to violent movies (in an aside, Sobchack points out that fans of cinematic violence tend to be male). In writing on this essay, students would do well to ground their arguments in specific examples of violent films. Question 4 has them do so by testing Sobchack's claim on a recent movie (of course, you could select one of those that she discusses as well), while question 2 invites them to take on her argument about why films like Beloved were disappointments at the box office. Sobchack doesn't directly discuss gangster films, which also are quite violent; a challenging question, number 5 asks students to argue whether the violence in a film like Boyz N the Hood is desensitizing or real. Finally, questions 1 and 3 ask students address broader issues of the effects of violence on audiences and of the possible need for restrictions of violence; if you assign these questions, you might first have the class brainstorm films that would provide relevant evidence for their arguments, no matter what position they take.

PATRICK GOLDSTEIN
THE TIME TO GET SERIOUS HAS COME (p. 384)

After the September 11 attacks, many a media pundit proclaimed that American media, particularly TV and film, would have to change their casual depiction of international violence and horrors, for no longer could audiences see hijackings and bombings as just entertainment. Patrick Goldstein would wish the same result — but he's skeptical about whether such a change will indeed happen, pointing to recent changes as being "cosmetic." What's useful about his piece is his grounding of this question within the context of cinematic history, looking at post–World War II and late 1960s responses to contemporary events. Ask your students what the cultural mood of those eras was (the answer is implicit in Goldstein's essay) and how that mood might have shaped cinematographers' creations. Then ask them about the mood before — and after — the 9/11 attacks: How might the nation's shock, resurgence of patriotism, and exhortations to "just get on with life" affected post-9/11 filmmaking? (Reading the Signs question 1 asks them to address this question, while question 4 has them analyze the cultural mood of one decade, the 1990s.) Since students have the benefit of hindsight that Goldstein didn't have (his article was published September 18, 2001), encourage them to refer to specific recent films as they discuss and write about this essay.

Goldstein's selection is ideal if you wish your students to consider the ethical dimensions of American popular culture. Reading the Signs question 2 has them take on the debatable question of whether films like *Collateral Damage* ever should have been released, while number 3 has them argue about Hollywood's abandonment of real-life issues (Tom Shales's "Resisting the False Security of TV" in Chapter Three could be a useful supplementary essay to assign for this topic). For both of these questions, students might want to research the box-office response to post–9/11 releases that went ahead anyway and showed as entertaining what many in real life found to be anything but.

PART TWO

Cultural Constructions

Chapter Five
POPULAR SPACES
Interpreting the Built Environment

If you want your students to enjoy the intellectual pleasure of analyzing something they probably have never studied in school, this chapter's for you. This chapter is among our favorites, because we've found that our students approach writing essays on both domestic and public places with incredible enthusiasm and zeal. If you're emphasizing the semiotic method, this chapter can help overcome any resistance you face among students who bristle, say, at interpreting their favorite film because they identify too closely with it. Students tend to feel less personally attached to the built environment (particularly to public spaces) and thus may find it easier to attain critical distance from the objects of their analysis. And there's plenty to analyze: buildings aren't just brick or stucco or glass; they are rich sign systems that define power structures and hierarchies (it was no accident that the September 11 attacks targeted edifices that symbolized American economic supremacy and military might), control visitors' behavior, and establish territorial boundaries. As the Discussing the Signs of Public Space boxed question suggests, you might start discussion with your own classroom: are chairs arranged in neat rows or in a circle, and how does the arrangement affect class dynamics? Are chairs bolted to the floor, and if so, what are the implications for pedagogical style? What sort of hierarchy is implied in the traditional lecture hall? You can extend this discussion to other parts of the campus: In which buildings do students feel more comfortable, and why? What messages are sent by your school's architecture? Ask your students to check your school's Web site to learn which buildings are featured: Why are *these* buildings and not others used to represent the campus? To stimulate your students' curiosity, assign the Exploring the Signs of Public Space boxed question, which has students reflect on their own use of public space for recreation or entertainment. Students taken by this topic might enjoy as well the Reading the Signs of Virtual Space on the Net boxed question, which asks them to consider how "virtual" space may alter our understanding and experience of space. You might pair this question with an analysis of the home-as-work-space photo on p. 394. In what ways does our increasing reliance on the Internet for business, research, and entertainment affect domestic relationships?

You'll see that many of the questions that accompany the readings in this chapter call for a kind of field research — that is, they ask students to visit a public place and analyze it. If you give such an assignment, you'll want to ascertain that your students have an equal ability to get to the place (it wouldn't be fair to expect students to drive fifty miles to an amusement park, for instance, especially when some may not have a car) and that the place is appropriate (we once counseled a novice instructor *not* to suggest a strip club as an assignment option). Since students may not have experience doing this sort of field research, you might spend some class time discussing note-taking techniques and observational strategies. We've found it useful to prepare observational guidelines with questions that help focus students' attention on important details. For instance, someone studying a public park might respond to questions such as "Are visitors primarily alone, in pairs, in large groups? Do people who seem to be strangers interact with each other? Do visitors walk slowly or quickly? Do they linger and relax? What is it about the physical design of the park that encourages this behavior?" Note that such assignments are ideal for small group projects and observational teams: Students may simply *see* more if they are with others, and they'll enjoy the camaraderie of the shared experience.

If you can't cover the entire chapter, we suggest you start with the introduction, which establishes a critical framework for analyzing public space, and then pick selections according to the type of space analyzed or the issues raised. Commerical and entertainment spaces are analyzed in the Susan Willis (Disney World), Anna McCarthy (NikeTown), and the Malcolm Gladwell (retail stores) selections. Lucy R. Lippard and Daphne Spain both address the gendered implications of architectural design, with Lippard considering urban space and Spain emphasizing the modern office environment. The Lippard piece also complements Camilo José Vergara's selection on the city itself as a space. For a first-person account of the dynamics of domestic space, assign Karen Karbo's "The Dining Room." Rina Swentzell examines the cultural values implicit in architecture in her comparision of Native American and mainstream school design. Finally, Eric Boehlert closes the chapter with a historical reading of the World Trade Center, a group of buildings that continues to demonstrate the enduring symbolic power of public space long after the rubble has been hauled away.

MALCOLM GLADWELL
The Science of Shopping (p. 403)

We've chosen to lead off the chapter with Gladwell's essay because we find students respond passionately to it. And you can have a lot of fun with this piece. It's a detailed description of the ways retailers use spatial design to manipulate consumers and to stimulate the urge to buy. Whether your students are city folk or suburbanites, well-off or struggling to make ends meet, you can assume that they're familiar with some sort of mall and that their consuming behavior has been affected by the mall's design. Thus this selection provides a good opportunity for combining discussion of personal experience with an analysis of a topic accessible to all students. Some students may resist the notion that one's behavior can be shaped by architecture and physical clues, but remind them that this is the assumption that successful retailers make: It's not just Gladwell's opinion. Indeed, Gladwell focuses his essay on Paco Underhill, a sort of retailers' anthropologist who studies consumer behavior. If students don't believe that Underhill's advice to retailers would have an effect, ask them to consider alternatives: If a huge shopping mall didn't have a food court, would shoppers behave in the same way? Why do college bookstores locate popular trade books, bestsellers, and merchandise such as calendars up front, near the cash registers, with the required textbooks relegated to the back? Have your students ever bought an unnecessary gee-gaw because of this arrangement? For more on Underhill's strategies, consult the Web site for Envirosell, his behavioral market research and consulting company (**www.envirosell.com**).

In varying ways, the Reading the Signs questions ask students to apply or respond to Gladwell's observations about the science behind customer manipulation. Question 1 invites students to respond to Gladwell's question, "Should we be afraid of Paco Underhill?" Be sure students note that, while at times Gladwell seems to suggest that his answer is yes, ultimately he decides that it is the shoppers who manipulate the retailers — a debatable point given his evidence. Two questions ask students to apply Gladwell's points to specific examples: Number 2 has them visit a local store (it could be one that Gladwell mentions, such as Banana Republic) or supermarket, and number 4 has them visit the Web site of a major retailer and study how the virtual space encourages them to buy. This topic is the more challenging of the two, for students may see some features of the Web site as mere functional conveniences (e.g., the "shopping carts" that allow you to pile up merchandise as you're "browsing" through the store), though, while they may be helpful to the virtual shopper, also stimulate additional consumption (it's easy to forget how much you've stashed in your cart). Your students may be disturbed by the invasion of personal privacy that's implicit in some of Paco Underhill's techniques; if that's the case, they may enjoy the class debate suggested in question 3 on the ethics of retail anthropology (Eric Schlosser's "Kid Kustomers" in Chapter Two could provide supplementary information for this topic).

ANNA MCCARTHY

BRAND IDENTITY AT NIKETOWN (p. 410)

Your students don't have to be familiar with a NikeTown outlet in order to appreciate this selection. Not only does McCarthy describe a sample outlet thoroughly; she offers ample comparison with other instances of supposed postmodern "shoppertainment." Your students will be familiar with the various in-store promotions, videos, and visual techniques that are so ubiquitous now, especially in stores that target the youth market; however, they may need a little help in grasping the subtleties of her argument. Be sure to ask them what she means by claiming that NikeTown's in-store marketing strategies produce a sense of disorientation. Why would a store, a brand name, want to establish a depersonalized relationship with its consumers? How does this strategy work to create a sense of mystique for the product line? Ask students as well about the image they associate with Nike products. What attitude does it convey? And how does that image influence consumer behavior, particularly for a product line (athletic shoes) that is competing in an oversaturated market (dozens of shoe companies manufacture hundreds of models).

A classic essay assignment (Reading the Signs number 2) asks students to visit a NikeTown and to write their own analysis of the outlet's in-store marketing techniques. Does McCarthy's critique still apply, or has NikeTown altered its strategies? If so, to what end? If a NikeTown is not located in your community, ask students to visit a retail outlet that employs similar layout and video displays. Or students could visit a single-brand store, such as Warner Bros. or Disney, that also sells a corporate and a brand image along with the products. The question suggests that students consult Gladwell's "The Signs of Shopping"; be sure students grasp that the disorienting effects of NikeTown displays are rather different than those engineered by Paco Underhill. To prepare students for a visit to a retail outlet, assign question number 3, which asks the class to brainstorm companies that promote brand image as a commodity (consider listing on the board all the items of clothing worn by your students that prominently display brand logos — the results may be amusing!). For argumentative topics, consider assigning question 1, which asks students to apply Kalle Lasn's strident critique of advertising from Chapter Two to NikeTown, or question 4, which has them take on McCarthy's assertion that NikeTown's marketing techniques are "Orwellian." This last question could also serve as the basis of an in-class debate about the effects and the ethics of modern marketing techniques.

SUSAN WILLIS

DISNEY WORLD: PUBLIC USE/PRIVATE STATE (p. 415)

Willis's essay is one of the more difficult in this book, and you may want to spend some time discussing critical reading strategies. You could ask students to outline her essay in their journals or to jot down a list of unfamiliar terms as they read and to propose, in their own words, definitions of those terms. Ask them to identify the argument and the wealth of support Willis offers (though occasionally abstract, this article is filled with specific details and anecdotes that students should have little trouble understanding). The Reading the Text questions all focus on Willis's main points, so you might also assign those questions as a reading log.

This selection is well worth the effort students may need to expend, however. Willis turns to a significant category of the built environment — the artificial world created by theme parks such as Disney World — and analyzes how the park's design encourages consumption. Be prepared for some resistance to her thesis: students often cling to childhood favorites, equating an analysis of them to an attack on themselves. If they do so, be sure to ask them the ever-useful question "Why?" Why did Disneyland, in a different venue, come up with "Disney Dollars"? Why don't we see kids playing spontaneously at Disney World? And make sure they don't rest content with the easy answer "Disney World is just fun." (Skeptical students may appreciate it if you assign Reading the Signs question 2, which invites students to support or refute one of Willis's central contentions.) If your students are unfamiliar with Disney World, ask them to apply her thesis to a local theme park they may have visited (see question 3). Although Willis focuses on Disney World, her argument extends to other theme parks and consumer products. Question 1 asks students to consider a related phenomenon, the plethora of Disney products, characters, and movies (here, too, expect a few students to defend Disney as if the company were equivalent to their own identity — a real sign of Disney's impact). A more challenging topic, number 5 calls for a comparison of the ways Disney World and a local shopping mall control spending behavior. Students will be prepared for this question if they read Anne Norton's "The Signs of Shopping" or Rachel Bowlby's "The Haunted Superstore" in Chapter One and Malcolm Gladwell's "The Science of Shopping" in this chapter. The question that demands the most creativity is 4, which asks students to design a theme park for the twenty-first century. As part of this question, ask students to articulate the rationale behind their design choices — a sure way to encourage them to see the ideological underpinnings of something so seemingly innocent as a child's fantasyland.

LUCY R. LIPPARD

ALTERNATING CURRENTS (p. 427)

We felt a chapter on the built environment practically required a discussion of the city and the country, and Lippard's selection fits the bill beautifully. The "alternating current" of her title is the push-pull that most Americans feel, at one time or another, between the high energy and drama of the city and the calming influence of a rural area. What we like about this selection is that Lippard goes beyond simply describing this dynamic to explore the symbolic (and semiotic) significances of each context, explaining, for instance, both the positive and negative associations attached to cities.

(Note that Lippard focuses more on cities and that her comments on the country are briefer and more implicit.) Before your students read this selection, ask them to brainstorm associations they have with the country and the city, then have them compare their results with the attributes Lippard describes. They may be interested in seeing how many of their prior attitudes are included in her discussion — and in recognizing that their own beliefs can fit into a full intellectual context. And encourage your students to relate their own experiences in different environments to Lippard's points. If your students are attending an urban college away from home, for instance, ask them to relate their experience of moving to school to Lippard's comments about the ways cities affect newcomers. If you're emphasizing gender issues, the Lippard article can be useful as well because she makes some debatable claims about what the city can represent to women in particular (Reading the Signs question 5 asks students to evaluate the validity of Lippard's gender-related claims). Question 1 is a journal topic that asks students to reflect on whether they have felt the alternating current that Lippard describes. Because some students may have lived in the same place all their lives, or because some may not be independent enough to see themselves as having options for where to live, you might encourage them to view this prompt broadly: Do they long for a camping vacation in the summer? How does a week-long wilderness hike make them feel? Lippard's focus on the binary poles of country and city largely excludes an environment that may in fact be more typical of where Americans live, the suburbs; thus, question 2 invites students to analyze the suburb's mythological significance. For focused questions that require students to handle specific evidence, consider assigning question 3, which invites them to conduct a survey on why urbanites are "lured" by their environment, and question 4, which asks students to test one of Lippard's claims about urban or rural landmarks.

KAREN KARBO
THE DINING ROOM (p. 434)

Expect your students — both male and female, young and older — to feel deeply moved by Karbo's selection. A memoir, this piece is a coming-of-age tale that charts Karbo's shifting relationship with her family, particularly with her mother; the changes in their relationship are paralleled by changes in the family's dining rooms as they move from house to house. Indeed, the dining rooms not only represent the family dynamic but also work to control it. This selection is ideal for discussing the often unrecognized influence of domestic space: ask your students to reflect on the ways their own homes' design affects family interactions. Do they have "neutral" space, where family members enjoy equal status? Or are some rooms marked as territory for one person? What happens if territorial boundaries are transgressed? You can develop this discussion by studying the photo of the father and son arguing at dinner on p. 442. What signs indicate that the characters are related, and what seems to be the dynamic among them? Beyond raising the issue of domestic space, this selection also is well-suited for teaching close reading techniques. Be sure to discuss Karbo's use of the second person: Why would a memoir writer elect this form of address, and what effect does it have on the reader? Ask students to pay attention to stylistic details as well. Why does Karbo capitalize some words, such as Special Occasion and Fancy, that normally are not capitalized? How does the capitalization work to create an image of Karbo's mother? One reason students find this selection engaging, we believe, is Karbo's subtle sense of humor. What makes some of the passages humorous, and why do students think Karbo includes humor in a tale that has a sad conclusion?

"The Dining Room" lends itself to both straightforward analytic essays and to more imaginative assignments. Reading the Signs question 1 has students analyze the ways the various dining tables and rooms symbolically represent Karbo's relationship with her mother; for a close textual analysis, assign question 4, which focuses on Karbo's characterization of her mother. For a more personal response, question 3 invites students to write their own memoir of a significant physical space; the question can be reformulated into an analytic essay if you prefer. Question 4 requires the most creativity, because it asks students to assume the role of Karbo's mother and to write her remembrance of the dining rooms the selection describes. To prepare students for this topic, you might discuss in class the dynamics among all the family members: What role does Karbo's father play? Why do we see so little of him? And what sort of relationship exists between Karbo's parents?

DAPHNE SPAIN

Spatial Segregation and Gender Stratification in the Workplace (p. 443)

This selection is perfect for addressing the ways in which the built environment can replicate cultural gender norms. Although the style of this selection is a tad dry, your students should find it easy to grasp Spain's main ideas about the gendered patterns in contemporary office environments. Be sure they focus on her distinction between "open floor" and "closed door," and encourage them to articulate the power relations that are implied by each type of office design. Ask them about their own experiences in work environments. Whether male or female, they most likely have occupied lower-level or intern positions and thus probably have experienced the hierarchical arrangements enforced by design. Why is a view office considered a sign of importance? Why, in the aftermath of John F. Kennedy Jr.'s death in 1999, did so many commentators note how remarkable it was that his office at *George* magazine was located on the same floor as those of the staffers? Then you can move to Spain's argument about gender stratification; you might note that, while women have moved into higher corporate spheres, the general patterns of employment that she describes still dominate the workplace.

Students should enjoy testing Spain's ideas on work environments with which they are familiar. Reading the Signs question 2 has students analyze the office where they work; as an alternative, students could study a staff office or even faculty offices at your college. For a topic that requires students to conduct interviews, assign question 3, which focuses on Spain's contention about the nature of women's work. An imaginative topic, question 1 invites students to work in groups to design a nonhierarchical office space. We suggest that you have each group present their proposal to the class, briefly outlining the rationale for their design. Your students can have some fun with question 4, which has them write a hypothetical response to the "ideal" boss-secretary relationship that Spain quotes in this selection. Expect a wide range of responses, especially in this post-Enron, post-Worldcom era, to the notion that the purpose of a secretarial job is to serve as custodian for the boss's "secrets."

RINA SWENTZELL

CONFLICTING LANDSCAPE VALUES: THE SANTA CLARA PUEBLO AND DAY SCHOOL (p. 450)

The first time we assigned this selection, we weren't sure whether our students, who are mostly urban Californians, would relate to Swentzell's topic. Our concerns proved baseless, however, as students seemed fascinated not only by Swentzell's comparison of Native American and mainstream worldviews but also by her discussion of the way a school's architectural design can embody a particular educational philosophy. Swentzell's writing is clear and accessible. You might organize your class discussion around the two worldviews that she describes. Ask students to brainstorm on the board the cultural values implicit in the Pueblo culture, for instance, and then to list the physical and architectural features common to traditional Pueblo communities. How do those features perpetuate traditional values? What approach to education and learning do they encourage? Then do the same for the Bureau of Indian Affairs school. What are the design features of this school, and what cultural and social values does it promote? What sort of pedagogy does the design dictate? Such questions can lead to a discussion of larger political issues as students consider the relation between the built environment, cultural dominance, and political power.

This selection can stimulate students to consider their own educational environment and the pedagogy that it encourages. We urge you to assign Reading the Signs question 1, which asks the class to analyze the design of your composition classroom (you could make this either a discussion topic or an essay assignment). Alternatively, students could compare two different sorts of classrooms — a lecture hall and a seminar room, for instance — addressing not only their physical layout but also the style of learning that each allows. We've created two questions that address the ideologies underlying school architectual design. Question 2 asks students to analyze the BIA Day School as a reflection of the myth of a manifest destiny, and question 3 sends them to Fan Shen's "The Classroom and the Wider Culture: Identity as a Key to Learning English Composition" (Chapter 7), prompting them to identify and evaluate the non-Western educational approaches that both authors describe. Question 4 focuses less on design than on pedagogy, inviting the class to debate the merits of hands-on learning at the university level. For this question, be sure that student consider how such learning could occur in a variety of disciplines, including the sciences, the humanities, and the arts.

CAMILO JOSÉ VERGARA

THE GHETTO CITYSCAPE (p. 461)

You should find this selection easy to teach, even if your students have little knowledge of the inner city. You might begin discussion by having students brainstorm their impressions of a ghetto environment (preferably before they have read the selection): don't be surprised if their impressions echo those of scholars to whom Vergara alludes early in the piece. Then move to his main point, which is that, rather than being uniform places of ruin, inner city environments can have quite different characters and are not necessarily places of total devastation. Vergara provides a handy paradigm for analyzing such environments; his triad of green ghettos, institutional ghettos, and new immigrant ghettos is accessible and tailor-made for applying to specific urban areas. If you teach in a city, ask your students to analyze it using this framework; if Vergara's categories don't quite fit, challenge students to modify them or to devise their own (see Reading the Signs question 1). Even if you don't teach in a city, this paradigm is still useful, for most suburbs and small towns have their older or relatively impoverished sections that reflect Vergara's distinctions. Indeed, this selection could be valuable in helping students observe spatial detail in any community, not just in the inner city.

This selection pairs well with Lippard's "Alternating Currents," for though these authors share the assumption that a sense of place has a profound effect on human consciousness, their focuses and concerns differ. Reading the Signs question 2 asks students to adopt Vergara's perspective and critique Lippard's reading of the city; alternatively, you could simply ask students to compare and contrast the two writers' views. One issue that emerges in this selection is the role that nature plays in shaping an urban environment; thus, question 3 asks students to explore this role. Note that this can be a rich, complex topic; you might assign the Lippard and the Swentzell selections to help trigger your students' thinking on the matter. If you want your students to do a little reseach, have them investigate the ways in which public parks affect urban life. Perhaps the most challenging topic is number 4, which has students argue for or against Vergara's basic premise that the city's physical environment is at least as influential as economic factors in shaping people's lives.

ERIC BOEHLERT

New York's Most Disliked Building? (p. 467)

We'd guess that most students have vivid memories of watching television on September 11, 2001, and etched in their minds is the terrible collapse of the famous twin towers. Indeed, that awful sight has often been likened to the assassination of John F. Kennedy or, to a lesser extent, the explosion of the space shuttle *Challenger* as an iconic part of cultural memory. You might begin discussion of this selection by discussing the World Trade Center's symbolic significance. How might that significance differ depending on one's perspective as an American? More specifically, as a New Yorker? Or as a militant terrorist? Why was it the target of terrorists, not just in 2001 but also in 1993? As you contemplate this question, study the photo of the WTC on p. 469 and the images of their destruction on pp. 20–23. Ask your students as well to consider the history of the WTC that Boehlert sketches. How was the WTC initially received, both by the public and by the architectural community? How did those responses evolve as the towers came to occupy what at one time seemed to be a permanent, anchoring role in the New York City skyline?

Boehlert's selection is flexible enough to invite assignments that focus either on the World Trade Center itself or on other buildings. Reading the Text question 1 asks students to assess the towers' posthumous symbolic significance; to develop support for their arguments, students could research the on-going debates over whether the towers should be rebuilt and over what sort of memorial would be appropriate for the WTC site. For a more focused topic, question 3 asks students to write an argumentative response to the claim that the WTC was an "arrogant" design. Question 2 extends the issues to your own community, asking students to analyze a local public building that has symbolic status. Beyond visiting the building, students might consult a local library or city hall for archival documents related to the planning and design of the building.

Alternatively, students could select a building that, like the World Trade Center, was initially greeted with skepticism if not outright hostility, and they could research the history of its public reception. Has the building's symbolic significance evolved, and, if so, how can the change be explained? Buildings or monuments that come to mind include the Transamerica pyramid in San Francisco, the Sears tower in Chicago, or the arch in St. Louis.

WE'VE COME A LONG WAY, MAYBE
Gender Codes in American Culture

If you want your course to focus on one far-ranging theme, you'd do well to select gender as your topic. Not only can students easily see how it shapes their everyday lives, but it affects every area of popular culture. Each chapter in this text has at least one selection that, at least in part, treats gender, so you should have no difficulty identifying a sufficient number of readings to cover a term (see p. 9 of this manual for suggested additional readings from *Signs of Life* for a gender-themed course). We have quite deliberately constructed this chapter to show students that gender is an issue for both women and men, that gender should not be confined to women's studies courses. Occasionally male students quietly — and sometimes not so quietly — tune out when gender becomes a focus in their courses, assuming, as Deborah Tannen points out in her essay, that they are not "marked" by gender as are their female peers. We wish to counter that assumption, for we believe males and females, heterosexuals and homosexuals, are equally subject to our culture's gender norms and mythologies, though the effects can differ radically for each group and for each individual. Accordingly, we treat gender issues broadly in this chapter, addressing both men and women in the chapter's introduction and including readings that explore the signs of both genders.

Assumptions about gender can be deeply rooted, so don't be surprised if your students react spontaneously or even emotionally to the topic. We've found that students usually enjoy discussing gender issues, but for some, just raising them seems to cast doubt on what's "normal." The Exploring the Signs of Gender topic thus is designed to allow students to explore their own assumptions about gender and how these assumptions were shaped. We've found it's most effective to structure class discussion to stimulate lively but controlled conversation about these issues. You can alternate between arranging students in same- and mixed-sex groups, for instance, to take advantage of gender dynamics. You might want to do that with the Discussing the Signs of Gender question, which asks students in small groups to study the gender roles depicted in popular magazines. If you have an ethnically diverse group, asking students to contribute perspectives that differ from "traditional" American gender norms can help show how they are culturally, not biologically, constructed. No matter what your students' backgrounds, we urge you to assume that all students are gender-marked, even if our culture assumes otherwise. We've deliberately made the Reading Gender on the Net exercise broad, inviting them to explore how the Net defines gender issues. If you assign your students this topic, encourage them to read their findings as a sign of what our culture identifies as "male" and "female" concerns.

Holly Devor's selection is essential for its theoretical argument that gender is socially constituted. It provides a framework for understanding the other selections in the chapter, as well as many selections throughout the text. Though one of the text's more difficult selections, it's extremely useful pedagogically. We include Kevin Jennings's memoir about growing up gay and coming to terms with his sexual orientation next, largely to counter the equation between gender and heterosexuality. Another counterpoint is offered by Deborah Blum, who contrasts with Devor in outlining the ways biology affects gender roles and behavior. Blum's piece, which talks about childhood development, can be paired with Jennifer Scanlon's selection, which discusses the ways in which board games socialize young girls to traditional gender norms. Children grow into teens, of course, and Andre Mayer follows by studying the very chauvinistic styles adopted by teen pop culture stars like Britney Spears. Next Naomi Wolf, Deborah Tannen, and James William Gibson address particular signs of gender identity: Wolf focuses on the pressure women face to be extravagantly slender; Tannen argues that women are always "marked" in our society; Gibson surveys popular culture to explain why the warrior has become a model for male identity. The chapter concludes with Laura Miller's selection on gender and cyberspace, which defends the Net against charges of being a mysogynistic environment.

HOLLY DEVOR

GENDER ROLE BEHAVIORS AND ATTITUDES (p. 484)

We highly recomend that you include Holly Devor's essay in your syllabus, for its overview of gender roles and the signs used to communicate them provides a basic critical framework for the chapter's remaining selections. But we warn you: Devor's writing style is somewhat academic and dense, and your students may find it tough going. We suggest that you use the essay as an occasion for discussing critical reading strategies and techniques for comprehending academic writing. You might ask your students to annotate the essay as they read it, and then, in small groups, to review their annotations — and their sense of what Devor's major points are. Or ask them to prepare review questions. At the beginning of class, have students write their questions on the board; you can quickly see which parts of the essay may have been confusing and warrant in-depth discussion.

Despite the difficulty, Devor's essay is well worth the effort. Not only does she chart the traditional cues of "masculinity" and "femininity," but she makes clear how they are cultural constructs, not biological necessities. You'll want to make sure students understand that, when talking about these cues, Devor is describing social norms, not her recommendations for how people should act (students might complain, for instance, that she wants women to be passive — quite the contrary). Her emphasis on social construction thus makes her essay a must-read if you're using a semiotic approach. Students tend not to dispute her general claims about the socially constructed nature of gender, but they do occasionally have trouble with two of her premises. First, they may resist the notion that signs of masculinity carry with them a position of social power and dominance — in other words, that gender norms can have some inequitable consequences. You might address this issue by discussing specific, concrete examples; the Deborah Tannen selection could help in this regard. Second, Devor suggests the possibility of mixing gender norms (the selection is excerpted from her book *Gender Blending*), and this may make some students uncomfortable. If you're game, you could broaden the terms of discussion to include the assumption that heterosexuality is the only morally acceptable sexual preference in America — but be prepared for hearing some strongly entrenched beliefs on this issue.

Because Devor provides a broad theoretical framework for viewing gender, her selection is ideal for applying to specific evidence. Consider doing the first Reading the Signs question in class before discussing the essay; that way you'll be able to refer back to students' presumptions about gender later. The question asks students to brainstorm gender traits in small groups and then to write their lists on the board. If students form same-sex groups, we can guarantee a lively discussion! Even students challenged by Devor's essay should be able to respond to most of the remaining questions. Question 2 allows students to assume the role of sociologist by asking them to use a friend's behavior as evidence they can analyze in terms of gender norms. Question 3 picks up on Devor's comments about body language and sends students to popular magazines to examine the gender-related postures of models (we've found that men in particular are allowed a limited range of postures in ads, with the limitations being greatest in men's magazines such as *GQ*). Finally, question 4 asks students to address the genuinely debatable issue of whether fashion continues to restrict the female body more than the male body.

KEVIN JENNINGS
AMERICAN DREAMS (p. 489)

Kevin Jennings's selection is one of our favorites, and not simply for its clear writing, mild sense of humor, and engaging individual voice. In this personal narrative, Jennings describes how he came to terms with being gay while growing up, combating not normative gender roles but also his own sense of insecurity. In the process, Jennings creates a whole cultural context for understanding why gays and lesbians are so often seen as the "other" in our society; indeed, as he describes his growing desires during adolescence to join the mainstream, to capture the traditional American dream, what emerges are multiple layers of "otherness." First Jennings became aware of geographical otherness and attempted to erase the signs that he was a southerner. What's interesting here is that he became an active participant in maintaining the distinction between mainstream and other (Reading the Signs question 2 asks students to write an essay in which they explore this issue further). What's even more interesting is that Jennings repeats this pattern, for a time, with his sexual orientation. That is, at first he tried to deny his homosexuality to himself, and this effort continued even when Jennings got to college. Note that when Jennings says that by accepting his identity as a gay man he has "done the most American thing of all," he is assuming a different definition of the American dream than the one he assumed in the beginning of the selection. Be sure to ask your students how the dream changes for Jennings thoughout his process of self-discovery. And encourage them to study the photo of the gay rights rally on p. 491. We deliberately include an image of gay senior citizens to counter the more common stereotype, so often projected in media today, of gays as hip and always young.

Although some students may feel that Jennings is a tad sentimental, expect that most students will respond positively to this very open, honest piece. Given the personal nature of this selection, students may enjoy responding to Reading the Signs question 1, a journal topic that has them reflect on the pressures of normative gender roles that they may have felt during their teens. Because both Jennings and Melissa Algranati (Chapter Seven) are young people who narrate their experiences growing up and struggling with their identity, question 4 poses a straightforward comparison and contrast assignment based on their selections. For a challenging argumentative topic, see question 3, which focuses on popular media's role in perpetuating a heterosexual norm. For this topic, be sure students look beyond the occasional media-hyped character or episode (Ellen DeGeneres, for instance, or Roseanne Barr's sharing a kiss with a woman) to consider the typical ways in which gender roles are defined.

DEBORAH BLUM

THE GENDER BLUR: WHERE DOES BIOLOGY END AND SOCIETY TAKE OVER? (p. 495)

As a clear explication of biology's influence on gender behaviors, Deborah Blum's piece serves as a direct response to Holly Devor's claim that gender is a social construct. As Blum herself points out, her argument is not exactly politically correct (readers familiar with the work of writers such as Emily Martin will bristle at her acceptance of the term "default sex" in reference to females). But don't expect her viewpoint to be reactionary: we like her essay precisely because it avoids the simplistic either-or thinking that often dominates the culture-versus-nature debate on gender matters. Indeed, Blum acknowledges that many of our gender codes are cultural constructs; what she argues, however, is that evidence suggests that biology has far more influence on gender behaviors than most humanists want to admit. To academics accustomed to social construction theories, that might seem like an untenable position, but another reason we like this piece is her careful approach to argumentation. In a nice Rogerian style, she begins with a personal anecdote that validates her readership's likely assumptions that gender is only a social construct (this piece originally appeared in the *Utne Reader*) and then explains how her thinking about gender evolved to include biological influence. Ask your students to chart the many ways in which she anticipates her readership's probable responses to her claims. Even though Blum occasionally talks about XX and XY chromosomes and Leydig cell hypoplasia, she is a Pulitzer Prize–winning science writer who knows how to make technical information accessible to the nonspecialist reader. You can use her piece as a model of clarity and specificity sans goopy jargon.

Particularly if you pair this selection with the Holly Devor essay, your students should be well equipped to write argumentative essays. The natural question to accompany this pairing is Reading the Signs question 2, which invites students to respond to Blum's challenge to the social construction view of gender. Because Blum talks a good deal about her own observations as a mother, it's likely your students will want to discuss child-rearing strategies; an imaginative topic, question 2 prompts students to suggest appropriate ways to raise boys given the biological evidence that Blum sets forth. To extend Blum's argument, question 4 invites students to research the current findings on the genetic basis of sexual orientation (recent studies have found that homosexuality may have some genetic influence). To allow students to respond personally to Blum's often personal essay, assign question 1, a journal entry on how one's upbringing affects one's understanding of gender norms.

We encourage you to study in class the photo of the stork and infants with male and females signs sitting in a shopping cart on p. 502. Ask your students: How is the gender of each baby indicated, and why are the babies — and the stork — sitting in a shopping cart? What is the photographer trying to suggest about gender roles in modern American society?

JENNIFER SCANLON

BOYS-R-US: BOARD GAMES AND THE SOCIALIZATION OF YOUNG ADOLESCENT GIRLS (p. 503)

Jennifer Scanlon's essay pairs nicely with Michael A. Messner's selection in Chapter Eight, for just as sports lead boys to adopt traditional male gender roles, the same-sex board games Scanlon describes socialize girls to embrace traditional female roles. We've found that students enjoy talking about their childhood experiences, and given the accessibility of Scanlon's writing, you should have no trouble triggering a lively discussion of this selection. You might start by dividing the board in two sections, one for girls and one for boys, and having the whole class come to the board and, in the appropriate section, identify a favorite toy or game from childhood (asking students to do this en masse will yield more candid responses). Then stand back and look for patterns: To what extent are the toys and games gender-specific? Are gender-neutral toys mentioned, and, if so, are they more common for girls or for boys? You may have some students complain that Scanlon makes "too much" out of games, saying, "I didn't think about these issues as a child." Use these objections as an opportunity to to to ask that handy question, "Why *this*?" Why is it that so few gender-neutral toys exist for children? Indeed, a provocative exercise would be to ask your students (either individually or as a group) to design a game that would avoid typical gender stereotypes (see Reading the Signs question 1). If some students have difficulty imagining such a game, they should discuss why the task is so hard.

Students often enjoy essays about childhood activities; to tap into this interest, Reading the Signs question 1 is a journal entry prompt that focuses on the games students played when young children. As Scanlon points out, board games are part of a pop cultural system that defines gender norms, a system that Naomi Wolf also studies in her selection. Accordingly, question 3 sends students to Wolf's "The Beauty Myth" to compare the games' influence on girls with that of the advertising and the beauty industries. We see as the most challenging question number 4, which asks students to use Scanlon's perspective in a response to Deborah Blum's selection in this chapter. In addition to addressing Blum's argument for the biological basis of gender behavior, students need to consider Blum's personal anecdotes about her own children's play habits.

ANDRE MAYER

THE NEW SEXUAL STONE AGE (p. 512)

We really think Mayer's argument is right on target — and we think you can expect it to trigger a lively class discussion. That's because many students may take issue with Mayer's biting indictment of today's pop culture stars, espcially musicians and singers, who have embraced sexist and chauvinistic gender roles. Often students see these stars, like Mariah Carey or Fred Durst, as cool and cutting-edge, not retrograde, and thus are likely to bristle at Mayer's attack. You might ask your class to list on the board a dozen or so current pop music stars, then consider the images they project. Do they follow the patterns Mayer describes? Alternatively, you could form small groups, each charged with the task of preparing two lists: five current stars who fit reflect Mayer's argument and five who in fact assume more progressive notions about gender. Have the groups write their lists on the board, and then analyze the results. If the lists demonstrate a consensus, discuss the particular details about the artists' images and behavior that led them to be so categorized; if the lists contradict each other, get students to discuss their assumptions about what constitutes outmoded or progressive attitudes toward gender. In either case, you may want to move from observing the phenomenon Mayer decries to addressing its larger significance. Why is a slutty appearance so prized for female stars, even for teen and preteen girls? While a group like Destiny's Child would like its audience to see them as champions of female empowerment, is their choice of clothing, makeup, and hair style really empowering or does it just make them sex objects? How can they account for this trend in pop music?

Students are likely to have plenty to say in response to Mayer's selection. For straightforward argument assignments, try Reading the Signs question 1, which invites students to support or oppose Mayer's central thesis, or number 5, which suggests students debate the degree of chauvinism or liberation that exists in pop music (an in-class debate, in which teams generate lots of specific evidence for their argument, could be the basis of an at-home essay assignment). Two questions narrow the assignment focus, with number 3 asking students to analyze *Maxim* in light of Mayer's charges and number 4 having them analyze the style of female rappers. The most speculative question is number 2, which challenges students to develop their own argument about why the trends that Mayer laments are so prevalent in popular music.

NAOMI WOLF

THE BEAUTY MYTH (p. 515)

In this selection, Naomi Wolf describes a fundamental component of our culture's gender mythology: the presumption that women should be judged and valued according to physical attractiveness. Wolf's presentation of this myth is particularly useful in that she distinguishes between biological and cultural imperatives, recognizes the historical fluctuations in this myth, and locates it in the context of power relations. That sounds like heady stuff, but her writing style is clear and direct and students should have little trouble understanding her points. As you discuss this essay, be aware that you may have some students who have struggled painfully with their own physical appearances: They may been tormented by years of failed dieting, they may have a sought a plastic surgeon's solution to a perceived facial defect, or they may be plagued by eating disorders. Although you want to establish a spirit of openness in class discussion, let students know that that openness does not obligate them to engage in confession. If they wish to respond personally to Wolf's essay (and it can trigger that sort of response), Reading the Signs question 1 invites them to do so in their journal (and we recommend that you keep this a private journal entry). One way to address these issues neutrally would be to study the beauty-parlor photo on p. 520: What are the images on the wall, and why are they there? Why does the photographer pose an older woman as a customer?

We particularly like assignments that ask students to apply Wolf's notion of the beauty myth to specific cases. Question 2, which directs them to a local art museum to analyze the representation of women's bodies, could be either an individual or a group project. We've made question 3, which asks students to study a woman's fashion magazine in light of Wolf's argument, a class exercise, but it could make an at-home essay assignment as well. If you prefer an argumentative topic, question 4 invites students to take on one of Wolf's major assertions. And to extend Wolf's thesis, try question 5, which asks students to debate whether men are trapped by standards of physical attractiveness as women are. For this topic, several other selections in the text, including the Diane Barthel (Chapter Two) and Mariah Burton Nelson (Chapter Eight) pieces, could help students generate ideas and arguments.

DEBORAH TANNEN

THERE IS NO UNMARKED WOMAN (p. 525)

This selection proved to be one of the most often used in the first three editions of *Signs of Life*, and we can understand why. In a clear, direct writing style, Tannen looks at nonlinguistic ways in which women are marked in our culture — a topic well suited to lots of lively classroom activities. You could have same-sex groups brainstorm ways in which both genders are marked among, say, students at your school; then you could ask the groups to write their lists on the board. How do the lists compare by gender? Are the lists themselves marked? Because this selection is extremely accessible, students should have no trouble recognizing the specifics of her argument. You may, however, want to spend a little time on her notion of being "marked." Some students may want to complicate her claim that men are normative (Tannen does tend to generalize broadly about males). You could, for instance, ask students to brainstorm ways in which men, too, can be marked — and then talk about how a marked status differs for men and women (see Reading the Signs question 1). This selection is particularly good for analytic assignments that ask students to apply Tannen's notion of marking to evidence they collect themselves (see questions 2 and 3). The final question allows students to use their imaginations in defining what an unmarked appearance for women would be like. We highly recommend that you ask your students to share their proposals with the class!

JAMES WILLIAM GIBSON

WARRIOR DREAMS (p. 531)

At first James William Gibson's selection may seem tangentially related to gender, for he opens with a "war" scene filled with "Communist battalions" assaulting victorious "Americans." But bear with Gibson. You'll quickly see that he's describing not a Vietnam War battle but a fantasy skirmish staged at a *Soldier of Fortune* convention, and you'll see that zeal for this sort of event reflects an increasingly influential model for male gender roles that Gibson dubs "warrior dreams." Gibson's writing is clear and lively, and his method for explaining warrior dreams is perfect for a class emphasizing semiotics and cultural analysis. He takes his reader through a wide range of popular culture, from movies to paintball to warrior magazines like *Gung-Ho*, demonstrating a pattern of paramilitary culture that, he claims, became the "ideal identity for *all* men." Expect that some students who enjoy the sort of entertainment Gibson describes may object to his not-entirely-positive depiction of paramilitary culture; be sure they understand that your use of this essay is to study a cultural systems and mythology and not to pass judgment on their personal lives. Alternately, some students may not have been exposed directly to paramilitary chic, and they might believe that Gibson's talking about a fringe element that has little to do with mainstream society. If you find that's the case, a discussion of 1999's shootings at Columbine High School might help them to see the on-going pervasiveness of what Gibson describes. Students interested in this may enjoy responding to Reading the Signs question 2, which invites them to explore the real-world implications of warrior dreams. In addition, Gibson's selection lends itself to argumentative and analytic topics. Question 1 sends students to Michael A. Messner's selection in Chapter Eight to compare sports ideology with warrior dreams (students should find plenty of parallels), while question 3 prompts students to use Gibson's argument as a framework for interpreting the attractions of professional wrestling. The broadest question, number 4 asks the class to brainstorm current media entertainment aimed at a male audience and then to discuss the prevalence of warrior dreams in pop culture today. Expect your class to compile a long list — one that both you and your students may find sobering.

LAURA MILLER

Women and Children First: Gender and the Settling of the Electronic Frontier (p. 539)

Even students who can't tell RAM from ROM are almost certainly aware of one of the controversies surrounding the Internet: the plethora of seedy and lecherous home pages, sexist diatribes, and pornographic garbage. This sort of material is often clearly identified for what it is, but sometimes it hides under an electronic disguise (for example, "cooking tips" might be a link to child pornography). As a result, many critics have wondered whether controls need to be placed on the Net to protect the innocent — who, in the main, are seen as women and children. Nonsense, says Laura Miller. She goes beyond describing the Net controversy to identify the larger implications surrounding gender roles within the context of American mythology. That is, she takes the common notion of the Net as a "frontier" and does a gender-based analysis of it, ultimately arguing that the calls for protection are themselves patronizing and reflect sexist assumptions. You may want to spend some time in class on her discussion of the "frontier" concept; Laurence Shames's "The More Factor" (Chapter One) could help your students grasp this point. You might also ask your students to consider the typical image of computer afficionados (in films, advertising, and so forth) — it's likely they'll see them as male. Then ask them to consider the implications of this image, for users and nonusers alike.

Your students are likely to have plenty to say in response to Miller's argument. Reading the Signs question 1 invites them to log onto a chat room and then to use their experience to support or to refute Miller's thesis; you might ask your students to do this in mixed-gender pairs so they can incorporate their partner's response into their argument. We highly recommend question 2, which asks the class to stage a debate on whether regulation to protect the innocent is necessary. Teams might first research any legislation on this matter that is before Congress. (We include the photo of a "Take Back the Night" rally on p. 545 to prompt students to consider the differences and similarities between online sexual abuse and the in-person variety. Can students imagine a way in which users can "take back the screen"?) If your students like controversial issues, they might enjoy responding to question 4, a journal topic on the possibility of online rape. Perhaps the most ambitious gender-related topic is number 5, which asks students to interview several women who are Net fans and to use the results of their interviews to argue about the construction of gender roles online. Finally, for a different focus, question 3 sidesteps the gender issue and sends students to Laurence Shames's selection to explain the extent to which the Net appeals to the American desire for more.

Chapter Seven
CONSTRUCTING RACE
Readings in Multicultural Semiotics

We consider this chapter crucial to any writing course with a cultural studies bent, largely because race and ethnicity have become such influential and, sometimes, divisive forces shaping popular culture, politics, education, and even one's personal identity. Race has always been important, of course, but many recent factors — for instance, successes in the civil rights movement, a political and legal backlash against those successes, increased immigration from non-European nations, and increased opposition to such immigration — have heightened Americans' sensitivity to race and racial conflict. Discussing multicultural issues in class can be tricky, especially if your campus has experienced racial tensions or if your students come from ethnic backgrounds that historically have been odds with each other. The potential for in-class conflict is not a reason to avoid the issue; in fact, it's probably the most compelling reason to address it. Students' ability to succeed in school may depend, in part, on their ability to handle those kinds of conflicts, and their writing class may be the only structured environment in which they can explore them.

You'll find that semiotic analysis is an optimal way to handle class discussion of race because, rather than focusing on private passions about race, it addresses the way race serves as a sign for the culture at large. This is not to say that students will feel divorced from discussion of race — indeed, we deliberately ask in the introduction to this chapter "Who are you?" to suggest the potency of race in shaping one's personal identity, and we make that question the focus of the Exploring the Signs of Race journal topic. But even when working on a personal level, a semiotic approach links the individual's views with that of the system, the larger society. The emphasis, then words, is on the cultural mythologies about race that shape our values and our worldviews.

That's not to say that those mythologies may not be changing. Indeed, the United States has passed through many phases in its racial history and, as the twenty-first century begins, it will pass through more. Accordingly, to encourage students to look into the future, the Discussing the Signs of Race question asks the class to consider the implications of an America where there is no majority race (a near-term prediction made by demographers). Since this question is future-oriented, we opted to focus on the present in the Reading Race on the Net exercise. This topic asks students to visit Web sites devoted to the culture of a particular ethnicity and to analyze the breadth of information available. You might want your students to share their findings in class, so they can assemble a composite description of Internet sources on ethnicities.

We feel reluctant to suggest cuts in this chapter, because the selections poignantly speak to the force race exerts both on our personal lives and on the American psyche. The essays do approach the issues from different perspectives, however, and you could choose selections according to those differences. Michael Omi's essay is the lead selection because he provides a broad theoretical overview of racial attitudes and explores how those attitudes are manifested in popular culture. If you've already discussed the media, Omi will provide you with a perfect transition to a unit on race; media focus continues in the next two selections, by Benjamin DeMott on the representation of blacks and whites and by Paul C. Taylor on ethnic crossovers. Jack Lopez follows with a memoir about his youth, when he enjoyed the best of two ethnic worlds; in contrast, Nell Bernstein, bell hooks, and Melissa Algranati next address conflicts experienced by individuals who don't comfortably "fit in" ethnically. Bernstein describes teens who "wear" a new racial identity, as if they were trying on a new pair of jeans; hooks writes a personal reflection that captures the affection a young black girl feels for a doll that is ethnically the same as she; and Algranati addresses the often-overlooked dilemmas faced by mixed-race individuals. Language and culture are the focus of the next selection, in which Fan Shen describes the usually unspoken, socially constituted assumptions governing conventions of writing and scholarship in American universities. Addressing the cross-cultural conflicts he experienced as a Chinese student of freshman composition, Shen's essay is perfect for a writing class. The chapter concludes with LynNell Hancock revealing the social and economic implications of Internet access for race relations in America and Randall Kennedy taking a provocative look at the recent controversy over racial profiling.

MICHAEL OMI

IN LIVING COLOR: RACE AND AMERICAN CULTURE (p. 557)

We've kept Omi's essay through three editions both for its clear exposition of the prevailing racial beliefs in America and for its focus on how those beliefs are manifested in popular culture. Thus, it is one of the more important selections in *Signs of Life:* it provides a critical framework for analyzing racial issues in selections found throughout the text. Students should find Omi challenging but accessible. Omi does not use the word *semiotics,* but essentially he provides a semiotic reading of race and racial images. His underlying assumption is that cultural myths about race are socially constructed but are seen as natural categories. Race and racism are, of course, sensitive issues, but it's particularly useful to begin class discussion of them with Omi because he focuses on the *process* whereby ideas about race are created, rather than evaluating individuals who believe the ideas. In class, be sure to discuss the concepts he advances for talking about race: overt and inferential racism, unexamined racial beliefs, the ideology of difference or otherness, situation context, and invisibility. Although Omi defines and explains these concepts, the terms may be foreign to students.

The essay lends itself to assignments extending and complicating Omi's analysis of the racial images that prevail in American popular culture. We highly recommend doing Reading the Signs question 1, which asks the class to brainstorm common racial stereotypes and then to discuss how these stereotypes are perpetuated in popular culture. If students have difficulty doing the second task, you might organize their discussion by medium (advertising, movies, and so forth) so that they can more easily focus on particular examples. You can use this discussion to speculate on the media's power to shape our understanding of the world. What difference does it make, for instance, if movies almost always depict gang members as black? What's wrong if advertising presents Asian students as hard-working and industrious? Don't be surprised if someone responds, "But isn't that true?" Such a question, of course, corroborates Omi's claims; we suggest that you invite other members of the class to respond. The remaining topics allow students to examine racial imagery and assumptions in various aspects of popular culture. Question 2 asks them to analyze how race operates as a sign in *Gone with the Wind*, while question 3 has them explore how films such as *Malcolm X* or *Mi Familia* may affect American attitudes toward racial identity. Students can have some fun with question 4, which asks them to analyze ethnicity in an ethnically targeted magazine. Have students work in teams so they can share insights, or ask that they present their findings in class.

BENJAMIN DEMOTT

PUT ON A HAPPY FACE: MASKING THE DIFFERENCES BETWEEN BLACKS AND WHITES (p. 569)

Don't be surprised if DeMott troubles some of your students, for he presents a controversial argument. DeMott deromanticizes Hollywood's tendency to depict friendly race relations, arguing that such fantasy works to perpetuate racial injustice, not to erase it. Students may wonder, "What's wrong with showing cordial race relations? Isn't that better than always depicting conflict?" It's important for students to realize that DeMott laments racial conflict as much as he opposes false images — it's just that he sees the false images as having serious social consequences. Such questions may well lead to a discussion of the effect of film, and the media more generally, on social consciousness. If that happens, you might refer students to Michael Omi's selection in this chapter. Students troubled by the implications of DeMott's position may enjoy responding to Reading the Signs question 3, which invites them to reflect in their journals on the impact of cinematic fantasy, or to question 5, which asks them to describe how they would depict race relations in film.

Whether your students buy DeMott's thesis, they will be able to write several different sorts of assignments in response to it. For a straightforward analysis assignment, try question 1, which asks students to analyze the race relations portrayed in one of the films DeMott mentions (or they can focus on a more recent film, such as *Men in Black II*). The issues this selection raises can be applied to ethnicities and media other than those addressed by DeMott. We've made question 2, which extends DeMott's concerns to other ethnic groups, a discussion topic, but it would be a workable essay assignment as well. Question 4 shifts to catalogues and advertising (you might assign Anne Norton's "The Signs of Shopping" in Chapter One to help students respond to this question).

PAUL C. TAYLOR

FUNKY WHITE BOYS AND HONORARY SOUL SISTERS (p. 579)

Don't let Taylor's hip title fool you: This selection is a challenging, at times philosophical reflection on racial identity and essentialism, ethnic "ownership" of cultural practices, and the tension between authentic and appropriated cultural products. This sounds like heady stuff, but with some help your students should be able to grasp Taylor's ideas about ethnic crossovers in popular culture. You might ask your students to prepare a list of Taylor's most important terms — for instance, cultural nationalism, metaphysical (or essentialist) nationalism, racial obligation, the Elvis effect — with definitions in students' own words. In small groups, students could compare their lists and select the most accurate definitions for class discussion; alternatively, you could collect the lists to determine students' comprehension levels. You could next focus on Taylor's personal narrative frame, his creation as a youth of The Funky White Boys Club, which is the most accessible part of the selection. Ask your students why Taylor is so careful to describe the evolution of his thinking about this club. Then be sure students are aware of the patterns of cultural borrowing that Taylor describes. You can extend his comments about blues and rap to other musical forms that originally were targeted to black audiences but that came to be embraced by mainstream white audiences (jazz and Motown come to mind). This may help students understand Taylor's assertion of the "historically racist trajectory of white American appetites for cultural commodities."

Taylor's selection creates opportunities for thoughtful, challenging analytic assignments. Reading the Signs question 1 allows students to addresses the central question that Taylor poses: whether whites can participate in African American cultural activities. Because your students' success in responding to this topic will depend, in part, on their discussion of specific artists and performers, this topic offers an occasion for a lesson on unsubstantiated generalizations. A somewhat broader topic, question 2 asks students to analyze the possibly racist basis of ethnic exclusivity in popular entertainment and sports. For a comparison topic, try question 3, which invites students to compare the history of rock-'n'-roll with that of rap; they should consider the extent to which each musical genre has gone mainstream and why. Question 4 extends Taylor's concerns to the more general question of preserving one's racial heritage; the Jack Lopez, Nell Bernstein, and bell hooks selections in this chapter can help students respond to this topic.

JACK LOPEZ
OF CHOLOS AND SURFERS (p. 592)

We've found that students have never failed to respond warmly to Jack Lopez, and it's easy to understand why. In this accessible memoir, Lopez describes growing up as a Mexican American in East Los Angeles, moving between *cholo* gang culture and the white surfer culture and, in the process, having "the best of both worlds." Students respond positively not only to his message that it's possible both to assimilate and to retain one's native culture; they also enjoy his friendly tone, mild self-deprecating humor, and resolutely nice persona. Students will want to discuss his message about assimilation, of course, but make sure they don't miss some of the subtleties of his narrative. Why, for instance, does his father ask other Mexican Americans if they are Mexican when he knows that they are — and why does that habit so irritate the young Lopez? What's the point Lopez makes about Victor VerHagen, his belligent schoolmate? This selection is also useful if you want to discuss persona and style: How do Lopez's diction and even sentence construction contribute to a reader's reponse?

Because this is a memoir, a natural journal topic is to have students write their own account of how they developed a sense of ethnic identity (see Reading the Signs question 1). A comparison assignment, question 2 asks students to compare Lopez's development of a sense of ethnic identity with that of Melissa Algranati, a mixed-race writer whose own memoir, "Being an Other," appears in this chapter. Lopez's reflections on his father's attitudes toward ethnicity raise the question of generational differences regarding this topic. Accordingly, question 3 has students interview friends and their parents about their sense of ethnic identity and asks the writers to assess the influence one's age can have on such attitudes. This is an ambitious topic, and you may want to prepare students by discussing interviewing strategies in advance. Finally, in describing his move from Mexican East L.A. to predominately white Huntington Beach, Lopez raises issues about ethnic geography and race relations that students can apply to their own neighborhoods (see question 4).

NELL BERNSTEIN

Goin' Gangsta, Choosin' Cholita (p. 599)

We find the phenomenon of "claiming" a remarkable social trend, and we hope your students are as intrigued as we are. In this easy-to-read selection, Bernstein describes teenagers who "claim," or adopt, a new racial identity. These teens have a variety of motives for doing so. Sometimes they want to emulate friends, other times they apparently want to irritate their parents, and often they just want to seem cool. Ask your class about these motives and whether they had friends in high school (or even now, in college) who were claimers. What does ethnic identity mean to these teens? How is ethnicity a sign for them? Because a few students in your class may be (or have been) claimers themselves, you'll want to make sure the discussion doesn't descend to ridicule of the teens whom Bernstein describes. To avoid that possibility, you might turn to the photo of four teens on p. 598. These people are not necessarily claimers, but they do strike a pose, one that some viewers may consider cool. Ask your students: How do these four teens relate to each other? How would students characterize their styles, and what messages do their styles communicate? In discussing Bernstein, you may want to cover several ethnicities; her essay is valuable in that it covers kids of different backgrounds adopting a variety of new racial identities. They don't claim being white, however, and that's worth discussing, too (see Reading the Signs question 4).

Bernstein's essay creates lots of opportunities for creative and argumentative assignments. Reading the Signs question 1 directs students to stage a conversation between one of the teens and her dad; through role-playing, this exercise could help students see how different generations may read ethnicity differently. The next two questions invite argumentative essays: Number 2 focuses on the media's role in stimulating the claiming trend, and number 3 asks students to take a position on whether claiming is an expression of tolerance or stereotyping (for more on how the notion of racial stereotyping can be slippery, refer students to Randall Kennedy's selection on racial profiling in this chapter). For a more open-ended topic, assign question 5, which sends students to the Jack Lopez selection in this chapter for help in assessing the motives behind claiming.

BELL HOOKS

Baby (p. 605)

If you know bell hooks's work, this selection may surprise you. Rather than engaging in her often-seeing analysis of gender and ethnic politics, hooks provides a poignant personal narrative relating her childhood experience with a doll — a brown doll — that looked like her. And students should find this selection quite easy to comprehend. But this is not to say that hooks isn't making a point about ethnic identity: a child needs to see herself reflected in not only her toys but also the culture that surrounds her. Be sure that your students don't overlook that point. Because this selection is short and tightly written, it's ideal for teaching some close reading strategies. You might ask your class why hooks labels herself her mother's "problem child." Why does she say Baby was "waiting" — and for what? Why does she point out that the newest Barbie at the time was "bald"?

Because this is a personal narrative, many instructors may wish their students to write their own reflections on the issues hooks raises (see Reading the Signs question

1 for a journal entry). Yet this selection can be the springboard for interesting analytic assignments as well. Question 2, which focuses on the construction of gender roles, sends students to Scanlon's selection in Chapter Six. (As a corollary, ask students to study the photo of the little girl playing with her doll on p. 606: In what ways is she engaged in role-playing?) To update hooks's reminiscences, question 3 has students visit a toy store and examine the ethnic identities of the dolls sold today. And, to extend the scope of hooks's piece, question 4 prompts them to study the ethnic patterns in other forms of children's entertainment, such as video games. Don't be surprised if your students find examples of extreme stereotyping in videos and toys; Omi's selection in this chapter can provide a useful critical framework for this topic.

MELISSA ALGRANATI

BEING AN OTHER (p. 608)

Algranati's essay is an important reminder of a fact often overlooked in discussions of ethnicity in which supposedly clear-cut terms like *Latino, white,* and *African American* are bandied about. That is, many people in America are not "pure" anything and may find it difficult (or choose not) to identify themselves as a member of a single racial group. How does ethnicity operate as a sign for biracial people? she answers that it's not easy. In this accessible selection, she describes the confusion occasioned by being a Puerto Rican, Egyptian, and Jewish mix — a confusion felt both by others, who expect a unitary ethnic identity, and by Algranati, who struggled with the question "Who am I?" Expect your students to respond positively to Algranati, who neither complains about her status nor indicts the evils of American racism. Instead, she matter-of-factly describes her family and the responses she receives to her mixed identity — and, in the process, creates a sympathetic response in her readers.

Given that sympathy is a likely response, our first Reading the Signs question is a journal topic that allows students to explore their own answer to "Who am I?" This selection creates opportunities for interesting, manageable analytic topics as well. Question 2 asks students to take a stand on whether official documents, such as school applications, should ask applicants to identify their ethnicity; in preparation for this assignment, find out if your college has a ethnic check-off list included in its application form and, if so, what ethnicities are listed. For a topic with open-ended possibilities, try question 3, which asks students how they would identify themselves if they had Algranati's background. For a challenging topic, see question 4, which asks students to assume Algranati's point of view in responding to the claiming fad described in Bernstein's article. Question 5 poses a potentially lively in-class activity; it has the class brainstorm biracial entertainers or other media figures and then discuss the media's tendency to pigeonhole people. What are the implications for people who don't quite fit ethnic categories?

FAN SHEN

THE CLASSROOM AND THE WIDER CULTURE: IDENTITY AS A KEY TO LEARNING ENGLISH COMPOSITION (p. 613)

Even if you don't use any other selection from Chapter Seven, we hope you cover this essay for its analysis of the link between culture and composition. Fan Shen describes the culture shock he experienced when he faced the expectation that he promote the self, not the group, in his writing. In so doing, he describes the ideological basis of English essay writing — a topic worth discussing with your class even if you don't focus on the multicultural issues. What are the conventions of academic writing, and what sorts of knowledge does it privilege? What's gained by a Western academic approach, and what's lost? Are conventions of English composition essays the same as the writing conventions in other disciplines? But the multicultural issues are significant as well, for in describing his initial expectations about what essays should be, Shen articulates an alternative to the norm with which your students are likely to be familiar. This revelation can create opportunities for students to explore their own expectations as writers; we heartily suggest you assign Reading the Signs question 4, which invites students to examine the aspects of writing that seem "natural" and "unnatural" to them. Indeed, you might raise the issue of how the writing class itself is a culture, one often at odds with mainstream university culture in its concern for student learning.

Shen's description of Western and non-Western styles of learning provides a heuristic that can be useful for a variety of assignments. Reading the Signs question 1 invites students to explore in their journal the extent to which they were raised with a Western concept of self; this question could also be an essay topic. Question 3 first asks the class to discuss whether their classes assume Western learning styles (as did Shen's, we're presuming that for the most part students' classes do). It then asks students to abandon that style by writing up the results of the discussion using the non-Western, or *yijing*, approach. We strongly recommend that, before asking students to attempt this task, you first discuss with them what Shen means by *yijing*; we also suggest that you ask students to read their work aloud so they can discuss how they attempted to achieve the *yijing* style. Question 2 is an accessible topic that asks students to compare Fan Shen's experiences with their own. Here, students could address the impact not only of cultural differences but of gender-based patterns.

LYNNELL HANCOCK

The Haves and the Have-Nots (p. 623)

Some of the most sweeping claims made for the Internet focus on its democratizing potential. The Net, its champions argue, will give all citizens direct access to government, make the fullest libraries available to any student, allow the curious to chat with renowned scientists, and so forth. Is this scenario realistic? No way, says Hancock. In this selection, Hancock outlines some of the very real obstacles to such visions: most important, economics, but also bureaucracy and age. And the lines between the haves and the have-nots often overlap with racial divisions (refer your students to the photo on p. 625 of an African American child using antiquated computer equipment). Some students who believe the "anyone-can-surf-the-Net" mantra will dispute Hancock's concerns, and that's fine. Challenge them to disprove Hancock's point, or, on a more local scale, to research ways in which your community has managed to bridge the gap between the haves and the have-nots. They might interview local schoolteachers or administrators, for instance, to learn the state of computer technology in the local school district — and if there are differences depending on the economic or ethnic status of schools within the district. If they discover deficiencies — which would not be surprising — invite the class to propose solutions (see Reading the Signs question 1). The issue of whether the Internet should be "realistic" also emerges in Hancock's discussion; students interested in this question may wish to respond to question 2 or 4.

We find Hancock's essay valuable for raising the question "Whose world is cyberspace, anyway?" What values and beliefs dominate, and why? We particularly recommend question 3, which asks students to interpret a computer magazine such as *Wired*. Ask your class to study details throughout the publication: the articles, the writing style, the ads, the layout. And urge them to consider the magazine's treatment of gender, ethnicity, class, and even age groupings. Based on our own sampling of such publications, we predict your students will find clear patterns emerging — patterns that, in most cases, will suggest the urgency of Hancock's concerns.

RANDALL KENNEDY
BLIND SPOT (p. 627)

Post–September 11, we feel it essential that a chapter on ethnicity address that most vexed of controversies, racial profiling. We particularly like Kennedy's treatment of this issue because he avoids the usual simplistic debate over whether the practice is necessary or harmful. Instead, he raises complex questions about the place of stereotyping in our culture and traces the contradictions inherent in the positions of both supporters and opponents. You'll want to make sure these contradictions are clear to your students. Supporters of racial profiling claim that the need to protect the public welfare supersedes the (to them, minor) infringement of individual rights, yet, Kennedy points out, the same people often oppose affirmative action as devaluing the achievement of individuals in favor of a broader social agenda. Opponents of profiling see it as discrimination and argue that race should not be used at all by law enforcement, yet they often support the use of race as a criterion in hiring or school admissions. We suggest that you steer your discussion away from which side is "right," for that question is moot as Kennedy presents the matter. Rather, you might raise some broader issues about the tensions between individual and community rights: when does the one supersede the other? (That thorny dilemma is the focus of a challenging question, Reading the Signs question 4.) In addition, you might encourage them to consider the act of stereotyping itself: When does a valid recognition of a pattern of behavior shade into invalid generalizations? Can there be a difference between "positive" profiling (as supporters of affirmative action would believe) and "negative," and how can we tell the difference? Does it matter who is doing the profiling? (Consider in this regard the habit of claiming as described in Bernstein's "Goin' Gangsta, Choosin' Cholita.") And to what extent does any form of profiling — by law enforcement, by employers, by school admissions officers — presume pure ethnic identities and ignore the multitude of bi- and multiethnic people in this country?

Don't be surprised if some of your students have their own tale about being subject to racial profiling; Reading the Signs question 1 invites students to write a journal entry on such an experience. For an analytic assignment, try question 2, which has students take on the central contradiction that Kennedy finds in the racial profiling debate, or question 4, which prompts them to consider the implications of racial profiling given that ethnic identity in America so often is mixed. The most contentious question is number 3, which has the class debate the merits of ethnic profiling in the wake of the September 11 attacks. Your students should take care to note the range of practices to which this term applies: as Kennedy suggests, a cop stopping a motorist for driving while black may not be the same as a flight attendant confronting a Richard Reid with smoke coming from his sneaker.

Chapter Eight

IT'S NOT JUST A GAME
Sports and American Culture

The academic study of sports did not begin with the advent of cultural studies; indeed, it has long been a mainstay of leisure studies scholarship and education. But while in the context of leisure studies sport is largely regarded as a form of recreation in which amateur participant-athletes play an active role, cultural studies views sports, especially American sports, as a form of entertainment, constituting a major part of what we are calling America's "sports-and-entertainment postindustrial complex." It's a long way, that is, from the neighborhood softball league to major league baseball, where shortstops can pull in quarter-billion-dollar contracts and television producers call the shots, and it is partly the purpose of this chapter to reveal just how far American sports has moved from the recreational playing field to the theatrical spectaculars of mass entertainment. (Striking evidence is that even as sports becomes a larger part of American popular culture, American obesity rates continue to rise.) The Exploring the Signs of Sports in American Culture boxed question accordingly asks students to consider their own relationship to sports, whether they were recreational participants or spectators and fans. If you have student-athletes in your class, you may want to conduct a class discussion in which they can share their motivations for pursuing athletics at the college level. Do they desire to become athlete-entertainers, celebrities who will perform for mass audiences, or do they have more traditional, amateur-oriented motivations? Or are they simply relying on their athletic scholarships to enable them to get a college education?

Whether your students are active participants in sports or passive spectators, they will be aware of the complex cultural codes to which American sports belong. The Discussing the Signs of Sports in American Culture boxed question thus asks your students to discuss the various images that different sports present. In your class discussion you will want to make sure that your students see that these images reflect such larger cultural issues as race, class, and gender. Basketball, for example, has become culturally coded as a black urban sports, while, as David Kamp's piece, "America's Spaz-Time," makes clear, soccer has become associated with the white suburbs. And you'll want your students to consider that athletes are not simply "jocks" (a word, you might point out, that carries its own gendered implications).

The Reading Sports on the Net question asks your students to surf the Net so that they can experience the ways in which contemporary sport has been integrated into a marketing-and-celebrity-driven culture in which consumption and image are everything. Your students could list on the board the Web addresses of the sites that they have found and can describe in the class the content that they discovered there (if you can schedule your class in a computer lab, students can visit and analyze the sites in class). Students can also bring in copies of the sports pages of your local newspaper to enhance a discussion of the similarities and differences between the two media.

As a topic for discussion and critical writing, sports may be a surprisingly controversial, or at least emotional, subject for your students if your university happens to be embroiled in one of the many debates over the proper place of athletics at the college level now roiling America's campuses. Whether the issue relates to Title IX enforcement, which has compelled some universities to cut back their men's programs to make room for more women's sports, or to the question of whether university athletes in such big-ticket sports as football should be paid for their performances, there is plenty of room for spirited debate. Try to make sure that your nonfan students feel free to express what they may think, especially if you teach at a large state university with a high-profile NCAA Division I program. Criticizing, say, the special scholarships set aside for athletes may not be easy in such a context, so you may have to make an effort to ensure an adequate comfort level for all your students.

If your interest in this chapter is primarily related to the current debates over college sports, you will certainly want to assign D. Stanley Eitzen's "The Contradictions of Big-Time College Sport" and Frank Deford's "Athletics 101." A prominent sports sociologist and sports fan, Eitzen takes a rigorous position against what he sees as the "compromising" influence that athletics have on higher education. Offering a rather different perspective, Deford, the well-known NPR sports commentator, advocates allowing college athletes professional status. Though much shorter than the Eitzen piece, Deford's offers a succinct counterpoint that many of your students, especially athletes, will almost certainly appreciate.

If you want to take a social-class based approach to sports, begin with the chapter introduction (especially the Interpreting the Signs of American Sports section), and then assign David Kamp's "America's Spaz-Time" and Henry Jenkins's "'Never Trust a Snake': WWF Wrestling as Masculine Melodrama." Kamp somewhat sardonically explores the suburban world of America's children's soccer leagues (the source of the near-notorious "soccer mom"), critiquing some of the rituals of contemporary middle-class parenting, while Jenkins takes a generally sympathetic, though hardly partisan, look at the largely working-class world of professional wrestling. The Deford selection could be a companion piece as well, for he takes a vigorous swipe at what he sees to be the upper-class-based biases that govern current university attitudes toward the amateur ideal. The selections by Michael A. Messner and Mariah Burton Nelson are essential readings should you focus on gender issues. Messner critically analyzes the role of sports as a male initiation ritual that encodes the patriarchal values of the traditional gender code. If that code drives men to be aggressively competitive, it also values female passivity, a gender trait that Nelson finds all too evident in the world of women's sports, where female athletes are forced to find a resolution to the cultural contradiction of being women in a masculinely defined world. The paradoxes of the apologetic competitor and the athletic fashion plate are just two of the solutions that Nelson critiques. And don't miss the famous, perhaps notorious, image of Brandi Chastain celebrating her winning goal in the 1999 Women's World Cup championship (p. 640). No one would have complained about a man ripping off his shirt in such circumstances; ask your class to interpret the furor over Chastain's performance from Nelson's perspective.

If you are doing a unit on the September 11 attacks, you will want to assign Gary Smith's "The Boys on the Bus," a personal reflection on sports that was written in the immediate aftermath of the disaster. Be sure to have your class look at the image on p. 24 of the September 11 Portfolio of the high school football team streaming onto the field waving an American flag. And if you are including an ethical component in your class study, you could assign E. M. Swift's and Don Yaeger's "Unnatural Selection," which directly and indirectly explores the problem of drug-enhanced athletic performance and the specter of future genetically engineered athletes.

D. STANLEY EITZEN

THE CONTRADICTIONS OF BIG-TIME COLLEGE SPORT (p. 642)

If you teach at a college or university with a high-profile sports program, this reading might lead to some fireworks in your class. From gender inequities, to the compromising (and perhaps corrupting) effects of the commercialization of college sport, to the low graduation rates of college athletes (especially African Americans), Eitzen sees a world of big-time college sports that comes dangerously close to contradicting the whole purpose of a university. Some students may resent this position, especially if they are athletes, and many, athletes and nonathletes alike, may take the often racially charged position that big-time college sports is the only way out of poverty for some athletes. Be sure to point out that Eitzen addresses this last argument explicitly, suggesting that the promise of riches and fame, especially to African American athletes, is something of a cheat that inhibits their education. More generally, emphasize the high level of empirical detail that Eitzen brings to his work, his statistical documentation and careful sociological research. He isn't just shooting from the hip, and you should make certain that your students understand the value of solid evidence in a debate of this kind.

Two Reading the Signs questions offer your students a chance to find some empirical evidence of their own in support of their arguments for or against Eitzen's proposition that "the pursuit of money has prostituted the university" (question 1) and his questioning whether "the athletic programs at big-time schools [are] consistent with the educational mission of U.S. colleges and universities" (question 2). Questions 3 and 4 each offer opportunities for gender analysis, leading your students to Nelson's and Messner's readings to analyze the role of sports in the construction of gender identities and to debate the Title IX mandates to establish gender parity in college sports spending and participation. Question 5 may be of particular interest to your students if you teach at a college or university that either doesn't have an intercollegiate athletic program or performs at the Division II or Division III level. Endorsing a kind of Division III program for everyone, Eitzen offers an opportunity for your students to discuss the athletic picture at *their* university. Conversely, if you teach at a Division I campus, the question will press your students to imagine what their university would be like without a big-time athletics department.

FRANK DEFORD

ATHLETICS 101: A CHANGE IN ELIGIBILITY RULES IS LONG OVERDUE (p. 659)

Should you be looking for a college-athlete-friendly piece, this one's for you. Deford not only heartily endorses the professionalization of college sports, he takes a swipe at the university administrators who have held the line on professionalization. Deford's essay should appeal to all of your students for its bouncy brevity as well. If you assign this reading with Eitzen's, you should discuss with your class the difference between the codes of academic analysis (Eitzen is a sociologist) and popular op-ed journalism (Deford is a virtual *Sports Illustrated* icon). Note that Deford relies more on ridicule and anecdote than he does on careful research and analysis. Ask your students whether Deford's comparisons between working professionally at a radio station and playing for pay is really an adequate basis for argument. After all, not every player on a college team is likely to be pursued by a professional "sponsor." You could ask your students to consider the effects on a team if only a few of its members are pulling in thousands, perhaps millions, of dollars. At the same time, your students may find Deford's entertaining, no-holds-barred approach to be more persuasive than Eitzen's careful analysis and argumentation. If they do, ask them to articulate what it is in such a rhetorical approach that makes it effective. If they don't, have them articulate the merits of the academic style.

Reading the Signs question 1 offers your students a chance to write an op-ed of their own and so experiment with Deford's techniques themselves. Conversely, question 2 asks your students to be more like Eitzen, sending them to the library to find evidence for or against Deford's charge that the amateur ideal was constituted in order to keep working-class athletes in their place. Reading the Signs questions 3 and 4 take your students directly to the Eitzen reading, the former inviting them to expand on Eitzen's concerns by imagining the further challenges that the professionalization of college sports might bring to university campuses, and the latter guiding them to a comparison and contrast essay on what both Deford and Eitzen see as the hypocrisies in current college athletics programs.

DAVID KAMP

AMERICA'S SPAZ-TIME (p. 661)

Pardon us for finding David Kamp's piece wickedly funny. With his sardonic take on the way the self-esteem movement seems to have taken over the U.S. Youth Soccer movement, Kamp takes aim at one of the newest sacred cows in American middle-class culture. Of course, if your students grew up playing in a suburban youth soccer league, or are soccer moms themselves, they may not find Kamp so funny. If so, make sure that they see that behind Kamp's barbs lies a serious student and fan of the game that the rest of the world calls football. He's not against youth soccer; he simply has a differerent vision of what it has to offer.

Any discussion of Kamp's article should begin with the overall place of soccer in the context not only of American sports but of global athletics as a whole. One of Kamp's main points is that though soccer, at long last, has taken its place in American culture, it is not only entirely different culturally from the game that produces British soccer hooligans and a well-nigh religious devotion to the sport in fans in the rest of the world, it also differs from most American sports in its unparallelled charge to be both "edifying and nurturing," as Kamp puts it. If you have students from other countries, ask them to share their view of soccer in comparison to the American view. Your students from immigrant communities may have particular opinions about Kamp's focus on suburban (read "middle-class white") youth soccer. Be sure your class understands that for many Americans, especially recent immigrants, soccer has nothing to do with the pieties of U.S. Youth Soccer and is regarded in just the same way as it is in the rest of the world. Thus it would be useful to point out that this article originally appeared in *GQ*. Ask your class how this might have affected Kamp's focus and tone.

Kamp does not ignore the gendered aspects of America's soccer history, and so Reading the Signs question 1 accordingly directs your students to Mariah Burton Nelson to help them analyze Kamp's citation of *Sports Illustrated* columnist Rick Reilly's breathtakingly traditionalist response to the U.S. Women's 1999 World Cup team. Questions 2 and 3 invite a more personal approach, one leading students to reflect on the meaning soccer (or any other youth sport) held for them when they were children, and the other calling for an essay arguing for or against Kamp's provocative assertion that American soccer is "a creepy perversion of a fun game." Question 4 calls for a semiotic interpretation of the place of soccer in the system of American popular and sporting culture. If you are taking a globalist approach to popular culture, you will want to be sure that your students take up the alternative assignment in question 4, which calls for a comparative analysis, contrasting the American image of soccer with that of the rest of the world.

MICHAEL A. MESSNER

POWER AT PLAY: SPORT AND GENDER RELATIONS (p. 668)

Be prepared for strong responses to this selection, especially if you have many athletes in class or if your school's sports teams have a devoted following. Messner presents a trenchant analysis of the gender roles that dominate the sports world, finding that an ideology of power and dominance controls the identities of the men who participate in sports. He believes that this pattern is damaging to men and serves to perpetuate social and institutional gender inequities. Although we buy Messner's argument, many students won't and may feel that their (or their friends') values are under attack. If that's the case, point out that Messner is as much concerned about the price athletes pay as he is about describing the dominant ideologies in the sports world. Students may not have thought much about the connection between sports and gender roles; Reading the Signs question 1, which asks them to explore this connection in their journals, can be a good place to start (and may help allay a defensive response). Whether your students agree or disagree with Messner, we've found that this selection can virtually guarantee a lively discussion among your students.

If your students are troubled by Messner's thesis, encourage them to develop counterarguments (Reading the Signs question 5 asks students to stage an in-class debate on his central point). To prepare for their debate, students might interview athletes, nonathletes, and coaches. Although Messner focuses primarily on male athletes, he does mention the place of female athletes in the world of sports; students may prefer to write an argument on this issue (see question 2 and question 3, which additionally raises the issue of ethnic patterns in professional sports). For a text-based assignment, ask your students to respond to question 4, which directs them to analyze the gender roles in a magazine such as *Sports Illustrated*. A reminder: *SI*'s swimsuit issue comes out each February!

MARIAH BURTON NELSON

I WON. I'M SORRY. (p. 679)

Here's a reading that will be especially poignant to your women students, particularly if they are athletes, but be prepared for some defensiveness from males and females alike when it comes to Nelson's questioning of the beauty demands made on women athletes, because Nelson strikes at the very heart of the gender codes that govern the world of sports. Your students may be surprised to realize that they are most comfortable with women athletes who, despite defying convention to the extent of entering what is traditionally regarded as a man's world, still abide by the old gender rules by muting their competitive drives and, so to speak, putting on high heels. You should draw your students' attention to the photo of Serena Williams on p. 681; here Williams appears physically powerful but also undeniably glamorous. (And you might remind them that Williams wore a silver, pearl-studded tiara throughout the 2002 Wimbledon match.) And what connection do students see between the photo of Williams and the 1903 lithograph of two women playing golf (p. 687)? By focusing on such refeminizing strategies, Nelson provides a kind of mirror image of the dilemma described by Diane Barthel in her analysis of the strategies to which advertisers resort when they are trying to pitch products like hairspray, which are traditionally coded as feminine, to men ("A Gentleman and a Consumer," Chapter Two). You might assign Barthel's essay in conjunction with Nelson's as preparation for a discussion of the ways in which those who challenge traditional gender codes often end up reinforcing them at the same time.

Reading the Signs questions 1, 3, and 5 are all useful assignments if your students object to Nelson's contentions. By asking them to observe some women athletes in action (question 1), analyze a women's sports magazine (question 2), or interview women athletes on their campus about the gender pressures they face (question 5), you will be guiding them not only to a sound basis for assessing Nelson's argument but also helping them to appreciate the value of empirical evidence. Question 2 offers a more personal and reflective exercise, which may be especially valued by female athletes, while question 4 presents an assignment in critical thinking and writing that requires your students to consider the arguments of other writers in constituting their own arguments about the role of sports in constructing heterosexual gender norms.

HENRY JENKINS

"NEVER TRUST A SNAKE": WWF WRESTLING AS MASCULINE MELODRAMA (p. 688)

We think your students will love Jenkins's uncondescending yet thoroughly academic analysis of the social significance of the World Wrestling Federation. A topic for semiotic analysis ever since Roland Barthes first tackled it in *Mythologies* (1957), professional wrestling appeals to a paradoxically wide range of fans, from the high-brow crowd who regard it as high-camp hilarity to the working-class men who take it more seriously. It is that latter audience that Jenkins is more concerned with, and his sympathetic analysis of the compensatory spectacles that professional wrestling provides for working-class men in a postindustrial, postfeminist era can be usefully paired with James William Gibson's related analysis in "Warrior Dreams" (Chapter Six). Though it might look like a rather long reading assignment, you might want to assign the Gibson piece alongside Jenkins's to show just how serious the semiotics of the apparently goofy world of the WWF can be.

For a basic exercise in semiotic interpretation, you can assign Reading the Signs question 1, which asks your students to decode some actual WWF contests (make sure your students realize that these are not real competitions but are entirely scripted theatrical productions). Question 2 presents a critical thinking and writing assignment that relates Jenkins's analysis to the larger themes presented in this chapter concerning the role of sport in the construction of gender identities. Questions 4 and 5 offer assignments that call for an analysis of class-based tastes (question 4) and of the way that fandom constructs a sense of group solidarity (question 5). For a more reflective assignment, question 3 provides an opportunity for any serious WWF fans in your class, who may feel embarrassed about speaking up in class, to express in their journals what professional wrestling means to them.

E. M. SWIFT AND DON YAEGER
UNNATURAL SELECTION (p. 704)

Beyond the current controversies over the use of performance-enhancing drugs in sports looms the potentially more controversial matter of performance-enhancing genetic engineering. Primarily informational in its approach and effect, Swift and Yaeger's piece nevertheless can stimulate far-ranging class debate, from the specific issue of using biology to get an edge on the competition to the larger issue of the ethics of genetic engineering. At a time when controversies over cloning, stem cell research, genetically engineered food crops, and the potential for terrorists to engineer deadly biological weapons are making headlines, this piece can help your students see how the ramifications of what may look on the surface to be rather trivial can be quite serious indeed.

Reading the Signs assignments 1 and 2 focus on the more limited issue of fairness, with question 1 calling for an op-ed essay about the legality of genetically engineered athletes and question 2 calling for a more personal reflection on the ethics of using genetic engineering to get a competitive edge. Question 3 offers a more imaginative assignment that invites your class to consider not only the possibility of genetically engineered intelligence but the different way in which our culture regards intelligence as opposed to athletic performance (it is our guess that your students will be far more upset by the prospect of artificial "brains" than by artificial athletes; if so, make sure that you discuss the reasons for this). Questions 4 and 5 both call for analytic essays that explore the cultural significance of the use of science in enhancing athletic performance, with question 4 focusing on the values that would lead a society to devote expensive scientific research to the creation of better athletes, and question 5 focusing on an analysis of the cultural pressures athletes face to increase their competitive edge.

GARY SMITH

THE BOYS ON THE BUS (p. 711)

Gary Smith's personal reflection in the immediate aftermath of the September 11 attacks may serve as an important reminder to your students of the profound cultural issues those attacks raised. There is no predicting what future terror America may face, but in the months since the attacks, American popular culture has pretty much returned to normal. Smith's piece reminds us of the soul-searching America went through in the dark days of September, wondering whether its obsessive devotion to sports and entertainment was really appropriate in what looked to be a dangerous new world. For that reason alone we feel that Smith's essay is worth assigning. Reading the Signs assignment 1 invites your students to reflect on their own response to the September 11 attacks, and to the changes, or perhaps lack of changes, in their daily routines that the disaster impelled. Question 2 calls for an opinion essay judging whether it was appropriate for Americans to return to popular-cultural business-as-usual so soon after the attacks, while question 3 focuses on the appropriateness of maintaining high school athletic schedules in the wake of the national tragedy. Assignment 4 calls for some critical analysis of four other readings in this text that are devoted to the September 11 attacks, guiding your students to analyze the values that each writer addresses and reflects.

Chapter Nine

AMERICAN ICONS
The Mythic Characters of Popular Culture

Pop culture personalities, media icons, folk heroes. Whatever you call them, America is populated with characters that reflect the nation's dreams, myths, and ideologies. Some may be real people and some fictional creations, but we've found they're perfect for analyzing semiotically. They serve as an accurate mirror of their times, symbolizing the values and interests of the era in which they are created. You can read pop culture characters in much the same way as you do fictional characters from literature. You can ask your students to analyze the values they hold, how they develop or change over time, how they compare with other characters, how they capture the hearts of their audience. And because such characters so closely reflect the interests of their culture, they create opportunities for addressing a host of serious issues such as gender, class, and ethnicity. Some of the very best student writing we've received has focused on popular characters. Perhaps it's the novelty of looking at culture in the same way one might look at literature; perhaps it's the immediacy of the subject matter; or perhaps it's the fun of exploring and explaining "people" who inhabit our daily lives but tend to be taken for granted. Whatever the reason, studying popular characters can be a fine way to develop your students' analytic skills while having some fun in the process.

The boxed questions in the introduction are designed to inspire a spirit of fun and serious critical inquiry in your students. We encourage you to try the Discussing the Signs of American Characters question, which asks the class to brainstorm a list of their favorite pop cultural icons and then to analyze the list. Not only will this question get all your students to participate, but it asks them to consider the cultural and social basis for their personal tastes. The Exploring the Signs of American Characters question is also personally reflective, asking students about the significance that characters from children's television had for them when they were young. The Reading American Characters on the Net exercise invites your students to look outward at the larger culture's values — and at America's cult of the celebrity — by investigating the role the Internet plays in fostering a celebrity's status. In doing so, your students may see how both the celebrity's image and an audience's response to that image are careful media constructs. Alternatively, you could ask students to investigate the backgrounds of historical figures that resonate in the American imagination; check **http://www.biography.com** for twenty thousand or so entries.

Because the chapter's introduction does the work of setting up a critical framework for analyzing characters, you could easily allow your students to pick which essays they'd like to read if you don't have time to cover them all. Michael Eric Dyson starts off with an analysis of a real-life superhero, Michael Jordan, with the next two selections, by Gary Engle and Andy Medhurst, focusing on fictional superheroes, Superman and Batman. A trio of selections on toys and games follows, with N'Gai Croal and Jane Hughes explaining Lara Croft, Emily Prager turning to the doll industry to critique Barbie, and Gary Cross moving from Barbie to G.I. Joe. Mark Caldwell returns to real life in his review of the queen of domesticity, Martha Stewart. In a humorous piece, Roy Rivenburg examines characters who have been used to peddle everything from cereal to paper towels. Jenny Lyn Bader follows, exploring whether today's twentysomethings can even believe in heroes anymore — a comprehensive essay that's crucial to include even if you use the chapter selectively. To conclude the chapter, Tim Layden provides an answer to Bader by recalling the firefighters and law enforcement officers who struggled to save whoever they could on September 11, 2001, and the days following.

A number of selections focus on toys as objects of analysis. Some students might wonder why: after all, isn't college where you study "serious" subjects? Our response: Toys are very serious business. In childhood we are conditioned to accept our culture's dominant mythologies, and toys and games are one of the primary "teachers" of those beliefs. We feel it essential that students see that dominant beliefs aren't "just in the air"; they are embodied in cultural artefacts that we usually take for granted. Toys aren't just fun; they help shape some of our most fundamental belief systems.

American mythmakers have not created an abundance of positive female pop culture characters. There are a few, but when asked, our students (both male and female) tend to think only of sex symbols, advertising characters (who are usually either a mom or an Elvira type), and romanticized historical figures such as Betsy Ross. Just as the introduction raises the issue of race, we suggest you ask your students about gender also. Why have female characters been limited to such a restricted range of roles? Are things changing? What sort of female characters, real or fictional, would your students like to see assume a greater role in American popular culture?

MICHAEL ERIC DYSON

BE LIKE MIKE? MICHAEL JORDAN AND THE PEDAGOGY OF DESIRE (p. 729)

This selection provides an opportunity to teach students the need to keep in check personal responses to a subject as they attempt to analyze it. Often in class discussion of American characters, Michael Jordan's name has come up, and with good reason. Not just a sports hero, he has an extremely attractive public persona (distinct from the bad-boy image of so many other athletes); details of his personal history, such as his father's murder, are tragic; his on-again, off-again retirement creates an aura of mystery and suspense. But expect your students to stick to a functional explanation for Jordan's popularity: "He's so much better than any other basketball player!" "He's just amazing!" If your students are Jordan fans, fine. They could benefit from this selection, though, because Dyson goes beyond the functional explanation to probe the cultural mythologies surrounding this larger-than-life hero. Dyson's unambiguous admiration for Jordan may be useful for students who resist analysis of their pop culture favorites because they equate analysis or criticism with negative commentary. And, to us at least, Dyson's argumentive base is sound: he locates Jordan within the context of black participation in sports, for instance, and he examines other parts of the system in which Jordan can be interpreted, including advertising and consumer culture. Some students may be put off by Dyson's rather academic style, but the diction is relatively jargon-free and students should grasp most of his points.

This selection creates opportunities for a variety of analytic and argumentative topics. A straightforward assignment is Reading the Signs question 1, an argument topic that focuses on one of the complaints about Jordan that Dyson mentions (note that it's not one that Dyson shares). For a more challenging question focused on ethnicity, try question 2, which has students respond to the belief, to which Dyson alludes, that basketball is primarily a black form of cultural expression. Students might do some research on the history of basketball for this topic; they'll find that the sport was invented by a white man. If you want your students to focus their attention on sports more generally, assign question 3, a class discussion prompt that gets students thinking about why sports personalities have become America's heroes, and question 4, an essay prompt that addresses Dyson's claims about athletics as a means for facilitating "white male bonding." For this last question, students should consult Messner's "Power at Play" in Chapter Eight.

GARY ENGLE

WHAT MAKES SUPERMAN SO DARNED AMERICAN? (p. 738)

This is a long selection, but it's clearly written and gives your students plenty to talk about. Engle's thesis is that Superman has succeeded as a superhero because he embodies a mythology dear to a land of immigrants. Superman, Engle asserts, has not just gone from rags to riches but has moved from being an alien to a quintessential American. That such an debatable thesis is well defended and thoroughly argued makes the selection a winner for class discussion. Why does Superman seem more patriotic than Batman? (If you want to pursue the "What is an American?" angle, Reading the Signs question 4 asks students to take on Engle's claim that Superman is more American than John Wayne.) Students would do well to consider whether the view of immigrants is always as romanticized as Engle suggests, either in our own era or in past decades. Engle here is asking that essential semiotic question, "Why Superman?" If your students don't buy his argument, ask them to propose alternative answers to the question "Why?" (Reading the Signs question 2 allows students to argue with Engle's thesis). If they don't see Superman as really being that important a character, again ask them why. Here, the fading of the assimilationist ideal in our multicultural era comes into play; Reading the Signs question 1 invites students to address this issue.

Engle's selection also works well when combined with other readings. Reading the Signs question 3 sends students to Robert B. Ray's definitions of heroic types (Chapter Four). Although Engle says little about race and gender, those issues are certainly relevant to Superman's success, so question 5 suggests that students consult the Michael Omi (Chapter Seven) and Holly Devor (Chapter Six) selections as they consider the significance of these issues. And finally, question 6 invites students to view a *Superman* movie to see if film has altered the comics' depiction of this superhero.

ANDY MEDHURST

BATMAN, DEVIANCE, AND CAMP (p. 746)

We find Medhurst's essay to be a lot of fun — and we hope you and your students do as well. Of course, Medhurst has a serious point to make: for him at least, the original Batman-and-Robin duo was gay, and it was the homophobic wave of the 1980s that eliminated Robin from the spate of *Batman* movies. Students often resist this thesis — they have real difficulty accepting the notion that such a popular character, and one intended to entertain children, could be homosexual. Medhurst uses a nice blend of evidence to support his claims, however, so challenge your students to refute that evidence if they dislike his argument (rather than simply denouncing it). Be sure they note his creation of a historical context, especially his discussion of Fredric Wertham's *Seduction of the Innocent* — skeptical students tend to find this discussion to be the most persuasive part of Medhurst's argument (Reading the Signs question 2 asks students to critique Wertham's argument). Discuss too Medhurst's reading of individual scenes from the 1960s *Batman* TV series. It's best if you can arrange to show at least part of a *Batman* episode in class; in fact, Reading the Signs question 1 suggests that students view tapes of the show in preparation for arguing for or against Medhurst's thesis. Check your college's media library to see if they have file tapes of old shows. One term that many students don't quite understand is *camp*; that's a central concept in Medhurst's essay and you may want to spend some class time discussing it. For a topic addressing *camp*, see question 4, which sends students to Susan Sontag (whom Medhurst discusses in his selection) for some further research. To bring Medhurst's argument up to date, question 3 asks students to buy some current Batman comics and to explain his current sexual orientation. As students work on this question, be sure they consider who the audience for comic books is and how that might affect decisions about Batman's sexuality.

N'GAI CROAL and JANE HUGHES
Lara Croft, the Bit Girl (p. 761)

Is Lara Croft a feminist model for girls to emulate? Or is she just a cyberBarbie? Let your students decide. In this accessible piece originally published in *Newsweek*, N'Gai Croal and Jane Hughes profile this virtual character and the reasons she has attracted so many fans. Ask your students whether she indeed is a "strong" woman, as some proponents claim, or simply a sexy body operating in a sexy technoevironment. And have them analyze the photo of Lara on p. 762: How is she depicted, and for whom? Ask them to locate Lara Croft within the larger context of female characters as well: How does she relate to a figure like Xena or Tank Girl, or to reach back a bit in time, Wonder Woman? Why is it that boys are among her most ardent fans (not so with Tank Girl)? For this last question, don't accept as an answer the fact that boys predominate in the videogame crowd: There have been plenty of attempts to launch female characters, but most have flopped. To ask that familiar semiotic question, why Lara?

We've created a variety of questions to accompany this piece. The first Reading the Signs question allows students to reflect on Lara's success in their journals; you could make this an essay topic as well. Shifting the focus to style, question 2 asks students to examine this selection as an instance of journalistic prose. For argumentative topics focused on gender, assign question 3, which poses the feminist-icon-or-cyberBarbie debate that we mention above, or question 5, which prompts students to interpret the gender roles in the film *Tomb Raider*. Question 4 shifts to male videogame characters and has students analyze the gender roles such games impose on them. Don't worry if you're not familiar with such characters: we're always surprised at how fluent our students are in the latest of videogame fare. Aren't they studying?

EMILY PRAGER
Our Barbies, Ourselves (p. 766)

Toys are much like cartoons. Students may never have stopped to think about the toys they played with as a child, but when they do, the sparks start flying. In fact, this accessible and clearly written selection has never failed to generate a lively discussion in our classes, and it has been one of instructors' favorite selections in the first three editions of this book. Prager takes a tongue-in-cheek look at Barbie and the role this doll has played in shaping the gender expectations of millions of children. Be sure that students recognize Prager's tone and discuss how it contributes to their response to it. Some students may respond defensively to this essay; when they perceive part of their upbringing to be under attack, they may feel they're under attack, too. They may want to do Reading the Signs question 3, which asks students to explore in their journal the significance of their Barbie doll to them as children. It's important that students notice that Prager includes herself, as a child, among Barbie's fans and that she distinguishes between the doll and its designer — whom she heartily attacks — and the children who play with it. If you had a Barbie once, you might want to confess the fact so students won't feel as if you, too, are judging them.

The assignments that you can generate with this essay will show your students that they can write serious analysis and have some fun at the same time. Be sure to analyze the photo on p. 767: How is Barbie continually being adapted to appeal to new generations of children? We highly recommend the first Reading the Signs question, which asks students to bring a toy to class and discuss its significance, first in same-sex groups, then with the whole class. Not only does this question broaden the issue beyond Barbie, but you can ask students to interpret the gender-related patterns in the whole class's collection of toys. Question 2 allows students to be more reflective, asking them to interpret a toy they played with as children. If students are not persuaded by Prager, they may want to respond to question 4, which allows them to consider how Jack Ryan, Barbie's creator, would defend himself against Prager's charges. The most challenging question is number 5, which sends students to Laurence Shames's "The More Factor" (Chapter One) to explore Barbie's consumerist ethos. Be sure your students visit a toy store as part of their research for this question; they'll find that Barbie's possessions are no longer limited to a car and a condo.

GARY CROSS

BARBIE, G.I. JOE, AND PLAY IN THE 1960S (p. 769)

This is a perfect companion piece to the Prager selection, for while Gary Cross discusses Barbie (and she occupies first place in his title), his main concern is G.I. Joe. What we like about this selection is that Cross charts Joe's shifting fortunes as cultural and social attitudes change — a perfect instance of the semiotic principle that a sign's meaning is historically conditioned. For an even broader cultural context, also assign bell hooks's short piece in Chapter Seven, "Baby," for an ethnic slant on these issues. As Cross points out, G.I. Joe eventually failed in his creators' attempts to adapt to changing times: How does he compare with the action-adventure toys in toy stores today?

You might also compare Cross's analysis of Barbie's appeal with Emily Prager's, since the selections differ substantially in tone, style, even substance (note that Cross attributes a different origin to Barbie than does Prager; we believe Cross is accurate). Which selection do they find more persuasive, and why? How might the intended audience affect each writer's presentation? This selection also raises gender issues: what's an appropriate toy for a girl or boy? Reading the Signs question 4 is a class exercise that would generate a lively discussion of this question.

You'll see that our questions for this selection push students to consider toys as culturally significant objects. Reading the Signs question 1 seems simple — it asks students to invent a toy of their own — but the challenge is writing an essay explaining the rationale for the creation. Be sure to assign this second part, because that's where the hard thinking (and perhaps rethinking of the design) comes in. For a topic that brings Cross's issues up to date, assign question 2, which asks students to survey current action-adventure toys and to analyze them in terms of the warrior dreams framework that James William Gibson describes in his selection (Chapter Six). We encourage students to see the larger cultural role that toys play in socializing kids to mainstream beliefs; question 3 invites them to address this issue.

MARK CALDWELL

THE ASSAULT ON MARTHA STEWART (p. 775)

As we write these words, Martha Stewart is under greater attack than Caldwell imagined when he wrote this piece, what with Kmart in bankruptcy and allegations of insider training plaguing the reigning queen of domesticity. What is it about Stewart's creation of a lifestyle industry has made her so popular that she's become, as Caldwell puts it, a "national symbol"? Is it the sheer ubiquity of her products, both actual and media? What does Caldwell mean by the "democratizing of good taste"? That point is especially important, because it is the key to Caldwell's explanation for Stewart's iconic status. Most students should be familiar with Stewart's industry, but if they're not, bring to class her magazine, *Living*; a videotape of Stewart's daily TV appearances, or a tape of her weekday radio broadcast (the schedules for both conveniently published in *Living*). Alternately, a visit to **www.marthastewart.com** will fill them in.

You'll find it easy to create focused, manageable assignments based on Caldwell's selection. We suggest several questions that prompt students to interpret Martha Stewart products directly: Reading the Signs question 1 asks students to analyze an issue of *Living* to see if it indeed has a democratizing effect, while question 3 sends them to a local KMart to examine the in-store Stewart display. For an investigative topic, try question 2, which asks students to interview Martha Stewart fans as the basis of their own arguments about her appeal. Perhaps the most challenging question is number 4, which sends students to "The Addictive Virus" in Chapter One and has them consider the connection between Stewart's popularity and Americans' increasing fondness for material goods.

ROY RIVENBURG

SNAP! CRACKLE! PLOT! (p. 780)

In this pleasantly tongue-in-cheek selection, Roy Rivenburg, a humor columnist for the *Los Angeles Times*, "investigates" the private lives of advertising characters such as Mrs. Paul and Mr. Clean (be sure to discuss the image of Mr. Clean on p. 784). In the process he notices a number of surprising patterns. Few characters, for instance, are married. Ask your students why that might be so, especially given that food products, which commonly are associated with a character, have a domestic function. Expect this selection to trigger a discussion of the power of advertising: Are consumers really so influenced by promotional characters? We strongly recommend Reading the Signs question 1, which asks the class to brainstorm and categorize as many advertising characters as they can (don't worry — while Rivenburg mentions lots of characters, there are plenty more out there). Be inventive with the categories, and study issues such as ethnicity, class, and gender. What patterns emerge? What do those patterns say about America's values and ideologies? If your students have resisted a semiotic approach thus far, this exercise ought surely to win them over.

We see Rivenburg's selection as ideal for either analytic or creative assignments. For an analytic research topic, question 2 asks students to investigate the controversy surrounding Joe Camel, that cigarette-peddaling creature who finally was retired as part of the tobacco industry's settlement with the federal government. Question 3 gives students a chance to be creative, asking them to invent a new representative for one of the products advertised in the second chapter's Portfolio of Advertisements. As an alternative, you could ask students to pick an ad of their own and then create a new character to represent the product. Finally, question 4 asks students to interpret the Taco Bell chihuahua.

JENNY LYN BADER

LARGER THAN LIFE (p. 785)

We highly recommend that you include Bader's essay in your syllabus, no matter how many other selections from this chapter you cover. Unlike the other selections, which interpret particular characters, Bader takes a broad view and contemplates the meaning and availability of mythic heroes for her twentysomething generation. Bader should strike a chord in many of your students, because she essentially argues that heroes no longer have a powerful influence over today's younger generation and that what is needed are realistic role models. This position should inspire plenty of debate among your students, who are likely to disagree with each other on the validity of Bader's thesis (Reading the Signs question 2 invites an argumentative essay in response to Bader's central argument, and question 4 triggers an in-class discussion of traditional American heroes). If you have nontraditional students in your class, take advantage of their perspective and ask them whether they believe Bader's position applies to older generations as well.

 Bader's argument is likely to touch some students personally. Consider assigning the journal topic mentioned in question 1, which allows students to explore à la Bader the heroes they admired when they were young. They may also enjoy question 3, which invites a creative response to Bader's call for "stories of spirit without apology." Bader's essay lends itself to direct analysis topics as well as more imaginative ones. Question 5 asks students to analyze Michael Jordan using Bader's perspective, but students could easily substitute another sports figure or a political figure if they prefer. Finally, question 6 has students consider Bader's argument in the light of the September 11 attacks on America, an event that caused many Americans to rethink what constitutes heroism.

TIM LAYDEN

A PATRIOT'S TALE (p. 795)

This short selection from *Sports Illustrated* is a perfect companion to Jenny Lyn Bader's piece, for while Bader questions whether heroes can exist for her generation Layden suggests a new category of hero: people like the New York City firefighters who risked their own lives to save victims of the September 11 attacks on the World Trade Center. What's interesting about Layden's article is that, early on, he focuses not on the firefighters themselves but on a brother of firefighters, a right guard for the New England Patriots who, by virtue of his profession, would be a typical candidate for the status of "hero" or "star." Ask your students: What is the attraction of professional sports players? What is it about them that prompts so many fans to idolize them? Then move to the description of the player's three brothers, the firefighters who worked the WTC disaster. What is the effect of the first-person narration? Why does Layden include it? And how does Layden attempt to redefine our sense of who a hero is? You'll note that this piece is designed to trigger an emotional response in readers, and you should discuss that with your class. Does that add to or detract from Layden's overall message?

 It remains to be seen whether America's apparent redefinition of heroes endures. The favorite costume for Halloween, 2001, was a firefighter's uniform. Will that trend prevail? Reading the Signs question 1 invites students to investigate this question. For a stylistic analysis, assign question 2, which asks students to analyze Layden's rhetorical strategies. The most complex question, number 3 has students argue whether the firefighters and other rescue personnel would satisfy Jenny Lyn Bader's call for "a new pantheon" of heroes.